Years

PEÑÍNGUIDE

TO
SPANISH
WINE
2015

www.guiapenin.com

9 788495 203175

Team:

Director: Carlos González
Editor in Chief: Javier Luengo
Tasting team: Carlos González, Javier Luengo and Pablo Vecilla
Texts: Javier Luengo and Carlos González
Database manager: Erika Laymuns
Advertising: Mª Carmen Hernández
Cover design, layout and desktop publishing: Raul Salgado and Luis Salgado
Supervising editor: José Peñín

PUBLISHED BY: PI&ERRE
Santa Leonor, 65 - Edificio A - Bajo A
28037 – MADRID
SPAIN
Tel.: 0034 914 119 464 - Fax: 0034 915 159 499
comunicacion@guiapenin.com
www.guiapenin.com

ISBN: 978-84-95203-17-5
Copyright library: M-24835-2014
Printed by: Gráficas Andalusí
Translation: John Mullen Connelly

DISTRIBUTED BY: GRUPO COMERCIAL ANAYA
Juan Ignacio Luca de Tena, 15
Tel: 0034 913 938 800
28027 MADRID
SPAIN

DISTRIBUTED BY: ACC PUBLISHING GROUP
Antique Collector's Club Ltd.
Sandy Jane, Old Martlesham
Woodbridge, Suffolk
IP12 45D, UNITED KINGDOM

CS DEL PENEDÈS (DO PENEDÈS)   MILMANDA (DO CONCA DE BARBERÀ)   PRIORAT (DOQ PRIORAT)

DELIGHT IN A DAY *of experiences*
DISCOVER BODEGAS **TORRES**.

dieta mediterránea

For more information:

Tel. 93 817 75 68 / 93 817 74 87 | reservas@torres.es

www.clubtorres.com | **www.facebook.com/bodegastorres**

WINEinMODERATION.eu
Art de Vivre

Wine, only appreciated in moderation.

014dietamediterranea.com

Guía Peñín,
chroniclers of Spanish wines over 25 years

t was in 1990 that this book you are holding came into being. What started as a Guidebook of Spanish Wines and Wine Cellars aimed especially at the at the final consumer was so well accepted in its first edition that it was only a question of time for its influence to reach the level the Guía Peñín brand. It has become an essential tool not only for consumers, avid for information which might help them to delve into this attractive world, but also for professionals all over the world who see it as the perfect tool for the purchase of Spanish wines beyond our frontiers.

The first edition in 1990 contained more than 3,000 wines tasted. Soon those 3,000 became 4,000 (1992-1993) and then 5,000 (2003) until it reached the amazing amount of 10,800, wines in this latest edition of 2015. The influence of the Guía continued to grow, which naturally led us to translate it into German and English and, by inertia, increase its dissemination in the international markets. In recent years we have observed a spectacular increase in the area of influence of the Guía Peñín.

More and more countries see that the scoring of the Guía is the perfect prescription for a deeper knowledge of Spanish wines. It is not by chance that, in recent years, the Guía Peñín has strengthened its presence in third countries through meetings aimed at specialised professionals and journalists. The success of the international meetings organized by the Guía Peñín in Miami, Mexico DF, Tokyo, Shanghai, Hong Kong, Moscow and New York is a response to the positioning which the Guía has achieved in these markets, which means that we must work harder in these areas.

The philosophy of the start of the Guía in its first year (1990) has remained inalterable throughout all its editions. All the wines tasted in the year continue to be described in it regardless of their final classification, which means that no classification is made by scoring or quality, but it simply shows the state of each wine and year at the time oftasting. In addition, the organoleptic analysis of the wines in their production areas together with similar wines is another of the unfailing methods of the Guía Peñín. Evaluating the wines in the framework of production of each zone is another way to efficiently measure wines which progressively seek to be linked to and identified with their areas, through their own varieties, soils and climates although not all achieve this.

Chronic le of Spanish wine in the last quarter of a century

According to the descriptions which the Guía Peñín has been able to make in its uncountable trips, the last 25 years have been of substantial importance in the development of wine growing in Spain. When the Guía began, most producers were trying hard to combat the defects of production, trying to minimize their effects, while taking advantage of the commercial yields of varieties which were being successful abroad, especially stocks originating in France with which the world learned to drink wine.

The passage of time led us to the era of the technical transformation of the wine cellars, which, little by little, assigned a substantial part of their income to technological development to such an extent that the production defects were disappearing. The globalisation which had been progressing since the commencement of the (1990) showed its effects in the world of wine years later, and transformed Spain into a factory of good, attractive and especially inexpensive wine, a burden we continue to carry although work is being done to invert this process.

The rejection generated by the globalization in capitalist societies gave way to an effort to seek differentiation with the cry "we are not all equal". This anxiety for differentiation meant studying our ancestors who had rationally cultivated the ideal varieties for each terrain, seeking the best adaptation to the prevailing soils and climate. Thus, the boom of the autochthonous varieties occurred and this led to a rational restructuring of the vineyards, a slow process which laid down the starting point for many production areas which had been drifting since then. The stage we are at now is perhaps the most interesting one we have experienced. Today, the vineyard is the only protagonist of the wine cellars. The days of the cult of oenology are long gone. Today the most important person is the wine grower. Wine Cellars and Regulatory Boards are assigning substantial financial resources to the study of the soils. They want to know everything about the base which makes their vines grow. The success of the wine cellars with the greatest international projection is based on the study and understanding of these soils and on less intromission through oenology which respects the grape.

In recent years, we have witnessed spectacular growth in wines termed "ecological", a trend which responds to the wish not to interfere in the correct growth of the vine and to guarantee the maximum expression of the grape while respecting the sustainability of the soil and guaranteeing its survival. Moreover, the consumer demands a certificate of those who work faithfully following these premises, however, not all the wine cellars which act ecologically have decided to include such a seal on their wines. For the first time, we have included an index of ecological wines in the Guía Peñín in order to respond to this demand from those consumers who are most aware.

It seems clear that the more immediate future of Spanish wine entails greater development of exports by the wine cellars. The conquest of the international markets must serve to be able to sell all the wine produced in Spain. Thus, we are entering an era in which international relations between wine producers and their markets will establish the commercial success where marketing and communication will play as important a role as the quality of the wine.

These have been our first 25 years of life as chroniclers of Spanish wines. Harvest by harvest we will continue to document the evolution of our wines as best we can: with respect, seriousness and a great deal of passion.

Guía Peñín

TEAM

Carlos González Sáez (Director)
cgonzalez@guiapenin.com

Born in Avila in 1979, Carlos Gonzalez is an Agricultural Engineer (University of Salamanca), with Masters in Enology and Viticulture (Torras and Associates) and a Masters in Wine Business Management (IE Business School). After practicing as a winemaker and vineyard technician, he undertook work as technical director for The Vintages of Spain. For the last eight years he has headed the Technical Department of the Peñín Guide, responsible for the coordination of staff assignments and development of wine tastings that appear in the various guides under the Peñín group.

Javier Luengo (Editor in Chief and taster)
jluengo@guiapenin.com

Born in Castellón de la Plana in 1976, Javier Luengo graduated with a degree in Journalism from the Universidad Complutense of Madrid and is also qualified in Integral Communications, University Francisco de Vitoria. After working as a journalist in different media agencies and publications, he joined the communication department of PI & ERRE as account director. Javier has been a professional taster for the Peñín team for six years, both wines and distillates. He is currently responsible for the different editorial publishing products covered by the Peñín Guide.

Pablo Vecilla (Taster)
pvecilla@guiapenin.com

Born in Madrid in 1985, Pablo studies agricultural technical engineering at the Polytechnic University of Madrid. He has been head of the Cultural Association of La Carrasca, an entity that promotes wine culture in the university, which was also under his responsibility during 2008 and 2009. Pablo joined the Peñín tasting team in 2010. He currently operates the tasting courses organized by the Peñín Tasting School.

ACKNOWLEDGMENTS

To all the Consejos Reguladores that have so readily collaborated with the Guide, providing their buildings and professional staff to make the tastings possible. In other cases it was not their fault but problems on our part that did not make them happen in the end. We have to thank also –and very especially– José Matás from Enoteca Casa Bernal, in El Palmar (Murcia); Juan Luis Pérez de Eulate from La Vinoteca, a wine shop in Palma de Mallorca; Quim Vila from Vila Viniteca, a wine shop in Barcelona; Casa del Vino La Baranda from El Sauzal, and particularly Jorge de Miguel García, as well as the Casa del Vino of Gran Canaria; the Parque Tecnológico del Vino (VITEC), in Falset (Tarragona), and Vinatería Pámpano in Almendralejo (Badajoz).

Ríás Baixas
HOME OF ALBARIÑO

DENOMINACIÓN DE ORIGEN

Ríás Baixas

CONSEJO REGULADOR

XUNTA DE GALICIA · FEADER: Europa inviste no rural · GOBIERNO DE ESPAÑA MINISTERIO DE AGRICULTURA, ALIMENTACIÓN Y MEDIO AMBIENTE

PEÑÍNGUIDE 25 years **to Spanish Wine**

EXCEPTIONAL WINES

Each year, the tasting of more than 10,000 wines provides us with a select group of brands which, due to their high scores, become part of the "exceptional wines" (Page 15) of the Guía Peñín. These are the wines which achieve 95 points and more, which come near to sensorial perfection and become essential references for those seeking wines throughout the world. Each one of these wines can be considered to be the portrait of a specific moment in time, from a particular soil, just like enclosing a moment in time in a bottle in order to enjoy it years later.

The approximately 200 highest scoring wines on this Podium have passed a double "exam" each year. One was the tasting of the wine carried out by each Regulating Board together with similar wines. The other process is the so-called Second Tasting of the Guía Peñín. This second tasting is now a ritual in this firm and is repeated annually in the month of July as a failsafe counter-analysis. I is carried out behind closed doors and our tasters hone the scoring of the wines, which, above 94 points, becomes a task involving millimetres.

The wines are positioned by score, style, variety, harvest and zones over a number of month. Each one of these wines has its glass in front so that after an organoleptic examination and a comparison with wines which have a similar style and scoring, it is possible determine whether the wine in question may rise, keep its initial score or drop if its quality does not settle at the level of the others. The possible improvement of the wine is the result of it improving over the possible tables, 94, 95, 96, 97, 98 in order to guarantee its splendid qualities as regards wines with higher scores so that it it finally perfectly fits one of these tables and obtains a definitive score. This is the fairest and most analytic way for a wine to achieve a high score.

Therefore, we invite you to let yourself be seduced by this exquisite world of grand Spanish wines, a podium which shows what a grand wine can achieve in each of its types.

The triumph of the soil and the vine over technological wines. The knowledge transmitted from grandparents to parents and from these to their children and so on.

EXCEPTIONAL WINES (SWEET WINES AND GENEROSOS)

POINTS	TYPE	DO	PAGE
98 POINTS			
Alvear Solera 1830 PX Reserva	Pedro Ximénez	Montilla-Moriles	311
Casta Diva Reserva Real 2002 B Reserva	Blanco Dulce	Alicante	31
La Bota de Fino (Bota nº 54) FI	Fino	Jerez	229
La Bota de Manzanilla Pasada Nº5 (Bota Punta) MZ	Manzanilla	Jerez	230
La Bota de Palo Cortado nº 47 "Bota NO" PC	Palo Cortado	Jerez	230
La Bota de Palo Cortado nº 51 "Bota GF" PC	Palo Cortado	Jerez	230
Reliquia AM	Amontillado	Jerez	224
97 POINTS			
La Bota de Palo Cortado nº 48 "Bota Punta" PC	Palo Cortado	Jerez	230
Old Mountain 2005 B	Blanco Dulce	Málaga y Sierras de Málaga	287
Osborne Solera BC 200 OL	Oloroso	Jerez	227
Reliquia PC	Palo Cortado	Jerez	224
Reliquia PX	Pedro Ximénez	Jerez	224
Allende Dulce 2011 B	Blanco Dulce	Rioja	614
96 POINTS			
Barbadillo Amontillado VORS AM	Amontillado	Jerez	223
Casta Diva Esencial 2012 B	BlancoDulce	Alicante	31
Don Gonzalo VOS OL	Oloroso	Jerez	235
El Tresillo 1874 Amontillado Viejo AM	Amontillado	Jerez	232
Gonzalez Byass Añada 1982 PC	Palo Cortado	Jerez	231
Jorge Ordóñez & Co. Nº3 Viñas Viejas 2010 B	Blanco Dulce	Málaga y Sierras de Málaga	288
La Cañada PX	Pedro Ximénez	Montilla-Moriles	314
La Diva 2011 B	Blanco Dulce	Alicante	31
Molino Real 2010 B	Blanco	Málaga y Sierras de Málaga	287
Osborne Solera AOS AM	Amontillado	Jerez	227
Reliquia OL	Oloroso	Jerez	224
Solear en Rama MZ	Manzanilla	Jerez	224
Solera de su Majestad VORS 37,5 cl. OL	Oloroso	Jerez	235
Teneguía Malvasía Dulce Estelar 1996 B Gran Reserva	Blanco Naturalmente Dulce	La Palma	273
95 POINTS			
Advent Samso Dulce Natural 2010 RD	Rosado	Penedès	370
Alvear Solera Fundación AM	Amontillado	Montilla-Moriles	311
Alvear Solera Fundación PC	Palo Cortado	Montilla-Moriles	311
Cantocuerdas Moscatel de Grano Menudo 2012 B	Blanco	Vinos de Madrid	797
Carballo Malvasía Dulce Añejo 2001 B Gran Reserva	Blanco	La Palma	271
Casta Diva Cosecha Miel 2013 B	Blanco Dulce	Alicante	31
Chivite Colección 125 Vendimia Tardía 2010 B	Blanco	Navarra	348
De Muller Garnacha Solera 1926 Solera	Solera	Tarragona	697
Dom Joan Fort 1865 Rancio	Rancio	Priorat	406
El Grifo Canari Dulce de Licor B	Blanco	Lanzarote	278
Fino en Rama Navazos, Saca Marzo 2014 FI	Fino	Jerez	229
Humboldt 1997 Blanco dulce	Blanco Dulce	Tacoronte-Acentejo	690
Jorge Ordóñez & Co Nº 2 Victoria 2013 B	Blanco Naturalmente Dulce	Málaga y Sierras de Málaga	288
La Bota de Palo Cortado 52 "Sanlúcar" PC	Palo Cortado	Jerez	230
La Ina FI	Fino	Jerez	233
Lustau VORS PX	Pedro Ximénez	Jerez	234
MR 2011 B	Blanco	Málaga y Sierras de Málaga	287
Oloroso Tradición VORS OL	Oloroso	Jerez	228
Osborne Rare Sherry PX VORS PX	Pedro Ximénez	Jerez	227

Recóndita Armonía 1987 Fondillón	Fondillón	Alicante	31
Recóndita Armonía 2002 Fondillón	Fondillón	Alicante	31
Sacristía AB MZ	Manzanilla	Jerez	236
San León Reserva de Familia MZ	Manzanilla	Jerez	232
Sibarita V.O.R.S. OL	Oloroso	Jerez	227
Tres Palmas FI	Fino	Jerez	232
Viñaredo Tostado 2011 B	Blanco Dulce	Valdeorras	765

95 POINTS

EXCEPTIONAL WINES (RED WINES)

POINTS	TYPE	DO	PAGE
Contador 2012 T	Red Wine	Rioja	547

99 POINTS

Artadi El Carretil 2012 T	Red Wine	Rioja	602
Pingus 2012 T	Red Wine	Ribera del Duero	509
Valbuena 5° 2010 T	Red Wine	Ribera del Duero	497
Victorino 2012 T	Red Wine	Toro	743

98 POINTS

Alabaster 2011 T	Red Wine	Toro	743
Artadi Valdeginés 2012 T	Red Wine	Rioja	602
Artadi Viña El Pisón 2012 T	Red Wine	Rioja	602
Avrvs 2010 T	Red Wine	Rioja	614
Cantos del Diablo 2012 T	Red Wine	Méntrida	302
Finca El Bosque 2011 T	Red Wine	Rioja	640
L'Ermita 2012 TC	Red Wine	Priorat	394
Termanthia 2011 T	Red Wine	Toro	726
Teso La Monja 2010 T	Red Wine	Toro	743
Vega Sicilia Reserva Especial 94/96/00 T	Red Wine	Ribera del Duero	497
Viña Sastre Pesus 2011 T	Red Wine	Ribera del Duero	483

97 POINTS

1902 Cariñena Centenaria 2009 T	Red Wine	Priorat	401
Alto Moncayo 2011 T	Red Wine	Campo de Borja	90
Altos de Lanzaga 2010 T	Red Wine	Rioja	608
Amancio 2010 T	Red Wine	Rioja	640
Artadi La Poza de Ballesteros 2012 T	Red Wine	Rioja	602
Bernabeleva "Carril del Rey" 2012 T	Red Wine	Vinos de Madrid	797
Breca 2012 T	Red Wine	Calatayud	86
Cirsion 2010 T	Red Wine	Rioja	592
Dalmau 2011 TR	Red Wine	Rioja	622
Dominio de Atauta La Mala 2011 TC	Red Wine	Ribera del Duero	509
Dominio de Atauta Llanos del Almendro 2011 T	Red Wine	Ribera del Duero	509
Dominio de Atauta Valdegatiles 2011 T	Red Wine	Ribera del Duero	509
Dominio del Aguila 2010 TR	Red Wine	Ribera del Duero	510
Dominio do Bibei 2011 T	Red Wine	Ribeira Sacra	446
Espectacle 2011 T	Red Wine	Montsant	325
Ferratus Sensaciones Décimo 2003 T	Red Wine	Ribera del Duero	477
Finca La Emperatriz Parcela nº 1 2011 T	Red Wine	Rioja	570
Finca Villacreces Nebro 2011 TC	Red Wine	Ribera del Duero	512
La Cueva del Contador 2012 T	Red Wine	Rioja	547
La Nieta 2012 T	Red Wine	Rioja	639
Las Beatas 2011 T	Red Wine	Rioja	608
Numanthia 2010 T	Red Wine	Toro	726
Pago de Carraovejas El Anejón de la Cuesta de las Liebres 2010 T	Red Wine	Ribera del Duero	518
Quincha Corral 2012 T	Red Wine	Vino de Pago El Terrerazo	818
Regina Vides 2011 T	Red Wine	Ribera del Duero	483
Rumbo al Norte 2012 T	Red Wine	VT CastyLe	879
San Vicente 2010 T	Red Wine	Rioja	631
Sierra Cantabria Colección Privada 2012 T	Red Wine	Rioja	641
Thalarn 2012 T	Red Wine	Costers del Segre	188
Victorino 2011 T	Red Wine	Toro	743

96 POINTS

95 POINTS

Aalto PS 2011 T	Red Wine	Ribera del Duero	463
Abadía Retuerta Pago Garduña Syrah 2011 T	Red Wine	VT CastyLe	868
Abadía Retuerta Pago Negralada 2011 T	Red Wine	VT CastyLe	868
Alabaster 2012 T	Red Wine	Toro	743
Algueira Brancellao 2012 T Roble	Red Wine	Ribeira Sacra	444
Alión 2011 T	Red Wine	Ribera del Duero	498
Aquilón 2011 T	Red Wine	Campo de Borja	90
Arínzano Gran Vino 2008 T	Red Wine	Pago Señorío de Arínzano	820
Aro 2010 T	Red Wine	Rioja	581
Artadi Pagos Viejos 2012 T	Red Wine	Rioja	602
Artuke K4 2012 T	Red Wine	Rioja	544
Blecua 2004 TR	Red Wine	Somontano	678
Bosque de Matasnos Edición Limitada 2010 T	Red Wine	Ribera del Duero	504
Calvario 2010 T	Red Wine	Rioja	614
Castillo Ygay 2005 TGR	Red Wine	Rioja	622
Cenit 2010 T	Red Wine	Tierra del Vino de Zamora	722
Chivite Colección 125 2010 TR	Red Wine	Navarra	348
Clos Erasmus 2012 T Barrica	Red Wine	Priorat	405
Clos Mogador 2011 T	Red Wine	Priorat	405
Congo 2009 T	Red Wine	Méntrida	300
Corteo 2010 T	Red Wine	Jumilla	242
Cortijo Los Aguilares Tadeo 2012 T	Red Wine	Málaga y Sierras de Málaga	288
Dalmau 2009 TR	Red Wine	Rioja	622
Doix 2010 TC	Red Wine	Priorat	401
Dominio de Atauta 2010 T	Red Wine	Ribera del Duero	509
Dominio de Es La Diva 2012 T	Red Wine	Ribera del Duero	509
Don Miguel Comenge 2010 T	Red Wine	Ribera del Duero	506
El Nido 2010 T	Red Wine	Jumilla	242
El Puntido 2010 T	Red Wine	Rioja	639
El Puntido 2011 T	Red Wine	Rioja	639
El Reventón 2012 T	Red Wine	VT CastyLe	879
El Titán del Bendito 2011 T	Red Wine	Toro	737
Finca Dofí 2012 TC	Red Wine	Priorat	394
Finca El Rincón de Clunia 2010 T	Red Wine	VT CastyLe	879
Finca La Emperatriz Terruño 2010 T	Red Wine	Rioja	570
Garnacha de Arrayán 2012 T	Red Wine	VT CastyLe	873
Gaudium Gran Vino 2009 TR	Red Wine	Rioja	576
Gran Reserva 904 Rioja Alta 2004 TGR	Red Wine	Rioja	619
Jiménez-Landi Piélago 2012 T	Red Wine	Méntrida	301
La Basseta 2011 T	Red Wine	Priorat	395
La Mejorada Las Cercas 2010 T	Red Wine	VT CastyLe	878
La Viña de Andrés Romeo 2012 T	Red Wine	Rioja	547
La Viña Escondida 2010 T	Red Wine	Méntrida	300
Lacima 2011 T	Red Wine	Ribeira Sacra	446
Las Lamas 2012 T	Red Wine	Bierzo	60
Les Manyes 2011 T	Red Wine	Priorat	413
Matallana 2010 T	Red Wine	Ribera del Duero	506
Pago de Mirabel 2013 T	Red Wine	VT Extremadura	888
Pasos de San Martín 2012 T	Red Wine	Navarra	346
PSI 2012 T	Red Wine	Ribera del Duero	509
Pujanza Norte 2011 T	Red Wine	Rioja	605
Ramblis Monastrell 2012 T	Red Wine	Alicante	37
Rejón 2012 T	Red Wine	VT CastyLe	876
San Vicente 2011 T	Red Wine	Rioja	631
Sierra Cantabria Colección Privada 2011 T	Red Wine	Rioja	640
Somni Magnum 2011 T	Red Wine	Priorat	404
St. Antoni de Scala Dei 2010 T	Red Wine	Priorat	403
Terreus 2011 T	Red Wine	VT CastyLe	875
Tros de Clos Magnum 2010 T	Red Wine	Priorat	404
Villa de Corullón 2012 T	Red Wine	Bierzo	61
Viña Sastre Pago de Santa Cruz 2011 T	Red Wine	Ribera del Duero	483

EXCEPTIONAL WINES (SPARKLING WINES)

POINTS	TYPE	DO	PAGE	
Gramona Enoteca Finca La Plana 2000 BN Gran Reserva	Brut Nature	Cava	135	**98** POINTS
Gramona Celler Batlle 2004 BR Gran Reserva	Brut	Cava	135	**97** POINTS
Enoteca Personal Manuel Raventos 1998 BN	Brut Nature	Vinos Espumosos	908	**96** POINTS
Gramona Enoteca Finca La Plana 2000 BR Gran Reserva	Brut	Cava	135	
Turo d'en Mota 2001 BN Gran Reserva	Brut Nature	Cava	159	
Cava Llopart Original 1887 2008 BN Gran Reserva	Brut Nature	Cava	149	**95** POINTS
Enoteca Personal Manuel Raventos 1999 BN	Brut Nature	Vinos Espumosos	909	
Recaredo Reserva Particular 2004 BN Gran Reserva	Brut Nature	Cava	159	
Reserva Real BR Gran Reserva	Brut	Cava	143	

EXCEPTIONAL WINES (WHITE WINES)

POINTS	TYPE	DO	PAGE	
Pazo Señorans Selección de Añada 2007 B	White Wine	Rias Baixas	434	**98** POINTS
Albariño de Fefiñanes III año 2011 B	White Wine	Rias Baixas	423	**97** POINTS
Mártires 2013 B	White Wine	Rioja	614	
As Sortes 2012 B	White Wine	Valdeorras	768	**96** POINTS
Chivite Colección 125 2012 BFB	White Wine	Navarra	348	
Mártires 2012 B	White Wine	Rioja	614	
Naiades 2011 BFB	White Wine	Rueda	658	
Qué Bonito Cacareaba 2013 B	White Wine	Rioja	547	
Branco de Santa Cruz 2011 B	White Wine	Valdeorras	767	**95** POINTS
Edetària 2011 B	White Wine	Terra Alta	708	
La Bota de Florpower "Mas allá" 2010 B	White Wine	Vino de Mesa/Vino	917	
La Comtesse 2010 B	White Wine	Rias Baixas	433	
Nisia 2013 B	White Wine	Rueda	659	
Nora da Neve 2010 BFB	White Wine	Rias Baixas	439	
Piesdescalzos 2012 B	White Wine	Vinos de Madrid	798	
Valdesil Godello sobre Lías 2007 B	White Wine	Valdeorras	769	

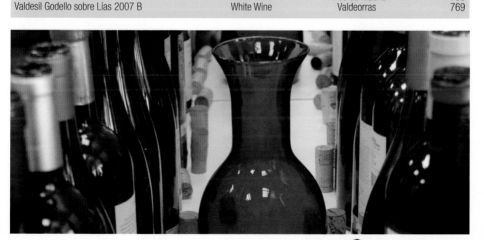

WINERIES and the TASTING of the WINES by DESIGNATION of ORIGIN

SCORING SYSTEM

95-100 EXCEPTIONAL
The wine excels among those of the same type, vintage and origin. It is in every sense extraordinary. It is full of complexity, with abundant sensory elements both on the nose and on the palate that arise from the combination of soil, grape variety, winemaking and ageing methods; elegant and utterly outstanding, it exceeds average commercial standards and in some cases it may still be unknown to the general public.

90-94 EXCELLENT
A wine with the same attributes as those indicated above but with less exceptional or significant characteristics.

85-89 VERY GOOD
The wine stands out thanks to features acquired through great winemaking and/or ageing standards, or an exceptional varietal character. It is a wine with unique features, although it may lack soil or terroir expression.

80-84 GOOD
Although not as distinctive, the wine expresses the basic characteristics of both its type and region of origin.

70-79 AVERAGE
The wine has no defects, but no virtues either.

60-69 NOT RECOMMENDED
It is a non-acceptable wine in which some faults are evident, although they may not spoil the overall flavour.

50-59 FAULTY
A non-acceptable wine from a sensory point of view that may be oxidised or have defects due to bad ageing or late racking; it may be an old wine past its best or a young wine with unfavourable fermentation off-odours.

ABBREVIATIONS

B	WHITE	AM	AMONTILLADO
BC	AGED WHITE	PX	PEDRO XIMÉNEZ(SWEET)
BFB	BARREL-FERMENTED WHITE	PC	PALO CORTADO
RD	ROSÉ	CR	CREAM
T	RED	PCR	PALE CREAM
TC	RED AGED (CRIANZA)	GE	GENEROSO (FORTIFIED)
TR	RED AGED (RESERVA)	ESP	SPARKLING
TGR	RED AGED (GRAN RESERVA)	BR	BRUT
FI	FINO	BN	BRUT NATURE
MZ	MANZANILLA	SC	DRY
OL	OLOROSO	SS	SEMI-DRY
OLV	OLOROSO VIEJO (OLD OLOROSO)	S/C	SIN COSECHA (NON-VINTAGE)

- 🗹 = ORGANIC WINES

- D.O.P. = DENOMINACIÓN DE ORIGEN PROTEGIDA

- I.G.P. = INDICACIÓN GEOGRÁFICA PROTEGIDA

- SC = Unrated

DO. ABONA

CONSEJO REGULADOR

Martín Rodríguez, 9
38588 Porís de Abona - Arico (Santa Cruz de Tenerife)
☎ :+34 922 164 241 - Fax: +34 922 164 135
@: vinosdeabona@vinosdeabona.com
www.vinosdeabona.com

LOCATION:

In the southern area of the island of Tenerife, with vineyards which occupy the slopes of the Teide down to the coast. It covers the municipal districts of Adeje, Arona, Vilaflor, San Miguel de Abona, Granadilla de Abona, Arico and Fasnia.

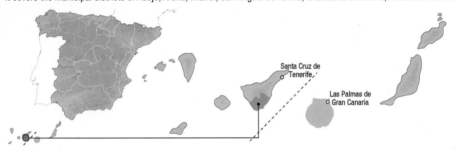

GRAPE VARIETIES:

White: albillo, marmajuelo, forastera blanca, güal, malvasía, moscatel alejandría, sabro, verdello, vijariego, baboso blanco, listán blanco, pedro ximénez and torrontés.
Red: castellana negra, listán negro, malvasía rosada, negramoll, tintilla, baboso negro, cabernet sauvignon, listán prieto, merlot, moscatel negro, pinot noir, ruby cabernet, syrah, tempranillo and vijariego negro.

FIGURES:

Vineyard surface: 946 – Wine-Growers: 1,228 – Wineries: 19 – 2013 Harvest rating: Very Good – Production 2013: 710,000 litres – Market percentages: 100% domestic

SOIL:

Distinction can be made between the sandy and calcareous soil inland and the more clayey, well drained soil of the higher regions, seeing as they are volcanic. The so-called 'Jable' soil is very typical, and is simply a very fine whitish volcanic sand, used by the local winegrower to cover the vineyards in order to retain humidity in the ground and to prevent weeds from growing. The vineyards are located at altitudes which range between 300 and 1,750 m (the better quality grapes are grown in the higher regions), which determines different grape harvesting dates in a period spanning the beginning of August up to October.

CLIMATE:

Mediterranean on the coastal belt, and gradually cools down inland as a result of the trade winds. Rainfall varies between 350 mm per year on the coast and 550 mm inland. In the highest region, Vilaflor, the vineyards do not benefit from these winds as they face slightly west. Nevertheless, the more than 200 Ha of this small plateau produce wines with an acidity of 8 g/l due to the altitude, but with an alcohol content of 13%, as this area of the island has the longest hours of sunshine.

VINTAGE RATING   PEÑINGUIDE

2009	2010	2011	2012	2013
GOOD	EXCELLENT	VERY GOOD	VERY GOOD	GOOD

 to Spanish Wine

ALTOS DE TR3VEJOS

La Iglesia, 1
San Miguel de Abona
(Santa Cruz de Tenerife)
☎: +34 650 937 340
www.altosdetrevejos.com
trevejos@altosdetrevejos.com

Altos de Tr3vejos BN
listán blanco, verdello
84

Altos de Tr3vejos 2012 T
baboso negro, syrah
86
Colour: black cherry, purple rim. Nose: powerfull, warm, scrubland, fruit preserve. Palate: good structure, concentrated, long.

Aromas de Tr3vejos 2013 B
malvasía, moscatel
89
Nose: powerfull, floral, honeyed notes, candied fruit, fragrant herbs. Palate: flavourful, sweet, fresh, fruity, good acidity, long.

BODEGA REVERÓN

Ctra. Gral. Vilaflor, Los Quemados, 8
38620 Vilaflor (Santa Cruz de Tenerife)
☎: +34 922 725 044
Fax: +34 922 725 044
www.bodegareveron.com
bodega@bodegareveron.com

Los Quemados 2013 B
100% albillo
85

Los Quemados 2013 BFB
100% albillo
88
Colour: bright yellow. Nose: powerfull, ripe fruit, sweet spices, creamy oak, fragrant herbs. Palate: rich, smoky aftertaste, flavourful, fresh, good acidity.

Los Quemados 2013 T
87
Colour: cherry, purple rim. Nose: expressive, fruit expression, balanced. Palate: good structure, fruity, flavourful.

Pago Reverón 2013 T
listán negro, tempranillo, castellana, otras
86 🌷
Colour: deep cherry, purple rim. Nose: medium intensity, red berry notes, balanced. Palate: correct, ripe fruit, good finish.

Pagos Reverón 2011 TC
86
Colour: very deep cherry, garnet rim. Nose: ripe fruit, spicy, balanced. Palate: fruity, good finish.

Pagos Reverón 2013 B
85 🌷

Pagos Reverón 2013 RD
listán negro, tempranillo, otras
84

Pagos Reverón Afrutado 2013 B
85

Pagos Reverón Naturalmente Dulce B
listán blanco
87
Colour: bright golden. Nose: powerfull, candied fruit, dried fruit, toasty. Palate: powerful, rich.

BODEGA SAN MIGUEL

Ctra. General del Sur, 5
38620 San Miguel de Abona
(Santa Cruz de Tenerife)
☎: +34 922 700 300
Fax: +34 922 700 301
bodega@casanmiguel.com

Chasnero 2013 B
86
Colour: bright straw. Nose: fresh, fresh fruit, white flowers, fragrant herbs. Palate: flavourful, fruity, good acidity, balanced.

Marqués de Fuente 2011 TC
87
Colour: cherry, garnet rim. Nose: spicy, creamy oak, toasty, balsamic herbs, ripe fruit. Palate: light-bodied, good finish, fruity.

Marqués de Fuente 2013 B
85

Marqués de Fuente 25 Aniversario 2013 B Roble
86
Colour: bright yellow. Nose: powerfull, ripe fruit, white flowers, sweet spices. Palate: rich, fruity, correct.

Marqués de Fuente s/c T
86
Colour: very deep cherry. Nose: medium intensity, ripe fruit. Palate: fruity, easy to drink, balsamic.

MENCEY CHASNA

Marta, 3 Chimiche
38594 Granadilla de Abona
(Santa Cruz de Tenerife)
☎: +34 922 777 285
Fax: +34 922 777 259
www.menceychasna.es
ventas@menceychasna.com

Los Tableros 2013 B Barrica
listán blanco, moscatel de alejandría, malvasía

85

Los Tableros 2013 T Barrica
vijariego negro, syrah

86

Colour: light cherry. Nose: medium intensity, sweet spices, balsamic herbs, ripe fruit. Palate: correct, easy to drink.

Los Tableros Afrutado 2013 B
listán blanco, moscatel de alejandría, malvasía

84

Los Tableros Ecológico 2013 B
listán blanco

86

Colour: bright straw. Nose: medium intensity, faded flowers, wild herbs. Palate: correct, balanced, long, fine bitter notes.

Los Tableros Ecológico 2013 T
tempranillo, ruby cabernet, syrah

86

Colour: bright cherry. Nose: ripe fruit, sweet spices, wild herbs. Palate: fruity, good acidity, correct.

Mencey Chasna 2013 B
listán blanco

86

Colour: bright straw. Nose: fresh, fresh fruit, white flowers, expressive. Palate: flavourful, fruity, good acidity, balanced.

Mencey Chasna 2013 T
listán negro, tempranillo, ruby cabernet, syrah

86

Colour: light cherry, garnet rim. Nose: medium intensity, scrubland, balanced. Palate: easy to drink, good finish.

S. COOP. CUMBRES DE ABONA

Camino del Viso, s/n Teguedite
38580 Arico (Santa Cruz de Tenerife)
☎: +34 922 768 604
Fax: +34 922 768 234
www.cumbresdeabona.es
bodega@cumbresdeabona.es

Cumbres de Abona 2013 T
listán negro, ruby cabernet, tempranillo

86

Colour: deep cherry, purple rim. Nose: red berry notes, ripe fruit, wild herbs. Palate: flavourful, balanced.

Flor de Chasna Cuatro Meses 2013 T Barrica
syrah

88

Colour: bright cherry, purple rim. Nose: violet drops, ripe fruit, expressive. Palate: spicy, good structure, round tannins.

Flor de Chasna Naturalmente Dulce 2010 T
syrah, tempranillo

82

Flor de Chasna Seco 2013 B
listán blanco

87

Colour: bright straw. Nose: wild herbs, medium intensity, balanced, fresh fruit. Palate: long, balsamic, fine bitter notes, good acidity.

Flor de Chasna Tradición 2013 T
tempranillo, ruby cabernet, listán negro

87

Colour: very deep cherry, purple rim. Nose: powerfull, characterful, ripe fruit, dried herbs. Palate: good structure, spicy.

Testamento Malvasía 2013 BFB
malvasía

88

Colour: bright yellow. Nose: powerfull, ripe fruit, sweet spices, creamy oak, fragrant herbs. Palate: rich, smoky aftertaste, flavourful, fresh, good acidity.

Testamento Malvasía Dry 2013 B
malvasía

87

Colour: bright yellow. Nose: white flowers, expressive, balanced, powerfull. Palate: fruity, flavourful, fine bitter notes.

Testamento Malvasía Dulce 2013 Blanco dulce
malvasía

86

Colour: bright yellow. Nose: white flowers, medium intensity. Palate: correct, balanced, easy to drink.

Testamento Malvasía Esencia 2008 B
malvasía

90

Colour: golden. Nose: powerfull, floral, honeyed notes, candied fruit, dried flowers, faded flowers. Palate: flavourful, sweet, fresh, fruity, long, good acidity.

TIERRA DE FRONTOS

Lomo Grande, 1- Los Blanquitos
38600 Granadilla de Abona
(Santa Cruz de Tenerife)
☎: +34 922 777 253
Fax: +34 922 777 246
www.frontos.es
bodega@frontos.es

Tierra de Frontos 2012 T
100% baboso negro

89

Colour: cherry, garnet rim. Nose: ripe fruit, spicy, complex, earthy notes. Palate: powerful, flavourful, toasty, round tannins.

Tierra de Frontos 2013 B
verdello, marmajuelo, albillo

86

Colour: bright straw. Nose: balanced, floral, dried herbs. Palate: fruity, easy to drink, fine bitter notes.

Tierra Frontos Blanco Seco Ecológico 2013 B
100% listán blanco

86 ⚘

Colour: bright straw. Nose: wild herbs, fresh fruit. Palate: balanced, fruity, light-bodied, easy to drink.

DO. ALELLA

CONSEJO REGULADOR

Avda. San Mateu, 2 - Masía Can Magarola
08328 Alella (Barcelona)
☎:+34 935 559 153 - Fax: +34 935 405 249
@: doalella@doalella.org
www.doalella.org

LOCATION:

It extends over the regions of El Maresme and el Vallès in Barcelona. It covers the municipal districts of Alella, Argentona, Cabrils, El Masnou, La Roca del Vallès, Martorelles, Montornès del Vallès, Montgat, Orrius, Premià de Dalt, Premià de Mar, Santa Mª de Martorelles, Sant Fost de Campsentelles, Teià, Tiana, Vallromanes, Vilanova del Vallès and Vilasar de Salt. The main feature of this region is the urban environment which surrounds this small stretch of vineyards; in fact, one of the smallest DO's in Spain.

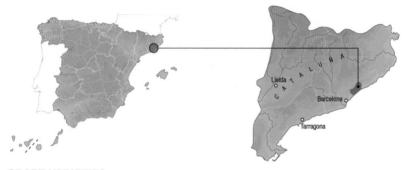

GRAPE VARIETIES:

White: Pansa Blanca (similar to the Xarel·lo from other regions in Catalonia), Garnatxa Blanca, Pansa Rosada, Picapoll, Malvasía, Macabeo, Parellada, Chardonnay, Sauvignon Blanc and Chenin Blanc.
Red (minority): Garnatxa Negra, Ull de Llebre (Tempranillo), Merlot, Pinot Noir, Syrah, Monastrell, Cabernet Sauvignon, Sumoll and Mataró.

FIGURES:

Vineyard surface: 227.91 – Wine-Growers: 57 – Wineries: 8 – 2013 Harvest rating: - – Production 12: 711,503 litres – Market percentages: 86% domestic - 14% export.

SOIL:

Distinction can be made between the clayey soils of the interior slope of the coastal mountain range and the soil situated along the coastline. The latter, known as Sauló, is the most typical. Almost white in colour, it is renowned for it high permeability and great capacity to retain sunlight, which makes for a better ripening of the grapes.

CLIMATE:

A typically Mediterranean microclimate with mild winters and hot dry summers. The coastal hills play an important role, as they protect the vines from cold winds and condense the humidity from the sea.

VINTAGE RATING   PEÑÍNGUIDE

2009	2010	2011	2012	2013
GOOD	VERY GOOD	VERY GOOD	VERY GOOD	VERY GOOD

ALELLA VINÍCOLA

Angel Guimerà, 62
08328 Alella (Barcelona)
☎: +34 935 403 842
Fax: +34 935 401 648
www.alellavinicola.com
xavi@alellavinicola.com

Costa del Maresme 2008 T
100% garnacha

89

Colour: cherry, garnet rim. Nose: ripe fruit, spicy, creamy oak, toasty, complex, tobacco. Palate: powerful, flavourful, toasty, round tannins.

Ivori 2012 B

87

Colour: bright yellow. Nose: ripe fruit, candied fruit, sweet spices, faded flowers. Palate: toasty, long, fine bitter notes, fruity.

Ivori Negre 2009 T

91

Colour: cherry, garnet rim. Nose: ripe fruit, spicy, creamy oak, toasty, complex, earthy notes, scrubland. Palate: powerful, flavourful, toasty, round tannins.

Marfil 2011 TC

85

Marfil Blanc de Noirs 2010 BR Reserva
100% garnacha

87

Colour: bright yellow. Nose: medium intensity, dried herbs. Palate: fresh, easy to drink.

Marfil Blanco Seco 2013 B
100% pansa blanca

85

Marfil Clàssic 2013 B

85

Marfil Generoso Seco Solera 1976 B
100% pansa blanca

91

Colour: light mahogany. Nose: complex, expressive, pungent, saline, dry nuts, aged wood nuances. Palate: rich, powerful, fresh, fine bitter notes, balanced.

Marfil Generoso Semi Solera 1976 B
100% pansa blanca

92

Colour: light mahogany. Nose: honeyed notes, candied fruit, fragrant herbs, acetaldehyde, spicy. Palate: flavourful, good acidity, long, sweetness, elegant.

Marfil Molt Dolç 2003 B
100% pansa blanca

93

Colour: dark mahogany. Nose: dry nuts, powerfull, toasty, aged wood nuances, dried fruit, pattiserie, honeyed notes. Palate: flavourful, fruity, spicy, toasty, long, balanced.

Marfil Moscatel 2010 ESP
100% moscatel

90

Colour: bright straw. Nose: white flowers, fresh, varietal, expressive. Palate: balanced, good acidity, fine bitter notes, sweet.

Marfil Rosado 2010 BR
100% garnacha

86

Colour: coppery red. Nose: floral, jasmine, fragrant herbs, candied fruit. Palate: fresh, fruity, flavourful, correct.

Marfil Rosat 2013 RD
100% merlot

84

Marfil Violeta 2003 T
100% garnacha

91

Colour: bright cherry, garnet rim. Nose: acetaldehyde, varnish, candied fruit. Palate: fruity, flavourful, sweet.

Mayla Rosado de Aguja Natural 2013 RD

83

Vallmora 2009 T
100% garnacha

87

Colour: deep cherry, garnet rim. Nose: powerfull, warm, ripe fruit, tobacco, wild herbs. Palate: correct, ripe fruit, long.

ALTA ALELLA S.L.

Camí Baix de Tiana s/n
08328 Alella (Barcelona)
☎: +34 934 693 720
Fax: +34 934 691 343
www.altaalella.cat
info@altaalella.cat

AA Blanc de Neu 2013 BFB
pansa blanca

91

Colour: golden. Nose: powerfull, floral, honeyed notes, candied fruit, fragrant herbs, acetaldehyde. Palate: flavourful, sweet, fresh, fruity, good acidity, long, balanced.

AA Dolç Mataró 2012 Tinto dulce
mataró

92

Colour: dark-red cherry, garnet rim. Nose: candied fruit, balsamic herbs, aromatic coffee, toasty. Palate: balanced, rich, flavourful, long, spicy.

AA Lanius 2013 BFB
pansa blanca

91 🌷

Colour: bright straw. Nose: fresh, fresh fruit, white flowers, expressive, spicy. Palate: flavourful, fruity, good acidity, balanced.

AA Orbus 2011 T
syrah

90 🌷

Colour: deep cherry, purple rim. Nose: expressive, balanced, ripe fruit, creamy oak. Palate: good structure, good finish, round tannins.

AA Pansa Blanca 2013 B
pansa blanca

87 🌷

Colour: bright straw. Nose: dried herbs, floral, ripe fruit. Palate: flavourful, fresh, easy to drink.

AA Parvus Chardonnay 2013 B
chardonnay

88 🌷

Colour: bright straw. Nose: white flowers, fragrant herbs, fruit expression. Palate: fresh, fruity, flavourful, balanced, elegant.

AA Parvus Rosé 2013 RD
cabernet sauvignon, syrah

86 🌷

Colour: light cherry. Nose: elegant, dried flowers, red berry notes, wild herbs. Palate: light-bodied, flavourful, good acidity, spicy.

AA Parvus Syrah 2012 T
syrah

87 🌷

Colour: bright cherry, purple rim. Nose: red berry notes, ripe fruit, floral, varietal. Palate: powerful, easy to drink, correct.

AA PS Xtrem 2012 TC
syrah

87 🌷

Colour: very deep cherry, purple rim. Nose: medium intensity, ripe fruit, scrubland. Palate: fruity, easy to drink, good finish.

AA Tallarol 2013 B
pansa blanca

88 🌷

Colour: bright straw. Nose: faded flowers, fresh fruit, wild herbs. Palate: light-bodied, easy to drink, good finish.

BODEGAS CASTILLO DE SAJAZARRA

Del Río, s/n
26212 Sajazarra (La Rioja)
☎: +34 941 320 066
Fax: +34 941 320 251
www.castillodesajazarra.com
bodega@castillodesajazarra.com

In Vita 2012 B

89

Colour: bright straw. Nose: white flowers, fragrant herbs, fruit expression, spicy. Palate: fresh, fruity, flavourful, elegant.

In Vita 2013 B

89

Colour: bright straw. Nose: white flowers, dried herbs, fresh. Palate: balanced, good acidity, fine bitter notes, long.

BODEGAS ROURA - JUAN ANTONIO PÉREZ ROURA

Valls de Rials
08328 Alella (Barcelona)
☎: +34 933 527 456
Fax: +34 933 524 339
www.roura.es
roura@roura.es

Roura Coupage 2012 T
87
Colour: cherry, garnet rim. Nose: ripe fruit, spicy, creamy oak, toasty, scrubland. Palate: powerful, flavourful, toasty, round tannins.

Roura Crianza Tres Ceps 2010 TC
88
Colour: dark-red cherry, garnet rim. Nose: ripe fruit, scrubland, spicy. Palate: balanced, spicy, balsamic, round tannins.

Roura Merlot 2010 T
100% merlot
86
Colour: dark-red cherry. Nose: scrubland, balanced, ripe fruit, old leather. Palate: flavourful, fruity, easy to drink.

Roura Merlot 2013 RD
merlot
84

Roura Sauvignon Blanc 2013 B
sauvignon blanc
88
Colour: bright straw. Nose: white flowers, fragrant herbs, fruit expression. Palate: fresh, fruity, flavourful, balanced.

Roura Xarel.lo 2013 B
xarel.lo
87
Colour: bright straw. Nose: white flowers, fresh fruit, expressive, wild herbs. Palate: flavourful, fruity, good acidity.

BOUQUET D'ALELLA

Sant Josep de Calassanç, 8
08328 Alella (Barcelona)
☎: +34 935 556 997
bouquetda@bouquetdalella.com

Bouquet D'A Blanc + 2012 BFB
pansa blanca, garnacha blanca
91
Colour: bright yellow. Nose: powerfull, ripe fruit, sweet spices, creamy oak, fragrant herbs. Palate: rich, flavourful, fresh, good acidity, long.

Bouquet D'A Blanc 2013 B
pansa blanca, garnacha blanca
87
Colour: bright straw. Nose: fresh, fresh fruit, white flowers, wild herbs, dry stone. Palate: flavourful, fruity, balanced.

Bouquet D'A Garnatxa Negra 2013 T
garnacha
89
Colour: cherry, garnet rim. Nose: ripe fruit, wild herbs, earthy notes, spicy, creamy oak. Palate: balanced, flavourful, long, balsamic.

Bouquet D'A Syrah 2011 T
syrah
87
Colour: cherry, garnet rim. Nose: fruit preserve, fruit liqueur notes, spicy, balsamic herbs. Palate: flavourful, pruney, correct.

MARQUÉS DE ALELLA

Camí de Can Garra, s/n
08391 Tiana (Barcelona)
☎: +34 935 153 100
www.marquesdealella.es
info@parxet.es

Galactica 2011 B
100% pansa blanca
90
Colour: bright yellow. Nose: powerfull, ripe fruit, sweet spices, creamy oak, fragrant herbs. Palate: rich, smoky aftertaste, flavourful, fresh, good acidity.

Marqués de Alella Allier 2011 BFB
chardonnay
91
Colour: bright yellow. Nose: ripe fruit, candied fruit, dried flowers, toasty, sweet spices. Palate: rich, long, toasty.

Marqués de Alella Pansa Blanca 2013 B
100% pansa blanca
89
Colour: bright straw. Nose: citrus fruit, fresh fruit, balanced. Palate: flavourful, varietal, full, balanced, fine bitter notes.

DO ALELLA / D.O.P

Marqués de Alella Pansa Rosada 2013 RD
100% pansa rosada

89 ☘

Colour: onion pink. Nose: elegant, candied fruit, dried flowers, fragrant herbs, red berry notes. Palate: light-bodied, flavourful, good acidity, long, spicy.

Marqués de Alella Viognier 2012 B
100% viognier

88 ☘

Colour: bright golden. Nose: ripe fruit, faded flowers, spicy, expressive. Palate: flavourful, dry, fine bitter notes.

Perfum de Pansa Blanca 2010 B
100% pansa blanca

87 ☘

Colour: old gold. Nose: ripe fruit, dried herbs, dried flowers, aged wood nuances. Palate: powerful, flavourful, dry, spicy.

Perfum Viognier Dulce 2011 B
100% viognier

90 ☘

Colour: bright golden. Nose: ripe fruit, dry nuts, powerfull, toasty, aged wood nuances. Palate: flavourful, fruity, spicy, toasty, long.

Sepo 2013 B
100% pansa blanca

87 ☘

Colour: yellow, greenish rim. Nose: fresh fruit, dried flowers, wild herbs. Palate: flavourful, balanced, good acidity, fine bitter notes.

TESTUAN
Carrer dels Roures, 3
08348 Cabrils (Barcelona)
☎: +34 679 448 722
www.testuan.com
info@testuan.com

3 de Testuan 2013 B
86

Colour: bright straw. Nose: fresh fruit, white flowers, dried herbs. Palate: flavourful, fruity, good acidity.

DO. ALICANTE

CONSEJO REGULADOR

Monjas, 6
03002 Alicante
☎:+34 965 984 478 - Fax: +34 965 229 295
@: crdo.alicante@crdo-alicante.org
www.crdo-alicante.org

LOCATION:

In the province of Alicante (covering 51 municipal districts), and a small part of the province of Murcia. The vineyards extend over areas close to the coast (in the surroundings of the capital city of Alicante, and especially in the area of La Marina, a traditional producer of Moscatel), as well as in the interior of the province.

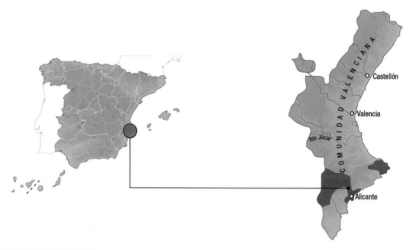

GRAPE VARIETIES:

White: Merseguera, Moscatel de Alejandría, Macabeo, Planta Fina, Verdil, Airén, Chardonnay and Sauvignon Blanc.
Red: Monastrell, Garnacha Tinta (Alicante or Giró), Garnacha Tintorera, Bobal, Tempranillo, Cabernet Sauvignon, Merlot, Pinot Noir, Syrah and Petit Verdot.

FIGURES:

Vineyard surface: 9,522 – Wine-Growers: 1,819 – Wineries: 39 – 2013 Harvest rating: Very Good – Production 13: 14,665,625 litres – Market percentages: 76.95% domestic - 23.05% export.

SOIL:

In general, the majority of the soils in the region are of a dun limestone type, with little clay and hardly any organic matter.

CLIMATE:

Distinction must be made between the vineyards situated closer to the coastline, where the climate is clearly Mediterranean and somewhat more humid, and those inland, which receive continental influences and have a lower level of rainfall.

VINTAGE RATING   PEÑÍNGUIDE

2009	2010	2011	2012	2013
VERY GOOD	VERY GOOD	VERY GOOD	VERY GOOD	VERY GOOD

BODEGA COOP, DE ALGUEÑA COOP. V.

Ctra. Rodriguillo, km. 29,5
03668 Algueña (Alicante)
☎: +34 965 476 113
Fax: +34 965 476 229
www.vinosdealguenya.com
bodega@vinosdealguenya.es

Alhenia 2011 T
monastrell
88 🌱
Colour: bright cherry. Nose: ripe fruit, sweet spices, creamy oak, expressive. Palate: flavourful, fruity, toasty, round tannins.

Casa Jiménez 2010 TC
monastrell
85

Dominio de Torreviñas 2013 B
verdil
84

Dominio de Torreviñas Doble Pasta 2012 T
monastrell
85

Fondillón 1980 Fondillón
monastrell
90
Colour: mahogany. Nose: complex, fruit liqueur notes, dried fruit, pattiserie, toasty. Palate: sweet, rich, unctuous, powerful.

Fondonet Vino de Licor Dulce 2010 T
monastrell
87
Colour: cherry, garnet rim. Nose: fruit preserve, ripe fruit, spicy, toasty, aged wood nuances, dark chocolate, aromatic coffee. Palate: powerful, flavourful, sweetness.

BODEGA NUESTRA SEÑORA DE LAS VIRTUDES COOP. V.

Ctra. de Yecla, 9
03400 Villena (Alicante)
☎: +34 965 802 187
www.coopvillena.com
coopvillena@coopvillena.com

Vinalopó 2008 TR
80

Vinalopó 2010 TC
86
Colour: cherry, garnet rim. Nose: ripe fruit, spicy, creamy oak, toasty. Palate: powerful, flavourful, toasty, round tannins.

Vinalopó 2013 RD
100% monastrell
87
Colour: rose, purple rim. Nose: powerfull, ripe fruit, red berry notes, floral, expressive. Palate: powerful, fruity, fresh.

Vinalopó 2013 T
87
Colour: cherry, purple rim. Nose: expressive, fresh fruit, red berry notes, floral. Palate: flavourful, fruity, good acidity, round tannins.

Vinalopó Sauvignon Blanc 2013 B
100% sauvignon blanc
83

Vinalopó Selección 2012 T
85

BODEGA SANTA CATALINA DEL MAÑÁN

Ctra. Monóvar-Pinoso, Km. 10,5
03649 Mañán Monóvar (Alicante)
☎: +34 966 960 096
Fax: +34 966 960 096
bodegamanan@gmail.com

Gran Mañán Moscatel
moscatel
86
Colour: bright straw. Nose: fruit liqueur notes, white flowers, powerfull, ripe fruit. Palate: fruity, flavourful, sweetness.

Torrent del Mañá RD
monastrell, tempranillo
88
Colour: onion pink. Nose: elegant, candied fruit, dried flowers, fragrant herbs, red berry notes. Palate: light-bodied, flavourful, good acidity, long, spicy.

Torrent del Mañá 2012 TR
86
Colour: cherry, purple rim. Nose: scrubland, ripe fruit, balanced. Palate: correct, ripe fruit, easy to drink.

Torrent del Mañá 2013 B
airén, merseguera
85

BODEGA VINESSENS

Ctra. de Caudete, Km. 1
03400 Villena (Alicante)
☎: +34 965 800 265
Fax: +34 965 800 265
www.vinessens.es
comercial@vinessens.es

El Telar 2011 TC
92
Colour: very deep cherry, garnet rim. Nose: powerfull, complex, ripe fruit, dark chocolate, creamy oak, scrubland.

Essens 2013 BFB
chardonnay
90
Colour: bright yellow. Nose: ripe fruit, sweet spices, creamy oak, fragrant herbs, balanced. Palate: rich, flavourful, fresh, elegant.

Sein 2011 TC
91
Colour: cherry, garnet rim. Nose: ripe fruit, spicy, creamy oak, toasty, complex, mineral. Palate: powerful, flavourful, toasty, round tannins, elegant.

Sein 2012 TC
90
Colour: cherry, garnet rim. Nose: spicy, creamy oak, toasty, complex, earthy notes, overripe fruit. Palate: powerful, flavourful, toasty, round tannins.

BODEGAS ANTONIO LLOBELL

Avda. Santa Catalina, 82
03725 Teulada (Alicante)
☎: +34 667 964 751
www.misteladeteulada.com
info@misteladeteulada.com

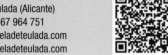

Cap d'Or 2013 B
moscatel de alejandría
90
Colour: golden. Nose: powerfull, floral, honeyed notes, candied fruit, fragrant herbs. Palate: flavourful, sweet, fresh, fruity, good acidity, long, balanced.

Cims del Mediterrani Mistela B
100% moscatel
90
Colour: golden. Nose: powerfull, floral, honeyed notes, white flowers. Palate: flavourful, sweet, fruity, good acidity, long.

BODEGAS BERNABÉ NAVARRO

Ctra. Villena-Cañada, Km. 3
03400 Villena (Alicante)
☎: +34 966 770 353
Fax: +34 966 770 353
www.bodegasbernabenavarro.com
info@bodegasbernabenavarro.com

Beryna 2012 TC
92
Colour: cherry, garnet rim. Nose: ripe fruit, wild herbs, earthy notes, spicy, creamy oak. Palate: balanced, flavourful, long, balsamic.

Casa Balaguer 2011 T
93
Colour: cherry, garnet rim. Nose: ripe fruit, spicy, creamy oak, complex, balsamic herbs, mineral, fine reductive notes. Palate: powerful, flavourful, toasty, round tannins, balanced.

Curro 2011 T
monastrell
92
Colour: cherry, garnet rim. Nose: balsamic herbs, floral, mineral, spicy, expressive, fruit preserve, fruit liqueur notes. Palate: flavourful, balsamic, spicy, long, balanced.

BODEGAS BOCOPA

Paraje Les Pedreres, Autovía A-31, km. 200 - 201
03610 Petrer (Alicante)
☎: +34 966 950 489
Fax: +34 966 950 406
www.bocopa.com
info@bocopa.com

Alcanta 2010 TC
monastrell, tempranillo
89
Colour: cherry, garnet rim. Nose: spicy, creamy oak, toasty, red berry notes, ripe fruit. Palate: powerful, flavourful, toasty, round tannins.

Alcanta Monastrell 2013 T
monastrell
88
Colour: deep cherry. Nose: red berry notes, ripe fruit, spicy. Palate: flavourful, fruity, good acidity.

Castillo de Alicante 2013 T
tempranillo, cabernet sauvignon, monastrell
88 ♣
Colour: cherry, purple rim. Nose: expressive, fresh fruit, red berry notes, floral. Palate: flavourful, fruity, good acidity, round tannins.

Dulcenegra Vino de Licor T
monastrell

89

Colour: cherry, garnet rim. Nose: fruit preserve, ripe fruit, spicy, toasty, aged wood nuances, dark chocolate, tar. Palate: powerful, flavourful, sweetness.

Fondillón Alone 1987
monastrell

88

Colour: pale ruby, brick rim edge. Nose: spicy, varnish, cocoa bean, dark chocolate, roasted almonds. Palate: fine bitter notes, unctuous, spirituous.

Laudum 2007 TR
monastrell, merlot, cabernet sauvignon

89

Colour: cherry, garnet rim. Nose: ripe fruit, spicy, creamy oak, toasty, complex. Palate: powerful, flavourful, toasty, round tannins.

Laudum 2009 TC
monastrell, merlot, cabernet sauvignon

87

Colour: cherry, garnet rim. Nose: ripe fruit, spicy, creamy oak, toasty, complex. Palate: powerful, flavourful, toasty, round tannins.

Laudum Barrica Especial 2010 T
monastrell, merlot, cabernet sauvignon

87

Colour: bright cherry. Nose: ripe fruit, dried herbs, toasty. Palate: flavourful, fruity, round tannins.

Laudum Cabernet Sauvignon 2010 T
cabernet sauvignon

86

Colour: cherry, garnet rim. Nose: spicy, toasty, balsamic herbs, ripe fruit. Palate: powerful, flavourful, toasty, warm.

Laudum Chardonnay 2013 BFB
chardonnay

87

Colour: bright yellow. Nose: powerfull, ripe fruit, sweet spices, creamy oak, fragrant herbs. Palate: rich, smoky aftertaste, flavourful, fresh, good acidity.

Laudum Nature 2013 T
monastrell, tempranillo, cabernet sauvignon

88

Colour: deep cherry, purple rim. Nose: balanced, powerfull, ripe fruit, balsamic herbs. Palate: fruity, good acidity.

Laudum Nature Tempranillo 2012 T
tempranillo

90

Colour: cherry, purple rim. Nose: expressive, fresh fruit, red berry notes, floral. Palate: flavourful, fruity, good acidity, round tannins.

Laudum Petit Verdot 2010 T
petit verdot

86

Colour: cherry, garnet rim. Nose: wild herbs, dried herbs. Palate: ripe fruit, spicy, round tannins.

Marina Alta 2013 B
moscatel de alejandría

87

Colour: bright straw. Nose: expressive, varietal, jasmine, fresh. Palate: balanced, easy to drink, good finish.

Marina Espumante B
moscatel de alejandría
87
Colour: bright straw. Nose: floral, expressive, balanced, fresh. Palate: flavourful, good acidity, spicy, easy to drink.

Marina Espumante BR
84

Marina Espumante RD
monastrell
82

Marina Espumante T
monastrell
83

Sol de Alicante Moscatel B
moscatel
89
Colour: golden. Nose: floral, honeyed notes, candied fruit, fragrant herbs, varietal. Palate: flavourful, sweet, fresh, fruity, good acidity, long.

Terreta Rosé 2013 RD
monastrell
88
Colour: rose, purple rim. Nose: powerfull, ripe fruit, red berry notes, floral, expressive. Palate: powerful, fruity, fresh.

BODEGAS E. MENDOZA
Partida El Romeral, s/n
03580 Alfaz del Pi (Alicante)
☎: +34 965 888 639
Fax: +34 965 889 232
www.bodegasmendoza.com
bodegas-mendoza@bodegasmendoza.com

Enrique Mendoza Cabernet - Shiraz 2010 TR
91
Colour: deep cherry, garnet rim. Nose: ripe fruit, sweet spices, balsamic herbs. Palate: fruity, balanced, easy to drink.

Enrique Mendoza Cabernet Monastrell 2011 TC
90
Colour: cherry, garnet rim. Nose: ripe fruit, spicy, complex, balsamic herbs. Palate: powerful, flavourful, toasty, round tannins.

Enrique Mendoza Chardonnay 2013 B
100% chardonnay
90
Colour: bright yellow. Nose: powerfull, ripe fruit, sweet spices, creamy oak, fragrant herbs. Palate: rich, smoky aftertaste, flavourful, fresh, good acidity.

Enrique Mendoza Dolç de Mendoza 2009 T
100% monastrell
90
Colour: deep cherry, garnet rim. Nose: candied fruit, fruit liqueur notes, balsamic herbs, complex. Palate: balanced, good structure, sweet, full.

Enrique Mendoza Merlot Monastrell 2011 T
91
Colour: bright cherry. Nose: ripe fruit, sweet spices, creamy oak, complex, toasty. Palate: flavourful, fruity, toasty, round tannins.

Enrique Mendoza Petit Verdot 2011 TC
100% petit verdot
93
Colour: cherry, garnet rim. Nose: ripe fruit, spicy, creamy oak, toasty, new oak. Palate: powerful, flavourful, toasty, round tannins.

Enrique Mendoza Santa Rosa 2010 T
93
Colour: cherry, garnet rim. Nose: ripe fruit, spicy, creamy oak, complex, balsamic herbs. Palate: powerful, flavourful, round tannins, balanced, spicy, balsamic.

Enrique Mendoza Shiraz 2011 TC
100% syrah

92

Colour: bright cherry. Nose: ripe fruit, sweet spices, creamy oak, expressive, powerfull. Palate: flavourful, fruity, toasty, round tannins.

Estrecho Monastrell 2010 TC
100% monastrell

92

Colour: cherry, garnet rim. Nose: ripe fruit, spicy, creamy oak, toasty, complex, earthy notes. Palate: powerful, flavourful, toasty, round tannins.

Las Quebradas 2010 TC
100% monastrell

94

Colour: bright cherry. Nose: sweet spices, creamy oak, expressive, cocoa bean, mineral. Palate: flavourful, fruity, toasty, round tannins.

BODEGAS FAELO
Cº de los Coves s/n Partida de Matola, Pol. 3 Nº 18
03296 Elche (Alicante)
☎: +34 655 856 898
www.vinosladama.com
info@vinosladama.com

L'Alba de Faelo 2012 RD
syrah

79

L'Alba del Mar 2013 B
chardonnay

84

La Dama 2010 TC

88

Colour: cherry, garnet rim. Nose: powerfull, warm, earthy notes, burnt matches, ripe fruit, toasty. Palate: flavourful, spicy, ripe fruit.

Palma Blanca 2013 B
moscatel

88

Colour: golden. Nose: powerfull, honeyed notes, candied fruit, fruit liqueur notes. Palate: flavourful, sweet, fresh, fruity, good acidity, long.

BODEGAS FRANCISCO GÓMEZ
Paraje Finca La Serrata Ctra.
Villena - Pinoso, Km. 8,8
03400 Villena (Alicante)
☎: +34 965 979 195
www.bodegasfranciscogomez.es
info@bodegasfranciscogomez.es

Boca Negra 2008 TC
monastrell

91

Colour: cherry, garnet rim. Nose: ripe fruit, spicy, creamy oak, toasty, complex, mineral. Palate: powerful, flavourful, toasty, round tannins.

Fruto Noble 2008 TC
cabernet sauvignon, monastrell, syrah

85

Fruto Noble 2013 RD
monastrell, syrah

88 ♣

Colour: rose, purple rim. Nose: powerfull, ripe fruit, red berry notes, floral, expressive. Palate: powerful, fruity, fresh.

Fruto Noble 2013 T
monastrell, syrah

89

Colour: cherry, purple rim. Nose: expressive, fresh fruit, red berry notes, floral. Palate: flavourful, fruity, good acidity, round tannins.

Fruto Noble 2013 T Roble
monastrell, syrah

86

Colour: cherry, purple rim. Nose: woody, roasted coffee. Palate: flavourful, spicy, ripe fruit.

Fruto Noble Sauvignon Blanc 2013 B
sauvignon blanc

84

Moratillas 2008 TC
monastrell, merlot, cabernet sauvignon

88

Colour: pale ruby, brick rim edge. Nose: wet leather, fruit liqueur notes, candied fruit, spicy. Palate: ripe fruit, classic aged character.

Serrata 2006 TR
merlot, petit verdot, cabernet sauvignon, monastrell

85

BODEGAS GUTIÉRREZ DE LA VEGA

Les Quintanes, 1
03792 Parcent (Alicante)
☎: +34 966 403 871
Fax: +34 966 405 257
www.castadiva.es
info@castadiva.es

Casta Diva Cosecha Miel 2013 B
moscatel

95

Colour: bright yellow. Nose: balsamic herbs, honeyed notes, floral, sweet spices, expressive. Palate: rich, fruity, powerful, flavourful, elegant.

Casta Diva Esencial 2012 B
moscatel

96

Colour: old gold, amber rim. Nose: ripe fruit, balsamic herbs, dried herbs, faded flowers, aged wood nuances. Palate: rich, flavourful, concentrated, spicy, long.

Casta Diva Reserva Real 2002 B Reserva
moscatel

98

Colour: old gold. Nose: pattiserie, spicy, honeyed notes, dry nuts, creamy oak, expressive, elegant. Palate: rich, flavourful, fruity, long, balanced.

Furtiva Lágrima 2013 B
moscatel

93

Colour: golden. Nose: powerfull, floral, honeyed notes, candied fruit, fragrant herbs. Palate: flavourful, sweet, fresh, fruity, good acidity, long.

La Diva 2011 B
moscatel

96

Colour: bright golden. Nose: ripe fruit, wild herbs, honeyed notes, balsamic herbs, spicy, balanced. Palate: powerful, flavourful, unctuous, round.

Recóndita Armonía 1987 Fondillón
monastrell

95

Colour: dark mahogany. Nose: powerfull, complex, elegant, dry nuts, toasty, aromatic coffee, expressive. Palate: rich, fine bitter notes, fine solera notes, long, spicy, balanced, elegant.

Recóndita Armonía 2002 Fondillón
monastrell

95

Colour: pale ruby, brick rim edge. Nose: ripe fruit, fruit liqueur notes, wild herbs, aged wood nuances, toasty, creamy oak. Palate: flavourful, fruity, spicy, long, balanced.

Recóndita Armonía 2010 T
monastrell

92

Colour: cherry, garnet rim. Nose: fruit preserve, ripe fruit, spicy, toasty, aged wood nuances, balsamic herbs, balanced. Palate: powerful, flavourful, spicy, long, elegant.

BODEGAS MURVIEDRO

Ampliación Pol. El Romeral, s/n
46340 Requena (Valencia)
☎: +34 962 329 003
Fax: +34 962 329 002
www.bodegasmurviedro.es
murviedro@murviedro.es

Cueva del Perdón 2011 TC
monastrell, syrah

90

Colour: cherry, garnet rim. Nose: ripe fruit, spicy, creamy oak, toasty, powerfull. Palate: powerful, flavourful, toasty, round tannins, concentrated.

DNA Murviedro Classic Monastrell 2013 T
monastrell

88

Colour: cherry, purple rim. Nose: expressive, red berry notes, wild herbs. Palate: flavourful, fruity, good acidity, easy to drink.

DNA Murviedro Signature Eko 2012 T
monastrell

90 🌷

Colour: bright cherry. Nose: ripe fruit, sweet spices, creamy oak, expressive. Palate: flavourful, fruity, toasty, round tannins.

Dulce de Murviedro 2012 B
moscatel

88

Colour: golden. Nose: honeyed notes, candied fruit, fragrant herbs, varietal. Palate: flavourful, sweet, fresh, fruity, good acidity, long.

BODEGAS PARCENT

Avda. Denia, 15
03792 Parcent (Alicante)
☎: +34 636 536 693
Fax: +34 966 405 173
www.bodegasparcent.com
armando@bodegasparcent.com

Auro 2013 B
moscatel, chardonnay

87

Colour: bright straw. Nose: expressive, powerfull, white flowers. Palate: fruity, flavourful, correct, varietal.

Comtat de Parcent 2012 TC
cabernet sauvignon, merlot

84

Dolç D'Art 2013 B
moscatel
88
Colour: bright straw. Nose: floral, citrus fruit, ripe fruit. Palate: flavourful, sweetness, spirituous.

Fruit D'Autor Rosado Vino de licor
87
Colour: light cherry. Nose: fruit liqueur notes, fruit preserve, spicy, acetaldehyde. Palate: sweet, powerful, concentrated.

Grà D'Or Blanco Seco 2013 B
moscatel
88
Colour: bright straw. Nose: ripe fruit, fruit expression, honeyed notes. Palate: balanced, spicy, ripe fruit.

Parcent 2012 BN
moscatel, chardonnay, macabeo
86
Colour: bright straw. Nose: medium intensity, fresh fruit, dried herbs, fine lees, floral. Palate: fresh, fruity, flavourful, good acidity.

Parcent Garnacha 2013 T
garnacha
88
Colour: bright cherry. Nose: medium intensity, fresh fruit, red berry notes. Palate: light-bodied, flavourful.

Rosat 2013 RD
syrah
86
Colour: rose, purple rim. Nose: powerfull, ripe fruit, red berry notes, floral. Palate: powerful, fruity, fresh.

BODEGAS SIERRA DE CABRERAS
La Molineta, s/n
03638 Salinas (Alicante)
☎: +34 647 515 590
www.carabibas.com
info@carabibas.com

Carabibas La Viña del Carpintero 2012 T
89
Colour: bright cherry. Nose: ripe fruit, expressive, balanced, scrubland. Palate: flavourful, fruity, round tannins.

Carabibas VS 2011 T
cabernet sauvignon, merlot, monastrell
89
Colour: cherry, garnet rim. Nose: spicy, creamy oak, toasty, fruit preserve. Palate: powerful, flavourful, toasty, round tannins.

Carabibas VS 2012 TC
cabernet sauvignon, merlot, monastrell
87
Colour: black cherry. Nose: powerfull, characterful, fruit preserve, macerated fruit, sweet spices. Palate: powerful, concentrated, grainy tannins.

Carabibas VS 21 meses 2010 TR
cabernet sauvignon, merlot, monastrell
92
Colour: cherry, garnet rim. Nose: ripe fruit, spicy, creamy oak, complex, balsamic herbs. Palate: powerful, flavourful, toasty, round tannins.

BODEGAS SIERRA SALINAS
Paraje del Puerto, s/n
(Ctra. Villena-Pinoso, km. 18)
30400 Villena (Alicante)
☎: +34 968 791 271
Fax: +34 968 791 900
www.sierrasalinas.com
comunicacion@sierrasalinas.com

Mira Salinas 2011 T
91
Colour: cherry, garnet rim. Nose: spicy, creamy oak, toasty, characterful. Palate: powerful, flavourful, toasty, round tannins.

Mo Salinas Monastrell 2012 T
91
Colour: bright cherry. Nose: ripe fruit, sweet spices, creamy oak, expressive, balsamic herbs. Palate: flavourful, fruity, toasty, round tannins.

Puerto Salinas 2011 T
92
Colour: bright cherry. Nose: ripe fruit, expressive, scrubland. Palate: flavourful, fruity, round tannins, balsamic.

Puerto Salinas Moscatel Chardonnay 2013 B
89
Colour: bright straw. Nose: fresh, fresh fruit, white flowers, expressive, sweet spices. Palate: flavourful, fruity, good acidity, balanced.

Salinas 1237 2010 T
93
Colour: cherry, garnet rim. Nose: ripe fruit, spicy, creamy oak, complex, dark chocolate, earthy notes. Palate: powerful, flavourful, toasty, round tannins.

BODEGAS VICENTE GANDÍA

Ctra. Cheste a Godelleta, s/n
46370 Chiva (Valencia)
☎: +34 962 524 242
Fax: +34 962 524 243
www.vicentegandia.es
info@vicentegandia.com

El Miracle Art 2011 T
88
Colour: cherry, garnet rim. Nose: ripe fruit, spicy, creamy oak, toasty. Palate: powerful, flavourful, toasty, round tannins.

El Miracle Fusión 2013 B
chardonnay, sauvignon blanc, moscatel
85

El Miracle Music 2013 RD
syrah, garnacha
85

El Miracle Planet Organic Wine 2012 T
100% monastrell
84 🌱

Puerto Alicante Chardonnay 2013 B
100% chardonnay
88
Colour: bright straw. Nose: fresh, fresh fruit, white flowers, expressive. Palate: flavourful, fruity, good acidity, balanced.

Puerto Alicante Syrah 2012 T
100% syrah
87
Colour: cherry, purple rim. Nose: ripe fruit, red berry notes, powerfull. Palate: fruity, flavourful, correct.

BODEGAS VIVANZA

Ctra. Jumilla Pinoso , Km. 13
30520 Jumilla (Murcia)
☎: +34 966 078 686
www.vivanza.es
agomez@vivanza.es

Vivanza 2009 T Barrica
monastrell, syrah, pinot noir
86
Colour: bright cherry. Nose: toasty, spicy, fruit preserve. Palate: fruity, spicy, warm.

Vivanza 2013 B
sauvignon blanc, chardonnay
86
Colour: bright straw. Nose: balanced, white flowers, powerfull. Palate: fruity, flavourful, correct.

Vivanza 2013 T
cabernet sauvignon, merlot
86
Colour: bright cherry. Nose: ripe fruit, grassy, spicy, medium intensity. Palate: flavourful, fruity, round tannins.

BODEGAS VOLVER

Ctra de Pinoso a Fortuna s/n
03658 Rodriguillo - Pinoso (Alicante)
☎: +34 966 185 624
Fax: +34 965 075 376
www.bodegasvolver.com
export@bodegasvolver.com

Tarima 2013 B
merseguera, macabeo, moscatel
90
Colour: bright straw. Nose: fresh, fresh fruit, white flowers. Palate: flavourful, fruity, good acidity, balanced.

Tarima 2013 RD
89
Colour: onion pink. Nose: candied fruit, dried flowers, fragrant herbs, red berry notes. Palate: light-bodied, flavourful, good acidity, long, spicy.

Tarima Hill 2012 T
monastrell
91
Colour: cherry, garnet rim. Nose: overripe fruit, dried fruit, sweet spices, toasty. Palate: ripe fruit, warm, powerful.

Tarima Monastrell 2013 T
monastrell
91
Colour: cherry, garnet rim. Nose: ripe fruit, spicy, creamy oak, toasty, complex, earthy notes, balsamic herbs. Palate: powerful, flavourful, toasty, concentrated.

Triga 2011 T
93
Colour: cherry, garnet rim. Nose: red berry notes, ripe fruit, spicy, creamy oak, toasty, complex, earthy notes. Palate: powerful, flavourful, toasty, concentrated, smoky aftertaste.

BODEGAS XALÓ

Ctra. Xaló Alcalali, s/n
03727 Xaló (Alicante)
☎: +34 966 480 034
Fax: +34 966 480 808
www.bodegasxalo.com
comercial@bodegasxalo.com

Bahía de Denia 2013 B Joven
moscatel
88
Colour: bright straw. Nose: fresh, fresh fruit, white flowers, expressive. Palate: fruity, good acidity, balanced, varietal.

Riu Rau 2012 B
89
Colour: old gold. Nose: candied fruit, pattiserie, sweet spices, honeyed notes. Palate: full, long, unctuous.

Serra de Bernia 2012 T Roble
garnacha, cabernet sauvignon
84

Vall de Pop Plaer 2013 B
moscatel
87
Colour: bright straw. Nose: fresh, fresh fruit, white flowers, expressive. Palate: flavourful, fruity, good acidity, balanced.

Vall de Xaló 2012 T
garnacha
86
Colour: cherry, purple rim. Nose: red berry notes, ripe fruit, balsamic herbs. Palate: correct, easy to drink, round tannins.

Vall de Xaló 2013 B
moscatel
89
Colour: bright straw. Nose: fresh, fresh fruit, white flowers, expressive. Palate: flavourful, fruity, good acidity, balanced.

Vall de Xaló 2013 Mistela
moscatel
87
Colour: bright straw. Nose: ripe fruit, tropical fruit, honeyed notes. Palate: flavourful, sweetness, fruity.

Vall de Xaló 2013 RD
giró
87
Colour: brilliant rose. Nose: elegant, candied fruit, dried flowers, red berry notes. Palate: light-bodied, flavourful, good acidity, long, spicy.

Vall de Xalón Vino de Licor T
90
Colour: cherry, garnet rim. Nose: fruit preserve, ripe fruit, spicy, toasty, aged wood nuances. Palate: powerful, flavourful, sweetness.

BODEGAS Y VIÑEDOS EL SEQUÉ
Casas de El Sequé, 59
03650 (Alicante)
☎: +34 945 600 119
Fax: +34 945 600 850
www.artadi.com/seque
elseque@artadi.com

El Sequé 2012 T
100% monastrell
94
Colour: cherry, garnet rim. Nose: ripe fruit, spicy, creamy oak, toasty, complex, dark chocolate, earthy notes. Palate: powerful, flavourful, toasty, round tannins.

El Sequé Dulce 2012 T
100% monastrell
93
Colour: cherry, garnet rim. Nose: fruit preserve, ripe fruit, spicy, toasty, aged wood nuances. Palate: powerful, flavourful, sweetness.

Laderas de El Sequé 2012 T
monastrell, syrah
91
Colour: bright cherry. Nose: ripe fruit, sweet spices, creamy oak, fresh. Palate: flavourful, fruity, toasty, round tannins.

BROTONS S.L.
Partida Culebrón, 74
03650 Pinoso (Alicante)
☎: +34 965 477 267
www.vinosculebron.com
info@vinosculebron.com

Culebrón 1998 TR
100% monastrell
76

Culebrón Edición Especial 1988 TGR
100% monastrell
72

Gran Fondillon 1964 Fondillón
Gran Reserva
100% monastrell
94
Colour: iodine, amber rim. Nose: powerfull, complex, elegant, toasty, dry nuts, fruit liqueur notes. Palate: rich, long, fine solera notes, spicy.

Robert's Macabo 2012 B
100% macabeo
79

Robert's Merlot 2012 T
100% merlot
88
Colour: cherry, garnet rim. Nose: powerfull, sulphur notes, ripe fruit, spicy. Palate: flavourful, good acidity, spicy.

Robert's Syrah 2012 T
100% syrah
82

COMERCIAL GRUPO FREIXENET

Joan Sala, 2
08770 Sant Sadurní D'Anoia (Barcelona)
☎: +34 938 917 000
Fax: +34 938 183 095
www.freixenet.es
freixenet@freixenet.es

Nauta 2010 TC
monastrell
86
Colour: very deep cherry, garnet rim. Nose: powerfull, ripe fruit, roasted coffee, smoky. Palate: powerful, toasty, roasted-coffee aftertaste.

FINCA COLLADO

Ctra. de Salinas a Villena, s/n
03638 Salinas (Alicante)
☎: +34 607 510 710
Fax: +34 962 878 818
www.fincacollado.com
info@fincacollado.com

Finca Collado 2011 B
chardonnay, moscatel
85

Finca Collado Merlot 2010 T
merlot
87
Colour: cherry, garnet rim. Nose: balanced, varietal, wild herbs, spicy. Palate: fruity, round tannins, balanced.

FINCA LA LAGUNILLA

Avda. Reyes Católicos 31 5ºA
03003 Alicante (Albacete)
☎: +34 965 928 857
www.fincalalagunilla.com
info@fincalalagunilla.com

Semsum 2 2013 B
macabeo, moscatel de alejandría
83

HERETAT ANTIGUA, CASA SICILIA 1707

Paraje Alcaydias, 4
03660 Novelda (Alicante)
☎: +34 965 605 385
Fax: +34 965 604 763
www.casasicilia1707.es
administracion@casasicilia1707.es

Ad 2012 T
90
Colour: cherry, garnet rim. Nose: fruit preserve, scrubland, expressive. Palate: good structure, flavourful, fine bitter notes. Personality.

Ad 2012 T Roble
87
Colour: cherry, garnet rim. Nose: warm, medium intensity, toasty, cocoa bean. Palate: flavourful, spicy.

Cardenal Álvarez 2008 T
92
Colour: cherry, garnet rim. Nose: overripe fruit, dried fruit, sweet spices, toasty. Palate: ripe fruit, warm, powerful.

IBERICA BRUNO PRATS

CV 830, km. 3,2
03640 Monovar (Alicante)
☎: +34 645 963 122
www.fidelisalliance.com
stephanepoint@hotmail.com

Alfynal 2010 T
monastrell
90
Colour: cherry, garnet rim. Nose: ripe fruit, spicy, wild herbs. Palate: powerful, flavourful, round tannins, balsamic.

Mosyca 2011 T
monastrell, syrah, cabernet sauvignon, otras
87
Colour: very deep cherry, purple rim. Nose: powerfull, fruit preserve, balsamic herbs, warm. Palate: round tannins, long, sweetness.

LA BODEGA DE PINOSO

Paseo de la Constitución, 82
03650 Pinoso (Alicante)
☎: +34 965 477 040
Fax: +34 966 970 149
www.labodegadepinoso.com
vanesa@labodegadepinoso.com

Pontos 1932 2009 TC
monastrell
87
Colour: pale ruby, brick rim edge. Nose: spicy, cocoa bean, fruit liqueur notes. Palate: spirituous, fine bitter notes.

Pontos Cepa 50 2012 T
monastrell
87
Colour: cherry, garnet rim. Nose: wild herbs, ripe fruit, powerfull, spicy. Palate: varietal, flavourful, round tannins.

Pontos Clasic 2009 TC
monastrell, merlot, cabernet sauvignon
84

Torre del Reloj 2013 B
airén, macabeo
83

Torre del Reloj 2013 RD
monastrell

86

Colour: rose, purple rim. Nose: ripe fruit, red berry notes, floral, expressive. Palate: powerful, fruity, fresh.

Torre del Reloj Monastrell 2012 T
monastrell

85

Vergel 2012 T
alicante bouschet, merlot, monastrell

88

Colour: bright cherry. Nose: ripe fruit, sweet spices, creamy oak, expressive. Palate: flavourful, fruity, toasty, round tannins.

Vergel Selección Barricas 2010 T
monastrell, syrah, merlot

91

Colour: cherry, garnet rim. Nose: ripe fruit, spicy, creamy oak, toasty, characterful, powerfull. Palate: powerful, flavourful, toasty, round tannins.

Vermador 2011 T Roble
monastrell

87

Colour: bright cherry. Nose: ripe fruit, expressive, balsamic herbs. Palate: flavourful, fruity, round tannins, balanced.

Vermador 2012 T
monastrell

83

Vermador 2013 B
airén, macabeo

84

Vermador 2013 RD
monastrell

88

Colour: onion pink. Nose: elegant, candied fruit, dried flowers, fragrant herbs, red berry notes. Palate: light-bodied, flavourful, good acidity, long, spicy.

PRIMITIVO QUILES
Mayor, 4
03640 Monóvar (Alicante)
☎: +34 965 470 099
Fax: +34 966 960 235
www.primitivoquiles.com
info@primitivoquiles.com

Gran Imperial GE
moscatel

92

Colour: dark mahogany. Nose: dark chocolate, sweet spices, pattiserie, candied fruit. Palate: balanced, round, long, sweet.

Primitivo Quiles Fondillón 1948 Fondillón
monastrell

92

Colour: iodine, amber rim. Nose: powerfull, complex, elegant, dry nuts, toasty. Palate: rich, long, fine solera notes, spicy.

Primitivo Quiles Monastrell 2010 TC
monastrell

85

Primitivo Quiles Monastrell-Merlot 2011 T Roble

82

Primitivo Quiles Moscatel Extra Vino de licor
moscatel

89

Colour: mahogany. Nose: pattiserie, caramel, sweet spices, powerfull, candied fruit. Palate: long, balanced.

Raspay 2008 TR
monastrell

85

VINS DEL COMTAT
Turballos, 11
03820 Cocentaina (Alicante)
☎: +34 667 669 287
Fax: +34 965 593 194
www.vinsdelcomtat.com
vinsdelcomtat@gmail.com

Cristalí 2013 B
moscatel de alejandría

92

Colour: bright straw. Nose: fresh, white flowers, expressive, candied fruit, citrus fruit. Palate: flavourful, fruity, good acidity, sweet.

Maigmó 2010 TR
monastrell

89

Colour: cherry, garnet rim. Nose: fruit preserve, ripe fruit, spicy, toasty, aged wood nuances. Palate: powerful, flavourful, sweetness.

Montcabrer 2006 TR
cabernet sauvignon

87

Colour: bright cherry. Nose: sweet spices, creamy oak, candied fruit. Palate: flavourful, fruity, toasty, round tannins.

Penya Cadiella Selecció 2011 T
monastrell, cabernet sauvignon, merlot, syrah

91

Colour: cherry, garnet rim. Nose: ripe fruit, spicy, creamy oak, toasty, complex. Palate: powerful, flavourful, toasty, round tannins.

Peña Cadiella 2011 TC
monastrell, cabernet sauvignon, merlot

87

Colour: cherry, garnet rím. Nose: powerfull, ripe fruit, toasty, dark chocolate. Palate: powerful, spirituous, concentrated.

Santa Bárbara 2012 T Roble

86

Colour: bright cherry. Nose: ripe fruit, expressive, wild herbs, varietal. Palate: flavourful, fruity, round tannins.

VIÑEDOS CULTURALES

Plaza Constitución, 8 - 1º

03380 Bigastro (Alicante)

☎: +34 966 770 353

Fax: +34 966 770 353

http://vinedosculturales.blogspot.com.es/
vinedosculturales@gmail.com

Los Cipreses de Usaldón 2012 T
garnacha peluda

94

Colour: light cherry. Nose: mineral, ripe fruit, fruit liqueur notes, fragrant herbs, balsamic herbs, spicy, creamy oak. Palate: flavourful, spicy, balsamic, balanced, elegant.

Ramblis del Arco 2012 T

91

Colour: cherry, garnet rim. Nose: fruit liqueur notes, balsamic herbs, wild herbs, earthy notes, mineral. Palate: flavourful, elegant, spicy, balsamic, balanced.

Ramblis Monastrell 2012 T
monastrell

95

Colour: light cherry. Nose: balsamic herbs, expressive, complex, mineral, red berry notes, fresh fruit. Palate: flavourful, fine bitter notes, light-bodied, easy to drink.

DO. ALMANSA

CONSEJO REGULADOR

Avda. Carlos III (Apdo. 158)
02640 Almansa (Albacete)
☎:+34 967 340 258 - Fax: +34 967 310 842
@: info@vinosdealmansa.com
www.vinosdealmansa.com

LOCATION:

In the South East region of the province of Albacete. It covers the municipal areas of Almansa, Alpera, Bonete, Corral Rubio, Higueruela, Hoya Gonzalo, Pétrola and the municipal district of El Villar de Chinchilla.

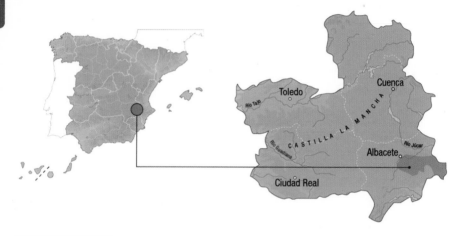

GRAPE VARIETIES:

White: Chardonnay, moscatel de grano menudo, Verdejo and Sauvignon Blanc.
Red: Garnacha Tintorera (most popular), Cencibel (Tempranillo), Monastrell (second most popular), Syrah, cabernet sauvignon, merlot, granacha, petit verdot and pinot noir.

FIGURES:

Vineyard surface: 7,200 – Wine-Growers: 760 – Wineries: 12 – 2013 Harvest rating: - – Production 13: 5,157,600 litres – Market percentages: 20% domestic - 80% export.

SOIL:

The soil is limy, poor in organic matter and with some clayey areas. The vineyards are situated at an altitude of about 700 m.

CLIMATE:

Of a continental type, somewhat less extreme than the climate of La Mancha, although the summers are very hot, with temperatures which easily reach 40 °C. Rainfall, on the other hand, is scant, an average of about 350 mm a year. The majority of the vineyards are situated on the plains, although there are a few situated on the slopes.

VINTAGE RATING   PEÑÍNGUIDE

2009	2010	2011	2012	2013
GOOD	VERY GOOD	VERY GOOD	VERY GOOD	GOOD

BODEGA SANTA CRUZ DE ALPERA

Cooperativa, s/n
02690 Alpera (Albacete)
☎: +34 967 330 108
www.bodegasantacruz.com
comercial@bodegasantacruz.com

Albarroble 2011 TC
88
Colour: bright cherry. Nose: ripe fruit, sweet spices, creamy oak, medium intensity. Palate: fruity, flavourful, toasty.

Rupestre de Alpera 2009 T Barrica
garnacha tintorera
90
Colour: bright cherry. Nose: ripe fruit, sweet spices, creamy oak, balsamic herbs, expressive. Palate: fruity, flavourful, toasty, balanced, elegant.

Santa Cruz de Alpera 2011 T Roble
100% garnacha tintorera
89
Colour: black cherry. Nose: toasty, cocoa bean, creamy oak, warm. Palate: good structure, flavourful, spicy.

Santa Cruz de Alpera 2013 B
100% verdejo
85

Santa Cruz de Alpera 2013 BFB
100% verdejo
88
Colour: bright yellow. Nose: ripe fruit, balsamic herbs, sweet spices, creamy oak. Palate: powerful, flavourful, fresh, fruity, spicy.

Santa Cruz de Alpera 2013 RD
100% syrah
86
Colour: light cherry. Nose: red berry notes, ripe fruit, floral, wild herbs. Palate: fresh, fruity, flavourful, easy to drink.

Santa Cruz de Alpera 2013 T
100% garnacha tintorera
86
Colour: cherry, purple rim. Nose: red berry notes, raspberry, floral, fragrant herbs. Palate: fresh, fruity, flavourful.

Santa Cruz de Alpera Blend 2013 T
87
Colour: bright cherry. Nose: ripe fruit, sweet spices, creamy oak, expressive. Palate: flavourful, fruity, toasty, round tannins.

Santa Cruz de Alpera Mosto Parcialmente Fermentado 2013 RD
100% syrah
85

BODEGAS ALMANSEÑAS

Ctra. de Alpera, CM 3201 Km. 98,6
02640 Almansa (Albacete)
☎: +34 967 098 116
Fax: +34 967 098 121
www.ventalavega.com
adaras@ventalavega.com

Adaras 2009 T
garnacha tintorera
92
Colour: cherry, garnet rim. Nose: ripe fruit, spicy, creamy oak, toasty, mineral. Palate: powerful, flavourful, toasty, balanced.

Aldea de Adaras 2013 T
monastrell
89
Colour: dark-red cherry, purple rim. Nose: warm, dried herbs, ripe fruit. Palate: flavourful, ripe fruit, long.

Calizo de Adaras 2013 T
garnacha tintorera, monastrell, syrah
88
Colour: cherry, purple rim. Nose: powerfull, red berry notes, ripe fruit, wild herbs, mineral. Palate: powerful, fresh, fruity, unctuous.

La Huella de Adaras 2011 T
garnacha tintorera, monastrell
90
Colour: bright cherry. Nose: ripe fruit, sweet spices, creamy oak, expressive. Palate: flavourful, fruity, toasty, round tannins.

La Huella de Adaras 2013 B
sauvignon blanc, verdejo
86
Colour: bright straw. Nose: fresh, fresh fruit, wild herbs. Palate: flavourful, fruity, good acidity, balanced.

Venta la Vega Old Vine 2011 T
garnacha tintorera, monastrell
90
Colour: cherry, garnet rim. Nose: spicy, creamy oak, toasty, complex, earthy notes, fruit liqueur notes. Palate: powerful, flavourful, toasty, balanced.

BODEGAS ATALAYA

Ctra. Almansa - Ayora, Km. 1
02640 Almansa (Albacete)
☎: +34 968 435 022
Fax: +34 968 716 051
www.orowines.com
info@orowines.com

Alaya 2011 T
100% garnacha tintorera
93
Colour: cherry, garnet rim. Nose: ripe fruit, spicy, creamy oak, toasty, balsamic herbs. Palate: powerful, flavourful, toasty, round tannins.

Alaya 2012 T
100% garnacha tintorera

89

Colour: black cherry. Nose: dark chocolate, roasted coffee, fruit liqueur notes, fruit preserve. Palate: powerful, sweetness, concentrated.

La Atalaya 2012 T
91

Colour: cherry, garnet rim. Nose: overripe fruit, sweet spices, ripe fruit, toasty. Palate: ripe fruit, warm, powerful.

Laya 2013 T
89

Colour: very deep cherry, garnet rim. Nose: fruit expression, grassy, spicy. Palate: flavourful, ripe fruit, long.

BODEGAS PIQUERAS
Zapateros, 11
02640 Almansa (Albacete)
☎: +34 967 341 482
www.bodegaspiqueras.es
info@bodegaspiqueras.es

Castillo de Almansa 2011 TC
monastrell, garnacha tintorera, cabernet sauvignon

86

Colour: cherry, garnet rim. Nose: balanced, ripe fruit, spicy, dried herbs. Palate: balanced, round tannins.

Castillo de Almansa 2011 TR
monastrell, garnacha tintorera, syrah

88

Colour: bright cherry. Nose: ripe fruit, sweet spices, creamy oak, medium intensity. Palate: fruity, flavourful, toasty.

Castillo de Almansa 2012 TC
monastrell, garnacha tintorera, cabernet sauvignon

87

Colour: bright cherry. Nose: ripe fruit, sweet spices, creamy oak. Palate: flavourful, fruity, toasty.

Castillo de Almansa 2013 RD
syrah

85

Castillo de Almansa Selección 2009 T
monastrell, syrah, garnacha tintorera, tempranillo

88

Colour: cherry, garnet rim. Nose: ripe fruit, wild herbs, spicy, creamy oak. Palate: balanced, flavourful, long, balsamic.

Castillo de Almansa Verdejo Sauvignon 2013 B
verdejo, sauvignon blanc

84

Valcanto 2011 T
monastrell

88

Colour: cherry, garnet rim. Nose: ripe fruit, spicy, creamy oak, toasty. Palate: powerful, flavourful, toasty.

Valcanto Syrah 2011 T Roble
100% syrah

86

Colour: very deep cherry. Nose: toasty, sweet spices, ripe fruit. Palate: correct, easy to drink, ripe fruit.

COOP. AGRARIA SANTA QUITERIA
Baltasar González Sáez, 34
02694 Higueruela (Albacete)
☎: +34 967 287 012
Fax: +34 967 287 031
www.tintoralba.com
direccion@tintoralba.com

Tintoralba 2010 TC
86

Colour: bright cherry. Nose: ripe fruit, sweet spices, creamy oak, balsamic herbs. Palate: flavourful, fruity, toasty, round tannins.

Tintoralba 2013 T Roble
85

Tintoralba Ecológico 2012 T
100% garnacha tintorera

86 🌱

Colour: very deep cherry, purple rim. Nose: powerfull, ripe fruit, fruit preserve, toasty. Palate: fruity, good finish.

Tintoralba Garnacha Tintorera 2013 T
100% garnacha tintorera

88

Colour: deep cherry, purple rim. Nose: fruit expression, red berry notes, grassy, balanced. Palate: fruity, easy to drink.

Tintoralba Selección 2011 T
garnacha tintorera, syrah

89

Colour: cherry, garnet rim. Nose: ripe fruit, spicy, creamy oak, toasty. Palate: powerful, flavourful, round tannins.

Tintoralba Syrah 2013 RD
100% syrah

87

Colour: rose, purple rim. Nose: powerfull, ripe fruit, red berry notes, floral, lactic notes, expressive. Palate: powerful, fruity, fresh.

DO. ARABAKO TXAKOLINA

CONSEJO REGULADOR
Dionisio Aldama, 7- 1ºD Apdo. 36
01470 Amurrio (Álava)
☎:+34 656 789 372 - Fax: +34 945 891 211
@: merino@txakolidealava.com
www.txakolidealava.com

LOCATION:

It covers the region of Aiara (Ayala), situated in the north west of the province of Alava on the banks of the Nervion river basin. Specifically, it is made up of the municipalities of Amurrio, Artziniega, Aiara (Ayala), Laudio (Llodio) and Okondo.

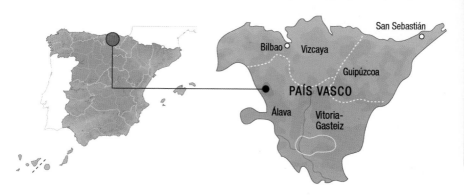

GRAPE VARIETIES:

Main: Hondarrabi Zuri (80%).
Authorized: Petit Manseng, Petit Corbu and Gross Manseng.

FIGURES:

Vineyard surface: 100 – Wine-Growers: 50 – Wineries: 8 – 2013 Harvest rating: Very Good – Production 13: 248,000 litres – Market percentages: 80% domestic - 20% export.

SOIL:

A great variety of formations are found, ranging from clayey to fundamentally stony, precisely those which to date are producing the best results and where fairly stable grape ripening is achieved.

CLIMATE:

Similar to that of the DO Bizkaiko Txakolina, determined by the influence of the Bay of Biscay, although somewhat less humid and slightly drier and fresher. In fact, the greatest risk in the region stems from frost in the spring. However, it should not be forgotten that part of its vineyards borders on the innermost plantations of the DO Bizkaiko Txakolina.

VINTAGE RATING

PEÑÍNGUIDE

2009	2010	2011	2012	2013
N/A	N/A	N/A	EXCELLENT	VERY GOOD

ARABAKO TXAKOLINA

Avda. Maskuribai s/n Edif. El Salvador
01470 Amurrio (Álava)
☎: +34 620 007 452
Fax: +34 945 891 211
www.xarmant.net
arabakotxakolina@euskalnet.net

Xarmant 2013 B
hondarrabi zuri, petit corbu, gros manseng
84

ARTOMAÑA TXAKOLINA

Masalarreina, s/n
01468 Artomaña (Alava)
www.eukeni.net
info@artomanatxakolina.com

Eukeni 2013 B
hondarrabi zuri, petit corbu, gros manseng
86

Colour: bright straw. Nose: fresh, fresh fruit, white flowers, expressive. Palate: good acidity, balanced, carbonic notes, fine bitter notes.

BODEGA SEÑORÍO DE ASTOBIZA

Barrio Jandiola, 16
01409 Okondo (Araba)
☎: +34 945 898 516
Fax: +34 945 898 447
www.senoriodeastobiza.com
jon.zubeldia@senoriodeastobiza.com

Malkoa Txakoli Edición Limitada 2013 B
100% hondarrabi zuri
88

Colour: bright straw, greenish rim. Nose: expressive, medium intensity, citrus fruit, fragrant herbs. Palate: flavourful, fresh.

Señorío de Astobiza 2013 B
87

Colour: bright straw. Nose: white flowers, fragrant herbs, fruit expression. Palate: fresh, fruity, flavourful.

GOIANEA KOOP E.

Pol. Ind. Kalzadako, 10 Pab. 3B
01470 Saratxo Amurrio (Alava)
☎: +34 656 714 709
Fax: +34 945 892 141
www.txakoliuno.com
info@txakoliuno.com

Uno 2012 B
92

Colour: bright straw. Nose: white flowers, fresh fruit, expressive, fine lees, dried herbs. Palate: flavourful, fruity, good acidity, balanced.

Uno 2013 B
90

Colour: bright straw. Nose: fresh, fresh fruit, white flowers, expressive. Palate: flavourful, fruity, good acidity, balanced.

DO. ARLANZA

CONSEJO REGULADOR

Ronda de la Cárcel, 4 - Edif. Arco de la Cárcel
09340 Lerma (Burgos)
☎ :+34 947 171 046 - Fax: +34 947 171 046
@: info@arlanza.org
www.arlanza.org

LOCATION:

With the medieval city of Lerma at the core of the region, Arlanza occupies the central and southern part of the province of Burgos, on the river valleys of the Arlanza and its subsidiaries, all the way westwards through 13 municipal districts of the province of Palencia until the Pisuerga River is reached.

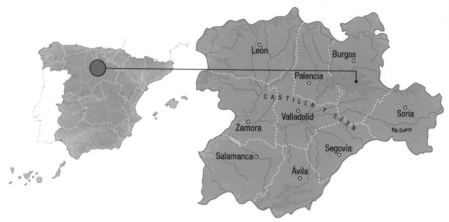

GRAPE VARIETIES:

White: Albillo and Viura.
Red: Tempranillo, Garnacha and Mencía.

FIGURES:

Vineyard surface: 450 – Wine-Growers: 280– Wineries: 16 – 2013 Harvest rating: - – Production 13: 1,000,000 litres – Market percentages: 85% domestic - 15%export.

SOIL:

Soil in the region is not particularly deep, with soft rocks underneath and good humidity levels. The landscape is one of rolling hills where vines are planted on varied soils, from limestone to calcareous, with abundant granite on certain areas.

CLIMATE:

The climate of this wine region is said to be one of the harshest within Castilla y León, with lower temperatures towards the western areas and rainfall higher on the eastern parts, in the highlands of the province of Soria.

VINTAGE RATING   PEÑÍNGUIDE

2009	2010	2011	2012	2013
GOOD	VERY GOOD	VERY GOOD	VERY GOOD	GOOD

ALONSO ANGULO

Mayor 14
09348 Castrillo de Solarana (Burgos)
☎: +34 647 628 148
www.alonsoangulo.com
info@alonsoangulo.com

Flor de Sanctus 2012 T
tempranillo
86
Colour: cherry, garnet rim. Nose: ripe fruit, wild herbs, spicy.
Palate: balanced, flavourful, long, balsamic, fine bitter notes.

BODEGA ESTEBAN ARAUJO

Pago Laredo
34230 Torquemada (Palencia)
☎: +34 620 479 142
bodegaestebanaraujo@gmail.com

El Monjío 2011 TC
100% tempranillo
86
Colour: cherry, garnet rim. Nose: ripe fruit, spicy, creamy oak,
toasty. Palate: powerful, flavourful, toasty, easy to drink.

El Monjío 2012 T Roble
tempranillo
83

El Monjío 2013 RD
100% tempranillo
85

BODEGAS ARLANZA

Ctra. Madrid-Irún km 203,800
09390 Villalmanzo (Burgos)
☎: +34 947 172 070
Fax: +34 947 170 259
www.bodegasarlanza.com
comercial@bodegasarlanza.com

Dominio de Manciles 12 meses 2012 T Barrica
100% tempranillo
87
Colour: deep cherry. Nose: spicy, toasty, ripe fruit, dried herbs.
Palate: good structure, round tannins.

Dominio de Manciles 2005 TR
100% tempranillo
89
Colour: dark-red cherry, garnet rim. Nose: spicy, fine reductive
notes, wet leather, aged wood nuances, toasty. Palate: spicy,
long, toasty.

Dominio de Manciles 2010 TR
100% tempranillo
88
Colour: cherry, garnet rim. Nose: ripe fruit, spicy, creamy oak,
toasty. Palate: powerful, flavourful, toasty, round tannins.

Dominio de Manciles 2012 T Fermentado en Barrica
90
Colour: rose. Nose: fresh fruit, red berry notes, floral, spicy,
creamy oak. Palate: flavourful, fruity, good acidity.

Dominio de Manciles 2013 B
83

Dominio de Manciles 2013 RD
89
Colour: rose, purple rim. Nose: powerfull, floral, red berry
notes, candied fruit, expressive. Palate: powerful, fruity, fresh,
easy to drink.

Dominio de Manciles 2013 T
86
Colour: cherry, purple rim. Nose: fresh fruit, red berry notes,
floral, balsamic herbs. Palate: flavourful, fruity, good acidity,
fine bitter notes.

Dominio de Manciles 4 meses 2012 T Roble
84

Dominio de Manciles Selección 2007 TC
100% tempranillo
88
Colour: very deep cherry, purple rim. Nose: ripe fruit, fruit preserve, sweet spices, cocoa bean. Palate: spicy, long.

Dominio de Manciles Selección Especial 2010 T
100% tempranillo
91
Colour: dark-red cherry, purple rim. Nose: red berry notes,
ripe fruit, dried herbs, cocoa bean, creamy oak. Palate: good
structure, concentrated, round tannins.

BODEGAS LERMA

Ctra. Madrid-Irún, Km. 202,5
09340 Lerma (Burgos)
☎: +34 947 177 030
Fax: +34 947 177 004
www.tintolerma.com
info@tintolerma.com

Gran Lerma 2010 T
tempranillo
92
Colour: cherry, garnet rim. Nose: ripe fruit, wild herbs, earthy
notes, spicy, creamy oak. Palate: balanced, flavourful, long,
balsamic.

Lerma Selección 2010 TR
tempranillo

91

Colour: cherry, garnet rim. Nose: red berry notes, ripe fruit, spicy, creamy oak, toasty, complex. Palate: powerful, flavourful, toasty, round tannins.

Nabal 2011 TC
tempranillo

86

Colour: very deep cherry, garnet rim. Nose: powerfull, ripe fruit, roasted coffee, dark chocolate. Palate: powerful, toasty, roasted-coffee aftertaste.

Risco 2013 RD
tempranillo, garnacha, albillo

83

Tinto Lerma 2011 TC
tempranillo

88

Colour: cherry, garnet rim. Nose: ripe fruit, wild herbs, earthy notes, spicy, creamy oak. Palate: flavourful, long, balsamic.

BODEGAS MONTE AMÁN
Ctra. Santo Domingo de Silos, s/n
09348 Castrillo de Solarana (Burgos)
☎: +34 947 173 304
Fax: +34 947 173 308
www.monteaman.com
bodegas@monteaman.com

Monte Amán 2009 TC
100% tempranillo

88

Colour: bright cherry. Nose: ripe fruit, sweet spices, creamy oak, balsamic herbs. Palate: fruity, flavourful, toasty, balanced.

Monte Amán 2013 RD
100% tempranillo

83

Monte Amán 2013 T
100% tempranillo

87

Colour: cherry, garnet rim. Nose: red berry notes, ripe fruit, balsamic herbs, spicy. Palate: powerful, flavourful, balsamic.

Monte Amán 5 meses de barrica 2012 T Roble
100% tempranillo

87

Colour: cherry, garnet rim. Nose: spicy, creamy oak, toasty, fruit liqueur notes, balsamic herbs. Palate: powerful, flavourful, toasty.

Monte Amán Pago de Valdeágueda Viñas Viejas 2004 T
100% tempranillo

89

Colour: pale ruby, brick rim edge. Nose: fruit liqueur notes, wild herbs, spicy, creamy oak. Palate: powerful, flavourful, spicy, classic aged character.

BODEGAS SIERRA
Ctra. Madrid-Irún km 203,7
09390 Villalmanzo (Burgos)
☎: +34 947 170 083
www.bodegassierra.com
info@bodegassierra.com

Cascajuelo 2010 T Roble
tempranillo

85

Cascajuelo 2012 T
tempranillo

83

Cascajuelo 2013 RD
tempranillo

82

Castillo de Ura 2004 TR
tempranillo

86

Colour: dark-red cherry, orangey edge. Nose: aged wood nuances, ripe fruit, tobacco. Palate: flavourful, spicy, round tannins.

Castillo de Ura 2008 TC
tempranillo

84

Castillo de Ura 2009 TC
tempranillo

87

Colour: ruby red. Nose: spicy, fine reductive notes, wet leather, aged wood nuances, toasty. Palate: spicy, long, toasty.

BUEZO
Paraje Valdeazadón, s/n
09342 Mahamud (Burgos)
☎: +34 947 616 899
Fax: +34 947 616 885
www.buezo.com
info@buezo.com

Buezo Nattan 2005 TR
tempranillo

91

Colour: dark-red cherry, garnet rim. Nose: toasty, ripe fruit, spicy, balanced. Palate: good structure, balanced, round tannins.

Buezo Petit Verdot 2005 TR
petit verdot, tempranillo
89
Colour: deep cherry, garnet rim. Nose: medium intensity, scrubland, spicy. Palate: flavourful, easy to drink, ripe fruit.

Buezo Tempranillo 2006 TR
tempranillo
87
Colour: dark-red cherry, garnet rim. Nose: balanced, medium intensity, varietal, sweet spices. Palate: correct, easy to drink.

Buezo Varietales 2006 TR
cabernet sauvignon, merlot, tempranillo
88
Colour: cherry, garnet rim. Nose: ripe fruit, wild herbs, earthy notes, spicy, creamy oak. Palate: balanced, flavourful, long, balsamic.

OLIVIER RIVIÈRE VINOS
Breton de los Herreros, 14 Entreplanta
26001 Logroño (La Rioja)
☎: +34 690 733 541
www.olivier-riviere.com
olivier@olivier-riviere.com

El Cadastro 2012 T
93
Colour: cherry, garnet rim. Nose: red berry notes, fruit liqueur notes, balsamic herbs, spicy, creamy oak, dry stone. Palate: powerful, flavourful, concentrated, spicy, long.

El Quemado 2011 T
90
Colour: cherry, garnet rim. Nose: red berry notes, ripe fruit, balsamic herbs, spicy, mineral. Palate: powerful, rich, flavourful, long, balanced.

PAGOS DE NEGREDO VIÑEDOS
Avda. Casado del Alisal, 26
34001 Palencia (Palencia)
☎: +34 979 700 450
Fax: +34 979 702 171
www.pagosdenegredo.com
administracion@pagosdenegredo.com

Pagos de Negredo Magnum 2010 TC
100% tinto fino
90
Colour: cherry, garnet rim. Nose: ripe fruit, spicy, creamy oak, toasty, complex. Palate: powerful, flavourful, toasty, round tannins, good acidity.

SABINARES
Vista Alegre, 21
09340 Lerma (Burgos)
☎: +34 983 406 212
www.vinoval.es
info@sabinares.com

Sabinares Blanco de Guarda 2012 B
viura, malvasía, chaselas, otras
89
Colour: yellow, greenish rim. Nose: powerfull, ripe fruit, sweet spices, characterful. Palate: flavourful, good structure, long.

Sabinares El Confin 2012 T
tempranillo, garnacha, mencía, otras
93
Colour: bright cherry. Nose: expressive, complex, dry stone, spicy, ripe fruit, fruit preserve. Palate: balanced, long, round tannins.

Sabinares El Temido 2012 T
tempranillo, garnacha, mencía, otras
93
Colour: cherry, garnet rim. Nose: red berry notes, ripe fruit, spicy, creamy oak, toasty, complex, earthy notes. Palate: powerful, flavourful, toasty, round tannins.

SEÑORÍO DE VALDESNEROS
Avda. La Paz, 4
34230 Torquemada (Palencia)
☎: +34 979 800 545
www.bodegasvaldesneros.com
sv@bodegasvaldesneros.com

Eruelo 2009 TC
tempranillo
86
Colour: dark-red cherry. Nose: ripe fruit, sweet spices. Palate: correct, round tannins, spicy, fruity.

Señorío de Valdesneros 2013 RD
tempranillo
87
Colour: rose, purple rim. Nose: red berry notes, fragrant herbs, lactic notes, floral. Palate: fresh, fruity, easy to drink.

Señorío de Valdesneros
6 meses 2011 T Roble
100% tempranillo
85

Señorío de Valdesneros Selección 2008 TC
tempranillo
86
Colour: dark-red cherry, garnet rim. Nose: tobacco, dried herbs, cocoa bean, ripe fruit. Palate: balanced, round tannins.

DO. ARRIBES

CONSEJO REGULADOR

La Almofea, 95
37175 Pereña de la Ribera (Salamanca)
☎ :+34 923 573 413 - Fax: +34 923 573 209
@: info@doarribes.es
www.vinoarribesduero.com

LOCATION:

In Las Arribes National Park, it comprises a narrow stretch of land along the southwest of Zamora and northeast of Salamanca. The vineyards occupy the valleys and steep terraces along the river Duero. Just a single municipal district, Fermoselle, has up to 90% of the total vineyard surface.

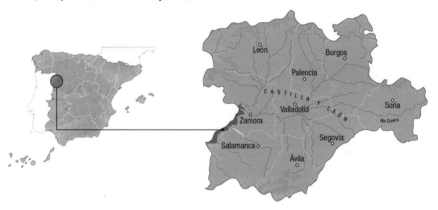

GRAPE VARIETIES:

White: Malvasía, Verdejo and Albillo.
Red: Juan García, Rufete, Tempranillo (preferential); Mencía, Garnacha (authorized).

FIGURES:

Vineyard surface: 400 – Wine-Growers:280 – Wineries: 13 – 2013 Harvest rating: - – Production 13: 607,116 litres – Market percentages: 80% domestic - 20% export.

SOIL:

The region has shallow sandy soils with abundant quartz and stones, even some granite found in the area of Fermoselle. In the territory which is part of the province of Salamanca it is quite noticeable the presence of slate, the kind of rock also featured on the Portuguese part along the Duero, called Douro the other side of the border. The slate subsoil works a splendid thermal regulator capable of accumulating the heat from the sunshine during the day and to slowly release it during the night time.

CLIMATE:

This wine region has a strong Mediterranean influence, given the prominent decrease in altitude that the territory features from the flat lands of the Sáyago area along the Duero valley until the river reaches Fermoselle, still in the province of Zamora. Rainfall is low all through the year, even during the averagely hot summer.

VINTAGE RATING

PEÑÍNGUIDE

2009	2010	2011	2012	2013
VERY GOOD	VERY GOOD	EXCELLENT	VERY GOOD	N/A

BODEGA ARRIBES DEL DUERO

Ctra. Masueco, s/n
37251 Corporario - Aldeadavila
(Salamanca)
☎: +34 923 169 195
Fax: +34 923 169 195
www.bodegasarribesdelduero.com
secretaria@bodegasarribesdelduero.com

Arribes de Vettonia 2006 TR
juan garcía
90
Colour: bright cherry. Nose: ripe fruit, sweet spices, creamy oak. Palate: fruity, flavourful, toasty, fine bitter notes, long.

Arribes de Vettonia 2007 BFB
malvasía
91
Colour: bright golden. Nose: ripe fruit, dry nuts, powerfull, toasty, aged wood nuances, honeyed notes. Palate: flavourful, fruity, spicy, toasty, long.

Arribes de Vettonia 2011 TC
juan garcía
87
Colour: cherry, garnet rim. Nose: spicy, toasty, overripe fruit, mineral. Palate: powerful, flavourful, toasty, round tannins.

Arribes de Vettonia 2012 T
84

Arribes de Vettonia 2013 B
malvasía
82

Arribes de Vettonia 2013 RD
juan garcía
79

Arribes de Vettonia Rufete 2011 T
rufete
87
Colour: cherry, garnet rim. Nose: spicy, toasty, overripe fruit, mineral. Palate: powerful, flavourful, toasty, round tannins.

Arribes de Vettonia Vendimia Selecionada 2007 T Roble
bruñal
90
Colour: cherry, garnet rim. Nose: ripe fruit, spicy, creamy oak, toasty, complex. Palate: powerful, flavourful, toasty, round tannins.

Hechanza Real 2010 TC
juan garcía
84

Secreto del Vetton 2009 T
bruñal
93
Colour: cherry, garnet rim. Nose: ripe fruit, wild herbs, earthy notes, spicy, creamy oak. Palate: balanced, flavourful, long, balsamic.

BODEGA COOP. VIRGEN DE LA BANDERA

Avda. General Franco, 24
49220 Fermoselle (Zamora)
☎: +34 692 682 682
vinosborbon@vinosborbon.com

Viña Borbon 2010 TC
juan garcía
87
Colour: dark-red cherry, garnet rim, orangey edge. Nose: powerfull, ripe fruit, fruit preserve, spicy, warm. Palate: balanced, round tannins.

Viña Borbon 2012 T
juan garcía
85

BODEGA DESCORCHANDO

La Colina, 9 N 417
29620 Torremolinos (Málaga)
☎: +34 634 676 868
www.descorchando.com
jgarcia@descorchando.com

JG 2008 T
100% juan garcía
87
Colour: cherry, garnet rim. Nose: fruit preserve, fruit liqueur notes, spicy. Palate: flavourful, pruney, balsamic.

BODEGA LA FONTANICAS

Requejo 222
49220 Fermoselle (Zamora)
☎: +34 629 548 774
info@arribesduero.com

Fontanicas 2011 TC
juan garcía
90
Colour: cherry, garnet rim. Nose: ripe fruit, spicy, creamy oak, toasty, complex. Palate: powerful, flavourful, toasty, round tannins.

BODEGA QUINTA LAS VELAS

Humilladero, 44
37248 Ahigal de los Aceiteros
(Salamanca)
☎: +34 619 955 735
Fax: +34 923 120 674
www.quintalasvelas.com
enrique@esla.com

Quinta las Velas 2010 TC
tempranillo

87

Colour: cherry, garnet rim. Nose: fruit preserve, fruit liqueur notes, spicy. Palate: flavourful, pruney, balsamic.

BODEGAS LAS GAVIAS
Avda. Constitución, 2
37175 Pereña de la Ribera (Salamanca)
☎: +34 902 108 031
Fax: +34 987 218 751
www.bodegaslasgavias.com
info@bodegaslasgavias.com

Aldana 2012 T Roble
juan garcía

85

BODEGAS PASTRANA
Toro, 9
49018 (Zamora)
☎: +34 664 546 131
www.bodegaspastrana.es
info@bodegaspastrana.es

Paraje de los Bancales 2010 T
100% juan garcía

90

Colour: cherry, garnet rim. Nose: ripe fruit, spicy, creamy oak, toasty, complex, mineral. Palate: powerful, flavourful, toasty, round tannins.

BODEGAS RIBERA DE PELAZAS
Camino de la Ermita, s/n
37175 Pereña de la Ribera (Salamanca)
☎: +34 902 108 031
Fax: +34 987 218 751
www.bodegasriberadepelazas.com
bodega@bodegasriberadepelazas.com

Abadengo 2010 TC
juan garcía

89

Colour: cherry, garnet rim. Nose: ripe fruit, spicy, creamy oak, toasty, complex. Palate: powerful, flavourful, toasty, round tannins.

Abadengo 2011 T Roble
juan garcía

88

Colour: bright cherry. Nose: ripe fruit, sweet spices, creamy oak, expressive, mineral. Palate: flavourful, fruity, toasty, round tannins.

Abadengo Malvasia 2013 B
malvasía

84

Abadengo Selección Especial 2004 T

88

Colour: cherry, garnet rim. Nose: ripe fruit, spicy, creamy oak, toasty, complex. Palate: powerful, flavourful, toasty, round tannins, long.

Bruñal 2007 T
bruñal

90

Colour: cherry, garnet rim. Nose: ripe fruit, wild herbs, earthy notes, spicy, creamy oak. Palate: balanced, flavourful, long, balsamic.

Gran Abadengo 2006 TR
juan garcía

89

Colour: cherry, garnet rim. Nose: fruit preserve, fruit liqueur notes, spicy. Palate: flavourful, pruney, balsamic.

GALLO VISCAY
Avda. San Amaro, 52
37160 Villarino de los Aires (Salamanca)
☎: +34 659 159 218
www.galloviscay.com
galloviscay@gmail.com

Eighteen 18 2010 T

90

Colour: cherry, garnet rim. Nose: ripe fruit, wild herbs, earthy notes, spicy, creamy oak. Palate: balanced, flavourful, long, balsamic.

HACIENDA ZORITA MARQUÉS DE LA CONCORDIA FAMILY OF WINES
Ctra. Zamora - fermoselle, km. 58
49220 Fermoselle (Zamora)
☎: +34 980 613 163
Fax: +34 980 613 163
www.the-haciendas.com
agarcia@the-haciendas.com

Hacienda Zorita 2011 TC

89

Colour: bright cherry, garnet rim. Nose: ripe fruit, sweet spices, creamy oak. Palate: fruity, flavourful, toasty.

LA SETERA
Calzada, 7
49232 Fornillos de Fermoselle (Zamora)
☎: +34 980 612 925
Fax: +34 980 612 925
www.lasetera.com
lasetera@lasetera.com

La Setera 2009 TC
juan garcía

88

Colour: bright cherry. Nose: ripe fruit, sweet spices, creamy oak, expressive. Palate: flavourful, fruity, toasty, round tannins.

La Setera 2012 T
juan garcía

87

Colour: cherry, purple rim. Nose: expressive, fresh fruit, red berry notes, floral. Palate: flavourful, fruity, good acidity, round tannins.

La Setera 2013 B
malvasía

84

La Setera Rosado de Lágrima 2013 RD
juan garcía

86

Colour: rose, purple rim. Nose: powerfull, ripe fruit, red berry notes, floral. Palate: powerful, fruity, fresh.

La Setera Selección Especial 2010 T Roble
touriga nacional

92

Colour: cherry, garnet rim. Nose: ripe fruit, wild herbs, earthy notes, spicy, creamy oak. Palate: balanced, flavourful, long, balsamic.

La Setera Tinaja Varietales 2011 T Roble
juan garcía, mencía, rufete, tinta madrid

93

Colour: cherry, garnet rim. Nose: ripe fruit, spicy, creamy oak, toasty, complex, dark chocolate, earthy notes. Palate: powerful, flavourful, toasty, round tannins.

OCELLVM DURII
San Juan 56 - 58
49220 Fermoselle (Zamora)
☎: +34 983 390 606
www.bodegasocellumdurii.es
ocellumdurii@hotmail.com

Ocila Condado de Fermosel 2012 T
juan garcía, tempranillo, rufete, bruñal

90

Colour: cherry, garnet rim. Nose: powerfull, scrubland, ripe fruit, spicy, creamy oak. Palate: flavourful, spicy, balanced, long.

Transitium Durii 2007 T
juan garcía, tempranillo, rufete, bruñal

90 🌷

Colour: very deep cherry. Nose: ripe fruit, balsamic herbs, earthy notes, spicy, expressive. Palate: rich, powerful, flavourful, balanced.

Transitium Durii 2008 T
juan garcía, tempranillo, rufete, bruñal

89

Colour: cherry, garnet rim. Nose: spicy, creamy oak, toasty, earthy notes, overripe fruit. Palate: powerful, flavourful, toasty, round tannins.

TERRAZGO BODEGAS DE CRIANZA S.L.
Portugal, 7
49323 Fornillos de Fermoselle (Zamora)
☎: +49 232 459 724
www.terrazgo.com
terrazgobc@hotmail.com

Terrazgo 2009 T
juan garcía, bruñal, rufete

91

Colour: cherry, garnet rim. Nose: red berry notes, fruit liqueur notes, spicy, toasty. Palate: flavourful, fruity, elegant.

VIÑA ROMANA

Pereña, 11
37160 Villarino de los Aires
(Salamanca)
☎: +34 629 756 328
www.vinaromana.com
joseluis@vinaromana.com

Harley 2010 T
juan garcía, bobal

91

Colour: bright cherry. Nose: ripe fruit, sweet spices, creamy oak, mineral. Palate: fruity, flavourful, toasty.

Heredad del Viejo Imperio 2009 T
juan garcía

87

Colour: cherry, garnet rim. Nose: fruit preserve, fruit liqueur notes, spicy. Palate: flavourful, pruney, balsamic.

Heredad del Viejo Imperio Homenaje Selección 2010 T
bruñal

93

Colour: very deep cherry. Nose: ripe fruit, spicy, creamy oak, toasty, characterful, balsamic herbs. Palate: powerful, flavourful, toasty, round tannins.

Solar de la Victoria 2012 T Roble
juan garcía

88

Colour: bright cherry. Nose: ripe fruit, sweet spices, creamy oak, mineral. Palate: flavourful, fruity, toasty, round tannins.

DO. BIERZO

CONSEJO REGULADOR

Mencía, 1
24540 Cacabelos (León)
☎:+34 987 549 408 - Fax: +34 987 547 077
@: info@crdobierzo.es
www.crdobierzo.es

LOCATION:

In the north west of the province of León. It covers 23 municipal areas and occupies several valleys in mountainous terrain and a flat plain at a lower altitude than the plateau of León, with higher temperatures accompanied by more rainfall. It may be considered an area of transition between Galicia, León and Asturias.

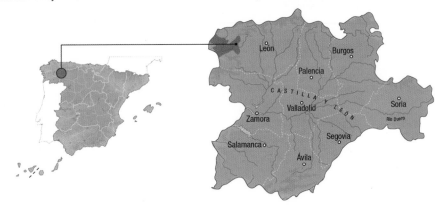

GRAPE VARIETIES:

White: Godello, Palomino, Dona Blanca and Malvasia.
Red: Mencía or Negra and Garnacha Tintorera.

FIGURES:

Vineyard surface: 3,009 – Wine-Growers: 2,484 – Wineries: 73 – 2013 Harvest rating: Very Good – Production 13: 9,804,100 litres – Market percentages: 72% domestic - 28% export.

SOIL:

In the mountain regions, it is made up of a mixture of fine elements, quartzite and slate. In general, the soil of the DO is humid, dun and slightly acidic. The greater quality indices are associated with the slightly sloped terraces close to the rivers, the half - terraced or steep slopes situated at an altitude of between 450 and 1,000 m.

CLIMATE:

Quite mild and benign, with a certain degree of humidity due to Galician influence, although somewhat dry like Castilla. Thanks to the low altitude, late frost is avoided quite successfully and the grapes are usually harvested one month before the rest of Castilla. The average rainfall per year is 721 mm.

VINTAGE RATING   PEÑÍNGUIDE

2009	2010	2011	2012	2013
GOOD	EXCELLENT	GOOD	VERY GOOD	VERY GOOD

AKILIA

Ctra. LE-142, PK. 54,7
24401 Ponferrada (León)
☎: +34 902 848 127
www.akiliawines.com
info@akiliawines.com

Akilia 2012 T
100% mencía

90

Colour: cherry, garnet rim. Nose: ripe fruit, wild herbs, earthy notes, spicy, varietal. Palate: balanced, flavourful, long, balsamic.

ÁLVAREZ DE TOLEDO VIÑEDOS Y GRUPO BODEGAS

Río Selmo, 8
24560 Toral de los Vados (León)
☎: +34 987 563 551
Fax: +34 987 563 532
www.bodegasalvarezdetoledo.com
admon@bodegasalvarezdetoledo.com

Álvarez de Toledo 2010 T Roble
100% mencía

89

Colour: bright cherry. Nose: red berry notes, ripe fruit, spicy, toasty, complex, balsamic herbs. Palate: powerful, flavourful, toasty, round tannins.

Álvarez de Toledo 2011 T Roble
100% mencía

88

Colour: cherry, garnet rim. Nose: ripe fruit, wild herbs, spicy, creamy oak. Palate: balanced, flavourful, long, balsamic.

MENCÍA ROBLE
Luis Varela
ALVAREZ DE TOLEDO

Desde el S.XV la dinastía de los Álvarez de Toledo
ha cultivado y vinificado cepas en el Bierzo.
Siguiendo con la vocación y tradición familiar,
descendientes de la familia han elaborado
este vino de forma cuidada y artesanal.

BIERZO
DENOMINACIÓN DE ORIGEN

Álvarez de Toledo Godello 2013 B
100% godello

88

Colour: bright straw. Nose: fresh, fresh fruit, white flowers, wild herbs. Palate: flavourful, fruity, good acidity.

AURELIO FEO VITICULTOR

El Oteiro, 7 San Andrés de Montejos
27791 Ponferrada (León)
☎: +34 987 401 865
Fax: +34 987 401 865
www.bodegafeo.es
bodega@bodegafeo.es

Buencomiezo 2011 T
mencía

87

Colour: cherry, garnet rim. Nose: ripe fruit, spicy, creamy oak, toasty. Palate: powerful, flavourful, toasty.

Cruz de San Andrés 2012 T
mencía

85

AXIAL

Pla-za Calle Castillo de Capua, 10 Nave 7
50197 (Zaragoza)
☎: +34 976 780 136
Fax: +34 976 303 035
www.axialvinos.com
info@axialvinos.com

La Mano Mencía 2012 T Roble
100% mencía

83

BODEGA ALBERTO LEDO

Estación, 6
24500 Villafranca del Bierzo (León)
☎: +34 636 023 676
www.albertoledo.com
aallrs@msn.com

Ledo Club de Barricas 1818 2007 TR
mencía

89

Colour: ruby red. Nose: spicy, fine reductive notes, wet leather, aged wood nuances, fruit liqueur notes. Palate: spicy, fine tannins, elegant, long, balanced.

Ledo Godello 2012 B
godello

86

Colour: bright straw. Nose: fresh, fresh fruit, white flowers, expressive. Palate: flavourful, fruity, good acidity, balanced.

Ledo Mencía 2012 T
mencía
86
Colour: cherry, garnet rim. Nose: ripe fruit, wild herbs. Palate: powerful, flavourful, ripe fruit.

Ledo Selección 2007 T
mencía
88
Colour: deep cherry, orangey edge. Nose: waxy notes, tobacco, ripe fruit, spicy, aged wood nuances. Palate: fine bitter notes, elegant, flavourful, fine tannins.

Ledo. 8 2008 T
mencía
89
Colour: ruby red. Nose: spicy, fine reductive notes, wet leather, aged wood nuances, toasty, ripe fruit. Palate: spicy, long, toasty.

Ledo. 8 2009 TC
mencía
87
Colour: bright cherry. Nose: ripe fruit, sweet spices, creamy oak, medium intensity, fine reductive notes. Palate: fruity, flavourful, toasty.

BODEGA ALMÁZCARA MAJARA
Calle de Las Eras, 5
24395 Almázcara (León)
☎: +34 609 322 194
www.almazcaramajara.com
javier.alvarez@alvarezmiras.com

Almázcara Majara 2010 T
90
Colour: cherry, garnet rim. Nose: red berry notes, ripe fruit, spicy, creamy oak, toasty, complex, earthy notes. Palate: powerful, flavourful, toasty, round tannins.

Amphora de Cobija del Pobre 2013 T
mencía
89
Colour: cherry, garnet rim. Nose: ripe fruit, spicy, dry stone. Palate: powerful, flavourful, round tannins.

Cobija del Pobre 2013 B
godello
89
Colour: bright straw. Nose: white flowers, fragrant herbs, fruit expression, mineral. Palate: fresh, fruity, flavourful, balanced, elegant.

Demasiado Corazón 2011 B
godello
88
Colour: bright straw. Nose: dried herbs, faded flowers, slightly evolved, spicy, creamy oak. Palate: ripe fruit, spicy, long.

Jarabe de Almázcara 2012 T
87
Colour: ruby red. Nose: spicy, fine reductive notes, wet leather, aged wood nuances, toasty. Palate: spicy, long, toasty, balsamic.

BODEGA ANTONIO JOSÉ SILVA BROCO
Lg. Paradones - Ctra. General, 4
24516 Toral Vados (León)
☎: +34 615 276 894
Fax: +34 987 553 043
antoniosilvabroco@hotmail.com

Lagar de Caxan 2012 T
mencía
87
Colour: bright cherry. Nose: ripe fruit, sweet spices, expressive, wild herbs. Palate: flavourful, fruity, toasty.

Viña Broco 2013 T
mencía
88
Colour: bright cherry. Nose: ripe fruit, sweet spices, creamy oak, expressive, balsamic herbs. Palate: flavourful, fruity, toasty, round tannins.

BODEGA DEL ABAD
Ctra. N-VI, km. 396
24549 Carracedelo (León)
☎: +34 987 562 417
Fax: +34 987 562 428
www.bodegadelabad.com
vinos@bodegadelabad.com

Abad Dom Bueno Godello 2013 B
godello
89
Colour: bright straw. Nose: white flowers, fragrant herbs, fruit expression, citrus fruit. Palate: fresh, fruity, flavourful, balanced, elegant.

Abad Dom Bueno Godello 2013 BFB
godello
90
Colour: bright yellow. Nose: ripe fruit, sweet spices, fragrant herbs. Palate: rich, flavourful, fresh, good acidity.

Abad Dom Bueno Señorío de Valcarce 2012 T Roble
mencía
89
Colour: cherry, garnet rim. Nose: ripe fruit, spicy, creamy oak, toasty, complex. Palate: powerful, flavourful, toasty, round tannins.

Carracedo 2011 TR
mencía

89

Colour: cherry, garnet rim. Nose: ripe fruit, spicy, creamy oak, toasty, complex. Palate: powerful, flavourful, toasty.

Gotín del Risc Essencia 2008 TR
mencía

91

Colour: cherry, garnet rim. Nose: balanced, complex, ripe fruit, spicy, mineral. Palate: good structure, flavourful, round tannins, balanced.

Gotín del Risc Godello de San Salvador 2012 B
godello

92

Colour: yellow, greenish rim. Nose: white flowers, expressive, fine lees, dried herbs, faded flowers. Palate: flavourful, fruity, good acidity, balanced.

BODEGA MARTÍNEZ YEBRA

San Pedro, 96
24530 Villadecanes (León)
☎: +34 987 562 082
Fax: +34 987 562 082
www.bodegamartinezyebra.es
info@bodegamartinezyebra.es

Canes 2013 B
godello

85

Canes 2013 T
100% mencía

84

Tres Racimos 2009 T
100% mencía

87

Colour: cherry, garnet rim. Nose: ripe fruit, wild herbs, earthy notes, spicy, creamy oak. Palate: balanced, flavourful, long, balsamic.

Viñadecanes 2009 TC
100% mencía

87

Colour: cherry, garnet rim. Nose: ripe fruit, wild herbs, earthy notes, spicy, creamy oak. Palate: balanced, flavourful, long, balsamic.

BODEGA Y VIÑEDOS LUNA BEBERIDE

Ant. Ctra. Madrid - Coruña, Km. 402
24540 Cacabelos (León)
☎: +34 987 549 002
Fax: +34 987 549 214
www.lunabeberide.es
info@lunabeberide.es

Art Luna Beberide 2011 TC
mencía

91

Colour: cherry, garnet rim. Nose: ripe fruit, spicy, creamy oak, toasty, complex, balsamic herbs. Palate: powerful, flavourful, toasty, round tannins.

Finca la Cuesta Luna Beberide 2011 TC
mencía

90

Colour: cherry, garnet rim. Nose: ripe fruit, spicy, creamy oak, complex. Palate: powerful, flavourful, toasty, round tannins.

Mencía Luna Beberide 2013 T
mencía

89

Colour: cherry, purple rim. Nose: red berry notes, raspberry, floral, expressive. Palate: fresh, fruity, flavourful, easy to drink.

BODEGA Y VIÑEDOS MAS ASTURIAS

Fueros de Leon nº 1
24400 Ponferrada (León)
☎: +34 650 654 492
www.bodegamasasturias.com
jose_mas_asturias@hotmail.com

Massuria 2010 T
mencía

90

Colour: cherry, garnet rim. Nose: ripe fruit, spicy, creamy oak, toasty. Palate: powerful, flavourful, toasty, round tannins, balanced.

BODEGAS ADRIÁ

Antigua Ctra. Madrid - Coruña, Km. 408
24500 Villafranca del Bierzo (León)
☎: +34 987 540 907
Fax: +34 987 540 347
www.bodegasadria.com
paco@bodegasadria.com

Vega Montán Adriá 2010 T
mencía

90

Colour: cherry, garnet rim. Nose: ripe fruit, spicy, creamy oak, toasty, complex. Palate: powerful, flavourful, toasty, round tannins.

Vega Montán Godello 2013 B
godello
89
Colour: bright straw. Nose: white flowers, fragrant herbs, fruit expression, dry stone. Palate: fresh, fruity, flavourful, balanced, elegant.

Vega Montán Mencía 2013 T
mencía
83

Vega Montán Silk 2012 T
mencía
89
Colour: bright cherry. Nose: ripe fruit, sweet spices, creamy oak, dark chocolate, expressive. Palate: flavourful, fruity, toasty, round tannins.

BODEGAS BERNARDO ÁLVAREZ
San Pedro, 75
24530 Villadecanes (León)
☎: +34 987 562 129
Fax: +34 987 562 129
www.bodegasbernardoalvarez.com
vinos@bodegasbernardoalvarez.com

Campo Redondo 2012 T Roble
100% mencía
89
Colour: cherry, garnet rim. Nose: ripe fruit, spicy, creamy oak, toasty, complex. Palate: powerful, flavourful, toasty, round tannins, balsamic.

Campo Redondo Godello 2013 B
100% godello
87
Colour: yellow, greenish rim. Nose: floral, citrus fruit, fresh fruit, balanced. Palate: balanced, correct, easy to drink.

Viña Migarrón 2008 TC
100% mencía
87
Colour: dark-red cherry. Nose: ripe fruit, spicy, toasty, old leather. Palate: powerful, flavourful, toasty, round tannins.

Viña Migarrón 2012 T
100% mencía
86
Colour: cherry, garnet rim. Nose: ripe fruit, fruit preserve, wild herbs. Palate: powerful, flavourful, fresh, balsamic.

Viña Migarrón 2013 B
dona blanca, jerez, godello
88
Colour: bright straw. Nose: fresh, fresh fruit, white flowers, expressive. Palate: flavourful, fruity, good acidity, balanced.

Viña Migarrón 2013 RD
100% mencía
87
Colour: light cherry, bright. Nose: red berry notes, balanced, fresh, medium intensity. Palate: fruity, easy to drink, good finish.

BODEGAS CUATRO PASOS
Santa María, 43
24540 Cacabelos (León)
☎: +34 987 548 089
Fax: +34 986 526 901
www.cuatropasos.es
bierzo@martincodax.com

Cuatro Pasos 2011 T
100% mencía
90
Colour: dark-red cherry, garnet rim. Nose: toasty, scrubland, ripe fruit, varietal. Palate: fruity, flavourful, round tannins.

Cuatro Pasos 2013 RD
100% mencía
88
Colour: rose, purple rim. Nose: ripe fruit, red berry notes, floral, expressive. Palate: powerful, fruity, fresh.

Cuatro Pasos Black 2011 T
100% mencía
90
Colour: bright cherry. Nose: ripe fruit, sweet spices, creamy oak, expressive, balsamic herbs. Palate: flavourful, fruity, toasty, round tannins.

Martín Sarmiento 2011 T
100% mencía
92
Colour: very deep cherry. Nose: varietal, ripe fruit, creamy oak, balsamic herbs, mineral. Palate: good structure, flavourful, full, round tannins.

Pizarras de Otero 2012 T
100% mencía
87
Colour: cherry, garnet rim. Nose: powerfull, wild herbs, ripe fruit, spicy. Palate: flavourful, fruity, balsamic.

BODEGAS GODELIA
Antigua Ctra. N-VI, NVI, Km. 403,5
24547 Pieros-Cacabelos (León)
☎: +34 987 546 279
Fax: +34 987 548 026
www.godelia.es
info@godelia.es

Godelia 2011 T Roble
mencía
89
Colour: deep cherry. Nose: smoky, toasty, spicy. Palate: fruity, flavourful, good structure, round tannins, balsamic.

Godelia 2012 B
91
Colour: bright straw. Nose: white flowers, fresh fruit, expressive, fine lees, dried herbs. Palate: flavourful, fruity, good acidity, balanced.

Godelia Blanco Selección 2012 B
100% godello
91
Colour: bright yellow. Nose: ripe fruit, sweet spices, creamy oak, fragrant herbs. Palate: rich, smoky aftertaste, flavourful, fresh, good acidity, balanced.

Godelia Tinto Selección 2011 T
100% mencía
91
Colour: cherry, garnet rim. Nose: ripe fruit, spicy, creamy oak, toasty, complex, mineral. Palate: powerful, flavourful, toasty, round tannins, balanced.

Viernes 2012 T
100% mencía
89
Colour: cherry, purple rim. Nose: fresh fruit, red berry notes, floral, balsamic herbs. Palate: flavourful, fruity, good acidity.

BODEGAS ORDÓÑEZ
Bartolomé Esteban Murillo, 11
29700 Vélez- Málaga (Málaga)
☎: +34 952 504 706
Fax: +34 951 284 796
www.grupojorgeordonez.com
info@jorgeordonez.es

Tritón Mencía 2013 T
100% mencía
91
Colour: cherry, garnet rim. Nose: ripe fruit, wild herbs, earthy notes, spicy, creamy oak. Palate: balanced, flavourful, long, balsamic.

BODEGAS PEIQUE
El Bierzo, s/n
24530 Valtuille de Abajo (León)
☎: +34 987 562 044
Fax: +34 987 562 044
www.bodegaspeique.com
bodega@bodegaspeique.com

Luis Peique 2009 T Fermentado en Barrica
mencía
91
Colour: cherry, garnet rim. Nose: balanced, complex, ripe fruit, spicy, roasted coffee. Palate: good structure, flavourful, balanced, roasted-coffee aftertaste.

Peique 2013 RD
moll
85

Peique Garnacha 2011 T
garnacha tintorera
91
Colour: cherry, garnet rim. Nose: ripe fruit, wild herbs, earthy notes, spicy, creamy oak. Palate: balanced, flavourful, long, balsamic.

Peique Godello 2013 B
godello
90
Colour: yellow. Nose: medium intensity, citrus fruit, white flowers, fresh fruit. Palate: fruity, good acidity, fine bitter notes, fresh.

Peique Ramón Valle 2012 T
mencía
89
Colour: dark-red cherry, garnet rim. Nose: fruit expression, balanced, wild herbs. Palate: flavourful, fruity aftestaste, easy to drink.

Peique Selección Familiar 2009 T
mencía
92
Colour: cherry, garnet rim. Nose: ripe fruit, spicy, creamy oak, toasty, complex. Palate: powerful, flavourful, toasty, round tannins, balsamic.

Peique Tinto Mencía 2013 T
mencía
88
Colour: bright cherry, purple rim. Nose: medium intensity, red berry notes, balsamic herbs, varietal. Palate: fruity, correct, easy to drink.

Peique Viñedos Viejos 2010 T Roble
mencía
92
Colour: bright cherry, garnet rim. Nose: scrubland, elegant, mineral. Palate: good structure, full, complex, balanced.

BODEGAS VIÑAS DE VIÑALES
Calle del Campo, s/n
24319 Viñales (León)
☎: +34 609 652 058
www.bodegasvinasdevinales.com
info@bodegasvinasdevinales.com

Interamnum Doce 2012 T
mencía
87
Colour: black cherry. Nose: ripe fruit, fruit preserve, sweet spices. Palate: flavourful, round tannins, spicy, good finish.

Interanum 2013 T
mencía
87
Colour: deep cherry, purple rim. Nose: scrubland, ripe fruit. Palate: correct, balanced, round tannins.

BODEGAS Y VIÑEDOS AMAYA

San Pedro, 49-53
24530 Villadecanes (León)
☎: +34 644 162 550
www.bodegasyvinedosamaya.es
byvamontuno@gmail.com

Montuno 2012 T
100% mencía
88

Colour: bright cherry. Nose: ripe fruit, sweet spices, creamy oak, dried herbs, toasty. Palate: flavourful, fruity, toasty, round tannins.

BODEGAS Y VIÑEDOS CASTROVENTOSA

Finca El Barredo, s/n
24530 Valtuille de Abajo (León)
☎: +34 987 562 148
Fax: +34 987 562 103
www.castroventosa.com
info@castroventosa.com

Castro Ventosa"Vintage" 2008 T
mencía
89

Colour: pale ruby, brick rim edge. Nose: elegant, spicy, fine reductive notes, wet leather, aged wood nuances. Palate: spicy, fine tannins, elegant, long.

El Castro de Valtuille 2011 T
mencía
92

Colour: very deep cherry. Nose: expressive, scrubland, spicy, ripe fruit, elegant. Palate: balanced, spicy.

El Castro de Valtuille Joven 2013 T
mencía
87

Colour: cherry, purple rim. Nose: scrubland, ripe fruit, varietal. Palate: balanced, balsamic, fruity.

Valtuille Cepas Centenarias 2011 T
mencía
93

Colour: very deep cherry, garnet rim. Nose: grassy, scrubland, spicy, ripe fruit. Palate: balanced, long, balsamic.

BODEGAS Y VIÑEDOS GANCEDO

Vistalegre, s/n
24548 Quilós (León)
☎: +34 987 134 980
Fax: +34 987 563 278
www.bodegasgancedo.com
info@bodegasgancedo.com

Gancedo 2012 T
mencía
91

Colour: bright cherry. Nose: ripe fruit, sweet spices, creamy oak, expressive, scrubland. Palate: flavourful, fruity, round tannins.

Herencia del Capricho 2008 BFB
93

Colour: bright yellow. Nose: powerfull, ripe fruit, sweet spices, creamy oak, fragrant herbs. Palate: rich, smoky aftertaste, flavourful, fresh, good acidity.

Ucedo Mencía 2008 T
mencía
87

Colour: very deep cherry, garnet rim. Nose: powerfull, ripe fruit, roasted coffee, dark chocolate. Palate: powerful, toasty, roasted-coffee aftertaste.

Val de Paxariñas Capricho 2013 B
92

Colour: bright straw. Nose: white flowers, fragrant herbs, fruit expression. Palate: fresh, fruity, flavourful, balanced, elegant.

Xestal 2008 T
mencía
90

Colour: cherry, garnet rim. Nose: ripe fruit, spicy, creamy oak, toasty, complex. Palate: powerful, flavourful, toasty, round tannins.

BODEGAS Y VIÑEDOS MENGOBA

Avda. del Parque, 7
24544 San Juan de Carracedo (León)
☎: +34 649 940 800
www.mengoba.com
gregory@mengoba.com

Brezo 2013 RD
mencía
87

Colour: light cherry. Nose: medium intensity, red berry notes, floral. Palate: fresh, correct, balanced, good acidity.

Brezo Godello y Doña Blanca 2013 B
godello, dona blanca

90

Colour: bright straw. Nose: white flowers, fresh fruit, expressive, fine lees, dried herbs. Palate: fruity, good acidity, balanced, fine bitter notes.

Flor de Brezo 2012 T
mencía, garnacha tintorera

90

Colour: cherry, garnet rim. Nose: ripe fruit, spicy, creamy oak, complex. Palate: powerful, flavourful, toasty, round tannins.

Mengoba 2012 T
mencía, garnacha tintorera

91

Colour: cherry, garnet rim. Nose: ripe fruit, spicy, creamy oak, toasty, complex, balsamic herbs. Palate: powerful, flavourful, toasty, round tannins, elegant.

Mengoba Godello sobre lías 2012 B
godello

93

Colour: golden. Nose: powerfull, ripe fruit, sweet spices, fragrant herbs, smoky. Palate: rich, smoky aftertaste, flavourful, fresh, good acidity.

Mengoba La Vigne de Sancho Martín 2012 T
mencía, garnacha tintorera

93

Colour: deep cherry. Nose: ripe fruit, spicy, creamy oak, toasty, complex, mineral, varietal. Palate: powerful, flavourful, toasty, round tannins.

BODEGAS Y VIÑEDOS MERAYO
Ctra. de la Espina, km. 6
Finca Miralmonte
24491 San Andrés de Montejos (León)
☎: +34 987 057 925
www.bodegasmerayo.com
info@byvmerayo.com

Aquiana 2011 T
100% mencía

92

Colour: cherry, garnet rim. Nose: ripe fruit, wild herbs, earthy notes, spicy, creamy oak. Palate: balanced, flavourful, long, balsamic.

Galbana 2012 T
100% mencía

91

Colour: cherry, garnet rim. Nose: ripe fruit, spicy, creamy oak, toasty, complex, dark chocolate, earthy notes. Palate: powerful, flavourful, toasty.

Las Tres Filas 2012 T
100% mencía

91

Colour: bright cherry. Nose: ripe fruit, sweet spices, creamy oak, expressive. Palate: flavourful, fruity, toasty, round tannins, balanced.

Merayo 2013 RD
100% mencía

88

Colour: coppery red, bright. Nose: medium intensity, red berry notes, floral. Palate: flavourful, good acidity, balanced, easy to drink.

Merayo Godello 2013 B
godello

88

Colour: yellow, greenish rim. Nose: medium intensity, white flowers, citrus fruit, fresh fruit. Palate: fresh, fine bitter notes, good acidity.

BODEGAS Y VIÑEDOS PAIXAR
Ribadeo, 56
24500 Villafranca del Bierzo (León)
☎: +34 987 549 002
Fax: +34 987 549 214
info@lunabeberide.es

Paixar Mencía 2011 T
mencía

90

Colour: bright cherry. Nose: ripe fruit, sweet spices, creamy oak, medium intensity. Palate: fruity, flavourful, toasty.

BODEGAS Y VIÑEDOS PUIL
La Estación, 17
24500 Villafranca del Bierzo (León)
☎: +34 677 420 392
vinospuil@gmail.com

Puil 2013 T
83

Puil Esencia de Godello 2013 B
godello
82

CASAR DE BURBIA
Travesia la Constitución, s/n
24549 Carracedelo (León)
☎: +34 987 562 910
Fax: +34 987 562 850
www.casardeburbia.com
info@casardeburbia.com

Casar de Burbia 2012 T
100% mencía

92

Colour: cherry, garnet rim. Nose: ripe fruit, wild herbs, spicy, creamy oak. Palate: powerful, flavourful, spicy, long.

Casar Godello 2012 BFB
100% godello

90

Colour: bright straw. Nose: fruit expression, ripe fruit, floral, spicy. Palate: fresh, fruity, flavourful, spicy, balanced.

Casar Godello 2013 B
100% godello

90

Colour: bright straw. Nose: white flowers, fragrant herbs, fruit expression. Palate: fresh, fruity, flavourful, balanced, elegant.

Hombros 2012 T
100% mencía

93

Colour: cherry, garnet rim. Nose: spicy, fragrant herbs, red berry notes, ripe fruit, mineral. Palate: flavourful, long, balsamic, balanced, elegant.

Tebaida 2012 T
100% mencía

93

Colour: cherry, garnet rim. Nose: red berry notes, ripe fruit, spicy, creamy oak, toasty, complex, earthy notes. Palate: powerful, flavourful, toasty, round tannins.

Tebaida Nemesio 2011 T
100% mencía

94

Colour: cherry, garnet rim. Nose: fragrant herbs, red berry notes, ripe fruit, spicy, creamy oak. Palate: powerful, flavourful, unctuous, balanced.

CEPAS DEL BIERZO
Ctra. de Sanabria, 111
24401 Ponferrada (León)
☎: +34 987 412 333
Fax: +34 987 412 912
coocebier@coocebier.e.telefonica.net

Don Osmundo 2009 T
mencía

88

Colour: bright cherry. Nose: ripe fruit, sweet spices, creamy oak, medium intensity. Palate: fruity, flavourful, toasty.

Don Osmundo 2011 T Barrica
mencía

85

CÍA. EXPORTADORA VINÍCOLA DEL BIERZO
Ctra. de Fabero, 83
24404 Cabañas Raras (León)
☎: +34 987 421 755
Fax: +34 987 421 755
bodega@vinicoladelbierzo.com

Lagarada Godello Edición Especial 2013 B
godello

82

Lagarada Mencia Edición Especial 2013 T
mencía

84

COBERTIZO DE VIÑA RAMIRO
Promadelo Pol. 33 Parcela 407
24530 Valtuille de Abajo (León)
☎: +34 987 562 157
Fax: +34 987 562 157
www.bodegacobertizo.com
vinos@bodegacobertizo.com

Cobertizo 2012 B
89

Colour: bright straw. Nose: white flowers, fresh fruit, expressive, fine lees, dried herbs. Palate: flavourful, fruity, good acidity, balanced.

Cobertizo 2012 T
84

Cobertizo Selección 2008 T Roble
83

DESCENDIENTES DE J. PALACIOS
Avda. Calvo Sotelo, 6
24500 Villafranca del Bierzo (León)
☎: +34 987 540 821
Fax: +34 987 540 851
info@djpalacios.com

Las Lamas 2012 T
95

Colour: cherry, garnet rim. Nose: wild herbs, earthy notes, spicy, creamy oak. Palate: balanced, flavourful, long, balsamic.

Moncerbal 2012 T
94

Colour: very deep cherry. Nose: ripe fruit, spicy, creamy oak, toasty, characterful, balsamic herbs. Palate: powerful, flavourful, toasty, round tannins.

Pétalos del Bierzo 2012 T
93
Colour: cherry, garnet rim. Nose: ripe fruit, wild herbs, earthy notes, spicy, creamy oak. Palate: balanced, flavourful, long, balsamic.

Villa de Corullón 2012 T
95
Colour: cherry, garnet rim. Nose: ripe fruit, wild herbs, earthy notes, spicy, creamy oak, red berry notes. Palate: balanced, flavourful, long, balsamic.

DIEGO LOSADA
Ctra. Cacabelos Sorribas, 11
24540 Sorribas (León)
☎: +34 674 608 232
diegolosada13@gmail.com

1984 2013 T
100% mencía
88
Colour: cherry, purple rim. Nose: red berry notes, floral, balsamic herbs, mineral. Palate: fresh, fruity, flavourful, balanced.

DOMINIO DE LOS CEREZOS
Camino de las Salgueras, s/n
24413 Molinaseca (León)
☎: +34 639 202 403
Fax: +34 987 405 779
www.dominiodeloscerezos.com
mariazv.bierzo@gmail.com

Van Gus Vana 2009 T
mencía
91
Colour: cherry, garnet rim. Nose: ripe fruit, wild herbs, earthy notes, spicy, creamy oak, tobacco. Palate: balanced, flavourful, long, balsamic.

HAMMEKEN CELLARS
Calle de la Muela, 16
3730 Jávea (Alicante)
☎: +34 965 791 967
Fax: +34 966 461 471
www.hammekencellars.com
cellars@hammekencellars.com

Viña Altamar 2013 T
mencía
89
Colour: deep cherry, purple rim. Nose: medium intensity, red berry notes, balsamic herbs, fresh. Palate: fruity, easy to drink.

Viña Altamar Mencía Barrel Select 2011 T
mencía
88
Colour: bright cherry. Nose: ripe fruit, sweet spices, creamy oak, expressive. Palate: flavourful, fruity, toasty, round tannins.

JOSE ANTONIO GARCÍA GARCÍA
El Puente s/n
24530 Valtuille de Abajo (León)
☎: +34 648 070 581
Fax: +34 987 562 223
info@g2wines.com

Aires de Vendimia 2012 T
mencía
89
Colour: cherry, garnet rim. Nose: overripe fruit, wild herbs, spicy, creamy oak, mineral. Palate: powerful, spicy, ripe fruit.

El Chuqueiro 2013 B
godello
88
Colour: bright straw. Nose: dried herbs, faded flowers, ripe fruit. Palate: ripe fruit, balsamic, balanced.

Unculin 2013 T
mencía
87
Colour: cherry, purple rim. Nose: red berry notes, medium intensity, scrubland. Palate: flavourful, fruity, good acidity, round tannins.

LA VIZCAINA DE VINOS

Bulevar Rey Juan Carlos 1º
Rey de España, 11 B
24400 Ponferrada (León)
☎: +34 679 230 480
www.raulperezbodegas.es
raulperez@raulperezbodegas.es

El Rapolao 2012 T

mencía, bastardo, alicante bouché

93

Colour: cherry, garnet rim. Nose: ripe fruit, wild herbs, earthy notes, spicy, creamy oak. Palate: balanced, flavourful, long, balsamic.

La Poulosa 2012 T

mencía

88

Colour: cherry, garnet rim. Nose: ripe fruit, spicy, creamy oak, toasty, scrubland. Palate: powerful, flavourful, toasty, fine bitter notes.

La Vitoriana 2012 T

mencía, bastardo negro, alicante bouché

92

Colour: cherry, garnet rim. Nose: red berry notes, ripe fruit, spicy, creamy oak, toasty, complex, earthy notes, balsamic herbs. Palate: powerful, flavourful, toasty, balanced.

Las Gundiñas 2012 T

mencía

89

Colour: bright cherry. Nose: ripe fruit, sweet spices, creamy oak, dried herbs, mineral. Palate: fruity, flavourful, toasty.

LOSADA VINOS DE FINCA

Ctra. a Villafranca LE-713, Km. 12
24540 Cacabelos (León)
☎: +34 987 548 053
www.losadavinosdefinca.com
bodega@losadavinosdefinca.com

Altos de Losada 2010 T

100% mencía

92

Colour: deep cherry, garnet rim. Nose: smoky, spicy, toasty, balsamic herbs, ripe fruit. Palate: balanced, complex, flavourful.

El Pájaro Rojo 2013 T

100% mencía

85

La Bienquerida 2012 T

94

Colour: very deep cherry. Nose: ripe fruit, spicy, creamy oak, toasty, complex, mineral. Palate: powerful, flavourful, toasty, round tannins.

Losada 2011 T

100% mencía

93

Colour: cherry, garnet rim. Nose: ripe fruit, spicy, creamy oak, toasty, balsamic herbs, mineral. Palate: powerful, flavourful, toasty, round tannins.

Losada 2012 T

100% mencía

91

Colour: black cherry. Nose: ripe fruit, wild herbs, spicy, creamy oak. Palate: balanced, flavourful, long, balsamic.

MENCÍA DE - DOS S.L.

La Reguera, 4
24540 Cacabelos (León)
☎: +34 616 920 648
alvaro.ollodegalo@gmail.com

Mencias de 2 2013 T

89

Colour: cherry, purple rim. Nose: expressive, fresh fruit, red berry notes, varietal. Palate: flavourful, fruity, good acidity, round tannins.

OTERO SANTÍN

Ortega y Gasset, 10
24402 Ponferrada (León)
☎: +34 987 410 101
Fax: +34 987 418 544
oterobenito@gmail.com

Otero Santín 2007 TC

100% mencía

87

Colour: dark-red cherry, orangey edge. Nose: candied fruit, pattiserie, cocoa bean. Palate: good structure, flavourful, long.

Otero Santín 2013 B

godello

89

Colour: bright straw. Nose: fresh, fresh fruit, white flowers. Palate: flavourful, fruity, good acidity, balanced.

Otero Santín 2013 RD

mencía, prieto picudo

86

Colour: onion pink. Nose: candied fruit, dried flowers, fragrant herbs, red berry notes. Palate: light-bodied, flavourful, good acidity, long, spicy.

Valdecampo 2012 T

100% mencía

84

PALACIO DE CANEDO

La Iglesia, s/n
24546 Canedo (León)
☎: +34 987 563 366
Fax: +34 987 567 000
www.pradaatope.es
info@pradaatope.es

Palacio de Canedo 2007 TR
mencía

87

Colour: pale ruby, brick rim edge. Nose: spicy, fine reductive notes, wet leather, aged wood nuances, fruit liqueur notes. Palate: spicy, fine tannins, elegant, long, correct.

Palacio de Canedo 2010 TR
mencía

90

Colour: cherry, garnet rim. Nose: red berry notes, ripe fruit, spicy, creamy oak, complex, earthy notes, balsamic herbs. Palate: flavourful, round tannins, varietal.

Palacio de Canedo 2013 RD
mencía, godello

86

Colour: light cherry, bright. Nose: fresh, red berry notes, fragrant herbs. Palate: fruity, easy to drink, good acidity.

Palacio de Canedo 2013 T
Maceración Carbónica
mencía

88

Colour: cherry, purple rim. Nose: expressive, fresh fruit, red berry notes, floral, balsamic herbs. Palate: fruity, correct, good finish.

Palacio de Canedo Godello 2013 B
godello

87

Colour: bright straw. Nose: fresh, fresh fruit, white flowers, dried herbs. Palate: flavourful, fruity, good acidity, correct.

Palacio de Canedo Mencía 2008 TC
mencía

86

Colour: cherry, garnet rim. Nose: old leather, spicy. Palate: flavourful, balsamic, good finish.

Palacio de Canedo Mencía 2011 T Roble
mencía

87

Colour: bright cherry. Nose: ripe fruit, sweet spices, creamy oak. Palate: flavourful, fruity, toasty.

Picantal 2010 T
mencía

89

Colour: cherry, garnet rim. Nose: ripe fruit, wild herbs, earthy notes, spicy, creamy oak. Palate: balanced, flavourful, long, balsamic.

Prada Godello 2013 B
100% godello

89

Colour: bright straw. Nose: fresh, fresh fruit, white flowers. Palate: flavourful, fruity, good acidity, balanced.

PÉREZ CARAMÉS

Peña Picón, s/n
24500 Villafranca del Bierzo (León)
☎: +34 987 540 197
Fax: +34 987 540 314
www.perezcarames.com
info@perezcarames.com

Valdaiga X 2013 T
mencía

87

Colour: very deep cherry, purple rim. Nose: medium intensity, scrubland, ripe fruit, varietal. Palate: fruity, flavourful.

Valdaiga X2 2013 T
mencía

89

Colour: black cherry, purple rim. Nose: varietal, mineral. Palate: balanced, fruity, ripe fruit, long, balsamic.

RIBAS DEL CÚA

Finca Robledo A.C. 83
24540 Cacabelos (León)
☎: +34 987 971 018
Fax: +34 987 971 016
www.ribasdelcua.com
bodega@ribasdelcua.com

Ribas del Cúa 2013 T
100% mencía

88

Colour: cherry, purple rim. Nose: red berry notes, ripe fruit, scrubland. Palate: ripe fruit, balsamic, easy to drink.

Ribas del Cúa Oncedo 2012 T
100% mencía

86

Colour: cherry, garnet rim. Nose: ripe fruit, spicy, creamy oak, toasty. Palate: powerful, flavourful, toasty, round tannins.

Ribas del Cúa Privilegio 2010 T
mencía

87

Colour: bright cherry. Nose: ripe fruit, sweet spices, wet leather, earthy notes. Palate: flavourful, toasty, round tannins.

SOTO DEL VICARIO

Ctra. Cacabelos- San Clemente,
Pol. Ind. 908 Parcela 155
24547 San Clemente (León)
☎: +34 670 983 534
Fax: +34 926 666 029
www.sotodelvicario.com
sandra.luque@pagodelvicario.com

Go de Godello 2009 BFB
100% godello

91

Colour: bright golden. Nose: smoky, toasty, candied fruit, floral. Palate: rich, toasty, long, spicy, fine bitter notes.

Soto del Vicario Men 2009 T
100% mencía

89

Colour: cherry, garnet rim. Nose: ripe fruit, spicy, creamy oak, toasty, complex. Palate: powerful, flavourful, toasty.

Soto del Vicario Men Selección 2009 T
100% mencía

91

Colour: cherry, garnet rim. Nose: ripe fruit, wild herbs, earthy notes, spicy, creamy oak, dry stone. Palate: balanced, flavourful, long, balsamic.

THE PEPE'S WINE CO.

Cl. Doligencia, 6-K, 5º A
28018
☎: +34 639 382 528
info@thepepeswine.com

Flor de Sil 2013 B
godello

87

Colour: bright straw. Nose: white flowers, fragrant herbs, citrus fruit, balanced. Palate: fresh, fruity, flavourful, elegant.

Opalo 2013 B
dona blanca, godello

86

Colour: bright straw. Nose: fresh, fresh fruit, white flowers. Palate: flavourful, fruity, good acidity, balanced.

VINOS DE ARGANZA

Río Ancares
24560 Toral de los Vados (León)
☎: +34 987 544 831
Fax: +34 987 563 532
www.vinosdearganza.com
admon@vinosdearganza.com

Caneiros 2009 T Roble
100% mencía

87

Colour: deep cherry. Nose: ripe fruit, sweet spices, creamy oak. Palate: flavourful, fruity, toasty, round tannins, balsamic.

Encanto Charm 2010 T
100% mencía

88

Colour: cherry, garnet rim. Nose: red berry notes, ripe fruit, spicy. Palate: powerful, flavourful, toasty, round tannins.

Encanto Charm Selección 2008 T
100% mencía

90

Colour: cherry, garnet rim. Nose: ripe fruit, wild herbs, earthy notes, spicy, creamy oak. Palate: balanced, flavourful, long, balsamic.

Flavium Mencía Premium 2011 T
100% mencía

87

Colour: cherry, garnet rim. Nose: spicy, creamy oak, toasty, red berry notes, ripe fruit. Palate: powerful, flavourful, toasty, easy to drink

Flavium Mencía Premium 2012 T
100% mencía

88

Colour: cherry, garnet rim. Nose: ripe fruit, spicy, creamy oak, earthy notes. Palate: powerful, flavourful, toasty, round tannins.

Século 2012 T Roble
100% mencía

87

Colour: cherry, garnet rim. Nose: ripe fruit, wild herbs, spicy, creamy oak. Palate: balanced, flavourful, long, balsamic, fine bitter notes.

Terra Única 2012 T Roble
100% mencía

88

Colour: cherry, garnet rim. Nose: ripe fruit, spicy, creamy oak, toasty, earthy notes. Palate: powerful, flavourful, toasty.

VINOS VALTUILLE
La Fragua, s/n
24530 Valtuille de Abajo (León)
☎: +34 987 562 165
www.vinosvaltuille.com
info@vinosvaltuille.com

Pago de Valdoneje 2013 T
mencía

88

Colour: cherry, purple rim. Nose: expressive, fresh fruit, red berry notes, floral, balsamic herbs. Palate: flavourful, fruity, good acidity.

Pago de Valdoneje 2013 T Roble
mencía

87

Colour: bright cherry. Nose: ripe fruit, creamy oak, spicy. Palate: flavourful, fruity, toasty, balsamic.

Pago de Valdoneje Viñas Viejas 2011 TC
mencía

90

Colour: cherry, garnet rim. Nose: ripe fruit, spicy, creamy oak, toasty, complex. Palate: powerful, flavourful, toasty, round tannins.

VIÑAS BIERZO
Ctra. Ponferrada a Cacabelos, s/n
24410 Camponaraya (León)
☎: +34 987 463 009
Fax: +34 987 450 323
www.granbierzo.com
vdelbierzo@granbierzo.com

Fundación 1963 2006 TR
100% mencía

86

Colour: dark-red cherry, garnet rim. Nose: scrubland, dried herbs, spicy, ripe fruit. Palate: correct, easy to drink.

Gran Bierzo 2006 TR
100% mencía

88

Colour: deep cherry, orangey edge. Nose: waxy notes, tobacco, ripe fruit, spicy, aged wood nuances. Palate: fine bitter notes, elegant, flavourful, fine tannins.

Gran Bierzo 2007 TC
100% mencía

86

Colour: dark-red cherry, orangey edge. Nose: ripe fruit, wild herbs, spicy, toasty, fine reductive notes. Palate: balanced, flavourful, long, balsamic.

Gran Bierzo Origen 2012 T
100% mencía

90

Colour: cherry, garnet rim. Nose: ripe fruit, scrubland, balsamic herbs, spicy, creamy oak. Palate: powerful, flavourful, spicy, long.

Marqués de Cornatel 2012 T Roble
100% mencía

89

Colour: bright cherry. Nose: ripe fruit, sweet spices, creamy oak. Palate: flavourful, fruity, toasty, round tannins.

Marqués de Cornatel 2013 B
godello

82

Marqués de Cornatel 2013 RD
100% mencía

85

Naraya 2013 B
100% valenciana

85

Naraya 2013 RD
100% mencía

84

Naraya 2013 T
100% mencía

86

Colour: dark-red cherry, purple rim. Nose: ripe fruit, scrubland, medium intensity. Palate: fruity, flavourful.

Valmagaz 2013 B
100% valenciana

84

Valmagaz 2013 RD
100% mencía

85

Valmagaz Mencía 2013 T
100% mencía

84

VIÑEDOS SINGULARES

Cuzco, 26 - 28, Nave 8
8030 (Barcelona)
☎: +34 934 807 041
Fax: +34 934 807 076
www.vinedossingulares.com
info@vinedossingulares.com

Corral del Obispo 2012 T
mencía
90
Colour: bright cherry. Nose: ripe fruit, sweet spices, creamy oak. Palate: flavourful, fruity, toasty, round tannins.

VIÑEDOS Y BODEGAS DOMINIO DE TARES

P.I. Bierzo Alto, Los Barredos, 4
24318 San Román de Bembibre (León)
☎: +34 987 514 550
Fax: +34 987 514 570
www.dominiodetares.com
info@dominiodetares.com

Baltos 2012 T
100% mencía
87
Colour: cherry, garnet rim. Nose: ripe fruit, spicy, toasty, balsamic herbs. Palate: powerful, flavourful, toasty, round tannins.

Bembibre 2009 T
100% mencía
91
Colour: cherry, garnet rim. Nose: red berry notes, ripe fruit, spicy, creamy oak, toasty, complex, earthy notes. Palate: powerful, flavourful, toasty, round tannins.

Dominio de Tares Cepas Viejas 2011 TC
100% mencía
92
Colour: cherry, garnet rim. Nose: ripe fruit, wild herbs, earthy notes, spicy, creamy oak. Palate: balanced, flavourful, long, balsamic.

Dominio de Tares Godello 2013 BFB
100% godello
91
Colour: yellow, greenish rim. Nose: spicy, floral, ripe fruit. Palate: fruity, flavourful, spicy, balanced, fine bitter notes, good acidity.

Tares P. 3 2009 T Roble
100% mencía
93
Colour: cherry, garnet rim. Nose: mineral, ripe fruit, balsamic herbs, spicy, creamy oak. Palate: balanced, powerful, flavourful, spicy, long.

VIÑEDOS Y BODEGAS PITTACUM

De la Iglesia, 11
24546 Arganza, El Bierzo (León)
☎: +34 987 548 054
Fax: +34 987 548 028
www.pittacum.com
pittacum@pittacum.com

Petit Pittacum 2013 T
100% mencía
89
Colour: black cherry, purple rim. Nose: ripe fruit, scrubland, varietal. Palate: flavourful, fruity, long, balsamic.

Pittacum 2009 T Barrica
100% mencía
91
Colour: cherry, garnet rim. Nose: ripe fruit, wild herbs, spicy, creamy oak, varietal. Palate: balanced, flavourful, long, balsamic.

Pittacum Aurea 2009 TC
100% mencía
92
Colour: cherry, garnet rim. Nose: ripe fruit, wild herbs, earthy notes, spicy, creamy oak, mineral. Palate: flavourful, long, balsamic, elegant.

Tres Obispos 2013 RD
100% mencía
83

DO. BINISSALEM MALLORCA

CONSEJO REGULADOR

Celler de Rei, 9-1º
07350 Binissalem (Mallorca)
☎ :+34 971 512 191 - Fax: +34 971 512 191
@: info@binissalemdo.com
www.binissalemdo.com

LOCATION:

In the central region on the island of Majorca. It covers the municipal areas of Santa María del Camí, Binissalem, Sencelles, Consell and Santa Eugenia.

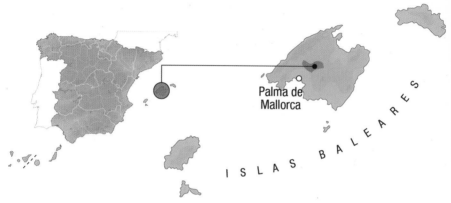

GRAPE VARIETIES:

White: Moll or Prensal Blanc (46 Ha), Macabeo, Parellada, Moscatel and Chardonnay.
Red: Manto Negro, Callet, Tempranillo, Syrah, Monastrell, Cabernet Sauvignon, Gorgollassa, Giró Ros and Merlot.

FIGURES:

Vineyard surface: 604.97 – Wine-Growers: 122 – Wineries: 15 – 2013 Harvest rating: - – Production 13: 1,866,077 litres – Market percentages: 86% domestic - 14% export.

SOIL:

The soil is of a brownish - grey or dun limey type, with limestone crusts on occasions. The slopes are quite gentle, and the vineyards are situated at an altitude ranging from 75 to 200 m.

CLIMATE:

Mild Mediterranean, with dry, hot summers and short winters. The average rainfall per year is around 450 mm. The production region is protected from the northerly winds by the Sierra de Tramuntana and the Sierra de Alfabia mountain ranges.

VINTAGE RATING   PEÑÍNGUIDE

2009	2010	2011	2012	2013
VERY GOOD	VERY GOOD	VERY GOOD	VERY GOOD	VERY GOOD

ANTONIO NADAL BODEGAS Y VIÑEDOS

Cami de Son Roig, s/n
07350 Binissalem (Illes Ballears)
☎: +34 630 914 511
Fax: +34 971 515 060
www.bodegasantonionadal.es
info@bodegasantonionadal.es

Blanc de Moll 2012 B
prensal, macabeo

83

BODEGAS JOSÉ LUIS FERRER

Conquistador, 103
07350 Binissalem (Illes Balears)
☎: +34 971 511 050
Fax: +34 971 870 084
www.vinosferrer.com
secretaria@vinosferrer.com

José L. Ferrer 2009 TR
manto negro, callet, cabernet sauvignon

89

Colour: bright cherry, orangey edge. Nose: balanced, toasty, spicy, dried herbs, tobacco. Palate: flavourful, good structure, balsamic.

José L. Ferrer 2011 TC
manto negro, callet, cabernet sauvignon, syrah

86

Colour: cherry, garnet rim. Nose: ripe fruit, spicy, toasty. Palate: powerful, flavourful, toasty, round tannins, balsamic.

José L. Ferrer Brut Veritas 2012 ESP
moll, moscatel, parellada

83

José L. Ferrer Pedra de Binissalem 2011 T
manto negro, cabernet sauvignon

89 ♣

Colour: cherry, garnet rim. Nose: medium intensity, dried herbs, dry stone. Palate: flavourful, balsamic, long.

José L. Ferrer Pedra de Binissalem 2012 B
moll

89

Colour: bright straw. Nose: fresh fruit, expressive, dried herbs, floral, dry stone. Palate: flavourful, fruity, good acidity, balanced.

José L. Ferrer Pedra de Binissalem Rosat 2013 RD
manto negro

86 ♣

Colour: light cherry. Nose: wild herbs, faded flowers, fresh. Palate: flavourful, fruity, fine bitter notes.

José L. Ferrer Veritas 2012 B
moll, chardonnay

90

Colour: bright yellow. Nose: expressive, balanced, sweet spices, ripe fruit, faded flowers. Palate: flavourful, rich, full, long.

José L. Ferrer Veritas Dolç 2013 Moscatel
moscatel

88

Colour: bright yellow. Nose: balanced, varietal, jasmine. Palate: flavourful, fruity, balanced, easy to drink.

José L. Ferrer Veritas Viñes Velles 2010 T
manto negro, cabernet sauvignon, syrah, callet

88

Colour: cherry, garnet rim. Nose: ripe fruit, spicy, creamy oak, complex. Palate: powerful, flavourful, toasty, round tannins.

José Luis Ferrer 2013 RD
manto negro, cabernet sauvignon, callet, tempranillo

86

Colour: light cherry. Nose: dry nuts, wild herbs, ripe fruit. Palate: flavourful, fruity, fine bitter notes.

José Luis Ferrer Blanc de Blancs 2013 B
moll, chardonnay, moscatel

86

Colour: bright yellow. Nose: medium intensity, fresh, dried herbs, floral. Palate: correct, good acidity, fine bitter notes.

José Luis Ferrer Manto Dolç 2011 T
manto negro

88

Colour: cherry, garnet rim. Nose: powerfull, candied fruit, faded flowers, balanced. Palate: full, flavourful.

José Luis Ferrer Reserva Especial Veritas 2005 T
manto negro, cabernet sauvignon, tempranillo, syrah

89

Colour: cherry, garnet rim. Nose: ripe fruit, spicy, toasty, complex, scrubland. Palate: powerful, flavourful, toasty, round tannins.

José Luis Ferrer Roig 2013 RD
manto negro, callet, syrah

87

Colour: coppery red, bright. Nose: powerfull, expressive, fragrant herbs, dried herbs. Palate: flavourful, balanced, fine bitter notes.

BODEGUES MACIÀ BATLE
Camí Coanegra, s/n
07320 Santa María del Camí
(Illes Balears)
☎: +34 971 140 014
Fax: +34 971 140 086
www.maciabatle.com
correo@maciabatle.com

Dos Marias 2013 T Roble

87

Colour: cherry, garnet rim. Nose: fresh fruit, citrus fruit, spicy. Palate: fruity, flavourful, easy to drink.

LLum 2013 B

90

Colour: bright straw. Nose: fresh, fresh fruit, white flowers, expressive, fragrant herbs. Palate: flavourful, fruity, good acidity, balanced.

Macià Batle 2011 TC
merlot, manto negro, cabernet sauvignon, syrah

89

Colour: light cherry, garnet rim. Nose: expressive, dry stone, ripe fruit, dried herbs. Palate: full, flavourful.

Macià Batle 2013 RD
manto negro, merlot, cabernet sauvignon

87

Colour: light cherry, coppery red. Nose: ripe fruit, wild herbs. Palate: flavourful, ripe fruit, long, good acidity.

Macià Batle 2013 T
manto negro, cabernet sauvignon, merlot, syrah

89

Colour: cherry, garnet rim. Nose: wild herbs, earthy notes, expressive. Palate: balanced, flavourful, long, balsamic, easy to drink.

Macià Batle Blanc de Blancs 2013 B

87

Colour: bright yellow. Nose: white flowers, fragrant herbs, fruit expression. Palate: fresh, fruity, flavourful, balanced, elegant.

Macià Batle Gustavo 75 Anys 2011 T

90

Colour: cherry, garnet rim. Nose: ripe fruit, spicy, toasty, warm, dry stone. Palate: powerful, flavourful, toasty, round tannins.

Macià Batle Margarita Llompart 2011 T
manto negro, merlot, cabernet sauvignon, syrah

88

Colour: bright cherry, garnet rim. Nose: balanced, ripe fruit, scrubland, spicy. Palate: flavourful, ripe fruit.

Macià Batle Reserva Privada 2010 TR
manto negro, merlot, cabernet sauvignon, syrah

89

Colour: cherry, garnet rim. Nose: closed, spicy, toasty, balsamic herbs. Palate: good structure, flavourful, long.

P. de Marìa 2009 T

94

Colour: cherry, garnet rim. Nose: expressive, ripe fruit, scrubland, spicy. Palate: good structure, long.

P. de Marìa 2011 T

92

Colour: cherry, garnet rim. Nose: ripe fruit, spicy, creamy oak, complex, earthy notes. Palate: flavourful, round tannins.

CA'N VERDURA VITICULTORS
S'Era, 6
07350 Binissalem (Balears)
☎: +34 695 817 038
tomeuverdura@gmail.com

Supernova 2012 TC
manto negro

90

Colour: cherry, garnet rim. Nose: ripe fruit, wild herbs, earthy notes, spicy, creamy oak. Palate: balanced, flavourful, long, balsamic.

Supernova Blanc 2013 B
prensal

88

Colour: bright straw. Nose: medium intensity, ripe fruit, white flowers. Palate: flavourful, fruity, fine bitter notes, good acidity.

CELLER TIANNA NEGRE
Camí des Mitjans
07340 Binissalem (Illes Balears)
☎: +34 971 886 826
www.tiannanegre.com
info@tiannanegre.com

Ses Nines Blanc 2013 B
prensal, chardonnay, moscatel

88

Colour: yellow, greenish rim. Nose: sweet spices, ripe fruit, creamy oak, faded flowers. Palate: balanced, fine bitter notes, good acidity.

Ses Nines Negre 2012 T
manto negro, cabernet sauvignon, syrah, callet

90

Colour: cherry, garnet rim. Nose: ripe fruit, spicy, complex. Palate: powerful, flavourful, toasty, round tannins.

Ses Nines Seleccio 07/9 2012 T
manto negro, cabernet sauvignon, syrah, callet

91

Colour: cherry, garnet rim. Nose: ripe fruit, wild herbs, earthy notes, spicy. Palate: balanced, flavourful, long, balsamic.

Tianna Bocchoris Negre 2012 T
manto negro, cabernet sauvignon, syrah, callet

92

Colour: deep cherry, garnet rim. Nose: ripe fruit, spicy, expressive, dried herbs. Palate: full, flavourful, round tannins.

Tianna Negre 2012 T
manto negro, callet, cabernet sauvignon, syrah

92

Colour: cherry, garnet rim. Nose: ripe fruit, wild herbs, earthy notes, spicy, creamy oak. Palate: balanced, flavourful, long, balsamic.

JAUME DE PUNTIRÓ
Pza. Nova, 23
07320 Santa María del Camí
(Illes Balears)
☎: +34 971 620 023
www.vinsjaumedepuntiro.com
pere@vinsjaumedepuntiro.com

Buc 2012 TC
manto negro, cabernet sauvignon

88 🌢

Colour: bright cherry, garnet rim. Nose: powerfull, ripe fruit, fruit preserve, sweet spices. Palate: balanced, ripe fruit, sweet tannins.

Daurat 2013 BFB
prensal

89 🌢

Colour: bright yellow. Nose: balanced, ripe fruit, sweet spices. Palate: fruity, rich, balanced, fine bitter notes.

J.P. 2008 TR
manto negro, cabernet sauvignon

90 🌢

Colour: dark-red cherry, orangey edge. Nose: ripe fruit, spicy, toasty, tobacco. Palate: spicy, long, round tannins.

Jaume de Puntiró Blanc 2013 B
prensal

87 🌢

Colour: bright straw. Nose: fresh, fresh fruit, expressive, faded flowers. Palate: flavourful, fruity, good acidity, balanced, rich.

Jaume de Puntiró Carmesí 2012 T
manto negro, callet

91 🌢

Colour: cherry, garnet rim. Nose: ripe fruit, wild herbs, earthy notes, spicy, creamy oak. Palate: balanced, flavourful, long, balsamic. Jaume de Puntiró Moscatel Dolç 2012 B moscatel

Jaume de Puntiró Moscatel Dolç 2012 B
manto negro, callet

86 🌢

Colour: bright straw. Nose: medium intensity, white flowers, balanced. Palate: flavourful, easy to drink, correct, good finish.

Jaume de Puntiró Rosat 2013 RD
manto negro

88 🌢

Colour: light cherry, bright. Nose: white flowers, red berry notes, medium intensity. Palate: fruity, fresh, easy to drink, good finish.

Porprat 2010 T
merlot, manto negro

87

Colour: light cherry, orangey edge. Nose: toasty, smoky, balsamic herbs. Palate: flavourful, round tannins.

VINS NADAL
Ramón Llull, 2
07350 Binissalem (Illes Balears)
☎: +34 971 511 058
Fax: +34 971 870 150
www.vinsnadal.com
albaflor@vinsnadal.com

Albaflor 2009 TR
manto negro, merlot, cabernet sauvignon

87

Colour: cherry, garnet rim. Nose: ripe fruit, fruit preserve, cocoa bean. Palate: spicy, round tannins, ripe fruit.

Albaflor 2010 TC
manto negro, merlot, cabernet sauvignon

88

Colour: cherry, garnet rim. Nose: ripe fruit, wild herbs, earthy notes, spicy, creamy oak. Palate: balanced, flavourful, long, balsamic.

Albaflor 2012 T
manto negro, cabernet sauvignon, merlot

86

Colour: bright cherry, purple rim. Nose: powerfull, fruit preserve. Palate: fruity, flavourful, long.

Albaflor 2013 B
prensal, moscatel

80

Albaflor 2013 RD
manto negro, merlot, cabernet sauvignon

87

Colour: rose. Nose: balanced, fresh, red berry notes, white flowers. Palate: fruity, fresh, fine bitter notes.

VINYA TAUJANA
Balanguera, 40
07142 Santa Eugenia (Illes Balears)
☎: +34 971 144 494
Fax: +34 971 144 494
www.vinyataujana.es
vinyataujana@gmail.com

Torrent Fals 2011 TC

88

Colour: cherry, garnet rim. Nose: ripe fruit, scrubland, spicy. Palate: flavourful, fruity, round tannins.

Vinya Taujana Blanc de Blanc 2013 B
100% moll

87

Colour: bright straw. Nose: medium intensity, dried herbs, dried flowers. Palate: easy to drink, fine bitter notes, good finish.

Vinya Taujana Rosat 2013 RD
100% manto negro

84

VINYES I VINS CA SA PADRINA
Camí dels Horts, s/n
07140 Sencelles (Illes Balears)
☎: +34 660 211 939
Fax: +34 971 874 370
cellermantonegro@gmail.com

Mollet Suñer Bibiloni 2013 B Joven
moll, prensal, chardonnay

90

Colour: bright straw. Nose: white flowers, fresh fruit, expressive, dried herbs, dry nuts. Palate: flavourful, fruity, good acidity, balanced.

Montenegro 2013 T Roble
manto negro, merlot, cabernet sauvignon, callet

89

Colour: light cherry, garnet rim. Nose: ripe fruit, sweet spices, cocoa bean. Palate: balanced, round tannins.

Rosat De Ca Sa Padrina 2013 RD
manto negro, merlot

87

Colour: coppery red, light cherry. Nose: medium intensity, dried herbs, balanced. Palate: fruity, flavourful, long.

DO. BIZKAIKO TXAKOLINA

CONSEJO REGULADOR

Bº Mendibile, 42
48940 Leioa (Bizkaia)
☎ :+34 946 076 071 - Fax: +34 946 076 072
@: info@bizkaikotxacolina.org
www.bizkaikotxakolina.org

LOCATION:

In the province of Vizcaya. The production region covers both coastal areas and other areas inland.

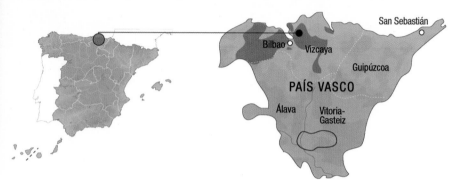

GRAPE VARIETIES:

White: Hondarrabi Zuri, Folle Blanche.
Red: Hondarrabi Beltza.

FIGURES:

Vineyard surface: 380 – Wine-Growers: 222 – Wineries: 46 – 2013 Harvest rating: - – Production 13: 999,807 litres – Market percentages: 96.8% domestic - 3.2% export.

SOIL:

Mainly clayey, although slightly acidic on occasions, with a fairly high organic matter content.

CLIMATE:

Quite humid and mild due to the influence of the Bay of Biscay which tempers the temperatures. Fairly abundant rainfall, with an average of 1,000 to 1,300 mm per year.

VINTAGE RATING

PEÑÍNGUIDE

2009	2010	2011	2012	2013
EXCELLENT	EXCELLENT	EXCELLENT	EXCELLENT	VERY GOOD

ABIO TXAKOLINA

Barrio Elexalde, 5 Caserío Basigo
48130 Bakio (Bizkaia)
☎: +34 657 794 754
www.abiotxakolina.com

Abio Txakolina 2013 B
100% hondarrabi zuri

87

Colour: bright straw. Nose: ripe fruit, floral, dried herbs. Palate: flavourful, fresh, fruity.

Gorena 2013 B
100% hondarrabi zuri

86

Colour: bright straw. Nose: white flowers, dried herbs, fruit expression, citrus fruit. Palate: powerful, flavourful, fresh, fruity.

BIZKAIBARNE

Bº Murueta s/n
48410 Orozko (Bizkaia)
☎: +34 946 330 709
bizkaibarne@gmail.com

Egiaenea Mahastia 2012 B
hondarrabi zuri zerratia

92

Colour: bright straw. Nose: white flowers, fresh fruit, expressive, fine lees, dried herbs. Palate: flavourful, fruity, good acidity, balanced.

Marko 2012 B
100% hondarrabi zuri zerratia

92

Colour: bright straw. Nose: white flowers, fragrant herbs, fruit expression. Palate: fresh, fruity, flavourful, balanced, elegant. Personality.

Mendiolagan 2013 B
hondarrabi zuri

87

Colour: bright straw. Nose: faded flowers, dried herbs, ripe fruit. Palate: flavourful, fresh, fruity.

Otxanduri Mahastia 2012 B

89

Colour: bright straw. Nose: ripe fruit, dried herbs, dried flowers, spicy. Palate: flavourful, fresh.

BODEGA ADOS BASARTE

Urkitzaurrealde, 4 Basarte
48130 Bakio (Bizkaia)
☎: +34 605 026 115
www.basarte.net
basarte@basarte.net

Ados 2013 B
100% hondarrabi zuri

89

Colour: bright straw. Nose: balsamic herbs, floral, ripe fruit, citrus fruit, fine lees. Palate: fresh, fruity, flavourful, round.

BODEGA AMUNATEGI

San Bartolomé, 57
48350 Busturia (Bizkaia)
☎: +34 685 737 398
www.amunategi.eu
info@amunategi.eu

Amunategi 2013 B
hondarrabi zuri, hondarrabi zuri zerratia, hondarrabi beltza, riesling

88

Colour: bright straw. Nose: white flowers, fragrant herbs, fruit expression, expressive. Palate: fresh, fruity, flavourful.

BODEGA BERROJA

48008 Bilbao (Bizkaia)
☎: +34 944 106 254
Fax: +34 946 309 390
www.bodegaberroja.com
txakoli@bodegaberroja.com

Txakoli Aguirrebeko 2013 B
hondarrabi zuri, riesling, folle blanch

89

Colour: bright straw. Nose: white flowers, fragrant herbs, fruit expression. Palate: fresh, fruity, flavourful, balanced, elegant.

Txakoli Berroja 2012 B
hondarrabi zuri, riesling

90

Colour: bright straw. Nose: white flowers, fresh fruit, expressive, fine lees, dried herbs. Palate: flavourful, fruity, good acidity, balanced.

BODEGA ELIZALDE

Barrio Mendraka, 1
48230 Elorrio (Bizkaia)
☎: +34 946 820 000
Fax: +34 946 820 000
www.mendraka.com
kerixa@gmail.com

Mendraka 2013 B

89

Colour: bright straw. Nose: fruit expression, dried flowers, dried herbs, mineral. Palate: flavourful, fresh, fruity.

BODEGA JON ANDER REKALDE

San Roke Bekoa, 11 (Artxanda)
48150 Sondika
☎: +34 944 458 631

Artxanda 2013 B
87
Colour: bright straw. Nose: saline, fruit expression, floral, wild herbs. Palate: fresh, fruity, balsamic.

BODEGA TALLERI

Barrio Erroteta s/n
48115 Morga (Bizkaia)
☎: +34 944 651 689
www.bodegatalleri.com
info@bodegatalleri.com

Bitxia 2013 B
hondarrabi zuri
88
Colour: bright straw. Nose: fresh, fresh fruit, white flowers, wild herbs. Palate: flavourful, fruity, good acidity, balanced.

Bitxia 2013 RD
hondarrabi beltza
81

BODEGA TXAKOLI URIARTE

Bº Acillcona-Cº Eguskiza
48113 Fika (Bizkaia)
☎: +34 659 674 595
Fax: +34 946 153 535
www.txakoli-uriarte.com
info@txakoli-uriarte.com

Uriarte 2013 B
hondarrabi zuri, folle blanch, chardonnay
87
Colour: bright straw. Nose: floral, citrus fruit, fragrant herbs. Palate: flavourful, fresh, fruity, balanced.

BODEGA ULIBARRI

Caserío Isuskiza Handi, 1 Barrio Zaldu
48192 Gordexola (Bizkaia)
☎: +34 665 725 735
ulibarriartzaiak@gmail.com

Artzai 2011 BFB
89
Colour: bright yellow. Nose: ripe fruit, sweet spices, creamy oak, fragrant herbs. Palate: rich, flavourful, fresh, good acidity.

Artzai 2012 BFB
88
Colour: bright straw. Nose: white flowers, fragrant herbs, sweet spices, toasty, ripe fruit. Palate: powerful, flavourful, balanced.

BODEGAS DE GALDAMES S.L.

El Bentorro, 4
48191 Galdames (Bizkaia)
☎: +34 627 992 063
Fax: +34 946 100 107
www.vinasulibarria.com
info@vinasulibarria.com

Torre de Loizaga Bigarren 2013 B
85

BODEGAS GORKA IZAGIRRE

Barrio Legina, s/n
48195 Larrabetzu (Bizkaia)
☎: +34 946 742 706
Fax: +34 946 741 221
www.gorkaizagirre.com
txakoli@gorkaizagirre.com

42 By Eneko Atxa 2012 B
100% hondarrabi zerratia
90
Colour: bright yellow. Nose: powerfull, ripe fruit, sweet spices, creamy oak, fragrant herbs. Palate: rich, smoky aftertaste, flavourful, fresh, good acidity.

Aretxondo s/c B
90
Colour: bright yellow. Nose: ripe fruit, white flowers, wild herbs. Palate: powerful, flavourful, spicy, long.

Arima de Gorka Izagirre Vendimia Tardía 2011 B
100% hondarrabi zerratia
91
Colour: golden. Nose: powerfull, floral, honeyed notes, candied fruit, fragrant herbs. Palate: flavourful, sweet, fresh, fruity, good acidity, long.

E-Gala 2013 B
89
Colour: bright straw. Nose: white flowers, fragrant herbs, fruit expression, wild herbs. Palate: fresh, fruity, flavourful.

G22 de Gorka Izagirre 2012 B
100% hondarrabi zerratia
90
Colour: bright yellow. Nose: citrus fruit, ripe fruit, wild herbs, fine lees. Palate: flavourful, fresh, fruity, round.

Garitza 2013 B
89
Colour: bright straw. Nose: floral, dried herbs, ripe fruit, citrus fruit. Palate: flavourful, fresh, fruity, powerful.

Gorka Izagirre 2013 B
90
Colour: bright yellow. Nose: floral, fragrant herbs, fresh fruit, tropical fruit, fine lees. Palate: powerful, flavourful, balanced, long.

Munetaberri 2013 B
87
Colour: bright straw. Nose: floral, ripe fruit, dried herbs. Palate: fresh, fruity, flavourful.

Saratsu 2013 B
100% hondarrabi zerratia
90
Colour: bright straw. Nose: white flowers, fresh fruit, expressive, fine lees, dried herbs. Palate: flavourful, fruity, balanced.

Torreko s/c B
86
Colour: bright straw. Nose: ripe fruit, faded flowers, dried herbs. Palate: flavourful, balsamic, powerful.

Uixar 2013 B
100% hondarrabi zerratia
89
Colour: bright straw. Nose: floral, fragrant herbs, candied fruit. Palate: fine bitter notes, fresh, fruity.

BODEGAS ITSASMENDI
Barrio Arane, 3 apartado correos 241
48300 Gernika (Bizkaia)
☎: +34 946 270 316
Fax: +34 946 251 032
www.bodegasitsasmendi.com
info@bodegasitsasmendi.com

Eklipse Itsas Mendi 2012 T
90
Colour: cherry, garnet rim. Nose: ripe fruit, spicy, creamy oak, toasty, complex, balsamic herbs. Palate: powerful, flavourful, toasty, round tannins.

Itsas Artizar 2011 B
hondarrabi zuri
88
Colour: bright yellow. Nose: powerfull, ripe fruit, sweet spices, creamy oak, roasted coffee. Palate: rich, smoky aftertaste, flavourful, fresh, good acidity.

Itsas Mendi Urezti 2011 B
93
Colour: bright yellow. Nose: wild herbs, floral, honeyed notes, ripe fruit, candied fruit, sweet spices. Palate: full, powerful, flavourful, spicy, long.

Itsasmendi 2013 B
hondarrabi zuri, hondarrabi zuri serratie
87
Colour: bright straw. Nose: white flowers, candied fruit, fragrant herbs. Palate: fresh, fruity, flavourful, easy to drink.

Itsasmendi nº 7 2012 B
91
Colour: bright yellow. Nose: powerfull, ripe fruit, sweet spices, creamy oak, fragrant herbs. Palate: rich, flavourful, fresh, good acidity.

Itsasmendi nº 7 Magnum 2011 B
93
Colour: bright yellow. Nose: ripe fruit, floral, fragrant herbs, spicy, creamy oak. Palate: powerful, flavourful, rich, long, toasty.

DONIENE GORRONDONA TXAKOLINA
Gibelorratzagako San Pelaio, 1
48130 Bakio (Bizkaia)
☎: +34 946 194 795
Fax: +34 946 195 831
www.donienegorrondona.com
gorrondona@donienegorrondona.com

Doniene 2012 BFB
hondarrabi zuri
90
Colour: bright yellow. Nose: powerfull, ripe fruit, sweet spices, creamy oak, fragrant herbs. Palate: rich, smoky aftertaste, flavourful, fresh, good acidity.

Doniene 2013 B
hondarrabi zuri
89
Colour: bright straw. Nose: white flowers, fruit expression, wild herbs, expressive. Palate: balanced, fresh, fruity, flavourful.

Doniene Apardune 2011 ESP
hondarrabi zuri, mune mahatsa
86
Colour: bright straw. Nose: medium intensity, fresh fruit, dried herbs, fine lees, floral. Palate: fresh, fruity, flavourful, good acidity.

Gorrondona 2013 B
hondarrabi zuri
88
Colour: bright straw. Nose: floral, wild herbs, citrus fruit, fruit expression. Palate: fresh, fruity, flavourful.

Gorrondona 2013 T
hondarrabi beltza
86
Colour: cherry, garnet rim. Nose: ripe fruit, grassy, herbaceous. Palate: balsamic, fine bitter notes, spicy, easy to drink.

ERDIKOETXE LANDETXEA

Goitioltza, 38
48196 Lezama (Bizkaia)
☎: +34 944 573 285
Fax: +34 944 573 285
erdikoetxelandetxea@hotmail.com

Erdikoetxe 2013 B

85

Erdikoetxe 2013 T

82

GARKALDE TXAKOLINA

Barrio Goitioltza, 8 - Caserio Garkalde
48196 Lezama
☎: +34 944 556 412
garkaldetxakolina@hotmail.com

Garkalde Txakolina 2013 B
hondarrabi zuri

86

Colour: bright straw. Nose: fresh fruit, white flowers, citrus fruit, fragrant herbs. Palate: fruity, fresh, fine bitter notes.

GURE AHALEGINAK

Barrio Ibazurra, 1
48460 Orduña (Bizkaia)
☎: +34 945 384 126
Fax: +34 945 384 126
www.gureahaleginak.com
maitedurana@gureahaleginak.com

Filoxera 2011 T
hondarrabi beltza

82

Filoxera 2012 T
hondarrabi beltza

81

Gure Ahaleginak 2013 B
hondarrabi zuri, hondarribia zuri zarratia, sauvignon blanc

84

JOSÉ ETXEBARRÍA URRUTIA

Txonebarri-C. Igartua, s/n
48110 Gatika (Bizkaia)
☎: +34 946 742 010

Txakoli Etxebarría 2013 B

85

M.B. ARESTI Y OTROS C.B.

Camino Etxebazarra-Mesone, 1
48950 Erandio (Vizcaya)
☎: +34 944 674 844

Txakoli Aresti 2013 B

84

MAGALARTE LEZAMA

B. Garaioltza, 92 B
48196 Lezama (Bizkaia)
☎: +34 636 621 455
Fax: +34 944 556 508
www.magalartelezamatxakolina.com

Magalarte Iñaki Aretxabaleta 2013 BFB

90

Colour: bright straw. Nose: ripe fruit, citrus fruit, floral, wild herbs. Palate: powerful, flavourful, spicy.

Magalarte Iñaki Aretxabaleta 2013 B

88

Colour: bright straw. Nose: fresh, fresh fruit, white flowers, fragrant herbs. Palate: flavourful, fruity, correct.

Sagastibeltza Karrantza 2013 B

87

Colour: bright straw. Nose: fruit expression, citrus fruit, floral, fragrant herbs. Palate: fresh, fruity, flavourful.

MAGALARTE ZAMUDIO

Arteaga Auzoa, 107
48170 Zamudio (Bizkaia)
☎: +34 944 521 431
Fax: +34 944 521 431
magalarte@hotmail.com

Magalarte 2013 B
hondarrabi zuri, petit manseng, riesling, folle blanch

89

Colour: bright straw. Nose: fresh, fresh fruit, white flowers, expressive. Palate: flavourful, fruity, good acidity, balanced.

Zabalondo 2013 B
hondarrabi zuri, petit manseng, riesling, petit corbu

87

Colour: bright straw. Nose: white flowers, fragrant herbs, fruit expression, citrus fruit. Palate: flavourful, fresh, fruity, balanced.

MERRUTXU

Caserío Merrutxu, Arboliz 15
48311 Ibarrangelu (Bizkaia)
☎: +34 946 276 435
www.txakolibizkaia.com
info@merrutxu.com

Merrutxu 2013 B
86
Colour: bright straw. Nose: citrus fruit, white flowers, dried herbs. Palate: correct, fresh, fruity.

TXAKOLI OXINBALTZA

Barrio Magunas, 27
48392 Muxika (Bizkaia)
☎: +34 686 345 131
www.oxinbaltza.com
oxinbaltza@oxinbaltza.com

Katan 2013 B
hondarrabi zuri
87
Colour: bright straw. Nose: fresh, fresh fruit, white flowers, expressive. Palate: flavourful, fruity, good acidity, balanced.

TXAKOLI TXABARRI

Juan Antonio del Yermo no1 4ºC
48860 Zalla (Bizkaia)
☎: +34 625 708 114
Fax: +34 946 390 947
www.txakolitxabarri.com
txabarri@txakolitxabarri.com

Txabarri 2013 RD
84

Txabarri 2013 T
100% Hondarrabi Beltza
83

Txakoli Txabarri Extra 2013 B
hondarrabi zuri, riesling, sauvignon blanc
87
Colour: bright straw. Nose: white flowers, fragrant herbs, fruit expression, citrus fruit. Palate: fresh, fruity, flavourful, balanced, elegant.

TXOÑE

Iguatua, 25
48110 Gatika
☎: +34 639 469 738
kepa@larrabeiti.com

Butroi 2013 B
100% hondarrabi zuri
88
Colour: bright straw. Nose: white flowers, fragrant herbs, fruit expression. Palate: fresh, fruity, flavourful, balanced, elegant.

VIRGEN DE LOREA

Barrio de Lorea s/n
48860 Otxaran-Zalla (Bizkaia)
☎: +34 944 242 680
Fax: +34 946 670 521
www.bodegasvirgendelorea.com
virgendelorea@spankor.com

Aretxaga 2013 B
hondarrabi zuri, folle blanch
89
Colour: bright straw. Nose: white flowers, fragrant herbs, fruit expression. Palate: fresh, fruity, flavourful, balanced, elegant.

Señorío de Otxaran 2013 B
hondarrabi zuri, folle blanch
90
Colour: bright straw. Nose: white flowers, fragrant herbs, fruit expression. Palate: fresh, fruity, flavourful, balanced.

DO. BULLAS

CONSEJO REGULADOR

Balsa, 26
30180 Bullas (Murcia)
☎ :+34 968 652 601 - Fax: +968 652 601
@: consejoregulador@vinosdebullas.es
www.vinosdebullas.es

LOCATION:

In the province of Murcia. It covers the municipal areas of Bullas, Cehegín, Mula and Ricote, and several vineyards in the vicinity of Calasparra, Moratalla and Lorca.

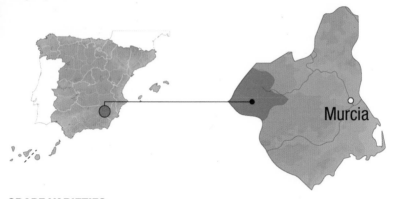

GRAPE VARIETIES:

White: Macabeo (main), Airén, Chardonnay, Malvasía, Moscatel de Grano Menudo and Sauvignon Blanc.
Red: Monastrell (main), Petit Verdot, Tempranillo, Cabernet Sauvignon, Syrah, Merlot and Garnacha.

FIGURES:

Vineyard surface: 2,500 – Wine-Growers: 497 – Wineries: 11 – 2013 Harvest rating: Good – Production 13: 2,442,796 litres – Market percentages: 50% domestic - 50% export.

SOIL:

Brownish - grey limey soil, with limestone crusts, and alluvial. The terrain is rugged and determined by the layout of the little valleys, each with their own microclimate. Distinction can be made between 3 areas: one to the north north - east with an altitude of 400 – 500 m; another in the central region, situated at an altitude of 500 – 600 m; and the third in the western and north - western region, with the highest altitude (500 – 810 m), the highest concentration of vineyards and the best potential for quality.

CLIMATE:

Mediterranean, with an average annual temperature of 15.6 °C and low rainfall (average of 300 mm per year). The heavy showers and storms which occur in the region are another defining element.

VINTAGE RATING   PEÑÍNGUIDE

2009	2010	2011	2012	2013
VERY GOOD	VERY GOOD	N/A	GOOD	GOOD

BODEGA BALCONA

Ctra. Bullas-Avilés, Km. 8
30180 Bullas (Murcia)
☎: +34 968 652 891
www.partal-vinos.com
info@partal-vinos.com

37 Barricas de Partal 2006 TC
monastrell, tempranillo, cabernet sauvignon
80

Partal de Autor 2006 T
85

BODEGA MONASTRELL

Ctra. Bullas-Avilés, km. 9,3
"Valle Aceniche"
30180 Bullas (Murcia)
☎: +34 648 702 412
Fax: +34 968 653 708
www.bodegamonastrell.com
info@bodegamonastrell.com

Almudí 2011 T
91 ♣

Colour: bright cherry. Nose: ripe fruit, sweet spices, creamy oak, expressive, earthy notes, mineral. Palate: flavourful, fruity, toasty, round tannins.

Chaveo 2010 TC
100% monastrell
91 ♣

Colour: cherry, garnet rim. Nose: ripe fruit, spicy, creamy oak, toasty, complex, dark chocolate, mineral. Palate: powerful, flavourful, toasty, round tannins.

Valché 2010 TC
100% monastrell
90 ♣

Colour: bright cherry. Nose: ripe fruit, sweet spices, creamy oak, roasted coffee, dark chocolate. Palate: fruity, flavourful, toasty.

BODEGA SAN ISIDRO BULLAS

Pol. Ind. Marimingo, Altiplano, s/n
Apdo. 61
30180 Bullas (Murcia)
☎: +34 968 654 991
Fax: +34 968 652 160
administracion@bodegasanisidrobullas.com

Cepas del Zorro 2011 TC
88

Colour: cherry, garnet rim. Nose: ripe fruit, spicy, creamy oak, toasty. Palate: powerful, flavourful, toasty, round tannins.

Cepas del Zorro 2012 T
100% monastrell
87

Colour: deep cherry. Nose: fresh fruit, red berry notes, fragrant herbs. Palate: flavourful, fine bitter notes, good acidity.

Cepas del Zorro 2013 RD
88

Colour: rose, purple rim. Nose: powerfull, ripe fruit, red berry notes, floral. Palate: powerful, fruity, fresh.

Cepas del Zorro 2013 T
89

Colour: cherry, purple rim. Nose: powerfull, red berry notes, ripe fruit, floral, varietal. Palate: powerful, fresh, fruity, unctuous.

Cepas del Zorro Macabeo 2013 B
100% macabeo
88

Colour: bright straw. Nose: expressive, powerfull, tropical fruit. Palate: flavourful, fruity.

BODEGA TERCIA DE ULEA

Tercia de Ulea, s/n
30440 Moratalla (Murcia)
☎: +34 968 433 213
Fax: +34 968 433 965
www.terciadeulea.com
info@terciadeulea.com

Rebeldía 2013 RD
80

Tercia de Ulea 2008 TC
90

Colour: deep cherry, orangey edge. Nose: spicy, toasty, over-ripe fruit, mineral, dry stone. Palate: powerful, flavourful, toasty, round tannins.

Viña Botial 2011 T Roble
84

BODEGAS DEL ROSARIO

Avda. de la Libertad, s/n
30180 Bullas (Murcia)
☎: +34 968 652 075
Fax: +34 968 653 765
www.bodegasdelrosario.com
ljp@bodegasdelrosario.com

3000 Años 2010 T
monastrell, syrah
93

Colour: cherry, garnet rim. Nose: ripe fruit, spicy, creamy oak, toasty, dark chocolate, earthy notes, characterful. Palate: powerful, flavourful, toasty, round tannins.

Las Reñas 2011 TC
monastrell, syrah

88

Colour: cherry, garnet rim. Nose: spicy, toasty, overripe fruit, mineral. Palate: powerful, flavourful, toasty, round tannins.

Las Reñas 2013 B
macabeo, malvasía

84

Las Reñas 2013 RD
monastrell, syrah

88

Colour: coppery red. Nose: candied fruit, dried flowers, fragrant herbs, red berry notes. Palate: light-bodied, flavourful, good acidity, long, spicy.

Las Reñas 2013 T
monastrell, syrah, tempranillo

88

Colour: cherry, purple rim. Nose: powerfull, red berry notes, ripe fruit, floral, expressive. Palate: powerful, fresh, fruity, unctuous.

Las Reñas Barrica 2012 T
monastrell, syrah, tempranillo

88

Colour: cherry, purple rim. Nose: expressive, fresh fruit, red berry notes, cocoa bean. Palate: flavourful, fruity, good acidity, round tannins.

Las Reñas Ecológico 2012 T
monastrell

90 🌷

Colour: cherry, purple rim. Nose: powerfull, red berry notes, ripe fruit, floral, complex, earthy notes. Palate: powerful, fresh, fruity, unctuous.

Las Reñas Monastrell - Shiraz 2010 TC
monastrell, syrah

88

Colour: deep cherry. Nose: toasty, sweet spices, dark chocolate, cocoa bean, ripe fruit. Palate: spicy, ripe fruit, round tannins.

Las Reñas Selección 2011 TC
monastrell, syrah

89

Colour: cherry, garnet rim. Nose: ripe fruit, spicy, creamy oak, complex, earthy notes, roasted coffee. Palate: powerful, flavourful, toasty, round tannins.

Lorca Selección 2012 T
monastrell

90

Colour: bright cherry. Nose: ripe fruit, sweet spices, creamy oak, medium intensity. Palate: fruity, flavourful, toasty.

Lorca Syrah 2012 T
syrah

89

Colour: cherry, garnet rim. Nose: ripe fruit, spicy, creamy oak, toasty, complex, earthy notes. Palate: powerful, flavourful, toasty, round tannins.

Niño de las Uvas 2012 T
monastrell, syrah, tempranillo

90

Colour: very deep cherry. Nose: floral, ripe fruit, fruit expression, balsamic herbs, scrubland. Palate: flavourful, fruity, spicy, good acidity.

Señorío de Bullas 2010 TR
monastrell, syrah

87

Colour: cherry, garnet rim. Nose: ripe fruit, spicy, creamy oak, complex, dark chocolate. Palate: powerful, flavourful, toasty, round tannins.

BODEGAS MERCADER-QUESADA
Paraje de Balamonte (C/Herrera)
30180 Bullas (Murcia)
☎: +34 609 121 647
Fax: +34 968 654 205
www.mundoenologico.com
pilarquesadagil@yahoo.es

Mercader Quesada Selección Monastrell Ecológico 2010 T
monastrell

87 🌷

Colour: very deep cherry. Nose: candied fruit, fruit preserve, warm. Palate: flavourful, spicy, pruney.

DOMINIO DE ANTARGU
Ronda de Atocha, 16
28012 (Madrid)
☎: +34 915 275 244
www.dominiodeantargu.es
dominiodeantargu@gmail.com

Da 2010 T

87

Colour: cherry, garnet rim. Nose: ripe fruit, spicy, creamy oak, toasty, balsamic herbs. Palate: powerful, flavourful, toasty.

FERNANDO CARREÑO PEÑALVER
Ginés de Paco, 22
30430 Cehegín (Murcia)
☎: +34 968 740 004
Fax: +34 968 740 004
www.bodegascarreno.com
info@bodegascarreno.com

Marmallejo 2011 TC

87

Colour: bright cherry. Nose: sweet spices, creamy oak, candied fruit. Palate: flavourful, fruity, toasty, round tannins.

Viña Azeniche 2011 T Roble

84

MOLINO Y LAGARES DE BULLAS

Paraje Venta del Pino, s/n - Parcela
38 km. 12 Camino del Portugalez
30430 Cehegín (Murcia)
☎: +34 638 046 694
Fax: +34 968 654 494
www.bodegaslavia.com
lavia@bodegaslavia.com

Lavia Monastrell Syrah 2010 TC

93

Colour: cherry, garnet rim. Nose: ripe fruit, spicy, creamy oak, complex, earthy notes, balsamic herbs, grassy. Palate: powerful, flavourful, toasty, round tannins.

Lavia+ 2009 TC
100% monastrell

93

Colour: deep cherry. Nose: expressive, elegant, balsamic herbs, fragrant herbs. Palate: flavourful, spicy, long, good acidity.

Lavia+ Paso Malo 2009 TC
100% monastrell

93

Colour: very deep cherry. Nose: balsamic herbs, scrubland, fresh fruit, red berry notes. Palate: flavourful, fruity, fresh, good acidity, fine bitter notes.

DO. CALATAYUD

CONSEJO REGULADOR
Ctra. de Valencia, 8
50300 Calatayud (Zaragoza)
☎:+34 976 884 260 - Fax: +34 976 885 912
@: administracion@docalatayud.com
www.docalatayud.com

LOCATION:

It is situated in the western region of the province of Zaragoza, along the foothills of the Sistema Ibérico, outlined by the network of rivers woven by the different tributaries of the Ebro: Jalón, Jiloca, Manubles, Mesa, Piedra and Ribota, and covers 46 municipal areas of the Ebro Valley.

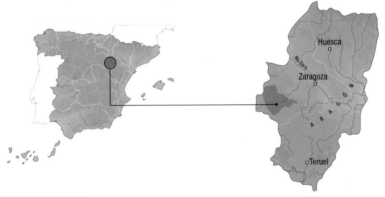

GRAPE VARIETIES:

White: Preferred: Macabeo (25%) and Malvasía.
Authorized: Moscatel de Alejandría, Garnacha Blanca, Sauvignon Blanc, Gewurztraiminer and Chardonnay.
Red: Preferred: Garnacha Tinta (61.9%), Tempranillo (10%) and Mazuela.
Authorized: Monastrell, Cabernet Sauvignon, Merlot, Bobal and Syrah.

FIGURES:

Vineyard surface: 3,280 – Wine-Growers: 900 – Wineries: 16 – 2013 Harvest rating: Very Good – Production 13: 7,078,979 litres – Market percentages: 15% domestic - 85% export.

SOIL:

In general, the soil has a high limestone content. It is formed by rugged stony materials from the nearby mountain ranges and is on many occasions accompanied by reddish clay. The region is the most rugged in Aragón, and the vineyards are situated at an altitude of between 550 and 880 m.

CLIMATE:

Semi - arid and dry, although somewhat cooler than Cariñena and Borja, with cold winters, an average annual temperature which ranges between 12 and 14 °C, and a period of frost of between 5 and 7 months which greatly affects the production. The average rainfall ranges between 300 – 550 mm per year, with great day/night temperature contrasts during the ripening season.

VINTAGE RATING   PEÑÍNGUIDE

2009	2010	2011	2012	2013
VERY GOOD	VERY GOOD	VERY GOOD	VERY GOOD	VERY GOOD

AGUSTÍN CUBERO

La Charluca, s/n
50300 Calatayud (Zaragoza)
☎: +34 976 882 332
Fax: +34 976 887 512
www.bodegascubero.com
calatayud@bodegascubero.com

Stylo 2012 T
garnacha

89

Colour: cherry, garnet rim. Nose: ripe fruit, creamy oak, toasty, cocoa bean, aromatic coffee. Palate: powerful, flavourful, toasty, roasted-coffee aftertaste.

Stylo 2013 T
garnacha

89

Colour: bright cherry. Nose: ripe fruit, sweet spices, creamy oak. Palate: flavourful, fruity, toasty, round tannins.

Unus 2013 B
macabeo

87

Colour: yellow, pale. Nose: balanced, medium intensity, fresh fruit, fragrant herbs. Palate: correct, fine bitter notes.

ALIANZA DE GARAPITEROS

Plaza España, 6 Planta 1ª
50001 (Zaragoza)
☎: +34 976 094 033
Fax: +34 976 094 033
www.alianzadegarapiteros.es
info@alianzadegarapiteros.es

Alquéz Garnacha Viñas Viejas 2012 T
100% garnacha

89

Colour: dark-red cherry, garnet rim. Nose: creamy oak, cocoa bean, sweet spices. Palate: fruity, flavourful, mineral, round tannins.

Nietro Garnacha Viñas Viejas 2013 T
100% garnacha

89

Colour: deep cherry. Nose: ripe fruit, sweet spices, cocoa bean. Palate: flavourful, fruity, toasty, round tannins.

Nietro Macabeo Viñas Viejas 2013 B
100% macabeo

88

Colour: bright straw. Nose: white flowers, fresh fruit, expressive, fine lees, dried herbs. Palate: flavourful, fruity, good acidity, balanced.

AXIAL

Pla-za Calle Castillo de Capua, 10 Nave 7
50197 (Zaragoza)
☎: +34 976 780 136
Fax: +34 976 303 035
www.axialvinos.com
info@axialvinos.com

Divina Lágrima 2012 T

89

Colour: cherry, garnet rim. Nose: ripe fruit, wild herbs, spicy, creamy oak. Palate: balanced, flavourful, long, balsamic, sweet tannins.

Marqués de Montañana Selección Especial 2013 T
100% garnacha

86

Colour: cherry, garnet rim. Nose: ripe fruit, wild herbs, spicy, creamy oak. Palate: balanced, flavourful, long, balsamic.

BODEGA CASTILLO DE MALUENDA

Avda. José Antonio, 61
50340 Maluenda (Zaragoza)
☎: +34 976 893 017
Fax: +34 976 546 969
www.castillodemaluenda.com
info@castillodemaluenda.com

Alto Las Pizarras 2011 T
100% garnacha
90
Colour: dark-red cherry. Nose: ripe fruit, wild herbs, spicy, creamy oak, mineral. Palate: balanced, flavourful, long, balsamic.

Castillo de Maluenda 2011 TC
86
Colour: deep cherry. Nose: ripe fruit, spicy, creamy oak, toasty, dry stone. Palate: powerful, flavourful, toasty, round tannins.

Claraval Selección Cuvée 2012 T
88
Colour: cherry, garnet rim. Nose: ripe fruit, spicy, creamy oak. Palate: balanced, flavourful, long, balsamic.

Claraval Syrah 2012 T
100% syrah
87
Colour: bright cherry. Nose: ripe fruit, sweet spices, creamy oak, expressive. Palate: flavourful, fruity, toasty, round tannins.

Las Pizarras 2011 T
100% garnacha
88
Colour: cherry, garnet rim. Nose: ripe fruit, wild herbs, spicy, creamy oak, varietal. Palate: balanced, flavourful, long, balsamic.

Las Pizarras Collection Fabla 2012 T
100% garnacha
90
Colour: cherry, garnet rim. Nose: ripe fruit, spicy. Palate: powerful, flavourful, toasty, round tannins, correct, easy to drink.

Las Pizarras Collection Siosy 2013 T
100% syrah
88
Colour: cherry, garnet rim. Nose: ripe fruit, wild herbs, earthy notes, spicy. Palate: balanced, flavourful, long, balsamic.

Las Pizarras Collection Volcán 2013 T
100% tempranillo
89
Colour: cherry, garnet rim. Nose: ripe fruit, spicy, toasty, complex, earthy notes, wild herbs, mineral. Palate: powerful, flavourful, toasty.

BODEGA COOP. VIRGEN DE LA SIERRA

Avda. de la Cooperativa, 21-23
50310 Villarroya de la Sierra (Zaragoza)
☎: +34 976 899 015
Fax: +34 976 899 132
www.bodegavirgendelasierra.com
oficina@bodegavirgendelasierra.com

Albada 2013 B
100% macabeo
88
Colour: bright straw. Nose: white flowers, fragrant herbs, fruit expression. Palate: fresh, fruity, flavourful, balanced, elegant.

Albada Finca 1 2012 T
garnacha
91
Colour: dark-red cherry, garnet rim. Nose: mineral, complex, ripe fruit, spicy. Palate: flavourful, ripe fruit, long.

Albada Finca 2 2012 T
garnacha
92
Colour: bright cherry. Nose: ripe fruit, sweet spices, creamy oak, mineral, balsamic herbs, expressive. Palate: flavourful, fruity, toasty, round tannins, balsamic, elegant.

Albada Viñas Viejas 2012 T
100% garnacha
88
Colour: cherry, garnet rim. Nose: red berry notes, ripe fruit, mineral, balsamic herbs. Palate: flavourful, spicy, balanced.

Cruz de Piedra 2013 B
100% macabeo
85

Cruz de Piedra 2013 RD
100% garnacha
87
Colour: brilliant rose. Nose: powerfull, ripe fruit, red berry notes, floral, expressive. Palate: powerful, fruity, fresh.

Cruz de Piedra 2013 T
100% garnacha
87
Colour: cherry, purple rim. Nose: expressive, fresh fruit, red berry notes, floral, wild herbs. Palate: flavourful, fruity, good acidity.

Cruz de Piedra Capricho 2010 TR
100% garnacha
90
Colour: cherry, garnet rim. Nose: ripe fruit, spicy, creamy oak, toasty, complex, balsamic herbs, mineral. Palate: powerful, flavourful, toasty, round tannins.

Cruz de Piedra Selección Especial 2012 T
100% garnacha

89

Colour: cherry, garnet rim. Nose: red berry notes, ripe fruit, mineral, wild herbs. Palate: flavourful, spicy, balsamic.

Cruz de Piedra Selección Especial 2013 T
100% garnacha

91

Colour: cherry, garnet rim. Nose: ripe fruit, wild herbs, spicy, creamy oak, mineral. Palate: balanced, flavourful, long, balsamic.

BODEGA SAN GREGORIO

Ctra. Villalengua, s/n
50312 Cervera de la Cañada (Zaragoza)
☎: +34 976 899 206
Fax: +34 976 896 240
www.bodegasangregorio.com
tresojos@bodegasangregorio.com

Armantes 2008 TR
89

Colour: dark-red cherry, garnet rim. Nose: spicy, wild herbs, cocoa bean. Palate: good acidity, balanced, long, balsamic.

Armantes 2010 TC
87

Colour: dark-red cherry. Nose: ripe fruit, earthy notes, spicy, scrubland. Palate: balanced, flavourful, balsamic, round tannins.

Armantes 2013 B
macabeo

85

Armantes 2013 BFB
macabeo

89

Colour: bright straw. Nose: ripe fruit, powerfull, toasty, aged wood nuances. Palate: flavourful, fruity, spicy, toasty, long, balanced, elegant.

Armantes 2013 RD
86

Colour: light cherry, bright. Nose: red berry notes, wild herbs. Palate: fresh, fruity, easy to drink, good acidity.

Armantes 2013 T
88

Colour: cherry, purple rim. Nose: powerfull, red berry notes, ripe fruit, floral, expressive. Palate: powerful, fresh, fruity, unctuous, correct.

Armantes Vendimia Seleccionada 2011 T
90

Colour: cherry, garnet rim. Nose: ripe fruit, spicy, creamy oak, toasty, mineral. Palate: powerful, flavourful, toasty, balsamic.

Tres Ojos Garnacha 2012 T
garnacha

86

Colour: dark-red cherry, garnet rim. Nose: ripe fruit, spicy, toasty, scrubland. Palate: correct, flavourful.

BODEGAS ATECA

Ctra. N-II, s/n
50200 Ateca (Zaragoza)
☎: +34 968 435 022
Fax: +34 968 716 051
www.orowines.com
info@orowines.com

Atteca 2012 T
100% garnacha

93

Colour: cherry, garnet rim. Nose: ripe fruit, spicy, creamy oak, toasty, complex, dark chocolate, earthy notes. Palate: powerful, flavourful, toasty, round tannins.

Atteca Armas 2010 T
100% garnacha

93

Colour: very deep cherry, garnet rim. Nose: powerfull, roasted coffee, dark chocolate, overripe fruit, warm. Palate: powerful, toasty, roasted-coffee aftertaste.

Atteca Armas 2011 T
100% garnacha

93

Colour: bright cherry. Nose: ripe fruit, sweet spices, creamy oak, medium intensity. Palate: fruity, flavourful, toasty, full.

Honoro Vera Garnacha 2013 T
100% garnacha

90

Colour: very deep cherry, garnet rim. Nose: warm, dried herbs, sweet spices, mineral, varietal. Palate: flavourful, ripe fruit, long.

BODEGAS AUGUSTA BILBILIS

Carramiedes, s/n
50331 Mara (Zaragoza)
☎: +34 677 547 127
www.bodegasaugustabilbilis.com
bodegasaugustabilbilis@hotmail.com

Samitier 2012 T Roble
100% garnacha

90

Colour: cherry, garnet rim. Nose: earthy notes, red berry notes, fruit expression, scrubland. Palate: good acidity, correct, round tannins.

Samitier Garnacha 2009 T
100% garnacha

93

Colour: cherry, garnet rim. Nose: ripe fruit, wild herbs, earthy notes, spicy, creamy oak. Palate: balanced, flavourful, long, balsamic.

BODEGAS BRECA

Ctra. Monasterio de Piedra, s/n
50219 Munébrega (Zaragoza)
☎: +34 976 895 071
Fax: +34 976 895 171
www.grupojorgeordonez.com
breca@jorgeordonez.es

Breca 2012 T
100% garnacha

96

Colour: cherry, garnet rim. Nose: ripe fruit, spicy, creamy oak, toasty, complex, dark chocolate, earthy notes. Palate: powerful, flavourful, toasty, round tannins.

BODEGAS DOMINIO MARÍA PILAR

Avda. Barón de Warsage, 27
50300 Calatayud (Zaragoza)
☎: + 34 976 886 606
Fax: +34 976 887 512

Dominio de María 2011 T
garnacha

90

Colour: bright cherry. Nose: sweet spices, creamy oak, toasty, smoky. Palate: flavourful, fruity, toasty, round tannins.

BODEGAS ESTEBAN CASTEJÓN

Portada, 13
50236 Ibdes (Zaragoza)
☎: +34 976 848 031
www.bodegasesteban.es
bodegasesteban@bodegasesteban.es

Tranquera 2013 RD
tempranillo, garnacha, cabernet sauvignon

85

Tranquera Garnacha 2012 T
100% garnacha

88

Colour: cherry, garnet rim. Nose: ripe fruit, spicy, toasty, complex, dried herbs. Palate: toasty, round tannins.

Tranquera Garnacha Blanca 2013 B
100% garnacha blanca

86

Colour: bright straw. Nose: fresh, fresh fruit, white flowers. Palate: flavourful, fruity, good acidity, balanced.

BODEGAS LANGA

Ctra. Nacional II, Km. 241,700
50300 Calatayud (Zaragoza)
☎: +34 976 881 818
Fax: +34 976 884 463
www.bodegas-langa.com
info@bodegas-langa.com

Langa Garnacha 2012 T
garnacha

89

Colour: cherry, garnet rim. Nose: ripe fruit, spicy, toasty, earthy notes. Palate: powerful, flavourful, toasty, round tannins.

Langa Merlot 2012 T
100% merlot

88

Colour: deep cherry, garnet rim. Nose: cocoa bean, sweet spices, ripe fruit, scrubland, balsamic herbs. Palate: flavourful, round tannins.

Langa Tradición 2012 T
100% garnacha

90

Colour: bright cherry. Nose: ripe fruit, sweet spices, scrubland. Palate: fruity, flavourful, toasty, mineral.

Real de Aragón Centenaria 2011 T
garnacha

90

Colour: cherry, garnet rim. Nose: ripe fruit, spicy, creamy oak, toasty, complex. Palate: powerful, flavourful, toasty, round tannins.

Reyes de Aragón Garnacha Cabernet 2011 TC
garnacha, cabernet sauvignon

90

Colour: cherry, garnet rim. Nose: ripe fruit, wild herbs, spicy, creamy oak. Palate: flavourful, long, balsamic.

BODEGAS SAN ALEJANDRO

Ctra. Calatayud - Cariñena, Km. 16
50330 Miedes de Aragón (Zaragoza)
☎: +34 976 892 205
Fax: +34 976 890 540
www.san-alejandro.com

Baltasar Gracián 2011 TC
garnacha, syrah, tempranillo

91

Colour: cherry, garnet rim. Nose: ripe fruit, spicy, creamy oak, toasty, mineral. Palate: powerful, flavourful, toasty, round tannins, balanced, elegant.

Baltasar Gracián 2010 TR
garnacha, syrah, tempranillo

91

Colour: dark-red cherry, garnet rim. Nose: expressive, red berry notes, ripe fruit, faded flowers, spicy. Palate: balanced.

Baltasar Gracián Garnacha 2013 RD
100% garnacha

88

Colour: rose, purple rim. Nose: powerfull, ripe fruit, red berry notes, floral, expressive. Palate: fruity, fresh, flavourful, good acidity.

Baltasar Gracián Garnacha Nativa 2011 T
100% garnacha

93

Colour: dark-red cherry, garnet rim. Nose: complex, balanced, balsamic herbs, scrubland, spicy. Palate: good structure, balanced, balsamic, mineral.

Baltasar Gracián Garnacha 2013 T
100% garnacha

90

Colour: cherry, garnet rim. Nose: ripe fruit, wild herbs, earthy notes, spicy, mineral. Palate: balanced, flavourful, long, balsamic.

Baltasar Gracián Garnacha Viñas Viejas 2012 T
100% garnacha

91

Colour: cherry, garnet rim. Nose: ripe fruit, wild herbs, spicy, creamy oak, mineral. Palate: balanced, flavourful, long, balsamic.

Baltasar Gracián Macabeo 2013 B
100% macabeo

86

Colour: bright straw. Nose: fresh, fresh fruit, white flowers, expressive. Palate: fruity, good acidity, balanced, good finish.

Las Rocas Garnacha 2011 T
garnacha

90

Colour: cherry, garnet rim. Nose: ripe fruit, spicy, creamy oak, toasty, complex, earthy notes. Palate: powerful, flavourful, toasty, round tannins.

Las Rocas Garnacha 2012 T
100% garnacha

91

Colour: cherry, garnet rim. Nose: ripe fruit, wild herbs, spicy, dry stone. Palate: balanced, flavourful, long, balsamic.

Las Rocas Garnacha Viñas Viejas 2012 T
100% garnacha

93

Colour: cherry, garnet rim. Nose: ripe fruit, spicy, creamy oak, toasty, dry stone, balsamic herbs. Palate: powerful, flavourful, toasty.

EL ESCOCÉS VOLANTE
Barrio La Rosa Bajo, 16
50300 Calatayud (Zaragoza)
☎: +34 637 511 133
www.escocesvolante.es
info@escocesvolante.es

El Puño 2011 T

93

Colour: cherry, garnet rim. Nose: spicy, creamy oak, toasty, fruit expression. Palate: powerful, flavourful, toasty, round tannins.

Manga del Brujo 2012 T

93

Colour: cherry, garnet rim. Nose: ripe fruit, wild herbs, earthy notes, spicy, creamy oak, expressive. Palate: balanced, flavourful, long, balsamic.

EMBUTIDOS GUERRERO SEBASTIÁN
Ctra. Daroca, s/n
50347 Acered (Zaragoza)
☎: +34 976 896 704
Fax: +34 976 896 704
www.bodegasguerrerosebastian.com
maguese1@gmail.com

Azeré 2012 TC
100% garnacha

85

Azeré 2013 B
100% macabeo

87

Colour: straw, pale. Nose: ripe fruit, medium intensity, dried herbs. Palate: full, flavourful, long, good acidity, fine bitter notes.

Azeré 2013 RD
100% garnacha

86

Colour: rose, purple rim. Nose: powerfull, ripe fruit, red berry notes, floral. Palate: powerful, fruity, fresh.

Azeré Garnacha + de 50 2010 T
100% garnacha

92

Colour: light cherry. Nose: ripe fruit, spicy, creamy oak, toasty, complex, dry stone. Palate: powerful, flavourful, toasty, round tannins, elegant.

FLORIS LEGERE

Ecuador, 5 2º 1ª
50012 Zaragoza (Zaragoza)
☎: +34 608 974 809
www.florislegere.com
contact@florislegere.com

Alaviana 2012 T
garnacha, syrah

92

Colour: cherry, garnet rim. Nose: red berry notes, balsamic herbs, dry stone, expressive. Palate: balanced, powerful, flavourful, long, spicy, round.

Atractylis 2012 T
syrah

92

Colour: cherry, garnet rim. Nose: ripe fruit, wild herbs, earthy notes, spicy, creamy oak. Palate: balanced, flavourful, long, balsamic.

NIÑO JESÚS

Las Tablas, s/n
50313 Aniñón (Zaragoza)
☎: +34 976 899 150
Fax: +34 976 896 160
www.satninojesus.com
gerencia@satninojesus.com

Estecillo 2013 B
macabeo

84

Estecillo 2013 T
garnacha, tempranillo

84

Legado Garnacha 2013 T
garnacha

85

Legado Garnacha Syrah 2012 T
garnacha, syrah

84

Legado Macabeo 2013 BFB
macabeo

86

Colour: bright yellow. Nose: powerfull, ripe fruit, sweet spices, creamy oak, fragrant herbs. Palate: rich, smoky aftertaste, flavourful, fresh, good acidity.

PAGOS ALTOS DE ACERED

Avda. Río Jalón, 62
50300 Calatayud (Zaragoza)
☎: +34 636 474 723
www.lajas.es
manuel@lajas.es

Lajas "Finca el Peñiscal" 2007 T
100% garnacha

93

Colour: cherry, garnet rim. Nose: ripe fruit, wild herbs, spicy, balsamic herbs, scrubland. Palate: balanced, flavourful, long, balsamic, elegant.

Lajas "Finca el Peñiscal" 2008 T
100% garnacha

92

Colour: dark-red cherry, garnet rim. Nose: fine reductive notes, spicy, dried herbs, mineral. Palate: flavourful, round tannins, long.

Lajas "Finca el Peñiscal" 2009 T
100% garnacha

94

Colour: cherry, garnet rim. Nose: expressive, red berry notes, ripe fruit, mineral, scrubland. Palate: ripe fruit, long, balanced, complex.

Lajas "Finca el Peñiscal" 2010 T
100% garnacha

93

Colour: cherry, garnet rim. Nose: ripe fruit, spicy, creamy oak, toasty, dry stone, wild herbs. Palate: powerful, flavourful, toasty, round tannins, balanced, round.

RESERVA Y CATA

Conde de Xiquena, 13
28004 (Madrid)
☎: +34 913 190 401
Fax: +34 913 190 401
www.reservaycata.com
info@reservaycata.com

Pagos Místicos 2011 T

89

Colour: cherry, garnet rim. Nose: ripe fruit, spicy, creamy oak, toasty, balsamic herbs. Palate: powerful, flavourful, toasty.

DO. CAMPO DE BORJA

CONSEJO REGULADOR

Subida de San Andrés, 6
50570 Ainzón (Zaragoza)
☎:+34 976 852 122 - Fax: +34 976 868 806
@: vinos@docampodeborja.com
www.docampodeborja.com

LOCATION:

The DO Campo de Borja is made up of 16 municipal areas, situated in the north west of the province of Zaragoza and 60 km from the capital city, in an area of transition between the mountains of the Sistema Ibérico (at the foot of the Moncayo) and the Ebro Valley: Agón, Ainzón, Alberite, Albeta, Ambel, Bisimbre, Borja, Bulbuente, Burueta, El Buste, Fuendejalón, Magallón, Malejan, Pozuelo de Aragón, Tabuenca and Vera del Moncayo.

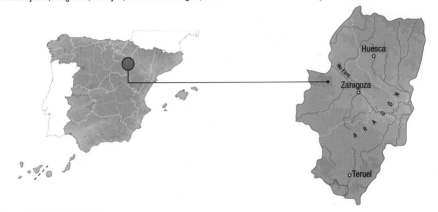

GRAPE VARIETIES:

White: Macabeo, Garnacha Blanca, Moscatel, Chardonnay, Sauvignon Blanc and Verdejo.
Red: Garnacha (majority with 75%), Tempranillo, Mazuela, Cabernet Sauvignon, Merlot and Syrah.

FIGURES:

Vineyard surface: 6,614.12 – Wine-Growers: 1,520 – Wineries: 17 – 2013 Harvest rating: - – Production 13: 13,386,915 litres – Market percentages: 63.12% domestic - 36.87% export.

SOIL:

The most abundant are brownish - grey limey soils, terrace soils and clayey ferrous soils. The vineyards are situated at an altitude of between 350 and 700 m on small slightly rolling hillsides, on terraces of the Huecha river and the Llanos de Plasencia, making up the Somontano del Moncayo.

CLIMATE:

A rather extreme continental climate, with cold winters and dry, hot summers. One of its main characteristics is the influence of the 'Cierzo', a cold and dry north - westerly wind. Rainfall is rather scarce, with an average of between 350 and 450 mm per year.

VINTAGE RATING   PEÑÍNGUIDE

2009	2010	2011	2012	2013
VERY GOOD	VERY GOOD	VERY GOOD	VERY GOOD	GOOD

PEÑÍNGUIDE 25 años **to Spanish Wine**

ARTIGA FUSTEL

Progres, 21 Bajos
08720 Vilafranca del Penedès
(Barcelona)
☎: +34 938 182 317
Fax: +34 938 924 499
www.artiga-fustel.com
info@artiga-fustel.com

Nostrada Syrah Monastrell 2013 T
86
Colour: bright cherry, purple rim. Nose: red berry notes, ripe fruit, balanced. Palate: fruity, flavourful, good acidity.

BODEGA PICOS

Ctra. Nacional 122, Km. 55'400
50520 Magallón (Zaragoza)
☎: +34 976 863 006
www.bodegapicos.com
info@bodegapicos.com

Gran Gregoriano 2012 T
garnacha, tempranillo, cabernet sauvignon, syrah
84

Gregoriano 2012 T Roble
garnacha, tempranillo, cabernet sauvignon
85

Gregoriano Blanco de Hielo 2013 B
moscatel, macabeo
83

Loteta 2013 T
garnacha, tempranillo, cabernet sauvignon
83

BODEGAS ALTO MONCAYO

Ctra. CV-606 Borja - El Buste, Km. 1,700
50540 Borja (Zaragoza)
☎: +34 976 868 098
Fax: +34 976 868 147
www.bodegasaltomoncayo.com
info@bodegasaltomoncayo.com

Alto Moncayo 2011 T
100% garnacha
96
Colour: cherry, garnet rim. Nose: ripe fruit, balsamic herbs, spicy, creamy oak, toasty, mineral. Palate: balanced, round, unctuous, spicy, long, elegant.

Alto Moncayo Veratón 2011 T
100% garnacha
93
Colour: cherry, garnet rim. Nose: ripe fruit, spicy, creamy oak, toasty, complex, cocoa bean. Palate: powerful, flavourful, toasty, round tannins.

Aquilón 2011 T
100% garnacha
95
Colour: cherry, garnet rim. Nose: red berry notes, ripe fruit, spicy, creamy oak, toasty, complex, earthy notes. Palate: powerful, flavourful, toasty, round tannins, balanced, elegant.

BODEGAS ARAGONESAS

Ctra. Magallón, s/n
50529 Fuendejalón (Zaragoza)
☎: +34 976 862 153
Fax: +34 976 862 363
www.bodegasaragonesas.com
vanesa@bodegasaragonesas.com

Aragonia Selección Especial 2011 T
100% garnacha
91
Colour: cherry, garnet rim. Nose: ripe fruit, spicy, creamy oak, toasty, complex. Palate: powerful, flavourful, toasty, round tannins.

Aragus 2013 T
87
Colour: deep cherry, purple rim. Nose: scrubland, ripe fruit. Palate: correct, balanced, fruity.

Aragus Ecológico 2013 T
100% garnacha
87 ♣
Colour: very deep cherry, purple rim. Nose: medium intensity, red berry notes, dried flowers. Palate: correct, ripe fruit, spicy.

Coto de Hayas 2010 TR
100% garnacha
89
Colour: cherry, garnet rim. Nose: red berry notes, ripe fruit, spicy, creamy oak, toasty, fine reductive notes. Palate: powerful, flavourful, toasty, round tannins.

Coto de Hayas 2011 TC
88
Colour: black cherry. Nose: ripe fruit, wild herbs, spicy, creamy oak. Palate: balanced, flavourful, long, balsamic.

Coto de Hayas 2013 RD
87
Colour: brilliant rose. Nose: powerfull, ripe fruit, red berry notes, floral, expressive. Palate: powerful, fruity, fresh.

Coto de Hayas Chardonnay 2013 B
chardonnay
84

Coto de Hayas Garnacha Centenaria 2012 T
garnacha
91
Colour: cherry, purple rim. Nose: ripe fruit, sweet spices, creamy oak, cocoa bean, dark chocolate, lactic notes, balsamic herbs. Palate: flavourful, fruity, toasty.

Coto de Hayas Garnacha Centenaria 2013 T
100% garnacha

90

Colour: bright cherry. Nose: ripe fruit, sweet spices. Palate: flavourful, fruity, toasty, round tannins.

Coto de Hayas Garnacha Syrah 2013 T
87

Colour: cherry, purple rim. Nose: ripe fruit, medium intensity. Palate: balanced, fruity, good finish.

Coto de Hayas Mistela 2013
Vino dulce natural
100% garnacha

90

Colour: ruby red. Nose: sweet spices, aromatic coffee, cocoa bean, balsamic herbs, floral, fruit liqueur notes. Palate: powerful, flavourful, spicy, spirituous, balanced.

Coto de Hayas Moscatel 2013 B
100% moscatel grano menudo

86

Colour: bright golden. Nose: floral, candied fruit, honeyed notes. Palate: flavourful, sweet, rich.

Coto de Hayas Tempranillo Cabernet 2013 T Roble
88

Colour: cherry, garnet rim. Nose: spicy, creamy oak, toasty, complex, dark chocolate, earthy notes, red berry notes. Palate: powerful, flavourful, toasty.

Don Ramón 2012 T Barrica
87

Colour: very deep cherry, garnet rim. Nose: powerfull, ripe fruit, dark chocolate. Palate: powerful, toasty, roasted-coffee aftertaste.

Don Ramón Garnacha Imperial 2012 T Roble
100% garnacha

89

Colour: bright cherry. Nose: ripe fruit, sweet spices, creamy oak, expressive, fruit preserve. Palate: flavourful, fruity, toasty, round tannins.

Ecce Homo 2013 T
100% garnacha

86

Colour: cherry, purple rim. Nose: powerfull, red berry notes, ripe fruit, floral, expressive. Palate: powerful, fresh, fruity, unctuous.

Ecce Homo Selección 2010 T
100% garnacha

87

Colour: very deep cherry, garnet rim. Nose: sweet spices, creamy oak, ripe fruit. Palate: fruity, round tannins.

Fagus de Coto de Hayas 2012 T
100% garnacha

93

Colour: cherry, garnet rim. Nose: red berry notes, ripe fruit, wild herbs, mineral, sweet spices, creamy oak. Palate: powerful, flavourful, long, toasty.

Galiano 2007 T
100% garnacha

92

Colour: pale ruby, brick rim edge. Nose: ripe fruit, spicy, creamy oak, toasty, complex, fine reductive notes. Palate: powerful, flavourful, toasty, round tannins, elegant.

Oxia 2010 TC
100% garnacha

91

Colour: pale ruby, brick rim edge. Nose: elegant, spicy, fine reductive notes, fruit preserve. Palate: spicy, fine tannins, elegant, long.

Solo Centifolia 2013 RD
100% garnacha

87

Colour: onion pink. Nose: elegant, dried flowers, fragrant herbs, red berry notes. Palate: light-bodied, flavourful, good acidity, long.

Solo Syrah 2013 T
100% syrah

87

Colour: bright cherry. Nose: sweet spices, creamy oak, balsamic herbs, violet drops. Palate: flavourful, fruity, toasty.

Solo Tiólico 2013 B
100% moscatel de alejandría

87

Colour: bright straw. Nose: fresh, fresh fruit, white flowers, expressive. Palate: flavourful, fruity, good acidity, balanced.

BODEGAS BORSAO
Ctra. N- 122, Km. 63
50540 Borja (Zaragoza)
☎: +34 976 867 116
Fax: +34 976 867 752
www.bodegasborsao.com
info@bodegasborsao.com

Borsao Berola 2010 T
92

Colour: bright cherry. Nose: ripe fruit, wild herbs, earthy notes, spicy, creamy oak, varietal. Palate: balanced, flavourful, long, balsamic.

Borsao Bole 2011 T
89

Colour: black cherry. Nose: ripe fruit, spicy, creamy oak, toasty, complex. Palate: powerful, flavourful, toasty, round tannins.

Borsao Selección 2011 TC

90

Colour: cherry, garnet rim. Nose: ripe fruit, wild herbs, earthy notes, spicy, creamy oak. Palate: balanced, flavourful, long, balsamic.

Borsao Selección 2013 B
macabeo

85

Borsao Selección 2013 RD
100% garnacha

86

Colour: rose. Nose: floral, red berry notes, balanced, dried herbs. Palate: fruity, easy to drink, fine bitter notes.

Borsao Selección 2013 T

86

Colour: cherry, garnet rim. Nose: ripe fruit, wild herbs, earthy notes. Palate: balanced, flavourful, long, balsamic.

Borsao Tres Picos 2012 T
100% garnacha

93

Colour: cherry, garnet rim. Nose: ripe fruit, spicy, creamy oak, toasty, complex, dark chocolate, earthy notes. Palate: powerful, flavourful, toasty, round tannins.

BODEGAS CARLOS VALERO

Castillo de Capúa, 10 Nave 1 Pol. PLA_ZA
50197 (Zaragoza)
☎: +34 976 180 634
Fax: +34 976 186 326
www.bodegasvalero.com
info@bodegasvalero.com

Heredad Asunción 2013 RD
100% garnacha

84

Heredad Garnacha Blanca y Radiante 2013 B
100% garnacha blanca

86

Colour: bright straw. Nose: medium intensity, fragrant herbs. Palate: fruity, easy to drink, fine bitter notes, good finish.

Heredad H Carlos Valero 2011 T
100% garnacha

88

Colour: very deep cherry, garnet rim. Nose: dark chocolate, creamy oak, ripe fruit, fruit preserve. Palate: good structure, flavourful.

Heredad Red Carlos Valero 2011 T
100% garnacha

91

Colour: cherry, garnet rim. Nose: ripe fruit, wild herbs, earthy notes, spicy, creamy oak. Palate: balanced, flavourful, long, balsamic.

BODEGAS ROMÁN

Ctra. Gallur - Agreda, 1
50546 Balbuente (Zaragoza)
☎: +34 976 852 936
www.bodegasroman.com
info@bodegasroman.es

Portal de Moncayo 2013 T
garnacha

88

Colour: very deep cherry, purple rim. Nose: red berry notes, balanced, dry stone. Palate: correct, fruity, flavourful, balanced.

Portal del Moncayo 2012 T Barrica
garnacha

87

Colour: bright cherry. Nose: ripe fruit, sweet spices, expressive, fruit preserve. Palate: flavourful, fruity, toasty, round tannins.

Román Cepas Viejas 2010 T
garnacha

92

Colour: bright cherry. Nose: ripe fruit, sweet spices, creamy oak, expressive. Palate: flavourful, fruity, toasty, round tannins.

Senda de Hoyas 2013 T
garnacha

85

CRIANZAS Y VIÑEDOS SANTO CRISTO

Ctra. Tabuenca, s/n
50570 Ainzón (Zaragoza)
☎: +34 976 869 696
Fax: +34 976 868 097
www.bodegas-santo-cristo.com
bodegas@bodegas-santo-cristo.com

Cayus Selección 2012 T Roble
100% garnacha

92

Colour: cherry, garnet rim. Nose: ripe fruit, wild herbs, earthy notes, spicy, creamy oak, dry stone. Palate: balanced, flavourful, long, balsamic.

Flor de Añon Verdejo 2013 B
100% verdejo

85

Moscatel Ainzón 2013 B
100% moscatel grano menudo

87

Colour: bright straw. Nose: powerfull, floral, honeyed notes, candied fruit. Palate: flavourful, sweet, fresh, fruity, good acidity, long.

Moscatel Ainzón 90 días 2013 B Barrica
100% moscatel grano menudo

92

Colour: bright straw. Nose: powerfull, floral, honeyed notes, candied fruit, fragrant herbs. Palate: flavourful, sweet, fresh, fruity, good acidity, long.

Peñazuela Selección 2012 T Roble
100% garnacha

86

Colour: black cherry. Nose: ripe fruit, sweet spices, creamy oak, fruit preserve. Palate: flavourful, fruity, toasty, round tannins.

Santo Cristo 2013 T Roble

86

Colour: very deep cherry, purple rim. Nose: ripe fruit, fruit preserve, scrubland. Palate: fruity, fruity afteistaste.

Terrazas del Moncayo Garnacha 2010 T Roble
100% garnacha

91

Colour: cherry, garnet rim. Nose: ripe fruit, spicy, creamy oak, toasty, complex. Palate: powerful, flavourful, toasty, round tannins, varietal.

Viña Ainzón 2011 TC

88

Colour: very deep cherry, garnet rim. Nose: balanced, ripe fruit, spicy, scrubland. Palate: flavourful, round tannins.

Viña Collado 2013 B
100% macabeo

85

Viña Collado 2013 RD
100% garnacha

86

Colour: rose, purple rim. Nose: ripe fruit, red berry notes, floral. Palate: powerful, fruity, fresh, easy to drink.

Viña Collado 2013 T
garnacha, syrah

87

Colour: cherry, purple rim. Nose: fresh fruit, red berry notes, floral. Palate: flavourful, fruity, good acidity, round tannins.

PAGOS DEL MONCAYO
Ctra. Z-372, Km. 1,6
50580 Vera de Moncayo (Zaragoza)
☎: +34 976 900 256
www.pagosdelmoncayo.com
info@pagosdelmoncayo.com

Pagos del Moncayo Garnacha 2012 T
100% garnacha

91

Colour: very deep cherry. Nose: ripe fruit, spicy, creamy oak, toasty, complex. Palate: powerful, flavourful, toasty, round tannins.

Pagos del Moncayo Garnacha Syrah 2013 T

88

Colour: cherry, purple rim. Nose: creamy oak, aromatic coffee, smoky, toasty. Palate: powerful, flavourful, toasty, roasted-coffee aftertaste.

Pagos del Moncayo Prados 2012 T
syrah

91

Colour: very deep cherry, garnet rim. Nose: powerfull, ripe fruit, roasted coffee, dry stone, balsamic herbs. Palate: powerful, toasty, roasted-coffee aftertaste, unctuous, round.

Pagos del Moncayo Syrah 2012 T
100% syrah

90

Colour: bright cherry. Nose: ripe fruit, sweet spices, creamy oak, dark chocolate, aromatic coffee. Palate: flavourful, fruity, toasty, round tannins.

RUBERTE HERMANOS
Tenor Fleta, s/n
50520 Magallón (Zaragoza)
☎: +34 976 858 106
Fax: +34 976 858 475
www.bodegasruberte.com
info@bodegasruberte.com

Aliana Carácter 2012 T
syrah

87

Colour: bright cherry, garnet rim. Nose: ripe fruit, fruit preserve, spicy, balanced. Palate: flavourful, round tannins.

Ruberte 2013 RD

86

Colour: rose. Nose: red berry notes, ripe fruit, raspberry, balsamic herbs, balanced. Palate: flavourful, fresh.

Ruberte Syrah 2010 T
syrah

85

Ruberte Tresor 2012 T

87

Colour: cherry, garnet rim. Nose: spicy, creamy oak, toasty, complex, fruit preserve. Palate: powerful, flavourful, toasty, harsh oak tannins.

DO. CARIÑENA

CONSEJO REGULADOR

Camino de la Platera, 7
50400 Cariñena (Zaragoza)
☎:+34 976 793 143 / +34 976 793 031 - Fax: +34 976 621 107
@: consejoregulador@docarinena.com
@: promocion@docarinena.com
www.docarinena.com

LOCATION:

In the province of Zaragoza, and occupies the Ebro valley covering 14 municipal areas: Aguarón, Aladrén, Alfamén, Almonacid de la Sierra, Alpartir, Cariñena, Cosuenda, Encinacorba, Longares, Mezalocha, Muel, Paniza, Tosos and Villanueva de Huerva.

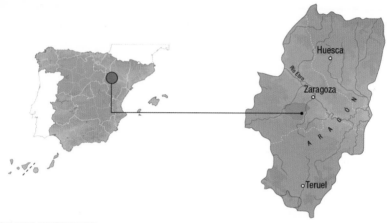

GRAPE VARIETIES:

White: Preferred: Macabeo (majority 20%).
Authorized: Garnacha Blanca, Moscatel Romano, Parellada and Chardonnay.
Red: Preferred: Garnacha Tinta (majority 55%), Tempranillo, Mazuela (or Cariñena).
Authorized: Juan Ibáñez, Cabernet Sauvignon, Syrah, Monastrell, Vidadillo and Merlot.

FIGURES:

Vineyard surface: 14,513 – Wine-Growers: 1,587– Wineries: 31 – 2013 Harvest rating: Very Good– Production 13: 59,363,647 litres – Market percentages: 24.88% domestic - 75.12% export.

SOIL:

Mainly poor; either brownish - grey limey soil, or reddish dun soil settled on rocky deposits, or brownish - grey soil settled on alluvial deposits. The vineyards are situated at an altitude of between 400 and 800 m.

CLIMATE:

A continental climate, with cold winters, hot summers and low rainfall. The viticulture is also influenced by the effect of the 'Cierzo'.

VINTAGE RATING   PEÑÍNGUIDE

2009	2010	2011	2012	2013
VERY GOOD	VERY GOOD	GOOD	GOOD	GOOD

AXIAL

Plaza Calle Castillo de Capua, 10 Nave 7
50197 (Zaragoza)
☎: +34 976 780 136
Fax: +34 976 303 035
www.axialvinos.com
info@axialvinos.com

La Granja 360 Garnacha Syrah 2013 T
85

La Granja 360 Tempranillo 2013 T
100% tempranillo
85

La Granja 360 Tempranillo Garnacha 2013 T
86
Colour: cherry, purple rim. Nose: powerfull, red berry notes, ripe fruit, floral. Palate: powerful, fresh, fruity, unctuous.

BIOENOS

Mayor, 88 Bajo
50400 Cariñena (Zaragoza)
☎: +34 976 620 045
Fax: +34 976 622 082
www.bioenos.com
bioenos@bioenos.com

Gorys Crespiello 2007 T
vidadilo, crespiello
92
Colour: ruby red. Nose: ripe fruit, wild herbs, earthy notes, spicy, creamy oak, balsamic herbs. Palate: balanced, flavourful, long, balsamic.

Gorys Crespiello 2008 T
vidadilo, crespiello
90
Colour: cherry, garnet rim. Nose: red berry notes, ripe fruit, balsamic herbs, spicy, earthy notes, cocoa bean. Palate: flavourful, complex, spicy, balsamic.

Pulchrum Crespiello 2010 T
vidadilo, crespiello
90
Colour: cherry, garnet rim. Nose: ripe fruit, spicy, creamy oak, toasty, complex, dried herbs. Palate: powerful, flavourful, toasty, round tannins, long.

Pulchrum Crespiello 2011 T
vidadilo, crespiello
92
Colour: cherry, garnet rim. Nose: ripe fruit, spicy, creamy oak, toasty, balsamic herbs. Palate: powerful, flavourful, toasty, round tannins.

BODEGA PAGO AYLÉS

Finca Aylés. Ctra. A-1101, Km. 24
50152 Mezalocha (Zaragoza)
☎: +34 976 140 473
Fax: +34 976 140 268
www.pagoayles.com
pagoayles@pagoayles.com

Aldeya de Aylés Garnacha 2013 T
garnacha
89
Colour: deep cherry, garnet rim. Nose: balanced, ripe fruit, sweet spices. Palate: balanced, ripe fruit, long.

Aldeya de Aylés Tinto 2013 T
syrah, tempranillo, merlot, cabernet sauvignon
87
Colour: cherry, purple rim. Nose: expressive, fresh fruit, red berry notes, floral, dried herbs. Palate: flavourful, fruity, good acidity, round tannins.

Aldeya de Aylés Tinto Barrica 2010 T
tempranillo, syrah, merlot
86
Colour: bright cherry. Nose: sweet spices, creamy oak, toasty. Palate: flavourful, fruity, toasty, round tannins.

Dorondón Chardonnay de Aylés 2013 B
chardonnay
87
Colour: straw. Nose: white flowers, fruit expression. Palate: fresh, fruity, flavourful, balanced, elegant.

Serendipia Chardonnay de Aylés 2013 B
chardonnay
90
Colour: bright yellow. Nose: powerfull, ripe fruit, sweet spices, creamy oak, fragrant herbs. Palate: rich, smoky aftertaste, flavourful, fresh, good acidity.

Serendipia Syrah 2012 T
syrah
90
Colour: cherry, garnet rim. Nose: spicy, creamy oak, toasty, complex, dark chocolate, earthy notes, ripe fruit. Palate: powerful, flavourful, toasty, round tannins.

BODEGAS AÑADAS

Ctra. Aguarón, km 47,100
50400 Cariñena (Zaragoza)
☎: +34 976 793 016
Fax: +34 976 620 448
www.carewines.com
bodega@carewines.com

Care 2013 B
macabeo, chardonnay
86
Colour: bright straw. Nose: white flowers, fragrant herbs, fruit expression. Palate: fresh, fruity, flavourful, balanced, elegant.

Care 2013 T
garnacha, syrah

88

Colour: cherry, purple rim. Nose: balanced, ripe fruit, dried flowers, dried herbs. Palate: fruity, flavourful, long.

Care 2012 TC
tempranillo, merlot

88

Colour: deep cherry, garnet rim. Nose: spicy, smoky, ripe fruit. Palate: flavourful, balsamic, ripe fruit, round tannins.

Care 2013 RD
tempranillo, cabernet sauvignon

86

Colour: rose, purple rim. Nose: ripe fruit, red berry notes, floral, expressive, fragrant herbs. Palate: fruity, fresh.

Care 2013 T Roble
garnacha, syrah

89

Colour: cherry, purple rim. Nose: ripe fruit, dried herbs, spicy, toasty. Palate: flavourful, fruity, long, balanced.

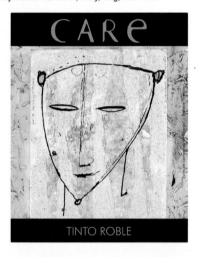

Care Finca Bancales 2011 TR
garnacha

91

Colour: cherry, garnet rim. Nose: red berry notes, ripe fruit, spicy, creamy oak, toasty, complex, earthy notes. Palate: powerful, flavourful, toasty, round tannins.

Care Moscatel de Alejandria 2013 B
moscatel de alejandría

89

Colour: golden. Nose: powerfull, floral, honeyed notes, candied fruit, fragrant herbs. Palate: flavourful, sweet, fresh, fruity, good acidity, long.

Care XCLNT 2010 T
syrah, garnacha, cabernet sauvignon

90

Colour: very deep cherry, garnet rim. Nose: characterful, powerfull, ripe fruit, fruit preserve, balsamic herbs. Palate: good structure, spicy, long.

Care Chardonnay 2013 B
chardonnay

88

Colour: bright straw. Nose: fresh, fresh fruit, white flowers, expressive. Palate: flavourful, fruity, good acidity, balanced.

BODEGAS CARLOS VALERO

Castillo de Capúa, 10 Nave 1 Pol. PLA_ZA
50197 (Zaragoza)
☎: +34 976 180 634
Fax: +34 976 186 326
www.bodegasvalero.com
info@bodegasvalero.com

Heredad X Carlos Valero 2012 T
100% garnacha
90
Colour: bright cherry. Nose: ripe fruit, sweet spices, creamy oak, expressive. Palate: flavourful, fruity, toasty, round tannins.

BODEGAS ESTEBAN MARTÍN

Camino Virgen de Lagunas, s/n
50461 Alfamén (Zaragoza)
☎: +34 976 628 490
Fax: +34 976 628 488
www.estebanmartin.com
carlosarnal@estebanmartin.es

Esteban Martín 2009 TR
garnacha, cabernet sauvignon
87
Colour: cherry, garnet rim. Nose: ripe fruit, wild herbs, spicy, creamy oak. Palate: balanced, flavourful, long, balsamic.

Esteban Martín 2010 T Roble
100% syrah
86
Colour: bright cherry. Nose: ripe fruit, sweet spices. Palate: flavourful, fruity, toasty, round tannins.

Esteban Martín 2011 TC
garnacha, syrah
86
Colour: bright cherry. Nose: ripe fruit, sweet spices, creamy oak, medium intensity. Palate: fruity, flavourful, toasty.

Esteban Martín 2013 B
chardonnay, macabeo
84

Esteban Martín 2013 RD
garnacha, syrah
82

Esteban Martín 2013 T
garnacha, syrah
86
Colour: cherry, garnet rim. Nose: ripe fruit, spicy. Palate: powerful, flavourful, round tannins, easy to drink.

BODEGAS GABARDA S.L.

Ctra. Valencia, km. 459
50460 Longarés (Zaragoza)
☎: +34 976 620 029
Fax: +34 976 621 031
www.gabardawines.com
contabilidad@gabardawines.comm

Gabarda Chardonnay 2013 B
chardonnay
84

Gabarda I 2013 T
garnacha, syrah
87
Colour: cherry, purple rim. Nose: red berry notes, ripe fruit, wild herbs, spicy. Palate: powerful, flavourful, correct.

Gabarda II 2011 T
garnacha, tempranillo, syrah
86
Colour: bright cherry. Nose: ripe fruit, sweet spices, creamy oak, expressive. Palate: flavourful, fruity, toasty, round tannins.

Gabarda III 2009 T
merlot, cabernet sauvignon, tempranillo
86
Colour: ruby red. Nose: spicy, fine reductive notes, wet leather, aged wood nuances, toasty. Palate: spicy, long, toasty.

Gabarda IV 2004 TGR
tempranillo, garnacha, merlot, cabernet sauvignon
85

BODEGAS IGNACIO MARÍN

San Valero, 1
50400 Cariñena (Zaragoza)
☎: +34 976 621 129
www.ignaciomarin.com
comercial@ignaciomarin.com

Ballad 2012 T
100% garnacha
88
Colour: cherry, garnet rim. Nose: ripe fruit, spicy, creamy oak, toasty. Palate: powerful, flavourful, toasty.

Barón de Lajoyosa 2005 TGR
garnacha, tempranillo, cariñena
86
Colour: pale ruby, brick rim edge. Nose: spicy, fine reductive notes, wet leather, aged wood nuances, fruit liqueur notes. Palate: spicy, fine tannins, elegant, long.

Campo Marín 2009 TR
tempranillo, garnacha, cariñena
86
Colour: cherry, garnet rim. Nose: ripe fruit, spicy, creamy oak, toasty. Palate: powerful, flavourful, toasty.

Duque de Medina 2013 T
garnacha, tempranillo, cariñena
86
Colour: black cherry. Nose: red berry notes, floral. Palate: flavourful, fruity, good acidity, round tannins, balsamic.

Marín Old Vine Garnacha 2010 T
garnacha
87
Colour: cherry, garnet rim. Nose: ripe fruit, spicy, creamy oak, toasty, complex. Palate: powerful, flavourful, toasty.

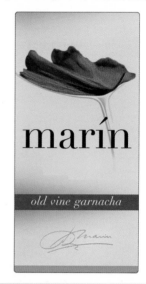

BODEGAS LALAGUNA

Ctra. A-1304 de Longares
a Alfamés, Km. 1,28
50460 Longares (Zaragoza)
☎: +34 657 804 783
Fax: +34 976 369 980
www.bodegaslalaguna.com
bodegaslalaguna@bodegaslalaguna.com

Lalaguna 2010 TC
85

Lalaguna 2012 T
84

BODEGAS PANIZA

Ctra. Valencia, Km. 53
50480 Paniza (Zaragoza)
☎: +34 976 622 515
Fax: +34 976 622 958
www.bodegaspaniza.com
info@bodegaspaniza.com

Artigazo 2008 T
90
Colour: ruby red. Nose: balanced, complex, ripe fruit, spicy, balsamic herbs, mineral. Palate: good structure, flavourful, round tannins.

Jabalí Garnacha-Cabernet 2013 RD
87
Colour: rose, purple rim. Nose: powerfull, ripe fruit, red berry notes, floral, expressive. Palate: powerful, fruity, fresh, confected.

Jabalí Garnacha-Syrah 2013 T
89
Colour: cherry, purple rim. Nose: expressive, fresh fruit, red berry notes, floral. Palate: flavourful, fruity, good acidity, round tannins.

Jabalí Tempranillo - Cabernet 2013 T
88
Colour: cherry, garnet rim. Nose: ripe fruit, wild herbs, earthy notes, spicy. Palate: balanced, flavourful, long.

Jabalí Viura & Chardonnay 2013 B
86
Colour: bright straw. Nose: white flowers, fragrant herbs, fruit expression. Palate: fresh, fruity, flavourful, confected.

Paniza 2008 TGR
87
Colour: cherry, garnet rim. Nose: balanced, complex, ripe fruit, spicy, fine reductive notes. Palate: good structure, flavourful, correct.

Paniza 2009 TR
88
Colour: cherry, garnet rim. Nose: ripe fruit, spicy, creamy oak, toasty, complex. Palate: powerful, flavourful, toasty, round tannins.

Paniza 2010 TC
88
Colour: cherry, garnet rim. Nose: ripe fruit, sweet spices, creamy oak, roasted coffee. Palate: flavourful, fruity, toasty.

Val de Paniza 2013 B
85

Val de Paniza 2013 RD
100% garnacha
87
Colour: rose, bright. Nose: ripe fruit, red berry notes, floral, expressive, lactic notes. Palate: powerful, fruity, fresh, correct.

Val de Paniza 2013 T
87
Colour: cherry, purple rim. Nose: expressive, fresh fruit, red berry notes, floral. Palate: flavourful, fruity, good acidity, easy to drink.

Viñas Viejas de Paniza 2012 T
100% garnacha
90
Colour: very deep cherry, garnet rim. Nose: powerfull, ripe fruit, roasted coffee. Palate: powerful, toasty, roasted-coffee aftertaste, round.

BODEGAS PRINUR
Ctra. N-330, Km. 449
50400 Cariñena (Zaragoza)
☎: +34 976 621 039
Fax: +34 976 620 714
www.bodegasprinur.com
info@bodegasprinur.com

Prinur Viñas Viejas s/c T
89
Colour: dark-red cherry, garnet rim. Nose: ripe fruit, fruit preserve, violet drops, sweet spices. Palate: flavourful, ripe fruit, long.

BODEGAS SAN VALERO
Ctra. N-330, Km. 450
50400 Cariñena (Zaragoza)
☎: +34 976 620 400
Fax: +34 976 620 398
www.sanvalero.com
bsv@sanvalero.com

Marqués de Tosos 2010 TR
garnacha, tempranillo, cabernet sauvignon
88
Colour: cherry, garnet rim. Nose: red berry notes, ripe fruit, spicy, creamy oak, toasty, complex. Palate: powerful, flavourful, toasty.

Marqués de Tosos 2011 TC
garnacha, tempranillo, cabernet sauvignon
89
Colour: cherry, garnet rim. Nose: ripe fruit, spicy, creamy oak, toasty, complex. Palate: powerful, flavourful, toasty, round tannins.

Monte Ducay 2013 RD
garnacha, cabernet sauvignon
87
Colour: rose, purple rim. Nose: powerfull, ripe fruit, red berry notes, floral, expressive. Palate: powerful, fruity, fresh.

Monte Ducay 2013 T
garnacha, cabernet sauvignon, tempranillo
85

Monte Ducay 2012 TC
garnacha, merlot, syrah
84

Monte Ducay 2013 B
macabeo, chardonnay
84

Monte Ducay Pergamino 2010 TR
garnacha, tempranillo, cabernet sauvignon

85

Sierra de Viento Moscatel Vendimia Tardía B
moscatel

93

Colour: old gold, amber rim. Nose: complex, fruit liqueur notes, dried fruit, pattiserie, toasty. Palate: sweet, rich, unctuous, powerful.

Sierra de Viento Tempranillo 2010 T
tempranillo

88

Colour: cherry, garnet rim. Nose: ripe fruit, wild herbs, spicy, toasty, smoky. Palate: balanced, flavourful, long, balsamic.

CAMPOS DE LUZ
Avda. Diagonal, 590, 5º - 1
8021 (Barcelona)
☎: +34 660 445 464
www.vinergia.com
vinergia@vinergia.com

Campos de Luz 2010 TC
100% garnacha

88

Colour: cherry, garnet rim. Nose: sweet spices, ripe fruit, fruit preserve. Palate: flavourful, balanced, correct.

Campos de Luz 2013 B
viura, chardonnay, moscatel

85

Campos de Luz 2013 RD
100% garnacha

87

Colour: rose. Nose: red berry notes, ripe fruit, rose petals. Palate: flavourful, full, fruity, powerful.

Campos de Luz Garnacha 2009 TR

88

Colour: light cherry, garnet rim. Nose: scrubland, spicy, tobacco. Palate: full, flavourful, round tannins.

Campos de Luz Garnacha 2013 T
100% garnacha

86

Colour: very deep cherry, purple rim. Nose: ripe fruit, fruit preserve, scrubland. Palate: easy to drink, correct.

COVINCA (COMPAÑÍA VITIVINÍCOLA)
Ctra, Valencia, s/n
50460 Longares (Zaragoza)
☎: +34 976 142 653
Fax: +34 976 142 402
www.covinca.es
info@covinca.es

Terrai OVG 2013 T
garnacha

87

Colour: bright cherry. Nose: ripe fruit, sweet spices, creamy oak. Palate: flavourful, fruity, toasty.

Torrelongares 2011 TC
garnacha, tempranillo

87

Colour: very deep cherry, garnet rim. Nose: medium intensity, ripe fruit, wild herbs. Palate: fruity, easy to drink, good finish.

Torrelongares Garnacha 2013 T
garnacha

85

Torrelongares Old Vine Garnacha 2013 T Roble
garnacha

86

Colour: bright cherry. Nose: ripe fruit, sweet spices, creamy oak, expressive. Palate: flavourful, fruity, toasty.

GRANDES VINOS Y VIÑEDOS
Ctra. Valencia Km 45,700
50400 Cariñena (Zaragoza)
☎: +34 976 621 261
Fax: +34 976 621 253
www.grandesvinos.com
info@grandesvinos.com

Anayón Cariñena 2011 T
cariñena

92

Colour: cherry, garnet rim. Nose: ripe fruit, spicy, creamy oak, toasty, complex, mineral. Palate: powerful, flavourful, toasty, round tannins.

Anayón Chardonnay 2011 B Barrica
chardonnay

89

Colour: bright yellow. Nose: ripe fruit, sweet spices, creamy oak. Palate: rich, smoky aftertaste, flavourful, fresh, good acidity.

Anayón Garnacha de Autor 2011 T
garnacha

90

Colour: bright cherry. Nose: sweet spices, creamy oak, expressive, fruit preserve. Palate: flavourful, fruity, toasty, round tannins.

Anayón Moscatel 2013 B
moscatel de alejandría

87

Colour: golden. Nose: powerfull, floral, honeyed notes, candied fruit, fragrant herbs. Palate: flavourful, sweet, fresh, fruity, good acidity, long.

Anayón Selección 2011 T
tempranillo, cabernet sauvignon, syrah

91

Colour: cherry, garnet rim. Nose: ripe fruit, wild herbs, earthy notes, spicy, creamy oak. Palate: balanced, flavourful, long, balsamic.

Beso de Vino Garnacha 2013 RD
garnacha

86

Colour: rose, bright. Nose: ripe fruit, red berry notes, floral, expressive. Palate: fruity, fresh, easy to drink.

Beso de Vino Macabeo 2013 B
macabeo

83

Beso de Vino Old Vine Garnacha 2013 T
garnacha

87

Colour: cherry, purple rim. Nose: red berry notes, ripe fruit, spicy, balsamic herbs. Palate: flavourful, balsamic, correct.

Beso de Vino Selección 2013 T
syrah, garnacha

88

Colour: bright cherry. Nose: ripe fruit, sweet spices, creamy oak. Palate: flavourful, fruity, toasty.

Corona de Aragón 2011 TC
garnacha, tempranillo, cabernet sauvignon, cariñena

88

Colour: cherry, garnet rim. Nose: ripe fruit, spicy, creamy oak, toasty. Palate: powerful, flavourful, toasty, round tannins.

Corona de Aragón 2004 TGR
garnacha, tempranillo, cabernet sauvignon, cariñena

87

Colour: pale ruby, brick rim edge. Nose: smoky, wet leather, spicy, toasty, fine reductive notes. Palate: powerful, flavourful, spicy.

Corona de Aragón 2009 TR
garnacha, tempranillo, cabernet sauvignon, cariñena

87

Colour: cherry, garnet rim. Nose: spicy, creamy oak, toasty. Palate: powerful, flavourful, toasty, round tannins.

Corona de Aragón Garnacha 2013 T
garnacha

84

Corona de Aragón Garnacha Cabernet Sauvignon 2013 RD
garnacha, cabernet sauvignon

85

Corona de Aragón Macabeo Chardonnay 2013 B
macabeo, chardonnay

85

Corona de Aragón Moscatel 2013 B
moscatel de alejandría

88

Colour: golden. Nose: powerfull, floral, honeyed notes, candied fruit, fragrant herbs. Palate: flavourful, sweet, fresh, fruity, good acidity, long.

Corona de Aragón Old Vine Garnacha 2012 T
garnacha

87

Colour: bright cherry. Nose: ripe fruit, sweet spices, creamy oak, expressive. Palate: flavourful, fruity, toasty, round tannins.

Corona de Aragón Special Selection 2012 T
garnacha, cariñena

90

Colour: cherry, garnet rim. Nose: ripe fruit, spicy, creamy oak, toasty. Palate: powerful, flavourful, toasty.

Don Vinico Edición Especial 2011 T
garnacha

86

Colour: very deep cherry. Nose: ripe fruit, wild herbs, sweet spices. Palate: balanced, flavourful, long, balsamic.

Don Vinico Tempranillo 2013 T
tempranillo

85

El Circo Bailarina Merlot 2013 T
merlot

85

El Circo Cabernet Sauvignon 2013 T
cabernet sauvignon

84

El Circo Cariñena 2013 T
cariñena

86

Colour: bright cherry, purple rim. Nose: balanced, red berry notes, ripe fruit. Palate: fruity, flavourful, good finish.

El Circo Garnacha 2013 RD
garnacha
86
Colour: rose, purple rim. Nose: powerfull, ripe fruit, red berry notes, floral, expressive, dried herbs. Palate: powerful, fruity, fresh.

El Circo Garnacha 2013 T
garnacha
85

El Circo Macabeo 2013 B
macabeo
84

El Circo Syrah 2013 T
syrah
85

El Circo Volatinero Tempranillo 2013 T
tempranillo
84

Hoy Celebration s/c TR
garnacha, tempranillo, cariñena
85

Hoy Chef s/c T Barrica
garnacha, cariñena
84

Hoy Friends 2013 T
garnacha, tempranillo
84

Hoy Love 2008 T
garnacha, tempranillo, cariñena
84

Hoy Party 2013 B
macabeo
84

Hoy Relax 2013 RD
garnacha
85

Monasterio de las Viñas 2008 TC
garnacha, tempranillo, cariñena, cabernet sauvignon
83

Monasterio de las Viñas 2013 B
macabeo
82

Monasterio de las Viñas 2005 TGR
garnacha, tempranillo, cariñena
87
Colour: pale ruby, brick rim edge. Nose: elegant, spicy, fine reductive notes, wet leather, aged wood nuances, fruit liqueur notes. Palate: spicy, fine tannins, elegant, long.

Monasterio de las Viñas 2006 TR
garnacha, tempranillo, cariñena
86
Colour: deep cherry, orangey edge. Nose: waxy notes, tobacco, ripe fruit, spicy, aged wood nuances. Palate: fine bitter notes, elegant, flavourful, fine tannins.

Monasterio de las Viñas 2013 RD
garnacha
86
Colour: rose. Nose: candied fruit, dried flowers, fragrant herbs, red berry notes. Palate: light-bodied, flavourful, good acidity.

Monasterio de las Viñas Garnacha Tempranillo 2013 T
garnacha, tempranillo
84

HACIENDA MOLLEDA
A-220 (Cariñena - Belchite, km 29,3
50154 Tosos (Zaragoza)
☎: +34 976 620 702
Fax: +34 976 620 702
www.haciendamolleda.com
hm@haciendamolleda.com

Finca La Matea Garnacha 2010 T
garnacha
90
Colour: cherry, garnet rim. Nose: ripe fruit, wild herbs, earthy notes, spicy, creamy oak. Palate: balanced, flavourful, long, balsamic.

Finca La Matea T + G 2011 TC
tempranillo, garnacha
89
Colour: bright cherry. Nose: ripe fruit, sweet spices, creamy oak, medium intensity. Palate: fruity, flavourful, toasty.

GHM Gran Hacienda Molleda 2009 T Roble
cariñena
88
Colour: very deep cherry. Nose: ripe fruit, spicy, creamy oak, toasty, characterful. Palate: powerful, flavourful, toasty, round tannins.

GHM Gran Hacienda Molleda Cariñena Garnacha 2011 T Roble
cariñena, garnacha
85

GHM Gran Hacienda Molleda Garnacha 2010 T Roble
garnacha
89
Colour: bright cherry. Nose: ripe fruit, sweet spices, creamy oak. Palate: flavourful, fruity, toasty.

Hacienda Molleda 2013 B
macabeo
83

Hacienda Molleda 2013 RD
garnacha
85

Hacienda Molleda 2013 T
tempranillo, garnacha
86
Colour: cherry, purple rim. Nose: fresh fruit, red berry notes, floral. Palate: flavourful, fruity, good acidity.

Hacienda Molleda 2013 T Roble
garnacha
86
Colour: cherry, purple rim. Nose: expressive, fresh fruit, red berry notes, floral. Palate: flavourful, fruity, good acidity, easy to drink.

Hacienda Molleda Viñas 2009 T Roble
garnacha
88
Colour: bright cherry. Nose: sweet spices, creamy oak, fruit preserve, scrubland. Palate: flavourful, fruity, toasty, round tannins.

Lleda 2013 T
tempranillo, garnacha
84

Tierra de Andros 2010 TC
garnacha
89
Colour: cherry, garnet rim. Nose: ripe fruit, spicy, creamy oak, toasty, wild herbs. Palate: powerful, flavourful, toasty, round tannins.

HAMMEKEN CELLARS
Calle de la Muela, 16
3730 Jávea (Alicante)
☎: +34 965 791 967
Fax: +34 966 461 471
www.hammekencellars.com
cellars@hammekencellars.com

Capa Garnacha 2013 T
100% garnacha
85

El Tocador Garnacha 2013 T
100% garnacha
84

Lumus Selección Nº 1 2013 T
100% garnacha
84

Montgó Garnacha 2013 T
100% garnacha
88
Colour: bright cherry. Nose: ripe fruit, sweet spices, creamy oak, expressive. Palate: flavourful, fruity, toasty, round tannins.

Picos del Montgó Old Vines Garnacha 2013 T
100% garnacha
85

HEREDAD ANSÓN
Camino Eras Altas, s/n
50450 Muel (Zaragoza)
☎: +34 976 141 133
Fax: +34 976 141 133
www.bodegasheredadanson.com
info@bodegasheredadanson.com

Heredad de Ansón 2007 TC
garnacha, syrah, tempranillo
80

Heredad de Ansón 2013 B
macabeo
81

Heredad de Ansón Merlot Syrah 2013 T
84

Heredad de Ansón Vendimia Seleccionada 2008 T
garnacha, syrah
80

Legum 2007 T
garnacha
86
Colour: pale ruby, brick rim edge. Nose: spicy, fine reductive notes, wet leather, aged wood nuances, fruit liqueur notes. Palate: spicy, fine tannins, long.

Liason Garnacha 2013 T
garnacha
80

JORDÁN DE ASSO

Cariñena, 55
50408 Aguarón (Zaragoza)
☎: +34 976 221 781
Fax: +34 976 230 270
www.jordandeasso.com
info@jordandeasso.com

Jordán de Asso BN
macabeo
84

Jordán de Asso 2007 TR
tempranillo, cabernet sauvignon, syrah
84

Jordán de Asso 2010 TC
garnacha, cariñena, cabernet sauvignon
85

Jordán de Asso Garnacha 2013 T
garnacha
83

Jordán de Asso Tempranillo 2012 T
tempranillo
83

MANUEL MONEVA E HIJOS

Avda. Zaragoza, 10
50108 Almonacid de la Sierra
(Zaragoza)
☎: +34 976 627 020
Fax: +34 976 627 334
www.bodegasmanuelmoneva.com
info@bodegasmanuelmoneva.com

Viña Vadina 2010 TC
100% garnacha
85

Viña Vadina Garnacha 2009 T
100% garnacha
84

NAVASCUÉS ENOLOGÍA

Avda. Ejército, 32
50400 Cariñena (Zaragoza)
☎: +34 651 845 176
www.cutio.es
info@navascuesenologia.es

Cutio 2013 T
garnacha
92
Colour: bright cherry. Nose: sweet spices, creamy oak, expressive, red berry notes. Palate: flavourful, fruity, toasty, round tannins.

SAN NICOLÁS DE TOLENTINO

San José, 8
50108 Almonacid de la Sierra
(Zaragoza)
☎: +34 976 627 019
Fax: +34 976 627 240
www.marquesdealmonacid.com
administracion@san-nicolas.es

Marqués de Almonacid 2013 B
100% macabeo
86
Colour: bright straw. Nose: fresh, fresh fruit, white flowers, expressive. Palate: flavourful, fruity, good acidity, balanced.

Marqués de Almonacid 2008 TR
86
Colour: cherry, garnet rim. Nose: ripe fruit, spicy, creamy oak, toasty, fine reductive notes. Palate: powerful, flavourful, toasty, round tannins.

Marqués de Almonacid 2013 RD
100% garnacha
88
Colour: rose, purple rim. Nose: powerfull, ripe fruit, red berry notes, floral, expressive. Palate: powerful, fruity, fresh, balanced.

Marqués de Almonacid 2013 T
100% garnacha
84

Marqués de Almonacid Vendimia Seleccionada 2012 T
87
Colour: very deep cherry, purple rim. Nose: toasty, woody, sweet spices, ripe fruit. Palate: flavourful, round tannins.

SOLAR DE URBEZO

San Valero, 14
50400 Cariñena (Zaragoza)
☎: +34 976 621 968
Fax: +34 976 620 549
www.solardeurbezo.es
info@solardeurbezo.es

Altius Garnacha Merlot 2013 T
merlot
90
Colour: bright cherry. Nose: ripe fruit, sweet spices, creamy oak, expressive. Palate: flavourful, fruity, toasty, round tannins.

Altius Syrah Cabernet 2011 TC
cabernet sauvignon, syrah
91
Colour: bright cherry. Nose: ripe fruit, sweet spices, creamy oak, complex. Palate: fruity, flavourful, toasty, balanced, elegant.

Urbezo 2008 TGR
garnacha, cabernet sauvignon

88

Colour: deep cherry, orangey edge. Nose: waxy notes, tobacco, ripe fruit, spicy, aged wood nuances. Palate: fine bitter notes, elegant, flavourful, fine tannins.

Urbezo 2009 TR
cabernet sauvignon, merlot, syrah

87

Colour: pale ruby, brick rim edge. Nose: spicy, fine reductive notes, wet leather, aged wood nuances, ripe fruit. Palate: spicy, fine tannins.

Urbezo 2011 TC
100% garnacha

90

Colour: cherry, garnet rim. Nose: creamy oak, spicy, balsamic herbs, red berry notes, ripe fruit. Palate: powerful, flavourful, fruity, long, toasty.

Urbezo Chardonnay 2013 B
100% chardonnay

90

Colour: bright straw. Nose: white flowers, fragrant herbs, fruit expression, tropical fruit. Palate: fresh, fruity, flavourful, balanced, elegant.

Urbezo Garnacha 2013 T
100% garnacha

90

Colour: cherry, garnet rim. Nose: ripe fruit, spicy, creamy oak, toasty, mineral. Palate: powerful, flavourful, toasty, round tannins.

Urbezo Merlot 2013 RD
100% merlot

89

Colour: rose, purple rim. Nose: powerfull, ripe fruit, red berry notes, floral, fragrant herbs. Palate: powerful, fruity, fresh.

Viña Urbezo 2013 T Maceración Carbónica
garnacha, merlot, syrah

89

Colour: cherry, purple rim. Nose: red berry notes, raspberry, floral, expressive. Palate: fresh, fruity, flavourful, easy to drink.

Ysiegas 2007 TGR
garnacha, cabernet sauvignon

87

Colour: deep cherry, orangey edge. Nose: waxy notes, tobacco, ripe fruit, spicy, aged wood nuances. Palate: fine bitter notes, elegant, flavourful, fine tannins.

Ysiegas 2008 TR
cabernet sauvignon, merlot, syrah

85

Ysiegas 2011 TC
syrah, merlot, cabernet sauvignon

89

Colour: ruby red. Nose: spicy, fine reductive notes, wet leather, aged wood nuances, toasty. Palate: spicy, long, toasty.

Ysiegas Chardonnay 2013 B
chardonnay

90

Colour: bright straw. Nose: white flowers, fresh fruit, fine lees, dried herbs. Palate: flavourful, fruity, good acidity, balanced.

Ysiegas Garnacha 2013 T
garnacha

88

Colour: bright cherry. Nose: red berry notes, spicy, balsamic herbs, scrubland. Palate: flavourful, fruity.

Ysiegas Merlot 2013 RD
merlot

88

Colour: rose, purple rim. Nose: powerfull, ripe fruit, red berry notes, floral, expressive. Palate: powerful, fruity, fresh.

Ysiegas Tempranillo Merlot 2013 T
tempranillo, merlot

88

Colour: bright cherry. Nose: ripe fruit, red berry notes, spicy. Palate: flavourful, good acidity.

Ysiegas Vendimia 2013 T
garnacha, merlot, syrah

89

Colour: cherry, purple rim. Nose: fresh fruit, red berry notes, floral. Palate: flavourful, fruity, good acidity, round tannins.

VIÑEDOS Y BODEGAS PABLO

Avda. Zaragoza, 16
50108 Almonacid de la Sierra
(Zaragoza)
☎: +34 976 627 037
Fax: +34 976 627 102
www.granviu.com
granviu@granviu.com

Gran Víu Garnacha del Terreno 2011 T
garnacha

90

Colour: cherry, garnet rim. Nose: ripe fruit, spicy, creamy oak, toasty, complex, earthy notes, dry stone. Palate: powerful, flavourful, toasty, round tannins.

Menguante Garnacha 2013 T
garnacha

85

Menguante Garnacha Blanca 2013 B
garnacha blanca

89

Colour: bright straw. Nose: white flowers, fragrant herbs, fruit expression. Palate: fresh, fruity, flavourful, balanced, elegant.

Menguante Selección Garnacha 2011 T
garnacha

90

Colour: deep cherry. Nose: ripe fruit, spicy, creamy oak, toasty, complex, smoky. Palate: powerful, flavourful, toasty, round tannins.

Menguante Tempranillo 2013 T Roble
tempranillo

83

Menguante Vidadillo 2011 T
vidadilo

88

Colour: bright cherry. Nose: ripe fruit, sweet spices, creamy oak, expressive, balsamic herbs. Palate: flavourful, fruity, toasty, harsh oak tannins.

DO. CATALUNYA

CONSEJO REGULADOR

Edifici de l'Estació Enológica Passeig Sunyer, 4-6 1º
43202 Reus (Tarragona)
☎:+34 977 328 103 - Fax: +34 977 321 357
@: info@do-catalunya.com
www.do-catalunya.com

LOCATION:

The production area covers the traditional vine - growing Catalonian regions, and practically coincides with the current DOs present in Catalonia plus a few municipal areas with vine - growing vocation.

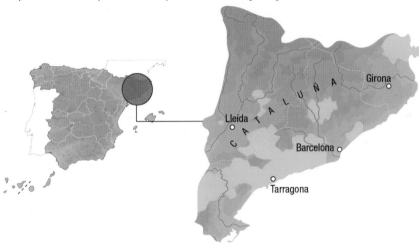

GRAPE VARIETIES:

White: Recommended: Chardonnay, Garnacha Blanca, Macabeo, Moscatel de Alejandría, Moscatel de Grano Menudo, Parellada, Riesling, Sauvignon Blanc and Xarel·lo.
Authorized: Gewürztraminer, Subirat Parent (Malvasía), Malvasía de Sitges, Picapoll, Pedro Ximénez, Chenin, Riesling and Sauvignon Blanc
Red: Recommended: Cabernet Franc, Cabernet Sauvignon, Garnacha, Garnacha Peluda, Merlot, Monastrell, Pinot Noir, Samsó (Cariñena), Trepat, Sumoll and Ull de Llebre (Tempranillo).
Authorized: Garnacha Tintorera and Syrah.

FIGURES:

Vineyard surface: 47,066 – Wine-Growers: 8,588 – Wineries: 205 – 2013 Harvest rating: Very Good – Production 12: 49,012,752 litres – Market percentages: 42% domestic - 58% export.

CLIMATE AND SOIL:

Depending on the location of the vineyard, the same as those of the Catalonian DO's, whose characteristics are defined in this guide. See Alella, Empordà, Conca de Barberà, Costers del Segre, Montsant, Penedès, Pla de Bages, Priorat, Tarragona and Terra Alta.

VINTAGE RATING

PEÑÍNGUIDE

2009	2010	2011	2012	2013
N/A	N/A	N/A	N/A	N/A

1898 RAMÓN ROQUETA

Ctra. de Vic, 81
8241 Manresa (Barcelona)
☎: +34 938 743 511
Fax: +34 938 737 204
www.1898ramonroqueta.com
info@1898ramonroqueta.com

Ramón Roqueta Chardonnay 2013 B
100% chardonnay

88

Colour: bright straw. Nose: white flowers, fragrant herbs, fruit expression. Palate: fresh, fruity, flavourful, balanced, elegant.

Ramón Roqueta Tempranillo 2013 T
100% tempranillo

88

Colour: cherry, purple rim. Nose: red berry notes, raspberry, floral, balsamic herbs. Palate: fresh, fruity, flavourful, easy to drink.

Synera 2010 TC

88

Colour: cherry, garnet rim. Nose: ripe fruit, spicy, creamy oak, toasty, complex. Palate: powerful, flavourful, toasty, round tannins, balanced.

Synera 2013 B

84

Synera 2013 RD

86

Colour: rose, purple rim. Nose: powerfull, ripe fruit, red berry notes, floral, expressive. Palate: powerful, fruity, fresh.

Synera 2013 T

86

Colour: bright cherry. Nose: ripe fruit, sweet spices, creamy oak. Palate: flavourful, fruity, toasty.

Vinya Nostra Nit de Tardor 2012 T

88

Colour: cherry, garnet rim. Nose: ripe fruit, spicy, creamy oak, toasty, balsamic herbs. Palate: powerful, flavourful, toasty, round tannins.

Vinya Nostra Xarel.lo 2012 B
100% xarel.lo

87 🌷

Colour: bright straw. Nose: fresh, fresh fruit, white flowers, expressive. Palate: flavourful, fruity, good acidity, balanced.

AGRÍCOLA SANT JOSEP

Estació, 2
43785 Bot (Tarragona)
☎: +34 977 428 352
Fax: +34 977 428 192
www.santjosepwines.com
info@santjosepwines.com

La Plana d'en Fonoll Selecció 2006 T

90

Colour: dark-red cherry, garnet rim. Nose: powerfull, ripe fruit, scrubland, expressive. Palate: spicy, ripe fruit, round tannins.

ALBET I NOYA

Can Vendrell de la Codina, s/n
8739 Sant Pau D'Ordal (Barcelona)
☎: +34 938 994 812
Fax: +34 938 994 930
www.albetinoya.cat
albetinoya@albetinoya.cat

Albet i Noya Aiguadines 2012 T
garnacha, merlot, cabernet sauvignon, syrah

87 🌷

Colour: cherry, garnet rim. Nose: ripe fruit, wild herbs, spicy, creamy oak. Palate: balanced, flavourful, long, balsamic.

Albet i Noya Aiguadines Superior 2012 T
merlot, syrah, cabernet sauvignon

90 🌷

Colour: bright cherry. Nose: ripe fruit, sweet spices, creamy oak, expressive. Palate: flavourful, fruity, toasty, round tannins, elegant.

Albet i Noya La Solana 2012 T
merlot, cabernet sauvignon, syrah

88 🌷

Colour: bright cherry. Nose: ripe fruit, sweet spices, creamy oak, expressive. Palate: flavourful, fruity, toasty, round tannins.

Albet i Noya Petit Albet Negre 2012 T
tempranillo, garnacha, cabernet sauvignon

85 🌷

Albet i Noya Pla de Morei 2012 T
merlot, syrah, cabernet sauvignon

87 🌷

Colour: cherry, garnet rim. Nose: ripe fruit, spicy, creamy oak, balsamic herbs. Palate: powerful, flavourful, toasty.

Albet i Noya Vinya Laia Negre 2012 T
merlot, garnacha, syrah, cabernet sauvignon

89 🌷

Colour: bright cherry. Nose: ripe fruit, sweet spices, creamy oak, expressive. Palate: flavourful, fruity, toasty, round tannins, balanced.

BODEGA EL GRIAL S.L.

Ctra. Perelló-Rasquera Km. 6
43519 El Perelló (Tarragona)
☎: +34 977 475 351
www.bodegaselgrial.com
b.elgrial@yahoo.es

Ariza 2013 T
100% cabernet franc
85 🌱

Blanc Ecologic 2012 B
84 🌱

Cabrafeixet 2013 T
100% cabernet franc
87 🌱
Colour: bright cherry. Nose: ripe fruit, sweet spices, creamy oak. Palate: flavourful, fruity, toasty.

El Grial Negre 2011 T
84 🌱

Lladoner 2012 T
86 🌱
Colour: cherry, garnet rim. Nose: ripe fruit, wild herbs, spicy. Palate: flavourful, long, balsamic, fine bitter notes.

Safraner 2013 B
sauvignon blanc, gewürztraminer
86 🌱
Colour: bright golden. Nose: ripe fruit, dry nuts, powerfull, aged wood nuances, roasted coffee. Palate: flavourful, fruity, spicy, toasty, long.

BODEGAS PUIGGRÒS

Ctra. de Manresa, Km. 13
8711 Odena (Barcelona)
☎: +34 629 853 587
www.bodegaspuiggros.com
bodegaspuiggros@telefonica.net

Mestre Vila Vell Vinyes Velles 2012 T
100% sumoll
88
Colour: cherry, garnet rim. Nose: spicy, tobacco, ripe fruit, balanced. Palate: balanced, balsamic, round tannins.

Sentits Negres Garnatxa Negra 2012 T
garnacha
93
Colour: cherry, garnet rim. Nose: ripe fruit, spicy, complex, earthy notes, scrubland. Palate: powerful, flavourful, toasty, round tannins.

Signes 2012 T
sumoll, garnacha
90
Colour: cherry, garnet rim. Nose: ripe fruit, spicy, toasty, complex. Palate: powerful, flavourful, toasty, round tannins.

BODEGAS TORRES

Miguel Torres i Carbó, 6
8720 Vilafranca del Penedès
(Barcelona)
☎: +34 938 177 400
Fax: +34 938 177 444
www.torres.com
mailadmin@torres.es

Coronas 2011 TC
tempranillo, cabernet sauvignon
87
Colour: cherry, garnet rim. Nose: ripe fruit, spicy, creamy oak, toasty. Palate: powerful, flavourful, toasty.

DeCasta 2013 RD
garnacha, merlot, syrah, cabernet sauvignon
87
Colour: rose, purple rim. Nose: powerfull, ripe fruit, red berry notes, floral, expressive. Palate: powerful, fruity, fresh.

Gran Sangre de Toro 2010 TR
garnacha, cariñena, syrah
87
Colour: cherry, garnet rim. Nose: ripe fruit, spicy, creamy oak, toasty, fine reductive notes, balsamic herbs. Palate: powerful, flavourful, toasty, correct.

Habitat 2012 B
xarel.lo, garnacha blanca
87 🌱
Colour: bright straw. Nose: white flowers, fragrant herbs, fruit expression. Palate: fresh, fruity, flavourful, balanced.

Habitat 2012 T
syrah, garnacha
88
Colour: bright cherry. Nose: ripe fruit, sweet spices, creamy oak, expressive. Palate: flavourful, fruity, toasty, easy to drink.

San Valentín 2013 B
parellada
85

Sangre de Toro 2012 T
garnacha, merlot, syrah, tempranillo
86
Colour: cherry, garnet rim. Nose: ripe fruit, balsamic herbs, creamy oak. Palate: spicy, long, balanced.

Viña Esmeralda 2013 B
moscatel, gewürztraminer
88
Colour: bright straw. Nose: white flowers, fragrant herbs, fruit expression, tropical fruit. Palate: fresh, fruity, flavourful, balanced, elegant.

Viña Sol 2013 B
parellada, garnacha blanca
87
Colour: bright straw. Nose: fresh, fresh fruit, white flowers, fragrant herbs. Palate: flavourful, fruity, good acidity, balanced.

CA N'ESTRUC
Ctra. C-1414, Km. 1,05
8292 Esparreguera (Barcelona)
☎: +34 937 777 017
Fax: +34 937 771 108
www.canestruc.com
canestruc@vilaviniteca.es

Ca N'Estruc 2013 T
88
Colour: very deep cherry, garnet rim. Nose: overripe fruit, warm, dried herbs. Palate: flavourful, ripe fruit, long.

Ca N'Estruc Blanc 2013 B
89
Colour: bright straw. Nose: white flowers, fragrant herbs, fruit expression. Palate: fresh, fruity, flavourful, elegant.

Ca N'Estruc Xarel.lo 2013 B
xarel.lo
90
Colour: bright straw. Nose: fresh, fresh fruit, white flowers, expressive. Palate: flavourful, fruity, good acidity, balanced.

Idoia 2012 T
90
Colour: cherry, garnet rim. Nose: red berry notes, ripe fruit, wild herbs, spicy, expressive. Palate: balanced, flavourful, spicy.

Idoia Blanc 2013 BFB
93
Colour: bright straw. Nose: white flowers, fresh fruit, expressive, fine lees, dried herbs. Palate: flavourful, fruity, good acidity.

L'Equilibrista 2012 T
90
Colour: bright cherry. Nose: ripe fruit, sweet spices, creamy oak, expressive. Palate: flavourful, fruity, toasty, round tannins.

L'Equilibrista 2013 B
92
Colour: bright straw. Nose: expressive, fresh fruit, citrus fruit, spicy. Palate: flavourful, good acidity.

L'Equilibrista Garnatxa 2011 T
garnacha
92
Colour: deep cherry. Nose: fruit liqueur notes, varietal, spicy, earthy notes. Palate: flavourful, ripe fruit, spicy, round tannins.

CAN GRAU VELL
Can Grau Vell, s/n
8781 Hostalets de Pierola (Barcelona)
☎: +34 676 586 933
Fax: +34 932 684 965
www.grauvell.cat
info@grauvell.cat

Alcor 2009 T
93
Colour: cherry, garnet rim. Nose: red berry notes, ripe fruit, wild herbs, mineral, expressive. Palate: powerful, flavourful, spicy, long.

CASTELL D'OR
Mare Rafols, 3- 1ºD
8720 Vilafranca del Penedès (Barcelona)
☎: +34 938 905 385
Fax: +34 938 905 455
www.castelldor.com
castelldor@castelldor.com

Flama D'Or 2010 TR
cabernet sauvignon
85

Flama D'Or 2012 T
tempranillo
82

Flama D'Or 2013 B
macabeo, parellada, xarel.lo
83

Flama D'Or 2013 RD
trepat
84

Puig de Solivella 2012 T
tempranillo
81

Puig de Solivella 2013 B
macabeo, parellada, xarel.lo
81

CAVES CONDE DE CARALT S.A.
Ctra. Sant Sadurní-Sant Pere de Riudebitlles, Km. 5
8775 Torrelavit (Barcelona)
☎: +34 938 917 070
Fax: +34 938 996 006
www.condedecaralt.com
condedecaralt@condedecaralt.es

Conde de Caralt 2013 B
macabeo, xarel.lo, parellada
85

Conde de Caralt 2013 RD
tempranillo, merlot
83

CELLER DE CAPÇANES
Llebaria, 4
43776 Capçanes (Tarragona)
☎: +34 977 178 319
Fax: +34 977 178 319
www.cellercapcanes.com
cellercapcanes@cellercapcanes.com

6/X Pinot Noir de Capçanes 2012 T
92
Colour: cherry, garnet rim. Nose: ripe fruit, wild herbs, earthy notes, spicy, creamy oak. Palate: flavourful, long, balsamic, balanced.

CLOS D'AGON
Afores, s/n
17251 Calonge (Girona)
☎: +34 972 661 486
Fax: +34 972 661 462
www.closdagon.com
info@closdagon.com

Clos D'Agon 2011 T
93
Colour: cherry, garnet rim. Nose: ripe fruit, spicy, creamy oak, toasty, complex, earthy notes, mineral. Palate: powerful, flavourful, toasty, round tannins, elegant.

Clos D'Agon 2012 B
93
Colour: bright yellow. Nose: powerfull, ripe fruit, sweet spices, creamy oak, fragrant herbs, balanced. Palate: rich, smoky aftertaste, flavourful, fresh, good acidity, elegant.

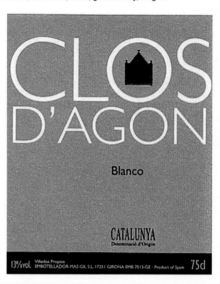

CLOS MONTBLANC
Ctra. Montblanc-Barbera, s/n
43422 Barberà de la Conca (Tarragona)
☎: +34 977 887 030
Fax: +34 977 887 032
www.closmontblanc.com
club@closmontblanc.com

Clos Montblanc Castell Macabeo Chardonnay 2013 B
macabeo, chardonnay
86
Colour: bright straw. Nose: white flowers, fragrant herbs, fruit expression. Palate: fresh, fruity, flavourful.

Clos Montblanc Castell Tempranillo 2013 T
tempranillo, cabernet sauvignon
86
Colour: very deep cherry, garnet rim. Nose: warm, ripe fruit, balsamic herbs. Palate: flavourful, ripe fruit, long.

Clos Montblanc Xipella 2011 TC
garnacha, monastrell, samsó, syrah
87
Colour: cherry, garnet rim. Nose: ripe fruit, spicy, creamy oak, toasty. Palate: powerful, flavourful, toasty, round tannins.

FERMI BOHIGAS

Finca Can Maciá s/n
8711 Ódena (Barcelona)
☎: +34 938 048 100
Fax: +34 938 032 366
www.bohigas.es
aministracio@bohigas.es

Bohigas 2010 TC
cabernet sauvignon, garnacha

90

Colour: cherry, garnet rim. Nose: ripe fruit, spicy, creamy oak, toasty, complex. Palate: powerful, flavourful, toasty, round tannins.

Bohigas Xarel.lo 2013 B
xarel.lo

88

Colour: bright straw. Nose: fresh, fresh fruit, white flowers, expressive. Palate: flavourful, fruity, good acidity, balanced.

Fermí de Fermí Bohigas 2009 TR
syrah, samsó

91

Colour: cherry, garnet rim. Nose: ripe fruit, spicy, creamy oak, toasty, complex. Palate: powerful, flavourful, toasty, round tannins, balanced.

Udina de Fermí Bohigas 2013 B
xarel.lo, garnacha blanca, chenin blanc

87

Colour: bright straw. Nose: white flowers, fragrant herbs, fruit expression. Palate: fresh, fruity, flavourful.

FRANCK MASSARD

Rambla Arnau de Vilanova, 6
8800 Vilanova i La Geltrú (Barcelona)
☎: +34 938 956 541
Fax: +34 938 956 541
www.epicure-wines.com
info@epicure-wines.com

Mas Amor 2013 RD
85

HEREDAD SEGURA VIUDAS

Ctra. Sant Sadurní a St. Pere
de Riudebitlles, Km. 5
8775 Torrelavit (Barcelona)
☎: +34 938 917 070
Fax: +34 938 996 006
www.seguraviudas.com
seguraviudas@seguraviudas.es

Viña Heredad 2013 RD
tempranillo, merlot

87

Colour: onion pink. Nose: elegant, candied fruit, dried flowers, fragrant herbs, red berry notes. Palate: light-bodied, flavourful, good acidity, long, spicy.

JAUME GRAU GRAU - VINS GRAU S.L.

Ctra. C-37, Km. 75,5 D'Igualada a
Manresa
8255 Maians (Barcelona)
☎: +34 938 356 002
www.vinsgrau.com
info@vinsgrau.com

Clos del Recó 2013 B
macabeo, xarel.lo, parellada, moscatel

85

Clos del Recó 2013 RD
tempranillo

85

Clos del Recó 2013 T
tempranillo

83

JAUME SERRA (J. GARCÍA CARRIÓN)

Ctra. de Vilanova a Vilafranca, Km. 2,5
8800 Vilanova i la Geltru (Barcelona)
☎: +34 938 936 404
Fax: +34 938 147 482
www.garciacarrion.es
jaumeserra@jgc.es

Vinya del Mar Seco 2013 B
80

Viña del Mar 2013 RD
83

Viña del Mar 2013 T
80

Viña del Mar Semidulce 2013 B
79

L'OLIVERA SCCL

La Plana, s/n
25268 Vallbona de les Monges (Lleida)
☎: +34 973 330 276
Fax: +34 973 330 276
www.olivera.org
olivera@olivera.org

Naltres 2013 T
cabernet sauvignon, garnacha, trepat

88 ♥

Colour: very deep cherry, garnet rim. Nose: powerfull, ripe fruit, dark chocolate. Palate: powerful, toasty, balanced.

LONG WINES

Avda. del Puente Cultural, 8 Bloque B Bajo 7
28702 San Sebastián de los Reyes
(Madrid)
☎: +34 916 221 305
Fax: +34 916 220 029
www.longwines.com
adm@longwines.com

Altos d'Oliva 2005 TGR

86

Colour: pale ruby, brick rim edge. Nose: spicy, fine reductive notes, wet leather, aged wood nuances, fruit liqueur notes. Palate: long, classic aged character, spicy.

MASET DEL LLEÓ

C-244, Km. 32,5
8792 La Granada del Penedès
(Barcelona)
☎: +34 902 200 250
Fax: +34 938 921 333
www.maset.com
info@maset.com

Maset del LLeó Cabernet Franc 2012 T
cabernet franc

90

Colour: cherry, garnet rim. Nose: ripe fruit, spicy, creamy oak, toasty, complex, mineral. Palate: powerful, flavourful, toasty, round tannins.

Maset del Lleó Roble 2011 T Roble
tempranillo

88

Colour: bright cherry. Nose: sweet spices, creamy oak, ripe fruit. Palate: flavourful, toasty, spicy.

Maset del LLeó Syrah 2011 TR
syrah

90

Colour: cherry, garnet rim. Nose: ripe fruit, spicy, creamy oak, toasty, complex. Palate: powerful, flavourful, toasty, round tannins.

MASIA VALLFORMOSA

La Sala, 45
8735 Vilobi del Penedès (Barcelona)
☎: +34 938 978 286
Fax: +34 938 978 355
www.domenechvidal.com
vallformosa@vallformosa.es

Laviña 2013 B
macabeo, garnacha blanca

83

Laviña 2013 RD
tempranillo, merlot

84

Laviña Semi Dulce 2013 B
macabeo, garnacha blanca

84

Laviña Tempranillo Merlot 2013 T
tempranillo, merlot

86

Colour: cherry, purple rim. Nose: red berry notes, raspberry, fruit expression, fragrant herbs. Palate: flavourful, light-bodied, good acidity.

PAGO DIANA

Pago Diana, s/n
17464 Sant Jordi Desvalls (Girona)
☎: +34 666 395 251
www.pagodiana.com
info@pagodiana.com

Clos Diana 2009 T
syrah

87

Colour: dark-red cherry, orangey edge. Nose: spicy, balsamic herbs, old leather, ripe fruit. Palate: correct, spicy, long.

Pago Diana Tempranillo 2010 T
tempranillo

82

Teria 2009 T
merlot, cabernet sauvignon, tempranillo

84

RENÉ BARBIER

Ctra. Sant Sadurní a St. Pere Riudebitlles, km. 5
8775 Torrelavit (Barcelona)
☎: +34 938 917 070
Fax: +34 938 996 006
www.renebarbier.com
renebarbier@renebarbier.es

René Barbier Kraliner 2013 B
macabeo, xarel.lo, parellada

85

René Barbier Rosado Tradición 2013 RD
tempranillo, merlot

84

René Barbier Viña Augusta 2012 B
macabeo, xarel.lo, parellada, moscatel

84

ROCAMAR

Major, 80
8755 Castellbisbal (Barcelona)
☎: +34 937 720 900
Fax: +34 937 721 495
www.rocamar.net
info@rocamar.net

Blanc de Palangre de Aguja B
macabeo, parellada

78

Masia Ribot 2013 B
macabeo, parellada

80

Masia Ribot 2013 RD
tempranillo, garnacha

81

Masia Ribot 2013 T
tempranillo, garnacha

80

Rosat de Palangre de Aguja RD
trepat

82

SPIRITUS BARCELONA

Domenech Soberano, 9
43203 Reus (Tarragona)
☎: +34 977 328 202
www.spiritusbarcelona.com
customer@spiritusbarcelona.com

Grand Vinafoc Cabernet Sauvignon 2010 TR
cabernet sauvignon

89

Colour: very deep cherry. Nose: ripe fruit, wild herbs, earthy notes, spicy, creamy oak. Palate: balanced, flavourful, long, balsamic.

Grand Vinafoc Merlot 2010 T
merlot

88

Colour: cherry, garnet rim. Nose: ripe fruit, wild herbs, spicy, creamy oak. Palate: flavourful, long, balsamic.

Grand Vinafoc Syrah 2010 T
syrah

88

Colour: cherry, garnet rim. Nose: ripe fruit, spicy, creamy oak, toasty, violets, balsamic herbs. Palate: powerful, flavourful, toasty, balanced.

Selección Vinafoc Cabernet Sauvignon 2011 T
cabernet sauvignon

87

Colour: cherry, garnet rim. Nose: ripe fruit, wild herbs, spicy, creamy oak, fine reductive notes. Palate: balanced, flavourful, long, balsamic.

Selection Vinafoc Merlot 2011 T
merlot

86

Colour: cherry, garnet rim. Nose: ripe fruit, spicy, toasty, fine reductive notes, scrubland. Palate: powerful, flavourful, toasty.

Selection Vinafoc Syrah 2011 T
syrah

87

Colour: cherry, garnet rim. Nose: ripe fruit, spicy, creamy oak, toasty, balsamic herbs, fine reductive notes. Palate: powerful, flavourful, toasty.

TOMÁS CUSINÉ

Plaça Sant Sebastià, 13
25457 El Vilosell (Lleida)
☎: +34 973 176 029
Fax: +34 973 175 945
www.tomascusine.com
info@tomascusine.com

Drac Màgic 2012 B
sauvignon blanc, macabeo, viognier

87

Colour: bright straw. Nose: fresh, fresh fruit, white flowers, expressive. Palate: flavourful, fruity, good acidity.

Drac Màgic 2012 T
tempranillo, garnacha, syrah

87

Colour: cherry, purple rim. Nose: red berry notes, ripe fruit, balsamic herbs, spicy. Palate: flavourful, balsamic, easy to drink.

VINALTIS

Passeig de Gracia, 56 6ª
8007 Barcelona (Barcelona)
☎: +34 934 673 575
Fax: +34 934 673 590
www.vinaltis.com
vinalti@vinaltis.com

Can Paloma - Montserrat 2010 TC
syrah, merlot

84

Can Paloma - Montserrat Muscat 2012 B
moscatel

83

Can Paloma - Montserrat
Ull de Llebre 2012 T
ull de llebre

85

VINS DEL MASSIS

Ctra. de Gava - Avimyonet, Km. 18,7
8795 Olesa de Bonesvails (Barcelona)
☎: +34 656 426 572
salesvinsdelmassis@gmail.com

Macizo 2013 B
93
Colour: bright golden. Nose: ripe fruit, powerfull, toasty, aged wood nuances, sweet spices, earthy notes. Palate: flavourful, fruity, spicy, toasty, long.

Massis 2013 B
90
Colour: bright straw. Nose: white flowers, dried herbs, ripe fruit, spicy, creamy oak. Palate: flavourful, fruity, good acidity, balanced, spicy.

VINYES DE L'ALBÀ

Carles Cardó, 31 2º 3ª
43800 Tarragona (Tarragona)
☎: +34 625 465 895
carles@vinyesdelalba.com

Vinyes de L'Alba Merlot 2013 T
merlot
84

Vinyes de L'Alba Sumoll 2013 T
sumoll
89
Colour: light cherry. Nose: mineral, spicy, red berry notes, ripe fruit, wild herbs. Palate: fresh, flavourful, balsamic, balanced.

DO. CAVA

CONSEJO REGULADOR

Avinguda Tarragona, 24
08720 Vilafranca del Penedès (Barcelona)
☎:+34 938 903 104 - Fax: +34 938 901 567
@: consejo@crcava.es
www.crcava.es

LOCATION:

The defined Cava region covers the sparkling wines produced according to the traditional method of a second fermentation in the bottle of 63 municipalities in the province of Barcelona, 52 in Tarragona, 12 in Lleida and 5 in Girona, as well as those of the municipal areas of Laguardia, Moreda de Álava and Oyón in Álava, Almendralejo in Badajoz, Mendavia and Viana in Navarra, Requena in Valencia, Ainzón and Cariñena in Zaragoza, and a further 18 municipalities of La Rioja.

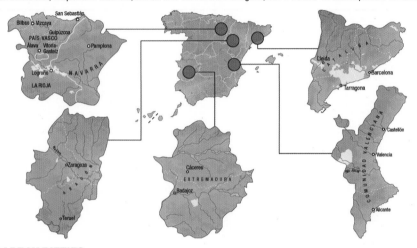

GRAPE VARIETIES:

White: Macabeo (Viura), Xarel.lo, Parellada, Subirat (Malvasía Riojana) and Chardonnay.
Red: Garnacha Tinta, Monastrell, Trepat and Pinot Noir.

FIGURES:

Vineyard surface: 32,913 – Wine-Growers: 6,365 – Wineries: 245 – 2013 Harvest rating: Excellent – Production 13: 209,203,262 litres – Market percentages: 33.6% domestic - 66.4% export.

SOIL:

This also depends on each producing region.

CLIMATE:

That of each producing region stated in the previous epigraph. Nevertheless, the region in which the largest part of the production is concentrated (Penedès) has a Mediterranean climate, with some production areas being cooler and situated at a higher altitude.

VINTAGE RATING   PEÑÍNGUIDE

2009	2010	2011	2012	2013

This denomination of origin, due to the wine-making process, does not make available single-year wines indicated by vintage, so the following evaluation refers to the overall quality of the wines that were tasted this year.

1 + 1 = 3
Masía Navinés
08736 Font-Rubí (Barcelona)
☎: +34 938 974 069
Fax: +34 938 974 724
www.umesufan3.com
umesu@umesufan3.com

1 + 1 = 3 BN
macabeo, xarel.lo, parellada
89
Colour: bright straw. Nose: medium intensity, fresh fruit, dried herbs, fine lees, floral. Palate: fresh, fruity, flavourful, good acidity.

1 + 1 = 3 BR
macabeo, xarel.lo, parellada
88
Colour: bright straw. Nose: medium intensity, fresh fruit, dried herbs, floral. Palate: fresh, fruity, flavourful, good acidity.

1 + 1 = 3 Especial 2008 BN Gran Reserva
xarel.lo, pinot noir
93
Colour: bright golden. Nose: fine lees, dry nuts, fragrant herbs, complex, toasty. Palate: powerful, flavourful, good acidity, fine bead, fine bitter notes.

1 + 1 = 3 Especial Blanc de Noirs BN Reserva
pinot noir
92
Colour: bright straw. Nose: fresh fruit, dried herbs, fine lees, floral, elegant. Palate: fresh, fruity, flavourful, good acidity.

1 + 1 = 3 Especial Xarel.lo s/c BN Reserva
xarel.lo
92
Colour: bright yellow. Nose: fine lees, dry nuts, fragrant herbs, complex, toasty. Palate: powerful, flavourful, good acidity, fine bead, fine bitter notes.

Cygnus 1 + 1 = 3 BN Reserva
macabeo, xarel.lo, parellada
90 🌷
Colour: bright yellow. Nose: ripe fruit, fine lees, balanced, dried herbs, fresh, citrus fruit. Palate: good acidity, flavourful, ripe fruit, long.

Julia & Navines Cava BN
macabeo, xarel.lo, parellada
89
Colour: bright straw. Nose: medium intensity, fresh fruit, dried herbs, fine lees, floral. Palate: fresh, fruity, flavourful, good acidity.

Julia & Navines Cava BR
macabeo, xarel.lo, parellada
85

Julia & Navines Cava Ecológico s/c BN
macabeo, xarel.lo, parellada
87 🌷
Colour: bright yellow. Nose: fine lees, balanced, dried herbs, citrus fruit. Palate: flavourful, long, fine bitter notes.

Julia & Navines Cava Rosé BR
pinot noir, garnacha, trepat
88
Colour: rose. Nose: floral, red berry notes, ripe fruit, fragrant herbs. Palate: powerful, flavourful, ripe fruit.

ADERNATS
Arrabal de Sant Joan, 7
43887 Nulles (Tarragona)
☎: +34 977 602 622
Fax: +34 977 609 798
www.vinicoladenulles.com
botiga@vinicoladenulles.com

Adernats 2009 BN Gran Reserva
macabeo, xarel.lo, chardonnay
91
Colour: bright golden. Nose: fine lees, dry nuts, fragrant herbs, complex, toasty. Palate: powerful, flavourful, good acidity, fine bead, fine bitter notes.

Adernats 2009 BR Gran Reserva
macabeo, xarel.lo, chardonnay
91
Colour: bright golden. Nose: fine lees, dry nuts, fragrant herbs, complex, toasty. Palate: powerful, flavourful, good acidity, fine bead, fine bitter notes.

Adernats 2011 BR Reserva
macabeo, xarel.lo, parellada
90
Colour: bright straw. Nose: fine lees, floral, fragrant herbs, expressive. Palate: powerful, flavourful, good acidity, fine bead, balanced.

Adernats Dolç 2011 Reserva
macabeo, xarel.lo, parellada
86
Colour: bright straw. Nose: medium intensity, fresh fruit, dried herbs, floral. Palate: flavourful, good acidity.

Adernats Reserva 2011 BN Reserva
macabeo, xarel.lo, parellada
90
Colour: bright yellow. Nose: ripe fruit, fine lees, balanced, dried herbs. Palate: good acidity, flavourful, ripe fruit, long.

Adernats Rosat 2011 BR Reserva
trepat
86
Colour: rose. Nose: floral, red berry notes, ripe fruit, fragrant herbs, expressive. Palate: powerful, balanced, flavourful.

Adernats XC 2006 BN Gran Reserva
xarel.lo

92

Colour: bright golden. Nose: fine lees, dry nuts, fragrant herbs, complex. Palate: powerful, flavourful, good acidity, fine bead, fine bitter notes.

AGUSTÍ TORELLÓ MATA

La Serra, s/n (Camí de Ribalta)
08770 Sant Sadurní D'Anoia (Barcelona)
☎: +34 938 911 173
Fax: +34 938 912 616
www.agustitorellomata.com
comunicacio@agustitorellomata.com

Agustí Torelló Mata 2008 BN Gran Reserva

92

Colour: bright golden. Nose: fine lees, fragrant herbs, complex, toasty, citrus fruit. Palate: powerful, flavourful, good acidity, fine bead, unctuous.

Agustí Torelló Mata 2009 BR Reserva

90

Colour: bright straw. Nose: fine lees, floral, fragrant herbs, pattiserie, sweet spices. Palate: powerful, flavourful, good acidity, fine bead, balanced.

Agustí Torelló Mata Gran Reserva Barrica 2008 BN
100% macabeo

90

Colour: bright golden. Nose: fine lees, dry nuts, spicy, pattiserie, cocoa bean, toasty. Palate: powerful, flavourful, good acidity, fine bead, fine bitter notes, toasty.

Agustí Torelló Mata Magnum 2007 BN Gran Reserva

94

Colour: bright golden. Nose: fine lees, fragrant herbs, complex, toasty, expressive, honeyed notes, dry nuts. Palate: flavourful, good acidity, fine bead, fine bitter notes, balanced, elegant.

Agustí Torelló Mata Rosat Trepat 2011 BR Reserva
100% trepat

89

Colour: rose. Nose: floral, red berry notes, ripe fruit, fragrant herbs, expressive. Palate: powerful, balanced, flavourful.

Bayanus 375ml 2009 BN Gran Reserva

91

Colour: bright yellow. Nose: fine lees, dry nuts, fragrant herbs, complex, toasty. Palate: powerful, flavourful, good acidity, fine bead, fine bitter notes.

Bayanus Rosat 375 2010 BR Reserva
100% trepat

87

Colour: coppery red. Nose: floral, jasmine, fragrant herbs, ripe fruit. Palate: fresh, fruity, flavourful, correct.

Kripta 2007 BN Gran Reserva

93

Colour: bright golden. Nose: characterful, ripe fruit, dry nuts, candied fruit, citrus fruit, pattiserie. Palate: powerful, flavourful, good acidity, fine bead, fine bitter notes, elegant.

ALSINA SARDÁ

08733 Pla del Penedès (Barcelona)
☎: +34 938 988 132
Fax: +34 938 988 671
www.alsinasarda.com
alsina@alsinasarda.com

Alsina & Sardá BR Reserva
macabeo, xarel.lo, parellada

89

Colour: bright straw. Nose: medium intensity, fresh fruit, dried herbs, fine lees, floral. Palate: fresh, fruity, flavourful, good acidity.

Alsina & Sardá 2011 BN Reserva
macabeo, xarel.lo, parellada

88

Colour: bright straw. Nose: fine lees, floral, fragrant herbs, expressive. Palate: powerful, flavourful, good acidity, fine bead, balanced.

Alsina & Sardá Gran Cuvée Vestigis 2007 BN Gran Reserva
macabeo, xarel.lo, parellada, pinot noir

91

Colour: bright straw. Nose: medium intensity, fresh fruit, dried herbs, fine lees, floral, elegant. Palate: fresh, fruity, flavourful, good acidity.

Alsina & Sardá Gran Reserva Especial 2009 BN Gran Reserva
chardonnay, xarel.lo

91

Colour: bright golden. Nose: fine lees, dry nuts, fragrant herbs, complex. Palate: powerful, flavourful, good acidity, fine bead, fine bitter notes.

Alsina & Sardá Mas D'Alsina BN Reserva
chardonnay, macabeo, xarel.lo, parraleta

88

Colour: bright yellow. Nose: spicy, smoky, dry nuts. Palate: flavourful, complex, good acidity, spicy.

Alsina & Sarda Pinot Noir BN
pinot noir

88

Colour: coppery red. Nose: floral, jasmine, fragrant herbs, candied fruit. Palate: fresh, fruity, flavourful, correct.

Alsina & Sardá Sello 2010 BN Gran Reserva
xarel.lo, macabeo, parellada

88

Colour: bright straw. Nose: fine lees, floral, fragrant herbs, expressive. Palate: powerful, flavourful, good acidity, fine bead, balanced.

ALTA ALELLA S.L.
Camí Baix de Tiana s/n
08328 Alella (Barcelona)
☎: +34 934 693 720
Fax: +34 934 691 343
www.altaalella.cat
info@altaalella.cat

AA Bruel 2012 BN
pansa blanca

88 🌿

Colour: bright yellow. Nose: ripe fruit, fine lees, balanced, dried herbs. Palate: good acidity, flavourful, ripe fruit, long.

AA Capsigrany 2008 BN
pansa rosada

86 🌿

Colour: bright yellow. Nose: ripe fruit, fruit liqueur notes, lees reduction notes, dried herbs. Palate: correct, powerful, flavourful.

AA Privat 2011 BN
pansa blanca, macabeo, parellada

88 🌿

Colour: bright straw. Nose: medium intensity, fresh fruit, dried herbs, fine lees, floral. Palate: fresh, fruity, flavourful, good acidity.

AA Privat Chardonnay 2011 BN Reserva
chardonnay

87 🌿

Colour: bright straw. Nose: medium intensity, fresh fruit, fine lees, floral. Palate: fresh, fruity, flavourful, good acidity.

AA Privat Laietà 2010 BN Gran Reserva
chardonnay, pinot noir

89 🌿

Colour: bright yellow. Nose: balanced, faded flowers, ripe fruit. Palate: balanced, fine bitter notes, good acidity.

AA Privat Laietà Rosé 2010 BN Reserva
mataró

90 🌿

Colour: coppery red. Nose: floral, jasmine, fragrant herbs, candied fruit. Palate: fresh, fruity, flavourful, correct.

AA Privat Mirgin BN Gran Reserva
chardonnay, pinot noir

91 🌿

Colour: bright yellow. Nose: balanced, ripe fruit, toasty, spicy, fine lees. Palate: balanced, fine bitter notes.

AA Privat Opus Evolutium 2009 BN Gran Reserva
chardonnay, pinot noir

93 🌿

Colour: bright golden. Nose: fine lees, dry nuts, fragrant herbs. Palate: powerful, flavourful, good acidity, fine bead, fine bitter notes, balanced, elegant.

AA Privat Rosé 2011 BN
pinot noir, mataró

87 🌿

Colour: coppery red. Nose: floral, jasmine, fragrant herbs, candied fruit. Palate: fresh, fruity, flavourful, correct.

ANTIGVA CIA. AGROALIMENTARIA ESPAÑOLA DEL MEDITERRANEO
Calle Pepe Martínez Molla, 2, Local 3
46800 Xátiva (Valencia)
☎: +34 962 280 555
www.antigvacava.com
info@antigvacava.com

Antigva White Label 2012 BN
xarel.lo, macabeo, parellada

82

Millesime Antigva 2010 BN Reserva
xarel.lo, macabeo, parellada, chardonnay

85

ARBOLEDA MEDITERRÁNEA BODEGAS
Ctra Sant Sadurni -
Piera BV-2242, km 10
08784 La Fortesa (Barcelona)
☎: +34 902 996 361
www.arboledamediterranean.com
arboleda@arboledamediterranean.com

Torrens & Moliner BR
macabeo, xarel.lo, parellada

86

Colour: bright straw. Nose: fine lees, floral, fragrant herbs, medium intensity. Palate: powerful, flavourful, good acidity, easy to drink.

Torrens & Moliner Premium BN Gran Reserva
macabeo, xarel.lo, parellada

88

Colour: bright golden. Nose: fine lees, fragrant herbs, characterful, ripe fruit, dry nuts. Palate: powerful, flavourful, good acidity, fine bead, fine bitter notes.

Torrens & Moliner Reserva Particular BN Reserva
macabeo, xarel.lo, parellada

87

Colour: bright straw. Nose: fine lees, floral, fragrant herbs. Palate: powerful, flavourful, good acidity, fine bead, balanced.

AVINYÓ CAVAS

Masia Can Fontanals
08793 Avinyonet del Penedès
(Barcelona)
☎: +34 938 970 055
Fax: +34 938 970 691
www.avinyo.com
avinyo@avinyo.com

Avinyó BN Reserva
macabeo, xarel.lo, parellada
89
Colour: bright yellow. Nose: ripe fruit, fine lees, balanced, dried herbs. Palate: good acidity, flavourful, ripe fruit, long.

Avinyó BR Reserva
macabeo, xarel.lo, parellada
88
Colour: bright straw. Nose: fine lees, floral, fragrant herbs, expressive. Palate: powerful, flavourful, good acidity, fine bead, balanced.

Avinyó Blanc de Noirs BN Reserva
100% pinot noir
88
Colour: bright straw. Nose: fine lees, floral, fragrant herbs. Palate: powerful, flavourful, good acidity, fine bead, balanced.

Avinyó Rosé Sublim BR Reserva
100% pinot noir
88
Colour: coppery red. Nose: floral, jasmine, fragrant herbs, candied fruit. Palate: fresh, fruity, flavourful, correct.

Avinyó Selecció La Ticota 2008 BN Gran Reserva
macabeo, xarel.lo
90
Colour: bright golden. Nose: fine lees, fragrant herbs, characterful, ripe fruit, dry nuts. Palate: powerful, flavourful, good acidity, fine bead, fine bitter notes.

AXIAL

Pla-za Calle Castillo de Capua, 10 Nave 7
050197 (Zaragoza)
☎: +34 976 780 136
Fax: +34 976 303 035
www.axialvinos.com
info@axialvinos.com

La Granja 360 Cava 2011 BR
86
Colour: bright straw. Nose: fragrant herbs, fresh, balanced. Palate: flavourful, good acidity, fine bead, balanced.

BODEGA SANSTRAVÉ

De la Conca, 10
43412 Solivella (Tarragona)
☎: +34 977 892 165
Fax: +34 977 892 073
www.sanstrave.com
bodega@sanstrave.com

Sanstravé BN Gran Reserva
macabeo, parellada, xarel.lo, chardonnay
88
Colour: bright golden. Nose: fine lees, dry nuts, fragrant herbs, complex. Palate: powerful, flavourful, good acidity, fine bead, fine bitter notes.

Sanstravé Rosat 2011 BR Reserva
trepat
89
Colour: coppery red. Nose: floral, jasmine, fragrant herbs, citrus fruit. Palate: fresh, fruity, flavourful, correct.

BODEGA SEBIRAN

Pérez Galdos, 1
46352 Campo Arcis - Requena
(Valencia)
☎: +34 962 303 321
Fax: +34 962 301 560
www.sebiran.es
info@sebiran.es

Coto D'Arcis BN
macabeo
88
Colour: bright yellow. Nose: candied fruit, pattiserie, spicy. Palate: flavourful, balanced, good acidity.

Coto D'Arcis Especial BR
macabeo
87
Colour: bright yellow. Nose: ripe fruit, medium intensity, spicy. Palate: correct, fine bitter notes.

BODEGAS ARRAEZ

Arcediano Ros, 35
46630 La Font de la Figuera (Valencia)
☎: +34 962 290 031
www.bodegasarraez.com
info@bodegasarraez.com

A-2 BR Reserva
87
Colour: bright straw. Nose: fine lees, floral, fragrant herbs, expressive. Palate: powerful, flavourful, good acidity, fine bead, balanced.

BODEGAS CA N'ESTELLA

Masia Ca N'Estella, s/n
08635 Sant Esteve Sesrovires
(Barcelona)
☎ +34 934 161 387
Fax: +34 934 161 620
www.fincacanestella.com
a.vidal@fincacanestella.com

Rabetllat i Vidal 2010 BN
chardonnay, macabeo

90

Colour: bright straw. Nose: fine lees, floral, fragrant herbs, expressive. Palate: powerful, flavourful, good acidity, fine bead, balanced.

Rabetllat i Vidal Brut Ca N'Estella 2012 BR
macabeo, xarel.lo, chardonnay

90

Colour: bright straw. Nose: fine lees, floral, fragrant herbs, expressive. Palate: powerful, flavourful, good acidity, fine bead, balanced.

Rabetllat i Vidal Gran Reserva de la Finca 2008 BN
trepat, garnacha

90

Colour: bright golden. Nose: dry nuts, fragrant herbs, fine lees, macerated fruit, sweet spices. Palate: powerful, flavourful, good acidity, fine bead, fine bitter notes.

Rabetllat i Vidal Rosado 2010 BR
trepat, garnacha

85

BODEGAS CAPITÀ VIDAL

Ctra. Villafranca-Igualada, Km. 21
08733 Pla del Penedès (Barcelona)
☎ +34 938 988 630
Fax: +34 938 988 625
www.capitavidal.com
helena@capitavidal.com

Fuchs de Vidal BR

86

Colour: bright straw. Nose: medium intensity, fresh fruit, dried herbs, fine lees, floral. Palate: fresh, fruity, flavourful, good acidity.

Fuchs de Vidal 2010 BN Gran Reserva

90

Colour: bright golden. Nose: fragrant herbs, characterful, ripe fruit, dry nuts. Palate: powerful, flavourful, good acidity, fine bead, fine bitter notes.

Fuchs de Vidal Cuvée BN Reserva

90

Colour: bright golden. Nose: fine lees, dry nuts, fragrant herbs, complex, toasty. Palate: powerful, flavourful, good acidity, fine bead, fine bitter notes.

Fuchs de Vidal Rosé Pinot Noir BN
100% pinot noir

86

Colour: rose. Nose: floral, red berry notes, ripe fruit, fragrant herbs, medium intensity. Palate: balanced, flavourful, fine bitter notes.

Fuchs de Vidal Unic BN

88

Colour: bright yellow. Nose: ripe fruit, fine lees, balanced, dried herbs. Palate: good acidity, flavourful, ripe fruit, long.

Gran Fuchs de Vidal BN

89

Colour: bright straw. Nose: fine lees, floral, fragrant herbs, expressive. Palate: powerful, flavourful, good acidity, fine bead, balanced.

Palau Solá BN

84

BODEGAS COVIÑAS

Avda. Rafael Duyos, s/n
46340 Requena (Valencia)
☎ +34 962 300 680
Fax: +34 962 302 651
www.covinas.es
covinas@covinas.es

Enterizo BR

87

Colour: bright straw. Nose: medium intensity, fresh fruit, fine lees, floral, citrus fruit. Palate: fresh, fruity, flavourful, good acidity.

Marqués de Plata BN

85

Marqués de Plata BR

88

Colour: bright straw. Nose: fresh fruit, dried herbs, fine lees, floral, citrus fruit. Palate: fresh, fruity, flavourful, good acidity.

BODEGAS ESCUDERO

Ctra. de Arnedo, s/n
26587 Grávalos (La Rioja)
☎ +34 941 398 008
Fax: +34 941 398 070
www.familiaescudero.com
info@familiaescudero.com

Benito Escudero BN
100% viura

84

Benito Escudero BR
100% viura

87

Colour: bright straw. Nose: medium intensity, fresh fruit, dried herbs, floral, fragrant herbs. Palate: fresh, fruity, flavourful, good acidity.

Dioro Baco BR

87

Colour: bright straw. Nose: fine lees, floral, fragrant herbs, expressive. Palate: powerful, flavourful, good acidity, fine bead, balanced.

Dioro Baco Extra Brut
100% chardonnay

84

Dioro Baco Rosado BR
100% pinot noir

84

BODEGAS FAUSTINO
Ctra. de Logroño, s/n
01320 Oyón (Álava)
☎: +34 945 622 500
Fax: +34 945 622 106
www.bodegasfaustino.com
info@bodegasfaustino.es

Cava Faustino BR Reserva
macabeo, chardonnay

84

BODEGAS HISPANO SUIZAS
Ctra. N-322, Km. 451,7 El Pontón
46357 Requena (Valencia)
☎: +34 661 894 200
www.bodegashispanosuizas.com
info@bodegashispanosuizas.com

Tantum Ergo Chardonnay Pinot Noir 2011 BN
chardonnay, pinot noir

93

Colour: bright straw. Nose: floral, fragrant herbs, expressive, candied fruit. Palate: powerful, flavourful, good acidity, fine bead, balanced.

Tantum Ergo Pinot Noir Rosé 2012 BN
pinot noir

91

Colour: coppery red. Nose: floral, jasmine, fragrant herbs, candied fruit, balsamic herbs. Palate: fresh, fruity, flavourful, correct, balanced.

Tantum Ergo Vintage 2010 BN
chardonnay, pinot noir

93

Colour: bright golden. Nose: dry nuts, fragrant herbs, complex, toasty, balsamic herbs, dried herbs. Palate: powerful, flavourful, good acidity, fine bead, fine bitter notes.

BODEGAS LANGA
Ctra. Nacional II, Km. 241,700
50300 Calatayud (Zaragoza)
☎: +34 976 881 818
Fax: +34 976 884 463
www.bodegas-langa.com
info@bodegas-langa.com

Reyes de Aragón BN Gran Reserva
chardonnay, macabeo

85

Reyes de Aragón BN Reserva
chardonnay, macabeo

85

Reyes de Aragón BR Reserva
macabeo, chardonnay

86

Colour: bright yellow. Nose: ripe fruit, fine lees, balanced, dried herbs. Palate: good acidity, flavourful, ripe fruit, long.

Reyes de Aragón Selección Familiar BN
macabeo, chardonnay

84

BODEGAS MUGA
Barrio de la Estación, s/n
26200 Haro (La Rioja)
☎: +34 941 311 825
www.bodegasmuga.com
marketing@bodegasmuga.com

Conde de Haro 2010 BR

92

Colour: bright straw. Nose: fresh fruit, dried herbs, fine lees, floral. Palate: fresh, fruity, flavourful, good acidity, balanced.

Conde de Haro Brut Vintage 2011 BR

91

Colour: bright yellow. Nose: fine lees, floral, fragrant herbs, expressive. Palate: powerful, flavourful, good acidity, fine bead, balanced.

Conde de Haro Rosado BR
100% garnacha

88

Colour: coppery red. Nose: floral, jasmine, fragrant herbs, candied fruit. Palate: fresh, fruity, flavourful, correct.

BODEGAS MUR BARCELONA

Rambla de la Generalitat, 1-9
08770 Sant Sadurni D'Anoia (Barcelona)
☎: +34 938 183 641
Fax: +34 938 911 662
www.mur-barcelona.com
info@mur-barcelona.com

Gran Montesquius 2012 BN Reserva
87
Colour: bright yellow. Nose: fine lees, fragrant herbs, floral, balanced. Palate: fresh, fruity, good acidity, fine bead.

Most Doré Objeto de deseo 2010 Extra Brut Reserva
87
Colour: bright golden. Nose: ripe fruit, dry nuts, dried herbs, floral. Palate: spicy, long, flavourful, good acidity.

Robert J. Mur Especial Tradició 2010 BN Reserva
88
Colour: bright straw. Nose: fine lees, fragrant herbs, complex, toasty, dried herbs. Palate: powerful, flavourful, good acidity, fine bead, fine bitter notes.

Robert J. Mur Especial Tradició Rosé 2010 BN Reserva
86
Colour: coppery red. Nose: faded flowers, dried herbs, ripe fruit, fruit liqueur notes, spicy, slightly evolved. Palate: fresh, fruity, balsamic.

BODEGAS MURVIEDRO

Ampliación Pol. El Romeral, s/n
46340 Requena (Valencia)
☎: +34 962 329 003
Fax: +34 962 329 002
www.bodegasmurviedro.es
murviedro@murviedro.es

Corolilla Chardonnay BR
chardonnay
85

Expresión Solidarity Cuvée Chardonnay BN
chardonnay
88
Colour: bright yellow. Nose: ripe fruit, fine lees, balanced, dried herbs. Palate: good acidity, flavourful, ripe fruit, long.

Luna de Murviedro BR
macabeo
88
Colour: bright yellow. Nose: ripe fruit, fine lees, balanced, dried herbs. Palate: good acidity, flavourful, ripe fruit, long.

Luna de Murviedro Rosé BR
garnacha
87
Colour: rose. Nose: floral, red berry notes, ripe fruit, fragrant herbs. Palate: powerful, balanced, flavourful.

BODEGAS OLARRA

Avda. de Mendavia, 30
26009 Logroño (La Rioja)
☎: +34 941 235 299
Fax: +34 941 253 703
www.bodegasolarra.es
bodegasolarra@bodegasolarra.es

Añares BN
100% viura
86
Colour: bright straw. Nose: medium intensity, fresh fruit, dried herbs, fine lees, floral. Palate: fresh, fruity, flavourful, good acidity.

Añares BR
100% viura
83

BODEGAS ONDARRE

Ctra. de Aras, s/n
31230 Viana (Navarra)
☎: +34 948 645 300
Fax: +34 948 646 002
www.bodegasondarre.es
bodegasondarre@bodegasondarre.es

Ondarre BN
100% viura
86
Colour: bright yellow. Nose: ripe fruit, fine lees, balanced, dried herbs. Palate: good acidity, flavourful, ripe fruit, long.

Ondarre Millennium BR
100% viura
85

BODEGAS ROMALE

Pol. Ind. Parc. 6, Manz. D
06200 Almendralejo (Badajoz)
☎: +34 924 665 877
Fax: +34 924 665 877
www.romale.com
romale@romale.com

Privilegio de Romale 2011 BN Reserva
macabeo, parellada
84

Viña Romale Rosado 2013 BN
garnacha
84

BODEGAS ROURA - JUAN ANTONIO PÉREZ ROURA

Valls de Rials
08328 Alella (Barcelona)
☎: +34 933 527 456
Fax: +34 933 524 339
www.roura.es
roura@roura.es

Roura BN
84

Roura BR
84

Roura 5 * BN
86
Colour: bright yellow. Nose: ripe fruit, fine lees, dried herbs. Palate: good acidity, ripe fruit.

Roura Rosat BN
100% trepat
85

BODEGAS TROBAT

Castelló, 10
17780 Garriguella (Girona)
☎: +34 972 530 092
Fax: +34 972 552 530
www.bodegastrobat.com
bodegas.trobat@bmark.es

Celler Trobat 2009 BN Gran Reserva
macabeo, xarel.lo, parellada, chardonnay
88
Colour: bright golden. Nose: fine lees, dry nuts, fragrant herbs. Palate: powerful, flavourful, good acidity, fine bead, fine bitter notes.

Celler Trobat 2009 BN Reserva
macabeo, xarel.lo, parellada, chardonnay
90
Colour: bright golden. Nose: fine lees, dry nuts, fragrant herbs, complex. Palate: powerful, flavourful, good acidity, fine bead, fine bitter notes.

Celler Trobat Rosat 2012 BR
monastrell, garnacha
83

Gran Amat 2013 BN
macabeo, xarel.lo, parellada
89
Colour: bright straw. Nose: fine lees, floral, fragrant herbs, expressive. Palate: powerful, flavourful, good acidity, fine bead, balanced.

BODEGAS VEGAMAR

Garcesa, s/n
46175 Calles (Valencia)
☎: +34 962 109 813
www.bodegasvegamar.com
info@bodegasvegamar.com

Privée 18 BN Reserva
chardonnay, macabeo
86
Colour: bright straw. Nose: fragrant herbs, toasty, spicy. Palate: powerful, flavourful, good acidity, balanced, fine bitter notes.

Vegamar BN
chardonnay, macabeo
86
Colour: bright straw. Nose: medium intensity, fresh fruit, floral. Palate: fresh, good acidity.

Vegamar Rosado BN
garnacha
88
Colour: rose. Nose: floral, red berry notes, ripe fruit, fragrant herbs, expressive. Palate: powerful, balanced, flavourful.

BODEGAS VICENTE GANDÍA

Ctra. Cheste a Godelleta, s/n
46370 Chiva (Valencia)
☎: +34 962 524 242
Fax: +34 962 524 243
www.vicentegandia.es
info@vicentegandia.com

El Miracle BR
macabeo, chardonnay
85

El Miracle Rosado BR
100% garnacha
85

Hoya de Cadenas BN
100% macabeo
87
Colour: bright yellow. Nose: ripe fruit, fine lees, dried herbs. Palate: good acidity, flavourful, good finish, fresh.

Hoya de Cadenas BR
macabeo, chardonnay
86
Colour: bright straw. Nose: medium intensity, fresh fruit, dried herbs, floral. Palate: fresh, fruity, good acidity, easy to drink.

Vicente Gandía BN
100% macabeo
87
Colour: bright yellow. Nose: fine lees, balanced, dried herbs, fresh fruit. Palate: good acidity, ripe fruit, long.

Vicente Gandía BR
macabeo, chardonnay
84

Vicente Gandía Rosado BR
100% garnacha
84

Whatever it Takes by Charlize Theron BR
macabeo, chardonnay
85

BODEGUES SUMARROCA
El Rebato, s/n
08739 Subirats (Barcelona)
☎: +34 938 911 092
Fax: +34 938 911 778
www.sumarroca.es
s-berrocal@selfoods.es

Sumarroca BR Reserva
macabeo, parellada, xarel.lo, chardonnay
89
Colour: bright straw. Nose: fine lees, floral, fragrant herbs, expressive. Palate: powerful, flavourful, good acidity, fine bead, balanced.

Sumarroca 2010 BN Gran Reserva
macabeo, parellada, xarel.lo, chardonnay
91
Colour: bright golden. Nose: fine lees, fragrant herbs, complex, toasty, expressive. Palate: powerful, flavourful, good acidity, fine bead, fine bitter notes.

Sumarroca Allier BR Gran Reserva
parellada, pinot noir, chardonnay
93
Colour: bright yellow. Nose: fine lees, dry nuts, fragrant herbs, complex, sweet spices, creamy oak. Palate: powerful, flavourful, good acidity, fine bead, fine bitter notes, elegant.

Sumarroca Cuvée BN Gran Reserva
chardonnay, parellada
91
Colour: yellow. Nose: fine lees, dry nuts, complex. Palate: powerful, flavourful, good acidity, fine bead, fine bitter notes, long.

Sumarroca Gran Brut Blanc de Negre BR Reserva
parellada, pinot noir, chardonnay
91
Colour: bright straw. Nose: fine lees, floral, fragrant herbs, expressive, spicy. Palate: powerful, flavourful, good acidity, fine bead, balanced.

Sumarroca IN SI TU Extra Brut Reserva
91
Colour: bright straw. Nose: fine lees, floral, fragrant herbs, expressive. Palate: powerful, flavourful, good acidity, fine bead, balanced.

Sumarroca Núria Claverol BR Gran Reserva
xarel.lo
93
Colour: bright yellow. Nose: fine lees, dry nuts, fragrant herbs, complex, toasty. Palate: powerful, flavourful, good acidity, fine bead, fine bitter notes, balanced, elegant.

Sumarroca Pinot Noir Rosé Brut BR Reserva
pinot noir
91
Colour: coppery red. Nose: floral, jasmine, fragrant herbs, candied fruit, spicy, expressive. Palate: fresh, fruity, flavourful, correct, balanced, elegant.

Sumarroca Rosat BR
pinot noir
88
Colour: rose. Nose: floral, red berry notes, ripe fruit, fragrant herbs, expressive. Palate: powerful, balanced, flavourful.

BOLET VINS I CAVAS ECOLÓGICOS
Finca Mas Lluet, s/n
08732 Castellvi de la Marca (Barcelona)
☎: +34 938 918 153
www.cavasbolet.com
cavasbolet@cavasbolet.com

Bolet 2008 BN Gran Reserva
86 🌿
Colour: bright golden. Nose: fine lees, dry nuts, fragrant herbs. Palate: flavourful, good acidity, fine bitter notes.

Bolet 2010 BN Reserva
xarel.lo, macabeo, parellada
86 🌿
Colour: bright yellow. Nose: ripe fruit, fine lees, dried herbs. Palate: good acidity, flavourful, ripe fruit, long.

Bolet 2010 BR
85 🌿

Bolet Classic 2011 BR
xarel.lo, macabeo, parellada
86 🌿
Colour: bright golden. Nose: fine lees, fragrant herbs, ripe fruit, dry nuts. Palate: powerful, flavourful, good acidity, fine bead, fine bitter notes.

Bolet Rosado 2012 BR
pinot noir
84 🌿

Bolet Selección Familiar
2007 BN Gran Reserva
87 🍷

Colour: bright yellow. Nose: ripe fruit, fine lees, balanced, dried herbs. Palate: good acidity, flavourful, ripe fruit, long.

CANALS & MUNNÉ
Plaza Pau Casals, 6
08770 Sant Sadurní D'Anoia (Barcelona)
☎: +34 938 910 318
Fax: +34 938 911 945
www.canalsimunne.com
info@canalsimunne.com

Canals & Munné "1915 by C y M"
2010 BN Gran Reserva
88

Colour: bright yellow. Nose: ripe fruit, fine lees, balanced, dried herbs. Palate: good acidity, flavourful, ripe fruit, long.

Canals & Munné 2011 BN Gran Reserva
88

Colour: bright yellow, greenish rim. Nose: ripe fruit, fine lees, dried herbs. Palate: good acidity, flavourful, ripe fruit, long.

Canals & Munné 2011 BR Gran Reserva
89

Colour: bright golden. Nose: fine lees, dry nuts, fragrant herbs, complex, spicy. Palate: powerful, flavourful, good acidity, fine bead, fine bitter notes.

Canals & Munné Gran Duc
2009 BN Gran Reserva
90

Colour: bright golden. Nose: fine lees, dry nuts, fragrant herbs, complex, toasty. Palate: powerful, flavourful, good acidity, fine bead, fine bitter notes, balanced.

Canals & Munné Insuperable
2012 BR Reserva
88

Colour: bright straw. Nose: medium intensity, fresh fruit, dried herbs, fine lees, floral. Palate: fresh, fruity, flavourful, good acidity.

Canals & Munné Reserva de
L'Avi 2010 BN Gran Reserva
89

Colour: bright yellow. Nose: fine lees, dry nuts, fragrant herbs, complex. Palate: powerful, flavourful, good acidity, fine bead, fine bitter notes.

Canals & Munné Reserva de L'Avi
Jeroboam (3 litros) 2009 BR Reserva
93

Colour: bright golden. Nose: fine lees, dry nuts, fragrant herbs, toasty. Palate: powerful, flavourful, good acidity, fine bead, fine bitter notes, elegant.

Canals & Munné Rosé 2012 BR Reserva
100% pinot noir
89

Colour: rose, bright. Nose: red berry notes, ripe fruit, floral, rose petals. Palate: fruity, flavourful, good acidity, long, fine bitter notes.

Dionysus Eco 2012 BN Reserva
89 🍷

Colour: bright straw. Nose: medium intensity, fresh fruit, dried herbs, fine lees, floral, sweet spices. Palate: fresh, fruity, flavourful, good acidity.

CANALS & NUBIOLA S.A.
Avda. Casetes Mir, 2
08770 Sant Sadurní D'Anoia (Barcelona)
☎: +34 938 917 025
Fax: +34 938 910 126
www.canalsnubiola.com
canalsnubiola@canalsnubiola.es

Canals & Nubiola Grapa Brut 2012 BR
84

Canals & Nubiola Grapa
Nature 2011 BN Reserva
87

Colour: bright yellow. Nose: ripe fruit, fine lees, balanced, dried herbs. Palate: good acidity, flavourful, ripe fruit, long.

CANALS CANALS
Avda. Montserrat, 9
08769 Castellví de Rosanes (Barcelona)
☎: +34 937 755 446
Fax: +34 937 741 719
www.canalscanals.com
cava@canalscanals.com

Canals Canals Reserva Numerada
2011 BN Reserva
xarel.lo, macabeo, parellada
90

Colour: bright golden. Nose: fine lees, dry nuts, fragrant herbs, toasty. Palate: powerful, flavourful, good acidity, fine bead, fine bitter notes.

Marta 2010 BN Reserva
xarel.lo, macabeo, parellada
88

Colour: bright straw. Nose: medium intensity, fresh fruit, dried herbs, fine lees, floral. Palate: fresh, fruity, flavourful, good acidity.

Marta Magnum 2007 BN Gran Reserva
xarel.lo, macabeo, parellada
91

Colour: bright yellow. Nose: ripe fruit, fine lees, balanced, dried herbs. Palate: good acidity, flavourful, ripe fruit, long.

Ramón Canals Gran Reserva Limitada 2008 BN Gran Reserva
xarel.lo, macabeo, parellada

89

Colour: bright yellow. Nose: ripe fruit, fine lees, balanced, dried herbs. Palate: good acidity, flavourful, ripe fruit, long.

CANALS NADAL
Ponent, 2
08733 El Pla del Penedès (Barcelona)
☎: +34 938 988 081
Fax: +34 938 989 050
www.canalsnadal.com
cava@canalsnadal.com

Antoni Canals Nadal Cupada Selecció 2010 BR Reserva

91

Colour: bright straw. Nose: fine lees, floral, fragrant herbs, expressive. Palate: powerful, flavourful, good acidity, fine bead, balanced.

Antoni Canals Nadal Cupada Selecció Magnum BN Gran Reserva

90

Colour: bright golden. Nose: fine lees, dry nuts, fragrant herbs, complex. Palate: powerful, flavourful, good acidity, fine bead, fine bitter notes.

Antoni Canals Nadal Gran Vintage 2010 BR Reserva

89

Colour: bright golden. Nose: fine lees, dry nuts, fragrant herbs, complex. Palate: powerful, flavourful, good acidity, fine bead, fine bitter notes.

Canals Nadal BR Reserva

87

Colour: bright straw. Nose: fine lees, expressive, medium intensity, dried herbs. Palate: flavourful, good acidity, fresh.

Canals Nadal 2009 BN Gran Reserva

89

Colour: bright yellow. Nose: ripe fruit, fine lees, balanced, dried herbs. Palate: good acidity, flavourful, ripe fruit, long.

Canals Nadal 2010 BN Reserva

88

Colour: bright straw. Nose: medium intensity, fresh fruit, dried herbs, fine lees, floral. Palate: fresh, fruity, flavourful, good acidity.

Canals Nadal 2012 BR

84

Canals Nadal Magnum 2009 BN

90

Colour: bright golden. Nose: fine lees, fragrant herbs, characterful, ripe fruit, dry nuts. Palate: powerful, flavourful, good acidity, fine bead, fine bitter notes.

Canals Nadal Rosé 2012 BR Reserva
100% trepat

88

Colour: rose. Nose: floral, red berry notes, ripe fruit, fragrant herbs. Palate: balanced, flavourful, easy to drink.

CASTELL D'AGE
Ctra. de Martorell a Capellades, 6-8
08782 La Beguda Baixa (Barcelona)
☎: +34 937 725 181
Fax: +34 937 727 061
www.castelldage.com
info@castelldage.com

Castell D'Age Anne Marie 2010 BN Reserva
xarel.lo, macabeo, parellada

90

Colour: bright golden. Nose: fine lees, dry nuts, fragrant herbs, complex, toasty. Palate: powerful, flavourful, good acidity, fine bead, fine bitter notes.

Castell D'Age Aurèlia 2009 BN Gran Reserva
xarel.lo, macabeo, parellada, chardonnay

88 🌱

Colour: bright golden. Nose: fine lees, fragrant herbs, characterful, ripe fruit, dry nuts. Palate: powerful, flavourful, fine bead, fine bitter notes.

Castell D'Age Olivia 2010 BN Reserva
chardonnay

86 🌱

Colour: bright yellow. Nose: ripe fruit, fruit liqueur notes, lees reduction notes, dried herbs. Palate: fine bitter notes, correct.

Castell D'Age Rosat 2011 BR
pinot noir

87

Colour: rose. Nose: floral, red berry notes, ripe fruit, fragrant herbs, expressive. Palate: powerful, balanced, flavourful.

Poculum Boni Geni 2006 BN Gran Reserva
pinot noir, chardonnay

90

Colour: bright golden. Nose: fine lees, dry nuts, fragrant herbs, complex, toasty. Palate: powerful, flavourful, good acidity, fine bead, fine bitter notes.

CASTELL D'OR

Mare Rafols, 3- 1ºD
08720 Vilafranca del Penedès
(Barcelona)
☎: +34 938 905 385
Fax: +34 938 905 455
www.castelldor.com
castelldor@castelldor.com

Castell de la Comanda BR
macabeo, parellada

84

Cautiu Imperial BR
macabeo, xarel.lo, parellada

88

Colour: bright straw. Nose: medium intensity, fresh fruit, dried herbs, fine lees, floral. Palate: fresh, fruity, flavourful, good acidity.

Cautiu Rosat BR
100% trepat

86

Colour: rose. Nose: floral, red berry notes, ripe fruit, fragrant herbs, expressive. Palate: powerful, balanced, flavourful.

Cossetània BN
macabeo, xarel.lo, parellada

87

Colour: bright yellow. Nose: ripe fruit, fine lees, balanced, dried herbs, sweet spices. Palate: good acidity, flavourful, ripe fruit, long.

Cossetània BR Reserva
macabeo, xarel.lo, parellada

87

Colour: bright straw. Nose: fine lees, floral, fragrant herbs, powerfull. Palate: powerful, flavourful, good acidity, fine bead.

Cossetània Rosado BR
trepat

85

Flama D'Or BN
xarel.lo, macabeo, parellada

84

Flama D'Or BR
xarel.lo, macabeo, parellada

85

Francoli BN
macabeo, parellada

86

Colour: bright yellow. Nose: ripe fruit, fruit liqueur notes, dried herbs, fine lees. Palate: correct, flavourful.

Francolí BR Reserva
macabeo, parellada

87

Colour: bright straw. Nose: fine lees, fragrant herbs, citrus fruit. Palate: powerful, flavourful, good acidity, fine bead, balanced.

Francolí Imperial BR
macabeo, parellada

87

Colour: bright straw. Nose: fresh fruit, dried herbs, fine lees, floral. Palate: fresh, fruity, flavourful, good acidity.

Francoli Rosat BR
trepat

85

Puig Solivella BN
macabeo, parellada

84

CASTELL SANT ANTONI

Passeig del Parc, 13
08770 Sant Sadurní D'Anoia (Barcelona)
☎: +34 938 183 099
Fax: +34 938 184 451
www.castellsantantoni.com
cava@castellsantantoni.com

Castell Sant Antoni 37.5 Brut BR Gran Reserva
macabeo, xarel.lo, parellada, chardonnay

91

Colour: bright golden. Nose: fine lees, dry nuts, fragrant herbs, complex. Palate: powerful, flavourful, good acidity, fine bead, fine bitter notes.

Castell Sant Antoni 37.5 Brut Nature BN Gran Reserva
macabeo, xarel.lo, parellada, chardonnay

90

Colour: bright golden. Nose: dry nuts, fragrant herbs, lees reduction notes. Palate: powerful, flavourful, good acidity, fine bead, fine bitter notes.

Castell Sant Antoni Brut de Postre BR Reserva
macabeo, xarel.lo, parellada, chardonnay

88

Colour: bright straw. Nose: fine lees, floral, fragrant herbs, expressive. Palate: powerful, flavourful, good acidity, fine bead, sweet.

Castell Sant Antoni Camí del Sot BN Reserva
macabeo, xarel.lo, parellada

93

Colour: bright golden. Nose: fine lees, dry nuts, fragrant herbs, complex. Palate: powerful, flavourful, good acidity, fine bead, fine bitter notes.

Castell Sant Antoni Camí del Sot Magnum BN Reserva
macabeo, xarel.lo, parellada, chardonnay
93
Colour: bright golden. Nose: fine lees, dry nuts, fragrant herbs, complex, toasty. Palate: powerful, flavourful, good acidity, fine bead, fine bitter notes.

Castell Sant Antoni Gran Barrica 2007 BN Gran Reserva
macabeo, xarel.lo, parellada, chardonnay
92
Colour: bright golden. Nose: dry nuts, fragrant herbs, complex, fine lees, macerated fruit, sweet spices. Palate: powerful, flavourful, good acidity, fine bead.

Castell Sant Antoni Gran Brut BR Gran Reserva
macabeo, xarel.lo, parellada, chardonnay
92
Colour: bright golden. Nose: fine lees, dry nuts, fragrant herbs, complex, toasty. Palate: powerful, flavourful, good acidity, fine bead, fine bitter notes.

Castell Sant Antoni Gran Brut Magnum BR Gran Reserva
macabeo, xarel.lo, parellada, chardonnay
91
Colour: bright golden. Nose: fragrant herbs, characterful, ripe fruit, dry nuts. Palate: powerful, flavourful, good acidity, fine bead, fine bitter notes.

Castell Sant Antoni Gran Reserva 2007 BN Gran Reserva
macabeo, xarel.lo, parellada, chardonnay
92
Colour: bright golden. Nose: fine lees, fragrant herbs, characterful, ripe fruit, dry nuts. Palate: powerful, flavourful, good acidity, fine bead, fine bitter notes.

Castell Sant Antoni Gran Reserva Magnum 2007 BN
macabeo, xarel.lo, parellada, chardonnay
88
Colour: bright golden. Nose: fine lees, dry nuts, fragrant herbs, aged wood nuances. Palate: powerful, flavourful, good acidity, fine bead, fine bitter notes.

Castell Sant Antoni Gran Rosat Pinot Noir BN Gran Reserva
pinot noir
88
Colour: rose. Nose: red berry notes, ripe fruit, fragrant herbs, expressive, toasty. Palate: powerful, balanced, flavourful.

Castell Sant Antoni Primvs Primvm BN Reserva
88
Colour: bright straw. Nose: medium intensity, fresh fruit, dried herbs, fine lees, floral. Palate: fresh, fruity, flavourful, good acidity.

Castell Sant Antoni Primvs Primvm BR Reserva
89
Colour: bright yellow. Nose: ripe fruit, fine lees, balanced, dried herbs. Palate: good acidity, flavourful, ripe fruit, long.

Castell Sant Antoni Primvs Rosado BR Reserva
88
Colour: rose. Nose: floral, ripe fruit, fragrant herbs, expressive. Palate: powerful, balanced, flavourful.

Castell Sant Antoni Torre de L'Homenatge 1999 BN
xarel.lo, macabeo, parellada
92
Colour: bright golden. Nose: dry nuts, fragrant herbs, complex, lees reduction notes. Palate: powerful, flavourful, good acidity, fine bead, fine bitter notes.

Castell Sant Antoni Torre de L'Homenatge 2003 BN Gran Reserva
xarel.lo, macabeo, parellada
94
Colour: bright golden. Nose: dry nuts, fragrant herbs, complex, fine lees, macerated fruit, sweet spices, expressive. Palate: powerful, flavourful, good acidity, fine bead, fine bitter notes, elegant.

CASTELLBLANCH
Avda. Casetes Mir, 2
08770 Sant Sadurní D'Anoia (Barcelona)
☎: +34 938 917 025
Fax: +34 938 910 126
www.castellblanch.com
castellblanch@castellblanch.es

Castellblanch Brut Zero 2010 BR Reserva
88
Colour: bright yellow. Nose: ripe fruit, fine lees, balanced, dried herbs. Palate: good acidity, flavourful, ripe fruit, long.

Castellblanch Dos Lustros 2008 BN Reserva
92
Colour: bright golden. Nose: fine lees, dry nuts, fragrant herbs, complex, toasty. Palate: powerful, flavourful, good acidity, fine bead, fine bitter notes.

Castellblanch Gran Cuveé 2009 BN Reserva
89
Colour: bright straw. Nose: fine lees, floral, fragrant herbs, expressive. Palate: powerful, flavourful, good acidity, fine bead, balanced.

Castellblanch Rosado Dulce 2012
86
Colour: rose. Nose: floral, red berry notes, ripe fruit, fragrant herbs, expressive. Palate: powerful, flavourful, sweet.

CASTELLROIG - FINCA SABATÉ I COCA
Ctra. De Sant Sadurní a Vilafranca (c-243a), km. 1
08739 Subirats (Barcelona)
☎: +34 938 911 927
Fax: +34 938 914 055
www.castellroig.com
info@castellroig.com

Castellroig 2011 BN Reserva
xarel.lo, macabeo, parellada
89
Colour: bright straw. Nose: fine lees, floral, fragrant herbs, expressive. Palate: powerful, flavourful, good acidity, fine bead, balanced.

Castellroig Xarel.lo BR
xarel.lo
88
Colour: bright yellow. Nose: fine lees, floral, fragrant herbs, expressive. Palate: powerful, flavourful, good acidity, fine bead, balanced.

Josep Coca Magnum BN Reserva
90
Colour: bright straw. Nose: scrubland, dried herbs, ripe fruit, fine lees. Palate: good acidity, balanced, powerful, fruity.

Sabaté i Coca Reserva Familiar BN Reserva
90
Colour: bright yellow. Nose: fine lees, dry nuts, fragrant herbs, complex, expressive. Palate: powerful, flavourful, good acidity, fine bead, fine bitter notes.

Sabaté i Coca Reserva Familiar 2010 BR
garnacha
87
Colour: rose. Nose: short, red berry notes. Palate: fruity, fresh, sweetness, good acidity.

CASTILLO PERELADA VINOS Y CAVAS
Avda. Barcelona, 78
08720 Vilafranca del Penedès
(Barcelona)
☎: +34 932 233 022
Fax: +34 932 231 370
www.castilloperelada.com
perelada@castilloperelada.com

Castillo Perelada BR
trepat, monastrell, pinot noir
87
Colour: rose. Nose: floral, red berry notes, ripe fruit, fragrant herbs, medium intensity. Palate: powerful, balanced, flavourful.

Castillo Perelada BR Reserva
macabeo, xarel.lo, parellada
89
Colour: bright golden. Nose: powerfull, ripe fruit, fragrant herbs, floral. Palate: spicy, fresh, fine bitter notes, good acidity.

Castillo Perelada 2011 BN
parellada, xarel.lo, macabeo
88
Colour: bright yellow. Nose: fine lees, balanced, dried herbs. Palate: good acidity, flavourful, ripe fruit, long.

Castillo Perelada Chardonnay 2011 BN
chardonnay
89
Colour: bright straw. Nose: fine lees, floral, fragrant herbs, sweet spices. Palate: powerful, flavourful, good acidity, fine bead, balanced.

Castillo Perelada Cuvée Especial 2012 BN
macabeo, parellada, xarel.lo, chardonnay
88
Colour: bright straw. Nose: medium intensity, fresh fruit, dried herbs, floral. Palate: fresh, fruity, flavourful.

Castillo Perelada Cuvée Especial Rosado 2012 BR
trepat
90
Colour: rose. Nose: floral, red berry notes, ripe fruit, fragrant herbs, expressive. Palate: powerful, balanced, flavourful.

Gran Claustro Cuvée Especial de Castillo Perelada 2008 BN Gran Reserva
chardonnay, pinot noir, parellada, xarel.lo

92

Colour: bright yellow. Nose: fine lees, dry nuts, fragrant herbs, complex, toasty. Palate: powerful, flavourful, good acidity, fine bead, fine bitter notes.

Gran Claustro de Castillo Perelada 2010 BN Reserva
chardonnay, pinot noir, parellada, macabeo

88

Colour: bright straw. Nose: fresh fruit, dried herbs, fine lees, floral. Palate: fresh, fruity, easy to drink, good finish.

Stars BN
parellada, xarel.lo, macabeo

89

Colour: bright yellow. Nose: ripe fruit, fine lees, balanced, dried herbs. Palate: good acidity, ripe fruit, long.

Torre Galatea Rosado BR
pinot noir, trepat, monastrell

86

Colour: rose. Nose: floral, red berry notes, ripe fruit, fragrant herbs. Palate: powerful, balanced, flavourful.

CAVA BERDIÉ
Les Conilleres (La Conillera Gran)
08732 Castellví de la Marca (Barcelona)
☎: +34 902 800 229
Fax: +34 938 919 738
www.cavaberdie.com
info@cavaberdie.com

Berdié Amor 2011 BR Reserva
macabeo, xarel.lo, parellada, garnacha

87

Colour: coppery red. Nose: floral, jasmine, fragrant herbs, candied fruit. Palate: fresh, fruity, flavourful, correct.

Berdié Fetish 2010 BR Reserva
garnacha, monastrell

86

Colour: rose. Nose: floral, red berry notes, ripe fruit, fragrant herbs. Palate: powerful, flavourful.

Berdié Gran Anyada 2004 Extra Brut Gran Reserva
macabeo, xarel.lo, parellada

86

Colour: bright golden. Nose: dry nuts, fragrant herbs, sweet spices, toasty. Palate: powerful, flavourful, good acidity, fine bead, fine bitter notes.

Berdié Gran Nature 2010 BN Gran Reserva
macabeo, xarel.lo, parellada

87

Colour: bright yellow. Nose: ripe fruit, fine lees, balanced, dried herbs. Palate: good acidity, flavourful, ripe fruit, long.

Berdié Nature 2011 BN Reserva
macabeo, xarel.lo, parellada

87

Colour: bright yellow. Nose: ripe fruit, fine lees, balanced, dried herbs. Palate: good acidity, flavourful, ripe fruit, long.

Berdié Rupestre 2011 BR Reserva
macabeo, xarel.lo, parellada

88

Colour: bright straw. Nose: fine lees, floral, fragrant herbs, expressive. Palate: powerful, flavourful, good acidity, fine bead, balanced.

CAVA CRISTINA COLOMER
Diputació, 58
08770 Sant Sadurní D'Anoia (Barcelona)
☎: +34 938 910 804
Fax: +34 938 913 034
www.cavescolomer.com
info@cavescolomer.com

1907 Colomer Costa Magnum BN Reserva
xarel.lo, macabeo, parellada

88

Colour: bright yellow. Nose: ripe fruit, fine lees, balanced, dried herbs, medium intensity. Palate: good acidity, flavourful, ripe fruit, long.

Colomer "er" BN Gran Reserva
xarel.lo, macabeo, parellada, chardonnay

90

Colour: bright yellow. Nose: ripe fruit, fine lees, balanced, dried herbs. Palate: good acidity, flavourful, ripe fruit, long.

Colomer "er" Magnum
2008 BN Gran Reserva
xarel.lo, macabeo, parellada, chardonnay
90
Colour: bright yellow. Nose: fine lees, dry nuts, fragrant herbs, complex, toasty. Palate: powerful, flavourful, good acidity, fine bead.

Colomer 1907 2012 BR Reserva
xarel.lo, macabeo, parellada
88
Colour: bright yellow. Nose: medium intensity, fresh fruit, dried herbs, fine lees, floral. Palate: fresh, fruity, flavourful, good acidity.

Colomer Brut D'Autor Homenatge Gaudí 2010 BR Gran Reserva
xarel.lo, macabeo, parellada, chardonnay
90
Colour: bright golden. Nose: fine lees, fragrant herbs, characterful, ripe fruit, dry nuts. Palate: powerful, flavourful, good acidity, fine bead, fine bitter notes.

Colomer Costa 1907 Cupatge BN Reserva
xarel.lo, macabeo, parellada
88
Colour: bright straw. Nose: medium intensity, fresh fruit, dried herbs, fine lees, floral. Palate: fresh, fruity, flavourful, good acidity.

Colomer Homenatge a Gaudí Pinot Noir Rosé BR Reserva
100% pinot noir
87
Colour: ochre. Nose: floral, ripe fruit, expressive, red berry notes, dried herbs, balsamic herbs. Palate: powerful, balanced, flavourful.

Colomer Prestige de Dali 2010 BN Gran Reserva
xarel.lo, macabeo, parellada, chardonnay
90
Colour: bright yellow. Nose: ripe fruit, fine lees, balanced, dried herbs. Palate: good acidity, flavourful, ripe fruit, long.

CAVA GUILERA
Ca l'Artigas, s/n
08739 Lavern-Subirats (Barcelona)
☎: +34 938 993 085
www.cavaguilera.com
info@cavaguilera.com

Guilera BN Reserva
macabeo, xarel.lo, parellada
88
Colour: bright straw. Nose: fine lees, floral, fragrant herbs, expressive. Palate: powerful, flavourful, good acidity, fine bead, balanced.

Guilera BR Reserva
macabeo, xarel.lo, parellada
86
Colour: bright yellow. Nose: ripe fruit, fine lees, balanced, dried herbs. Palate: good acidity, flavourful, ripe fruit, long.

Guilera 2006 BN Gran Reserva
macabeo, xarel.lo, parellada
90
Colour: bright golden. Nose: fine lees, fragrant herbs, characterful, ripe fruit, dry nuts. Palate: powerful, flavourful, good acidity, fine bead, fine bitter notes.

Guilera 2007 BN Gran Reserva
macabeo, xarel.lo, parellada
87
Colour: bright golden. Nose: fragrant herbs, characterful, ripe fruit, dry nuts. Palate: powerful, flavourful, good acidity, fine bead, fine bitter notes.

Guilera Rosado BR Reserva
garnacha, pinot noir
85

CAVA JOSEP M. FERRET GUASCH
Barri L'Alzinar, 68
08736 Font-Rubí (Barcelona)
☎: +34 938 979 037
Fax: +34 938 979 414
www.ferretguasch.com
ferretguasch@ferretguasch.com

Josep M. Ferret Guasch 2009 BN Reserva
89
Colour: bright yellow. Nose: ripe fruit, fine lees, balanced, dried herbs. Palate: good acidity, flavourful, long, fresh.

Josep M. Ferret Guasch Au79 2006 BR Reserva
87
Colour: bright straw. Nose: medium intensity, floral. Palate: fresh, fruity, flavourful, good acidity.

Josep M. Ferret Guasch Rosat 2007 BN Gran Reserva
84

CAVA MARTÍN SOLER

Finca La Serra de Sabanell, s/n
08736 Font-Rubí (Barcelona)
☎: +34 938 988 220
www.cavamartinsoler.com
info@cavamartinsoler.com

Margarita de Soler 2010 BN Gran Reserva
macabeo, xarel.lo, parellada
88
Colour: bright golden. Nose: fine lees, dry nuts, fragrant herbs, pattiserie. Palate: flavourful, good acidity, fine bead, fine bitter notes.

Martin Soler 2011 BR Reserva
macabeo, xarel.lo, parellada
89
Colour: bright yellow. Nose: fine lees, balanced, dried herbs, citrus fruit, candied fruit. Palate: good acidity, flavourful, easy to drink.

Martin Soler Rosado 2012 BN
trepat
87
Colour: rose. Nose: red berry notes, ripe fruit, dried herbs, dried flowers. Palate: powerful, balanced, flavourful, fine bitter notes.

CAVA MASTINELL

Ctra. de Vilafranca a St. Martí Sarroca, Km. 0,5
08720 Vilafranca del Penedès
(Barcelona)
☎: +34 938 170 586
Fax: +34 938 170 500
www.mastinell.com
info@mastinell.com

MasTinell Brut Real BR Reserva
88
Colour: bright straw. Nose: fine lees, fragrant herbs, expressive. Palate: powerful, flavourful, good acidity, fine bead, balanced.

MasTinell Brut Rosé 2008 BR Reserva
100% trepat
90
Colour: coppery red. Nose: floral, jasmine, fragrant herbs, candied fruit. Palate: fresh, fruity, flavourful, correct.

MasTinell Carpe Diem 2006 BN Reserva
91
Colour: bright yellow. Nose: ripe fruit, fine lees, balanced, faded flowers. Palate: good acidity, flavourful, ripe fruit, long.

MasTinell Cristina 2006 Extra Brut Gran Reserva
90
Colour: bright golden. Nose: fine lees, dry nuts, fragrant herbs, complex. Palate: powerful, flavourful, good acidity, fine bead, fine bitter notes.

MasTinell Nature Real 2006 BN Gran Reserva
89
Colour: bright yellow. Nose: fine lees, dry nuts, fragrant herbs, complex, toasty. Palate: powerful, flavourful, good acidity, fine bead, fine bitter notes.

CAVA MESTRES

Plaça Ajuntament, 8
08770 Sant Sadurní D'Anoia (Barcelona)
☎: +34 938 910 043
Fax: +34 938 911 611
www.mestres.es
cava@mestres.es

Mestre Clos Nostre Senyor 2004 BN Gran Reserva
93
Colour: bright golden. Nose: fine lees, dry nuts, fragrant herbs, complex, spicy, toasty. Palate: powerful, flavourful, good acidity, fine bead, fine bitter notes.

Mestres 1312 Resreva Especial BR Reserva
87
Colour: bright straw. Nose: medium intensity, fresh fruit, dried herbs, fine lees, dried flowers. Palate: fresh, fruity, flavourful, good acidity, easy to drink.

Mestres Coquet 2008 BN Gran Reserva
90
Colour: bright yellow. Nose: ripe fruit, fine lees, balanced, dried herbs, floral. Palate: good acidity, flavourful, long, elegant.

Mestres Visol 2007 BN Gran Reserva
90
Colour: bright yellow. Nose: fine lees, dry nuts, fragrant herbs, complex, toasty, sweet spices. Palate: powerful, flavourful, good acidity, fine bead, fine bitter notes.

CAVA REVERTÉ

Paseo Tomás García Rebull, 4
43885 Salomó (Tarragona)
☎: +34 977 629 246
Fax: +34 977 629 246
www.cavareverte.com
reverte@cavareverte.com

Cava Reverté "Electe" 2009 BN Reserva
88
Colour: bright yellow. Nose: balanced, dried herbs, floral, fine lees. Palate: good acidity, flavourful, long, fine bitter notes.

Cava Reverté 2010 BN Reserva
87
Colour: bright straw. Nose: ripe fruit, fine lees, balanced, dried herbs. Palate: good acidity, flavourful, ripe fruit, long.

CAVA VIDAL I FERRÉ
Nou, 2
43815 Les Pobles (Tarragona)
☎: +34 977 638 554
Fax: +34 977 638 554
www.vidaliferre.com
vidaliferre@vidaliferre.com

Vidal i Ferré 2010 BN Gran Reserva
macabeo, xarel.lo, parellada
88
Colour: bright yellow. Nose: fine lees, dry nuts, fragrant herbs, complex. Palate: powerful, flavourful, good acidity, fine bead, fine bitter notes.

Vidal i Ferré 2010 BN Reserva
macabeo, xarel.lo, parellada
87
Colour: bright yellow. Nose: ripe fruit, fine lees, balanced, dried herbs. Palate: good acidity, flavourful, ripe fruit, long.

Vidal i Ferré 2010 BR Reserva
macabeo, xarel.lo, parellada
86
Colour: bright straw. Nose: medium intensity, fresh fruit, dried herbs, fine lees, floral. Palate: fresh, fruity, flavourful, good acidity.

Vidal i Ferré 2010 SS Reserva
macabeo, xarel.lo, parellada
84

Vidal i Ferré Rosado 2011 BR Reserva
pinot noir
87
Colour: rose. Nose: floral, red berry notes, ripe fruit, fragrant herbs, expressive. Palate: powerful, balanced, flavourful.

BRUT
Reserva • Mètode Tradicional
CAVA
Vidal i Ferré

CAVAS FERRET
Avda. de Catalunya, 36
08736 Guardiola de Font-Rubí (Barcelona)
☎: +34 938 979 148
Fax: +34 938 979 285
www.cavasferret.com
comercial@cavasferret.com

Celia de Ferret Rosado 2003 BN Gran Reserva
pinot noir, garnacha
89
Colour: rose. Nose: floral, red berry notes, fragrant herbs, expressive. Palate: powerful, balanced, flavourful, fresh, fruity.

Celler del Mingo BR
88
Colour: bright straw. Nose: fresh fruit, dried herbs, fine lees, floral. Palate: fresh, fruity, flavourful, good acidity.

Ezequiel Ferret BN Gran Reserva
xarel.lo, parellada, macabeo
89
Colour: bright golden. Nose: fine lees, dry nuts, fragrant herbs, sweet spices. Palate: powerful, flavourful, good acidity, fine bead, fine bitter notes.

Ferret BN Gran Reserva
macabeo, parellada, xarel.lo
90
Colour: bright yellow. Nose: fine lees, dry nuts, fragrant herbs, complex, toasty. Palate: powerful, flavourful, good acidity, fine bead, elegant.

Ferret BN Reserva
macabeo, parellada, xarel.lo
90
Colour: bright yellow. Nose: ripe fruit, fine lees, balanced, fragrant herbs. Palate: good acidity, flavourful, ripe fruit, long.

Ferret BR Reserva
macabeo, parellada, xarel.lo
89
Colour: bright yellow. Nose: ripe fruit, fine lees, balanced, dried herbs, floral. Palate: good acidity, flavourful, ripe fruit, long.

Ferret Barrica 2005 BN Gran Reserva
parellada, xarel.lo, macabeo, chardonnay
87
Colour: bright yellow. Nose: fine lees, dry nuts, fragrant herbs, creamy oak. Palate: powerful, flavourful, good acidity, fine bead, fine bitter notes.

Ferret Magnum BN
90
Colour: bright straw. Nose: fine lees, floral, fragrant herbs, expressive. Palate: powerful, flavourful, good acidity, fine bead, balanced.

Ferret Petit 37,5 cl BN
85

Ferret Rosado BN Gran Reserva
88
Colour: rose. Nose: floral, red berry notes, ripe fruit, fragrant herbs, expressive. Palate: powerful, balanced, flavourful.

Ferret Rosado BR Reserva
trepat, garnacha, monastrell
87
Colour: coppery red. Nose: floral, jasmine, fragrant herbs, candied fruit. Palate: fresh, fruity, flavourful, correct.

CAVAS GRAMONA
Industria, 36
08770 Sant Sadurní D'Anoia (Barcelona)
☎: +34 938 910 113
Fax: +34 938 183 284
www.gramona.com
comunicacion@gramona.com

Gramona Argent 2009 BR Gran Reserva
100% chardonnay
93
Colour: bright straw. Nose: fine lees, floral, fragrant herbs, expressive, jasmine. Palate: powerful, flavourful, good acidity, fine bead, balanced.

Gramona Argent Rosé 2010 BN Gran Reserva
100% pinot noir
91
Colour: onion pink. Nose: elegant, candied fruit, dried flowers, fragrant herbs, red berry notes, medium intensity. Palate: light-bodied, flavourful, good acidity, long, spicy.

Gramona Celler Batlle 2002 BR Gran Reserva
xarel.lo, macabeo
93
Colour: bright golden. Nose: fine lees, dry nuts, fragrant herbs, complex. Palate: powerful, flavourful, good acidity, fine bead, fine bitter notes.

Gramona Celler Batlle 2004 BR Gran Reserva
97
Colour: bright golden. Nose: fine lees, dry nuts, fragrant herbs, complex, toasty, lactic notes, spicy. Palate: powerful, flavourful, good acidity, fine bead, fine bitter notes.

Gramona Enoteca Finca La Plana 2000 BN Gran Reserva
98
Colour: bright golden. Nose: dry nuts, fragrant herbs, complex, fine lees, macerated fruit, sweet spices, expressive. Palate: powerful, flavourful, good acidity, fine bead, fine bitter notes, elegant.

Gramona Enoteca Finca La Plana 2000 BR Gran Reserva
96
Colour: bright golden. Nose: dry nuts, fragrant herbs, complex, fine lees, macerated fruit, sweet spices, expressive. Palate: powerful, flavourful, good acidity, fine bead, fine bitter notes, elegant.

Gramona III Lustros 2006 BN Gran Reserva
93
Colour: bright golden. Nose: fragrant herbs, characterful, ripe fruit, dry nuts. Palate: powerful, flavourful, good acidity, fine bead, fine bitter notes.

Gramona Imperial 2007 BR Gran Reserva
91
Colour: bright golden. Nose: fine lees, dry nuts, fragrant herbs, toasty. Palate: powerful, flavourful, good acidity, fine bead, fine bitter notes.

Gramona Imperial Magnum 2009 BR Gran Reserva
92
Colour: bright yellow. Nose: fine lees, fragrant herbs, ripe fruit, dry nuts. Palate: flavourful, good acidity, fine bead, fine bitter notes.

CAVAS HILL

Bonavista, 2
08734 Moja-Olérdola (Barcelona)
☎: +34 938 900 588
Fax: +34 938 170 246
www.cavashill.com
cavashill@cavashill.com

Cavas Hill 1887 BR
macabeo, xarel.lo, chardonnay
84

Cavas Hill 1887 Rosado BR
garnacha, monastrell
85

Cavas Hill Artesanía BR Reserva
macabeo, xarel.lo, chardonnay
86
Colour: bright straw. Nose: medium intensity, fresh fruit, dried herbs, fine lees, floral. Palate: fresh, fruity, flavourful, good acidity.

Cavas Hill Vintage BR Reserva
macabeo, xarel.lo, chardonnay
87
Colour: bright yellow. Nose: ripe fruit, fine lees, balanced, dried herbs. Palate: good acidity, flavourful, ripe fruit, long.

Cavas Hill Vintage 2008 BN Gran Reserva
macabeo, xarel.lo, chardonnay
90
Colour: bright golden. Nose: fine lees, fragrant herbs, characterful, ripe fruit, dry nuts. Palate: powerful, flavourful, good acidity, fine bead, fine bitter notes.

CAVAS LAVERNOYA

Masia La Porxada
08729 Sant Marçal (Barcelona)
☎: +34 938 912 202
www.lavernoya.com
lavernoya@lavernoya.com

Lácrima Baccus BN
xarel.lo, macabeo, parellada
87
Colour: bright yellow. Nose: ripe fruit, fine lees, balanced, dried herbs. Palate: good acidity, flavourful, ripe fruit, long.

Lácrima Baccus BR
84

Lácrima Baccus Heretat BN Reserva
87
Colour: bright straw. Nose: medium intensity, fresh fruit, dried herbs, fine lees. Palate: fresh, fruity, flavourful, good acidity.

Lácrima Baccus Heretat BR
82

Lácrima Baccus Primerísimo BR Gran Reserva
87
Colour: bright straw. Nose: fine lees, floral, fragrant herbs. Palate: powerful, flavourful, good acidity, fine bead, balanced.

Lácrima Baccus Summum BN Gran Reserva
89
Colour: bright golden. Nose: fine lees, dry nuts, fragrant herbs, complex. Palate: powerful, flavourful, good acidity, fine bead, fine bitter notes.

CAVES EL MAS FERRER

Caves El Mas Ferrer
08739 Subirats (Barcelona)
☎: +34 938 988 292
www.elmasferrer.com
info@elmasferrer.com

El Mas Ferrer 2011 BR Reserva
89
Colour: bright straw. Nose: fine lees, floral, fragrant herbs, expressive. Palate: powerful, flavourful, good acidity, fine bead, balanced.

El Mas Ferrer 2012 BN Reserva
87
Colour: bright straw. Nose: fine lees, floral, fragrant herbs, expressive. Palate: powerful, flavourful, good acidity, fine bead, balanced.

El Mas Ferrer Familiar 2009 BN Gran Reserva
89
Colour: bright straw. Nose: fine lees, floral, fragrant herbs, expressive. Palate: powerful, flavourful, good acidity, fine bead, balanced.

El Mas Ferrer Rosat 2011 BR Reserva
85

El Mas Ferrer Segle XXI 2010 Extra Brut Gran Reserva
90
Colour: bright golden. Nose: fine lees, fragrant herbs, characterful, ripe fruit, dry nuts. Palate: powerful, flavourful, good acidity, fine bead, fine bitter notes.

CAVES MUSCÀNDIA

Avernó, 4
08770 Sant Sadurní D'Anoia (Barcelona)
☎: +34 937 428 239
www.muscandia.com
info@cavamuscandia.com

Cava Muscàndia 2008 BN Gran Reserva
86
Colour: bright yellow. Nose: fine lees, dry nuts, fragrant herbs, complex. Palate: powerful, flavourful, good acidity, fine bead, fine bitter notes.

Cava Muscàndia 2011 BR Reserva
86
Colour: bright straw. Nose: fine lees, floral, fragrant herbs. Palate: powerful, flavourful, good acidity, fine bead, balanced.

Cava Muscàndia Magnum 2010 BR Gran Reserva
89
Colour: bright yellow. Nose: ripe fruit, fine lees, balanced, dried herbs. Palate: good acidity, flavourful, ripe fruit, long.

Cava Muscàndia Rosé 2010 BR Reserva
100% pinot noir
87
Colour: coppery red. Nose: floral, jasmine, fragrant herbs, candied fruit. Palate: fresh, fruity, flavourful, correct.

CAVES NAVERÁN

Can Parellada
08775 Torrelavit (Barcelona)
☎: +34 938 988 274
Fax: +34 938 989 027
www.naveran.com
naveran@naveran.com

Naveran Millesime 2011 BN
macabeo, chardonnay, parellada, xarel.lo
92
Colour: bright yellow. Nose: floral, balanced, ripe fruit, citrus fruit. Palate: rich, flavourful, long, good acidity, fine bitter notes.

Naveran Perles Blanques 2011 BR
chardonnay, pinot noir
91
Colour: bright straw. Nose: fine lees, fragrant herbs, expressive, smoky. Palate: powerful, flavourful, good acidity, fine bead, balanced.

Naverán Perles Roses Pinot Noir 2011 BR
pinot noir
93
Colour: coppery red. Nose: floral, jasmine, fragrant herbs, candied fruit, balanced. Palate: fresh, fruity, flavourful, correct, elegant.

Odisea Naverán 2011 BN
chardonnay, parellada
91
Colour: bright yellow. Nose: balanced, dry nuts, dried flowers, elegant, citrus fruit. Palate: balanced, fine bitter notes, good acidity, spicy.

CELLER CARLES ANDREU

Sant Sebastià, 19
43423 Pira (Tarragona)
☎: +34 977 887 404
Fax: +34 977 887 427
www.cavandreu.com
celler@cavandreu.com

Cava Brut Carles Andreu BR
parellada, macabeo
90
Colour: bright straw. Nose: medium intensity, fresh fruit, dried herbs, fine lees, floral. Palate: fresh, fruity, flavourful, good acidity.

Cava Brut Nature Carles Andreu BN
parellada, macabeo
88
Colour: bright yellow. Nose: ripe fruit, fine lees, balanced, dried herbs. Palate: good acidity, flavourful, ripe fruit, long.

Cava Reserva Barrica Brut Nature Carles Andreu BN Reserva
parellada, macabeo, chardonnay
91
Colour: bright golden. Nose: fine lees, dry nuts, fragrant herbs, complex, toasty. Palate: powerful, flavourful, good acidity, fine bead, fine bitter notes.

Cava Reserva Brut Nature Carles Andreu 2010 BN
parellada, macabeo, chardonnay
90
Colour: bright yellow. Nose: ripe fruit, fine lees, balanced, dried herbs. Palate: good acidity, flavourful, ripe fruit, long.

Cava Rosado Trepat Brut Carles Andreu BR
trepat
87
Colour: light cherry. Nose: medium intensity, ripe fruit, faded flowers. Palate: flavourful, good acidity, fruity.

Cava Rosado Trepat Reserva Barrica Brut Carles Andreu BR
trepat
91
Colour: coppery red. Nose: floral, jasmine, fragrant herbs, candied fruit, spicy. Palate: fresh, fruity, flavourful. Personality.

Semiseco Carles Andreu SS
parellada, macabeo

86
Colour: bright yellow. Nose: powerfull, ripe fruit, dried flowers. Palate: fruity, flavourful, easy to drink, correct.

CELLER DEL RAVAL
Vinyals, 161
08223 Terrassa (Barcelona)
☎: +34 937 330 695
Fax: +34 937 333 605
www.angelcava.com
jcernuda@asociadis.com

Ángel Brut De Bruts 2011 BR Reserva
xarel.lo, macabeo, parellada

87
Colour: bright straw. Nose: fine lees, floral, fragrant herbs, sweet spices. Palate: powerful, flavourful, good acidity, fine bead, balanced.

Ángel Cupatge 2012 BN Reserva
chardonnay, macabeo, xarel.lo, parellada

86
Colour: bright yellow. Nose: balanced, dried herbs, fresh. Palate: good acidity, flavourful, long.

Ángel Noir 2010 BR
pinot noir, garnacha, trepat

86
Colour: rose. Nose: floral, red berry notes, ripe fruit, fragrant herbs. Palate: powerful, balanced, flavourful.

CELLER VELL
Partida Mas Solanes, s/n
08770 Sant Sadurní D'Anoia (Barcelona)
☎: +34 938 910 290
Fax: +34 938 183 246
www.cellervell.com
info@cellervell.com

Celler Vell 2010 BN Reserva
xarel.lo, macabeo, parellada

90
Colour: bright straw. Nose: fine lees, floral, fragrant herbs, expressive. Palate: powerful, flavourful, good acidity, fine bead, balanced.

Celler Vell Cuvèe Les Solanes 2008 BN Reserva
xarel.lo, chardonnay, pinot noir

90
Colour: bright straw. Nose: medium intensity, fresh fruit, dried herbs, fine lees, spicy, grassy. Palate: fresh, fruity, flavourful, good acidity.

Estruch Eco 2010 BN Gran Reserva
pinot noir, chardonnay

89 ❀
Colour: bright straw. Nose: floral, jasmine, fragrant herbs, candied fruit, citrus fruit. Palate: fresh, fruity, flavourful, correct.

CELLERS CAROL VALLÈS
Can Parellada, s/n - Corral del Mestre
08739 Subirats (Barcelona)
☎: +34 938 989 078
Fax: +34 938 988 413
www.cellerscarol.com
info@cellerscarol.com

Guillem Carol 2009 BN Gran Reserva
90
Colour: bright straw. Nose: fresh fruit, dried herbs, fine lees, floral. Palate: fresh, fruity, flavourful, good acidity.

Guillem Carol 2009 Extra Brut Gran Reserva
87
Colour: bright straw. Nose: fresh fruit, dried herbs, fine lees, floral, citrus fruit. Palate: fresh, fruity, flavourful, good acidity.

Guillem Carol Barrica 2008 BN Gran Reserva
91
Colour: bright golden. Nose: fine lees, dry nuts, fragrant herbs, complex. Palate: powerful, flavourful, good acidity, fine bead, fine bitter notes.

Guillem Carol Millenium 2005 BR Gran Reserva
91
Colour: bright golden. Nose: fine lees, fragrant herbs, characterful, ripe fruit, dry nuts. Palate: powerful, flavourful, good acidity, fine bead, fine bitter notes, rich.

Parellada i Faura 2012 BN Reserva
87
Colour: bright yellow. Nose: ripe fruit, fine lees, balanced, dried herbs. Palate: good acidity, flavourful, long, fruity.

Parellada i Faura Millenium 2011 BN Reserva
84

CELLERS GRAU DÒRIA
Plaza Eliseo Oliver, 4 bis
08811 Canyelles (Barcelona)
☎: +34 938 973 263
Fax: +34 938 973 263
www.graudoria.com
info@graudoria.com

Grau Dòria Rosado 2012 BR
garnacha, monastrell, pinot noir
87
Colour: rose. Nose: floral, red berry notes, ripe fruit, fragrant herbs, expressive. Palate: powerful, balanced, flavourful.

Mercè Grau Doria 2008 BN Gran Reserva
xarel.lo, macabeo, parellada
90
Colour: bright golden. Nose: fine lees, dry nuts, fragrant herbs, complex, citrus fruit. Palate: powerful, flavourful, good acidity, fine bead, fine bitter notes.

Nature Reserva de Grau Dòria BN Reserva
xarel.lo, chardonnay, parellada
88
Colour: bright yellow. Nose: ripe fruit, fine lees, balanced, dried herbs. Palate: good acidity, flavourful, ripe fruit, long.

CELLERS PLANAS ALBAREDA
Ctra. Guardiola, Km. 3
08735 Vilobí del Penedès (Barcelona)
☎: +34 938 922 143
Fax: +34 938 922 143
www.planasalbareda.com
planasalbareda@yahoo.es

Planas Albareda 2010 BN Reserva
macabeo, xarel.lo, parellada
88
Colour: bright straw. Nose: fine lees, floral, fragrant herbs, expressive. Palate: powerful, flavourful, good acidity, fine bead, balanced.

Planas Albareda 2011 BN
macabeo, xarel.lo, parellada
83

Planas Albareda Rosat 2012 BR
84

CHOZAS CARRASCAL
Vereda San Antonio POl. Ind. Catastral,
16 Parcelas 136-138
46340 San Antonio de Requena
(Valencia)
☎: +34 963 410 395
Fax: +34 963 168 067
www.chozascarrascal.es
chozas@chozascarrascal.es

El Cava de Chozas Carrascal 2012 BN Reserva
chardonnay, macabeo
93 ⚜
Colour: bright straw. Nose: fine lees, dry nuts, fragrant herbs, complex, toasty. Palate: powerful, flavourful, good acidity, fine bead, fine bitter notes.

CODORNÍU
Avda. Jaume Codorníu, s/n
08770 Sant Sadurní D'Anoia (Barcelona)
☎: +34 938 183 232
www.codorniu.com
codinfo@codorniu.com

Anna de Codorníu BR
87
Colour: bright straw. Nose: medium intensity, dried herbs, fine lees, dry nuts. Palate: fresh, fruity, flavourful, good acidity.

Anna de Codorníu Blanc de Blancs BR
pinot noir
90
Colour: bright yellow. Nose: medium intensity, fresh fruit, dried herbs, fine lees, floral. Palate: fresh, fruity, flavourful, good acidity, balanced.

Anna de Codorníu Blanc de Noirs BR
100% pinot noir
88
Colour: yellow. Nose: fine lees, floral, expressive. Palate: powerful, flavourful, good acidity, fine bead, balanced, easy to drink.

Anna de Codorníu Rosé BR
87
Colour: light cherry. Nose: floral, red berry notes, expressive, medium intensity. Palate: balanced, flavourful, easy to drink.

Gran Codorníu Chardonnay BN Reserva
100% chardonnay
89
Colour: bright yellow. Nose: ripe fruit, fine lees, balanced, dried herbs. Palate: good acidity, flavourful, ripe fruit, long.

Gran Codorníu Chardonnay
2007 BN Gran Reserva
100% chardonnay

92

Colour: bright golden. Nose: fine lees, dry nuts, fragrant herbs, complex, toasty, faded flowers. Palate: powerful, flavourful, good acidity, fine bead, fine bitter notes.

Gran Codorníu Pinot Noir
2007 BR Gran Reserva
100% pinot noir

93

Colour: bright golden. Nose: fine lees, fragrant herbs, characterful, ripe fruit, dry nuts. Palate: powerful, flavourful, good acidity, fine bead, fine bitter notes.

Gran Codorníu Pinot Noir Vintage 2012 BR
100% pinot noir

89

Colour: light cherry. Nose: fresh fruit, dried herbs, fine lees, floral. Palate: fresh, fruity, flavourful, good acidity.

Gran Codorníu Xarel.lo
2007 BR Gran Reserva
100% xarel.lo

93

Colour: bright yellow. Nose: fine lees, ripe fruit, dry nuts, expressive. Palate: powerful, flavourful, good acidity, fine bead, fine bitter notes.

Jaume Codorníu 2009 BR Gran Reserva
pinot noir, chardonnay

92

Colour: bright golden. Nose: fine lees, dry nuts, fragrant herbs, complex, toasty. Palate: powerful, flavourful, good acidity, fine bead, fine bitter notes.

Non Plus Ultra BN
parellada, macabeo, xarel.lo

89

Colour: bright yellow. Nose: ripe fruit, fine lees, balanced, dried herbs. Palate: good acidity, flavourful, ripe fruit, long.

Reina Mª Cristina Blanc de Noirs
Vintage 2011 BR Reserva
pinot noir

91

Colour: bright yellow. Nose: fine lees, floral, fragrant herbs, expressive. Palate: powerful, flavourful, good acidity, fine bead, balanced.

COOPERATIVA AGRÍCOLA DE BARBERÀ

Carrer Comerç, 40
43422 Barberà de la Conca (Tarragona)
☎: +34 977 887 035
www.coop-barbera.com
cobarbera@doconcadebarbera.com

Castell Comanda 2011 BN Reserva
85

Castell de la Comanda 2011 BR Reserva
85

CUM LAUDE

08770 Sant Sadurní D'Anoia (Barcelona)
☎: +34 941 454 050
Fax: +34 941 454 529
www.bodegasriojanas.com
bodega@bodegasriojanas.com

Cum Laude BN Reserva
85

DOMINIO DE LA VEGA

Ctra. Madrid - Valencia, N-III Km. 270,6
46390 Requena (Valencia)
☎: +34 962 320 570
Fax: +34 962 320 330
www.dominiodelavega.com
dv@dominiodelavega.com

Artemayor IV BN
chardonnay, macabeo

91

Colour: bright yellow. Nose: ripe fruit, fine lees, balanced, dried herbs. Palate: good acidity, flavourful, ripe fruit, long.

Dominio de la Vega BN
macabeo

88

Colour: bright yellow. Nose: fine lees, dried herbs, dry nuts, sweet spices. Palate: good acidity, flavourful, ripe fruit.

Dominio de la Vega BR
macabeo

87

Colour: bright yellow. Nose: ripe fruit, fine lees, balanced, dried herbs, floral. Palate: good acidity, flavourful, ripe fruit, long.

Dominio de la Vega 2011 BN Reserva
macabeo, chardonnay

89

Colour: bright straw. Nose: fresh fruit, dried herbs, fine lees, floral. Palate: fresh, fruity, flavourful, good acidity.

Dominio de la Vega Pinot Noir 2009 BR
pinot noir

87

Colour: rose. Nose: floral, red berry notes, ripe fruit, fragrant herbs, expressive. Palate: powerful, balanced, flavourful.

Dominio de la Vega Reserva Especial 2011 BR Reserva
macabeo, chardonnay

90

Colour: bright golden. Nose: dry nuts, fragrant herbs, complex, fine lees, macerated fruit, sweet spices. Palate: powerful, flavourful, good acidity, fine bead, fine bitter notes.

EMENDIS
Barrio de Sant Marçal, 67
08732 Castellet i La Gornal (Barcelona)
☎: +34 938 919 790
Fax: +34 938 918 169
www.emendis.es
avalles@emendis.es

Emendis BN Gran Reserva
90

Colour: yellow. Nose: fine lees, dry nuts, fragrant herbs, complex, toasty. Palate: powerful, flavourful, good acidity, fine bead, fine bitter notes.

Emendis BR
88

Colour: bright straw. Nose: medium intensity, fresh fruit, dried herbs, fine lees, floral. Palate: fresh, fruity, flavourful, good acidity.

Emendis Imum BN Reserva
89

Colour: bright yellow. Nose: ripe fruit, fine lees, dried herbs, slightly evolved. Palate: good acidity, flavourful.

Emendis Rosé BR
pinot noir

87

Colour: light cherry, bright. Nose: balanced, red berry notes, floral. Palate: fruity, correct, good finish, good acidity.

EMW GRANDES VINOS DE ESPAÑA
Sánchez Picazo, 53
30332 Balsapintada (Fuente Alamo)
(Murcia)
☎: +34 968 151 520
Fax: +34 968 151 539
www.emw.es
info@emw.es

Casa Rojo Macabeo Chardonnay BN
macabeo, chardonnay

88 🌼

Colour: bright yellow. Nose: ripe fruit, fine lees, balanced, faded flowers. Palate: good acidity, flavourful.

EPILENSE DE VINOS Y VIÑEDOS, THE GARAGE WINE
San Agustín, 7
50019 Epila (Zaragoza)
☎: +34 669 148 771
www.thegaragewine.com
info@thegaragewine.com

Latidos de Vino I Love Barrica 2010 T Barrica
85

FERMI BOHIGAS
Finca Can Maciá s/n
08711 Òdena (Barcelona)
☎: +34 938 048 100
Fax: +34 938 032 366
www.bohigas.es
aministracio@bohigas.es

Bohigas BN Gran Reserva
macabeo, xarel.lo, parellada, chardonnay

89

Colour: bright yellow. Nose: ripe fruit, fine lees, balanced, dried herbs. Palate: good acidity, flavourful, ripe fruit, long.

Bohigas BN Reserva
macabeo, xarel.lo, parellada

89

Colour: bright straw. Nose: fine lees, floral, fragrant herbs, expressive. Palate: powerful, flavourful, good acidity, fine bead, balanced.

BOHIGAS
BRUT NATURE
CAVA

Les vinyes i caves de Bohigas es troben en l'entorn privilegiat de la conca de l'Anoia.
Los viñedos y casas de Bohigas se encuentran en el entorno privilegiado de la cuenca del Anoia.

RESERVA

Bohigas BR Reserva
macabeo, xarel.lo, parellada

88

Colour: bright straw. Nose: fresh fruit, dried herbs, fine lees, floral. Palate: fresh, fruity, flavourful, good acidity.

Noa de Fermí Bohigas BN
pinot noir, xarel.lo

89

Colour: bright yellow. Nose: ripe fruit, fine lees, balanced, white flowers. Palate: good acidity, flavourful, ripe fruit, long.

FERRE I CATASUS
Masía Gustems s/n Ctra. Sant Sadurní, Km. 8
08792 La Granada (Barcelona)
☎: +34 647 806 896
Fax: +34 938 974 708
www.ferreicatasus.com
info@ferreicatasus.com

Ferré i Catasús 2011 BN Reserva
macabeo, xarel.lo, parellada, chardonnay

89

Colour: bright yellow. Nose: ripe fruit, fine lees, balanced, dried herbs. Palate: good acidity, flavourful, ripe fruit, long.

Ferré i Catasús 2011 BR Reserva
macabeo, xarel.lo, parellada, chardonnay

87

Colour: bright golden. Nose: fine lees, fragrant herbs, characterful, ripe fruit, dry nuts. Palate: powerful, flavourful, fine bead, fine bitter notes.

Ferré i Catasús Rosé 2011 BR
pinot noir

83

Mas Suau 2012 BN
macabeo, xarel.lo, parellada

88

Colour: bright straw. Nose: medium intensity, fresh fruit, dried herbs, fine lees, floral. Palate: fresh, fruity, flavourful, good acidity.

Mas Suau Rose 2012 BR
trepat, monastrell

78

FINCA TORREMILANOS
Finca Torremilanos
09400 Aranda de Duero (Burgos)
☎: +34 947 512 852
Fax: +34 947 508 044
www.torremilanos.com
reservas@torremilanos.com

Peñalba-López 2012 BN
84 🌷

FINCA VALLDOSERA
Masia Les Garrigues, Urb. Can Trabal
08734 Olèrdola (Barcelona)
☎: +34 938 143 047
Fax: +34 938 935 590
www.fincavalldosera.com
general@fincavalldosera.com

Cava Subirat Parent 2010 BN
subirat parent

92

Colour: bright straw. Nose: fresh fruit, dried herbs, fine lees, floral, sweet spices, honeyed notes. Palate: fresh, fruity, flavourful, good acidity. Personality.

Cava Valldosera 2010 BN Reserva

88

Colour: bright yellow. Nose: ripe fruit, fine lees, balanced, dried herbs. Palate: good acidity, flavourful, ripe fruit, long.

MS 4.7 2009 BN Gran Reserva

89

Colour: bright golden. Nose: fine lees, dry nuts, fragrant herbs, complex, toasty. Palate: powerful, flavourful, good acidity, fine bead, fine bitter notes.

FREIXA RIGAU
Santa Llucía, 15
17750 Capmany (Girona)
☎: +34 972 549 012
Fax: +34 972 549 106
www.grupoliveda.com
comercial@grupoliveda.com

Familia Oliveda 2011 BN Reserva

87

Colour: bright straw. Nose: medium intensity, fresh fruit, dried herbs, fine lees, floral. Palate: fresh, fruity, flavourful, good acidity.

Familia Oliveda 2012 BR

86

Colour: bright straw. Nose: fine lees, floral, fragrant herbs, expressive. Palate: powerful, flavourful, good acidity.

Freixa Rigau Nature Mil.lèssima Reserva Familiar 2010 BN

87

Colour: bright yellow. Nose: ripe fruit, fine lees, balanced. Palate: good acidity, flavourful, ripe fruit, long.

Gran Rigau 2009 BN Reserva

86

Colour: bright straw. Nose: medium intensity, fresh fruit, dried herbs, fine lees, floral. Palate: fresh, fruity, flavourful, good acidity.

Gran Rigau Chardonnay 2009 BN
100% chardonnay

86

Colour: bright yellow. Nose: ripe fruit, fine lees, balanced, white flowers. Palate: good acidity, flavourful, ripe fruit, long.

Gran Rigau Pinot Noir 2009 BN
100% pinot noir

87

Colour: rose. Nose: floral, red berry notes, ripe fruit, fragrant herbs, expressive. Palate: powerful, balanced, flavourful.

FREIXENET
Joan Sala, 2
08770 Sant Sadurní D'Anoia (Barcelona)
☎: +34 938 917 000
Fax: +34 938 183 095
www.freixenet.es
freixenet@freixenet.es

Casa Sala 2005 BR Gran Reserva
parellada, xarel.lo

93

Colour: bright golden. Nose: fine lees, fragrant herbs, characterful, ripe fruit, dry nuts. Palate: powerful, flavourful, good acidity, fine bead, fine bitter notes.

Cordón Negro BR
parellada, macabeo, xarel.lo

88

Colour: bright straw. Nose: medium intensity, fresh fruit, dried herbs, fine lees, floral. Palate: fresh, fruity, flavourful, good acidity.

Cuvée D.S. 2007 BR Gran Reserva
macabeo, xarel.lo, parellada

90

Colour: bright yellow. Nose: ripe fruit, fine lees, balanced, dried herbs. Palate: good acidity, flavourful, ripe fruit, long.

Elyssia Gran Cuvée BR Reserva
chardonnay, macabeo, parellada, pinot noir

88

Colour: bright straw. Nose: fine lees, floral, fragrant herbs, expressive. Palate: powerful, flavourful, good acidity, fine bead, balanced.

Elyssia Pinot Noir Rosé BR Reserva
pinot noir

88

Colour: coppery red. Nose: fragrant herbs, fruit preserve. Palate: fresh, fruity, flavourful, correct.

Freixenet 2009 BN Reserva
macabeo, xarel.lo, parellada

89

Colour: bright yellow. Nose: ripe fruit, fine lees, balanced, dried herbs. Palate: good acidity, flavourful, ripe fruit, long.

Freixenet Carta Nevada BR
macabeo, xarel.lo, parellada

87

Colour: bright straw. Nose: medium intensity, fresh fruit, dried herbs, fine lees, floral. Palate: fresh, fruity, flavourful, good acidity.

Freixenet Malvasía B Gran Reserva
malvasía

87

Colour: bright golden. Nose: characterful, fruit preserve, honeyed notes. Palate: sweetness, flavourful.

Freixenet Monastrell Xarel.lo
2009 BR Gran Reserva
monastrell, xarel.lo

91

Colour: bright straw. Nose: fine lees, floral, fragrant herbs, expressive. Palate: powerful, flavourful, good acidity, fine bead, balanced.

Freixenet Trepat 2011 BR Reserva
trepat

90

Colour: coppery red. Nose: floral, jasmine, fragrant herbs, candied fruit. Palate: fresh, fruity, flavourful, correct.

Meritum 2008 BR Gran Reserva xarel.lo, macabeo, parellada

92

Colour: bright golden. Nose: fine lees, dry nuts, fragrant herbs, complex, toasty. Palate: powerful, flavourful, good acidity, fine bead, fine bitter notes.

Reserva Real BR Gran Reserva
macabeo, xarel.lo, parellada

95

Colour: bright golden. Nose: fine lees, dry nuts, fragrant herbs, complex, toasty. Palate: powerful, flavourful, good acidity, fine bead, fine bitter notes.

GASTÓN COTY S.A.
Avernó, 28-30
08770 Sant Sadurní D'Anoia (Barcelona)
☎: +34 938 183 602
Fax: +34 938 913 461
www.lorigancava.com
lorigan@lorigancava.com

Aire de L'O de L'Origan BN

91

Colour: bright straw. Nose: medium intensity, fresh fruit, dried herbs, fine lees, floral. Palate: fresh, fruity, flavourful, good acidity.

L'Origan BN

93

Colour: bright golden. Nose: fine lees, dry nuts, fragrant herbs, complex, toasty. Palate: powerful, flavourful, good acidity, fine bead, fine bitter notes.

L'Origan Rosat BN
90
Colour: coppery red. Nose: floral, jasmine, fragrant herbs, candied fruit. Palate: fresh, fruity, flavourful, correct.

GIRÓ DEL GORNER
Finca Giró del Gorner, s/n
08797 Puigdálber (Barcelona)
☎: +34 938 988 032
www.girodelgorner.com
gorner@girodelgorner.com

Giró del Gorner 2006
BN Gran Reserva
macabeo, xarel.lo, parellada
88
Colour: bright yellow. Nose: fine lees, dry nuts, fragrant herbs, sweet spices. Palate: powerful, flavourful, good acidity, fine bead, fine bitter notes.

Giró del Gorner 2006 BR Gran Reserva
macabeo, xarel.lo, parellada
88
Colour: bright golden. Nose: fine lees, dry nuts, fragrant herbs, toasty. Palate: powerful, flavourful, good acidity, fine bead, fine bitter notes.

Giró del Gorner 2010 BN Reserva
macabeo, xarel.lo, parellada
87
Colour: bright straw. Nose: fine lees, floral, fragrant herbs, dry nuts. Palate: powerful, flavourful, good acidity, fine bead.

Giró del Gorner 2010 BR Reserva
macabeo, xarel.lo, parellada
89
Colour: bright straw. Nose: medium intensity, fresh fruit, dried herbs, fine lees, floral. Palate: fresh, fruity, flavourful, good acidity, easy to drink.

Pinot Noir Giró del Gorner Rosado 2013 BR
100% pinot noir
88
Colour: coppery red. Nose: floral, jasmine, fragrant herbs, candied fruit. Palate: fresh, fruity, flavourful, correct, easy to drink.

GIRÓ RIBOT, S.L.
Finca El Pont, s/n
08792 Santa Fe del Penedès (Barcelona)
☎: +34 938 974 050
Fax: +34 938 974 311
www.giroribot.es
giroribot@giroribot.es

Excelsus 100 Magnum
2004 BN Gran Reserva
93
Colour: bright golden. Nose: fine lees, dry nuts, fragrant herbs, complex, toasty. Palate: powerful, flavourful, good acidity, fine bead, fine bitter notes.

Giró Ribot AB Origine 2009
BN Gran Reserva
88
Colour: bright yellow. Nose: medium intensity, citrus fruit, white flowers, spicy, dry nuts. Palate: fruity, spicy, good acidity.

Giró Ribot AB Origine 2011 BR Reserva
86
Colour: bright straw. Nose: floral, fragrant herbs, medium intensity. Palate: flavourful, good acidity, balanced, correct.

Giró Ribot AB Origine Rosé 2012 BR
89
Colour: rose, light cherry. Nose: floral, red berry notes, ripe fruit, expressive. Palate: powerful, balanced, flavourful.

Giró Ribot Avant 2010 BR Reserva
93
Colour: bright yellow. Nose: fine lees, floral, fragrant herbs, expressive, balsamic herbs. Palate: powerful, flavourful, good acidity, fine bead, balanced, elegant.

Giró Ribot Divinis Magnum
2008 BN Reserva
93
Colour: bright golden. Nose: fine lees, dry nuts, fragrant herbs, complex, toasty. Palate: powerful, flavourful, good acidity, fine bead, fine bitter notes.

Giró Ribot Mare 2008 BN Gran Reserva
92
Colour: bright straw. Nose: fine lees, dry nuts, fragrant herbs, complex, toasty. Palate: powerful, flavourful, good acidity, fine bead, fine bitter notes, balanced.

Giró Ribot Mare Magnum
2008 BN Gran Reserva
92
Colour: bright yellow. Nose: fine lees, dry nuts, fragrant herbs, complex, toasty. Palate: powerful, flavourful, good acidity, fine bead, fine bitter notes.

Giró Ribot Tendencias 2010 Extra Brut
87
Colour: bright straw. Nose: medium intensity, fresh fruit, dried herbs, fine lees, floral. Palate: fresh, fruity, flavourful, good acidity.

Giró Ribot Unplugged Rosado 2011 BR Reserva
pinot noir
93
Colour: coppery red. Nose: floral, jasmine, fragrant herbs, candied fruit, expressive. Palate: fresh, fruity, flavourful, correct, balanced, elegant. Personality.

Paul Cheneau 2011 BR Reserva
88
Colour: bright straw. Nose: medium intensity, fresh fruit, dried herbs, fine lees, floral. Palate: fresh, fruity, flavourful, good acidity.

GRIMAU DE PUJADES

Barri Sant Sepulcre s/n
08734 Olerdola (Barcelona)
☎: +34 938 918 031
www.grimau.com
grimau@grimau.com

Grimau BN
xarel.lo, macabeo, parellada
89
Colour: bright yellow. Nose: ripe fruit, fine lees, balanced, spicy. Palate: good acidity, flavourful, ripe fruit, long.

Grimau BR
xarel.lo, macabeo, parellada
88
Colour: bright yellow. Nose: balanced, expressive, ripe fruit, citrus fruit, faded flowers. Palate: flavourful, fine bitter notes, good acidity.

Grimau Reserva Familiar BN
chardonnay, xarel.lo, macabeo, parellada
89
Colour: bright yellow. Nose: ripe fruit, fine lees, balanced, dried herbs. Palate: good acidity, flavourful, ripe fruit, long.

Trencadís BN
xarel.lo, macabeo, parellada, chardonnay
88
Colour: bright straw. Nose: medium intensity, fresh fruit, fine lees. Palate: fresh, fruity, flavourful, good acidity.

Trencadís Rosat BN
85

HEREDAD SEGURA VIUDAS
Ctra. Sant Sadurní a St. Pere de Riudebitlles, Km. 5
08775 Torrelavit (Barcelona)
☎: +34 938 917 070
Fax: +34 938 996 006
www.seguraviudas.com
seguraviudas@seguraviudas.es

Aria BN Reserva
macabeo, xarel.lo
88
Colour: bright straw. Nose: fresh fruit, dried herbs, fine lees, floral. Palate: fresh, fruity, flavourful, good acidity.

Conde de Caralt BR
macabeo, xarel.lo, parellada
87
Colour: bright straw. Nose: medium intensity, fresh fruit, dried herbs, fine lees, floral. Palate: fresh, fruity, flavourful, good acidity.

Conde de Caralt Blanc de Blancs BR
macabeo, xarel.lo, parellada
91
Colour: bright golden. Nose: fine lees, dry nuts, fragrant herbs, complex, toasty. Palate: powerful, flavourful, good acidity, fine bead, fine bitter notes.

Lavit 2011 BN
macabeo, parellada
88
Colour: bright yellow. Nose: ripe fruit, fine lees, balanced, fragrant herbs. Palate: good acidity, flavourful, ripe fruit, long.

Lavit Rosado BR
trepat, monastrell, garnacha
87
Colour: light cherry, bright. Nose: fine lees, citrus fruit, fresh fruit. Palate: fresh, easy to drink, good acidity.

Segura Viudas BR Reserva
macabeo, xarel.lo, parellada
87
Colour: bright straw. Nose: fine lees, floral, fragrant herbs. Palate: powerful, flavourful, good acidity, fine bead, balanced.

Segura Viudas Brut Vintage 2008 BN Gran Reserva
macabeo, parellada
90
Colour: bright straw. Nose: fine lees, dry nuts, fragrant herbs, complex, toasty. Palate: powerful, flavourful, good acidity, fine bead, fine bitter notes.

Segura Viudas Reserva
Heredad BR Reserva
macabeo, parellada

92

Colour: bright golden. Nose: fine lees, dry nuts, fragrant herbs, complex, toasty. Palate: powerful, flavourful, good acidity, fine bead, fine bitter notes.

JANÉ VENTURA

Ctra. Calafell, 2
43700 El Vendrell (Tarragona)
☎: +34 977 660 118
Fax: +34 977 661 239
www.janeventura.com
janeventura@janeventura.com

"Do" de Jané Ventura Vintage
2009 BN Gran Reserva

91

Colour: bright golden. Nose: fine lees, dry nuts, fragrant herbs, complex, toasty. Palate: powerful, flavourful, good acidity, fine bead, fine bitter notes.

Cava 1914 de Jané Ventura 2007 BN

93

Colour: bright golden. Nose: fine lees, dry nuts, fragrant herbs, complex. Palate: powerful, flavourful, good acidity, fine bead, fine bitter notes, elegant.

Jané Ventura de L'Orgue 2006 BN Gran Reserva 93

Colour: bright golden. Nose: fine lees, fragrant herbs, characterful, ripe fruit, dry nuts. Palate: powerful, flavourful, good acidity, fine bead, fine bitter notes.

Jané Ventura Reserva de la
Música 2011 BN Reserva

90

Colour: bright straw. Nose: fine lees, floral, fragrant herbs, expressive. Palate: powerful, flavourful, good acidity, fine bead, balanced.

Jané Ventura Reserva de la
Música 2011 BR Reserva

89

Colour: bright straw. Nose: medium intensity, fresh fruit, dried herbs, fine lees, floral. Palate: fresh, fruity, flavourful, good acidity.

Jané Ventura Reserva de la
Música Rosé 2011 BR
100% garnacha

88

Colour: rose. Nose: floral, red berry notes, ripe fruit, fragrant herbs, expressive. Palate: powerful, balanced, flavourful.

JAUME GIRÓ I GIRÓ

Montaner i Oller, 5
08770 Sant Sadurní D'Anoia (Barcelona)
☎: +34 938 910 165
Fax: +34 938 911 271
www.cavagiro.com
cavagiro@cavagiro.com

Jaume Giró i Giró 2010 BR Reserva

88

Colour: bright yellow. Nose: fine lees, floral, fragrant herbs. Palate: powerful, flavourful, good acidity, fine bead, balanced.

Jaume Giró i Giró Bombonetta
2008 BR Gran Reserva

90

Colour: bright straw. Nose: fine lees, floral, fragrant herbs, expressive. Palate: powerful, flavourful, good acidity, fine bead, balanced.

Jaume Giró i Giró Elaboración
Artesana 2011 BN Reserva

88

Colour: bright straw. Nose: medium intensity, fresh fruit, dried herbs, fine lees, floral. Palate: fresh, fruity, flavourful, good acidity.

Jaume Giró i Giró Grandalla
2010 BR Gran Reserva

91

Colour: bright golden. Nose: fine lees, dry nuts, fragrant herbs, complex, toasty. Palate: powerful, flavourful, good acidity, fine bead, fine bitter notes.

Jaume Giró i Giró Grandalla de
Luxe 2007 BR Gran Reserva

92

Colour: bright golden. Nose: fine lees, fragrant herbs, characterful, ripe fruit, dry nuts. Palate: powerful, flavourful, good acidity, fine bead, fine bitter notes.

Jaume Giró i Giró Homenatge Cal
Rei 2006 BR Gran Reserva

90

Colour: bright golden. Nose: fine lees, fragrant herbs, characterful, ripe fruit, dry nuts. Palate: powerful, flavourful, good acidity, fine bead, fine bitter notes.

Jaume Giró i Giró Montaner
2008 BN Gran Reserva

88

Colour: bright yellow. Nose: ripe fruit, fine lees, balanced, dried herbs. Palate: good acidity, flavourful, ripe fruit, long.

Jaume Giró i Giró Premium
2006 BN Gran Reserva
88
Colour: bright golden. Nose: fragrant herbs, characterful, ripe fruit, dry nuts. Palate: powerful, flavourful, good acidity, fine bead, fine bitter notes.

Jaume Giró i Giró Rosat de Cal Rei 2011 BR
100% trepat
87
Colour: rose. Nose: floral, red berry notes, ripe fruit, fragrant herbs, expressive. Palate: powerful, balanced, flavourful.

Jaume Giró i Giró Selecte
2007 BN Gran Reserva
91
Colour: bright golden. Nose: fine lees, fragrant herbs, characterful, ripe fruit, dry nuts. Palate: powerful, flavourful, good acidity, fine bead, fine bitter notes.

JAUME LLOPART ALEMANY
Font Rubí, 9
08736 Font-Rubí (Barcelona)
☎: +34 938 979 133
Fax: +34 938 979 133
www.jaumellopartalemany.com
info@jaumellopartalemany.com

Aina Jaume Llopart Alemany
Rosado 2011 BR Reserva
pinot noir
85

Jaume Llopart Alemany 2009 BN Reserva
macabeo, xarel.lo, parellada
90
Colour: bright straw. Nose: medium intensity, fresh fruit, dried herbs, fine lees, floral. Palate: fresh, fruity, flavourful, good acidity.

Jaume Llopart Alemany
2008 BN Gran Reserva
macabeo, xarel.lo, parellada
92
Colour: bright golden. Nose: fine lees, dry nuts, fragrant herbs, complex, toasty. Palate: powerful, flavourful, good acidity, fine bead, fine bitter notes, balanced.

Vinya d'en Ferran Jaume Llopart
Alemany 2007 BN Gran Reserva
pinot noir, chardonnay
91
Colour: bright golden. Nose: fine lees, dry nuts, fragrant herbs, complex. Palate: powerful, flavourful, good acidity, fine bead, fine bitter notes.

JAUME SERRA (J. GARCÍA CARRIÓN)
Ctra. de Vilanova, Km. 2,5
08800 Vilanova i la Geltrú (Barcelona)
☎: +34 938 936 404
Fax: +34 938 147 482
www.garciacarrion.es
jaumeserra@jgc.es

Cristalino Jaume Serra BR
86
Colour: bright straw. Nose: medium intensity, fresh fruit, dried herbs, fine lees, floral. Palate: fresh, fruity, flavourful, good acidity.

Cristalino Jaume Serra Rosado BR
84

Heretat el Padruell BR
84

Heretat El Padruell Rosé BR
trepat, pinot noir
85

Jaume Serra BN
87
Colour: bright yellow. Nose: ripe fruit, fine lees, balanced, dried herbs. Palate: good acidity, flavourful, ripe fruit, long.

Jaume Serra BN Reserva
83

Jaume Serra BR
80

Jaume Serra SS
83

Jaume Serra Chardonnay
2010 BN Gran Reserva
100% chardonnay
88
Colour: bright straw. Nose: fine lees, floral, fragrant herbs, expressive. Palate: powerful, flavourful, good acidity, fine bead, balanced.

Jaume Serra Rosado BR
84

Jaume Serra Vintage 2010
BR Gran Reserva
85

Pata Negra BR
83

Pata Negra SS
84

Pata Negra Rosado BR
83

Pata Negra Vintage 2010 BN Reserva
macabeo, chardonnay, parellada
85

JOAN SARDÀ
Ctra. Vilafranca a St. Jaume dels Domenys, Km. 8,1
08732 Castellvi de la Marca (Barcelona)
☎: +34 937 720 900
Fax: +34 937 721 495
www.joansarda.com
joansarda@joansarda.com

Joan Sardà BN Reserva
macabeo, xarel.lo, parellada
87
Colour: bright golden. Nose: powerfull, ripe fruit, spicy. Palate: ripe fruit, long, fine bitter notes.

Joan Sardà BR Reserva
macabeo, xarel.lo, parellada
88
Colour: bright straw. Nose: medium intensity, fresh fruit, dried herbs, fine lees, floral. Palate: fresh, fruity, flavourful, good acidity.

Joan Sardà Millenium BN Gran Reserva
macabeo, xarel.lo, parellada
88
Colour: bright yellow. Nose: ripe fruit, fine lees, balanced, dried herbs. Palate: good acidity, flavourful, ripe fruit, long.

Joan Sardá Rosé BR Reserva
86
Colour: rose. Nose: powerfull, ripe fruit, rose petals. Palate: correct, fine bitter notes.

JUVÉ Y CAMPS
Sant Venat, 1
08770 Sant Sadurní D'Anoia (Barcelona)
☎: +34 938 911 000
Fax: +34 938 912 100
www.juveycamps.com
juveycamps@juveycamps.com

Essential Xarel.lo 2012 BR
100% xarel.lo
89
Colour: bright straw. Nose: fine lees, floral, fragrant herbs, expressive. Palate: powerful, flavourful, fine bead, sweetness.

Gran Juvé Camps 2010 BR Gran Reserva
94
Colour: bright yellow. Nose: fine lees, fragrant herbs, characterful, ripe fruit, dry nuts. Palate: powerful, flavourful, good acidity, fine bead, fine bitter notes.

Gran Juvé Camps Rosé 2010 BN Gran Reserva
100% pinot noir
92
Colour: coppery red. Nose: floral, jasmine, fragrant herbs, candied fruit, fine lees. Palate: fresh, fruity, flavourful, correct.

Juvé & Camps Blanc de Noirs 2012 BR Reserva
89
Colour: bright straw. Nose: fine lees, fragrant herbs, expressive. Palate: flavourful, good acidity, fine bead, balanced.

Juvé & Camps Cinta Púrpura BR Reserva
89
Colour: bright straw. Nose: fine lees, floral, fragrant herbs, expressive. Palate: powerful, flavourful, good acidity, fine bead, balanced.

Juvé & Camps Milesimé Chardonnay 2007 BR
100% chardonnay
93
Colour: bright golden. Nose: dry nuts, fragrant herbs, fine lees, macerated fruit, expressive. Palate: powerful, flavourful, good acidity, fine bead, fine bitter notes.

Juvé & Camps Milesimé Chardonnay 2011 BR Reserva
100% chardonnay
91
Colour: bright yellow. Nose: fine lees, floral, fragrant herbs, expressive. Palate: flavourful, good acidity, fine bead, balanced.

Juvé & Camps Milesimé Magnum 2010 BR Reserva
100% chardonnay
93
Colour: bright yellow. Nose: fine lees, floral, fragrant herbs, expressive. Palate: powerful, flavourful, good acidity, fine bead, balanced.

Juvé & Camps Reserva de la Familia 2010 BN Gran Reserva
91
Colour: bright yellow. Nose: fine lees, dry nuts, fragrant herbs, complex, toasty. Palate: powerful, flavourful, good acidity, fine bead, fine bitter notes.

Juvé & Camps Reserva de la Familia Magnum 2010 BN Gran Reserva
93
Colour: bright golden. Nose: fine lees, dry nuts, fragrant herbs, toasty, floral. Palate: powerful, flavourful, good acidity, fine bead, fine bitter notes, elegant.

Juvé & Camps Rosé BR Reserva
100% pinot noir
87
Colour: light cherry. Nose: red berry notes, ripe fruit, fragrant herbs, expressive. Palate: powerful, balanced, flavourful.

Juvé & Camps Viña La Capella 2005 BN Gran Reserva
100% xarel.lo
94
Colour: bright golden. Nose: fine lees, dry nuts, fragrant herbs, complex, toasty. Palate: powerful, flavourful, good acidity, fine bead, fine bitter notes.

Juvé Camps Sweet Reserva
89
Colour: bright straw. Nose: medium intensity, fresh fruit, fine lees, floral. Palate: fresh, fruity, flavourful, good acidity.

LLOPART
Ctra. de Sant Sadurni - Ordal, Km. 4 Els Casots
08739 Subirats (Barcelona)
☎: +34 938 993 125
Fax: +34 938 993 038
www.llopart.com
llopart@llopart.com

Cava Llopart 2011 BN Reserva
88
Colour: bright straw. Nose: medium intensity, fresh fruit, dried herbs, fine lees, floral. Palate: fresh, fruity, flavourful, good acidity.

Cava Llopart Ex-Vite 2007 BR Gran Reserva
93
Colour: bright yellow. Nose: fresh fruit, dried herbs, fine lees, floral, citrus fruit, balanced. Palate: fresh, fruity, flavourful, good acidity, elegant.

Cava Llopart Imperial 2010 BR Gran Reserva
89
Colour: bright yellow. Nose: fine lees, fragrant herbs, ripe fruit, dry nuts. Palate: flavourful, good acidity, fine bead, fine bitter notes.

Cava Llopart Integral (375 ml) 2012 BN Reserva
87
Colour: bright straw. Nose: fresh, balanced, floral. Palate: good acidity, correct, fine bitter notes.

Cava Llopart Integral 2012 BN Reserva
88
Colour: bright straw. Nose: medium intensity, fresh fruit, dried herbs, fine lees, floral. Palate: fresh, fruity, flavourful, good acidity, easy to drink.

Cava Llopart Leopardi 2009 BN Gran Reserva
92
Colour: bright yellow. Nose: fine lees, fragrant herbs, characterful, ripe fruit, dry nuts. Palate: powerful, flavourful, good acidity, fine bead, fine bitter notes.

Cava Llopart Magnum 2010 BR Gran Reserva
91
Colour: bright yellow. Nose: fine lees, dry nuts, fragrant herbs. Palate: powerful, flavourful, good acidity, fine bead, fine bitter notes.

Cava Llopart Microcosmos Rosé 2010 BN Reserva
90
Colour: onion pink. Nose: medium intensity, dried herbs, fine lees, floral, candied fruit. Palate: fresh, fruity, flavourful, good acidity.

Cava Llopart Néctar Terrenal 2011 Semidulce Reserva
86
Colour: bright yellow. Nose: medium intensity, white flowers, fresh. Palate: fruity, easy to drink, correct.

Cava Llopart Original 1887 2008 BN Gran Reserva
95
Colour: bright golden. Nose: fine lees, dry nuts, fragrant herbs, complex, sweet spices, pattiserie. Palate: flavourful, good acidity, fine bead, rich, good structure.

Cava Llopart Rosé (375 ml) 2011 BR Reserva
89
Colour: light cherry. Nose: medium intensity, red berry notes, floral. Palate: fruity, easy to drink, fine bitter notes.

Cava Llopart Rosé 2011 BR Reserva
90
Colour: light cherry. Nose: floral, jasmine, fragrant herbs, red berry notes. Palate: fresh, fruity, flavourful, correct, fine bead, good acidity.

LONG WINES

Avda. del Puente Cultural, 8 Bloque B Bajo 7
28702 San Sebastián de los Reyes
(Madrid)
☎: +34 916 221 305
Fax: +34 916 220 029
www.longwines.com
adm@longwines.com

De Pró BR
85

De Pró Rosé BR
100% trepat
85

Escapada BR
88
Colour: bright straw. Nose: fine lees, floral, fragrant herbs, expressive. Palate: powerful, flavourful, good acidity, fine bead, balanced.

Escapada Rosé BR
100% trepat
88
Colour: rose. Nose: floral, red berry notes, fragrant herbs, expressive. Palate: powerful, balanced, flavourful.

MARÍA CASANOVAS

Ctra. BV-2242, km. 7,5
08160 Sant Jaume Sesoliveres
(Barcelona)
☎: +34 938 910 812
www.mariacasanovas.com
mariacasanovas@brutnature.com

María Casanovas 2011 BN Gran Reserva
93
Colour: bright golden. Nose: fine lees, fragrant herbs, characterful, ripe fruit, sweet spices. Palate: powerful, flavourful, good acidity, fine bead, fine bitter notes, balanced, elegant.

María Casanovas Glaç 2012 BN Reserva
86
Colour: bright yellow. Nose: fine lees, dried herbs, citrus fruit, floral. Palate: good acidity, flavourful, long.

MARIA OLIVER PORTÍ

Passatge Menorca, 4
08770 Sant Sadurní d'Anoia (Barcelona)
☎: +34 938 912 043
Fax: +34 938 912 043
www.mariaoliverporti.com
angelscaldu@hotmail.com

María Oliver Portí 2011 BN Reserva
macabeo, xarel.lo, parellada
86
Colour: bright straw. Nose: fresh fruit, dried herbs, floral. Palate: fresh, fruity, flavourful, good acidity.

María Oliver Portí Gran Brut 2011 BR Reserva
macabeo, xarel.lo, parellada
87
Colour: bright straw. Nose: fine lees, floral, fragrant herbs. Palate: powerful, flavourful, good acidity, fine bead, balanced.

MARÍA RIGOL ORDI

Fullerachs, 9
08770 Sant Sadurní D'Anoia (Barcelona)
☎: +34 938 910 194
Fax: +34 938 912 736
www.mariarigolordi.com
cava@mariarigolordi.com

Maria Rigol Ordi 2007 BN Gran Reserva
macabeo, xarel.lo, parellada
90
Colour: bright golden. Nose: fine lees, dry nuts, fragrant herbs, toasty. Palate: powerful, flavourful, good acidity, fine bead, fine bitter notes.

María Rigol Ordi 2009 BN Reserva
macabeo, xarel.lo, parellada
88
Colour: bright yellow. Nose: ripe fruit, fine lees, balanced, dried herbs. Palate: good acidity, flavourful, ripe fruit, long.

María Rigol Ordi 2011 BN
macabeo, xarel.lo, parellada
87
Colour: bright straw. Nose: medium intensity, fresh fruit, dried herbs, citrus fruit. Palate: fresh, fruity, flavourful, good acidity.

MARQUÉS DE LA CONCORDIA

Monistrol D'Anoia, s/n
08770 Sant Sadurní D'Anoia (Barcelona)
☎: +34 914 365 900
www.haciendas-espana.com

MM Reserva de la Familia Brut Millesime 2009 BN Reserva
chardonnay, macabeo, xarel.lo, parellada
88
Colour: bright yellow. Nose: ripe fruit, fine lees, balanced, faded flowers. Palate: good acidity, flavourful, ripe fruit, long.

MM Reserva de la Familia Brut Millesime Rosé 2010 BR
88
Colour: raspberry rose. Nose: floral, jasmine, fragrant herbs, candied fruit. Palate: fresh, fruity, flavourful, correct.

MM Selección Especial BR
85

MM Selección Especial Rosé 2012 BR
85

MARQUÉS DE MONISTROL
Monistrol d'Anoia s/n
08770 Sant Sadurní D'Anoia (Barcelona)
☎: +34 914 365 924

Clos de Monistrol BN
chardonnay, macabeo, xarel.lo, parellada
86
Colour: bright yellow. Nose: ripe fruit, fine lees, balanced, dried herbs. Palate: good acidity, ripe fruit.

Monistrol Premium Cuvée 2010 BN
85

Monistrol Premium Cuvée Rosé 2011 BR
87
Colour: raspberry rose. Nose: medium intensity, fresh fruit, dried herbs, fine lees, floral. Palate: fresh, fruity, flavourful, good acidity.

Monistrol Selección Especial BR
85

Monistrol Selección Especial BR
macabeo, xarel.lo, parellada
84

Monistrol Winemakers Select BN
chardonnay, macabeo, xarel.lo, parellada
87
Colour: bright straw. Nose: medium intensity, fresh fruit, dried herbs, fine lees, floral. Palate: fresh, fruity, flavourful, good acidity.

MARQUÉS DE TOMARES
Ctra. de Cenicero, s/n
26360 Fuenmayor (La Rioja)
☎: +34 676 433 820
Fax: +34 941 450 297
www.marquesdetomares.com
info@marquesdetomares.com

Don Román ESP
macabeo, xarel.lo, parellada
84

Don Román Imperial ESP Reserva
macabeo, xarel.lo, chardonnay
87
Colour: bright straw, greenish rim. Nose: fresh fruit, dried herbs, fine lees, floral. Palate: fresh, fruity, flavourful, good acidity.

MARRUGAT S.A. (BODEGAS PINORD)
Doctor Pasteur, 6
08776 Vilafranca del Penedès (Barcelona)
☎: +34 938 903 066
www.pinord.com
visites@pinord.com

Marrugat + Natura Vintage BN Reserva
macabeo, xarel.lo, parellada
88 ✿
Colour: bright golden. Nose: fine lees, fragrant herbs, ripe fruit. Palate: powerful, flavourful, good acidity, fine bead, fine bitter notes.

Marrugat Brut Imperial BR Reserva
macabeo, xarel.lo, parellada
85

Marrugat Brut Nature Milesime 2009 BN Gran Reserva
xarel.lo, macabeo, parellada
85

Rima 32 2008 BN Reserva
chardonnay, pinot noir
90
Colour: bright yellow. Nose: ripe fruit, fine lees, balanced, dried herbs, citrus fruit. Palate: good acidity, flavourful, long.

Suspirum 2006 BN Gran Reserva
xarel.lo, macabeo, chardonnay
83

MARTÍ SERDÀ
Camí Mas del Pont s/n
08792 Santa Fe del Penedès (Barcelona)
☎: +34 938 974 411
Fax: +34 938 974 405
www.martiserda.com
info@martiserda.com

El Secret de Martí Serdà BN Reserva
86
Colour: bright straw. Nose: medium intensity, fresh fruit, dried herbs, fine lees, floral. Palate: fresh, fruity, flavourful, good acidity.

Martí Serdà BN Reserva
86
Colour: bright straw. Nose: fine lees, floral, fragrant herbs, expressive. Palate: powerful, flavourful, good acidity, fine bead, balanced.

Martí Serdà BR
88
Colour: bright yellow. Nose: medium intensity, dry nuts, faded flowers. Palate: balanced, fine bitter notes, good acidity, easy to drink.

Martí Serdà Brut Rosé
85

Martí Serdà SS
87
Colour: bright yellow. Nose: ripe fruit, white flowers, fine lees. Palate: fine bitter notes, easy to drink.

Martí Serdà 2007 BN Gran Reserva
90
Colour: bright yellow. Nose: ripe fruit, fine lees, balanced, toasty. Palate: good acidity, flavourful, ripe fruit, long.

Martí Serdà Chardonnay BR
100% chardonnay
88
Colour: bright straw. Nose: medium intensity, fresh fruit, dried herbs, fine lees, floral. Palate: fresh, fruity, flavourful, good acidity.

Martí Serdà Cuvée Real 2006 BN Gran Reserva
91
Colour: bright golden. Nose: fine lees, dry nuts, fragrant herbs, complex, toasty. Palate: powerful, flavourful, good acidity, fine bead, fine bitter notes.

Masía D'Or BN
86
Colour: bright yellow. Nose: ripe fruit, balanced, dried herbs. Palate: good acidity, flavourful, ripe fruit, long.

Masía D'Or BR
84

MAS CODINA
Barri El Gorner, s/n - Mas Codina
08797 Puigdalber (Barcelona)
☎: +34 938 988 166
Fax: +34 938 988 166
www.mascodina.com
info@mascodina.com

Mas Codina 2008 BN Gran Reserva
chardonnay, xarel.lo, macabeo, pinot noir
90
Colour: bright golden. Nose: fine lees, dry nuts, fragrant herbs, complex. Palate: powerful, flavourful, good acidity, fine bead, fine bitter notes.

Mas Codina 2009 BN Reserva
chardonnay, xarel.lo, macabeo, pinot noir
88
Colour: bright straw. Nose: fine lees, floral, fragrant herbs. Palate: powerful, flavourful, good acidity, fine bead, balanced.

Mas Codina 2009 BR Reserva
chardonnay, xarel.lo, macabeo, pinot noir
84

Mas Codina Rosé 2010 BR
pinot noir
85

MAS GOMÀ 1724
Torras i Bages, 21
08794 Les Cabanyes (Barcelona)
☎: +34 626 160 162
www.masgoma1724.com
jvendrell@masgomas1724.com

Vendrell Olivella Organic 2009 BN
macabeo, xarel.lo, parellada
90
Colour: bright straw. Nose: fresh fruit, dried herbs, fine lees, floral. Palate: fresh, fruity, flavourful, good acidity, balanced.

Vendrell Olivella Organic 2009 BR
xarel.lo, macabeo, parellada
90
Colour: bright yellow. Nose: dry nuts, fragrant herbs, fine lees, sweet spices. Palate: powerful, flavourful, good acidity, fine bead, fine bitter notes, elegant.

Vendrell Olivella Original 2009 BN
xarel.lo, macabeo, parellada
88
Colour: bright straw. Nose: ripe fruit, fine lees, balanced, dried herbs. Palate: good acidity, flavourful, ripe fruit, long.

Vendrell Olivella Original 2011 BR
xarel.lo, macabeo, parellada
88
Colour: bright straw. Nose: fine lees, floral, fragrant herbs, expressive. Palate: powerful, flavourful, good acidity, fine bead, balanced.

MASCARÓ
Casal, 9
08720 Vilafranca del Penedès (Barcelona)
☎: +34 938 901 628
Fax: +34 938 901 358
www.mascaro.es
mascaro@mascaro.es

Mascaro Cuvée Antonio Mascaró 2007 BN Gran Reserva
90
Colour: bright yellow. Nose: fine lees, fragrant herbs, characterful, ripe fruit, dry nuts. Palate: powerful, flavourful, good acidity, fine bead, fine bitter notes.

Mascaró Nigrum 2011 BR Reserva
86
Colour: bright straw. Nose: fine lees, floral, fragrant herbs. Palate: powerful, flavourful.

Mascaró Pure 2011 BN Reserva
88
Colour: bright straw. Nose: medium intensity, fresh fruit, dried herbs, fine lees, floral. Palate: fresh, fruity, flavourful, good acidity.

Mascaró Rosado "Rubor Aurorae" 2012 BR
100% trepat
88
Colour: light cherry, bright. Nose: balanced, medium intensity, dried flowers, red berry notes. Palate: fruity, flavourful, fine bitter notes.

MASET DEL LLEÓ
C-244, Km. 32,5
08792 La Granada del Penedès
(Barcelona)
☎: +34 902 200 250
Fax: +34 938 921 333
www.maset.com
info@maset.com

Maset del Lleó BR Reserva
macabeo, xarel.lo, parellada
87
Colour: bright straw. Nose: fine lees, floral, fragrant herbs, citrus fruit. Palate: flavourful, good acidity, balanced.

Maset del Lleó Aurum BN Reserva
chardonnay, xarel.lo
85

Maset del Lleó Colección Privada 1917 2010 BN Reserva
90
Colour: bright yellow. Nose: ripe fruit, fine lees, balanced, dried herbs, smoky. Palate: good acidity, flavourful, ripe fruit, long.

Maset del Lleó L'Avi Pau BN Reserva
macabeo, xarel.lo, parellada, chardonnay
88
Colour: bright yellow. Nose: white flowers, citrus fruit, balanced. Palate: correct, fine bitter notes, fruity, good acidity.

Maset del Lleó Rosé BR
garnacha, trepat
84

Maset del Lleó Vintage BN Reserva
macabeo, xarel.lo, parellada
85

Nu Brut de Maset del Lleó BR Reserva
macabeo, parellada, xarel.lo
87
Colour: coppery red. Nose: floral, jasmine, fragrant herbs, candied fruit. Palate: fresh, fruity, flavourful, correct.

MASIA VALLFORMOSA
La Sala, 45
08735 Vilobí del Penedès (Barcelona)
☎: +34 938 978 286
Fax: +34 938 978 355
www.domenechvidal.com
vallformosa@vallformosa.es

Gala de Vallformosa Vintage 2008 BR Gran Reserva
macabeo, xarel.lo, parellada, chardonnay
90
Colour: bright yellow. Nose: fine lees, dry nuts, fragrant herbs, complex. Palate: powerful, flavourful, good acidity, fine bead, fine bitter notes.

Origen 2012 SC
macabeo, xarel.lo, parellada
86
Colour: bright yellow. Nose: medium intensity, fresh, balanced, dried flowers. Palate: fresh, flavourful.

Vallformosa Col.lecció 2011 BN Reserva
macabeo, xarel.lo, parellada, chardonnay
87
Colour: bright yellow. Nose: ripe fruit, fruit liqueur notes, lees reduction notes, dried herbs. Palate: correct, easy to drink.

Vallformosa Col.lecció 2011 BR Reserva
macabeo, xarel.lo, parellada, chardonnay
87
Colour: bright yellow. Nose: fine lees, fragrant herbs, characterful, ripe fruit. Palate: powerful, flavourful, good acidity, fine bead, fine bitter notes.

Vallformosa Col.lecció Pinot Noir Rosado 2012 BR
pinot noir
90
Colour: raspberry rose. Nose: floral, jasmine, fragrant herbs, candied fruit. Palate: fresh, fruity, flavourful, correct.

Vallformosa Origen 2011 BN
macabeo, xarel.lo, parellada
88
Colour: bright straw. Nose: medium intensity, fresh fruit, dried herbs, fine lees, floral. Palate: fresh, fruity, flavourful, good acidity.

Vallformosa Origen 2011 BR
macabeo, xarel.lo, parellada
86
Colour: bright yellow. Nose: fine lees, fragrant herbs, dry nuts. Palate: flavourful, good acidity, fine bead, fine bitter notes.

Vallformosa Origen 2012 SS
macabeo, xarel.lo, parellada

87

Colour: bright straw. Nose: fine lees, floral, fragrant herbs, expressive. Palate: powerful, flavourful, good acidity, fine bead, balanced.

Vallformosa Origen Rosado 2011 BR
garnacha, monastrell

89

Colour: coppery red. Nose: floral, jasmine, fragrant herbs, candied fruit. Palate: fresh, fruity, flavourful, correct.

MATA I COLOMA
Ctra. St. Boi-La Llacuna, km. 10
08770 Sant Sadurní D'Anoia (Barcelona)
☎: +34 938 183 968
www.matacoloma.com
info@matacoloma.com

Pere Mata Cupada Nº 10 2010 BN Reserva
macabeo, xarel.lo, parellada

90

Colour: bright straw. Nose: fresh fruit, dried herbs, fine lees, floral. Palate: fresh, fruity, flavourful, good acidity.

Pere Mata Cupada Rosat 2010 Reserva
monastrell

91

Colour: coppery red. Nose: floral, jasmine, fragrant herbs, candied fruit. Palate: fresh, fruity, flavourful, correct.

Pere Mata Cuvée Barcelona
2008 BR Gran Reserva
macabeo, xarel.lo, parellada

90

Colour: bright golden. Nose: dry nuts, fragrant herbs, complex, expressive. Palate: powerful, flavourful, good acidity, fine bead, fine bitter notes.

Pere Mata Gran Coloma
2008 BR Gran Reserva
macabeo, xarel.lo, parellada

90

Colour: bright straw. Nose: fine lees, floral, fragrant herbs, expressive, toasty. Palate: powerful, flavourful, good acidity, fine bead, balanced.

Pere Mata L'Ensamblatge
2007 BN Gran Reserva
macabeo, xarel.lo, parellada

89

Colour: bright golden. Nose: fine lees, dry nuts, fragrant herbs, complex, toasty. Palate: powerful, flavourful, good acidity, fine bead, fine bitter notes.

Pere Mata L'Origen 2009 BR Gran Reserva
macabeo, xarel.lo, parellada

89

Colour: bright golden. Nose: fine lees, dry nuts, fragrant herbs, complex. Palate: powerful, flavourful, good acidity, fine bead, fine bitter notes.

Pere Mata Reserva Familia
2007 BN Gran Reserva
macabeo, xarel.lo, parellada

90

Colour: bright straw. Nose: fine lees, floral, fragrant herbs, expressive. Palate: powerful, flavourful, good acidity, fine bead, balanced.

MIQUEL PONS
Baix Llobregat, 5
08792 La Granada del Penedès
(Barcelona)
☎: +34 938 974 541
Fax: +34 938 974 710
www.cavamiquelpons.com
miquelpons@cavamiquelpons.com

Miquel Pons 2008 BN Gran Reserva

90

Colour: bright golden. Nose: fine lees, dry nuts, fragrant herbs, smoky. Palate: powerful, flavourful, good acidity, fine bead, fine bitter notes.

Miquel Pons 2010 BN Reserva

88

Colour: bright yellow. Nose: ripe fruit, fine lees, balanced, dried herbs, spicy. Palate: good acidity, flavourful, ripe fruit, long.

Miquel Pons 2010 BR Reserva

86

Colour: bright straw. Nose: fine lees, floral, fragrant herbs, citrus fruit. Palate: powerful, flavourful, good acidity, fine bead.

Miquel Pons Eulàlia Rosé 2011 BN Reserva
trepat

85

Miquel Pons Xarel.lo 2008 BN
xarel.lo

91

Colour: bright golden. Nose: fine lees, characterful, ripe fruit, dry nuts, sweet spices. Palate: powerful, flavourful, good acidity, fine bead, fine bitter notes.

MONT MARÇAL

Finca Manlleu
08732 Castellví de la Marca (Barcelona)
☎: +34 938 918 281
Fax: +34 938 919 045
www.mont-marcal.com
mont-marcal@mont-marcal.com

Aureum de Mont Marçal BN Gran Reserva
91
Colour: bright golden. Nose: fine lees, dry nuts, fragrant herbs, complex. Palate: powerful, flavourful, good acidity, fine bead, fine bitter notes.

Gran Portaceli BR
89
Colour: bright straw. Nose: fine lees, floral, fragrant herbs, expressive. Palate: powerful, flavourful, good acidity, fine bead, balanced.

La Perla de Santa Mónica BR
89
Colour: bright straw. Nose: fine lees, floral, fragrant herbs, expressive, toasty, spicy. Palate: powerful, flavourful, good acidity, fine bead, balanced.

Mont Marçal BR Reserva
88
Colour: bright straw. Nose: medium intensity, fresh fruit, dried herbs, fine lees, floral. Palate: fresh, fruity, flavourful, good acidity.

Mont Marçal Brut Rosado
100% trepat
86
Colour: light cherry. Nose: ripe fruit, powerfull, rose petals, red berry notes. Palate: good structure, flavourful, ripe fruit.

Mont Marçal Extremarium BR Reserva
87
Colour: bright straw. Nose: medium intensity, fresh fruit, dried herbs, fine lees, floral. Palate: fresh, fruity, flavourful, good acidity.

Mont Marçal Extremarium Rosado BN
100% pinot noir
88
Colour: coppery red. Nose: floral, jasmine, fragrant herbs, candied fruit. Palate: fresh, fruity, flavourful, correct.

Mont Marçal Gran Cuvée BR Reserva
86
Colour: bright yellow. Nose: fresh fruit, floral, citrus fruit, balanced. Palate: good acidity, fine bitter notes.

Mont Marçal Gran Cuvée Rosado BR
100% pinot noir
89
Colour: light cherry. Nose: floral, red berry notes, ripe fruit, fragrant herbs, expressive. Palate: balanced, flavourful, good acidity.

Mont Marçal Palau BR
87
Colour: bright straw. Nose: medium intensity, fresh fruit, dried herbs, fine lees, floral. Palate: fresh, fruity, flavourful, good acidity.

Portaceli BR
86
Colour: bright yellow. Nose: ripe fruit, fine lees, balanced, dried herbs. Palate: good acidity, flavourful, ripe fruit, long.

Santa Mónica BR
86
Colour: bright yellow. Nose: ripe fruit, dried herbs, medium intensity, fresh. Palate: correct, light-bodied, fresh.

MONT-FERRANT

Abad Escarré, 1 Cantonada
Mont-Ferrant
17300 Blanes (Girona)
☎: +34 934 191 000
www.montferrant.com
jcivit@montferrant.com

Agustí Vilaret 2007 Extra Brut Reserva
macabeo, xarel.lo, parellada, chardonnay
88
Colour: bright straw. Nose: fine lees, floral, fragrant herbs, fruit liqueur notes. Palate: powerful, flavourful, good acidity, fine bitter notes.

Berta Bouzy Extra Brut Reserva
macabeo, xarel.lo, parellada, chardonnay
92
Colour: bright yellow. Nose: dry nuts, fragrant herbs, complex, fine lees, macerated fruit, sweet spices. Palate: powerful, flavourful, fine bead, fine bitter notes.

Blanes Nature Extra Brut Reserva
macabeo, xarel.lo, parellada, chardonnay
87
Colour: bright yellow. Nose: fine lees, floral, fragrant herbs, sweet spices. Palate: powerful, flavourful, good acidity, fine bead, balanced.

L´Americano BR Reserva
macabeo, xarel.lo, parellada, chardonnay
89
Colour: bright yellow. Nose: dry nuts, fragrant herbs, fine lees, sweet spices. Palate: flavourful, good acidity, fine bead, fine bitter notes, elegant.

Mont Ferrant Tradició BR Reserva
macabeo, xarel.lo, parellada, chardonnay

88

Colour: bright straw. Nose: fine lees, floral, fragrant herbs, expressive. Palate: powerful, flavourful, good acidity, fine bead, balanced.

Mont-Ferrant Gran Cuvée BR Gran Reserva
macabeo, xarel.lo, parellada, chardonnay

89

Colour: bright golden. Nose: fine lees, dry nuts, fragrant herbs, complex. Palate: powerful, flavourful, good acidity, fine bead, fine bitter notes.

Mont-Ferrant Rosé BR
garnacha, monastrell

87

Colour: rose. Nose: floral, red berry notes, ripe fruit, fragrant herbs. Palate: powerful, balanced, flavourful, ripe fruit.

MOST DORÉ
Rambla de la Generalitat, 8
08770 Sant Sadurní d'Anoia (Barcelona)
☎: +34 938 181 662
Fax: +34 939 183 641
www.objetodedeseo.eu
lodeseo@objetodedeseo.si

Most - Doré "Objeto de Deseo Rosé 2010 Extra Brut Reserva
monastrell, pinot noir, trepat

88

Colour: coppery red. Nose: floral, jasmine, fragrant herbs, candied fruit. Palate: fresh, fruity, flavourful, correct.

OLIVELLA I BONET
Casetes Puigmoltó, 15
43720 L'Arboç del Penedès (Tarragona)
☎: +34 977 670 433
Fax: +34 977 670 433
www.olivellaibonet.com
olivellaibonet@gmail.com

Mont Caranac Chardonnay BR Gran Reserva
chardonnay

84

Mont Caranac S/C BN Gran Reserva
xarel.lo, macabeo, parellada

88

Colour: bright golden. Nose: fine lees, dry nuts, fragrant herbs, complex, toasty. Palate: powerful, flavourful, good acidity, fine bead, fine bitter notes.

Olivella i Bonet 2013 BN
xarel.lo, macabeo, parellada

86

Colour: yellow. Nose: medium intensity, fresh fruit, dried herbs, fine lees, faded flowers. Palate: fresh, fruity, flavourful, good acidity.

Olivella i Bonet 2013 BR
xarel.lo, macabeo, parellada

83

Olivella i Bonet 2013 SS
xarel.lo, macabeo, parellada

84

Olivella i Bonet Especial Artesà S/C BN Reserva
xarel.lo, macabeo, parellada

88

Colour: bright golden. Nose: fine lees, dry nuts, fragrant herbs, floral. Palate: powerful, flavourful, good acidity, fine bead, fine bitter notes.

Olivella i Bonet Especial Artesà S/C Extra Brut Reserva
xarel.lo, macabeo, parellada

86

Colour: bright straw. Nose: ripe fruit, fine lees, dried herbs. Palate: good acidity, flavourful, fresh.

ORIOL ROSSELL
Masia Can Cassanyes
08729 Sant Marçal (Barcelona)
☎: +34 977 671 061
Fax: +34 977 671 050
www.oriolrossell.com
oriolrossell@oriolrossell.com

Oriol Rossell 2010 BN Gran Reserva
macabeo, xarel.lo

88

Colour: bright yellow. Nose: ripe fruit, fine lees, balanced, dried herbs. Palate: good acidity, flavourful, ripe fruit, long.

Oriol Rossell 2011 BN Reserva
macabeo, xarel.lo, parellada

88

Colour: bright yellow. Nose: ripe fruit, fine lees, dried herbs. Palate: good acidity, flavourful, ripe fruit, long.

Oriol Rossell 2011 BR
macabeo, xarel.lo, parellada

87

Colour: bright straw. Nose: medium intensity, fresh fruit, dried herbs, fine lees, floral. Palate: fresh, fruity, flavourful, good acidity.

Oriol Rossell Reserva de la Propietat 2009 BN Gran Reserva
macabeo, xarel.lo, parellada

92

Colour: bright yellow. Nose: balanced, expressive, ripe fruit, spicy, fine lees. Palate: flavourful, fine bitter notes, good acidity.

Oriol Rossell Rosat 2011 BR
trepat

88

Colour: rose. Nose: floral, red berry notes, ripe fruit, fragrant herbs, expressive. Palate: powerful, balanced, flavourful.

OSBORNE MALPICA DE TAJO
Ctra. Malpica - Pueblanueva, km. 6
45692 Malpica del Tajo (Toledo)
☎: +34 925 860 990
Fax: +34 925 860 905
www.osborne.es
carolina.cerrato@osborne.es

Abadia de Montserrat BR Reserva
macabeo, xarel.lo, parellada

89

Colour: bright straw. Nose: fine lees, floral, fragrant herbs, expressive. Palate: powerful, flavourful, good acidity, fine bead, balanced.

PAGO DE THARSYS
Ctra. Nacional III, km. 274
46340 Requena (Valencia)
☎: +34 962 303 354
Fax: +34 962 329 000
www.pagodetharsys.com
pagodetharsys@pagodetharsys.com

Carlota Suria 2012 BN
macabeo, parellada

88

Colour: bright straw. Nose: fine lees, floral, fragrant herbs, expressive. Palate: powerful, flavourful, good acidity, fine bead, balanced.

Pago de Tharsys 2011 BN
macabeo, chardonnay

89

Colour: bright yellow. Nose: ripe fruit, fine lees, balanced, dried herbs. Palate: good acidity, flavourful, ripe fruit, long.

Pago de Tharsys Millesime 2008 BN Gran Reserva
macabeo, parellada, chardonnay

91

Colour: bright golden. Nose: fine lees, dry nuts, fragrant herbs, complex. Palate: powerful, flavourful, good acidity, fine bead, fine bitter notes.

PARATÓ
Can Respall de Renardes s/n
08733 El Pla del Penedès (Barcelona)
☎: +34 938 988 182
Fax: +34 938 988 510
www.parato.es
info@parato.es

Ática 2009 Extra Brut Gran Reserva
macabeo, xarel.lo, parellada, chardonnay

89

Colour: bright golden. Nose: fine lees, dry nuts, fragrant herbs, complex. Palate: powerful, flavourful, good acidity, fine bead, fine bitter notes, balanced.

Ática Pinot Noir 2011 RD Reserva
pinot noir

87

Colour: rose, purple rim. Nose: powerfull, ripe fruit, red berry notes, floral, expressive, balsamic herbs. Palate: powerful, fruity, fresh.

Elias i Terns 2005 BN Gran Reserva
xarel.lo, macabeo, chardonnay, parellada

90

Colour: bright golden. Nose: fine lees, dry nuts, fragrant herbs. Palate: powerful, flavourful, good acidity, fine bead, fine bitter notes.

Parató 2010 BN Reserva
macabeo, xarel.lo, parellada

86

Colour: bright yellow. Nose: ripe fruit, fine lees, balanced, dried herbs, floral. Palate: good acidity, flavourful, ripe fruit, spicy.

Parató 2011 BR Reserva
macabeo, xarel.lo, parellada, chardonnay

84

Renardes 2011 BN
macabeo, xarel.lo, parellada, chardonnay

83

PARÉS BALTÀ
Masía Can Baltá, s/n
08796 Pacs del Penedès (Barcelona)
☎: +34 938 901 399
Fax: +34 938 901 143
www.paresbalta.com
paresbalta@paresbalta.com

Blanca Cusiné 2009 BR Gran Reserva
chardonnay, pinot noir

93 ✿

Colour: bright golden. Nose: fine lees, fragrant herbs, characterful, ripe fruit, dry nuts. Palate: powerful, flavourful, good acidity, fine bead, fine bitter notes.

Blanca Cusiné 2010 BN
chardonnay, pinot noir

93

Colour: bright golden. Nose: fine lees, dry nuts, fragrant herbs, complex, toasty. Palate: powerful, flavourful, good acidity, fine bead, fine bitter notes.

Parés Baltà BN
macabeo, xarel.lo, parellada

88

Colour: bright straw. Nose: fine lees, floral, fragrant herbs, expressive. Palate: powerful, flavourful, good acidity, fine bead, balanced.

Parés Baltà Selectio BR
macabeo, xarel.lo, parellada, chardonnay

91

Colour: bright golden. Nose: fine lees, fragrant herbs, characterful, ripe fruit, dry nuts. Palate: powerful, flavourful, good acidity, fine bead, fine bitter notes.

Rosa Cusine Rosado 2010 BR
100% garnacha

90

Colour: coppery red. Nose: floral, jasmine, fragrant herbs, candied fruit. Palate: fresh, fruity, flavourful, correct, fine bitter notes.

PARXET
Torrent, 38
08391 Tiana (Barcelona)
☎: +34 933 950 811
www.parxet.es
info@parxet.es

Parxet Aniversari 92 BN
chardonnay, pinot noir

93

Colour: bright golden. Nose: fine lees, dry nuts, fragrant herbs, complex, toasty. Palate: powerful, flavourful, good acidity, fine bead, fine bitter notes.

Parxet BR
pansa blanca, macabeo, parellada

90

Colour: bright yellow. Nose: ripe fruit, fine lees, balanced, dried herbs. Palate: good acidity, flavourful, ripe fruit, long.

Parxet SS Reserva
pansa blanca, macabeo, parellada

88

Colour: bright straw. Nose: fine lees, floral, fragrant herbs, expressive. Palate: powerful, flavourful, fine bead, sweetness.

Parxet 2010 BN
pansa blanca, macabeo, parellada

88

Colour: bright straw. Nose: fine lees, floral, fragrant herbs, expressive. Palate: powerful, flavourful, good acidity, fine bead, balanced.

Parxet 2011 BR Reserva
pansa blanca, macabeo, parellada

88

Colour: bright straw. Nose: medium intensity, fresh fruit, dried herbs, fine lees, floral. Palate: fresh, fruity, flavourful, good acidity.

Parxet Cuvée 21 Ecológico BR
pansa blanca, macabeo, parellada

91

Colour: bright golden. Nose: fine lees, dry nuts, fragrant herbs, complex, toasty. Palate: powerful, flavourful, good acidity, fine bead, fine bitter notes.

Parxet Cuvée Dessert 375 ml. RD
pinot noir

88

Colour: onion pink. Nose: candied fruit, dried flowers, fragrant herbs, red berry notes. Palate: light-bodied, flavourful, good acidity, long, spicy.

Parxet María Cabané 2009 Extra Brut Gran Reserva
pansa blanca, macabeo, parellada

92

Colour: bright golden. Nose: fine lees, fragrant herbs, characterful, ripe fruit, dry nuts. Palate: powerful, flavourful, good acidity, fine bead, fine bitter notes.

Parxet Rosé BR
pinot noir

88

Colour: coppery red. Nose: floral, jasmine, fragrant herbs, candied fruit. Palate: fresh, fruity, flavourful, correct.

RAIMAT
Ctra. Lleida, s/n
25111 Raimat (Lleida)
☎: +34 973 724 000
www.raimat.com
info@raimat.es

Raimat Brut BR

88

Colour: yellow. Nose: fine lees, floral, fragrant herbs, expressive. Palate: powerful, flavourful, good acidity, fine bead, balanced.

Raimat Chardonnay BR
100% chardonnay

89

Colour: bright yellow. Nose: ripe fruit, fine lees, balanced, dried flowers. Palate: good acidity, flavourful, ripe fruit, long.

RECAREDO

Tamarit, 10 Apartado 15
08770 Sant Sadurní D'Anoia (Barcelona)
☎: +34 938 910 214
Fax: +34 938 911 697
www.recaredo.es
cava@recaredo.es

Recaredo Brut de Brut
2005 BN Gran Reserva
93

Colour: bright yellow. Nose: complex, fine lees, spicy, ripe fruit, expressive, dried herbs. Palate: balanced, fine bead, fine bitter notes.

Recaredo Brut Nature
2008 BN Gran Reserva
93

Colour: bright yellow. Nose: fine lees, dry nuts, fragrant herbs, toasty, floral, balsamic herbs. Palate: powerful, flavourful, good acidity, fine bead, fine bitter notes. Personality.

Recaredo Intens Rosat
2010 BN Gran Reserva
84

Recaredo Reserva Particular
2004 BN Gran Reserva
95

Colour: bright golden. Nose: fine lees, fragrant herbs, characterful, ripe fruit, dry nuts, elegant. Palate: powerful, flavourful, good acidity, fine bead, fine bitter notes, balanced.

Recaredo Subtil 2007 BN Gran Reserva
91

Colour: bright yellow. Nose: elegant, dry nuts, fine lees, faded flowers. Palate: balanced, good acidity, fine bitter notes.

Turo d'en Mota 2001 BN Gran Reserva
100% xarel.lo
96

Colour: bright golden. Nose: fine lees, dry nuts, fragrant herbs, complex, floral, candied fruit. Palate: flavourful, good acidity, fine bead, fine bitter notes. Personality.

REXACH BAQUES

Santa María, 12
08736 Guardiola de Font-Rubí
(Barcelona)
☎: +34 938 979 170
www.rexachbaques.com
info@rexachbaques.com

P. Baqués 100 Aniversari
2006 BR Gran Reserva
xarel.lo, macabeo, parellada, pinot noir
91

Colour: bright golden. Nose: fine lees, dry nuts, fragrant herbs, complex. Palate: powerful, flavourful, good acidity, fine bead, fine bitter notes, toasty.

Rexach Baques 2009 BN Gran Reserva
xarel.lo, macabeo, parellada
88

Colour: bright yellow. Nose: ripe fruit, fine lees, balanced, dried herbs. Palate: good acidity, flavourful, ripe fruit, long.

Rexach Baques Brut Imperial
2010 BR Reserva
xarel.lo, macabeo, parellada
89

Colour: bright straw. Nose: fine lees, floral, fragrant herbs, expressive, citrus fruit. Palate: powerful, flavourful, good acidity, fine bead, balanced.

Rexach Baques Gran Carta
2011 BR Reserva
macabeo, xarel.lo, parellada
86

Colour: bright straw. Nose: medium intensity, fresh fruit, dried herbs. Palate: fresh, fruity, flavourful, good acidity.

Rexach Rosado BR
pinot noir
85

RIMARTS

Avda. Cal Mir, 44
08770 Sant Sadurní D'Anoia (Barcelona)
☎: +34 938 912 775
Fax: +34 938 912 775
www.rimarts.net
rimarts@rimarts.net

Rimarts 2012 BR Reserva
xarel.lo, macabeo, parellada
91

Colour: bright golden. Nose: fine lees, dry nuts, fragrant herbs, complex, toasty. Palate: powerful, flavourful, good acidity, fine bead, fine bitter notes.

Rimarts 24 BN Reserva
xarel.lo, macabeo, parellada

92

Colour: bright golden. Nose: fine lees, fragrant herbs, characterful, ripe fruit, dry nuts. Palate: powerful, flavourful, good acidity, fine bead, fine bitter notes.

Rimarts 40 2009 BN Gran Reserva
xarel.lo, macabeo, parellada, chardonnay

92

Colour: bright golden. Nose: dry nuts, fragrant herbs, complex. Palate: powerful, flavourful, good acidity, fine bead, fine bitter notes.

Rimarts Chardonnay 2009 BN Reserva Especial
chardonnay

93

Colour: bright yellow. Nose: ripe fruit, fine lees, balanced, dried herbs, floral, complex. Palate: good acidity, flavourful, ripe fruit, long.

Rimarts Magnum 2009 BN Gran Reserva
xarel.lo, macabeo, parellada, chardonnay

93

Colour: bright golden. Nose: fine lees, dry nuts, fragrant herbs, complex, toasty. Palate: powerful, flavourful, good acidity, fine bead, fine bitter notes.

Rimarts Uvae BN Reserva
xarel.lo, chardonnay

87

Colour: bright golden. Nose: dry nuts, fragrant herbs, lees reduction notes, toasty. Palate: powerful, flavourful, fine bitter notes.

ROCAMAR
Major, 80
08755 Castellbisbal (Barcelona)
☎: +34 937 720 900
Fax: +34 937 721 495
www.rocamar.net
info@rocamar.net

Castell de Ribes BN
macabeo, xarel.lo, parellada

86

Colour: bright yellow. Nose: medium intensity, ripe fruit, citrus fruit. Palate: fruity, balanced, fine bitter notes, good acidity.

ROGER GOULART
Major, 6
08635 Sant Esteve Sesrovires (Barcelona)
☎: +34 937 714 003
Fax: +34 937 713 759
www.rogergoulart.com
sac@rogergoulart.com

Roger Goulart 2010 BN Reserva

90

Colour: bright golden. Nose: fine lees, dry nuts, fragrant herbs, complex, toasty. Palate: powerful, flavourful, good acidity, fine bead, fine bitter notes.

Roger Goulart 2011 BR Reserva

88

Colour: bright yellow. Nose: ripe fruit, fine lees, balanced, dried herbs. Palate: good acidity, flavourful, ripe fruit, long.

Roger Goulart Gran Cuvée Josep Valls 2008 Extra Brut Gran Reserva

90

Colour: bright golden. Nose: fine lees, dry nuts, fragrant herbs, complex. Palate: powerful, flavourful, good acidity, fine bead, fine bitter notes.

Roger Goulart Rosé 2011 BR

88

Colour: rose. Nose: floral, red berry notes, ripe fruit, fragrant herbs, expressive. Palate: powerful, balanced, flavourful.

ROSELL & FORMOSA
Rambla de la Generalitat, 14
08770 Sant Sadurní D'Anoia (Barcelona)
☎: +34 938 911 013
Fax: +34 938 911 967
www.roselliformosa.com
rformosa@roselliformosa.com

Rosell & Formosa Daurat "Brut de Bruts" 2008 BN Gran Reserva

89

Colour: bright yellow. Nose: ripe fruit, fine lees, balanced, dried herbs, spicy. Palate: good acidity, flavourful, ripe fruit, long, toasty.

Rosell i Formosa BR Reserva

87

Colour: bright straw. Nose: fine lees, fragrant herbs, expressive. Palate: flavourful, good acidity, balanced, easy to drink.

Rosell i Formosa 2009 BN Gran Reserva

88

Colour: bright yellow. Nose: dry nuts, fragrant herbs, fine lees, sweet spices. Palate: powerful, flavourful, good acidity, fine bead, fine bitter notes, elegant.

Rosell i Formosa Rosat BR Reserva
84

ROSELL GALLART
Montserrat, 56
08770 Sant Sadurní D'Anoia (Barcelona)
☎: +34 938 912 073
Fax: +34 938 183 539
www.rosellgallart.com
info@rosellgallart.com

Rosell Gallart 2009 BN Reserva
xarel.lo, macabeo, parellada, chardonnay
87
Colour: bright yellow. Nose: fine lees, balanced, dried herbs. Palate: good acidity, flavourful, ripe fruit, long.

Rosell Raventós Cristal 2007 BN Reserva
xarel.lo, macabeo, parellada, chardonnay
82

Teresa Mata Garriga 2010 BN Reserva
xarel.lo, macabeo, parellada, chardonnay
88
Colour: bright yellow. Nose: ripe fruit, fine lees, dried herbs, sweet spices. Palate: good acidity, flavourful, ripe fruit, long.

ROVELLATS
Finca Rovellats - Bº La Bleda
08731 Sant Marti Sarroca (Barcelona)
☎: +34 934 880 575
Fax: +34 934 880 819
www.rovellats.com
rovellats@cavasrovellats.com

Rovellats 2012 BR
macabeo, xarel.lo, parellada
87
Colour: bright straw. Nose: medium intensity, fresh fruit, dried herbs, fine lees, floral. Palate: fresh, fruity, flavourful, good acidity.

Rovellats Col.lecció 2007 Extra Brut
macabeo, xarel.lo, parellada
90
Colour: bright yellow. Nose: fresh fruit, dried herbs, fine lees, floral, pattiserie. Palate: fresh, fruity, flavourful, good acidity, elegant.

Rovellats Gran Reserva 2008 BN Gran Reserva
macabeo, xarel.lo, parellada
88
Colour: bright golden. Nose: fine lees, dry nuts, fragrant herbs, complex. Palate: powerful, flavourful, good acidity, fine bead, fine bitter notes.

Rovellats Imperial 2011 BR Reserva
macabeo, xarel.lo, parellada
86
Nose: fine lees, floral, fragrant herbs, expressive. Palate: powerful, flavourful, good acidity, fine bead, balanced.

Rovellats Imperial 37,5 cl. 2011 BR Reserva
macabeo, xarel.lo, parellada
84

Rovellats Imperial Rosé 2011 BR Reserva
garnacha
82

Rovellats Magnum 2007 BN Gran Reserva
macabeo, xarel.lo, parellada
90
Colour: bright golden. Nose: fine lees, dry nuts, fragrant herbs, complex, sweet spices. Palate: powerful, flavourful, good acidity, fine bead, fine bitter notes.

Rovellats Masia S. XV 2005 BN Gran Reserva
macabeo, xarel.lo, parellada, chardonnay
88
Colour: bright yellow. Nose: ripe fruit, fine lees, balanced, dried herbs. Palate: good acidity, flavourful, ripe fruit, long.

Rovellats Premier 2012 BN
macabeo, parellada
86
Colour: bright yellow. Nose: medium intensity, fresh fruit, dried herbs, fine lees, floral, jasmine. Palate: fresh, fruity, flavourful, good acidity.

Rovellats Premier Brut 2012 BR
macabeo, parellada
86
Colour: bright yellow. Nose: fine lees, dry nuts, fragrant herbs. Palate: powerful, flavourful, fine bitter notes.

SIGNAT
Torrent 38
08391 Tiana (Barcelona)
☎: +34 935 403 400
info@signatcava.com

Signat BN
xarel.lo, macabeo, parellada
89
Colour: bright yellow. Nose: ripe fruit, fine lees, dried herbs, floral. Palate: good acidity, flavourful, ripe fruit, long.

Signat BR
xarel.lo, macabeo, parellada
88
Colour: bright straw. Nose: fine lees, floral, fragrant herbs, expressive. Palate: powerful, flavourful, good acidity, fine bead, balanced.

Signat Magenta Rosé BR
pinot noir

89

Colour: rose. Nose: floral, red berry notes, ripe fruit, fragrant herbs, expressive. Palate: powerful, balanced, flavourful.

SOGAS MASCARÓ
Amalia Soler, 35
08720 Vilafranca del Penedès
(Barcelona)
☎: +34 931 184 107
www.sogasmascaro.com
info@sogasmascaro.com

Sogas Mascaró BN

89

Colour: bright yellow. Nose: ripe fruit, fine lees, balanced, dried herbs. Palate: good acidity, flavourful, ripe fruit, long.

Sogas Mascaró BR

88

Colour: bright straw. Nose: fine lees, floral, fragrant herbs, expressive. Palate: powerful, flavourful, good acidity, fine bead, balanced.

Sogas Mascaró 2010 BN Reserva

85

SURIOL
Can Suriol del Castell
08736 Font-Rubí (Barcelona)
☎: +34 938 978 426
Fax: +34 938 978 426
www.suriol.com
cansuriol@suriol.com

Castell de Grabuac 2007 BN Fermentado en Barrica
macabeo, xarel.lo

85 ♣

Castell de Grabuac Millesime 2001 BN Reserva
macabeo, xarel.lo, parellada

90

Colour: bright golden. Nose: fine lees, dry nuts, fragrant herbs, complex, petrol notes. Palate: powerful, flavourful, good acidity, fine bead, fine bitter notes, balanced.

Castell de Grabuac Millesime 2005 BN Reserva
macabeo, xarel.lo, parellada

75

Castell de Grabuac Millesime 2006 BN Reserva
macabeo, xarel.lo, parellada

85

Castell de Grabuac Xarel.lo 2012 BN
xarel.lo

86

Colour: bright yellow. Nose: ripe fruit, fruit liqueur notes, lees reduction notes, dried herbs, pattiserie. Palate: correct, powerful, spicy, toasty.

Suriol 2011 BN Reserva
macabeo, xarel.lo, parellada

86

Colour: bright yellow. Nose: ripe fruit, fine lees, dried herbs. Palate: good acidity, flavourful.

Suriol 2012 BN Reserva
macabeo, xarel.lo, parellada

85

Suriol Rosado 2010 BR Reserva
pinot noir, garnacha

84

Suriol Rosado 2011 BR Reserva
garnacha, monastrell

86

Colour: coppery red. Nose: floral, dried herbs, fine lees, fruit liqueur notes. Palate: flavourful, spicy, ripe fruit.

Suriol Rosado 2012 BR Reserva
garnacha, monastrell

85

THE GRAND WINES
Ramón y Cajal 7, 1ºA
01007 Vitoria (Alava)
☎: +34 945 158 282
Fax: +34 945 158 283
www.thegrandwines.com
araex@araex.com

Villa Conchi BR Reserva

87

Colour: bright straw. Nose: fine lees, floral, fragrant herbs. Palate: flavourful, good acidity, fine bead.

Villa Conchi Brut Imperial BR

89

Colour: bright yellow. Nose: fine lees, dry nuts, fragrant herbs, complex, toasty. Palate: powerful, flavourful, good acidity, fine bead, fine bitter notes.

Villa Conchi Brut Selección BR

86

Colour: bright yellow. Nose: ripe fruit, fine lees, dried herbs. Palate: good acidity, flavourful, balsamic.

Villa Conchi Rosado BR
100% trepat

84

TITIANA

Torrente, 38
08391 Tiana (Barcelona)
☎: +34 933 950 811
info@parxet.es

Titiana Pansa Blanca 2010 BR
pansa blanca

91

Colour: bright golden. Nose: dry nuts, fragrant herbs, complex, toasty, white flowers. Palate: powerful, flavourful, good acidity, fine bead, fine bitter notes.

Titiana Pinot Noir Rosé 2011 BR
pinot noir

89

Colour: coppery red. Nose: floral, jasmine, fragrant herbs, candied fruit. Palate: fresh, fruity, flavourful, correct.

Titiana Vintage 2010 BN
chardonnay

90

Colour: bright straw. Nose: fine lees, floral, fragrant herbs, expressive. Palate: powerful, flavourful, good acidity, fine bead, balanced.

TORELLÓ

Can Martí de Baix (Apartado Correos nº8)
08770 Sant Sadurní D'Anoia (Barcelona)
☎: +34 938 910 793
Fax: +34 938 910 877
www.torello.com
torello@torello.es

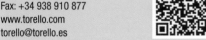

Gran Torelló 2008 BN Gran Reserva
macabeo, xarel.lo, parellada

93

Colour: bright golden. Nose: fragrant herbs, characterful, ripe fruit, dry nuts. Palate: powerful, flavourful, good acidity, fine bead, fine bitter notes.

Gran Torelló Magnum 2008 BN Gran Reserva
macabeo, xarel.lo, parellada

93

Colour: bright yellow. Nose: candied fruit, fruit expression, dried herbs. Palate: fine bitter notes, good acidity, fine bitter notes.

Jeroboam Torelló 2010 BN Gran Reserva
macabeo, xarel.lo, parellada

94

Colour: bright golden. Nose: fine lees, dry nuts, fragrant herbs, complex, toasty. Palate: powerful, flavourful, good acidity, fine bead, fine bitter notes.

Torelló 2009 BN Gran Reserva
macabeo, xarel.lo, parellada

91

Colour: bright straw. Nose: fine lees, floral, fragrant herbs, expressive. Palate: powerful, flavourful, good acidity, fine bead, balanced.

Torelló 2010 BR Reserva
macabeo, xarel.lo, parellada

88

Colour: bright yellow. Nose: ripe fruit, fine lees, balanced, dried herbs. Palate: good acidity, flavourful, ripe fruit, long.

Torelló 225 2009 BN Gran Reserva
macabeo, xarel.lo, parellada

94

Colour: bright golden. Nose: fine lees, fragrant herbs, characterful, ripe fruit, dry nuts. Palate: powerful, flavourful, good acidity, fine bead, fine bitter notes.

Torelló by Custo 3D 2008 BR Gran Reserva
macabeo, xarel.lo, parellada

91

Colour: bright golden. Nose: fine lees, dry nuts, fragrant herbs, complex, toasty. Palate: powerful, flavourful, good acidity, fine bead, fine bitter notes.

Torelló Magnum 2009 BN Gran Reserva
macabeo, xarel.lo, parellada

92

Colour: bright straw. Nose: candied fruit, spicy. Palate: flavourful, fruity, fresh, spicy.

Torelló Reserva Especial Edition 2010 BR Reserva
macabeo, xarel.lo, parellada

90
Colour: bright straw. Nose: medium intensity, fresh fruit, dried herbs, fine lees, floral. Palate: fresh, fruity, flavoured, good acidity.

Torelló Rosé 2011 BR Reserva
monastrell, garnacha

88
Colour: rose. Nose: floral, red berry notes, ripe fruit, fragrant herbs, expressive. Palate: powerful, balanced, flavourful.

TRIAS BATLLE
Pere El Gran, 21
08720 Vilafranca del Penedès (Barcelona)
☎: +34 677 497 892
www.triasbatlle.com
peptrias@jtrias.com

Trias Batlle BN Reserva

88
Colour: bright straw. Nose: medium intensity, fresh fruit, dried herbs, floral, citrus fruit. Palate: fresh, fruity, flavourful, good acidity.

Trias Batlle 2007 BN Gran Reserva

90
Colour: bright straw. Nose: medium intensity, fresh fruit, dried herbs, fine lees, floral. Palate: fresh, fruity, flavourful, good acidity.

Trias Batlle Rosado 2010 BR
100% trepat

88
Colour: coppery red. Nose: floral, jasmine, fragrant herbs, candied fruit. Palate: fresh, fruity, flavourful, correct.

UNIÓN VINÍCOLA DEL ESTE
Pl. Ind. El Romeral- Construcción, 74
46340 Requena (Valencia)
☎: +34 962 323 343
Fax: +34 962 349 413
www.uveste.es
cava@uveste.es

Beso de Rechenna BN

85

Nasol de Rechenna BN

88
Colour: bright straw. Nose: fine lees, floral, fragrant herbs, expressive. Palate: powerful, flavourful, good acidity, fine bead, balanced.

Vega Medien BN

86
Colour: bright straw. Nose: fine lees, floral, fragrant herbs, expressive. Palate: powerful, flavourful, good acidity, fine bead, balanced.

Vega Medien BR

87
Colour: bright straw. Nose: fine lees, floral, fragrant herbs, expressive. Palate: powerful, flavourful, good acidity, fine bead, balanced.

VALLDOLINA
Plaça de la Creu, 1
08795 Olesa de Bonesvalls (Barcelona)
☎: +34 938 984 181
Fax: +34 938 984 181
www.valldolina.com
info@valldolina.com

Tutusaus ECO 2010 BN Gran Reserva
macabeo, xarel.lo, parellada, chardonnay

89 ❦
Colour: bright yellow. Nose: ripe fruit, fine lees, balanced, dried herbs. Palate: good acidity, flavourful, ripe fruit, long.

VallDolina Eco 2009 BR Gran Reserva
macabeo, xarel.lo, parellada, chardonnay

91 ❦
Colour: bright golden. Nose: fine lees, dry nuts, fragrant herbs, complex, toasty. Palate: powerful, flavourful, good acidity, fine bead, fine bitter notes.

VallDolina Eco 2011 BN Reserva
macabeo, xarel.lo, parellada, chardonnay

89 ❦
Colour: bright yellow. Nose: ripe fruit, fine lees, balanced, dried herbs. Palate: good acidity, flavourful, ripe fruit, long.

VILARNAU
Ctra. d'Espiells, Km. 1,4 Finca "Can Petit"
08770 Sant Sadurní D'Anoia (Barcelona)
☎: +34 938 912 361
Fax: +34 938 912 913
www.vilarnau.es
vilarnau@vilarnau.es

Albert de Vilarnau Chardonnay Pinot Noir 2010 BN Gran Reserva

89
Colour: bright yellow. Nose: ripe fruit, macerated fruit, sweet spices, dried herbs. Palate: fine bitter notes, powerful, flavourful, toasty.

Albert de Vilarnau Fermentado en Barrica 2010 BN Gran Reserva
91
Colour: bright golden. Nose: dry nuts, fragrant herbs, complex, fine lees, macerated fruit, sweet spices. Palate: powerful, flavourful, fine bead, fine bitter notes.

Vilarnau 2011 BN Reserva
89
Colour: bright yellow. Nose: ripe fruit, fine lees, balanced, dried herbs. Palate: good acidity, flavourful, ripe fruit, long.

Vilarnau Brut Rosé BR
86
Colour: coppery red. Nose: floral, red berry notes, ripe fruit, fragrant herbs. Palate: powerful, balanced, flavourful.

Vilarnau Vintage 2010 BN Gran Reserva
91
Colour: bright golden. Nose: fine lees, dry nuts, fragrant herbs, complex, expressive. Palate: powerful, flavourful, good acidity, fine bead, elegant.

VINÍCOLA DE SARRAL Í SELECCIÓ DE CREDIT
Avinguda de la Conca, 33
43424 Sarral (Tarragona)
☎: +34 977 890 031
Fax: +34 977 890 136
www.cava-portell.com
cavaportell@covisal.es

Portell 2011 BN
86
Colour: greenish rim, bright yellow. Nose: dried herbs, citrus fruit, fresh. Palate: correct, good acidity, toasty.

Portell 2012 BR
86
Colour: bright straw. Nose: fine lees, floral, fragrant herbs. Palate: flavourful, good acidity, fine bead.

Portell 2012 SS
84

Portell Petrignano 2008 BN Gran Reserva
88
Colour: bright golden. Nose: fine lees, dry nuts, fragrant herbs, complex. Palate: powerful, flavourful, good acidity, fine bead, fine bitter notes, balanced.

Portell Rosat 2012 SS
100% trepat
85

VINS DEL SUD
Raval del Roser, 3
43886 Vilabella (Tarragona)
☎: +34 625 408 974
www.vinsdelsud.com
oriol@vinsdelsud.com

Gasela s/c BN
87
Colour: bright yellow. Nose: ripe fruit, fine lees, balanced, dried herbs. Palate: good acidity, flavourful, ripe fruit, long.

VINS EL CEP
Can Llopart de Les Alzines, Espiells
08770 Sant Sadurní D'Anoia (Barcelona)
☎: +34 938 912 353
Fax: +34 938 183 956
www.vinselcep.com
info@vinselcep.com

Claror 2009 BN Gran Reserva
xarel.lo, macabeo, parellada
87
Colour: bright straw. Nose: fine lees, floral, fragrant herbs, expressive. Palate: powerful, flavourful, good acidity, fine bead, balanced.

L'Alzinar 2010 BN Reserva
xarel.lo, macabeo, parellada
88
Colour: bright straw. Nose: medium intensity, fresh fruit, dried herbs, fine lees, floral. Palate: fresh, fruity, flavourful, good acidity.

L'Alzinar 2011 BR Reserva
xarel.lo, macabeo, parellada
88
Colour: bright straw. Nose: fine lees, floral, fragrant herbs, expressive. Palate: powerful, flavourful, good acidity, fine bead, balanced.

Marqués de Gelida 4 Heretats 2009 BN Gran Reserva
macabeo, xarel.lo, parellada, chardonnay
86
Colour: bright straw. Nose: medium intensity, fresh fruit, dried herbs, fine lees, floral. Palate: fresh, fruity, flavourful, good acidity.

Marqués de Gelida Brut Ecològic 2010 BR Reserva
macabeo, xarel.lo, parellada, chardonnay
90 🌸
Colour: bright straw. Nose: medium intensity, fresh fruit, dried herbs, fine lees, floral. Palate: fresh, fruity, flavourful, good acidity.

**Marqués de Gelida Exclusive
2010 BR Reserva**
macabeo, xarel.lo, parellada, chardonnay
88
Colour: bright straw. Nose: fine lees, floral, fragrant herbs, expressive. Palate: powerful, flavourful, good acidity, fine bead, balanced.

**Marqués de Gelida Gran Selecció
2009 BN Gran Reserva**
xarel.lo, macabeo, parellada, chardonnay
90
Colour: bright golden. Nose: fine lees, dry nuts, fragrant herbs, complex. Palate: powerful, flavourful, good acidity, fine bead, fine bitter notes.

**Marqués de Gelida Pinot
Noir 2011 BR Reserva**
pinot noir
87
Colour: rose. Nose: floral, red berry notes, ripe fruit, fragrant herbs, expressive. Palate: powerful, balanced, flavourful.

VINS I CAVES CUSCÓ BERGA
Esplugues, 7
08793 Avinyonet del Penedès
(Barcelona)
☎: +34 938 970 164
www.cuscoberga.com
cuscoberga@cuscoberga.com

Cuscó Berga 2010 BN Reserva
86
Colour: bright yellow. Nose: ripe fruit, fine lees, balanced, dried herbs. Palate: good acidity, flavourful, ripe fruit, long, correct.

Cuscó Berga 2010 BR Gran Reserva
87
Colour: bright yellow. Nose: fine lees, dry nuts, fragrant herbs. Palate: flavourful, good acidity, fine bead, fine bitter notes.

Cuscó Berga 2011 BR
85

Cuscó Berga Ecològic 2011 BN Reserva
88
Colour: bright yellow. Nose: fine lees, balanced, dried herbs, floral. Palate: good acidity, flavourful, ripe fruit, long, spicy.

Cuscó Berga Rosé 2012 BR
100% trepat
87
Colour: rose. Nose: floral, red berry notes, ripe fruit, fragrant herbs, expressive. Palate: powerful, balanced, flavourful.

VIÑA TORREBLANCA
Masia Torreblanca, s/n
08734 Olérdola (Barcelona)
☎: +34 938 915 066
Fax: +34 938 900 102
www.vinatorreblanca.com
info@vinatorreblanca.com

Torreblanca BN
macabeo, xarel.lo, parellada
86
Colour: bright yellow. Nose: ripe fruit, fine lees, balanced, dried herbs. Palate: good acidity, flavourful, long.

Torreblanca BR
macabeo, xarel.lo, parellada
86
Colour: bright yellow. Nose: ripe fruit, fruit liqueur notes, lees reduction notes, dried herbs. Palate: correct, slightly evolved.

Torreblanca 2008 Extra Brut Reserva
macabeo, xarel.lo, parellada, chardonnay
86
Colour: bright golden. Nose: fine lees, dry nuts, fragrant herbs. Palate: flavourful, good acidity, fine bead, fine bitter notes.

VIÑEDOS Y BODEGAS MAYO GARCÍA
La Font 116
12192 Vilafamés (Castellón)
☎: +34 964 329 312
www.mayocasanova.com
mail@mayogarcia.com

Magnanimvs 2011 BR Reserva
chardonnay, macabeo
85

VIÑEDOS Y BODEGAS VEGALFARO

Ctra. Pontón - Utiel, Km. 3
46390 Requena (Valencia)
☎: +34 962 320 680
Fax: +34 962 321 126
www.vegalfaro.com
rodolfo@vegalfaro.com

Vegalfaro 2009 BN Reserva
chardonnay, macabeo

90

Colour: bright yellow. Nose: ripe fruit, fine lees, balanced, dried herbs, citrus fruit. Palate: good acidity, flavourful, ripe fruit, long.

VIVES AMBRÒS

Mayor, 39
43812 Montferri (Tarragona)
☎: +34 639 521 652
Fax: +34 977 606 579
www.vivesambros.com
mail@vivesambros.com

Vives Ambròs 2008 BN Gran Reserva

90

Colour: bright golden. Nose: fine lees, dry nuts, fragrant herbs. Palate: powerful, flavourful, good acidity, fine bead, fine bitter notes.

Vives Ambròs 2010 BR Reserva

88

Colour: bright straw. Nose: fine lees, floral, fragrant herbs, expressive. Palate: powerful, flavourful, good acidity, fine bead, balanced.

Vives Ambròs Jujol 2009 BN Gran Reserva
100% xarel.lo

92

Colour: bright golden. Nose: fine lees, dry nuts, fragrant herbs, complex. Palate: powerful, flavourful, good acidity, fine bead, fine bitter notes.

Vives Ambròs Tradició 2007 BN Gran Reserva

91

Colour: bright straw. Nose: fine lees, dry nuts, fragrant herbs, complex, toasty. Palate: powerful, flavourful, good acidity, fine bead, fine bitter notes, elegant.

Vives Ambròs Tradició Magnum 2007 BN Gran Reserva

91

Colour: bright golden. Nose: fine lees, fragrant herbs, ripe fruit, dry nuts. Palate: powerful, flavourful, good acidity, fine bead, fine bitter notes.

DO. CIGALES

CONSEJO REGULADOR
Pza. Corro Vaca, 5
47270 Cigales (Valladolid)
☎ :+34 983 580 074 - Fax: +34 983 586 590
@: consejo@do-cigales.es
www.do-cigales.es

LOCATION:

The region stretches to the north of the Duero depression and on both sides of the Pisuerga, bordered by the Cérvalos and the Torozos hills. The vineyards are situated at an altitude of 750 m; the DO extends from part of the municipal area of Valladolid (the wine estate known as 'El Berrocal') to the municipality of Dueñas in Palencia, also including Cabezón de Pisuerga, Cigales, Corcos del Valle, Cubillas de Santa Marte, Fuensaldaña, Mucientes, Quintanilla de Trigueros, San Martín de Valvení, Santovenia de Pisuerga, Trigueros del Valle and Valoria la Buena.

GRAPE VARIETIES:

White: Verdejo, Albillo, Sauvignon Blanc and Viura.
Red: Tinta del País (Tempranillo), Garnacha Tinta, Garnacha Gris, Merlot, Syrah and Cabernet Sauvignon.

TYPES OF WINE:

Rosés: Cigales Nuevo. Produced with at least 60% of the Tinta del País variety and at least 20% of white varieties. The vintage must be displayed on the label. Cigales. Produced with at least 60% of the Tinta del País variety and at least 20% of white varieties. Marketed from 31st December of the following year. reds: Produced with at least 85% of the Tinta del País and the Garnacha Tinta varieties.

FIGURES:

Vineyard surface: 2,100 – Wine-Growers: 445 – Wineries: 34 – 2013 Harvest rating (Rosés and Reds): Very Good – Production 13: 5,740,000 litres – Market percentages: 80% domestic - 20% export.

SOIL:

The soil is sandy and limy with clay loam which is settled on clay and marl. It has an extremely variable limestone content which, depending on the different regions, ranges between 1% and 35%.

CLIMATE:

The climate is continental with Atlantic influences, and is marked by great contrasts in temperature, both yearly and day/night. The summers are extremely dry; the winters are harsh and prolonged, with frequent frost and fog; rainfall is irregular.

VINTAGE RATING   PEÑÍNGUIDE

2009	2010	2011	2012	2013
GOOD	EXCELLENT	EXCELLENT	VERY GOOD	GOOD

AVELINO VEGAS

Calvo Sotelo, 8
40460 Santiuste (Segovia)
☎: +34 921 596 002
Fax: +34 921 596 035
www.avelinovegas.com
ana@avelinovegas.com

Zarzales 2013 RD
tempranillo, garnacha, albillo, verdejo

88

Colour: rose, purple rim. Nose: powerfull, ripe fruit, red berry notes, floral, expressive. Palate: powerful, fruity, fresh, easy to drink.

BODEGA CÉSAR PRÍNCIPE

Ctra. Fuensaldaña-Mucientes, s/n
47194 Fuensaldaña (Valladolid)
☎: +34 983 663 123
www.cesarprincipe.es
cesarprincipe@cesarprincipe.es

César Príncipe 2011 TC
100% tempranillo

93

Colour: very deep cherry. Nose: ripe fruit, creamy oak, toasty, characterful, sweet spices, earthy notes. Palate: powerful, flavourful, toasty, round tannins.

BODEGA COOPERATIVA DE CIGALES

Las Bodegas, s/n
47270 Cigales (Valladolid)
☎: +34 983 580 135
Fax: +34 983 580 682
www.bodegacooperativacigales.com
bcc@bodegacooperativacigales.com

Torondos 2013 RD
87

Colour: rose, purple rim. Nose: powerfull, ripe fruit, red berry notes. Palate: powerful, fruity, fresh.

BODEGA HIRIART

Avda. Los Cortijos, 38
47270 Cigales (Valladolid)
☎: +34 983 580 094
Fax: +34 983 100 701
www.bodegahiriart.es
info@bodegahiriart.es

Candiles de Hiriart 2011 TC
tinta del país

88

Colour: bright cherry. Nose: ripe fruit, sweet spices, creamy oak, medium intensity. Palate: fruity, flavourful, toasty.

Hiriart 2010 TC
tinta del país

90

Colour: cherry, garnet rim. Nose: ripe fruit, spicy, creamy oak, toasty, complex. Palate: powerful, flavourful, toasty, round tannins.

Hiriart 2012 T Roble
tinta del país

87

Colour: very deep cherry, garnet rim. Nose: overripe fruit, warm, dried herbs. Palate: flavourful, ripe fruit, long.

Hiriart Élite 2013 RD
tinta del país, garnacha, verdejo

90

Colour: raspberry rose. Nose: elegant, candied fruit, dried flowers, fragrant herbs, red berry notes. Palate: light-bodied, flavourful, good acidity, long, spicy.

Hiriart Lágrima 2013 RD
tinta del país, garnacha, verdejo

88

Colour: rose, purple rim. Nose: ripe fruit, red berry notes, floral, expressive, medium intensity. Palate: powerful, fruity, fresh.

Hiriart sobre Lías 2013 RD
tinta del país, garnacha, verdejo

89

Colour: raspberry rose. Nose: ripe fruit, red berry notes, sweet spices. Palate: flavourful, fruity, good acidity.

Juana de Hiriart 2011 TC
tinta del país

88

Colour: cherry, garnet rim. Nose: fruit preserve, fruit liqueur notes, spicy. Palate: flavourful, pruney, balsamic.

BODEGA MUSEUM

Ctra. Cigales - Corcos, Km. 3
47270 Cigales (Valladolid)
☎: +34 983 581 029
Fax: +34 983 581 030
www.bodegasmuseum.com
info@bodegasmuseum.com

Museum 2010 TR
tempranillo

92

Colour: very deep cherry. Nose: ripe fruit, spicy, creamy oak, toasty, characterful. Palate: powerful, flavourful, toasty, round tannins.

Vinea 2010 TC
tempranillo

91

Colour: bright cherry. Nose: ripe fruit, sweet spices, creamy oak, expressive. Palate: flavourful, fruity, toasty, round tannins.

Vinea 2013 RD
tempranillo
89
Colour: raspberry rose. Nose: elegant, candied fruit, dried flowers, fragrant herbs, red berry notes. Palate: light-bodied, flavourful, good acidity, long, spicy.

BODEGA VALDELOSFRAILES
Camino de Cubillas, s/n
47290 Cubillas de Santa Marta (Valladolid)
☎: +34 983 485 028
Fax: +34 983 107 104
www.valdelosfrailes.es
valdelosfrailes@matarromera.es

Valdelosfrailes 2013 RD
89
Colour: rose, purple rim. Nose: powerfull, ripe fruit, red berry notes, floral, expressive. Palate: powerful, fruity, fine bitter notes.

Valdelosfrailes Prestigio 2006 TR
100% tempranillo
93
Colour: very deep cherry. Nose: ripe fruit, spicy, creamy oak, toasty, characterful, powerfull, dark chocolate. Palate: powerful, flavourful, toasty, round tannins.

Valdelosfrailes Tempranillo 2013 T
100% tempranillo
87
Colour: very deep cherry, garnet rim. Nose: overripe fruit, warm, dried herbs. Palate: flavourful, ripe fruit, long.

Valdelosfrailes Vendimia Seleccionada 2010 TC
100% tempranillo
91
Colour: cherry, garnet rim. Nose: ripe fruit, spicy, creamy oak, toasty, complex. Palate: powerful, flavourful, toasty, round tannins.

BODEGAS C.H. VINOS DE CUBILLAS
Paseo Fuente la Teja, 31
47290 Cubillas de Santa Marta (Valladolid)
☎: +34 983 585 203
Fax: +34 983 585 203
www.bodegaschvinosdecubillas.com
info@bodegaschvinosdecubillas.com

Valcabado 2009 TC
100% tempranillo
87
Colour: cherry, garnet rim. Nose: fruit preserve, fruit liqueur notes, spicy. Palate: flavourful, pruney, balsamic.

Valdecabado 2011 T Barrica
100% tempranillo
85

Valdecabado 2013 RD
85

BODEGAS FERNÁNDEZ CAMARERO
Don Alvaro de Bazán, 1 4ºB
28003 Madrid (Madrid)
☎: +34 677 682 426
www.balvinar.com
javier.fernandez@balvinar.com

Balvinar Pagos Seleccionados 2009 T
100% tempranillo
89
Colour: bright cherry. Nose: ripe fruit, sweet spices, creamy oak, aged wood nuances. Palate: fruity, flavourful, toasty.

BODEGAS HIJOS DE FÉLIX SALAS
Corrales, s/n
47280 Corcos del Valle (Valladolid)
☎: +34 685 783 213
Fax: +34 983 580 262
www.bodegasfelixsalas.com
bodega@bodegasfelixsalas.com

Viña Picota 2013 RD
tempranillo, albillo, verdejo, garnacha
82

BODEGAS LEZCANO-LACALLE
Ctra. de Valoria, s/n
47282 Trigueros del Valle (Valladolid)
☎: +34 629 280 515
www.lezcano-lacalle.com
info@lezcano-lacalle.com

Docetañidos 2013 RD
tempranillo
87
Colour: rose, purple rim. Nose: powerfull, ripe fruit, red berry notes, floral. Palate: powerful, fruity, fresh.

Lezcano-Lacalle 2010 TR
tempranillo, merlot
89
Colour: cherry, garnet rim. Nose: spicy, toasty, overripe fruit, mineral. Palate: powerful, flavourful, toasty, round tannins.

Maudes 2011 TC
tempranillo, merlot
86
Colour: very deep cherry. Nose: powerfull, aged wood nuances, woody, ripe fruit, grassy. Palate: fine bitter notes, warm, sweetness.

BODEGAS OVIDIO GARCÍA

Malpique, s/n
47270 Cigales (Valladolid)
☎: +34 628 509 475
Fax: +34 983 474 085
www.ovidiogarcia.com
info@ovidiogarcia.com

Ovidio García 2007 TR
100% tempranillo

88

Colour: cherry, garnet rim. Nose: fruit preserve, fruit liqueur notes, spicy. Palate: flavourful, pruney, balsamic.

Ovidio García Esencia 2009 TC
100% tempranillo

89

Colour: cherry, garnet rim. Nose: ripe fruit, spicy, creamy oak, toasty, complex. Palate: powerful, flavourful, toasty, round tannins.

Ovidio García Esencia 2010 TC
100% tempranillo

88

Colour: cherry, garnet rim. Nose: spicy, toasty, overripe fruit, mineral. Palate: powerful, flavourful, toasty, round tannins.

BODEGAS REMIGIO DE SALAS JALÓN

Carril de Vinateras, s/n
34210 Dueñas (Palencia)
☎: +34 979 780 056
Fax: +34 979 780 056
www.remigiodesalasjalon.com
amada@remigiodesalasjalon.com

Las Luceras 2012 T
tempranillo

87

Colour: very deep cherry, garnet rim. Nose: overripe fruit, warm, dried herbs. Palate: flavourful, ripe fruit, long.

Las Luceras 2013 RD

87

Colour: rose, purple rim. Nose: powerfull, ripe fruit, red berry notes, floral. Palate: powerful, fruity, fresh.

BODEGAS SANTA RUFINA

Pago Fuente La Teja. Pol. Ind. 3 - Parcela 102
47290 Cubillas de Santa Marta
(Valladolid)
☎: +34 983 585 202
Fax: +34 983 585 202
www.bodegassantarufina.com
info@bodegassantarufina.com

A Solas 2013 B
100% verdejo

82

Viña Rufina 2010 TC
100% tempranillo

87

Colour: bright cherry. Nose: ripe fruit, sweet spices, creamy oak. Palate: flavourful, fruity, toasty, round tannins.

Viña Rufina 2013 RD

80

BODEGAS Y VIÑEDOS ALFREDO SANTAMARÍA

Poniente, 18
47290 Cubillas de Santa Marta
(Valladolid)
☎: +34 983 585 006
Fax: +34 983 440 770
www.bodega-santamaria.com
info@bodega-santamaria.com

Alfredo Santamaría 2010 TC
tempranillo

89

Colour: bright cherry. Nose: ripe fruit, sweet spices, creamy oak, expressive. Palate: flavourful, fruity, toasty, round tannins.

Trascasas 2010 TR

89

Colour: very deep cherry. Nose: ripe fruit, spicy, creamy oak, toasty, characterful. Palate: powerful, flavourful, toasty, round tannins.

Valvinoso 2013 RD

86

Colour: rose, purple rim. Nose: ripe fruit, red berry notes, floral, medium intensity. Palate: powerful, fruity, fresh.

BODEGAS Y VIÑEDOS ROSAN

Santa María, 6
47270 Cigales (Valladolid)
☎: +34 983 580 006
Fax: +34 983 580 006
rodriguezsanz@telefonica.net

Albéitar 2012 T
100% tinta del país

88

Colour: cherry, purple rim. Nose: expressive, fresh fruit, red berry notes, floral, balsamic herbs. Palate: flavourful, fruity, good acidity, unctuous.

Rosan 2013 RD

83

BODEGAS Y VIÑEDOS SINFORIANO VAQUERO
San Pedro, 12
47194 Mucientes (Valladolid)
☎: +34 983 663 008
Fax: +34 983 660 465
www.sinforianobodegas.com
sinfo@sinforianobodegas.com

Sinfo 2012 RD Fermentado en Barrica
87
Colour: rose, purple rim. Nose: powerfull, ripe fruit, red berry notes, floral, sweet spices, creamy oak. Palate: powerful, fruity, fresh.

Sinfo 2012 T Roble
100% tempranillo
87
Colour: bright cherry. Nose: ripe fruit, sweet spices, creamy oak, expressive. Palate: flavourful, fruity, toasty, round tannins.

Sinforiano 2009 TR
100% tempranillo
92
Colour: very deep cherry. Nose: ripe fruit, spicy, creamy oak, toasty, characterful. Palate: powerful, flavourful, toasty, round tannins.

Sinforiano 2010 TC
100% tempranillo
91
Colour: cherry, garnet rim. Nose: ripe fruit, spicy, creamy oak, toasty, complex. Palate: powerful, flavourful, toasty, round tannins.

BODEGAS Y VIÑEDOS VALERIANO
Camino de las Bodegas, s/n
47290 Cubillas de Santa Marta (Valladolid)
☎: +34 983 585 085
Fax: +34 983 585 186
www.bodegasvaleriano.com
info@bodegasvaleriano.com

Valeriano 2010 TC
100% tempranillo
84

Valeriano 2012 T Roble
100% tempranillo
88
Colour: bright cherry. Nose: ripe fruit, sweet spices, creamy oak. Palate: flavourful, fruity, toasty, round tannins.

Valeriano 2013 B
100% verdejo
82

Viña Sesmero 2013 RD
tempranillo
80

CONCEJO BODEGAS
Ctra. Valoria, Km. 3.6
47200 Valoria La Buena (Valladolid)
☎: +34 983 502 263
Fax: +34 983 502 253
www.concejobodegas.com
info@concejobodegas.com

Carredueñas 2013 RD
tempranillo
88
Colour: coppery red. Nose: elegant, candied fruit, dried herbs. Palate: flavourful, light-bodied, fruity.

Carredueñas 2013 RD Fermentado en Barrica
tempranillo
89
Colour: coppery red. Nose: ripe fruit, violet drops, cocoa bean, creamy oak. Palate: sweetness, powerful.

Carredueñas Dolce 2013 RD
tempranillo
88
Colour: rose, purple rim. Nose: powerfull, ripe fruit, red berry notes, floral, expressive. Palate: powerful, fruity, fresh, good acidity, sweetness.

Concejo 2011 T
tempranillo
90
Colour: cherry, garnet rim. Nose: fruit preserve, fruit liqueur notes, spicy. Palate: flavourful, pruney, balsamic.

FARRÁN DIEZ BODEGAS Y VIÑEDOS S.L.
Ctra. Cubillas, Km. 1
47290 Cubillas de Santa María (Valladolid)
☎: +34 696 441 185
Fax: +34 983 400 114
www.bodegasfarran.com
farrandiez@gmail.com

Ajedrez 2013 RD
87
Colour: rose, purple rim. Nose: powerfull, ripe fruit, red berry notes, floral. Palate: powerful, fruity, fresh.

Malvanegra 2013 RD
88
Colour: rose, purple rim. Nose: powerfull, ripe fruit, red berry notes, floral, expressive. Palate: powerful, fruity, fresh.

Viña Farrán 2013 RD
87
Colour: rose, purple rim. Nose: powerfull, ripe fruit, red berry notes, floral. Palate: powerful, fruity, fresh.

FRUTOS VILLAR
Camino Los Barreros, s/n
47270 Cigales (Valladolid)
☎: +34 983 586 868
Fax: +34 983 580 180
www.bodegasfrutosvillar.com
bodegasfrutosvillar@bodegasfrutosvillar.com

Calderona 2012 T
100% tempranillo
87
Colour: very deep cherry, garnet rim. Nose: overripe fruit, warm, dried herbs. Palate: flavourful, ripe fruit, long.

Calderona 2008 TR
100% tempranillo
86
Colour: ruby red. Nose: spicy, fine reductive notes, wet leather, aged wood nuances, toasty, ripe fruit. Palate: spicy, long, toasty.

Calderona 2009 TC
100% tempranillo
89
Colour: bright cherry. Nose: ripe fruit, sweet spices, creamy oak, expressive. Palate: flavourful, fruity, toasty, round tannins.

Conde Ansúrez 2009 TC
100% tempranillo
87
Colour: bright cherry. Nose: ripe fruit, sweet spices. Palate: flavourful, fruity, toasty, round tannins.

Conde Ansúrez 2012 T
100% tempranillo
87
Colour: cherry, garnet rim. Nose: red berry notes, ripe fruit, balsamic herbs, spicy. Palate: powerful, flavourful, ripe fruit.

Conde Ansúrez 2013 RD
100% tempranillo
84

Viña Calderona 2013 RD
100% tempranillo
86
Colour: rose, purple rim. Nose: powerfull, ripe fruit, red berry notes. Palate: powerful, fruity, fresh.

HIJOS DE CRESCENCIA MERINO
Corrales s/n
47280 Corcos del Valle (Valladolid)
☎: +34 983 580 118
Fax: +34 983 580 118
www.bodegashcmerino.com
eugenio@bodegashcmerino.com

Viña Catajarros "Élite" 2013 RD
88
Colour: brilliant rose. Nose: elegant, candied fruit, dried flowers, fragrant herbs, red berry notes. Palate: light-bodied, flavourful, good acidity, long, spicy.

HIJOS DE MARCOS GÓMEZ S.L.
Cuarto San Pedro s/n
47194 Mucientes (Valladolid)
☎: +34 625 115 619
Fax: +34 983 587 764
www.salvueros.com
bodegas@salvueros.com

Salvueros 2013 RD
90
Colour: rose, purple rim. Nose: powerfull, ripe fruit, red berry notes, floral, expressive. Palate: powerful, fruity, fresh.

HIJOS DE RUFINO IGLESIAS
La Canoniga, 25
47194 Mucientes (Valladolid)
☎: +34 983 587 778
Fax: +34 983 587 778
www.hijosderufinoiglesias.com
bodega@hijosderufinoiglesias.com

Carratraviesa 2013 RD
87
Colour: rose, purple rim. Nose: ripe fruit, red berry notes, floral. Palate: powerful, fruity, fresh.

LA LEGUA
Ctra. Cigales, km. 1
47161 Fuensaldaña (Valladolid)
☎: +34 983 583 244
Fax: +34 983 583 172
www.lalegua.com
lalegua@lalegua.com

7L Rosado de una Noche 2013 RD
tempranillo, garnacha, cabernet sauvignon
89
Colour: coppery red. Nose: elegant, candied fruit, dried flowers, fragrant herbs, red berry notes. Palate: light-bodied, flavourful, good acidity, long, spicy.

La Legua 2010 TR
tempranillo
88
Colour: very deep cherry. Nose: ripe fruit, spicy, creamy oak, toasty, characterful. Palate: powerful, flavourful, toasty, round tannins.

La Legua 2011 TC
tempranillo

87

Colour: cherry, garnet rim. Nose: ripe fruit, spicy, creamy oak, toasty, complex. Palate: powerful, flavourful, toasty, round tannins.

La Legua 2012 T Roble
tempranillo

87

Colour: cherry, garnet rim. Nose: red berry notes, ripe fruit, spicy, creamy oak, toasty. Palate: powerful, flavourful, toasty, round tannins.

La Legua 2013 T
tempranillo

86

Colour: very deep cherry, garnet rim. Nose: dried herbs, ripe fruit. Palate: flavourful, ripe fruit, long.

La Legua Capricho 2009 TR
tempranillo

90

Colour: very deep cherry, garnet rim. Nose: powerfull, ripe fruit, roasted coffee, dark chocolate. Palate: powerful, toasty, roasted-coffee aftertaste.

La Legua Garnacha 2013 T
garnacha

88

Colour: cherry, purple rim. Nose: expressive, fresh fruit, red berry notes, floral. Palate: flavourful, fruity, good acidity, round tannins.

TRASLANZAS
Barrio de las Bodegas, s/n
47194 Mucientes (Valladolid)
☎: +34 639 641 123
Fax: +34 946 020 263
www.traslanzas.com
traslanzas@traslanzas.com

Traslanzas 2009 TC
100% tempranillo

91

Colour: very deep cherry. Nose: ripe fruit, spicy, creamy oak, toasty, characterful, earthy notes. Palate: powerful, flavourful, toasty, round tannins.

DO. CONCA DE BARBERÀ

CONSEJO REGULADOR

Torre del Portal de Sant Antoni De la Volta, 2
43400 Montblanc
☎ :+34 977 926 905 - Fax: +34 977 926 906
@: cr@doconcadebarbera.com
www.doconcadebarbera.com

LOCATION:

In the north of the province of Tarragona with a production area covering 14 municipalities, to which two new ones have recently been added: Savallà del Comtat and Vilanova de Prades.

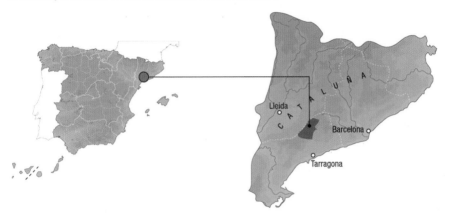

GRAPE VARIETIES:

White: Macabeo, Parellada (majority 3,300 Ha) Chardonnay, Sauvignon Blanc and Viognier.
Red: Trepat, Ull de Llebre (Tempranillo), Garnatxa, Cabernet Sauvignon, Merlot, Syrah and Pinot Noir.

FIGURES:

Vineyard surface: 3,807 – Wine-Growers: 957 – Wineries: 23 – 2013 Harvest rating: - – Production 12: 1,491,000 litres – Market percentages: 80% domestic - 20% export.

SOIL:

The soil is mainly brownish-grey and limy. The vines are cultivated on slopes protected by woodland. An important aspect is the altitude which gives the wines a fresh, light character.

CLIMATE:

Mediterranean and continental influences, as the vineyards occupy a river valley surrounded by mountain ranges without direct contact with the sea.

VINTAGE RATING

PEÑÍNGUIDE

2009	2010	2011	2012	2013
GOOD	GOOD	GOOD	VERY GOOD	GOOD

ABADÍA DE POBLET

Passeig de l'Abat Conill, 6
43448 Poblet (Tarragona)
☎: +34 977 870 358
www.grupocodorniu.com
info@abadiadepoblet.es

Abadía de Poblet 2010 T
100% pinot noir

88

Colour: light cherry. Nose: ripe fruit, spicy, creamy oak, toasty, complex. Palate: powerful, flavourful, toasty, round tannins.

Intramurs 2012 T
ull de llebre, syrah

87

Colour: bright cherry. Nose: ripe fruit, sweet spices, creamy oak. Palate: flavourful, fruity, toasty.

Intramurs 2013 B
100% chardonnay

88

Colour: bright straw. Nose: white flowers, fragrant herbs, fruit expression. Palate: fresh, fruity, flavourful, balanced, elegant.

Les Masies de Poblet 2010 T
100% pinot noir

87

Colour: ruby red. Nose: spicy, fine reductive notes, aged wood nuances, toasty, smoky, balsamic herbs. Palate: spicy, long, toasty.

BODEGA SANSTRAVÉ

De la Conca, 10
43412 Solivella (Tarragona)
☎: +34 977 892 165
Fax: +34 977 892 073
www.sanstrave.com
bodega@sanstrave.com

Sanstravé Finca Gasset Crepuscle 2012 T Fermentado en Barrica
syrah, merlot

89

Colour: very deep cherry, garnet rim. Nose: powerfull, ripe fruit, roasted coffee, dark chocolate. Palate: toasty, roasted-coffee aftertaste.

Sanstravé Finca Gasset Muscat 2012 BFB
moscatel

90

Colour: bright straw. Nose: white flowers, fragrant herbs, fruit expression. Palate: fresh, fruity, flavourful, balanced, elegant.

Sanstravé Finca Gasset Syrah 2006 TR
syrah

88

Colour: ruby red. Nose: ripe fruit, fragrant herbs, wild herbs, mineral, fine reductive notes. Palate: spicy, long, balanced, fine tannins.

Sanstravé Partida dels Jueus 2011 TC
merlot, trepat, cabernet sauvignon, tempranillo

90

Colour: cherry, garnet rim. Nose: ripe fruit, spicy, creamy oak, toasty, complex, balanced. Palate: powerful, flavourful, toasty, round tannins, elegant.

BODEGAS TORRES

Miguel Torres i Carbó, 6
08720 Vilafranca del Penedès (Barcelona)
☎: +34 938 177 400
Fax: +34 938 177 444
www.torres.com
mailadmin@torres.es

Grans Muralles 2006 TR
monastrell, garnacha, garró, samsó

93

Colour: cherry, garnet rim. Nose: balanced, complex, ripe fruit, spicy. Palate: good structure, flavourful, round tannins.

Milmanda 2011 B
chardonnay

91

Colour: bright yellow. Nose: powerfull, ripe fruit, sweet spices, creamy oak, fragrant herbs. Palate: rich, smoky aftertaste, flavourful, fresh, good acidity, elegant.

CARA NORD

25457 El Vilosell (Lleida)
☎: +34 973 176 029
Fax: +34 973 175 945
www.caranordceller.com
hola@caranordceller.com

Cara Nord 2013 B
macabeo, chardonnay

92

Colour: bright straw. Nose: white flowers, fresh fruit, expressive, fine lees, dried herbs, mineral. Palate: flavourful, fruity, good acidity, balanced.

Cara Nord Negre 2012 T
garnacha, syrah, garrut

94

Colour: cherry, garnet rim. Nose: ripe fruit, spicy, creamy oak, toasty, dark chocolate, earthy notes. Palate: powerful, flavourful, toasty, round tannins.

CARLANIA CELLER

Hort d'en Cirera, 23
43422 Barberà de la Conca (Tarragona)
☎: +34 977 887 375
www.carlania.com
info@carlania.com

Carlania 2008 TR
merlot, trepat

87 🌷

Colour: cherry, garnet rim. Nose: ripe fruit, spicy, creamy oak, toasty, complex, earthy notes. Palate: powerful, flavourful, toasty.

Carlania 2010 TC
tempranillo, trepat

84 🌷

El Petit Carlania 2012 T
100% trepat

86 🌷

Colour: cherry, garnet rim. Nose: warm, ripe fruit, balsamic herbs. Palate: flavourful, ripe fruit, long.

El Petit Carlania 2013 T
100% trepat

87

Colour: light cherry. Nose: expressive, fresh fruit, red berry notes, floral. Palate: flavourful, fruity, good acidity, round tannins.

CASTELL D'OR

Mare Rafols, 3- 1ºD
08720 Vilafranca del Penedès
(Barcelona)
☎: +34 938 905 385
Fax: +34 938 905 455
www.castelldor.com
castelldor@castelldor.com

Castell de la Comanda 2009 TR
cabernet sauvignon

86

Colour: cherry, garnet rim. Nose: balanced, complex, ripe fruit, spicy. Palate: good structure, flavourful.

Castell de la Comanda 2011 TC
cabernet sauvignon, cabernet franc

82

Castell de la Comanda 2013 T
tempranillo, cabernet sauvignon

84

Francoli 2009 TR
cabernet sauvignon

86

Colour: cherry, garnet rim. Nose: balanced, complex, ripe fruit, spicy. Palate: good structure, flavourful.

Francoli 2011 TC
cabernet sauvignon, cabernet franc

83

Francoli 2013 B
macabeo

82

Francoli 2013 RD
trepat

84

Francoli 2013 T
tempranillo, cabernet sauvignon

84

CELLER CARLES ANDREU

Sant Sebastià, 19
43423 Pira (Tarragona)
☎: +34 977 887 404
Fax: +34 977 887 427
www.cavandreu.com
celler@cavandreu.com

Vino Tinto Trepat Carles Andreu 2012 T
100% trepat

90

Colour: light cherry. Nose: elegant, candied fruit, dried flowers, fragrant herbs, red berry notes. Palate: light-bodied, flavourful, good acidity, long, spicy.

CELLER ESCODA SANAHUJA

Camí de Lilla a Prenafeta, s/n
43400 Montblanc (Tarragona)
☎: +34 659 478 198
Fax: +34 977 314 897
www.celler-escodasanahuja.com
jre@celler-escodasanahuja.com

Coll del Sabater 2007 TC

89 🌷

Nose: balanced, complex, ripe fruit, spicy, cigar, earthy notes, scrubland. Palate: good structure, flavourful, round tannins, elegant.

Els Bassots B

89 🌷

Colour: old gold, amber rim. Nose: dried herbs, faded flowers, slightly evolved, saline, dry nuts. Palate: ripe fruit, spicy, flavourful. Personality.

La Llopetera 2012 TC

90

Colour: cherry, garnet rim. Nose: ripe fruit, wild herbs, earthy notes, spicy, creamy oak. Palate: balanced, flavourful, long, balsamic, good structure.

Nas del gegant 2012 T

89

Colour: cherry, purple rim. Nose: ripe fruit, spicy, scrubland, creamy oak. Palate: powerful, flavourful, spicy, long.

CELLER MAS FORASTER

Camino Ermita de Sant Josep, s/n
43400 Montblanc (Tarragona)
☎: +34 977 860 229
Fax: +34 977 875 037
www.josepforaster.com
ricard@josepforaster.com

Josep Foraster 2011 TC
cabernet sauvignon, tempranillo, syrah, trepat

87

Colour: bright cherry. Nose: ripe fruit, sweet spices, creamy oak, balsamic herbs. Palate: fruity, flavourful, toasty.

Josep Foraster Blanc del Coster 2013 B

84

Josep Foraster Blanc Selecció 2012 B

86

Colour: bright yellow. Nose: powerfull, ripe fruit, creamy oak, fragrant herbs, smoky. Palate: rich, smoky aftertaste, flavourful, fresh, good acidity.

Josep Foraster Collita 2013 T

86

Colour: cherry, purple rim. Nose: fresh fruit, red berry notes, floral, balsamic herbs. Palate: flavourful, fruity, good acidity.

Josep Foraster Rosat Trepat 2013 RD
trepat

88

Colour: raspberry rose. Nose: elegant, dried flowers, fragrant herbs, red berry notes. Palate: light-bodied, flavourful, good acidity, long, spicy.

Josep Foraster Selecció 2011 TC
garnacha, cabernet sauvignon

90

Colour: cherry, garnet rim. Nose: ripe fruit, spicy, creamy oak, toasty, complex, earthy notes, balsamic herbs. Palate: powerful, flavourful, toasty, balanced.

Josep Foraster Trepat 2012 T
trepat

87

Colour: light cherry. Nose: fruit liqueur notes, fragrant herbs, mineral, spicy. Palate: flavourful, spicy, balsamic.

CELLER MOLÍ DELS CAPELLANS

Celler de Viveristes de
Barberà de la Conca
43422 Barberà de la Conca (Tarragona)
☎: +34 651 034 221
www.molidelscapellans.com
info@molidelscapellans.com

Molí dels Capellans BFB
chardonnay

87

Colour: bright yellow. Nose: powerfull, ripe fruit, sweet spices, creamy oak, fragrant herbs. Palate: rich, smoky aftertaste, flavourful, fresh, good acidity.

Molí dels Capellans 2012 T
trepat

88 🏵

Colour: light cherry. Nose: spicy, creamy oak, fragrant herbs, fruit liqueur notes. Palate: balanced, flavourful, balsamic.

Molí dels Capellans Premium 2010 TC
100% trepat

88

Colour: light cherry. Nose: fruit liqueur notes, wild herbs, spicy, creamy oak. Palate: round tannins, flavourful, balsamic, spicy.

Molí dels Capellans Selecció 2011 T

87

Colour: bright cherry, garnet rim. Nose: ripe fruit, sweet spices, creamy oak, expressive. Palate: flavourful, fruity, toasty, round tannins.

CELLER TINTORÉ DE VIMBODÍ I POBLET

Copèrnic, 44 Baixos
08021 (Barcelona)
☎: +34 932 096 101
www.tinto-re.com
info@tinto-re.com

Re 2011 TC
garnacha, cariñena, cabernet sauvignon

89

Colour: bright cherry. Nose: ripe fruit, sweet spices, creamy oak, medium intensity, fragrant herbs. Palate: fruity, flavourful, toasty.

CELLER VEGA AIXALÁ

De la Font, 11
43439 Vilanova de Prades (Barcelona)
☎: +34 636 519 821
Fax: +34 977 869 019
www.vegaaixala.com
info@vegaaixala.com

Vega Aixalá Barrau 2012 T
tempranillo, garnacha, syrah

87

Colour: light cherry. Nose: ripe fruit, spicy, creamy oak, toasty, characterful. Palate: powerful, flavourful, toasty, balsamic.

Vega Aixalá La Bauma 2012 B
garnacha blanca, chardonnay

87

Colour: bright straw. Nose: white flowers, fresh fruit, expressive, dried herbs. Palate: flavourful, fruity, good acidity, balanced.

Vega Aixalá Viern 2009 TC
cabernet sauvignon, garnacha, cariñena, syrah

86

Colour: ruby red. Nose: spicy, fine reductive notes, wet leather, aged wood nuances, toasty. Palate: spicy, long, toasty.

CELLERS DOMENYS
Plaça del Sindicat, s/n
43411 Blancafort (Tarragona)
☎: +34 977 892 115
Fax: +34 977 892 115
www.latevacooperativa.com

Comanglora 2013 RD
100% trepat

86

Colour: rose, purple rim. Nose: powerfull, ripe fruit, red berry notes, floral. Palate: powerful, fruity, fresh.

CELLERS ROSET
Ctra. N-240 km. 38,8 Pol. Ind. Plans de Jori
43400 Montblanc (Tarragona)
☎: +34 977 862 663
Fax: +34 977 862 333
www.cellersroset.cat
info@brescat.cat

Ambari 2012 B
macabeo, parellada

84

Brescat 2008 TC
cabernet sauvignon, merlot, syrah

84

Rogent 2012 T
cabernet sauvignon, ull de llebre

84

CLOS MONTBLANC
Ctra. Montblanc-Barbera, s/n
43422 Barberà de la Conca (Tarragona)
☎: +34 977 887 030
Fax: +34 977 887 032
www.closmontblanc.com
club@closmontblanc.com

Clos Montblanc Castell Rosat 2013 RD
garnacha

84

Clos Montblanc Masía Les Comes 2008 TR
cabernet sauvignon, merlot

87

Colour: deep cherry, orangey edge. Nose: waxy notes, tobacco, ripe fruit, spicy. Palate: fine bitter notes, elegant, flavourful, fine tannins.

Clos Montblanc Merlot 2011 TC
100% merlot

86

Colour: cherry, garnet rim. Nose: ripe fruit, spicy, creamy oak, toasty, balsamic herbs. Palate: powerful, flavourful, toasty, good acidity.

Clos Montblanc Pinot Noir 2012 TC
100% pinot noir

87

Colour: very deep cherry, garnet rim. Nose: powerfull, ripe fruit, fruit liqueur notes, spicy. Palate: powerful, toasty, spicy.

Clos Montblanc Sauvignon Blanc 2013 B
100% sauvignon blanc

85

Clos Montblanc Syrah 2011 T
100% syrah

86

Colour: deep cherry. Nose: powerfull, red berry notes, ripe fruit, floral, balsamic herbs, creamy oak. Palate: powerful, toasty, balsamic.

Clos Montblanc Xipella Blanc 2013 B
macabeo, parellada

87

Colour: bright straw. Nose: fresh, fresh fruit, white flowers, balsamic herbs. Palate: flavourful, fruity, good acidity, balanced.

Gran Clos Montblanc Unic Trepat 2011 T
100% trepat

89

Colour: cherry, garnet rim. Nose: ripe fruit, spicy, creamy oak, toasty, complex. Palate: powerful, flavourful, toasty, round tannins, balanced.

GERIDA VITICULTORS
Fortuny, 2
43411 Blancafort (Tarragona)
☎: +34 659 405 419
info@geridavins.cat

Cuvic 2012 T
syrah, ull de llebre, cabernet sauvignon

87

Colour: bright cherry. Nose: ripe fruit, sweet spices, creamy oak, balsamic herbs. Palate: fruity, flavourful, toasty.

Encantats 2013 T Maceración Carbónica
ull de llebre

88

Colour: cherry, purple rim. Nose: red berry notes, raspberry, fruit expression, fragrant herbs. Palate: flavourful, light-bodied, good acidity, fresh, fruity.

Poal 2012 B
chardonnay, macabeo

86

Colour: bright straw. Nose: white flowers, fresh fruit, expressive, dried herbs. Palate: flavourful, fruity, good acidity, balanced.

RENDÉ MASDÉU
Avda. Catalunya, 44
43440 L'Espluga de Francolí
(Tarragona)
☎: +34 977 871 361
Fax: +34 977 871 361
www.rendemasdeu.cat
celler@rendemasdeu.cat

Arnau syrah de Rendé Masdeu 2011 T
syrah

90

Colour: cherry, garnet rim. Nose: ripe fruit, spicy, creamy oak, toasty, complex. Palate: powerful, flavourful, toasty, round tannins.

inQuiet de Rendé Masdeu 2012 T
cabernet sauvignon

87 🌢

Colour: cherry, garnet rim. Nose: ripe fruit, wild herbs, spicy, creamy oak. Palate: balanced, flavourful, long, balsamic.

Rendé Masdeu 2007 TR

88

Colour: cherry, garnet rim. Nose: balanced, complex, ripe fruit, spicy. Palate: good structure, flavourful, round tannins.

Rendé Masdeu 2010 TC

88

Colour: cherry, garnet rim. Nose: ripe fruit, spicy, creamy oak, toasty, complex. Palate: powerful, flavourful, toasty, round tannins.

Rendé Masdéu Manuela Ventosa 2009 T Fermentado en Barrica

90

Colour: very deep cherry. Nose: ripe fruit, spicy, creamy oak, toasty, characterful. Palate: powerful, flavourful, toasty, round tannins, balanced.

Rendé Masdeu Rosat 2013 RD
syrah

87 🌢

Colour: brilliant rose. Nose: floral, red berry notes, wild herbs. Palate: fresh, fruity, flavourful.

ROSA MARÍA TORRES
Avda. Anguera, 2
43424 Sarral (Tarragona)
☎: +34 977 890 013
www.rosamariatorres.com
info@rosamariatorres.com

Rd Roure 2012 T
cabernet sauvignon, merlot

84

Saüc 2011 TC
cabernet franc

89

Colour: cherry, garnet rim. Nose: ripe fruit, wild herbs, spicy, creamy oak, mineral. Palate: balanced, flavourful, long, balsamic.

Susel 2013 RD
pinot noir

89

Colour: onion pink. Nose: elegant, candied fruit, dried flowers, fragrant herbs, red berry notes. Palate: light-bodied, flavourful, good acidity, long, spicy.

Susel 2013 T
cabernet sauvignon

86

Colour: very deep cherry, garnet rim. Nose: dried herbs, ripe fruit, floral. Palate: flavourful, ripe fruit, long.

Vinya Plans 2011 TC
cabernet sauvignon, cabernet franc, syrah

86

Colour: cherry, garnet rim. Nose: ripe fruit, spicy, creamy oak, toasty, grassy. Palate: powerful, flavourful, toasty.

Viognier 2011 BFB
viognier

89

Colour: bright golden. Nose: ripe fruit, dry nuts, powerfull, toasty, aged wood nuances, sweet spices. Palate: flavourful, fruity, spicy, toasty, long.

SUCCÉS VINÍCOLA
Vinyols, 3
43400 Montblanc (Tarragona)
☎: +34 677 144 629
www.succesvinicola.com
succesvinicola@gmail.com

Feedback de Succés Vinícola 2011 T
cabernet sauvignon, tempranillo, merlot, garrut

89

Colour: cherry, garnet rim. Nose: ripe fruit, spicy, creamy oak, toasty, fine reductive notes. Palate: powerful, flavourful, toasty, balanced.

Succés El Mentider 2012 T
trepat

91

Colour: bright cherry. Nose: sweet spices, creamy oak, red berry notes, ripe fruit, expressive. Palate: flavourful, fruity, toasty, round tannins.

Succés Experiència Parellada 2013 B
parellada

88

Colour: bright straw. Nose: fresh, fresh fruit, white flowers, expressive. Palate: flavourful, fruity, good acidity, balanced.

Succés La Cuca de LLum 2013 T
trepat

90

Colour: light cherry. Nose: mineral, fragrant herbs, spicy, balanced. Palate: flavourful, fruity, balsamic.

VINÍCOLA DE SARRAL Í SELECCIÓ DE CREDIT

Avinguda de la Conca, 33
43424 Sarral (Tarragona)
☎: +34 977 890 031
Fax: +34 977 890 136
www.cava-portell.com
cavaportell@covisal.es

Portell 2006 TR
merlot, cabernet sauvignon, tempranillo

85

Portell 2010 TC
cabernet sauvignon, merlot, tempranillo

82

Portell Agulla Blanc 2013 Blanco de Aguja
macabeo, parellada

83

Portell Blanc de Blancs 2013 B
macabeo, parellada

85

Portell Blanc Semi dolç 2013 B
macabeo, parellada

85

Portell Rosat Trepat 2013 RD
trepat

85

VINS DE PEDRA

Sant Josep, 13
43400 Montblanc (Tarragona)
☎: +34 630 405 118
www.vinsdepedra.es
celler@vinsdepedra.es

L'Orni 2012 B
chardonnay

89

Colour: bright straw. Nose: white flowers, fresh fruit, expressive, fine lees, dried herbs. Palate: flavourful, fruity, good acidity, balanced.

La Musa 2011 T
merlot, cabernet sauvignon

86

Colour: cherry, garnet rim. Nose: ripe fruit, spicy, creamy oak, toasty, complex, balsamic herbs, fine reductive notes. Palate: powerful, flavourful, toasty.

DO / D.O.P. CONDADO DE HUELVA / VINO NARANJA DEL CONDADO DE HUELVA

CONSEJO REGULADOR

Plaza Ildefonso Pinto, s/n.
21710 Bollullos Par del Condado (Huelva)
☎:+34 959 410 322 - Fax: +34 959 413 859
@: cr@condadodehuelva.es
www.condadodehuelva.es

LOCATION:

In the south east of Huelva. It occupies the plain of Bajo Guadalquivir. The production area covers the municipal areas of Almonte, Beas, Bollullos Par del Condado, Bonares, Chucena, Gibraleón, Hinojos, La Palma del Condado, Lucena del Puerto, Manzanilla, Moguer, Niebla, Palos de la Frontera, Rociana del Condado, San Juan del Puerto, Villalba del Alcor, Villarrasa and Trigueros.

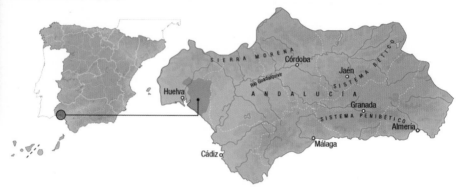

GRAPE VARIETIES:

WHITE: Zalema (majority with 86% of vineyards), Palomino, Listán de Huelva, Garrido Fino, Moscatel de Alejandría and Pedro Ximénez.
RED: Merlot, Syrah, Tempranillo, Cabernet Sauvignon and Cabernet Franc.

FIGURES:

Vineyard surface: 2,530 – Wine-Growers: 1,474 – Wineries: 30 – 2013 Harvest rating: Very Good – Production 13: 18,327,658 litres – Market percentages: 98% domestic - 2% export.

SOIL:

In general, flat and slightly rolling terrain, with fairly neutral soils of medium fertility. The soil is mainly reddish, brownish-grey with alluvium areas in the proximity of the Guadalquivir.

CLIMATE:

Mediterranean in nature, with certain Atlantic influences. The winters and springs are fairly mild, with long hot summers. The average annual temperature is 18 °C, and the average rainfall per year is around 550 mm, with a relative humidity of between 60% and 80%.

VINTAGE RATING

PEÑÍNGUIDE

2009	2010	2011	2012	2013
GOOD	GOOD	GOOD	VERY GOOD	AVERAGE

1ER. CONSORCIO DE BODEGUEROS ESPAÑOLES

Dirección Polígono Industrial
El Palmar calle Torno, 27
11500 El Puerto de Santa María (Cádiz)
☎: +34 956 056 642
www.vinodenaranja.com
admin@emc3.es

Orange Tree (Vino Naranja)
zalema

87

Colour: coppery red. Nose: fruit liqueur notes, fruit liqueur notes, citrus fruit, cocoa bean, caramel. Palate: powerful, flavourful, fruity.

AGROALIMENTARIA VIRGEN DEL ROCÍO

Avda. de Cabezudos, 1
21730 Almonte (Huelva)
☎: +34 959 406 146
www.raigal.es
administracion@raigal.com

Raigal 2013 B
zalema

87

Colour: bright straw. Nose: white flowers, fruit expression, wild herbs. Palate: fresh, fruity, flavourful, elegant.

BODEGAS ANDRADE

Avda. Coronación, 35
21710 Bollullos del Condado (Huelva)
☎: +34 959 410 106
Fax: +34 959 410 305
www.bodegasandrade.es
informacion@bodegasandrade.es

Andrade PX Gran Reserva
100% pedro ximénez

87

Colour: dark mahogany. Nose: dried fruit, pattisserie, toasty. Palate: sweet, rich, unctuous, powerful.

Andrade Pedro Ximénez 1985 GE Reserva
100% pedro ximénez

87

Colour: mahogany. Nose: dried fruit, aged wood nuances, creamy oak, sweet spices, varnish, caramel. Palate: rich, powerful, flavourful.

Andrade Syrah T Roble
100% syrah

85

Andrade Vino de Naranja 1985
pedro ximénez

88

Colour: mahogany. Nose: powerfull, characterful, citrus fruit, fruit liqueur notes, spicy, caramel. Palate: flavourful, powerful, fruity, complex.

Andrade Vino Naranja GE
zalema

87

Colour: light mahogany. Nose: candied fruit, citrus fruit, ripe fruit, wild herbs, spicy. Palate: fruity, powerful, flavourful.

Castillo de Andrade 2013 B
100% zalema

83

Doceañero CR
pedro ximénez, zalema

88

Nose: powerfull, complex, elegant, dry nuts, toasty. Palate: rich, fine bitter notes, fine solera notes, long, spicy.

Doceañero Oloroso OL
zalema

86

Colour: light mahogany. Nose: powerfull, dry nuts, toasty, aged wood nuances. Palate: rich, long, fine solera notes.

Fino Palmarejo Condado Pálido
palomino

84

Murallas de Niebla 2013 Semidulce
moscatel, zalema

80

BODEGAS DE DIEZMO NUEVO BODEGA SAENZ

Sor Ángela de la Cruz, 56
21800 Moguer (Huelva)
☎: +34 959 370 004
Fax: +34 959 371 840
www.bodegadiezmonuevo.com
info@bodegadiezmonuevo.com

Melquiades Saenz "Vino de Naranja" B

85

Viña El Patriarca 2011 T
syrah, cabernet sauvignon

81

Viña El Patriarca 2012 T
syrah, cabernet sauvignon

83

Viña El Patriarca Semidulce 2013 B

80

BODEGAS IGLESIAS

Teniente Merchante, 2
21710 Bollullos del Condado (Huelva)
☎: +34 959 410 439
Fax: +34 959 410 463
www.bodegasiglesias.com
bodegasiglesias@bodegasiglesias.com

% UZ Cien x Cien Uva Zalema 2013 B Joven
100% zalema

87

Colour: bright straw. Nose: fragrant herbs, saline, candied fruit, floral. Palate: fruity, flavourful, good structure.

Letrado Solera 1992 GE Solera
100% zalema

86

Colour: mahogany. Nose: acetaldehyde, roasted almonds, aged wood nuances, sweet spices, creamy oak. Palate: fine bitter notes, powerful, flavourful, long.

Par Vino Naranja Vino de licor

88

Colour: light mahogany. Nose: candied fruit, citrus fruit, wild herbs, spicy. Palate: rich, powerful, flavourful, fruity.

Ricahembra Solera 1980 GE

88

Colour: dark mahogany. Nose: fruit preserve, dry nuts, dried fruit, aromatic coffee, toasty. Palate: balanced, flavourful, long, creamy.

BODEGAS OLIVEROS

Rábida, 12
21710 Bollullos Par del Condado
(Huelva)
☎: +34 959 410 057
Fax: +34 959 410 057
www.bodegasoliveros.com
info@bodegasoliveros.com

Oliveros Oloroso OL

82

Oliveros Pedro Ximénez PX
pedro ximénez

89

Colour: dark mahogany. Nose: fruit liqueur notes, dried fruit, toasty, dark chocolate. Palate: sweet, rich, unctuous, powerful.

Oliveros Vino Naranja B

86

Colour: mahogany. Nose: fruit liqueur notes, citrus fruit, spicy, sweet spices. Palate: powerful, flavourful, rich, fruity.

BODEGAS SAUCI

Doctor Fleming, 1
21710 Bollullos del Condado (Huelva)
☎: +34 959 410 524
Fax: +34 959 410 331
www.bodegassauci.es
sauci@bodegassauci.es

Espinapura Condádo Pálido
100% palomino

89

Colour: bright yellow. Nose: complex, expressive, pungent, saline, faded flowers, dried herbs. Palate: rich, powerful, fresh, fine bitter notes, balanced.

Riodiel Solera 1980 Condádo Viejo
100% palomino

86

Colour: mahogany. Nose: dry nuts, spicy, acetaldehyde, sweet spices. Palate: powerful, flavourful, spicy, long.

S' Naranja Vino de licor

88

Colour: mahogany. Nose: fruit liqueur notes, candied fruit, caramel, pattiserie, expressive. Palate: powerful, flavourful, spirituous, complex.

S' Px Dulce Natural Vino de licor
100% pedro ximénez

90

Colour: mahogany. Nose: dried fruit, dry nuts, sweet spices, pattiserie, toasty. Palate: powerful, rich, flavourful, spicy, long.

S' Px Solera 1989 PX
100% pedro ximénez

91

Colour: dark mahogany. Nose: complex, fruit liqueur notes, dried fruit, pattiserie, toasty. Palate: sweet, rich, unctuous, powerful.

S' Vino Dulce Vino de licor
palomino, pedro ximénez

85

Sauci 2013 B Joven
100% zalema

88

Colour: bright straw. Nose: white flowers, fragrant herbs, fruit expression, expressive. Palate: fresh, fruity, flavourful, elegant.

Sauci Cream Solera 1980 CR

85

Sauci Vendimia Tardía Semidulce 2013 B Joven
100% zalema

84

CONVENTO DE MORAÑINA

Avda. de la Paz, 43
21710 Bollullos Par del Condado
(Huelva)
☎: +34 959 412 250
www.bodegasconvento.com
bodega@bodegasconvento.com

Amaranto Generoso de Licor Dulce
100% moscatel
85

Convento PX Reserva
100% pedro ximénez
90
Colour: dark mahogany. Nose: fruit liqueur notes, dried fruit, pattiserie, toasty. Palate: sweet, rich, unctuous, powerful.

Convento de Morañina 2013 B
100% zalema
86
Colour: bright straw. Nose: fresh, fresh fruit, white flowers, fruit expression. Palate: flavourful, fruity, good acidity.

Convento Naranja Semidulce
zalema
89
Colour: light mahogany. Nose: fruit liqueur notes, candied fruit, citrus fruit, fresh, powerfull. Palate: powerful, flavourful, complex, long.

Convento Sureño Viejo Condado Viejo Oloroso
listán blanco, zalema
85

Secreto del Convento 1960 OL
listán blanco, palomino, pedro ximénez
92
Colour: dark mahogany. Nose: powerfull, complex, elegant, dry nuts, toasty, dried fruit, acetaldehyde. Palate: rich, long, fine solera notes, spicy, unctuous, round.

COOPERATIVA VIT. NTRA. SRA. DEL SOCORRO S.C.A.

Carril de los Moriscos, 72
21720 Rociana del Condado (Huelva)
☎: +34 959 416 069
Fax: +34 959 092 900
jl63@nuestrasenoradelsocorro.com

Don Frede 2011 TC
86
Colour: deep cherry. Nose: ripe fruit, spicy, creamy oak, toasty, wild herbs. Palate: powerful, flavourful, toasty.

Don Frede 2013 RD
100% tempranillo
81

Don Frede 2013 T
100% tempranillo
82

El Gamo 2013 B
100% zalema
84

Viñagamo Seco 2013 B
100% zalema
85

Viñagamo Semidulce 2013 B
100% zalema
84

MARQUÉS DE VILLALÚA

Ctra. A-472, Km. 25,2
21860 Villalba del Alcor (Huelva)
☎: +34 959 420 905
www.marquesdevillalua.com
bodega@marquesdevillalua.com

Aguadulce de Villalúa 2013 Semidulce
zalema, moscatel
83

Marqués de Villalúa 2013 B
zalema, moscatel
88
Colour: bright straw. Nose: fresh, fresh fruit, white flowers. Palate: flavourful, fruity, good acidity, balanced.

Marqués de Villalúa Colección 1000 2013 B
zalema, moscatel, sauvignon blanc
89
Colour: bright straw. Nose: white flowers, fragrant herbs, fruit expression. Palate: fresh, fruity, flavourful, balanced.

Santa Agueda Vino Naranja
zalema, moscatel
87
Colour: mahogany. Nose: candied fruit, citrus fruit, floral, sweet spices, creamy oak, toasty. Palate: powerful, flavourful.

VINÍCOLA DEL CONDADO, S. COOP. AND.

San José, 2
21710 Bollullos del Condado (Huelva)
☎: +34 959 410 261
Fax: +34 959 410 171
www.vinicoladelcondado.com
comercial@vinicoladelcondado.com

Lantero Roble Syrah 2011 T Roble
syrah
84

Mioro 2013 B
100% zalema

84

Mioro Gran Selección 2013 B

86

Colour: bright straw. Nose: powerfull, honeyed notes, candied fruit, dried herbs. Palate: flavourful, fresh, fruity.

Misterio Dulce PX
100% zalema

85

Misterio Oloroso Seco OL
100% zalema

87

Colour: iodine, amber rim. Nose: powerfull, elegant, dry nuts, toasty, varnish. Palate: rich, long, spicy.

VDM Orange

88

Colour: old gold. Nose: fruit liqueur notes, citrus fruit, wild herbs, pattiserie, sweet spices. Palate: powerful, flavourful, spicy, long, fruity.

DO. COSTERS DEL SEGRE

CONSEJO REGULADOR
Complex de la Caparrella, 97
25192 Lleida
☎ :+34 973 264 583 - Fax: +34 973 264 583
@: secretari@costersdelsegre.es
www.costersdelsegre.es

LOCATION:

In the southern regions of Lleida, and a few municipal areas of Tarragona. It covers the sub-regions of: Artesa de Segre, Garrigues, Pallars Jussà, Raimat, Segrià and Valls del Riu Corb.

SUB-REGIONS:

Artesa de Segre: Located on the foothills of the Sierra de Montsec, just north of the Noguera region, it has mainly limestone soils. **Urgell**: Located in the central part of the province of Lleida, at an average altitude of 350 meters, its climate is a mix of mediterranean and continental features. **Garrigues**: To the southeast of the province of Lleida, it is a region with a complex topography and marl soils. Its higher altitude is near 700 meters. **Pallars Jussà**: Located in the Pyrinees, it is the northernmost sub-zone. Soils are predominantly limestone and its type of climate mediterranean with strong continental influence. **Raimat**: Located in the province of Lleida and with predominantly limestone soils, it has a mediterranean climate with continental features, with predominantly cold winters and very hot summers. **Segrià**: Is the central sub-zone of the DO, with limestone soils. **Valls del Riu Corb**: Located in the southeast of the DO, its climate is primarily mediterranean-continental softened by both the beneficial effect of the sea breezes (called marinada in the region) and "el Seré", a dry sea-bound inland wind.

GRAPE VARIETIES:

White: Preferred: Macabeo, Xarel·lo, Parellada, Chardonnay, Garnacha Blanca, Moscatel de Grano Menudo, Malvasía, Gewürztztraminer, Albariño, Riesling and Sauvignon Blanc.
Red: Preferred: Garnacha Negra, Ull de Llebre (Tempranillo), Cabernet Sauvignon, Merlot, Monastrell, Trepat, Samsó, Pinot Noir and Syrah.

FIGURES:

Vineyard surface: 4,346 – Wine-Growers: 583 – Wineries: 41 – 2013 Harvest rating: Excellent – Production 13: 8,175,600 litres – Market percentages: 60% domestic - 40% export.

SOIL:

The soil is mainly calcareous and granitic in nature. Most of the vineyards are situated on soils with a poor organic matter content, brownish-grey limestone, with a high percentage of limestone and very little clay.

CLIMATE:

Rather dry continental climate in all the sub-regions, with minimum temperatures often dropping below zero in winter, summers with maximum temperatures in excess of 35° on occasions, and fairly low rainfall figures: 385 mm/year in Lleida and 450 mm/year in the remaining regions.

VINTAGE RATING   PEÑÍNGUIDE

2009	2010	2011	2012	2013
AVERAGE	GOOD	VERY GOOD	VERY GOOD	VERY GOOD

DO COSTERS DEL SEGRE / D.O.P

BREGOLAT
Crta L - 512 Km 13.75 Les Pletes
25738 Montmagastre (Lérida)
☎: +34 973 091 130
www.bregolat.com
info@bregolat.com

Bregolat 2008 TR
cabernet sauvignon, merlot, garnacha
84

Bregolat 2009 TR
cabernet sauvignon, merlot, garnacha
88
Colour: pale ruby, brick rim edge. Nose: spicy, sweet spices, creamy oak, fine reductive notes. Palate: spicy, fine tannins, long.

Bregolat 2011 BFB
macabeo
87
Colour: bright yellow. Nose: powerfull, ripe fruit, sweet spices, creamy oak, fragrant herbs. Palate: rich, flavourful, fresh, good acidity.

Petit Bregolat 2011 TC
merlot, garnacha, cabernet sauvignon
85

Petit Bregolat 2012 B
macabeo, gewürztraminer, sauvignon blanc
85

CAL CABO CELLER
Castell, 30
25344 Sant Martí de Malda (Lérida)
☎: +34 639 887 836
www.calcaboceller.cat
celler@calcaboceller.cat

Un Onzé 2013 RD
syrah
87
Colour: rose, purple rim. Nose: powerfull, ripe fruit, red berry notes, floral, wild herbs, lactic notes. Palate: powerful, fruity, fresh, flavourful.

CASTELL D'ENCUS
Ctra. Tremp a Santa Engracia, Km. 5
25630 Talarn (Lleida)
☎: +34 973 252 974
www.castelldencus.com
rbobet@encus.org

Acusp 2012 T
pinot noir
94
Colour: light cherry. Nose: ripe fruit, fruit liqueur notes, fragrant herbs, spicy, expressive, mineral. Palate: balanced, elegant, balsamic, spicy.

Ekam 2013 B
riesling, albariño
90
Colour: bright straw. Nose: fresh, fresh fruit, white flowers, expressive. Palate: flavourful, fruity, good acidity, balanced.

Quest 2012 T
cabernet sauvignon, cabernet franc, merlot, petit verdot
94
Colour: bright cherry. Nose: ripe fruit, sweet spices, creamy oak, expressive, balsamic herbs, dry stone. Palate: flavourful, fruity, toasty, round tannins, balanced, elegant.

Taleia 2013 B
sauvignon blanc, semillón
91
Colour: bright straw. Nose: white flowers, fragrant herbs, fruit expression, lactic notes, elegant. Palate: fresh, fruity, flavourful, balanced, elegant.

Thalarn 2012 T
syrah
96
Colour: cherry, garnet rim. Nose: ripe fruit, spicy, creamy oak, toasty, cocoa bean, complex. Palate: powerful, flavourful, toasty, long, balanced, elegant, round.

CASTELL DEL REMEI
Finca Castell del Remei
25333 Castell del Remei (Lérida)
☎: +34 973 580 200
Fax: +34 973 718 312
www.castelldelremei.com
info@castelldelremei.com

Castell del Remei 1780 2008 T
cabernet sauvignon, tempranillo, garnacha, merlot
90
Colour: ruby red. Nose: spicy, fine reductive notes, wet leather, aged wood nuances, toasty, fruit liqueur notes. Palate: spicy, long, toasty.

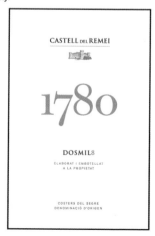

Castell del Remei Gotim Blanc 2013 B
sauvignon blanc, macabeo

88

Colour: bright straw. Nose: fresh, fresh fruit, white flowers, expressive. Palate: flavourful, fruity, good acidity, balanced.

Castell del Remei Gotim Bru 2012 T
tempranillo, garnacha, cabernet sauvignon, merlot

90

Colour: cherry, garnet rim. Nose: spicy, toasty, overripe fruit, mineral. Palate: powerful, flavourful, toasty, round tannins.

Castell del Remei Oda 2010 T
merlot, cabernet sauvignon, tempranillo, garnacha

89

Colour: ruby red. Nose: ripe fruit, spicy, creamy oak, toasty, complex, fine reductive notes. Palate: powerful, flavourful, toasty, round tannins.

Castell del Remei Oda Blanc 2013 BFB
macabeo, chardonnay

91

Colour: bright yellow. Nose: ripe fruit, sweet spices, creamy oak, fragrant herbs. Palate: rich, smoky aftertaste, flavourful, fresh, good acidity.

Castell del Remei Punt Zero 2013 T
tempranillo, merlot, syrah

88

Colour: very deep cherry. Nose: powerfull, candied fruit. Palate: flavourful, spicy, ripe fruit.

Castell del Remei Sícoris 2011 T
cabernet sauvignon, garnacha, tempranillo, syrah

87

Colour: bright cherry. Nose: ripe fruit, creamy oak, spicy. Palate: fruity, flavourful, toasty.

CELLER ANALEC
Ctra. a Nalec, s/n
25341 Nalec (Lleida)
☎: +34 973 303 190
www.analec.net
elcelleranalec@gmail.com

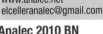

Analec 2010 BN
84

Analec Sort Abril 2009 ESP Reserva
86

Colour: bright golden. Nose: dry nuts, fragrant herbs, complex, lees reduction notes. Palate: powerful, flavourful, good acidity, fine bead, fine bitter notes.

Gualech Reserva Especial 2009 ESP Gran Reserva
90

Colour: bright yellow. Nose: fresh fruit, dried herbs, fine lees, floral, sweet spices. Palate: fresh, fruity, flavourful, good acidity, fine bead, elegant.

La Creu 2012 RD
85

La Creu Blanc 2012 B
88

Colour: bright yellow. Nose: fragrant herbs, ripe fruit, sweet spices, creamy oak. Palate: powerful, flavourful, spicy.

La Creu Negro 2011 T
100% tempranillo

87

Colour: cherry, garnet rim. Nose: ripe fruit, spicy, toasty, complex, earthy notes. Palate: powerful, flavourful, toasty.

La Romiguera 2010 TC
89

Colour: cherry, garnet rim. Nose: ripe fruit, spicy, creamy oak, toasty. Palate: powerful, flavourful, toasty, round tannins.

CELLER CASA PATAU
Costa del Senyor, s/n
25139 Menarguens (Lérida)
☎: +34 973 180 367
www.casapatau.com
info@casapatau.com

Casa Patau 2005 TR
cabernet sauvignon, merlot, ull de llebre

86

Colour: pale ruby, brick rim edge. Nose: ripe fruit, spicy, creamy oak, toasty, wild herbs. Palate: powerful, flavourful, toasty.

Casa Patau 2010 TC
cabernet sauvignon, garnacha, ull de llebre

84

Casa Patau 2012 TC
garnacha, merlot, cabernet sauvignon

86

Colour: cherry, garnet rim. Nose: ripe fruit, spicy, creamy oak, toasty, scrubland. Palate: powerful, flavourful, toasty.

CELLER CERCAVINS

Ctra. LV-2101, km. 0,500
25340 Verdú (Lleida)
☎: +34 973 348 114
Fax: +34 973 347 197
www.cellercercavins.com
info@cellercercavins.com

Bru de Verdú 14 2010 T
cabernet sauvignon, tempranillo, syrah, merlot

89

Colour: cherry, garnet rim. Nose: ripe fruit, spicy, creamy oak, toasty, complex. Palate: powerful, flavourful, toasty, round tannins.

Bru de Verdú 2011 T
tempranillo, syrah, merlot

88

Colour: bright cherry, garnet rim. Nose: ripe fruit, sweet spices, creamy oak. Palate: fruity, flavourful, toasty.

Guilla 2012 BFB
macabeo

87

Colour: bright yellow. Nose: powerfull, ripe fruit, sweet spices, creamy oak. Palate: rich, smoky aftertaste, flavourful.

Guillamina 2013 B
sauvignon blanc, garnacha blanca, gewürztraminer, albariño

84

Lo Virol 2012 T
tempranillo, merlot

87

Colour: bright cherry, garnet rim. Nose: sweet spices, creamy oak, ripe fruit, balsamic herbs. Palate: flavourful, toasty, spicy, easy to drink.

Lo Virol 2013 B
garnacha blanca, chardonnay, sauvignon blanc, gewürztraminer

88

Colour: bright straw. Nose: white flowers, fragrant herbs, fruit expression. Palate: fresh, fruity, flavourful, balanced, elegant.

Lo Virol 2013 RD
syrah

88

Colour: onion pink. Nose: elegant, candied fruit, dried flowers, fragrant herbs, red berry notes. Palate: light-bodied, flavourful, good acidity, long, spicy.

CELLER COMALATS

Major, 40
25217 L'Ametlla de Segarra (Lérida)
☎: +34 676 293 332
www.comalats.cat
info@comalats.cat

Comalats 2013 T
cabernet sauvignon

88 🌷

Colour: cherry, purple rim. Nose: fresh fruit, red berry notes, floral, balsamic herbs. Palate: flavourful, fruity, good acidity.

Comalats Rosat 2013 RD
cabernet sauvignon

84 🌷

Comalats sin sulfitos añadidos 2013 T
cabernet sauvignon

89 🌷

Colour: cherry, purple rim. Nose: red berry notes, fruit liqueur notes, wild herbs, mineral. Palate: balsamic, fine bitter notes, powerful, flavourful.

CELLER MAS GARCÍA MURET

Ctra. Masos de Llimiana s/n
25639 Masos de Llimiana (Lérida)
☎: +34 973 651 748
Fax: +34 973 651 748
www.masgarciamuret.com
info@masgarciamuret.com

Colomina 2013 RD
tempranillo, pinot noir

88

Colour: onion pink. Nose: elegant, candied fruit, dried flowers, fragrant herbs. Palate: light-bodied, flavourful, good acidity, long, spicy.

Mas García Muret 2012 T
tempranillo, cabernet sauvignon

89

Colour: bright cherry. Nose: ripe fruit, sweet spices, creamy oak, expressive. Palate: flavourful, fruity, toasty, round tannins.

Muriac 2011 T
syrah

91

Colour: cherry, garnet rim. Nose: ripe fruit, spicy, creamy oak, toasty, complex, mineral. Palate: powerful, flavourful, toasty, round tannins, balanced.

Unua 2011 T
tempranillo

90

Colour: bright cherry. Nose: ripe fruit, sweet spices, creamy oak, balsamic herbs. Palate: flavourful, fruity, toasty, round tannins.

CELLER MATALLONGA

Raval, 8
25411 Fulleda (Lleida)
☎: +34 660 840 791
http://cellermatallonga.blogspot.com
matallonga60@gmail.com

Escorça 2012 B
87
Colour: bright straw. Nose: white flowers, fragrant herbs, fruit expression, sweet spices. Palate: fresh, fruity, flavourful, balanced.

Vi del Banya 2012 T
88
Colour: cherry, garnet rim. Nose: ripe fruit, spicy, creamy oak, toasty, complex, balsamic herbs. Palate: powerful, flavourful, toasty, round tannins.

CELLER VILA CORONA

Camí els Nerets, s/n
25654 Vilamitjana (Lérida)
☎: +34 973 652 638
Fax: +34 973 652 638
www.vilacorona.cat
vila-corona@avired.com

Llabustes Cabernet Sauvignon 2009 TC
cabernet sauvignon
84

Llabustes Chardonnay 2013 B
chardonnay
85

Llabustes Merlot 2012 T
merlot
88
Colour: light cherry. Nose: ripe fruit, spicy, complex, earthy notes, fragrant herbs, mineral. Palate: powerful, flavourful, balsamic.

Llabustes Riesling 2013 B
riesling
88
Colour: bright straw. Nose: white flowers, fragrant herbs, fruit expression. Palate: fresh, fruity, flavourful, balanced, good acidity.

Llabustes Ull de Llebre 2010 TC
ull de llebre
84

Tu Rai 2012 T
monastrell, ull de llebre, garnacha
86
Colour: cherry, garnet rim. Nose: ripe fruit, earthy notes, spicy, grassy. Palate: balanced, flavourful, long, balsamic.

CÉRVOLES CELLER

Avda. Les Garrigues, 26
25471 La Pobla de Cèrvoles (Lleida)
☎: +34 973 175 101
Fax: +34 973 718 312
www.cervoles.com
info@cervoles.com

Cérvoles 2013 BFB
macabeo, chardonnay
92
Colour: bright yellow. Nose: powerfull, ripe fruit, sweet spices, creamy oak. Palate: rich, flavourful, fresh, good acidity.

Cérvoles Colors 2011 T
tempranillo, cabernet sauvignon, garnacha, merlot
86
Colour: cherry, garnet rim. Nose: fruit preserve, fruit liqueur notes, spicy, wild herbs. Palate: flavourful, pruney, balsamic.

Cérvoles Colors Blanc 2013 B
macabeo, chardonnay
90
Colour: bright straw. Nose: white flowers, fresh fruit, expressive, fine lees. Palate: flavurful, fruity, good acidity, balanced.

Cérvoles Estrats 2008 T
cabernet sauvignon, tempranillo, garnacha, merlot
94
Colour: cherry, garnet rim. Nose: ripe fruit, spicy, creamy oak, toasty, complex, dark chocolate, earthy notes. Palate: powerful, flavourful, toasty, round tannins.

Cérvoles Negre 2008 T
cabernet sauvignon, tempranillo, garnacha, merlot
91
Colour: cherry, garnet rim. Nose: ripe fruit, spicy, creamy oak, toasty, complex, earthy notes. Palate: powerful, flavourful, toasty, round tannins.

2008

COSTERS DEL SEGRE | LA POBLA DE CÉRVOLES
LLEIDA | ESPAÑA

Cérvoles

CLOS PONS

Ctra. LV-7011, km. 4,5
25155 L'Albagés (Lérida)
☎: +34 973 070 737
Fax: +34 973 070 738
www.clospons.com
clospons@grup-pons.com

Clos Pons 811 2011 T
marcelan

91

Colour: cherry, garnet rim. Nose: fruit preserve, scrubland, spicy, creamy oak. Palate: powerful, flavourful, spicy, balsamic, long.

Clos Pons Alges 2011 TC
garnacha, syrah, tempranillo

87

Colour: very deep cherry, garnet rim. Nose: powerfull, ripe fruit, creamy oak, smoky. Palate: powerful, toasty, balsamic.

Clos Pons Roc de Foc 2011 B
macabeo

90

Colour: bright golden. Nose: ripe fruit, powerfull, toasty, aged wood nuances. Palate: flavourful, fruity, spicy, toasty, long, smoky aftertaste.

Clos Pons Roc Nu 2010 TC
cabernet sauvignon, garnacha, tempranillo

91

Colour: bright cherry, garnet rim. Nose: ripe fruit, sweet spices, creamy oak, medium intensity, mineral. Palate: fruity, flavourful, toasty.

Clos Pons Sisquella 2012 B
garnacha blanca, albariño, moscatel de alejandría

89

Colour: bright yellow. Nose: powerfull, ripe fruit, sweet spices, creamy oak, fragrant herbs. Palate: rich, smoky aftertaste, flavourful, fresh, good acidity, roasted-coffee aftertaste.

COSTERS DEL SIÓ

Ctra. de Agramunt, Km. 4,2
25600 Balaguer (Lérida)
☎: +34 973 424 062
Fax: +34 973 424 112
www.costersio.com
administracio@costersio.com

Alto Siós 2010 T
syrah, tempranillo, garnacha

92

Colour: cherry, garnet rim. Nose: ripe fruit, spicy, creamy oak, toasty, dry stone. Palate: powerful, flavourful, toasty, round tannins, elegant.

Finca Siós 2010 T
cabernet sauvignon, syrah, tempranillo, garnacha

91

Colour: bright cherry. Nose: ripe fruit, sweet spices, creamy oak, wild herbs, mineral. Palate: fruity, flavourful, toasty, balanced.

Siós Blanc de Noirs 2011 BR
pinot noir

92

Colour: bright straw. Nose: fine lees, floral, citrus fruit, fresh fruit, fragrant herbs. Palate: fresh, fruity, flavourful, good acidity, elegant.

Siós Cau del Gat 2012 T
syrah, garnacha

89

Colour: cherry, garnet rim. Nose: spicy, toasty, mineral, overripe fruit. Palate: powerful, flavourful, toasty, harsh oak tannins.

Siós Pla del LLadoner 2013 B
chardonnay, viognier

89

Colour: bright straw. Nose: white flowers, fragrant herbs, candied fruit. Palate: fresh, fruity, flavourful, balanced, elegant.

Siós Rosé 2011 BR Reserva
pinot noir

90

Colour: coppery red. Nose: floral, jasmine, fragrant herbs, candied fruit. Palate: fresh, fruity, flavourful, correct, balanced.

L'OLIVERA SCCL

La Plana, s/n
25268 Vallbona de les Monges (Lleida)
☎: +34 973 330 276
Fax: +34 973 330 276
www.olivera.org
olivera@olivera.org

Agaliu 2012 BFB
100% macabeo

89 🌱

Colour: bright straw. Nose: floral, wild herbs, ripe fruit, spicy, creamy oak. Palate: powerful, flavourful, spicy.

Blanc de Marges 2011 BFB
parellada, moscatel, sauvignon blanc

89 🌷

Colour: bright yellow. Nose: mineral, citrus fruit, ripe fruit, creamy oak. Palate: powerful, flavourful, spicy, easy to drink.

Blanc de Roure 2013 B
macabeo, parellada, chardonnay

87 🌱

Colour: bright yellow. Nose: ripe fruit, powerfull, toasty, aged wood nuances. Palate: flavourful, fruity, spicy, toasty, long.

Blanc de Serè 2013 B

macabeo, parellada, chardonnay

86 ☙

Colour: bright straw. Nose: fresh, fresh fruit, white flowers, dried herbs. Palate: flavourful, fruity, good acidity.

Eixaders 2011 BFB

chardonnay

91 ☙

Colour: bright yellow. Nose: ripe fruit, sweet spices, dried flowers, wild herbs. Palate: powerful, flavourful, rich.

L'Olivera 2009 BN

macabeo, parellada, chardonnay

87

Colour: bright yellow. Nose: ripe fruit, fine lees, dried herbs. Palate: good acidity, flavourful, ripe fruit, long.

L'Olivera Gran Reserva 2008 BN

macabeo, parellada, chardonnay

88

Colour: bright golden. Nose: fine lees, dry nuts, fragrant herbs, complex, toasty. Palate: powerful, flavourful, good acidity, fine bead, fine bitter notes.

Missenyora 2012 BFB

100% macabeo

90

Colour: bright yellow. Nose: powerfull, ripe fruit, sweet spices, creamy oak, fragrant herbs. Palate: rich, smoky aftertaste, flavourful, fresh.

Rasim Negre Vimadur 2012 T Barrica

garnacha

90

Colour: deep cherry. Nose: overripe fruit, dried fruit, sweet spices, toasty. Palate: ripe fruit, powerful, spicy, long.

Rasim Vi Pansit 2012 B

garnacha blanca, malvasía, xarel.lo

90

Colour: golden. Nose: powerfull, floral, honeyed notes, candied fruit, fragrant herbs. Palate: flavourful, sweet, fresh, fruity, good acidity, long.

Vallisbona 89 2011 BFB

chardonnay

93

Colour: bright yellow. Nose: powerfull, ripe fruit, sweet spices, creamy oak, fragrant herbs. Palate: rich, smoky aftertaste, flavourful, fresh, good acidity, elegant.

LAGRAVERA

Ctra. de Tamarite, 9
25120 Alfarrás (Lérida)
☎: +34 973 761 374
Fax: +34 973 760 218
www.lagravera.com
info@lagravera.com

La Pell Puresa Blanc 2012 B

88 ☙

Colour: bright straw. Nose: white flowers, fragrant herbs, fruit expression, sweet spices, dry stone. Palate: fresh, fruity, flavourful, balanced, elegant. Personality.

La Pell Puresa Negre 2012 T

88

Colour: light cherry. Nose: ripe fruit, wild herbs, jasmine, spicy, dry stone. Palate: flavourful, spicy, mineral.

La Pell Saviesa Blanc 2012 BFB

macabeo

91 ☙

Colour: bright yellow. Nose: powerfull, ripe fruit, sweet spices, creamy oak, fragrant herbs, saline. Palate: rich, smoky aftertaste, flavourful, fresh, good acidity.

La Pell Saviesa Negre 2012 TR

garnacha, monastrell, mandó, trobat

93 ☙

Colour: light cherry. Nose: red berry notes, dry stone, earthy notes, fragrant herbs, balsamic herbs, spicy. Palate: flavourful, complex, spicy, long, balsamic.

Laltre 2013 T

88 ☙

Colour: cherry, garnet rim. Nose: ripe fruit, spicy, creamy oak, toasty, dark chocolate, earthy notes. Palate: powerful, flavourful, toasty, round tannins.

Ònra Blanc 2013 B

88 ☙

Colour: bright straw. Nose: white flowers, fresh fruit, expressive, dried herbs. Palate: flavourful, fruity, good acidity, balanced.

Ònra Molta Honra Blanc 2012 BFB

89 ☙

Colour: bright yellow. Nose: powerfull, ripe fruit, sweet spices, creamy oak, fragrant herbs. Palate: rich, smoky aftertaste, flavourful, fresh, good acidity.

Ònra Molta Honra Negre 2011 T

92 ☙

Colour: cherry, garnet rim. Nose: ripe fruit, wild herbs, earthy notes, spicy, creamy oak. Palate: balanced, flavourful, long, balsamic, elegant.

Ònra Negre GN+ME+CS 2011 T

90 🏆

Colour: bright cherry, garnet rim. Nose: ripe fruit, sweet spices, creamy oak, dry stone, balsamic herbs. Palate: fruity, flavourful, toasty, balanced.

Ònra Vi de Pedra Solera Gran Reserva

garnacha blanca

93 🏆

Colour: bright yellow. Nose: ripe fruit, floral, dry stone, sweet spices, aged wood nuances, creamy oak. Palate: rich, powerful, flavourful, complex, fine solera notes.

MAS BLANCH I JOVÉ

Paratge Llinars. Pol. Ind. 9- Parc. 129
25471 La Pobla de Cérvoles (Lleida)
☎: +34 973 050 018
Fax: +34 973 391 151
www.masblanchijove.com
sara@masblanchijove.com

Petit Saó 2010 T

tempranillo, garnacha, cabernet sauvignon

86

Colour: cherry, garnet rim. Nose: balanced, complex, ripe fruit, spicy, fine reductive notes. Palate: good structure, flavourful.

Petit Saó 2011 T

tempranillo, garnacha, cabernet sauvignon

88

Colour: cherry, garnet rim. Nose: red berry notes, ripe fruit, spicy, creamy oak, toasty, complex. Palate: powerful, flavourful, toasty.

Saó Abrivat 2010 TC

tempranillo, garnacha, cabernet sauvignon

89

Colour: cherry, garnet rim. Nose: ripe fruit, wild herbs, earthy notes, spicy. Palate: balanced, flavourful, long, balsamic.

Saó Blanc 2013 B

macabeo, garnacha blanca

88

Colour: bright straw. Nose: fresh, white flowers, candied fruit. Palate: flavourful, fruity, good acidity, balanced.

Saó Expressiu 2008 TC

garnacha, cabernet sauvignon, tempranillo

90

Colour: cherry, garnet rim. Nose: ripe fruit, spicy, creamy oak, toasty, complex. Palate: powerful, flavourful, toasty, round tannins, balanced.

Saó Expressiu 2009 T

garnacha, cabernet sauvignon, tempranillo

91

Colour: ruby red. Nose: spicy, fine reductive notes, toasty, balsamic herbs, balanced. Palate: spicy, long, toasty, elegant.

Saó Rosat 2013 RD

garnacha, syrah

86

Colour: rose, purple rim. Nose: powerfull, ripe fruit, red berry notes, floral, balsamic herbs. Palate: powerful, fruity, fresh.

RAIMAT

Ctra. Lleida, s/n
25111 Raimat (Lleida)
☎: +34 973 724 000
www.raimat.com
info@raimat.es

Castell de Raimat Albariño 2013 B

100% albariño

87

Colour: bright straw. Nose: fresh, fresh fruit, white flowers. Palate: flavourful, fruity, good acidity.

Castell de Raimat Cabernet Sauvignon 2009 TC

100% cabernet sauvignon

88

Colour: cherry, garnet rim. Nose: ripe fruit, spicy, creamy oak, toasty. Palate: powerful, flavourful, toasty.

Castell de Raimat Chardonnay 2013 B

100% chardonnay

89

Colour: bright straw. Nose: ripe fruit, fragrant herbs, floral. Palate: powerful, flavourful, unctuous.

Castell de Raimat Syrah 2011 T

100% syrah

87

Colour: bright cherry. Nose: ripe fruit, sweet spices, creamy oak, medium intensity. Palate: fruity, flavourful, toasty.

Raimat Abadía 2011 TC

cabernet sauvignon, tempranillo

85

Raimat Terra Chardonnay 2013 B

100% chardonnay

90 🏆

Colour: bright yellow. Nose: dried flowers, wild herbs, ripe fruit, expressive. Palate: round, powerful, flavourful.

Raimat Vallcorba 2011 T

89

Colour: cherry, garnet rim. Nose: ripe fruit, wild herbs, earthy notes, creamy oak. Palate: balanced, flavourful, long, balsamic.

RUBIÓ DE SÓLS

Camí LV 9138, Parc. 28
25737 Foradada (Lérida)
☎: +34 690 872 356
juditsogas@gmail.com

Xarel 15 2012 B
xarel.lo

90

Colour: bright yellow. Nose: powerfull, ripe fruit, sweet spices, creamy oak, fragrant herbs. Palate: rich, smoky aftertaste, flavourful, fresh.

TOMÁS CUSINÉ

Plaça Sant Sebastià, 13
25457 El Vilosell (Lleida)
☎: +34 973 176 029
Fax: +34 973 175 945
www.tomascusine.com
info@tomascusine.com

Auzells 2013 B
macabeo, sauvignon blanc, riesling, chardonnay

93

Colour: bright straw. Nose: white flowers, fragrant herbs, fruit expression. Palate: fresh, fruity, flavourful, balanced, elegant.

Finca Comabarra 2010 T
cabernet sauvignon, garnacha, syrah

91

Colour: ruby red. Nose: ripe fruit, spicy, creamy oak, toasty, complex, mineral. Palate: powerful, flavourful, toasty, round tannins, round.

Finca La Serra 2013 B
chardonnay

94

Colour: bright straw. Nose: citrus fruit, wild herbs, spicy, floral. Palate: fresh, fruity, good structure, balanced.

Geol 2009 TR
merlot, cabernet sauvignon, garnacha, samsó

94

Colour: cherry, garnet rim. Nose: ripe fruit, spicy, creamy oak, toasty, dark chocolate, earthy notes. Palate: powerful, flavourful, toasty, round tannins.

Geol 2011 T

93

Colour: cherry, garnet rim. Nose: ripe fruit, spicy, creamy oak, toasty, complex, dark chocolate, earthy notes. Palate: powerful, flavourful, toasty, round tannins.

Llebre 2012 T
tempranillo, garnacha, merlot, samsó

90

Colour: cherry, garnet rim. Nose: ripe fruit, spicy, creamy oak, toasty, complex. Palate: powerful, flavourful, toasty, round tannins, balanced.

Macabeu Finca Racons 2013 B
macabeo

92

Colour: bright straw. Nose: white flowers, fresh fruit, expressive, fine lees. Palate: flavourful, fruity, good acidity, balanced.

Vilosell 2011 T
tempranillo, syrah, merlot, cabernet sauvignon

89

Colour: cherry, garnet rim. Nose: ripe fruit, wild herbs, earthy notes, spicy, creamy oak, toasty. Palate: balanced, flavourful, long, balsamic.

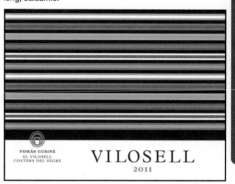

TOMÁS CUSINÉ
EL VILOSELL
COSTERS DEL SEGRE

VILOSELL
2011

VALL DE BALDOMAR

Ctra. de Alós de Balaguer, s/n
25737 Baldomar (Lleida)
☎: +34 973 402 205
www.valldebaldomar.com
info@valldebaldomar.com

Baldomà Selecció 2012 T
merlot, cabernet sauvignon, tempranillo

86

Colour: cherry, garnet rim. Nose: red berry notes, fruit preserve, wild herbs, spicy. Palate: powerful, flavourful, ripe fruit.

Cristiari 2013 RD
merlot, cabernet sauvignon

85

Cristiari d'Alòs Merlot 2012 T Roble
merlot

85

VINYA ELS VILARS

Camí de Puiggrós, s/n
25140 Arbeca (Lleida)
☎: +34 973 149 144
Fax: +34 973 160 719
www.vinyaelsvilars.com
vinyaelsvilars@vinyaelsvilars.com

Gerar 2010 T
merlot
86
Colour: cherry, garnet rim. Nose: spicy, toasty, mineral, fruit preserve. Palate: powerful, flavourful, toasty.

Leix 2009 T
syrah
88
Colour: bright cherry. Nose: ripe fruit, sweet spices, creamy oak, medium intensity, balsamic herbs. Palate: fruity, flavourful, toasty, unctuous.

Tallat de Lluna 2009 T
syrah
89
Colour: cherry, garnet rim. Nose: fruit preserve, fruit liqueur notes, spicy, balsamic herbs, mineral. Palate: flavourful, pruney, balsamic.

Vilars 2009 TC
merlot, syrah
86
Colour: cherry, garnet rim. Nose: ripe fruit, spicy, creamy oak, toasty. Palate: powerful, flavourful, toasty, harsh oak tannins.

VINYA L'HEREU DE SERÓ

Molí, s/n
25739 Seró-Artesa de Segre (Lérida)
☎: +34 639 311 175
Fax: +34 973 400 472
www.vinyalhereu.com
vinyalhereu@vinyalhereu.com

Flor de Grealó 2006 T
merlot, syrah, cabernet sauvignon
86 �️
Colour: deep cherry, orangey edge. Nose: waxy notes, tobacco, ripe fruit, spicy. Palate: fine bitter notes, flavourful, reductive nuances.

Petit Grealó 2011 T
syrah, merlot, cabernet sauvignon
86 🌷
Colour: deep cherry, orangey edge. Nose: ripe fruit, scrubland, spicy, damp earth. Palate: long, balsamic, flavourful.

DO. EL HIERRO

CONSEJO REGULADOR

Oficina de Agricultura. El Matorral, s/n
38911 Frontera (El Hierro)
☎:+34 922 556 064 / +34 922 559 744 - Fax: +34 922 559 691
@: doelhierro@hotmail.com
www.elhierro.tv

LOCATION:

On the island of El Hierro, part of the Canary Islands. The production area covers the whole island, although the main growing regions are Valle del Golfo, Sabinosa, El Pinar and Echedo.

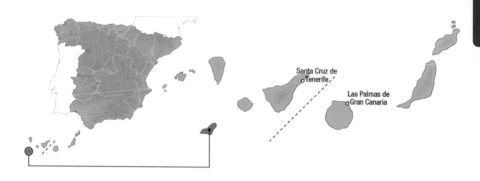

GRAPE VARIETIES:

White: Verijadiego (majority with 50% of all white varieties), Listán Blanca, Bremajuelo, Uval (Gual), Pedro Ximénez, Baboso and Moscatel.
Red: Listán Negro, Negramoll, Baboso Negro and Verijadiego Negro.

FIGURES:

Vineyard surface: 120 – Wine-Growers: 209 – Wineries: 9 – 2012 Harvest rating: Very Good – Production 13: 206,778 litres – Market percentages: 100% domestic.

SOIL:

Volcanic in origin, with a good water retention and storage capacity. Although the vineyards were traditionally cultivated in the higher regions, at present most of them are found at low altitudes, resulting in an early ripening of the grapes.

CLIMATE:

Fairly mild in general, although higher levels of humidity are recorded in high mountainous regions. Rainfall is relatively low.

VINTAGE RATING   PEÑÍNGUIDE

2009	2010	2011	2012	2013
GOOD	VERY GOOD	N/A	N/A	N/A

DO. EMPORDÀ

CONSEJO REGULADOR

Avda. Marignane, 2
17600 Figueres (Girona)
☎:+34 972 507 513 - Fax: +34 972 510 058
@: info@doemporda.cat
www.doemporda.cat

LOCATION:

In the far north west of Catalonia, in the province of Girona. The production area covers 40 municipal areas and is situated the slopes of the Rodes and Alberes mountain ranges forming an arch which leads from Cape Creus to what is known as the Garrotxa d'Empordà.

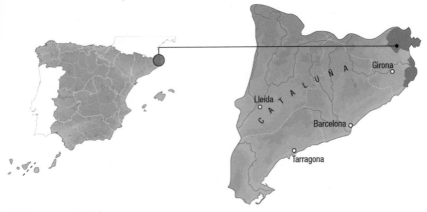

GRAPE VARIETIES:

WHITE:Preferred: Garnacha Blanca, Macabeo (Viura) and Moscatel de Alejandría.
Authorized: Xarel.lo, Chardonnay, Gewürztraminer, Malvasía, Moscatel de Gra Petit, Picapoll Blanc and Sauvignon Blanc.
RED:Preferred: Cariñena and Garnacha Tinta.
Authorized: Cabernet Sauvignon, Cabernet Franc, Merlot, Monastrell, Tempranillo, Syrah, Garnacha Roja (lledoner roig) and Garnacha Peluda.

FIGURES:

Vineyard surface: 1,795 – Wine-Growers: 330 – Wineries: 50 – 2013 Harvest rating: Very Good – Production 13: 6,092,300 litres – Market percentages: 84% domestic - 16% export.

SOIL:

The soil is in general poor, of a granitic nature in the mountainous areas, alluvial in the plains and slaty on the coastal belt.

CLIMATE:

The climatology is conditioned by the 'Tramontana', a strong north wind which affects the vineyards. Furthermore, the winters are mild, with hardly any frost, and the summers hot, although somewhat tempered by the sea breezes. The average rainfall is around 600 mm.

VINTAGE RATING   PEÑÍNGUIDE

2009	2010	2011	2012	2013
GOOD	VERY GOOD	VERY GOOD	GOOD	GOOD

AGRÍCOLA DE GARRIGUELLA

Ctra. de Roses, s/n
17780 Garriguella (Gerona)
☎: +34 972 530 002
Fax: +34 972 531 747
www.cooperativagarriguella.com
marta@cooperativagarriguella.com

Dinarells Blanc 2013 B
macabeo, garnacha blanca, moscatel
84

Dinarells Negre 2013 T
garnacha, merlot, cabernet sauvignon
85

Dinarells Rosat 2013 RD
garnacha
85

Dolç de Gerisena 2005 Vino de licor
garnacha, cariñena
91
Colour: very deep cherry. Nose: candied fruit, toasty, varnish, sweet spices. Palate: full, flavourful, balanced, spicy, long.

Essencia de Gerisena 2012 B
moscatel, moscatel de alejandría
90
Colour: bright yellow. Nose: varietal, balanced, white flowers, jasmine, expressive. Palate: ripe fruit, long, good acidity.

Garriguella 2010 TC
cariñena, cabernet sauvignon, garnacha
87
Colour: bright cherry. Nose: ripe fruit, sweet spices, creamy oak, expressive. Palate: flavourful, fruity, toasty, round tannins, balsamic.

Garriguella Garnatxa D'Empordá Negra 2007 T
garnacha
85

Garriguella Garnatxa D'Empordá Roja 2008 Vino del licor
garnacha rosada
85

Garriguella Moscatel D'Empordá 2012 B
moscatel
84

Garriguella Novell 2013 T
garnacha, cariñena
89
Colour: light cherry, purple rim. Nose: red berry notes, medium intensity, floral. Palate: flavourful, balanced, easy to drink, fresh.

Gerisena Blanc 2013 B
garnacha blanca
88
Colour: coppery red. Nose: medium intensity, balanced, floral, ripe fruit. Palate: flavourful, fruity, fine bitter notes, full, spicy.

Gerisena Rosat 2013 RD
garnacha rosada
87
Colour: coppery red, bright. Nose: fresh fruit, floral, wild herbs. Palate: fruity, flavourful, easy to drink, good finish.

Gerisena Sel.lecció 2012 T
cabernet sauvignon, merlot, garnacha
88
Colour: dark-red cherry, garnet rim. Nose: expressive, balsamic herbs, ripe fruit, spicy. Palate: good structure, flavourful, round tannins.

Puntils Blanc 2013 B
garnacha blanca, moscatel
85

Puntils Negre 2013 T
cabernet sauvignon, garnacha, merlot
86
Colour: bright cherry, purple rim. Nose: red berry notes, dried herbs. Palate: powerful, flavourful, ripe fruit.

Puntils Rosat 2013 RD
garnacha, tempranillo, syrah
85

AV BODEGUERS

Sant Baldiri, 23
17781 Vilamaniscle (Girona)
☎: +34 676 231 199
www.avbodeguers.com
info@avbodeguers.com

Nereus Garnacha Negra 2011 T
garnacha
87
Colour: cherry, garnet rim. Nose: ripe fruit, spicy, toasty, balsamic herbs. Palate: powerful, flavourful, toasty, round tannins.

Nereus Selección 2010 T
merlot, syrah, garnacha
86
Colour: cherry, garnet rim. Nose: ripe fruit, wild herbs, spicy, medium intensity. Palate: balanced, flavourful, long, balsamic.

Petit Suneus 2013 T
merlot, garnacha
87
Colour: light cherry. Nose: expressive, fresh fruit, red berry notes, dried herbs. Palate: flavourful, fruity, good acidity, round tannins.

Suneus 2012 T
garnacha, syrah

87

Colour: bright cherry. Nose: sweet spices, creamy oak. Palate: flavourful, fruity, toasty, round tannins, long, spicy.

Suneus 2013 B
garnacha blanca

87

Colour: bright straw. Nose: white flowers, fresh fruit, expressive, fine lees, dried herbs. Palate: flavourful, fruity, good acidity, balanced.

Suneus 2013 RD
merlot

83

BODEGAS MAS VIDA
Afores, s/n
17741 Cistella (Gerona)
☎: +34 659 548 512
Fax: +34 932 045 598
www.bodegasmasvida.com
info@bodegasmasvida.com

Mas Vida 117 2013 B Roble
chardonnay

86

Colour: bright yellow. Nose: sweet spices, toasty, dried flowers, ripe fruit. Palate: fruity, flavourful, spicy.

Mas Vida 17 2013 B
chardonnay

84

Mas Vida 23 2011 T
merlot, tempranillo

84

Mas Vida 32 2010 T Roble
merlot

86

Colour: bright cherry. Nose: ripe fruit, medium intensity, dried herbs. Palate: fruity, flavourful, toasty.

BODEGAS TROBAT
Castelló, 10
17780 Garriguella (Girona)
☎: +34 972 530 092
Fax: +34 972 552 530
www.bodegastrobat.com
bodegas.trobat@bmark.es

Amat Blanc 2013 B
100% xarel.lo

85

Amat Merlot 2013 RD
100% merlot

86

Colour: raspberry rose. Nose: white flowers, fresh fruit, medium intensity. Palate: balanced, fine bitter notes, fine bead.

Amat Negre Coupage 2011 TC
merlot, syrah, samsó

87

Colour: dark-red cherry, orangey edge. Nose: ripe fruit, fruit preserve, sweet spices. Palate: flavourful, fruity, long, round tannins.

Amat Sauvignon Blanc 2013 B
100% sauvignon blanc

86

Colour: bright straw. Nose: fresh, fresh fruit, fragrant herbs. Palate: flavourful, fruity, good acidity, balanced.

Noble Chardonnay 2013 B
100% chardonnay

85

Noble Negre 2011 T
cabernet sauvignon, syrah, samsó

89

Colour: cherry, garnet rim. Nose: ripe fruit, spicy, creamy oak, toasty, complex. Palate: powerful, flavourful, toasty, round tannins.

CASTILLO PERELADA VINOS Y CAVAS
Pl. del Carmen, 1
17491 Perelada (Girona)
☎: +34 972 538 011
Fax: +34 932 231 370
www.castilloperelada.com
perelada@castilloperelada.com

Castillo de Perelada 3 Fincas 2011 TC
86

Colour: deep cherry, garnet rim. Nose: cocoa bean, sweet spices, ripe fruit. Palate: flavourful, fruity.

Castillo de Perelada 5 Fincas 2009 TR
90

Colour: cherry, garnet rim. Nose: complex, creamy oak, cocoa bean, ripe fruit. Palate: ripe fruit, balsamic, round tannins

Castillo de Perelada 5 Fincas 2010 TR
88
Colour: cherry, garnet rim. Nose: ripe fruit, spicy, creamy oak, toasty, complex. Palate: powerful, flavourful, toasty, round tannins.

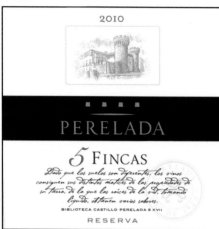

Castillo Perelada 2013 RD
87
Colour: light cherry. Nose: medium intensity, dried flowers, red berry notes. Palate: fruity, good acidity, fine bitter notes.

Castillo Perelada Blanc de Blancs 2013 B
87
Colour: bright straw. Nose: fresh, fresh fruit, white flowers, expressive, fragrant herbs. Palate: flavourful, fruity, good acidity, balanced.

Castillo Perelada Cabernet Sauvignon 2013 RD
100% cabernet sauvignon
87
Colour: rose, purple rim. Nose: ripe fruit, red berry notes, floral, expressive, balanced. Palate: fruity, fresh, flavourful.

Castillo Perelada Cigonyes 2013 RD
garnacha
87
Colour: raspberry rose. Nose: elegant, white flowers, red berry notes, dried herbs. Palate: flavourful, fruity, fine bitter notes.

Castillo Perelada Collection 2013 B
91
Colour: bright yellow. Nose: dried herbs, faded flowers, balanced, sweet spices, expressive. Palate: flavourful, complex, long, balanced.

Castillo Perelada Finca Espolla 2010 T
94
Colour: very deep cherry, garnet rim. Nose: expressive, complex, closed, fragrant herbs, ripe fruit. Palate: full, flavourful, complex.

Castillo Perelada Finca Malaveïna 2010 T
91
Colour: cherry, garnet rim. Nose: ripe fruit, wild herbs, earthy notes, spicy, elegant, cocoa bean. Palate: balanced, flavourful, long, balsamic.

Castillo Perelada Finca Malaveïna 2011 T
90
Colour: bright cherry. Nose: ripe fruit, sweet spices, creamy oak, medium intensity, fragrant herbs. Palate: fruity, flavourful, toasty.

Castillo Perelada Garnatxa Blanca B
100% garnacha blanca
88
Colour: bright straw. Nose: white flowers, fresh fruit, balsamic herbs. Palate: fruity, long, balsamic.

Castillo Perelada Garnatxa de l'Empordà B
92
Colour: light mahogany. Nose: sweet spices, cocoa bean, candied fruit, acetaldehyde, varnish. Palate: flavourful, full, complex, long, unctuous, spicy.

Castillo Perelada Gran Claustro 2009 T
92
Colour: dark-red cherry, garnet rim. Nose: scrubland, ripe fruit, spicy, complex. Palate: long, round tannins, ripe fruit.

Castillo Perelada Jardins Blanc 2013 B
86
Colour: bright straw. Nose: medium intensity, white flowers, dried herbs. Palate: fruity, correct, balanced.

Castillo Perelada Jardins Negre 2013 T
87
Colour: cherry, purple rim. Nose: red berry notes, grassy, medium intensity. Palate: flavourful, fruity, balsamic, balanced.

Castillo Perelada Jardins Rosé 2013 RD
86
Colour: coppery red, bright. Nose: medium intensity, fresh, floral. Palate: fruity, good acidity, balanced.

Castillo Perelada La Garriga 2010 T
100% samsó
90
Colour: black cherry, garnet rim. Nose: complex, dark chocolate, tobacco, ripe fruit. Palate: spicy, long, round tannins, good structure.

Castillo Perelada La Garriga 2012 B
91
Colour: bright yellow. Nose: ripe fruit, sweet spices, creamy oak, fragrant herbs, elegant. Palate: rich, smoky aftertaste, flavourful, fresh, good acidity.

Cigonyes 2012 T
87
Colour: bright cherry, garnet rim. Nose: powerfull, ripe fruit, fruit preserve, sweet spices. Palate: flavourful, round tannins.

Cigonyes 2013 B
100% macabeo
88
Colour: yellow, greenish rim. Nose: expressive, varietal, floral. Palate: full, fine bitter notes, good acidity, long.

Finca Garbet 2007 T
100% syrah
93
Colour: very deep cherry, garnet rim. Nose: closed, ripe fruit, complex, cocoa bean, creamy oak. Palate: full, ripe fruit, balanced, round tannins.

FINCA
GARBET
2007
D.O. EMPORDÀ

CELLER ARCHÉ PAGÈS

Sant Climent, 31
17750 Capmany (Girona)
☎: +34 626 647 251
Fax: +34 972 549 229
www.cellerarchepages.com
bonfill@capmany.com

Bonfill 2009 T
garnacha, cariñena
89
Colour: cherry, garnet rim. Nose: ripe fruit, spicy, creamy oak, toasty, complex, balsamic herbs. Palate: powerful, flavourful, toasty, round tannins.

Cartesius Blanc 2012 B
garnacha blanca
85

Cartesius Negre 2009 T
garnacha, merlot, cabernet sauvignon
88
Colour: ruby red. Nose: ripe fruit, old leather, spicy, wild herbs. Palate: balanced, spicy, balsamic.

Sàtirs Blanc 2013 B
macabeo
85

Sàtirs Negre 2008 T
garnacha, cariñena, cabernet sauvignon
86
Colour: ruby red. Nose: spicy, fine reductive notes, aged wood nuances, toasty, dried herbs. Palate: spicy, long, toasty.

Ull de Serp Carinyena 2011 T
cariñena
91
Colour: cherry, garnet rim. Nose: ripe fruit, spicy, creamy oak, toasty, complex, dark chocolate, earthy notes. Palate: powerful, flavourful, toasty, round tannins.

Ull de Serp Garnatxa 2010 T
garnacha
89
Colour: very deep cherry, garnet rim. Nose: powerfull, scrubland, ripe fruit, toasty. Palate: full, flavourful, round tannins.

Ull de Serp Macabeu 2012 B
macabeo
90
Colour: bright straw. Nose: white flowers, fresh fruit, expressive, fine lees, dried herbs. Palate: flavourful, fruity, good acidity, balanced, elegant.

CELLER COOPERATIU D'ESPOLLA

Ctra. Roses, s/n
17773 Espolla (Gerona)
☎: +34 972 563 178
www.cellerespolla.com
info@cellerespolla.com

Castell de Panissars 2011 TC
cariñena, lledoner, merlot

85

Clos de les Dòmines 2010 TR
merlot, cabernet sauvignon, cariñena

87

Colour: dark-red cherry, garnet rim. Nose: ripe fruit, wild herbs, spicy, creamy oak. Palate: balanced, flavourful, long, balsamic.

Clos de les Dòmines 2012 BFB
lladoner blanco, cariñena blanca, moscatel de alejandría

86

Colour: bright yellow. Nose: ripe fruit, sweet spices, faded flowers. Palate: flavourful, fruity, rich.

Garnatxa D'Empordà Espolla
lledoner blanc, lledoner roig

88

Colour: light mahogany. Nose: powerfull, aged wood nuances, rancio notes, candied fruit, honeyed notes. Palate: unctuous, flavourful, spicy.

Moscatell D'Empordà Espolla 2013 B
4,5% moscatel de alejandría

83

Negre Jove 2013 T
lladoner blanco, lladoner roig, lledoner

86

Colour: light cherry, purple rim. Nose: medium intensity, violets, red berry notes. Palate: fruity, easy to drink, balsamic.

Panissars 2013 B
lladoner blanco, lladoner roig, sauvignon blanc

85

Panissars 2013 RD

87

Colour: light cherry. Nose: fresh, white flowers, balanced, medium intensity, red berry notes. Palate: fruity, easy to drink, fresh.

Solera Garnatxa d'Empordà
lledoner roig, lladoner blanco

89

Colour: light mahogany. Nose: expressive, rancio notes, sweet spices, dry nuts, pattiserie, honeyed notes. Palate: flavourful, toasty, unctuous.

SoliSerena Garnatxa d'Empordà Dulce Natural
lladoner blanco, lledoner roig

90

Colour: light mahogany. Nose: candied fruit, pattiserie, cocoa bean, dry nuts. Palate: balanced, good acidity, sweet, full.

Vinya Orlina Negre 2013 T
lledoner, cariñena

86

Colour: cherry, purple rim. Nose: ripe fruit, sweet spices. Palate: fruity, flavourful, good acidity.

CELLER HUGAS DE BATLLE

Francesc Rivera, 28-30
17469 Colera (Gerona)
☎: +34 972 389 149
www.cellerhugasdebatlle.com
info@cellerhugasdebatlle.com

30.70 2013 B
89

Colour: bright yellow. Nose: balanced, expressive, dried herbs, faded flowers. Palate: flavourful, balanced.

Coma de Vaixell 2012 T
88

Colour: deep cherry, garnet rim. Nose: ripe fruit, fruit preserve, balsamic herbs. Palate: flavourful, balanced, good acidity, good structure.

CELLER LA VINYETA

Ctra. de Mollet de Peralada
a Masarac, s/n
17770 Mollet de Peralada (Girona)
☎: +34 647 748 809
www.lavinyeta.es
celler@lavinyeta.es

Heus Blanc 2013 B
macabeo, xarel.lo, malvasía, moscatel

86

Colour: bright straw. Nose: medium intensity, dried flowers, faded flowers. Palate: flavourful, fruity, fine bitter notes.

Heus Negre 2013 T
cariñena, syrah, garnacha, merlot

88

Colour: cherry, purple rim. Nose: red berry notes, floral, medium intensity. Palate: fresh, fruity, unctuous, fruity aftestaste.

Heus Rosat 2013 RD
garnacha, merlot, syrah, samsó

85

Llavors 2012 TC
merlot, cariñena, cabernet sauvignon, syrah

86

Colour: dark-red cherry, garnet rim. Nose: warm, scrubland, ripe fruit. Palate: flavourful, long, round tannins.

Microvins Negre 2011 T
cariñena

92

Colour: cherry, garnet rim. Nose: ripe fruit, elegant, balanced, complex, spicy, fragrant herbs. Palate: good structure, fine tannins, ripe fruit.

Puntiapart 2011 T
cabernet sauvignon, cariñena

88

Colour: dark-red cherry, garnet rim. Nose: powerfull, warm, fruit preserve, sweet spices. Palate: good structure, full, flavourful, round tannins.

Sols 2010 Dulce
garnacha roja, garnacha blanca

86

Colour: light mahogany. Nose: candied fruit, dried fruit, wild herbs, faded flowers, honeyed notes. Palate: balanced, rich, flavourful.

CELLER MARIÀ PAGÈS

Pujada, 6
17750 Capmany (Girona)
☎: +34 972 549 160
Fax: +34 972 549 160
www.cellermpages.com
info@cellermpages.com

Celler Marià Pagès Moscat d'Empordà 2012 B
moscatel de alejandría

89

Colour: bright golden. Nose: balanced, expressive, candied fruit, faded flowers, sweet spices, pattiserie. Palate: rich, full, flavourful, long.

Marià Pagès Garnatxa d'Empordà B Reserva
garnacha blanca, garnacha

87

Colour: light mahogany. Nose: candied fruit, pattiserie, cocoa bean, caramel. Palate: balanced, spicy, long, unctuous.

Marià Pagès Garnatxa d'Empordà 2012 B
garnacha blanca, garnacha

89

Colour: old gold, amber rim. Nose: sweet spices, pattiserie, candied fruit, faded flowers. Palate: fruity, flavourful.

Serrasagué 2007 TC
garnacha, merlot, cabernet sauvignon

86

Colour: dark-red cherry, orangey edge. Nose: spicy, tobacco, old leather. Palate: flavourful, balsamic, ripe fruit.

Serrasagué 2013 B
garnacha blanca, chardonnay, moscatel

84

Serrasagué 2013 RD
tempranillo, garnacha, merlot

83

Serrasagué 2013 T
garnacha, merlot, cabernet sauvignon

87

Colour: very deep cherry, purple rim. Nose: powerfull, ripe fruit, dried herbs. Palate: flavourful, balanced, round tannins, long.

Serrasagué Rosa - T 2013 RD
garnacha, merlot

87

Colour: light cherry, bright. Nose: powerfull, ripe fruit, red berry notes, floral, expressive, fresh. Palate: fruity, fresh, good acidity.

Serrasagué Taca Negra 2011 T
garnacha, merlot, cabernet franc

86

Colour: deep cherry, garnet rim. Nose: spicy, scrubland, ripe fruit. Palate: flavourful, round tannins, long.

Serrasagué Vinya de L'Hort 2013 B
garnacha blanca, chardonnay, moscatel

85

CELLER MARTÍN FAIXÓ

Ctra. de Cadaqués s/n
17488 Cadaqués (Girona)
☎: +34 682 107 142
www.saperafita.com
tastos@cellermartinfaixo.com

Cadac 2007 TR
cabernet sauvignon, garnacha

89

Colour: black cherry, garnet rim. Nose: fine reductive notes, scrubland, ripe fruit. Palate: spicy, fine tannins, flavourful, toasty, smoky aftertaste, reductive nuances.

Perafita 2009 TC
cabernet sauvignon, garnacha, merlot

88

Colour: deep cherry, garnet rim. Nose: spicy, creamy oak, scrubland, ripe fruit. Palate: flavourful, good structure.

Perafita Picapoll 2013 B
picapoll

87 🌱

Colour: bright straw. Nose: fresh, fresh fruit, white flowers. Palate: flavourful, fruity, good acidity, balanced, fine bitter notes.

Perafita Rosat 2013 RD
merlot, garnacha

87 🍷

Colour: coppery red, bright. Nose: medium intensity, fresh fruit, floral, dried herbs. Palate: flavourful, easy to drink, fine bitter notes.

CELLER MAS ROMEU
Gregal, 1
17495 Palau-Saverdera (Gerona)
☎: +34 687 744 056
www.cellermasromeu.cat
info@cellermasromeu.cat

Blanc Fitó 2013 B
chardonnay

84

Finca Malesa 2009 TR
garnacha, merlot

87

Colour: cherry, garnet rim. Nose: powerfull, balsamic herbs, cocoa bean, ripe fruit. Palate: flavourful, slightly dry, soft tannins.

Malesa Rosat 2013 RD
garnacha, merlot

86

Colour: raspberry rose. Nose: medium intensity, fresh fruit, floral. Palate: fruity, easy to drink, good finish.

Senglar 2012 T
garnacha, merlot, cabernet sauvignon

87

Colour: dark-red cherry. Nose: ripe fruit, wild herbs, earthy notes, spicy, creamy oak. Palate: balanced, flavourful, long, balsamic.

CELLERS D'EN GUILLA
Camí de Perelada s/n, Delfià
17754 Rabós d'Empordà (Gerona)
☎: +34 660 001 622
www.cellersdenguilla.com
info@cellersdenguilla.com

Edith 2012 BC
garnacha blanca, garnacha roja

87

Colour: bright yellow. Nose: toasty, smoky, ripe fruit. Palate: balanced, fruity, toasty, spicy.

Garnacha dels Cellers D'en Guilla
garnacha roja

88

Colour: coppery red. Nose: complex, balanced, sweet spices, candied fruit, pattiserie. Palate: flavourful, full, long.

Magenc 2013 B
garnacha blanca, garnacha roja, macabeo, moscatel

88

Colour: bright straw. Nose: fresh, fresh fruit, expressive, fragrant herbs. Palate: flavourful, fruity, good acidity, balanced.

Rec de Brau 2012 T
cariñena, garnacha

87

Colour: very deep cherry, purple rim. Nose: ripe fruit, sweet spices, balanced, powerfull. Palate: good structure, flavourful, round tannins.

Vinya del Metge 2013 RD
garnacha roja, garnacha

88

Colour: raspberry rose. Nose: medium intensity, dried flowers, dried herbs, ripe fruit. Palate: fruity, long, good acidity.

CELLERS SANTAMARÍA
Pza. Mayor, 6
17750 Capmany (Girona)
☎: +34 972 549 033
Fax: +34 972 549 022
www.granrecosind.com
info@granrecosind.com

Gran Recosind 2007 TC
garnacha, tempranillo, merlot, syrah

84

Gran Recosind 2008 TR
syrah, cabernet sauvignon

86

Colour: dark-red cherry, orangey edge. Nose: ripe fruit, tobacco, old leather. Palate: correct, spicy, easy to drink.

Gran Recosind Cabernet Sauvignon Merlot 2004 TR
cabernet sauvignon, merlot

85

CLOS D'AGON
Afores, s/n
17251 Calonge (Girona)
☎: +34 972 661 486
Fax: +34 972 661 462
www.closdagon.com
info@closdagon.com

Amic de Clos D'Agon 2012 T

90

Colour: dark-red cherry, garnet rim. Nose: ripe fruit, sweet spices, expressive. Palate: flavourful, fruity, toasty, round tannins, long.

Amic de Clos D'Agon 2013 B
87
Colour: bright straw. Nose: fresh, fresh fruit, white flowers, expressive. Palate: fruity, good acidity, fine bitter notes.

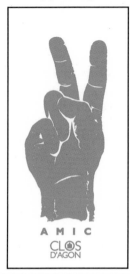

Amic de Clos D'Agon 2013 RD
100% garnacha
87
Colour: onion pink. Nose: elegant, dried flowers, fragrant herbs, red berry notes. Palate: flavourful, good acidity, long, spicy.

COCA I FITÓ & ROIG PARALS
Garriguella, 8
17752 Mollet de Peralada (Girona)
☎: +34 636 223 919
Fax: +34 935 457 092
www.cocaifito.cat
info@cocaifito.cat

Tocat de l'Ala 2012 TC
90
Colour: dark-red cherry, garnet rim. Nose: balanced, fragrant herbs, ripe fruit, spicy. Palate: fruity, balsamic, balanced.

Tocat i Posat 2011 TC
89
Colour: cherry, garnet rim. Nose: ripe fruit, spicy, toasty, cocoa bean, balsamic herbs. Palate: powerful, flavourful, toasty, round tannins, balsamic.

COLL DE ROSES
Ctra. de les Arenes, s/n
17480 Roses (Girona)
Fax: +34 972 531 741
www.collderoses.es
info@collderoses.es

Coll de Roses 2013 B
86
Colour: bright straw. Nose: fresh, fresh fruit, white flowers, expressive. Palate: flavourful, fruity, good acidity, balanced.

Coll de Roses 2013 T
88
Colour: cherry, purple rim. Nose: expressive, fresh fruit, red berry notes, floral. Palate: flavourful, fruity, good acidity, round tannins.

Coll de Roses Finca del Mar 2011 T
90
Colour: cherry, garnet rim. Nose: ripe fruit, spicy, creamy oak, complex, cocoa bean. Palate: powerful, flavourful, toasty, round tannins.

COMERCIAL VINÍCOLA DEL NORDEST
Empolla, 9
17752 Mollet de Peralada (Gerona)
☎: +34 972 563 150
Fax: +34 972 545 134
www.vinicoladelnordest.com
vinicola@vinicoladelnordest.com

Anubis 2008 TR
cabernet sauvignon, merlot
86
Colour: dark-red cherry. Nose: spicy, wet leather, aged wood nuances, scrubland. Palate: spicy, flavourful, ripe fruit, reductive nuances.

Covest 2013 RD
86
Colour: coppery red, bright. Nose: red berry notes, floral, jasmine. Palate: fruity, easy to drink, flavourful, correct.

Covest Cabernet Sauvignon 2013 T
cabernet sauvignon
87
Colour: bright cherry, purple rim. Nose: red berry notes, ripe fruit, balanced, scrubland. Palate: flavourful, round tannins.

Covest Chardonnay 2013 B
chardonnay
84

Covest Garnatxa de L'Emporda B Reserva
garnacha roja
88
Colour: coppery red. Nose: rancio notes, candied fruit, roasted almonds, spicy, honeyed notes. Palate: unctuous, flavourful, spicy, complex.

Covest Moscatel de L'Emporda B
100% moscatel de alejandría

87

Colour: bright golden. Nose: candied fruit, pattiserie, sweet spices. Palate: unctuous, flavourful, long.

Covest Negre 2013 T

85

Garrigal 2009 TC

82

Vinya Farriol Semidulce T
samsó

84

Vinya Farriol Semidulce s/c B
macabeo, garnacha roja

82

Vinya Farriol Semidulce s/c RD
garnacha, cariñena

83

COSMIC
Plaça M. Teresa Palleja, 3
17707 Agullana (Girona)
☎: +34 639 338 176
www.cosmic.cat
info@cosmic.cat

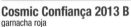

Cosmic Confiança 2013 B
garnacha roja

83 🌷

Cosmic Llibertat 2013 T
cariñena

86 🌷

Colour: cherry, purple rim. Nose: red berry notes, faded flowers, dry nuts. Palate: fruity, good acidity, round tannins, good finish.

Cosmic Valentía 2013 B
cariñena blanca

85 🌷

DIGUEM NO S.L.U.
Ctra. de Llança, s/n
17489 El Port de la Selva (Girona)
☎: +34 630 875 649
genis@elportdelaselva.cat

Ruixim de Mar 2012 ESP
100% macabeo

83

Vinya de L'Aví Genís 2010 T
100% cabernet sauvignon

90

Colour: cherry, garnet rim. Nose: ripe fruit, wild herbs, earthy notes, spicy, creamy oak. Palate: flavourful, long, balsamic, balanced, elegant.

Vinya de L'Aví Genís 2012 T
100% cabernet sauvignon

89

Colour: bright cherry. Nose: ripe fruit, sweet spices, creamy oak, expressive. Palate: flavourful, fruity, toasty, round tannins.

EMPORDÀLIA
Ctra. de Roses, s/n
17600 Pau (Girona)
☎: +34 972 530 140
Fax: +34 972 530 528
www.empordalia.com
info@empordalia.com

Sinols 2010 TR
cariñena, garnacha, cabernet sauvignon, merlot

86

Colour: cherry, garnet rim. Nose: medium intensity, dried herbs, spicy. Palate: correct, ripe fruit, balsamic.

Sinols 2011 TC
cariñena, garnacha, cabernet sauvignon, syrah

87

Colour: cherry, garnet rim. Nose: ripe fruit, wild herbs, earthy notes, spicy, creamy oak. Palate: balanced, flavourful, long, balsamic.

Sinols Antima 2009 T
cariñena, garnacha

87

Colour: cherry, garnet rim. Nose: ripe fruit, wild herbs, earthy notes, spicy. Palate: balanced, flavourful, long, balsamic.

Sinols Blanc 2013 B
macabeo, garnacha blanca

85

Sinols Coromina 2010 T
cariñena, garnacha

86

Colour: cherry, garnet rim. Nose: medium intensity, ripe fruit, spicy. Palate: correct, easy to drink.

Sinols Garnatxa Dulce Solera
garnacha

87

Colour: ochre. Nose: white flowers, dark chocolate, pattiserie, candied fruit. Palate: fruity, flavourful, balanced.

Sinols Moscatell 2013 Blanco dulce
moscatel de alejandría

85

Sinols Negre 2013 T
cariñena, garnacha, syrah, cabernet sauvignon
86
Colour: cherry, purple rim. Nose: balanced, scrubland, red berry notes. Palate: flavourful, fruity, good structure.

Sinols Rosat 2013 RD
cariñena, garnacha, syrah, merlot
85

ESPELT VITICULTORS
Mas Espelt s/n
17493 Vilajuiga (Gerona)
☎: +34 972 531 727
Fax: +34 972 531 741
www.espeltviticultors.com
info@espeltviticultors.com

Espelt Airam Solera 1997 Dulce Solera
88
Colour: old gold, amber rim. Nose: expressive, complex, sweet spices, candied fruit. Palate: flavourful, full, long.

Espelt ComaBruna 2010 T
100% cariñena
91
Colour: very deep cherry. Nose: toasty, spicy, ripe fruit, expressive. Palate: good structure, good acidity, round tannins.

Espelt Corali 2013 RD
100% lladoner
88
Colour: raspberry rose. Nose: medium intensity, fresh, floral, rose petals. Palate: fruity, long, good acidity.

Espelt Lledoner Rosat 2013 RD
100% lledoner
87
Colour: rose, purple rim. Nose: powerfull, ripe fruit, red berry notes, floral, expressive. Palate: powerful, fruity, fresh.

Espelt Mareny 2013 B
86
Colour: bright straw. Nose: balanced, fresh, dried herbs, fresh fruit, citrus fruit. Palate: good acidity, correct, easy to drink.

Espelt Quinze Roures 2013 BFB
89
Colour: bright yellow. Nose: fresh fruit, wild herbs, spicy, balanced. Palate: flavourful, elegant, fine bitter notes.

Espelt Sauló 2013 T
86
Colour: dark-red cherry, purple rim. Nose: powerfull, balsamic herbs, ripe fruit. Palate: correct, flavourful, fruity.

Espelt Solivent Eco 2013 T
87
Colour: bright cherry, purple rim. Nose: expressive, fresh fruit, red berry notes, floral, medium intensity. Palate: flavourful, fruity, good acidity, round tannins.

Espelt Terres Negres 2012 T
89
Colour: very deep cherry, garnet rim. Nose: creamy oak, sweet spices, ripe fruit. Palate: good structure, flavourful, good acidity, balanced.

Espelt Vailet 2013 B
84

Espelt Vidiví 2012 T
85

JOAN SARDÀ
Ctra. Vilafranca a St. Jaume dels Domenys, Km. 8,1
8732 Castellvi de la Marca (Barcelona)
☎: +34 937 720 900
Fax: +34 937 721 495
www.joansarda.com
joansarda@joansarda.com

Cap de Creus Corall 2013 T
lladoner, samsó
86
Colour: cherry, purple rim. Nose: ripe fruit, balanced, mineral. Palate: fruity, flavourful, round tannins.

Cap de Creus Nacre 2013 B
lladoner, lladoner blanco
84

LORDINA
Burgos, 4
8440 Cardedeu (Barcelona)
☎: +34 629 578 001
www.lordina.net
lordina@lordina.es

Lordina "Amphora" 2011 TC
90
Colour: bright cherry, garnet rim. Nose: expressive, balanced, earthy notes, ripe fruit, balsamic herbs. Palate: good structure, flavourful, good acidity.

Lordina Message 2012 TC
garnacha, samsó, syrah
87
Colour: cherry, garnet rim. Nose: ripe fruit, spicy, fragrant herbs. Palate: powerful, flavourful, round tannins, long.

Lordina Message 2013 B
sauvignon blanc, moscatel
86
Colour: bright straw. Nose: fresh, fresh fruit, white flowers, scrubland. Palate: flavourful, fruity, good acidity.

Lordina Message 2013 RD
garnacha
85

MAS ESTELA
Mas Estela
17489 Selva de Mar (Girona)
☎: +34 972 126 176
Fax: +34 972 388 011
www.masestela.com
masestela@hotmail.com

Quindals 2008 T
84 🌿

Quindals 2011 T
87 🌿
Colour: deep cherry, purple rim. Nose: powerfull, fragrant herbs, ripe fruit. Palate: flavourful, spicy, round tannins.

Vinya Selva de Mar 2007 TR
87 🌿
Colour: dark-red cherry, garnet rim. Nose: balanced, sweet spices, cocoa bean, balsamic herbs. Palate: good structure, flavourful, round tannins.

Vinya Selva de Mar 2008 TR
garnacha, syrah, samsó
88 🌿
Colour: cherry, garnet rim. Nose: balanced, ripe fruit, scrubland, spicy, expressive. Palate: good structure, flavourful.

MAS LLUNES
Ctra. de Vilajuiga, s/n
17780 Garriguella (Gerona)
☎: +34 972 552 684
Fax: +34 972 530 112
www.masllunes.es
masllunes@masllunes.es

Cercium 2012 T
88
Colour: cherry, garnet rim. Nose: ripe fruit, wild herbs, earthy notes, spicy. Palate: balanced, flavourful, long, balsamic.

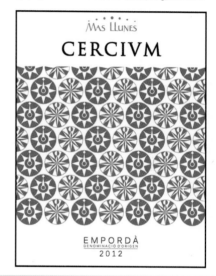

Empórion 2008 T
87
Colour: black cherry, garnet rim. Nose: ripe fruit, wild herbs, spicy. Palate: balanced, flavourful, long, balsamic.

Maragda 2013 B
86
Colour: bright straw. Nose: fresh fruit, wild herbs, faded flowers. Palate: fruity, flavourful, good acidity, fine bitter notes.

Maragda Rosa 2013 RD
86
Colour: light cherry, bright. Nose: medium intensity, fresh fruit. Palate: fruity, easy to drink, good finish, fine bitter notes.

Mas Llunes Dolç Moscat 2012 B
100% moscatel grano menudo
85

Mas llunes Garnatxa D'Emporda Soleres B Solera
100% garnacha roja

92

Colour: light mahogany. Nose: spicy, toasty, acetaldehyde, candied fruit, varnish, dark chocolate. Palate: rich, flavourful, powerful, long.

Nivia 2012 BFB

89

Colour: bright yellow. Nose: ripe fruit, sweet spices, fragrant herbs, powerfull, toasty. Palate: rich, flavourful, good acidity.

Rhodes 2009 T

89

Colour: cherry, garnet rim. Nose: ripe fruit, spicy, creamy oak, toasty, complex. Palate: powerful, flavourful, toasty, round tannins.

MAS OLLER
Ctra. GI-652, Km. 0,23
17123 Torrent (Gerona)
☎: +34 972 300 001
Fax: +34 972 300 001
www.masoller.es
info@masoller.es

Mas Oller Mar 2013 B
picapoll, malvasía

91

Colour: bright straw. Nose: white flowers, fresh fruit, expressive, fine lees, dried herbs. Palate: flavourful, fruity, good acidity, balanced.

Mas Oller Plus 2012 T
syrah, garnacha

93

Colour: cherry, garnet rim. Nose: ripe fruit, spicy, creamy oak, toasty, complex, dark chocolate, earthy notes. Palate: powerful, flavourful, toasty, round tannins.

Mas Oller Pur 2013 T
syrah, garnacha, cabernet sauvignon

91

Colour: cherry, garnet rim. Nose: spicy, toasty, overripe fruit, mineral. Palate: powerful, flavourful, toasty, round tannins.

MASETPLANA
Paratge Pedreguers, s/n
17780 Garriguella (Gerona)
☎: +34 972 530 090
Fax: +34 972 501 948
www.masetplana.com
info@masetplana.com

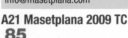

A21 Masetplana 2009 TC
85

El Nen de Can Maset 2013 T
85

MASIA SERRA
Dels Solés, 20
17708 Cantallops (Girona)
☎: +34 689 604 905
www.masiaserra.com
masiaserra@masiaserra.com

Aroa 2008 T
89

Colour: very deep cherry. Nose: characterful, tobacco, cocoa bean, ripe fruit, wild herbs. Palate: concentrated, round tannins.

Ctònia 2013 BFB
100% garnacha blanca

90

Colour: yellow. Nose: ripe fruit, faded flowers, sweet spices, dried herbs. Palate: balanced, fruity, full, rich.

Gneis 2007 T
87

Colour: deep cherry. Nose: ripe fruit, acetaldehyde, balsamic herbs, spicy, aged wood nuances, dry nuts. Palate: flavourful, spirituous, ripe fruit.

INO Garnatxa de L'Empordà Vino dulce natural
100% garnacha roja

94

Colour: mahogany. Nose: acetaldehyde, aged wood nuances, pattiserie, sweet spices, dry nuts, honeyed notes, expressive. Palate: powerful, flavourful, spicy, balsamic, long.

IO Masia Serra 2011 T
90

Colour: cherry, garnet rim. Nose: ripe fruit, wild herbs, earthy notes, spicy, creamy oak. Palate: balanced, flavourful, long, balsamic.

Mosst 2013 B
87

Colour: bright straw. Nose: white flowers, fresh fruit, balanced. Palate: correct, fine bitter notes, balsamic.

OLIVEDA S.A.
La Roca, 3
17750 Capmany (Girona)
☎: +34 972 549 012
Fax: +34 972 549 106
www.grupoliveda.com
comercial@grupoliveda.com

Masia Oliveda "Mo" Blanc de Blancs 2013 B
macabeo, chardonnay

86

Colour: bright straw. Nose: white flowers, jasmine, expressive. Palate: fruity, fine bitter notes, good acidity.

Masia Oliveda "Mo" Negre Jove 2013 T
garnacha, cabernet sauvignon

86

Colour: cherry, purple rim. Nose: expressive, fresh fruit, red berry notes, balsamic herbs. Palate: fruity, good acidity, easy to drink.

Masia Oliveda "Mo" Rosat Flor 2013 RD
samsó, garnacha, cabernet sauvignon

87

Colour: light cherry, bright. Nose: red berry notes, wild herbs, fresh. Palate: flavourful, fruity, long, good acidity.

OLIVER CONTI
Puignau, s/n
17750 Capmany (Gerona)
☎: +34 972 193 161
www.oliverconti.com
ocvi@oliverconti.com

Oliver Conti Ara 2010 T
cabernet sauvignon, garnacha

88

Colour: dark-red cherry, garnet rim. Nose: medium intensity, dried herbs, ripe fruit. Palate: fruity, round tannins.

Oliver Conti Carlota 2010 TR
cabernet franc

90

Colour: cherry, garnet rim. Nose: ripe fruit, wild herbs, earthy notes, spicy. Palate: balanced, flavourful, long, balsamic, spicy.

Oliver Conti Etiqueta Negra 2010 B Reserva
90

Colour: bright yellow. Nose: expressive, faded flowers, ripe fruit, candied fruit, spicy. Palate: rich, flavourful, long.

Oliver Conti Etiqueta Negra 2010 TR
cabernet sauvignon, merlot, cabernet franc

89

Colour: cherry, garnet rim. Nose: balanced, expressive, fragrant herbs, spicy. Palate: fruity, easy to drink, balsamic.

Oliver Conti Treyu 2012 B
89

Colour: bright yellow. Nose: faded flowers, ripe fruit, balanced, expressive. Palate: rich, flavourful, spicy.

Turó Negre d'Oliver Conti 2011 T
garnacha, cabernet sauvignon, merlot, cabernet franc

90

Colour: cherry, garnet rim. Nose: expressive, ripe fruit, fragrant herbs, spicy. Palate: flavourful, full. Personality.

PERE GUARDIOLA
Ctra. GI-602, Km. 2,9
17750 Capmany (Gerona)
☎: +34 972 549 096
Fax: +34 972 549 097
www.pereguardiola.com
marta@pereguardiola.com

Anhel d'Empordà 2013 B
xarel.lo, garnacha blanca

85

Anhel d'Empordà 2013 RD
garnacha

86

Colour: onion pink. Nose: elegant, dried flowers, fragrant herbs, red berry notes. Palate: flavourful, good acidity, long.

Floresta 2005 TR
merlot, garnacha, syrah, cabernet sauvignon

87

Colour: cherry, garnet rim. Nose: ripe fruit, wild herbs, spicy. Palate: balanced, flavourful, balsamic, spicy.

Floresta 2009 TC
cabernet sauvignon, garnacha, merlot

87

Colour: deep cherry, garnet rim. Nose: scrubland, ripe fruit, warm. Palate: flavourful, ripe fruit, round tannins.

Floresta 2012 T
merlot, syrah, garnacha

85

Floresta 2013 B
macabeo, chardonnay, sauvignon blanc, xarel.lo

85

Floresta 2013 RD
garnacha, merlot, cabernet sauvignon, samsó

85

Floresta 2013 T
garnacha, merlot, cabernet sauvignon, syrah

87

Colour: cherry, purple rim. Nose: red berry notes, ripe fruit, balsamic herbs, balanced. Palate: powerful, flavourful, spicy, long.

Joncària Moscatel 2012 BFB
moscatel de alejandría

88

Colour: bright yellow. Nose: expressive, varietal, white flowers, jasmine, fresh. Palate: flavourful, long, balanced.

Torre de Capmany Garnatxa d'Empordà B Gran Reserva
garnacha blanca

88

Colour: light mahogany. Nose: sweet spices, roasted almonds, dry nuts, candied fruit. Palate: balanced, long, good acidity.

ROIG PARALS
Garriguella, 8
17752 Mollet de Peralada (Girona)
☎: +34 972 634 320
www.roigparals.cat
info@roigparals.cat

Camí de Cormes Vinyes Centenàries 2008 T
100% samsó

89

Colour: dark-red cherry, orangey edge. Nose: tobacco, old leather, ripe fruit. Palate: spicy, flavourful, balanced.

Finca Pla del Molí 2008 T
cabernet sauvignon, merlot

87

Colour: very deep cherry. Nose: ripe fruit, spicy, dried herbs, tobacco. Palate: balanced, flavourful, long, balsamic.

La Botera 2011 TC
samsó, garnacha

86

Colour: cherry, garnet rim. Nose: ripe fruit, wild herbs, spicy, medium intensity. Palate: balanced, flavourful, balsamic.

Mallolet 2013 T
samsó, garnacha

87

Colour: cherry, purple rim. Nose: red berry notes, ripe fruit, expressive, balsamic herbs, medium intensity. Palate: fresh, fruity.

SOTA ELS ÀNGELS
Veinat de Rabiosas
17116 Cruïlles (Girona)
☎: +34 872 006 976
www.sotaelsangels.com
mariajpolanco@sotaelsangels.com

Desea 2009 TC
carménère, carignan, cabernet sauvignon, merlot

89

Colour: cherry, garnet rim. Nose: balanced, scrubland, sweet spices. Palate: good structure, flavourful, spicy, long.

Sota els Àngels 2008 TC
carignan, carménère, cabernet sauvignon

90

Colour: cherry, garnet rim. Nose: ripe fruit, wild herbs, earthy notes, spicy, creamy oak. Palate: balanced, flavourful, long, balsamic.

Sota els Àngels 2012 B
picapoll, viognier

90

Colour: bright yellow. Nose: ripe fruit, dry nuts, powerfull, toasty, sweet spices. Palate: flavourful, fruity, spicy, toasty, long.

VINALTIS
Passeig de Gracia, 56 6ª
8007 Barcelona (Barcelona)
☎: +34 934 673 575
Fax: +34 934 673 590
www.vinaltis.com
vinalti@vinaltis.com

Claret de Tardor 2013 T
garnacha, cabernet sauvignon

85

Finca els 3 Frares 2009 TC
cariñena, cabernet sauvignon

87

Colour: cherry, garnet rim. Nose: balsamic herbs, ripe fruit, spicy. Palate: fruity, spicy, round tannins.

Finca els 3 Frares 2013 B
macabeo, chardonnay, moscatel

84

VINOS JOC - JORDI OLIVER CONTI
Mas Marti
17467 Sant Mori (Girona)
☎: +34 607 222 002
www.vinojoc.com
info@vinojoc.com

JOC Blanc Empordà 2012 B
87

Colour: bright yellow. Nose: dried flowers, dried herbs, ripe fruit, dry stone. Palate: flavourful, ripe fruit.

JOC Negre Empordà 2012 T
87

Colour: dark-red cherry, garnet rim. Nose: dried herbs, ripe fruit, sweet spices. Palate: good structure, flavourful, long, fruity.

VINYES D'OLIVARDOTS
Paratge Olivadots, s/n
17750 Capmany (Girona)
☎: +34 650 395 627
www.olivardots.com
vdo@olivardots.com

Blanc de Gresa 2012 B
garnacha blanca, garnacha rosada, cariñena blanca

91

Colour: bright yellow. Nose: powerfull, ripe fruit, sweet spices, creamy oak, fragrant herbs. Palate: rich, smoky aftertaste, flavourful, good acidity, long.

Finca Olivardots Groc D'Anfora 2013 B
garnacha rosada, garnacha blanca, macabeo

88

Colour: yellow. Nose: balanced, dried herbs, fresh, fresh fruit. Palate: flavourful, long, balsamic. Personality.

Finca Olivardots Vermell 2012 T
syrah, garnacha, cariñena, cabernet sauvignon

90

Colour: deep cherry, garnet rim. Nose: red berry notes, ripe fruit, sweet spices, cocoa bean, balanced. Palate: flavourful, fruity.

Gresa 2008 T

93

Colour: deep cherry, garnet rim. Nose: expressive, ripe fruit, creamy oak, balsamic herbs. Palate: good structure, balanced, round tannins.

Troç d'en Ros Garnatxa 2011 T
100% garnacha

89

Colour: cherry, garnet rim. Nose: elegant, expressive, balsamic herbs, ripe fruit. Palate: flavourful, good acidity, balanced, spicy.

Troç d'en Ros Xarel.lo 2012 B
100% xarel.lo

89

Colour: bright yellow. Nose: powerfull, faded flowers, balanced, ripe fruit, dried herbs. Palate: flavourful, fruity, rich.

Vd'O 1.09 2009 T
100% cariñena

92

Colour: dark-red cherry, garnet rim. Nose: ripe fruit, scrubland, spicy, complex. Palate: good structure, flavourful, round tannins.

Vd'O 2.09 2009 T
100% cariñena

93

Colour: very deep cherry, garnet rim. Nose: complex, balanced, wild herbs, sweet spices, creamy oak. Palate: full, spicy, long, round tannins.

Vd'O 5.10 2010 T
100% garnacha

91

Colour: deep cherry, garnet rim. Nose: ripe fruit, creamy oak, sweet spices, balsamic herbs. Palate: good structure, full, long.

VINYES DELS ASPRES
Requesens, 7
17708 Cantallops (Girona)
☎: +34 619 741 442
Fax: +34 972 420 662
www.vinyesdelsaspres.cat
dmolas@vinyesdelsaspres.cat

Bac de les Ginesteres Vino dulce Natural 2004 Dulce
100% garnacha gris

92

Colour: light mahogany. Nose: acetaldehyde, candied fruit, varnish, spicy, dry nuts. Palate: spirituous, flavourful, fine bitter notes.

Blanc dels Aspres 2012 BFB
100% garnacha blanca

87

Colour: bright yellow. Nose: medium intensity, sweet spices, toasty, ripe fruit. Palate: flavourful, ripe fruit, long, toasty.

Negre dels Aspres 2010 TC

90

Colour: cherry, garnet rim. Nose: ripe fruit, spicy, creamy oak, toasty, complex, dried herbs, dry stone. Palate: powerful, flavourful, toasty, round tannins.

Oriol Blanc 2013 B
100% garnacha gris

85

Oriol dels Aspres Negre 2013 T

89

Colour: cherry, purple rim. Nose: medium intensity, fresh fruit, scrubland, expressive. Palate: flavourful, long, round tannins.

Oriol dels Aspres Rosat 2013 RD

86

Colour: rose, bright. Nose: medium intensity, fresh fruit, red berry notes. Palate: flavourful, powerful, fruity, long.

S'Alou 2010 TC

92

Colour: cherry, garnet rim. Nose: ripe fruit, wild herbs, earthy notes, spicy, creamy oak. Palate: balanced, flavourful, long, balsamic, full, toasty.

Vi de Panses dels Aspres 2006 B
100% garnacha gris

87

Colour: light mahogany. Nose: expressive, balanced, candied fruit, floral, varnish, dry nuts. Palate: full, flavourful, sweet.

DO. GETARIAKO TXAKOLINA

CONSEJO REGULADOR
Parque Aldamar, 4 bajo
20808 Getaria (Gipuzkoa)
☎ :+34 943 140 383 - Fax: +34 943 896 030
@: info@getariakotxakolina.com
www.getariakotxakolina.com

LOCATION:

Mainly on the coastal belt of the province of Guipuzcoa, covering the vineyards situated in the municipal areas of Aia, Getaria and Zarauz, at a distance of about 25 km from San Sebastián.

GRAPE VARIETIES:

White: hondarrabi zuri, gros manseng, riesling, chardonnay y petit courbu.
Red: Hondarrabi Beltza.

FIGURES:

Vineyard surface: 402 – Wine-Growers: 96 – Wineries: 29 – 2013 Harvest rating: Good – Production 13: 1,031,000 litres – Market percentages: 92% domestic - 8% export.

SOIL:

The vineyards are situated in small valleys and gradual hillsides at altitudes of up to 200 m. They are found on humid brownish-grey limy soil, which are rich in organic matter.

CLIMATE:

Fairly mild, thanks to the influence of the Bay of Biscay. The average annual temperature is 13°C, and the rainfall is plentiful with an average of 1,600 mm per year.

VINTAGE RATING   PEÑÍNGUIDE

2009	2010	2011	2012	2013
VERY GOOD	VERY GOOD	VERY GOOD	EXCELLENT	GOOD

ADUR

Ferrerias, 3 8ºF
20011 Donostia (Gipuzkoa)
☎: +34 617 216 617
www.adurtxakolina.com
info@adurtxakolina.com

Adur 2013 B
100% hondarrabi zuri

87

Colour: bright straw. Nose: fresh, medium intensity, citrus fruit, grassy. Palate: fresh, fruity, balsamic, correct.

AGERRE

Agerre Baserria - Bº Askizu
20808 Getaria (Gipuzkoa)
☎: +34 943 140 446
Fax: +34 943 140 446
www.agerretxakolina.com
agerre@agerretxakolina.com

Agerre 2013 B
hondarrabi zuri

86

Colour: bright straw. Nose: fresh fruit, citrus fruit, medium intensity, floral. Palate: fresh, fruity.

AIZPURUA

Ctra. de Meagas
20808 Getaria (Gipuzkoa)
☎: +34 943 140 696
www.txakoliaizpurua.com
aialleaizpurua@gmx.es

Aialle 2012 B
hondarrabi zuri

83

Aizpurua. B 2013 B
hondarrabi zuri, hondarrabi beltza

86

Colour: bright straw. Nose: white flowers, fresh fruit, citrus fruit. Palate: correct, easy to drink, good finish.

AMEZTOI

Barrio Eitzaga, 10
20808 Getaria (Gipuzkoa)
☎: +34 943 140 918
Fax: +34 943 140 169
www.txakoliameztoi.com
ameztoi@txakoliameztoi.com

Rubentis Ameztoi 2013 RD
hondarrabi zuri, hondarrabi beltza

87

Colour: onion pink. Nose: elegant, candied fruit, dried flowers, fragrant herbs, red berry notes. Palate: light-bodied, flavourful, good acidity, long, spicy.

Txakoli Ameztoi 2013 B
hondarrabi zuri

88

Colour: bright straw. Nose: medium intensity, white flowers, balanced. Palate: balanced, fine bitter notes, correct.

BODEGA REZABAL

Itsas Begi Etxea, 628
20800 Zarautz (Gipuzkoa)
☎: +34 943 580 899
Fax: +34 943 580 775
www.txakolirezabal.com
info@txakolirezabal.com

Txakoli Rezabal 2013 B
hondarrabi zuri

88

Colour: bright straw. Nose: balanced, floral, medium intensity. Palate: carbonic notes, fresh, fruity, easy to drink, fine bitter notes.

Txakoli Rezabal Rosé 2013 RD
hondarrabi beltza

86

Colour: onion pink. Nose: faded flowers, dried herbs, candied fruit. Palate: fresh, fruity, fine bitter notes.

BODEGAS JUAN CELAYA LETAMENDI

Upaingoa-Zañartuko
20560 Oñati (Gipuzkoa)
☎: +34 670 288 086
Fax: +34 948 401 182
www.upain.es
administracion@naparralde.com

Upaingoa 2010 B
hondarrabi zuri, riesling

84

Upaingoa 2011 B
hondarrabi zuri, riesling

84

Upaingoa 2012 B
hondarrabi zuri, riesling

86

Colour: bright yellow. Nose: faded flowers, balanced, fresh fruit, citrus fruit. Palate: slightly acidic.

Upaingoa 2013 B
hondarrabi zuri, riesling

87

Colour: bright yellow. Nose: white flowers, balanced, fresh fruit. Palate: easy to drink, long, good acidity.

GAÑETA

Agerre Goikoa Baserria
20808 Getaria (Gipuzkoa)
☎: +34 943 140 174
Fax: +34 943 140 174
gainetatxakolina@gmail.com

Gañeta 2013 B
hondarrabi zuri
84

GOROSTI

Barrio Elorriaga, 35
20820 Deba (Gipuzkoa)
☎: +34 670 408 439
www.flyschtxakolina.com
gorostibodega@hotmail.com

Flysch Txakolina 2013 B
88

Colour: bright straw. Nose: fresh fruit, citrus fruit, balanced. Palate: carbonic notes, fresh, light-bodied, easy to drink, good acidity, correct.

HIRUZTA

Barrio Jaizubia, 266
20280 Hondarribia (Gipuzkoa)
☎: +34 943 646 689
Fax: +34 943 260 801
www.hiruzta.com
info@hiruzta.com

Hiruzta Berezia 2013 B
89

Colour: bright straw. Nose: fresh, fresh fruit, white flowers, expressive. Palate: flavourful, fruity, good acidity, balanced.

Hiruzta Txakolina 2013 B
86

Colour: bright straw, greenish rim. Nose: fresh fruit, citrus fruit, grassy. Palate: correct, easy to drink, light-bodied.

SAGARMIÑA

Sagarmiña Baserria
20830 Mitriku (Gipuzcoa)
☎: +34 943 603 225
www.txakolisagarmina.com
txakolisagarmina@live.com

Sagarmiña 2013 B
hondarrabi zuri
83

TALAI BERRI

Talaimendi, 728
20800 Zarautz (Gipuzkoa)
☎: +34 943 132 750
Fax: +34 943 132 750
www.talaiberri.com
info@talaiberri.com

Txakoli Finca Jakue 2013 B
hondarrabi zuri
87

Colour: yellow, greenish rim. Nose: scrubland, wild herbs, fresh. Palate: good acidity, fresh, good finish.

Txakoli Talai Berri 2013 B
hondarrabi zuri
86

Colour: bright straw. Nose: fresh, grassy, medium intensity, citrus fruit. Palate: fresh, light-bodied, fine bitter notes.

TXAKOLI ARREGI

Talaimendi, 727- Bajo
20800 Zarautz (Gipuzkoa)
☎: +34 943 580 835
www.txakoliarregi.com
info@txakoliarregi.com

Arregi 2013 B
hondarrabi zuri
86

Colour: bright straw. Nose: fragrant herbs, grassy, fresh fruit, medium intensity. Palate: correct, fine bitter notes.

TXAKOLI ELKANO

Elkano Etxea Nº24 Eitzaga Auzoa
20808 Getaria (Gipuzkoa)
☎: +34 600 800 259
www.txakolielkano.com
txakolielkano@hotmail.com

Txakoli Elkano 2013 B
hondarrabi zuri, hondarrabi beltza
86

Colour: bright straw. Nose: fresh, fresh fruit, expressive, grassy, damp undergrowth. Palate: fruity, good acidity.

TXAKOLI GAINTZA S.L.

Barrio San Prudentzio 26, Ctra. Meagas
20808 Getaria (Gipuzkoa)
☎: +34 943 140 032
www.gaintza.com
info@gaintza.com

Aitako 2012 B
hondarrabi zuri, hondarrabi beltza, chardonnay
85

Gaintza 2013 B
hondarrabi zuri, hondarrabi beltza, gros manseng
87

Colour: bright straw, greenish rim. Nose: white flowers, medium intensity, fruit expression. Palate: carbonic notes, correct.

Gaintza Roses 2012 RD
hondarrabi zuri, hondarrabi beltza

82

TXAKOLI ULACIA
San Prudentzio Auzoa, 41
20808 Getaria (Gipuzkoa)
☎: +34 943 140 893
Fax: +34 943 140 893
www.txakoliulacia.com
nicolasulacia@euskalnet.net

Izaro 2013 B
hondarrabi zuri

88

Colour: bright straw. Nose: fresh, fresh fruit, white flowers, citrus fruit, dried flowers. Palate: good acidity, balanced.

Txakoli Ulacia 2013 B
hondarrabi zuri, hondarrabi beltza

86

Colour: bright straw. Nose: grassy, balanced, medium intensity, faded flowers. Palate: fresh, easy to drink.

TXAKOLI ZUDUGARAI
Ctra. Zarautz - Aia Bº Laurgain
20810 Aia (Guipuzcoa)
☎: +34 943 830 386
Fax: +34 943 835 952
www.txakolizudugarai.com
txakolizudugarai@euskalnet.net

Amats 2013 B
100% hondarrabi zuri

85

Antxiola 2013 B
100% hondarrabi zuri

84

Zudugarai 2013 B
100% hondarrabi zuri

84

TXOMIN ETXANIZ
Txomin Etxaniz Barrio Eitzaiga, 13
20808 Getaria (Gipuzkoa)
☎: +34 943 140 702
www.txominetxaniz.com
txakoli@txominetxaniz.com

Eugenia Txomín Etxaníz Blanco ESP
100% hondarrabi zuri

86

Colour: bright straw. Nose: medium intensity, fresh, dried flowers. Palate: easy to drink, correct.

Eugenia Txomín Etxaníz Rosado ESP
88

Colour: raspberry rose. Nose: balanced, medium intensity, dry nuts, fragrant herbs, dried flowers. Palate: fresh, easy to drink, correct, fine bitter notes, good acidity.

Txomín Etxaníz 2013 B
100% hondarrabi zuri

89

Colour: bright straw. Nose: medium intensity, fresh, floral, citrus fruit. Palate: flavourful, balanced, fine bitter notes, correct, good acidity.

Txomín Etxaníz 2013 RD
86

Colour: light cherry. Nose: candied fruit, dried flowers, fragrant herbs. Palate: light-bodied, flavourful, spicy.

Txomín Etxaníz Berezia 2013 B
91

Colour: bright straw. Nose: floral, citrus fruit, wild herbs, expressive. Palate: light-bodied, fresh, fruity, easy to drink, balanced.

Uydi 2012 B
100% hondarrabi zuri

88

Colour: bright straw. Nose: fresh, fresh fruit, white flowers, expressive. Palate: flavourful, fruity, good acidity, balanced.

DO. GRAN CANARIA

CONSEJO REGULADOR
Calvo Sotelo, 26
35300 Santa Brígida (Las Palmas)
☎ :+34 928 640 462
@: crdogc@yahoo.es
www.vinosdegrancanaria.es

LOCATION:

The production region covers 99% of the island of Gran Canaria, as the climate and the conditions of the terrain allow for the cultivation of grapes at altitudes close to sea level up to the highest mountain tops. The DO incorporates all the municipal areas of the island, except for the Tafira Protected Landscape which falls under an independent DO, Monte de Lentiscal, also fully covered in this Guide.

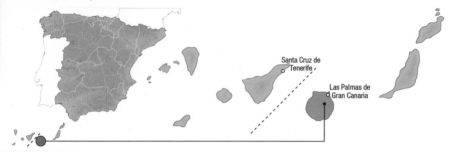

GRAPE VARIETIES:

White: Preferred: Malvasía, Güal, Marmajuelo (Bermejuela), Vijariego, Albillo and Moscatel.
Authorized: Listán Blanco, Burrablanca, Torrontés, Pedro Ximénez, Brebal and Bastardo Blanco.
Red: Preferred: Listán Negro, Negramoll, Tintilla, Malvasía Rosada.
Authorized: Moscatel Negra, Bastardo Negro, Listán Prieto, Vijariego Negro, Bastardo Negro, Listón Prieto und Vijariego Negro.

FIGURES:

Vineyard surface: 241 – Wine-Growers: 353 – Wineries: 70 – 2013 Harvest rating: - – Production 11: 271,973 litres – Market percentages: 99% domestic - 1% export.

SOIL:

The vineyards are found both in coastal areas and on higher grounds at altitudes of up to 1500 m, resulting in a varied range of soils.

CLIMATE:

As with the other islands of the archipelago, the differences in altitude give rise to several microclimates which create specific characteristics for the cultivation of the vine. Nevertheless, the climate is conditioned by the influence of the trade winds which blow from the east and whose effect is more evident in the higher-lying areas.

VINTAGE RATING				PEÑÍNGUIDE
2009	**2010**	**2011**	**2012**	**2013**
N/A	VERY GOOD	VERY GOOD	VERY GOOD	GOOD

BENTAYGA

El Alberconcillo, s/n
35360 Tejeda (Las Palmas)
☎: +34 649 941 098
Fax: +34 928 418 795
www.bodegasbentayga.com
info@bodegasbentayga.com

Agala 2012 TC
tintilla, vijariego negro

89

Colour: cherry, garnet rim. Nose: ripe fruit, spicy, creamy oak, toasty, complex, scrubland. Palate: powerful, flavourful, toasty, round tannins.

Agala Altitud 1318 Semi 2013 B
vijariego blanco, albillo, moscatel de alejandría

87

Colour: bright yellow. Nose: fresh fruit, expressive, white flowers. Palate: flavourful, fruity, good acidity, balanced.

Agala Dulce Dulcena 2012 B Barrica
moscatel de alejandría

87

Colour: bright golden. Nose: medium intensity, white flowers, faded flowers, ripe fruit, honeyed notes. Palate: fruity, sweet, correct.

BODEGA LOS BERRAZALES

León y Castillo, 43
35480 Agaete (Las Palmas)
☎: +34 628 922 588
Fax: +34 928 898 154
www.bodegalosberrazales.com
lugojorge3@hotmail.com

Los Berrazales 2013 RD
listán negro

85

Los Berrazales 2013 T Barrica
tintilla, listán negro

86

Colour: bright cherry. Nose: ripe fruit, sweet spices, creamy oak. Palate: flavourful, fruity, toasty, round tannins.

Los Berrazales Dulce Natural 2013 B
moscatel, malvasía

88

Colour: golden. Nose: powerfull, floral, fragrant herbs, jasmine. Palate: flavourful, sweet, fresh, fruity, good acidity, long.

Los Berrazales Seco 2013 B
malvasía, moscatel

86

Colour: bright yellow. Nose: powerfull, varietal, fresh fruit, jasmine. Palate: fruity, flavourful, good acidity, fine bitter notes.

Los Berrazales Semiseco 2013 B
moscatel, malvasía

88

Colour: bright yellow. Nose: fresh, fresh fruit, white flowers, expressive. Palate: flavourful, fruity, good acidity, balanced.

BODEGA PLAZA PERDIDA

Ctra. a Los Hoyod, 271
35017 Las Palmas de Gran Canaria
(Las Palmas)
☎: +34 669 680 910
Fax: +34 928 355 871
www.bodegaplazaperdida.com
vidlavica@hotmail.com

La Vica 2013 T
86

Colour: bright cherry, purple rim. Nose: roasted coffee, ripe fruit, violets, dried herbs. Palate: flavourful, toasty, good finish.

Plaza Perdida 2013 T
listán negro

86

Colour: dark-red cherry, garnet rim. Nose: ripe fruit, violet drops, sweet spices. Palate: fruity, flavourful, long.

BODEGAS LAS TIRAJANAS

Las Lagunas s/n
35290 San Bartolomé de Tirajana
(Gran Canaria)
☎: +34 928 155 978
www.bodegaslastirajanas.com
info@bodegaslastirajanas.com

Blanco Las Tirajanas 2013 B
albillo, verdello, listán blanco, marmajuelo

86

Colour: bright straw. Nose: fresh, fresh fruit, white flowers, expressive. Palate: flavourful, fruity, good acidity, balanced.

Las Tirajanas 2012 BFB
malvasía

85

Las Tirajanas 2012 T Barrica
tintilla, listán negro, castellana, vijariego negro

85

Malvasía Volcánica Las Tirajanas 2013 B
malvasía

85

Tinto Las Tirajanas 2013 T
listán negro, vijariego negro, castellana

86

Colour: cherry, garnet rim. Nose: medium intensity, dried herbs, red berry notes, ripe fruit. Palate: fruity, easy to drink, fruity aftestaste.

Verijadiego Las Tirajanas 2013 B
verijadiego
84

LA HIGUERA MAYOR

Ctra. de Telde a Santa Brígida, GC 80,P.K., 7,5
35200 El Palmital de Telde
(Las Palmas)
☎: +34 630 285 454
Fax: +34 928 275 281
www.lahigueramayor.com
lahigueramayor@gmail.com

La Higuera Mayor 2011 T
listán negro, tintilla, castellana, negramoll
83

La Higuera Mayor 2012 T
listán negro, tintilla, castellana, negramoll
84

LA MONTAÑA

La Solana, 89 (Utiaca)
35328 Vega de San Mateo (Las Palmas)
☎: +34 678 800 164
conjema@yahoo.es

La Montaña 2013 B
listán blanco, malvasía, verdello, albillo
83

LA SAVIA ECOLÓGICA

Pío XII, 221
35460 Galdar (Las Palmas)
☎: +34 617 455 863
ondina@ondinasurf.com

Caletón 2012 T Barrica
listán negro, castellana, baboso negro
85

Caletón Dulce 2012 T
listán negro, castellana, baboso negro
87
Colour: dark-red cherry, orangey edge. Nose: toasty, spicy, ripe fruit, dried herbs, scrubland. Palate: balanced, easy to drink.

SEÑORÍO DE CABRERA

Barranco García Ruiz, 5
35200 Telde (Las Palmas)
☎: +34 928 572 124
agustincabrera@sunandbeachhotels.com

Señorío de Cabrera 2012 T
84

Señorío de Cabrera 2013 B
86
Colour: bright yellow. Nose: expressive, balanced, floral, ripe fruit. Palate: fruity, correct, fine bitter notes, flavourful.

VEGA DE GÁLDAR

La Longuera s/n - La Vega
35460 Gáldar (Las Palmas)
☎: +34 605 043 047
lamenora1960@yahoo.es

El Convento de la Vega 2012 T Roble
listán negro, castellana
84

Nubia 2013 B
malvasía, listán blanco
84

Viña Amable 2013 T Roble
listán negro, castellana
88
Colour: deep cherry, purple rim. Nose: powerfull, ripe fruit, creamy oak, violet drops. Palate: fruity, round tannins.

VIÑA MONTEALTO

Avda. de Escaleritas, 112
35011 Las Palmas de Gran Canaria
(Gran Canaria)
☎: +34 928 289 055
Fax: +34 928 206 512
www.grupoflick.com
jflick@grupoflick.com

Montealto 2012 T
87
Colour: cherry, garnet rim. Nose: balanced, wild herbs, spicy, ripe fruit. Palate: good structure, round tannins.

DO. JEREZ-XÈRÉS-SHERRY- MANZANILLA DE SANLÚCAR DE BARRAMEDA

CONSEJO REGULADOR

Avda. Álvaro Domecq, 2
11405 Jerez de la Frontera (Cádiz)
☎ :+34 956 332 050 - Fax: +34 956 338 908
@: vinjerez@sherry.org
www.sherry.org

LOCATION:

In the province of Cádiz. The production area covers the municipal districts of Jerez de la Frontera, El Puerto de Santa María, Chipiona, Trebujena, Rota, Puerto Real, Chiclana de la Frontera and some estates in Lebrija.

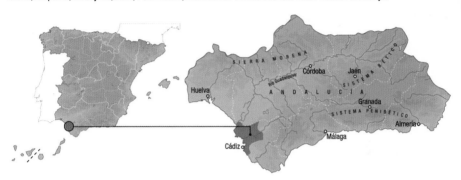

GRAPE VARIETIES:

White: Palomino (90%), Pedro Ximénez, Moscatel, Palomino Fino and Palomino de Jerez.

FIGURES:

Vineyard surface: 6,937.71 – Wine-Growers: 1,723 – Wineries: 30 – 2013 Harvest rating: - – Production 13: 44,555,000 litres – Market percentages: 28% domestic - 72% export.

SOIL:

The so-called 'Albariza' soil is a key factor regarding quality. This type of soil is practically white and is rich in calcium carbonate, clay and silica. It is excellent for retaining humidity and storing winter rainfall for the dry summer months. Moreover, this soil determines the so-called 'Jerez superior'. It is found in Jerez de la Frontera, Puerto de Santa María, Sanlúcar de Barrameda and certain areas of Trebujena. The remaining soil, known as 'Zona', is muddy and sandy.arenas.

CLIMATE:

Warm with Atlantic influences. The west winds play an important role, as they provide humidity and help to temper the conditions. The average annual temperature is 17.5°C, with an average rainfall of 600 mm per year.

VINTAGE RATING   PEÑÍNGUIDE

2009	2010	2011	2012	2013

This denomination of origin, due to the wine-making process, does not make available single-year wines indicated by vintage, so the following evaluation refers to the overall quality of the wines that were tasted this year.

AECOVI-JEREZ

Urb. Pie de Rey, 3- Local Izquierda
11407 Jerez de la Frontera (Cádiz)
☎: +34 956 180 873
Fax: +34 956 180 301
www.aecovi-jerez.com
crecio@aecovi-jerez.com

Alexandro MZ
palomino
90
Colour: bright yellow. Nose: saline, candied fruit. Palate: flavourful, spicy, fine solera notes.

Alexandro OL
palomino
87
Colour: iodine, amber rim. Nose: powerfull, dry nuts, toasty, fruit liqueur notes. Palate: rich, long, spicy.

Alexandro PC
palomino
88
Colour: light mahogany. Nose: acetaldehyde, medium intensity, sweet spices, toasty. Palate: balanced, fine bitter notes, long.

Alexandro PX
pedro ximénez
87
Colour: mahogany. Nose: dried fruit, sun-drenched nuances, pattiserie. Palate: concentrated, flavourful, creamy, sweet, spicy.

ALVARO DOMECQ

Madre de Dios s/n
11401 Jerez de la Frontera (Cádiz)
☎: +34 956 339 634
Fax: +34 956 340 402
www.alvarodomecq.com
alvarodomecqsl@alvarodomecq.com

1730 VORS AM
100% palomino
93
Colour: light mahogany. Nose: elegant, sweet spices, acetaldehyde, dry nuts, cocoa bean. Palate: full, dry, spicy, long, fine bitter notes, complex.

1730 VORS OL
100% palomino
94
Colour: iodine, amber rim. Nose: powerfull, complex, dry nuts, toasty, acetaldehyde, iodine notes. Palate: rich, long, fine solera notes, spicy.

1730 VORS PC
100% palomino
94
Colour: light mahogany. Nose: fruit liqueur notes, dry nuts, dark chocolate, aromatic coffee, caramel, roasted almonds. Palate: fine bitter notes, spirituous, balanced.

Alburejo OL
100% palomino
91
Colour: iodine, amber rim. Nose: powerfull, complex, dry nuts, toasty, sweet spices, characterful. Palate: rich, long, fine solera notes, spicy.

Aranda Cream CR
palomino, pedro ximénez
87
Colour: iodine, amber rim. Nose: sweet spices, pattiserie, dry nuts. Palate: sweetness, spirituous.

La Jaca MZ
100% palomino
90
Colour: bright yellow. Nose: complex, expressive, pungent, saline. Palate: rich, powerful, fresh, fine bitter notes.

La Janda FI
100% palomino
92
Colour: bright yellow. Nose: complex, expressive, pungent, saline, powerfull. Palate: rich, powerful, fresh, fine bitter notes, complex.

Pedro Ximénez 1730 PX
100% pedro ximénez
92
Colour: dark mahogany. Nose: complex, fruit liqueur notes, dried fruit, pattiserie, toasty. Palate: sweet, rich, unctuous, powerful.

BEAM SPAIN, S.L.

San Ildefonso, 3
11403 Jerez de la Frontera (Cádiz)
☎: +34 956 151 500
Fax: +34 956 338 674
www.bodegasharveys.com
bodegasdejerez@beamglobal.com

Harveys Bristol Cream CR
87
Colour: light mahogany. Nose: medium intensity, dried fruit, cocoa bean, tobacco. Palate: light-bodied, easy to drink, correct, sweetness.

Harveys Fine Old VORS AM
100% palomino
93
Colour: iodine, amber rim. Nose: expressive, balanced, sweet spices, aged wood nuances. Palate: balanced, fine bitter notes, rich.

Harveys Medium VORS OL
91
Colour: mahogany. Nose: balanced, sweet spices, acetaldehyde, animal reductive notes. Palate: fine bitter notes, spicy, good acidity, balanced.

Harveys Medium VORS PC
94
Colour: light mahogany. Nose: expressive, characterful, aromatic coffee, spicy. Palate: fine bitter notes, good acidity, spirituous.

Harveys VORS PX
100% pedro ximénez
91
Colour: dark mahogany. Nose: aromatic coffee, caramel, dried fruit. Palate: sweet, long, creamy, fine solera notes.

Terry Amontillado AM
100% palomino
90
Colour: old gold, amber rim. Nose: powerfull, expressive, sweet spices, acetaldehyde. Palate: flavourful, balanced, dry.

Terry Fino FI
100% palomino
91
Colour: bright yellow. Nose: complex, expressive, pungent, saline. Palate: rich, powerful, fresh, fine bitter notes.

Terry Oloroso OL
100% palomino
90
Colour: light mahogany. Nose: acetaldehyde, spicy, dry nuts, varnish, balanced. Palate: good structure, fine bitter notes, long, fine solera notes.

Terry Pedro Ximénez PX
100% pedro ximénez
91
Colour: dark mahogany. Nose: complex, dried fruit, pattiserie, toasty. Palate: sweet, rich, unctuous, powerful.

BODEGA CÉSAR FLORIDO
Padre Lerchundi, 35-37
11550 Chipiona (Cádiz)
☎: +34 956 371 285
Fax: +34 956 370 222
www.bodegasflorido.com
florido@bodegasflorido.com

César Florido Moscatel Dorado Moscatel
100% moscatel de alejandría
89
Colour: old gold, amber rim. Nose: candied fruit, acetaldehyde, sweet spices. Palate: flavourful, fruity, rich.

César Florido Moscatel Especial Moscatel
100% moscatel de alejandría
91
Colour: dark mahogany. Nose: powerfull, dried fruit, pattiserie, dark chocolate, citrus fruit. Palate: full, flavourful, long.

César Florido Moscatel Pasas Moscatel
100% moscatel
89
Colour: mahogany. Nose: powerfull, honeyed notes, pattiserie, dried fruit. Palate: rich, flavourful, sweet.

Cruz del Mar CR
75% palomino, moscatel de alejandría
86
Colour: dark mahogany. Nose: dried fruit, toasty, rancio notes, pattiserie. Palate: flavourful, powerful, correct, sweetness.

Cruz del Mar OL
100% palomino
87
Colour: light mahogany. Nose: medium intensity, spicy. Palate: flavourful, fine bitter notes, balanced, easy to drink.

Fino César Florido FI
100% palomino
91
Colour: bright yellow. Nose: balanced, fresh, saline, expressive, pungent. Palate: flavourful, fine bitter notes, long.

Palo Cortado Reserva de Familia "Peña del Águila" PC
100% palomino
93
Colour: iodine, amber rim. Nose: elegant, balanced, acetaldehyde, sweet spices. Palate: full, good structure, complex, fine solera notes.

BODEGAS BARBADILLO
Luis de Eguilaz, 11
11540 Sanlúcar de Barrameda (Cádiz)
☎: +34 956 385 500
Fax: +34 956 385 501
www.barbadillo.com
barbadillo@barbadillo.com

Barbadillo Amontillado VORS AM
100% palomino
96
Colour: iodine, amber rim. Nose: expressive, powerfull, acetaldehyde, sweet spices, dry nuts. Palate: complex, fine bitter notes, spicy.

Barbadillo Medium Oloroso Dulce VORS OL
palomino, pedro ximénez
92
Colour: iodine, amber rim. Nose: powerfull, complex, elegant, dry nuts. Palate: rich, long, fine solera notes, spicy, sweetness.

Barbadillo Oloroso Seco VORS OL
palomino

93

Colour: iodine, amber rim. Nose: powerfull, expressive, varnish, acetaldehyde, dry nuts. Palate: full, flavourful, fine bitter notes.

Barbadillo Palo Cortado VORS PC
palomino

94

Colour: iodine, amber rim. Nose: acetaldehyde, pungent, roasted almonds, aromatic coffee, toasty. Palate: spicy, long, fine solera notes, good acidity, fine bitter notes.

Cuco Oloroso Seco OL
100% palomino

91

Colour: iodine, amber rim. Nose: powerfull, complex, dry nuts, creamy oak, varnish. Palate: rich, long, fine solera notes, spicy.

Eva Cream CR
pedro ximénez, palomino

90

Colour: mahogany. Nose: dark chocolate, candied fruit, balanced, cocoa bean. Palate: good structure, flavourful, full.

La Cilla PX
pedro ximénez

88

Colour: dark mahogany. Nose: complex, dried fruit, pattiserie, fruit liqueur notes. Palate: sweet, rich, unctuous, powerful.

Laura Moscatel
moscatel

88

Colour: iodine, amber rim. Nose: sweet spices, honeyed notes. Palate: sweet, concentrated.

Obispo Gascón PC
100% palomino

94

Colour: iodine, amber rim. Nose: acetaldehyde, fruit liqueur notes, spicy, varnish. Palate: round, balanced, spirituous, fine bitter notes.

Príncipe AM
100% palomino

91

Colour: iodine, amber rim. Nose: complex, dry nuts, toasty, cocoa bean. Palate: rich, fine bitter notes, fine solera notes, long, spicy.

Reliquia AM

98

Colour: iodine, amber rim. Nose: powerfull, complex, dry nuts, toasty, acetaldehyde, pungent. Palate: rich, fine bitter notes, fine solera notes, long, spicy.

Reliquia OL

96

Colour: iodine, amber rim. Nose: powerfull, complex, elegant, dry nuts, toasty, acetaldehyde, pungent. Palate: rich, long, fine solera notes, spicy, powerful, fine bitter notes.

Reliquia PC

97

Colour: light mahogany. Nose: fruit liqueur notes, dry nuts, complex, characterful, spicy. Palate: powerful, complex, full, spirituous.

Reliquia PX
pedro ximénez

97

Colour: dark mahogany. Nose: complex, fruit liqueur notes, dried fruit, pattiserie, toasty, acetaldehyde, tar, dark chocolate. Palate: sweet, rich, unctuous, powerful, flavourful.

San Rafael OL

90

Colour: old gold, amber rim. Nose: caramel, aromatic coffee, sweet spices. Palate: spirituous, sweetness.

Solear MZ
100% palomino

92

Colour: bright yellow. Nose: complex, expressive, pungent, saline. Palate: rich, powerful, fresh, fine bitter notes.

Solear en Rama MZ
100% palomino

96

Colour: bright yellow. Nose: powerfull, characterful, dry nuts, pungent. Palate: spirituous, good acidity, round, fine solera notes.

BODEGAS DIOS BACO

Tecnología, A-14
11407 Jerez de la Frontera (Cádiz)
☎: +34 956 333 337
Fax: +34 956 333 825
www.bodegasdiosbaco.com
comercial@bodegasdiosbaco.com

Baco de Élite Medium OL
palomino

90

Colour: iodine, amber rim. Nose: powerfull, complex, elegant, dry nuts, toasty. Palate: rich, long, fine solera notes, sweetness.

Baco Imperial 30 años VORS PC
100% palomino

92

Colour: old gold, amber rim. Nose: cocoa bean, spicy, dry nuts, varnish. Palate: flavourful, good acidity, balanced, long.

Bulería FI
100% palomino

90

Colour: bright yellow. Nose: complex, expressive, pungent, saline, powerfull, characterful. Palate: rich, powerful, fresh, fine bitter notes.

Dios Baco CR

92

Colour: mahogany. Nose: toasty, caramel, cocoa bean, dried fruit, aged wood nuances. Palate: flavourful, fine solera notes, balanced.

Oxford 1970 PX
100% pedro ximénez

90

Colour: light mahogany. Nose: dried fruit, aromatic coffee, dark chocolate. Palate: powerful, concentrated.

Riá Pitá MZ
100% palomino

90

Colour: bright yellow. Nose: powerfull, pungent, saline, expressive, complex. Palate: long, fine bitter notes, good structure, dry.

BODEGAS GUTIÉRREZ COLOSÍA
Avda. Bajamar, 40
11500 El Puerto de Santa María (Cádiz)
☎: +34 956 852 852
Fax: +34 956 542 936
www.gutierrezcolosia.com
info@gutierrezcolosia.com

Campo de Guía FI
palomino

87

Colour: bright straw. Nose: medium intensity, saline, balanced. Palate: fresh, balanced, good acidity, correct.

Gutiérrez Colosía AM
palomino

90

Colour: iodine, amber rim. Nose: powerfull, complex, dry nuts, toasty. Palate: rich, fine bitter notes, fine solera notes, long, spicy.

Gutiérrez Colosía CR
palomino, pedro ximénez

88

Colour: iodine, amber rim. Nose: creamy oak, spicy, caramel. Palate: fine solera notes, good finish.

Gutiérrez Colosía FI
palomino

91

Colour: bright yellow. Nose: complex, expressive, pungent, saline, powerfull, characterful. Palate: rich, powerful, fresh, fine bitter notes.

Gutiérrez Colosía MZ
palomino

91

Colour: bright yellow. Nose: complex, expressive, pungent, saline. Palate: rich, powerful, fresh, fine bitter notes.

Gutiérrez Colosía OL
palomino

90

Colour: iodine, amber rim. Nose: powerfull, dry nuts, toasty, acetaldehyde. Palate: rich, long, fine solera notes, spicy.

Gutiérrez Colosía PX
pedro ximénez

89

Colour: iodine, amber rim. Nose: sweet spices, dark chocolate, caramel. Palate: sweet, concentrated.

Gutiérrez Colosía Fino en Rama 3 años FI
palomino

90

Colour: bright yellow. Nose: complex, expressive, pungent, saline. Palate: rich, powerful, fresh, fine bitter notes.

Gutiérrez Colosía Fino en Rama 5 años FI
palomino

93

Colour: bright yellow. Nose: complex, expressive, pungent, saline, toasty. Palate: rich, powerful, fine bitter notes, full.

Gutiérrez Colosía Moscatel
Soleado Moscatel
moscatel

88

Colour: dark mahogany. Nose: dried fruit, varietal, honeyed notes, pattisserie. Palate: unctuous, sweet, flavourful.

Gutiérrez Colosía Solera Familiar AM
palomino

91

Colour: iodine, amber rim. Nose: powerfull, complex, dry nuts, toasty, saline, roasted almonds. Palate: rich, fine bitter notes, fine solera notes, long, spicy.

Gutiérrez Colosía Solera Familiar OL
palomino

93

Colour: iodine, amber rim. Nose: powerfull, complex, elegant, dry nuts, toasty, acetaldehyde. Palate: rich, spicy, long.

Gutiérrez Colosía Solera Familiar PC
palomino

92

Colour: iodine, amber rim. Nose: acetaldehyde, pungent, fruit liqueur notes, varnish. Palate: sweetness, spirituous, good acidity.

Gutiérrez Colosía Solera Familiar PX
pedro ximénez

93

Colour: dark mahogany. Nose: complex, fruit liqueur notes, dried fruit, pattiserie, toasty. Palate: sweet, rich, unctuous, powerful.

Mari Pepa CR
palomino, pedro ximénez

88

Colour: old gold, amber rim. Nose: cocoa bean, aromatic coffee, roasted almonds. Palate: spicy, spirituous.

Sangre y Trabajadero OL
100% palomino

90

Colour: iodine, amber rim. Nose: powerfull, complex, elegant, dry nuts, toasty. Palate: rich, long, fine solera notes, spicy.

BODEGAS HIDALGO-LA GITANA
Banda de Playa, 42
11540 Sanlúcar de Barrameda (Cádiz)
☎: +34 956 385 304
Fax: +34 956 363 844
www.lagitana.es
bodegashidalgo@lagitana.es

Alameda CR
87

Colour: light mahogany. Nose: caramel, dried fruit, sweet spices. Palate: good structure, flavourful, spicy, fine bitter notes.

Faraón OL
100% palomino

89

Colour: iodine, amber rim. Nose: dry nuts, balanced, spicy. Palate: flavourful, fine bitter notes, fine solera notes.

Faraón 30 años VORS 50 cl. OL
100% palomino

91

Colour: iodine, amber rim. Nose: elegant, dry nuts, toasty, expressive. Palate: rich, long, fine solera notes, spicy.

La Gitana MZ
palomino

92

Colour: bright yellow. Nose: complex, expressive, pungent, saline. Palate: rich, powerful, fresh, fine bitter notes.

La Gitana en Rama (Saca de Invierno) MZ
100% palomino

93

Colour: bright golden. Nose: spicy, dry nuts, saline, complex. Palate: balanced, fine bitter notes, fine solera notes, spicy, rich.

Napoleón AM
100% palomino

91

Colour: iodine, amber rim. Nose: powerfull, complex, elegant, dry nuts. Palate: rich, fine bitter notes, fine solera notes, long, spicy.

Napoleón 30 años VORS 50 cl. AM
100% palomino

93

Colour: iodine, amber rim. Nose: powerfull, complex, elegant, dry nuts, toasty. Palate: rich, fine bitter notes, fine solera notes, long, spicy.

Pastrana Manzanilla Pasada MZ
100% palomino

94

Colour: bright yellow. Nose: saline, iodine notes, dry nuts, powerfull. Palate: fine bitter notes, spirituous, round.

Triana PX
100% pedro ximénez

90

Colour: dark mahogany. Nose: complex, fruit liqueur notes, dried fruit, toasty, dark chocolate, varnish. Palate: sweet, rich, unctuous, powerful.

Triana 30 años VORS PX
100% pedro ximénez

92

Colour: dark mahogany. Nose: complex, fruit liqueur notes, dried fruit, pattiserie, toasty. Palate: sweet, rich, unctuous, powerful.

Wellington 30 años VORS PC
palomino

92

Colour: light mahogany. Nose: acetaldehyde, fruit liqueur notes, dry nuts, smoky, aromatic coffee, spicy. Palate: fine bitter notes, good acidity.

Wellington Jerez Cortado 20 años VOS 50 cl. PC
100% palomino

91

Colour: old gold, amber rim. Nose: spicy, dry nuts, acetaldehyde, cocoa bean. Palate: balanced, good acidity, full, flavourful.

BODEGAS LA CIGARRERA
Pza. Madre de Dios, s/n
11540 Sanlúcar de Barrameda (Cádiz)
☎: +34 956 381 285
www.bodegaslacigarrera.com
lacigarrera@bodegaslacigarrera.com

La Cigarrera AM
100% palomino

92

Colour: iodine, amber rim. Nose: dry nuts, spicy, fruit liqueur notes. Palate: rich, flavourful, balanced, fine bitter notes, dry.

La Cigarrera Moscatel
100% moscatel

91

Colour: iodine, amber rim. Nose: caramel, overripe fruit, honeyed notes. Palate: sweetness, spirituous, complex.

La Cigarrera MZ
100% palomino

86

Colour: bright yellow. Nose: powerfull, fresh fruit. Palate: fruity, correct, fine bitter notes.

La Cigarrera OL
100% palomino

87

Colour: old gold, amber rim. Nose: medium intensity, cocoa bean. Palate: correct, spicy, balanced, fine bitter notes.

La Cigarrera PX
pedro ximénez

89

Colour: dark mahogany. Nose: complex, fruit liqueur notes, dried fruit, dark chocolate. Palate: sweet, rich, unctuous, powerful, good structure.

BODEGAS OSBORNE
Fernán Caballero, 7
11500 El Puerto de Santa María (Cádiz)
☎: +34 956 869 000
Fax: +34 925 869 026
www.osborne.es
carolina.cerrato@osborne.es

10 RF OL
palomino, pedro ximénez

90

Colour: light mahogany. Nose: balanced, caramel, sweet spices, candied fruit. Palate: balanced, fine bitter notes.

Amontillado 51-1ª V.O.R.S AM
palomino

94

Colour: iodine, amber rim. Nose: powerfull, complex, elegant, dry nuts, toasty, saline, pungent. Palate: rich, fine bitter notes, fine solera notes, long, spicy.

Bailén OL
100% palomino

88

Colour: iodine, amber rim. Nose: powerfull, complex, dry nuts. Palate: rich, long, fine solera notes, spicy.

Capuchino V.O.R.S PC
palomino

94

Colour: old gold, amber rim. Nose: elegant, complex, dry nuts, roasted almonds, sweet spices. Palate: full, long, fine solera notes.

Fino Quinta FI
100% palomino

92

Colour: bright yellow. Nose: complex, expressive, pungent, saline. Palate: rich, powerful, fresh, fine bitter notes.

Osborne Pedro Ximénez 1827 PX
100% pedro ximénez

91

Colour: dark mahogany. Nose: complex, fruit liqueur notes, dried fruit, pattiserie, toasty. Palate: sweet, rich, unctuous, powerful.

Osborne Rare Sherry PX VORS PX
pedro ximénez

95

Colour: dark mahogany. Nose: complex, fruit liqueur notes, dried fruit, pattiserie, toasty, roasted coffee, tar. Palate: sweet, rich, unctuous, powerful.

Osborne Solera AOS AM
palomino

96

Colour: iodine, amber rim. Nose: complex, elegant, dry nuts, toasty, acetaldehyde, pungent, saline. Palate: rich, fine bitter notes, fine solera notes, long, spicy.

Osborne Solera BC 200 OL
pedro ximénez, palomino

97

Colour: iodine, amber rim. Nose: powerfull, complex, elegant, dry nuts, toasty, acetaldehyde. Palate: rich, long, fine solera notes, spicy, elegant.

Osborne Solera India OL
pedro ximénez, palomino

94

Colour: light mahogany. Nose: powerfull, pungent, fruit liqueur notes, dry nuts, sweet spices. Palate: flavourful, rich, full, long, complex.

Santa María Cream CR
pedro ximénez, palomino

87

Colour: iodine, amber rim. Nose: candied fruit, spicy, cocoa bean. Palate: sweetness, flavourful.

Sibarita V.O.R.S. OL

95

Colour: iodine, amber rim. Nose: powerfull, complex, dry nuts, toasty, acetaldehyde. Palate: rich, long, fine solera notes, spicy, good acidity, round.

BODEGAS REY FERNANDO DE CASTILLA

Jardinillo, 7-11
11404 Jerez de la Frontera (Cádiz)
☎ +34 956 182 454
Fax: +34 956 182 222
www.fernandodecastilla.com
bodegas@fernandodecastilla.com

Fernando de Castilla "Amontillado Antique" AM
100% palomino

94

Colour: light mahogany. Nose: complex, sweet spices, acetaldehyde, dry nuts, powerfull. Palate: rich, flavourful, full, long.

Fernando de Castilla "Fino Antique" FI
100% palomino

94

Colour: bright golden. Nose: powerfull, fruit liqueur notes, dry nuts, acetaldehyde, saline. Palate: flavourful, fine bitter notes, good acidity, round.

Fernando de Castilla "Oloroso Antique" OL
100% palomino

92

Colour: iodine, amber rim. Nose: complex, dry nuts, toasty, characterful. Palate: rich, long, fine solera notes, spicy.

Fernando de Castilla "P.X. Antique" PX
pedro ximénez

94

Colour: dark mahogany. Nose: complex, aromatic coffee, sweet spices, cocoa bean, balanced. Palate: flavourful, full, complex, spicy, long.

Fernando de Castilla "Palo Cortado Antique" PC
100% palomino

94

Colour: iodine, amber rim. Nose: aged wood nuances, sweet spices, fruit liqueur notes. Palate: spicy, fine bitter notes, full, powerful, flavourful.

Fernando de Castilla "PX Classic" PX
pedro ximénez

89

Colour: dark mahogany. Nose: dried fruit, powerfull, fruit liqueur notes. Palate: unctuous, sweet, flavourful.

Fernando de Castilla Fino Classic FI
100% palomino

90

Colour: bright yellow. Nose: complex, expressive, pungent, saline. Palate: rich, powerful, fresh, fine bitter notes.

Fernando de Castilla Fino en Rama FI
100% palomino

93

Colour: bright yellow. Nose: powerfull, dry nuts, fruit liqueur notes, saline, flor yeasts. Palate: flavourful, powerful, fine bitter notes, round.

Fernando de Castilla Oloroso Classic OL
100% palomino

90

Colour: iodine, amber rim. Nose: powerfull, complex, elegant, dry nuts, toasty. Palate: rich, long, fine solera notes, spicy.

BODEGAS TRADICIÓN

Cordobeses, 3
11408 Jerez de la Frontera (Cádiz)
☎: +34 956 168 628
Fax: +34 956 331 963
www.bodegastradicion.com
visitas@bodegastradicion.com

Amontillado Tradición VORS AM
palomino

94

Colour: iodine, amber rim. Nose: powerfull, complex, elegant, dry nuts, dark chocolate, acetaldehyde. Palate: rich, fine bitter notes, fine solera notes, long, spicy.

Fino Tradición FI
palomino

90

Colour: bright golden. Nose: dry nuts, spicy, balsamic herbs, complex, expressive. Palate: flavourful, fine bitter notes, balanced.

Oloroso Tradición VORS OL
palomino

95

Colour: old gold, amber rim. Nose: acetaldehyde, complex, sweet spices, cocoa bean, varnish, dry nuts. Palate: flavourful, full, fine bitter notes, fine solera notes.

Palo Cortado Tradición VORS PC
palomino

94

Colour: old gold, amber rim. Nose: complex, spicy, acetaldehyde, dry nuts. Palate: full, flavourful, complex, long, fine bitter notes, fine solera notes.

Pedro Ximénez Tradición VOS PX
pedro ximénez

93

Colour: dark mahogany. Nose: complex, fruit liqueur notes, dried fruit, pattiserie, toasty, characterful, powerfull. Palate: sweet, rich, unctuous, powerful.

DELGADO ZULETA

Avda. Rocío Jurado, s/n
11540 Sanlúcar de Barrameda (Cádiz)
☎: +34 956 361 107
Fax: +34 956 360 780
www.delgadozuleta.com
jfcarvajal@delgadozuleta.com

Barbiana MZ
palomino
88
Colour: bright yellow. Nose: expressive, pungent, saline. Palate: rich, powerful, fresh, fine bitter notes.

La Goya MZ
palomino
92
Colour: bright yellow. Nose: complex, pungent, saline, expressive. Palate: rich, powerful, fresh, fine bitter notes, full, long.

Monteagudo AM
palomino
90
Colour: iodine, amber rim. Nose: powerfull, complex, elegant, dry nuts, fruit liqueur notes. Palate: rich, fine bitter notes, fine solera notes, long, spicy.

Zuleta AM
palomino
88
Colour: iodine, amber rim. Nose: spicy, dry nuts, balanced. Palate: correct, fine bitter notes.

DIEZ - MÉRITO

Ctra. Jerez Lebrija (Morabita, Km. 2)
11407 Jerez de la Frontera (Cádiz)
☎: +34 956 186 112
Fax: +34 956 303 500
www.diezmerito.com
info@diezmerito.com

Fino Imperial 30 años VORS AM
palomino
92
Colour: iodine, amber rim. Nose: complex, elegant, dry nuts, toasty. Palate: rich, fine bitter notes, fine solera notes, long.

Pemartín AM
palomino
91
Colour: iodine, amber rim. Nose: medium intensity, dry nuts, toasty. Palate: flavourful, full, long.

Pemartín CR
palomino
85

Pemartín FI
palomino
86
Colour: bright yellow. Nose: medium intensity, dry nuts, saline. Palate: light-bodied, easy to drink.

Pemartín OL
palomino
87
Colour: light mahogany. Nose: medium intensity, sweet spices, dry nuts. Palate: correct, balanced, spicy, flavourful.

Pemartín PX
pedro ximénez
87
Colour: mahogany. Nose: candied fruit, sweet spices, cocoa bean, medium intensity. Palate: rich, flavourful, easy to drink.

Victoria Regina VORS OL
palomino
93
Colour: iodine, amber rim. Nose: powerfull, complex, elegant, dry nuts, toasty, spicy, acetaldehyde. Palate: rich, long, fine solera notes, spicy, spirituous.

Vieja Solera 30 años PX
pedro ximénez
92
Colour: dark mahogany. Nose: complex, dark chocolate, sweet spices, dried fruit. Palate: balanced, unctuous, long.

EQUIPO NAVAZOS

11403 Jerez de la Frontera (Cádiz)
www.equiponavazos.com
equipo@navazos.com

Fino en Rama Navazos, Saca Marzo 2014 FI
palomino
95
Colour: bright yellow. Nose: flor yeasts, lees reduction notes, pungent. Palate: good acidity, fine bitter notes, spicy, long.

La Bota de Fino (Bota nº 54) FI
palomino
98
Colour: bright yellow. Nose: fine lees, powerfull, characterful, complex, expressive. Palate: powerful, spicy, long, fine bitter notes.

La Bota de Manzanilla (Bota nª 55) MZ
palomino
94
Colour: bright yellow. Nose: powerfull, characterful, petrol notes, lees reduction notes, wet leather, waxy notes. Palate: spicy, fine bitter notes, good acidity.

La Bota de Manzanilla Pasada Nº5 (Bota Punta) MZ
palomino

98

Colour: bright yellow. Nose: candied fruit, spicy, varnish, acetaldehyde, pungent, saline. Palate: fine bitter notes, good acidity, rich, long.

La Bota de Palo Cortado 52 "Sanlúcar" PC
palomino

95

Colour: light mahogany. Nose: spicy, candied fruit, fruit liqueur notes. Palate: powerful, sweetness, spicy, long.

La Bota de Palo Cortado nº 47 "Bota NO" PC
palomino

98

Colour: light mahogany. Nose: powerfull, characterful, complex, fruit liqueur notes, toasty, spicy. Palate: powerful, concentrated, complex, spicy.

La Bota de Palo Cortado nº 48 "Bota Punta" PC
palomino

97

Colour: iodine, amber rim. Nose: powerfull, complex, elegant, dry nuts, toasty. Palate: rich, fine solera notes, spicy.

La Bota de Palo Cortado nº 51 "Bota GF" PC
palomino

98

Colour: light mahogany. Nose: complex, elegant, dry nuts, toasty, mineral, pungent, saline. Palate: rich, long, fine solera notes, spicy, toasty, powerful.

Manzanilla en Rama I Think. Saca Abril 2014 MZ
palomino

92

Colour: bright yellow. Nose: lees reduction notes, candied fruit, scrubland, fragrant herbs. Palate: sweetness, good acidity, fine bitter notes.

GARVEY
Ctra. Circunvalación, s/n (Complejo Bellavista)
11407 Jerez de la Frontera (Cádiz)
☎: +34 956 319 650
Fax: +34 956 319 824
www.grupogarvey.com
info@grupogarvey.com

Asalto Amoroso

90

Colour: mahogany. Nose: toasty, caramel, spicy, fruit liqueur notes. Palate: sweetness, powerful, flavourful, spicy.

Don José María AM
100% palomino

91

Colour: light mahogany. Nose: aged wood nuances, dry nuts, spicy, creamy oak. Palate: powerful, flavourful, spicy, fine bitter notes.

Don José María CR

87

Colour: dark mahogany. Nose: dried fruit, aromatic coffee, caramel, creamy oak, toasty. Palate: spicy, long, toasty, unctuous.

Don José María FI
100% palomino

91

Colour: bright yellow. Nose: complex, expressive, pungent, saline, dry nuts. Palate: rich, powerful, fresh, fine bitter notes, balanced, elegant.

Don José María OL
100% palomino

92

Colour: mahogany. Nose: acetaldehyde, varnish, spicy, creamy oak, sweet spices, aged wood nuances. Palate: rich, powerful, flavourful, spicy, long.

Flor de Jerez CR

88

Colour: iodine, amber rim. Nose: powerfull, complex, elegant, dry nuts, toasty, caramel, sweet spices. Palate: rich, long, fine solera notes, spicy, sweet.

Flor del Museo CR

89

Colour: mahogany. Nose: dried fruit, sweet spices, creamy oak, toasty, expressive. Palate: sweetness, spicy, long.

Garvey PX
100% pedro ximénez

87

Colour: dark mahogany. Nose: complex, fruit liqueur notes, dried fruit, pattiserie, toasty, sweet spices, aromatic coffee. Palate: sweet, rich, unctuous, powerful.

Garvey VORS OL
100% palomino

93

Colour: mahogany. Nose: pungent, acetaldehyde, honeyed notes, dry nuts, dark chocolate, sweet spices, creamy oak, aged wood nuances. Palate: balanced, elegant, spicy, toasty, fine bitter notes.

Garvey VORS PX
100% pedro ximénez

94

Colour: dark mahogany. Nose: complex, fruit liqueur notes, dried fruit, pattiserie, toasty, varnish, spicy, aromatic coffee. Palate: sweet, rich, unctuous, powerful, balanced, elegant.

Garvey VOS PX
100% pedro ximénez

92

Colour: dark mahogany. Nose: acetaldehyde, dried fruit, dry nuts, dark chocolate, aromatic coffee, expressive. Palate: powerful, rich, spicy, toasty, long.

Gran Orden PX
100% pedro ximénez

94

Colour: dark mahogany. Nose: complex, fruit liqueur notes, dried fruit, pattiserie, toasty, smoky, aromatic coffee. Palate: sweet, rich, unctuous, powerful, balanced, elegant.

Jauna PC
100% palomino

94

Colour: mahogany. Nose: acetaldehyde, dry nuts, balsamic herbs, spicy, creamy oak, elegant. Palate: balanced, spicy, long, flavourful, unctuous, good structure.

Ochavico OL
100% palomino

88

Colour: light mahogany. Nose: powerfull, complex, dry nuts, toasty, caramel. Palate: rich, long, fine solera notes, spicy.

Oñana AM
100% palomino

93

Colour: light mahogany. Nose: varnish, dry nuts, acetaldehyde, spicy, pattiserie, cocoa bean, balanced. Palate: powerful, flavourful, spicy, long.

Puerta Real OL
100% palomino

93

Colour: old gold, amber rim. Nose: dark chocolate, cocoa bean, acetaldehyde, pattiserie, expressive. Palate: flavourful, spicy, toasty, balanced.

San Patricio FI
100% palomino

91

Colour: bright yellow. Nose: ripe fruit, dry nuts, floral, aged wood nuances, spicy. Palate: spicy, fine bitter notes, easy to drink.

Tio Guillermo AM
100% palomino

85

GONZÁLEZ BYASS

Manuel María González, 12
11403 Jerez de la Frontera (Cádiz)
☎: +34 956 357 000
Fax: +34 956 357 043
www.bodegastiopepe.es
elrincondegb@gonzalezbyass.es

Alfonso OL
100% palomino

90

Colour: iodine, amber rim. Nose: powerfull, elegant, dry nuts, toasty, dark chocolate. Palate: rich, long, spicy.

Amontillado del Duque VORS AM
100% palomino

94

Colour: iodine, amber rim. Nose: acetaldehyde, elegant, expressive, varnish, dry nuts. Palate: balanced, fine bitter notes, long, fine solera notes.

Apóstoles VORS PC

92

Colour: iodine, amber rim. Nose: petrol notes, candied fruit, spicy, toasty. Palate: fine bitter notes, good acidity, spicy, sweetness.

Gonzalez Byass Añada 1982 PC
100% palomino

96

Colour: old gold, amber rim. Nose: expressive, elegant, sweet spices, roasted almonds. Palate: complex, long, fine solera notes, fine bitter notes.

Leonor PC
100% palomino

92

Colour: iodine, amber rim. Nose: elegant, balanced, cocoa bean, sweet spices. Palate: full, flavourful, complex, long.

Matusalem VORS OL

94

Colour: iodine, amber rim. Nose: powerfull, complex, elegant, dry nuts, toasty. Palate: rich, long, fine solera notes, spicy, sweetness.

Néctar PX
100% pedro ximénez

91

Colour: dark mahogany. Nose: fruit liqueur notes, dried fruit, pattiserie, dark chocolate. Palate: sweet, rich, unctuous, powerful.

Noé VORS PX
100% pedro ximénez

94

Colour: dark mahogany. Nose: complex, fruit liqueur notes, dried fruit, pattiserie, toasty. Palate: sweet, rich, unctuous, powerful.

Solera 1847 CR
palomino, pedro ximénez

88

Colour: mahogany. Nose: cocoa bean, sweet spices, rancio notes, dried fruit. Palate: fruity, flavourful, sweetness, fine bitter notes.

Tío Pepe FI
100% palomino

94

Colour: bright yellow. Nose: complex, expressive, pungent, saline, fresh, powerfull. Palate: rich, powerful, fresh, fine bitter notes.

Tío Pepe en Rama FI
palomino

94

Colour: bright yellow. Nose: complex, expressive, saline, powerfull. Palate: rich, powerful, fresh, fine bitter notes.

Tres Palmas FI
palomino

95

Colour: bright yellow. Nose: complex, pungent, saline, spicy. Palate: rich, powerful, fresh, fine bitter notes.

Viña AB AM
100% palomino

91

Colour: old gold, amber rim. Nose: balanced, expressive, saline, dry nuts, complex, elegant. Palate: flavourful, spicy.

HEREDEROS DE ARGÜESO S.A.
Mar, 8
11540 Sanlúcar de Barrameda (Cádiz)
☎: +34 956 385 116
Fax: +34 956 368 169
www.argueso.es
argueso@argueso.es

Argüeso AM
palomino

90

Colour: light mahogany. Nose: balanced, acetaldehyde, spicy, dry nuts. Palate: good structure, full, fine bitter notes, long.

Argüeso PX
pedro ximénez

87

Colour: iodine, amber rim. Nose: overripe fruit, candied fruit, spicy. Palate: sweet, good acidity.

Argüeso Cream CR
palomino, pedro ximénez

87

Colour: iodine, amber rim. Nose: spicy, fruit liqueur notes, toasty. Palate: spicy, fine bitter notes, good acidity.

San León "Clásica" MZ
palomino

93

Colour: bright yellow. Nose: complex, expressive, pungent, saline. Palate: rich, powerful, fresh, fine bitter notes.

San León Reserva de Familia MZ
palomino

95

Colour: bright yellow. Nose: complex, pungent, saline, dry nuts, acetaldehyde. Palate: rich, powerful, fresh, fine bitter notes.

HIDALGO
Clavel, 29
11402 Jerez de la Frontera (Cádiz)
☎: +34 956 341 078
Fax: +34 956 320 922
www.hidalgo.com
info@hidalgo.com

El Tresillo 1874 Amontillado Viejo AM
palomino

96

Colour: iodine, amber rim. Nose: elegant, dry nuts, toasty, pungent, characterful, complex. Palate: rich, fine bitter notes, fine solera notes, long, spicy.

El Tresillo Amontillado Fino AM
palomino

93

Colour: bright golden. Nose: powerfull, complex, elegant, dry nuts, toasty. Palate: rich, fine bitter notes, fine solera notes, long, spicy.

Gobernador OL
palomino

90

Colour: mahogany. Nose: smoky, dry nuts, balanced, sweet spices, creamy oak, expressive. Palate: powerful, flavourful, spicy, unctuous, long.

La Panesa Especial Fino FI
palomino

94

Colour: bright golden. Nose: complex, expressive, pungent, saline, iodine notes, dry nuts. Palate: rich, powerful, fresh, fine bitter notes.

Villapanés OL
palomino

94

Colour: iodine, amber rim. Nose: powerfull, complex, elegant, dry nuts, toasty, fruit liqueur notes. Palate: rich, long, fine solera notes, spicy.

HIJOS DE RAINERA PÉREZ MARÍN

Ctra. Nacional IV, Km. 640
11404 Jerez de la Frontera (Cádiz)
☎: +34 956 321 004
Fax: +34 956 340 216
www.laguita.com
info@grupoestevez.com

La Guita MZ
100% palomino
92
Colour: bright yellow. Nose: complex, expressive, pungent, saline, fresh, white flowers. Palate: rich, powerful, fresh, fine bitter notes.

LUIS CABALLERO

San Francisco, 32
11500 El Puerto de Santa María (Cádiz)
☎: +34 956 851 751
Fax: +34 956 859 204
www.caballero.es
marketing@caballero.es

Pavón Fl
palomino
94
Colour: bright yellow. Nose: complex, expressive, pungent, saline, dry nuts, iodine notes. Palate: rich, powerful, fresh, fine bitter notes.

LUSTAU

Arcos, 53
11402 Jerez de la Frontera (Cádiz)
☎: +34 956 341 597
www.lustau.es
lustau@lustau.es

Botaina AM
palomino
89
Colour: iodine, amber rim. Nose: balanced, sweet spices, dry nuts, acetaldehyde. Palate: good structure, flavourful, spicy.

La Ina Fl
palomino
95
Colour: bright yellow. Nose: complex, expressive, pungent, saline, elegant, dry nuts. Palate: rich, powerful, fresh, fine bitter notes.

Lustau Almacenista Amontillado de Sanlúcar Cuevas Jurado 50 cl. AM
palomino
91
Colour: iodine, amber rim. Nose: powerfull, complex, dry nuts, toasty, saline, iodine notes, elegant. Palate: rich, fine bitter notes, fine solera notes, long, spicy.

Lustau Almacenista Oloroso del Puerto González Obregón 50 cl. OL
palomino
93
Colour: iodine, amber rim. Nose: complex, elegant, dry nuts, toasty, creamy oak, sweet spices. Palate: rich, long, fine solera notes, spicy.

Lustau Almacenista Palo Cortado Vides PC
palomino
93
Colour: iodine, amber rim. Nose: powerfull, complex, elegant, dry nuts, toasty, saline, acetaldehyde. Palate: rich, long, fine solera notes, spicy.

Lustau Añada 1997 Oloroso Dulce OL
palomino
92
Colour: iodine, amber rim. Nose: powerfull, elegant, dry nuts, caramel. Palate: rich, long, fine solera notes, spicy.

Lustau East India CR
palomino, pedro ximénez
91
Colour: mahogany. Nose: caramel, sweet spices, dried fruit, acetaldehyde. Palate: flavourful, powerful, good structure.

Lustau Emilín Moscatel
moscatel
90
Colour: iodine, amber rim. Nose: sweet spices, fruit liqueur notes, white flowers. Palate: flavourful, good acidity, balanced.

Lustau Escuadrilla AM
palomino
91
Colour: iodine, amber rim. Nose: spicy, dry nuts, acetaldehyde, iodine notes. Palate: full, long, complex, fine bitter notes.

Lustau Jarana Fl
palomino
93
Colour: bright yellow. Nose: complex, expressive, pungent, saline, powerfull, characterful. Palate: rich, powerful, fresh, fine bitter notes.

Lustau Papirusa MZ
palomino
94
Colour: bright yellow. Nose: complex, pungent, saline, toasty. Palate: rich, powerful, fresh, fine bitter notes.

Lustau Penísula PC
palomino
90
Colour: old gold, amber rim. Nose: balanced, cocoa bean, sweet spices, candied fruit, roasted almonds. Palate: flavourful, spicy.

Lustau Puerto Fino FI
palomino

94

Colour: bright yellow. Nose: complex, pungent, expressive, saline. Palate: rich, full, fine bitter notes, round, long. Personality.

Lustau San Emilio PX
pedro ximénez

92

Colour: dark mahogany. Nose: complex, fruit liqueur notes, dried fruit, pattiserie, dark chocolate. Palate: sweet, rich, unctuous, powerful.

Lustau VORS AM
palomino

93

Colour: iodine, amber rim. Nose: powerfull, complex, cocoa bean, sweet spices, expressive. Palate: complex, full, spicy, fine solera notes, long.

Lustau VORS OL
palomino

94

Colour: iodine, amber rim. Nose: balanced, sweet spices, cocoa bean, acetaldehyde. Palate: full, balanced, fine bitter notes, fine solera notes.

Lustau VORS PX
pedro ximénez

95

Colour: dark mahogany. Nose: dried fruit, pattiserie, toasty, balanced, cocoa bean. Palate: sweet, rich, unctuous, powerful.

Río Viejo OL
palomino

90

Colour: light mahogany. Nose: dry nuts, medium intensity, caramel. Palate: long, fine solera notes, spicy.

MARQUÉS DEL REAL TESORO
Ctra. Nacional IV, Km. 640
11404 Jerez de la Frontera (Cádiz)
☎: +34 956 321 004
Fax: +34 956 340 216
www.grupoestevez.com
info@grupoestevez.com

Del Príncipe AM
100% palomino

93

Colour: iodine, amber rim. Nose: elegant, dry nuts, toasty. Palate: rich, fine bitter notes, fine solera notes, long, spicy.

Tío Mateo FI
100% palomino

93

Colour: bright yellow. Nose: complex, pungent, saline, floral, fresh. Palate: rich, powerful, fresh, fine bitter notes.

ROMATE
Lealas, 26
11404 Jerez de la Frontera (Cádiz)
☎: +34 956 182 212
Fax: +34 956 185 276
www.romate.com
comercial@romate.com

Cardenal Cisneros PX
100% pedro ximénez

91

Colour: dark mahogany. Nose: complex, fruit liqueur notes, dried fruit, pattiserie, toasty. Palate: sweet, rich, unctuous, powerful.

Don José OL
100% palomino

91

Colour: light mahogany. Nose: balanced, acetaldehyde, sweet spices, varnish. Palate: rich, fine solera notes, spicy, long.

Duquesa PX
100% pedro ximénez

90

Colour: dark mahogany. Nose: expressive, fruit liqueur notes, dried fruit, powerfull. Palate: varietal, sweet, flavourful, creamy.

Iberia CR

89

Colour: dark mahogany. Nose: sweet spices, dried fruit, varnish, fruit liqueur notes. Palate: good structure, flavourful, fine bitter notes.

Marismeño FI
100% palomino

90

Colour: bright yellow. Nose: medium intensity, balanced, saline, dry nuts. Palate: rich, flavourful, fine bitter notes.

NPU AM
100% palomino

93

Colour: iodine, amber rim. Nose: powerfull, complex, elegant, dry nuts, toasty. Palate: rich, fine bitter notes, fine solera notes, long, spicy.

Old & Plus Amontillado VORS AM
100% palomino

92

Colour: iodine, amber rim. Nose: candied fruit, fruit liqueur notes, spicy, varnish. Palate: fine solera notes, fine bitter notes, spirituous.

Old & Plus Oloroso OL
100% palomino

93

Colour: iodine, amber rim. Nose: powerfull, complex, elegant, dry nuts. Palate: rich, long, fine solera notes, spicy.

Old & Plus P.X. PX
100% pedro ximénez

93

Colour: dark mahogany. Nose: complex, dried fruit, pattiserie, toasty, sweet spices, aromatic coffee. Palate: sweet, rich, unctuous, powerful.

Regente PC
100% palomino

91

Colour: light mahogany. Nose: cocoa bean, sweet spices, candied fruit, dry nuts. Palate: flavourful, fine bitter notes, good acidity.

SANDEMAN JEREZ

Porvera, 3 of.-8 y 11
11403 Jerez de la Frontera (Cádiz)
☎: +34 956 151 700
Fax: +34 956 300 007
www.sandeman.eu
jose.moreno@sogrape.pt

Sandeman Armada Premium CR
palomino, pedro ximénez

90

Colour: iodine, amber rim. Nose: candied fruit, caramel, aromatic coffee. Palate: flavourful, spirituous, sweetness.

Sandeman Character Premium AM
palomino, pedro ximénez

91

Colour: iodine, amber rim. Nose: powerfull, complex, elegant, dry nuts, toasty. Palate: rich, fine bitter notes, fine solera notes, long, spicy.

Sandeman Classic FI
palomino

88

Colour: bright straw. Nose: medium intensity, candied fruit, saline. Palate: flavourful, fine bitter notes, good acidity.

Sandeman Classic Medium Dry
palomino, pedro ximénez

87

Colour: light mahogany. Nose: medium intensity, balanced, dry nuts, spicy. Palate: correct, fine bitter notes.

Sandeman Don Fino Premium FI
palomino

90

Colour: bright yellow. Nose: balanced, saline, fresh, dry nuts. Palate: flavourful, fine bitter notes, spicy.

Sandeman Medium Sweet
palomino, pedro ximénez

89

Colour: old gold. Nose: candied fruit, cocoa bean, sweet spices, medium intensity. Palate: rich, fruity, sweet, ripe fruit, balanced.

Sandeman Pedro Ximénez Premium PX
pedro ximénez

92

Colour: dark mahogany. Nose: complex, fruit liqueur notes, dried fruit, pattiserie, toasty. Palate: sweet, rich, unctuous, powerful.

Sandeman Royal Ambrosante VOS PX
pedro ximénez

93

Colour: dark mahogany. Nose: complex, elegant, dried fruit, aromatic coffee, varietal. Palate: rich, full, complex, unctuous, spicy.

VALDESPINO

Ctra. Nacional IV, Km. 640
11408 Jerez de la Frontera (Cádiz)
☎: +34 956 321 004
Fax: +34 956 340 216
www.grupoestevez.com
info@grupoestevez.com

Don Gonzalo VOS OL
100% palomino

96

Colour: iodine, amber rim. Nose: powerfull, complex, elegant, dry nuts. Palate: rich, long, fine solera notes, spicy, fine bitter notes, spirituous.

El Candado PX
pedro ximénez

91

Colour: dark mahogany. Nose: fruit liqueur notes, dried fruit, pattiserie, toasty. Palate: sweet, rich, unctuous, powerful.

Moscatel Promesa Moscatel
moscatel

93

Colour: iodine, amber rim. Nose: sweet spices, honeyed notes, fruit liqueur notes. Palate: good acidity, fine bitter notes.

Solera 1842 VOS OL
100% palomino

94

Colour: mahogany. Nose: ripe fruit, cocoa bean, sweet spices, complex, dry nuts. Palate: full, good structure, spicy, long, fine solera notes. Personality.

Solera de su Majestad VORS 37,5 cl. OL
100% palomino

96

Colour: iodine, amber rim. Nose: complex, elegant, dry nuts, toasty, acetaldehyde, iodine notes. Palate: rich, fine solera notes, spicy.

Tío Diego AM
100% palomino
91
Colour: iodine, amber rim. Nose: powerfull, complex, elegant, dry nuts, toasty. Palate: rich, fine bitter notes, fine solera notes, long, spicy.

Ynocente FI
100% palomino
93
Colour: bright yellow. Nose: complex, expressive, pungent, saline, elegant, flor yeasts. Palate: rich, powerful, fresh, fine bitter notes.

VINOS DE SACRISTÍA
Sevilla, 2 1º Izq.
11540 Sanlúcar de Barrameda (Cádiz)
☎: +34 607 920 337
www.sacristiaab.com
sacristiaab@sacristiaab.com

Sacristía AB MZ
palomino
95
Colour: bright yellow. Nose: complex, expressive, fresh fruit, spicy. Palate: rich, long, fine solera notes, fine bitter notes. Personality.

WILLIAMS & HUMBERT S.A.
Ctra. N-IV, Km. 641,75
11408 Jerez de la Frontera (Cádiz)
☎: +34 956 353 400
Fax: +34 956 353 408
www.williams-humbert.com
williams@williams-humbert.com

Canasta OL
palomino, pedro ximénez
88
Colour: dark mahogany. Nose: powerfull, aromatic coffee, dark chocolate, roasted coffee, dry nuts. Palate: balanced, sweetness, powerful, flavourful, spicy.

Don Guido Solera Especial 20 años VOS PX
pedro ximénez
93
Colour: dark mahogany. Nose: dried fruit, aromatic coffee, spicy, creamy oak, toasty, acetaldehyde, pungent, balanced. Palate: rich, flavourful, spicy, long.

Dos Cortados PC
palomino
94
Colour: light mahogany. Nose: acetaldehyde, pungent, varnish, aged wood nuances, creamy oak. Palate: powerful, flavourful, spicy, long, balanced.

Dry Sack Medium Dry CR
88
Colour: old gold, amber rim. Nose: ripe fruit, sweet spices, creamy oak, toasty. Palate: sweetness, flavourful, spicy.

Fino Pando FI
palomino
90
Colour: bright yellow. Nose: pungent, saline, dried herbs, faded flowers, dry nuts. Palate: powerful, flavourful, spicy, long.

Jalifa VORS "30 years" AM
93
Colour: mahogany. Nose: varnish, acetaldehyde, sweet spices, cocoa bean, roasted almonds, dark chocolate, creamy oak. Palate: balanced, elegant, spicy, long.

DO. JUMILLA

CONSEJO REGULADOR

San Roque, 15
30520 Jumilla (Murcia)
☎:+34 968 781 761 - Fax: +34 968 781 900
@: info@vinosdejumilla.org
www.vinosdejumilla.org

LOCATION:

Midway between the provinces of Murcia and Albacete, this DO spreads over a large region in the southeast of Spain and covers the municipal areas of Jumilla (Murcia) and Fuente Álamo, Albatana, Ontur, Hellín, Tobarra and Montealegre del Castillo (Albacete).

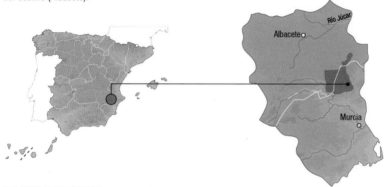

GRAPE VARIETIES:

Red: Monastrell (main 35,373 Ha), Garnacha Tinta, Garnacha Tintorera, Cencibel (Tempranillo), Cabernet Sauvignon, Merlot, Petit Verdot and Syrah.
White: Airén (3,751 Ha), Macabeo, Malvasía, Pedro Ximénez, Chardonnay, Sauvignon Blanc and Moscatel de Grano Menudo.

FIGURES:

Vineyard surface: 25,000 – Wine-Growers: 2,100 – Wineries: 45 – 2013 Harvest rating: - – Production 13: 26,000,000 litres – Market percentages: 53% domestic - 47% export.

SOIL:

The soil is mainly brownish-grey, brownish-grey limestone and limy. In general, it is poor in organic matter, with great water retention capacity and medium permeability.

CLIMATE:

Continental in nature with Mediterranean influences. It is characterized by its aridity and low rainfall (270 mm) which is mainly concentrated in spring and autumn. The winters are cold and the summers dry and quite hot.

VINTAGE RATING				PEÑÍNGUIDE
2009	**2010**	**2011**	**2012**	**2013**
GOOD	VERY GOOD	VERY GOOD	VERY GOOD	GOOD

AROMAS EN MI COPA
Pza. Médico Luis Martínez Pérez, 2
30520 Jumilla (Murcia)
☎: +34 676 492 477
www.aromasenmicopa.com
elisa@aromasenmicopa.com

Evol 2012 T
100% monastrell
91
Colour: bright cherry. Nose: ripe fruit, sweet spices, creamy oak, medium intensity, varietal. Palate: fruity, flavourful, toasty.

ARTIGA FUSTEL
Progres, 21 Bajos
8720 Vilafranca del Penedès
(Barcelona)
☎: +34 938 182 317
Fax: +34 938 924 499
www.artiga-fustel.com
info@artiga-fustel.com

Ariola Espíritu Monastrell Tempranillo 2013 T
86
Colour: cherry, purple rim. Nose: expressive, red berry notes, violets. Palate: flavourful, fruity, good acidity, round tannins.

Camino de Seda 2013 T
84

Castillo de la Peña Syrah Monastrell 2013 T
84

Dominio de Artiga 2009 TR
87
Colour: cherry, garnet rim. Nose: ripe fruit, spicy, creamy oak, toasty, complex. Palate: powerful, flavourful, toasty, round tannins.

El Campeador 2009 TR
87
Colour: dark-red cherry, garnet rim. Nose: ripe fruit, scrubland, sweet spices. Palate: ripe fruit, easy to drink, good finish.

Mas Delmera 2009 TR
87
Colour: cherry, garnet rim. Nose: ripe fruit, spicy, creamy oak, toasty, complex. Palate: powerful, flavourful, toasty, round tannins.

Ossiam 2013 T
100% monastrell
86
Colour: cherry, purple rim. Nose: powerfull, red berry notes, ripe fruit, floral, expressive. Palate: powerful, fresh, fruity, easy to drink.

ASENSIO CARCELÉN N.C.R.
Ctra. RM-714, km. 8
30520 Jumilla (Murcia)
☎: +34 968 435 543
Fax: +34 968 435 542
www.facebook.com/AsensioCarcelen
bodegascarcelen@gmail.com

100 x 100 Monastrell Ecológico 4 Lunas 2011 T Roble
100% monastrell
84 🌱

100 x 100 Syrah Ecológico 4 Lunas 2012 T
100% syrah
84 🌱

Pura Sangre 2006 TGR
100% monastrell
83 🌱

BARÓN DEL SOLAR
Paraje El Jurado s/n
30520 Jumilla (Murcia)
☎: +34 968 066 002
Fax: +34 968 716 472
www.barondelsolar.com
info@barondelsolar.com

Barón del Solar 2011 T
monastrell, petit verdot
87
Colour: bright cherry. Nose: ripe fruit, sweet spices, creamy oak, medium intensity. Palate: fruity, flavourful, toasty.

Barón del Solar Colección Privada 2011 T
monastrell
89
Colour: cherry, garnet rim. Nose: ripe fruit, spicy, creamy oak, toasty, complex. Palate: powerful, flavourful, toasty, round tannins.

BODEGA ARTESANAL VIÑA CAMPANERO
Ctra. de Murcia, s/n- Apdo. 346
30520 Jumilla (Murcia)
☎: +34 968 780 754
Fax: +34 968 780 754
www.vinacampanero.com
bodegas@vinacampanero.com

Vegardal Cuco del Ardal Edición Especial 2010 T
100% monastrell
84

Vegardal Monastrell Cepas Nuevas 2013 T
100% monastrell
84

Vegardal Monastrell Cepas Viejas 2013 T
100% monastrell

87

Colour: cherry, purple rim. Nose: powerfull, red berry notes, ripe fruit, floral, expressive. Palate: powerful, fresh, fruity, unctuous.

Vegardal Naturally Sweet Wine 2010 T
100% monastrell

83

BODEGA SAN JOSÉ
Camino de Hellín, s/n
2652 Ontur (Albacete)
☎: +34 967 324 212
Fax: +34 967 324 186
www.bodegasanjose.com
comercial@bodegasanjose.com

Dominio de Ontur Merlot 2012 T
merlot

86

Colour: cherry, purple rim. Nose: powerfull, red berry notes, ripe fruit, expressive, scrubland, fragrant herbs. Palate: fruity, unctuous, round tannins.

Dominio de Ontur Monastrell 2012 T
monastrell

85

Dominio de Ontur Selección 2010 T
syrah, monastrell

88

Colour: cherry, garnet rim. Nose: ripe fruit, spicy, complex, varietal. Palate: powerful, flavourful, toasty, round tannins.

Dominio de Ontur Syrah 2012 T
syrah

79

Dominio de Ontur Verdejo 2013 B
verdejo

82

Patre 2010 TC
monastrell, syrah

87

Colour: cherry, garnet rim. Nose: ripe fruit, spicy, creamy oak, toasty. Palate: powerful, flavourful, toasty, round tannins, easy to drink.

Raven & Bull 2010 T
monastrell

86

Colour: cherry, garnet rim. Nose: varietal, scrubland, ripe fruit. Palate: fruity, easy to drink, good finish.

BODEGA TORRECASTILLO
Ctra. de Bonete, s/n
2650 Montealegre del Castillo
(Albacete)
☎: +34 967 582 188
Fax: +34 967 582 339
www.torrecastillo.com
bodega@torrecastillo.com

TorreCastillo 2013 B
sauvignon blanc

87

Colour: bright straw. Nose: fresh, fresh fruit, white flowers, expressive, wild herbs, grassy. Palate: flavourful, fruity, good acidity, balanced.

TorreCastillo 2013 RD
monastrell

85

TorreCastillo 2013 T Roble
monastrell

87

Colour: bright cherry. Nose: ripe fruit, sweet spices, creamy oak, expressive. Palate: flavourful, fruity, toasty, round tannins.

TorreCastillo Ello 2011 TC
monastrell

90

Colour: bright cherry. Nose: ripe fruit, sweet spices, creamy oak, medium intensity, balsamic herbs. Palate: fruity, flavourful, toasty.

BODEGA VIÑA ELENA S.L.
Estrecho Marín, s/n
30520 Jumilla (Murcia)
☎: +34 968 781 340
www.vinaelena.com
info@vinaelena.com

Familia Pacheco 2012 T Roble
monastrell, cabernet sauvignon, syrah

85

Familia Pacheco Cuvée 2010 T
cabernet sauvignon, monastrell, syrah

86

Colour: cherry, garnet rim. Nose: fruit preserve, warm, powerfull. Palate: rich, flavourful, round tannins.

Familia Pacheco Orgánico 2012 T
monastrell, syrah

87

Colour: bright cherry. Nose: ripe fruit, sweet spices, creamy oak, expressive. Palate: flavourful, fruity, toasty, round tannins.

Los Cucos de la Alberquilla 2012 T
cabernet sauvignon

89

Colour: bright cherry. Nose: ripe fruit, sweet spices, creamy oak, medium intensity. Palate: fruity, flavourful, toasty.

BODEGAS 1890
Ctra. Venta del Olivo, Km. 2,5
30520 Jumilla (Murcia)
☎: +34 968 757 099
Fax: +34 968 757 099
www.garciacarrion.es
bodegas1890@jgc.es

Castillo San Simón 2008 TGR
monastrell, tempranillo

86

Colour: cherry, garnet rim. Nose: ripe fruit, spicy, medium intensity. Palate: flavourful, toasty, round tannins, balsamic.

Castillo San Simón 2009 TR
monastrell, tempranillo

82

Mayoral 2013 T Joven
monastrell, syrah, cabernet sauvignon

87

Colour: cherry, purple rim. Nose: powerfull, red berry notes, ripe fruit, expressive, balsamic herbs. Palate: powerful, fresh, fruity, unctuous.

BODEGAS ALCEÑO
Duque s/n
30520 Jumilla (Murcia)
☎: +34 968 780 142
Fax: +34 968 716 256
www.alceno.com
plmsa@alceno.com

Alceño 2013 B
sauvignon blanc

85

Alceño 2013 RD
monastrell, syrah

88

Colour: light cherry, bright. Nose: ripe fruit, red berry notes, floral, expressive. Palate: fruity, fresh, easy to drink, fruity aftestaste.

Alceño 12 meses 2011 TC
monastrell, syrah

92

Colour: cherry, garnet rim. Nose: ripe fruit, spicy, creamy oak, toasty, complex, dark chocolate, earthy notes. Palate: powerful, flavourful, toasty, round tannins.

Alceño 2012 T
monastrell, syrah

89

Colour: bright cherry. Nose: ripe fruit, sweet spices, creamy oak, powerfull, violets. Palate: flavourful, fruity, toasty, round tannins.

Alceño 2013 T
monastrell, syrah, tempranillo, garnacha

89

Colour: very deep cherry, purple rim. Nose: ripe fruit, expressive. Palate: flavourful, fruity, round tannins.

Alceño Dulce 2012 T
monastrell

90

Colour: cherry, garnet rim. Nose: fruit preserve, spicy, toasty, aged wood nuances, balsamic herbs. Palate: powerful, flavourful. Personality.

Alceño Organic 2013 T
monastrell, syrah, garnacha

89

Colour: deep cherry. Nose: powerfull, violets, ripe fruit, sweet spices. Palate: fruity, round tannins.

Alceño Premium 2012 T
syrah, monastrell

91

Colour: bright cherry. Nose: ripe fruit, sweet spices, creamy oak, medium intensity. Palate: fruity, flavourful, toasty.

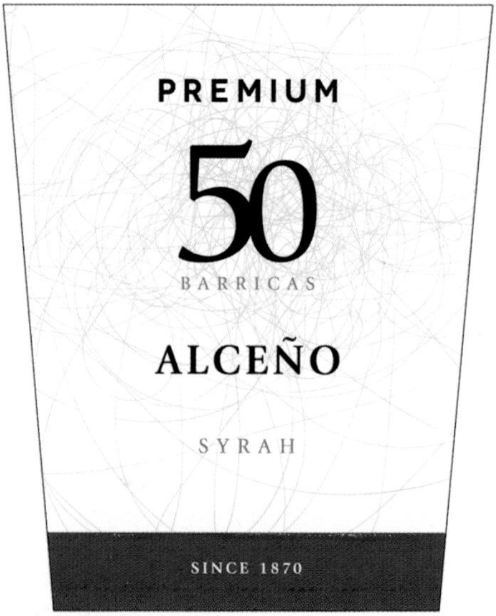
PREMIUM
50
BARRICAS
ALCEÑO
SYRAH
SINCE 1870

Alceño Selección 2010 TC
monastrell, syrah, tempranillo

87

Colour: cherry, garnet rim. Nose: roasted coffee, smoky, spicy, ripe fruit. Palate: flavourful, smoky aftertaste, ripe fruit.

Genio Español 2013 T
monastrell, syrah, garnacha, tempranillo

86

Colour: cherry, purple rim. Nose: expressive, powerfull, ripe fruit, toasty. Palate: flavourful, fruity, good acidity, round tannins.

Hilanda 2012 T
monastrell

87

Colour: bright cherry. Nose: sweet spices, creamy oak, ripe fruit. Palate: flavourful, fruity, toasty, round tannins.

Hilanda de Arriba 2011 T
monastrell

89

Colour: bright cherry. Nose: ripe fruit, sweet spices, creamy oak, expressive. Palate: flavourful, fruity, toasty, round tannins.

BODEGAS ARLOREN
Ctra. del Puerto. Cañada del Trigo
30579 Jumilla (Murcia)
☎: +34 968 821 096
Fax: +34 968 821 096
www.arloren.es
bodegas.arloren@arloren.com

Miriar Rubí 2008 T
monastrell

83

Vegacañada 2010 T
monastrell

82

BODEGAS ARRAEZ
Arcediano Ros, 35
46630 La Font de la Figuera (Valencia)
☎: +34 962 290 031
www.bodegasarraez.com
info@bodegasarraez.com

Vivir sin Dormir 2013 T Roble
monastrell

86 🌿

Colour: cherry, garnet rim. Nose: ripe fruit, spicy, creamy oak, toasty, dark chocolate, earthy notes. Palate: powerful, flavourful, toasty.

BODEGAS BLEDA
Ctra. Jumilla - Ontur, Km. 2.
30520 Jumilla (Murcia)
☎: +34 968 780 012
Fax: +34 968 782 699
www.bodegasbleda.com
vinos@bodegasbleda.com

Amatus Dulce 2011 T
monastrell

89

Colour: black cherry. Nose: dried fruit, sweet spices, toasty, balsamic herbs, expressive. Palate: ripe fruit, powerful, flavourful, long, rich, toasty.

Castillo de Jumilla 2009 TR

85

Castillo de Jumilla 2010 TC

87

Colour: cherry, garnet rim. Nose: ripe fruit, spicy, creamy oak, toasty. Palate: powerful, flavourful, toasty.

Castillo de Jumilla 2013 B
sauvignon blanc, macabeo, airén

88

Colour: bright straw. Nose: white flowers, fragrant herbs, fruit expression. Palate: fresh, fruity, flavourful, balanced.

Castillo de Jumilla 2013 RD
monastrell

84

Castillo de Jumilla Monastrell - Tempranillo 2013 T

87

Colour: cherry, purple rim. Nose: powerfull, red berry notes, ripe fruit. Palate: fruity, unctuous, powerful.

Castillo de Jumilla Monastrell 2013 T
monastrell

86

Colour: cherry, garnet rim. Nose: ripe fruit, grassy, herbaceous. Palate: balsamic, fine bitter notes, ripe fruit.

Divus 2011 T
monastrell

90

Colour: cherry, garnet rim. Nose: ripe fruit, spicy, creamy oak, toasty, earthy notes, complex. Palate: powerful, flavourful, toasty, round tannins.

Flor del Carche 2012 T
monastrell

85

Pinodoncel 2012 T
monastrell, syrah, merlot

87

Colour: cherry, garnet rim. Nose: fruit preserve, balsamic herbs, floral, powerfull. Palate: warm, flavourful, good structure.

Pinodoncel Cinco Meses 2012 T
monastrell, syrah, petit verdot

89

Colour: cherry, garnet rim. Nose: ripe fruit, spicy, creamy oak, toasty, complex, dark chocolate. Palate: powerful, flavourful, toasty, round tannins.

BODEGAS CARCHELO
Casas de la Hoya, s/n
30520 Jumilla (Murcia)
☎: +34 968 435 137
Fax: +34 968 435 200
www.carchelo.com
comex@carchelo.com

Altico Syrah 2011 T
100% syrah

89

Colour: cherry, garnet rim. Nose: ripe fruit, spicy, creamy oak, toasty, powerfull. Palate: powerful, flavourful, toasty, round tannins.

Canalizo 2009 TR

91

Colour: cherry, garnet rim. Nose: ripe fruit, spicy, creamy oak, toasty, complex, dry stone. Palate: powerful, flavourful, toasty, round tannins.

Carchelo 2012 T

89

Colour: bright cherry. Nose: ripe fruit, sweet spices, medium intensity, toasty. Palate: fruity, flavourful, toasty.

Sierva 2011 T

91

Colour: cherry, garnet rim. Nose: spicy, toasty, mineral, ripe fruit, fruit preserve. Palate: powerful, flavourful, toasty, round tannins, balsamic.

Vedré 2011 T

88

Colour: cherry, garnet rim. Nose: ripe fruit, spicy, creamy oak, varnish, dark chocolate. Palate: powerful, flavourful, toasty, round tannins, fruity aftestaste.

BODEGAS EL NIDO
Ctra. de Fuentealamo -
Paraje de la Aragona
30520 Jumilla (Murcia)
☎: +34 968 435 022
Fax: +34 968 435 653
www.orowines.com
info@bodegaselnido.com

Clío 2010 T

93

Colour: deep cherry, garnet rim. Nose: complex, ripe fruit, creamy oak, powerfull, balsamic herbs. Palate: good structure, long, spicy, round tannins.

Clío 2011 T
monastrell, cabernet sauvignon

94

Colour: cherry, garnet rim. Nose: ripe fruit, spicy, creamy oak, balanced. Palate: balanced, flavourful, long, balsamic, complex.

Corteo 2010 T
100% syrah

95

Colour: very deep cherry. Nose: spicy, creamy oak, toasty, complex, fruit expression, ripe fruit. Palate: powerful, flavourful, toasty, fruity aftestaste, full.

Corteo 2011 T
100% syrah

94

Colour: cherry, garnet rim. Nose: ripe fruit, spicy, creamy oak, toasty, complex, earthy notes. Palate: powerful, flavourful, toasty, round tannins.

El Nido 2010 T

95

Colour: cherry, garnet rim. Nose: ripe fruit, spicy, creamy oak, toasty, complex, dark chocolate, earthy notes. Palate: powerful, flavourful, toasty, round tannins.

El Nido 2011 T
cabernet sauvignon, monastrell

93

Colour: deep cherry, garnet rim. Nose: cocoa bean, creamy oak, ripe fruit. Palate: good structure, concentrated, rich, full, powerful.

BODEGAS FERNÁNDEZ
30520 Jumilla (Murcia)
☎: +34 968 780 559
Fax: +34 968 780 024
www.bodegafernandez.es
export@bodegafernandez.es

Campolargo 2012 T
100% monastrell

83

Perla Real 2011 T
100% monastrell

86

Colour: cherry, purple rim. Nose: powerfull, ripe fruit, expressive. Palate: fresh, fruity, unctuous.

Vega Jimena 2010 T
100% monastrell

85

BODEGAS HACIENDA DEL CARCHE
Ctra. del Carche, Km. 8,3
30520 Jumilla (Murcia)
☎: +34 968 975 942
Fax: +34 968 975 935
www.haciendadelcarche.com
fran@haciendadelcarche.com

Hacienda del Carche Cepas Viejas 2010 TC
88

Colour: bright cherry. Nose: ripe fruit, fruit preserve, cocoa bean, sweet spices. Palate: fruity, flavourful, long.

Hacienda del Carche Cepas Viejas 2011 T
monastrell, cabernet sauvignon

89

Colour: cherry, garnet rim. Nose: ripe fruit, spicy, creamy oak, toasty, complex, dark chocolate, mineral. Palate: powerful, flavourful, toasty, round tannins.

Tavs 2013 T
90

Colour: cherry, purple rim. Nose: expressive, fresh fruit, red berry notes, floral. Palate: flavourful, fruity, good acidity, round tannins.

Tavs Selección 2012 T
90

Colour: bright cherry. Nose: ripe fruit, sweet spices, creamy oak, expressive, balsamic herbs. Palate: flavourful, fruity, toasty, round tannins.

BODEGAS JUAN GIL
Ctra. Fuentealamo - Paraje de la Aragona
30520 Jumilla (Murcia)
☎: +34 968 435 022
Fax: +34 968 716 051
www.juangil.es
info@juangil.es

Honoro Vera Organic 2013 T
100% monastrell

91 ❦

Colour: cherry, purple rim. Nose: powerfull, red berry notes, ripe fruit, expressive, dried herbs, varietal. Palate: powerful, fresh, fruity, unctuous.

Juan Gil 12 meses 2011 T
100% monastrell

93

Colour: cherry, garnet rim. Nose: ripe fruit, spicy, creamy oak, toasty, complex, dark chocolate, earthy notes. Palate: powerful, flavourful, toasty, round tannins.

Juan Gil 12 meses 2012 T
100% monastrell

91

Colour: deep cherry, garnet rim. Nose: cocoa bean, toasty, ripe fruit, warm. Palate: good structure, powerful, sweet tannins.

Juan Gil 18 meses 2011 T
92

Colour: cherry, garnet rim. Nose: spicy, toasty, ripe fruit, dark chocolate. Palate: powerful, flavourful, toasty, round tannins.

Juan Gil 4 meses 2013 T
100% monastrell

90

Colour: bright cherry. Nose: ripe fruit, sweet spices, creamy oak, expressive, floral. Palate: flavourful, fruity, toasty, round tannins.

Juan Gil Moscatel 2013 B
100% moscatel

90

Colour: bright straw. Nose: fresh, fresh fruit, white flowers, expressive, jasmine. Palate: flavourful, fruity, good acidity, balanced, fine bitter notes.

BODEGAS LUZÓN
Ctra. Jumilla-Calasparra, Km. 3,1
30520 Jumilla (Murcia)
☎: +34 968 784 135
Fax: +34 968 781 911
www.bodegasluzon.com
info@bodegasluzon.com

Altos de Luzón 2010 T
90
Colour: cherry, garnet rim. Nose: ripe fruit, spicy, creamy oak, toasty, complex, balsamic herbs. Palate: powerful, flavourful, toasty, round tannins.

Luzón 2013 T
91
Colour: cherry, purple rim. Nose: powerfull, red berry notes, ripe fruit, floral, expressive. Palate: powerful, fresh, fruity, unctuous, long.

Luzón 2012 T Roble
monastrell
88
Colour: bright cherry. Nose: ripe fruit, sweet spices, creamy oak, expressive. Palate: flavourful, fruity, toasty, round tannins.

Luzón 2013 B
87
Colour: bright yellow. Nose: balanced, ripe fruit, floral, citrus fruit. Palate: fruity, flavourful, fine bitter notes, rich.

Luzón Crianza Selección 12 2011 TC
90
Colour: cherry, garnet rim. Nose: ripe fruit, spicy, creamy oak, toasty, complex. Palate: powerful, flavourful, toasty, round tannins.

Luzón Verde Organic 2013 T
monastrell
90
Colour: bright cherry. Nose: ripe fruit, expressive, spicy, balsamic herbs, varietal. Palate: flavourful, fruity, toasty, round tannins.

BODEGAS MADROÑO
Ctra., Jumilla-Ontur, km. 16
30520 Jumilla (Murcia)
☎: +34 662 380 985
gmartinez@vinocrapula.com

Madroño 2012 T Roble
100% syrah
90
Colour: bright cherry. Nose: ripe fruit, sweet spices, expressive, toasty. Palate: flavourful, fruity, toasty, round tannins, good structure.

Madroño Chardonnay 2013 B
100% chardonnay
86
Colour: bright straw. Nose: fresh, fresh fruit, white flowers. Palate: flavourful, fruity, good acidity, balanced, easy to drink.

Madroño Petit Verdot 2011 T
100% petit verdot
89
Colour: black cherry, garnet rim. Nose: powerfull, characterful, ripe fruit, wild herbs, dried herbs. Palate: good structure, fruity, flavourful.

Viña Marcelino 2012 T
100% monastrell
89
Colour: bright cherry. Nose: ripe fruit, expressive, spicy, balsamic herbs. Palate: flavourful, fruity, toasty, round tannins.

BODEGAS MONTEREBRO
Barrio Iglesias, 55
30520 Jumilla (Murcia)
☎: +34 669 359 647
www.monterebro.com
info@monterebro.com

Monterebro 2011 TC
89
Colour: very deep cherry. Nose: creamy oak, cocoa bean, ripe fruit, powerfull. Palate: good structure, long, round tannins.

Monterebro 2012 T Barrica
90
Colour: cherry, garnet rim. Nose: ripe fruit, spicy, creamy oak, complex, balsamic herbs. Palate: powerful, flavourful, toasty, round tannins.

Monterebro 2013 B
100% sauvignon blanc
85

Monterebro 2013 RD
86
Colour: rose, purple rim. Nose: powerfull, red berry notes, floral, expressive. Palate: fruity, fresh, fine bitter notes.

Monterebro 2013 T
88
Colour: cherry, purple rim. Nose: powerfull, red berry notes, ripe fruit, floral, expressive, varietal. Palate: powerful, fresh, fruity, unctuous.

Monterebro Barrica 2013 T
88
Colour: cherry, garnet rim. Nose: ripe fruit, wild herbs, spicy, creamy oak. Palate: powerful, flavourful, roasted-coffee aftertaste.

Monterebro Selección 2012 T
90
Colour: cherry, garnet rim. Nose: ripe fruit, spicy, creamy oak, toasty, complex, dark chocolate, red berry notes. Palate: powerful, flavourful, toasty, round tannins.

Monterebro Selección 2013 T
88
Colour: cherry, garnet rim. Nose: spicy, creamy oak, toasty, fruit preserve. Palate: powerful, flavourful, toasty, round tannins.

BODEGAS OLIVARES
Vereda Real, s/n
30520 Jumilla (Murcia)
☎: +34 968 780 180
Fax: +34 968 756 474
www.bodegasolivares.com
correo@bodegasolivares.com

Altos de la Hoya 2012 T
monastrell
89
Colour: bright cherry. Nose: ripe fruit, sweet spices, creamy oak, expressive. Palate: flavourful, fruity, toasty, round tannins, powerful, long.

Olivares 2010 TC
monastrell
90
Colour: cherry, garnet rim. Nose: ripe fruit, spicy, creamy oak, toasty, cocoa bean. Palate: powerful, flavourful, toasty, round tannins.

Olivares 2013 RD
83

BODEGAS PÍO DEL RAMO
Ctra. Almanza, s/n
2652 Ontur (Albacete)
☎: +34 967 323 230
www.piodelramo.com
admin@piodelramo.com

Pío 2012 T Roble
90
Colour: bright cherry. Nose: ripe fruit, sweet spices, expressive. Palate: flavourful, fruity, toasty, round tannins.

Pío del Ramo 2011 TC
90
Colour: bright cherry. Nose: ripe fruit, sweet spices, creamy oak, medium intensity, balsamic herbs. Palate: fruity, flavourful, toasty.

Pío Ecológico 2012 T
100% monastrell
88 ♥
Colour: bright cherry. Nose: ripe fruit, medium intensity, balsamic herbs, spicy. Palate: fruity, flavourful, round tannins, balsamic.

Viña Betola 2013 B
86
Colour: bright straw. Nose: fresh, fresh fruit, white flowers, expressive. Palate: flavourful, fruity, good acidity, balanced.

Viña Betola 2013 T
87
Colour: cherry, purple rim. Nose: powerfull, red berry notes, ripe fruit, expressive, balsamic herbs. Palate: powerful, fresh, fruity.

BODEGAS SAN DIONISIO, S. COOP,
Ctra. Higuera, s/n
2651 Fuenteálamo (Albacete)
☎: +34 967 543 032
Fax: +34 967 543 136
www.bodegassandinisio.es
sandionisio@bodegassandionisio.es

Mainetes Petit Verdot 2011 T Roble
100% petit verdot
88
Colour: cherry, garnet rim. Nose: ripe fruit, spicy, toasty, complex, balsamic herbs. Palate: powerful, flavourful, toasty, round tannins.

Señorío de Fuenteálamo 2013 T
100% monastrell
84

Señorío de Fuenteálamo Monastrell Syrah 2011 TC
86
Colour: bright cherry, garnet rim. Nose: ripe fruit, fruit preserve, spicy. Palate: good structure, ripe fruit.

Señorío de Fuenteálamo Sauvignon Blanc 2013 B
100% sauvignon blanc

84

Señorío de Fuenteálamo Syrah 2013 RD
100% syrah

88

Colour: rose, bright. Nose: fresh, balanced, dried flowers, red berry notes. Palate: flavourful, fruity, good acidity, fine bitter notes.

BODEGAS SILVANO GARCÍA S.L.
Avda. de Murcia, 29
30520 Jumilla (Murcia)
☎: +34 968 780 767
Fax: +34 968 716 125
www.silvanogarcia.com
bodegas@silvanogarcia.com

Silvano García Dulce Monastrell 2011 T
100% monastrell

90

Colour: cherry, garnet rim. Nose: overripe fruit, dried fruit, sweet spices, toasty, pattiserie. Palate: ripe fruit, warm, powerful.

Silvano García Dulce Moscatel 2012 B
100% moscatel

89

Colour: bright yellow. Nose: warm, white flowers, jasmine, honeyed notes, fruit liqueur notes. Palate: flavourful, sweet, ripe fruit.

Viñahonda 2013 B
100% macabeo

85

Viñahonda 2013 RD
100% monastrell

86

Colour: light cherry, bright. Nose: fresh, red berry notes, floral, citrus fruit. Palate: fresh, fruity, easy to drink, long.

BODEGAS SIMÓN
Madrid, 15
2653 Albatana (Albacete)
☎: +34 967 323 340
Fax: +34 967 323 340
www.bodegassimon.com
info@bodegassimon.com

Galán del Siglo Monastrell Syrah 2011 T
monastrell, syrah

78

Galán del Siglo Petit Verdot 2008 T
petit verdot

85

Galán del Siglo Selección 2009 T
petit verdot, monastrell, tempranillo

84

Galán del Siglo Tradición Familiar 2009 T
monastrell

84

BODEGAS VOLVER
Ctra de Pinoso a Fortuna s/n
3658 Rodriguillo - Pinoso (Alicante)
☎: +34 966 185 624
Fax: +34 965 075 376
www.bodegasvolver.com
export@bodegasvolver.com

Wrongo Dongo 2013 T
monastrell

90

Colour: deep cherry. Nose: overripe fruit, spicy, dark chocolate. Palate: powerful, sweetness, fine bitter notes.

BODEGAS Y VIÑEDOS CASA DE LA ERMITA
Ctra. El Carche, Km. 11,5
30520 Jumilla (Murcia)
☎: +34 968 783 035
Fax: +34 968 716 063
www.casadelaermita.com
bodega@casadelaermita.com

Altos del Cuco 2013 T
87

Colour: cherry, purple rim. Nose: fresh fruit, red berry notes, floral. Palate: flavourful, fruity, good acidity, round tannins, fruity aftestaste.

Altos del Cuco Garnacha Monastrell 2013 T
87

Colour: cherry, purple rim. Nose: expressive, fresh fruit, red berry notes, medium intensity, dried herbs. Palate: flavourful, fruity, good acidity, round tannins.

Altos del Cuco Monastrell Ecológico 2013 T
100% monastrell

86 🌷

Colour: black cherry, purple rim. Nose: medium intensity, ripe fruit, violets. Palate: fruity, correct, easy to drink.

Caracol Serrano 2013 T
monastrell, syrah, cabernet sauvignon

86

Colour: cherry, purple rim. Nose: scrubland, ripe fruit. Palate: fruity, correct, balanced.

Casa de la Ermita 2010 TC
89 🌷

Colour: cherry, garnet rim. Nose: ripe fruit, spicy, creamy oak, dried herbs. Palate: powerful, flavourful, toasty, round tannins.

Casa de la Ermita 2013 B
87

Colour: bright straw. Nose: fresh, fresh fruit, white flowers, expressive, jasmine, tropical fruit. Palate: flavourful, fruity, good acidity, balanced.

Casa de la Ermita 2013 T
87 �

Colour: deep cherry, purple rim. Nose: ripe fruit, balsamic herbs, balanced. Palate: fruity, correct, easy to drink.

Casa de la Ermita 2013 T Roble
89

Colour: bright cherry. Nose: ripe fruit, sweet spices, creamy oak, expressive, dried herbs. Palate: flavourful, fruity, toasty, round tannins.

Casa de la Ermita Crianza Ecológico 2010 TC
monastrell

88 🌿

Colour: bright cherry. Nose: ripe fruit, sweet spices, creamy oak, medium intensity. Palate: fruity, flavourful, easy to drink.

Casa de la Ermita Dulce 2012 B
88

Colour: old gold. Nose: pattiserie, sweet spices, honeyed notes, floral, overripe fruit. Palate: balanced, unctuous, flavourful.

Casa de la Ermita Dulce Monastrell 2012 T
100% monastrell

85

Casa de la Ermita Ecológico Monastrell 2013 T
100% monastrell

89 🌿

Colour: cherry, purple rim. Nose: medium intensity, wild herbs, ripe fruit, balanced. Palate: fruity, easy to drink, ripe fruit.

Casa de la Ermita Idílico 2010 TC
89

Colour: very deep cherry. Nose: dry stone, wild herbs, ripe fruit. Palate: good structure, fruity, spicy.

Casa de la Ermita Petit Verdot 2010 T
100% petit verdot

87

Colour: cherry, garnet rim. Nose: spicy, balsamic herbs, ripe fruit, fruit preserve. Palate: flavourful, round tannins.

Monasterio de Santa Ana Monastrell 2012 T
100% monastrell

87

Colour: bright cherry. Nose: ripe fruit, sweet spices, medium intensity. Palate: fruity, flavourful, toasty.

Monasterio de Santa Ana Tempranillo Monastrell Ecológico 2013 T
85 🌿

BSI BODEGAS SAN ISIDRO
Ctra. Murcia, s/n
30250 Jumilla (Murcia)
☎: +34 968 780 700
Fax: +34 968 782 351
www.bsi.es
bsi@bsi.es

Gémina Cuvée Selección 2011 T
100% monastrell

87

Colour: deep cherry, garnet rim. Nose: powerfull, ripe fruit, characterful, creamy oak. Palate: good structure, flavourful.

Gémina Monastrell 2013 T
100% monastrell

87

Colour: very deep cherry. Nose: spicy, ripe fruit, dried herbs. Palate: good structure, flavourful, round tannins.

Genus 2012 T Roble
100% monastrell

85

Genus Monastrell Syrah 2011 T
86

Colour: cherry, garnet rim. Nose: ripe fruit, toasty. Palate: flavourful, spicy, easy to drink.

Numun Monastrell 2013 T
100% monastrell

84

Numun Syrah 2013 T
100% syrah

86

Colour: cherry, purple rim. Nose: red berry notes, floral, ripe fruit. Palate: flavourful, fruity, good acidity, round tannins.

Sabatacha 2010 TC
100% monastrell

87

Colour: cherry, garnet rim. Nose: ripe fruit, spicy, creamy oak, toasty, complex. Palate: powerful, flavourful, toasty, round tannins.

Sabatacha Monastrell 2013 T
100% monastrell

88

Colour: cherry, purple rim. Nose: expressive, ripe fruit, balsamic herbs. Palate: flavourful, fruity, good acidity, round tannins.

Sabatacha Syrah 2013 T
syrah
86
Colour: cherry, purple rim. Nose: red berry notes, floral, medium intensity. Palate: flavourful, fruity, good acidity, round tannins.

CAMPOS DE RISCA
Avda. Diagonal, 590, 5º 1ª
8021 (Barcelona)
☎: +34 660 445 464
www.vinergia.com
vinergia@vinergia.com

Campos de Risca 2012 T
87 🌷
Colour: bright cherry. Nose: ripe fruit, sweet spices, expressive. Palate: flavourful, fruity, toasty, round tannins.

CORTIJO TRIFILLAS
Finca Trifillas Ctra. Rincón del Moro, km. 10
2410 Liétor (Albacete)
☎: +34 967 680 009
Fax: +34 967 681 165
www.cortijodetrifillas.com
info@cortijotrifillas.com

CT Monastrell Syrah 2013 T
89
Colour: bright cherry. Nose: ripe fruit, sweet spices, creamy oak, medium intensity. Palate: fruity, flavourful, toasty.

CRAPULA WINES, S.L.
Avda. de la Asunción, 42 2D
30520 Jumilla (Murcia)
☎: +34 682 172 052
gmartinez@vinocrapula.com

Barinas Roble 2012 T Roble
monastrell
88
Colour: black cherry. Nose: creamy oak, sweet spices, ripe fruit, toasty. Palate: good structure, flavourful, round tannins, spicy.

Cármine 2011 T
monastrell, syrah
90
Colour: very deep cherry, garnet rim. Nose: creamy oak, toasty, sweet spices. Palate: round tannins, ripe fruit, fruity aftestaste.

Cármine 3 meses 2012 T
monastrell
89
Colour: bright cherry. Nose: ripe fruit, sweet spices, creamy oak, medium intensity. Palate: fruity, flavourful, toasty.

Celebre 2010 TC
monastrell, syrah
91
Colour: very deep cherry, garnet rim. Nose: cocoa bean, creamy oak, ripe fruit. Palate: flavourful, full, long, round tannins.

Celebre 2012 T Roble
monastrell, syrah
90
Colour: black cherry, purple rim. Nose: ripe fruit, violets, powerfull, toasty, sweet spices. Palate: balanced, round tannins.

Crápula 2011 T
91
Colour: very deep cherry. Nose: toasty, sweet spices, cocoa bean, ripe fruit. Palate: good structure, concentrated, round tannins.

Crápula Gold 2012 T
87
Colour: very deep cherry. Nose: roasted coffee, sweet spices, powerfull. Palate: flavourful, good structure, round tannins.

Crápula Petit Verdot 2011 T
petit verdot
92
Colour: black cherry. Nose: ripe fruit, fruit preserve, dark chocolate, balsamic herbs, expressive. Palate: balanced, ripe fruit, round tannins.

Crápula Soul 2011 T
monastrell, petit verdot, cabernet sauvignon, syrah
93
Colour: cherry, garnet rim. Nose: ripe fruit, spicy, creamy oak, toasty, complex, scrubland. Palate: powerful, flavourful, toasty, round tannins.

Dulce Crápula 2011 T
100% monastrell
88
Colour: cherry, garnet rim. Nose: fruit preserve, ripe fruit, spicy, toasty, aged wood nuances, dried herbs. Palate: powerful, flavourful, sweetness.

G Wine 2012 T
90
Colour: bright cherry. Nose: ripe fruit, sweet spices, creamy oak, medium intensity. Palate: fruity, flavourful, toasty, powerful.

NdQ (Nacido del Quorum) 2012 T
90
Colour: cherry, garnet rim. Nose: ripe fruit, spicy, creamy oak, toasty, complex. Palate: powerful, flavourful, round tannins.

NdQ (Nacido del Quorum) Selección 2011 T
monastrell, syrah, petit verdot

92

Colour: black cherry, garnet rim. Nose: powerfull, dark chocolate, ripe fruit, fruit preserve. Palate: good structure, full, long, round tannins.

EGO BODEGAS

Plaza Santa Gertrudis, Nº 1, Entresuelo A
30001 (Murcia)
☎: +34 968 964 326
Fax: +34 968 964 205
www.egobodegas.com
ioana.paunescu@egobodegas.com

Fuerza 2011 TC
91

Colour: cherry, garnet rim. Nose: ripe fruit, spicy, creamy oak, toasty, complex. Palate: powerful, flavourful, toasty, round tannins.

Goru Monastrell 2011 TC
91

Colour: cherry, garnet rim. Nose: ripe fruit, spicy, creamy oak, toasty, complex, dark chocolate, earthy notes. Palate: powerful, flavourful, toasty, round tannins.

Infinito 2011 T
91

Colour: cherry, garnet rim. Nose: ripe fruit, spicy, creamy oak, toasty, complex, earthy notes, dried herbs. Palate: powerful, flavourful, toasty, round tannins.

EMW GRANDES VINOS DE ESPAÑA

Sánchez Picazo, 53
30332 Balsapintada (Fuente Alamo) (Murcia)
☎: +34 968 151 520
Fax: +34 968 151 539
www.emw.es
info@emw.es

MMM Macho Man Monastrell 2012 T
100% monastrell

88

Colour: bright cherry, garnet rim. Nose: balanced, varietal, balsamic herbs, ripe fruit. Palate: fruity, flavourful, full, round tannins.

ORO WINES

Ctra. de Fuentealamo - Paraje de la Aragona
30520 Jumilla (Murcia)
☎: +34 968 435 022
Fax: +34 968 716 051
www.orowines.com
info@orowines.com

Comoloco 2012 T
100% monastrell

89

Colour: cherry, garnet rim. Nose: ripe fruit, balsamic herbs, balanced, expressive. Palate: flavourful, fruity, spicy, round tannins, easy to drink.

Comoloco 2013 T
100% monastrell

89

Colour: deep cherry, purple rim. Nose: balanced, ripe fruit, varietal, wild herbs. Palate: balanced, good structure.

PROPIEDAD VITÍCOLA CASA CASTILLO

Ctra. Jumilla - Hellín, RM-428, Km. 8
30520 Jumilla (Murcia)
☎: +34 968 781 691
Fax: +34 968 716 238
www.casacastillo.es
info@casacastillo.es

Casa Castillo Monastrell 2013 T
100% monastrell

91

Colour: bright cherry. Nose: ripe fruit, sweet spices, creamy oak, expressive, balsamic herbs. Palate: flavourful, fruity, toasty, round tannins.

Casa Castillo Pie Franco 2011 T
100% monastrell

94

Colour: bright cherry, garnet rim. Nose: varietal, expressive, balsamic herbs, ripe fruit, balanced, complex. Palate: fruity, round tannins, balsamic, spicy.

El Molar 2012 T
100% garnacha

93

Colour: bright cherry. Nose: ripe fruit, sweet spices, scrubland. Palate: flavourful, round tannins.

Las Gravas 2011 T
monastrell, syrah, garnacha

94

Colour: bright cherry, garnet rim. Nose: complex, balanced, expressive, spicy. Palate: good structure, flavourful, good acidity, balanced, round tannins.

Valtosca 2012 T
100% syrah

93

Colour: bright cherry. Nose: ripe fruit, sweet spices, balanced. Palate: fruity, toasty, full, good structure, round tannins.

VIÑAS DE LA CASA DEL RICO
Poeta Andrés Bolarin, 1- 5ºB
30011 Murcia (Murcia)
☎: +34 609 197 353
Fax: +34 968 782 400
www.casadelrico.com
produccion@casadelrico.com

Gorgocil Monastrell 2010 T
monastrell

90

Colour: bright cherry. Nose: ripe fruit, sweet spices, creamy oak, medium intensity. Palate: fruity, flavourful, toasty, balsamic.

Gorgocil Tempranillo 2010 T
tempranillo

91

Colour: cherry, garnet rim. Nose: ripe fruit, spicy, toasty, complex. Palate: powerful, flavourful, toasty, round tannins.

DO. LA GOMERA

CONSEJO REGULADOR

Avda. Guillermo Ascanio,16
38840 Vallehermoso (La Gomera)
☎ :+34 922 800 801 - Fax: +34 922 801 146
@: crdolagomera@922800801.e.telefonica.net
www.vinosdelagomera.es

LOCATION:

The majority of the vineyards are found in the north of the island, in the vicinity of the towns of Vallehermoso (some 385 Ha) and Hermigua. The remaining vineyards are spread out over Agulo, Valle Gran Rey –near the capital city of La Gomera, San Sebastián– and Alajeró, on the slopes of the Garajonay peak.

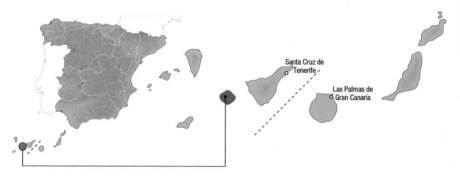

GRAPE VARIETIES:

White: Forastera (90%), Gomera Blanca, Listán Blanca, Marmajuelo, Malvasía and Pedro Ximenez.
Red: Listán Negra (5%), Negramoll (2%); Experimental: Tintilla Castellana, Cabernet Sauvignon and Rubí Cabernet.

FIGURES:

Vineyard surface: 125 – Wine-Growers: 250 – Wineries: 16 – 2013 Harvest rating: - – Production 13: 70,000 litres – Market percentages: 100% domestic.

SOIL:

The most common soil in the higher mountain regions is deep and clayey, while, as one approaches lower altitudes towards the scrubland, the soil is more Mediterranean with a good many stones and terraces similar to those of the Priorat.

CLIMATE:

The island benefits from a subtropical climate together with, as one approaches the higher altitudes of the Garajonay peak, a phenomenon of permanent humidity known as 'mar de nubes' (sea of clouds) caused by the trade winds. This humid air from the north collides with the mountain range, thereby creating a kind of horizontal rain resulting in a specific ecosystem made up of luxuriant valleys. The average temperature is 20°C all year round.

VINTAGE RATING   PEÑÍNGUIDE

2009	2010	2011	2012	2013
N/A	N/A	N/A	N/A	N/A

DO. LA MANCHA

CONSEJO REGULADOR

Avda. de Criptana, 73
13600 Alcázar de San Juan (Ciudad Real)
☎:+34 926 541 523 - Fax: +34 926 588 040
@: consejo@lamanchawines.com
www.lamanchawines.com

LOCATION:

On the southern plateau in the provinces of Albacete, Ciudad Real, Cuenca and Toledo. It is the largest wine-growing region in Spain and in the world.

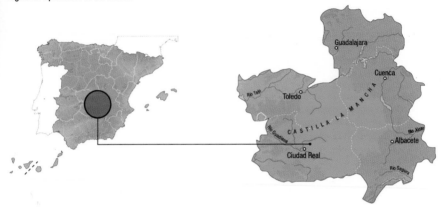

GRAPE VARIETIES:

White: Airén (majority), Macabeo, Pardilla, Chardonnay, Sauvignon Blanc, Verdejo, Moscatel de Grano Menudo, Gewürztraminer, Parellada, Pero Ximénez, Riesling and Torrontés.
Red: Cencibel (majority amongst red varieties), Garnacha, Moravia, Cabernet Sauvignon, Merlot, Syrah, Cabernet Franc, Graciano, Malbec, Mencía, Monastrell, Pinot Noir, Petit Verdot and Bobal.

FIGURES:

Vineyard surface: 162,625 – Wine-Growers: 16,257 – Wineries: 265 – 2013 Harvest rating: Good – Production 13: 166,833,489 litres – Market percentages: 42% domestic - 58% export.

SOIL:

The terrain is flat and the vineyards are situated at an altitude of about 700 m above sea level. The soil is generally sandy, limy and clayey.

CLIMATE:

Extreme continental, with temperatures ranging between 40/45°C in summer and –10/12°C in winter. Rather low rainfall, with an average of about 375 mm per year.

VINTAGE RATING			PEÑÍNGUIDE	
2009	**2010**	**2011**	**2012**	**2013**
VERY GOOD	VERY GOOD	VERY GOOD	GOOD	AVERAGE

¡EA! VINOS

Avda. Jose prat 14 Esc 3. 1º D1
2008 (Albacete)
☎: +34 967 278 578
Fax: +34 967 278 578
www.eavinos.com
info@eavinos.com

¡Ea! 2012 T
cencibel

87

Colour: deep cherry, purple rim. Nose: ripe fruit, fruit preserve, sweet spices. Palate: flavourful, round tannins.

BACO, BODEGAS ASOCIADAS

Avda. de los Vinos, s/n
13600 Alcázar de San Juan
(Ciudad Real)
☎: +34 926 547 404
www.grupobaco.com
info@grupobaco.com

Dominio de Baco Airén 2013 B
100% airén

87

Colour: bright straw. Nose: medium intensity, expressive, varietal, fresh fruit. Palate: fruity, balanced, fine bitter notes, good acidity.

Dominio de Baco Tempranillo 2013 T
100% tempranillo

84

Dominio de Baco Verdejo 2013 B
100% verdejo

84

BODEGA CENTRO ESPAÑOLAS

Ctra. Alcázar, s/n
13700 Tomelloso (Ciudad Real)
☎: +34 926 505 653
Fax: +34 926 505 652
www.allozo.com
allozo@allozo.com

Allozo 2009 TC
100% tempranillo

86

Colour: cherry, garnet rim. Nose: ripe fruit, spicy, creamy oak, toasty, grassy. Palate: powerful, flavourful, toasty, spicy.

Allozo 2006 TGR
100% tempranillo

87

Colour: cherry, garnet rim. Nose: spicy, toasty, medium intensity, ripe fruit. Palate: good structure, flavourful, round tannins, good acidity.

Allozo 2008 TR
100% tempranillo

87

Colour: dark-red cherry, garnet rim. Nose: fruit preserve, sweet spices, balanced. Palate: fruity, flavourful, round tannins.

Allozo 927 2010 T
tempranillo, merlot, syrah

87

Colour: cherry, garnet rim. Nose: ripe fruit, spicy. Palate: ripe fruit, correct, flavourful.

Allozo Cabernet 2012 T
100% cabernet sauvignon

85

Allozo Merlot 2012 T
100% merlot

82

Allozo Shyraz 2012 T
100% syrah

87

Colour: bright cherry. Nose: ripe fruit, sweet spices, creamy oak, expressive. Palate: flavourful, fruity, toasty, round tannins.

Allozo Tempranillo 2013 T
100% tempranillo

85

Allozo Verdejo 2013 B
100% verdejo

85

Flor de Allozo 2010 T
garnacha, tempranillo

85

BODEGA Y VIÑAS ALDOBA S.A.

Crta. Alcazar, s/n, 130
13700 Tomelloso (Ciudad Real)
☎: +34 926 50 56 53
Fax: +34 926 50 56 52
www.allozo.com
aldoba@allozo.com

Aldoba 2009 TC
100% tempranillo
84

Aldoba 2013 B
100% verdejo
82

Aldoba 2008 TR
100% tempranillo
87
Colour: cherry, garnet rim. Nose: ripe fruit, spicy, creamy oak, toasty, complex. Palate: powerful, flavourful, toasty, round tannins.

Aldoba 2013 T
100% tempranillo
85

BODEGAS ALCARDET

Mayor, 130
45810 Villanueva de Alcardete (Toledo)
☎: +34 925 166 375
Fax: +34 925 166 611
www.alcardet.com
alcardet@alcardet.com

Alcardet Brut Natura 2012 ESP
chardonnay, macabeo, airén
83 🌷

Alcardet Natura Red 2013 T
tempranillo, petit verdot
88 🌷
Colour: cherry, purple rim. Nose: expressive, fresh fruit, red berry notes, dried herbs. Palate: flavourful, fruity, good acidity, round tannins.

Alcardet Natura White 2013 B
airén, chardonnay
85 🌷

Alcardet Sommelier 2010 TC
tempranillo, petit verdot
86
Colour: bright cherry. Nose: ripe fruit, sweet spices, medium intensity, scrubland. Palate: fruity, flavourful, toasty.

Alcardet Sommelier 2013 B
airén, verdejo, sauvignon blanc
84

Alcardet Sommelier 2013 RD
tempranillo, syrah, garnacha
83

Alcardet Sommelier 2013 T
tempranillo, cabernet sauvignon, merlot
86
Colour: deep cherry, purple rim. Nose: ripe fruit, balsamic herbs, balanced. Palate: fruity, easy to drink, good finish.

Grumier 2008 TC
tempranillo, syrah
85

BODEGAS AYUSO

2600 Villarrobledo (Albacete)
☎: +34 967 140 458
Fax: +34 967 144 925
www.bodegasayuso.es
comercial@bodegasayuso.es

Armiño 2013 B
85

Castillo de Benizar Cabernet Sauvignon 2013 RD
100% cabernet sauvignon
83

Castillo de Benizar Macabeo 2013 B
100% macabeo
85

Castillo de Benizar Tempranillo 2013 T
100% tempranillo
85

Estola 2004 TGR
85

Estola 2008 TR
84

Estola 2009 TC
100% tempranillo
84

Estola Verdejo 2013 B
100% verdejo
85

Finca Los Azares Cabernet Merlot 2007 T
86
Colour: dark-red cherry, orangey edge. Nose: toasty, sweet spices, balsamic herbs, old leather. Palate: toasty, round tannins, ripe fruit.

Finca Los Azares Petit Verdot 2009 T
100% petit verdot

88

Colour: dark-red cherry, orangey edge. Nose: tobacco, spicy, ripe fruit. Palate: full, flavourful, round tannins, good acidity, balanced.

Finca Los Azares Sauvignon Blanc 2013 B
100% sauvignon blanc

85

BODEGAS CAMPOS REALES

Castilla La Mancha, 4
16670 El Provencio (Cuenca)
☎: +34 967 166 066
Fax: +34 967 165 032
www.bodegascamposreales.com
info@bodegascamposreales.com

Canforrales 2011 TC
cabernet sauvignon

89

Colour: cherry, garnet rim. Nose: ripe fruit, spicy, creamy oak, toasty, complex. Palate: powerful, flavourful, toasty, round tannins, balanced.

Canforrales Chardonnay 2013 B
chardonnay

88

Colour: bright straw. Nose: fresh, fresh fruit, white flowers, expressive. Palate: flavourful, fruity, good acidity, balanced.

Canforrales Clásico Tempranillo 2013 T
tempranillo

86

Colour: bright cherry, purple rim. Nose: red berry notes, ripe fruit, balanced. Palate: fruity, easy to drink, correct.

Canforrales Edición Especial Chardonnay 2013 B
chardonnay

91

Colour: bright straw. Nose: white flowers, fragrant herbs, fruit expression, expressive. Palate: fresh, fruity, flavourful, balanced, elegant.

Canforrales Garnacha 2013 RD
garnacha

84

Canforrales Lucía 2013 B
airén

84

Canforrales Sauvignon Blanc 2013 B
sauvignon blanc

87

Colour: bright straw. Nose: white flowers, fragrant herbs, fruit expression. Palate: fresh, fruity, flavourful, balanced, easy to drink.

Canforrales Selección 2012 T
tempranillo

86

Colour: bright cherry. Nose: ripe fruit, sweet spices, creamy oak, expressive. Palate: flavourful, fruity, toasty, round tannins.

Canforrales Selección 2013 T
tempranillo

87

Colour: cherry, garnet rim. Nose: ripe fruit, spicy, creamy oak, balsamic herbs. Palate: powerful, flavourful, toasty.

Canforrales Syrah 2012 T Roble
syrah

88

Colour: bright cherry, garnet rim. Nose: sweet spices, ripe fruit, balanced. Palate: balanced, round tannins, spicy.

Gladium Viñas Viejas 2011 TC
tempranillo

90

Colour: cherry, garnet rim. Nose: ripe fruit, spicy, creamy oak, toasty, complex, dark chocolate, earthy notes. Palate: powerful, flavourful, toasty, round tannins, balanced.

BODEGAS DE ALORT - DE ALORT PREMIUM WINES

Ctra. de Herencia km 2,5
13600 Alcázar de San Juan (Ciudad Real)
☎: +34 607 740 885
www.dealortwines.com
contacta@dealortwines.com

Pétrola 2009 TC
cabernet franc

88

Colour: very deep cherry, garnet rim. Nose: spicy, scrubland, ripe fruit. Palate: balanced, round tannins, balsamic.

Pétrola Sauvignon Blanc 2013 B
sauvignon blanc

86

Colour: bright straw. Nose: powerfull, candied fruit, fragrant herbs, white flowers, jasmine. Palate: flavourful, fresh, fruity, good acidity. Personality.

Pétrola Tempranillo 2011 T Roble
tempranillo

90

Colour: bright cherry. Nose: ripe fruit, sweet spices, creamy oak, expressive. Palate: flavourful, fruity, toasty, round tannins.

BODEGAS DEL SAZ

Maestro Manzanares, 57
13610 Campo de Criptana
(Ciudad Real)
☎: +34 926 562 424
Fax: +34 926 562 659
www.bodegasdelsaz.com
bodegasdelsaz@bodegasdelsaz.com

Vidal del Saz 2011 TC
100% tempranillo
85

Vidal del Saz 2012 T Roble
100% tempranillo
84

Vidal del Saz Selección Rosé 2013 RD
85

Vidal del Saz Selección White 2013 B
86
Colour: bright straw, greenish rim. Nose: medium intensity, balanced, white flowers. Palate: fresh, fruity, fine bitter notes.

BODEGAS LAHOZ

Ctra. N-310 Tomelloso-Villarrobledo Km. 108,5
13630 Socuéllamos (Ciudad Real)
☎: +34 926 699 083
Fax: +34 926 514 929
www.bodegaslahoz.com
info@bodegaslahoz.com

Vega Córcoles 2013 RD
100% tempranillo
86
Colour: light cherry, bright. Nose: fresh, red berry notes, floral. Palate: light-bodied, good acidity, fresh.

Vega Córcoles Airén 2013 B
100% airén
85

Vega Córcoles Sauvignon Blanc 2013 B
100% sauvignon blanc
87
Colour: bright straw. Nose: fresh, fresh fruit, white flowers, expressive. Palate: flavourful, fruity, good acidity, balanced.

Vega Córcoles Tempranillo 2011 T Roble
100% tempranillo
89
Colour: bright cherry. Nose: sweet spices, creamy oak, expressive, red berry notes, fruit liqueur notes. Palate: flavourful, fruity, toasty, round tannins.

Vega Córcoles Tempranillo 2013 T
100% tempranillo
86
Colour: bright cherry, purple rim. Nose: balanced, fruit expression, fresh. Palate: fruity, flavourful, good acidity.

BODEGAS LATÚE

Camino Esperilla, s/n
45810 Villanueva de Alcardete (Toledo)
☎: +34 925 166 350
Fax: +34 925 166 673
www.latue.com
info@latue.com

Latúe 2013 RD
88
Colour: rose, purple rim. Nose: powerfull, ripe fruit, red berry notes, floral, expressive. Palate: powerful, fruity, fresh.

Latúe Brut Nature ESP
86 🏆
Colour: bright straw. Nose: dried herbs, faded flowers. Palate: fruity, balanced, easy to drink.

Latúe Cabernet Sauvignon & Syrah 2010 T
cabernet sauvignon, syrah
89 🏆
Colour: bright cherry. Nose: ripe fruit, sweet spices, creamy oak, expressive. Palate: flavourful, fruity, toasty, round tannins.

Pingorote 2008 TR
89
Colour: cherry, garnet rim. Nose: ripe fruit, spicy, creamy oak, toasty. Palate: powerful, flavourful, toasty, round tannins.

Pingorote 2009 TC
tempranillo
87
Colour: bright cherry. Nose: ripe fruit, sweet spices, creamy oak, medium intensity, balsamic herbs. Palate: fruity, flavourful, toasty.

Pingorote s/c T
tempranillo
87
Colour: deep cherry, garnet rim. Nose: ripe fruit, balanced. Palate: flavourful, full, ripe fruit.

Pingorote Sauvignon Blanc 2013 B
sauvignon blanc
88
Colour: bright straw. Nose: fresh, fresh fruit, white flowers, expressive. Palate: flavourful, fruity, good acidity, balanced.

BODEGAS LOZANO

Avda. Reyes Católicos, 156
2600 Villarrobledo (Albacete)
☎: +34 967 141 907
Fax: +34 967 145 843
www.bodegas-lozano.com
jlozano@bodegas-lozano.com

Añoranza 2013 RD
100% tempranillo
87
Colour: onion pink. Nose: elegant, candied fruit, dried flowers, fragrant herbs, red berry notes. Palate: light-bodied, flavourful, good acidity, long, spicy.

Añoranza Cabernet Shiraz 2013 T
87
Colour: cherry, purple rim. Nose: expressive, fresh fruit, red berry notes, floral. Palate: flavourful, fruity, good acidity, round tannins.

Añoranza Sauvignon Blanc 2013 B
100% sauvignon blanc
85

Añoranza Tempranillo 2010 TC
100% tempranillo
85

Gran Oristán 2008 TGR
88
Colour: dark-red cherry, garnet rim. Nose: ripe fruit, fruit preserve, dried herbs, old leather. Palate: flavourful, spicy, ripe fruit.

Oristán 2010 TR
86
Colour: cherry, garnet rim. Nose: medium intensity, spicy, dried herbs. Palate: ripe fruit, correct, round tannins.

Oristán 2011 TC
90
Colour: cherry, garnet rim. Nose: ripe fruit, spicy, creamy oak, toasty, complex. Palate: powerful, flavourful, toasty, round tannins.

BODEGAS NARANJO

Felipe II, 5
13150 Carrión de Calatrava
(Ciudad Real)
☎: +34 926 814 155
Fax: +34 926 815 335
www.bodegasnaranjo.com
info@bodegasnaranjo.com

Casa de la Dehesa 2010 TC
tempranillo
89
Colour: cherry, garnet rim. Nose: ripe fruit, spicy, creamy oak, toasty, complex. Palate: powerful, flavourful, toasty.

Viña Cuerva 2013 RD
tempranillo
84

Viña Cuerva 2010 TC
tempranillo
87
Colour: cherry, garnet rim. Nose: ripe fruit, spicy, creamy oak, toasty. Palate: powerful, flavourful, toasty.

Viña Cuerva 2012 T Roble
tempranillo, syrah
86
Colour: bright cherry, garnet rim. Nose: sweet spices, creamy oak. Palate: flavourful, toasty, spicy, harsh oak tannins.

Viña Cuerva 2013 T
tempranillo, syrah
87
Colour: cherry, purple rim. Nose: red berry notes, raspberry, fruit expression, fragrant herbs. Palate: flavourful, light-bodied, good acidity, fruity.

Viña Cuerva Airén B
airén
84

BODEGAS ROMERO DE ÁVILA SALCEDO

Avda. Constitución, 4
13240 La Solana (Ciudad Real)
☎: +34 926 631 426
www.bodegasromerodeavila.com
sales@bras1960.com

Portento 2008 TC
79

Portento Tempranillo 2011 T Roble
100% tempranillo
86
Colour: cherry, garnet rim. Nose: ripe fruit, balsamic herbs, spicy, creamy oak. Palate: powerful, flavourful, toasty.

BODEGAS SAN ANTONIO ABAD

Afueras, 17
45860 Villacañas (Toledo)
☎: +34 925 160 414
Fax: +34 925 162 015
www.sanantonioabad.es
export@sanantonioabad.es

Albardiales 2013 B
airén
83

Albardiales 2013 T
tempranillo
88
Colour: cherry, purple rim. Nose: expressive, fresh fruit, red berry notes, floral. Palate: flavourful, fruity, good acidity, round tannins.

Espanillo 2013 B
100% verdejo
84

Espanillo Semi Dulce 2013 RD
tempranillo
83

Villa Abad 2010 TC
tempranillo
83

Villa Abad 2013 B
100% macabeo
82

Villa Abad Tempranillo 2013 T Roble
tempranillo
87
Colour: bright cherry. Nose: ripe fruit, sweet spices, creamy oak, expressive. Palate: flavourful, fruity, toasty, round tannins

Villa Abad Tempranillo Semiseco 2013 T
tempranillo
85

BODEGAS SAN ISIDRO DE PEDRO MUÑOZ
Ctra. El Toboso, 1
13620 Pedro Muñoz (Ciudad Real)
☎: +34 926 586 057
Fax: +34 926 568 380
www.viacotos.com
mail@viacotos.com

Gran Amigo Sancho 2011 TC
100% tempranillo
86
Colour: cherry, garnet rim. Nose: ripe fruit, spicy, creamy oak, toasty. Palate: powerful, flavourful, toasty.

La Hijuela Airén 2013 B
100% airén
79

La Hijuela Tempranillo s/c T
100% tempranillo
82

BODEGAS VERDÚGUEZ
Los Hinojosos, 1
45810 Villanueva de Alcardete (Toledo)
☎: +34 925 167 493
Fax: +34 925 166 148
www.bodegasverduguez.com
export@bodegasverduguez.com

Hidalgo Castilla 2009 TR
tempranillo
89
Colour: bright cherry, garnet rim. Nose: ripe fruit, scrubland, spicy. Palate: flavourful, round tannins, good structure.

Hidalgo Castilla Verdejo 2013 B
verdejo
88
Colour: bright straw. Nose: fresh, fresh fruit, white flowers, expressive. Palate: flavourful, fruity, good acidity, balanced.

Imperial Toledo 2007 TGR
tempranillo
89
Colour: cherry, garnet rim. Nose: ripe fruit, spicy, creamy oak, toasty, complex. Palate: powerful, flavourful, toasty, round tannins.

Imperial Toledo Oaked Selection 2012 T
tempranillo, merlot, syrah
86
Colour: bright cherry. Nose: ripe fruit, sweet spices, smoky. Palate: flavourful, fruity, toasty, round tannins.

Imperial Toledo Tempranillo 2013 T
tempranillo
86
Colour: bright cherry. Nose: ripe fruit, sweet spices. Palate: flavourful, fruity, toasty, round tannins.

Palacios Reales Chardonnay 2013 B
chardonnay
84

BODEGAS VOLVER
Ctra de Pinoso a Fortuna s/n
3658 Rodriguillo - Pinoso (Alicante)
☎: +34 966 185 624
Fax: +34 965 075 376
www.bodegasvolver.com
export@bodegasvolver.com

Volver 2012 T
tempranillo
93
Colour: very deep cherry. Nose: earthy notes, overripe fruit, warm, roasted coffee. Palate: flavourful, powerful, fine bitter notes, good acidity.

BODEGAS Y VIÑEDOS BRO VALERO

Ctra. Las Mesas, Km. 11
2600 Villarrobledo (Albacete)
☎: +34 649 985 103
Fax: +34 914 454 675
www.brovalero.es
bodegas@brovalero.es

Bro Valero 2012 BFB
macabeo, chardonnay

86

Colour: bright yellow. Nose: powerfull, ripe fruit, sweet spices, creamy oak, dried herbs, dried flowers. Palate: rich, flavourful, fresh.

Bro Valero Syrah 2011 T
syrah

85

Bro Valero Tempranillo 2013 T
tempranillo

85

BODEGAS Y VIÑEDOS FONTANA

O'Donnell, 18 1ºG
28009 Madrid (Madrid)
☎: +34 915 783 197
Fax: +34 915 783 072
www.bodegasfontana.com
gemag@bodegasfontana.com

Fontal 2010 TC
tempranillo, cabernet sauvignon

89

Colour: cherry, garnet rim. Nose: ripe fruit, spicy, creamy oak, toasty, complex. Palate: powerful, flavourful, toasty, round tannins.

Fontal 2013 B

89

Colour: bright straw. Nose: fresh, fresh fruit, white flowers, expressive. Palate: flavourful, fruity, good acidity, balanced.

Fontal Tempranillo 2012 T Roble
tempranillo

87

Colour: bright cherry. Nose: ripe fruit, sweet spices, creamy oak. Palate: flavourful, fruity, toasty, round tannins, roasted-coffee aftertaste.

BODEGAS Y VIÑEDOS LADERO S.L.

Ctra. Alcázar, s/n
13700 Tomelloso (Ciudad Real)
☎: +34 926 505 653
Fax: +34 926 505 652
www.allozo.com
ladero@allozo.com

Ladero 2007 TR
100% tempranillo

86

Colour: dark-red cherry, garnet rim. Nose: ripe fruit, warm, sweet spices, toasty. Palate: flavourful, round tannins, easy to drink.

Ladero 2008 TC
100% tempranillo

84

Ladero 2013 T
100% tempranillo

86

Colour: cherry, purple rim. Nose: fresh fruit, red berry notes, floral. Palate: flavourful, fruity, good acidity, round tannins.

Ladero Selección 2013 B
100% airén

86

Colour: bright straw. Nose: fresh, fresh fruit, white flowers. Palate: flavourful, fruity, good acidity, easy to drink.

BOGARVE 1915

Reyes Católicos, 10
45710 Madridejos (Toledo)
☎: +34 925 460 820
Fax: +34 925 467 006
www.bogarve1915.com
bogarve@bogarve1915.com

100 Vendimias 2013 T
100% tempranillo

84

100 Vendimias Syrah 2013 T
100% syrah

86

Colour: cherry, purple rim. Nose: red berry notes, violets, spicy. Palate: flavourful, ripe fruit, spicy.

Lacruz Vega 2013 B
100% sauvignon blanc

84

Lacruz Vega Syrah 2013 T
100% syrah

84

Lacruz Vega Tempranillo 2013 T
100% tempranillo

85

Lacruz Vega Terroir 2012 T Roble
86
Colour: dark-red cherry. Nose: ripe fruit, sweet spices, creamy oak, expressive. Palate: flavourful, fruity, toasty, round tannins.

Lacruz Vega Verdejo 2013 B
100% verdejo
83

CAMPOS DE VIENTO
Avda. Diagonal, 590 - 5º 1ª
8021 (Barcelona)
☎: +34 660 445 464
www.vinergia.com
vinergia@vinergia.com

Campos de Viento 2012 T
100% tempranillo
86
Colour: cherry, purple rim. Nose: red berry notes, dried herbs, balanced. Palate: correct, ripe fruit, easy to drink.

COOPERATIVA EL PROGRESO
Avda. de la Virgen, 89
13670 Villarubia de los Ojos
(Ciudad Real)
☎: +34 926 896 135
www.bodegaselprogreso.com
administracion@bodegaselprogreso.com

Ojos del Guadiana 2007 TGR
tempranillo
89
Colour: cherry, garnet rim. Nose: ripe fruit, spicy, creamy oak, toasty, complex. Palate: powerful, flavourful, toasty, round tannins.

Ojos del Guadiana 2009 TC
tempranillo
86
Colour: bright cherry. Nose: ripe fruit, sweet spices, creamy oak, medium intensity. Palate: fruity, flavourful, toasty.

Ojos del Guadiana 2009 TR
tempranillo
87
Colour: cherry, garnet rim. Nose: red berry notes, ripe fruit, sweet spices. Palate: flavourful, toasty, round tannins.

Ojos del Guadiana 2012 BR
chardonnay
84

Ojos del Guadiana Airén 2013 B
airén
84

Ojos del Guadiana Cencibel 2013 T
cencibel
88
Colour: cherry, purple rim. Nose: expressive, fresh fruit, red berry notes, floral. Palate: flavourful, fruity, good acidity, round tannins.

Ojos del Guadiana Chardonnay 2013 B
chardonnay
87
Colour: bright straw. Nose: fresh, fresh fruit, white flowers. Palate: flavourful, fruity, good acidity, balanced.

Ojos del Guadiana Selección 2012 T
cabernet sauvignon, merlot, syrah
87
Colour: cherry, garnet rim. Nose: sweet spices, cocoa bean, ripe fruit. Palate: ripe fruit, good acidity.

Ojos del Guadiana Syrah 2013 T Roble
syrah
88
Colour: deep cherry, purple rim. Nose: red berry notes, ripe fruit, violets, expressive. Palate: balanced, spicy, good acidity, round tannins, fruity aftestaste.

Ojos del Guadiana Verdejo 2013 B
verdejo
84

CORDIS TERRA HISPANIA
Gamonal, 16 2ºC
28031 Madrid (Madrid)
☎: +34 911 610 024
Fax: +34 913 316 047
www.cordisterra.com
info@cordisterra.com

Cordis Terra 2013 B
macabeo
85

Cordis Terra 2013 T
tempranillo
84

Cordis Terra Semidulce 2013 RD
tempranillo
87
Colour: rose, purple rim. Nose: powerfull, ripe fruit, red berry notes, floral, expressive. Palate: powerful, fruity, fresh.

CRISTO DE LA VEGA BODEGAS

General Goded, 8
13630 Socuéllamos (Ciudad Real)
☎: +34 926 530 388
Fax: +34 926 530 024
www.bodegascrisve.com
info@bodegascrisve.com

El Yugo 2008 TR
tempranillo
87
Colour: cherry, garnet rim. Nose: ripe fruit, spicy, creamy oak, toasty. Palate: powerful, flavourful, toasty, round tannins.

El Yugo 2010 TC
tempranillo
86
Colour: bright cherry. Nose: ripe fruit, sweet spices, creamy oak, balsamic herbs. Palate: fruity, flavourful, toasty.

El Yugo 2012 BR
airén, chardonnay
82

El Yugo 2013 RD
garnacha, tempranillo
88
Colour: rose, purple rim. Nose: powerfull, ripe fruit, red berry notes, floral, expressive. Palate: powerful, fruity, fresh.

El Yugo 2013 T
tempranillo, syrah, merlot
87
Colour: cherry, purple rim. Nose: fresh fruit, red berry notes, floral, medium intensity. Palate: flavourful, fruity, good acidity, round tannins.

El Yugo Airén 2013 B
airén
86
Colour: bright straw. Nose: medium intensity, fresh fruit, citrus fruit. Palate: correct, balanced, easy to drink.

Marqués de Castilla 2009 TC
tempranillo
85

Marqués de Castilla 2009 TR
tempranillo, cabernet sauvignon
86
Colour: dark-red cherry, garnet rim. Nose: fruit preserve, sweet spices. Palate: fruity, balsamic, round tannins.

Marqués de Castilla 2010 T Barrica
merlot, cabernet sauvignon
86
Colour: dark-red cherry, garnet rim. Nose: toasty, spicy, dried herbs. Palate: flavourful, fruity, round tannins.

Marqués de Castilla 2013 RD
garnacha, tempranillo
84

Marqués de Castilla 2013 T
tempranillo, syrah, merlot
85

Marqués de Castilla Airén 2013 B
airén
84

Marqués de Castilla Sauvignon Blanc 2013 B
sauvignon blanc, chardonnay
80

DOMINIO DE PUNCTUM ORGANIC & BIODYNAMIC WINES

Finca Fabian, s/n - Aptdo. 71
16660 Las Pedroñeras (Cuenca)
☎: +34 912 959 998
Fax: +34 912 959 997
www.dominiodepunctum.com
export@dominiodepunctum.com

Nortesur Chardonnay 2013 B
100% chardonnay
87 🌷
Colour: bright straw. Nose: fine lees, dried herbs, citrus fruit, ripe fruit. Palate: flavourful, fruity, easy to drink.

Nortesur Tempranillo Cabernet Sauvignon 2013 T
88 ❦
Colour: bright cherry. Nose: balsamic herbs, fresh fruit. Palate: fruity, long, balanced, fruity aftestaste.

Uno de Mil Tempranillo Petit Verdot 2011 T Barrica
88 ❦
Colour: cherry, garnet rim. Nose: powerfull, ripe fruit, balanced, wild herbs. Palate: fruity, spicy, balsamic.

Uno de Mil Viognier 2011 B
100% viognier
89 ❦
Colour: bright yellow. Nose: powerfull, ripe fruit, sweet spices, creamy oak, white flowers. Palate: rich, smoky aftertaste, flavourful.

Viento Aliseo Graciano Cabernet Sauvignon 2011 TC
88 ❦
Colour: cherry, garnet rim. Nose: ripe fruit, fruit preserve, balsamic herbs, sweet spices. Palate: powerful, round tannins, long.

Viento Aliseo Tempranillo
Petit Verdot 2013 T

88 🍷

Colour: cherry, purple rim. Nose: medium intensity, red berry notes, wild herbs. Palate: fruity, balanced, good acidity.

Viento Aliseo Viognier 2013 B
100% viognier

86 🍷

Colour: bright golden. Nose: white flowers, fragrant herbs, candied fruit, mineral. Palate: fruity, flavourful, balanced.

FÉLIX SOLÍS S.L.
Otumba, 2
45840 La Puebla de Almoradiel (Toledo)
☎: +34 925 178 626
Fax: +34 925 178 626
www.felixsolis.com
lamancha@felixsolis.com

Caliza 2013 B
chardonnay, verdejo, viura
85

Caliza 2013 RD
tempranillo
85

Caliza 2013 T
merlot, syrah, tempranillo
86

Colour: cherry, purple rim. Nose: fresh fruit, red berry notes, floral, medium intensity. Palate: fruity, good acidity.

Viña San Juan 2013 B
chardonnay, verdejo, viura
85

Viña San Juan 2013 RD
tempranillo
85

Viña San Juan 2013 T
merlot, syrah, tempranillo
86

Colour: bright cherry, purple rim. Nose: floral, red berry notes, fresh fruit. Palate: fruity, good acidity, easy to drink.

FINCA ANTIGUA
Ctra. Quintanar - Los Hinojosos, Km. 11,5
16417 Los Hinojosos (Cuenca)
☎: +34 969 129 700
Fax: +34 969 129 496
www.familiamartinezbujanda.com
comunicacion@bujanda.com

Ciclos de Finca Antigua 2005 TR
88

Colour: pale ruby, brick rim edge. Nose: spicy, toasty, overripe fruit, mineral. Palate: powerful, flavourful, toasty, round tannins.

Clavis 2006 TR
92

Colour: cherry, garnet rim. Nose: ripe fruit, spicy, creamy oak, dark chocolate, expressive, wild herbs, tobacco. Palate: powerful, flavourful, toasty, round tannins, good structure, balsamic.

Finca Antigua 2010 TC
90

Colour: cherry, garnet rim. Nose: ripe fruit, spicy, creamy oak, complex, balsamic herbs. Palate: powerful, flavourful, toasty, round tannins.

Finca Antigua Cabernet
Sauvignon 2011 T Roble
100% cabernet sauvignon
85

Finca Antigua Garnacha 2011 T
100% garnacha
89

Colour: bright cherry. Nose: ripe fruit, sweet spices, creamy oak, expressive. Palate: flavourful, fruity, toasty, round tannins, balanced.

Finca Antigua Merlot 2011 T Roble
100% merlot
87

Colour: light cherry. Nose: fragrant herbs, creamy oak, sweet spices, balsamic herbs. Palate: powerful, flavourful, spicy.

Finca Antigua Moscatel 2012 B
100% moscatel
91

Colour: golden. Nose: powerfull, floral, honeyed notes, candied fruit, fragrant herbs. Palate: flavourful, sweet, fresh, fruity, good acidity, long. Personality.

Finca Antigua Syrah 2011 T
100% syrah
90

Colour: cherry, garnet rim. Nose: ripe fruit, spicy, creamy oak, toasty, complex. Palate: powerful, flavourful, toasty, round tannins.

Finca Antigua Tempranillo 2011 T
100% tempranillo

88

Colour: bright cherry. Nose: ripe fruit, sweet spices, creamy oak, expressive. Palate: flavourful, fruity, toasty, round tannins.

Finca Antigua Viura 2013 B
100% viura

86

Colour: bright straw. Nose: fresh, fresh fruit, white flowers. Palate: flavourful, fruity, good acidity, balanced.

FINCA LA BLANCA
Princesa, 84
45840 Puebla de Almoradiel (Toledo)
☎: +34 669 995 315
Fax: +34 968 897 675
www.fincalablanca.es
export@fincalablanca.es

Monte Don Lucio 2007 TR
tempranillo, cabernet sauvignon

84

Monte Don Lucio Cabernet Sauvignon 2012 T
cabernet sauvignon

83

Monte Don Lucio Sauvignon Blanc 2013 B
sauvignon blanc

82

Monte Don Lucio Tempranillo 2013 T
tempranillo

82

Ribera de los Molinos 2013 B
airén, sauvignon blanc, macabeo

82

Ribera de los Molinos 2013 T
tempranillo, cabernet sauvignon, garnacha, merlot

83

HERMANOS MATEOS HIGUERA
Ctra. La Solana - Villanueva de los Infantes, km. 7,1
13240 La Solana (Ciudad Real)
☎: +34 676 920 905
www.vegamara.es
info@vegamara.es

Vega Demara 2010 TC

88

Colour: cherry, garnet rim. Nose: ripe fruit, spicy, creamy oak, toasty, complex. Palate: powerful, flavourful, toasty.

Vega Demara 2011 T Roble
tempranillo

82

Vega Demara Tempranillo 2013 T
tempranillo

83

Vega Demara Verdejo 2013 B
verdejo

80

Ylirum Tempranillo s/c T
tempranillo

84

Ylirum Verdejo 2013 B
verdejo

82

J. GARCÍA CARRIÓN
Pol. Guarnicionero - Daimel
13250 Daimiel (Ciudad Real)
☎: +34 926 260 104
www.garciacarrion.es
daimiel@jgc.es

Don Luciano 2009 TR
tempranillo

85

Don Luciano 2010 TC
tempranillo

81

Don Luciano Tempranillo 2013 T Joven
tempranillo

84

JESÚS DEL PERDÓN - BODEGAS YUNTERO
Pol. Ind., Ctra. Alcázar de San Juan s/n
13200 Manzanares (Ciudad Real)
☎: +34 926 610 309
Fax: +34 926 610 516
www.yuntero.com
yuntero@yuntero.com

Epílogo 2011 TC
tempranillo, merlot

87

Colour: cherry, garnet rim. Nose: ripe fruit, spicy, creamy oak, toasty. Palate: powerful, flavourful, toasty.

Epílogo 2013 B
sauvignon blanc, moscatel

87

Colour: bright straw. Nose: powerfull, floral, candied fruit, fragrant herbs. Palate: flavourful, fresh, fruity.

Mundo de Yuntero 2013 T
tempranillo, merlot, syrah
84

Mundo de Yuntero 2013 B
verdejo, sauvignon blanc
85

Yuntero 2008 TR
tempranillo
84

Yuntero 2010 TC
tempranillo, petit verdot
86
Colour: cherry, garnet rim. Nose: red berry notes, ripe fruit, scrubland, creamy oak. Palate: powerful, flavourful, spicy.

Yuntero 2013 RD
tempranillo
82

Yuntero 2013 T
tempranillo, syrah
85

JOSÉ LUIS GUILLERMO MENDIETA S.L.
Avda. de La Mancha, 42
45860 Villacañas (Toledo)
☎: +34 925 160 439
Fax: +34 925 160 912
bodegasguillermo@wanadoo.es

Cibelino 2009 TC
84

Viña Cibelina 2010 T
86
Colour: deep cherry, garnet rim. Nose: ripe fruit, fruit preserve, balsamic herbs. Palate: flavourful, spicy.

Viña La Ria s/c B
airén
81

LA REMEDIADORA S.C.L. DE CASTILLA LA MANCHA
Alfredo Atieza, 149
2630 La Roda (Albacete)
☎: +34 967 440 600
Fax: +34 967 441 465
www.laremediadora.com
export@laremediadora.com

La Villa Real 2008 TC
89
Colour: cherry, garnet rim. Nose: spicy, scrubland, toasty, ripe fruit. Palate: balanced, round tannins.

La Villa Real 2008 TR
85

La Villa Real 2011 T Roble
87
Colour: bright cherry. Nose: ripe fruit, sweet spices, creamy oak, expressive. Palate: flavourful, fruity, toasty, round tannins.

La Villa Real 2013 RD
tempranillo
87
Colour: raspberry rose. Nose: floral, balanced. Palate: fresh, fruity, easy to drink, fine bitter notes.

La Villa Real Macabeo 2013 B
100% macabeo
83

La Villa Real Vendimia Seleccionada 2013 T
85

NTRA. SRA. DE MANJAVACAS SOC. COOP. DE CLM
Camino del Campo de Criptana, s/n
16630 Mota del Cuervo (Cuenca)
☎: +34 967 180 025
Fax: +34 967 181 120
www.zagarron.com
info@zagarron.com

Zagarron Sauvignon Blanc 2013 B
100% sauvignon blanc
87
Colour: bright straw. Nose: fresh, fresh fruit, white flowers. Palate: flavourful, fruity, good acidity, balanced.

Zagarron Tempranillo 2013 T
100% tempranillo
86
Colour: cherry, purple rim. Nose: medium intensity, violets, fresh fruit. Palate: balanced, good acidity, fruity.

Zagarron Verdejo 2013 B
100% verdejo
85

NUESTRA SEÑORA DE LA CABEZA S.C.
Tapias, 8
16708 Pozoamargo (Cuenca)
☎: +34 969 387 173
www.casagualda.com
info@casagualda.com

Casa Gualda 2010 TC
tempranillo, cabernet sauvignon
89
Colour: bright cherry. Nose: sweet spices, creamy oak, medium intensity. Palate: fruity, flavourful, toasty, balsamic.

Casa Gualda Sauvignon Blanc 2013 B
sauvignon blanc
85

Casa Gualda Selección
50 Aniversario 2011 T
tempranillo, petit verdot, syrah
87
Colour: cherry, garnet rim. Nose: ripe fruit, spicy, creamy oak, toasty, complex, dried herbs. Palate: powerful, flavourful, toasty, round tannins.

Casa Gualda Selección C&J 2009 T
tempranillo
85

Casa Gualda Tempranillo 2013 T
tempranillo
86
Colour: cherry, purple rim. Nose: fresh fruit, red berry notes, medium intensity. Palate: easy to drink, balanced, fruity aftestaste.

NUESTRA SEÑORA DE LA PIEDAD, S. COOP. DE C. L-M
Ctra. Circunvalación, s/n
45800 Quintanar de la Orden (Toledo)
☎: +34 925 180 237
Fax: +34 925 560 092
comercial@bodegasentremontes.com

Clavelito 2012 RD
100% tempranillo
82

Clavelito Airén 2013 B
airén
83

Clavelito Macabeo 2013 B
100% macabeo
80

Clavelito Sauvignon Blanc 2013 B
100% sauvignon blanc
80

Clavelito Verdejo 2013 B
100% verdejo
78

Entremontes BN
84

Entremontes SS
100% airén
82

Entremontes 2002 TGR
100% tempranillo
85

Entremontes 2003 TR
100% tempranillo
82

Entremontes 2005 TC
100% tempranillo
81

Entremontes 2009 T Roble
100% tempranillo
84

Entremontes Cabernet Sauvignon 2013 T
100% cabernet sauvignon
83

Entremontes Merlot 2013 T
100% merlot
78

Entremontes Tempranillo 2012 T
100% tempranillo
82

PAGO DE LA JARABA
Ctra. Nacional 310, Km. 142,7
2600 Villarrobledo (Albacete)
☎: +34 967 138 250
Fax: +34 967 138 252
www.lajaraba.com
info@lajaraba.com

Pago de la Jaraba 2012 TC
87
Colour: cherry, garnet rim. Nose: ripe fruit, spicy, complex, scrubland. Palate: powerful, flavourful, toasty, round tannins.

Viña Jaraba Selección 2010 TC
86
Colour: cherry, garnet rim. Nose: ripe fruit, spicy, creamy oak, toasty, scrubland. Palate: powerful, flavourful, toasty.

SANTA CATALINA
Cooperativa, 2
13240 La Solana (Ciudad Real)
☎: +34 926 632 194
Fax: +34 926 631 085
www.santacatalina.es
central@santacatalina.es

Campechano 2012 T Roble
tempranillo
85

Campechano 2013 T
tempranillo
86
Colour: bright cherry, purple rim. Nose: red berry notes, ripe fruit, balanced, floral. Palate: flavourful, fruity.

Campechano Airén 2013 B
airén
85

Campechano Verdejo 2013 B
verdejo
83

Los Galanes 2010 TR
tempranillo
85

Los Galanes 2011 TC
tempranillo
87
Colour: bright cherry. Nose: ripe fruit, sweet spices, creamy oak, balsamic herbs. Palate: fruity, flavourful, toasty.

Los Galanes 2013 T
tempranillo
84

Los Galanes Airén 2013 B
airén
85

Los Galanes Macabeo 2013 B
macabeo
85

SANTA RITA S.A.T.
San Agustín, 14
16630 Mota del Cuervo (Cuenca)
☎: +34 967 180 071
Fax: +34 967 182 277
satsantarita@hotmail.com

Varones 1998 TR
87
Colour: pale ruby, brick rim edge. Nose: elegant, spicy, fine reductive notes, wet leather, aged wood nuances, fruit liqueur notes. Palate: spicy, fine tannins, elegant, long.

Varones 2000 TC
tempranillo
86
Colour: dark-red cherry, garnet rim. Nose: tobacco, old leather, spicy, fruit liqueur notes. Palate: fruity, spicy, balanced.

Varones 2000 TC
tempranillo, cabernet sauvignon
85

Varones 2000 TR
cabernet sauvignon, tempranillo
84

Varones 2001 TR
cabernet sauvignon
84

VIHUCAS
Mayor, 3
45860 Villacañas (Toledo)
☎: +34 925 160 309
Fax: +34 925 160 176
www.vihucas.com
patricia@vihucas.com

Vihucas Borealis 2008 TR
merlot
88
Colour: dark-red cherry, garnet rim. Nose: scrubland, fine reductive notes, spicy. Palate: flavourful, ripe fruit, spicy.

Vihucas Cencibel 2013 T
cencibel
85

Vihucas Colección Familiar 2009 TC
100% merlot
89
Colour: very deep cherry, garnet rim. Nose: balanced, wild herbs, ripe fruit. Palate: good structure, balanced.

Vihucas Colección Familiar 2010 T
merlot
89
Colour: cherry, garnet rim. Nose: ripe fruit, spicy, creamy oak, toasty, complex, balsamic herbs. Palate: powerful, flavourful, toasty, balanced.

Vihucas Doble 10/11 TC
tempranillo, merlot
87
Colour: light cherry, orangey edge. Nose: ripe fruit, balsamic herbs, spicy, creamy oak, tobacco, wet leather. Palate: powerful, flavourful, spicy.

VINÍCOLA DE CASTILLA
Pol. Ind. Calle I, s/n
13200 Manzanares (Ciudad Real)
☎: +34 926 647 800
Fax: +34 926 610 466
www.vinicoladecastilla.com
nacional@vinicoladecastilla.com

Señorío de Guadianeja 2013 RD
tempranillo
83

Señorío de Guadianeja 2006 TR
tempranillo
84

Señorío de Guadianeja 2009 TC
tempranillo
85

Señorío de Guadianeja Cabernet Sauvignon 2013 T
cabernet sauvignon
84

Señorío de Guadianeja Chardonnay 2013 B
chardonnay
86
Colour: bright straw. Nose: tropical fruit, ripe fruit, balsamic herbs. Palate: easy to drink, fresh, fruity.

Señorío de Guadianeja Macabeo 2013 B
macabeo
84

Señorío de Guadianeja Merlot 2013 T
merlot
84

Señorío de Guadianeja Petit Verdot 2013 T
petit verdot
88
Colour: cherry, purple rim. Nose: fresh fruit, red berry notes, floral, wild herbs. Palate: flavourful, fruity, fine bitter notes.

Señorío de Guadianeja Sauvignon Blanc 2013 B
sauvignon blanc
84

Señorío de Guadianeja Syrah 2013 T
syrah
87
Colour: cherry, purple rim. Nose: expressive, fresh fruit, red berry notes, floral. Palate: flavourful, fruity, good acidity, round tannins.

Señorío de Guadianeja Tempranillo 2013 T
tempranillo
86
Colour: bright cherry, purple rim. Nose: balanced, expressive, red berry notes, floral, lactic notes. Palate: flavourful, good acidity, fruity aftestaste.

Señorío de Guadianeja Verdejo 2013 B
verdejo
85

VINÍCOLA DE TOMELLOSO
Ctra. Toledo - Albacete, Km. 130,8
13700 Tomelloso (Ciudad Real)
☎: +34 926 513 004
Fax: +34 926 538 001
www.vinicolatomelloso.com
vinicola@vinicolatomelloso.com

Añil 2013 B
macabeo, chardonnay
88
Colour: bright straw. Nose: fresh, fresh fruit, white flowers, expressive. Palate: flavourful, fruity, good acidity, sweetness.

MACABEO-CHARDONNAY

Finca Cerrada 2006 TR
tempranillo, cabernet sauvignon
82

Finca Cerrada 2007 TC
tempranillo, cabernet sauvignon, syrah
84

Finca Cerrada 2013 RD
tempranillo
84

Finca Cerrada Tempranillo 2013 T
tempranillo
85

Finca Cerrada Viura 2013 B
viura
83

Mantolán ESP
macabeo
83

Torre de Gazate 2002 TGR
cabernet sauvignon
83

Torre de Gazate 2006 TR
tempranillo, cabernet sauvignon
85

Torre de Gazate 2008 TC
tempranillo, cabernet sauvignon

86

Colour: bright cherry. Nose: ripe fruit, sweet spices, creamy oak, medium intensity. Palate: fruity, flavourful, toasty, correct.

Torre de Gazate 2010 T Roble
tempranillo

88

Colour: cherry, purple rim. Nose: expressive, fresh fruit, red berry notes, floral, sweet spices. Palate: flavourful, fruity, good acidity, round tannins.

Torre de Gazate Airén 2013 B
airén

80

Torre de Gazate Cabernet Sauvignon 2013 RD
cabernet sauvignon

84

Torre de Gazate Syrah Merlot Cabernet Sauvignon 2013 T
syrah, merlot, cabernet sauvignon

86

Colour: bright cherry. Nose: fresh fruit, citrus fruit, floral. Palate: good acidity, fruity, flavourful, good finish.

Torre de Gazate Tempranillo 2013 T
tempranillo

87

Colour: cherry, purple rim. Nose: expressive, fresh fruit, red berry notes, floral. Palate: flavourful, fruity, good acidity, round tannins.

Torre de Gazate Verdejo Sauvignon Blanc 2013 B
verdejo, sauvignon blanc

84

VINOS COLOMAN S.A.T.
Goya, 17
13620 Pedro Muñoz (Ciudad Real)
☎: +34 926 586 410
Fax: +34 926 586 656
www.satcoloman.com
coloman@satcoloman.com

Besana Real 2009 TC
tempranillo

88

Colour: dark-red cherry, garnet rim. Nose: balanced, ripe fruit, cocoa bean, spicy. Palate: balanced, round tannins.

Besana Real 2013 RD
tempranillo

83

Besana Real Cabernet Sauvignon 2011 T Roble
cabernet sauvignon

83

Besana Real Macabeo 2013 B
macabeo

82

Besana Real Verdejo 2013 B
verdejo

82

VIÑA MAGUA
Doña Berenguela, 59
28011 Madrid (Madrid)
☎: +34 659 583 020
http://vinoecologicomagua.blogspot.com
vino.magua@gmail.com

Viña Magua 2012 T
tempranillo

84

VIÑEDOS MEJORANTES S.L.
Ctra. de Villafranca, km. 2
45860 Villacañas (Toledo)
☎: +34 925 200 023
Fax: +34 925 200 023
www.portillejo.es
portillejo@portillejo.com

Portillejo 2003 TR
100% cabernet sauvignon

82

Portillejo 2006 TC
100% cabernet sauvignon
84

Portillejo Cabernet Sauvignon 2009 T Roble
100% cabernet sauvignon
79

Portillejo Merlot 2009 T Roble
100% merlot
84

VIÑEDOS Y BODEGAS MUÑOZ

Ctra. Villarrubia, 11
45350 Noblejas (Toledo)
☎: +34 925 140 070
Fax: +34 925 141 334
www.bodegasmunoz.com
c.calidad@bodegasmunoz.com

Artero 2009 TR
tempranillo, merlot
86
Colour: cherry, garnet rim. Nose: medium intensity, ripe fruit, dried herbs. Palate: ripe fruit, correct.

Artero 2011 TC
tempranillo, merlot, syrah
88
Colour: cherry, garnet rim. Nose: ripe fruit, spicy, creamy oak, toasty, complex. Palate: powerful, flavourful, toasty, round tannins.

Artero 2013 RD
tempranillo
85

Artero Macabeo Verdejo 2013 B
macabeo, verdejo
83

Artero Tempranillo 2013 T
tempranillo
86
Colour: cherry, purple rim. Nose: fresh fruit, red berry notes, floral. Palate: flavourful, fruity, good acidity, round tannins.

Blas Muñoz Chardonnay 2012 BFB
chardonnay
90
Colour: bright yellow. Nose: creamy oak, roasted coffee, sweet spices, faded flowers. Palate: rich, flavourful, spicy, long, smoky aftertaste.

VIRGEN DE LAS VIÑAS BODEGA Y ALMAZARA S.C. CLM

Ctra. Argamasilla de Alba, 1
13700 Tomelloso (Ciudad Real)
☎: +34 926 510 865
Fax: +34 926 512 130
www.vinostomillar.com
atencion.cliente@vinostomillar.com

Tomillar 2008 TR
86
Colour: cherry, garnet rim. Nose: woody, ripe fruit, dried herbs. Palate: correct, ripe fruit, good finish.

Tomillar Chardonnay 2013 B
100% chardonnay
85

Tomillar Tempranillo 2013 T
100% tempranillo
86
Colour: bright cherry. Nose: wild herbs, red berry notes, expressive. Palate: flavourful, good acidity, round tannins, easy to drink.

DO. LA PALMA

CONSEJO REGULADOR

Esteban Acosta Gómez, 7
38740 Fuencaliente (La Palma)
☎ :+34 922 444 404
Fax: +34 922 444 432
@: vinoslapalma@vinoslapalma.com
www.vinoslapalma.com

LOCATION:

The production area covers the whole island of San Miguel de La Palma, and is divided into three distinct sub-regions: Hoyo de Mazo, Fuencaliente and Northern La Palma.

SUB-REGIONS:

Hoyo de Mazo: It comprises the municipal districts of Villa de Mazo, Breña Baja, Breña Alta and Santa Cruz de La Palma, at altitudes of between 200 m and 700 m. The vines grow over the terrain on hillsides covered with volcanic stone ('Empedrados') or with volcanic gravel ('Picón Granado'). White and mainly red varieties are grown.

Fuencaliente: It comprises the municipal districts of Fuencaliente, El Paso, Los Llanos de Aridane and Tazacorte. The vines grow over terrains of volcanic ash at altitudes of between 200 m and 1900 m. The white varieties and the sweet Malvasia stand out.

Northern La Palma: Situated at an altitude of between 100 m and 200 m, It comprises the municipal areas of Puntallana, San Andrés and Sauces, Barlovento, Garafía, Puntagorda and Tijarafe. The region is richer in vegetation and the vines grow on trellises and using the goblet system. The traditional 'Tea' wines are produced here.

GRAPE VARIETIES:

White: Malvasía, Güal and Verdello (main); Albillo, Bastardo Blanco, Bermejuela, Bujariego, Burra Blanca, Forastera Blanca, Listán Blanco, Moscatel, Pedro Ximénez, Sabro and Torrontés.
Red: Negramol (main), Listán Negro (Almuñeco), Bastardo Negro, Malvasía Rosada, Moscatel Negro, Tintilla, Castellana, Listán Prieto and Vijariego Negro.

FIGURES:

Vineyard surface: 620 – Wine-Growers: 1,151 – Wineries: 20 – 2013 Harvest rating: N/A – Production 13: 554,390 litres – Market percentages: 99% domestic - 1% export.

SOIL:

The vineyards are situated at altitudes of between 200 m and 1,400 m above sea level in a coastal belt ranging in width which surrounds the whole island. Due to the ragged topography, the vineyards occupy the steep hillsides in the form of small terraces. The soil is mainly of volcanic origin.

CLIMATE:

This is the most north-westerly island of the archipelago of the Canary Islands. Its complex orography with altitudes which reach 2,400 metres above sea level make it a micro-continent with a wide variety of climates. The influence of the anti-cyclone of the Azores and the trade winds condition the thermal variables and the rainfall registered throughout the year. The greatest amount of rainfall is registered in the more easterly and northern parts of the island due to the entry of the trade winds.

Throughout the north-east, from Mazo to Barlovento, the climate is milder and fresher, while the western part of the island has drier and warmer weather. The average rainfall increases from the coast as the terrain ascends. The greatest amount of rainfall is in the north and east of the island.

VINTAGE RATING   PEÑÍNGUIDE

2009	2010	2011	2012	2013
GOOD	GOOD	VERY GOOD	VERY GOOD	N/A

BODEGA JOSÉ DAVID RODRIGUEZ PEREZ

Barranquito hondo Nº 4
El Pinar - Puntagorda
☎: +34 636 918 839
vinarda@hotmail.com

Viñarda 2013 B
85

Viñarda 2013 T
85

BODEGA JUAN MATÍAS TORRES

Fuencaliente de Ciudad Real, s/n Los
Canarios
38740 Fuentecaliente de la Palma
(Santa Cruz de Tenerife)
☎: +34 617 967 499
www.matiastorres.com
bodega@matiasitorres.com

Colección Minúscula de Matías Torres 2010 B
100% malvasía
93
Colour: bright golden. Nose: expressive, candied fruit, dried fruit, powerfull. Palate: flavourful, concentrated, sweet.

Las Machuqueras 2013 B
100% listán blanco
91
Colour: bright yellow. Nose: expressive, elegant, dried herbs. Palate: balanced, easy to drink, fine bitter notes, elegant, good acidity.

Matias i Torres Diego 2013 B
87
Colour: greenish rim. Nose: balanced, floral, dry nuts, fresh fruit. Palate: balanced, fine bitter notes, good finish.

Matias i Torres Malvasía Aromática 2011 B
100% malvasía
94
Colour: golden. Nose: powerfull, floral, honeyed notes, candied fruit, fragrant herbs. Palate: flavourful, sweet, fresh, fruity, good acidity, long.

Vid Sur Dulce 2006 B
100% malvasía
94
Colour: old gold. Nose: sweet spices, toasty, fruit expression, honeyed notes, cocoa bean. Palate: flavourful, unctuous, long.

Vid Sur Dulce 2008 B
100% malvasía
93
Colour: light mahogany. Nose: fruit liqueur notes, candied fruit, powerfull, expressive. Palate: flavourful, full, balanced, good acidity, long.

BODEGA PERDOMO S.A.T.

Joaquina, 12 (Las Tricias)
38738 Garafia (La Palma)
☎: +34 922 400 089
Fax: +34 922 400 689

Piedra Jurada 2013 B
albillo
86
Colour: bright straw, greenish rim. Nose: fresh fruit, white flowers. Palate: fruity, fine bitter notes, good acidity.

Piedra Jurada Albillo 2013 B
albillo
86
Colour: bright straw, greenish rim. Nose: medium intensity, white flowers, fresh fruit. Palate: correct, flavourful, fine bitter notes.

BODEGAS CARBALLO

Ctra. a Las Indias, 74
38740 Fuencaliente de La Palma
(Santa Cruz de Tenerife)
☎: +34 922 444 140
Fax: +34 922 211 744
www.bodegascarballo.com
info@bodegascarballo.com

Carballo Malvasia Dulce 2011 B
malvasía
92 🌺
Colour: old gold. Nose: candied fruit, honeyed notes, powerfull, faded flowers. Palate: flavourful, varietal, unctuous, long.

Carballo Malvasía Dulce Añejo 2001 B Gran Reserva
malvasía
95 🌺
Colour: old gold, amber rim. Nose: toasty, spicy, dried herbs, dried fruit, faded flowers. Palate: full, good structure, complex.

Carballo Seco 2013 B
79 🌺

BODEGAS NOROESTE DE LA PALMA

Camino de Bellido, s/n
38780 Tijarafe (Santa Cruz de Tenerife)
☎: +34 922 491 075
Fax: +34 922 491 075
www.vinosveganorte.com
administracion@vinosveganorte.com

Vega Norte 2013 T
negramoll, listán negro, listán priet
86
Colour: light cherry. Nose: medium intensity, spicy, red berry notes, faded flowers. Palate: fruity, flavourful.

Vega Norte "Vino de Tea" 2013 T
88
Colour: cherry, garnet rim. Nose: expressive, complex, scrubland, dried flowers. Palate: flavourful, spicy, long.

Vega Norte 2013 B
88
Colour: bright straw. Nose: fresh, fresh fruit, expressive. Palate: flavourful, fruity, good acidity, balanced, long, fine bitter notes.

Vega Norte 2013 RD
95% negramoll, listan prieto, almuñeco
88
Colour: rose, bright. Nose: fresh, expressive, red berry notes, balanced, rose petals. Palate: fresh, fruity, easy to drink, long.

Vega Norte Albillo 2013 B
100% albillo
89
Colour: bright straw. Nose: elegant, dried flowers, expressive, fresh. Palate: flavourful, good acidity, balanced, long, fine bitter notes.

Vega Norte Listán Prieto 2012 T
listan prieto
88
Colour: cherry, garnet rim. Nose: ripe fruit, wild herbs, spicy. Palate: balanced, flavourful, long, balsamic, slightly dry, soft tannins.

Vega Norte Vendimia Seleccionada X Aniversario 2012 T
100% listán prieto
89
Colour: bright cherry. Nose: ripe fruit, sweet spices, creamy oak, expressive. Palate: flavourful, fruity, toasty, round tannins.

BODEGAS TAMANCA S.L.
Las Manchas - San Nicolás
38750 El Paso (Santa Cruz de Tenerife)
☎: +34 922 494 155
Fax: +34 922 494 296
bodegas_tamanca@hotmail.com

Tamanca 2013 RD
negramoll
85

Tamanca 2013 T Roble
negramoll, almuñeco, vijariego negro, baboso negro
87
Colour: bright cherry. Nose: expressive, red berry notes, ripe fruit, spicy. Palate: flavourful, fruity, toasty, round tannins.

Tamanca Malvasía Dulce 2005 B Barrica
malvasía
93
Colour: golden. Nose: powerfull, floral, honeyed notes, candied fruit, pattiserie. Palate: flavourful, sweet, fresh, fruity, good acidity, long.

Tamanca Malvasía Dulce 2012 B
malvasía
87
Colour: golden. Nose: powerfull, floral, honeyed notes, candied fruit, fragrant herbs. Palate: flavourful, sweet, fresh, fruity, good acidity, long.

Tamanca Sabro Dulce B
sabro
87
Colour: old gold. Nose: candied fruit, honeyed notes, floral. Palate: correct, fruity, rich, long.

Tamanca Selección 2013 B
albillo, vijariego blanco, malvasía, marmajuelo
86
Colour: yellow, greenish rim. Nose: balanced, ripe fruit, tropical fruit, floral. Palate: fruity, flavourful, good acidity.

BODEGAS TENEGUÍA
Plazoleta García Escamez, 1
38740 Fuencaliente de La Palma
(Santa Cruz de Tenerife)
☎: +34 922 444 078
Fax: +34 922 444 394
www.vinosteneguia.com
enologia@vinosteneguia.com

Teneguía 2013 B
listán blanco, vijariego blanco, albillo, gual
85

Teneguía La Gota 2013 B
listán blanco, vijariego blanco, albillo, negramoll
86
Colour: yellow, greenish rim. Nose: expressive, balanced, floral. Palate: fruity, easy to drink, good finish, fine bitter notes.

Teneguía Malvasía Aromática 2012 B
malvasía
90
Colour: bright yellow. Nose: balanced, expressive, varietal, white flowers. Palate: balanced, rich, ripe fruit.

Teneguía Malvasía Aromática Dulce 2006 B Reserva
malvasía
94
Colour: old gold, amber rim. Nose: complex, expressive, balanced, sweet spices, varnish, dried fruit. Palate: balanced, long, good acidity, unctuous.

Teneguía Malvasía Aromática Seco 2012 BFB
malvasía

88

Colour: bright yellow. Nose: balanced, candied fruit, sweet spices, jasmine, toasty, spicy, ripe fruit.

Teneguía Malvasía Dulce Estelar 1996 B Gran Reserva
malvasía

96

Colour: mahogany. Nose: expressive, complex, balanced, honeyed notes, faded flowers, cocoa bean. Palate: full, concentrated, flavourful, long.

Teneguía Sabro/Gual Dulce 2012 B
sabro, gual

89

Colour: bright golden. Nose: complex, grassy, faded flowers, honeyed notes. Palate: fruity, balanced, long.

Teneguía Varietales 2013 T
negramoll, castellana, vijariego negro, baboso negro

84

Teneguía Zeus Negramoll 2012 Tinto Dulce
negramoll

88

Colour: dark-red cherry, garnet rim. Nose: ripe fruit, dried herbs. Palate: rich, flavourful, long, good acidity.

ONÉSIMA PÉREZ RODRÍGUEZ

Las Tricias
38738 Garafia (La Palma)
☎: +34 922 463 481
Fax: +34 922 463 481
vinosvitega@terra.es

Vitega Tea 2013 T
86

Colour: light cherry, garnet rim. Nose: expressive, balsamic herbs, balanced. Palate: light-bodied, easy to drink, correct. Personality.

VINOS EL NÍSPERO

Briesta, 3
38787 Villa de Garafia
(Santa Cruz de Tenerife)
☎: +34 639 080 712
Fax: +34 922 400 447
adali_12@msn.com

El Níspero 2012 T Roble
87

Colour: bright cherry. Nose: ripe fruit, sweet spices, creamy oak, expressive. Palate: flavourful, fruity, toasty, round tannins.

El Níspero 2013 B
albillo

88

Colour: bright straw. Nose: expressive, jasmine, white flowers, tropical fruit. Palate: fruity, fresh, easy to drink.

DO. LANZAROTE

CONSEJO REGULADOR

Arrecife, 9
35550 San Bartolomé (Lanzarote)
☎ :+34 928 521 313 - Fax: +34 928 521 049
@: info@dolanzarote.com
www.dolanzarote.com

LOCATION:

On the island of Lanzarote. The production area covers the municipal areas of Tinajo, Yaiza, San Bartolomé, Haría and Teguise.

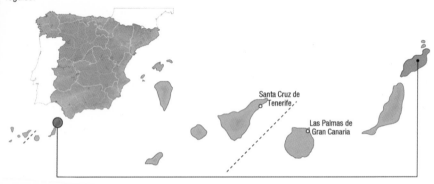

GRAPE VARIETIES:

White: Malvasía (majority 75%), Pedro Ximénez, Diego, Listán Blanco, Moscatel, Burrablanca, Breval.
Red: Listán Negra (15%) and Negramoll.

FIGURES:

Vineyard surface: 1,828 – Wine-Growers: 1,742 – Wineries: 14 – 2013 Harvest rating: Excellent – Production 13: 1,523,532 litres – Market percentages: 95% domestic - 5% export.

SOIL:

Volcanic in nature (locally known as 'Picón'). In fact, the cultivation of vines is made possible thanks to the ability of the volcanic sand to perfectly retain the water from dew and the scant rainfall. The island is relatively flat (the maximum altitude is 670 m) and the most characteristic form of cultivation is in 'hollows' surrounded by semicircular walls which protect the plants from the wind. This singular trainig system brings about an extremaly low density.

CLIMATE:

Dry subtropical in nature, with low rainfall (about 200 mm per year) which is spread out irregularly throughout the year. On occasions, the Levante wind (easterly), characterised by its low humidity and which carries sand particles from the African continent, causes a considerable increase in the temperatures.

VINTAGE RATING   PEÑÍNGUIDE

2009	2010	2011	2012	2013
GOOD	EXCELLENT	VERY GOOD	VERY GOOD	VERY GOOD

BODEGA LA FLORIDA

Calle de la Florida, 89
35559 San Bartolomé de Lanzarote
(Las Palmas)
☎: +34 928 593 001

La Florida 2012 T
82

La Florida Malvasía Volcánica 2013 B
86
Colour: bright yellow. Nose: ripe fruit, jasmine, powerfull. Palate: flavourful, fruity, rich, fine bitter notes.

La Florida Moscatel 2012 B
moscatel
88
Colour: golden. Nose: powerfull, floral, honeyed notes, candied fruit, fragrant herbs. Palate: flavourful, sweet, fresh, fruity, good acidity, long.

La Florida Moscatel Essence B
moscatel
89
Colour: golden. Nose: powerfull, floral, honeyed notes, candied fruit, fragrant herbs, toasty. Palate: flavourful, sweet, fresh, fruity, good acidity, long.

BODEGA LA GERIA

Ctra. de la Geria, Km. 19
35570 Yaiza
(Las Palmas de Gran Canaria)
☎: +34 928 173 178
Fax: +34 928 511 370
www.lageria.com
bodega@lageria.com

La Geria 2013 RD
listán negro
86
Colour: light cherry. Nose: red berry notes, wild herbs, balanced. Palate: flavourful, correct, easy to drink.

La Geria 2013 T
syrah, tintilla, merlot, listán negro
86
Colour: bright cherry. Nose: ripe fruit, scrubland. Palate: flavourful, fruity, toasty, round tannins.

La Geria Malvasía 2013 Dulce
malvasía
86
Colour: bright straw, greenish rim. Nose: white flowers, faded flowers, fresh fruit. Palate: fruity, flavourful, good finish.

Manto Seco 2013 B
malvasía
88
Colour: bright straw. Nose: white flowers, fresh fruit, expressive, fine lees, dried herbs. Palate: flavourful, fruity, good acidity, balanced.

Manto Semidulce 2013 B
malvasía
87
Colour: yellow. Nose: expressive, elegant, varietal, fresh. Palate: fruity, easy to drink, good finish, good acidity.

BODEGA MARTINON

Camino del Mentidero, 2
35572 Masdache Tías (Las Palmas)
☎: +34 928 834 160
Fax: +34 928 834 160
www.bodegasmartinon.com
info@bodegasmartinon.com

Martinón Malvasía Seco s/c B
100% malvasía
87
Colour: yellow, greenish rim. Nose: floral, fresh, expressive. Palate: flavourful, fruity, fine bitter notes.

BODEGA VULCANO DE LANZAROTE

Victor Fernández, 5
35572 Tías
(Las Palmas de Gran Canaria)
☎: +34 928 524 469
www.bodegavulcano.es
info@bodegavulcano.es

Vulcano de Lanzarote 2013 RD
85

Vulcano de Lanzarote 2013 T Barrica
87
Colour: bright cherry. Nose: ripe fruit, sweet spices, expressive. Palate: flavourful, fruity, toasty, round tannins.

Vulcano de Lanzarote Malvasía Volcánica Seco 2013 B
100% malvasía volcánica
88
Colour: bright straw. Nose: fresh, expressive, faded flowers. Palate: flavourful, fruity, good acidity, balanced.

Vulcano de Lanzarote Malvasía Volcánica Semidulce 2013 B
86
Colour: bright straw, greenish rim. Nose: medium intensity, fresh, varietal, white flowers. Palate: easy to drink, good finish, fruity.

Vulcano Dolce 2013 B
100% moscatel de alejandría

91

Colour: bright golden. Nose: candied fruit, honeyed notes, expressive, varietal. Palate: long, rich, sweet, complex, balanced.

BODEGAS GUIGUAN
Avda. Los Volcanes, 116
35560 Tinajo (Las Palmas)
☎: +34 928 840 715
Fax: +34 928 840 715
www.bodegasguiguan.com
bodegaguiguan@hotmail.com

Guiguan 2013 T
listán negro

88

Colour: cherry, garnet rim. Nose: ripe fruit, wild herbs, earthy notes, spicy, creamy oak. Palate: balanced, flavourful, long, balsamic.

Guiguan Malvasía Seco 2013 B
malvasía

85

Guiguan Moscatel Dulce 2013 B
moscatel

87

Colour: bright yellow. Nose: powerfull, floral, honeyed notes, fragrant herbs. Palate: flavourful, sweet, fruity, good acidity, long.

Guiguan Semidulce 2013 B
malvasía

84

BODEGAS LOS BERMEJOS
Camino a Los Bermejos, 7
35550 San Bartolomé de Lanzarote
(Las Palmas)
☎: +34 928 522 463
Fax: +34 928 522 641
www.losbermejos.com
bodega@losbermejos.com

Bermejo 2013 RD
listán negro

86

Colour: coppery red. Nose: floral, jasmine, fragrant herbs, faded flowers. Palate: fresh, fruity, flavourful, correct.

Bermejo Diego 2013 B
diego

87

Colour: bright straw. Nose: medium intensity, faded flowers, fresh. Palate: fruity, balanced.

Bermejo Diego Ecológico 2013 B
diego

89 ❦

Colour: bright straw. Nose: fresh fruit, balanced, expressive, floral. Palate: fruity, good acidity, easy to drink, fresh.

Bermejo Listán 2013 RD
listán negro

86 ❦

Colour: coppery red, bright. Nose: balanced, faded flowers, medium intensity, red berry notes. Palate: full, good acidity, long.

Bermejo Listán Negro 2013 T Barrica
listán negro

87

Colour: cherry, garnet rim. Nose: ripe fruit, wild herbs, earthy notes, spicy, creamy oak. Palate: balanced, flavourful, long, balsamic, smoky aftertaste.

Bermejo Listán Negro 2013 T Maceración Carbónica
listán negro

88

Colour: cherry, purple rim. Nose: red berry notes, raspberry, floral, expressive. Palate: fresh, fruity, flavourful, easy to drink.

Bermejo Malvasía 2013 BFB
malvasía

87

Colour: bright yellow. Nose: medium intensity, ripe fruit. Palate: fruity, rich, correct, fine bitter notes.

Bermejo Malvasia 2012 BN
malvasía

88

Colour: bright yellow, greenish rim. Nose: ripe fruit, fine lees, balanced, dried herbs. Palate: good acidity, flavourful, ripe fruit, long.

Bermejo Malvasia Naturalmente Dulce B
malvasía

93

Colour: old gold, amber rim. Nose: complex, expressive, sweet spices, acetaldehyde. Palate: long, complex, balanced.

Bermejo Malvasía Seco 2013 B
malvasía

85

Bermejo Malvasía Seco 2013 B
malvasía

88 ❦

Colour: bright straw. Nose: fresh, balanced, floral, wild herbs. Palate: balanced, good acidity, fine bitter notes, long.

Bermejo Malvasía Semidulce 2013 B
manto negro

87

Colour: bright straw, greenish rim. Nose: balanced, expressive, white flowers. Palate: correct, fruity, flavourful.

Bermejo Moscatel Naturalmente Dulce 2013 B
moscatel

89

Colour: bright yellow. Nose: powerfull, floral, candied fruit, fragrant herbs. Palate: flavourful, sweet, fresh, fruity, good acidity, long.

BODEGAS REYMAR
Pza. Virgen de Los Dolores, 19 Mancha Blanca

35560 Tinajo (Las Palmas)

☎: +34 649 993 096

Fax: +34 928 840 737

www.bodegasreymar.com

reymarmalvasia@terra.com

Los Perdomos 2013 RD
85

Los Perdomos Diego 2013 B
diego

86

Colour: bright yellow, greenish rim. Nose: floral, citrus fruit, balanced, medium intensity. Palate: flavourful, rich, balsamic.

Los Perdomos Listán Negro T
listán negro

89

Colour: very deep cherry, garnet rim. Nose: wild herbs, ripe fruit, candied fruit. Palate: full, flavourful, balsamic.

Los Perdomos Listán Negro 2012 T Barrica
listán negro

84

Los Perdomos Malvasia Dulce 2012 B
malvasía

89

Colour: golden. Nose: powerfull, floral, honeyed notes, candied fruit, sweet spices, creamy oak. Palate: flavourful, sweet, fresh, fruity, good acidity, long.

Los Perdomos Malvasía Moscatel 2013 B
malvasía, moscatel

86

Colour: bright straw. Nose: white flowers, fragrant herbs, fruit expression. Palate: fresh, fruity, flavourful.

Los Perdomos Malvasía Seco 2013 B
86

Colour: bright yellow. Nose: ripe fruit, jasmine. Palate: fruity, flavourful, long, balanced.

Los Perdomos Moscatel Diego 2013 B
86

Colour: bright yellow. Nose: expressive, balanced, varietal, floral. Palate: fruity, easy to drink, correct, good finish.

Los Perdomos Moscatel Dulce 2012 B
moscatel

88

Colour: golden. Nose: powerfull, floral, honeyed notes, candied fruit, sweet spices. Palate: flavourful, sweet, fresh, fruity, good acidity, long.

BODEGAS RUBICÓN
Ctra. Teguise - Yaiza, 2

35570 La Geria - Yaiza (Las Palmas)

☎: +34 928 173 708

www.vinosrubicon.com

bodegasrubicon@gmail.com

Amalia 2013 T
listán negro, tinto conejera, syrah

90

Colour: cherry, garnet rim. Nose: ripe fruit, spicy, creamy oak, toasty, balsamic herbs. Palate: powerful, flavourful, toasty, round tannins.

Amalia Malvasía Seco 2013 B
malvasía

88

Colour: bright yellow. Nose: fresh, fresh fruit, white flowers, expressive. Palate: flavourful, fruity, good acidity, balanced.

Rubicón Malvasía Seco 2013 B
87

Colour: bright yellow. Nose: white flowers, fresh fruit, medium intensity. Palate: flavourful, correct, fine bitter notes.

Rubicón Malvasía Semidulce 2013 B
87

Colour: bright yellow. Nose: medium intensity, white flowers, jasmine. Palate: fruity, flavourful, balanced, long.

Rubicón Moscatel 2013 B
moscatel de alejandría

87

Colour: bright yellow. Nose: white flowers, jasmine, powerfull. Palate: fruity, flavourful, sweet.

EL GRIFO

Lugar de El Grifo, s/n Apdo. Correos, 6
35500 San Bartolomé
(Las Palmas de Gran Canaria)
☎: +34 928 524 036
Fax: +34 928 832 634
www.elgrifo.com
enologo@elgrifo.com

Ariana 2012 T

91

Colour: bright cherry. Nose: ripe fruit, creamy oak, expressive, toasty, scrubland. Palate: flavourful, fruity, toasty, round tannins.

El Grifo 2013 RD

listán negro

87

Colour: rose. Nose: medium intensity, balanced, fresh fruit, wild herbs. Palate: easy to drink, fine bitter notes.

El Grifo Canari Dulce de Licor B

malvasía

95

Colour: old gold. Nose: cocoa bean, varnish, sweet spices, candied fruit, faded flowers, complex, expressive. Palate: long, toasty, ripe fruit, fine solera notes.

El Grifo Listán Negro 2013 T

listán negro

89

Colour: cherry, purple rim. Nose: dry nuts, red berry notes, scrubland, expressive. Palate: fruity, fruity aftestaste, long.

El Grifo Malvasía 2013 BFB

malvasía

89

Colour: bright yellow. Nose: powerfull, ripe fruit, sweet spices, varietal, faded flowers. Palate: rich, flavourful, fresh, good acidity.

El Grifo Malvasía Seco Colección 2013 B

malvasía

90

Colour: bright straw. Nose: expressive, varietal, white flowers. Palate: fresh, fruity, good acidity, balanced.

El Grifo Malvasía Semidulce Colección 2013 B

malvasía

88

Colour: bright straw. Nose: white flowers, fragrant herbs. Palate: fresh, fruity, flavourful, balanced, elegant.

George Glass Dulce de Licor 1999 TC

listán negro

92

Colour: dark-red cherry, orangey edge. Nose: sweet spices, creamy oak, expressive, pattiserie. Palate: flavourful, fruity, toasty.

DO. MÁLAGA Y SIERRAS DE MÁLAGA

CONSEJO REGULADOR
Plaza de los Viñeros,1
29008 Málaga
☎ :+34 952 227 990 - Fax: +34 952 227 990
@: info@vinomalaga.com
www.vinomalaga.com

LOCATION:

In the province of Málaga. It covers 54 municipal areas along the coast (in the vicinity of Málaga and Estepona) and inland (along the banks of the river Genil), together with the new sub-region of Serranía de Ronda, a region to which the two new municipal districts of Cuevas del Becerro and Cortes de la Frontera have been added.

GRAPE VARIETIES:

White: DO Málaga: Pedro Ximénez and Moscatel; DO Sierras de Málaga: Chardonnay, Moscatel, Pedro Ximénez, Macabeo, Sauvignon Blanc and Colombard.
Red (only DO Sierras de Málaga): Romé, Cabernet Sauvignon, Merlot, Syrah, Tempranillo, Petit Verdot.

TYPOLOGY OF CLASSIC WINES:

a) Liqueur wines: from 15 to 22% vol.
b) Natural sweet wines: from 15 to 22 % vol. obtained from the Moscatel or Pedro Ximénez varieties, from musts with a minimum sugar content of 244 grams/litre.
C) Naturally sweet wines (with the same varieties, over 13% vol. and from musts with 300 grams of sugar/litre) and still wines (from 10 to 15% vol.).
Depending on their ageing:
- Málaga Joven: Unaged still wines.- Málaga Pálido: Unaged non-still wines.
- Málaga: Wines aged for between 6 and 24 months.- Málaga Noble: Wines aged for between 2 and 3 years.
- Málaga Añejo: Wines aged for between 3 and 5 years.- Málaga Trasañejo: Wines aged for over 5 years.

FIGURES:

Vineyard surface: 1,000.341 – Wine-Growers: 478 – Wineries: 45 – 2013 Harvest rating: - – Production 13: 2,513,943 litres – Market percentages: 74% domestic - 36% export.

SOIL:

It varies from red Mediterranean soil with limestone components in the northern region to decomposing slate on steep slopes of the Axarquía.

CLIMATE:

Varies depending on the production area. In the northern region, the summers are short with high temperatures, and the average rainfall is in the range of 500 mm; in the region of Axarquía, protected from the northerly winds by the mountain ranges and facing south, the climate is somewhat milder due to the influence of the Mediterranean; whilst in the west, the climate can be defined as dry subhumid.

VINTAGE RATING

PEÑÍNGUIDE

2009	2010	2011	2012	2013
GOOD	GOOD	VERY GOOD	VERY GOOD	VERY GOOD

BODEGA ANTONIO MUÑOZ CABRERA (DIMOBE)

Ctra. Almachar, s/n
29738 Moclinejo (Málaga)
☎: +34 952 400 594
Fax: +34 952 400 743
www.dimobe.es
bodega@dimobe.es

El Lagar de Cabrera Moscatel 2013 B
moscatel de alejandría

83

El Lagar de Cabrera Syrah 2012 T
syrah

88

Colour: cherry, garnet rim. Nose: red berry notes, ripe fruit, floral, fragrant herbs. Palate: powerful, flavourful, spicy, long.

Finca La Indiana 2011 TC
petit verdot

88

Colour: cherry, garnet rim. Nose: ripe fruit, wild herbs, earthy notes, spicy, creamy oak. Palate: balanced, flavourful, long, balsamic.

Lagar de Cabrera 2010 TC
syrah

86

Colour: dark-red cherry, garnet rim. Nose: dark chocolate, sweet spices, ripe fruit. Palate: flavourful, good structure, good acidity, long.

Piamater 2013 B
moscatel de alejandría

88

Colour: bright yellow. Nose: white flowers, jasmine, balanced, varietal. Palate: flavourful, sweet, balanced.

Rujaq Andalusi Trasañejo
moscatel de alejandría

87

Colour: light mahogany. Nose: candied fruit, dried fruit, sweet spices, pattiserie. Palate: flavourful, unctuous, long.

Señorío de Broches 2013 Moscatel
moscatel de alejandría

87

Colour: bright yellow, greenish rim. Nose: medium intensity, white flowers, varietal. Palate: fruity, sweet, rich.

Viña Axarkia Vino de Licor B
moscatel de alejandría

85

Zumbral Moscatel
moscatel de alejandría

85

Zumbral Conarte B
moscatel de alejandría

87

Colour: light mahogany. Nose: balanced, candied fruit, pattiserie, toasty. Palate: flavourful, full, unctuous, long.

BODEGA DOÑA FELISA

Cordel del Puerto s/n
29400 Ronda (Málaga)
☎: +34 951 166 033
Fax: +34 951 166 033
www.chinchillawine.com
info@chinchillawine.com

Chinchilla 2012 T Roble
tempranillo, cabernet sauvignon

88

Colour: bright cherry. Nose: ripe fruit, sweet spices, creamy oak, dried herbs. Palate: flavourful, fruity, round tannins.

Chinchilla 2013 RD
merlot, tempranillo

87

Colour: light cherry. Nose: fresh, medium intensity, dried flowers, red berry notes. Palate: flavourful, long.

Chinchilla Conarte 2008 T
cabernet sauvignon, merlot, syrah

88

Colour: cherry, garnet rim. Nose: ripe fruit, spicy, creamy oak, toasty, complex, scrubland. Palate: powerful, flavourful, toasty, round tannins.

Chinchilla Doble Doce 2008 T
cabernet sauvignon, merlot

88

Colour: cherry, garnet rim. Nose: ripe fruit, wild herbs, spicy, creamy oak. Palate: balanced, flavourful, long, balsamic.

Chinchilla Seis + Seis 2010 T Roble
tempranillo, syrah

89

Colour: bright cherry. Nose: ripe fruit, sweet spices, creamy oak, medium intensity. Palate: fruity, flavourful, toasty.

BODEGA ECOLÓGICA JOAQUÍN FERNÁNDEZ

Paraje Los Frontones s/n
29400 Ronda (Málaga)
☎: +34 951 166 043
Fax: +34 951 166 043
www.bodegajf.com
info@bodegajf.es

Finca Los Frutales Garnacha 2011 T
garnacha, cabernet sauvignon

88

Colour: cherry, garnet rim. Nose: ripe fruit, wild herbs, earthy notes, spicy, creamy oak. Palate: balanced, flavourful, long, balsamic.

Finca Los Frutales Igualados 2008 T
cabernet sauvignon, garnacha, merlot, syrah

87 🌸

Colour: bright cherry. Nose: ripe fruit, creamy oak, medium intensity, spicy, balsamic herbs. Palate: fruity, flavourful, toasty.

Finca Los Frutales Merlot Syrah 2009 TC
merlot, syrah

87 🌸

Colour: cherry, garnet rim. Nose: ripe fruit, spicy, creamy oak, toasty, scrubland. Palate: flavourful, round tannins, correct, easy to drink.

Hacienda Vizcondesa 2010 TC

88 🌸

Colour: cherry, garnet rim. Nose: ripe fruit, spicy, creamy oak, toasty, complex. Palate: powerful, flavourful, toasty, round tannins.

Rosado Finca Los Frutales 2012 RD Roble
merlot, syrah, cabernet sauvignon

86 🌸

Colour: rose, purple rim. Nose: powerfull, ripe fruit, red berry notes, floral, expressive. Palate: powerful, fruity, fresh.

BODEGA F. SCHATZ
Finca Sanguijuela, s/n
29400 Ronda (Málaga)
☎: +34 952 871 313
Fax: +34 952 871 313
www.f-schatz.com
bodega@f-schatz.com

Finca Sanguijuela 2008 TC
89 🌸

Colour: cherry, garnet rim. Nose: ripe fruit, wild herbs, spicy, creamy oak, fine reductive notes. Palate: balanced, flavourful, long, balsamic.

Finca Sanguijuela 2009 T
89 🌸

Colour: dark-red cherry, garnet rim. Nose: expressive, ripe fruit, dried herbs, cocoa bean. Palate: good structure, flavourful, round tannins.

Finca Sanguijuela 2010 T
91 🌸

Colour: cherry, garnet rim. Nose: ripe fruit, fruit liqueur notes, wild herbs, spicy, mineral. Palate: powerful, flavourful, balsamic, balanced.

Finca Sanguijuela 2011 T
90 🌸

Colour: dark-red cherry, garnet rim. Nose: balanced, ripe fruit, spicy, fragrant herbs. Palate: fruity, easy to drink, round tannins.

Schatz Chardonnay 2013 B
100% chardonnay

82 🌸

Schatz Petit Verdot 2007 TC
100% petit verdot

90 🌸

Colour: cherry, garnet rim. Nose: ripe fruit, wild herbs, spicy, creamy oak, fine reductive notes. Palate: balanced, flavourful, long, balsamic.

Schatz Petit Verdot 2008 T
100% petit verdot

85 🌸

Schatz Petit Verdot 2009 T
100% petit verdot

91 🌸

Colour: dark-red cherry. Nose: complex, ripe fruit, elegant, balanced, balsamic herbs, creamy oak. Palate: good structure, flavourful, spicy.

Schatz Petit Verdot 2010 T
100% petit verdot

89 🌸

Colour: bright cherry, purple rim. Nose: balanced, expressive, scrubland, ripe fruit, spicy. Palate: flavourful, balanced.

Schatz Petit Verdot 2011 T
100% petit verdot

88 🌸

Colour: bright cherry, purple rim. Nose: powerfull, ripe fruit, fruit preserve, dried herbs. Palate: balanced, flavourful.

Schatz Pinot Noir 2008 TC
100% pinot noir

91 🌸

Colour: cherry, garnet rim. Nose: fruit liqueur notes, cocoa bean, sweet spices, expressive. Palate: flavourful, balsamic, fine tannins.

Schatz Pinot Noir 2009 T
100% pinot noir

90 🌸

Colour: dark-red cherry, garnet rim. Nose: fruit preserve, powerfull, cocoa bean. Palate: good structure, flavourful, round tannins.

Schatz Pinot Noir 2010 T
100% pinot noir

93 🌸

Colour: dark-red cherry, garnet rim. Nose: red berry notes, ripe fruit, fine reductive notes, balsamic herbs, varietal. Palate: balanced, ripe fruit, round tannins, balsamic.

Schatz Pinot Noir 2011 T

100% pinot noir

92 🌷

Colour: cherry, garnet rim. Nose: ripe fruit, wild herbs, earthy notes, spicy, creamy oak. Palate: balanced, flavourful, long, balsamic.

BODEGA GONZALO BELTRÁN

Finca La Nogalera, Hoya de los Molinos
29400 Ronda (Málaga)
☎: +34 629 455 558
www.bodegagonzalobeltran.com
info@bodegagonzalobeltran.com

Perezoso 2011 T

100% syrah

90

Colour: cherry, garnet rim. Nose: ripe fruit, wild herbs, earthy notes, creamy oak, toasty. Palate: flavourful, spicy, balsamic, long.

BODEGA KIENINGER

Los Frontones, 67 (Apdo. Correos 215)
29400 Ronda (Málaga)
☎: +34 952 879 554
www.bodegakieninger.com
martin@bodegakieninger.com

Vinana Cuvé 2012 T

merlot, cabernet sauvignon, cabernet franc, malbec

91

Colour: cherry, garnet rim. Nose: ripe fruit, wild herbs, earthy notes, spicy, creamy oak. Palate: balanced, flavourful, long, balsamic.

Vinana Pinot Noir 2012 T

100% pinot noir

90 🌷

Colour: light cherry. Nose: medium intensity, floral, red berry notes, balanced, expressive. Palate: fruity, round tannins.

BODEGA LASCAS DE PEDERNAL

Limonar s/n (Nueva Aljaima)
29570 Cartama (Málaga)
☎: +34 952 366 400
www.bodegalascas.com
marketing2@bodegalascas.com

Lascas de Pedernal 2012 B

100% moscatel

88

Colour: bright straw. Nose: fresh, fresh fruit, white flowers, expressive. Palate: flavourful, fruity, good acidity, balanced.

Lascas de Pedernal 2012 T

89

Colour: black cherry. Nose: fruit preserve, dried fruit, sweet spices, creamy oak, toasty, balsamic herbs. Palate: powerful, flavourful, rich, balanced.

Lascas de Pedernal Naturalmente Dulce 2012 B

89

Colour: golden. Nose: powerfull, floral, honeyed notes, candied fruit, fragrant herbs. Palate: flavourful, sweet, fresh, fruity, good acidity, long.

BODEGA PASOSLARGOS

Ctra. Ronda El Burgo, Km 1
29400 Ronda (Málaga)
☎: +34 673 235 072
Fax: +34 952 161 309
www.hoteleljuncalronda.com
bodegapasoslargos@gmail.com

A Pasos 2010 T

90

Colour: cherry, garnet rim. Nose: fruit preserve, fruit liqueur notes, spicy. Palate: flavourful, pruney, balsamic.

Pasos Largos 2008 T Roble

91

Colour: cherry, garnet rim. Nose: ripe fruit, spicy, creamy oak, toasty, complex. Palate: powerful, flavourful, toasty, round tannins.

BODEGA VETAS

Con Nador Finca El Baco
29350 Arriate (Málaga)
☎: +34 647 177 620
www.bodegavetas.com
info@bodegavetas.com

Vetas Petit Verdot 2004 T

100% petit verdot

92

Colour: dark-red cherry, garnet rim. Nose: balanced, cocoa bean, balsamic herbs, ripe fruit. Palate: spicy, ripe fruit, long.

Vetas Petit Verdot 2006 T

100% petit verdot

93

Colour: very deep cherry, garnet rim. Nose: complex, scrubland, creamy oak. Palate: good structure, ripe fruit, balsamic.

Vetas Selección 2008 T

cabernet sauvignon, cabernet franc, petit verdot

93

Colour: cherry, garnet rim. Nose: ripe fruit, spicy, creamy oak, toasty, complex, dark chocolate, earthy notes. Palate: powerful, flavourful, toasty, round tannins.

BODEGA Y VIÑEDOS DE LA CAPUCHINA

Cortijo La Capuchina, Apdo. Correos 26
29532 Mollina (Málaga)
☎: +34 952 111 565
www.bodegalacapuchina.es
info@bodegalacapuchina.es

Capuchina Vieja 2009 T
91
Colour: cherry, garnet rim. Nose: ripe fruit, spicy, creamy oak, complex, scrubland. Palate: powerful, flavourful, toasty, round tannins.

Capuchina Vieja Moscatel Seco 2012 B
100% moscatel de alejandría
87
Colour: bright straw. Nose: fresh, fresh fruit, white flowers, expressive. Palate: flavourful, fruity, good acidity, balanced.

Capuchina Vieja Sol 2013 Blanco dulce
100% moscatel de alejandría
89
Colour: bright yellow. Nose: ripe fruit, white flowers, expressive, varietal. Palate: balanced, good acidity, long, flavourful.

BODEGAS BENTOMIZ

Finca Almendro - Pago Cuesta Robano
29752 Sayalonga (Málaga)
☎: +34 658 845 285
www.bodegasbentomiz.com
info@bodegasbentomiz.com

Ariyanas Naturalmente Dulce 2008 Blanco Dulce
moscatel de alejandría
91
Colour: bright golden. Nose: complex, faded flowers, honeyed notes, balanced. Palate: long, rich, flavourful, sweet.

Ariyanas Romé 2012 RD
100% romé
88
Colour: raspberry rose. Nose: dried flowers, fragrant herbs, red berry notes, ripe fruit. Palate: light-bodied, flavourful, good acidity, long, spicy. Personality.

Ariyanas Seco sobre lías 2012 B
moscatel de alejandría
89
Colour: bright straw. Nose: white flowers, fragrant herbs, fruit expression. Palate: fresh, fruity, flavourful, balanced, elegant. Personality.

Ariyanas Terruño Pizarroso 2008 B
moscatel de alejandría
94
Colour: old gold. Nose: expressive, balanced, sweet spices, cocoa bean, candied fruit, honeyed notes. Palate: spicy, complex, rich.

Ariyanas Tinto de Ensamblaje 2011 T
petit verdot, tempranillo, romé, cabernet franc
88
Colour: dark-red cherry. Nose: ripe fruit, sweet spices, creamy oak, medium intensity, macerated fruit. Palate: fruity, flavourful, toasty, balsamic.

BODEGAS CONRAD

Ctra. El Burgo, Km. 4,0
29400 Ronda (Málaga)
☎: +34 951 166 035
Fax: +34 951 166 035
www.vinosconrad.com
conrad@vinosconrad.com

Creación Conrad Cristina 2011 T
malbec, petit verdot
90
Colour: bright cherry. Nose: ripe fruit, creamy oak, medium intensity, spicy, scrubland. Palate: fruity, flavourful, toasty.

Creación Conrad El Niño León 2011 T
tempranillo, cabernet sauvignon, cabernet franc
88
Colour: cherry, garnet rim. Nose: ripe fruit, spicy, toasty, complex, dried herbs. Palate: powerful, flavourful, toasty, round tannins.

Creación Conrad El Pinsapo 2011 T
cabernet franc, tempranillo
87
Colour: cherry, garnet rim. Nose: ripe fruit, spicy, toasty, complex, dried herbs. Palate: powerful, flavourful, toasty, round tannins.

Creación Conrad Leona Hermosa 2013 B
moscatel grano menudo, viognier, sauvignon blanc
87
Colour: bright straw. Nose: fresh fruit, dried herbs, faded flowers. Palate: fruity, fresh, fine bitter notes.

Creación Conrad San Lorenzo 2011 T
pinot noir, tempranillo
87
Colour: bright cherry. Nose: ripe fruit, sweet spices, creamy oak, expressive, toasty. Palate: flavourful, fruity, toasty, round tannins.

Creación Conrad Soleón 2010 T
merlot, cabernet sauvignon, petit verdot
88
Colour: dark-red cherry, garnet rim. Nose: dried herbs, ripe fruit, spicy, neat. Palate: fruity, good structure, round tannins.

BODEGAS EXCELENCIA

Almendra, 40-42
29004 Ronda (Málaga)
☎: +34 952 870 960
Fax: +34 952 877 002
www.bodegasexcelencia.com
joseluis.lopez@bodegasexcelencia.com

Los Frontones 2009 TC
cabernet sauvignon, cabernet franc, tempranillo, syrah
87
Colour: cherry, garnet rim. Nose: ripe fruit, spicy, creamy oak, toasty, scrubland. Palate: powerful, flavourful, toasty, round tannins.

Tagus 2012 T
100% cabernet franc
88
Colour: bright cherry. Nose: scrubland, toasty, spicy, ripe fruit. Palate: good structure, flavourful, round tannins.

BODEGAS GARCÍA HIDALGO

Partido Rural Los Morales-
LLano de la Cruz s/n
29400 Ronda (Málaga)
☎: +34 600 487 284
www.bodegasgarciahidalgo.es
info@bodegasgarciahidalgo.es

Alcobazín 2012 T Roble
cabernet sauvignon, syrah, merlot
84

Alcobazín 2013 RD
syrah
84

Alcobazín Chardonnay 2013 B
chardonnay
82

Zabel de Alcobazín 2011 TC
cabernet sauvignon, syrah, merlot
86
Colour: cherry, garnet rim. Nose: ripe fruit, spicy, balsamic herbs. Palate: powerful, flavourful, toasty, round tannins.

BODEGAS GOMARA

Diseminado Maqueda Alto, 59
29590 Campanillas (Málaga)
☎: +34 952 434 195
Fax: +34 952 626 312
www.gomara.com
bodegas@gomara.com

Gomara Pedro Ximénez PX
100% pedro ximénez
86
Colour: dark mahogany. Nose: fruit liqueur notes, dried fruit, pattiserie, toasty. Palate: sweet, rich, unctuous, powerful.

Gran Gomara Vino de Licor
pedro ximénez, moscatel de alejandría
91
Colour: iodine, amber rim. Nose: candied fruit, powerfull, dry nuts, sweet spices, toasty. Palate: powerful, flavourful, sweet.

Lacrimae Christi Noble Solera
87
Colour: dark mahogany. Nose: dried fruit, sweet spices, hon-eyed notes. Palate: powerful, flavourful, sweet.

Málaga Cream Noble
90
Colour: light mahogany. Nose: varnish, cocoa bean, caramel. Palate: good structure, flavourful, complex.

Málaga Dulce Gomara B
91
Colour: dark mahogany. Nose: candied fruit, fruit liqueur notes, dark chocolate, sweet spices. Palate: flavourful, sweet, concentrated.

Málaga Trasañejo Gomara Vino de Licor
100% pedro ximénez
91
Colour: mahogany. Nose: cocoa bean, dried fruit, caramel, aged wood nuances. Palate: full, flavourful, long, balanced, toasty.

Pajarete Gomara
100% pedro ximénez
85

Seco Añejo Gomara OL
100% pedro ximénez
86
Colour: bright golden. Nose: ripe fruit, dry nuts, creamy oak. Palate: powerful, flavourful.

BODEGAS JOSÉ MOLINA

Fresca, 4
29170 Colmenar (Málaga)
☎: +34 952 730 956
www.bodegasjosemolina.es
contactar@bodegasjosemolina.es

Primera Intención 2009 T
tempranillo, syrah
85

Primera Intención "Mountain" Naturalmente Dulce B
pedro ximénez
86
Colour: old gold, amber rim. Nose: caramel, varnish, cocoa bean, dry nuts, candied fruit. Palate: spicy, correct.

Primera Intención Seco B
pedro ximénez
85

Primera Intención Tempranillo de Montaña 2011 T
tempranillo
86
Colour: light cherry, garnet rim. Nose: medium intensity, ripe fruit, balanced, spicy. Palate: fruity, fine bitter notes, round tannins.

BODEGAS LUNARES DE RONDA
Ctra. Ronda-Elburgo, km 1,2
29400 Ronda (Málaga)
☎: +34 649 690 847
Fax: +34 952 190 170
www.bodegaslunares.com
pmorales@bodegaslunares.com

Altocielo 2011 T
syrah, cabernet sauvignon
88
Colour: bright cherry. Nose: ripe fruit, sweet spices, creamy oak, medium intensity. Palate: fruity, flavourful, toasty.

Lunares 2012 T
garnacha, syrah
88
Colour: bright cherry. Nose: ripe fruit, sweet spices, creamy oak, expressive, balsamic herbs. Palate: flavourful, fruity, toasty, round tannins.

BODEGAS MÁLAGA VIRGEN
Autovía A-92, Km. 132
29520 Fuente de Piedra (Málaga)
☎: +34 952 319 454
Fax: +34 952 359 819
www.bodegasmalagavirgen.com
bodegas@bodegasmalagavirgen.com

Barón de Rivero 2013 RD
syrah
86
Colour: rose, purple rim. Nose: powerfull, ripe fruit, red berry notes, floral, expressive. Palate: powerful, fruity, fresh.

Barón de Rivero Chardonnay 2013 B
chardonnay
84

Barón de Rivero Verdejo 2013 B
verdejo
87
Colour: bright straw, greenish rim. Nose: fresh, fresh fruit, white flowers, expressive. Palate: flavourful, fruity, good acidity, balanced.

Cartojal Pálido
moscatel de alejandría, moscatel morisco
85

Don Salvador Moscatel 30 años Moscatel
moscatel
93
Colour: mahogany. Nose: cocoa bean, sweet spices, expressive, complex, candied fruit, honeyed notes. Palate: unctuous, balanced, complex, full.

Don Salvador Pedro Ximénez 30 años PX
pedro ximénez
92
Colour: dark mahogany. Nose: complex, fruit liqueur notes, dried fruit, pattiserie, toasty. Palate: sweet, rich, unctuous, powerful.

El Vivillo 2013 T
syrah
86
Colour: cherry, purple rim. Nose: red berry notes, ripe fruit, floral, expressive. Palate: powerful, fresh, fruity, balanced.

Málaga Virgen PX
pedro ximénez
87
Colour: dark mahogany. Nose: complex, fruit liqueur notes, dried fruit, pattiserie, toasty. Palate: sweet, rich, unctuous, powerful.

Moscatel Iberia Malaga
moscatel
85

Moscatel Reserva de Familia Moscatel
moscatel
90
Colour: light mahogany. Nose: expressive, varietal, candied fruit, honeyed notes, jasmine. Palate: flavourful, complex, spicy, long.

Pedro Ximénez Reserva de Familia PX
pedro ximénez
92
Colour: mahogany. Nose: complex, expressive, cocoa bean, pattiserie, dried fruit, honeyed notes. Palate: unctuous, balanced, full.

Pernales Syrah 2010 T
syrah
88
Colour: bright cherry. Nose: ripe fruit, sweet spices, expressive, violet drops. Palate: flavourful, fruity, toasty, round tannins.

Seco Trasañejo B
pedro ximénez

92

Colour: dark mahogany. Nose: expressive, balanced, candied fruit, honeyed notes. Palate: complex, flavourful, spicy, long.

Sol de Málaga Vino de Licor
pedro ximénez, moscatel de alejandría

88

Colour: dark mahogany. Nose: toasty, aromatic coffee, dark chocolate, fruit liqueur notes. Palate: creamy, balanced, fruity, sweet.

Trajinero Añejo
pedro ximénez

89

Colour: old gold, amber rim. Nose: aged wood nuances, dry nuts, spicy, pattiserie. Palate: balanced, powerful, flavourful.

Tres Leones B
moscatel de alejandría

85

BODEGAS MOROSANTO
Ctra. Arriate - Setenil, Km. 1,6
29400 Ronda (Málaga)
☎: +34 619 124 208
www.bodegasmorosanto.com
bodega@bogasmorosanto.com

Morosanto Cabernet Sauvignon 2010 TC
cabernet sauvignon

91

Colour: cherry, garnet rim. Nose: ripe fruit, wild herbs, earthy notes, spicy, creamy oak, expressive. Palate: balanced, flavourful, long, balsamic.

BODEGAS QUITAPENAS
Ctra. de Guadalmar, 12
29004 Málaga (Málaga)
☎: +34 952 247 595
Fax: +34 952 105 138
www.quitapenas.es
ventas@quitapenas.es

BT. Málaga Oro Viejo 2009 Trasañejo

86

Colour: mahogany. Nose: caramel, fruit liqueur notes, dried fruit, sweet spices. Palate: flavourful, rich, long.

Guadalvin 2012 T
syrah

82

Málaga PX 2010 Noble
pedro ximénez

87

Colour: light mahogany. Nose: powerfull, fruit liqueur notes, pattiserie, honeyed notes. Palate: long, creamy, toasty.

Quitapenas Málaga Dulce Malaga
pedro ximénez

88

Colour: dark mahogany. Nose: caramel, cocoa bean, pattiserie. Palate: flavourful, balanced, unctuous, sweet.

Quitapenas Moscatel Dorado
moscatel

85

Vegasol 2013 B
moscatel

83

BODEGAS SÁNCHEZ ROSADO
Pacífico, 3 5ºC
29004 Málaga (Málaga)
☎: +34 600 504 302
Fax: +34 952 213 644
www.bodegassanchezrosado.com
info@bodegassanchezrosado.com

Cartima Siglo XXI (CSXXI) 2012 T
tempranillo, garnacha, merlot, syrah

85

Cartima Siglo XXI (CSXXI) 2013 B
moscatel

85

BODEGAS VILORIA
Avda. Málaga, 50 Fase 11, 2ºC
29400 Ronda (Málaga)
☎: +34 637 531 800
www.bodegasviloria.es
bodegasviloria@hotmail.es

Lagarejo 2005 T
tempranillo, cabernet sauvignon, syrah, merlot

86

Colour: dark-red cherry, orangey edge. Nose: spicy, fine reductive notes, wet leather, aged wood nuances, toasty. Palate: spicy, long, toasty.

Lagarejo 2012 RD Roble
petit verdot, syrah

84

Lagarejo Cabernet Sauvignon S/C T
cabernet sauvignon

80

Lagarejo Selección 2007 T
tempranillo, cabernet sauvignon, syrah, merlot

87

Colour: dark-red cherry, garnet rim. Nose: balanced, balsamic herbs, spicy, toasty. Palate: correct, balanced, round tannins.

Lagarejo Selección 2008 TR
tempranillo, cabernet sauvignon, syrah, merlot

87

Colour: dark-red cherry. Nose: spicy, dried herbs, ripe fruit. Palate: balanced, round tannins, balsamic.

Lagarejo Tempranillo 2012 T
tempranillo

85

COMPAÑÍA DE VINOS TELMO RODRÍGUEZ
El Monte
01308 Lanciego (Álava)
☎: +34 945 628 315
Fax: +34 945 628 314
www.telmorodriguez.com
contact@telmorodriguez.com

Molino Real 2010 B
moscatel de alejandría

96

Colour: golden. Nose: powerfull, floral, honeyed notes, candied fruit, fragrant herbs. Palate: flavourful, sweet, fresh, fruity, good acidity, long.

Mountain 2012 B
moscatel

92

Colour: bright straw. Nose: candied fruit, expressive, dried herbs, grassy. Palate: powerful, good acidity, fine bitter notes.

MR 2011 B
moscatel de alejandría

95

Colour: bright yellow. Nose: white flowers, ripe fruit, candied fruit, petrol notes. Palate: good acidity, sweetness, balanced.

Old Mountain 2005 B
moscatel de alejandría

97

Colour: golden. Nose: powerfull, honeyed notes, candied fruit, fragrant herbs, acetaldehyde. Palate: flavourful, sweet, fresh, fruity, good acidity, long.

CORTIJO LA FUENTE
Avda. La Fuente, 10
29532 Mollina (Málaga)
☎: +34 663 045 906
www.bodegacortijolafuente.es
cortijolafuente@terra.com

Cortijo La Fuente 2012 Blanco Afrutado
moscatel grano menudo

86

Colour: bright yellow. Nose: floral, balanced, varietal, fresh fruit. Palate: fresh, easy to drink, good finish.

Cortijo La Fuente 2012 T Roble
cabernet sauvignon, syrah

87

Colour: very deep cherry, garnet rim. Nose: powerfull, ripe fruit, roasted coffee, dark chocolate. Palate: powerful, toasty, fruity aftestaste.

Cortijo La Fuente Blanco Pedro Ximénez PX
pedro ximénez

85

Cortijo La Fuente Montes Solera Semidulce
moscatel, pedro ximénez

84

CORTIJO LOS AGUILARES
Paraje Cortijo El Calero s/n Apdo. 119
29400 Ronda (Málaga)
☎: +34 952 874 457
Fax: +34 951 166 000
www.cortijolosaguilares.com
bodega@cortijolosaguilares.com

Cortijo Los Aguilares 2013 RD
89

Colour: light cherry, bright. Nose: floral, fresh fruit, elegant, balanced. Palate: fruity, fresh, balanced, good acidity.

Cortijo Los Aguilares 2013 T
89

Colour: very deep cherry, purple rim. Nose: violet drops, red berry notes, balanced. Palate: fruity, flavourful, fruity aftestaste.

Cortijo Los Aguilares Pago El Espino 2010 T
92

Colour: cherry, garnet rim. Nose: ripe fruit, spicy, creamy oak, complex, cocoa bean. Palate: flavourful, toasty, round tannins, spicy.

Cortijo Los Aguilares Pago El Espino 2011 T
petit verdot, tempranillo, merlot

92

Colour: cherry, garnet rim. Nose: ripe fruit, earthy notes, spicy, creamy oak, scrubland. Palate: flavourful, long, balsamic, balanced.

Cortijo Los Aguilares Pinot Noir 2012 T
100% pinot noir

92

Colour: light cherry. Nose: wild herbs, earthy notes, spicy, creamy oak, fruit liqueur notes. Palate: balanced, flavourful, long, balsamic.

Cortijo Los Aguilares Pinot Noir 2013 T
100% pinot noir

94

Colour: light cherry. Nose: expressive, varietal, red berry notes, elegant, floral. Palate: flavourful, good structure, round tannins, balanced, good acidity.

Cortijo Los Aguilares Tadeo 2012 T
100% petit verdot

95

Colour: cherry, garnet rim. Nose: ripe fruit, spicy, creamy oak, toasty, complex, dark chocolate, earthy notes. Palate: flavourful, round tannins, good structure, balsamic.

FINCA LA MELONERA
Paraje Los Frontones,
Camino Ronda-Setenil s/n
29400 Ronda (Malaga)
☎: +34 951 194 018
www.lamelonera.com
info@lamelonera.com

Embajador Gálvez 2012 T
tintilla de rota, romé, melonera

93

Colour: cherry, garnet rim. Nose: ripe fruit, spicy, creamy oak, toasty, complex, dark chocolate, earthy notes, balsamic herbs. Palate: powerful, flavourful, toasty, round tannins.

La Encina del Inglés 2013 B
88

Colour: bright straw. Nose: fresh, fresh fruit, white flowers. Palate: flavourful, fruity, good acidity, balanced.

Payoya Negra 2011 T
syrah, tintilla de rota, cabernet sauvignon

93

Colour: cherry, garnet rim. Nose: ripe fruit, spicy, creamy oak, complex, cocoa bean, dried herbs. Palate: powerful, flavourful, toasty, round tannins.

Yo sólo 2011 T
100% romé

91

Colour: bright cherry. Nose: ripe fruit, sweet spices, creamy oak, expressive. Palate: flavourful, fruity, toasty, round tannins.

JORGE ORDÓÑEZ & CO
Bartolome Esteban Murillo, 11
29700 Velez-Málaga (Málaga)
☎: +34 952 504 706
Fax: +34 951 284 796
www.jorgeordonez.es
info@jorgeordonez.es

Jorge Ordóñez & Co Botani 2013 B
100% moscatel de alejandría

92

Colour: bright straw. Nose: fresh, fresh fruit, white flowers, expressive. Palate: flavourful, fruity, good acidity.

Jorge Ordóñez & Co Botani Garnacha 2013 T
100% garnacha

91

Colour: cherry, purple rim. Nose: red berry notes, balsamic herbs, fragrant herbs. Palate: flavourful, ripe fruit, good acidity.

Jorge Ordóñez & Co Nº 1 Selección Especial 2013 B
moscatel de alejandría

94

Colour: golden. Nose: powerfull, floral, honeyed notes, candied fruit, fragrant herbs. Palate: flavourful, sweet, fresh, fruity, good acidity, long.

Jorge Ordóñez & Co Nº 2 Victoria 2013 B
moscatel de alejandría

95

Colour: golden. Nose: powerfull, floral, honeyed notes, candied fruit, fragrant herbs. Palate: flavourful, sweet, fresh, fruity, good acidity, long.

Jorge Ordóñez & Co. Nº3 Viñas Viejas 2010 B
100% moscatel de alejandría

96

Colour: bright golden. Nose: acetaldehyde, fruit preserve, faded flowers. Palate: good acidity, balanced, round, unctuous.

LAGAR DE BAILLO
Pasaje Parroco Juan Estrada, 2
29014 Málaga (Málaga)
☎: +34 687 952 350
lagardebaillo@hotmail.es

Baillalto 2010 TC
cabernet sauvignon, tempranillo, romé

88

Colour: cherry, garnet rim. Nose: ripe fruit, spicy, toasty, complex, scrubland. Palate: powerful, flavourful, toasty, round tannins.

SAMSARA WINES
Partida Los Molinos s/n
29400 Ronda (Málaga)
☎: +34 697 911 440
www.samsarawines.com
pablochaconv@gmail.com

Samsara 2011 TC
100% petit verdot

93 ❀

Colour: cherry, garnet rim. Nose: ripe fruit, spicy, creamy oak, complex, elegant, scrubland. Palate: powerful, flavourful, toasty, round tannins.

SEDELLA VINOS

Término Las Viñuelas, s/n
29715 Sedella (Málaga)
☎: +34 687 463 082
Fax: +34 967 140 723
www.sedellavinos.com
info@sedellavinos.com

Laderas de Sedella 2013 T
romé, garnacha, Jaen tinto, cabernet sauvignon

89

Colour: bright cherry, purple rim. Nose: red berry notes, balanced, balsamic herbs, floral. Palate: powerful, flavourful, toasty, round tannins.

Sedella 2012 T
romé, garnacha, Jaen tinto, moscatel romano

91

Colour: cherry, purple rim. Nose: red berry notes, balanced, faded flowers, fresh. Palate: fruity, flavourful, good acidity, round tannins.

TIERRAS DE MOLLINA

Avda. de las Américas, s/n (Cortijo Colarte)
29532 Mollina (Málaga)
☎: +34 952 841 451
Fax: +34 952 842 555
www.tierrasdemollina.net
administracion@tierrasdemollina.net

Carpe Diem Málaga Añejo
pedro ximénez

89

Colour: dark mahogany. Nose: candied fruit, varnish, sweet spices, cocoa bean. Palate: flavourful, full, spicy, long.

Carpe Diem Dulce Natural B
moscatel

88

Colour: golden. Nose: powerfull, floral, honeyed notes, candied fruit. Palate: flavourful, sweet, fresh, fruity, good acidity, long.

Carpe Diem Málaga Trasañejo Málaga
pedro ximénez

91

Colour: dark mahogany. Nose: candied fruit, roasted almonds, sweet spices, pattiserie. Palate: flavourful, full, balanced.

Montespejo 2012 T
syrah

85

Montespejo 2012 T Roble
syrah, merlot

85

Montespejo 2013 B
lairén, doradilla, moscatel

81

Montespejo Cepas Viejas 2012 BFB
doradilla

87

Colour: bright yellow. Nose: powerfull, ripe fruit, sweet spices, toasty. Palate: rich, smoky aftertaste, flavourful, good acidity.

DO. MANCHUELA

CONSEJO REGULADOR

Avda. San Agustín, 9
02270 Villamalea (Albacete)
☎ :+34 967 090 694 - Fax: +34 967 090 696
@: domanchuela@lamanchuela.es
www.do-manchuela.com

LOCATION:

The production area covers the territory situated in the southeast of the province of Cuenca and the northeast of Albacete, between the rivers Júcar and Cabriel. It comprises 70 municipal districts, 26 of which are in Albacete and the rest in Cuenca.

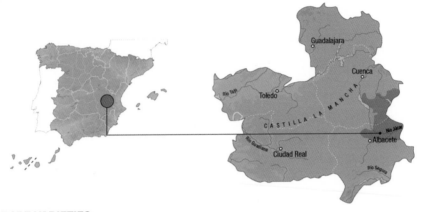

GRAPE VARIETIES:

White: Albillo, Chardonnay, Macabeo, Sauvignon Blanc, Verdejo, Pardillo, Viognier and Moscatel de Grano Menudo.
Red: Bobal, Cabernet Sauvignon, Cencibel (Tempranillo), Garnacha, Merlot, Monastrell, Moravia Dulce, Syrah, Garnacha Tintorera, Malbec, Moravia agria, Mazuelo, Graciano, Rojal, Frasco (Tinto Velasco), Petit Verdot, Cabernet Franc and Pinot Noir.

FIGURES:

Vineyard surface: 5,201 – Wine-Growers: 774 – Wineries: 32 – 2013 Harvest rating: Good – Production 13: 1,300,000 litres – Market percentages: 10% domestic - 90% export.

SOIL:

The vineyards are situated at an altitude ranging between 600 and 700 m above sea level. The terrain is mainly flat, except for the ravines outlined by the rivers. Regarding the composition of the terrain, below a clayey surface of gravel or sand, the soil is limy, which is an important quality factor for the region.

CLIMATE:

The climate is continental in nature, with cold winters and hot summers, although the cool and humid winds from the Mediterranean during the summer help to lower the temperatures at night, so creating favourable day-night temperature contrasts for a slow ripening of the grapes.

VINTAGE RATING

PEÑINGUIDE

2009	2010	2011	2012	2013
VERY GOOD	VERY GOOD	VERY GOOD	VERY GOOD	GOOD

ALTOLANDÓN

Ctra. N-330, km. 242
16330 Landete (Cuenca)
☎: +34 677 228 974
Fax: +34 962 300 662
www.altolandon.com
altolandon@altolandon.com

Altolandón 2009 T
syrah, garnacha, cabernet franc

92 🌷

Colour: cherry, garnet rim. Nose: ripe fruit, spicy, creamy oak, toasty, roasted coffee. Palate: powerful, flavourful, toasty, round tannins.

Altolandón White 2011 BFB
chardonnay, petit manseng

91 🌷

Colour: bright golden. Nose: ripe fruit, dry nuts, powerfull, toasty, aged wood nuances. Palate: flavourful, spicy, toasty, fine bitter notes.

CF de Altolandón 2011 T
cabernet franc

93 🌷

Colour: cherry, garnet rim. Nose: ripe fruit, wild herbs, earthy notes, spicy, creamy oak. Palate: balanced, flavourful, long, balsamic.

Irrepetible 2012 T
syrah, malbec

91 🌷

Colour: bright cherry. Nose: ripe fruit, sweet spices, creamy oak, expressive. Palate: flavourful, fruity, toasty, round tannins.

Rayuelo 2011 T
100% bobal

93 🌷

Colour: cherry, garnet rim. Nose: wild herbs, earthy notes, spicy, creamy oak, candied fruit. Palate: balanced, flavourful, long, balsamic.

BODEGA INIESTA

Ctra. Fuentealbilla Villamalea, km. 1,5
02260 Fuentealbilla (Albacete)
☎: +34 967 090 650
Fax: +34 967 090 651
www.bodegainiesta.es
info@bodegainiesta.com

Corazón Loco 2012 T
tempranillo, syrah

89

Colour: bright cherry. Nose: ripe fruit, sweet spices. Palate: flavourful, fruity, toasty, round tannins.

Corazón Loco 2013 B
verdejo, sauvignon blanc

84

Corazón Loco 2013 RD
bobal

87

Colour: brilliant rose. Nose: fresh fruit, balsamic herbs, red berry notes. Palate: flavourful, fruity, fresh.

Corazón Loco Nature 2012 T
tempranillo, syrah

84 🌷

Corazón Loco Premium 2010 T
syrah, petit verdot, cabernet sauvignon

91

Colour: cherry, garnet rim. Nose: ripe fruit, spicy, creamy oak, toasty, complex. Palate: powerful, flavourful, toasty, round tannins.

Corazón Loco Selección 2010 T
syrah, petit verdot, tempranillo, cabernet sauvignon

88

Colour: cherry, garnet rim. Nose: spicy, creamy oak, toasty, complex. Palate: powerful, flavourful, toasty, round tannins.

Dulce Corazón 2013 B
moscatel

90

Colour: bright straw. Nose: powerfull, floral, honeyed notes, candied fruit, fragrant herbs. Palate: flavourful, sweet, fruity, good acidity.

Dulce Corazón Semidulce 2013 RD
bobal

88

Colour: coppery red. Nose: elegant, candied fruit, dried flowers, fragrant herbs. Palate: light-bodied, flavourful, good acidity, long, balanced.

Finca El Carril 2011 TC
tempranillo, petit verdot, syrah

90

Colour: cherry, garnet rim. Nose: ripe fruit, spicy, creamy oak, toasty, mineral. Palate: powerful, flavourful, toasty, round tannins.

Finca El Carril 2012 B
macabeo, chardonnay

86

Colour: bright straw. Nose: white flowers, fragrant herbs. Palate: fresh, fruity, fine bitter notes.

Finca El Carril Hechicero 2010 TC
syrah, petit verdot, tempranillo, cabernet sauvignon

90

Colour: bright cherry. Nose: ripe fruit, sweet spices, creamy oak, mineral. Palate: fruity, flavourful, toasty.

Finca El Carril Valeria 2012 BFB
chardonnay, viognier

88

Colour: bright yellow. Nose: powerfull, ripe fruit, sweet spices, creamy oak, fragrant herbs. Palate: rich, smoky aftertaste, good acidity.

BODEGA PARDO TOLOSA
Villatoya, 26
02215 Alborea (Albacete)
☎: +34 963 517 067
Fax: +34 963 517 091
www.bodegapardotolosa.com
export@bodegapardotolosa.com

La Sima 2013 T
bobal, tempranillo

85

Mizaran Bobal 2013 RD
100% bobal

83

Mizaran Tempranillo 2009 T
100% tempranillo

84

Senda de las Rochas 2008 TC
100% tempranillo

88

Colour: very deep cherry, garnet rim. Nose: powerfull, ripe fruit, roasted coffee, dark chocolate. Palate: powerful, toasty, roasted-coffee aftertaste.

Senda de las Rochas Bobal 2011 T
100% bobal

85

BODEGA VIRGEN DE LAS NIEVES
Paseo Virgen de las Nieves
02247 Cenizate (Albacete)
☎: +34 967 482 006
Fax: +34 967 482 805
www.virgendelasnieves.com
comercial@virgendelasnives.com

Artesones de Cenizate 2008 TR
tempranillo

85

Artesones de Cenizate 2010 TC

84

Artesones de Cenizate 2013 B
macabeo

85

Artesones de Cenizate 2013 RD
bobal

87

Colour: rose, purple rim. Nose: powerfull, ripe fruit, red berry notes, floral, expressive. Palate: powerful, fruity, fresh.

Artesones de Cenizate Petit Verdot 2012 T
petit verdot

84

Artesones de Cenizate Semidulce 2013 B
macabeo

86

Colour: bright straw. Nose: candied fruit, citrus fruit, floral. Palate: flavourful, sweetness.

Artesones de Cenizate Semidulce 2013 RD
bobal

88

Colour: rose, purple rim. Nose: powerfull, ripe fruit, red berry notes. Palate: powerful, fruity, sweet, balanced.

Artesones de Cenizate Tempranillo 2012 T
tempranillo

86

Colour: cherry, garnet rim. Nose: ripe fruit, balsamic herbs, powerfull. Palate: flavourful, balanced, easy to drink.

BODEGAS EL MOLAR
Finca El Molar de Rus
02260 Fuentealbilla (Albacete)
☎: +34 647 075 371
www.elmolarderus.com
info@elmolarderus.com

Quantum 2012 TC
cabernet sauvignon, merlot, syrah

87

Colour: cherry, garnet rim. Nose: spicy, creamy oak, toasty, complex, ripe fruit. Palate: powerful, flavourful, toasty, round tannins.

Quantum Multi-variety 2011 T

87

Colour: cherry, garnet rim. Nose: fruit preserve, fruit liqueur notes, spicy. Palate: flavourful, pruney, balsamic.

Quantum Syrah 2011 T Roble
syrah

86

Colour: bright cherry. Nose: ripe fruit, sweet spices, creamy oak, expressive. Palate: flavourful, fruity, toasty, round tannins.

BODEGAS RECIAL

Libertad, 1
02154 Pozo Lorente (Albacete)
☎: +34 630 418 264
Fax: +34 967 572 063
www.bodegasrecial.com
gerencia@bodegasrecial.com

Divina Putea 2009 TR
garnacha tintorera
89
Colour: very deep cherry. Nose: ripe fruit, spicy, creamy oak, toasty, characterful. Palate: powerful, flavourful, toasty, round tannins.

Púrpura 2013 B
sauvignon blanc
80

Púrpura Pozo Lorente 2009 TC
garnacha tintorera
87
Colour: bright cherry. Nose: ripe fruit, sweet spices, creamy oak, medium intensity. Palate: fruity, flavourful, toasty.

BODEGAS VILLAVID, D.N.J. S. COOP. DE CLM

Niño Jesús, 25
16280 Villarta (Cuenca)
☎: +34 962 189 006
Fax: +34 962 189 125
www.villavid.com
export@villavid.com

Villavid 2011 TC
100% syrah
85

Villavid 2013 B
100% macabeo
81

Villavid 2013 RD
100% bobal
87
Colour: rose. Nose: candied fruit, floral. Palate: spicy, ripe fruit.

Villavid 2013 T
100% tempranillo
84

BODEGAS VITIVINOS

Camino de Cabezuelas, s/n
02270 Villamalea (Albacete)
☎: +34 967 483 114
Fax: +34 967 483 964
www.vitivinos.com
info@vitivinos.com

Azua 2008 TC
bobal
87
Colour: bright cherry. Nose: sweet spices, creamy oak, medium intensity, ripe fruit. Palate: flavourful, fruity, toasty, round tannins.

Azua 2008 TR
bobal
87
Colour: pale ruby, brick rim edge. Nose: spicy, fine reductive notes, wet leather, aged wood nuances, fruit liqueur notes. Palate: spicy, fine tannins.

Azua Bobal 2012 T Roble
bobal
88
Colour: cherry, purple rim. Nose: expressive, fresh fruit, red berry notes, floral. Palate: flavourful, fruity, good acidity, round tannins.

Azua Bobal 2013 RD
bobal
86
Colour: rose, purple rim. Nose: powerfull, ripe fruit, red berry notes, floral, expressive. Palate: powerful, fruity, fresh.

Azua Macabeo 2013 B
macabeo
84

Azua Verdejo 2013 B
verdejo
85

BODEGAS Y VIÑEDOS PONCE

Ctra. San Clemente s/n
16230 Villanueva de la Jara (Cuenca)
☎: +34 677 434 523
Fax: +34 967 220 876
bodegasponce@gmail.com

Clos Lojen 2013 T
bobal
92
Colour: cherry, purple rim. Nose: red berry notes, raspberry, fragrant herbs, balsamic herbs. Palate: flavourful, light-bodied, good acidity, fresh, fruity.

P.F. 2012 T
100% bobal
93
Colour: cherry, garnet rim. Nose: spicy, complex, earthy notes, creamy oak. Palate: powerful, flavourful, toasty, round tannins.

Pino 2012 T
100% bobal
94
Colour: cherry, garnet rim. Nose: ripe fruit, wild herbs, earthy notes, spicy, creamy oak, balsamic herbs. Palate: balanced, flavourful, long, balsamic.

CIEN Y PICO
San Francisco, 19
02240 Mahora (Albacete)
☎: +34 610 239 186
www.cienypico.com
caterina@cienypico.com

En Vaso 2012 T
100% bobal
90
Colour: bright cherry. Nose: sweet spices, creamy oak, expressive, ripe fruit. Palate: flavourful, fruity, toasty, round tannins.

Knights Errant 2008 T
100% garnacha tintorera
91
Colour: cherry, garnet rim. Nose: ripe fruit, spicy, creamy oak, toasty, complex. Palate: powerful, flavourful, toasty, round tannins.

Knights Errant 2009 T
100% garnacha tintorera
88
Colour: very deep cherry, garnet rim. Nose: powerfull, ripe fruit, roasted coffee, dark chocolate. Palate: powerful, toasty, roasted-coffee aftertaste.

Winemaker's Gallant 2011 T
100% bobal
87
Colour: very deep cherry, garnet rim. Nose: powerfull, ripe fruit, roasted coffee, dark chocolate. Palate: powerful, toasty, roasted-coffee aftertaste.

COOP. DEL CAMPO SAN ISIDRO
Extramuros, s/n
02215 Alborea (Albacete)
☎: +34 967 477 067
Fax: +34 967 477 096
www.vinosalborea.com
coopalborea@telefonica.net

Alterón 2010 TC
cencibel
83

Alterón 2013 B
macabeo
80

Alterón 2013 RD
100% bobal
87
Colour: rose, purple rim. Nose: powerfull, ripe fruit, red berry notes, expressive. Palate: powerful, fruity, fresh.

COOPERATIVA SAN ANTONIO ABAD BODEGAS SAAC
Valencia, 41
02270 Villamalea (Albacete)
☎: +34 967 483 023
Fax: +34 967 483 536
www.bodegas-saac.com
saac@bodegas-saac.com

Altos del Cabriel 2013 B
macabeo
84

Altos del Cabriel 2013 RD
bobal
88
Colour: rose, purple rim. Nose: powerfull, ripe fruit, red berry notes, floral. Palate: powerful, fruity, fresh.

Altos del Cabriel 2013 T
tempranillo
87
Colour: cherry, purple rim. Nose: expressive, fresh fruit, red berry notes, floral. Palate: flavourful, fruity, good acidity, round tannins.

Altos del Cabriel Semidulce 2013 B
macabeo
87
Colour: bright straw. Nose: ripe fruit, tropical fruit. Palate: flavourful, fruity, fresh, sweetness.

Gredas Viejas 2009 TR
syrah
88
Colour: cherry, garnet rim. Nose: ripe fruit, spicy, toasty. Palate: powerful, flavourful, toasty, round tannins.

Viñamalea 2008 TC
tempranillo, syrah
83

FINCA SANDOVAL

Ctra. CM-3222, Km. 26,800
16237 Ledaña (Cuenca)
☎: +34 696 910 769
www.grandespagos.com
fincasandoval@gmail.com

Finca Sandoval 2009 T
syrah, monastrell, bobal

93

Colour: cherry, garnet rim. Nose: creamy oak, toasty, complex, overripe fruit. Palate: powerful, flavourful, toasty, round tannins.

Finca Sandoval Cuvée Cecilia 2012 T
syrah, moscatel de alejandría

91

Colour: cherry, garnet rim. Nose: fruit preserve, ripe fruit, spicy, toasty, aged wood nuances. Palate: powerful, flavourful, sweetness.

Salia 2010 T
syrah, garnacha tintorera, garnacha

92

Colour: cherry, garnet rim. Nose: ripe fruit, spicy, creamy oak, toasty. Palate: powerful, flavourful, toasty, round tannins.

Signo Bobal 2011 T
bobal, syrah

92

Colour: very deep cherry. Nose: spicy, creamy oak, toasty, characterful, candied fruit, ripe fruit. Palate: powerful, flavourful, toasty, round tannins.

NUESTRA SEÑORA DE LA CABEZA DE CASAS IBÁÑEZ SOC. COOP. DE CLM

Avda. del Vino, 10
02200 Casas Ibáñez (Albacete)
☎: +34 967 460 266
Fax: +34 967 460 105
www.coop-cabeza.com
info@coop-cabeza.com

Viaril 2012 BFB
macabeo

90

Colour: bright yellow. Nose: powerfull, ripe fruit, sweet spices, creamy oak, fragrant herbs. Palate: rich, flavourful, fresh, good acidity.

Viaril 2011 T

84

Viaril 2013 RD

86

Colour: brilliant rose. Nose: ripe fruit, red berry notes, floral, expressive. Palate: powerful, fruity, fresh.

Viaril Cabernet Sauvignon 2011 T
cabernet sauvignon

85

Viaril Selección 2013 T

84

NUESTRA SEÑORA DE LA ESTRELLA S.COOP.

Elías Fernández, 10
16290 El Herrumbar (Cuenca)
☎: +34 962 313 029
Fax: +34 962 313 232
info@antaresvinos.es

Antares 2012 T Fermentado en Barrica
syrah

87

Colour: bright cherry. Nose: ripe fruit, sweet spices, creamy oak, expressive. Palate: flavourful, fruity, toasty, round tannins.

Antares 2012 TC
syrah

89

Colour: bright cherry. Nose: sweet spices, creamy oak, fruit expression. Palate: flavourful, fruity, toasty, round tannins.

Antares 2013 RD
bobal

88

Colour: brilliant rose. Nose: candied fruit, dried flowers, fragrant herbs, red berry notes. Palate: light-bodied, flavourful, good acidity, long, spicy.

Antares Macabeo 2013 B
macabeo

87

Colour: bright straw. Nose: fresh, fresh fruit, white flowers, expressive. Palate: flavourful, fruity, good acidity, balanced.

Antares Sauvignon Blanc 2013 B
sauvignon blanc

85

Antares Sauvignon Blanc 2013 BFB
sauvignon blanc

87

Colour: bright yellow. Nose: sweet spices, creamy oak, tropical fruit. Palate: rich, smoky aftertaste, good acidity.

SAN ISIDRO SC DE CLM

Ctra. Valencia, 6
02240 Mahora (Albacete)
☎: +34 967 494 058
www.vinosmahora.com
joseangel.montero@gmail.com

Mahora 2010 TC
tempranillo
87
Colour: bright cherry. Nose: ripe fruit, sweet spices, creamy oak, medium intensity. Palate: fruity, flavourful, toasty.

SOC. COOP. AGRARIA DE CLM SAN ISIDRO

Ctra. de Albacete, s/n
16220 Quintanar del Rey (Cuenca)
☎: +34 967 495 052
Fax: +34 967 496 750
www.bodegasanisidro.es
gerencia@bodegasanisidro.es

Monte de las Mozas 2013 B
100% macabeo
86
Colour: bright straw. Nose: citrus fruit, medium intensity. Palate: flavourful, light-bodied.

Monte de las Mozas 2013 RD
bobal
86
Colour: rose, purple rim. Nose: powerfull, ripe fruit, red berry notes, floral, expressive. Palate: powerful, fruity, fresh.

Quinta Regia 2012 T
100% bobal
88
Colour: cherry, garnet rim. Nose: fruit liqueur notes, mineral, dry stone. Palate: spicy, ripe fruit.

Zaíno 2011 T Roble
tempranillo
85

Zaíno Syrah 2012 T
syrah
85

UNION CAMPESINA INIESTENSE

San Idefonso, 1
16235 Iniesta (Cuenca)
☎: +34 967 490 120
Fax: +34 967 490 777
www.cooperativauci.com
aurora@cooperativauci.com

Realce Bobal 2013 RD
bobal
87
Colour: rose, purple rim, rose, brilliant rose. Nose: powerfull, ripe fruit, red berry notes, floral, expressive. Palate: powerful, fruity, fresh.

Realce Tempranillo 2009 TC
tempranillo
84

Realce Tempranillo 2012 T
tempranillo
86
Colour: cherry, garnet rim. Nose: ripe fruit, grassy. Palate: balsamic, fine bitter notes, soft tannins.

VEGA TOLOSA

Pol. Ind. Calle B, 11
02200 Casas Ibáñez (Albacete)
☎: +34 967 461 331
www.vegatolosa.com
info@vegatolosa.com

11 Pinos Bobal Old Vines 2013 T Roble
bobal
91
Colour: bright cherry. Nose: ripe fruit, sweet spices, creamy oak, expressive, earthy notes. Palate: flavourful, fruity, toasty, round tannins.

Bobal Icon 2012 T Roble
bobal
88 🌷
Colour: bright cherry. Nose: creamy oak, balsamic herbs, spicy, ripe fruit. Palate: fruity, flavourful, toasty.

Finca Los Halcones 2013 T
87 🌷
Colour: cherry, garnet rim. Nose: red berry notes, ripe fruit, spicy, creamy oak, toasty, complex, earthy notes. Palate: powerful, flavourful, toasty, round tannins.

Secreto di Vino Viognier Semiseco 2013 B
viognier
85 🌷

Secreto di Vinon Lágrima de Syrah Semiseco 2013 RD
syrah

87 🌷

Colour: rose, purple rim. Nose: powerfull, red berry notes, floral, candied fruit. Palate: powerful, fruity, fresh.

Vega Tolosa Bobal 2011 TC
100% bobal

87 🌷

Colour: cherry, garnet rim. Nose: ripe fruit, spicy, creamy oak, toasty, complex. Palate: powerful, flavourful, toasty, round tannins.

Vega Tolosa Bobal Viñas Viejas 2010 TC
bobal

89

Colour: cherry, garnet rim. Nose: ripe fruit, spicy, complex. Palate: powerful, flavourful, toasty, round tannins.

Vega Tolosa Cabernet Sauvignon Merlot 2009 TC

89

Colour: cherry, garnet rim. Nose: ripe fruit, wild herbs, spicy. Palate: powerful, flavourful, ripe fruit.

Vega Tolosa Nature 2012 T
syrah, tempranillo

84 🌷

Vega Tolosa Selección 2013 B
macabeo, sauvignon blanc, chardonnay

86 🌷

Colour: bright straw. Nose: white flowers, fragrant herbs, fruit expression. Palate: fresh, fruity, balanced, elegant.

Vega Tolosa Syrah 2009 TR
100% syrah

90

Colour: bright cherry, garnet rim. Nose: ripe fruit, spicy, smoky. Palate: flavourful, round tannins, balanced.

DO. MÉNTRIDA

CONSEJO REGULADOR

Avda. Cristo del Amparo, 16. Piso 1 Of. 1-2.
45510 Fuensalida (Toledo)
☎ :+34 925 785 185 - Fax: +34 925 784 154
@: administracion@domentrida.es
www.domentrida.es

LOCATION:

In the north of the province of Toledo. It borders with the provinces of Ávila and Madrid to the north, with the Tajo to the south, and with the Sierra de San Vicente to the west. It is made up of 51 municipal areas of the province of Toledo.

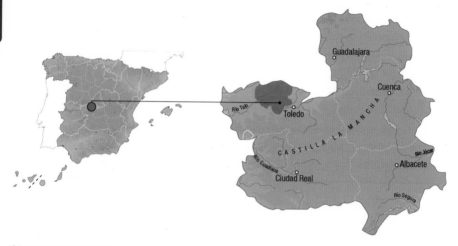

GRAPE VARIETIES:

White: Albillo, Macabeo, Sauvignon Blanc, Chardonnay and Moscatel de Grano Menudo.
Red: Garnacha (majority 85% of total), Cencibel (Tempranillo), Cabernet Sauvignon, Merlot, Syrah, Petit Verdot, Cabernet Franc and Graciano.

FIGURES:

Vineyard surface: 5,466.82 – Wine-Growers: 1,200 – Wineries: 27 – 2013 Harvest rating: Good – Production 13: 399,736 litres – Market percentages: 80% domestic - 20% export.

SOIL:

The vineyards are at an altitude of between 400 m and 600 m, although some municipal districts of the Sierra de San Vicente reach an altitude of 800 m. The soil is mainly sandy-clayey, with a medium to loose texture.

CLIMATE:

Continental, dry and extreme, with long, cold winters and hot summers. Late frosts in spring are quite common. The average rainfall is between 300 mm and 500 mm, and is irregularly distributed throughout the year.

VINTAGE RATING

PEÑÍNGUIDE

2009	2010	2011	2012	2013
AVERAGE	VERY GOOD	GOOD	GOOD	GOOD

AGROVILLARTA

Ctra. Toledo-Ávila, Km. 48
45910 Escalona (Toledo)
☎: +34 913 441 990
comunicacion@haciendavillarta.com

Besanas 2008 TR
tempranillo, cabernet sauvignon, syrah

87

Colour: dark-red cherry, garnet rim. Nose: tobacco, spicy, ripe fruit, scrubland. Palate: balanced, flavourful, long.

Besanas 2009 TC
tempranillo, cabernet sauvignon, syrah

87

Colour: cherry, garnet rim. Nose: ripe fruit, spicy, creamy oak, scrubland. Palate: flavourful, toasty, round tannins.

Besanas 2013 B
chardonnay, sauvignon blanc

86

Colour: bright straw. Nose: fresh, fresh fruit, white flowers, expressive. Palate: flavourful, fruity, good acidity, balanced.

Rose 5 2013 RD
garnacha, petit verdot

86

Colour: coppery red, bright. Nose: fresh, medium intensity, dried flowers, fragrant herbs, balanced. Palate: fruity, good acidity, fine bitter notes.

ALONSO CUESTA

Pza. de la Constitución, 4
45920 La Torre de Esteban Hambrán (Toledo)
☎: +34 925 795 742
Fax: +34 925 795 742
www.alonsocuesta.com
comercial@alonsocuesta.com

Alonso Cuesta 2011 T
garnacha, cabernet sauvignon, tempranillo

92

Colour: cherry, garnet rim. Nose: spicy, creamy oak, toasty, complex, balsamic herbs, fruit preserve. Palate: powerful, flavourful, toasty, round tannins.

Alonso Cuesta 2013 B
verdejo, sauvignon blanc

86

Colour: bright straw. Nose: fresh, fresh fruit, white flowers, wild herbs. Palate: fruity, good acidity, balanced.

Camarus 2013 T
garnacha

90

Colour: light cherry, purple rim. Nose: balanced, red berry notes, medium intensity. Palate: fruity, flavourful, easy to drink, long.

BODEGA SANTO DOMINGO DE GUZMÁN

Alameda del Fresno, 14
28054 Valmojado (Toledo)
☎: +34 918 170 904
www.santodomingodeguzman.es
info@santodomingodeguzman.es

Valdejuana Syrah 2012 TC
syrah

88

Colour: bright cherry. Nose: sweet spices, creamy oak, ripe fruit, fruit preserve. Palate: flavourful, fruity, toasty, round tannins.

Valdejuana Syrah 2013 T
syrah

87

Colour: bright cherry, purple rim. Nose: balanced, varietal, red berry notes, dried herbs. Palate: fruity, easy to drink, correct.

BODEGAS ARRAYÁN

Finca La Verdosa, s/n
45513 Santa Cruz del Retamar (Toledo)
☎: +34 916 633 131
Fax: +34 916 632 796
www.arrayan.es
comercial@arrayan.es

Arrayán 2013 RD
syrah, merlot

88

Colour: rose, purple rim. Nose: powerfull, ripe fruit, red berry notes, floral, expressive. Palate: powerful, fruity, fresh.

Arrayán Petit Verdot 2010 T
petit verdot

90

Colour: cherry, garnet rim. Nose: ripe fruit, wild herbs, spicy. Palate: balanced, flavourful, long, balsamic.

Arrayán Premium 2010 T
syrah, merlot, cabernet sauvignon, petit verdot

92

Colour: cherry, garnet rim. Nose: ripe fruit, spicy, creamy oak, toasty, complex, wild herbs. Palate: powerful, flavourful, toasty, round tannins.

Arrayán Selección 2010 T
syrah, merlot, cabernet sauvignon, petit verdot

87

Colour: bright cherry. Nose: ripe fruit, sweet spices, creamy oak, medium intensity, scrubland. Palate: fruity, flavourful, toasty.

Arrayán Syrah 2010 T
syrah

88

Colour: bright cherry. Nose: ripe fruit, sweet spices, creamy oak. Palate: flavourful, fruity, toasty, round tannins.

Estela de Arrayán 2010 T
93
Colour: cherry, garnet rim. Nose: scrubland, spicy, ripe fruit, powerfull. Palate: spicy, long, round tannins, balsamic.

La Suerte de Arrayán 2011 T
garnacha
92
Colour: cherry, garnet rim. Nose: ripe fruit, spicy, creamy oak, complex. Palate: powerful, flavourful, toasty, round tannins, ripe fruit, long.

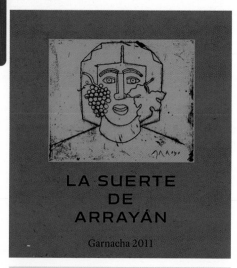

Garnacha 2011

BODEGAS CANOPY
Ctra. Toledo-Valmojado, km. 23
45180 Camarena (Toledo)
☎: +34 619 244 878
Fax: +34 925 283 680
achacon@bodegascanopy.com

Castillo de Berlarfonso 2013 T
garnacha
92
Colour: bright cherry. Nose: ripe fruit, sweet spices, expressive. Palate: flavourful, fruity, toasty, round tannins.

Congo 2009 T
garnacha
95
Colour: cherry, garnet rim. Nose: red berry notes, ripe fruit, spicy, creamy oak, toasty, complex, mineral. Palate: powerful, flavourful, toasty, round tannins.

Gonzo Garnachas Felices 2011 T
100% garnacha
91
Colour: cherry, garnet rim. Nose: balanced, fruit expression, balsamic herbs. Palate: fruity, easy to drink, correct, good finish.

La Viña Escondida 2010 T
garnacha
95
Colour: cherry, garnet rim. Nose: ripe fruit, spicy, creamy oak, toasty, complex, balsamic herbs, mineral. Palate: powerful, flavourful, toasty, round tannins.

Loco 2013 B
garnacha blanca
91
Colour: bright straw. Nose: balanced, white flowers, fresh fruit. Palate: rich, fruity, flavourful, easy to drink, long, good acidity.

Malpaso 2012 T
syrah
94
Colour: dark-red cherry, garnet rim. Nose: spicy, scrubland, closed, expressive, mineral. Palate: good structure, full, round tannins.

Tres Patas 2010 T
garnacha
93
Colour: light cherry. Nose: dry stone, wild herbs, spicy, scrubland. Palate: flavourful, long, balsamic, good acidity.

BODEGAS GONZALO VALVERDE
Río Tajo, 19
45523 Alcabón (Toledo)
☎: +34 659 452 512
www.bodegasgonzalovalverde.es
info@bodegasgonzalovalverde.es

Mensagallo 2012 T
garnacha
90
Colour: bright cherry. Nose: ripe fruit, sweet spices, creamy oak, smoky. Palate: fruity, flavourful, toasty, round tannins, long.

Vallelobo 2012 T
tempranillo, cabernet sauvignon, syrah
84

BODEGAS JIMÉNEZ LANDI

Avda. Solana, 39
45930 Méntrida (Toledo)
☎: +34 918 178 213
www.jimenezlandi.com
info@jimenezlandi.com

Jiménez-Landi Ataulfos 2012 T
garnacha

94

Colour: bright cherry. Nose: ripe fruit, spicy, complex, mineral, expressive. Palate: flavourful, toasty, round tannins, full.

Jiménez-Landi Bajondillo 2013 T

89 ♣

Colour: light cherry, purple rim. Nose: medium intensity, fruit expression, balanced. Palate: flavourful, fruity, fruity aftertaste.

Jiménez-Landi Piélago 2012 T
garnacha

95

Colour: light cherry. Nose: ripe fruit, wild herbs, earthy notes, spicy, creamy oak. Palate: balanced, flavourful, long, balsamic.

Jiménez-Landi Sotorrondero 2012 T

93

Colour: light cherry, cherry, garnet rim. Nose: mineral, balanced, elegant, ripe fruit. Palate: flavourful, complex, fine tannins, balanced.

BODEGAS LA CERCA

Lepanto, 15
45950 Casarrubios del Monte (Toledo)
☎: +34 918 172 456
bodegaslacerca@yahoo.es

Molino Viejo 2010 TC
tempranillo

83

Molino Viejo Tempranillo 2011 T Roble
tempranillo

83

BODEGAS TORRESTEBAN

Ctra. Méntrida, s/n
45920 La Torre de Esteban Hambrán (Toledo)
☎: +34 925 795 114
coopcristo@gmail.com

Remuri 2012 T Roble
100% tempranillo

84

Remuri 2013 RD
100% garnacha

85

Remuri 2013 T

84

Remuri Syrah 2012 T Fermentado en Barrica
100% syrah

87

Colour: cherry, purple rim. Nose: creamy oak, lactic notes, ripe fruit. Palate: fruity, flavourful, round tannins, spicy.

Remuri Verdejo 2013 B
100% verdejo

78

BODEGAS Y VIÑEDOS TAVERA S.L.

Ctra. Valmojado - Toledo, Km. 22
45182 Arcicóllar (Toledo)
☎: +34 637 847 777
www.bodegastavera.com
info@bodegastavera.com

Tavera 2013 T Maceración Carbónica

86

Colour: cherry, purple rim. Nose: expressive, fresh fruit, red berry notes, floral. Palate: flavourful, fruity, good acidity, round tannins.

Tavera Antiguos Viñedos 2012 T
garnacha

86

Colour: light cherry. Nose: ripe fruit, fruit preserve, spicy, wild herbs. Palate: correct, balanced.

Tavera Edición Syrah 2010 T Fermentado en Barrica
100% syrah

87

Colour: bright cherry. Nose: ripe fruit, sweet spices, creamy oak, medium intensity. Palate: fruity, flavourful, toasty.

Tavera Rosado Antiguos Viñedos 2013 RD

86

Colour: light cherry. Nose: floral, violet drops, red berry notes. Palate: fruity, correct, easy to drink, good finish.

Tavera Vendimia Seleccionada 2010 T
tempranillo, syrah

88

Colour: bright cherry. Nose: ripe fruit, spicy, toasty, complex. Palate: powerful, flavourful, toasty, round tannins.

CARTEMA

Finca Las Cañadas - Montes de Alamin
45513 Santa Cruz del Retamar (Toledo)
☎: +34 629 431 950
www.cartema.es
info@cartema.es

Cartema 2009 TR
cabernet sauvignon, tempranillo, syrah
86
Colour: deep cherry, garnet rim. Nose: creamy oak, sweet spices, ripe fruit. Palate: fruity, correct, fine bitter notes.

CÉSAR & CIPRIANO S.L.

Adolfo Suárez, 4
45542 El Casar de Escalona (Toledo)
☎: +34 618 951 853
www.unvinobenayas.es
info@unvinobenayas.es

Encastao 2013 TC
garnacha
86
Colour: bright cherry, purple rim. Nose: spicy, wild herbs, ripe fruit, balanced. Palate: flavourful, rich, round tannins.

COOPERATIVA CONDES DE FUENSALIDA

Avda. San Crispín, 129
45510 Fuensalida (Toledo)
☎: +34 925 784 823
Fax: +34 925 784 823
www.condesdefuensalida.iespana.es
condesdefuensalida@hotmail.com

Condes de Fuensalida 2011 TC
82

Condes de Fuensalida 2013 T
garnacha, tempranillo
81

Condes de Fuensalida 2013 RD
84

Condes de Fuensalida Fruit Rose 2013 RD
83

COOPERATIVA NUESTRA SEÑORA DE LA NATIVIDAD

San Roque, 1
45930 Méntrida (Toledo)
☎: +34 918 177 004
Fax: +34 918 177 004
www.cooperativamentrida.es
coopnatividad@gmail.com

Vega Berciana 2013 RD
garnacha
84

Vega Berciana 2013 T
garnacha
85

COOPERATIVA NUESTRA SEÑORA DE LINARES

Inmaculada, 95
45920 Torre de Esteban Hambrán (Toledo)
☎: +34 925 795 452
Fax: +34 925 795 452
cooplina@futurnet.es

Fortitudo 2013 RD
garnacha
82

Fortitudo 2013 T
garnacha
83

DANI LANDI

Constitución, 23
28640 Cadalso de los Vidrios (Madrid)
☎: +34 696 366 555
www.danilandi.com
daniel@danilandi.com

Cantos del Diablo 2012 T
garnacha
97
Colour: very deep cherry. Nose: balsamic herbs, scrubland, red berry notes, fruit expression. Palate: flavourful, good acidity, long, spicy.

Las Uvas de la Ira 2012 T
garnacha
92
Colour: deep cherry. Nose: red berry notes, fruit expression, floral. Palate: flavourful, fruity, grainy tannins.

UNVINOBENAYAS

Adolfo Suárez, 4
45542 El Casar de Escalona (Toledo)
☎: +34 655 907 640
www.unvinobenayas.es
unvinobenayas@gmail.com

Codicioso 2011 TC
syrah
84

VIÑEDOS DE CAMARENA, SDAD. COOP. DE CLM

Ctra. Toledo - Valmojado, km. 24,6
45180 Camarena (Toledo)
☎: +34 918 174 347
Fax: +34 918 174 632
www.vdecamarena.com
vdecamarena@hotmail.com

Bastión de Camarena 2012 T Roble
cabernet sauvignon
84

Bastión de Camarena 2013 B
verdejo
81

Bastión de Camarena 2013 RD
garnacha, tempranillo
87
Colour: light cherry, bright. Nose: red berry notes, fragrant herbs, citrus fruit, fresh. Palate: fruity, flavourful, balanced, fine bitter notes.

Bastión de Camarena 2013 T
garnacha, tempranillo
86
Colour: cherry, purple rim. Nose: expressive, fresh fruit, red berry notes, floral. Palate: flavourful, fruity, good acidity, round tannins, easy to drink.

VIÑEDOS Y BODEGAS GONZÁLEZ

Real, 86
45180 Camarena (Toledo)
☎: +34 918 174 063
Fax: +34 918 174 063
www.vinobispo.com
bodegasgonzalez@yahoo.es

Viña Bispo 2013 B
sauvignon blanc, verdejo
82

Viña Bispo 2013 RD
garnacha
85

Viña Bispo 2013 T
syrah, merlot
84

DO. MONDÉJAR

CONSEJO REGULADOR

Pza. Mayor, 10
19110 Mondéjar (Guadalajara)
☎ :+34 949 385 284 - Fax: +34 949 385 284
@: crdom@crdomondejar.com
www.crdomondejar.com

LOCATION:

In the southwest of the province of Guadalajara. It is made up of the municipal districts of Albalate de Zorita, Albares, Almoguera, Almonacid de Zorita, Driebes, Escariche, Escopete, Fuenteovilla, Illana, Loranca de Tajuña, Mazuecos, Mondéjar, Pastrana, Pioz, Pozo de Almoguera, Sacedón, Sayatón, Valdeconcha, Yebra and Zorita de los Canes.

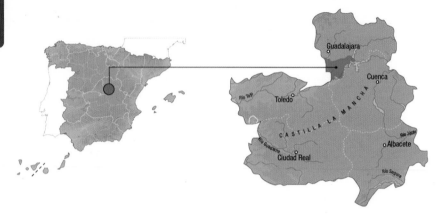

GRAPE VARIETIES:

White (40%): Malvar (majority 80% of white varieties), Macabeo and Torrontés.
Red (60%): Cencibel (Tempranillo – represents 95% of red varieties), Cabernet Sauvignon (5%) and Syrah.

FIGURES:

Vineyard surface: 3,000 – Wine-Growers: 300 – Wineries: 2 – 2011 Harvest rating: N/A – Production 11: 421,130 litres – Market percentages: 100% domestic.

SOIL:

The south of the Denomination is characterized by red soil on lime-clayey sediments, and the north (the municipal districts of Anguix, Mondéjar, Sacedón, etc.) has brown limestone soil on lean sandstone and conglomerates.

CLIMATE:

Temperate Mediterranean. The average annual temperature is around 18°C and the average rainfall is 500 mm per year.

VINTAGE RATING   PEÑÍNGUIDE

2009	2010	2011	2012	2013
N/A	N/A	N/A	N/A	N/A

DO. MONTERREI

CONSEJO REGULADOR

Avenida Luis Espada, 73 bajo
32600 Verín (Ourense)
☎ :+34 988 410 634 - Fax: +34 988 410 634
@: info@domonterrei.com
www.domonterrei.com

LOCATION:

In the east of the province of Orense, on the border with Portugal. The vineyards occupy the valley of Monterrei, and it is made up of the municipal districts of Verín, Monterrei, Oimbra and Castrelo do Vall.

SUB-REGIONS:

Val de Monterrei. Comprising the vineyards situated in the valley region (therefore, more level terrains) and covering the parishes and municipal districts belonging to the following city councils: Castrelo do Val (Castrelo do Val, Pepín and Nocedo); Monterrei (Albarellos, Infesta, Monterrei and Vilaza); Oimbra (Oimbra, Rabal, O Rosal and San Cibrao); Verín (Abedes, Cabreiroa, Feces da Baixo, Feces de Cima, Mandín, Mourazos, Pazos, Queizás, A Rasela, Tamagos, Tamaguelos, Tintores, Verín, Vilela and Vilamaior do Val).
Ladeira de Monterrei. These vineyards occupy the hills. The parishes and municipal districts that make up this sub-region are: Castrelo do Val (Gondulfes and Servoi), Oimbra (As Chas and A Granxa), Monterrey (Flariz, Medeiros, Mixós, Estevesiños and Vences) and Verín (Queirugas).

GRAPE VARIETIES:

White: Dona Blanca, Verdello (Godello) and Treixadura (Verdello Louro), Albariño, Caiño Blanco, Loureira and Blanca de Monterrei.
Red: Aranxa (Tempranillo), Caiño Tinto, Mencía, Bastardo (or María Ardoña) and Sousón.

FIGURES:

Vineyard surface: 432 – Wine-Growers: 364 – Wineries: 23 – 2013 Harvest rating: Very Good – Production 13: 1,583,380 litres – Market percentages: 88% domestic - 12% export.

SOIL:

The vineyard extends over the sides of the hills and valleys irrigated by the River Támega and its tributaries. There are three types of soils in the area: slate and shale, granite and sandy, from the degradation of the granite rocks, and sediment type soils.

CLIMATE:

Midway between the Atlantic and Continental influences. Drier than in the rest of Galicia, with maximum temperatures of 35°C in summer and minimum of –5°C in winter.

VINTAGE RATING   PEÑÍNGUIDE

2009	2010	2011	2012	2013
EXCELLENT	VERY GOOD	VERY GOOD	VERY GOOD	VERY GOOD

PEÑÍNGUIDE 25 Years to Spanish Wine

ADEGA ABELEDOS

Avda. Portugal, 110 2ºA
32600 Verín (Ourense)
☎: +34 988 414 075
Fax: +34 988 414 075
adegaabeledos@gmail.com

Abeledo 2013 B
godello, treixadura
85

Abeledo 2013 T
mencía, tempranillo
85

ADEGA VALDERELLO

Rua Máximo 1 Albarellos de Monterrey
32618 Monterrei (Ourense)
☎: +34 606 767 005
valderello@yahoo.es

Valderello 2012 T
mencía
88

Colour: dark-red cherry, garnet rim. Nose: balanced, red berry notes, ripe fruit, dry stone, spicy. Palate: flavourful, balsamic, balanced.

Valderello 2013 B
godello
86

Colour: bright straw. Nose: fresh, fresh fruit, white flowers, expressive. Palate: flavourful, fruity, good acidity.

ADEGAS PAZO DAS TAPIAS

Finca As Tapias - Pazos
32619 Verin (Ourense)
☎: +34 988 261 256
Fax: +34 988 261 264
www.pazodastapias.com
info@pazodomar.com

Alma de Blanco Godello 2013 B
godello
88

Colour: bright straw. Nose: white flowers, fragrant herbs. Palate: flavourful, fine bitter notes, long.

Alma de Tinto Mencía 2013 T
mencía
89

Colour: cherry, purple rim. Nose: dry stone, ripe fruit, expressive. Palate: balanced, good structure, flavourful.

ADEGAS TRIAY

Rua Ladairo, 36
32613 O'Rosal Oimbra (Ourense)
☎: +34 988 422 776
Fax: +34 988 422 776
www.bodegastriay.com
triayadegas@gmail.com

Triay 2013 B
godello
87

Colour: bright straw. Nose: white flowers, fragrant herbs, fruit expression. Palate: fresh, fruity, flavourful.

Triay 2013 T
mencía
89

Colour: bright cherry, purple rim. Nose: red berry notes, ripe fruit, balanced, wild herbs. Palate: good structure, flavourful, good finish.

ALMA ATLÁNTICA

Burgáns, 91
36633 Vilariño - Cambados
(Pontevedra)
☎: +34 986 526 040
Fax: +34 986 526 901
www.martincodax.com
comercial@martincodax.com

Mara Martin Godello 2013 B
100% godello
88

Colour: bright straw. Nose: white flowers, fragrant herbs, fruit expression. Palate: fresh, fruity, flavourful, balanced.

BODEGA BOO-RIVERO

Touza, 22
32618 Villaza (Ourense)
☎: +34 988 425 950
Fax: +34 988 425 950
bodegaboorivero@yahoo.es

Fragas do Lecer 2012 T
83

Fragas do Lecer 2013 B
godello, treixadura
86

Colour: bright straw. Nose: floral, dried herbs, fruit expression. Palate: fresh, fruity, thin.

BODEGA COUTO MIXTO

Rua Principal, 46 Mandin
32698 Verin (Ourense)
☎: +34 636 762 200

Couto Mixto 2012 B
84

Couto Mixto 2012 T
mencía, caiño, bastardo negro

87

Colour: cherry, garnet rim. Nose: ripe fruit, spicy, complex, earthy notes, balsamic herbs. Palate: powerful, flavourful, toasty.

BODEGA TABÚ
Plaza A Carreira, 6 O Rosal
32613 Oimbra (Ourense)
☎: +34 665 644 500
www.bodegatabu.com
bodegatabu@gmail.com

Stibadía 2011 T Barrica
mencía, tempranillo

89

Colour: cherry, garnet rim. Nose: ripe fruit, spicy, creamy oak, toasty, complex. Palate: powerful, flavourful, toasty, round tannins.

Stibadía 2012 B Barrica
godello, treixadura

88

Colour: bright yellow. Nose: powerfull, ripe fruit, sweet spices, creamy oak, fragrant herbs. Palate: rich, smoky aftertaste, flavourful, fresh, good acidity.

Stibadía 2013 B
godello, treixadura

87

Colour: bright straw. Nose: fresh, fresh fruit, white flowers, expressive. Palate: flavourful, fruity, good acidity.

Stibadía 2013 T
mencía, tempranillo

86

Colour: cherry, garnet rim. Nose: grassy, herbaceous, red berry notes. Palate: balsamic, fine bitter notes.

BODEGAS GARGALO
Rua Do Castelo, 59
32619 Verín (Ourense)
☎: +34 988 590 203
Fax: +34 988 590 295
www.gargalo.es
gargalo@verino.es

Gargalo Albariño & Treixadura 2013 B
albariño, treixadura

89

Colour: bright straw. Nose: fresh, fresh fruit, white flowers, expressive. Palate: fruity, good acidity, balanced, fine bitter notes.

Gargalo Godello 2013 B
godello

90

Colour: bright straw. Nose: fragrant herbs, fruit expression, mineral, citrus fruit, floral. Palate: correct, flavourful, fresh, fruity, balanced.

Gargalo Mencía & Arauxa 2013 T
mencía, arauxa

90

Colour: cherry, garnet rim. Nose: ripe fruit, spicy, complex, balsamic herbs, mineral. Palate: powerful, flavourful, toasty, round tannins.

Terra do Gargalo Carballo 2010 TC
mencía

91

Colour: cherry, garnet rim. Nose: red berry notes, ripe fruit, spicy, creamy oak, toasty, complex, mineral. Palate: powerful, flavourful, toasty, round tannins.

Terra do Gargalo sobre Lías 2012 B
godello, treixadura

91

Colour: yellow. Nose: expressive, fine lees, dried herbs, faded flowers. Palate: flavourful, fruity, good acidity, balanced.

Terra Rubia Godello-Treixadura 2013 B
godello, treixadura

86

Colour: bright straw. Nose: white flowers, fresh fruit, citrus fruit. Palate: fresh, easy to drink, good finish, light-bodied.

Viña Verino 2012 BFB
100% godello

93

Colour: bright golden. Nose: floral, fruit expression, fragrant herbs, mineral, spicy, expressive. Palate: flavourful, rich, complex, balsamic, balanced, elegant.

BODEGAS LADAIRO
Ctra. Ladairo, 42
32613 O'Rosal (Oimbra) (Ourense)
☎: +34 988 422 757
Fax: +34 988 422 757
www.ladairo.com
info@bodegasladairo.com

Ladairo 2011 T Barrica

89

Colour: bright cherry. Nose: ripe fruit, sweet spices, creamy oak, expressive. Palate: flavourful, fruity, toasty, round tannins.

Ladairo 2013 B

88

Colour: bright straw. Nose: fresh, fresh fruit, white flowers, fragrant herbs. Palate: flavourful, fruity, good acidity, thin.

Ladairo 2013 T

86

Colour: cherry, purple rim. Nose: expressive, fresh fruit, red berry notes, floral, balsamic herbs. Palate: flavourful, fruity, good acidity.

BODEGAS Y VIÑEDOS QUINTA DA MURADELLA

Avda. Luis Espada, 99- Entresuelo, dcha.
32600 Verín (Ourense)
☎: +34 988 411 724
Fax: +34 988 590 427
bodega@muradella.com

Alanda 2012 T Barrica
mencía, bastardo negro, mouratón, garnacha tintorera

90

Colour: cherry, garnet rim. Nose: ripe fruit, wild herbs, earthy notes, spicy, creamy oak. Palate: balanced, flavourful, long, balsamic.

Alanda 2013 B Barrica
dona blanca, verdello, treixadura

90

Colour: bright straw. Nose: floral, dried herbs, earthy notes, ripe fruit, balsamic herbs, creamy oak. Palate: powerful, flavourful, spicy, long.

Gorvia 2012 T

91

Colour: cherry, garnet rim. Nose: red berry notes, ripe fruit, spicy, creamy oak, toasty, complex, earthy notes, wild herbs, elegant. Palate: powerful, flavourful, toasty, balanced.

Gorvia Fermentado en Barrica 2011 BFB
100% dona blanca

93

Colour: bright yellow. Nose: powerfull, ripe fruit, sweet spices, creamy oak, fragrant herbs, mineral. Palate: rich, smoky aftertaste, flavourful, fresh.

Muradella 2010 B
100% treixadura

90

Colour: bright yellow. Nose: white flowers, fragrant herbs, fruit expression, dry stone, expressive. Palate: fresh, fruity, flavourful, balanced, elegant.

Quinta da Muradella Berrande T
100% mencía

93

Colour: cherry, garnet rim. Nose: ripe fruit, spicy, balsamic herbs, expressive, mineral. Palate: powerful, flavourful, round tannins, long, balsamic, spicy, elegant, balanced.

CREGO E MONAGUILLO S.L.

Rua Nova s/n
32618 Salgueira (Ourense)
☎: +34 988 418 164
Fax: +34 988 418 164
www.cregoemonaguillo.com
tito@cregoemonaguillo.com

Crego e Monaguillo Godello 2013 B

88

Colour: bright straw. Nose: fresh, fresh fruit, white flowers, wild herbs. Palate: flavourful, fruity, good acidity, balanced.

Crego e Monaguillo Mencía 2013 T

87

Colour: cherry, purple rim. Nose: red berry notes, raspberry, fruit expression, fragrant herbs. Palate: flavourful, light-bodied, good acidity, easy to drink.

MANUEL GUERRA JUSTO

Ctra. Albarellos, 61
32618 Villaza (Monterrei) (Ourense)
☎: +34 687 409 618
Fax: +34 988 590 108
viaarxentea@viaarxentea.com

Vía Arxéntea 2013 B
treixadura, godello

88

Colour: bright yellow. Nose: dried flowers, wild herbs, dry stone, ripe fruit. Palate: flavourful, fine bitter notes, correct.

PAZO BLANCO NÚÑEZ, S.L. (ADEGAS TAPIAS-MARIÑÁN)

Ctra. N-525, Km. 170,4
32619 Pazos - Verín (Ourense)
☎: +34 988 411 693
Fax: +34 988 411 693
www.tapiasmarinhan.com
info@tapiasmarinhan.com

Colleita Propia 2013 B
godello, albariño

87

Colour: bright yellow. Nose: white flowers, fresh fruit, fragrant herbs. Palate: fruity, correct, good acidity.

Colleita Propia 2013 T
mencía

86

Colour: cherry, purple rim. Nose: expressive, fresh fruit, red berry notes, floral, balsamic herbs. Palate: flavourful, fruity, good acidity.

Pazo de Mariñan 2013 B
godello, treixadura, albariño

87

Colour: bright straw. Nose: fresh, fresh fruit, white flowers, mineral. Palate: flavourful, fruity, good acidity, balanced.

Pazo de Mariñan 2013 T
mencía, tempranillo

86

Colour: light cherry, purple rim. Nose: balanced, red berry notes, wild herbs, spicy. Palate: fruity, good finish.

Quintas das Tapias 2012 T
mencía

87

Colour: cherry, garnet rim. Nose: ripe fruit, wild herbs, spicy, creamy oak. Palate: balanced, flavoured, long, balsamic.

Quintas das Tapias 2013 B
treixadura

90

Colour: bright straw. Nose: white flowers, fragrant herbs, fruit expression. Palate: fresh, fruity, flavourful, balanced, elegant.

PAZOS DEL REY
Carrero Blanco, 33
32618 Albarellos de Monterrei
(Ourense)
☎: +34 988 425 959
www.pazosdelrey.com
info@pazosdelrey.com

Pazo de Monterrey 2013 B
100% godello

90

Colour: bright straw. Nose: white flowers, fragrant herbs, fruit expression. Palate: fresh, fruity, flavourful, balanced, elegant.

Sila Mencía 2012 T Barrica
100% mencía

89

Colour: bright cherry, garnet rim. Nose: ripe fruit, sweet spices, creamy oak, expressive. Palate: flavourful, fruity, toasty, round tannins, balanced.

QUINTA DO BUBLE
Ladeira A Machada s/n
Casas dos Montes
32613 Oimbra (Ourense)
☎: +34 988 422 960
www.quintadobuble.com
info@quintadobuble.com

Quinta do Buble 2013 B
godello

89

Colour: bright straw. Nose: white flowers, fresh fruit, expressive, fine lees, dried herbs. Palate: flavourful, fruity, good acidity, balanced.

TERRAS DE CIGARRÓN
Ctra. de Albarellos, km. 525
32618 Albarellos de Monterrei
(Ourense)
☎: +34 988 418 703
www.terrasdocigarron.com
bodega@terrasdocigarron.com

Terras do Cigarrón 2013 B
100% godello

89

Colour: bright straw. Nose: fresh fruit, balanced, floral, fragrant herbs, citrus fruit. Palate: fruity, easy to drink, good acidity.

VINIGALICIA
Ctra. Antigua Santiago, km. 3
27500 Chantada (Lugo)
☎: +34 982 454 005
Fax: +34 982 454 094
www.vinigalicia.es
vinigalicia@vinigalicia.es

Lagar de Deuses Godello 2012 B
godello, treixadura

88

Colour: bright yellow. Nose: faded flowers, ripe fruit, balanced, dry stone. Palate: rich, flavourful, fine bitter notes.

Lagar de Deuses Mencía 2012 T
mencía, tempranillo

87

Colour: deep cherry, purple rim. Nose: scrubland, ripe fruit, balanced, spicy. Palate: fruity, round tannins.

DO. MONTILLA - MORILES

CONSEJO REGULADOR

Rita Pérez, s/n
14550 Montilla (Córdoba)
☎:+34 957 652 110 - Fax: +34 957652 407
@: consejo@montillamoriles.es
www.montilla-moriles.org

LOCATION:

To the south of Córdoba. It covers all the vineyards of the municipal districts of Montilla, Moriles, Montalbán, Puente Genil, Montruque, Nueva Carteya and Doña Mencía, and part of the municipal districts of Montemayor, Fernán-Núñez, La Rambla, Santaella, Aguilar de la Frontera, Lucena, Cabra, Baena, Castro del Río and Espejo.

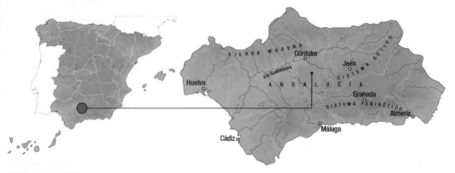

SUB-REGIONS:

We have to differentiate between the vineyards in the flatlands and those in higher areas –such as Sierra de Montilla and Moriles Alto–, prominently limestone soils of higher quality and hardly 2000 hectares planted.

GRAPE VARIETIES:

White: Pedro Ximénez (main variety), Airén, Baladí, Moscatel, Torrontés and Verdejo.
Red: Tempranillo, Syrah and Cabernet Sauvignon.

FIGURES:

Vineyard surface: 5,239 – Wine-Growers: 2,218 – Wineries: 63 – 2013 Harvest rating: Good – Production 13: 41,031,300 litres – Market percentages: 90% domestic - 10% export.

SOIL:

The vineyards are situated at an altitude of between 125 m and 640 m. The soils are franc, franc-sandy and, in the higher regions, calcareous ('Albarizas'), which are precisely those of best quality, and which predominate in what is known as the Upper Sub-Region, which includes the municipal districts of Montilla, Moriles, Castro del Río, Cabra and Aguilar de la Frontera.

CLIMATE:

Semi-continental Mediterranean, with long, hot, dry summers and short winters. The average annual temperature is 16.8°C and the average rainfall is between 500 mm and 1,000 mm per year.

VINTAGE RATING   PEÑÍNGUIDE

2009	2010	2011	2012	2013
VERY GOOD	GOOD	N/A	N/A	N/A

ALVEAR

María Auxiliadora, 1
14550 Montilla (Córdoba)
☎: +34 957 650 100
Fax: +34 957 650 135
www.alvear.es
info@alvear.es

Alvear Dulce Viejo 2000 PX Reserva
100% pedro ximénez

94

Colour: dark mahogany. Nose: complex, fruit liqueur notes, dried fruit, pattiserie, toasty, acetaldehyde, aged wood nuances. Palate: sweet, rich, unctuous, powerful, balanced, elegant.

Alvear Fino En Rama 2008 FI
100% pedro ximénez

90

Colour: bright yellow. Nose: complex, expressive, pungent, saline, iodine notes, ripe fruit. Palate: rich, powerful, fresh, fine bitter notes, elegant.

Alvear PX 1927 PX
100% pedro ximénez

92

Colour: dark mahogany. Nose: complex, fruit liqueur notes, dried fruit, pattiserie, toasty, aromatic coffee. Palate: sweet, rich, unctuous, powerful, roasted-coffee aftertaste.

Alvear PX de Añada 2011 PX
100% pedro ximénez

92

Colour: mahogany. Nose: complex, fruit liqueur notes, dried fruit, pattiserie, toasty, acetaldehyde. Palate: sweet, rich, unctuous, fine solera notes, balanced.

Alvear Solera 1830 PX Reserva
100% pedro ximénez

98

Colour: dark mahogany. Nose: powerfull, expressive, aromatic coffee, spicy, dark chocolate, acetaldehyde, dry nuts. Palate: balanced, elegant, powerful, spicy, toasty, long. Personality.

Alvear Solera Fundación AM
100% pedro ximénez

95

Colour: light mahogany. Nose: powerfull, complex, elegant, dry nuts, toasty, saline. Palate: rich, fine bitter notes, fine solera notes, long, spicy, balanced, elegant.

Alvear Solera Fundación PC

95

Colour: iodine, amber rim. Nose: powerfull, complex, elegant, dry nuts, toasty, fine lees. Palate: rich, long, fine solera notes, spicy.

Asunción OL
100% pedro ximénez

91

Colour: iodine, amber rim. Nose: powerfull, complex, elegant, toasty, sweet spices. Palate: rich, long, fine solera notes, spicy, elegant.

C.B. FI
100% pedro ximénez

90

Colour: bright yellow. Nose: complex, expressive, pungent, saline. Palate: rich, powerful, fresh, fine bitter notes.

BODEGAS CRUZ CONDE

Ronda Canillo, 4
14550 Montilla (Córdoba)
☎: +34 957 651 250
Fax: +34 957 653 619
www.bodegascruzconde.es
info@bodegascruzconde.es

Cream Cruz Conde 1902 CR
100% pedro ximénez

84

Cruz Conde PC
100% pedro ximénez

86

Colour: mahogany. Nose: cocoa bean, dark chocolate, sweet spices, creamy oak, balsamic herbs. Palate: powerful, flavourful, toasty, sweetness.

Cruz Conde Solera Fundación PX
100% pedro ximénez

92

Colour: dark mahogany. Nose: fruit liqueur notes, dried fruit, pattiserie, toasty, acetaldehyde. Palate: sweet, rich, unctuous, powerful, balanced.

Fino Cruz Conde 1902 FI
100% pedro ximénez

87

Colour: bright yellow. Nose: complex, expressive, pungent, saline, dry nuts. Palate: rich, fine bitter notes, balanced.

Pedro Ximénez Cruz Conde 1902 PX
100% pedro ximénez

90

Colour: mahogany. Nose: dried fruit, aged wood nuances, pattiserie, spicy, dry nuts, dark chocolate. Palate: powerful, flavourful, complex, balanced.

BODEGAS DELGADO

Cosano, 2
14500 Puente Genil (Córdoba)
☎: +34 957 600 085
Fax: +34 957 604 571
www.bodegasdelgado.com
fino@bodegasdelgado.com

Abuelamaría OL
100% pedro ximénez
84

Delgado 1874 PX
100% pedro ximénez
91
Colour: dark mahogany. Nose: complex, fruit liqueur notes, dried fruit, pattiserie, toasty. Palate: sweet, rich, unctuous, powerful.

Delgado 1874 Amontillado Natural muy Viejo s/c AM
100% pedro ximénez
92
Colour: iodine, amber rim. Nose: powerfull, dry nuts, toasty, dark chocolate, acetaldehyde. Palate: rich, fine bitter notes, fine solera notes, long, spicy, balanced.

Segunda Bota FI
100% pedro ximénez
90
Colour: bright yellow. Nose: complex, expressive, pungent, saline, floral, ripe fruit. Palate: rich, powerful, fresh, fine bitter notes, elegant.

BODEGAS JESÚS NAZARENO

Avda. Cañete de las Torres, 33
14850 Baena (Córdoba)
☎: +34 957 670 225
Fax: +34 957 690 873
www.bjn1963.com
bjn@bjn1963.com

Cancionero de Baena FI
palomino
84

Pedro Ximénez PX Crianza
pedro ximénez
88
Colour: dark mahogany. Nose: complex, fruit liqueur notes, dried fruit, pattiserie, toasty. Palate: sweet, rich, unctuous, powerful.

BODEGAS SILLERO

Ctra. de La Redonda, s/n
14540 La Rambla (Córdoba)
☎: +34 957 684 464
www.bodegassillero.com
sillero@bodegassillero.com

Las Cármenes FI
pedro ximénez
86
Colour: bright yellow. Nose: complex, expressive, pungent, saline, ripe fruit. Palate: rich, powerful, fresh, fine bitter notes.

Sillero PX
pedro ximénez
87
Colour: dark mahogany. Nose: dried fruit, pattiserie, toasty. Palate: sweet, rich, unctuous.

Viejo Rondalla OL
pedro ximénez
87
Colour: iodine, amber rim. Nose: powerfull, complex, elegant, dry nuts, toasty. Palate: rich, long, fine solera notes, spicy.

CÍA. VINÍCOLA DEL SUR - TOMÁS GARCÍA

Avda. Luis de Góngora y Argote, s/n
14550 Montilla (Córdoba)
☎: +34 957 650 204
Fax: +34 957 652 335
www.vinicoladelsur.com
info@vinicoladelsur.com

Monte Cristo FI
100% pedro ximénez
90
Colour: bright yellow. Nose: complex, expressive, pungent, saline, ripe fruit. Palate: rich, powerful, fine bitter notes.

Monte Cristo PX
100% pedro ximénez
91
Colour: dark mahogany. Nose: complex, fruit liqueur notes, dried fruit, pattiserie, toasty. Palate: sweet, rich, unctuous, powerful.

Monte Cristo AM
100% pedro ximénez
90
Colour: mahogany. Nose: acetaldehyde, cocoa bean, sweet spices, creamy oak, expressive. Palate: powerful, flavourful, complex, balanced.

Monte Cristo OL
100% pedro ximénez
92
Colour: iodine, amber rim. Nose: powerfull, complex, elegant, dry nuts, toasty. Palate: rich, fine solera notes, spicy, elegant.

Pedro Ximénez Viejo Tomás García PX
pedro ximénez

89

Colour: dark mahogany. Nose: complex, fruit liqueur notes, dried fruit, pattiserie, toasty. Palate: sweet, rich, unctuous, powerful.

Verbenera FI
100% pedro ximénez

88

Colour: bright yellow. Nose: complex, expressive, pungent, saline, medium intensity. Palate: rich, powerful, fresh, fine bitter notes.

COOP. AGRÍCOLA LA AURORA
Avda. Europa, 7
14550 Montilla (Córdoba)
☎: +34 957 650 362
Fax: +34 957 654 642
www.bodegaslaaurora.com
administracion@bodegaslaaurora.com

Amanecer AM
100% pedro ximénez

88

Colour: light mahogany. Nose: aged wood nuances, sweet spices, creamy oak, saline, balanced. Palate: powerful, flavourful, spicy, long.

Amanecer PX
100% pedro ximénez

87

Colour: dark mahogany. Nose: fruit liqueur notes, dried fruit, pattiserie, toasty. Palate: sweet, rich, unctuous.

GRACIA HERMANOS
Avda. Luis de Góngora y Argote, s/n
14550 Montilla (Córdoba)
☎: +34 957 650 162
Fax: +34 957 652 335
www.bodegasgracia.com
info@bodegasgracia.com

Dulce Viejo Pedro Ximénez Gracia PX
100% pedro ximénez

88

Colour: dark mahogany. Nose: roasted coffee, aromatic coffee, dried fruit. Palate: creamy, powerful, flavourful, toasty.

Fino Corredera FI
pedro ximénez

86

Colour: bright yellow. Nose: pungent, saline, ripe fruit, dry nuts. Palate: powerful, fresh, fine bitter notes, thin.

Solera Fina María del Valle FI
100% pedro ximénez

87

Colour: bright yellow. Nose: pungent, saline, dry nuts. Palate: rich, powerful, fresh, fine bitter notes, balanced.

Solera Fina Tauromaquia FI
100% pedro ximénez

89

Colour: bright yellow. Nose: expressive, pungent, saline, ripe fruit. Palate: rich, powerful, fresh, fine bitter notes, long.

Tauromaquia OL
100% pedro ximénez

88

Colour: iodine, amber rim. Nose: powerfull, elegant, dry nuts, toasty. Palate: rich, long, fine solera notes, spicy, toasty.

Tauromaquia PX
pedro ximénez

91

Colour: dark mahogany. Nose: complex, fruit liqueur notes, dried fruit, pattiserie, toasty. Palate: sweet, rich, unctuous, powerful.

Tauromaquia Amontillado Viejo AM
100% pedro ximénez

91

Colour: old gold, amber rim. Nose: acetaldehyde, saline, spicy, creamy oak. Palate: powerful, spicy, long, elegant.

Viñaverde 2013 B
pedro ximénez, moscatel, verdejo, torrontés

85

NAVISA INDUSTRIAL VINÍCOLA ESPAÑOLA S.A.
Avda. José Padillo, s/n
14550 Montilla (Córdoba)
☎: +34 957 650 554
Fax: +34 957 651 747
www.navisa.es
navisa@navisa.es

Cobos FI
pedro ximénez

85

Dos Pasas PX
pedro ximénez

86

Colour: dark mahogany. Nose: dried herbs, sweet spices, creamy oak, medium intensity. Palate: toasty, rich, correct.

Montulia OL
pedro ximénez

86

Colour: iodine, amber rim. Nose: powerfull, dry nuts, toasty. Palate: rich, long, fine solera notes, spicy.

Tres Pasas PX
pedro ximénez

88

Colour: dark mahogany. Nose: fruit liqueur notes, dried fruit, pattiserie, toasty. Palate: sweet, rich, unctuous.

Vega María 2013 B
chardonnay
81

PÉREZ BARQUERO S.A.

Avda. Andalucía, 27
14550 Montilla (Córdoba)
☎: +34 957 650 500
Fax: +34 957 650 208
www.perezbarquero.com
info@perezbarquero.com

Fino Los Amigos FI
pedro ximénez
86
Colour: bright straw. Nose: medium intensity, dried herbs, ripe fruit, saline. Palate: fine bitter notes, flavourful, balanced.

Gran Barquero AM
100% pedro ximénez
90
Colour: light mahogany. Nose: acetaldehyde, saline, spicy, roasted almonds, expressive. Palate: fine bitter notes, flavourful, spicy, balanced.

Gran Barquero FI
100% pedro ximénez
91
Colour: bright yellow. Nose: complex, expressive, pungent, saline. Palate: rich, powerful, fresh, fine bitter notes, balanced, elegant.

Gran Barquero OL
100% pedro ximénez
90
Colour: iodine, amber rim. Nose: acetaldehyde, saline, sweet spices, creamy oak. Palate: balanced, fine bitter notes, flavourful, oaky, fine solera notes.

Gran Barquero PX
100% pedro ximénez
91
Colour: dark mahogany. Nose: complex, dried fruit, pattiserie, toasty, spicy, aromatic coffee. Palate: sweet, rich, powerful, roasted-coffee aftertaste.

La Cañada PX
100% pedro ximénez
96
Colour: dark mahogany. Nose: complex, dried fruit, pattiserie, toasty, caramel, dark chocolate, acetaldehyde, expressive. Palate: sweet, rich, unctuous, powerful, balanced, elegant.

Pérez Barquero Pedro Ximénez de Cosecha 2011 PX
100% pedro ximénez
91
Colour: light mahogany. Nose: dried fruit, pattiserie, toasty, sweet spices, cocoa bean. Palate: sweet, rich, unctuous, elegant.

Viña Amalia 2013 B
pedro ximénez, moscatel, verdejo, torrontés
85

TORO ALBALÁ

Avda. Antonio Sánchez, 1
14920 Aguilar de la Frontera (Córdoba)
☎: +34 957 660 046
Fax: +34 957 661 494
www.toroalbala.com
r.sanchez@toroalbala.com

Don P.X. 1983 PX Gran Reserva
pedro ximénez
94
Colour: dark mahogany. Nose: complex, fruit liqueur notes, dried fruit, pattiserie, toasty, aromatic coffee. Palate: sweet, rich, unctuous, powerful, roasted-coffee aftertaste, balanced.

Don P.X. 2010 PX
pedro ximénez
90
Colour: light mahogany. Nose: complex, fruit liqueur notes, dried fruit, pattiserie, toasty. Palate: sweet, rich, unctuous.

Eléctrico Fino del Lagar FI
pedro ximénez
87
Colour: bright golden. Nose: ripe fruit, dried herbs, faded flowers, powerfull, dry nuts, toasty. Palate: powerful, flavourful, spicy.

Marqués de Poley OL
100% pedro ximénez
89
Colour: light mahogany. Nose: powerfull, complex, elegant, dry nuts, toasty, acetaldehyde. Palate: rich, long, fine solera notes, spicy.

Marqués de Poley Dulce CR
100% pedro ximénez
87
Colour: light mahogany. Nose: varnish, caramel, sweet spices, creamy oak. Palate: powerful, flavourful, spicy, long.

DO. MONTSANT

CONSEJO REGULADOR

Plaça de la Quartera, 6
43730 Falset (Tarragona)
☎ :+34 977 831 742 - Fax: +34 977 830 676
@: info@domontsant.com
www.domontsant.com

LOCATION:

In the region of Priorat (Tarragona). It is made up of Baix Priorat, part of Alt Priorat and various municipal districts of Ribera d'Ebre that were already integrated into the Falset sub-region. In total, 16 municipal districts: La Bisbal de Falset, Cabaces, Capçanes, Cornudella de Montsant, La Figuera, Els Guiamets, Marçá, Margalef, El Masroig, Pradell, La Torre de Fontaubella, Ulldemolins, Falset, El Molar, Darmós and La Serra d'Almos. The vineyards are located at widely variable altitudes, ranging between 200 m to 700 m above sea level.

GRAPE VARIETIES:

White: Chardonnay, Garnacha Blanca, Macabeo, Moscatel, Pansal, Parellada.
Red: Cabernet Sauvignon, Cariñena, Garnacha Tinta, Garnacha Peluda, Merlot, Monastrell, Picapoll, Syrah, Tempranillo and Mazuela.

FIGURES:

Vineyard surface: 1,890 – Wine-Growers: 772 – Wineries: 63 – 2013 Harvest rating: Very Good – Production 13: 5,806,800 litres – Market percentages: 55% domestic - 45% export.

SOIL:

There are mainly three types of soil: compact calcareous soils with pebbles on the borders of the DO; granite sands in Falset; and siliceous slate (the same stony slaty soil as Priorat) in certain areas of Falset and Cornudella.

CLIMATE:

Although the vineyards are located in a Mediterranean region, the mountains that surround the region isolate it from the sea to a certain extent, resulting in a somewhat more Continental climate. Due to this, it benefits from the contrasts in day/night temperatures, which is an important factor in the ripening of the grapes. However, it also receives the sea winds, laden with humidity, which help to compensate for the lack of rainfall in the summer. The average rainfall is between 500 and 600 mm per year.

VINTAGE RATING

PEÑÍNGUIDE

2009	2010	2011	2012	2013
VERY GOOD	VERY GOOD	VERY GOOD	GOOD	VERY GOOD

PEÑÍNGUIDE to Spanish Wine

315

ACÚSTIC CELLER

Progrés s/n
43775 Marça (Tarragona)
☎: +34 672 432 691
Fax: +34 977 660 867
www.acusticceller.com
acustic@acusticceller.com

Acústic 2011 T Roble
cariñena, garnacha

92 🏆

Colour: very deep cherry, garnet rim. Nose: complex, ripe fruit, spicy, scrubland. Palate: full, flavourful, long, fruity.

Acústic 2012 T Roble
garnacha, cariñena

91 🏆

Colour: black cherry, garnet rim. Nose: ripe fruit, sweet spices, creamy oak, expressive. Palate: flavourful, fruity, toasty, round tannins.

Acústic Blanc 2011 BFB
garnacha blanca, macabeo, garnacha roja, pansal

93 🏆

Colour: bright yellow. Nose: ripe fruit, sweet spices, creamy oak, dry stone, expressive. Palate: rich, flavourful, fresh, roasted-coffee aftertaste, balanced, elegant.

Acústic Blanc 2012 BFB
garnacha blanca, macabeo, garnacha roja, pansal

90 🏆

Colour: bright straw. Nose: toasty, spicy, powerfull, ripe fruit. Palate: balanced, toasty, spicy, fine bitter notes.

Acústic Blanc 2013 BFB
garnacha blanca, macabeo, garnacha roja, pansal

88 🏆

Colour: bright yellow. Nose: ripe fruit, sweet spices, creamy oak, dried herbs. Palate: rich, flavourful, fresh, good acidity, toasty.

Auditori 2010 T
garnacha

94 🏆

Colour: deep cherry, garnet rim. Nose: closed, balsamic herbs, spicy, dry stone. Palate: full, complex, balanced, round.

Auditori 2011 T
garnacha

93 🏆

Colour: cherry, garnet rim. Nose: spicy, creamy oak, toasty, complex, red berry notes, ripe fruit. Palate: flavourful, round tannins, good structure.

Braó 2011 T
garnacha, cariñena

93 🏆

Colour: cherry, garnet rim. Nose: ripe fruit, wild herbs, earthy notes, spicy, creamy oak, complex. Palate: balanced, flavourful, long, balsamic, full.

Braó 2012 T
garnacha, cariñena

91 🏆

Colour: bright cherry, purple rim. Nose: expressive, complex, ripe fruit, wild herbs, spicy. Palate: balanced, long, round tannins.

AGRÍCOLA D'ULLDEMOLINS SANT JAUME

Saltadora, 17
43363 Ulldemolins (Tarragona)
☎: +34 977 561 640
Fax: +34 977 561 613
www.coopulldemolins.com
info@coopulldemolins.com

Les Pedrenyeres 2011 T
garnacha

89

Colour: dark-red cherry, garnet rim. Nose: ripe fruit, fruit preserve, creamy oak. Palate: good structure, flavourful, round tannins.

Les Pedrenyeres 2013 B
garnacha blanca, macabeo

87

Colour: bright straw. Nose: medium intensity, fresh, white flowers, spicy. Palate: fruity, correct, fine bitter notes.

Ulldemolins 2013 T
garnacha

87

Colour: cherry, purple rim. Nose: balanced, red berry notes, ripe fruit. Palate: flavourful, easy to drink, good finish.

AGRÍCOLA I SC DE LA SERRA D'ALMOS

Avinguda de la Cooperativa, s/n
43746 La Serra D'Almos (Tarragona)
☎: +34 977 418 125
Fax: +34 977 418 399
www.serradalmos.com
coopserra@telefonica.net

L'OM 2013 T
cariñena, garnacha, syrah

87

Colour: cherry, purple rim. Nose: expressive, fresh fruit, red berry notes, mineral. Palate: flavourful, fruity, good acidity, round tannins.

Mussefres 2013 B
macabeo, garnacha blanca

80

Mussefres Negre 2013 T
cariñena, garnacha, syrah

85

Mussefres Rosat 2013 RD
garnacha

84

ALFREDO ARRIBAS
Sort dels Capellans, 23
43730 Falset (Tarragona)
☎: +34 932 531 760
Fax: +34 934 173 591
www.portaldelpriorat.com
info@portaldelpriorat.com

Gotes del Montsant 2012 T
garnacha, cariñena

90

Colour: cherry, garnet rim. Nose: ripe fruit, earthy notes, spicy, fragrant herbs, mineral. Palate: flavourful, long, balsamic, balanced.

Trossos Sants 2013 B
garnacha blanca

91

Colour: bright straw. Nose: white flowers, fragrant herbs, fruit expression, dry stone. Palate: fresh, fruity, flavourful, balanced.

Trossos Tros Blanc 2012 B
garnacha blanca

92

Colour: bright straw. Nose: white flowers, fragrant herbs, fruit expression. Palate: fresh, fruity, flavourful, balanced, elegant.

Trossos Tros Blanc Magnum 2011 B
garnacha blanca

94

Colour: bright straw. Nose: white flowers, fragrant herbs, fruit expression, sweet spices, creamy oak, mineral. Palate: fresh, fruity, flavourful, balanced, elegant.

Trossos Tros Negre 2011 T
garnacha

93

Colour: deep cherry. Nose: ripe fruit, wild herbs, spicy, creamy oak, mineral. Palate: complex, spicy, long, balsamic, elegant, fine tannins.

Trossos Tros Negre 2012 T
garnacha

94

Colour: cherry, garnet rim. Nose: ripe fruit, wild herbs, earthy notes, spicy, creamy oak, mineral. Palate: flavourful, long, balsamic, balanced, elegant.

Trossos Vells 2012 T
cariñena

91

Colour: cherry, garnet rim. Nose: ripe fruit, spicy, creamy oak, toasty, complex, earthy notes, balsamic herbs. Palate: powerful, flavourful, toasty, balanced.

ANGUERA DOMENECH
Sant Pere, 2
43743 Darmós (Tarragona)
☎: +34 654 382 633
www.vianguera.com
angueradomenech@gmail.com

Reclot 2013 T
tempranillo, garnacha, monastrell

87

Colour: cherry, purple rim. Nose: red berry notes, raspberry, floral, expressive. Palate: fresh, fruity, flavourful, easy to drink.

BODEGAS ORDÓÑEZ
Bartolomé Esteban Murillo, 11
29700 Vélez- Málaga (Málaga)
☎: +34 952 504 706
Fax: +34 951 284 796
www.grupojorgeordonez.com
info@jorgeordonez.es

Zerrán 2012 T
mazuelo, syrah

93

Colour: cherry, garnet rim. Nose: wild herbs, earthy notes, spicy, creamy oak, mineral. Palate: balanced, flavourful, long, balsamic, elegant.

Zerrán Garnatxa Blanca 2013 B
100% garnacha blanca

89

Colour: bright straw. Nose: white flowers, fragrant herbs, fruit expression, mineral. Palate: fresh, fruity, flavourful, balanced, elegant, fine bitter notes.

CAPAFONS OSSÓ
Finca Masía Esplanes s/n
43730 Falset (Tarragona)
☎: +34 977 831 201
www.capafons-osso.cat
cellers@capafons-osso.com

Masia Esplanes 2005 T
merlot, cabernet sauvignon, garnacha, cariñena

90

Colour: pale ruby, brick rim edge. Nose: complex, ripe fruit, spicy, balanced, fine reductive notes. Palate: good structure, flavourful, round tannins, elegant.

Roigenc 2013 RD
syrah

82

Vessants 2008 T
garnacha, cariñena, cabernet sauvignon, merlot

86

Colour: pale ruby, brick rim edge. Nose: spicy, toasty, overripe fruit, mineral, fine reductive notes. Palate: powerful, flavourful, toasty.

Vessants Xic 2010 T
garnacha, cabernet sauvignon, zalema

86

Colour: cherry, garnet rim. Nose: ripe fruit, scrubland, mineral, spicy, fine reductive notes. Palate: powerful, flavourful, spicy, balanced.

CARA NORD
25457 El Vilosell (Lleida)
☎: +34 973 176 029
Fax: +34 973 175 945
www.caranordceller.com
hola@caranordceller.com

Mineral 2012 T

90

Colour: cherry, garnet rim. Nose: wild herbs, mineral, red berry notes, ripe fruit, spicy, creamy oak. Palate: flavourful, spicy, balanced.

CELLER CEDÓ ANGUERA
Ctra. La Serra d'Almos-Darmós, Km. 0,2
43746 La Serra d'Almos (Tarragona)
☎: +34 699 694 728
Fax: +34 977 417 369
www.cedoanguera.com
celler@cedoanguera.com

Anexe 2013 T
84

Anexe Syrah 2013 T
100% syrah

86

Colour: dark-red cherry, purple rim. Nose: powerfull, red berry notes. Palate: correct, fruity, flavourful.

Anexe Vinyes Velles de Samso 2013 T
100% samsó

89

Colour: cherry, purple rim. Nose: balanced, scrubland, wild herbs. Palate: flavourful, correct, good acidity, varietal.

Clònic 2009 TC

90

Colour: cherry, garnet rim. Nose: ripe fruit, spicy, creamy oak, toasty. Palate: powerful, flavourful, toasty, round tannins, elegant.

Clònic Vinyes Velles de Samso 2012 T
100% samsó

87

Colour: black cherry, garnet rim. Nose: toasty, dark chocolate, spicy. Palate: flavourful, powerful, round tannins.

CELLER CORNUDELLA DE MONTSANT
Carrer Comte de Rius, 2
43360 Cornudella de Montsant
(Tarragona)
☎: +34 977 821 329
Fax: +34 977 821 329
www.cornudella.net
info@cornudella.net

Castell de Siurana Garnatxa del Montsant 2012 RD
100% garnacha

90

Colour: coppery red. Nose: powerfull, ripe fruit, red berry notes, floral, expressive, aged wood nuances. Palate: powerful, fruity, sweet.

Castella de Siurana Mistela 2011 Vino de licor
100% garnacha

88

Colour: cherry, garnet rim. Nose: red berry notes, ripe fruit, balsamic herbs, expressive. Palate: powerful, flavourful, sweet, correct.

El Codolar 2012 T

90

Colour: cherry, garnet rim. Nose: ripe fruit, wild herbs, earthy notes, spicy, creamy oak, dry stone. Palate: balanced, flavourful, long, balsamic.

Les Troies 2013 B

87

Colour: yellow. Nose: white flowers, powerfull, fresh fruit. Palate: fresh, easy to drink, correct.

Les Troies 2013 RD
cariñena, garnacha

88

Colour: light cherry, bright. Nose: grassy, citrus fruit, red berry notes. Palate: balanced, fine bitter notes, good acidity, long.

Les Troies 2013 T

87

Colour: cherry, purple rim. Nose: red berry notes, raspberry, fruit expression, fragrant herbs, mineral. Palate: flavourful, light-bodied, good acidity, fresh, fruity.

CELLER DE CAPÇANES

Llebaria, 4
43776 Capçanes (Tarragona)
☎: +34 977 178 319
Fax: +34 977 178 319
www.cellercapcanes.com
cellercapanes@cellercapanes.com

2 Pájaros 2012 T
100% cariñena

92

Colour: very deep cherry. Nose: ripe fruit, wild herbs, earthy notes, spicy. Palate: balanced, flavourful, long, balsamic.

7/X Pinot Noir de Capçanes 2012 T
100% pinot noir

91

Colour: ruby red, garnet rim. Nose: fruit liqueur notes, ripe fruit, fragrant herbs, spicy, mineral. Palate: balanced, flavourful, spicy, long.

Cabrida 2012 T
100% garnacha

90

Colour: very deep cherry. Nose: wild herbs, ripe fruit, wild herbs. Palate: flavourful, good structure, round tannins.

Costers del Gravet 2012 TC

89

Colour: cherry, garnet rim. Nose: ripe fruit, wild herbs, earthy notes, spicy, creamy oak. Palate: balanced, flavourful, long, balsamic.

Lasendal Garnatxa 2013 T Barrica
garnacha, syrah

87

Colour: bright cherry. Nose: creamy oak, ripe fruit, wild herbs. Palate: flavourful, spicy, harsh oak tannins.

Mas Collet 2012 T Barrica
garnacha, cariñena, ull de llebre, cabernet sauvignon

87

Colour: bright cherry. Nose: ripe fruit, sweet spices, creamy oak, expressive. Palate: flavourful, fruity, toasty, round tannins, balsamic.

Mas Donís 2013 T
garnacha, syrah

85

Mas Tortó 2012 T
garnacha, syrah, cabernet sauvignon, merlot

89

Colour: cherry, garnet rim. Nose: ripe fruit, spicy, creamy oak, toasty, complex, balsamic herbs. Palate: powerful, flavourful, toasty, round tannins.

Peraj Ha'Abib 2012 T
garnacha, cabernet sauvignon, cariñena

91

Colour: very deep cherry, purple rim. Nose: mineral, expressive, ripe fruit, scrubland. Palate: flavourful, good structure.

Vall del Calàs 2012 T
merlot, garnacha, ull de llebre

88

Colour: cherry, purple rim. Nose: powerfull, ripe fruit, balsamic herbs, characterful. Palate: flavourful, round tannins, spicy.

CELLER DE L'ERA

Mas de las Moreras s/n
43360 Cornudella de Montsant (Tarragona)
☎: +34 977 262 031
www.cellerdelera.com
info@cellerdelera.com

Bri Celler de L'Era 2010 T

91

Colour: cherry, garnet rim. Nose: ripe fruit, spicy, toasty, tobacco. Palate: powerful, flavourful, toasty, round tannins.

CELLER EL MASROIG

Passeig de L'Arbre, 3
43736 El Masroig (Tarragona)
☎: +34 977 825 026
Fax: +34 977 825 489
www.cellermasroig.com
celler@cellermasroig.com

Castell de les Pinyeres 2011 TC

89

Colour: dark-red cherry, garnet rim. Nose: ripe fruit, warm, wild herbs, toasty. Palate: flavourful, correct, round tannins.

Etnic 2009 TC

93

Colour: deep cherry, garnet rim. Nose: complex, varietal, balsamic herbs, fresh fruit, mineral. Palate: good structure, full, flavourful, complex.

Etnic 2011 BFB
100% garnacha blanca

90

Colour: bright yellow. Nose: ripe fruit, powerfull, toasty, aged wood nuances. Palate: flavourful, fruity, spicy, toasty, long.

Finca Cucó 2013 T

86

Colour: cherry, purple rim. Nose: red berry notes, floral, wild herbs. Palate: flavourful, fruity, good acidity.

Finca Cucó Selecció 2011 T

88

Colour: very deep cherry. Nose: ripe fruit, spicy, creamy oak, toasty, characterful. Palate: powerful, flavourful, toasty, round tannins.

Les Sorts 2012 BFB
100% garnacha blanca

88

Colour: bright yellow. Nose: ripe fruit, sweet spices, creamy oak, fragrant herbs. Palate: rich, flavourful, fresh, good acidity, roasted-coffee aftertaste.

Les Sorts 2013 T Maceración Carbónica
cariñena, garnacha, syrah

89

Colour: cherry, purple rim. Nose: red berry notes, raspberry, floral, expressive. Palate: fresh, fruity, flavourful, easy to drink.

Les Sorts Rosat 2013 RD

90

Colour: onion pink. Nose: elegant, dried flowers, fragrant herbs, red berry notes. Palate: light-bodied, flavourful, good acidity, long, spicy.

Les Sorts Sycar 2011 T

91

Colour: black cherry. Nose: toasty, powerfull, ripe fruit, fragrant herbs, spicy, tobacco. Palate: flavourful, balanced.

Les Sorts Vinyes Velles 2009 TC

91

Colour: cherry, garnet rim. Nose: ripe fruit, spicy, creamy oak, toasty, complex. Palate: powerful, flavourful, toasty, round tannins.

Sola Fred 2013 B

86

Colour: bright straw. Nose: fresh, fresh fruit, white flowers. Palate: flavourful, fruity, good acidity, balanced.

Solà Fred 2013 T

87

Colour: cherry, purple rim. Nose: expressive, fresh fruit, red berry notes, floral. Palate: flavourful, fruity, good acidity.

Sola Fred Rosat 2013 RD

87

Colour: light cherry, bright. Nose: fresh fruit, red berry notes, floral, dried herbs. Palate: correct, balanced, easy to drink.

CELLER LAURONA
Ctra. Bellmunt, s/n
43730 Falset (Tarragona)
☎: +34 977 830 221
Fax: +34 977 831 797
www.cellerlaurona.com
laurona@cellerlaurona.com

Blanc de Laurona 2013 B

90

Colour: bright straw. Nose: white flowers, fragrant herbs, fruit expression. Palate: fresh, fruity, flavourful, balanced, elegant.

Laurona 2009 T
garnacha, cariñena, syrah, merlot

91

Colour: cherry, garnet rim. Nose: ripe fruit, spicy, creamy oak, toasty, complex. Palate: powerful, flavourful, toasty, round tannins.

CELLER MALONDRO
Miranda, 27
43360 Cornudella del Montsant
(Tarragona)
☎: +34 977 821 451
Fax: +34 977 821 451
www.malondro.es
celler@malondro.es

Latria 2011 T

88

Colour: cherry, garnet rim. Nose: ripe fruit, spicy, creamy oak, toasty, complex, dark chocolate, earthy notes. Palate: powerful, flavourful, toasty, round tannins.

Malondro 2012 T

91

Colour: cherry, garnet rim. Nose: ripe fruit, spicy, creamy oak, toasty, complex, balsamic herbs, mineral. Palate: powerful, flavourful, toasty, balanced.

Malondro Coelum 2010 TC

93

Colour: cherry, garnet rim. Nose: red berry notes, ripe fruit, spicy, creamy oak, toasty, complex, dry stone. Palate: powerful, flavourful, toasty, balsamic, balanced, elegant.

CELLER MAS DE LES VINYES
Mas de les Vinyes, s/n
43373 Cabacés (Tarragona)
☎: +34 652 568 848
Fax: +34 977 719 690
www.masdelesvinyes.com
josep@masdelesvinyes.com

Mas de les Vinyes 2013 B
100% macabeo

87

Colour: bright straw. Nose: fresh fruit, grassy, wild herbs. Palate: flavourful, good acidity, fine bitter notes, long.

Mas de les Vinyes Negre 2012 T

84

CELLER SERRA MAJOR

Alfons El Cast, s/n
43363 Ulldemolins (Tarragona)
☎: +34 647 986 960
santi@sarroges.com

Sarroges 2010 T
garnacha, cabernet sauvignon, syrah, merlot

90

Colour: black cherry, garnet rim. Nose: ripe fruit, expressive, powerfull, spicy. Palate: balanced, good structure, long.

Teix 2011 T
garnacha, cabernet sauvignon, syrah, merlot

85

CELLER VENDRELL RIVED

Bassa, 10
43775 Marçà (Tarragona)
☎: +34 977 263 053
www.vendrellrived.com
celler@vendrellrived.com

L'Alleu 2011 TC
garnacha, cariñena

90 🍷

Colour: cherry, garnet rim. Nose: ripe fruit, spicy, creamy oak, toasty, complex. Palate: powerful, flavourful, toasty, round tannins.

Miloca Garnacha 2013 T
100% garnacha

90 🍷

Colour: cherry, purple rim. Nose: floral, red berry notes, ripe fruit, balsamic herbs, spicy, dry stone. Palate: flavourful, concentrated, balanced, round.

Miloca Samso 2013 T
100% cariñena

88 🍷

Colour: cherry, purple rim. Nose: red berry notes, fruit preserve, scrubland, mineral, spicy. Palate: powerful, flavourful, complex.

Serè 2012 T
garnacha, cariñena

88 🍷

Colour: bright cherry. Nose: ripe fruit, sweet spices, creamy oak. Palate: flavourful, fruity, toasty.

CELLER VERMUNVER

Ricard Pique, 15
43775 Marçà (Tarragona)
☎: +34 977 178 288
Fax: +34 977 178 288
www.genesi.cat
info@genesi.cat

Gènesi Selecció 2009 T
garnacha, cariñena

92

Colour: cherry, garnet rim. Nose: ripe fruit, spicy, creamy oak, toasty, complex, dark chocolate, earthy notes. Palate: powerful, flavourful, toasty, round tannins.

CELLERS AT ROCA

Pol. La Sort dels Capellans, 13
43730 Falset (Tarragona)
☎: +34 935 165 043
www.cellersatroca.com
info@cellersatroca.com

Sileo 2013 T

89

Colour: cherry, purple rim. Nose: balanced, balsamic herbs, ripe fruit, spicy. Palate: fruity, flavourful, long.

CELLERS BARONÍA DEL MONTSANT

Comte de Rius, 1
43360 Cornudella de Montsant (Tarragona)
☎: +34 977 821 483
Fax: +34 977 821 483
www.baronia-m.com
englora@baronia-m.com

Cims del Montsant 2011 T
garnacha, cariñena

89

Colour: dark-red cherry, garnet rim. Nose: scrubland, dried herbs, ripe fruit, spicy. Palate: balanced, round tannins.

Clos D'Englora AV 14 2009 T
garnacha, garnacha peluda, cariñena

92

Colour: cherry, garnet rim. Nose: ripe fruit, spicy, toasty, complex, earthy notes. Palate: powerful, flavourful, toasty, round tannins, long.

Clos D'Englora Blanc 2012 B
garnacha blanca, viognier

86

Colour: bright straw. Nose: ripe fruit, tropical fruit. Palate: flavourful, fruity, easy to drink.

Còdols del Montsant 2013 T
garnacha

87

Colour: deep cherry, purple rim. Nose: dried herbs, ripe fruit, balanced. Palate: fruity, flavourful, easy to drink.

Englora 2010 TC
garnacha, cariñena, merlot, syrah

92

Colour: dark-red cherry. Nose: scrubland, cocoa bean, ripe fruit. Palate: good structure, flavourful, balanced, long, good acidity, round tannins.

Flor D'Englora Garnatxa 2013 T
garnacha

89

Colour: cherry, purple rim. Nose: expressive, fresh fruit, red berry notes, toasty, scrubland. Palate: flavourful, fruity, good acidity, round tannins.

Flor D'Englora Roure 2011 T
garnacha, cariñena

88

Colour: cherry, garnet rim. Nose: ripe fruit, spicy, toasty. Palate: powerful, flavourful, toasty, round tannins, easy to drink.

CELLERS CAN BLAU
Ctra. Bellmunt, s/n
43730 Falset (Tarragona)
☎: +34 629 261 379
Fax: +34 968 716 051
www.orowines.com
info@orowines.com

Blau 2012 T
89

Colour: bright cherry. Nose: ripe fruit, sweet spices, creamy oak, toasty. Palate: flavourful, fruity, toasty, round tannins.

Can Blau 2012 T
91

Colour: very deep cherry, purple rim. Nose: spicy, smoky, ripe fruit. Palate: good structure, full, round tannins, spicy.

Mas de Can Blau 2010 T
94

Colour: cherry, garnet rim. Nose: ripe fruit, spicy, creamy oak, toasty, complex, mineral. Palate: powerful, flavourful, toasty, round tannins.

Mas de Can Blau 2011 T
92

Colour: cherry, garnet rim. Nose: ripe fruit, spicy, creamy oak, toasty, complex, dark chocolate, earthy notes. Palate: powerful, flavourful, toasty, round tannins.

CELLERS SANT RAFEL
Ctra. La Torre, Km. 1,7
43774 Pradell (Tarragona)
☎: +34 689 792 305
www.cellerssantrafel.com
xavi@cellerssantrafel.com

Joana 2013 T
89

Colour: cherry, purple rim. Nose: expressive, fresh fruit, red berry notes, floral. Palate: flavourful, fruity, good acidity.

Solpost Blanc 2012 B
garnacha blanca

92

Colour: yellow. Nose: ripe fruit, white flowers, sweet spices, creamy oak. Palate: full, flavourful, long, good acidity, rich.

CELLERS TERRA I VINS
Av. Falset, 17 Bajos
43006 Reus (Tarragona)
☎: +34 633 289 267
cterraivins@gmail.com

Clos del Gos 2013 T
87

Colour: bright cherry, purple rim. Nose: red berry notes, wild herbs, balanced. Palate: ripe fruit, flavourful, easy to drink.

CELLERS UNIÓ
Joan Oliver, 16-24
43206 Reus (Tarragona)
☎: +34 977 330 055
Fax: +34 977 330 070
www.cellersunio.com
info@cellersunio.com

Dairo 2012 TC
garnacha, mazuelo, syrah

88

Colour: cherry, garnet rim. Nose: ripe fruit, spicy, creamy oak, toasty. Palate: powerful, flavourful, toasty.

El Toro Avanzado Bag in box 3l 2012 T
garnacha

84

Mas dels Mets 2013 T
merlot, garnacha, tempranillo, mazuelo

87

Colour: black cherry, garnet rim. Nose: ripe fruit, dried herbs. Palate: flavourful, fruity, easy to drink.

Perlat Syrah 2012 T
syrah

88

Colour: bright cherry. Nose: ripe fruit, sweet spices, creamy oak, expressive. Palate: flavourful, fruity, toasty, round tannins.

Roca Blanca 2012 TC
garnacha, mazuelo, syrah
89
Colour: very deep cherry. Nose: ripe fruit, wild herbs, spicy, creamy oak, mineral. Palate: balanced, flavourful, long, balsamic.

CHARMIAN
Avda. Baix Penedès 77-81, 1º 1ª esc. A
43700 El Vendrell (Tarragona)
☎: +34 977 661 862
Fax: +34 977 661 862
www.cataloniacava.net
j.murillo@cataloniacava.net

Charmian 2013 T
88
Colour: cherry, purple rim. Nose: red berry notes, ripe fruit, balsamic herbs, mineral, spicy. Palate: powerful, flavourful, fruity, concentrated.

Charmian Garnatxa Blanca 2012 B
100% garnacha blanca
86
Colour: yellow. Nose: ripe fruit, dried flowers. Palate: fruity, good finish, easy to drink.

Charmian Grenache Old Vines 2008 T
87
Colour: pale ruby, brick rim edge. Nose: elegant, spicy, fine reductive notes, wet leather, aged wood nuances. Palate: spicy, fine tannins, long.

CINGLES BLAUS
Mas de les Moreres - Afueras de Cornudella
43360 Cornudella de Montsant
(Tarragona)
☎: +34 977 310 382
Fax: +34 977 323 928
www.cinglesblaus.com
info@cinglesblaus.com

Cingles Blaus Aurí 2007 AM
garnacha roja
90
Colour: iodine, amber rim. Nose: powerfull, complex, dry nuts, toasty, rancio notes. Palate: rich, fine bitter notes, fine solera notes, long, spicy.

Cingles Blaus Mas de les Moreres 2010 T
garnacha, cariñena, cabernet sauvignon, merlot
89
Colour: dark-red cherry, garnet rim. Nose: spicy, fine reductive notes, wet leather, toasty. Palate: spicy, long, toasty, good acidity.

Cingles Blaus Octubre 2011 T
garnacha, cariñena
88
Colour: bright cherry. Nose: ripe fruit, sweet spices, expressive. Palate: flavourful, fruity, toasty, round tannins.

Cingles Blaus Octubre 2013 B
macabeo, garnacha blanca, chardonnay
89
Colour: straw. Nose: fresh, fresh fruit, white flowers, citrus fruit. Palate: flavourful, fruity, good acidity, fine bitter notes.

Cingles Blaus Octubre 2013 RD
garnacha, cariñena
88
Colour: raspberry rose. Nose: powerfull, ripe fruit, red berry notes, floral, expressive. Palate: powerful, fruity, fresh.

Cingles Blaus Selecció 2009 T
garnacha, cariñena
88
Colour: dark-red cherry. Nose: old leather, tobacco, scrubland. Palate: flavourful, round tannins.

COCA I FITÓ
Avda. Onze de Setembre s/n
43736 El Masroig (Tarragona)
☎: +34 619 776 948
Fax: +34 935 457 092
www.cocaifito.com
info@cocaifito.cat

Coca i Fitó Negre 2010 T
91
Colour: cherry, garnet rim. Nose: ripe fruit, wild herbs, earthy notes, spicy, creamy oak, fine reductive notes. Palate: balanced, flavourful, long, balsamic.

Coca i Fitó Rosa 2013 RD
100% syrah
89
Colour: light cherry. Nose: ripe fruit, red berry notes, floral, expressive, balsamic herbs. Palate: powerful, fruity, fresh, balanced.

Jaspi Maragda 2011 T
91
Colour: cherry, garnet rim. Nose: red berry notes, ripe fruit, balsamic herbs, dry stone, balanced. Palate: flavourful, powerful, balsamic, correct.

Jaspi Negre 2011 T
87
Colour: bright cherry. Nose: ripe fruit, sweet spices, creamy oak, scrubland. Palate: fruity, flavourful, toasty.

COOPERATIVA FALSET MARÇA

Miquel Barceló, 31
43730 Falset (Tarragona)
☎: +34 977 830 105
www.la-cooperativa.cat
info@etim.cat

Ètim 2013 B
garnacha blanca
86
Colour: bright straw. Nose: fresh, fresh fruit, dried flowers. Palate: flavourful, fruity, good acidity.

Ètim L'Esparver 2009 T
garnacha, samsó, cabernet sauvignon, syrah
87
Colour: ruby red. Nose: spicy, fine reductive notes, wet leather, aged wood nuances, toasty. Palate: spicy, long, toasty.

Ètim Negre 2012 T
garnacha, samsó, syrah
89
Colour: cherry, purple rim. Nose: red berry notes, floral, wild herbs, spicy, expressive. Palate: flavourful, fresh, fruity, spicy, balsamic.

Ètim Old Vines Grenache 2010 T
garnacha
90
Colour: cherry, garnet rim. Nose: ripe fruit, wild herbs, earthy notes, spicy. Palate: balanced, flavourful, long, balsamic.

Ètim Ranci AM
garnacha, samsó
92
Colour: light mahogany. Nose: acetaldehyde, aged wood nuances, spicy, roasted almonds, candied fruit. Palate: full, spicy, fine bitter notes.

Ètim Rosat 2013 RD
garnacha, syrah
84

Ètim Syrah 2010 T
syrah
89
Colour: cherry, garnet rim. Nose: ripe fruit, spicy, creamy oak, toasty, fine reductive notes. Palate: powerful, flavourful, toasty, round tannins.

Ètim Verema Tardana Negre 2011 T
garnacha
90
Colour: cherry, garnet rim. Nose: balanced, expressive, candied fruit, fruit liqueur notes, toasty. Palate: good acidity, flavourful.

Imus Selecció de Vinyes 2013 T
garnacha, samsó, cabernet sauvignon, merlot
84

La Dama de Blanc 2010 BFB
100% garnacha blanca
90
Colour: bright yellow. Nose: powerfull, ripe fruit, sweet spices, creamy oak, fragrant herbs. Palate: rich, smoky aftertaste, flavourful, fresh, good acidity.

Lo Dolç Joglar 2013 T
samsó
87
Colour: black cherry. Nose: candied fruit, pattiserie, honeyed notes, toasty. Palate: flavourful, balsamic.

Lo Foc del Castell 2010 T
garnacha, samsó, syrah, cabernet sauvignon
88
Colour: cherry, garnet rim. Nose: balanced, complex, ripe fruit, spicy, wet leather, tobacco. Palate: good structure, flavourful, round tannins.

Lo Senyor del Castell 2012 T
garnacha, samsó, syrah
89
Colour: cherry, garnet rim. Nose: ripe fruit, spicy, creamy oak, toasty, complex, earthy notes. Palate: powerful, flavourful, toasty.

EDICIONES I-LIMITADAS

Claravall, 2
8021 (Barcelona)
☎: +34 932 531 760
Fax: +34 934 173 591
www.edicionesi-limitadas.com
info@edicionesi-limitadas.com

Faunus 2012 T
syrah, tempranillo, cariñena, merlot
88
Colour: bright cherry. Nose: ripe fruit, sweet spices, creamy oak, medium intensity. Palate: fruity, flavourful, toasty.

Luno 2012 T
garnacha, cariñena, syrah, cabernet sauvignon
92
Colour: cherry, garnet rim. Nose: spicy, toasty, complex, fruit expression. Palate: powerful, flavourful, toasty, round tannins.

Núvol 2013 B
garnacha blanca, macabeo
89
Colour: bright yellow. Nose: balanced, expressive, wild herbs, ripe fruit. Palate: balanced, fine bitter notes.

Terrícola 2012 T
garnacha, cariñena, syrah, cabernet sauvignon

93

Colour: cherry, garnet rim. Nose: ripe fruit, spicy, complex, earthy notes, scrubland. Palate: powerful, flavourful, toasty, round tannins.

EL VI A PUNT
Raval del Roser, 3
43886 Vilabella (Tarragona)
☎: +34 625 408 974
www.elviapunt.com
comercial@elviapunt.com

Qua Bag in box (3 litros) 2013 T
84

ESPECTACLE VINS
Crat. Bellmunt – sort dels Capellans
43730 Falset (Tarragona)
☎: +34 977 839 171
Fax: +34 977 839 326
www.espectaclevins.com
closmogador@closmogador.com

Espectacle 2011 T
100% garnacha

96

Colour: cherry, garnet rim. Nose: ripe fruit, expressive, fresh, balsamic herbs, complex, spicy. Palate: balanced, round tannins, full.

ESTONES
Pl. Sort dels Capellans, Nau Bahaus
43740 Falset (Tarragona)
☎: +34 666 415 735
www.massersal.com
vins@massersal.com

Estones 2011 T
87

Colour: very deep cherry. Nose: dark chocolate, sweet spices, ripe fruit, fruit preserve. Palate: balanced, round tannins.

Estones de Mishima "Set Tota la Vida" 2012 T
89

Colour: cherry, garnet rim. Nose: ripe fruit, spicy, creamy oak, toasty, complex. Palate: powerful, flavourful, toasty.

Petit Estones 2012 T
88

Colour: cherry, garnet rim. Nose: ripe fruit, wild herbs, earthy notes, spicy, creamy oak. Palate: balanced, flavourful, long, balsamic.

FRANCK MASSARD
Rambla Arnau de Vilanova, 6
08800 Vilanova i La Geltrú (Barcelona)
☎: +34 938 956 541
Fax: +34 938 956 541
www.epicure-wines.com
info@epicure-wines.com

El Brindis 2012 T
89

Colour: cherry, garnet rim. Nose: ripe fruit, spicy, closed. Palate: powerful, flavourful, toasty, round tannins, balanced.

Finca El Romero 2011 TC
100% cariñena

89

Colour: cherry, garnet rim. Nose: ripe fruit, wild herbs, earthy notes, spicy, creamy oak. Palate: balanced, flavourful, long, balsamic.

I TANT VINS
Passeig del Ferrocarril, 337 Baixos
08860 Castelldefels (Barcelona)
☎: +34 936 628 253
www.aribau.es
albert@aribau.es

I Tant Garnatxa Negra 2013 T
100% garnacha

87

Colour: deep cherry. Nose: ripe fruit, red berry notes, scrubland. Palate: good acidity, fine bitter notes.

Que Si 2013 T
88

Colour: cherry, purple rim. Nose: red berry notes, ripe fruit, balsamic herbs, dry stone. Palate: powerful, flavourful, spicy, long.

JOSEP GRAU VITICULTOR
Polígono 7 Parcela 27
43775 Marça (Tarragona)
☎: +34 977 054 071
Fax: +34 977 054 071
www.josepgrauviticultor.com
exec@josepgrauviticultor.com

Dosterras 2012 T
100% garnacha

91

Colour: cherry, garnet rim. Nose: ripe fruit, spicy, creamy oak, toasty, complex, earthy notes. Palate: powerful, flavourful, toasty, balanced, balsamic.

L'Efecte Volador 2013 T
90

Colour: very deep cherry, purple rim. Nose: balanced, red berry notes, ripe fruit, dried herbs. Palate: balanced, easy to drink, fruity.

Vespres 2013 T

90

Colour: deep cherry, purple rim. Nose: expressive, wild herbs. Palate: flavourful, ripe fruit, balanced, round tannins.

MAS DE L'ABUNDÀNCIA VITICULTORS

Camí de Gratallops, s/n
43736 El Masroig (Tarragona)
☎: +34 627 471 444
www.masdelabundancia.com
info@masdelabundancia.com

De Calpino 2013 B

garnacha blanca

89

Colour: bright yellow. Nose: fresh, floral, fragrant herbs. Palate: rich, flavourful, balanced, long, complex.

Flvminis 2012 T

87

Colour: bright cherry. Nose: ripe fruit, sweet spices, creamy oak, earthy notes. Palate: flavourful, fruity, toasty.

Mas de l'Abundància 2012 T

89

Colour: cherry, garnet rim. Nose: ripe fruit, spicy, creamy oak, wild herbs, mineral. Palate: powerful, flavourful, toasty, balanced.

NOGUERALS

Tou, 5
43360 Cornudella de Montsant
(Tarragona)
☎: +34 650 033 546
www.noguerals.com
cellernoguerals@gmail.com

Corbatera 2011 T

89

Colour: bright cherry. Nose: ripe fruit, sweet spices, creamy oak, expressive. Palate: flavourful, fruity, toasty.

ORIGAMI WINES

Els Guiamets
Els Guiamets (Tarragona)
☎: +34 902 800 229
Fax: +34 938 919 735
www.origamiwines.com
info@origamiwines.com

Mysti Garnatxa 2013 T

garnacha

86

Colour: cherry, purple rim. Nose: red berry notes, ripe fruit, wild herbs, mineral. Palate: flavourful, balsamic, good finish.

Mysti Syrah 2011 T

100% syrah

85

ORTO VINS

Passeig de l'Arbre, s/n
43736 El Masroig (Tarragona)
☎: +34 629 171 246
www.ortovins.com
info@ortovins.com

Blanc D'Orto 2013 B

garnacha blanca

87

Colour: bright yellow. Nose: medium intensity, faded flowers. Palate: balanced, correct, fine bitter notes, rich.

Blanc D'Orto Brisat 2011 B

100% garnacha blanca

90

Colour: bright golden. Nose: ripe fruit, dry nuts, powerfull, toasty, aged wood nuances. Palate: flavourful, fruity, spicy, toasty, long.

Dolç D'Orto 2013 B

93

Colour: golden. Nose: powerfull, floral, honeyed notes, candied fruit, fragrant herbs. Palate: flavourful, sweet, fresh, fruity, good acidity, long, balanced, elegant.

La Carrerada 2012 T

100% samsó

93

Colour: bright cherry. Nose: ripe fruit, sweet spices, creamy oak, mineral, balsamic herbs, balanced. Palate: flavourful, fruity, spicy, balanced, elegant.

Les Comes D'Orto 2012 T

87

Colour: bright cherry. Nose: ripe fruit, sweet spices, creamy oak, medium intensity. Palate: fruity, flavourful, toasty.

Les Pujoles 2012 TC

100% ull de llebre

92

Colour: cherry, garnet rim. Nose: ripe fruit, spicy, creamy oak, toasty, complex, mineral, balsamic herbs. Palate: powerful, flavourful, toasty, balanced.

Les Tallades de Cal Nicolau 2012 TC

picapoll

93

Colour: cherry, garnet rim. Nose: ripe fruit, spicy, creamy oak, toasty, complex, earthy notes, fragrant herbs, dry stone. Palate: powerful, flavourful, toasty, balsamic.

Orto 2012 T

89

Colour: cherry, garnet rim. Nose: red berry notes, balsamic herbs, mineral, spicy, balanced. Palate: elegant, flavourful, fresh, fruity.

Palell 2012 TC
100% garnacha peluda

93

Colour: bright cherry. Nose: creamy oak, fruit liqueur notes, balsamic herbs, dry stone. Palate: fruity, flavourful, balanced, elegant.

PORTAL DEL MONTSANT
Carrer de Dalt, s/n
43775 Marçà (Tarragona)
☎: +34 933 950 811
Fax: +34 933 955 500
www.portaldelmontsant.com
tsoler@parxet.es

Bruberry 2012 T
cariñena, garnacha

90

Colour: cherry, garnet rim. Nose: ripe fruit, spicy, creamy oak, toasty, complex, mineral. Palate: powerful, flavourful, toasty.

Bruberry 2013 B
garnacha blanca, garnacha gris

90

Colour: bright straw. Nose: white flowers, fragrant herbs, fruit expression. Palate: fresh, fruity, flavourful, balanced, elegant.

Brunus 2011 T
cariñena, garnacha

92

Colour: very deep cherry. Nose: red berry notes, fruit expression, floral, fruit liqueur notes, earthy notes. Palate: good structure, long, good acidity.

Brunus Rosé 2013 RD
garnacha

89

Colour: brilliant rose. Nose: rose petals, floral, fragrant herbs, mineral, expressive. Palate: fresh, fruity, flavourful.

Santbru 2009 T
cariñena, garnacha

93

Colour: cherry, garnet rim. Nose: spicy, earthy notes, mineral, scrubland. Palate: spicy, ripe fruit, balsamic, good finish, fine tannins.

Santbru 2010 T
cariñena, garnacha

93

Colour: cherry, garnet rim. Nose: red berry notes, ripe fruit, creamy oak, balsamic herbs, mineral. Palate: balanced, flavourful, fruity.

Santbru Blanc 2012 B

92

Colour: bright yellow. Nose: powerfull, ripe fruit, sweet spices, creamy oak, fragrant herbs. Palate: rich, smoky aftertaste, flavourful, fresh, good acidity, elegant.

SOMSIS
Apartado 96
43730 Falset (Tarragona)
☎: +34 662 214 291
www.somsis.es
info@somsis.es

Somsis 2010 TC

90

Colour: cherry, garnet rim. Nose: red berry notes, ripe fruit, spicy, creamy oak, toasty, complex, earthy notes. Palate: powerful, flavourful, toasty, round tannins.

Somsis 2012 T

87

Colour: black cherry, garnet rim. Nose: powerfull, dried herbs, spicy. Palate: ripe fruit, round tannins.

TERRA PERSONAS
www.terrapersonas.festis.cat
ruud@terrapersonas.com

Terra Negra 2010 T

88

Colour: deep cherry, garnet rim. Nose: smoky, toasty, spicy. Palate: flavourful, round tannins, good acidity.

Terra Vermella 2012 T

87

Colour: dark-red cherry, purple rim. Nose: scrubland, spicy, ripe fruit. Palate: balanced, correct.

TERRASSES DEL MONTSANT
Major, 14
43746 La Serra d'Almos (Tarragona)
☎: +34 932 051 009
Fax: +34 932 051 120
www.heretatnavas.com
info@heretatnavas.com

Heretat Navas 2012 T

87

Colour: bright cherry. Nose: ripe fruit, sweet spices. Palate: flavourful, fruity, toasty, round tannins.

VENUS LA UNIVERSAL
Ctra. Porrera, s/n
43730 Falset (Tarragona)
☎: +34 699 354 135
www.venuslauniversal.com
info@venuslauniversal.com

Dido 2012 T
garnacha, syrah, cabernet sauvignon, merlot

92 ♣

Colour: deep cherry, purple rim. Nose: powerfull, dried herbs, ripe fruit, spicy, mineral. Palate: complex, long, balsamic.

Dido Blanc 2013 B
macabeo, garnacha blanca, xarel.lo

92

Colour: bright yellow. Nose: balsamic herbs, dry stone, floral, citrus fruit, fruit expression, expressive. Palate: flavourful, rich, complex, spicy, elegant.

Venus 2010 T
cariñena, syrah, garnacha

94 🌷

Colour: cherry, garnet rim. Nose: ripe fruit, wild herbs, spicy, closed. Palate: balanced, flavourful, long, balsamic, full, complex, good acidity.

VINYES DOMÈNECH
Camí del Collet, km. 3,8
43776 Capçanes (Tarragona)
☎: +34 670 297 395
www.vinyesdomenech.com
jidomenech@vinyesdomenech.com

Bancal del Bosc 2012 T
88

Colour: very deep cherry, garnet rim. Nose: wild herbs, dried herbs, ripe fruit. Palate: correct, round tannins.

Bancal del Bosc Blanc 2013 B
garnacha blanca

90

Colour: bright straw. Nose: fresh, fresh fruit, white flowers, mineral. Palate: flavourful, fruity, good acidity, balanced, elegant.

Furvus 2011 T
92

Colour: cherry, garnet rim. Nose: scrubland, spicy, ripe fruit, earthy notes, dry stone, expressive. Palate: powerful, flavourful, spicy, long, balanced.

Rita 2013 B
100% garnacha blanca

93

Colour: bright straw. Nose: white flowers, fresh fruit, expressive, fine lees, dried herbs, spicy, elegant. Palate: flavourful, fruity, good acidity, balanced.

Teixar 2011 T
100% garnacha peluda

94

Colour: cherry, garnet rim. Nose: ripe fruit, wild herbs, earthy notes, spicy, creamy oak, mineral. Palate: balanced, flavourful, long, balsamic, elegant.

VIÑAS DEL MONTSANT
Partida Coll de Mora , s/n
43775 Marça (Tarragona)
☎: +34 977 831 309
Fax: +34 977 831 356
www.morlanda.com
mariajose.bajon@morlanda.com

Amor Loco 2013 RD
syrah, garnacha

86

Colour: raspberry rose. Nose: candied fruit, dried flowers, fragrant herbs. Palate: light-bodied, flavourful, good acidity, long, spicy.

Fra Guerau 2011 TC
merlot, tempranillo

84

VIÑEDOS SINGULARES
Cuzco, 26 - 28, Nave 8
08030 (Barcelona)
☎: +34 934 807 041
Fax: +34 934 807 076
www.vinedossingulares.com
info@vinedossingulares.com

El Veïnat 2013 T
garnacha

89

Colour: cherry, garnet rim. Nose: red berry notes, ripe fruit, balsamic herbs, spicy, mineral. Palate: powerful, flavourful, spicy, long, correct.

VIRÀMIDUS
Navas de Tolosa 255, 3º-3ª
08026 Barcelona (Barcelona)
☎: +34 696 321 120
www.viramidus.es
viramidus.eph@gmail.com

Viràmidus 2006 TR
garnacha, cariñena, cabernet sauvignon

87

Colour: black cherry. Nose: spicy, fine reductive notes, wet leather, aged wood nuances, toasty. Palate: spicy, long, toasty, flavourful.

Viràmidus Garnatxa 2008 T
garnacha, cabernet sauvignon

86

Colour: dark-red cherry. Nose: smoky, toasty, spicy. Palate: flavourful, good acidity, round tannins.

Viràmidus Grand Selecció 2005 T
garnacha, cariñena, syrah, cabernet sauvignon

88

Colour: pale ruby, brick rim edge. Nose: elegant, spicy, fine reductive notes, wet leather, aged wood nuances, fruit liqueur notes. Palate: spicy, fine tannins, elegant, long.

Viràmidus Negre 2011 TC
garnacha, cariñena, syrah

87

Colour: cherry, garnet rim. Nose: ripe fruit, spicy, creamy oak, toasty, balsamic herbs. Palate: powerful, flavourful, toasty.

Viràmidus Syrah 2006 T
syrah

86

Colour: very deep cherry. Nose: ripe fruit, fruit preserve, sweet spices, cocoa bean. Palate: good structure, powerful.

XIROI VINS
Plaça Europa, 3 5o 3a
43205 Reus (Tarragona)
☎: +34 669 486 713
www.xiroi-vins.com
teretr@yahoo.com

Xiroi 2013 T Barrica
garnacha, cariñena, cabernet sauvignon, syrah

89

Colour: cherry, garnet rim. Nose: ripe fruit, wild herbs, earthy notes, spicy. Palate: flavourful, long, balsamic.

DO. NAVARRA

CONSEJO REGULADOR

Rúa Romana, s/n
31390 Olite (Navarra)
☎ :+34 948 741 812 - Fax: +34 948 741 776
@: consejoregulador@vinonavarra.com
@: info@navarrawine.com
www.navarrawine.com

LOCATION:

In the province of Navarra. It draws together areas of different climates and soils, which produce wines with diverse characteristics.

SUB-REGIONS:

Baja Montaña. Situated northeast of Navarra, it comprises 22 municipal districts with around 2,500 Ha under cultivation.
Tierra Estella. In western central Navarra, it stretches along the Camino de Santiago. It has 1,800 Ha of vineyards in 38 municipal districts.
Valdizarbe. In central Navarra. It is the key centre of the Camino de Santiago. It comprises 25 municipal districts and has 1,100 Ha of vineyards.
Ribera Alta. In the area around Olite, it takes in part of central Navarra and the start of the southern region. There are 26 municipal districts and 3,300 Ha of vineyards.
Ribera Baja. In the south of the province, it is the most important in terms of size (4,600 Ha). It comprises 14 municipal districts.

GRAPE VARIETIES:

White: Chardonnay (2%), Garnacha Blanca, Malvasía, Moscatel de Grano Menudo, Viura (6% of total) and Sauvignon Blanc.
Red: Cabernet Sauvignon (9%), Garnacha Tinta (majority 42% of total), Graciano, Mazuelo, Merlot, Tempranillo (29%), Syrah and Pinot Noir.

FIGURES:

Vineyard surface: 11,400 – Wine-Growers: 2,716 – Wineries: 100 – 2013 Harvest rating: Good – Production 13: 46,743,758 litres – Market percentages: 64% domestic - 36% export.

SOIL:

The diversity of the different regions is also reflected in the soil. Reddish or yellowish and stony in the Baja Montaña, brownish-grey limestone and limestone in Valdizarbe and Tierra Estella, limestone and alluvium marl in the Ribera Alta, and brown and grey semi-desert soil, brownish-grey limestone and alluvium in the Ribera Baja.

CLIMATE:

Typical of dry, sub-humid regions in the northern fringe, with average rainfall of between 593 mm and 683 mm per year. The climate in the central region is transitional and changes to drier conditions in southern regions, where the average annual rainfall is a mere 448 mm.

VINTAGE RATING

PEÑÍNGUIDE

2009	2010	2011	2012	2013
GOOD	VERY GOOD	VERY GOOD	VERY GOOD	GOOD

ADEGA Y VIÑEDOS PACO & LOLA

Valdamor, 18 - XII
36986 Meaño (Pontevedra)
☎: +34 986 747 779
Fax: +34 986 748 940
www.pacolola.com
comercial@pacolola.com

Paco by Paco & Lola 2012 T
87
Colour: cherry, garnet rim. Nose: ripe fruit, spicy, dried herbs.
Palate: powerful, flavourful, correct, easy to drink.

ASENSIO VIÑEDOS Y BODEGAS

Mayor, 84
31293 Sesma (Navarra)
☎: +34 948 698 078
Fax: +34 948 698 097
www.bodegasasensio.com
info@bodegasasensio.com

Javier Asensio 2006 TR
cabernet sauvignon, tempranillo
86
Colour: cherry, garnet rim. Nose: ripe fruit, wild herbs, spicy,
creamy oak. Palate: balanced, flavourful, long, balsamic.

Javier Asensio 2010 TC
syrah, merlot, tempranillo
85

Javier Asensio 2013 B
chardonnay, sauvignon blanc
87
Colour: bright yellow. Nose: citrus fruit, ripe fruit, fragrant
herbs, white flowers. Palate: fresh, fruity, flavourful.

AZUL Y GARANZA BODEGAS

San Juan, 19
31310 Carcastillo (Navarra)
☎: +34 659 857 979
Fax: +34 949 115 185
www.azulygaranza.com
fernando@azulygaranza.com

Graciano de Azul y Garanza 2011 T Barrica
89 ♣
Colour: cherry, garnet rim. Nose: ripe fruit, wild herbs, earthy
notes, spicy. Palate: balanced, flavourful, long, balsamic.

Seis de Azul y Garanza 2011 T
88 ♣
Colour: cherry, garnet rim. Nose: ripe fruit, fruit preserve, dried
herbs, powerfull. Palate: good structure, flavourful, balsamic.

BODEGA DE SADA

Arrabal, 2
31491 Sada (Navarra)
☎: +34 948 877 013
Fax: +34 948 877 433
www.bodegadesada.com
bodega@bodegadesada.com

Palacio de Sada 2011 TC
garnacha
88
Colour: cherry, garnet rim. Nose: ripe fruit, spicy, creamy oak,
floral. Palate: powerful, flavourful, toasty, round tannins.

Palacio de Sada 2013 RD
garnacha
89
Colour: rose, bright. Nose: red berry notes, rose petals, fresh.
Palate: flavourful, long, balsamic, good acidity, fruity.

Palacio de Sada Garnacha 2013 T
garnacha
87
Colour: bright cherry, garnet rim. Nose: wild herbs, balanced,
floral, ripe fruit. Palate: fruity, flavourful, easy to drink.

BODEGA DE SARRÍA

Finca Señorío de Sarría, s/n
31100 Puente La Reina (Navarra)
☎: +34 948 202 200
Fax: +34 948 172 164
www.bodegadesarria.com
info@taninia.com

Señorío de Sarría 2009 TR
cabernet sauvignon, merlot
88
Colour: very deep cherry. Nose: ripe fruit, spicy, creamy oak,
toasty, characterful. Palate: powerful, flavourful, toasty, round
tannins.

Señorío de Sarría 2011 TC
cabernet sauvignon, tempranillo
87
Colour: cherry, garnet rim. Nose: ripe fruit, spicy, creamy oak,
toasty, grassy. Palate: powerful, flavourful, toasty.

Señorío de Sarría 2013 RD
garnacha
87
Colour: rose, purple rim. Nose: ripe fruit, red berry notes, floral, expressive. Palate: powerful, fruity, fresh.

Señorío de Sarría Chardonnay 2013 B
chardonnay
86
Colour: bright straw. Nose: medium intensity, faded flowers.
Palate: fruity, correct, fine bitter notes.

Señorío de Sarría Moscatel 2013 Blanco dulce
moscatel

88

Colour: bright straw. Nose: white flowers, honeyed notes, ripe fruit, wild herbs. Palate: powerful, flavourful, rich, balanced.

Señorío de Sarría Viñedo Nº 5 2013 RD
garnacha

87

Colour: rose, bright. Nose: expressive, balanced, rose petals, ripe fruit. Palate: fruity, flavourful.

Señorío de Sarría Viñedo Sotés 2010 TC
tempranillo, merlot, cabernet sauvignon, graciano

90

Colour: cherry, garnet rim. Nose: ripe fruit, creamy oak, complex, balsamic herbs, toasty. Palate: powerful, flavourful, toasty, round tannins.

BODEGA INURRIETA
Ctra. Falces-Miranda de Arga, km. 30
31370 Falces (Navarra)
☎: +34 948 737 309
Fax: +34 948 737 310
www.bodegainurrieta.com
info@bodegainurrieta.com

Altos de Inurrieta 2010 TR
cabernet sauvignon, merlot

91

Colour: cherry, garnet rim. Nose: ripe fruit, spicy, creamy oak, earthy notes, dried herbs. Palate: powerful, flavourful, toasty, round tannins.

Inurrieta Cuatrocientos 2011 TC
cabernet sauvignon, merlot, graciano, garnacha

87

Colour: cherry, garnet rim. Nose: ripe fruit, wild herbs, earthy notes, spicy, creamy oak. Palate: balanced, flavourful, long, balsamic.

Inurrieta Mediodía 2013 RD
garnacha, cabernet sauvignon, syrah, merlot

90

Colour: rose, purple rim. Nose: powerfull, ripe fruit, red berry notes, floral, expressive. Palate: powerful, fruity, fresh, balanced.

Inurrieta Norte 2012 T Roble
merlot, cabernet sauvignon

89

Colour: bright cherry, garnet rim. Nose: ripe fruit, red berry notes, scrubland, sweet spices. Palate: fruity, flavourful.

Inurrieta Orchídea 2013 B
sauvignon blanc

89

Colour: bright yellow. Nose: powerfull, ripe fruit, sweet spices, fragrant herbs. Palate: rich, smoky aftertaste, flavourful, fresh, good acidity.

Inurrieta Orchídea Cuvée 2012 B
sauvignon blanc

89

Colour: bright yellow. Nose: sweet spices, creamy oak, fragrant herbs, citrus fruit, ripe fruit. Palate: rich, smoky aftertaste, flavourful, powerful.

Inurrieta Sur 2012 T Roble
garnacha, syrah

88

Colour: deep cherry, garnet rim. Nose: creamy oak, ripe fruit, spicy. Palate: flavourful, full, round tannins.

Laderas de Inurrieta 2010 T
graciano

91

Colour: cherry, garnet rim. Nose: ripe fruit, spicy, creamy oak, toasty, complex. Palate: powerful, flavourful, toasty, round tannins, balanced.

BODEGA MARQUÉS DE MONTECIERZO
San José, 62
31590 Castejón (Navarra)
☎: +34 948 814 414
Fax: +34 948 814 420
www.marquesdemontecierzo.com
info@marquesdemontecierzo.com

Emergente 2010 TC
tempranillo, cabernet sauvignon, merlot

86

Colour: bright cherry. Nose: ripe fruit, spicy, dried herbs. Palate: powerful, flavourful, round tannins.

Emergente 2011 T Roble
tempranillo, cabernet sauvignon, merlot

84

Emergente 2012 T
tempranillo, cabernet sauvignon

86

Colour: bright cherry, garnet rim. Nose: powerfull, ripe fruit, sweet spices, dried herbs. Palate: flavourful, fruity, correct.

Emergente 2013 B
chardonnay

83

Emergente Garnacha 2011 T Roble
garnacha

86

Colour: bright cherry. Nose: ripe fruit, sweet spices, creamy oak. Palate: flavourful, fruity, toasty.

Emergente Garnacha Selección 2010 T Roble
garnacha

90

Colour: light cherry, garnet rim. Nose: expressive, red berry notes, ripe fruit, balanced, balsamic herbs. Palate: fruity, spicy, good acidity.

Emergente Moscatel 2013 B
moscatel

86

Colour: golden. Nose: floral, honeyed notes, candied fruit, medium intensity. Palate: flavourful, sweet, fresh, fruity.

Emergente Reserva Numerada 2006 TR
tempranillo, merlot, cabernet sauvignon

86

Colour: cherry, garnet rim. Nose: balanced, ripe fruit, tobacco, scrubland. Palate: good structure, round tannins.

Emergente Rosado de Lágrima 2013 RD
83

Marques de Montecierzo Merlot Selección 2006 TC
merlot

88

Colour: pale ruby, brick rim edge. Nose: spicy, fine reductive notes, wet leather, aged wood nuances, fruit liqueur notes. Palate: spicy, fine tannins, elegant, long.

BODEGA MÁXIMO ABETE
Ctra. Estella-Sangüesa, Km. 43,5
31495 San Martín de Unx (Navarra)
☎: +34 948 738 120
www.bodegasmaximoabete.com
info@bodegasmaximoabete.com

Guerinda 2010 TC
garnacha, merlot, cabernet sauvignon

88

Colour: cherry, garnet rim. Nose: ripe fruit, wild herbs, earthy notes, spicy, creamy oak. Palate: balanced, flavourful, long, balsamic.

Guerinda Casalasierra 2013 RD
100% garnacha

87

Colour: brilliant rose. Nose: floral, fresh fruit, red berry notes. Palate: balanced, fruity, easy to drink, fine bitter notes, good acidity, balsamic.

Guerinda La Cruzica 2010 T
100% tempranillo

87

Colour: cherry, garnet rim. Nose: ripe fruit, sweet spices, balanced, expressive. Palate: good structure, good acidity, balanced.

Guerinda Navasentero 2011 T
100% graciano

89

Colour: very deep cherry, garnet rim. Nose: balanced, dried herbs, ripe fruit. Palate: full, round tannins, flavourful, long.

Guerinda Tres Partes 2012 T
100% garnacha

88

Colour: bright cherry. Nose: ripe fruit, sweet spices, creamy oak, expressive. Palate: flavourful, fruity, toasty.

La Blanca Guerinda Chardonnay 2013 B
100% chardonnay

89

Colour: bright straw. Nose: fresh, fresh fruit, white flowers, expressive. Palate: flavourful, fruity, good acidity, balanced.

BODEGA OTAZU
Señorío de Otazu, s/n
31174 Etxauri (Navarra)
☎: +34 948 329 200
Fax: +34 948 329 353
www.otazu.com
otazu@otazu.com

Otazu Chardonnay 2013 B
chardonnay

90

Colour: bright straw. Nose: white flowers, fragrant herbs, fruit expression. Palate: fresh, fruity, flavourful, balanced.

Otazu Premium Cuvee 2010 TC
89

Colour: cherry, garnet rim. Nose: ripe fruit, spicy, creamy oak, toasty. Palate: powerful, flavourful, toasty.

BODEGA PAGO DE CIRSUS
Ctra. de Ablitas a Ribafora, Km. 5
31523 Ablitas (Navarra)
☎: +34 948 386 427
Fax: +34 948 386 420
www.pagodecirsus.com
laura.dominguez@pagodecirsus.com

Pago de Cirsus Chardonnay 2012 BFB
chardonnay
89
Colour: bright yellow. Nose: white flowers, sweet spices, candied fruit. Palate: fruity, spicy, ripe fruit, fine bitter notes.

Pago de Cirsus Chardonnay 2013 B
chardonnay
90
Colour: bright straw. Nose: white flowers, fresh fruit, expressive, dried herbs. Palate: flavourful, fruity, good acidity, balanced.

Pago de Cirsus Cuvée Especial 2010 TR
tempranillo, merlot, syrah
91
Colour: cherry, garnet rim. Nose: balanced, complex, cocoa bean, spicy. Palate: balanced, long, round tannins.

Pago de Cirsus Moscatel Vendimia Tardía 2007 BFB
moscatel grano menudo
92
Colour: old gold, amber rim. Nose: ripe fruit, dry nuts, powerfull, toasty, aged wood nuances, wild herbs. Palate: flavourful, fruity, spicy, toasty, long.

Pago de Cirsus Selección de Familia 2009 T
tempranillo, syrah
91
Colour: cherry, garnet rim. Nose: ripe fruit, wild herbs, earthy notes, spicy, creamy oak. Palate: balanced, flavourful, long, balsamic.

Pago de Cirsus Vendimia Seleccionada 2011 TC
tempranillo, merlot, syrah
89
Colour: cherry, garnet rim. Nose: ripe fruit, spicy, creamy oak, toasty, dark chocolate. Palate: powerful, flavourful, toasty.

BODEGA SAN MARTÍN S. COOP.

Ctra. de Sanguesa, s/n
31495 San Martín de Unx (Navarra)
☎: +34 948 738 294
Fax: +34 948 738 297
www.bodegasanmartin.com
enologia@bodegasanmartin.com

Alma de Unx 2010 T
garnacha

89

Colour: bright cherry. Nose: fresh fruit, balanced, balsamic herbs, spicy, tobacco. Palate: balanced, spicy, good acidity, round tannins.

Alma de Unx 2012 B Barrica
garnacha blanca

87

Colour: yellow, pale. Nose: ripe fruit, faded flowers, toasty, sweet spices. Palate: correct, fine bitter notes.

Ilagares 2013 B
viura

82

Ilagares 2013 RD
garnacha

86

Colour: light cherry, bright. Nose: floral, expressive, fresh fruit, balanced. Palate: correct, fine bitter notes, good acidity.

Ilagares 2013 T
tempranillo, garnacha

83

Señorío de Unx 2008 TR
tempranillo, garnacha

86

Colour: cherry, garnet rim. Nose: ripe fruit, spicy, creamy oak, toasty. Palate: powerful, flavourful, spicy.

Señorío de Unx 2011 TC
tempranillo, garnacha

87

Colour: bright cherry, garnet rim. Nose: balanced, ripe fruit, balsamic herbs. Palate: fruity, ripe fruit, long.

Señorío de Unx 2013 B
garnacha blanca

86

Colour: bright straw. Nose: fresh, fresh fruit, white flowers, expressive. Palate: flavourful, fruity, good acidity, balanced.

Señorío de Unx Garnacha 2013 T
garnacha

86

Colour: bright cherry, purple rim. Nose: red berry notes, ripe fruit, dried herbs. Palate: easy to drink, fruity.

BODEGA TÁNDEM

Ctra. Pamplona - Logroño Km. 35,9
31292 Lácar (Navarra)
☎: +34 948 536 031
Fax: +34 948 536 068
www.tandem.es
bodega@tandem.es

Ars In Vitro 2011 T
tempranillo, merlot

87

Colour: bright cherry. Nose: ripe fruit, sweet spices, balsamic herbs. Palate: flavourful, fruity, toasty, round tannins.

Ars Memoria 2008 T
cabernet sauvignon

89

Colour: cherry, garnet rim. Nose: balanced, complex, ripe fruit, spicy, scrubland. Palate: good structure, flavourful, round tannins.

Ars Nova 2008 T
tempranillo, merlot, cabernet sauvignon

88

Colour: bright cherry. Nose: ripe fruit, sweet spices, creamy oak, medium intensity, grassy. Palate: fruity, flavourful, toasty.

Mácula 2006 T
cabernet sauvignon, merlot

89

Colour: cherry, garnet rim. Nose: ripe fruit, wild herbs, spicy. Palate: balanced, flavourful, long, balsamic.

BODEGA Y VIÑAS VALDELARES

Ctra. Eje del Ebro, km. 60
31579 Carcar (Navarra)
☎: +34 656 849 602
www.valdelares.com
valdelares@valdelares.com

Valdelares 2011 TC
cabernet sauvignon, merlot, tempranillo

88

Colour: cherry, garnet rim. Nose: ripe fruit, wild herbs, spicy, creamy oak, toasty. Palate: powerful, flavourful, spicy.

Valdelares 2013 RD
merlot

88

Colour: rose, purple rim. Nose: powerfull, ripe fruit, red berry notes, floral, expressive. Palate: powerful, fruity, fresh.

Valdelares Cabernet 2011 TC
cabernet sauvignon

89

Colour: cherry, garnet rim. Nose: ripe fruit, spicy, creamy oak, toasty, complex, wild herbs. Palate: powerful, flavourful, toasty, round tannins.

Valdelares Chardonnay 2013 B
chardonnay
85

Valdelares Dulce 2013 B
100% moscatel
86
Colour: golden. Nose: floral, honeyed notes, dried herbs. Palate: flavourful, sweet, good acidity, long.

BODEGAS AGUIRRE
Placeta de Añorbe 1
31370 Falces (Navarra)
☎: +34 948 734 155
Fax: +34 948 714 773
info@bodegasaguirre.es

Castillo de Falces 2013 RD
100% garnacha
84

BODEGAS AZPEA
Camino Itúrbero, s/n
31440 Lumbier (Navarra)
☎: +34 948 880 433
Fax: +34 948 880 433
www.bodegasazpea.com
info@bodegasazpea.com

Azpea 2013 RD
garnacha
83 🌷

Azpea Garnacha 2006 T
garnacha
84 🌷

Azpea Garnacha 2012 T
garnacha
78 🌷

Azpea Joven 2013 T
82 🌷

Azpea Selección 2010 T
81 🌷

Azpea Vino Dulce de Moscatel 2012 B
moscatel grano menudo
90 🌷
Colour: golden. Nose: powerfull, floral, honeyed notes, candied fruit, fragrant herbs. Palate: flavourful, sweet, fresh, fruity, good acidity, long.

Azpea Viura 2013 B
viura
75 🌷

BODEGAS BERAMENDI
Ctra. Tafalla, s/n
31495 San Martín de Unx (Navarra)
☎: +34 948 738 262
Fax: +34 948 738 080
www.bodegasberamendi.com
info@bodegasberamendi.com

Beramendi 2013 RD
garnacha, tempranillo
85

Beramendi 3F 2013 B
chardonnay, moscatel
84

Beramendi 3F 2013 RD
garnacha
86
Colour: rose, purple rim. Nose: powerfull, ripe fruit, red berry notes, fragrant herbs. Palate: powerful, fruity, fresh.

Beramendi Tempranillo 2010 TC
tempranillo
86
Colour: cherry, garnet rim. Nose: ripe fruit, spicy, creamy oak, toasty, complex. Palate: powerful, flavourful, toasty.

BODEGAS CAMILO CASTILLA
Santa Bárbara, 40
31591 Corella (Navarra)
☎: +34 948 780 006
Fax: +34 948 780 515
www.bodegasab.com
info@camilocastilla.com

Capricho de Goya Dulce PX Gran Reserva
moscatel grano menudo
93
Colour: dark mahogany. Nose: complex, fruit liqueur notes, dried fruit, pattiserie, toasty, acetaldehyde. Palate: sweet, rich, unctuous, powerful.

Montecristo 2013 B
moscatel grano menudo
85

Montecristo Dulce 2013 B
100% moscatel grano menudo
86
Colour: golden. Nose: floral, honeyed notes, candied fruit, fragrant herbs. Palate: flavourful, sweet, fresh, fruity, good acidity, long.

BODEGAS CASTILLO DE MONJARDÍN

Viña Rellanada, s/n
31242 Villamayor de Monjardín
(Navarra)
☎: +34 948 537 412
Fax: +34 948 537 436
www.monjardin.es
sonia@monjardin.es

Castillo de Monjardín 2011 TC
cabernet sauvignon, merlot, tempranillo

87

Colour: bright cherry. Nose: ripe fruit, sweet spices, creamy oak, balsamic herbs. Palate: fruity, flavourful, toasty.

Castillo de Monjardín Chardonnay 2009 B Reserva
chardonnay

92

Colour: bright yellow. Nose: sweet spices, creamy oak, candied fruit, expressive, balanced, complex. Palate: rich, flavourful.

Castillo de Monjardín Chardonnay 2011 BFB
chardonnay

93

Colour: bright yellow. Nose: powerfull, sweet spices, creamy oak, fragrant herbs, faded flowers. Palate: rich, smoky aftertaste, flavourful, fresh, good acidity.

Castillo de Monjardín Chardonnay 2013 B
chardonnay

83

Castillo de Monjardín Deyo 2009 TC
merlot

88

Colour: cherry, garnet rim. Nose: ripe fruit, wild herbs, earthy notes, spicy, creamy oak. Palate: balanced, balsamic, easy to drink.

Castillo de Monjardín Finca los Carasoles 2008 TR
cabernet sauvignon, tempranillo

90

Colour: very deep cherry. Nose: ripe fruit, spicy, creamy oak, toasty. Palate: powerful, flavourful, toasty, round tannins.

Castillo de Monjardín Garnacha Old Vines 2012 T
garnacha

90

Colour: bright cherry. Nose: fresh fruit, raspberry, red berry notes, fragrant herbs, expressive. Palate: fresh, fruity, flavourful, spicy, balsamic.

Castillo de Monjardín Rosado de Lágrima 2013 RD
cabernet sauvignon

88

Colour: light cherry. Nose: powerfull, red berry notes, floral, balsamic herbs. Palate: powerful, fruity, fresh, easy to drink.

Castillo de Monjardín Tempranillo 2013 T
tempranillo

85

Esencia Monjardín 2007 B
chardonnay

93

Colour: bright golden. Nose: ripe fruit, citrus fruit, honeyed notes, fruit liqueur notes, wild herbs. Palate: long, spicy, balsamic, fruity, flavourful.

BODEGAS CAUDALIA

San Francisco, 7
26300 Najera (La Rioja)
☎: +34 670 833 340
www.bodegascaudalia.com
info@bodegascaudalia.com

Paal 01 2012 T
syrah

88

Colour: cherry, garnet rim. Nose: ripe fruit, spicy, creamy oak, toasty, balsamic herbs. Palate: powerful, flavourful, toasty.

Xi'Ipal 2012 T
syrah

89

Colour: deep cherry, purple rim. Nose: fruit expression, ripe fruit, powerfull. Palate: balanced, round tannins, fruity.

BODEGAS CORELLANAS

Santa Bárbara, 29
31591 Corella (Navarra)
☎: +34 948 780 029
Fax: +34 948 781 542
www.bodegascorellanas.com
info@bodegascorellanas.com

Moscatel Sarasate Expresión 2013 B
moscatel grano menudo
86
Colour: bright straw. Nose: fresh, fresh fruit, white flowers.
Palate: flavourful, fruity, good acidity, balanced.

Viña Rubicán 2010 TC
tempranillo, cabernet sauvignon
85

Viña Rubicán 2013 B
moscatel
86
Colour: bright straw. Nose: white flowers, fragrant herbs, fruit
expression. Palate: fresh, fruity, flavourful, balanced.

Viña Rubicán Tempranillo 2012 T Roble
tempranillo
82

Viña Rubicán Único 2007 TC
garnacha, tempranillo
88
Colour: cherry, garnet rim. Nose: fruit preserve, fruit liqueur
notes, spicy. Palate: flavourful, pruney, balsamic.

BODEGAS DE LA CASA DE LÚCULO

Ctra. Larraga, s/n
31150 Mendigorría (Navarra)
☎: +34 948 343 148
www.luculo.es
bodega@luculo.es

Jardín de Lúculo 2012 T
100% garnacha
92
Colour: cherry, garnet rim. Nose: ripe fruit, spicy, creamy oak,
toasty, complex, dark chocolate, earthy notes. Palate: powerful, flavourful, toasty, round tannins, elegant.

Jardín de Lúculo Los Bohemios 2012 T
100% garnacha
90
Colour: cherry, garnet rim. Nose: expressive, balanced, ripe
fruit, wild herbs. Palate: fruity, flavourful, long.

Jardín de Lúculo Los Bohemios 2013 RD
100% garnacha
87
Colour: rose, bright. Nose: red berry notes, fragrant herbs,
floral. Palate: fruity, fresh, good acidity.

BODEGAS FERNÁNDEZ DE ARCAYA

La Serna, 31
31210 Los Arcos (Navarra)
☎: +34 948 640 811
www.fernandezdearcaya.com
info@fernandezdearcaya.com

Fernández de Arcaya 2010 TR
100% cabernet sauvignon
89
Colour: cherry, garnet rim. Nose: red berry notes, ripe fruit,
spicy, creamy oak, toasty, complex. Palate: powerful, flavourful, toasty.

Viña Perguita 2011 TC
88
Colour: cherry, garnet rim. Nose: ripe fruit, spicy, creamy oak,
toasty, complex. Palate: powerful, flavourful, toasty.

Viña Perguita 2013 T Roble
83

BODEGAS GRAN FEUDO

Ribera, 34
31592 Cintruénigo (Navarra)
☎: +34 948 811 000
Fax: +34 948 811 407
www.granfeudo.com
info@granfeudo.com

Gran Feudo 2009 TR
tempranillo, cabernet sauvignon, merlot
88
Colour: bright cherry, garnet rim. Nose: powerfull, ripe fruit,
dried herbs. Palate: flavourful, fine bitter notes, round tannins.

Gran Feudo 2010 TC
tempranillo, garnacha, cabernet sauvignon, merlot
89
Colour: cherry, garnet rim. Nose: ripe fruit, spicy, creamy oak,
toasty. Palate: powerful, flavourful, toasty.

Gran Feudo 2012 T Roble
tempranillo
86
Colour: bright cherry. Nose: ripe fruit, sweet spices, creamy
oak. Palate: flavourful, fruity, toasty, round tannins.

Gran Feudo 2013 RD
garnacha
89
Colour: rose, purple rim. Nose: powerfull, ripe fruit, red berry
notes, floral, expressive. Palate: powerful, fruity, fresh, easy
to drink.

Gran Feudo Chardonnay 2013 B
chardonnay

88

Colour: yellow. Nose: varietal, ripe fruit, floral. Palate: good acidity, correct, ripe fruit.

Gran Feudo Edición 2013 RD
garnacha, tempranillo, merlot

89

Colour: coppery red. Nose: elegant, dried flowers, red berry notes. Palate: light-bodied, flavourful, good acidity, long, spicy.

Gran Feudo Edición Dulce de Moscatel 2012 B
moscatel grano menudo

92

Colour: golden. Nose: powerfull, floral, honeyed notes, candied fruit, fragrant herbs. Palate: flavourful, sweet, fresh, fruity, good acidity, long.

BODEGAS IRACHE
Monasterio de Irache, 1
31240 Ayegui (Navarra)
☎: +34 948 551 932
Fax: +34 948 554 954
www.irache.com
irache@irache.com

Castillo Irache 2013 B
chardonnay

82

Castillo Irache 2013 RD
garnacha

84

Gran Irache 2010 TC
tempranillo, cabernet sauvignon, merlot

84

Irache 2004 TR
tempranillo, cabernet sauvignon, merlot

82

BODEGAS ITURBIDE
Término la Torre, s/n
31350 Peralta (Navarra)
☎: +34 948 750 537
Fax: +34 647 742 368
www.bodegasiturbide.com
bodegasiturbide@bodegasiturbide.com

Iturbide 2013 T
tempranillo, cabernet sauvignon, garnacha

84

Novem 2012 T
tempranillo, garnacha, cabernet sauvignon

84 🌷

BODEGAS LEZAUN
Egiarte, 1
31292 Lakar (Navarra)
☎: +34 948 541 339
www.lezaun.com
info@lezaun.com

Egiarte 2009 TR
tempranillo, cabernet sauvignon, merlot

87 🌷

Colour: deep cherry, garnet rim. Nose: ripe fruit, dried herbs, cocoa bean. Palate: good structure, flavourful, round tannins.

Egiarte 2010 TC
tempranillo, cabernet sauvignon, merlot

87 🌷

Colour: cherry, garnet rim. Nose: ripe fruit, spicy, creamy oak, toasty, complex. Palate: powerful, flavourful, toasty.

Egiarte 2013 T

84 🌷

Egiarte Rosado 2013 RD
garnacha, tempranillo

88

Colour: coppery red. Nose: elegant, candied fruit, dried flowers, fragrant herbs. Palate: light-bodied, flavourful, good acidity, long, spicy.

Lezaun 0,0 Sulfitos 2013 T
tempranillo

87 🌷

Colour: cherry, purple rim. Nose: balanced, red berry notes, fresh. Palate: flavourful, correct, long.

Lezaun 2009 TR
tempranillo, graciano, garnacha

89 🌷

Colour: cherry, garnet rim. Nose: red berry notes, ripe fruit, spicy, creamy oak, toasty, complex, earthy notes. Palate: powerful, flavourful, toasty, round tannins.

Lezaun 2010 TC
tempranillo, cabernet sauvignon, graciano

89 🌷

Colour: bright cherry, garnet rim. Nose: expressive, complex, balanced, ripe fruit, sweet spices. Palate: ripe fruit, good structure, flavourful.

Lezaun Gazaga 2012 T Roble
tempranillo, cabernet sauvignon

88 🌷

Colour: bright cherry. Nose: ripe fruit, sweet spices, creamy oak. Palate: flavourful, fruity, toasty.

Lezaun Tempranillo 2013 T
tempranillo

89 🌷

Colour: cherry, purple rim. Nose: powerfull, red berry notes, ripe fruit, floral, lactic notes. Palate: powerful, fresh, fruity, unctuous, balanced.

Lezaun Txuria 2013 B
garnacha blanca

84 🌷

BODEGAS MACAYA
Ctra. Berbinzana, 74
31251 Larraga (Navarra)
☎: +34 948 711 549
Fax: +34 948 711 788
www.bodegasmacaya.com
info@bodegasmacaya.com

Almara Cabernet Sauvignon Vendimia Seleccionada 2009 TR
100% cabernet sauvignon

88

Colour: cherry, garnet rim. Nose: ripe fruit, spicy, creamy oak, toasty. Palate: powerful, flavourful, toasty.

Condado de Almara Crianza 2009 TC
87

Colour: bright cherry. Nose: ripe fruit, sweet spices, creamy oak, medium intensity. Palate: fruity, flavourful, toasty.

Condado de Almara Reserva 2008 TR
88

Colour: cherry, garnet rim. Nose: ripe fruit, spicy, creamy oak, toasty. Palate: powerful, flavourful, toasty.

Condado de Almara Selección 2010 T
100% tempranillo

88

Colour: bright cherry. Nose: red berry notes, ripe fruit, spicy, creamy oak, toasty. Palate: powerful, flavourful, toasty, round tannins.

Finca Linte 2012 T
100% tempranillo

86

Colour: bright cherry, purple rim. Nose: fruit expression, medium intensity. Palate: correct, balanced, good acidity, good finish.

BODEGAS MALON DE ECHAIDE
Ctra. de Tarazona, 33
31520 Cascante (Navarra)
☎: +34 948 851 411
Fax: +34 948 844 504
www.malondeechaide.com
info@bodegasdelromero.com

Malón de Echaide 2009 TC
100% tempranillo

86

Colour: cherry, garnet rim. Nose: ripe fruit, spicy, creamy oak, toasty, fine reductive notes. Palate: powerful, flavourful, toasty.

Malón de Echaide 2013 RD
100% garnacha

85

Malón de Echaide Chardonnay 2013 B
100% chardonnay

86

Colour: bright straw. Nose: fresh, fresh fruit, white flowers, expressive. Palate: flavourful, fruity, good acidity, balanced.

Torrecilla 2013 RD
85

Torrecilla 2013 T
84

BODEGAS MARCO REAL
Ctra. Pamplona-Zaragoza, Km. 38
31390 Olite (Navarra)
☎: +34 948 712 193
Fax: +34 948 712 343
www.familiabelasco.com
info@familiabelasco.com

Homenaje 2010 TC
tempranillo, merlot, syrah

89

Colour: cherry, garnet rim. Nose: ripe fruit, spicy, creamy oak, toasty, complex. Palate: powerful, flavourful, toasty, round tannins, balanced.

Homenaje 2012 T
tempranillo, cabernet sauvignon

85

Homenaje 2013 B
viura, chardonnay, moscatel

88

Colour: bright straw. Nose: fresh, fresh fruit, white flowers, expressive. Palate: flavourful, fruity, good acidity, balanced.

Homenaje 2013 RD
garnacha

88

Colour: rose, purple rim. Nose: powerfull, ripe fruit, red berry notes, expressive, rose petals. Palate: powerful, fruity, fresh.

Marco Real Colección Privada 2011 TC
tempranillo, cabernet sauvignon, merlot, graciano

89

Colour: cherry, garnet rim. Nose: ripe fruit, spicy, creamy oak, toasty, complex, earthy notes, dried herbs. Palate: powerful, flavourful, toasty, round tannins.

Marco Real Pequeñas Producciones Garnacha Corraliza de los Roncaleses 2012 T
garnacha

91

Colour: bright cherry. Nose: ripe fruit, sweet spices, creamy oak, fragrant herbs. Palate: flavourful, fruity, toasty, round tannins.

Marco Real Pequeñas Producciones Syrah 2012 TC
syrah

89

Colour: cherry, garnet rim. Nose: ripe fruit, red berry notes, wild herbs, expressive. Palate: ripe fruit, fruity aftestaste, balanced.

Marco Real Pequeñas Producciones Tempranillo 2012 TC
tempranillo

89

Colour: cherry, garnet rim. Nose: ripe fruit, spicy, varietal, floral. Palate: powerful, flavourful, toasty, round tannins, fruity.

Marco Real Reserva de Familia 2009 TR
tempranillo, cabernet sauvignon, merlot, graciano

91

Colour: cherry, garnet rim. Nose: ripe fruit, wild herbs, earthy notes, spicy, creamy oak. Palate: balanced, flavourful, long, balsamic.

BODEGAS NAPARRALDE
Crtra. de Madrid s/n
31591 Corella (Navarra)
☎: +34 948 782 255
Fax: +34 948 401 182
www.upain.es
administracion@naparralde.com

Upain 2013 RD
100% garnacha

87

Colour: rose, purple rim. Nose: powerfull, ripe fruit, red berry notes, floral, expressive. Palate: powerful, fruity, fresh.

Upain Selección Privada 2008 T

86

Colour: bright cherry, orangey edge. Nose: balanced, tobacco, ripe fruit, spicy. Palate: flavourful, correct, spicy.

Upain Selección Privada 2009 T
garnacha

87

Colour: cherry, garnet rim. Nose: ripe fruit, spicy, creamy oak, toasty. Palate: powerful, flavourful, toasty.

Upain Syrah Selección Privada 2010 T
100% syrah

86

Colour: cherry, garnet rim. Nose: ripe fruit, spicy, creamy oak, toasty, complex. Palate: powerful, flavourful, toasty, round tannins.

Upain Tempranillo Merlot 2008 TC

82

Upainberri 2011 T Roble

84

BODEGAS OCHOA
Alcalde Maillata, 2
31390 Olite (Navarra)
☎: +34 948 740 006
Fax: +34 948 740 048
www.bodegasochoa.com
info@bodegasochoa.com

Moscato de Ochoa 2013 B
moscatel grano menudo

87

Colour: bright straw. Nose: ripe fruit, white flowers. Palate: flavourful, sweetness.

Ochoa 2008 TR
tempranillo, merlot, cabernet sauvignon

88

Colour: cherry, garnet rim. Nose: balanced, complex, ripe fruit, spicy, creamy oak. Palate: good structure, flavourful, round tannins.

Ochoa Calendas 2013 B
moscatel grano menudo, chardonnay

86

Colour: bright straw. Nose: ripe fruit, faded flowers, dried herbs. Palate: easy to drink, ripe fruit.

Ochoa Moscatel Vendimia Tardía 2013 Blanco dulce
moscatel grano menudo

88

Colour: bright yellow. Nose: floral, ripe fruit, candied fruit, honeyed notes. Palate: powerful, spirituous, ripe fruit.

Ochoa Rosado de Lágrima 2013 RD
garnacha, cabernet sauvignon

88

Colour: rose, purple rim. Nose: powerfull, ripe fruit, red berry notes, floral, fragrant herbs. Palate: powerful, fruity, fresh.

Ochoa Serie 8A Mil Gracias 2010 TC
graciano

88

Colour: bright cherry. Nose: red berry notes, ripe fruit, spicy, creamy oak, toasty, complex, earthy notes. Palate: powerful, flavourful, toasty.

Ochoa Tempranillo 2011 TC
tempranillo

89

Colour: cherry, garnet rim. Nose: ripe fruit, spicy, toasty, balsamic herbs. Palate: powerful, flavourful, toasty, round tannins.

BODEGAS OLIMPIA
Avda. Río Aragón, 1
31490 Cáseda (Navarra)
☎: +34 948 186 262
Fax: +34 948 186 565
www.bodegasolimpia.com
info@bodegasolimpia.com

Bodegas Artajona 2010 TC
cabernet sauvignon, merlot, tempranillo

86

Colour: bright cherry, garnet rim. Nose: balanced, dried herbs, sweet spices, ripe fruit. Palate: correct, ripe fruit.

F. Olimpia 15 de Abril 2013 RD
100% garnacha

85

F. Olimpia Garnacha Blanca 2013 B
100% garnacha blanca

84

F. Olimpia Legado de Familia 2010 T
100% garnacha

90

Colour: cherry, garnet rim. Nose: ripe fruit, spicy, toasty, balsamic herbs, dark chocolate. Palate: powerful, flavourful, toasty, round tannins.

BODEGAS ORVALAIZ
Ctra. Pamplona-Logroño, s/n
31151 Óbanos (Navarra)
☎: +34 948 344 437
Fax: +34 948 344 401
www.orvalaiz.es
bodega@orvalaiz.es

8:00 AM 2010 TC
tempranillo, merlot, cabernet sauvignon

85

8:00 AM 2013 RD
cabernet sauvignon

88

Colour: onion pink. Nose: elegant, candied fruit, dried flowers, fragrant herbs, red berry notes. Palate: light-bodied, flavourful, good acidity, long, spicy.

8:00 AM Chardonnay 2013 B
chardonnay

84

8:00 AM Devoción 2010 T
merlot, tempranillo

86

Colour: cherry, garnet rim. Nose: ripe fruit, spicy, creamy oak, toasty, complex. Palate: powerful, flavourful, toasty.

Orvalaiz 2007 TR
tempranillo, cabernet sauvignon

87

Colour: cherry, garnet rim. Nose: balanced, complex, ripe fruit, spicy. Palate: good structure, flavourful, round tannins.

Orvalaiz 2010 TC
tempranillo, merlot, cabernet sauvignon

86

Colour: ruby red. Nose: spicy, fine reductive notes, wet leather, aged wood nuances, toasty. Palate: spicy, long, toasty.

Orvalaiz Chardonnay 2013 B
chardonnay

84

Orvalaiz Rosado de Lágrima 2013 RD
cabernet sauvignon
88
Colour: light cherry. Nose: powerfull, ripe fruit, red berry notes, floral, expressive. Palate: powerful, fruity, fresh.

Septentrión 2010 TC
merlot, tempranillo
88
Colour: cherry, garnet rim. Nose: ripe fruit, spicy, creamy oak, toasty, complex. Palate: powerful, flavourful, toasty, round tannins, balanced.

BODEGAS PAGOS DE ARÁIZ
Camino de Araiz, s/n
31390 Olite (Navarra)
☎: +34 948 399 182
www.bodegaspagosdearaiz.com
info@bodegaspagosdearaiz.com

Blaneo by Pagos de Aráiz 2012 T
100% syrah
88
Colour: very deep cherry, garnet rim. Nose: powerfull, ripe fruit, roasted coffee, dark chocolate. Palate: powerful, toasty, roasted-coffee aftertaste, correct.

Pagos de Aráiz 2011 TC
89
Colour: cherry, garnet rim. Nose: ripe fruit, spicy, creamy oak, toasty, complex. Palate: powerful, flavourful, toasty, round tannins.

Pagos de Aráiz 2013 RD
100% garnacha
88
Colour: rose, purple rim. Nose: powerful, ripe fruit, red berry notes, floral, expressive. Palate: powerful, fruity, fresh.

BODEGAS PIEDEMONTE
Rua Romana, s/n
31390 Olite (Navarra)
☎: +34 948 712 406
Fax: +34 948 740 090
www.piedemonte.com
bodega@piedemonte.com

Piedemonte +dQuince 2009 T
merlot
88
Colour: bright cherry, orangey edge. Nose: fruit preserve, ripe fruit, cocoa bean, creamy oak. Palate: full, round tannins.

Piedemonte 2008 TR
merlot, tempranillo, cabernet sauvignon
86
Colour: bright cherry, orangey edge. Nose: scrubland, grassy, spicy. Palate: flavourful, round tannins.

Piedemonte 2009 TC
merlot, tempranillo, cabernet sauvignon
85

Piedemonte 2013 RD
garnacha
85

Piedemonte Cabernet Sauvignon 2009 TC
cabernet sauvignon
87
Colour: cherry, garnet rim. Nose: scrubland, ripe fruit, spicy. Palate: good structure, flavourful, round tannins.

Piedemonte Chardonnay 2013 B
chardonnay
85

Piedemonte Gamma 2012 T
merlot, cabernet sauvignon, tempranillo
81

Piedemonte Gamma 2013 B
chardonnay, viura, moscatel
83

Piedemonte Merlot 2009 TC
merlot
84

Piedemonte Moscatel 2012 B
moscatel grano menudo
87
Colour: bright yellow. Nose: citrus fruit, ripe fruit, honeyed notes, balsamic herbs. Palate: powerful, flavourful, correct.

BODEGAS PRÍNCIPE DE VIANA
Mayor, 191
31521 Murchante (Navarra)
☎: +34 948 838 640
Fax: +34 948 818 574
www.principedeviana.com
info@principedeviana.com

Príncipe de Viana 2009 TR
88
Colour: cherry, garnet rim. Nose: ripe fruit, spicy, aged wood nuances, dried herbs. Palate: fruity, flavourful, long, round tannins.

Príncipe de Viana 1423 2009 TR
86
Colour: bright cherry, garnet rim. Nose: ripe fruit, dried herbs. Palate: flavourful, spicy, balanced.

Príncipe de Viana Chardonnay 2013 B
100% chardonnay

88

Colour: bright straw. Nose: white flowers, fresh fruit, expressive, dried herbs, sweet spices. Palate: flavourful, fruity, good acidity, balanced.

Príncipe de Viana Edición Limitada 2010 TC

90

Colour: cherry, garnet rim. Nose: ripe fruit, wild herbs, earthy notes, spicy, creamy oak. Palate: balanced, flavourful, long, balsamic.

Príncipe de Viana Garnacha 2013 RD
100% garnacha

86

Colour: rose, purple rim. Nose: ripe fruit, red berry notes, floral. Palate: powerful, fruity, fresh.

Príncipe de Viana Garnacha Viñas Viejas 2013 T
100% garnacha

87

Colour: bright cherry, purple rim. Nose: red berry notes, violets, sweet spices. Palate: balanced, flavourful, fine bitter notes.

Príncipe de Viana Syrah 2013 T Roble
100% syrah

88

Colour: bright cherry. Nose: ripe fruit, sweet spices, expressive, floral. Palate: flavourful, fruity, toasty, round tannins.

Príncipe de Viana Tempranillo 2013 T Roble
100% tempranillo

89

Colour: cherry, purple rim. Nose: red berry notes, wild herbs, sweet spices. Palate: fruity, balsamic, fresh, fruity aftestaste.

Príncipe de Viana Vendimia Seleccionada 2011 TC

88

Colour: bright cherry. Nose: ripe fruit, sweet spices, creamy oak, balsamic herbs. Palate: powerful, flavourful, spicy, balanced.

BODEGAS VALCARLOS

Ctra. Circunvalación, s/n
31210 Los Arcos (Navarra)
☎: +34 948 640 806
Fax: +34 948 640 866
www.bodegasvalcarlos.com
info@bodegasvalcarlos.com

Élite de Fortius 2009 TR

88

Colour: bright cherry. Nose: ripe fruit, sweet spices, creamy oak, medium intensity. Palate: fruity, flavourful, toasty.

Fortius 2001 TGR
tempranillo, cabernet sauvignon

89

Colour: cherry, garnet rim. Nose: balanced, complex, ripe fruit, spicy, balsamic herbs. Palate: good structure, flavourful, round tannins.

Fortius 2006 TR
tempranillo, cabernet sauvignon

86

Colour: pale ruby, brick rim edge. Nose: spicy, fine reductive notes, wet leather, aged wood nuances. Palate: spicy, fine tannins, long.

Fortius 2013 B
viura, chardonnay

83

Fortius 2013 RD
tempranillo, merlot

88

Colour: rose, purple rim. Nose: powerfull, ripe fruit, red berry notes, floral, expressive. Palate: powerful, fruity, fresh.

Fortius Chardonnay 2013 B
chardonnay

85

Fortius Merlot 2009 TC
merlot

86

Colour: bright cherry. Nose: ripe fruit, sweet spices, creamy oak, medium intensity. Palate: fruity, flavourful, toasty.

Fortius Tempranillo 2009 TC
tempranillo

84

Fortius Tempranillo 2011 T Roble
100% tempranillo

86

Colour: bright cherry. Nose: ripe fruit, spicy. Palate: flavourful, fruity, round tannins, easy to drink, balanced.

Marqués de Valcarlos 2009 TC
tempranillo, cabernet sauvignon

86

Colour: cherry, garnet rim. Nose: ripe fruit, spicy, creamy oak, toasty. Palate: powerful, flavourful, toasty, round tannins.

Marqués de Valcarlos 2013 B
chardonnay, viura

84

Marqués de Valcarlos 2013 RD
tempranillo, merlot

85

Marqués de Valcarlos Chardonnay 2013 B
chardonnay
85

Marqués de Valcarlos Tempranillo 2011 T Roble
tempranillo
84

BODEGAS VEGA DEL CASTILLO

Rua Romana, 7
31390 Olite (Navarra)
☎: +34 948 740 012
info@vegadelcastillo.com

Capa Roja 2011 T
tempranillo
89
Colour: cherry, garnet rim. Nose: ripe fruit, spicy, creamy oak, toasty, complex. Palate: powerful, flavourful, toasty, round tannins.

Crianza Vega del Castillo 2010 TC
merlot, cabernet sauvignon, tempranillo
88
Colour: bright cherry. Nose: ripe fruit, sweet spices, creamy oak, medium intensity. Palate: fruity, flavourful, toasty.

Dubhe 2008 T
merlot, cabernet sauvignon, tempranillo
90
Colour: cherry, garnet rim. Nose: ripe fruit, spicy, creamy oak, toasty, complex, dark chocolate, earthy notes. Palate: powerful, flavourful, toasty, round tannins.

Galimatias 2011 T
cabernet sauvignon
88
Colour: cherry, garnet rim. Nose: ripe fruit, spicy, creamy oak, toasty. Palate: powerful, flavourful, toasty.

Merak 2008 T
merlot, cabernet sauvignon, tempranillo
89
Colour: cherry, garnet rim. Nose: powerfull, toasty, ripe fruit, spicy. Palate: fruity, long, balsamic, round tannins.

Rosado Vega del Castillo 2013 RD
garnacha
88
Colour: brilliant rose. Nose: powerfull, ripe fruit, red berry notes, floral, expressive. Palate: powerful, fruity, fresh.

Vega del Castillo Chardonnay 2013 B
chardonnay
87
Colour: bright straw. Nose: fresh, fresh fruit, white flowers, expressive. Palate: flavourful, fruity, good acidity, balanced.

BODEGAS VINÍCOLA NAVARRA

Avda. Pamplona, 25
31398 Tiebas (Navarra)
☎: +34 948 360 131
Fax: +34 948 360 544
www.bodegasvinicolanavarra.com
vinicolanavarra@pernod-ricard.com

Castillo de Javier 2013 RD
garnacha
87
Colour: rose, purple rim. Nose: powerfull, ripe fruit, red berry notes, floral, expressive. Palate: powerful, fruity, fresh.

Las Campanas 2009 TC
tempranillo, merlot, cabernet sauvignon
84

Las Campanas 2013 RD
garnacha
87
Colour: rose, purple rim. Nose: powerfull, red berry notes, floral, expressive, fresh fruit. Palate: fruity, fresh, easy to drink.

Las Campanas Chardonnay 2013 B
chardonnay, viura
88
Colour: bright straw. Nose: fresh, fresh fruit, white flowers, expressive. Palate: flavourful, fruity, good acidity, balanced.

BODEGAS VIÑA MAGAÑA

San Miguel, 9
31523 Barillas (Navarra)
☎: +34 948 850 034
Fax: +34 948 851 536
www.vinamagana.com
bodegas@vinamagana.com

Magaña Calchetas 2006 T
91
Colour: deep cherry, garnet rim. Nose: elegant, spicy, fine reductive notes, aged wood nuances, mineral, ripe fruit. Palate: spicy, fine tannins, elegant, long, balsamic.

Magaña Merlot 2007 TR
merlot
87
Colour: pale ruby, brick rim edge. Nose: spicy, fine reductive notes, wet leather, aged wood nuances, ripe fruit, scrubland. Palate: spicy, fine tannins.

BODEGAS Y VIÑEDOS ARTAZU

Mayor, 3
31109 Artazu (Navarra)
☎: +34 945 600 119
Fax: +34 945 600 850
artazu@artadi.com

Pasos de San Martín 2012 T
100% garnacha
95
Colour: cherry, garnet rim. Nose: wild herbs, earthy notes, creamy oak, fruit expression, balsamic herbs, scrubland. Palate: balanced, flavourful, long, balsamic.

Santa Cruz de Artazu 2012 T
100% garnacha
94
Colour: cherry, garnet rim. Nose: wild herbs, earthy notes, spicy, creamy oak, fruit expression. Palate: balanced, flavourful, long, balsamic.

CAMPOS DE ENANZO

Mayor, 189
31521 Murchante (Navarra)
☎: +34 948 838 030
Fax: +34 948 838 677
www.enanzo.com
info@enanzo.com

Enanzo 2007 TR
89
Colour: cherry, garnet rim. Nose: red berry notes, ripe fruit, spicy, creamy oak, toasty, complex, balsamic herbs. Palate: powerful, flavourful, toasty.

Enanzo 2009 TC
85

Enanzo 2013 RD
100% garnacha
86
Colour: light cherry. Nose: red berry notes, lactic notes, wild herbs. Palate: fresh, fruity, flavourful.

Enanzo Chardonnay 2013 B Barrica
100% chardonnay
86
Colour: bright straw. Nose: sweet spices, white flowers. Palate: flavourful, fruity, spicy, fine bitter notes.

Remonte 2009 TC
89
Colour: bright cherry, garnet rim. Nose: balanced, expressive, balsamic herbs. Palate: fruity, round tannins, flavourful, spicy.

Remonte 2013 RD
100% garnacha
87
Colour: rose, purple rim. Nose: ripe fruit, red berry notes, floral, expressive. Palate: powerful, fruity, fresh.

Remonte Chardonnay 2013 B
100% chardonnay
87
Colour: bright straw. Nose: ripe fruit, powerfull, toasty, floral. Palate: flavourful, fruity, spicy, long, rich.

Remonte Juntos 2012 T
86
Colour: bright cherry. Nose: ripe fruit, sweet spices, creamy oak, expressive. Palate: flavourful, fruity, toasty, round tannins.

COSECHEROS BODEGAS Y VIÑEDOS

Pza. San Antón, 1
31390 Olite (Navarra)
☎: +34 948 740 067
Fax: +34 948 740 067
www.bodegacosecheros.com
info@bodegacosecheros.com

Viña Juguera 2009 TC
tempranillo, garnacha
84

Viña Juguera 2013 B
100% viura
85

Viña Juguera 2013 RD
100% garnacha
87
Colour: rose, purple rim. Nose: powerfull, ripe fruit, red berry notes, floral, expressive. Palate: powerful, fruity, fresh.

Viña Juguera Selección 2009 T
tempranillo, cabernet sauvignon
84

CRIANZAS Y VIÑEDOS R. REVERTE

Lejalde, 43
31593 Fitero (Navarra)
☎: +34 948 780 617
Fax: +34 948 401 894
www.rafaelreverte.es
odipus@rafaelreverte.es

Cistum 2011 T
garnacha
85

Odipus Garnacha 2012 T
garnacha

88

Colour: cherry, garnet rim. Nose: ripe fruit, fruit liqueur notes, balsamic herbs, balanced. Palate: fine bitter notes, powerful, flavourful, balanced.

DOMAINES LUPIER
Monseñor Justo Goizueta, 4
31495 San Martín de Unx (Navarra)
☎: +34 639 622 111
www.domaineslupier.com
info@domaineslupier.com

Domaines Lupier El Terroir 2011 T
100% garnacha

93

Colour: very deep cherry. Nose: characterful, overripe fruit, scrubland, balsamic herbs, sweet spices. Palate: powerful, sweetness.

Domaines Lupier La Dama Viñas Viejas 2011 T
100% garnacha

94

Colour: cherry, garnet rim. Nose: wild herbs, earthy notes, spicy, creamy oak, candied fruit, fruit expression. Palate: balanced, flavourful, long, balsamic.

EMILIO VALERIO - LADERAS DE MONTEJURRA
Paraje de Argonga
31263 Dicastillo (Navarra)
www.laderasdemontejurra.com
info@laderasdemontejurra.com

Amburza 2010 T

92 🌱

Colour: bright cherry. Nose: red berry notes, fruit liqueur notes, wild herbs, mineral, spicy, creamy oak, expressive. Palate: balanced, spicy, balsamic.

Emilio Valerio Laderas de Montejurra 2012 T

92 🌱

Colour: cherry, garnet rim. Nose: ripe fruit, spicy, creamy oak, toasty, complex, earthy notes, wild herbs. Palate: powerful, flavourful, toasty, balanced.

La Merced 2012 B
malvasía

92 🌱

Colour: bright yellow. Nose: powerfull, ripe fruit, sweet spices, fragrant herbs. Palate: rich, smoky aftertaste, flavourful, fresh, good acidity.

Usuaran 2011 T

92 🌱

Colour: bright cherry. Nose: sweet spices, ripe fruit, mineral, complex. Palate: good structure, flavourful, round tannins, balsamic.

Viña de San Martín 2011 T
garnacha

93 🌱

Colour: cherry, garnet rim. Nose: ripe fruit, spicy, creamy oak, complex, earthy notes. Palate: powerful, flavourful, toasty, round tannins.

Viña de San Martín 2012 T
garnacha

94 🌱

Colour: bright cherry. Nose: complex, expressive, wild herbs, red berry notes, ripe fruit, spicy. Palate: good structure, full.

FINCA ALBRET
Ctra. Cadreita-Villafranca, s/n
31515 Cadreita (Navarra)
☎: +34 948 406 806
Fax: +34 948 406 699
www.fincaalbret.com
info@fincaalbret.com

Albret 2009 TR

90

Colour: cherry, garnet rim. Nose: elegant, balanced, ripe fruit, red berry notes, dried herbs. Palate: good structure, spicy.

Albret 2013 RD
100% garnacha

89

Colour: rose, purple rim. Nose: powerfull, ripe fruit, red berry notes, floral, expressive. Palate: powerful, fruity, fresh.

Albret Chardonnay 2013 BFB
100% chardonnay

90

Colour: bright yellow. Nose: fruit expression, honeyed notes, sweet spices, creamy oak. Palate: powerful, flavourful, spicy, long.

Albret Garnacha 2013 T
100% garnacha

88

Colour: bright cherry. Nose: ripe fruit, sweet spices, creamy oak, expressive. Palate: flavourful, fruity, toasty, round tannins.

Albret La Viña de mi Madre 2009 TR
92

Colour: cherry, garnet rim. Nose: ripe fruit, spicy, toasty, complex, scrubland. Palate: powerful, flavourful, toasty, round tannins.

Juan de Albret 2011 TC
89

Colour: bright cherry, garnet rim. Nose: expressive, balanced, ripe fruit, red berry notes. Palate: fruity, round tannins.

GARCÍA BURGOS
Finca La Cantera de Santa Ana, s/n
31521 Murchante (Navarra)
☎: +34 948 847 734
Fax: +34 948 847 734
www.bodegasgarciaburgos.com
info@bodegasgarciaburgos.com

Finca La Cantera de Santa Ana 2010 T
cabernet sauvignon

91

Colour: cherry, garnet rim. Nose: wild herbs, dry stone, red berry notes, ripe fruit, creamy oak. Palate: powerful, flavourful, spicy, long.

García Burgos Sh 2010 T
syrah

90

Colour: cherry, garnet rim. Nose: spicy, ripe fruit, smoky. Palate: full, fruity, rich, round tannins, long.

García Burgos Vendimia Seleccionada 2011 T
cabernet sauvignon, merlot, syrah

87

Colour: cherry, garnet rim. Nose: ripe fruit, wild herbs, earthy notes, spicy. Palate: balanced, flavourful, long, balsamic.

Lola García 2009 TR
merlot

90

Colour: cherry, garnet rim. Nose: ripe fruit, wild herbs, earthy notes, spicy, creamy oak, complex. Palate: balanced, flavourful, long, balsamic.

J. CHIVITE FAMILY ESTATE
Ctra. NA-132, Km. 3
31264 Aberin (Navarra)
☎: +34 948 555 285
Fax: +34 948 555 415
www.chivite.com
info@bodegaschivite.com

Chivite Colección 125 2010 TR
100% tempranillo

95

Colour: cherry, garnet rim. Nose: ripe fruit, spicy, creamy oak, toasty, dark chocolate, earthy notes. Palate: powerful, flavourful, toasty, round tannins.

Chivite Colección 125 2012 BFB
chardonnay

96

Colour: bright straw. Nose: expressive, fine lees, dried herbs, white flowers. Palate: flavourful, fruity, good acidity, balanced.

Chivite Colección 125 2012 RD Fermentado en Barrica
tempranillo

93

Colour: onion pink. Nose: elegant, candied fruit, dried flowers, fragrant herbs, red berry notes. Palate: flavourful, good acidity, long, spicy.

Chivite Colección 125 Vendimia Tardía 2010 B
moscatel grano menudo

95

Colour: bright straw. Nose: powerfull, honeyed notes, candied fruit, fragrant herbs. Palate: flavourful, sweet, fresh, fruity, good acidity, long.

Chivite Finca de Villatuerta Chardonnay sobre Lías 2012 B
chardonnay

92

Colour: bright straw. Nose: white flowers, fine lees, dried herbs. Palate: flavourful, fruity, good acidity, balanced.

Chivite Finca de Villatuerta Selección Especial 2010 T
92

Colour: bright cherry. Nose: sweet spices, creamy oak. Palate: flavourful, fruity, toasty, round tannins.

Chivite Finca de Villatuerta Syrah 2011 T
syrah

93

Colour: very deep cherry. Nose: powerfull, ripe fruit, earthy notes, toasty, aromatic coffee, tobacco. Palate: flavourful, good acidity, fine bitter notes.

LA CALANDRIA. PURA GARNACHA

Camino de Aspra, s/n
31521 Murchante (Navarra)
☎: +34 630 904 327
www.puragarnacha.com
javier@lacalandria.org

Cientruenos 2012 T Barrica
100% garnacha

92

Colour: bright cherry, garnet rim. Nose: complex, expressive, varietal, wild herbs, earthy notes. Palate: balanced, spicy, long.

Sonrojo 2013 RD
100% garnacha

88

Colour: rose, purple rim. Nose: powerfull, ripe fruit, red berry notes, floral, expressive. Palate: powerful, fruity, fresh.

Volandera 2013 T
100% garnacha

88

Colour: cherry, purple rim. Nose: red berry notes, raspberry, floral. Palate: fresh, fruity, flavourful, easy to drink.

NEKEAS

Las Huertas, s/n
31154 Añorbe (Navarra)
☎: +34 948 350 296
Fax: +34 948 350 300
www.nekeas.com
nekeas@nekeas.com

El Chaparral de Vega Sindoa Old Vine Garnacha 2012 T
100% garnacha

88

Colour: cherry, garnet rim. Nose: ripe fruit, wild herbs, sweet spices, toasty. Palate: balanced, flavourful, long, balsamic.

Izar de Nekeas 2009 TR
cabernet sauvignon, merlot

89

Colour: deep cherry, garnet rim. Nose: scrubland, spicy, ripe fruit. Palate: good structure, harsh oak tannins.

Nekeas Chardonnay Barrel Fermented 2013 BFB
100% chardonnay

86

Colour: bright yellow. Nose: sweet spices, white flowers, ripe fruit. Palate: flavourful, good acidity, correct.

Nekeas 2010 TC
tempranillo, cabernet sauvignon

89

Colour: cherry, garnet rim. Nose: ripe fruit, spicy, creamy oak, toasty, complex, dark chocolate. Palate: powerful, flavourful, toasty, round tannins.

Nekeas 2013 RD
garnacha, tempranillo, merlot

86

Colour: light cherry. Nose: medium intensity, fresh, citrus fruit, floral, fragrant herbs. Palate: fresh, good acidity.

Nekeas Cabernet Sauvignon Merlot 2009 TR
cabernet sauvignon, merlot

88

Colour: cherry, garnet rim. Nose: red berry notes, ripe fruit, spicy, creamy oak, toasty, complex. Palate: powerful, flavourful, toasty.

Nekeas Cepa x Cepa (CXC) 2012 T
100% garnacha

89

Colour: bright cherry. Nose: balanced, red berry notes, floral, expressive. Palate: easy to drink, fruity, balsamic, fruity aftertaste.

Nekeas Chardonnay 2013 B
100% chardonnay

88

Colour: yellow. Nose: ripe fruit, dried flowers, expressive. Palate: balanced, fine bitter notes, good acidity.

Nekeas Viura/ Chardonnay 2013 B
viura, chardonnay

87

Colour: bright straw. Nose: medium intensity, dried herbs, fresh fruit. Palate: fruity, fresh, balsamic, good acidity.

NUEVOS VINOS

Alfafara, 12 Entlo.
3803 Alcoy (Alicante)
☎: +34 965 549 172
Fax: +34 965 549 173
www.nuevosvinos.es
josecanto@nuevosvinos.es

Terraplen Blanco Viura 2013 B
100% viura

81

Terraplen Rosado Garnacha 2013 RD
100% garnacha

86

Colour: rose. Nose: powerfull, floral, red berry notes. Palate: balanced, flavourful, good acidity, easy to drink.

Terraplen Tinto Garnacha 2013 T
100% garnacha

84

PAGO DE LARRÁINZAR
Camino de la Corona, s/n
31240 Ayegui (Navarra)
☎: +34 948 550 421
Fax: +34 948 556 120
www.pagodelarrainzar.com
info@pagodelarrainzar.com

Pago de Larrainzar 2008 T
92

Colour: cherry, garnet rim. Nose: ripe fruit, spicy, creamy oak, toasty, complex. Palate: powerful, flavourful, toasty, round tannins.

Pago de Larrainzar Cabernet Sauvignon 2011 T
100% cabernet sauvignon

93

Colour: cherry, garnet rim. Nose: ripe fruit, wild herbs, earthy notes, spicy, creamy oak, elegant. Palate: balanced, flavourful, long, balsamic.

Raso de Larrainzar 2010 T
91

Colour: cherry, garnet rim. Nose: ripe fruit, spicy, creamy oak, toasty, complex, earthy notes. Palate: powerful, flavourful, toasty, round tannins.

PROYECTO ZORZAL
Ctra. del Villar, s/n
31591 Corella (Navarra)
☎: +34 948 780 617
Fax: +34 948 401 894
www.vinazorzal.com
xabi@vinazorzal.com

Viña Zorzal Garnacha Viñas Viejas 2012 T
garnacha

88

Colour: bright cherry. Nose: ripe fruit, balsamic herbs, spicy, creamy oak. Palate: powerful, flavourful, good structure.

Viña Zorzal Graciano 2012 T
graciano

87

Colour: cherry, garnet rim. Nose: dried herbs, ripe fruit, closed. Palate: flavourful, good structure, good acidity, balanced.

Viña Zorzal La Señora de las Alturas 2010 T
93

Colour: cherry, garnet rim. Nose: ripe fruit, wild herbs, earthy notes, spicy, creamy oak, expressive. Palate: balanced, flavourful, long, balsamic.

SEÑORÍO DE ANDIÓN
Ctra. Pamplona-Zaragoza, Km. 38
31390 Olite (Navarra)
☎: +34 948 712 193
Fax: +34 948 712 343
www.familiabelasco.com
info@familiabelasco.com

Señorío de Andión 2009 T
tempranillo, cabernet sauvignon, merlot, graciano

91

Colour: cherry, garnet rim. Nose: ripe fruit, spicy, creamy oak, complex, dried herbs. Palate: powerful, flavourful, toasty, round tannins.

Señorío de Andión Moscatel Vendimia Tardía 2007 B
moscatel grano menudo

94

Colour: golden. Nose: powerfull, floral, honeyed notes, candied fruit, fragrant herbs. Palate: flavourful, sweet, fresh, fruity, good acidity, long.

VINOS Y VIÑEDOS DOMINIO LASIERPE

Ribera, s/n
31592 Cintruénigo (Navarra)
☎: +34 948 811 033
Fax: +34 948 815 160
www.dominiolasierpe.com
comercial@dominiolasierpe.com

Dominio Lasierpe 2011 TC
garnacha, graciano
85

Finca Lasierpe Blanco de Viura 2013 B
100% viura
84

Finca Lasierpe Chardonnay 2013 B
100% chardonnay
88
Colour: bright straw. Nose: fresh, fresh fruit, white flowers, expressive. Palate: flavourful, fruity, good acidity, balanced.

Finca Lasierpe Garnacha 2013 RD
100% garnacha
85

Finca Lasierpe Garnacha Tempranillo 2013 T
garnacha, tempranillo
85

VIÑA ALIAGA

Camino del Villar. N-161, Km. 3
31591 Corella (Navarra)
☎: +34 948 401 321
Fax: +34 948 781 414
www.vinaaliaga.com
sales@vinaaliaga.com

Aliaga Carlantonio 2011 B
100% sauvignon blanc
89
Colour: bright yellow. Nose: powerfull, ripe fruit, sweet spices, creamy oak, fragrant herbs. Palate: rich, smoky aftertaste, flavourful, fresh, good acidity.

Aliaga Colección Privada 2009 TC
87
Colour: cherry, garnet rim. Nose: ripe fruit, spicy, creamy oak, toasty, fine reductive notes. Palate: powerful, flavourful, toasty.

Aliaga Cuvée 2010 T
87
Colour: cherry, garnet rim. Nose: ripe fruit, spicy, creamy oak, toasty, complex. Palate: powerful, flavourful, toasty, round tannins.

Aliaga Doscarlos 2013 B
100% sauvignon blanc
86
Colour: bright straw. Nose: floral, candied fruit, fragrant herbs. Palate: fresh, flavourful, balanced.

Aliaga Garnacha Vieja 2010 T
100% garnacha
84

Aliaga Lágrima de Garnacha 2013 RD
100% garnacha
86
Colour: light cherry. Nose: candied fruit, dried flowers, fragrant herbs. Palate: light-bodied, flavourful, good acidity, spicy.

Aliaga Moscatel Vendimia Tardía 2012 B
100% moscatel grano menudo
90
Colour: bright yellow. Nose: floral, candied fruit, honeyed notes, fragrant herbs. Palate: fresh, flavourful, balanced.

Aliaga Reserva de la Familia 2008 TR
86
Colour: pale ruby, brick rim edge. Nose: spicy, fine reductive notes, wet leather, aged wood nuances, ripe fruit. Palate: spicy, balanced.

Aliaga Syrha 2009 T
100% syrah
87
Colour: bright cherry. Nose: ripe fruit, sweet spices, creamy oak, expressive. Palate: flavourful, fruity, toasty, round tannins.

Aliaga Tempranillo 2012 T
100% tempranillo
83

VIÑA VALDORBA

Ctra. de la Estación, s7n
31395 Garinoain (Navarra)
☎: +34 948 720 505
Fax: +34 948 720 505
www.bodegasvaldorba.com
bodegasvaldorba@bodegasvaldorba.com

Cauro 2002 TR
cabernet sauvignon, graciano
87
Colour: very deep cherry. Nose: spicy, creamy oak, toasty, characterful, fruit preserve. Palate: powerful, flavourful, toasty, round tannins.

Eolo 2010 TC
cabernet sauvignon, tempranillo, garnacha, graciano
86
Colour: bright cherry. Nose: ripe fruit, sweet spices, creamy oak, medium intensity. Palate: fruity, flavourful, toasty.

Eolo Chardonnay 2013 B
chardonnay
87
Colour: bright yellow. Nose: balanced, expressive, dried flowers, citrus fruit. Palate: fruity, long, fine bitter notes, good acidity.

Eolo Garnacha 2012 T
garnacha
85

Eolo Moscatel 2012 B
moscatel
89
Colour: golden. Nose: powerfull, floral, honeyed notes, candied fruit, fragrant herbs. Palate: flavourful, sweet, fresh, fruity, good acidity.

Eolo Roble 2011 T
tempranillo, garnacha
84

Eolo Rosado Sangrado 2013 RD
garnacha
84

Eolo Syrah 2011 T
syrah
88
Colour: cherry, garnet rim. Nose: ripe fruit, wild herbs, earthy notes, spicy. Palate: balanced, flavourful, long, balsamic.

Gran Eolo 2009 TR
cabernet sauvignon, merlot, garnacha
88
Colour: cherry, garnet rim. Nose: ripe fruit, spicy, creamy oak, toasty, complex. Palate: powerful, flavourful, toasty, round tannins.

VIÑEDOS DE CALIDAD
Ctra. Tudela, s/n
31591 Corella (Navarra)
☎: +34 948 782 014
Fax: +34 948 782 164
www.vinosalex.com
javier@vinosalex.com

Alex 2007 TR
tempranillo, merlot
85

Alex 2010 TC
tempranillo, merlot, graciano
88
Colour: bright cherry, garnet rim. Nose: ripe fruit, dried herbs, spicy. Palate: good structure, flavourful, round tannins.

Alex Garnacha 2013 RD
garnacha
89
Colour: light cherry. Nose: candied fruit, floral, fragrant herbs, expressive. Palate: fresh, fruity, easy to drink.

Alex Tempranillo 2013 T
tempranillo
86
Colour: cherry, purple rim. Nose: fresh fruit, red berry notes, floral, balsamic herbs. Palate: flavourful, fruity, good acidity.

Alex Viura 2013 B
viura
86
Colour: bright straw. Nose: white flowers, fragrant herbs, fruit expression. Palate: fresh, fruity, flavourful.

Ontinar 2009 T
merlot, tempranillo
87
Colour: cherry, garnet rim. Nose: ripe fruit, spicy, creamy oak, toasty, fine reductive notes. Palate: powerful, flavourful, toasty.

VIÑEDOS Y BODEGAS ALCONDE
Ctra. de Calahorra, s/n
31260 Lerín (Navarra)
☎: +34 948 530 058
Fax: +34 948 530 589
www.bodegasalconde.com
gerente@bodegasalconde.com

Bodegas Alconde 2005 TR
merlot, cabernet sauvignon, tempranillo, garnacha
89
Colour: cherry, garnet rim. Nose: ripe fruit, wild herbs, spicy, creamy oak, tobacco. Palate: balanced, flavourful, long, balsamic.

PRODUCTO DE ESPAÑA

ALCONDE

RESERVA

NAVARRA
Denominación de Origen

Bodegas Alconde Sauvignon Blanc Selección 2013 B
sauvignon blanc

86

Colour: bright straw. Nose: fresh, fresh fruit, white flowers. Palate: flavourful, fruity, good acidity, balanced.

Bodegas Alconde Selección 2009 TC
tempranillo, garnacha, cabernet sauvignon

87

Colour: bright cherry, garnet rim. Nose: creamy oak, cocoa bean, sweet spices. Palate: powerful, ripe fruit, round tannins.

Viña Sardasol 2007 TR
tempranillo, cabernet sauvignon

86

Colour: very deep cherry. Nose: ripe fruit, spicy, toasty, wild herbs, fine reductive notes. Palate: powerful, flavourful, toasty.

Viña Sardasol 2010 TC
tempranillo

86

Colour: cherry, garnet rim. Nose: balanced, complex, ripe fruit, spicy. Palate: good structure, flavourful, round tannins.

Viña Sardasol Tempranillo Merlot 2012 T Roble
tempranillo, merlot

86

Colour: bright cherry, garnet rim. Nose: balanced, balsamic herbs, ripe fruit. Palate: flavourful, correct, fruity.

DO. PENEDÉS

CONSEJO REGULADOR
Plaça Àgora. s/n. Pol. Ind. Domenys, II
08720 Vilafranca del Penedès (Barcelona)
☎:+34 938 904 811 - Fax: +34 938 904 754
@: dopenedes@dopenedes.cat
www.dopenedes.es

LOCATION:

In the province of Barcelona, between the pre-coastal Catalonian mountain range and the plains that lead to the Mediterranean coast. There are three different areas: Penedès Superior, Penedès Central or Medio and Bajo Penedès.

SUB-REGIONS:

Penedès Superior. The vineyards reach an altitude of 800 m; the traditional, characteristic variety is the Parellada, which is better suited to the cooler regions.

Penedès Central or Medio. Cava makes up a large part of the production in this region; the most abundant traditional varieties are Macabeo and Xarel·lo.

Bajo Penedès. This is the closest region to the sea, with a lower altitude and wines with a markedly Mediterranean character.

GRAPE VARIETIES:

White: Macabeo, Xarel·lo, Parellada, Chardonnay, Riesling, Gewürztraminer, Chenin Blanc, Moscatel de Alejandría, Garnacha Blanca and Vioquier.
Red: Garnacha, Merlot, Cariñena, Ull de Llebre (Tempranillo), Pinot Noir, Monastrell, Cabernet Sauvignon, Petit Verdot, Syrah and Sumoll.

FIGURES:

Vineyard surface: 18,376 – Wine-Growers: 2,620 – Wineries: 170 – 2013 Harvest rating: Very Good – Production 13: 12,392,735 litres – Market percentages: 69% domestic - 31% export.

SOIL:

There is deep soil, not too sandy or too clayey, permeable, which retains the rainwater well. The soil is poor in organic matter and not very fertile.

CLIMATE:

Mediterranean, in general warm and mild; warmer in the Bajo Penedès region due to the influence of the Mediterranean Sea, with slightly lower temperatures in Medio Penedès and Penedès Superior, where the climate is typically pre-coastal (greater contrasts between maximum and minimum temperatures, more frequent frosts and annual rainfall which at some places can reach 990 litres per square metre).

VINTAGE RATING   PEÑÍNGUIDE

2009	2010	2011	2012	2013
EXCELLENT	VERY GOOD	VERY GOOD	GOOD	VERY GOOD

1 + 1 = 3

Masía Navinés
08736 Font-Rubí (Barcelona)
☎: +34 938 974 069
Fax: +34 938 974 724
www.umesufan3.com
umesu@umesufan3.com

1+1=3 Xarel.lo 2013 B
xarel.lo
89 ♣
Colour: bright straw. Nose: fresh, fresh fruit, expressive, dried flowers. Palate: flavourful, fruity, good acidity, balanced.

Dahlia 1 + 1 = 3 2012 B
91
Colour: bright straw. Nose: white flowers, fragrant herbs, fruit expression. Palate: fresh, fruity, flavourful, balanced, elegant.

Défora 1 + 1 = 3 2011 T
garnacha, samsó
90
Colour: cherry, garnet rim. Nose: ripe fruit, spicy, toasty, complex, earthy notes, balsamic herbs. Palate: powerful, flavourful, toasty, round tannins.

AGUSTÍ TORELLÓ MATA

La Serra, s/n (Camí de Ribalta)
08770 Sant Sadurní D'Anoia (Barcelona)
☎: +34 938 911 173
Fax: +34 938 912 616
www.agustitorellomata.com
comunicacio@agustitorellomata.com

Aptià d'Agustí Torelló Mata "Col.lecció Terrers" 2012 BFB
macabeo
92 ♣
Colour: bright yellow. Nose: candied fruit, faded flowers, sweet spices, mineral. Palate: flavourful, fruity, long, spicy.

Xarel.lo d'Agustí Torelló Mata XIC 2013 B
xarel.lo
85

XII Subirat Parent d'Agustí Torelló Mata "Col.lecció Terrers" 2013 B
100% subirat parent
90
Colour: bright straw. Nose: white flowers, fragrant herbs, fruit expression, mineral. Palate: fresh, fruity, flavourful, balanced, elegant.

ALBET I NOYA

Can Vendrell de la Codina, s/n
08739 Sant Pau D'Ordal (Barcelona)
☎: +34 938 994 812
Fax: +34 938 994 930
www.albetinoya.cat
albetinoya@albetinoya.cat

Albet i Noya 2011 BR Reserva
xarel.lo, chardonnay, parellada, macabeo
87
Colour: bright straw. Nose: fine lees, floral, fragrant herbs, expressive. Palate: powerful, flavourful, good acidity, fine bead, balanced, easy to drink.

Albet i Noya 3 Macabeus 2013 B
macabeo
89 ♣
Colour: bright straw. Nose: floral, dried herbs, earthy notes, citrus fruit. Palate: powerful, flavourful, fruity, spicy.

Albet i Noya Brut 21 2011 BR
chardonnay, parellada
91 ♣
Colour: bright yellow. Nose: fine lees, floral, fragrant herbs, expressive. Palate: powerful, flavourful, good acidity, fine bead, balanced, dry.

Albet i Noya Brut 21 Barrica 2007 BR Gran Reserva
pinot noir, chardonnay
92 ♣
Colour: bright yellow. Nose: dried herbs, fine lees, floral, toasty, ripe fruit. Palate: fruity, flavourful, good acidity, long.

Albet i Noya Col.lecció Chardonnay 2013 B
chardonnay
92 ♣
Colour: bright yellow. Nose: sweet spices, creamy oak, ripe fruit, balanced. Palate: flavourful, complex, long.

Albet i Noya Col.lecció Syrah 2009 T
syrah
92 ♣
Colour: bright cherry. Nose: ripe fruit, sweet spices, creamy oak, violets, balsamic herbs. Palate: fruity, flavourful, toasty, balanced.

Albet i Noya Dolç Adrià 2007 Tinto dulce Reserva
syrah, merlot
91 ♣
Colour: pale ruby, brick rim edge. Nose: ripe fruit, fruit liqueur notes, tar, aromatic coffee, toasty, powerfull. Palate: powerful, flavourful, rich, sweet, balanced.

Albet i Noya El Blanc XXV "ecológico" 2013 B

viognier, vidal, marina rion

92 🌷

Colour: bright straw. Nose: balanced, elegant, fresh fruit, floral. Palate: long, good acidity, fine bitter notes, flavourful, balanced.

Albet i Noya EL Fanio 2012 B

xarel.lo

92 🌷

Colour: bright yellow. Nose: expressive, dry stone, faded flowers, balanced. Palate: full, flavourful, rich, long, good acidity, fine bitter notes.

Albet i Noya Lignum 2012 T

cabernet sauvignon, garnacha, merlot, syrah

89 🌷

Colour: dark-red cherry, purple rim. Nose: smoky, ripe fruit, balanced, powerfull. Palate: flavourful, round tannins.

Albet i Noya Lignum 2013 B

chardonnay, xarel.lo, sauvignon blanc

89 🌷

Colour: bright yellow. Nose: ripe fruit, sweet spices, fragrant herbs, toasty. Palate: rich, smoky aftertaste, flavourful, good acidity.

Albet i Noya Petit Albet 2013 B

xarel.lo, macabeo, chardonnay

88 🌷

Colour: bright straw. Nose: fresh, fresh fruit, white flowers. Palate: flavourful, fruity, good acidity, easy to drink.

Albet i Noya Petit Albet Brut 2011 BR

macabeo, xarel.lo, parellada

89 🌷

Colour: bright straw. Nose: fresh fruit, dried herbs, fine lees, floral. Palate: fresh, fruity, flavourful, good acidity.

Albet i Noya Pinot Noir Brut Rosat 2011 BR

pinot noir

88 🌷

Colour: rose. Nose: floral, red berry notes, ripe fruit, fragrant herbs, expressive. Palate: powerful, flavourful.

Albet i Noya Pinot Noir Merlot Clàssic 2013 RD

pinot noir, merlot

88 🌷

Colour: light cherry. Nose: powerfull, ripe fruit, red berry notes, floral, expressive. Palate: fruity, good finish, easy to drink, good acidity.

Albet i Noya Reserva 3 2010 BN

xarel.lo, parellada, chardonnay, macabeo

87 🌷

Colour: bright yellow. Nose: ripe fruit, fine lees, balanced, dried herbs. Palate: good acidity, flavourful, ripe fruit, long.

Albet i Noya Reserva Martí 2008 TR

tempranillo, cabernet sauvignon, syrah, merlot

93 🌷

Colour: cherry, garnet rim. Nose: red berry notes, ripe fruit, spicy, creamy oak, toasty, complex, earthy notes. Palate: powerful, flavourful, toasty, round tannins.

Albet i Noya Ull de Llebre Clàssic 2013 T

tempranillo

89 🌷

Colour: cherry, purple rim. Nose: powerfull, red berry notes, ripe fruit, floral, balsamic herbs. Palate: powerful, fresh, fruity, unctuous.

Albet i Noya Xarel.lo Nosodos + 2013 B

xarel.lo

85 🌷

Albet i Noya Xarel-lo Clàssic 2013 B

xarel.lo

89 🌷

Colour: bright straw. Nose: varietal, fresh, dried flowers. Palate: fruity, easy to drink, balsamic, good acidity.

Belat 2009 T

belat

93 🌷

Colour: ruby red. Nose: red berry notes, fruit liqueur notes, balsamic herbs, mineral, spicy, creamy oak. Palate: flavourful, round, complex, spicy, balanced, elegant. Personality.

Finca La Milana 2011 T

caladoc, tempranillo, cabernet sauvignon, merlot

91 🌷

Colour: cherry, garnet rim. Nose: ripe fruit, spicy, creamy oak, toasty, complex, characterful. Palate: powerful, flavourful, toasty, round tannins.

Marina Rion "ecológico" 2013 B

marina rión

90 🌷

Colour: bright straw. Nose: fresh fruit, dry nuts, white flowers, fine lees. Palate: balanced, flavourful, full.

Ocell de Foc 2012 T
arinarnoa, caladoc, marselan

91 ♣

Colour: cherry, garnet rim. Nose: ripe fruit, spicy, creamy oak, toasty, complex, earthy notes. Palate: powerful, flavourful, toasty, round tannins.

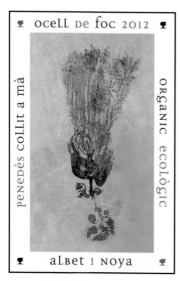

ALEMANY I CORRIO

Melió, 78
08720 Vilafranca del Penedès (Barcelona)
☎: +34 938 180 949
sotlefriec@sotlefriec.com

Cargol Treu Vi 2013 B
xarel.lo

90 ♣

Colour: bright straw. Nose: fresh, fresh fruit, white flowers, dried herbs. Palate: flavourful, fruity, good acidity, balanced.

Pas Curtei 2012 T
merlot, cariñena

90 ♣

Colour: cherry, garnet rim. Nose: ripe fruit, wild herbs, earthy notes, spicy, creamy oak. Palate: balanced, flavourful, long, balsamic.

Principia Mathematica 2013 B
xarel.lo

90 ♣

Colour: bright straw. Nose: fresh, fresh fruit, white flowers, expressive. Palate: flavourful, fruity, good acidity, balanced.

ALSINA SARDÁ

08733 Pla del Penedès (Barcelona)
☎: +34 938 988 132
Fax: +34 938 988 671
www.alsinasarda.com
alsina@alsinasarda.com

Alsina & Sardá Blanc de Blancs 2013 B

87

Colour: bright straw. Nose: fruit expression, floral, fragrant herbs. Palate: fresh, fruity, flavourful.

Alsina & Sardá Chardonnay Xarel.lo 2013 B

85

Alsina & Sardá Finca Cal Janes 2010 T
100% merlot

88

Colour: bright cherry. Nose: sweet spices, smoky, toasty, dried herbs. Palate: flavourful, fruity, toasty, round tannins.

Alsina & Sardá Finca La Boltana 2013 B
100% xarel.lo

89

Colour: bright straw. Nose: fresh, fresh fruit, white flowers, expressive. Palate: flavourful, fruity, good acidity, balanced.

Alsina & Sardá Finca Olerdola 2009 TR

90

Colour: bright cherry. Nose: ripe fruit, sweet spices, creamy oak, medium intensity. Palate: fruity, toasty, easy to drink.

Alsina & Sardá Merlot Llàgrima 2013 RD
100% merlot

85

Alsina & Sardá Muscat Llàgrima 2013 B
100% moscatel de alejandría

87

Colour: yellow. Nose: medium intensity, varietal, white flowers. Palate: fresh, fruity, easy to drink.

Alsina & Sardá Reserva de Familia 2008 T
100% merlot

90

Colour: cherry, garnet rim. Nose: ripe fruit, wild herbs, earthy notes, spicy. Palate: balanced, flavourful, long, balsamic.

Arnau 2013 T
100% merlot

86

Colour: dark-red cherry, purple rim. Nose: varietal, scrubland, ripe fruit. Palate: correct, easy to drink, good finish.

AT ROCA

La Vinya, 15
08770 Sant Sadurní D'Anoia (Barcelona)
☎: +34 935 165 043
www.cellersatroca.com
info@cellersatroca.com

At Roca 2012 BR Reserva
87 🍷

Colour: bright straw. Nose: medium intensity, fresh fruit, dried herbs, fine lees, floral. Palate: fresh, fruity, flavourful, good acidity.

At Roca Rosat 2012 ESP Reserva
macabeo, monastrell
87

Colour: raspberry rose. Nose: floral, red berry notes, fragrant herbs. Palate: fresh, fruity, flavourful, easy to drink.

Xarel.lo D'At Roca 2013 B
xarel.lo
90 🌷

Colour: bright straw. Nose: fresh, fresh fruit, white flowers, mineral, dry stone. Palate: flavourful, fruity, good acidity, balanced.

BODEGA J. MIQUEL JANÉ

Masia Cal Costas, s/n
08736 Guardiola de Font-Rubí (Barcelona)
☎: +34 934 140 948
Fax: +34 934 140 948
www.jmiqueljane.com
info@jmiqueljane.com

J. Miquel Jané Blanc Baltana 2013 B
88

Colour: bright straw. Nose: fresh fruit, white flowers, wild herbs. Palate: fruity, flavourful, fine bitter notes.

J. Miquel Jané Cabernet Sauvignon 2013 RD
86

Colour: rose, purple rim. Nose: powerfull, ripe fruit, red berry notes, floral. Palate: powerful, fruity, fresh, easy to drink.

J. Miquel Jané Sauvignon Blanc 2013 B
100% sauvignon blanc
89

Colour: bright straw. Nose: ripe fruit, tropical fruit, white flowers. Palate: balanced, fine bitter notes, fruity, long.

Miquel Jané Baltana Negre 2012 T
86

Colour: dark-red cherry, garnet rim. Nose: powerfull, fruit preserve, cocoa bean, sweet spices. Palate: ripe fruit, correct.

Miquel Jané Baltana Selecció 2011 T
merlot, cabernet sauvignon, tempranillo
88

Colour: cherry, garnet rim. Nose: spicy, creamy oak, toasty, fruit preserve. Palate: powerful, flavourful, toasty, round tannins.

BODEGAS CA N'ESTELLA

Masia Ca N'Estella, s/n
08635 Sant Esteve Sesrovires (Barcelona)
☎: +34 934 161 387
Fax: +34 934 161 620
www.fincacanestella.com
a.vidal@fincacanestella.com

Clot dels Oms 2011 TR
ull de llebre, samsó, merlot
88

Colour: cherry, garnet rim. Nose: ripe fruit, wild herbs, spicy. Palate: balanced, flavourful, long, balsamic.

Clot dels Oms 2013 B
chardonnay, malvasía
87

Colour: bright yellow. Nose: dried flowers, citrus fruit. Palate: correct, good acidity, fruity.

Clot dels Oms Cabernet Sauvignon 2006 T
cabernet sauvignon
85

Clot dels Oms Rosat 2013 RD
merlot
88

Colour: rose, purple rim. Nose: powerfull, ripe fruit, red berry notes, floral, expressive. Palate: powerful, fruity, fresh.

Clot dels Oms Vi Dolç de Fred Rosat 2012 RD
merlot
85

Gran Clot dels Oms 2011 BFB
chardonnay
89

Colour: bright yellow. Nose: powerfull, ripe fruit, sweet spices, creamy oak, fragrant herbs. Palate: rich, smoky aftertaste, flavourful, fresh, good acidity.

Gran Clot dels Oms Negre 2008 TGR
merlot, cabernet sauvignon
87

Colour: dark-red cherry, garnet rim. Nose: powerfull, fruit preserve, scrubland, spicy. Palate: flavourful, round tannins, balanced.

Gran Clot dels Oms Xarel.lo 2011 BFB
xarel.lo
90
Colour: bright yellow. Nose: citrus fruit, ripe fruit, wild herbs, dry stone, floral, toasty. Palate: flavourful, fruity, rich, spicy.

Petit Clot dels Oms 2012 T
merlot, cabernet sauvignon
86
Colour: dark-red cherry, garnet rim. Nose: grassy, ripe fruit, characterful, toasty. Palate: correct, flavourful.

Petit Clot dels Oms 2013 RD
cabernet sauvignon
85

Petit Clot dels Oms Blanc 2013 B
macabeo, xarel.lo, chardonnay
86
Colour: bright straw. Nose: fresh, fresh fruit, white flowers. Palate: flavourful, fruity, good acidity, balanced.

BODEGAS CAPITÀ VIDAL
Ctra. Villafranca-Igualada, Km. 21
08733 Pla del Penedès (Barcelona)
☎: +34 938 988 630
Fax: +34 938 988 625
www.capitavidal.com
helena@capitavidal.com

Clos Vidal Blanc de Blancs 2013 B
86
Colour: bright straw. Nose: ripe fruit, floral, dried herbs. Palate: correct, balanced, fine bitter notes.

Clos Vidal Cabernet Sauvignon 2009 T Roble
87
Colour: bright cherry. Nose: ripe fruit, sweet spices, creamy oak, balsamic herbs. Palate: flavourful, fruity, toasty, balanced.

Clos Vidal Merlot 2010 TC
87
Colour: cherry, garnet rim. Nose: ripe fruit, creamy oak, toasty. Palate: powerful, flavourful, toasty.

Clos Vidal Rosé Cuvée 2013 RD
88
Colour: brilliant rose. Nose: medium intensity, balanced, white flowers, fresh fruit. Palate: fruity, easy to drink, fine bitter notes.

BODEGAS TORRE DEL VEGUER
Urb. Torre de Veguer, s/n
08810 Sant Pere de Ribes (Barcelona)
☎: +34 938 963 190
Fax: +34 938 962 967
www.torredelveguer.com
torredelveguer@torredelveguer.com

Torre del Veguer Eclèctic 2010 T
90
Colour: ruby red. Nose: spicy, fine reductive notes, toasty, wild herbs, creamy oak. Palate: spicy, long, balsamic.

Torre del Veguer Gala 2013 B
86
Colour: bright straw. Nose: white flowers, fruit expression. Palate: fresh, fruity, flavourful, balanced.

Torre del Veguer Muscat 2013 B
100% moscatel de frontignan
88
Colour: bright straw. Nose: white flowers, fragrant herbs, fruit expression. Palate: fresh, fruity, flavourful, elegant.

Torre del Veguer Raïms de la Inmortalitat 2005 TR
87
Colour: dark-red cherry. Nose: ripe fruit, scrubland, spicy, balanced. Palate: good structure, flavourful, round tannins.

Torre del Veguer Raïms de la Inmortalitat 2013 BFB
xarel.lo
86
Colour: yellow, pale. Nose: smoky, roasted coffee. Palate: smoky aftertaste, correct, spicy.

Torre del Veguer Xarel.lo 2013 B
100% xarel.lo
87
Colour: yellow. Nose: fresh fruit, faded flowers, fragrant herbs. Palate: fruity.

BODEGAS TORRES
Miguel Torres i Carbó, 6
08720 Vilafranca del Penedès (Barcelona)
☎: +34 938 177 400
Fax: +34 938 177 444
www.torres.com
mailadmin@torres.es

Atrium Merlot 2012 T
merlot
88
Colour: black cherry, garnet rim. Nose: fruit preserve, sweet spices, characterful. Palate: good structure, fruity, flavourful.

Fransola 2012 B
sauvignon blanc, parellada

90

Colour: bright yellow. Nose: sweet spices, citrus fruit, ripe fruit, tropical fruit. Palate: flavourful, fruity, balanced.

Gran Coronas 2010 TR
cabernet sauvignon, tempranillo

90

Colour: cherry, garnet rim. Nose: ripe fruit, spicy, creamy oak, toasty, complex, earthy notes. Palate: powerful, flavourful, toasty, round tannins, balanced.

Mas La Plana Cabernet Sauvignon 2010 TGR
cabernet sauvignon

93

Colour: cherry, garnet rim. Nose: ripe fruit, wild herbs, earthy notes, spicy, creamy oak. Palate: balanced, flavourful, long, balsamic.

Reserva Real 2009 TGR
cabernet sauvignon, merlot, cabernet franc

94

Colour: very deep cherry, garnet rim. Nose: complex, expressive, elegant, balsamic herbs. Palate: good structure, full, spicy, balanced, round tannins.

Waltraud 2013 B
riesling

90

Colour: bright straw. Nose: white flowers, fragrant herbs, fruit expression. Palate: fresh, fruity, flavourful, balanced, elegant.

BODEGUES AMETLLER CIVILL
Caspe, 139 Entr 1ª
08013 (Barcelona)
☎: +34 933 208 439
Fax: +34 933 208 437
www.ametller.com
ametller@ametller.com

Ametller Blanc Floral 2013 B
xarel.lo, chardonnay, moscatel

90

Colour: bright straw. Nose: white flowers, fragrant herbs, fruit expression. Palate: fresh, fruity, flavourful, balanced, elegant.

BODEGUES SUMARROCA
El Rebato, s/n
08739 Subirats (Barcelona)
☎: +34 938 911 092
Fax: +34 938 911 778
www.sumarroca.es
s-berrocal@selfoods.es

Bòria 2011 T
syrah, merlot, cabernet sauvignon

91

Colour: cherry, garnet rim. Nose: red berry notes, ripe fruit, spicy, creamy oak, toasty, earthy notes. Palate: flavourful, toasty, round tannins, balanced.

Sumarroca Blanc de Blancs 2013 B
xarel.lo, macabeo, moscatel, parellada

88

Colour: bright straw. Nose: fresh, fresh fruit, white flowers, expressive. Palate: flavourful, fruity, good acidity, balanced.

Sumarroca Chardonnay 2013 B
100% chardonnay

91

Colour: bright yellow. Nose: white flowers, fragrant herbs, fruit expression. Palate: fresh, fruity, flavourful, balanced, elegant, rich.

Sumarroca Gewürztraminer 2013 B
100% gewürztraminer

87

Colour: bright straw. Nose: white flowers, fragrant herbs, fruit expression, tropical fruit. Palate: fresh, fruity, flavourful.

Sumarroca HUMM Dolc de Fred B
moscatel

88

Colour: golden. Nose: honeyed notes, candied fruit, fragrant herbs, slightly evolved. Palate: flavourful, sweet, fresh, fruity, good acidity, long.

Sumarroca Muscat 2013 B
100% moscatel

87

Colour: bright straw. Nose: white flowers, varietal, expressive. Palate: balanced, fruity, easy to drink.

Sumarroca Negre 2013 T
tempranillo, merlot, syrah

88

Colour: cherry, purple rim. Nose: fresh fruit, red berry notes, floral, balsamic herbs. Palate: flavourful, fruity, good acidity, balanced.

Sumarroca Pinot Noir 2013 RD
100% pinot noir

88

Colour: light cherry. Nose: elegant, candied fruit, fragrant herbs, red berry notes. Palate: light-bodied, flavourful, good acidity, long, spicy.

Sumarroca Rosat 2013 RD
merlot, tempranillo, cabernet sauvignon

87

Colour: onion pink. Nose: candied fruit, dried flowers, fragrant herbs, red berry notes. Palate: light-bodied, flavourful, good acidity, spicy.

Sumarroca Santa Creu de Creixà 2011 T
garnacha, syrah, cabernet franc, cabernet sauvignon

89

Colour: bright cherry. Nose: ripe fruit, sweet spices, creamy oak, medium intensity. Palate: fruity, flavourful, toasty.

Sumarroca Tempranillo 2012 T
tempranillo

87

Colour: bright cherry. Nose: ripe fruit, sweet spices, creamy oak, expressive. Palate: flavourful, fruity, toasty.

Sumarroca Temps de Flors 2013 B
xarel.lo, moscatel, gewürztraminer

88

Colour: bright straw. Nose: white flowers, fragrant herbs, fruit expression. Palate: fresh, fruity, flavourful, balanced.

Sumarroca Temps de Fruits 2013 T
pinot noir, carménère, malbec, pinot gris

87

Colour: cherry, purple rim. Nose: expressive, fresh fruit, red berry notes, balsamic herbs. Palate: flavourful, fruity, good acidity, round tannins.

Sumarroca Viognier 2013 B
100% viognier

87

Colour: bright straw. Nose: citrus fruit, fruit expression, fragrant herbs. Palate: flavourful, fresh, fruity.

Sumarroca Xarel.lo 2013 B
100% xarel.lo

89

Colour: bright straw. Nose: white flowers, fragrant herbs, fresh fruit. Palate: fresh, fruity, flavourful, elegant.

Terral 2011 T
cabernet franc, syrah, merlot, cabernet sauvignon

91

Colour: bright cherry. Nose: ripe fruit, sweet spices, creamy oak, expressive, balsamic herbs. Palate: flavourful, fruity, toasty, round tannins.

BOLET VINS I CAVAS ECOLÓGICOS
Finca Mas Lluet, s/n
08732 Castellvi de la Marca (Barcelona)
☎: +34 938 918 153
www.cavasbolet.com
cavasbolet@cavasbolet.com

Bolet 2013 B

87

Colour: bright straw. Nose: white flowers, fragrant herbs, fruit expression. Palate: fresh, fruity, flavourful.

Bolet 2013 RD
100% pinot noir

80

Bolet 2013 T

86

Colour: cherry, garnet rim. Nose: ripe fruit, grassy. Palate: balsamic, fine bitter notes, flavourful.

Bolet Cabernet Sauvignon 2006 T
cabernet sauvignon

84

Bolet Sàpiens Merlot 2007 TC
100% merlot

86

Colour: deep cherry, orangey edge. Nose: old leather, tobacco, ripe fruit. Palate: flavourful, correct, balanced.

Bolet Xarel.lo 2013 B
100% xarel.lo

83

CAN RÀFOLS DELS CAUS
Finca Can Rafols del Caus s/n
08792 Avinyonet del Penedès (Barcelona)
☎: +34 938 970 013
Fax: +34 938 970 370
www.canrafolsdelscaus.com
info@causgrup.com

Ad Fines 2008 T
100% pinot noir

91

Colour: pale ruby, brick rim edge. Nose: wet leather, fruit liqueur notes, earthy notes. Palate: good acidity, fine bitter notes, long.

Can Rafols Sumoll 2010 T
100% sumoll

90

Colour: bright cherry, orangey edge. Nose: ripe fruit, wild herbs, earthy notes, spicy. Palate: flavourful, long, balsamic, slightly acidic.

Caus Lubis 2001 T
100% merlot
92
Colour: pale ruby, brick rim edge. Nose: elegant, spicy, fine reductive notes, wet leather, aged wood nuances, fruit liqueur notes. Palate: spicy, fine tannins, elegant, long.

El Rocallís 2010 BFB
100% incrocio manzoni
93
Colour: bright golden. Nose: ripe fruit, dry nuts, powerfull, toasty, aged wood nuances. Palate: flavourful, fruity, spicy, toasty, long.

Gran Caus 2005 TR
cabernet franc, merlot, cabernet sauvignon
93
Colour: deep cherry, garnet rim. Nose: elegant, complex, scrubland, spicy, balsamic herbs. Palate: good structure, long, round tannins.

Gran Caus 2012 B
xarel.lo, chenin blanc, chardonnay
89
Colour: bright straw. Nose: dried flowers, dried herbs, balanced, spicy. Palate: balanced, fine bitter notes, long, good acidity.

Gran Caus 2013 RD
100% merlot
89
Colour: rose, purple rim. Nose: powerfull, ripe fruit, red berry notes, floral, expressive. Palate: powerful, fruity, fresh.

Pedradura 2006 TR
garnacha, cabernet sauvignon, petit verdot
89
Colour: cherry, garnet rim. Nose: spicy, toasty, overripe fruit, mineral, old leather. Palate: powerful, flavourful, toasty, round tannins.

Petit Caus 2013 B
xarel.lo, macabeo, chardonnay, chenin blanc
87
Colour: bright straw. Nose: white flowers, fresh fruit, dried herbs, expressive. Palate: flavourful, fruity, good acidity, balanced.

Petit Caus 2013 RD
merlot, tempranillo, syrah, cabernet sauvignon
89
Colour: light cherry. Nose: ripe fruit, red berry notes, floral, expressive, balanced. Palate: fruity, fresh, flavourful, fine bitter notes.

Petit Caus 2013 T
merlot, syrah, cabernet franc
86
Colour: dark-red cherry, purple rim. Nose: balanced, red berry notes, ripe fruit, dried herbs. Palate: fruity, easy to drink.

Terraprima 2011 T
cabernet franc, garnacha, syrah
89
Colour: cherry, garnet rim. Nose: ripe fruit, spicy, creamy oak, toasty, scrubland. Palate: powerful, flavourful, toasty, balsamic.

Terraprima 2013 B
xarel.lo, riesling
91
Colour: bright straw. Nose: white flowers, fragrant herbs, fruit expression, dry stone. Palate: fresh, fruity, flavourful, balanced, elegant.

Vinya La Calma 2011 BFB
100% chenin blanc
92
Colour: bright straw. Nose: white flowers, fresh fruit, expressive, fine lees, dried herbs. Palate: flavourful, fruity, good acidity, fine bitter notes.

CANALS & MUNNÉ
Plaza Pau Casals, 6
08770 Sant Sadurní D'Anoia (Barcelona)
☎: +34 938 910 318
Fax: +34 938 911 945
www.canalsimunne.com
info@canalsimunne.com

Blanc Prínceps Ecologic 2013 B
86
Colour: bright straw. Nose: fresh, fresh fruit, white flowers, expressive. Palate: flavourful, fruity, good acidity, fine bitter notes.

Blanc Prínceps Muscat 2013 B
moscatel
88
Colour: bright straw. Nose: fresh, fresh fruit, white flowers, expressive, varietal. Palate: flavourful, fruity, good acidity, balanced.

Gran Blanc Prínceps 2013 BFB
xarel.lo
89
Colour: bright straw. Nose: white flowers, fragrant herbs, spicy. Palate: fresh, fruity, flavourful, balanced, elegant.

Gran Prínceps 2008 TR
84

Noir Prínceps 2008 TC
tempranillo, cabernet sauvignon, merlot
85

Rose Prínceps Merlot 2013 RD
merlot
86
Colour: rose. Nose: red berry notes, ripe fruit, floral, medium intensity. Palate: correct, fine bitter notes, easy to drink.

CASA RAVELLA
Casa Ravella, 1
08739 Ordal - Subirats (Barcelona)
☎: +34 938 179 173
Fax: +34 938 179 245
www.casaravella.com
bodega@casaravella.com

Casa Ravella 2011 BFB
100% xarel.lo
88
Colour: bright yellow. Nose: ripe fruit, sweet spices, creamy oak, fragrant herbs. Palate: rich, flavourful, fresh.

Casa Ravella 2013 B
100% xarel.lo
87
Colour: bright straw. Nose: fresh, fresh fruit, white flowers. Palate: flavourful, fruity, good acidity, balanced.

Casa Ravella 2013 RD
100% merlot
85

Casa Ravella 2013 T Roble
100% merlot
84

CASTELL D'AGE
Ctra.de Martorell a Capellades, 6-8
08782 La Beguda Baixa (Barcelona)
☎: +34 937 725 181
Fax: +34 937 727 061
www.castelldage.com
info@castelldage.com

Castell D'Age Blanc de Blancs 2013 B
100% macabeo
86
Colour: bright straw. Nose: fresh, fresh fruit, white flowers. Palate: fruity, good acidity, balanced, easy to drink.

Castell D'Age Cabernet Sauvignon 2010 T
100% cabernet sauvignon
88 🍸
Colour: cherry, garnet rim. Nose: ripe fruit, wild herbs, earthy notes, spicy. Palate: flavourful, long, balsamic.

Castell D'Age Merlot 2010 T
100% merlot
84

Castell D'Age Rosat Merlot 2013 RD
100% merlot
87
Colour: light cherry, bright. Nose: medium intensity, fresh fruit, floral, rose petals. Palate: balanced, fresh, good acidity.

Castell D'Age Tempranillo 2011 T
100% tempranillo
86 🍸
Colour: dark-red cherry, garnet rim. Nose: powerfull, ripe fruit, fruit preserve, creamy oak. Palate: powerful, toasty.

L'Essència del Xarel·lo 2013 B
100% xarel.lo
88
Colour: bright straw. Nose: fresh, balanced, white flowers, dried flowers. Palate: flavourful, good acidity, correct.

CASTELL D'OR
Mare Rafols, 3- 1°D
08720 Vilafranca del Penedès
(Barcelona)
☎: +34 938 905 385
Fax: +34 938 905 455
www.castelldor.com
castelldor@castelldor.com

Cossetània 2009 TR
cabernet sauvignon
89
Colour: deep cherry. Nose: ripe fruit, wild herbs, earthy notes, spicy, creamy oak. Palate: balanced, flavourful, long, balsamic.

Cossetània 2010 TC
merlot, cabernet sauvignon
87
Colour: bright cherry. Nose: ripe fruit, sweet spices, creamy oak, scrubland. Palate: fruity, flavourful, toasty.

Cossetània 2012 T
cabernet sauvignon, merlot
87
Colour: cherry, garnet rim. Nose: ripe fruit, wild herbs, earthy notes, spicy. Palate: balanced, flavourful, long, balsamic.

Cossetània 2013 RD
merlot
85

Cossetània Chardonnay 2013 B
chardonnay
88
Colour: bright straw. Nose: fresh, fresh fruit, white flowers. Palate: flavourful, fruity, good acidity.

Cossetània Vi Blanc 2013 B
xarel.lo, macabeo, parellada
85

CASTELLROIG - FINCA SABATÉ I COCA

Ctra. De Sant Sadurní a Vilafranca (c-243a), km. 1
08739 Subirats (Barcelona)
☎: +34 938 911 927
Fax: +34 938 914 055
www.castellroig.com
info@castellroig.com

Castellroig Negre Ull de Llebre 2011 T
ull de llebre
88
Colour: cherry, garnet rim. Nose: ripe fruit, spicy, creamy oak, toasty, balsamic herbs, mineral. Palate: powerful, flavourful, toasty.

Castellroig Xarel.lo 2013 B
xarel.lo
87
Colour: bright straw. Nose: white flowers, fragrant herbs, fruit expression. Palate: fresh, fruity, flavourful.

Terroja de Sabaté i Coca 2012 B
xarel.lo
92
Colour: bright yellow. Nose: expressive, varietal, faded flowers, balanced, spicy, dry nuts. Palate: flavourful, complex, balanced.

Terroja de Sabaté i Coca Magnum 2010 B
93
Colour: bright golden. Nose: ripe fruit, dry nuts, powerfull, toasty, aged wood nuances, mineral. Palate: flavourful, fruity, spicy, toasty, long, balanced.

CAVA MASTINELL

Ctra. de Vilafranca a St. Martí Sarroca, Km. 0,5
08720 Vilafranca del Penedès
(Barcelona)
☎: +34 938 170 586
Fax: +34 938 170 500
www.mastinell.com
info@mastinell.com

Mas Tinell Arte 2007 TR
cabernet sauvignon, merlot, cabernet franc
88
Colour: deep cherry. Nose: ripe fruit, wild herbs, spicy, creamy oak. Palate: balanced, flavourful, long, balsamic.

Mas Tinell Chardonnay 2013 B
chardonnay
88
Colour: bright yellow. Nose: powerfull, ripe fruit, sweet spices, fragrant herbs. Palate: rich, flavourful, fresh, good acidity.

Mas Tinell Clos Sant Pau 2012 B
moscatel
87
Colour: bright straw. Nose: fresh, white flowers, varietal. Palate: fruity, easy to drink.

Mas Tinell L' Alba Blanc de Lluna 2013 B
87
Colour: bright straw. Nose: fresh, fresh fruit, grassy. Palate: flavourful, fruity, good acidity, balanced.

CAVAS FERRET

Avda. de Catalunya, 36
08736 Guardiola de Font-Rubí
(Barcelona)
☎: +34 938 979 148
Fax: +34 938 979 285
www.cavasferret.com
comercial@cavasferret.com

Abac 2012 B
xarel.lo
88
Colour: bright straw. Nose: medium intensity, balanced, faded flowers, varietal. Palate: correct, fine bitter notes, flavourful.

Ferret Selecció de Barriques 2010 TGR
tempranillo, cabernet sauvignon, merlot
86
Colour: dark-red cherry. Nose: old leather, spicy, characterful, animal reductive notes. Palate: correct, flavourful.

Ferret Selecció de Barriques 2011 BFB
xarel.lo, chardonnay
89
Colour: bright yellow. Nose: powerfull, ripe fruit, sweet spices, creamy oak, fragrant herbs. Palate: rich, smoky aftertaste, flavourful, fresh, good acidity.

Marmediterraneo 2012 T
merlot, cabernet sauvignon, tempranillo
84

Marmediterraneo 2013 B
parellada, xarel.lo, moscatel
84

Marmediterraneo 2013 RD
merlot, tempranillo
85

CAVAS HILL
Bonavista, 2
08734 Moja-Olérdola (Barcelona)
☎: +34 938 900 588
Fax: +34 938 170 246
www.cavashill.com
cavashill@cavashill.com

Blanc Bruc 2013 BFB
88
Colour: bright straw. Nose: white flowers, fragrant herbs, mineral, spicy. Palate: fresh, fruity, flavourful, balanced.

Gran Civet 2011 TC
86
Colour: cherry, garnet rim. Nose: ripe fruit, wild herbs, toasty, herbaceous. Palate: flavourful, balsamic.

Gran Toc 2010 TR
90
Colour: cherry, garnet rim. Nose: balanced, complex, ripe fruit, spicy, mineral. Palate: good structure, flavourful, correct.

Oro Penedès 2013 B
moscatel, xarel.lo
87
Colour: bright straw. Nose: white flowers, fragrant herbs, fruit expression. Palate: fresh, fruity, flavourful, balanced, elegant.

Reserva Hill 2008 TR
89
Colour: cherry, garnet rim. Nose: balanced, complex, ripe fruit, spicy. Palate: good structure, flavourful, round tannins, correct.

CAVAS LAVERNOYA
Masia La Porxada
08729 Sant Marçal (Barcelona)
☎: +34 938 912 202
www.lavernoya.com
lavernoya@lavernoya.com

Lácrima Baccus 2013 B
86
Colour: bright straw. Nose: white flowers, fragrant herbs, fruit expression. Palate: fresh, fruity, flavourful.

Lácrima Baccus 2013 RD
84

Lácrima Baccus 2013 T
89
Colour: dark-red cherry, purple rim. Nose: scrubland, ripe fruit, balanced, expressive. Palate: fruity, good acidity.

Lácrima Baccus Blanc de Blancs 2013 B
87
Colour: bright straw. Nose: fresh fruit, white flowers, wild herbs. Palate: flavourful, fruity.

CAVES NAVERÁN
Can Parellada
08775 Torrelavit (Barcelona)
☎: +34 938 988 274
Fax: +34 938 989 027
www.naveran.com
naveran@naveran.com

Manuela de Naverán 2013 B
chardonnay
86
Colour: bright straw. Nose: faded flowers, medium intensity. Palate: correct, easy to drink.

Naverán Clos dels Angels 2013 T
75% syrah, 15% merlot, 10% cabernet sauvignon
93
Colour: cherry, purple rim. Nose: red berry notes, raspberry, floral, fragrant herbs, balanced. Palate: fresh, fruity, flavourful, easy to drink, elegant.

CELLER CREDO
Tamarit, 10
08770 Sant Sadurní D'Anoia (Barcelona)
☎: +34 938 910 214
Fax: +34 938 911 697
www.cellercredo.cat
vins@cellercredo.cat

Aloers 2012 B
xarel.lo
91
Colour: bright yellow. Nose: balanced, expressive, wild herbs, dried flowers. Palate: balanced, fine bitter notes, elegant, long.

Aloers 2013 B
100% xarel.lo
90
Colour: bright straw. Nose: white flowers, fresh fruit, fine lees, dried herbs. Palate: flavourful, fruity, good acidity, balanced.

Can Credo 2010 B
xarel.lo
93
Colour: bright golden. Nose: expressive, complex, ripe fruit, spicy, fine lees, faded flowers. Palate: rich, full, balanced, elegant. Personality.

Can Credo 2011 B
100% xarel.lo
93
Colour: bright yellow. Nose: faded flowers, spicy, dry nuts, complex. Palate: rich, flavourful, long, balanced, good acidity, complex.

Cap ficat 2013 B
90
Colour: bright straw. Nose: white flowers, fragrant herbs, fruit expression, mineral. Palate: fresh, fruity, flavourful, balanced, elegant.

Estrany 2012 B

90

Colour: bright yellow. Nose: ripe fruit, faded flowers, dried herbs, dry stone. Palate: fine bitter notes, powerful, flavourful, long.

Miranius 2013 B

89

Colour: yellow, pale. Nose: faded flowers, medium intensity, fresh fruit, fragrant herbs. Palate: fresh, good acidity.

Ratpenat 2013 B

90

Colour: bright straw. Nose: white flowers, fine lees, dried herbs. Palate: flavourful, fruity, good acidity, balanced.

CELLERS AVGVSTVS FORVM

Ctra. Sant Vicenç, s/n Apartado Correos 289
43700 El Vendrell (Tarragona)
☎ : +34 977 666 910
Fax: +34 977 666 590
www.avgvstvs.es
avgvstvs@avgvstvsforvm.com

Avgvstvs Cabernet Franc 2011 T Roble

cabernet franc

89

Colour: dark-red cherry, garnet rim. Nose: wild herbs, ripe fruit. Palate: flavourful, balsamic, spicy, good finish.

Avgvstvs Cabernet Sauvignon-Merlot 2011 T Roble

cabernet sauvignon, merlot

89

Colour: black cherry, garnet rim. Nose: balsamic herbs, wild herbs, ripe fruit, powerfull. Palate: elegant, balanced, varietal.

Avgvstvs Chardonnay 2013 BFB

chardonnay

92

Colour: bright yellow. Nose: powerfull, ripe fruit, sweet spices, creamy oak, fragrant herbs. Palate: rich, flavourful, good acidity, balanced, elegant.

Avgvstvs Chardonnay Magnum 2012 B

chardonnay

93

Colour: bright yellow. Nose: powerfull, ripe fruit, sweet spices, creamy oak, fragrant herbs, faded flowers. Palate: rich, smoky aftertaste, flavourful, fresh, good acidity.

Avgvstvs Merlot Syrah 2012 T

merlot, syrah

87

Colour: cherry, garnet rim. Nose: ripe fruit, sweet spices, creamy oak. Palate: flavourful, fruity, toasty.

Avgvstvs Trajanvs 2009 TR

cabernet sauvignon, merlot, cabernet franc, garnacha

90

Colour: cherry, garnet rim. Nose: ripe fruit, spicy, creamy oak, toasty, complex, earthy notes, balsamic herbs. Palate: powerful, flavourful, toasty, balanced.

Avgvstvs Trajanvs 2010 T

cabernet sauvignon, merlot, cabernet franc, garnacha

91

Colour: deep cherry, garnet rim. Nose: spicy, ripe fruit, fine reductive notes, complex, dried herbs. Palate: good structure, full, flavourful.

Avgvstvs VI Varietales Magnum 2011 TC

cabernet sauvignon, cabernet franc, tempranillo, garnacha

90

Colour: deep cherry, garnet rim. Nose: balanced, complex, balsamic herbs, spicy. Palate: good structure, flavourful, round tannins.

Avgvstvs Xarel.lo 2011 BFB

xarel.lo

89

Colour: bright yellow. Nose: ripe fruit, creamy oak, fragrant herbs. Palate: rich, flavourful, fresh, good acidity, round.

Avgvstvs Xarel.lo 2013 BFB

xarel.lo

91

Colour: bright yellow. Nose: dried herbs, floral, mineral, spicy, citrus fruit, fruit expression, expressive. Palate: flavourful, fruity, spicy, balsamic.

Avgvstvs Xarel.lo Vermell 2013 B

xarel.lo, vermell

89

Colour: yellow, pale. Nose: scrubland, grassy, dried flowers, characterful. Palate: flavourful, complex, good acidity.

Look 2013 B

xarel.lo, moscatel de alejandría, sauvignon blanc, subirat parent

87

Colour: bright straw. Nose: fresh, fresh fruit, white flowers, expressive. Palate: flavourful, fruity, good acidity, balanced.

CLOS LENTISCUS

Masía Can Ramón del Montgros, s/n
08810 Sant Pere de Ribes (Barcelona)
☎ : +34 667 517 659
www.closlentiscus.com
manel@closlentiscus.com

Clos Lentiscus 41ºN Rosé 2009 BN Gran Reserva

samsó

89

Colour: coppery red. Nose: floral, jasmine, fragrant herbs, candied fruit. Palate: fresh, fruity, flavourful, correct, balanced.

Clos Lentiscus Blanc 2011 BN
xarel.lo, malvasía

87

Colour: bright yellow. Nose: ripe fruit, fine lees, balanced, dried herbs. Palate: good acidity, flavourful, ripe fruit, long.

Clos Lentiscus Malvasia de Sitges 2009 BN
malvasía

85

Clos Lentiscus Syrah Colection Rosé 2009 BN
syrah

84

Sumoll Reserva Familia de Clos Lentiscus Blanc de Noir 2009 BN
sumoll

87

Colour: coppery red. Nose: candied fruit, faded flowers. Palate: fruity, good acidity, fine bitter notes, long.

X-Pressio de Clos Lentiscus 2008 BN
xarel.lo, vermell

93

Colour: bright golden. Nose: dry nuts, fragrant herbs, complex, fine lees, macerated fruit, sweet spices, expressive. Palate: powerful, flavourful, good acidity, fine bead, fine bitter notes, elegant.

COLET
Salinar, s/n
08796 Pacs del Penedès (Barcelona)
☎: +34 938 170 809
Fax: +34 938 170 809
www.colet.cat
info@colet.cat

A Posteriori Rosat ESP

87

Colour: coppery red, bright. Nose: faded flowers, medium intensity, wild herbs. Palate: flavourful, correct, fine bitter notes.

A Priori ESP
macabeo, chardonnay, riesling, gewürztraminer

90

Colour: bright straw. Nose: fresh fruit, dried herbs, fine lees, floral. Palate: fresh, fruity, flavourful, good acidity.

Colet Assemblage Blanc de Noir ESP
pinot noir, chardonnay

90

Colour: coppery red. Nose: dry nuts, ripe fruit, faded flowers, toasty, pattiserie, fine lees. Palate: fine bitter notes, rich, flavourful.

Colet Grand Cuveé ESP
chardonnay, macabeo, xarel.lo

90

Colour: bright golden. Nose: fine lees, dry nuts, fragrant herbs, complex. Palate: powerful, flavourful, good acidity, fine bead, fine bitter notes.

Colet Navazos 2010 Extra Brut
xarel.lo

93

Colour: bright golden. Nose: fine lees, fragrant herbs. Palate: powerful, flavourful, good acidity, fine bead, fine bitter notes.

Colet Navazos 2011 ESP
xarel.lo

91

Colour: bright golden. Nose: fine lees, dry nuts, fragrant herbs, complex, toasty. Palate: powerful, flavourful, good acidity, fine bead, fine bitter notes.

Colet Tradicional ESP
xarel.lo, macabeo, parellada

92

Colour: bright yellow. Nose: toasty, dry nuts, fine lees, pungent, saline, expressive. Palate: flavourful, fine bitter notes, good acidity.

Vatua ! ESP
moscatel, parellada, gewürztraminer

90

Colour: bright straw. Nose: fruit expression, citrus fruit, wild herbs, spicy, pattiserie. Palate: fine bitter notes, balsamic, balanced, elegant.

COMA ROMÀ
Can Guilera, s/n
08739 Sant Pau D'Ordal (Barcelona)
☎: +34 938 993 094
Fax: +34 938 993 094
www.comaroma.net
canguilera@comaroma.net

Coma Romà Merlot 2011 T
merlot

83

Coma Romà Ull Llebre 2013 RD
ull de llebre

87

Colour: onion pink. Nose: dried flowers, fragrant herbs, red berry notes, elegant. Palate: light-bodied, flavourful, good acidity, long, spicy.

Coma Romà Xarel.lo 2013 B
xarel.lo

86

Colour: bright straw. Nose: fresh, fresh fruit, white flowers, medium intensity. Palate: flavourful, fruity, good acidity, balanced.

Coma Romà Xarel.lo macerat 2012 B
xarel.lo

87

Colour: bright straw. Nose: fresh, fresh fruit, white flowers. Palate: flavourful, fruity, good acidity.

EMENDIS
Barrio de Sant Marçal, 67
08732 Castellet i La Gornal (Barcelona)
☎: +34 938 919 790
Fax: +34 938 918 169
www.emendis.es
avalles@emendis.es

Emendis Duet Varietal 2012 T
syrah, ull de llebre

88

Colour: bright cherry. Nose: ripe fruit, sweet spices, creamy oak, medium intensity, scrubland. Palate: fruity, flavourful, spicy.

Emendis Mater 2006 TR
100% merlot

89

Colour: cherry, garnet rim. Nose: ripe fruit, wild herbs, earthy notes, spicy. Palate: balanced, flavourful, long, balsamic.

Emendis Nox 2013 RD
pinot noir, syrah

85

Emendis Trío Varietal 2013 B
macabeo, chardonnay, moscatel

87

Colour: bright straw. Nose: white flowers, fragrant herbs, fruit expression. Palate: fresh, fruity, flavourful, balanced, elegant.

ENRIC SOLER
Barri Sabanell, 11
08736 Font Rubí (Barcelona)
☎: +34 607 262 779
info@calraspallet.cat

Improvisació 2012 B
xarel.lo

91

Colour: bright straw. Nose: fresh, fresh fruit, white flowers, spicy, expressive. Palate: flavourful, fruity, good acidity, balanced.

Nun Vinya dels Taus 2012 B
xarel.lo

94

Colour: bright straw. Nose: white flowers, fresh fruit, expressive, fine lees, dried herbs. Palate: flavourful, fruity, good acidity, balanced.

ESTEVE I GIBERT VITICULTORS
Masia Cal Panxa s/n – Els Casots
08739 Subirats (Barcelona)
☎: +34 650 665 953
www.esteveigibert.com
info@esteveigibert.com

L'Antana 2009 T
merlot

85

Origen 2012 B
xarel.lo

86

Colour: yellow. Nose: wild herbs, faded flowers. Palate: flavourful, fine bitter notes, correct.

FERRE I CATASUS
Masía Gustems s/n Ctra. Sant Sadurní, Km. 8
08792 La Granada (Barcelona)
☎: +34 647 806 896
Fax: +34 938 974 708
www.ferreicatasus.com
info@ferreicatasus.com

Cap de Trons 2013 T
cabernet sauvignon, merlot, syrah

88

Colour: black cherry, purple rim. Nose: balsamic herbs, ripe fruit, balanced. Palate: flavourful, fruity, easy to drink.

Ferré i Catasús Gall Negre 2009 T
merlot

89

Colour: ruby red. Nose: spicy, fine reductive notes, wet leather, aged wood nuances, toasty, wild herbs. Palate: spicy, long, toasty.

Ferré i Catasús Xarel.lo 2012 B
xarel.lo

89

Colour: bright yellow. Nose: faded flowers, spicy, characterful. Palate: flavourful, long, balanced, fine bitter notes, rich.

Somiatruites 2013 B
chenin blanc, xarel.lo, sauvignon blanc, chardonnay

88

Colour: bright yellow. Nose: expressive, balanced, sweet spices, white flowers. Palate: flavourful, balanced, fine bitter notes.

Sonat de l'ala 2012 T
merlot, syrah, garnacha

85

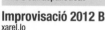

FINCA VILADELLOPS

Celler Gran Viladellops
08734 Olérdola (Barcelona)
☎: +34 938 188 371
Fax: +34 938 188 371
www.viladellops.com
info@viladellops.com

Finca Viladellops Xarel.lo 2012 BFB
100% xarel.lo

90

Colour: bright yellow. Nose: floral, fragrant herbs, fruit expression, mineral, expressive. Palate: powerful, flavourful, long, balanced.

Finca Viladellops Xarel.lo 2013 B
100% xarel.lo

87

Colour: bright straw. Nose: floral, fragrant herbs, mineral, fruit expression. Palate: flavourful, fresh, fruity.

Finca Viladellops 2011 TC

87

Colour: dark-red cherry, garnet rim. Nose: wild herbs, ripe fruit, dried herbs. Palate: spicy, good finish, round tannins.

Turó de les Abelles 2010 T

92

Colour: cherry, garnet rim. Nose: ripe fruit, wild herbs, earthy notes, spicy, creamy oak. Palate: balanced, flavourful, long, balsamic.

Viladellops Garnatxa 2013 T
100% garnacha

88

Colour: dark-red cherry, purple rim. Nose: ripe fruit, dried herbs, medium intensity. Palate: correct, easy to drink.

GIRÓ RIBOT, S.L.

Finca El Pont, s/n
08792 Santa Fe del Penedès (Barcelona)
☎: +34 938 974 050
Fax: +34 938 974 311
www.giroribot.es
giroribot@giroribot.es

AIKARAI Muscat de Frontignac 2013 B
100% moscatel de frontignan

89

Colour: bright straw. Nose: white flowers, fragrant herbs, tropical fruit. Palate: fresh, fruity, flavourful, balanced.

Giró Ribot Blanc de Blancs 2013 B

85

Giró Ribot Giro 2 s/c B
giró

90

Colour: bright straw. Nose: medium intensity, fresh, wild herbs. Palate: fresh, easy to drink, good acidity, fruity.

GRAMONA

Industria, 36
08770 Sant Sadurní D'Anoia (Barcelona)
☎: +34 938 910 113
Fax: +34 938 183 284
www.gramona.com
comunicacion@gramona.com

Gramona Sauvignon Blanc 2012 BFB
100% sauvignon blanc

90

Colour: bright yellow. Nose: ripe fruit, dried flowers, wild herbs, mineral. Palate: powerful, flavourful, balsamic, correct, ripe fruit.

Gramona Xarel.lo Font Jui 2013 B
100% xarel.lo

93

Colour: bright straw. Nose: white flowers, fresh fruit, spicy, fragrant herbs. Palate: flavourful, fruity, good acidity, balanced.

Gramona Xarel.lo Ovum 2013 B
100% xarel.lo

92

Colour: bright yellow. Nose: wild herbs, citrus fruit, fruit expression, dry stone, white flowers. Palate: round, flavourful, spicy, long, balanced, elegant.

Gramona Xarel.lo Roent 2013 RD
100% xarel.lo

91

Colour: bright straw. Nose: floral, wild herbs, fruit expression, dry stone, expressive. Palate: powerful, flavourful, complex, balanced, elegant.

Vi de Glass Gewürztraminer 0,375 2010 B
100% gewürztraminer

93

Colour: iodine, amber rim. Nose: powerfull, floral, honeyed notes, candied fruit, fragrant herbs. Palate: flavourful, sweet, fresh, fruity, good acidity, long, elegant.

Vi de Glass Gewürztraminer 0,75 2007 BC
100% gewürztraminer

94

Colour: bright golden. Nose: candied fruit, honeyed notes, faded flowers, expressive, complex, spicy. Palate: balanced, complex, long.

GRIMAU DE PUJADES

Barri Sant Sepulcre s/n
08734 Olerdola (Barcelona)
☎: +34 938 918 031
www.grimau.com
grimau@grimau.com

Grimau Blanc de Blancs 2013 B
xarel.lo, parellada, chardonnay

84

Grimau Cabernet Sauvignon 2007 TR
cabernet sauvignon

89

Colour: cherry, garnet rim. Nose: ripe fruit, spicy, creamy oak, toasty, complex, wild herbs. Palate: flavourful, toasty, round tannins.

Grimau Chardonnay 2013 B
chardonnay

88

Colour: bright straw. Nose: white flowers, fragrant herbs, fruit expression. Palate: fresh, fruity, flavourful.

Grimau Merlot 2013 RD
merlot

86

Colour: onion pink. Nose: candied fruit, dried flowers, fragrant herbs, red berry notes. Palate: light-bodied, flavourful, good acidity, spicy.

Rubicundus 2010 T

89

Colour: cherry, garnet rim. Nose: ripe fruit, spicy, creamy oak, toasty, complex. Palate: powerful, flavourful, toasty, round tannins.

HEREDAD SEGURA VIUDAS
Ctra. Sant Sadurní a St. Pere de Riudebitlles, Km. 5
08775 Torrelavit (Barcelona)
☎: +34 938 917 070
Fax: +34 938 996 006
www.seguraviudas.com
seguraviudas@seguraviudas.es

Creu de Lavit 2012 BFB
xarel.lo

87

Colour: yellow, greenish rim. Nose: toasty, dried flowers, ripe fruit, dried herbs. Palate: spicy, rich, smoky aftertaste.

Viña Heredad 2013 B
macabeo, xarel.lo, parellada

84

Viña Heredad Cabernet Sauvignon 2012 T
cabernet sauvignon

85

HERETAT MONT-RUBÍ
L'Avellà, 1
08736 Font- Rubí (Barcelona)
☎: +34 938 979 066
Fax: +34 938 979 066
www.montrubi.com
hmr@montrubi.com

Advent Samso Dulce Natural 2010 RD
samsó

95

Colour: light mahogany. Nose: acetaldehyde, varnish, candied fruit, complex, expressive, balanced. Palate: full, flavourful.

Advent Sumoll Dulce 2010 RD
100% sumoll

94

Colour: coppery red. Nose: ripe fruit, dried herbs, acetaldehyde, varnish, dry nuts, dark chocolate, creamy oak, toasty. Palate: long, creamy, powerful, flavourful, complex, balanced, elegant.

Advent Xarel.lo 2010 B
xarel.lo

93

Colour: old gold, amber rim. Nose: acetaldehyde, ripe fruit, balsamic herbs, spicy, aged wood nuances, toasty. Palate: powerful, flavourful, spicy, long, balanced, elegant.

Black Hmr 2013 T
garnacha

89

Colour: cherry, purple rim. Nose: red berry notes, raspberry, floral, expressive, wild herbs. Palate: fresh, fruity, flavourful, easy to drink.

Durona 2006 T
sumoll, garnacha, samsó

90

Colour: very deep cherry. Nose: ripe fruit, spicy, creamy oak, toasty, characterful, scrubland. Palate: powerful, flavourful, toasty, round tannins.

Finca Durona 2013 B
100% parellada

87

Colour: bright straw. Nose: medium intensity, fresh fruit, citrus fruit. Palate: fresh, fruity, easy to drink.

Gaintus 2010 T
100% sumoll

91

Colour: ruby red. Nose: ripe fruit, wild herbs, earthy notes, spicy, creamy oak. Palate: balanced, flavourful, long, balsamic.

Vinodelaluna Magnum 2010 T
garnacha

91

Colour: cherry, garnet rim. Nose: red berry notes, ripe fruit, balsamic herbs, damp earth, mineral, spicy. Palate: powerful, flavourful, balsamic, balanced.

White Hmr 2013 B
100% xarel.lo

89

Colour: bright straw. Nose: white flowers, fragrant herbs, fruit expression. Palate: fresh, fruity, flavourful, elegant.

HERETAT SABARTÉS

Ctra. TP-2125
43711 Banyeres del Penedès
☎: +34 934 750 125
www.heretatsabartes.com
sabartes@sumarroca.com

Heretat Sabartés 2013 B
gewürztraminer, sauvignon blanc, macabeo

87

Colour: bright straw. Nose: fresh, fresh fruit, white flowers, expressive. Palate: flavourful, fruity, good acidity, easy to drink.

Heretat Sabartés 2013 RD
tempranillo, merlot

87

Colour: raspberry rose. Nose: medium intensity, floral, balanced, dried flowers. Palate: correct, fine bitter notes, easy to drink.

Heretat Sabartés Negre 2012 T
pinot noir, syrah

92

Colour: ruby red. Nose: ripe fruit, wild herbs, earthy notes, spicy, creamy oak. Palate: balanced, flavourful, long, balsamic, elegant.

JANÉ VENTURA

Ctra. Calafell, 2
43700 El Vendrell (Tarragona)
☎: +34 977 660 118
Fax: +34 977 661 239
www.janeventura.com
janeventura@janeventura.com

Jané Ventura "Finca Els Camps" Macabeu 2012 BFB
100% macabeo

92

Colour: bright yellow. Nose: toasty, smoky, ripe fruit. Palate: flavourful, rich, spicy, ripe fruit, balanced.

Jané Ventura "Mas Vilella" Costers del Rotllan 2011 T

90

Colour: very deep cherry, purple rim. Nose: powerfull, ripe fruit, spicy, dried herbs. Palate: balanced, ripe fruit, long, balsamic.

Jané Ventura Blanc Selecció 2013 B

90

Colour: bright straw. Nose: fresh, fresh fruit, white flowers. Palate: flavourful, fruity, good acidity.

Jané Ventura Malvasía de Sitges 2013 B Barrica
100% malvasía

93

Colour: bright straw. Nose: white flowers, fragrant herbs, fruit expression, spicy. Palate: fresh, fruity, flavourful, balanced, elegant. Personality.

Jané Ventura Negre Selecció 2012 T

90

Colour: bright cherry. Nose: ripe fruit, sweet spices, creamy oak, expressive. Palate: flavourful, fruity, toasty, round tannins, balanced.

Jané Ventura Rosat Selecció 2013 RD

89

Colour: light cherry, bright. Nose: red berry notes, floral, expressive, fresh. Palate: powerful, fruity, fresh, flavourful, long.

Jané Ventura Sumoll 2012 T
100% sumoll

93

Colour: deep cherry, garnet rim. Nose: ripe fruit, wild herbs, earthy notes, spicy, creamy oak. Palate: balanced, flavourful, long, balsamic.

JAUME SERRA

Ctra. de Vilanova a Vilafranca, Km. 2,5
08800 Vilanova i la Geltru (Barcelona)
☎: +34 938 936 404
Fax: +34 938 147 482
www.garciacarrion.es
jaumeserra@jgc.es

Jaume Serra 2011 TC
80

Jaume Serra 2013 B
84

Jaume Serra Chardonnay 2013 BFB
100% chardonnay

87

Colour: bright yellow. Nose: ripe fruit, sweet spices, creamy oak, dried herbs. Palate: rich, flavourful, fresh.

Jaume Serra Merlot 2013 RD
100% merlot

84

Jaume Serra Semidulce 2013 B
80

Jaume Serra Tempranillo 2012 T
tempranillo

82

JEAN LEON

Pago Jean León, s/n
08775 Torrelavit (Barcelona)
☎: +34 938 995 512
Fax: +34 938 995 517
www.jeanleon.com
jeanleon@jeanleon.com

Jean León 3055 2013 RD
merlot, cabernet sauvignon

89

Colour: light cherry, bright. Nose: ripe fruit, red berry notes, floral, expressive, dried herbs. Palate: powerful, fruity, fresh.

Jean León 3055 Chardonnay 2013 B
100% chardonnay

91 🌷

Colour: bright yellow. Nose: white flowers, fruit expression, expressive. Palate: fresh, fruity, flavourful, balanced, elegant.

Jean León 3055 Merlot Petit Verdot 2013 T Roble
merlot, petit verdot

89 🌷

Colour: dark-red cherry, purple rim. Nose: ripe fruit, scrubland, balanced. Palate: fruity, balanced, balsamic.

Jean León Vinya La Scala Cabernet Sauvignon 2003 TGR
100% cabernet sauvignon

93

Colour: deep cherry, orangey edge. Nose: elegant, spicy, fine reductive notes, wet leather, aged wood nuances. Palate: spicy, fine tannins, elegant, long.

Jean León Vinya Le Havre 2006 TR
cabernet sauvignon, cabernet franc

91

Colour: cherry, garnet rim. Nose: ripe fruit, spicy, creamy oak, toasty, fine reductive notes, balsamic herbs. Palate: powerful, flavourful, toasty.

Jean León Vinya Palau Merlot 2009 TC
100% merlot

91

Colour: cherry, garnet rim. Nose: ripe fruit, spicy, toasty, complex, earthy notes. Palate: powerful, flavourful, toasty, round tannins.

Jean León Viña Gigi Chardonnay 2012 BC
100% chardonnay

92

Colour: bright straw. Nose: white flowers, fresh fruit, expressive, fine lees, dried herbs, spicy. Palate: flavourful, fruity, good acidity, balanced, elegant.

JOAN SARDÀ

Ctra. Vilafranca a St. Jaume dels Domenys, Km. 8,1
08732 Castellví de la Marca (Barcelona)
☎: +34 937 720 900
Fax: +34 937 721 495
www.joansarda.com
joansarda@joansarda.com

Blanc Mariner 2013 B
xarel.lo, chardonnay

88

Colour: bright straw. Nose: fresh, fresh fruit, white flowers, citrus fruit. Palate: flavourful, fruity, good acidity, balanced.

Joan Sardà 2009 TR
cabernet sauvignon, tempranillo, merlot

89

Colour: cherry, garnet rim. Nose: ripe fruit, spicy, toasty, complex, wild herbs. Palate: powerful, flavourful, toasty, round tannins.

Joan Sardà 2011 TC
merlot, syrah

86

Colour: dark-red cherry, garnet rim. Nose: wild herbs, scrubland, ripe fruit. Palate: flavourful, fruity.

Joan Sardà Cabernet Sauvignon 2012 TC
cabernet sauvignon

87

Colour: cherry, garnet rim. Nose: ripe fruit, wild herbs, earthy notes, spicy, creamy oak. Palate: balanced, flavourful, long, balsamic.

Joan Sardà Cabernet Sauvignon 2013 RD
cabernet sauvignon

87

Colour: light cherry. Nose: ripe fruit, red berry notes, floral, balsamic herbs. Palate: powerful, fruity, fresh, easy to drink.

Joan Sardà Chardonnay 2013 B
chardonnay

88

Colour: bright straw. Nose: white flowers, fresh fruit, expressive, dried herbs. Palate: flavourful, fruity, good acidity, balanced.

Vinya Sardà 2013 B
xarel.lo

85

Vinya Sardà 2013 RD
merlot

83

Vinya Sardà 2013 T
merlot, tempranillo

86

Colour: cherry, purple rim. Nose: scrubland, ripe fruit. Palate: correct, easy to drink, good finish, fruity.

JUVÉ Y CAMPS

Sant Venat, 1
08770 Sant Sadurní D'Anoia (Barcelona)
☎: +34 938 911 000
Fax: +34 938 912 100
www.juveycamps.com
juveycamps@juveycamps.com

Aurora D'Espiells Rosé 2013 RD

89

Colour: onion pink. Nose: elegant, candied fruit, dried flowers, fragrant herbs, red berry notes. Palate: light-bodied, flavourful, good acidity, long, spicy.

Casa Vella D'Espiells 2009 T

91

Colour: cherry, garnet rim. Nose: ripe fruit, spicy, creamy oak, toasty, complex. Palate: powerful, flavourful, toasty, round tannins, balanced.

Ermita D'Espiells 2013 B

87

Colour: yellow. Nose: fresh, white flowers, expressive. Palate: flavourful, fruity, good acidity, balanced.

Ermita D'Espiells Rosé 2013 RD

88

Colour: light cherry. Nose: powerfull, ripe fruit, red berry notes, floral, expressive. Palate: powerful, fruity, fresh, unctuous.

Flor D'Espiells 2013 BFB
100% chardonnay

90

Colour: bright straw. Nose: white flowers, fragrant herbs, fruit expression, spicy. Palate: fresh, fruity, flavourful, balanced, elegant.

Gregal D'Espiells 2013 B

89

Colour: bright straw. Nose: white flowers, fragrant herbs, fruit expression. Palate: fresh, fruity, flavourful, balanced, elegant.

Iohannes 2008 T

92

Colour: deep cherry, brick rim edge. Nose: elegant, spicy, fine reductive notes, wet leather, aged wood nuances, fruit liqueur notes. Palate: spicy, fine tannins, elegant, long.

Miranda D'Espiells 2013 B
100% chardonnay

91

Colour: bright straw. Nose: white flowers, fresh fruit, expressive, fine lees, dried herbs. Palate: flavourful, fruity, good acidity, balanced.

Viña Escarlata 2010 T
100% merlot

91

Colour: cherry, garnet rim. Nose: ripe fruit, wild herbs, earthy notes, spicy, creamy oak. Palate: balanced, flavourful, long, balsamic.

LLOPART

Ctra. de Sant Sadurni - Ordal, Km. 4 Els Casots
08739 Subirats (Barcelona)
☎: +34 938 993 125
Fax: +34 938 993 038
www.llopart.com
llopart@llopart.com

Llopart Castell de Subirats 2011 TC

89

Colour: cherry, garnet rim. Nose: ripe fruit, spicy, creamy oak, toasty, complex. Palate: powerful, flavourful, toasty, round tannins.

Llopart Clos dels Fòssils 2013 B

88

Colour: bright yellow. Nose: powerfull, ripe fruit, sweet spices, creamy oak, fragrant herbs, citrus fruit. Palate: rich, flavourful, fresh.

Llopart Vitis 2013 B

84

LOXAREL

Can Mayol, s/n
08735 Vilobí del Penedès (Barcelona)
☎: +34 938 978 001
www.loxarel.com
loxarel@loxarel.com

790 Loxarel 2008 T
cabernet sauvignon

89

Colour: ruby red. Nose: spicy, fine reductive notes, wet leather, toasty. Palate: spicy, long, toasty, balsamic.

Eos de Loxarel Syrah 2012 T
cabernet sauvignon

87 🌷

Colour: bright cherry, garnet rim. Nose: ripe fruit, sweet spices, creamy oak. Palate: flavourful, fruity, toasty.

Garnatxa Blanca de Loxarel 2013 B
garnacha blanca

91 🏆

Colour: bright straw. Nose: white flowers, fresh fruit, expressive, dried herbs. Palate: flavourful, fruity, good acidity, balanced.

Loxarel Vintage 2009 ESP Reserva
xarel.lo, macabeo, chardonnay

90 🏆

Colour: yellow. Nose: medium intensity, dried herbs, fine lees, floral, ripe fruit. Palate: fresh, fruity, flavourful, good acidity.

Loxarel Vintage 2012 ESP Reserva
xarel.lo, macabeo, chardonnay

89 🏆

Colour: bright straw. Nose: medium intensity, fresh fruit, dried herbs, fine lees, floral, expressive. Palate: fresh, fruity, flavourful, good acidity, balanced.

LXV de Loxarel Xarel.lo Vermell 2013 B
xarel.lo, vermell

88

Colour: coppery red, bright. Nose: medium intensity, dried herbs, dried flowers, fresh fruit. Palate: fine bitter notes, easy to drink, balanced.

MM de Loxarel 2008 ESP Gran Reserva
pinot noir, xarel.lo

88 🏆

Colour: yellow, coppery red. Nose: fine lees, dry nuts, fragrant herbs, complex. Palate: powerful, flavourful, good acidity, fine bead, fine bitter notes.

Refugi de Loxarel 2009 ESP Reserva
xarel.lo, chardonnay

86

Colour: bright yellow. Nose: dried herbs, fine lees, faded flowers. Palate: fresh, fruity, flavourful, good acidity.

Xarel.lo de Loxarel 2013 B
xarel.lo

91

Colour: bright straw. Nose: white flowers, fragrant herbs, fruit expression. Palate: fresh, fruity, flavourful, balanced, elegant.

MARRUGAT S.A. (BODEGAS PINORD)
Doctor Pasteur, 6
08776 Vilafranca del Penedès
(Barcelona)
☎: +34 938 903 066
www.pinord.com
visites@pinord.com

Pinord Chateldon 2007 TR
100% cabernet sauvignon

80

Pinord Clos de Torribas 2010 TC
tempranillo, cabernet sauvignon, merlot

82

Pinord Clos de Torribas 2013 B
gewürztraminer, macabeo, xarel.lo

86 🏆

Colour: bright straw. Nose: fresh, fresh fruit, white flowers. Palate: flavourful, fruity, good acidity.

Pinord Diorama Cabernet Sauvignon 2013 RD
cabernet sauvignon

80 🏆

Pinord Diorama Merlot 2011 T
merlot

85

Pinord Mireia 2013 B
gewürztraminer, moscatel, sauvignon blanc

85

MAS BERTRAN
Ctra. BP-2121 Km.7,7
08731 St. Martí Sarroca (Barcelona)
☎: +34 938 990 859
www.masbertran.com
info@masbertran.com

Argila 2009 BN Gran Reserva
100% xarel.lo

88

Colour: bright golden. Nose: fine lees, dry nuts, fragrant herbs, pattiserie. Palate: powerful, flavourful, good acidity, fine bead, fine bitter notes.

Argila 2010 BN Gran Reserva
100% xarel.lo

91

Colour: bright golden. Nose: fine lees, dry nuts, fragrant herbs, complex, toasty. Palate: powerful, flavourful, good acidity, fine bead, fine bitter notes.

Argila Rosé 2011 BN Reserva
100% sumoll

89

Colour: coppery red. Nose: floral, jasmine, fragrant herbs, candied fruit. Palate: fruity, flavourful, balanced.

Balma 2011 BN Reserva

88

Colour: bright yellow. Nose: ripe fruit, fine lees, balanced, dried herbs. Palate: good acidity, flavourful, ripe fruit, long.

Balma 2011 BR Reserva

86

Colour: bright straw. Nose: fine lees, floral, fragrant herbs, expressive. Palate: powerful, flavourful, good acidity, fine bead, balanced.

Nutt 2013 B
xarel.lo

89

Colour: bright straw. Nose: fragrant herbs, fresh fruit, white flowers, mineral. Palate: fresh, fruity, flavourful.

Nutt Rosé Sumoll 2013 RD
100% sumoll

87

Colour: light cherry. Nose: elegant, candied fruit, dried flowers, fragrant herbs. Palate: light-bodied, good acidity, carbonic notes.

MAS CAN COLOMÉ

Masies Sant Marçal s/n
08729 Castellet i La Gornal (Barcelona)
☎: +34 938 918 203
Fax: +34 938 918 203
www.mascancolome.com
info@mascancolome.com

Mas Can Colome Viticultors 2011 BN Reserva
xarel.lo, macabeo, parellada

86

Colour: bright yellow. Nose: ripe fruit, fine lees, balanced, dried herbs. Palate: good acidity, flavourful, ripe fruit, long.

Petit Serenor Mas can Colome Viticultors 2011 ESP Reserva
xarel.lo, macabeo, parellada, chardonnay

87

Colour: bright yellow. Nose: medium intensity, dried herbs, fine lees, floral, dry nuts. Palate: fresh, fruity, flavourful, good acidity.

Rosadenc Mas Can Colomé Viticultors 2013 RD
syrah, garnacha, pinot noir

85

Serenor Mas Can Colome Viticultors 2010 ESP Reserva
xarel.lo, chardonnay, macabeo, parellada

90

Colour: bright straw. Nose: medium intensity, fresh fruit, dried herbs, fine lees, floral, expressive. Palate: fresh, fruity, flavourful, good acidity, elegant.

Turo Mas can Colomé Viticultors 2011 T
garnacha, syrah, samsó

89

Colour: deep cherry, garnet rim. Nose: balanced, expressive, ripe fruit, floral, spicy. Palate: flavourful, round tannins.

Turonet Mas Can Colomé Viticultors 2013 B
chardonnay, xarel.lo, sauvignon blanc

89

Colour: bright straw. Nose: white flowers, fragrant herbs, fruit expression. Palate: fresh, fruity, flavourful, balanced, elegant, easy to drink.

MAS CANDÍ

Ctra. de Les Gunyoles, s/n
08793 Les Gunyoles (Barcelona)
☎: +34 680 765 275
www.mascandi.com
info@mascandi.com

Mas Candi Cova de L'Ometlló Dulce 2011
cabernet sauvignon

87

Colour: light mahogany. Nose: candied fruit, fruit liqueur notes, acetaldehyde, aged wood nuances, rancio notes. Palate: flavourful, unctuous, long.

Mas Candi Desig 2013 B
xarel.lo

87

Colour: bright straw. Nose: white flowers, fragrant herbs, fruit expression. Palate: fresh, fruity, flavourful.

Mas Candi Les Forques 2010 T
cabernet sauvignon, sumoll, otras

91

Colour: cherry, garnet rim. Nose: ripe fruit, wild herbs, earthy notes, spicy, creamy oak. Palate: balanced, flavourful, long, balsamic.

Mas Candi Pecat Noble 2013 BFB
malvasía

90

Colour: bright yellow. Nose: floral, fragrant herbs, citrus fruit. Palate: flavourful, sweet, fresh, fruity, good acidity, long.

Mas Candí Quatre Xarel.lo 2012 BFB
100% xarel.lo

91

Colour: bright yellow. Nose: ripe fruit, sweet spices, creamy oak, fragrant herbs. Palate: rich, flavourful, good acidity.

Mas Candí Sol+Sol 2010 T
cabernet sauvignon, sumoll, otras

91

Colour: cherry, garnet rim. Nose: earthy notes, spicy, creamy oak, balsamic herbs, dry stone, ripe fruit. Palate: balanced, flavourful, balsamic.

MAS CODINA

Barri El Gorner, s/n - Mas Codina
08797 Puigdalber (Barcelona)
☎: +34 938 988 166
Fax: +34 938 988 166
www.mascodina.com
info@mascodina.com

Mas Codina 2010 T
merlot, cabernet sauvignon, syrah
88
Colour: cherry, garnet rim. Nose: ripe fruit, spicy, creamy oak, toasty, complex. Palate: powerful, flavourful, toasty, round tannins.

Mas Codina 2013 B
chardonnay, macabeo, xarel.lo, moscatel
89
Colour: bright straw. Nose: fresh, fresh fruit, white flowers, expressive. Palate: flavourful, fruity, good acidity, balanced.

Mas Codina 2013 RD
merlot, cabernet sauvignon, syrah
84

Mas Codina Vinya Ferrer 2009 TR
cabernet sauvignon
86
Colour: pale ruby, brick rim edge. Nose: ripe fruit, wild herbs, spicy, creamy oak. Palate: balanced, balsamic, spicy.

Mas Codina Vinya Miquel 2009 TC
syrah
87
Colour: very deep cherry, garnet rim. Nose: powerfull, ripe fruit, roasted coffee, dark chocolate. Palate: powerful, toasty, balsamic.

MAS COMTAL

Mas Comtal, 1
08793 Avinyonet del Penedès
(Barcelona)
☎: +34 938 970 052
Fax: +34 938 970 591
www.mascomtal.com
mascomtal@mascomtal.com

Antistiana Merlot 2010 T
100% merlot
91
Colour: cherry, garnet rim. Nose: ripe fruit, earthy notes, scrubland, creamy oak, toasty. Palate: balanced, flavourful, long, balsamic.

Antistiana Xarel.lo 2012 B
100% xarel.lo
90
Colour: bright yellow. Nose: complex, faded flowers, balanced, expressive. Palate: flavourful, good acidity, fine bitter notes, ripe fruit, spicy.

Mas Comtal 20 Aniversari Rosado 2012 ESP Reserva
100% merlot
86
Colour: light cherry, bright. Nose: ripe fruit, fragrant herbs, spicy, dried flowers. Palate: flavourful, fine bitter notes, good acidity.

Mas Comtal Cuvèe Prestige Joan Milà 2009 ESP
89
Colour: bright golden. Nose: fine lees, fragrant herbs, complex. Palate: powerful, flavourful, good acidity, fine bead.

Mas Comtal Negre D'Anyada 2012 T
87
Colour: dark-red cherry, garnet rim. Nose: spicy, ripe fruit, wild herbs. Palate: flavourful, balanced, round tannins.

Mas Comtal Pomell de Blancs 2013 B
88
Colour: bright straw. Nose: fresh, fresh fruit, white flowers, expressive. Palate: flavourful, fruity, good acidity, balanced.

Mas Comtal Premium 2011 BR
87
Colour: bright yellow. Nose: ripe fruit, fine lees, balanced, dried herbs, expressive. Palate: good acidity, flavourful, ripe fruit, long.

Mas Comtal Rosat de Llàgrima 2013 RD
100% merlot
87 ❁
Colour: rose. Nose: red berry notes, balanced, ripe fruit, dried herbs. Palate: flavourful, fruity, long.

Pétrea 2008 BFB
100% chardonnay
89
Colour: bright golden. Nose: cocoa bean, creamy oak, toasty, candied fruit. Palate: powerful, rich, long, spicy, toasty, fine bitter notes.

MAS DEL PUIG BONANS

Mas Bonans s/n
08784 Piera (Barcelona)
☎: +34 622 207 500
www.bonans.cat
bonans@bonans.cat

Mas del Puig Bonans Xarel.lo 2013 B
100% xarel.lo
88 ❁
Colour: bright straw. Nose: white flowers, fragrant herbs, fruit expression. Palate: fruity, flavourful, balanced.

Vi Escumós Mas Bonans 2012 ESP
macabeo, xarel.lo, parellada
84

MAS RODÓ

Km. 2 Ctra. Sant Pere Sacarrera a
Sant Joan de Mediona (Alto Penedès)
08773 Barcelona (Barcelona)
☎: +34 932 385 780
Fax: +34 932 174 356
www.masrodo.com
info@masrodo.com

Mas Rodó Cabernet Sauvignon 2010 T
cabernet sauvignon
90
Colour: cherry, garnet rim. Nose: ripe fruit, spicy, creamy oak, balsamic herbs. Palate: powerful, flavourful, toasty, round tannins.

Mas Rodó Macabeo 2013 B
macabeo
88
Colour: yellow. Nose: faded flowers, sweet spices, ripe fruit, toasty. Palate: rich, flavourful, ripe fruit, toasty.

Mas Rodó Merlot 2011 TR
merlot
88
Colour: bright cherry. Nose: ripe fruit, sweet spices, creamy oak, balsamic herbs. Palate: flavourful, fruity, toasty, round tannins.

Mas Rodó Montonega 2012 B
100% montonega
90
Colour: bright straw. Nose: white flowers, fresh fruit, expressive, fine lees, dried herbs. Palate: flavourful, fruity, good acidity, balanced.

Mas Rodó Reserva de la Propietat 2008 T
cabernet sauvignon
88
Colour: cherry, garnet rim. Nose: ripe fruit, wild herbs, spicy, tobacco. Palate: balanced, flavourful, fine bitter notes.

Mas Rodó Riesling 2013 B
riesling
88
Colour: bright straw. Nose: white flowers, fragrant herbs, fruit expression. Palate: fresh, fruity, flavourful, balanced, sweetness.

MASET DEL LLEÓ

C-244, Km. 32,5
08792 La Granada del Penedès
(Barcelona)
☎: +34 902 200 250
Fax: +34 938 921 333
www.maset.com
info@maset.com

Maset del Lleó Cabernet Sauvignon 2010 TR
cabernet sauvignon
86
Colour: cherry, garnet rim. Nose: ripe fruit, wild herbs, spicy, creamy oak. Palate: balanced, flavourful, long, balsamic.

Maset del Lleó Cabernet Sauvignon 2011 TC
cabernet sauvignon
84

Maset del Lleó Chardonnay Flor de Mar 2013 B
chardonnay
87
Colour: bright straw. Nose: fresh fruit, white flowers, dried herbs. Palate: flavourful, fruity, balanced.

Maset del Lleó Merlot 2013 RD
merlot
85

Maset del Lleó Merlot Foc 2011 TC
merlot
89
Colour: bright cherry. Nose: ripe fruit, sweet spices, creamy oak, wild herbs. Palate: fruity, flavourful, toasty, balsamic, correct.

Maset del Lleó Selección 2012 T
ull de llebre
90
Colour: cherry, garnet rim. Nose: red berry notes, raspberry, fruit expression, fragrant herbs, spicy, mineral. Palate: flavourful, light-bodied, good acidity, fresh, fruity, balanced.

Maset del Lleó Xarel.lo Blanc de Blancs 2013 B
xarel.lo
88
Colour: bright straw. Nose: fresh fruit, balanced, floral, fresh. Palate: fruity, fine bitter notes, easy to drink, flavourful.

MASIA VALLFORMOSA

La Sala, 45
08735 Vilobi del Penedès (Barcelona)
☎: +34 938 978 286
Fax: +34 938 978 355
www.domenechvidal.com
vallformosa@vallformosa.es

La.Sala Tempranillo Cabernet Sauvignon 2012 T
tempranillo, cabernet sauvignon

89

Colour: bright cherry. Nose: ripe fruit, sweet spices, creamy oak, expressive, balsamic herbs. Palate: flavourful, fruity, toasty, round tannins.

MAS LA.ROCA 2012 T
tempranillo, cabernet sauvignon

88

Colour: cherry, garnet rim. Nose: ripe fruit, spicy, creamy oak, toasty, balsamic herbs. Palate: powerful, flavourful, toasty.

MAS LA.ROCA 2013 B
xarel.lo, macabeo, chardonnay

86

Colour: bright straw. Nose: white flowers, fragrant herbs, fruit expression. Palate: fresh, fruity, flavourful.

MAS LA.ROCA 2013 RD
merlot, sumoll, tempranillo

85

Masia Freyè Merlot Sumoll 2013 RD
merlot, sumoll

87

Colour: coppery red, bright. Nose: fresh, red berry notes, citrus fruit, floral. Palate: flavourful, balanced, fine bitter notes, fruity.

Masia Freyè Parellada Muscat 2013 B
parellada, moscatel

88

Colour: bright straw. Nose: floral, fragrant herbs, tropical fruit. Palate: fresh, fruity, easy to drink.

Masia Freyè Syrah Tempranillo 2012 T
tempranillo, syrah

89

Colour: cherry, garnet rim. Nose: spicy, complex, dark chocolate, earthy notes, red berry notes, ripe fruit, violets. Palate: powerful, flavourful, toasty.

Masia Freyè Xarel.lo Chardonnay 2013 B
xarel.lo, chardonnay

88

Colour: yellow, greenish rim. Nose: white flowers, dried herbs, balanced. Palate: fruity, correct, fine bitter notes.

Masia La.Sala 2013 RD
merlot, sumoll, tempranillo

89

Colour: onion pink. Nose: elegant, candied fruit, dried flowers, fragrant herbs, red berry notes. Palate: light-bodied, flavourful, good acidity, long, spicy.

Masia La.Sala Xarel.lo Macabeo Chardonnay 2013 B
xarel.lo

88

Colour: bright straw. Nose: fresh, fresh fruit, white flowers. Palate: flavourful, fruity, good acidity, balanced.

MONT MARÇAL

Finca Manlleu
08732 Castellví de la Marca (Barcelona)
☎: +34 938 918 281
Fax: +34 938 919 045
www.mont-marcal.com
mont-marcal@mont-marcal.com

Mont Marçal 2011 TC

87

Colour: deep cherry, purple rim. Nose: ripe fruit, violets, sweet spices. Palate: fruity, spicy, easy to drink.

Mont Marçal 2013 B

87

Colour: bright straw. Nose: fresh, fresh fruit, white flowers, fragrant herbs. Palate: flavourful, fruity, good acidity, balanced.

Mont Marçal 2013 RD

85

Mont Marçal 2013 T

86

Colour: cherry, purple rim. Nose: medium intensity, balanced, red berry notes, ripe fruit, scrubland. Palate: correct, easy to drink.

NADAL

Finca Nadal de la Boadella, s/n
08775 Torrelavit (Barcelona)
☎: +34 938 988 011
Fax: +34 938 988 443
www.nadal.com
comunicacio@nadal.com

Nadal Xarel.lo 2013 B
100% xarel.lo

87

Colour: bright straw. Nose: white flowers, fragrant herbs, fruit expression, balsamic herbs. Palate: fresh, fruity, flavourful.

ORIOL ROSSELL

Masia Can Cassanyes
08729 Sant Marçal (Barcelona)
☎: +34 977 671 061
Fax: +34 977 671 050
www.oriolrossell.com
oriolrossell@oriolrossell.com

Les Cerveres Xarel.lo 2012 B
xarel.lo

90

Colour: bright yellow. Nose: powerfull, ripe fruit, sweet spices, creamy oak, fragrant herbs. Palate: rich, smoky aftertaste, flavourful, fresh, good acidity.

Rocaplana 2012 TC
100% syrah

87

Colour: black cherry, purple rim. Nose: fruit preserve, spicy. Palate: flavourful, ripe fruit, balanced, round tannins.

Virolet Xarel.lo 2013 B
xarel.lo

90

Colour: straw, pale. Nose: dry nuts, faded flowers, varietal, dry stone, fine lees. Palate: flavourful, fine bitter notes, long, good acidity.

PARATÓ

Can Respall de Renardes s/n
08733 El Pla del Penedès (Barcelona)
☎: +34 938 988 182
Fax: +34 938 988 510
www.parato.es
info@parato.es

Finca Renardes 2012 T
tempranillo, cariñena, cabernet sauvignon

90

Colour: bright cherry. Nose: ripe fruit, creamy oak, medium intensity, wild herbs. Palate: fruity, flavourful, toasty.

Parató Ática Tres x Tres 2012 B
xarel.lo, macabeo, chardonnay

86

Colour: bright yellow. Nose: dry nuts, dried flowers, balsamic herbs, mineral. Palate: powerful, flavourful, ripe fruit.

Parató Pinot Noir 2013 RD

86

Colour: rose, bright. Nose: balanced, medium intensity, red berry notes. Palate: fruity, long, easy to drink, good acidity.

Parató Samsó 2009 TR
cariñena

89

Colour: black cherry. Nose: ripe fruit, fruit preserve, sweet spices, balsamic herbs. Palate: balanced, round tannins.

Parató Xarel.lo 2013 B
xarel.lo

87

Colour: bright straw. Nose: fresh, fresh fruit, white flowers. Palate: flavourful, fruity, good acidity.

PARDAS

Finca Can Comas, s/n
08775 Torrelavit (Barcelona)
☎: +34 938 995 005
www.cellerpardas.com
pardas@cancomas.com

Pardas Aspriu 2011 T
100% cabernet franc

93

Colour: cherry, garnet rim. Nose: scrubland, ripe fruit, toasty. Palate: fine bitter notes, good acidity, round tannins.

Pardas Collita Roja 2012 T
100% sumoll

90

Colour: cherry, garnet rim. Nose: red berry notes, raspberry, balsamic herbs, spicy, creamy oak. Palate: flavourful, fruity, spicy, balanced.

Pardas Negre Franc 2010 T

93

Colour: cherry, garnet rim. Nose: ripe fruit, spicy, creamy oak, complex, dark chocolate, mineral. Palate: powerful, flavourful, toasty, round tannins.

Pardas Rupestris 2013 B

89

Colour: bright straw. Nose: fresh, fresh fruit, white flowers, fragrant herbs. Palate: flavourful, fruity, good acidity, balanced.

Pardas Xarel.lo 2010 B
100% xarel.lo

91

Colour: bright yellow. Nose: powerfull, ripe fruit, sweet spices, creamy oak, fragrant herbs. Palate: rich, smoky aftertaste, flavourful, fresh, good acidity.

Pardas Xarel.lo Aspriu 2011 B
100% xarel.lo

93

Colour: bright yellow. Nose: powerfull, ripe fruit, sweet spices, creamy oak. Palate: rich, smoky aftertaste, flavourful, fresh, good acidity.

PARÉS BALTÀ

Masía Can Baltá, s/n
08796 Pacs del Penedès (Barcelona)
☎: +34 938 901 399
Fax: +34 938 901 143
www.paresbalta.com
paresbalta@paresbalta.com

Amphora 2013 B
xarel.lo

90

Colour: bright straw. Nose: expressive, dry nuts, balanced, complex, saline, flor yeasts. Palate: flavourful, long. Personality.

Blanc de Pacs 2013 B
parellada, macabeo, xarel.lo

88

Colour: bright straw. Nose: white flowers, fresh fruit, dried herbs. Palate: flavourful, fruity, good acidity, balanced.

Calcari Xarel.lo 2013 B
xarel.lo

91

Colour: bright straw. Nose: white flowers, fresh fruit, expressive, fine lees, dried herbs, dry stone. Palate: flavourful, fruity, good acidity, balanced.

Cosmic Parés Baltà 2013 B
xarel.lo, sauvignon blanc

89

Colour: bright yellow. Nose: faded flowers, dry nuts, ripe fruit, complex, tropical fruit. Palate: balanced, fine bitter notes.

Electio Xarel.lo 2012 B
xarel.lo

90

Colour: bright golden. Nose: sweet spices, expressive, ripe fruit. Palate: flavourful, rich, balanced, fine bitter notes.

Ginesta 2013 B
gewürztraminer

88

Colour: bright yellow. Nose: white flowers, fine lees, ripe fruit, faded flowers. Palate: flavourful, fruity, good acidity, balanced.

Hisenda Miret Garnatxa 2011 T
garnacha

88

Colour: dark-red cherry, garnet rim. Nose: fruit preserve, powerfull, spicy, dried herbs. Palate: flavourful, fruity, round tannins.

Indígena 2012 T
garnacha

90

Colour: cherry, garnet rim. Nose: red berry notes, ripe fruit, wild herbs, mineral, spicy. Palate: flavourful, fruity, long, balsamic.

Indígena 2013 B
garnacha blanca

93

Colour: bright straw. Nose: floral, fruit expression, wild herbs, mineral, spicy. Palate: powerful.

Indígena 2013 RD
garnacha

90

Colour: onion pink. Nose: elegant, dried flowers, fragrant herbs, red berry notes. Palate: flavourful, good acidity, long, balsamic, fine bitter notes.

Marta de Baltà 2009 T
syrah

90

Colour: cherry, garnet rim. Nose: ripe fruit, spicy, creamy oak, toasty, earthy notes, mineral. Palate: powerful, flavourful, toasty, round tannins, balanced.

Mas Elena 2011 T
merlot, cabernet franc, cabernet sauvignon

90

Colour: dark-red cherry, garnet rim. Nose: powerfull, balsamic herbs, warm, spicy, ripe fruit. Palate: flavourful, good structure, balanced.

Mas Irene 2010 T
merlot, cabernet franc

92

Colour: cherry, garnet rim. Nose: ripe fruit, wild herbs, earthy notes, spicy, creamy oak. Palate: balanced, flavourful, long, balsamic, elegant.

Mas Petit 2012 T
cabernet sauvignon, garnacha

89

Colour: cherry, garnet rim. Nose: red berry notes, ripe fruit, balsamic herbs, earthy notes, dry stone, expressive. Palate: powerful, flavourful, spicy, good finish.

RAVENTÓS I BLANC

Plaça del Roure, s/n
08770 Sant Sadurní D'Anoia (Barcelona)
☎: +34 938 183 262
Fax: +34 938 912 500
www.raventos.com
raventos@raventos.com

11 de Isabel Negra 2007 T
monastrell, cabernet sauvignon

92

Colour: deep cherry, garnet rim. Nose: elegant, complex, spicy, dried herbs, tobacco. Palate: balanced, long, round tannins.

11 de Isabel Negra 2008 T
monastrell
89
Colour: pale ruby, brick rim edge. Nose: elegant, spicy, fine reductive notes, wet leather, aged wood nuances, fruit liqueur notes. Palate: spicy, fine tannins, elegant, long.

Extrem 2013 B
xarel.lo
89
Colour: straw, pale. Nose: fresh fruit, elegant, dried herbs. Palate: flavourful, fine bitter notes, complex, long, balanced, good acidity.

Isabel Negra 2011 T
89
Colour: cherry, garnet rim. Nose: ripe fruit, spicy, creamy oak, toasty, wild herbs. Palate: powerful, flavourful, toasty, balanced.

Silencis 2013 B
xarel.lo
91
Colour: bright straw. Nose: white flowers, fragrant herbs, fruit expression. Palate: fresh, fruity, flavourful, balanced, elegant.

ROCAMAR
Major, 80
08755 Castellbisbal (Barcelona)
☎: +34 937 720 900
Fax: +34 937 721 495
www.rocamar.net
info@rocamar.net

Rocamar Tempranillo 2013 T
tempranillo
86
Colour: cherry, garnet rim. Nose: wild herbs, red berry notes, floral. Palate: balsamic, fine bitter notes, flavourful.

ROS MARINA VITICULTORS
Camino Puigdàlber a las Cases Noves
08736 Guardiola de Font-Rubí
(Barcelona)
☎: +34 938 988 185
Fax: +34 938 988 185
rosmarina@rosmarina.es

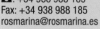

Mas Uberni Blanc de Blanc 2013 B
xarel.lo, chardonnay
87
Colour: bright straw. Nose: fresh, fresh fruit, white flowers, expressive. Palate: flavourful, fruity, good acidity, balanced.

Mas Uberni Chardonnay 2013 B
chardonnay
89
Colour: bright yellow. Nose: citrus fruit, ripe fruit, wild herbs, floral. Palate: powerful, flavourful, round.

Mas Uberni Negre Selecció 2012 T
cabernet sauvignon, ull de llebre
86
Colour: cherry, garnet rim. Nose: ripe fruit, wild herbs, spicy, creamy oak, scrubland. Palate: balanced, flavourful, long, balsamic.

Mas Uberni Rosat Llágrima 2013 RD
cabernet sauvignon, merlot
88
Colour: rose, purple rim. Nose: powerfull, ripe fruit, red berry notes, floral, expressive. Palate: powerful, fruity, fresh.

Ros Marina Cabernet Merlot 2010 T Roble
cabernet sauvignon, merlot
88
Colour: pale ruby, brick rim edge. Nose: ripe fruit, scrubland, spicy, creamy oak. Palate: powerful, flavourful, spicy, long.

Ros Marina Cupatge 3.4 2011 T Barrica
cabernet sauvignon, merlot, ull de llebre
86
Colour: cherry, garnet rim. Nose: ripe fruit, spicy, grassy. Palate: flavourful, long, balsamic.

Ros Marina Merlot 2010 T
merlot
87
Colour: pale ruby, brick rim edge. Nose: ripe fruit, balsamic herbs, powerfull, spicy, creamy oak. Palate: correct, flavourful, spicy.

Ros Marina Xarel.lo 2013 BFB
xarel.lo
88
Colour: bright straw. Nose: white flowers, fresh fruit, dried herbs. Palate: flavourful, fruity, good acidity, balanced.

SURIOL
Can Suriol del Castell
08736 Font-Rubí (Barcelona)
☎: +34 938 978 426
Fax: +34 938 978 426
www.suriol.com
cansuriol@suriol.com

Castell de Grabuac Els Bancals "Castanyer" 2010 B
xarel.lo
89
Colour: bright yellow. Nose: powerfull, ripe fruit, sweet spices, creamy oak, fragrant herbs. Palate: rich, smoky aftertaste, flavourful, fresh, good acidity.

Castell de Grabuac Els Bancals 2011 B
xarel.lo
87
Colour: bright yellow. Nose: ripe fruit, dry nuts, toasty, aged wood nuances. Palate: flavourful, fruity, spicy, toasty.

Suriol 2012 T
garnacha, cariñena, ull de llebre, monastrell
86
Colour: cherry, garnet rim. Nose: ripe fruit, spicy, wild herbs. Palate: powerful, flavourful, balsamic.

Suriol 2013 B
macabeo, malvasía
84

Suriol 2013 RD
garnacha
85

Suriol Donzella 2011 B
xarel.lo
87
Colour: bright yellow. Nose: powerfull, ripe fruit, sweet spices, fragrant herbs, toasty. Palate: rich, smoky aftertaste, flavourful, fresh, good acidity, long.

Suriol Donzella 2013 B
xarel.lo
85

Suriol Sang de Drac 2009 T
ull de llebre
83

Suriol Sang de Drac 2010 T
ull de llebre
85

Suriol Sang de Drac 2011 T
ull de llebre
84

TON RIMBAU
Casa Rimbau, s/n
08735 Vilobí del Penedès (Barcelona)
☎: +34 938 978 121
Fax: +34 938 978 121
www.tonrimbau.com
tonrimbau@tonrimbau.com

Espurnejant 2011 ESP
xarel.lo, macabeo
90
Colour: yellow. Nose: expressive, complex, varietal, dry nuts, fine reductive notes. Palate: complex, flavourful, fine bitter notes. Personality.

Porcellànic 2011 B
93
Colour: golden. Nose: powerfull, floral, honeyed notes, candied fruit, fragrant herbs, cocoa bean, dark chocolate, sweet spices. Palate: flavourful, sweet, fresh, fruity, good acidity, long. Personality.

Porcellànic Xarel.lo 2011 B
xarel.lo
75

Porcellànic Xarel.lo Sur Lie 2011 B
xarel.lo
88
Colour: bright yellow. Nose: pungent, acetaldehyde, lees reduction notes, citrus fruit, dry nuts. Palate: powerful, flavourful, rich, spicy, fine bitter notes. Personality.

TORELLÓ
Can Martí de Baix (Apartado Correos nº8)
08770 Sant Sadurní D'Anoia (Barcelona)
☎: +34 938 910 793
Fax: +34 938 910 877
www.torello.com
torello@torello.es

Crisalys 2013 BFB
100% xarel.lo
89
Colour: bright straw. Nose: fresh, fresh fruit, white flowers, expressive. Palate: flavourful, fruity, good acidity, balanced.

Gran Crisalys 2012 B
91
Colour: bright yellow. Nose: powerfull, ripe fruit, sweet spices, creamy oak, fragrant herbs. Palate: rich, smoky aftertaste, flavourful, fresh, good acidity.

Petjades 2013 RD
merlot
88
Colour: rose, purple rim. Nose: ripe fruit, red berry notes, floral, expressive. Palate: powerful, fruity, fresh.

Raimonda 2008 TR
91
Colour: cherry, garnet rim. Nose: ripe fruit, spicy, creamy oak, toasty. Palate: powerful, flavourful, toasty, round tannins.

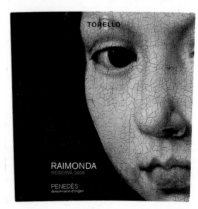

Vittios Vendimia Tardía 2013 B
xarel.lo
89
Colour: bright straw. Nose: fresh fruit, citrus fruit, white flowers. Palate: fruity, fresh, easy to drink.

VILARNAU
Ctra. d'Espiells, Km. 1,4 Finca "Can Petit"
08770 Sant Sadurní D'Anoia (Barcelona)
☎: +34 938 912 361
Fax: +34 938 912 913
www.vilarnau.es
vilarnau@vilarnau.es

Els Capricis de Vilarnau 2013 B
100% xarel.lo
90
Colour: bright yellow. Nose: white flowers, expressive, dried herbs, dry nuts, spicy, ripe fruit. Palate: flavourful, fruity, good acidity, balanced.

VINYA OCULTA
Cal Banyeres s/n
08731 La Bleda (Barcelona)
☎: +34 607 597 655
www.vinyaoculta.com
amos@vinyaoculta.com

V.O. Vinya Oculta 2011 B
xarel.lo
90
Colour: bright golden. Nose: sweet spices, creamy oak, candied fruit, faded flowers. Palate: rich, fruity, long, toasty, fine bitter notes.

V.O. Vinya Oculta MSX 2012 B
91
Colour: bright yellow. Nose: balanced, ripe fruit, medium intensity, faded flowers. Palate: rich, complex.

VIÑA TORREBLANCA
Masia Torreblanca, s/n
08734 Olérdola (Barcelona)
☎: +34 938 915 066
Fax: +34 938 900 102
www.vinatorreblanca.com
info@vinatorreblanca.com

Torreblanca 2012 T
100% cabernet sauvignon
84

Torreblanca Les Atzavares 2013 B
xarel.lo, macabeo, parellada
86
Colour: bright straw. Nose: white flowers, fresh fruit, balanced. Palate: correct, easy to drink.

Torreblanca Merlot 2013 RD
100% merlot
89
Colour: rose, purple rim. Nose: powerfull, ripe fruit, red berry notes, floral, expressive. Palate: powerful, fruity, fresh.

DO. PLA DE BAGES

CONSEJO REGULADOR
Casa de La Culla - La Culla, s/n
08240 Manresa (Barcelona)
☎ :+34 938 748 236 - Fax: +34 938 748 094
@: info@dopladebages.com
www.dopladebages.com

LOCATION:

Covering one of the eastern extremes of the Central Catalonian Depression; it covers the natural region of Bages, of which the city of Manresa is the urban centre. To the south the region is bordered by the Montserrat mountain range, the dividing line which separates it from Penedés. It comprises the municipal areas of Fonollosa, Monistrol de Caldres, Sant Joan de Vilatorrada, Artés, Avinyó, Balsareny, Calders, Callús, Cardona, Castellgalí, Castellfollit del Boix, Castellnou de Bages, Manresa, Mura, Navarcles, Navàs, El Pont de Vilomara, Rajadell, Sallent, Sant Fruitós de Bages, Sant Mateu de Bages, Sant Salvador de Guardiola, Santpedor, Santa María d'Oló, Súria and Talamanca.

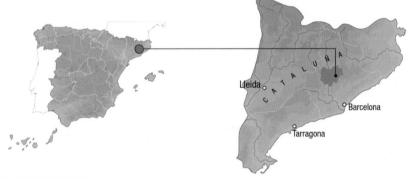

GRAPE VARIETIES:

White: Chardonnay, Gewürztraminer, Macabeo, Picapoll, Parellada, Sauvignon Blanc.
Red: Sumoll, Ull de Llebre (Tempranillo), Merlot, Cabernet Franc, Cabernet Sauvignon, Syrah and Garnacha.

FIGURES:

Vineyard surface: 500 – Wine-Growers: 90 – Wineries: 11 – 2013 Harvest rating: Very Good – Production 13: 875,981 litres – Market percentages: 75% domestic - 25% export.

SOIL:

The vineyards are situated at an altitude of about 400 m. The soil is franc-clayey, franc-sandy and franc-clayey-sandy.

CLIMATE:

Mid-mountain Mediterranean, with little rainfall (500 mm to 600 mm average annual rainfall) and greater temperature contrasts than in the Penedès.

VINTAGE RATING   PEÑÍNGUIDE

2009	2010	2011	2012	2013
VERY GOOD	GOOD	VERY GOOD	GOOD	VERY GOOD

ABADAL

Santa María d'Horta d'Avinyó s/n
08279 Santa María D'Horta D'Avinyó
(Barcelona)
☎: +34 938 743 511
Fax: +34 938 737 204
www.abadal.net
info@abadal.net

Abadal 2010 TC
88

Colour: cherry, garnet rim. Nose: ripe fruit, wild herbs, earthy notes, spicy, creamy oak. Palate: balanced, flavourful, long, balsamic.

Abadal 3.9 2009 TR
91

Colour: cherry, garnet rim. Nose: ripe fruit, wild herbs, earthy notes, spicy, creamy oak. Palate: balanced, flavourful, long, balsamic, round.

Abadal 5 Merlot 2010 TR
100% merlot
89

Colour: deep cherry. Nose: ripe fruit, wild herbs, earthy notes, spicy, creamy oak, varietal. Palate: balanced, flavourful, long, balsamic.

Abadal Cabernet Sauvignon 2013 RD
88

Colour: rose, purple rim. Nose: powerfull, ripe fruit, red berry notes, floral, expressive. Palate: powerful, fruity, fresh.

Abadal Nuat 2011 B
91

Colour: bright yellow. Nose: ripe fruit, fine lees, spicy, faded flowers, dry nuts. Palate: correct, fine bitter notes, easy to drink.

Abadal Picapoll 2013 B
100% picapoll
89

Colour: bright straw. Nose: white flowers, fragrant herbs, fruit expression. Palate: fresh, fruity, flavourful, balanced, elegant.

Abadal Selecció 2007 TR
92

Colour: cherry, garnet rim. Nose: balanced, complex, ripe fruit, spicy, fine reductive notes. Palate: good structure, flavourful, round tannins, balanced, elegant.

CELLER SOLERGIBERT

Barquera, 40
08271 Artés (Barcelona)
☎: +34 938 305 084
Fax: +34 938 305 763
www.cellersolergibert.com
josep@cellersolergibert.com

Pd'a de Solergilabert 2012 B
picapoll
91

Colour: bright golden. Nose: ripe fruit, powerfull, toasty, aged wood nuances, balsamic herbs. Palate: flavourful, fruity, spicy, toasty, long, balanced, elegant.

Pic Solergibert 2013 B
picapoll
90

Colour: bright yellow. Nose: fresh, fresh fruit, white flowers, fragrant herbs. Palate: flavourful, fruity, good acidity, balanced, elegant.

Solergibert de Matacans 2012 T
89

Colour: cherry, garnet rim. Nose: ripe fruit, wild herbs, creamy oak, toasty. Palate: powerful, flavourful, spicy, long.

COLLBAIX - CELLER EL MOLI

Cami de Rajadell, km. 3
08241 Manresa (Barcelona)
☎: +34 931 021 965
www.cellerelmoli.com
collbaix@cellerelmoli.com

Collbaix Cupatge 2009 T
cabernet sauvignon, merlot, ull de llebre, cabernet franc
91 ♣

Colour: light cherry. Nose: spicy, fine reductive notes, wet leather, aged wood nuances, toasty, ripe fruit. Palate: spicy, long, toasty, correct, elegant.

Collbaix La Llobeta 2009 T
cabernet sauvignon, merlot, cabernet franc
88 ♣

Colour: pale ruby, brick rim edge. Nose: elegant, spicy, fine reductive notes, wet leather, aged wood nuances, fruit liqueur notes. Palate: spicy, fine tannins, elegant, long.

Collbaix Merlot 2013 RD
merlot, sumoll

87

Colour: rose, purple rim. Nose: powerfull, ripe fruit, red berry notes, floral, expressive, balsamic herbs. Palate: powerful, fruity, fresh.

Collbaix Picapoll Macabeo 2013 B
picapoll, macabeo

88

Colour: bright yellow. Nose: floral, ripe fruit, citrus fruit, wild herbs. Palate: fresh, fruity, easy to drink.

Collbaix Singular 2010 T
cabernet sauvignon

93

Colour: cherry, garnet rim. Nose: ripe fruit, spicy, creamy oak, toasty, complex, balsamic herbs, mineral. Palate: powerful, flavourful, toasty, round tannins.

Collbaix Singular 2012 B Barrica
macabeo, picapoll

92

Colour: bright yellow. Nose: powerfull, ripe fruit, sweet spices, creamy oak, fragrant herbs. Palate: rich, flavourful, fresh, good acidity.

El Sagal 2013 T
merlot, cabernet franc

88

Colour: cherry, purple rim. Nose: expressive, fresh fruit, red berry notes, floral. Palate: flavourful, fruity, good acidity, balanced.

U D'Urpina 2011 T
cabernet sauvignon

90

Colour: cherry, garnet rim. Nose: scrubland, damp earth, mineral, fruit preserve, fine reductive notes. Palate: powerful, flavourful, concentrated, balanced.

HERETAT OLLER DEL MAS
Ctra. de Igualada (C-37), km. 91
08241 Manresa (Barcelona)
☎: +34 938 768 315
Fax: +34 932 056 949
www.ollerdelmas.com
info@ollerdelmas.com

Arnau Oller 2009 T
merlot, picapoll negro

91

Colour: dark-red cherry, garnet rim. Nose: fine reductive notes, spicy, ripe fruit, wild herbs. Palate: balanced, spicy, round tannins.

Bernat Oller 2012 T
merlot, picapoll negro

88

Colour: dark-red cherry, garnet rim. Nose: warm, ripe fruit, spicy, balsamic herbs. Palate: correct, ripe fruit, long.

Bernat Oller Blanc de Picapolls 2013 B
picapoll, picapoll negro

88

Colour: bright straw. Nose: ripe fruit, spicy, dried flowers, dried herbs. Palate: rich, flavourful, spicy, long.

Bernat Oller Rosat 2013 RD
merlot, picapoll negro

85

Heretat Oller del Mas Especial Picapoll 2012 T
100% picapoll negro

87

Colour: light cherry. Nose: scrubland, balanced, ripe fruit, spicy, medium intensity. Palate: light-bodied, easy to drink, balsamic.

Petit Bernat 2013 T
merlot, syrah, cabernet franc, cabernet sauvignon

86

Colour: dark-red cherry, purple rim. Nose: wild herbs, toasty, spicy. Palate: flavourful, correct, balsamic.

Petit Bernat Blanc 2013 B
picapoll, macabeo

87

Colour: bright straw. Nose: fresh, fresh fruit, white flowers, expressive. Palate: flavourful, fruity, good acidity, balanced.

JAUME GRAU GRAU - VINS GRAU S.L.
Ctra. C-37, Km. 75,5
D'Igualada a Manresa
08255 Maians (Barcelona)
☎: +34 938 356 002
www.vinsgrau.com
info@vinsgrau.com

Jaume Grau i Grau Avrvm 2013 B
sauvignon blanc, chardonnay, macabeo

85

Jaume Grau i Grau Merlot 2013 RD
merlot

86

Colour: light cherry. Nose: ripe fruit, wild herbs, lactic notes. Palate: fresh, fruity, easy to drink.

Jaume Grau i Grau Negre Sumoll Cent - Kat 2013 T
sumoll, merlot, tempranillo

86

Colour: light cherry, garnet rim. Nose: red berry notes, fruit liqueur notes, wild herbs. Palate: fresh, fruity, flavourful, easy to drink.

Jaume Grau i Grau Picapoll Cent - Kat 2013 B
picapoll

88

Colour: bright straw. Nose: fresh, fresh fruit, white flowers, balanced. Palate: flavourful, fruity, good acidity, elegant.

Jaume Grau i Grau Rosat Sumoll Cent - Kat 2013 RD
sumoll, tempranillo, merlot

87

Colour: rose, purple rim. Nose: powerfull, ripe fruit, red berry notes, floral, lactic notes. Palate: powerful, fruity, fresh, balanced.

Jaume Grau i Grau Selección Especial 2012 T
tempranillo, merlot, cabernet franc, syrah

87

Colour: cherry, garnet rim. Nose: ripe fruit, wild herbs, spicy, creamy oak. Palate: powerful, flavourful, long.

DO. PLA I LLEVANT

CONSEJO REGULADOR

Molí de N'Amengual. Dusai, 3
07260 Porreres (Illes Balears)
☎ :+34 971 168 569 - Fax: +34 971 184 49 34
@: info@plaillevantmallorca.es
www.plaillevantmallorca.es

LOCATION:

The production region covers the eastern part of Majorca and consists of 18 municipal districts: Algaida, Ariany, Artá, Campos, Capdepera, Felanitx, Lluchamajor, Manacor, Mª de la Salud, Montuiri, Muro, Petra, Porreres, Sant Joan, Sant Llorens des Cardasar, Santa Margarita, Sineu and Vilafranca de Bonany.

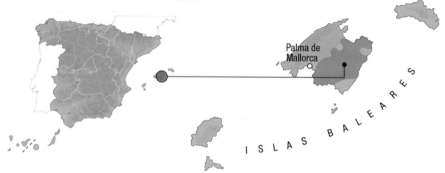

GRAPE VARIETIES:

White: Prensal Blanc, Macabeo, Parellada, Moscatel and Chardonnay.
Red: Callet (majority), Manto Negro, Fogoneu, Tempranillo, Monastrell, Cabernet Sauvignon, Merlot and Syrah.

FIGURES:

Vineyard surface: 362.76 – Wine-Growers: 75 – Wineries: 13 – 2013 Harvest rating: - – Production 13: 1,053,600 litres – Market percentages: 89% domestic - 11% export.

SOIL:

The soil is made up of limestone rocks, which give limy-clayey soils. The reddish Colour: of the terrain is due to the presence of iron oxide. The clays and calcium and magnesium carbonates, in turn, provide the whitish Colour: which can also be seen in the vineyards.

CLIMATE:

Mediterranean, with an average temperature of 16°C and with slightly cool winters and dry, hot summers. The constant sea breeze during the summer has a notable effect on these terrains close to the coast. The wet season is in autumn and the average annual rainfall is between 450 mm and 500 mm.

VINTAGE RATING   PEÑÍNGUIDE

2009	2010	2011	2012	2013
EXCELLENT	VERY GOOD	VERY GOOD	VERY GOOD	GOOD

ARMERO I ADROVER

Camada Real s/n
07200 Mallorca (Illes Ballears)
☎: +34 971 827 103
Fax: +34 971 580 305
www.armeroiadrover.com
luisarmero@armeroiadrover.com

Armero Adrover 2011 T
cabernet sauvignon, syrah, merlot

88

Colour: cherry, garnet rim. Nose: scrubland, spicy, balanced. Palate: flavourful, long, round tannins.

Armero Adrover Syrah-Callet Rosat 2013 RD
cabernet sauvignon, syrah, callet

86

Colour: raspberry rose. Nose: medium intensity, fresh fruit, fragrant herbs. Palate: easy to drink, fine bitter notes.

Armero i Adrover Collita de Fruits 2011 T
89

Colour: bright cherry, garnet rim. Nose: expressive, red berry notes, ripe fruit, wild herbs. Palate: balanced, good acidity, round tannins.

Armero i Adrover Collita de Fruits Callet 2013 RD
87

Colour: raspberry rose. Nose: medium intensity, dried herbs, dried flowers. Palate: fruity, fine bitter notes, good acidity.

Armero i Adrover Seleccion Familiar 2009 T
88

Colour: cherry, garnet rim. Nose: ripe fruit, spicy, creamy oak, toasty, complex. Palate: powerful, flavourful, toasty, round tannins.

BODEGA MESQUIDA MORA

Camí Pas des Frare,s/n
(antigua carretera PorreresSant Joan)
07260 Porreres (Illes Balears)
☎: +34 687 971 457
www.mesquidamora.com
info@mesquidamora.com

Trispol 2012 T
cabernet sauvignon, syrah, merlot, callet

91 🌿

Colour: bright cherry. Nose: ripe fruit, sweet spices, creamy oak, expressive, scrubland. Palate: flavourful, fruity, toasty, round tannins.

BODEGAS BORDOY

Pérez Galdos, 29
07006 Palma Mallorca (Illes Ballears)
☎: +34 646 619 776
www.bodegasbordoy.es
sarota@bodegasbordoy.com

Sa Rota 2009 TC
merlot, cabernet sauvignon, syrah

89

Colour: cherry, garnet rim. Nose: ripe fruit, spicy, toasty, scrubland. Palate: flavourful, toasty, round tannins.

Sa Rota 2009 TR
syrah, merlot, cabernet sauvignon

89

Colour: bright cherry. Nose: ripe fruit, spicy, creamy oak. Palate: powerful, flavourful, toasty, round tannins.

Sa Rota 2012 T
cabernet sauvignon, callet

87

Colour: cherry, garnet rim. Nose: dried herbs, scrubland, balanced. Palate: flavourful, ripe fruit, balsamic.

Sa Rota Blanc 2013 B
chardonnay, prensal

88

Colour: bright straw. Nose: faded flowers, fresh fruit, fragrant herbs. Palate: fresh, easy to drink, good acidity.

Sa Rota Blanc Chardonnay 2012 BFB
chardonnay

88

Colour: bright yellow. Nose: balanced, ripe fruit, sweet spices, creamy oak, faded flowers. Palate: flavourful, rich, toasty.

Sa Rota Dulce 2012 T
merlot

86

Colour: bright cherry, garnet rim. Nose: powerfull, ripe fruit, candied fruit, scrubland. Palate: fruity, flavourful.

Sa Rota Rosat 2013 RD
merlot, syrah, callet

86

Colour: rose, bright. Nose: medium intensity, fresh, red berry notes. Palate: good acidity, fine bitter notes, easy to drink.

Terra de Marés 2010 T
cabernet sauvignon, syrah, merlot

92

Colour: cherry, garnet rim. Nose: ripe fruit, wild herbs, earthy notes, spicy, creamy oak. Palate: balanced, flavourful, long, balsamic.

BODEGAS PERE SEDA

Cid Campeador, 22
07500 Manacor (Illes Balleares)
☎: +34 971 550 219
Fax: +34 971 844 934
www.pereseda.com
pereseda@pereseda.com

Chardonnay Pere Seda 2013 B
chardonnay
86
Colour: bright straw. Nose: fresh fruit, white flowers, balanced. Palate: fresh, easy to drink.

Gvivm Blanc 2013 B
moscatel, chardonnay, prensal
87
Colour: bright straw. Nose: fresh, fresh fruit, white flowers. Palate: flavourful, fruity, good acidity, balanced.

Gvivm Merlot-Callet 2010 T
90
Colour: cherry, garnet rim. Nose: ripe fruit, creamy oak, toasty, complex, earthy notes. Palate: powerful, flavourful, toasty, round tannins.

Gvivm Rosat 2013 RD
85

L'Arxiduc Pere Seda Negre 2011 T
tempranillo, cabernet sauvignon, merlot, manto negro
86
Colour: cherry, garnet rim. Nose: ripe fruit, wild herbs, earthy notes, spicy. Palate: balanced, flavourful, long, balsamic.

Mossèn Alcover 2010 T
89
Colour: cherry, garnet rim. Nose: ripe fruit, spicy, creamy oak, complex, waxy notes. Palate: powerful, flavourful, toasty, round tannins.

Pere Seda 2009 TR
merlot, cabernet sauvignon, syrah, callet
86
Colour: cherry, garnet rim. Nose: ripe fruit, spicy. Palate: fruity, spicy, correct, balsamic.

Pere Seda 2012 BN
85

Pere Seda 2010 TC
merlot, cabernet sauvignon, syrah, callet
90
Colour: cherry, garnet rim. Nose: spicy, ripe fruit, toasty. Palate: flavourful, long, fine tannins.

Pere Seda Rosat 2011 BN
100% callet
84

Pere Seda Rosat Novell 2013 RD
cabernet sauvignon, merlot, syrah, callet
86
Colour: rose, purple rim. Nose: powerfull, ripe fruit, red berry notes, floral. Palate: fruity, fresh, fine bitter notes.

MIQUEL OLIVER VINYES I BODEGUES

Font, 26
07520 Petra-Mallorca (Illes Balleares)
☎: +34 971 561 117
Fax: +34 971 561 117
www.miqueloliver.com
bodega@miqueloliver.com

1912 Miquel Oliver 2010 T
cabernet sauvignon, merlot
92
Colour: bright cherry, garnet rim. Nose: complex, spicy, creamy oak, balsamic herbs. Palate: fruity, flavourful, spicy.

Aia 2010 T
merlot
91
Colour: cherry, garnet rim. Nose: red berry notes, ripe fruit, wild herbs, spicy. Palate: flavourful, long, balsamic.

Original Muscat Miquel Oliver 2013 B
moscatel

90

Colour: bright straw. Nose: white flowers, fragrant herbs, fruit expression. Palate: fresh, fruity, flavourful, balanced, elegant.

Ses Ferritges 2010 TR
callet, cabernet sauvignon, merlot, syrah

91

Colour: cherry, garnet rim. Nose: ripe fruit, wild herbs, earthy notes, spicy, creamy oak. Palate: balanced, flavourful, long, balsamic.

Syrah Negre Miquel Oliver 2011 T
syrah

88

Colour: bright cherry. Nose: ripe fruit, sweet spices, creamy oak, expressive. Palate: flavourful, fruity, toasty, round tannins.

Xperiment 2011 T
callet

91

Colour: bright cherry, cherry, garnet rim. Nose: creamy oak, sweet spices, ripe fruit. Palate: balanced, spicy, long.

VID'AUBA
Quinta Volta, 2
07200 Felanitx (Mallorca)
☎: +34 699 096 295
www.vidauba.com
vidauba@vidauba.com

Vid'Auba Can Vetla 2011 T
callet

87

Colour: light cherry, garnet rim. Nose: ripe fruit, dried herbs, spicy. Palate: light-bodied, easy to drink, correct.

Vid'Auba Picot Blanc 2013 B
prensal, chardonnay, giró, moscatel

87 🌿

Colour: bright straw. Nose: fresh, fresh fruit, medium intensity, fragrant herbs. Palate: flavourful, fruity, good acidity, balanced.

Vid'Auba Picot Negre 2011 T
cabernet sauvignon, callet, merlot, syrah

89

Colour: cherry, garnet rim. Nose: ripe fruit, spicy, creamy oak, toasty, complex. Palate: powerful, flavourful, toasty, round tannins, balsamic.

Vid'Auba Singlo 2011 B
chardonnay, giró

90

Colour: bright yellow. Nose: candied fruit, faded flowers, sweet spices. Palate: flavourful, smoky aftertaste, long, spicy.

VINS MIQUEL GELABERT
Salas, 50
07500 Manacor (Illes Balears)
☎: +34 971 821 444
www.vinsmiquelgelabert.com
vinsmg@vinsmiquelgelabert.com

Chardonnay Roure 2012 BFB
chardonnay

91

Colour: bright yellow. Nose: powerfull, ripe fruit, sweet spices, creamy oak, fragrant herbs. Palate: rich, flavourful, fresh, good acidity.

Golós 2013 RD
pinot noir

86

Colour: coppery red, bright. Nose: medium intensity, white flowers, balanced. Palate: fruity, easy to drink, fine bitter notes.

Golós Blanc 2012 B
riesling, moscatel

87

Colour: bright yellow. Nose: ripe fruit, jasmine, balanced, faded flowers. Palate: flavourful, fruity, long, ripe fruit.

Golós Negre 2011 T
callet, manto negro, fogoneu

91

Colour: bright cherry, garnet rim. Nose: dry stone, scrubland, smoky, spicy, expressive. Palate: good structure, round tannins.

Gran Vinya Son Caules 2007 T
callet

90

Colour: dark-red cherry, orangey edge. Nose: spicy, ripe fruit, fruit liqueur notes, old leather. Palate: flavourful, spicy, long.

Sa Vall Selecció Privada 2010 BFB
chardonnay, prensal, moscatel

90

Colour: bright yellow. Nose: powerfull, ripe fruit, sweet spices, creamy oak, fragrant herbs. Palate: rich, flavourful, fresh, good acidity.

Torrent Negre 2007 T
cabernet sauvignon, merlot, syrah

88

Colour: dark-red cherry, orangey edge. Nose: warm, ripe fruit, scrubland. Palate: good structure, spicy, long.

Torrent Negre Selecció Privada Cabernet 2006 T
cabernet sauvignon

90

Colour: deep cherry, orangey edge. Nose: powerfull, complex, scrubland, varietal, warm. Palate: full, powerful, round tannins.

Torrent Negre Selecció Privada Syrah 2007 T
syrah

90

Colour: cherry, garnet rim. Nose: closed, medium intensity, ripe fruit, spicy. Palate: full, good structure, round tannins.

Vinya des Moré 2008 T
pinot noir

90

Colour: light cherry, orangey edge. Nose: ripe fruit, faded flowers, sweet spices. Palate: balanced, flavourful, fruity aftertaste.

DO. Ca. PRIORAT

CONSEJO REGULADOR
Major, 2
43737 Torroja del Priorat (Tarragona)
☎:+34 977 839 495 - Fax. +34 977 839 472
@: info@doqpriorat.org
www.doqpriorat.org

LOCATION:

In the province of Tarragona. It is made up of the municipal districts of La Morera de Montsant, Scala Dei, La Vilella, Gratallops, Bellmunt, Porrera, Poboleda, Torroja, Lloá, Falset and Mola.

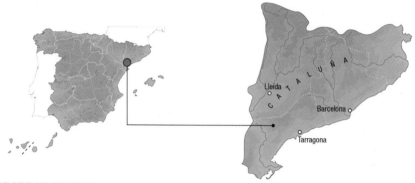

GRAPE VARIETIES:

White: Chenin Blanc, Macabeo, Garnacha Blanca, Pedro Ximénez.
Red: Cariñena, Garnacha, Garnacha Peluda, Cabernet Sauvignon, Merlot, Syrah.

FIGURES:

Vineyard surface: 1,901 – Wine-Growers: 606 – Wineries: 99 – 2013 Harvest rating: - – Production 13: 3,100,000 litres – Market percentages: 49% domestic - 51% export.

SOIL:

This is probably the most distinctive characteristic of the region and precisely what has catapulted it to the top positions in terms of quality, not only in Spain, but around the world. The soil, thin and volcanic, is composed of small pieces of slate (llicorella), which give the wines a markedly mineral character. The vineyards are located on terraces and very steep slopes.

CLIMATE:

Although with Mediterranean influences, it is temperate and dry. One of the most important characteristics is the practical absence of rain during the summer, which ensures very healthy grapes. The average rainfall is between 500 and 600 mm per year.

VINTAGE RATING

PEÑÍNGUIDE

2009	2010	2011	2012	2013
EXCELLENT	GOOD	VERY GOOD	VERY GOOD	VERY GOOD

ALTA ALELLA PRIVAT

Ctra. de Falset a Vilella Baixa, Km 11,1
43737 Gratallops (Tarragona)
☎: +34 977 262 259
www.masigneus.com
celler@masigneus.com

Barranc Blanc 2012 B
90 🏆

Colour: bright straw. Nose: toasty, ripe fruit, spicy, faded flowers, mineral. Palate: flavourful, full, fine bitter notes, ripe fruit.

Barranc Negre 2012 T
89 🏆

Colour: cherry, purple rim. Nose: ripe fruit, red berry notes, sweet spices, smoky, cocoa bean. Palate: powerful, ripe fruit, good acidity.

FA 104 Blanc 2013 B
100% garnacha blanca
93 🏆

Colour: bright straw. Nose: white flowers, expressive, dried herbs, ripe fruit, spicy. Palate: flavourful, fruity, good acidity, balanced.

FA 112 2011 T
93 🏆

Colour: cherry, garnet rim. Nose: ripe fruit, spicy, creamy oak, toasty, complex, earthy notes, varnish. Palate: powerful, flavourful, toasty, round tannins.

FA 206 Negre 2010 T
91 🏆

Colour: deep cherry, garnet rim. Nose: ripe fruit, expressive, balanced, wild herbs. Palate: full, balanced, round tannins.

ALVARO PALACIOS

Afores, s/n
43737 Gratallops (Tarragona)
☎: +34 977 839 195
Fax: +34 977 839 197
info@alvaropalacios.com

Camins del Priorat 2013 T
91

Colour: bright cherry. Nose: ripe fruit, sweet spices, creamy oak, expressive, earthy notes. Palate: flavourful, fruity, toasty, round tannins.

Finca Dofí 2012 TC
95

Colour: cherry, garnet rim. Nose: red berry notes, ripe fruit, balsamic herbs, balanced, spicy, mineral. Palate: fresh, powerful, elegant, rich, flavourful, balanced.

Gratallops Vi de la Vila 2012 T
94

Colour: light cherry, garnet rim. Nose: ripe fruit, fruit liqueur notes, wild herbs, balsamic herbs, spicy. Palate: fresh, fruity, flavourful, complex, balanced, elegant.

L'Ermita 2012 TC
97

Colour: cherry, garnet rim. Nose: mineral, expressive, spicy. Palate: flavourful, ripe fruit, fine bitter notes, good acidity.

Les Terrasses 2012 T
92

Colour: deep cherry, garnet rim. Nose: medium intensity, balanced, ripe fruit, mineral. Palate: good structure, full, flavourful, long, balsamic, mineral.

BODEGA PUIG PRIORAT

Ctra. T-710, km. 8,3 Mas del Ros
43737 Gratallops (Tarragona)
☎: +34 977 054 032
www.puigpriorat.com
mail@puigpriorat.com

Akyles 2010 TC
45% garnacha, garnacha peluda, 40% cariñena, 15% cabernet sauvignon
92

Colour: cherry, garnet rim. Nose: ripe fruit, wild herbs, earthy notes, spicy, creamy oak. Palate: balanced, flavourful, long, balsamic.

Dominicus 2010 TC
87

Colour: bright cherry. Nose: ripe fruit, sweet spices, creamy oak, medium intensity. Palate: fruity, flavourful, toasty.

Odysseus Garnacha Blanca 2013 B
100% garnacha blanca
87

Colour: bright yellow. Nose: balanced, fragrant herbs, fresh fruit, dried flowers. Palate: balanced, fine bitter notes, good acidity, long, ripe fruit.

Odysseus Pedro Ximénez 2013 B
100% pedro ximénez
88

Colour: bright straw. Nose: fresh, fresh fruit, white flowers. Palate: flavourful, fruity, good acidity.

Odysseus Único 2009 TR
89

Colour: cherry, garnet rim. Nose: ripe fruit, spicy, creamy oak, toasty, complex. Palate: powerful, flavourful, toasty, round tannins.

Penelope Dulce 2011 T
100% garnacha peluda

90

Colour: cherry, garnet rim. Nose: dried fruit, sweet spices, toasty. Palate: ripe fruit, warm, powerful, flavourful, spicy, balsamic.

BODEGAS BORDALÁS GARCÍA (BG)
Ctra. T-710, Km. 9,5
43737 Gratallops (Tarragona)
☎: +34 977 839 434
Fax: +34 977 839 434
www.bodegasbg.es
bodegasbg@yahoo.es

El Si del Molí 2013 B
garnacha blanca, macabeo

85

Fra Fort 2010 T
garnacha, cariñena

85

Gueta Lupia 2009 T
garnacha, cariñena, cabernet sauvignon, merlot

88

Colour: very deep cherry. Nose: wild herbs, spicy, old leather. Palate: flavourful, round tannins, long, balsamic.

Gueta Lupia 2010 T
garnacha, cariñena, cabernet sauvignon, merlot

86 ♥

Colour: cherry, garnet rim. Nose: ripe fruit, spicy, creamy oak, toasty, fine reductive notes. Palate: powerful, flavourful, toasty, oaky.

Pamatura Vi de Familia 2011 T
garnacha, cariñena, merlot

85 ♥

BODEGAS MAS ALTA
Ctra. T-702, Km. 16,8
43375 La Vilella Alta (Tarragona)
☎: +34 977 054 151
Fax: +34 977 817 194
www.bodegasmasalta.com
info@bodegasmasalta.com

Artigas 2011 T
93
Colour: cherry, garnet rim. Nose: ripe fruit, spicy, creamy oak, toasty, complex, dark chocolate, earthy notes. Palate: powerful, flavourful, toasty, round tannins.

Artigas 2013 B
92
Colour: bright straw. Nose: fresh, fresh fruit, white flowers, expressive. Palate: flavourful, fruity, good acidity, balanced.

Cirerets 2011 T
94
Colour: cherry, garnet rim. Nose: spicy, toasty, overripe fruit, mineral. Palate: powerful, flavourful, toasty, round tannins.

Els Pics 2012 T
garnacha, cariñena, syrah, cabernet sauvignon

92

Colour: cherry, purple rim. Nose: red berry notes, raspberry, balsamic herbs, spicy, expressive. Palate: powerful, flavourful, spicy, balanced.

La Basseta 2011 T
95
Colour: cherry, garnet rim. Nose: ripe fruit, spicy, creamy oak, complex, dark chocolate, earthy notes. Palate: powerful, flavourful, toasty, round tannins.

BODEGAS VICENTE GANDÍA
Ctra. Cheste a Godelleta, s/n
46370 Chiva (Valencia)
☎: +34 962 524 242
Fax: +34 962 524 243
www.vicentegandia.es
info@vicentegandia.com

Xibrana 2009 T
mazuelo, syrah, garnacha

86

Colour: cherry, garnet rim. Nose: ripe fruit, spicy, creamy oak, toasty. Palate: powerful, flavourful, toasty, round tannins.

BUIL & GINÉ
Ctra. de Gratallops - Vilella Baixa, Km. 11,5
43737 Gratallops (Tarragona)
☎: +34 977 839 810
Fax: +34 977 839 811
www.builgine.com
info@builgine.com

Giné Giné 2012 T
garnacha, cariñena

91

Colour: cherry, garnet rim. Nose: ripe fruit, wild herbs, earthy notes, spicy, creamy oak. Palate: balanced, flavourful, long, balsamic.

Giné Rosat 2013 RD
88
Colour: light cherry. Nose: powerfull, ripe fruit, red berry notes, floral, expressive. Palate: powerful, fruity, fresh.

Joan Giné 2010 T
88
Colour: dark-red cherry. Nose: fine reductive notes, toasty, ripe fruit, balsamic herbs. Palate: spicy, long, toasty, easy to drink.

Joan Giné 2013 B
88
Colour: bright straw. Nose: fresh, fresh fruit, white flowers, expressive. Palate: flavourful, fruity, good acidity, balanced.

Pleret 2007 T
89
Colour: very deep cherry. Nose: ripe fruit, sweet spices, creamy oak, medium intensity, mineral. Palate: fruity, flavourful, toasty.

Pleret Blanc Dolç 2010 B
90
Colour: golden. Nose: powerfull, floral, honeyed notes, candied fruit, fragrant herbs. Palate: flavourful, sweet, fresh, fruity, good acidity, long.

BURGOS PORTA
Finca Mas Sinén, s/n
43202 Poboleda (Tarragona)
☎: +34 696 094 509
www.massinen.com
burgosporta@massinen.com

Mas Sinén Coster 2009 TC
garnacha, cariñena
93 ❦
Colour: cherry, garnet rim. Nose: ripe fruit, wild herbs, earthy notes, spicy, creamy oak, dry stone. Palate: flavourful, long, balsamic, balanced, elegant.

Mas Sinén Negre 2007 T
garnacha, cariñena, cabernet sauvignon, syrah
89 ❦
Colour: deep cherry, garnet rim. Nose: ripe fruit, wild herbs, spicy, creamy oak, fine reductive notes, cigar. Palate: powerful, flavourful, spicy, long.

Mas Sinén Negre 2008 T
garnacha, cariñena, cabernet sauvignon, syrah
91 ❦
Colour: very deep cherry, garnet rim. Nose: powerfull, fine reductive notes, tobacco, dried herbs. Palate: spicy, long, flavourful, fruity.

Petit Mas Sinén 2010 T
garnacha, cariñena, cabernet sauvignon, syrah
89 ❦
Colour: cherry, garnet rim. Nose: ripe fruit, spicy, creamy oak, toasty, earthy notes. Palate: powerful, flavourful, toasty, round tannins.

CASA GRAN DEL SIURANA
Mayor, 3
43738 Bellmunt del Priorat (Tarragona)
☎: +34 932 233 022
Fax: +34 932 231 370
www.castilloperelada.com
perelada@castilloperelada.com

Cruor 2010 T
garnacha, syrah, cabernet sauvignon, cariñena
92
Colour: cherry, garnet rim. Nose: ripe fruit, spicy, creamy oak, toasty, complex, earthy notes, wild herbs. Palate: powerful, flavourful, toasty, round tannins.

GR-174 2013 T
garnacha, cariñena, cabernet sauvignon, syrah
89
Colour: deep cherry, purple rim. Nose: red berry notes, fresh, scrubland. Palate: fruity, balanced, easy to drink.

Gran Cruor 2010 T
93
Colour: cherry, garnet rim. Nose: red berry notes, ripe fruit, spicy, creamy oak, toasty, complex, earthy notes, mineral. Palate: powerful, flavourful, toasty, round tannins, balsamic.

CASTELL D'OR
Mare Rafols, 3- 1ºD
08720 Vilafranca del Penedès (Barcelona)
☎: +34 938 905 385
Fax: +34 938 905 455
www.castelldor.com
castelldor@castelldor.com

Esplugen 2012 T
garnacha, cariñena
89
Colour: bright cherry. Nose: ripe fruit, sweet spices, creamy oak, expressive. Palate: flavourful, fruity, toasty.

CELLER AIXALÀ I ALCAIT
Balandra, 43
43737 Torroja del Priorat (Tarragona)
☎: +34 629 507 807
www.pardelasses.com
pardelasses@gmail.com

Destrankis 2012 T
87
Colour: black cherry. Nose: powerfull, ripe fruit, fruit preserve, toasty, warm. Palate: flavourful, correct, round tannins.

El Coster de L'Alzina 2011 TC
cariñena
89 ❦
Colour: deep cherry. Nose: fine reductive notes, balsamic herbs, cocoa bean. Palate: ripe fruit, flavourful, long, round tannins.

Pardelasses 2011 T
90
Colour: deep cherry, garnet rim. Nose: balsamic herbs, mineral, spicy, complex. Palate: full, round tannins, spicy, long.

CELLER BALAGUER I CABRÉ
La Font, 8
43737 Gratallops
☎: +34 977 839 004
www.cellerbalaguercabre.blogspot.com
vins.jaume@yahoo.com

Cèrcol Daurat 2010 T
garnacha
90
Colour: cherry, garnet rim. Nose: red berry notes, ripe fruit, spicy, creamy oak, toasty, complex, earthy notes. Palate: powerful, flavourful, toasty, round tannins.

La Guinardera 2010 T
garnacha
89
Colour: cherry, garnet rim. Nose: ripe fruit, earthy notes, spicy, creamy oak, balsamic herbs. Palate: balanced, flavourful, long.

Lluna Vella 2010 T
garnacha
88
Colour: cherry, garnet rim. Nose: ripe fruit, spicy, earthy notes. Palate: good structure, flavourful, round tannins.

CELLER BARTOLOMÉ
Major, 23
43738 Bellmunt del Priorat (Tarragona)
☎: +34 977 320 448
www.cellerbartolome.com
cellerbartolome@hotmail.com

Clos Bartolome 2010 T
91
Colour: deep cherry, garnet rim. Nose: balanced, closed, mineral, ripe fruit. Palate: balanced, round tannins, ripe fruit, long.

Primitiu de Bellmunt 2008 T
93
Colour: deep cherry, garnet rim. Nose: expressive, balanced, tobacco, cocoa bean, ripe fruit, mineral. Palate: good structure, flavourful, fruity, full.

Primitiu de Bellmunt 2010 T
90
Colour: cherry, garnet rim. Nose: ripe fruit, spicy, creamy oak, toasty, complex, scrubland. Palate: powerful, flavourful, toasty, round tannins.

CELLER CAL PLA
Prat de la Riba, 1
43739 Porrera (Tarragona)
☎: +34 977 828 125
Fax: +34 977 828 125
www.cellercalpla.com
info@cellercalpla.com

Mas D'en Compte 2010 B
garnacha blanca, xarel.lo, picapoll
85

Planots 2009 TC
garnacha, cariñena
88
Colour: cherry, garnet rim. Nose: ripe fruit, spicy, creamy oak, warm. Palate: powerful, flavourful, toasty, sweet tannins.

CELLER CASTELLET
Font de Dalt, 11
43739 Porrera (Tarragona)
☎: +34 977 828 044
www.cellercastellet.cat
info@cellercastellet.cat

Empit 2011 TC
garnacha, cabernet sauvignon, cariñena
89
Colour: bright cherry. Nose: ripe fruit, sweet spices, creamy oak, balsamic herbs, dry stone. Palate: flavourful, fruity, toasty, round tannins, balanced.

Empit Selecció 2011 TC
91
Colour: cherry, garnet rim. Nose: ripe fruit, spicy, creamy oak, toasty, complex, cocoa bean, mineral. Palate: powerful, flavourful, toasty, round tannins.

Ferral 2011 T
garnacha, cabernet sauvignon, syrah, merlot
88
Colour: cherry, garnet rim. Nose: ripe fruit, wild herbs, earthy notes, spicy, creamy oak, mineral. Palate: flavourful, long, balsamic.

CELLER CECILIO

Piró, 28
43737 Gratallops (Tarragona)
☎: +34 977 839 181
Fax: +34 977 839 507
www.cellercecilio.com
celler@cellercecilio.com

Celler Cecilio Negre 2011 T
garnacha, cariñena, syrah, cabernet sauvignon
85

L'Espill 2010 TC
garnacha, cariñena, cabernet sauvignon
87
Colour: very deep cherry, garnet rim. Nose: powerfull, ripe fruit, roasted coffee, aromatic coffee. Palate: powerful, toasty, roasted-coffee aftertaste.

L'Udol 2013 B
garnacha
87
Colour: bright straw. Nose: white flowers, fragrant herbs, fruit expression. Palate: fresh, fruity, flavourful, balanced, elegant.

CELLER DE L'ABADÍA

Font, 38
43737 Gratallops (Tarragona)
☎: +34 627 032 134
www.cellerabadia.com
jeroni@cellerabadia.com

Alice 2008 TR
garnacha, cariñena, syrah, cabernet sauvignon
89 🌷
Colour: cherry, garnet rim. Nose: ripe fruit, spicy, toasty. Palate: powerful, flavourful, toasty.

Clos Clara 2008 TGR
garnacha, cariñena, syrah, cabernet sauvignon
88 🌷
Colour: pale ruby, brick rim edge. Nose: elegant, spicy, fine reductive notes, wet leather, aged wood nuances, fruit liqueur notes. Palate: spicy, fine tannins, elegant, long.

Sant Jeroni "Garnatxa de L'Hort 2013 T
garnacha, syrah
87 🌷
Colour: cherry, purple rim. Nose: ripe fruit, fruit preserve, grassy, floral. Palate: fresh, fruity, flavourful.

Sant Jeroni Blanc 2013 B
pedro ximénez, garnacha blanca
86 🌷
Colour: bright straw. Nose: fragrant herbs, fresh fruit, wild herbs. Palate: flavourful, balanced, easy to drink, fruity.

Sant Jeroni Dolç 2010 TGR
cariñena, cabernet sauvignon
87
Colour: cherry, garnet rim. Nose: ripe fruit, wild herbs, spicy, varnish, aged wood nuances. Palate: balanced, flavourful, long, balsamic, spicy.

Sant Jeroni Negre 2009 TC
garnacha, syrah, cariñena
90
Colour: cherry, garnet rim. Nose: ripe fruit, wild herbs, creamy oak, cocoa bean. Palate: balanced, flavourful, long, balsamic.

CELLER DE L'ENCASTELL

Castell, 7
43739 Porrera (Tarragona)
☎: +34 630 941 959
www.roquers.com
roquers@roquers.com

Marge 2012 T
89
Colour: bright cherry. Nose: ripe fruit, sweet spices, creamy oak, medium intensity. Palate: fruity, flavourful, toasty.

Roquers de Porrera 2011 TR
91
Colour: bright cherry. Nose: ripe fruit, sweet spices, creamy oak, medium intensity, dried herbs. Palate: fruity, flavourful, toasty.

CELLER DEVINSSI

De les Valls, 14
43737 Gratallops (Tarragona)
☎: +34 977 839 523
www.devinssi.com
devinssi@il-lia.com

Cupatge Devinssi 2013 T
garnacha, cariñena
89
Colour: deep cherry, purple rim. Nose: wild herbs, fresh fruit, medium intensity, grassy. Palate: correct, fruity.

Il.lia 2011 T
cariñena, garnacha, cabernet sauvignon
90
Colour: deep cherry. Nose: ripe fruit, wild herbs, earthy notes, spicy, creamy oak, mineral. Palate: balanced, flavourful, long, balsamic.

Mas de les Valls 2011 B
pedro ximénez, garnacha blanca
86
Colour: bright golden. Nose: ripe fruit, dry nuts, powerfull, toasty, aged wood nuances. Palate: flavourful, fruity, spicy, toasty, long, roasted-coffee aftertaste.

Mas de les Valls 2011 TC
garnacha, cariñena, cabernet sauvignon

87

Colour: bright cherry. Nose: ripe fruit, sweet spices, creamy oak, balsamic herbs. Palate: fruity, flavourful, toasty.

Rocapoll 2010 TC
100% cariñena

91

Colour: cherry, garnet rim. Nose: red berry notes, ripe fruit, spicy, toasty, complex, earthy notes. Palate: powerful, flavourful, toasty, balsamic, long, balanced.

CELLER ESCODA PALLEJÀ
La Font, 16
43737 Torroja del Priorat (Tarragona)
☎: +34 977 839 200
rescoda@hotmail.com

Palet 2012 T
garnacha, cariñena, cabernet sauvignon, syrah

89

Colour: deep cherry, purple rim. Nose: ripe fruit, balsamic herbs, cocoa bean. Palate: flavourful, fruity, good acidity, round tannins.

Palet Most de Flor 2012 T
garnacha, cariñena, cabernet sauvignon, syrah

91

Colour: bright cherry. Nose: ripe fruit, sweet spices, creamy oak, expressive, balsamic herbs, cocoa bean. Palate: flavourful, fruity, toasty, round tannins.

CELLER HIDALGO ALBERT
Poligono 14, Parcela 102
43141 Poboleda (Tarragona)
☎: +34 977 842 064
Fax: +34 977 842 064
www.cellerhidalgoalbert.es
hialmi@yahoo.es

1270 a Vuit 2008 T
garnacha, syrah, cabernet sauvignon, cariñena

91

Colour: ruby red. Nose: elegant, spicy, fine reductive notes, wet leather, aged wood nuances, fruit liqueur notes. Palate: spicy, fine tannins, elegant, long.

1270 a Vuit 2009 T
garnacha, syrah, cabernet sauvignon, cariñena

90

Colour: cherry, garnet rim. Nose: red berry notes, ripe fruit, spicy, creamy oak, complex, earthy notes. Palate: powerful, flavourful, toasty, round tannins.

Fina 2010 TR
garnacha, syrah, cabernet sauvignon, merlot

90

Colour: cherry, garnet rim. Nose: ripe fruit, earthy notes, spicy, creamy oak, balsamic herbs. Palate: flavourful, long, spicy, balanced.

CELLER JOAN SIMÓ
11 de Setembre, 5-7
43739 Porrera (Tarragona)
☎: +34 627 563 713
Fax: +34 977 830 993
www.cellerjoansimo.com
leseres@cellerjoansimo.com

Les Eres 2010 T

93

Colour: deep cherry, garnet rim. Nose: expressive, balanced, complex, balsamic herbs, cocoa bean. Palate: flavourful, balanced, round tannins, spicy, balsamic.

Les Eres Especial dels Carners 2010 T

93

Colour: cherry, garnet rim. Nose: balanced, complex, ripe fruit, spicy, mineral. Palate: good structure, flavourful, round tannins, mineral, elegant.

Sentius 2010 T

89

Colour: cherry, garnet rim. Nose: ripe fruit, wild herbs, earthy notes, spicy, creamy oak. Palate: balanced, flavourful, long, balsamic.

CELLER JORDI DOMENECH
Finca Les Comes
43376 Poboleda (Tarragona)
☎: +34 646 169 210
www.cellerjordidomenech.com
jordidomenech@live.com

Clos Penat 2010 TC
garnacha, syrah

89

Colour: cherry, garnet rim. Nose: ripe fruit, spicy, creamy oak, toasty, scrubland, fine reductive notes. Palate: powerful, flavourful, toasty.

Petit Clos Penat 2011 T
garnacha, syrah

88

Colour: cherry, garnet rim. Nose: ripe fruit, spicy, creamy oak, toasty, complex, earthy notes. Palate: powerful, flavourful, toasty, round tannins, concentrated.

CELLER L'INFERNAL

Del Pont, 9
43739 Porrera (Tarragona)
☎: +34 977 828 057
Fax: +34 977 828 380
contact@linfernal.es

L'Infernal Aguilera 2008 TC
100% cariñena

91

Colour: deep cherry, garnet rim. Nose: spicy, fine reductive notes, wet leather, toasty. Palate: spicy, long, toasty, reductive nuances.

L'Infernal El Casot 2012 T
100% garnacha

91

Colour: cherry, garnet rim. Nose: mineral, wild herbs, balanced, fruit liqueur notes. Palate: flavourful, good structure, spicy, easy to drink.

L'Infernal Face Nord 2012 T
100% syrah

90

Colour: dark-red cherry, purple rim. Nose: creamy oak, toasty, spicy, ripe fruit. Palate: good structure, flavourful, round tannins.

L'Infernal Fons Clar 2012 T
100% cariñena

92

Colour: deep cherry, garnet rim. Nose: grassy, balanced, ripe fruit, mineral. Palate: flavourful, balanced, long, good acidity.

Riu by Trío Infernal 2011 T
garnacha, cariñena, syrah

90

Colour: cherry, garnet rim. Nose: ripe fruit, scrubland, spicy, creamy oak, balanced. Palate: powerful, flavourful, spicy, long.

CELLER MAS BASTE

Font, 38
43737 Gratallops (Tarragona)
☎: +34 622 060 136
www.cellermasbaste.com
info@cellermasbaste.com

Clos Peites 2008 T
cariñena, syrah, cabernet sauvignon

91 🍃

Colour: cherry, garnet rim. Nose: balanced, complex, ripe fruit, spicy, fine reductive notes, balsamic herbs. Palate: good structure, flavourful, round tannins.

Peites 2010 TC
cariñena, syrah, cabernet sauvignon

89 🍃

Colour: cherry, garnet rim. Nose: ripe fruit, spicy, creamy oak, toasty, balsamic herbs. Palate: powerful, flavourful, toasty, balanced.

Peites 2012 T
garnacha, syrah

90 🍃

Colour: cherry, garnet rim. Nose: ripe fruit, wild herbs, earthy notes, spicy, creamy oak. Palate: balanced, flavourful, long, balsamic.

CELLER MAS DE LES PERERES

Mas de Les Pereres, s/n
43376 Poboleda (Tarragona)
☎: +34 977 827 257
Fax: +34 977 827 257
www.nunci.com
dirk@nunci.com

Nunci Abocat 2011 B
macabeo, garnacha, moscatel de alejandría, moscatel grano menudo

88

Colour: bright yellow. Nose: white flowers, balanced, ripe fruit. Palate: correct, balanced, flavourful.

Nunci Abocat 2012 B
macabeo, pedro ximénez, moscatel de alejandría, moscatel grano menudo

90

Colour: bright straw. Nose: faded flowers, dried herbs, spicy, dry stone. Palate: flavourful, fresh, fruity, balsamic.

Nunci Blanc 2010 BFB
garnacha, macabeo

92

Colour: bright yellow.

Nunci Blanc 2011 BFB
garnacha, macabeo

91

Colour: bright yellow. Nose: powerfull, ripe fruit, sweet spices, creamy oak, fragrant herbs. Palate: rich, smoky aftertaste, flavourful, fresh, good acidity.

Nunci Costero 2006 T
mazuelo, grenache, merlot

90

Colour: cherry, garnet rim. Nose: ripe fruit, wild herbs, spicy, creamy oak, fine reductive notes. Palate: flavourful, long, balsamic.

Nunci Costero 2007 T
mazuelo, grenache, merlot

89

Colour: deep cherry. Nose: ripe fruit, spicy, toasty, complex, cocoa bean. Palate: powerful, flavourful, toasty, round tannins, balsamic.

Nunci Negre 2007 T
syrah, grenache, merlot, cabernet franc

89

Colour: deep cherry, garnet rim. Nose: spicy, tobacco, balsamic herbs, balanced. Palate: flavourful, ripe fruit, long.

to Spanish Wine

Nunci Negre 2008 T

syrah, grenache, cabernet franc, mazuelo

90

Colour: bright cherry, garnet rim. Nose: ripe fruit, balanced, cocoa bean, expressive. Palate: fruity, round tannins.

Nuncito 2009 T Barrica

grenache, cabernet franc, syrah, mazuelo

91

Colour: bright cherry, garnet rim. Nose: ripe fruit, sweet spices, creamy oak, expressive, balsamic herbs, mineral. Palate: flavourful, fruity, toasty, round tannins, spirituous.

Nuncito 2010 T Barrica

syrah, grenache, mazuelo, cabernet franc

91

Colour: deep cherry, garnet rim. Nose: expressive, balanced, ripe fruit, spicy, fresh. Palate: correct, easy to drink.

Nunsweet 2011 Tinto dulce

merlot, grenache, syrah

89

Colour: cherry, garnet rim. Nose: red berry notes, fruit preserve, wild herbs, balsamic notes, toasty, sweet spices. Palate: long, balanced, flavourful, spirituous.

CELLER MAS DOIX

Carme, 115
43376 Poboleda (Tarragona)
☎: +34 639 356 172
www.masdoix.com
info@masdoix.com

1902 Cariñena Centenaria 2009 T

cariñena

96

Colour: very deep cherry. Nose: expressive, characterful, mineral, earthy notes. Palate: flavourful, powerful, fine bitter notes, good acidity, round.

Doix 2010 TC

95

Colour: cherry, garnet rim. Nose: ripe fruit, spicy, creamy oak, toasty, complex, dark chocolate, earthy notes. Palate: powerful, flavourful, toasty, round tannins.

Les Crestes 2012 T

92

Colour: cherry, purple rim. Nose: expressive, fresh fruit, red berry notes. Palate: flavourful, fruity, good acidity, round tannins.

Salanques 2011 T

93

Colour: deep cherry, garnet rim. Nose: ripe fruit, wild herbs, spicy, creamy oak, dry stone. Palate: balanced, flavourful, long, balsamic.

CELLER MAS GARRIAN

Camí Rieres, s/n Mas del Camperol
43736 El Molar (Tarragona)
☎: +34 977 262 118
Fax: +34 977 262 118
www.masgarrian.com
masgarrian@gmail.com

Clos Severi 2005 T

cabernet sauvignon, syrah

89

Colour: pale ruby, brick rim edge. Nose: elegant, spicy, fine reductive notes, wet leather, aged wood nuances, fruit liqueur notes. Palate: spicy, fine tannins, long, correct.

Mas del Camperol 2003 T

cabernet sauvignon, syrah

87

Colour: deep cherry, orangey edge. Nose: waxy notes, tobacco, ripe fruit, spicy, aged wood nuances. Palate: fine bitter notes, flavourful, spirituous.

CELLER PAHÍ

Carrer del Carme, 57
43376 Poboleda (Tarragona)
☎: +34 977 762 042
www.celler-pahi.com
ramon@cellerpahi.com

Gaubança 2013 B

86

Colour: bright straw. Nose: dried flowers, fresh fruit, fragrant herbs. Palate: fruity, good acidity, correct, easy to drink.

Gaubança 2013 RD

87

Colour: rose, purple rim. Nose: powerfull, ripe fruit, red berry notes, floral. Palate: powerful, fruity, fresh.

Gaubança 2013 T

87

Colour: bright cherry. Nose: ripe fruit, sweet spices, expressive. Palate: flavourful, fruity, toasty, round tannins.

CELLER PASANAU

La Bassa, s/n
43361 La Morera de Montsant
(Tarragona)
☎: +34 977 827 202
Fax: +34 977 827 202
www.cellerpasanau.com
informacion@cellerpasanau.com

Pasanau Ceps Nous 2011 T

garnacha, syrah

86

Colour: cherry, garnet rim. Nose: fruit preserve, scrubland, floral. Palate: correct, flavourful, concentrated.

Pasanau Dànae 2013 B
viognier, pedro ximénez, otras

87

Colour: golden. Nose: powerfull, floral, honeyed notes, candied fruit, fragrant herbs. Palate: flavourful, sweet, fresh, fruity, good acidity, long, sweetness.

Pasanau Finca La Planeta 2008 T
cabernet sauvignon, garnacha

92

Colour: cherry, garnet rim. Nose: balanced, complex, ripe fruit, spicy, scrubland. Palate: good structure, flavourful, round tannins.

Ten Nezasu Dulce Natural 2011 T
garnacha

86

Colour: deep cherry. Nose: powerfull, warm, fruit preserve, scrubland, fruit liqueur notes. Palate: fruity, sweet, correct.

CELLER PRIOR PONS
Rei, 4
43375 La Vilella Alta (Tarragona)
☎: +34 606 547 865
www.priorpons.com
info@priorpons.com

Planets de Prior Pons 2011 T
89

Colour: cherry, garnet rim. Nose: ripe fruit, fruit preserve, balsamic herbs, spicy, creamy oak. Palate: powerful, flavourful, spicy, long.

Prior Pons 2011 T
92

Colour: cherry, garnet rim. Nose: ripe fruit, spicy, creamy oak, toasty, dry stone. Palate: powerful, flavourful, toasty, round tannins, balanced.

CELLER SABATÉ
Nou, 6
43374 La Vilella Baixa (Tarragona)
☎: +34 977 839 209
www.cellersabate.com
cellersabate@cellersabate.com

Mas Plantadeta 2009 TC
89

Colour: cherry, garnet rim. Nose: ripe fruit, spicy, toasty, scrubland. Palate: powerful, flavourful, toasty, round tannins.

Mas Plantadeta 2011 T Roble
garnacha

87

Colour: bright cherry. Nose: ripe fruit, sweet spices, creamy oak. Palate: flavourful, fruity, toasty.

Mas Plantadeta 2013 BFB
garnacha blanca, moscatel

88

Colour: yellow. Nose: ripe fruit, white flowers, expressive, powerfull. Palate: spicy, fruity, balanced, fine bitter notes.

Mas Plantadeta Solera
35 años Rancio Solera
garnacha

93

Colour: light mahogany. Nose: powerfull, complex, elegant, dry nuts, toasty, acetaldehyde, spicy. Palate: rich, fine bitter notes, fine solera notes, long, spicy, balanced.

Pètals de Garnatxa 2013 RD
garnacha

88

Colour: onion pink. Nose: elegant, candied fruit, dried flowers, fragrant herbs, red berry notes. Palate: light-bodied, flavourful, good acidity, long, spicy.

CELLER VALL-LLACH
Pont, 9
43739 Porrera (Tarragona)
☎: +34 977 828 244
Fax: +34 977 828 325
www.vallllach.com
celler@vallllach.com

Embruix de Vall-Llach 2012 T
92

Colour: deep cherry, garnet rim. Nose: balanced, cocoa bean, ripe fruit, balsamic herbs. Palate: flavourful, good structure, round tannins.

Idus de Vall-Llach 2012 T
91

Colour: very deep cherry, garnet rim. Nose: expressive, balanced, scrubland, ripe fruit, cocoa bean. Palate: flavourful, round tannins, spicy.

Porrera Vi de Vila de Vall Llach 2012 TC
93

Colour: cherry, garnet rim. Nose: ripe fruit, wild herbs, earthy notes, spicy, creamy oak, expressive, mineral. Palate: balanced, flavourful, long, balsamic.

Vall Llach vi de Finca Qualificada
Mas de la Rosa 2012 TC
93

Colour: cherry, garnet rim. Nose: ripe fruit, spicy, creamy oak, toasty, complex, earthy notes, cocoa bean. Palate: powerful, flavourful, toasty, round tannins.

CELLERS DE SCALA DEI

Rambla de la Cartoixa, s/n
43379 Scala Dei (Tarragona)
☎: +34 977 827 027
Fax: +34 977 827 044
www.grupocodorniu.com
codinfo@codorniu.es

Artigots de Scala Dei 2010 T
100% garnacha

93

Colour: cherry, garnet rim. Nose: ripe fruit, fruit liqueur notes, scrubland, earthy notes, spicy, creamy oak. Palate: powerful, flavourful, spicy, balanced.

La Creueta de Scala Dei 2010 T
garnacha

93

Colour: cherry, purple rim. Nose: red berry notes, ripe fruit, balsamic herbs, mineral, creamy oak, sweet spices. Palate: powerful, flavourful, mineral, balanced, round.

Masdeu de Scala Dei 2011 T
100% garnacha

94

Colour: cherry, garnet rim. Nose: ripe fruit, fruit liqueur notes, balsamic herbs, scrubland, earthy notes. Palate: powerful, flavourful, spicy, long.

Scala Dei Cartoixa 2007 TR

90

Colour: cherry, garnet rim. Nose: ripe fruit, wild herbs, spicy, creamy oak, mineral, tobacco. Palate: balanced, flavourful, long, balsamic.

Scala Dei Negre 2012 T

87

Colour: very deep cherry. Nose: powerfull, characterful, ripe fruit, mineral, grassy. Palate: flavourful, green, spicy.

Scala Dei Prior 2012 TC

91

Colour: cherry, garnet rim. Nose: ripe fruit, wild herbs, earthy notes, spicy, creamy oak. Palate: balanced, flavourful, long, balsamic.

St. Antoni de Scala Dei 2010 T
100% garnacha

95

Colour: cherry, garnet rim. Nose: ripe fruit, wild herbs, balsamic herbs, mineral, dry stone, creamy oak, spicy. Palate: spicy, balsamic, balanced, elegant.

CELLERS UNIÓ

Joan Oliver, 16-24
43206 Reus (Tarragona)
☎: +34 977 330 055
Fax: +34 977 330 070
www.cellersunio.com
info@cellersunio.com

Roureda Llicorella Blanc Pedro Ximénez 2012 B
pedro ximénez

89

Colour: bright yellow. Nose: spicy, toasty, dried flowers, ripe fruit. Palate: flavourful, fine bitter notes, correct.

Roureda Llicorella Classic 2010 T
garnacha, mazuelo, merlot

90

Colour: cherry, garnet rim. Nose: ripe fruit, wild herbs, earthy notes, spicy, creamy oak, fine reductive notes. Palate: balanced, flavourful, long, balsamic.

Roureda Llicorella Vitis 60 2009 T
garnacha, mazuelo, cabernet sauvignon, syrah

89

Colour: dark-red cherry, garnet rim. Nose: toasty, cocoa bean, ripe fruit, smoky. Palate: good structure, round tannins, spicy.

Tendral Selección 2011 T
mazuelo, garnacha

88

Colour: bright cherry. Nose: ripe fruit, sweet spices, creamy oak, medium intensity. Palate: fruity, flavourful, toasty.

CLOS 93

Nou, 26
43737 El Lloar (Tarragona)
☎: +34 620 215 770
www.clos93.com
clos93@clos93.com

L'Interrogant 2012 T

91

Colour: cherry, garnet rim. Nose: ripe fruit, wild herbs, earthy notes, spicy, creamy oak. Palate: balanced, flavourful, long, balsamic.

CLOS DE L'OBAC

Camí Manyetes, s/n
43737 Gratallops (Tarragona)
☎: +34 977 839 276
Fax: +34 977 839 371
www.obac.es
info@obac.es

Clos de L'Obac 2010 TC
garnacha, cariñena, cabernet sauvignon, merlot

93

Colour: bright cherry. Nose: ripe fruit, wild herbs, spicy, creamy oak, mineral. Palate: balanced, flavourful, long, balsamic.

Kyrie 2010 BC
garnacha blanca, macabeo, xarel.lo, moscatel de alejandría

90

Colour: bright golden. Nose: ripe fruit, dry nuts, powerfull, toasty, aged wood nuances. Palate: flavourful, fruity, spicy, toasty, long.

Miserere 2010 TC
garnacha, cariñena, tempranillo, merlot

93

Colour: very deep cherry, garnet rim. Nose: expressive, complex, mineral, balsamic herbs, balanced. Palate: full, flavourful, round tannins.

CLOS DEL PORTAL
Pista del Lloar a Bellmunt
43376 Vila del Lloar (Tarragona)
☎: +34 932 531 760
Fax: +34 934 173 591
www.portaldelpriorat.com
info@portaldelpriorat.com

Gotes Blanques 2013 B
garnacha blanca

91

Colour: bright straw. Nose: fresh, fresh fruit, white flowers, expressive. Palate: flavourful, fruity, good acidity, balanced, full.

Gotes del Priorat 2013 T
garnacha, cariñena

89

Colour: cherry, garnet rim. Nose: ripe fruit, fruit liqueur notes, wild herbs, mineral, spicy. Palate: powerful, flavourful, fruity, balsamic.

Gotes del Priorat Magnum 2012 T
garnacha, cariñena

91

Colour: bright cherry, garnet rim. Nose: ripe fruit, sweet spices, creamy oak, mineral. Palate: flavourful, fruity, toasty, round tannins.

Negre de Negres 2012 T
garnacha, cariñena, syrah, cabernet sauvignon

93 🌷

Colour: cherry, garnet rim. Nose: dry stone, balsamic herbs, red berry notes, ripe fruit, creamy oak. Palate: balanced, flavourful, long, balsamic, concentrated, elegant.

Negre de Negres Magnum 2011 T
garnacha, cariñena, syrah, cabernet sauvignon

94

Colour: cherry, garnet rim. Nose: spicy, creamy oak, toasty, dry stone, red berry notes, fruit liqueur notes. Palate: powerful, flavourful, toasty, round tannins, balanced.

Somni 2012 T
cariñena, syrah

93 🌷

Colour: cherry, garnet rim. Nose: red berry notes, violets, fragrant herbs, dry stone, expressive, balanced. Palate: elegant, fresh, fruity, flavourful, balsamic, balanced.

Somni Magnum 2011 T
cariñena, syrah

95

Colour: cherry, garnet rim. Nose: red berry notes, ripe fruit, violets, dry stone, fragrant herbs, expressive, balanced, creamy oak. Palate: spicy, long, balsamic, mineral, round, elegant.

Tros de Clos 2012 T
cariñena

91 🌷

Colour: cherry, garnet rim. Nose: ripe fruit, dry stone, fragrant herbs, spicy. Palate: balanced, flavourful, spicy, balsamic, elegant.

Tros de Clos Magnum 2010 T
cariñena

95

Colour: cherry, garnet rim. Nose: red berry notes, ripe fruit, spicy, creamy oak, toasty, complex, mineral, wild herbs. Palate: powerful, flavourful, toasty, balanced, fine tannins.

Tros de Clos Magnum 2011 T
cariñena

93

Colour: very deep cherry, garnet rim. Nose: floral, mineral, red berry notes, fruit liqueur notes, creamy oak, expressive. Palate: fresh, fruity, flavourful, balanced, elegant.

CLOS FIGUERAS
Carrer La Font, 38
43737 Gratallops (Tarragona)
☎: +34 627 471 732
Fax: +34 977 830 422
www.desfigueras.com
info@closfigueras.com

Clos Figueres 2010 T
garnacha, cariñena, cabernet sauvignon, syrah

90 🌷

Colour: deep cherry. Nose: ripe fruit, dried herbs, tobacco, spicy. Palate: balanced, round tannins, flavourful.

Font de la Figuera 2011 T
garnacha, cariñena, cabernet sauvignon, syrah

88 🌷

Colour: cherry, garnet rim. Nose: fruit preserve, spicy, powerfull. Palate: flavourful, pruney, balsamic, round tannins.

Font de la Figuera 2013 B
viognier, garnacha blanca, chenin blanc

88 🌷

Colour: yellow, pale. Nose: fragrant herbs, faded flowers, balanced, spicy. Palate: flavourful, easy to drink, good finish.

Serras del Priorat 2013 T
garnacha, cariñena, cabernet sauvignon, syrah

90

Colour: cherry, purple rim. Nose: expressive, fresh fruit, red berry notes, floral, mineral, balsamic herbs. Palate: flavourful, fruity, good acidity, round tannins.

Sweet Clos Figueras Dulce 2012 T
garnacha

87

Colour: cherry, garnet rim. Nose: fruit preserve, ripe fruit, spicy, toasty. Palate: powerful, flavourful, sweetness.

CLOS GALENA
Camino de la Solana, s/n
43736 El Molar (Tarragona)
☎: +34 619 790 956
www.closgalena.com
info@closgalena.com

Clos Galena 2010 TC

93

Colour: cherry, garnet rim. Nose: ripe fruit, spicy, creamy oak, toasty, complex, cocoa bean, mineral. Palate: powerful, flavourful, toasty, round tannins, good structure.

Crossos 2011 T

87

Colour: deep cherry. Nose: ripe fruit, medium intensity, tobacco. Palate: flavourful, good structure, round tannins.

Formiga 2012 T

90

Colour: cherry, purple rim. Nose: expressive, fresh fruit, red berry notes, floral, spicy. Palate: flavourful, fruity, good acidity, round tannins.

Galena 2010 T

91

Colour: cherry, garnet rim. Nose: red berry notes, ripe fruit, spicy, creamy oak, toasty, complex, earthy notes. Palate: powerful, flavourful, toasty, round tannins.

CLOS I TERRASSES
La Font, 1
43737 Gratallops (Tarragona)
☎: +34 977 839 022
Fax: +34 977 839 179
info@closerasmus.com

Laurel 2012 T

92

Colour: cherry, garnet rim. Nose: ripe fruit, wild herbs, earthy notes, spicy, creamy oak. Palate: balanced, flavourful, long, balsamic.

Clos Erasmus 2012 T Barrica

95

Colour: deep cherry. Nose: ripe fruit, sweet spices, toasty, mineral. Palate: ripe fruit, spicy, long, round tannins.

CLOS MOGADOR
Camí Manyetes, s/n
43737 Gratallops (Tarragona)
☎: +34 977 839 171
Fax: +34 977 839 426
closmogador@closmogador.com

Clos Mogador 2011 T

95

Colour: cherry, garnet rim. Nose: ripe fruit, spicy, toasty, complex, earthy notes, mineral. Palate: powerful, flavourful, toasty, round tannins, spicy, balsamic, elegant.

Manyetes 2011 T

93

Colour: very deep cherry, garnet rim. Nose: balanced, expressive, sweet spices, cocoa bean, scrubland. Palate: flavourful, round tannins.

Nelin 2012 B

90

Colour: yellow, pale. Nose: mineral, faded flowers, dry nuts, complex. Palate: correct, long, flavourful, balanced.

COSTERS DEL PRIORAT
Finca Sant Martí
43738 Bellmunt del Priorat (Tarragona)
☎: +34 610 203 473
www.costersdelpriorat.com
info@costersdelpriorat.com

Blanc de Pissarres 2013 B
100% macabeo

90

Colour: bright yellow. Nose: powerfull, ripe fruit, sweet spices, fragrant herbs, mineral. Palate: rich, fresh, good acidity.

Clos Cypres 2012 T
100% cariñena

90

Colour: deep cherry, purple rim. Nose: spicy, ripe fruit, toasty, mineral. Palate: flavourful, round tannins, long.

Elios 2012 T

90

Colour: cherry, garnet rim. Nose: ripe fruit, spicy, creamy oak, toasty, complex, balsamic herbs. Palate: flavourful, toasty, round tannins.

Pissarres 2012 T

92

Colour: very deep cherry. Nose: spicy, toasty, ripe fruit, wild herbs. Palate: balanced, flavourful, easy to drink.

DE MULLER
Camí Pedra Estela, 34
43205 Reus (Tarragona)
☎: +34 977 757 473
Fax: +34 977 771 129
www.demuller.es
lab@demuller.es

Dom Joan Fort 1865 Rancio
garnacha, garnacha blanca
95
Colour: old gold, amber rim. Nose: balanced, expressive, candied fruit, varnish, acetaldehyde, powerfull. Palate: balanced, spicy, long.

Les Pusses De Muller 2011 TC
merlot, syrah
89
Colour: cherry, garnet rim. Nose: ripe fruit, spicy, creamy oak, toasty, fine reductive notes. Palate: powerful, flavourful, toasty.

Lo Cabaló 2008 TR
garnacha, merlot, syrah, mazuelo
89
Colour: ruby red. Nose: ripe fruit, spicy, creamy oak, toasty, complex, fine reductive notes. Palate: powerful, flavourful, toasty, round tannins.

Priorat Legitim 2011 TC
garnacha, merlot, syrah, mazuelo
86
Colour: cherry, garnet rim. Nose: powerfull, scrubland, toasty, spicy. Palate: correct, flavourful.

EDICIONES I-LIMITADAS
Claravall, 2
8021 (Barcelona)
☎: +34 932 531 760
Fax: +34 934 173 591
www.edicionesi-limitadas.com
info@edicionesi-limitadas.com

Flors 2012 T
cariñena, garnacha, syrah
89
Colour: dark-red cherry, purple rim. Nose: powerfull, ripe fruit, dried herbs. Palate: correct, round tannins, spicy, balsamic.

ELVIWINES
Finca Clos Mesorah, Ctra. T-300
43775 Falset-Marça (Tarragona)
☎: +34 618 792 963
www.elviwines.com
victor@elviwines.com

EI26 2010 TR
91
Colour: black cherry, garnet rim. Nose: ripe fruit, fruit preserve, powerfull, sweet spices. Palate: flavourful, balanced, long, full.

EMW GRANDES VINOS DE ESPAÑA
Sánchez Picazo, 53
30332 Balsapintada (Fuente Alamo) (Murcia)
☎: +34 968 151 520
Fax: +34 968 151 539
www.emw.es
info@emw.es

Maquinon 2013 T
100% garnacha
90
Colour: cherry, garnet rim. Nose: ripe fruit, wild herbs, earthy notes, spicy, creamy oak. Palate: balanced, flavourful, long, balsamic.

FAMILIA NIN ORTIZ
Finca Planetes, Pol Partida Masis Parcela 288
Falset (Tarragona)
☎: +34 686 467 579
fnovins.blogspot.com.es
carlesov@gmail.com

Nit de Nin 2011 T
94
Colour: deep cherry, purple rim. Nose: closed, complex, wild herbs, spicy. Palate: full, fruity, fine tannins, good acidity, complex, round.

Planetes de Nin 2011 T
91
Colour: bright cherry. Nose: expressive, wild herbs, spicy, ripe fruit. Palate: flavourful, spicy, round tannins, elegant, long.

FERRER BOBET
Ctra. Falset a Porrera, Km. 6,5
43730 Falset (Tarragona)
☎: +34 609 945 532
Fax: +34 935 044 265
www.ferrerbobet.com
eguerre@ferrerbobet.com

Ferrer Bobet Selecció Especial Vinyes Velles 2011 T
100% cariñena
94
Colour: cherry, garnet rim. Nose: ripe fruit, spicy, creamy oak, toasty, complex, cocoa bean, mineral. Palate: powerful, flavourful, toasty, round tannins.

Ferrer Bobet Vinyes Velles 2012 T
93
Colour: very deep cherry, garnet rim. Nose: powerfull, ripe fruit, roasted coffee, dark chocolate, aromatic coffee. Palate: powerful, toasty, balanced.

FINCA TOBELLA

Les Aubagues
43737 Gratallops (Tarragona)
☎: +34 977 684 403
Fax: +34 977 684 403
www.fincatobella.com
info@fincatobella.com

Finca Tobella 2012 T
88
Colour: cherry, garnet rim. Nose: ripe fruit, wild herbs, earthy notes, spicy, creamy oak. Palate: balanced, flavourful, long, balsamic.

Finca Tobella Selecció Especial 2008 T
91
Colour: cherry, garnet rim. Nose: ripe fruit, wild herbs, earthy notes, creamy oak. Palate: balanced, flavourful, long, balsamic.

GENIUM CELLER

Nou, 92- Bajos
43376 Poboleda (Tarragona)
☎: +34 977 827 146
Fax: +34 977 827 146
www.geniumceller.com
genium@geniumceller.com

Genium Celler 2009 TC
88
Colour: cherry, garnet rim. Nose: ripe fruit, spicy, creamy oak, toasty, cigar, wet leather. Palate: powerful, flavourful, toasty.

Genium Costers Vinyes Velles 2009 T
87
Colour: cherry, garnet rim. Nose: ripe fruit, wild herbs, spicy, creamy oak, warm. Palate: balanced, flavourful, long, balsamic.

Genium Ecològic 2009 TC
89 🌱
Colour: black cherry. Nose: wild herbs, ripe fruit, mineral, balanced, warm. Palate: flavourful, good structure, long.

Genium Rosat 2013 RD
100% merlot
82 🌱

Genium Ximenis 2012 BFB
88
Colour: bright yellow. Nose: fresh, fresh fruit, white flowers, mineral. Palate: flavourful, fruity, good acidity, balanced.

Poboleda Vi de Vila 2009 TR
89
Colour: cherry, garnet rim. Nose: ripe fruit, wild herbs, earthy notes, spicy. Palate: balanced, flavourful, long, balsamic.

GRAN CLOS

Montsant, 2
43738 Bellmunt del Priorat (Tarragona)
☎: +34 977 830 675
www.granclos.com
info@granclos.com

Cartus 2006 T
93
Colour: ruby red. Nose: ripe fruit, fruit liqueur notes, wild herbs, balsamic herbs, mineral, spicy, creamy oak. Palate: balanced, flavourful, spicy, long, elegant.

Finca El Puig 2010 T
garnacha, syrah, cabernet sauvignon
89
Colour: cherry, garnet rim. Nose: ripe fruit, spicy, creamy oak, toasty, earthy notes. Palate: powerful, flavourful, toasty.

Gran Clos 2007 T
garnacha, cariñena, cabernet sauvignon
92
Colour: very deep cherry, garnet rim. Nose: fine reductive notes, ripe fruit, dried herbs, spicy, cocoa bean, mineral. Palate: flavourful, round tannins, good acidity.

Gran Clos 2011 BFB
garnacha blanca, macabeo
90
Colour: bright golden. Nose: ripe fruit, dried herbs, faded flowers, spicy, creamy oak. Palate: rich, flavourful, spicy, long, balsamic, balanced.

Les Mines 2011 T
garnacha, cariñena, merlot
87
Colour: bright cherry, garnet rim. Nose: ripe fruit, sweet spices, creamy oak, earthy notes, balsamic herbs. Palate: fruity, flavourful, toasty.

Solluna 2011 T
garnacha, cariñena, merlot
88
Colour: bright cherry. Nose: ripe fruit, sweet spices, creamy oak, medium intensity, dried herbs. Palate: flavourful, toasty, balsamic, fine bitter notes.

GRATAVINUM

Mas d'en Serres s/n
43737 Gratallops (Tarragona)
☎: +34 938 901 399
Fax: +34 938 901 143
www.gratavinum.com
gratavinum@gratavinum.com

Dolç D'En Piqué Dulce 2011 T
garnacha, cariñena, cabernet sauvignon

89 🌱

Colour: cherry, garnet rim. Nose: fruit preserve, ripe fruit, spicy, toasty, aged wood nuances. Palate: powerful, flavourful, sweetness.

Gratavinum Coster 2010 T
cariñena

90 🌱

Colour: black cherry, garnet rim. Nose: characterful, powerfull, ripe fruit, fruit preserve, wild herbs, varnish. Palate: good structure, flavourful, round tannins.

Gratavinum Silvestris 2012 T
cariñena, syrah

88 🌱

Colour: cherry, garnet rim. Nose: ripe fruit, wild herbs, earthy notes, spicy, creamy oak, powerfull. Palate: balanced, flavourful, long, balsamic.

HAMMEKEN CELLARS

Calle de la Muela, 16
3730 Jávea (Alicante)
☎: +34 965 791 967
Fax: +34 966 461 471
www.hammekencellars.com
cellars@hammekencellars.com

Tosalet 2013 T

89

Colour: cherry, purple rim. Nose: expressive, fresh fruit, red berry notes, scrubland, mineral. Palate: flavourful, fruity, good acidity, round tannins.

JOAN AMETLLER

Ctra. La Morera de Monsant - Cornudella, km. 3,2
43361 La Morera de Monsant
(Tarragona)
☎: +34 933 208 439
Fax: +34 933 208 437
www.ametller.com
info@ametller.com

Clos Corriol 2011 T
garnacha, cabernet sauvignon, merlot

87

Colour: cherry, garnet rim. Nose: ripe fruit, spicy, toasty. Palate: powerful, flavourful, toasty, round tannins.

Clos Corriol 2013 B
100% garnacha blanca

88

Colour: bright straw. Nose: fresh, fresh fruit, white flowers, expressive. Palate: flavourful, fruity, good acidity, balanced.

Clos Mustardó 2006 TC
garnacha, cabernet sauvignon, merlot

91

Colour: cherry, garnet rim. Nose: earthy notes, spicy, creamy oak, scrubland, fruit liqueur notes. Palate: balanced, flavourful, long, balsamic, spicy.

Clos Mustardó 2010 B
garnacha blanca

89

Colour: bright yellow. Nose: powerfull, ripe fruit, sweet spices, creamy oak, fragrant herbs. Palate: rich, flavourful, fresh, good acidity.

Clos Mustardó 2011 BFB
100% garnacha blanca

90

Colour: bright yellow. Nose: floral, ripe fruit, dried herbs, dry stone, creamy oak. Palate: balanced, mineral, spicy, long.

Clos Mustardó 2012 BFB
100% garnacha blanca

90

Colour: bright straw. Nose: white flowers, fresh fruit, expressive, fine lees, dried herbs, spicy. Palate: flavourful, fruity, good acidity, balanced.

Clos Socarrat 2011 T
garnacha, merlot, cabernet sauvignon

86

Colour: very deep cherry, garnet rim. Nose: powerfull, ripe fruit, roasted coffee, dark chocolate. Palate: powerful, toasty, roasted-coffee aftertaste.

Els Igols 2005 TR
garnacha, cabernet sauvignon, merlot

90

Colour: pale ruby, brick rim edge. Nose: balanced, complex, ripe fruit, spicy, creamy oak, balsamic herbs. Palate: good structure, flavourful, round tannins, balanced.

LA CONRERIA D'SCALA DEI

Carrer Mitja Galta, 32
43379 Scala Dei (Tarragona)
☎: +34 977 827 055
Fax: +34 977 827 055
www.vinslaconreria.com
laconreria@vinslaconreria.com

Iugiter 2010 T
garnacha, merlot, samsó, cabernet sauvignon
89
Colour: black cherry. Nose: ripe fruit, sweet spices, creamy oak, fruit preserve. Palate: flavourful, fruity, toasty, round tannins.

Iugiter Selecció Vinyes Velles 2008 TC
garnacha, samsó, cabernet sauvignon
91
Colour: cherry, garnet rim. Nose: ripe fruit, wild herbs, earthy notes, spicy, creamy oak. Palate: balanced, flavourful, long, balsamic.

La Conreria 2012 T Roble
garnacha, syrah, merlot, samsó
90
Colour: cherry, garnet rim. Nose: ripe fruit, wild herbs, earthy notes, spicy, creamy oak. Palate: balanced, flavourful, long, balsamic.

Les Brugueres 2013 B
garnacha blanca
90
Colour: bright straw. Nose: white flowers, fragrant herbs, fruit expression. Palate: fresh, fruity, flavourful, balanced, elegant.

MAIUS

Santa María, 17
43361 La Morera de Montsant
(Tarragona)
☎: +34 696 998 575
Fax: +34 936 752 897
www.maiusviticultors.com
jgomez@maiusviticultors.com

Maius Assemblage 2011 T
garnacha, cariñena
90
Colour: deep cherry, garnet rim. Nose: spicy, dried herbs, ripe fruit. Palate: full, flavourful, powerful, mineral.

Maius Barranc de la Bruixa 2011 T
garnacha, cariñena, cabernet sauvignon
90
Colour: deep cherry, garnet rim. Nose: powerfull, ripe fruit, fruit preserve, creamy oak, sweet spices. Palate: good structure, flavourful.

MARCO ABELLA

Ctra. de Porrera a Cornudella del Montsant, Km. 0,7
43739 Porrera (Tarragona)
☎: +34 933 712 407
Fax: +34 932 755 538
www.marcoabella.com
admin@marcoabella.com

Clos Abella 2009 T
91
Colour: cherry, garnet rim. Nose: ripe fruit, wild herbs, earthy notes, violets. Palate: balanced, flavourful, long, balsamic.

Loidana 2010 T
88
Colour: bright cherry. Nose: ripe fruit, sweet spices, creamy oak, earthy notes. Palate: fruity, flavourful, toasty.

Mas Mallola 2009 TR
91
Colour: cherry, garnet rim. Nose: ripe fruit, wild herbs, spicy, creamy oak, mineral. Palate: balanced, flavourful, long, balsamic.

Olbia 2013 B
macabeo, garnacha blanca, pedro ximénez
88
Colour: bright yellow. Nose: balanced, expressive, white flowers, fragrant herbs. Palate: flavourful, mineral, good finish.

MAS BLANC PINORD PRIORAT

Dr. Pasteur, 6
08720 Vilafranca del Penedès
(Barcelona)
☎: +34 938 903 066
Fax: +34 938 170 979
www.pinord.com
visites@pinord.es

Clos del Mas 2010 T
90
Colour: deep cherry, garnet rim. Nose: fruit preserve, scrubland, damp earth, spicy, creamy oak. Palate: powerful, flavourful, spicy, balsamic.

Clos del Music 2009 T
91
Colour: cherry, garnet rim. Nose: ripe fruit, wild herbs, spicy, mineral. Palate: elegant, flavourful, balsamic, spicy, balanced.

MAS D'EN BLEI

Mas d'en Blei s/n
43361 La Morera de Montsant
(Tarragona)
☎: +34 977 262 031
www.masdenblei.com
info@masdenblei.com

Blei 2010 T
89
Colour: cherry, garnet rim. Nose: ripe fruit, spicy, creamy oak, toasty, complex, tobacco. Palate: powerful, flavourful, toasty, round tannins.

Clos Martina 2012 B
86
Colour: bright yellow. Nose: powerfull, sweet spices, creamy oak, smoky. Palate: rich, smoky aftertaste, flavourful, good acidity.

MAS LA MOLA

Raval, 4
43376 Poboleda (Tarragona)
☎: +34 651 034 215
www.maslamola.com
info@maslamola.com

L'Expressió del Priorat 2012 T
garnacha, mazuelo
88
Colour: deep cherry, purple rim. Nose: dried herbs, ripe fruit, spicy. Palate: flavourful, fruity, round tannins.

Mas la Mola 2011 B
85

Mas la Mola Negre 2009 T
90
Colour: cherry, garnet rim. Nose: red berry notes, ripe fruit, spicy, creamy oak, toasty, complex, earthy notes, balsamic herbs. Palate: powerful, flavourful, toasty, round tannins.

MAS MARTINET VITICULTORS

Ctra. Falset - Gratallops, Km. 6
43730 Falset (Tarragona)
☎: +34 629 238 236
Fax: +34 977 262 348
www.masmartinet.com
masmartinet@masmartinet.com

Cami Pesseroles 2011 T
garnacha, cariñena
93
Colour: cherry, garnet rim. Nose: ripe fruit, spicy, creamy oak, toasty, balsamic herbs, dry stone. Palate: powerful, flavourful, toasty, round tannins, balanced.

Clos Martinet 2011 T
garnacha, cariñena, syrah, cabernet sauvignon
94
Colour: cherry, garnet rim. Nose: red berry notes, ripe fruit, spicy, creamy oak, toasty, complex, dry stone, balanced. Palate: powerful, flavourful, toasty, round tannins, long, elegant.

Els Escurçons 2011 T
garnacha
93
Colour: cherry, garnet rim. Nose: ripe fruit, spicy, creamy oak, toasty, complex, scrubland, candied fruit. Palate: powerful, flavourful, toasty, round tannins.

Martinet Bru 2011 T
garnacha, syrah, merlot, cabernet sauvignon
90
Colour: black cherry. Nose: medium intensity, ripe fruit, balanced, scrubland, mineral. Palate: flavourful, fruity, spicy, reductive nuances.

MERITXELL PALLEJÀ

Carrer Major, 32
43737 Gratallops (Tarragona)
☎: +34 670 960 735
www.nita.cat
info@nita.cat

Nita 2012 T
89
Colour: deep cherry, purple rim. Nose: ripe fruit, scrubland, balanced. Palate: flavourful, round tannins.

RITME CELLER

Camí Sindicat s/n
43375 La Vilella Alta (Tarragona)
☎: +34 672 432 691
Fax: +34 977 660 867
www.acusticceller.com
ritme@ritmeceller.com

+ Ritme Blanc 2011 B
garnacha blanca, macabeo
91 🍷
Colour: bright yellow. Nose: balanced, faded flowers, spicy, ripe fruit, mineral. Palate: rich, flavourful, fruity.

+ Ritme Blanc 2012 B
garnacha blanca, macabeo
93 🍷
Colour: bright yellow. Nose: powerfull, ripe fruit, sweet spices, creamy oak, fragrant herbs, mineral. Palate: rich, smoky aftertaste, flavourful, fresh, good acidity, balanced.

Etern 2011 T
garnacha, cariñena
92 🍷
Colour: very deep cherry, garnet rim. Nose: balanced, elegant, cocoa bean, balsamic herbs, mineral. Palate: good structure, spicy, long, round tannins.

Plaer 2011 T
garnacha, cariñena

93

Colour: cherry, garnet rim. Nose: ripe fruit, spicy, creamy oak, toasty, dry stone. Palate: powerful, flavourful, toasty, round tannins, balanced.

Plaer 2012 T
garnacha, cariñena

89

Colour: cherry, garnet rim. Nose: fruit preserve, spicy, dried herbs, mineral. Palate: pruney, balsamic, full, flavourful, round tannins.

Ritme Negre 2011 T
garnacha, cariñena

90

Colour: bright cherry, garnet rim. Nose: sweet spices, creamy oak, ripe fruit, fruit preserve, balsamic herbs. Palate: fruity, flavourful, toasty, balanced.

Ritme Negre 2012 T
garnacha, cariñena

91

Colour: cherry, garnet rim. Nose: ripe fruit, wild herbs, earthy notes, spicy, creamy oak. Palate: balanced, flavourful, long, balsamic.

ROCA DE LES DOTZE
Ctra. La Morera de Montsant-
Cornudella de Montsant, Km. 4
43361 La Morera de Montsant
(Tarragona)
☎: +34 662 302 214
www.rocadelesdotze.cat
info@rocadelesdotze.cat

Noray 2007 T
garnacha, cabernet sauvignon, syrah, samsó

91

Colour: cherry, garnet rim. Nose: ripe fruit, balsamic herbs, mineral, spicy, creamy oak, balanced. Palate: powerful, flavourful, balsamic, spicy, long.

Noray 2008 T
garnacha, cabernet sauvignon, syrah, samsó

92

Colour: dark-red cherry. Nose: ripe fruit, powerfull, mineral, scrubland, balsamic herbs. Palate: flavourful, good acidity, fine tannins, spicy.

Roca Bruixa 2007 T
garnacha, syrah

89

Colour: cherry, garnet rim. Nose: red berry notes, ripe fruit, spicy, creamy oak, toasty, complex, earthy notes. Palate: powerful, flavourful, toasty.

Roca Bruixa 2008 T
garnacha, syrah

90

Colour: cherry, garnet rim. Nose: mineral, spicy, balanced, ripe fruit. Palate: powerful, full, concentrated, round tannins.

RODRÍGUEZ SANZO
Manuel Azaña, 9
47014 (Valladolid)
☎: +34 983 150 150
Fax: +34 983 150 151
www.rodriguezsanzo.com
comunicacion@valsanzo.com

Nassos 2010 T
garnacha

93

Colour: cherry, garnet rim. Nose: ripe fruit, wild herbs, spicy, creamy oak, dry stone. Palate: balanced, flavourful, long, balsamic.

ROTLLAN TORRA
Balandra, 6
43737 Torroja del Priorat (Tarragona)
☎: +34 933 134 347
www.rotllantorra.com
administracion@rotllantorra.com

Autor 2009 TR

90

Colour: cherry, garnet rim. Nose: red berry notes, ripe fruit, spicy, creamy oak, toasty, complex, earthy notes. Palate: powerful, flavourful, toasty, round tannins, balanced.

Autor 2011 TC

88

Colour: cherry, garnet rim. Nose: ripe fruit, wild herbs, spicy, creamy oak, toasty, mineral. Palate: balanced, flavourful, long, balsamic.

Balandra 2007 TR

86

Colour: very deep cherry, garnet rim. Nose: fruit preserve, spicy, aromatic coffee. Palate: flavourful, toasty, spicy.

Mistik 2008 TR

90

Colour: cherry, garnet rim. Nose: red berry notes, ripe fruit, spicy, creamy oak, toasty, complex, earthy notes. Palate: powerful, flavourful, toasty, round tannins.

Mistik 2010 TC

89

Colour: cherry, garnet rim. Nose: red berry notes, ripe fruit, spicy, toasty, complex, mineral. Palate: powerful, flavourful, toasty, round tannins.

SANGENÍS I VAQUÉ

Pl. Catalunya, 3
43739 Porrera (Tarragona)
☎: +34 977 828 252
www.sangenisivaque.com
celler@sangenisivaque.com

Clos Monlleó 2011 TR
garnacha, cariñena

89

Colour: cherry, garnet rim. Nose: ripe fruit, spicy, toasty, earthy notes, mineral, smoky. Palate: powerful, toasty, round tannins.

Dara 2009 TC
garnacha, cariñena, merlot

90

Colour: cherry, garnet rim. Nose: ripe fruit, spicy, creamy oak, toasty. Palate: powerful, flavourful, toasty, round tannins, balanced.

Lo Coster Blanc 2012 B
garnacha blanca, macabeo

90

Colour: bright yellow. Nose: powerfull, ripe fruit, sweet spices, creamy oak, fragrant herbs. Palate: rich, smoky aftertaste, flavourful, fresh, good acidity.

SAÓ DEL COSTER

Calle Valls, 28
43737 Gratallops (Tarragona)
☎: +34 606 550 825
www.saodelcoster.com
info@saodelcoster.com

"S" de Saó Coster 2012 T
garnacha, merlot, cabernet sauvignon, syrah

87 🌷

Colour: bright cherry. Nose: ripe fruit, sweet spices, creamy oak, earthy notes. Palate: flavourful, fruity, toasty.

Pim Pam Poom 2013 T
100% garnacha

88 🌷

Colour: cherry, purple rim. Nose: expressive, fresh fruit, red berry notes, wild herbs. Palate: flavourful, fruity, good acidity, round tannins.

Terram 2010 TR
garnacha, cariñena, cabernet sauvignon, syrah

89 🌷

Colour: bright cherry. Nose: ripe fruit, sweet spices, creamy oak, medium intensity. Palate: fruity, flavourful, toasty, balsamic, balanced.

SOLA CLASSIC

Nou, 15
43738 Bellmunt del Priorat (Tarragona)
☎: +34 686 115 104
www.solaclassic.com
info@solaclassic.com

Solà Classic 2011 T

84

Solà2 Classic 2012 T

88

Colour: deep cherry, purple rim. Nose: fruit preserve, spicy, dried herbs. Palate: concentrated, flavourful, round tannins.

Vinyes Josep 2009 T

89

Colour: cherry, garnet rim. Nose: spicy, toasty, fruit preserve, dried herbs. Palate: powerful, flavourful, toasty, round tannins.

TERRA DE VEREMA

Baix de St. Pere, 1
43374 La Vilella Baixa (Tarragona)
☎: +34 656 607 867
Fax: +34 934 159 698
www.terradeverema.com
admin@terradeverema.com

Corelium 2008 T

90

Colour: cherry, garnet rim. Nose: ripe fruit, wild herbs, earthy notes, spicy, creamy oak, fine reductive notes. Palate: balanced, flavourful, long, balsamic, smoky aftertaste.

Triumvirat 2009 T

90

Colour: dark-red cherry, garnet rim. Nose: powerfull, warm, spicy, scrubland. Palate: full, flavourful, round tannins, balsamic.

TERROIR AL LIMIT

Baixa Font, 10
43737 Torroja del Priorat (Tarragona)
☎: +34 699 732 707
Fax: +34 977 839 391
www.terroir-al-limit.com
dominik@terroir-al-limit.com

Arbossar 2011 T
100% cariñena

94 🌷

Colour: cherry, purple rim. Nose: expressive, wild herbs, balsamic herbs, complex, varietal, spicy, tobacco. Palate: flavourful, spicy, long, balanced.

Dits del Terra 2011 T
100% cariñena

93

Colour: cherry, garnet rim. Nose: ripe fruit, spicy, creamy oak, toasty, earthy notes, scrubland, mineral. Palate: powerful, flavourful, toasty, round tannins, balanced.

Les Manyes 2011 T
100% garnacha

95

Colour: cherry, garnet rim. Nose: fruit liqueur notes, red berry notes, floral, fragrant herbs, spicy, dry stone, earthy notes. Palate: balanced, fresh, fruity, flavourful, balsamic, long, round.

Les Tosses 2011 T
100% cariñena

93

Colour: dark-red cherry, garnet rim. Nose: complex, balanced, scrubland, spicy. Palate: good structure, flavourful, good acidity, balsamic.

Pedra de Guix 2011 B
93

Colour: yellow. Nose: ripe fruit, dried herbs, dry nuts, spicy, faded flowers, mineral. Palate: flavourful, fine bitter notes, long.

Terra de Cuques 2012 B
91

Colour: bright straw. Nose: white flowers, fragrant herbs, fruit expression, tropical fruit. Palate: fresh, fruity, flavourful, balanced, elegant.

Torroja Vi de la Vila 2012 T
94

Colour: cherry, garnet rim. Nose: ripe fruit, wild herbs, earthy notes, spicy, creamy oak, mineral. Palate: balanced, flavourful, long, balsamic.

TORRES PRIORAT
Finca La Soleta, s/n
43737 El Lloar (Tarragona)
☎: +34 938 177 400
Fax: +34 938 177 444
www.torres.es
admin@torres.es

Perpetual 2011 TC
garnacha, cariñena

92

Colour: cherry, garnet rim. Nose: ripe fruit, spicy, creamy oak, toasty, complex, wild herbs, mineral. Palate: powerful, flavourful, toasty, round tannins.

Salmos 2011 TC
cariñena, garnacha, syrah

89

Colour: cherry, garnet rim. Nose: ripe fruit, wild herbs, earthy notes, spicy, creamy oak. Palate: balanced, flavourful, long, balsamic.

Secret del Priorat Dulce 2011 T
garnacha, cariñena

92

Colour: cherry, garnet rim. Nose: fruit preserve, ripe fruit, spicy, toasty, aged wood nuances. Palate: powerful, flavourful, sweetness, fine solera notes, elegant.

TROSSOS DEL PRIORAT
Ctra. Gratallops a La Vilella
Baixa, Km. 10,65
43737 Gratallops (Tarragona)
☎: +34 670 590 788
www.trossosdelpriorat.com
celler@trossosdelpriorat.com

Abracadabra 2012 B
93

Colour: bright yellow. Nose: floral, balsamic herbs, spicy, creamy oak, dry stone. Palate: balanced, good acidity, flavourful, fruity, rich, spicy, elegant.

Lo Món 2010 T
92

Colour: cherry, garnet rim. Nose: ripe fruit, spicy, creamy oak, toasty, complex, mineral. Palate: powerful, flavourful, toasty, round tannins, balanced.

Lo Petit de la Casa 2011 TC
90

Colour: deep cherry, garnet rim. Nose: powerfull, balanced, scrubland, spicy, dry stone. Palate: flavourful, balanced.

Pam de Nas 2010 T
93

Colour: very deep cherry. Nose: ripe fruit, spicy, creamy oak, toasty, complex, mineral, cocoa bean. Palate: powerful, flavourful, toasty, round tannins.

VINÍCOLA DEL PRIORAT
Piró, s/n
43737 Gratallops (Tarragona)
☎: +34 977 839 167
Fax: +34 977 839 201
www.vinicoladelpriorat.com
info@vinicoladelpriorat.com

Clos Gebrat 2011 TC
garnacha, mazuelo, cabernet sauvignon

90

Colour: cherry, garnet rim. Nose: ripe fruit, spicy, creamy oak, toasty, complex. Palate: powerful, flavourful, toasty, round tannins.

Clos Gebrat 2013 T
garnacha, mazuelo, cabernet sauvignon, merlot

88

Colour: cherry, purple rim. Nose: red berry notes, ripe fruit, wild herbs, mineral, spicy. Palate: powerful, flavourful, toasty, balanced.

L'Obaga 2013 T
garnacha, syrah, mazuelo

90

Colour: cherry, purple rim. Nose: red berry notes, raspberry, floral, expressive. Palate: fresh, fruity, flavourful, easy to drink, balanced.

Nadiu 2011 TC
mazuelo, garnacha, cabernet sauvignon, merlot

88

Colour: bright cherry. Nose: ripe fruit, sweet spices, creamy oak, medium intensity. Palate: fruity, flavourful, toasty, correct.

Nadiu 2013 T
mazuelo, garnacha, cabernet sauvignon, merlot

89

Colour: cherry, purple rim. Nose: red berry notes, ripe fruit, balsamic herbs, creamy oak. Palate: flavourful, fruity, spicy, good finish.

Ònix Clássic 2013 B
viura, garnacha blanca, pedro ximénez

90

Colour: bright straw. Nose: white flowers, fragrant herbs, fruit expression, dry stone. Palate: fresh, fruity, flavourful, balanced, elegant.

Ònix Clássic 2013 T
garnacha, mazuelo

89

Colour: cherry, purple rim. Nose: expressive, fresh fruit, red berry notes, floral, balsamic herbs. Palate: flavourful, fruity, good acidity, round tannins, easy to drink.

Ònix Evolució 2011 T
mazuelo, garnacha, cabernet sauvignon

91

Colour: black cherry. Nose: closed, scrubland, spicy, toasty. Palate: flavourful, balanced, round tannins, long.

Ònix Fusió 2012 T
garnacha, syrah, mazuelo

90

Colour: very deep cherry. Nose: balsamic herbs, balanced, ripe fruit, spicy. Palate: flavourful, spicy, easy to drink, ripe fruit.

VITICULTORS DEL PRIORAT
Partida Palells, s/n - Mas Subirat
43738 Bellmunt del Priorat (Tarragona)
☎: +34 977 262 268
Fax: +34 977 831 356
www.morlanda.com
mariajose.bajon@morlanda.com

Costers del Prior 2011 T
garnacha, cariñena

88

Colour: bright cherry. Nose: ripe fruit, sweet spices, creamy oak, scrubland. Palate: flavourful, fruity, toasty.

Morlanda 2009 T

89

Colour: bright cherry. Nose: sweet spices, smoky, ripe fruit, fruit preserve. Palate: flavourful, fruity, toasty, round tannins.

VITICULTORS MAS D'EN GIL
Finca Mas d'en Gil s/n
43738 Bellmunt del Priorat (Tarragona)
☎: +34 977 830 192
Fax: +34 977 830 152
www.masdengil.com
mail@masdengil.com

Clos Fontà 2010 TR

94

Colour: cherry, garnet rim. Nose: ripe fruit, wild herbs, earthy notes, spicy, creamy oak, mineral. Palate: balanced, flavourful, long, balsamic.

Coma Blanca 2010 BC

90

Colour: yellow, pale. Nose: spicy, dried flowers, faded flowers, toasty. Palate: toasty, rich, complex, spicy, mineral, long, ripe fruit.

Nus 2011 Dulce Natural

93

Colour: very deep cherry. Nose: complex, balanced, candied fruit, spicy, varnish, cocoa bean. Palate: balanced, long.

DO. RÍAS BAIXAS

CONSEJO REGULADOR
Edif. Pazo de Mugartegui
36002 Pontevedra
☎ :+34 986 854 850 / +34 864 530 - Fax: +34 986 864 546
@: consejo@doriasbaixas.com
www.doriasbaixas.com

LOCATION:

In the southwest of the province of Pontevedra, covering five distinct sub-regions: Val do Salnés, O Rosal, Condado do Tea, Soutomaior and Ribeira do Ulla.

SUB-REGIONS:

Val do Salnés. This is the historic sub-region of the Albariño (in fact, here, almost all the white wines are produced as single-variety wines from this variety) and is centred around the municipal district of Cambados. It has the flattest relief of the four sub-regions.
Condado do Tea. The furthest inland, it is situated in the south of the province on the northern bank of the Miño. It is characterized by its mountainous terrain. The wines must contain a minimum of 70% of Albariño and Treixadura.
O Rosal. In the extreme southwest of the province, on the right bank of the Miño river mouth. The warmest sub-region, where river terraces abound. The wines must contain a minimum of 70% of Albariño and Loureira.
Soutomaior. Situated on the banks of the Verdugo River, about 10 km from Pontevedra, it consists only of the municipal district of Soutomaior. It produces only single-varietals of Albariño.
Ribeira do Ulla. A new sub-region along the Ulla River, which forms the landscape of elevated valleys further inland. It comprises the municipal districts of Vedra and part of Padrón, Deo, Boquixon, Touro, Estrada, Silleda and Vila de Cruce. Red wines predominate.

GRAPE VARIETIES:

White: Albariño (majority), Loureira Blanca or Marqués, Treixadura and Caíño Blanco (preferred); Torrontés and Godello (authorized). Red: Caíño Tinto, Espadeiro, Loureira Tinta and Sousón (preferred); Tempranillo, Mouratón, Garnacha Tintorera, Mencía and Brancellao (authorized).

FIGURES:

Vineyard surface: 4,064 – Wine-Growers: 6,677 – Wineries: 178 – 2013 Harvest rating: Very Good – Production 12: 22,989,997 litres – Market percentages: 69% domestic - 31% export.

SOIL:

Sandy, shallow and slightly acidic, which makes fine soil for producing quality wines. The predominant type of rock is granite, and only in the Concellos of Sanxenxo, Rosal and Tomillo is it possible to find a narrow band of metamorphic rock. Quaternary deposits are very common in all the sub-regions.

CLIMATE:

Atlantic, with moderate, mild temperatures due to the influence of the sea, high relative humidity and abundant rainfall (the annual average is around 1600 mm). There is less rainfall further downstream of the Miño (Condado de Tea), and as a consequence the grapes ripen earlier.

VINTAGE RATING

PEÑÍNGUIDE

2009	2010	2011	2012	2013
EXCELLENT	GOOD	VERY GOOD	VERY GOOD	VERY GOOD

A. PAZOS DE LUSCO

Lg. Grixó - Alxén s/n
36458 Salvaterra do Miño (Pontevedra)
☎: +34 987 514 550
Fax: +34 987 514 570
www.lusco.es
info@lusco.es

Lusco 2012 B
100% albariño
94
Colour: yellow. Nose: faded flowers, ripe fruit, fine lees, complex, expressive. Palate: flavourful, balanced, fine bitter notes.

Zios de Lusco 2013 B
100% albariño
92
Colour: bright straw. Nose: white flowers, fresh fruit, expressive, dried herbs, elegant. Palate: flavourful, fruity, good acidity, balanced.

ADEGA CONDES DE ALBAREI

Lugar a Bouza, 1 Castrelo
36639 Cambados (Pontevedra)
☎: +34 986 543 535
Fax: +34 986 524 251
www.condesdealbarei.com
inf@condesdealbarei.com

Albariño Condes de Albarei 2013 B
100% albariño
88
Colour: straw. Nose: white flowers, balanced, fresh fruit. Palate: correct, good acidity, easy to drink, good finish.

Albariño Condes de Albarei Carballo Galego 2012 BFB
100% albariño
92
Colour: bright straw. Nose: jasmine, sweet spices, faded flowers. Palate: ripe fruit, flavourful, good acidity, rich.

Albariño Condes de Albarei En Rama 2010 B
100% albariño
93
Colour: bright yellow. Nose: expressive, balanced, ripe fruit, faded flowers, complex, spicy. Palate: rich, full, fine bitter notes.

Albariño Condes de Albarei Enxebre 2012 B Maceración Carbónica
100% albariño
89
Colour: bright straw. Nose: fresh fruit, white flowers, balanced, ripe fruit. Palate: flavourful, fruity, balanced, good finish.

ADEGA EIDOS

Padriñán, 65
36960 Sanxenxo (Pontevedra)
☎: +34 986 690 009
Fax: +34 986 720 307
www.adegaeidos.com
info@adegaeidos.com

Contraaparede 2009 B
albariño
93
Colour: bright yellow. Nose: expressive, dried flowers, ripe fruit, complex. Palate: balanced, rich, ripe fruit, complex.

Eidos de Padriñán 2013 B
100% albariño
92
Colour: yellow, greenish rim. Nose: expressive, balanced, white flowers, faded flowers, citrus fruit. Palate: balanced, complex, long.

Veigas de Padriñán 2011 B
100% albariño
93
Colour: bright yellow, greenish rim. Nose: complex, expressive, faded flowers, balanced. Palate: fruity, rich, spicy, long.

ADEGA Y VIÑEDOS PACO & LOLA

Valdamor, 18 - XII
36986 Meaño (Pontevedra)
☎: +34 986 747 779
Fax: +34 986 748 940
www.pacolola.com
comercial@pacolola.com

Follas Novas 2013 B
100% albariño
90
Colour: bright straw. Nose: fresh, fresh fruit, white flowers, expressive. Palate: flavourful, fruity, good acidity, balanced.

FOLLAS NOVAS
ALBARIÑO

Paco & Lola 2013 B
100% albariño

92

Colour: bright straw. Nose: white flowers, fragrant herbs, fruit expression. Palate: fresh, fruity, flavourful, balanced, elegant.

Paco & Lola Prime 2011 B
100% albariño

94

Colour: bright straw. Nose: white flowers, fresh fruit, expressive, fine lees, dried herbs. Palate: flavourful, fruity, good acidity, balanced.

ADEGAS AROUSA
Tirabao, 15 - Baión
36614 Vilanova de Arousa (Pontevedra)
☎: +34 986 506 113
Fax: +34 986 715 454
www.adegasarousa.com
info@adegasarousa.com

Pazo da Bouciña 2013 B
albariño

92

Colour: bright straw. Nose: white flowers, fresh fruit, expressive, dried herbs. Palate: flavourful, fruity, good acidity, balanced, long, rich.

Pazo da Bouciña Expresión 2013 B
albariño

91

Colour: bright straw. Nose: white flowers, fragrant herbs, fruit expression. Palate: fresh, fruity, flavourful, balanced, elegant.

Valdemonxes 2013 B
albariño

89

Colour: yellow. Nose: varietal, fresh, floral, citrus fruit. Palate: balanced, fine bitter notes, easy to drink.

ADEGAS CASTROBREY
Camanzo, s/n
36587 Vila de Cruces (Pontevedra)
☎: +34 986 583 643
Fax: +34 986 411 612
www.castrobrey.com
bodegas@castrobrey.com

Nice to Meet You Castrobrey 2012 B
albariño, treixadura, godello

89

Colour: bright straw. Nose: floral, ripe fruit, balanced, expressive, dried herbs. Palate: fruity, rich, flavourful, balanced.

Señorío de Cruces 2013 B
100% albariño

88

Colour: bright straw. Nose: fresh fruit, white flowers. Palate: fresh, fruity, flavourful, balanced, elegant.

Sin Palabras 2013 B
100% albariño

92

Colour: bright straw. Nose: white flowers, fresh fruit, expressive, dried herbs, elegant. Palate: flavourful, fruity, good acidity, balanced.

ADEGAS GALEGAS
Meder, s/n
36457 Salvaterra de Miño (Pontevedra)
☎: +34 986 657 143
Fax: +34 986 526 901
www.adegasgalegas.es
comercial@adegasgalegas.es

Bago Amarelo 2013 B
100% albariño

88

Colour: bright straw. Nose: white flowers, fragrant herbs, dried herbs. Palate: fresh, fruity, flavourful.

Dionisos 2013 B
100% albariño

86

Colour: bright straw. Nose: citrus fruit, fresh fruit, floral, dried herbs. Palate: fine bitter notes, fresh.

Don Pedro Soutomaior 2013 B
100% albariño

89

Colour: bright straw. Nose: fresh, fresh fruit, white flowers. Palate: flavourful, fruity, good acidity.

Don Pedro Soutomaior Macerado en Neve Carbónica 2013 B Maceración Carbónica
100% albariño

88

Colour: bright straw. Nose: white flowers, fresh fruit, fine lees, dried herbs. Palate: flavourful, fruity, good acidity, balanced.

O Deus Dionisos 2013 B
albariño

87

Colour: bright straw. Nose: fresh, fresh fruit, white flowers, dried herbs. Palate: flavourful, fruity, good acidity.

Veigadares 2012 B

90

Colour: bright yellow. Nose: powerfull, ripe fruit, sweet spices, creamy oak, fragrant herbs. Palate: rich, smoky aftertaste, flavourful, fresh, good acidity.

ADEGAS GRAN VINUM
Fermín Bouza Brei, 9 - 5ºB
36600 Vilagarcía de Arousa (Pontevedra)
☎: +34 986 555 742
Fax: +34 986 555 742
www.granvinum.com
info@adegasgranvinum.com

Esencia Diviña 2013 B
100% albariño

90

Colour: bright straw. Nose: fresh fruit, citrus fruit, fragrant herbs, white flowers, expressive. Palate: flavourful, fresh, fruity, balanced.

Gran Vinum 2013 B
100% albariño

89

Colour: bright straw. Nose: medium intensity, white flowers, jasmine, fresh. Palate: correct, fine bitter notes, good acidity, easy to drink.

Mar de Viñas 2013 B
100% albariño

87

Colour: bright straw. Nose: fresh, fresh fruit, white flowers. Palate: flavourful, fruity, balanced.

Nessa 2013 B
100% albariño

87

Colour: bright straw. Nose: dried flowers, wild herbs, citrus fruit. Palate: flavourful, fresh, fruity, easy to drink.

ADEGAS MORGADÍO
Albeos
36429 Creciente (Pontevedra)
☎: +34 988 261 212
Fax: +34 988 261 213
www.gruporeboredamorgadio.com
info@gruporeboredamorgadio.com

Morgadío 2013 B
albariño

89

Colour: bright straw. Nose: fresh, fresh fruit, white flowers, fragrant herbs. Palate: flavourful, fruity, balanced.

ADEGAS TOLLODOURO
Estrada Tui-A Guardia km. 45
36760 Eiras (O Rosal) (Pontevedra)
☎: +34 986 609 810
Fax: +34 986 609 811
www.tollodouro.com
oscarmartinez@hogomar.es

Pontellón Albariño 2013 B
100% albariño

89

Colour: bright straw. Nose: white flowers, fragrant herbs, fruit expression, tropical fruit. Palate: fresh, fruity, flavourful.

Tollodouro 2012 B
albariño, loureiro, treixadura

89

Colour: bright straw. Nose: white flowers, fresh fruit, expressive, fine lees, dried herbs. Palate: flavourful, fruity, good acidity, balanced.

ADEGAS VALMIÑOR
A Portela, s/n – San Juan de Tabagón
36370 O'Rosal (Pontevedra)
☎: +34 986 609 060
Fax: +34 986 609 313
www.adegasvalminor.com
valminor@valminorebano.com

Davila 2013 B
albariño, loureiro, treixadura

90

Colour: bright yellow. Nose: white flowers, fragrant herbs, fruit expression. Palate: fresh, fruity, flavourful, balanced, elegant.

Davila L-100 2011 B
loureiro

93

Colour: bright yellow. Nose: balsamic herbs, expressive, citrus fruit, floral. Palate: flavourful, good acidity, fine bitter notes, long. Personality.

Davila M-100 2011 B
loureiro, caíño blanco, albariño

92

Colour: bright yellow. Nose: floral, wild herbs, balsamic herbs, ripe fruit, spicy. Palate: correct, unctuous, flavourful, balsamic, spicy, long.

Serra da Estrela 2013 B
albariño

86

Colour: bright straw. Nose: fresh, fresh fruit, floral. Palate: flavourful, fruity, fine bitter notes.

Torroxal 2013 B
albariño

87

Colour: bright yellow. Nose: dried herbs, faded flowers, ripe fruit. Palate: powerful, flavourful, correct.

Valmiñor 2013 B
albariño

90

Colour: bright straw. Nose: white flowers, fragrant herbs, varietal. Palate: fresh, fruity, flavourful, balanced, elegant.

ADEGAS VALTEA
Lg. Portela, 14
36429 Crecente (Pontevedra)
☎: +34 986 666 344
Fax: +34 986 644 914
www.vilarvin.com
vilarvin@vilarvin.com

C de V 2013 B
albariño, treixadura, loureiro

90

Colour: bright yellow. Nose: floral, ripe fruit, dried herbs, balanced. Palate: fresh, fruity, flavourful, elegant.

Finca Garabato 2012 B
100% albariño

90

Colour: bright yellow. Nose: powerfull, ripe fruit, faded flowers. Palate: good structure, flavourful, rich, complex, long.

Marexías 2013 B
albariño, treixadura, loureiro

87

Colour: bright straw. Nose: fresh, fresh fruit, white flowers, expressive. Palate: flavourful, fruity, good acidity.

Valtea 2012 B
100% albariño

91

Colour: bright yellow. Nose: floral, dried herbs, ripe fruit, honeyed notes. Palate: rich, flavourful, complex, long.

Valtea 2013 B
100% albariño

89

Colour: bright straw. Nose: fresh fruit, fine lees, dried herbs, dried flowers, faded flowers. Palate: flavourful, fruity, good acidity, balanced.

AGRO DE BAZÁN
Tremoedo, 46
36628 Vilanova de Arousa (Pontevedra)
☎: +34 986 555 562
Fax: +34 986 555 799
www.agrodebazan.com
agrodebazan@agrodebazan.com

Contrapunto 2013 B
100% albariño

87

Colour: bright straw. Nose: medium intensity, fresh, floral, citrus fruit. Palate: correct, good acidity, easy to drink.

Granbazán Ámbar 2013 B
100% albariño

90

Colour: bright straw. Nose: white flowers, fragrant herbs, fruit expression, balsamic herbs. Palate: fresh, fruity, flavourful, elegant.

Granbazán Don Alvaro de Bazán 2013 B
100% albariño

91

Colour: bright straw. Nose: fresh fruit, fragrant herbs, floral, expressive, balanced. Palate: flavourful, rich, fruity, balanced.

Granbazán Etiqueta Verde 2013 B
100% albariño

89

Colour: bright yellow. Nose: balanced, floral, ripe fruit. Palate: fruity, flavourful, fine bitter notes, good finish.

ALDEA DE ABAIXO
Novas, s/n
36778 O'Rosal (Pontevedra)
☎: +34 986 626 121
Fax: +34 986 626 121
www.bodegasorosal.com
senoriodatorre@grannovas.com

Gran Novas Albariño 2013 B
100% albariño

87

Colour: bright yellow. Nose: white flowers, fresh, medium intensity, fragrant herbs. Palate: correct, easy to drink, good finish.

Señorío da Torre Rosal 2013 B

85

Señorío da Torre Rosal sobre Lías 2010 B
92
Colour: bright yellow. Nose: expressive, fine lees, dried herbs, dried flowers, mineral. Palate: flavourful, fruity, good acidity, balanced.

ALMA ATLÁNTICA
Burgáns, 91
36633 Vilariño - Cambados
(Pontevedra)
☎: +34 986 526 040
Fax: +34 986 526 901
www.martincodax.com
comercial@martincodax.com

Alba Martín 2013 B
albariño
91
Colour: bright straw. Nose: fragrant herbs, floral, fresh fruit, citrus fruit. Palate: fresh, fruity, flavourful, balanced, elegant.

Anxo Martín 2013 B
92
Colour: bright straw. Nose: fragrant herbs, fresh fruit, wild herbs, balanced. Palate: fresh, good acidity, fine bitter notes, long.

ATTIS BODEGAS Y VIÑEDOS
Lg. Morouzos, 16D - Dena
36967 Meaño (Pontevedra)
☎: +34 986 744 790
Fax: +34 986 744 790
www.attisbyv.com
info@attisbyv.com

Attis 2013 B
100% albariño
90
Colour: bright straw. Nose: white flowers, fragrant herbs, fruit expression. Palate: fresh, fruity, flavourful, balanced, elegant.

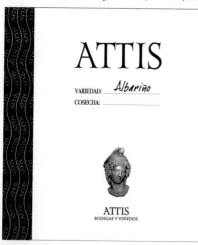

Attis Caiño 2012 T
100% caiño
89
Colour: light cherry. Nose: fresh, damp undergrowth, scrubland. Palate: complex, spicy, ripe fruit, fine tannins.

Attis Espadeiro 2012 T
100% espadeiro
87
Colour: cherry, garnet rim. Nose: grassy, spicy, wild herbs. Palate: correct, complex, balsamic.

Attis Sousón 2012 T
100% sousón
91
Colour: cherry, purple rim. Nose: spicy, balsamic herbs, ripe fruit, scrubland. Palate: balanced, good acidity.

Nana 2012 BFB
100% albariño
91 ⚘
Colour: bright golden. Nose: ripe fruit, wild herbs, spicy, creamy oak. Palate: powerful, flavourful, spicy, concentrated, long.

Xión 2013 B
100% albariño
87 ⚘
Colour: bright straw. Nose: white flowers, fragrant herbs, fruit expression. Palate: fresh, fruity, flavourful, balanced.

BENJAMÍN MIGUEZ NOVAL
Porto de Abaixo, 10 - Porto
36458 Salvaterra de Miño (Pontevedra)
☎: +34 636 014 506
www.mariabargiela.com
enoturismo@mariabargiela.com

María Bargiela 2012 B
87
Colour: bright yellow. Nose: ripe fruit, honeyed notes, dried herbs, floral. Palate: fresh, fruity, flavourful.

BODEGA CASTRO BAROÑA
Cabeiro - San Martín de Meis
36637 Meis (Pontevedra)
☎: +34 986 680 868
www.castrobarona.com
castrobarona@castrobarona.com

Castro Baroña 2013 B
100% albariño
91
Colour: bright straw. Nose: white flowers, fragrant herbs, fruit expression, balsamic herbs. Palate: fresh, fruity, flavourful, elegant.

Lagar do Castelo 2013 B
100% albariño

89

Colour: bright straw. Nose: fresh, fresh fruit, white flowers, expressive. Palate: flavourful, fruity, good acidity, balanced.

BODEGA FORJAS DEL SALNÉS

As Covas, 5
36968 Meaño (Pontevedra)
☎: +34 699 446 113
Fax: +34 986 744 428
goliardovino@gmail.com

Bastión de la Luna 2012 T
caiño, espadeiro, loureiro

92

Colour: cherry, garnet rim. Nose: ripe fruit, spicy, creamy oak, complex, earthy notes, balsamic herbs, powerfull. Palate: powerful, flavourful, toasty, round tannins.

Goliardo A Telleira 2012 B Barrica
100% albariño

91

Colour: yellow. Nose: dry stone, expressive, ripe fruit, medium intensity. Palate: fresh, spicy, correct, good acidity, long.

Goliardo Espadeiro 2012 T
100% espadeiro

92

Colour: deep cherry, purple rim. Nose: expressive, wild herbs, grassy, ripe fruit. Palate: balanced, long.

Goliardo Loureiro 2012 T
100% loureiro

93

Colour: very deep cherry. Nose: grassy, saline, fresh, ripe fruit. Palate: spicy, good acidity, balanced, easy to drink. Personality.

Leirana 2013 B
albariño

91

Colour: bright straw. Nose: white flowers, fragrant herbs, fruit expression, mineral. Palate: fresh, fruity, flavourful, balanced, fine bitter notes.

Leirana Finca Genoveva 2012 BFB
100% albariño

94

Colour: yellow. Nose: white flowers, expressive, fine lees, dried herbs, ripe fruit. Palate: flavourful, fruity, good acidity, balanced.

BODEGA PAZO QUINTEIRO DA CRUZ

A Cruz 12, Lois
36635 Ribadumia (Pontevedra)
☎: +34 635 592 215
www.pazoquinteirodacruz.es
pedropinheirolago@yahoo.es

Quinteiro Da Cruz 2013 B
albariño

87

Colour: bright straw. Nose: fresh fruit, white flowers, citrus fruit, medium intensity. Palate: correct, good acidity, fine bitter notes.

BODEGA Y VIÑEDOS VEIGA DA PRINCESA

32619 Arbo (Pontevedra)
☎: +34 988 261 256
Fax: +34 988 261 264
www.pazodomar.com
info@pazodomar.com

Veiga da Princesa 2013 B
albariño

91

Colour: bright straw. Nose: fresh, fresh fruit, white flowers, expressive, balanced. Palate: flavourful, fruity, good acidity, balanced.

BODEGAS ABANICO

Pol. Ind Ca l'Avellanet - Susany, 6
08553 Seva (Barcelona)
☎: +34 938 125 676
Fax: +34 938 123 213
www.bodegasabanico.com
info@exportiberia.com

Diluvio 2013 B
100% albariño

90

Colour: bright straw. Nose: white flowers, fruit expression, mineral, balsamic herbs, saline. Palate: fresh, flavourful, balanced, elegant.

BODEGAS ALBAMAR

O Adro, 11 - Castrelo
36639 Cambados (Pontevedra)
☎: +34 660 292 750
Fax: +34 986 520 048
info@bodegasalbamar.com

Albamar 2012 B
100% albariño

88

Colour: bright straw. Nose: fresh, white flowers, expressive. Palate: flavourful, fruity, balanced, correct.

Albamar 2013 B
100% albariño

87

Colour: bright straw. Nose: fresh, fresh fruit, white flowers, expressive. Palate: flavourful, fruity, good acidity, balanced.

Albamar Edición Especial 2012 B
100% albariño

89

Colour: yellow, pale. Nose: expressive, complex, dried flowers, fine lees. Palate: fresh, fruity, correct, fine bitter notes.

Albamar Finca O Pereiro 2013 B
100% albariño

89

Colour: bright straw, greenish rim. Nose: fresh fruit, citrus fruit, white flowers, balanced. Palate: correct, easy to drink, fine bitter notes, fresh.

Alma de Mar sobre Lías 2011 B
100% albariño

91

Colour: bright yellow. Nose: powerfull, ripe fruit, sweet spices, creamy oak, fragrant herbs, citrus fruit. Palate: rich, flavourful, fruity, balanced, elegant.

Pepe Luis 2012 BFB
100% albariño

93

Colour: bright yellow. Nose: powerfull, ripe fruit, sweet spices, fragrant herbs. Palate: rich, smoky aftertaste, flavourful, fresh, good acidity.

Sesenta e Nove Arrobas 2012 B
100% albariño

93

Colour: bright straw, greenish rim. Nose: ripe fruit, faded flowers, spicy. Palate: rich, fruity, good finish.

BODEGAS ALTOS DE TORONA
Estrada Tui-A Guardia km. 45
36760 Eiras (O Rosal) (Pontevedra)
☎: +34 986 288 212
Fax: +34 986 401 185
www.altosdetorona.com
oscarmartinez@hogomar.es

Albanta 2013 B
100% albariño

86

Colour: bright yellow. Nose: ripe fruit, citrus fruit, floral, dried herbs. Palate: fresh, fruity, flavourful.

Altos de Torona Lías 2013 B
100% albariño

90

Colour: bright yellow. Nose: fresh fruit, fragrant herbs, dried flowers. Palate: flavourful, balanced, fine bitter notes, fruity.

Altos de Torona Rosal 2013 B

89

Colour: bright straw. Nose: floral, wild herbs, dry stone, expressive. Palate: balsamic, easy to drink, flavourful, fresh, fruity.

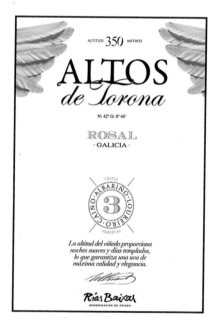

BODEGAS AQUITANIA

Bouza, 17 Castrelo
36639 Cambados (Pontevedra)
☎: +34 610 288 450
Fax: +34 986 520 895
www.bodegasaquitania.es
info@bodegasaquitania.com

Aquitania 2013 B
100% albariño
89
Colour: bright straw. Nose: white flowers, citrus fruit, medium intensity. Palate: balanced, good acidity, fresh.

Aquitania 2013 T
100% mencía
80

Bernon 2013 B
100% albariño
88
Colour: bright straw. Nose: fresh, fresh fruit, expressive, citrus fruit, dried flowers. Palate: flavourful, fruity, balanced.

Raiolas D'Outono 2013 B
100% albariño
85

BODEGAS AS LAXAS

As Laxas, 16
36430 Arbo (Pontevedra)
☎: +34 986 665 444
Fax: +34 986 665 554
www.bodegasaslaxas.com
info@bodegasaslaxas.com

Bágoa do Miño 2013 B
100% albariño
90
Colour: bright straw. Nose: fresh, fresh fruit, white flowers, dried herbs, medium intensity. Palate: fruity, good acidity.

Condado Laxas 2013 B
89
Colour: bright yellow. Nose: floral, balanced, expressive, ripe fruit. Palate: balanced, fine bitter notes, flavourful.

Laxas 2013 B
100% albariño
90
Colour: bright straw. Nose: fresh, fresh fruit, white flowers, expressive, elegant. Palate: flavourful, fruity, balanced.

Sensum Laxas ESP
100% albariño
85

Val Do Sosego 2013 B
100% albariño
89
Colour: bright straw. Nose: white flowers, fragrant herbs. Palate: fresh, fruity, balanced, elegant, fine bitter notes.

BODEGAS DEL PALACIO DE FEFIÑANES

Pza. de Fefiñanes, s/n
36630 Cambados (Pontevedra)
☎: +34 986 542 204
Fax: +34 986 524 512
www.fefinanes.com
fefinanes@fefinanes.com

1583 Albariño de Fefiñanes 2013 BFB
100% albariño
93
Colour: bright yellow. Nose: ripe fruit, fragrant herbs, floral, sweet spices. Palate: rich, flavourful, fresh, good acidity, balanced, elegant.

Albariño de Fefiñanes 2013 B
100% albariño
91
Colour: bright straw. Nose: fresh fruit, white flowers, fragrant herbs, expressive, elegant. Palate: fruity, rich, flavourful, balanced.

ALBARIÑO D FEFIÑANEſ

Albariño de Fefiñanes III año 2011 B
100% albariño
97
Colour: bright yellow. Nose: sweet spices, creamy oak, fragrant herbs, honeyed notes, fruit expression. Palate: rich, smoky aftertaste, flavourful, fresh, good acidity, balanced, elegant.

BODEGAS EIDOSELA

Eidos de Abaixo, s/n - Sela
36494 Arbo (Pontevedra)
☎: +34 986 665 550
Fax: +34 986 665 299
www.bodegaseidosela.com
info@bodegaseidosela.com

Arbastrum 2013 B
91
Colour: bright straw. Nose: white flowers, fresh fruit, expressive, dried herbs, floral. Palate: flavourful, fruity, good acidity, balanced.

Eidosela 2013 B
100% albariño
90
Colour: bright straw. Nose: fresh, fresh fruit, white flowers, wild herbs. Palate: flavourful, fruity, balanced, correct.

Eidosela Burbujas del Atlántico BN
100% albariño
88
Colour: bright straw. Nose: medium intensity, fresh fruit, fine lees, floral. Palate: fresh, fruity, flavourful, good acidity.

Eidosela Burbujas del Atlántico Extra Brut ESP
100% albariño
86
Colour: bright straw. Nose: medium intensity, fresh fruit, dried herbs, fine lees, floral. Palate: fresh, fruity, flavourful, easy to drink.

Etra Albariño 2013 B
100% albariño
88
Colour: bright straw. Nose: fresh, fresh fruit, white flowers, dried herbs. Palate: flavourful, fruity, fine bitter notes, correct.

Etra Burbujas del Atlántico Extra Brut ESP
100% albariño
87
Colour: bright straw, greenish rim. Nose: fresh, white flowers, medium intensity, fragrant herbs. Palate: correct, balanced, fine bitter notes.

Etra Condado 2013 B
88
Colour: bright straw. Nose: dried herbs, floral, fresh fruit, citrus fruit. Palate: light-bodied, fresh, fruity, flavourful, correct.

BODEGAS EL INICIO

San Vicente, 22
47300 Peñafiel (Valladolid)
☎: +34 947 515 884
Fax: +34 947 515 886
www.bodegaselinicio.com
rbi@redbottleint.com

Elas 2013 B
100% albariño
89
Colour: bright straw. Nose: balanced, fragrant herbs, floral, medium intensity. Palate: fruity, flavourful, easy to drink.

BODEGAS FILLABOA

Lugar de Fillaboa, s/n
36450 Salvaterra do Miño (Pontevedra)
☎: +34 986 658 132
www.bodegasfillaboa.com
info@bodegasfillaboa.com

Fillaboa 2013 B
100% albariño
91
Colour: bright yellow. Nose: expressive, balanced, white flowers, fresh fruit, varietal. Palate: flavourful, good acidity, fine bitter notes.

BODEGAS GERARDO MÉNDEZ

Galiñanes, 10 - Lores
36968 Meaño (Pontevedra)
☎: +34 986 747 046
Fax: +34 986 748 915
www.bodegasgerardomendez.com
info@bodegasgerardomendez.com

Albariño Do Ferreiro 2013 B
100% albariño
91
Colour: bright straw, greenish rim. Nose: fresh fruit, floral. Palate: fresh, easy to drink, correct.

BODEGAS GÓMEZ Y RIAL

Piro, 15 - Oza
15886 Teo (A Coruña)
☎: +34 629 885 371
www.gomezrial.com
aagorial@yahoo.es

Alargo 2013 B
100% albariño
86
Colour: bright yellow. Nose: faded flowers, ripe fruit. Palate: correct, fruity, flavourful.

Compostelae 2013 B
100% albariño
87
Colour: bright yellow. Nose: ripe fruit, faded flowers, fine lees. Palate: rich, fine bitter notes.

BODEGAS LA CANA

Camiño Novo, 36
29700 Zamar - Villagarcía de Arousa
(Pontevedra)
☎: +34 986 686 811
Fax: +34 952 504 706
www.lacana.es
lacana@jorgeordonez.es

La Caña 2013 B
100% albariño

89

Colour: bright straw. Nose: fresh fruit, white flowers, dried herbs, mineral. Palate: flavourful, fruity, good acidity, balanced.

La Caña Navia 2010 B
100% albariño

93

Colour: bright yellow. Nose: powerfull, ripe fruit, sweet spices, creamy oak, fragrant herbs, mineral. Palate: rich, flavourful, fresh, good acidity, spicy.

BODEGAS LA VAL

Lugar Muguiña, s/n - Arantei
36458 Salvaterra de Miño (Pontevedra)
☎: +34 986 610 728
Fax: +34 986 611 635
www.bodegaslaval.com
laval@bodegaslaval.com

Finca Arantei 2013 B
100% albariño

90

Colour: bright straw. Nose: fragrant herbs, citrus fruit, fresh fruit, floral. Palate: fresh, fruity, flavourful, balanced, elegant.

La Val Albariño 2011 BFB
100% albariño

93

Colour: bright yellow. Nose: powerfull, ripe fruit, sweet spices, creamy oak, fragrant herbs, citrus fruit, balsamic herbs. Palate: rich, flavourful, fresh, good acidity, balanced.

La Val Albariño 2013 B
100% albariño

91

Colour: bright straw. Nose: fresh, fresh fruit, white flowers, expressive. Palate: flavourful, fruity, good acidity, balanced.

La Val Crianza sobre Lías 2007 BC
100% albariño

94

Colour: yellow. Nose: complex, expressive, spicy, faded flowers, balanced. Palate: full, flavourful, long, fine bitter notes, good acidity.

Mas que Dos 2013 B
albariño, treixadura, loureiro

87

Colour: bright straw. Nose: fresh, fresh fruit, expressive. Palate: flavourful, fruity, good acidity, balanced.

Orballo 2013 B
100% albariño

90

Colour: bright straw. Nose: fragrant herbs, fruit expression, floral, dried herbs. Palate: fresh, fruity, flavourful, balanced, elegant.

Taboexa 2013 B
100% albariño

88

Colour: bright yellow. Nose: fresh, white flowers, fresh fruit. Palate: fresh, correct, easy to drink, good finish.

Viña Ludy 2013 B
100% albariño

90

Colour: bright straw. Nose: dried herbs, dried flowers. Palate: fruity, balanced, fine bitter notes, good acidity, easy to drink.

BODEGAS MAR DE FRADES

Lg. Arosa, 16 - Finca Valiñas
36637 Meis (Pontevedra)
☎: +34 986 680 911
Fax: +34 986 680 926
www.mardefrades.es
info@mardefrades.es

Finca Valiñas "crianza sobre lías" 2012 B
albariño

93

Colour: bright straw. Nose: white flowers, expressive, fine lees, dried herbs, candied fruit. Palate: flavourful, fruity, good acidity, balanced.

Mar de Frades BN
albariño

86

Colour: bright straw. Nose: medium intensity, dried herbs, fine lees, floral, candied fruit, citrus fruit. Palate: fresh, fruity, flavourful, good acidity.

Mar de Frades 2013 B

albariño

89

Colour: bright straw. Nose: citrus fruit, white flowers. Palate: flavourful, fruity, good acidity, balanced.

BODEGAS MARQUÉS DE VIZHOJA

Finca La Moreira s/n
36438 Arbo (Pontevedra)
☎: +34 986 665 825
Fax: +34 986 665 960
www.marquesdevizhoja.com
informacion@marquesdevizhoja.com

Señor da Folla Verde 2013 B

89

Colour: bright straw. Nose: white flowers, fragrant herbs, fruit expression. Palate: fresh, fruity, flavourful, balanced, elegant.

Torre La Moreira 2013 B

100% albariño

90

Colour: bright straw. Nose: white flowers, citrus fruit, fresh fruit, expressive. Palate: balanced, good acidity, fine bitter notes.

BODEGAS MARTÍN CÓDAX

Burgáns, 91
36633 Vilariño-Cambados (Pontevedra)
☎: +34 986 526 040
Fax: +34 986 526 901
www.martincodax.com
comercial@martincodax.com

Burgáns 2013 B

100% albariño

89

Colour: straw. Nose: fruit expression, tropical fruit, fragrant herbs, white flowers. Palate: fresh, fruity, flavourful, easy to drink.

Marieta 2013 B

100% albariño

87

Colour: bright straw. Nose: fresh, fresh fruit, white flowers, expressive. Palate: flavourful, fruity, sweetness, easy to drink.

Martín Códax 2013 B

100% albariño

88

Colour: bright straw. Nose: fresh, fresh fruit, white flowers. Palate: flavourful, fruity, good acidity, balanced.

Martín Códax Gallaecia 2009 B

100% albariño

94

Colour: bright golden. Nose: ripe fruit, dry nuts, powerfull, toasty, aged wood nuances, honeyed notes, pattiserie. Palate: flavourful, fruity, spicy, toasty, long.

Martin Codax Lías 2011 B

100% albariño

93

Colour: bright straw. Nose: white flowers, fresh fruit, expressive, fine lees, dried herbs, balanced. Palate: flavourful, fruity, good acidity, balanced, elegant.

Organistrum 2011 B

100% albariño

89

Colour: bright yellow. Nose: sweet spices, ripe fruit, faded flowers. Palate: ripe fruit, rich, good structure.

BODEGAS NANCLARES

Castriño, 13 - Castrelo
36639 Cambados (Pontevedra)
☎: +34 986 520 763
www.bodegasnanclares.com
bodega@bodegasnanclares.es

Alberto Nanclares sobre Lías 2012 B

albariño

89

Colour: bright straw. Nose: fresh fruit, white flowers, fragrant herbs. Palate: flavourful, fruity, balanced.

Soverribas de Nanclares 2011 BFB
albariño
84

Tempus Vivendi 2012 B
albariño
86
Colour: bright yellow. Nose: dried flowers, faded flowers, ripe fruit. Palate: rich, flavourful, fine bitter notes.

BODEGAS PABLO PADÍN
Ameiro, 24 - Dena
36967 Meaño (Pontevedra)
☎: +34 986 743 231
Fax: +34 986 745 791
www.pablopadin.com
info@pablopadin.com

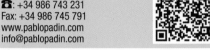

Albariño Eiral 2013 B
100% albariño
89
Colour: yellow. Nose: balanced, white flowers, faded flowers, ripe fruit. Palate: good acidity, balanced, fine bitter notes, flavourful.

Albariño Segrel 2013 B
100% albariño
89
Colour: bright straw. Nose: fragrant herbs, fresh fruit, white flowers. Palate: fresh, fruity, flavourful, elegant.

Feitizo da Noite 2013 ESP
albariño
89
Colour: bright straw. Nose: medium intensity, fresh fruit, dried herbs, fine lees, floral. Palate: fresh, fruity, flavourful, good acidity.

Segrel Ámbar 2013 B
100% albariño
90
Colour: bright straw. Nose: white flowers, fragrant herbs, fruit expression, balsamic herbs. Palate: fresh, fruity, flavourful, balanced, good finish.

BODEGAS SANTIAGO ROMA
Catariño, 5 - Besomaño
36636 Ribadumia (Pontevedra)
☎: +34 679 469 218
www.santiagoroma.com
bodega@santiagoroma.com

Albariño Santiago Roma 2013 B
albariño
91
Colour: bright yellow. Nose: scrubland, faded flowers, powerfull, wild herbs. Palate: flavourful, fresh, long.

Albariño Santiago Roma Selección Albariño 2013 B
albariño
91
Colour: straw. Nose: dried herbs, wild herbs, dried flowers, expressive, saline. Palate: balanced, flavourful, long.

Colleita de Martis Albariño 2013 B
albariño
90
Colour: bright straw. Nose: fresh, fresh fruit, white flowers, expressive. Palate: flavourful, fruity, good acidity, balanced.

BODEGAS SEÑORÍO DE VALEI
La Granja, 65
36494 Sela - Arbo (Pontevedra)
☎: +34 698 146 950
Fax: +34 986 665 390
www.senoriodevalei.com
info@senoriodevalei.com

Estela 2013 B
100% albariño
87
Colour: bright straw. Nose: fresh, fresh fruit, white flowers, varietal. Palate: flavourful, fruity, good acidity, balanced.

Frailes do Mar 2013 B
100% albariño
90
Colour: bright straw. Nose: white flowers, fresh fruit, expressive, fine lees, dried herbs. Palate: flavourful, fruity, good acidity, balanced.

Gran Muiño 2013 B
100% albariño
87
Colour: bright straw. Nose: medium intensity, fresh, white flowers, citrus fruit. Palate: fresh, easy to drink, good finish.

Oro Valei 2013 B
100% albariño
86
Colour: bright straw. Nose: ripe fruit, tropical fruit, dried herbs. Palate: fine bitter notes, fresh, fruity, easy to drink.

Señorío de Valei 2013 B
100% albariño
89
Colour: bright straw. Nose: fresh fruit, citrus fruit, floral. Palate: balanced, fine bitter notes, good acidity, easy to drink.

BODEGAS TERRAS GAUDA

Ctra. Tui - A Guarda, Km. 55
36760 O'Rosal (Pontevedra)
☎: +34 986 621 001
Fax: +34 986 621 084
www.terrasgauda.com
terrasgauda@terrasgauda.com

Abadía de San Campio 2013 B
100% albariño
88
Colour: bright yellow. Nose: medium intensity, fresh fruit, floral. Palate: flavourful, fine bitter notes, balanced.

La Mar 2012 B
91
Colour: bright yellow. Nose: powerfull, ripe fruit, sweet spices, creamy oak, fragrant herbs. Palate: rich, flavourful, fresh, good acidity, elegant.

Terras Gauda 2013 B
92
Colour: bright yellow. Nose: expressive, complex, varietal, dried flowers. Palate: flavourful, rich, complex, balanced, fine bitter notes.

Terras Gauda Etiqueta Negra 2012 BFB
92
Colour: bright yellow. Nose: ripe fruit, sweet spices, creamy oak, fragrant herbs, expressive. Palate: rich, flavourful, fresh, good acidity, balanced, elegant.

BODEGAS TORRES

Miguel Torres i Carbó, 6
8720 Vilafranca del Penedès
(Barcelona)
☎: +34 938 177 400
Fax: +34 938 177 444
www.torres.com
mailadmin@torres.es

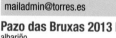

Pazo das Bruxas 2013 B
albariño
88
Colour: bright yellow. Nose: medium intensity, dried flowers, dried herbs. Palate: easy to drink, good acidity, fine bitter notes, good finish.

BODEGAS VICENTE GANDÍA

Ctra. Cheste a Godelleta, s/n
46370 Chiva (Valencia)
☎: +34 962 524 242
Fax: +34 962 524 243
www.vicentegandia.es
info@vicentegandia.com

Con un Par Albariño 2013 B
100% albariño
90
Colour: bright yellow. Nose: floral, fruit expression, wild herbs, mineral. Palate: powerful, rich, flavourful, balanced.

BODEGAS VIONTA S.L.

Lugar de Axis - Simes, s/n
36968 Meaño (Pontevedra)
☎: +34 986 747 566
Fax: +34 986 747 621
www.freixenet.es
david.martinez@vionta.com

Agnusdei Albariño 2013 B
100% albariño
91
Colour: bright yellow. Nose: white flowers, fresh fruit, balanced. Palate: long, good acidity, fine bitter notes, balanced.

Vionta 2013 B
100% albariño
88
Colour: bright straw, greenish rim. Nose: white flowers, varietal, medium intensity. Palate: correct, easy to drink, fine bitter notes.

You & Me White Experience 2013 B
100% albariño
90
Colour: bright straw. Nose: fresh fruit, floral, fresh, expressive. Palate: fresh, easy to drink, good acidity, fine bitter notes, fruity aftestaste.

BODEGAS Y VIÑEDOS DON OLEGARIO

Refoxos, s/n - Corbillón
36634 Cambados (Pontevedra)
☎: +34 986 520 886
www.donolegario.com
info@donolegario.com

Don Olegario Albariño 2013 B
100% albariño
92
Colour: bright straw. Nose: white flowers, medium intensity, ripe fruit. Palate: flavourful, fruity, good acidity, balanced.

BODEGAS Y VIÑEDOS RODRIGO MÉNDEZ S.L.

Pza. de Compostola, 22
36201 Vigo (Pontevedra)
☎: +34 699 446 113
goliardovino@gmail.com

Cies 2012 BFB
100% albariño
92
Colour: bright straw. Nose: white flowers, fresh fruit, expressive, dried herbs, spicy. Palate: flavourful, fruity, good acidity, balanced.

Sálvora 2011 BFB
100% albariño
93

Colour: bright straw, greenish rim. Nose: expressive, elegant, spicy, ripe fruit, dried flowers. Palate: balanced, fine bitter notes, long.

BOUZA DE CARRIL

Avda. Caponiñas, 14 - Barrantes
36636 Ribadumia (Pontevedra)
☎: +34 600 020 627
Fax: +34 986 710 471
www.bouzadecarril.com
bodega@bouzacarril.com

Bouza de Carril Albariño 2013 B
100% albariño
87

Colour: straw. Nose: ripe fruit, tropical fruit, floral. Palate: correct, fine bitter notes, flavourful.

BOUZA DO REI

Lugar de Puxafeita, s/n
36636 Ribadumia (Pontevedra)
☎: +34 986 710 257
Fax: +34 986 718 393
www.bouzadorei.com
bouzadorei@bouzadorei.com

Albariño Bouza Do Rei 2013 B
100% albariño
90

Colour: bright yellow. Nose: white flowers, expressive, fresh fruit. Palate: flavourful, good acidity, fine bitter notes.

Albariño Gran Lagar de Bouza 2013 B
100% albariño
87

Colour: bright straw. Nose: white flowers, fragrant herbs, fruit expression. Palate: fresh, fruity, flavourful, balanced, elegant.

Albariño Pazo da Torre 2013 B
100% albariño
85

Bouza do Rei Albariño Gran Selección 2012 B
100% albariño
90

Colour: bright yellow. Nose: spicy, complex, balanced, faded flowers. Palate: flavourful, good structure, long, good acidity.

Castel de Bouza 2013 B
100% albariño
89

Colour: bright straw. Nose: white flowers, fragrant herbs. Palate: fresh, fruity, flavourful, balanced, elegant.

CARMEN ALVAREZ OUBIÑA

Cristimil 5 Padrenda
36968 Meaño (Pontevedra)
☎: +34 616 643 559
altosdecristimil@gmail.com

Altos de Cristimil 2013 B
100% albariño
88

Colour: bright straw. Nose: white flowers, fragrant herbs, fruit expression, citrus fruit. Palate: fresh, fruity, flavourful, balanced, elegant.

EMW GRANDES VINOS DE ESPAÑA

Sánchez Picazo, 53
30332 Balsapintada (Fuente Alamo) (Murcia)
☎: +34 968 151 520
Fax: +34 968 151 539
www.emw.es
info@emw.es

La Marimorena 2013 B
100% albariño
89

Colour: bright yellow. Nose: balanced, fresh fruit. Palate: fruity, easy to drink, good finish, fine bitter notes, correct.

EULOGIO GONDAR GALIÑANES

Pereira, 6
36968 Meaño (Pontevedra)
☎: +34 986 747 241
Fax: +34 986 747 742
www.lagardecandes.com
albarino@lagardecandes.com

Lagar de Candes Albariño 2013 B
100% albariño
88

Colour: bright straw. Nose: medium intensity, dried flowers, fragrant herbs. Palate: correct, balanced, fine bitter notes.

Quinta Vide 2013 B
100% albariño
86

Colour: bright straw. Nose: dried herbs, dried flowers, powerfull. Palate: rich, good finish.

FRORE DE CARME

Sobrán, 38
36611 Vilagarcía de Arousa
(Pontevedra)
☎: +34 986 501 218
Fax: +34 986 501 218
www.eladiopineiro.es
eladiopineiro@froredecarme.es

Envidiacochina 2012 B
100% albariño

90

Colour: bright yellow. Nose: balanced, dried flowers, faded flowers, ripe fruit. Palate: flavourful, rich, long, balanced.

Frore de Carme 2010 B
100% albariño

91

Colour: bright yellow. Nose: candied fruit, faded flowers, expressive, spicy, complex. Palate: rich, flavourful, good structure.

GENUS DE VINUM

32003 Ourense (Ourense)
☎: +34 988 100 120
www.genusdevinum.es
info@genusdevinum.es

Cellarium 2012 B
100% albariño

89

Colour: yellow, pale. Nose: dried flowers, faded flowers, ripe fruit. Palate: fruity, fine bitter notes, long.

GRUPO VINÍCOLA MARQUÉS DE VARGAS

Pombal, 3 - Lugar de Porto
36458 Salvaterra de Miño (Pontevedra)
☎: +34 986 658 285
Fax: +34 986 664 208
www.marquesdevargas.com
info@pazosanmauro.com

Pazo San Mauro 2013 B
albariño

90

Colour: bright straw. Nose: medium intensity, fresh, white flowers, varietal. Palate: fruity, correct, fine bitter notes, easy to drink.

Sanamaro 2010 B
albariño, loureiro

91

Colour: bright straw. Nose: white flowers, fresh fruit, expressive, fine lees, dried herbs, sweet spices. Palate: flavourful, fruity, good acidity, balanced, spicy.

HROS. ANTÓN BÉRTOLO LOSADA

Estación, s/n - Sela
36494 Arbo (Pontevedra)
☎: +34 986 853 366
Fax: +34 986 661 522

Don Ramón 2013 B
albariño

88

Colour: bright straw. Nose: white flowers, fragrant herbs, fruit expression, tropical fruit. Palate: fresh, fruity, flavourful.

JULIÁN GONZÁLEZ AREAL

Finca Lavandeira - Rebordans
36712 Tui (Pontevedra)
☎: +34 629 837 509
Fax: +34 986 601 414
canonigoareal@canonigoareal.com

Canónigo Areal 2013 B
100% albariño

86

Colour: bright yellow. Nose: dried flowers, ripe fruit, wild herbs. Palate: fresh, fruity, easy to drink.

KATAME

Berlin, 5 1ºC
28850 Torrejón de Ardo (Madrid)
☎: +34 916 749 427
katame@katamesl.com

Pekado Mortal 2013 B
100% albariño

90

Colour: bright straw. Nose: white flowers, fragrant herbs, fruit expression. Palate: fresh, fruity, flavourful.

LA MALETA HAND MADE FINE WINES

Julio Prieto Nespereira, 21
32005 Ourense (Ourense)
☎: +34 988 614 234
lamaletawines.com
hola@lamaletawines.com

El Príncipe y el Birrete 2013 B
100% albariño

89

Colour: bright straw. Nose: white flowers, medium intensity, varietal. Palate: balanced, fine bitter notes, good finish.

El Rubio Infante 2013 B
100% albariño

88

Colour: bright straw. Nose: white flowers, fragrant herbs, fruit expression, expressive. Palate: fresh, fruity, flavourful, easy to drink.

LAGAR DA CONDESA

Lugar de Maran s/n Arcos da Condesa
36650 Caldas de Reis (Pontevedra)
☎: +34 968 435 022
Fax: +34 968 716 051
www.orowines.com
info@orowines.com

Lagar da Condesa 2013 B
100% albariño
91
Colour: bright straw. Nose: white flowers, fragrant herbs, fruit expression, spicy. Palate: fresh, fruity, flavourful, rich, easy to drink.

LAGAR DE BESADA

Pazo, 11
36968 Xil-Meaño (Pontevedra)
☎: +34 986 747 473
Fax: +34 986 747 826
www.lagardebesada.com
info@lagardebesada.com

Añada de Baladiña 2006 B
100% albariño
90
Colour: bright yellow. Nose: dried flowers, saline, dry nuts, expressive, tobacco. Palate: spicy, balanced, fine bitter notes, long.

Baladiña 2012 B
100% albariño
89
Colour: bright straw. Nose: medium intensity, varietal, fresh fruit. Palate: fruity, easy to drink.

Lagar de Besada 2013 B
100% albariño
86
Colour: bright straw. Nose: fresh, fresh fruit, white flowers. Palate: flavourful, fruity, good acidity.

LAGAR DE CERVERA

Estrada de Loureza, 86
36770 O Rosal (Pontevedra)
☎: +34 986 625 875
Fax: +34 986 625 011
www.riojalta.com
lagar@riojalta.com

Lagar de Cervera 2013 B
100% albariño
90
Colour: bright straw. Nose: citrus fruit, fresh fruit, wild herbs, mineral, expressive. Palate: powerful, flavourful, rich, long, balsamic, fine bitter notes.

LAGAR DE CERVERA

ALBARIÑO 2013

A brisa do mar, unha terra única, a fina chuvia de Galicia sobre as nosas viñas, a última mirada do sol antes de deitarse, crean esta marabilla da natureza: o albariño Lagar de Cervera.

RIAS BAIXAS
Denominación de Origen

LAGAR DE COSTA

Sartaxes, 8 - Castrelo
36639 Cambados (Pontevedra)
☎: +34 986 543 526
Fax: +34 986 982 342
www.lagardecosta.com
contacto@lagardecosta.com

Lagar de Costa 2012 B Barrica
100% albariño
91
Colour: bright yellow. Nose: ripe fruit, sweet spices, creamy oak, fragrant herbs. Palate: rich, smoky aftertaste, flavourful, fresh, good acidity.

Lagar de Costa 2013 B
100% albariño
87
Colour: bright straw. Nose: fresh, fresh fruit, white flowers, expressive. Palate: flavourful, fruity, good acidity, balanced.

Maio5 de Lagar Costa 2012 B
100% albariño
90
Colour: bright yellow. Nose: floral, jasmine, fragrant herbs, balsamic herbs, ripe fruit. Palate: balanced, fine bitter notes, unctuous, flavourful.

M. CONSTANTINA SOTELO ARES

Castriño, 9
36639 Cambados (Pontevedra)
☎: +34 639 835 073
adegasotelo@yahoo.es

Rosalía 2013 B
albariño
92
Colour: bright straw. Nose: white flowers, fresh fruit, fine lees, dried herbs, expressive. Palate: flavourful, fruity, good acidity, balanced.

Rosalía de Castro 2013 B
albariño
91
Colour: straw. Nose: white flowers, fragrant herbs, balanced. Palate: balanced, fine bitter notes, flavourful, long.

MAIOR DE MENDOZA

Rúa de Xiabre, 58
36600 Villagarcía de Arosa (Pontevedra)
☎: +34 986 508 896
Fax: +34 986 507 924
www.maiordemendoza.com
maiordemendoza@hotmail.es

Fulget 2013 B
albariño
87
Colour: bright straw. Nose: fresh, fresh fruit, citrus fruit. Palate: good acidity, balanced, good finish.

Maior de Mendoza 3 Crianzas 2012 B
albariño
90
Colour: yellow. Nose: ripe fruit, spicy, dried flowers, faded flowers. Palate: flavourful, fruity, rich, correct, fine bitter notes.

Maior de Mendoza Maceración Carbónica 2013 B
albariño
86
Colour: bright straw. Nose: medium intensity, fresh, floral. Palate: correct, easy to drink, good finish.

Maior de Mendoza sobre Lías 2013 B
albariño
88
Colour: bright straw. Nose: white flowers, fresh fruit, expressive, dried herbs. Palate: fruity, good acidity, balanced.

MAR DE ENVERO

Concepción Arenal 1, bajo
36620 Vilanova de Arousa (Pontevedra)
☎: +34 981 566 329
Fax: +34 981 569 552
www.mardeenvero.es
bodega@mardeenvero.es

Mar de Envero 2012 B
albariño
92
Colour: bright straw. Nose: fragrant herbs, fruit expression, dried flowers, citrus fruit. Palate: fresh, fruity, flavourful, balanced, elegant.

Troupe 2013 B
albariño
91
Colour: bright straw. Nose: white flowers, fragrant herbs, fruit expression, mineral. Palate: fresh, fruity, flavourful, balanced, elegant.

MARCOS LOJO

Pza. Clemencio Fernández Pulido, P2 2ºF
36630 Cambados (Pontevedra)
☎: +34 633 538 802
www.chanderosas.com
info@chanderosas.com

Chan de Rosas 2013 B
albariño
87
Colour: yellow, pale. Nose: dried flowers, fragrant herbs, citrus fruit. Palate: correct, good finish, easy to drink.

Chan de Rosas Cuvée Especial 2013 B
albariño
90
Colour: bright straw. Nose: white flowers, fragrant herbs, fruit expression. Palate: fresh, fruity, flavourful, balanced, elegant.

MARÍA VICTORIA DOVALO MÉNDEZ

Estación, 1-21
26350 Cenicero (La Rioja)
☎: +34 941 454 050
Fax: +34 941 454 529
www.bodegasriojanas.com
bodega@bodegasriojanas.com

Veiga Naúm 2013 B
100% albariño
87
Colour: bright straw. Nose: fresh, fresh fruit, white flowers, expressive. Palate: fruity, good acidity, balanced, easy to drink.

NUBORI
Avda. del Ebro s/n
26540 Alfaro (La Rioja)
☎: +34 941 183 502
Fax: +34 941 183 157
www.bodegasnubori.com
nubori@nubori.es

Pazo de Nubori 2012 B
albariño
89
Colour: bright yellow. Nose: ripe fruit, dried herbs, powerfull, mineral. Palate: powerful, flavourful, long, balsamic.

SELECCIONADO POR NUBORI, S. L.

PAZO DE NUBORI

Rías Baixas
DENOMINACIÓN DE ORIGEN

ALBARIÑO 2012

ORO WINES
Ctra. de Fuentealamo - Paraje de la Aragona
30520 Jumilla (Murcia)
☎: +34 968 435 022
Fax: +34 968 716 051
www.orowines.com
info@orowines.com

Kentia 2013 B
100% albariño
91
Colour: bright straw. Nose: white flowers, fragrant herbs, citrus fruit, mineral. Palate: fresh, fruity, flavourful, balanced, elegant.

PALACIOS VINOTECA
Ctra. de Nalda a Viguera, 46
26190 Nalda (La Rioja)
☎: +34 941 444 418
www.palaciosvinoteca.com
info@palaciosvinoteca.com

A Calma 2013 B
100% albariño
91
Colour: bright yellow. Nose: citrus fruit, fruit expression, floral, fragrant herbs, expressive. Palate: fresh, fruity, flavourful, spicy, balsamic, balanced.

Sete Bois 2013 B
albariño
90
Colour: bright straw. Nose: fresh, white flowers, expressive, varietal. Palate: flavourful, fruity, good acidity, long, complex.

PAZO BAIÓN
Abelleira 4, 5, 6 - Baión
36614 Vilanova de Arousa (Pontevedra)
☎: +34 986 543 535
Fax: +34 986 524 251
www.pazobaion.com
inf@pazobaion.com

Pazo Baión 2013 B
100% albariño
92
Colour: bright straw. Nose: fragrant herbs, fruit expression, white flowers, mineral. Palate: fresh, fruity, flavourful, elegant.

PAZO DE BARRANTES
Finca Pazo de Barrantes
36636 Barrantes (Pontevedra)
☎: +34 986 718 211
Fax: +34 986 710 424
www.pazodebarrantes.com
bodega@pazodebarrantes.com

La Comtesse 2010 B
100% albariño
95
Colour: bright yellow. Nose: expressive, candied fruit, citrus fruit, sweet spices, cocoa bean. Palate: flavourful, good acidity, fine bitter notes, long.

La Comtesse 2011 B
100% albariño

93

Colour: bright straw. Nose: spicy, ripe fruit, dried herbs, white flowers. Palate: flavourful, good acidity, round.

Pazo de Barrantes Albariño 2012 B
albariño

93

Colour: bright straw. Nose: white flowers, fresh fruit, expressive, fine lees, dried herbs. Palate: flavourful, fruity, good acidity, balanced.

Pazo de Barrantes Albariño 2013 B
100% albariño

92

Colour: bright straw. Nose: fresh, fresh fruit, white flowers. Palate: flavourful, fruity, good acidity, balanced.

PAZO DE SEÑORANS
Vilanoviña, s/n
36616 Meis (Pontevedra)
☎: +34 986 715 373
Fax: +34 986 715 569
www.pazodesenorans.com
info@pazodesenorans.com

Pazo Señorans 2013 B
100% albariño

92

Colour: bright straw. Nose: white flowers, fragrant herbs, fruit expression. Palate: fresh, fruity, flavourful, balanced, elegant.

Pazo Señorans Selección de Añada 2007 B
100% albariño

98

Colour: bright yellow. Nose: complex, petrol notes, ripe fruit, spicy, dry nuts, faded flowers. Palate: round, rich, flavourful, fine bitter notes.

PAZO DE VILLAREI
Arousa s/n San Martiño
36637 Meis (Pontevedra)
☎: +34 986 710 827
Fax: +34 986 710 827
www.pazodevillarei.com
info@hgabodegas.com

Pazo de Villarei 2013 B
100% albariño

91

Colour: bright straw. Nose: wild herbs, balsamic herbs, floral, citrus fruit, fresh fruit. Palate: flavourful, rich, fruity, complex, elegant.

Pazo de Villarei 2012 B
100% albariño

92

Colour: bright yellow. Nose: floral, dried herbs, ripe fruit, mineral. Palate: flavourful, rich, fruity, spicy, balsamic, round.

PAZO PONDAL
Coto, s/n - Cabeiras
36436 Arbo (Pontevedra)
☎: +34 986 665 551
Fax: +34 986 665 949
www.pazopondal.com
mktg@pazopondal.com

Leira 2013 B
100% albariño

89

Colour: bright straw. Nose: dried flowers, fresh fruit. Palate: fruity, easy to drink, flavourful, balanced, correct.

Pazo Pondal Albariño 2013 B
100% albariño

88

Colour: bright straw. Nose: varietal, medium intensity, white flowers, citrus fruit. Palate: correct, easy to drink.

PONTECABALEIROS
As Laxas, 16
36430 Arbo (Pontevedra)
☎: +34 986 665 444
Fax: +34 986 665 554
www.pontecabaleiros.com
info@pontecabaleiros.com

Alvinte 2013 B
100% albariño

88

Colour: bright straw. Nose: fresh, fresh fruit, white flowers, balsamic herbs. Palate: flavourful, fruity, good acidity, easy to drink.

Ferrum 2013 B
100% albariño

87

Colour: bright straw. Nose: fruit expression, tropical fruit, balanced. Palate: correct, fine bitter notes.

Valdocea 2013 B
100% albariño

87

Colour: bright straw. Nose: fresh, fresh fruit, white flowers, medium intensity. Palate: fruity, good acidity, balanced, easy to drink.

PRIMA VINIA
Soutelo, 3
36750 Goián (Pontevedra)
☎: +34 986 620 137
Fax: +34 986 620 071
info@primavinia.com

Gaudila 2010 B
albariño

92

Colour: bright straw. Nose: white flowers, fresh fruit, expressive, fine lees, dried herbs. Palate: flavourful, fruity, good acidity, balanced.

Leira Vella 2013 B
albariño

89

Colour: yellow. Nose: varietal, dry stone, balanced. Palate: correct, fine bitter notes, balanced, easy to drink.

QUINTA COUSELO
Couselo, 13
36770 O'Rosal (Pontevedra)
☎: +34 986 625 051
Fax: +34 986 626 267
www.quintacouselo.com
quintacouselo@quintacouselo.com

Quinta de Couselo 2013 B
albariño, loureiro, caíño blanco

92 🌷

Colour: bright straw. Nose: white flowers, fragrant herbs, fruit expression, expressive. Palate: fresh, fruity, flavourful, balanced, elegant.

Turonia 2013 B
albariño

90

Colour: bright yellow. Nose: floral, balsamic herbs, fresh fruit, citrus fruit. Palate: fresh, fruity, flavourful, balanced.

QUINTA DE LA ERRE
Eiras s/n
36778 Eiras O'Rosal (Pontevedra)
☎: +34 693 622 429
Fax: +34 693 622 429
www.quintadelaerre.com
labodega@quintadelaerre.com

Quinta de la Erre 2013 B
albariño

90

Colour: bright straw. Nose: white flowers, fragrant herbs, fruit expression. Palate: fresh, fruity, flavourful, balanced, elegant.

Quinta de la Erre Rosal 2011 B Barrica
albariño, loureiro, caíño

91

Colour: bright yellow. Nose: powerfull, ripe fruit, sweet spices, creamy oak, fragrant herbs. Palate: rich, smoky aftertaste, flavourful, fresh, good acidity.

RECTORAL DO UMIA

Rua do Pan, Polígono industrial de Ribadumia
36636 Ribadumia (Pontevedra)
☎: +34 988 384 200
Fax: +34 988 384 068
www.rectoraldoumia.com
jania@bodegasgallegas.com

Miudiño 2013 B
100% albariño

87

Colour: yellow. Nose: fresh fruit, white flowers. Palate: flavourful, easy to drink, good finish, fine bitter notes.

Pórtico da Ria 2013 B
100% albariño

87

Colour: bright yellow. Nose: fragrant herbs, floral, medium intensity. Palate: fruity, good acidity, correct.

Rectoral do Umia 2013 B
100% albariño

88

Colour: yellow. Nose: white flowers, fresh fruit, citrus fruit, floral. Palate: fresh, fruity, flavourful, balanced, correct.

RICARDO ABAL PADIN

Avda. La Pastora, 24
36630 Cambados (Pontevedra)
☎: +34 670 452 929
Fax: +34 986 542 882
lagardacachada@gmail.com

Don Ricardo 2013 B
100% albariño

84

Lagar da Cachada 2013 B
100% albariño

84

RODRÍGUEZ SANZO

Manuel Azaña, 9
47014 (Valladolid)
☎: +34 983 150 150
Fax: +34 983 150 151
www.rodriguezsanzo.com
comunicacion@valsanzo.com

María Sanzo 2013 B
100% albariño

89

Colour: bright straw. Nose: white flowers, fragrant herbs, fruit expression. Palate: fresh, fruity, flavourful, balanced.

SANTIAGO RUIZ

Rua do Vinicultor Santiago Ruiz
36760 San Miguel de Tabagón -
O Rosal (Pontevedra)
☎: +34 986 614 083
Fax: +34 986 614 142
www.bodegasantiagoruiz.com
info@bodegasantiagoruiz.com

Santiago Ruiz 2013 B

91

Colour: bright straw. Nose: medium intensity, citrus fruit, fresh fruit, floral. Palate: fresh, correct, easy to drink, good finish.

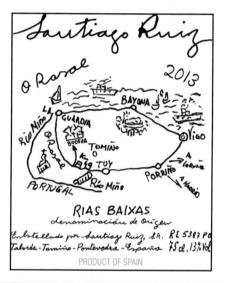

SEÑORÍO DE RUBIÓS

Bouza do Rato, s/n - Rubiós
36449 As Neves (Pontevedra)
☎: +34 986 667 212
Fax: +34 986 648 279
www.srubios.com
info@srubios.com

Liñar de Vides 2013 B
100% albariño

90

Colour: bright straw. Nose: fresh, fresh fruit, white flowers. Palate: flavourful, fruity, good acidity, balanced, fine bitter notes.

Manuel D'Amaro Pedral 2011 T
100% pedral

89

Colour: cherry, garnet rim. Nose: ripe fruit, wild herbs, earthy notes, spicy, creamy oak. Palate: balanced, flavourful, long, balsamic.

Señorío de Rubiós Albariño 2013 B
100% albariño

91

Colour: bright straw. Nose: balsamic herbs, dried herbs, citrus fruit, fresh fruit, expressive. Palate: rich, powerful, flavourful, balanced.

Señorío de Rubiós Condado Blanco 2012 ESP
treixadura, albariño, loureiro, godello

89

Colour: bright straw. Nose: fresh fruit, dried herbs, fine lees, floral. Palate: fresh, fruity, flavourful, good acidity, balanced.

Señorío de Rubiós Condado Blanco do Tea 2013 B
treixadura, albariño, loureiro, godello

89

Colour: bright yellow. Nose: fresh fruit, floral, dried herbs, citrus fruit. Palate: correct, light-bodied, easy to drink.

Señorío de Rubiós Condado do Tea Barrica 2010 B Roble
treixadura, albariño, loureiro, godello

91

Colour: bright yellow. Nose: ripe fruit, sweet spices, creamy oak, fragrant herbs, balanced. Palate: rich, flavourful, fresh, good acidity.

Señorío de Rubiós Condado Tinto 2013 T
sousón, espadeiro, caíño, mencía

83

Señorío de Rubiós Mencía 2013 T
100% mencía

86

Colour: cherry, garnet rim. Nose: ripe fruit, grassy, herbaceous. Palate: balsamic, fine bitter notes, slightly green tannins.

Señorío de Rubiós Sousón 2013 T
100% sousón

90

Colour: cherry, purple rim. Nose: red berry notes, raspberry, fruit expression, fragrant herbs, dry stone. Palate: flavourful, light-bodied, good acidity, fresh, fruity.

Señorío de Rubiós Vino Novo 2012 T Maceración Carbónica
sousón, espadeiro, caíño, mencía

87

Colour: dark-red cherry, garnet rim. Nose: medium intensity, wild herbs, red berry notes. Palate: correct, balsamic.

SEÑORÍO DE SOBRAL
Lg. Porto - Finca Sobral
36458 Salvaterra do Miño (Pontevedra)
☎: +34 986 415 144
Fax: +34 986 421 744
www.ssobral.net
info@ssobral.net

Señorío de Sobral 2013 B
100% albariño

86

Colour: bright yellow. Nose: citrus fruit, dried flowers, fragrant herbs. Palate: correct, easy to drink.

SPANISH STORY
Espronceda, 27 1ºD
28003 Madrid (Madrid)
☎: +34 915 356 184
Fax: +34 915 363 796
paul@globalwinefood.com

Spanish Story Black Pulpo 2013 B
albariño

87

Colour: bright yellow. Nose: floral, ripe fruit, dried herbs. Palate: balanced, flavourful, balsamic, long.

SUCESORES DE BENITO SANTOS
Currás, 46 Caleiro
36629 Vilanova de Arousa (Pontevedra)
☎: +34 986 554 435
Fax: +34 986 554 200
www.benitosantos.com
nacional@benitosantos.com

Benito Santos Igrexario de Saiar 2013 B
100% albariño

89

Colour: bright straw. Nose: fresh fruit, white flowers, balsamic herbs. Palate: flavourful, fruity, good acidity, balanced.

Benito Santos Pago de Bemil 2008 B
100% albariño

85

Pago de Xoan 2010 B
100% albariño

84

Terra de Cálago 2013 B
100% albariño

88

Colour: bright straw. Nose: fresh, fresh fruit, white flowers, balsamic herbs, mineral. Palate: flavourful, fruity, good acidity, balanced.

TERRA DE ASOREI

San Francisco, 2 - 1º C-D
36630 Cambados (Pontevedra)
☎: +34 986 198 882
Fax: +34 986 520 813
www.terradeasorei.com
info@terradeasorei.com

Nai e Señora 2013 B
100% albariño
88
Colour: bright straw. Nose: medium intensity, fresh fruit, floral. Palate: fresh, correct, easy to drink.

Pazo Torrado 2013 B
100% albariño
87
Colour: bright straw. Nose: white flowers, fragrant herbs, citrus fruit. Palate: fresh, fruity, flavourful.

Terra de Asorei 2013 B
100% albariño
89
Colour: bright straw. Nose: white flowers, fragrant herbs, fresh fruit. Palate: fresh, fruity, flavourful.

TOMADA DE CASTRO

Travesía do Freixo, 3
36636 Ribadumia (Pontevedra)
☎: +34 986 710 550
Fax: +34 986 718 552
www.tomadadecastro.com
info@tomadadecastro.com

Gran Ribad 2013 B
100% albariño
88
Colour: bright yellow. Nose: balanced, fruit expression, floral. Palate: flavourful, fruity, balanced.

Ría de Arosa 2013 B
100% albariño
87
Colour: bright straw. Nose: fresh, fresh fruit, white flowers, expressive. Palate: flavourful, fruity, fine bitter notes.

Silfide 2013 B
100% albariño
89
Colour: bright straw. Nose: ripe fruit, honeyed notes, dried herbs, white flowers. Palate: powerful, flavourful, rich, correct.

Tomada de Castro 2013 B
100% albariño
86
Colour: bright straw. Nose: floral, fresh fruit, dried herbs, medium intensity. Palate: fresh, fruity, easy to drink.

UNESDI DISTRIBUCIONES

Aurora, 11
11500 El Puerto de Santa María (Cádiz)
☎: +34 956 541 329
www.unesdi.com
info@unesdi.com

Finca Lobeira 2013 B
albariño
88
Colour: bright yellow. Nose: ripe fruit, dried flowers, wild herbs. Palate: powerful, flavourful, spicy, correct.

UVAS FELICES

Agullers, 7
08003 Barcelona (Barcelona)
☎: +34 902 327 777
www.vilaviniteca.es

El Jardín de Lucia 2013 B
91
Colour: bright straw. Nose: fresh, fresh fruit, white flowers. Palate: flavourful, fruity, good acidity, balanced.

La Locomotora 2008 T
90
Colour: ruby red. Nose: balanced, complex, ripe fruit, spicy, fine reductive notes. Palate: good structure, flavourful, round tannins.

VINIGALICIA

Ctra. Antigua Santiago, km. 3
27500 Chantada (Lugo)
☎: +34 982 454 005
Fax: +34 982 454 094
www.vinigalicia.es
vinigalicia@vinigalicia.es

Terramundi 2012 B
100% albariño
86
Colour: bright straw. Nose: fruit expression, jasmine. Palate: fresh, fruity, flavourful, balanced.

VIÑA ALMIRANTE

Peroxa, 5
36658 Portas (Pontevedra)
☎: +34 620 294 293
Fax: +34 986 541 471
www.vinaalmirante.com
info@vinaalmirante.com

Pionero Maccerato 2013 B
100% albariño
89
Colour: bright straw. Nose: fresh, fresh fruit, white flowers, dried herbs, balsamic herbs. Palate: flavourful, fruity, balanced, good acidity.

Pionero Mundi 2013 B
100% albariño

90

Colour: bright straw. Nose: fresh fruit, floral, fragrant herbs, citrus fruit. Palate: balanced, flavourful, long.

Vanidade 2013 B
100% albariño

90

Colour: bright straw. Nose: white flowers, fragrant herbs, fruit expression. Palate: fresh, fruity, flavourful, balanced, elegant.

VIÑA CARTIN
Baceiro, 1 - Lantaño
36657 Portas (Pontevedra)
☎: +34 615 646 442
www.terrasdelantano.com
bodegas@montino.es

Ruta 49 2013 B
100% albariño

87

Colour: bright straw. Nose: white flowers, fragrant herbs, fruit expression, citrus fruit. Palate: fresh, fruity, flavourful, elegant.

Terras de Lantaño 2013 B
100% albariño

92

Colour: bright straw. Nose: balanced, citrus fruit, fresh fruit, floral, scrubland. Palate: balanced, long, good acidity.

Viña Cartin 2013 B
100% albariño

90

Colour: bright straw. Nose: fresh, fresh fruit, white flowers, expressive. Palate: flavourful, fruity, good acidity, balanced.

VIÑA NORA
Bruñeiras, 7
36440 As Neves (Pontevedra)
☎: +34 986 667 210
www.vinanora.com
sperez@avanteselecta.com

Carqueixal Albariño 2013 B
100% albariño

86

Colour: bright straw. Nose: dried herbs, floral, citrus fruit, medium intensity. Palate: fresh, fruity, easy to drink.

Nora 2013 B
100% albariño

92

Colour: bright straw. Nose: white flowers, fragrant herbs, fruit expression. Palate: fresh, fruity, flavourful, balanced, long.

Nora da Neve 2010 BFB
100% albariño

95

Colour: bright yellow. Nose: ripe fruit, sweet spices, creamy oak, fragrant herbs, dry stone. Palate: rich, flavourful, fresh, good acidity.

Peitán 2013 B
100% albariño

87

Colour: bright straw. Nose: white flowers, fresh fruit, expressive, dried herbs. Palate: flavourful, fruity, balanced, fine bitter notes.

Val de Nora 2013 B
100% albariño

90

Colour: straw. Nose: fresh, white flowers, citrus fruit. Palate: fruity, balanced, fine bitter notes, good acidity.

VIÑEDOS SINGULARES
Cuzco, 26 - 28, Nave 8
08030 (Barcelona)
☎: +34 934 807 041
Fax: +34 934 807 076
www.vinedossingulares.com
info@vinedossingulares.com

Luna Creciente 2013 B
albariño

89

Colour: bright straw. Nose: fresh, fresh fruit, white flowers, expressive. Palate: fruity, good acidity, balanced.

ZÁRATE

Bouza, 23
36638 Padrenda - Meaño (Pontevedra)
☎: +34 986 718 503
Fax: +34 986 718 549
www.albarino-zarate.com
info@zarate.es

Zárate 2013 B
100% albariño

90

Colour: bright straw. Nose: fresh, fresh fruit, white flowers, expressive. Palate: flavourful, fruity, good acidity, balanced.

Zárate Caiño Tinto 2012 T
100% caiño

90

Colour: bright cherry. Nose: scrubland, fragrant herbs, balsamic herbs. Palate: light-bodied, fine bitter notes, good acidity.

Zárate El Palomar 2012 BFB
100% albariño

93

Colour: bright straw. Nose: white flowers, fresh fruit, fine lees, dried herbs. Palate: flavourful, fruity, good acidity, balanced.

Zárate Espadeiro Tinto 2012 T
100% espadeiro

91

Colour: deep cherry. Nose: fragrant herbs, balsamic herbs, ripe fruit. Palate: ripe fruit, spicy, good acidity.

Zárate Loureiro Tinto 2012 T
100% loureiro

90

Colour: cherry, garnet rim. Nose: ripe fruit, wild herbs, earthy notes, spicy, creamy oak. Palate: balanced, flavourful, long, balsamic.

Zárate Tras da Viña 2011 B
100% albariño

92

Colour: bright straw. Nose: white flowers, fresh fruit, expressive, fine lees, dried herbs. Palate: flavourful, fruity, good acidity, balanced.

DO. RIBEIRA SACRA

CONSEJO REGULADOR
Rúa do Comercio, 6-8
27400 Monforte de Lemos (Lugo)
☎:+34 982 410 968 - Fax: +34 982 411 265
@: info@ribeirasacra.org
www.ribeirasacra.org

LOCATION:
The region extends along the banks of the rivers Miño and Sil in the south of the province of Lugo and the northern region of the province of Orense; it is made up of 17 municipal districts in this region.

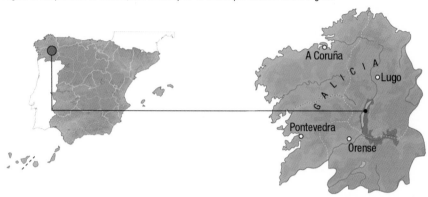

SUB-REGIONS:
Amandi, Chantada, Quiroga-Bibei, Ribeiras do Miño (in the province of Lugo) and Ribeiras do Sil.

GRAPE VARIETIES:
White: Albariño, Loureira, Treixadura, Godello, Dona Blanca and Torrontés.
Red: Main: Mencía, Brancellao Merenzao, Garnacha Tintorera, Tempranillo, Sausón, Caiño Tinto and Mouratón.

FIGURES:
Vineyard surface: 1,250.47 – Wine-Growers: 2,817 – Wineries: 90 – 2013 Harvest rating: Very Good – Production 13: 3,103,268 litres – Market percentages: 90% domestic - 10% export.

SOIL:
In general, the soil is highly acidic, although the composition varies greatly from one area to another. The vineyards are located on steep terraces and are no higher than 400 m to 500 m above sea level.

CLIMATE:
Quite variable depending on the specific area. Less rain and slightly cooler climate and greater Continental influence in the Sil valley, and greater Atlantic character in the Miño valley. Altitude, on the other hand, also has an effect, with the vineyards closer to the rivers and with a more favourable orientation (south-southeast) being slightly warmer.

VINTAGE RATING
PEÑÍNGUIDE

2009	2010	2011	2012	2013
VERY GOOD	VERY GOOD	VERY GOOD	EXCELLENT	VERY GOOD

ADEGA CACHÍN

Abeleda, s/n
32764 A Texeira (Ourense)
☎: +34 619 859 281
adegacachin@adegacachin.es

Noite Pecha 2011 T
87
Colour: cherry, garnet rim. Nose: ripe fruit, wild herbs, spicy, smoky. Palate: balanced, long, balsamic.

Peza Do Rei 2011 T Barrica
mencía
88
Colour: bright cherry, garnet rim. Nose: balanced, ripe fruit, spicy, dried herbs. Palate: balsamic, ripe fruit.

Peza Do Rei 2013 B
godello, treixadura, albariño
86
Colour: bright straw. Nose: fresh, fresh fruit, wild herbs, grassy, citrus fruit. Palate: fruity, good acidity, fine bitter notes.

Peza Do Rei 2013 T
mencía
87
Colour: bright cherry, purple rim. Nose: fresh fruit, violets, varietal. Palate: fruity, easy to drink, good finish.

ADEGA DON RAMÓN

Rubín - Rozabales, 3
27413 Monforte de Lemos (Lugo)
☎: +34 982 404 237
donramonsl@gmail.com

Don Ramón Mencía 2013 T
mencía
86
Colour: cherry, purple rim. Nose: fruit expression, fragrant herbs, balsamic herbs, mineral. Palate: flavourful, light-bodied, fresh, fruity.

Don Ramón Mencía Vendimia Seleccionada 2010 T Roble
mencía
86
Colour: bright cherry. Nose: ripe fruit, sweet spices, creamy oak, medium intensity, fine reductive notes. Palate: fruity, flavourful, toasty.

ADEGA PENA DAS DONAS

Lg. Ribas de Sil, 1 Pombeiro
27470 Pantón (Lugo)
☎: +34 988 200 045
Fax: +34 988 200 045
www.penadasdonas.com
adega@penadasdonas.com

Almalarga 2012 B Barrica
godello
92
Colour: bright straw. Nose: white flowers, fresh fruit, expressive, dried herbs, spicy. Palate: flavourful, fruity, good acidity, balanced.

Almalarga 2013 B
godello
91
Colour: yellow, greenish rim. Nose: citrus fruit, scrubland, expressive. Palate: full, flavourful, varietal, fine bitter notes, good acidity, long.

Verdes Matas Mencía 2013 T
mencía
87
Colour: cherry, garnet rim. Nose: ripe fruit, wild herbs, medium intensity. Palate: balanced, long, balsamic.

ADEGAS CONDADO DE SEQUEIRAS

Sequeiras, 1
27500 Chantada (Lugo)
☎: +34 618 815 135
Fax: +34 944 120 227
www.condadodesequeiras.com
condadodesequeiras@grupopeago.com

Condado de Sequeiras 2010 T Barrica
100% mencía
87
Colour: bright cherry. Nose: ripe fruit, sweet spices, medium intensity, tobacco. Palate: fruity, flavourful, toasty.

Condado de Sequeiras 2012 T
100% mencía
86
Colour: dark-red cherry, garnet rim. Nose: medium intensity, ripe fruit, dried herbs. Palate: good structure, ripe fruit.

Condado de Sequeiras 2013 B
godello, treixadura
90
Colour: bright straw. Nose: fresh, fresh fruit, white flowers, balsamic herbs, mineral. Palate: flavourful, fruity, good acidity, balanced.

ADEGAS E VIÑEDOS VÍA ROMANA

A Ermida - Belesar, s/n
27500 Chantada (Lugo)
☎: +34 982 454 005
Fax: +34 982 454 094
www.viaromana.es
viaromana@viaromana.es

Vía Romana Godello 2012 B
100% godello

88

Colour: bright straw. Nose: white flowers, fragrant herbs, fruit expression, spicy. Palate: fresh, fruity, flavourful, good finish.

Vía Romana Mencía 2011 T Barrica
100% mencía

90

Colour: cherry, garnet rim. Nose: red berry notes, ripe fruit, spicy, creamy oak, toasty, complex, earthy notes. Palate: powerful, flavourful, toasty, round tannins.

Vía Romana Mencía 2012 T
100% mencía

88

Colour: deep cherry, garnet rim. Nose: balanced, ripe fruit, dried herbs, dry stone. Palate: flavourful, fruity, long.

ADEGAS GUIMARO

Sanmil, 43 - Santa Cruz de Brosmos
27425 Sober (Lugo)
☎: +34 982 152 508
Fax: +34 982 402 000
adegasguimaro@gmail.com

Guimaro 2013 B
godello, treixadura

89

Colour: bright yellow. Nose: faded flowers, earthy notes, spicy, dried herbs. Palate: rich, powerful, flavourful, spicy.

Guimaro Finca Meixeman 2011 T
mencía

93

Colour: cherry, garnet rim. Nose: ripe fruit, wild herbs, earthy notes, spicy, creamy oak. Palate: balanced, flavourful, long, balsamic.

Guimaro Mencía 2013 T
mencía

90

Colour: light cherry. Nose: floral, fruit liqueur notes, mineral, balsamic herbs, spicy. Palate: good acidity, flavourful, spicy.

ADEGAS MOURE

Avda. Buenos Aires, 12
27540 Escairón (Lugo)
☎: +34 982 452 031
Fax: +34 982 452 700
www.adegasmoure.com
abadiadacova@adegasmoure.com

A Fuga 2013 T

86

Colour: cherry, purple rim. Nose: fruit expression, fragrant herbs, floral, mineral. Palate: flavourful, light-bodied, fresh, fruity.

Abadía Da Cova 2011 T Barrica
mencía

93

Colour: bright cherry. Nose: ripe fruit, sweet spices, creamy oak, expressive, scrubland. Palate: flavourful, fruity, toasty, round tannins.

Abadía Da Cova 2013 B

90

Colour: bright straw. Nose: white flowers, fragrant herbs, fruit expression, mineral. Palate: fresh, fruity, flavourful, balanced, elegant.

Abadía da Cova de Autor 2011 T
100% mencía

94

Colour: very deep cherry. Nose: expressive, creamy oak, wild herbs, mineral. Palate: flavourful, fruity, good structure.

Abadía Da Cova Mencía 2013 T
mencía
89
Colour: cherry, purple rim. Nose: red berry notes, wild herbs, balanced, varietal, wild herbs. Palate: easy to drink, fruity, correct.

Cepa Vella 2013 T
87
Colour: cherry, purple rim. Nose: wild herbs, dry stone, expressive. Palate: fresh, fruity, mineral, easy to drink.

ADEGAS VIÑA GAROÑA S.L.
Nogueira de Abaixo
27515 Chantada (Lugo)
☎: +34 982 171 636
Fax: +34 982 162 373
www.vinagarona.com
adegasvinagarona@gmail.com

Viña Garoña 2013 B
88
Colour: bright straw. Nose: fresh, fresh fruit, white flowers, expressive. Palate: flavourful, fruity, good acidity, balanced.

ALGUEIRA
Doade, s/n
27424 Sober (Lugo)
☎: +34 982 410 299
Fax: +34 982 410 299
www.algueira.com
info@algueira.com

Algueira Brancellao 2012 T Roble
100% brancellao
95
Colour: ruby red. Nose: fruit expression, fruit liqueur notes, fragrant herbs, spicy, creamy oak, expressive. Palate: balanced, elegant, spicy, long, toasty.

Algueira Cortezada 2013 B
godello, albariño, treixadura
91
Colour: bright straw. Nose: white flowers, fragrant herbs, fruit expression, mineral. Palate: fresh, fruity, flavourful, balanced, elegant.

Algueira Escalada 2011 B
100% godello
93
Colour: bright yellow. Nose: balsamic herbs, scrubland, expressive, balanced, elegant, mineral. Palate: flavourful, full, complex.

Algueira Fincas 2011 T Roble
94
Colour: cherry, garnet rim. Nose: expressive, complex, grassy, scrubland, spicy. Palate: flavourful, easy to drink, balanced. Personality.

Algueira Madialeva 2012 T
mencía
91
Colour: cherry, garnet rim. Nose: red berry notes, wild herbs, spicy, dry stone, floral. Palate: balanced, elegant, unctuous, spicy, long, balsamic.

Algueira Merenzao 2012 T Roble
100% merenzao
94
Colour: light cherry. Nose: ripe fruit, spicy, creamy oak, toasty, earthy notes, balsamic herbs, dry stone. Palate: powerful, flavourful, toasty, round tannins, balanced, elegant.

Algueira Pizarra 2011 T Roble
mencía
92
Colour: cherry, garnet rim. Nose: scrubland, dry stone, spicy, earthy notes, expressive. Palate: flavourful, rich, spicy, balanced, elegant.

Brandán Godello 2013 B
godello
89
Colour: bright straw. Nose: white flowers, fruit expression, mineral, balsamic herbs. Palate: fresh, fruity, flavourful, balanced.

Carballo Galego 2011 T
garnacha
92
Colour: dark-red cherry, garnet rim. Nose: ripe fruit, expressive, smoky, toasty. Palate: good structure, ripe fruit, round tannins.

AMEDO
Lg. Tarrio, s/n Sanfiz de Asma
27516 Chantada (Lugo)
☎: +34 610 846 686
www.adegasamedo.com
bodegasamedo@gmail.com

As Glorias 2013 B
60% godello, treixadura, torrontés, alariño
86
Colour: bright yellow. Nose: ripe fruit, faded flowers, dried herbs. Palate: correct, fine bitter notes.

Pero Bernal 2013 T
84

Pero Bernal Selección 2011 T
83

ARACELI VÁZQUEZ RODRÍGUEZ
Rosende
27466 Sober (Lugo)
☎: +34 630 908 338

Malcavada Selección 2013 T
100% mencía
89
Colour: deep cherry, purple rim. Nose: red berry notes, ripe fruit, scrubland, balanced. Palate: flavourful, long, balsamic.

BODEGA RECTORAL DE AMANDI
Santa Cruz de Arrabaldo, 49
32990 Ourense
☎: +34 988 384 200
Fax: +34 988 384 068
www.bodegasgallegas.com
export@bodegasgallegas.com

Rectoral de Amandi 2013 T
mencía
90
Colour: cherry, purple rim. Nose: red berry notes, ripe fruit, floral, balsamic herbs, dry stone. Palate: powerful, fresh, fruity, unctuous.

BODEGA RIBADA
San Fiz
27500 Chantada (Lugo)
☎: +34 629 830 893
www.bogaribada.com
manuel.calvo.mendez@gmail.com

Ribada Godello 2013 B
godello
89
Colour: bright yellow. Nose: white flowers, fragrant herbs, balanced. Palate: correct, fruity, easy to drink.

Ribada Seleccion 2010 T
mencía
88
Colour: deep cherry, garnet rim. Nose: powerfull, fruit preserve, cocoa bean. Palate: flavourful, powerful, balanced, round tannins.

Viña Ribada 2013 T
mencía
88
Colour: cherry, purple rim. Nose: ripe fruit, floral, mineral, scrubland. Palate: powerful, fresh, fruity, correct.

BODEGA VICTORINO ÁLVAREZ
Lugar Os Vazquez, s/n
32765 A Teixeira (Ourense)
☎: +34 639 787 665
adegasollio@yahoo.es

Sollío Mencía 2013 T
87
Colour: very deep cherry. Nose: powerfull, ripe fruit, dry stone. Palate: good structure, flavourful, ripe fruit.

BODEGAS ALBAMAR
O Adro, 11 - Castrelo
36639 Cambados (Pontevedra)
☎: +34 660 292 750
Fax: +34 986 520 048
info@bodegasalbamar.com

Fusco 2012 T
mencía
87
Colour: bright cherry. Nose: ripe fruit, medium intensity, tobacco, spicy, balsamic herbs. Palate: fruity, flavourful, toasty.

Fusco 2013 T
mencía
89
Colour: light cherry, purple rim. Nose: medium intensity, red berry notes, wild herbs. Palate: correct, good acidity, easy to drink.

Fusco Edición Especial 2012 T
100% mencía
90
Colour: dark-red cherry, purple rim. Nose: elegant, balanced, scrubland. Palate: fruity, easy to drink, fine tannins.

CASA MOREIRAS

San Martín de Siós, s/n
27430 Pantón (Pontevedra)
☎: +34 982 456 129
Fax: +34 982 456 129
www.casamoreiras.com
bodega@casamoreiras.com

Casa Moreiras 2013 B
89

Colour: bright straw. Nose: white flowers, fragrant herbs, mineral. Palate: fresh, fruity, flavourful, balanced, elegant.

Casa Moreiras 2013 T
90

Colour: cherry, purple rim. Nose: expressive, fresh fruit, red berry notes, floral, mineral. Palate: flavourful, fruity, good acidity, round tannins.

DOMINGO LÓPEZ FERNÁNDEZ

Doade, 54
27424 Sober (Lugo)
☎: +34 982 152 458

Viña Cichón 2013 T
85

DOMINIO DO BIBEI

Langullo, s/n
32781 Manzaneda (Ourense)
☎: +34 988 294 483
Fax: +34 988 519 494
www.dominiodobibei.com
info@dominiodobibei.com

Dominio do Bibei 2011 T
100% brancellao
96

Colour: ruby red, garnet rim. Nose: red berry notes, ripe fruit, fragrant herbs, spicy, floral, mineral, expressive. Palate: balanced, flavourful, spicy, balsamic, round, elegant.

Lacima 2011 T
100% mencía
95

Colour: cherry, garnet rim. Nose: red berry notes, ripe fruit, spicy, creamy oak, toasty, complex, dry stone. Palate: powerful, flavourful, toasty, round tannins, elegant.

Lalama 2011 T
mencía, brancellao, mouraton, garnacha
93

Colour: cherry, garnet rim. Nose: ripe fruit, wild herbs, spicy, creamy oak, mineral. Palate: balanced, flavourful, long, balsamic.

Lapena 2011 B
100% godello
93

Colour: bright straw. Nose: powerfull, ripe fruit, sweet spices, creamy oak, fragrant herbs. Palate: rich, flavourful, fresh, good acidity.

Lapola 2012 B
92

Colour: bright straw. Nose: floral, balsamic herbs, dry stone, fruit expression, spicy. Palate: powerful, flavourful, balanced.

ENVINATE

Gran Vía, 2 1ºC
27600 Sarría (Lugo)
☎: +34 682 207 160
asesoria@envinate.es

Lousas Parcela Camiño Novo 2013 T
93

Colour: cherry, purple rim. Nose: balsamic herbs, mineral, red berry notes, ripe fruit, spicy, expressive. Palate: flavourful, fruity, balanced, balsamic.

Lousas Parcela Seoane 2013 T
94

Colour: cherry, purple rim. Nose: red berry notes, fruit liqueur notes, wild herbs, spicy, mineral, expressive. Palate: fresh, fruity, spicy, balanced, elegant.

Lousas Viño de Aldeas 2013 T
93

Colour: bright cherry. Nose: ripe fruit, sweet spices, expressive, fragrant herbs. Palate: flavourful, fruity, toasty, balsamic, spicy.

ERNESTO RODRÍGUEZ PÉREZ

Barrio Figueiroá, 13
27460 Sober (Lugo)
☎: +34 600 687 107
ernestoribadent@yahoo.es

Viña Peón 2012 T
83

FINCA MILLARA

Lugar Millara s/n
27430 Pantón (Lugo)
☎: +34 981 110 181
info@fincamillara.com

Finca Millara 2010 T Barrica
100% mencía
87

Colour: bright cherry. Nose: ripe fruit, sweet spices, creamy oak, medium intensity. Palate: fruity, toasty, balsamic, easy to drink.

Lagariza 2012 T
100% mencía

86

Colour: deep cherry, garnet rim. Nose: ripe fruit, dried herbs. Palate: correct, good finish.

JAVIER FERNÁNDEZ GONZÁLEZ

Espasantes-Pantón
27450 Espasantes-Pantón (Lugo)
☎: +34 670 739 470
Fax: +34 982 456 228
javier.fdez@hotmail.com

Javier Fernández Vendimia Seleccionada 2013 T

87

Colour: cherry, garnet rim. Nose: red berry notes, ripe fruit, complex, earthy notes, wild herbs. Palate: powerful, flavourful, toasty, round tannins.

Saiñas 2013 T
mencía

90

Colour: deep cherry, purple rim. Nose: expressive, fresh, mineral, balanced. Palate: balanced, flavourful, easy to drink.

JOSÉ BLANCO LÓPEZ

A Ermida, 8 - Belesar
27514 Chantada (Lugo)
☎: +34 625 475 677
Fax: +34 982 440 281

Adega do Veiga Mencía 2013 T
mencía

84

JOSÉ IGNACIO RODRÍGUEZ PÉREZ

Barantes de Arriba
27421 Sober (Lugo)
☎: +34 669 880 532
bodegasregueiral@gmail.com

Viña Regueiral 2012 T
100% mencía

85

JOSÉ MANUEL VIDAL LÓPEZ

Carballeda, 4 Lobios
27423 Sober (Lugo)
☎: +34 679 328 546
jmvle@yahoo.es

Viña Mezquita 2013 T
100% mencía

85

LEIRABELLA

Leirabella - Sacardebois
32747 Parada do Sil (Ourense)
☎: +34 630 882 558
martin.lagaron@hotmal.es

Martín Lagarón 2012 TC
mencía, tempranillo, garnacha, sousón

91

Colour: cherry, garnet rim. Nose: ripe fruit, wild herbs, spicy, creamy oak. Palate: balanced, flavourful, long, balsamic.

MARCELINO ÁLVAREZ GONZÁLEZ

A Carqueixa - Proendos
27460 Sober (Lugo)
☎: +34 982 460 043
eapsober@hotmail.com

Marcelino I 2013 T

79

MOURE VIÑOS ARTESANS

Serreira, 8
27540 Escairon (Lugo)
☎: +34 982 452 031
moure@vinosartesans.com

Moure Tradición 2012 B
albariño, godello

92

Colour: bright yellow. Nose: ripe fruit, sweet spices, creamy oak, fragrant herbs, dried flowers, expressive, mineral, citrus fruit. Palate: rich, smoky aftertaste, flavourful, fresh, good acidity.

Moure Tradición 2012 T Barrica
mencía, garnacha, tempranillo, merenzao

93

Colour: very deep cherry, purple rim. Nose: balanced, expressive, scrubland, mineral. Palate: flavourful, good structure, spicy, round tannins.

Moure Tradición 2013 B
albariño, godello

93

Colour: bright yellow. Nose: ripe fruit, sweet spices, creamy oak, fragrant herbs. Palate: rich, smoky aftertaste, flavourful, fresh, good acidity.

Moure Tradición 2013 T
mencía, garnacha, tempranillo, merenzao

92

Colour: cherry, purple rim. Nose: ripe fruit, spicy, toasty, complex, earthy notes, dry stone, balsamic herbs. Palate: powerful, flavourful, toasty, round tannins.

NOVA TOURAL

Santo Estevo de Ribas de Miño
27594 O Saviñao (Lugo)
☎: +34 620 825 362
info@novatoural.es

Sombrero 2012 T Roble
mencía, tempranillo

85

Sombrero Mencía 2013 T
mencía, tempranillo, garnacha tintorera

89

Colour: ruby red. Nose: powerfull, red berry notes, ripe fruit, floral, mineral, grassy. Palate: powerful, fresh, fruity, unctuous.

PONTE DA BOGA

Lugar do Couto - Sampaio
32764 Castro Caldelas (Ourense)
☎: +34 988 203 306
Fax: +34 988 203 299
www.pontedaboga.es
info@pontedaboga.es

Ponte Da Boga Bancales Olvidados Mencía 2011 T
mencía

92

Colour: cherry, garnet rim. Nose: red berry notes, raspberry, violets, mineral, spicy, creamy oak. Palate: balanced, flavourful, fruity, complex, balsamic, elegant.

Ponte Da Boga Capricho DE Merenzao 2012 T
merenzao

92

Colour: cherry, garnet rim. Nose: ripe fruit, wild herbs, spicy, mineral. Palate: balanced, flavourful, long, balsamic.

Ponte Da Boga Expresión Gótica 2012 T
sousón, brancellao, merenzao

92

Colour: cherry, purple rim. Nose: red berry notes, balsamic herbs, mineral, spicy, balanced, expressive. Palate: powerful, flavourful, fruity, spicy.

Ponte Da Boga Godello 2013 B
godello, albariño, dona blanca

90

Colour: bright yellow. Nose: wild herbs, fresh fruit, wild herbs, dry stone. Palate: flavourful, good acidity, fine bitter notes.

Ponte Da Boga Mencía 2013 T
mencía

88

Colour: deep cherry, purple rim. Nose: red berry notes, scrubland, varietal. Palate: fruity, easy to drink, good finish.

Porto de Lobos 2011 T
brancellao

93

Colour: cherry, garnet rim. Nose: ripe fruit, wild herbs, earthy notes, spicy, creamy oak, expressive. Palate: balanced, flavourful, long, balsamic.

PRIOR DE PANTÓN

Santa Mariña de Eire, 17
27430 Ferreira de Pantón (Lugo)
☎: +34 982 456 211
www.priordepanton.com
info@priordepanton.com

Finca Cuarta 2012 T
mencía

91

Colour: cherry, garnet rim. Nose: ripe fruit, spicy, toasty, complex, earthy notes, balsamic herbs, dry stone. Palate: powerful, flavourful, toasty, round tannins.

Finca Cuarta 2013 B
godello

87

Colour: bright yellow. Nose: white flowers, fresh fruit, expressive, fine lees, dried herbs. Palate: flavourful, fruity.

Finca Cuarta Edición Especial 2012 T

92

Colour: bright cherry, garnet rim. Nose: ripe fruit, sweet spices, creamy oak, scrubland, mineral. Palate: fruity, flavourful, toasty, balanced.

RAMÓN MARCOS FERNÁNDEZ

Vilachá de Doade, 140
27424 Sober (Lugo)
☎: +34 609 183 352
www.adegacruceiro.es
info@adegacruceiro.es

Cruceiro 2013 T
mencía, merenzao

89

Colour: cherry, garnet rim. Nose: ripe fruit, wild herbs, earthy notes. Palate: balanced, flavourful, long, balsamic.

Cruceiro Rexio 2011 T
mencía, albarello, caíño

89

Colour: cherry, garnet rim. Nose: floral, wild herbs, dry stone, spicy. Palate: balanced, flavourful, fruity, balsamic.

REGINA VIARUM

Doade, s/n
27424 Sober (Lugo)
☎: +34 982 096 031
www.reginaviarum.es
info@reginaviarum.es

Regina Expresión 2011 T Barrica
mencía
89
Colour: cherry, garnet rim. Nose: ripe fruit, spicy, toasty, complex, earthy notes, scrubland. Palate: powerful, flavourful, toasty, round tannins.

Regina Viarum Godello 2013 B
godello
91
Colour: bright straw. Nose: white flowers, fragrant herbs, fruit expression, scrubland, sweet spices. Palate: fresh, fruity, flavourful, balanced, spicy.

Regina Viarum Mencía 2013 T
mencía
89
Colour: cherry, purple rim. Nose: balanced, red berry notes, medium intensity. Palate: balanced, balsamic, ripe fruit.

Regina Viarum Mencía Ecológico en Barrica 2011 T
mencía
88
Colour: deep cherry, garnet rim. Nose: scrubland, varietal, red berry notes, ripe fruit. Palate: flavourful, toasty.

RONSEL DO SIL

Sacardebois
32740 Parada de Sil (Ourense)
☎: +34 988 984 923
www.ronseldosil.com
info@ronseldosil.com

Alpendre 2012 T
100% merenzao
94
Colour: light cherry. Nose: expressive, elegant, ripe fruit, balsamic herbs, balanced. Palate: complex, full, flavourful.

Arpegio 2012 T
100% mencía
91
Colour: cherry, garnet rim. Nose: red berry notes, ripe fruit, fragrant herbs. Palate: easy to drink, fruity, spicy, good finish.

Ourive Dona Branca 2012 B
dona blanca
90
Colour: bright straw. Nose: white flowers, fragrant herbs, fruit expression, sweet spices. Palate: fresh, fruity, flavourful, balanced, elegant.

Ourive Godello 2012 B
100% godello
91
Colour: bright straw. Nose: white flowers, fresh fruit, expressive, dried herbs, spicy. Palate: flavourful, fruity, good acidity, balanced.

Vel'Uveyra Godello 2012 B
godello, treixadura, dona blanca
89
Colour: bright straw. Nose: white flowers, fresh fruit, expressive, dried herbs. Palate: flavourful, fruity, good acidity, balanced.

Vel'Uveyra Mencía 2012 T
100% mencía
90
Colour: light cherry. Nose: red berry notes, fruit liqueur notes, dry stone, fragrant herbs, expressive. Palate: correct, flavourful, balsamic, spicy, balanced.

SAT VIRXEN DOS REMEDIOS

Diomondi, 56
27548 O Saviñao (Lugo)
☎: +34 982 171 720
Fax: +34 982 171 720
www.virxendosremedios.es
info@virxendosremedios.es

Bail Mencía 2012 T
100% mencía
89
Colour: bright cherry. Nose: ripe fruit, sweet spices, creamy oak, expressive, wild herbs, mineral. Palate: flavourful, fruity, toasty, round tannins.

Viña Vella 2013 B
86
Colour: straw, greenish rim. Nose: white flowers, fragrant herbs, medium intensity, balanced. Palate: correct, easy to drink.

Viña Vella Mencía 2013 T

100% mencía

89

Colour: light cherry. Nose: balsamic herbs, dry stone, spicy, creamy oak. Palate: flavourful, fresh, fruity, balsamic, balanced.

TOMÁS ARIAS FERNÁNDEZ

Sanxillao - Proendos
27460 Sober (Lugo)
☎: +34 982 460 055
proencia1@gmail.com

Proencia Amandi 2009 T Barrica

91

Colour: dark-red cherry, garnet rim. Nose: red berry notes, ripe fruit, scrubland, spicy. Palate: balanced, spicy, long, balsamic.

Proencia Amandi 2013 T

87

Colour: light cherry, purple rim. Nose: ripe fruit, balsamic herbs, balanced. Palate: balanced, good acidity, balsamic, easy to drink.

TOMÁS RODRÍGUEZ GONZÁLEZ

Proendos, 104
27460 Sober (Lugo)
☎: +34 982 460 252
Fax: +34 982 460 489

Adega Barbado 2011 T Barrica

86

Colour: dark-red cherry, garnet rim. Nose: scrubland, powerfull, ripe fruit. Palate: fruity, flavourful, correct, spicy.

Adega Barbado 2013 T

87

Colour: cherry, purple rim. Nose: medium intensity, red berry notes, fresh, mineral. Palate: correct, balanced, easy to drink, balsamic.

As Muras 2013 T

88

Colour: cherry, purple rim, garnet rim. Nose: medium intensity, red berry notes, ripe fruit, scrubland. Palate: correct, easy to drink, fruity.

VÍCTOR MANUEL RODRÍGUEZ LÓPEZ

Cantón, 22 Amandi
27400 Sober (Lugo)
☎: +34 629 679 639
www.valdalenda.com
info@valdalenda.com

Val Da Lenda 2013 T

mencía

89

Colour: cherry, purple rim. Nose: mineral, red berry notes, balanced, scrubland. Palate: flavourful, fruity, easy to drink.

DO. RIBEIRO

CONSEJO REGULADOR

Salgado Moscoso, 9
32400 Ribadavia (Ourense)
☎:+34 988 477 200 - Fax: +34 988 477 201
@: info@ribeiro.es
www.ribeiro.es

LOCATION:

In the west of the province of Ourense. The region comprises 13 municipal districts marked by the Miño and its tributaries.

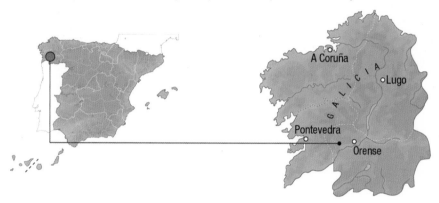

GRAPE VARIETIES:

White: Preferred: Treixadura, Torrontés, Palomino, Godello, Macabeo, Loureira and Albariño. Authorized: Albilla, Macabeo, Jerez. Experimental: Lado.
Red: Preferred: Caíño, Alicante, Sousón, Ferrón, Mencía, Tempranillo, Brancellao.
Authorized: Tempranillo, Garnacha.

FIGURES:

Vineyard surface: 2,761.63 – Wine-Growers: 5,960 – Wineries: 101– 2013 Harvest rating: Excellent – Production 13: 9,166,653 litres – Market percentages: 95% domestic - 5% export.

SOIL:

Predominantly granite, deep and rich in organic matter, although in some areas clayey soils predominate. The vineyards are on the slopes of the mountains (where higher quality wines are produced) and on the plains.

CLIMATE:

Atlantic, with low temperatures in winter, a certain risk of spring frosts, and high temperatures in the summer months. The average annual rainfall varies between 800 mm and 1,000 mm.

VINTAGE RATING   PEÑÍNGUIDE

2009	2010	2011	2012	2013
EXCELLENT	VERY GOOD	VERY GOOD	VERY GOOD	VERY GOOD

ADEGA DONA ELISA

Santo André, 110
32415 Ribadavia (Ourense)
☎: +34 609 281 616
adega.donaelisa@gmail.com

Canción de Elisa 2013 B
treixadura, albariño, godello
90
Colour: bright yellow. Nose: floral, fruit expression, ripe fruit, wild herbs, expressive. Palate: fresh, fruity, flavourful, balanced.

ADEGA MANUEL FORMIGO

Ctra. Ribadavia Carballiño, km. 4,27
32431 Beade (Ourense)
☎: +34 627 569 885
www.fincateira.com
info@fincateira.com

Finca Teira 2013 B
treixadura, godello, torrontés
89
Colour: bright straw. Nose: medium intensity, fresh fruit, floral. Palate: good acidity, fine bitter notes, balanced.

Finca Teira 2013 T
caiño, sousón, brancellao
85

Formigo 2013 B
treixadura, palomino, godello, torrontés
88
Colour: bright straw. Nose: white flowers, fragrant herbs, fruit expression, dry stone. Palate: fresh, fruity, flavourful, elegant.

Teira X 2013 B
treixadura, loureiro, albariño, albillo
86
Colour: bright straw. Nose: white flowers, fragrant herbs, fruit expression, spicy. Palate: fresh, fruity, flavourful, elegant.

ADEGA MANUEL ROJO

Chaos s/n
32417 Arnoia (Pontevedra)
☎: +34 670 309 688
www.adegamanuelrojo.es
aroa@adegamanuelrojo.es

Manuel Rojo 2013 B
treixadura, godello, lado
91
Colour: bright straw. Nose: floral, fruit expression, fragrant herbs, balsamic herbs, mineral, citrus fruit. Palate: fresh, fruity, flavourful, balanced.

ADEGA MARÍA DO PILAR

Casardeita, 14 Macendo
32430 Castrelo de Miño (Ourense)
☎: +34 687 532 088
Fax: +34 988 475 236
www.adegamariadopilar.com
adega@adegamariadopilar.com

Porta da Raiña 2013 B
treixadura
90
Colour: bright straw. Nose: expressive, elegant, balanced, fresh fruit, neat, fresh. Palate: full, long, complex, good acidity.

Rechamante 2013 T
mencía, brancellao
84

ADEGA POUSADOIRO

A Capela, 3, Barral
32430 Castrelo de Miño (Ourense)
☎: +34 667 568 029
www.pousadoiro.com
pousadoiro@gmail.com

Pousadoiro 2013 B
treixadura, torrontés, godello, loureiro
86
Colour: bright straw. Nose: faded flowers, dried herbs, fresh. Palate: light-bodied, easy to drink, good finish.

ADEGA RAMÓN DO CASAR

Lg. Sansebastián s/n Prado-Vide
32430 Castrelo de Miño (Orense)
☎: +34 638 433 611
adega@ramondocasar.es

Ramón Do Casar 2013 B
treixadura, albariño, godello
91
Colour: bright straw, greenish rim. Nose: white flowers, balanced, citrus fruit. Palate: flavourful, fruity, long, good acidity, complex.

Ramón Do Casar Treixadura 2013 B
treixadura
90
Colour: bright straw. Nose: fresh, white flowers, expressive. Palate: flavourful, fruity, good acidity, balanced.

ADEGAS PAZO DO MAR

Ctra. Ourense-Castrelo, Km. 12,5
32940 Toén (Ourense)
☎: +34 988 261 256
Fax: +34 988 261 264
www.pazodomar.com
info@pazodomar.com

Expresión de Pazo do Mar 2013 B

treixadura

88

Colour: bright straw. Nose: white flowers, fragrant herbs, fruit expression, citrus fruit. Palate: fresh, fruity, flavourful, balanced, elegant.

Pazo do Mar 2013 B

treixadura, torrontés, godello

87

Colour: bright straw. Nose: fresh, fresh fruit, white flowers. Palate: flavourful, fruity, good acidity.

ADEGAS VALDAVIA

Cuñas, s/n
32454 Cenlle (Ourense)
☎: +34 669 892 681
www.adegasvaldavia.com
comercial@adegasvaldavia.com

Cuñas Davia 2012 BFB

treixadura, albariño

89

Colour: bright yellow. Nose: powerfull, ripe fruit, sweet spices, creamy oak, fragrant herbs. Palate: rich, flavourful, fresh, good acidity.

Cuñas Davia 2013 B

87

Colour: yellow, greenish rim. Nose: white flowers, ripe fruit, balanced, dry stone. Palate: flavourful, correct, good acidity.

AILALA-AILALELO

Barro de Gomariz s/n
32429 Leiro (Ourense)
☎: +34 695 220 256
Fax: +34 988 488 741
www.ailalawine.com
export@ailalawine.com

Ailalá 2013 B

100% treixadura

90

Colour: bright straw. Nose: medium intensity, fresh, floral, citrus fruit. Palate: flavourful, balanced, fine bitter notes, long.

ANTONIO CAJIDE GULIN (ADEGA SAMEIRÁS)

San Andrés, 98
32415 Ribadavia (Ourense)
☎: +34 678 894 963
a.sameiras@gmail.com

1040 Sameirás 2013 B

treixadura, albariño, godello, lado

92

Colour: bright yellow. Nose: ripe fruit, sweet spices, creamy oak, fragrant herbs. Palate: rich, flavourful, fresh, good acidity.

Sameirás 2013 B

treixadura, albariño, godello, lado

90

Colour: bright straw. Nose: fresh, fresh fruit, white flowers, expressive. Palate: flavourful, fruity, good acidity, balanced.

Sameirás 2013 T

sousón, caíño, brancellao

90

Colour: light cherry, garnet rim. Nose: scrubland, balsamic herbs, red berry notes. Palate: fruity, easy to drink, good acidity.

Viña Do Avó 2013 B

treixadura, albariño, godello, torrontés

86

Colour: bright straw. Nose: fresh, fresh fruit, white flowers. Palate: flavourful, fruity, good acidity, balanced.

Viña Do Avó 2013 T

sousón, caíño, brancellao, mencía

82

ANTONIO MONTERO

Santa María, 7
32430 Castrelo do Miño (Ourense)
☎: +34 607 856 002
www.antoniomontero.com
antoniomontero@antoniomontero.com

Antonio Montero "Autor" 2013 B

89

Colour: bright yellow. Nose: white flowers, ripe fruit, tropical fruit. Palate: rich, flavourful, balanced, good acidity, fine bitter notes.

ARCO DA VELLA A ADEGA DE ELADIO

Pza. de España, 1
32431 Beade (Ourense)
☎: +34 607 487 060
Fax: +34 986 376 800
www.bodegaeladio.com
bodega@bodegaeladio.com

Tarabelo 2011 TC
86
Colour: cherry, garnet rim. Nose: ripe fruit, spicy, creamy oak, toasty, complex. Palate: powerful, flavourful, toasty, round tannins.

Torques do Castro 2013 B
87
Colour: bright straw. Nose: fresh, fresh fruit, white flowers, dried herbs. Palate: flavourful, fruity, fine bitter notes.

ÁUREA LUX

Barrio de abaixo, s/n
32454 Esposende (Ourense)
☎: +34 698 166 665
www.aurealux.com
info@aurealux.com

Leive Paradigma 2013 B
90
Colour: bright straw. Nose: white flowers, fresh fruit, expressive, fine lees, dried herbs. Palate: flavourful, fruity, good acidity, balanced.

Leive Reliquia 2012 BFB
89
Colour: bright yellow. Nose: powerfull, ripe fruit, sweet spices, creamy oak, fragrant herbs. Palate: rich, smoky aftertaste, flavourful, fresh, good acidity.

Leive Treixadura 2013 B
100% treixadura
83

Preto de Leive 2012 T
84

BODEGA A PORTELA

Piñeiros, s/n
32431 Beade (Ourense)
☎: +34 988 480 050
Fax: +34 988 480 050
www.beadeprimacia.com
beade@beadeprimacia.com

Beade Primacía 2013 B
91
Colour: bright straw. Nose: white flowers, fragrant herbs, fruit expression. Palate: fresh, fruity, flavourful, balanced, elegant.

Señorío de Beade 2013 B
treixadura, godello, torrontés
86
Colour: bright straw. Nose: fresh, medium intensity, dried flowers. Palate: fresh, easy to drink, good finish.

Señorío de Beade 2013 T
mencía, caíño
88
Colour: cherry, garnet rim. Nose: ripe fruit, wild herbs, earthy notes, spicy, creamy oak. Palate: balanced, flavourful, long, balsamic.

BODEGA ALANÍS

Barbantes Estación
32450 Cenlle (Ourense)
☎: +34 988 384 200
Fax: +34 988 384 068
www.bodegasgallegas.com
jania@bodegasgallegas.com

Gran Alanís 2013 B
91
Colour: bright straw. Nose: white flowers, fragrant herbs, fruit expression, mineral. Palate: fresh, fruity, flavourful, elegant.

San Trocado 2013 B
100% treixadura
85

BODEGAS EL PARAGUAS

Lugar de Esmelle, 111
15594 Ferrol (A Coruña)
☎: +34 636 161 479
www.bodegaselparaguas.com
info@bodegaselparaguas.com

El Paraguas Atlántico 2011 B
treixadura, godello, albariño
93
Colour: bright straw. Nose: white flowers, fresh fruit, expressive, fine lees, dried herbs, mineral. Palate: flavourful, fruity, good acidity, balanced. Personality.

BODEGAS NAIROA

A Ponte, 2
32417 Arnoia (Ourense)
☎: +34 988 492 867
www.bodegasnairoa.com
info@bodegasnairoa.com

Alberte 2013 B
89
Colour: bright straw. Nose: fresh fruit, white flowers, dried herbs. Palate: flavourful, fruity, fine bitter notes.

Nairoa 2013 B
treixadura, torrontés, palomino
86
Colour: bright straw. Nose: fresh, fresh fruit, white flowers, mineral. Palate: flavourful, fruity, good acidity, balanced.

Val de Nairoa 2012 B
91
Colour: bright straw. Nose: white flowers, fresh fruit, dried herbs, mineral, honeyed notes. Palate: flavourful, fruity, good acidity, balanced.

Val do Couso 2013 B
treixadura, torrontés, otras
88
Colour: bright straw. Nose: fragrant herbs, faded flowers. Palate: balanced, fine bitter notes, easy to drink.

BODEGAS O'VENTOSELA
Ctra. Ribadavia - Carballiño, km. 8,8 San Clodio
32420 Leiro (Ourense)
☎: +34 981 635 829
Fax: +34 981 635 870
www.oventosela.com
bodegasydestilerias@oventosela.com

Viña Leiriña 2013 B
90
Colour: bright yellow. Nose: expressive, balanced, fresh fruit, floral. Palate: flavourful, good acidity, fine bitter notes, balanced.

CASAL DE ARMÁN
O Cotiño, s/n
32415 San Andrés- Ribadavia (Ourense)
☎: +34 699 060 464
www.casaldearman.net
bodega@casaldearman.net

7 Cupos 2013 B
100% treixadura
90
Colour: bright straw. Nose: medium intensity, fresh fruit, citrus fruit. Palate: fruity, flavourful, fresh, good acidity, fine bitter notes.

Casal de Armán 2013 B
91
Colour: bright straw. Nose: white flowers, fresh fruit, expressive, dried herbs, mineral. Palate: flavourful, fruity, good acidity, balanced, elegant.

Finca Misenhora 2012 B
90
Colour: bright yellow. Nose: expressive, fine lees, dried herbs, ripe fruit, faded flowers. Palate: flavourful, fruity, balanced, rich.

Finca Os Loureiros 2012 B
100% treixadura
92
Colour: bright yellow. Nose: expressive, fine lees, dried herbs, dried flowers. Palate: flavourful, fruity, good acidity, balanced, spicy.

CASTRO REI
Camino Torre, Sampaio
32414 Ribadavia (Ourense)
☎: +34 988 472 069
www.bodegacastrorei.com
bodegacastrorei@bodegacastrorei.com

Divino Rei 2013 B
treixadura, albariño, loureiro
88
Colour: bright straw. Nose: white flowers, fragrant herbs, fruit expression. Palate: fresh, fruity, flavourful.

COTO DE GOMARIZ
Barro de Gomariz s/n
32429 Leiro (Ourense)
☎: +34 988 101 733
Fax: +34 988 488 174
www.cotodegomariz.com
mmontoto@cotodegomariz.com

Abadía de Gomariz 2011 T
sousón, brancellao, ferrol, mencía
91
Colour: cherry, garnet rim. Nose: ripe fruit, wild herbs, spicy, creamy oak, mineral. Palate: balanced, flavourful, long, balsamic.

Coto de Gomariz 2013 B
treixadura, godello, loureiro, albariño
92
Colour: bright straw. Nose: white flowers, fragrant herbs, fruit expression. Palate: fresh, fruity, flavourful, balanced, elegant.

Coto de Gomariz Colleita Seleccionada 2011 B
treixadura, godello, albariño, lado
94
Colour: bright straw. Nose: white flowers, fragrant herbs, fruit expression, sweet spices, creamy oak. Palate: fresh, fruity, flavourful, balanced, elegant, spicy.

Gomariz X 2013 B
89
Colour: bright yellow. Nose: white flowers, citrus fruit, fresh fruit. Palate: correct, fine bitter notes, easy to drink.

Hush 2009 T
ferrol, sousón, caíño, bastardo negro
90
Colour: cherry, garnet rim. Nose: ripe fruit, wild herbs, earthy notes, spicy, creamy oak. Palate: balanced, flavourful, long, balsamic.

Salvaxe 2011 B
lado, treixadura, godello, albariño
93
Colour: bright yellow. Nose: expressive, fine lees, dried herbs, faded flowers, spicy. Palate: flavourful, fruity, good acidity, balanced.

Super Héroe 2010 T
ferrol, sousón, caíño, bastardo negro
89
Colour: bright cherry. Nose: ripe fruit, sweet spices, creamy oak, expressive. Palate: flavourful, fruity, toasty, round tannins.

The FLower and The Bee Sousón 2012 T
sousón
87
Colour: bright cherry. Nose: ripe fruit, sweet spices, creamy oak, expressive, balsamic herbs. Palate: flavourful, fruity, toasty, spicy.

The FLower and The Bee Treixadura 2013 B
treixadura
90
Colour: bright straw. Nose: white flowers, fruit expression, dried herbs, mineral. Palate: fresh, fruity, flavourful, balanced, elegant.

CUNQUEIRO
Prado de Miño, 4
32430 Castrelo de Miño (Ourense)
☎: +34 988 489 023
Fax: +34 988 489 082
www.bodegascunqueiro.es
info@bodegascunqueiro.es

Cunqueiro III Milenium 2013 B
treixadura, godello, albariño, loureiro
90
Colour: bright straw. Nose: white flowers, fragrant herbs, fruit expression. Palate: fresh, fruity, flavourful, elegant.

Cuqueira 2013 B
treixadura, torrontés, godello
87
Colour: bright straw. Nose: fresh, fresh fruit, white flowers, expressive. Palate: flavourful, fruity, good acidity.

Mais de Cunqueiro 2012 B
torrontés
89
Colour: bright yellow. Nose: fruit expression, honeyed notes, dried herbs. Palate: fresh, fruity, flavourful, spicy, balsamic.

DOCAMPO S.A.
San Paio s/n
32400 Ribadavia (Ourense)
☎: +34 988 470 258
Fax: +34 988 470 421
www.bodegasdocampo.com
admin@bodegasdocampo.com

Señorío da Vila 2012 B
treixadura
92
Colour: bright straw. Nose: fresh fruit, expressive, fine lees, dried herbs, faded flowers. Palate: flavourful, fruity, good acidity, balanced.

Viña Do Campo 2013 B
treixadura, torrontés
87
Colour: bright straw. Nose: white flowers, fragrant herbs, fruit expression, citrus fruit, mineral. Palate: fresh, fruity, flavourful, good acidity.

Viña Do Campo Mencía 2013 T
mencía
88
Colour: cherry, purple rim. Nose: red berry notes, raspberry, floral, balsamic herbs. Palate: fresh, fruity, flavourful, easy to drink.

EDUARDO PEÑA
Barral s/n
32430 Castelo de Miño (Ourense)
☎: +34 629 872 130
Fax: +34 988 239 704
www.bodegaeduardopenha.es
bodega@bodegaeduardopenha.es

Eduardo Peña 2013 B
treixadura, albariño, godello, loureiro
91
Colour: yellow, greenish rim. Nose: fragrant herbs, fresh, dried flowers. Palate: balanced, fine bitter notes, good acidity.

ELISA COLLARTE BERNÁRDEZ
Santo Andrés
32415 Ribadavia (Ourense)
☎: +34 670 473 266
elisacollarte@gmail.com

Cordón de Santo André 2013 B
treixadura, godello, loureiro
88
Colour: bright straw. Nose: fresh, fresh fruit, white flowers, expressive. Palate: flavourful, fruity, good acidity, balanced.

Elisa Collarte 2012 T Barrica
mencía, sousón, caíño, brancellao
85

ELOI LORENZO
A Ponte, 37
32417 Arnoia (Ourense)
☎: +34 640 376 007
www.eloilorenzo.es
gerente@eloilorenzo.es

Eloi Lorenzo 2013 B
85

Villa Paz 2013 B
86
Colour: yellow, greenish rim. Nose: fresh fruit, citrus fruit, balanced, medium intensity. Palate: light-bodied, easy to drink, good finish.

EMILIO ROJO

Lugar de Remoiño, s/n
32233 Arnoia (Ourense)
☎: +34 600 522 812
vinoemiliorojo@hotmail.com

Emilio Rojo 2012 B
93
Colour: bright straw. Nose: white flowers, fresh fruit, expressive, fine lees, dried herbs. Palate: flavourful, fruity, good acidity, balanced.

FINCA VIÑOA

Colón, 18 4ºC
32201 O Carballiño (Ourense)
☎: +34 986 625 051
Fax: +34 986 626 267
www.fincavinoa.com
fincavinoa@fincavinoa.com

Finca Viñoa 2013 B
treixadura, godello, albariño, loureiro
93
Colour: bright yellow. Nose: fruit expression, floral, fragrant herbs, dry stone, expressive. Palate: powerful, flavourful, fruity, balsamic, balanced.

FRANCISCO FERNÁNDEZ SOUSA

Prado, 14
32430 Castrelo do Miño (Ourense)
☎: +34 678 530 898
www.terraminei.com
info@terraminei.com

Lagar de Brais 2012 B
85

Terra Minei 2013 B
100% treixadura
89
Colour: bright straw. Nose: fresh fruit, expressive, floral, dry stone. Palate: flavourful, fruity, good acidity, balanced.

FRANCISCO GARCÍA PÉREZ

Trasmesones, 13
32400 Rivadavia (Ourense)
☎: +34 650 105 723
www.adegadomoucho.com
adegadomoucho@gmail.com

Adega do Moucho 2012 B
90
Colour: bright yellow. Nose: powerfull, ripe fruit, sweet spices, creamy oak, fragrant herbs. Palate: rich, smoky aftertaste, flavourful, fresh, good acidity.

GENUS DE VINUM

32003 Ourense (Ourense)
☎: +34 988 100 120
www.genusdevinum.es
info@genusdevinum.es

Versatus 2012 B
treixadura, godello, loureiro, torrontés
91
Colour: bright straw. Nose: white flowers, fresh fruit, expressive, fine lees, dried herbs. Palate: flavourful, fruity, good acidity, balanced, elegant.

JOSÉ ESTÉVEZ FERNÁNDEZ

Ponte, 21
32417 Arnoia (Ourense)
☎: +34 696 402 970
joseestevezarnoia@gmail.com

Auxía da Ponte 2012 B
lado
92
Colour: bright straw. Nose: floral, wild herbs, scrubland, balsamic herbs, mineral. Palate: flavourful, fresh, fruity, complex, balanced, elegant, balsamic.

Mauro Estevez 2013 B
treixadura, lado, albariño, loureiro
93
Colour: bright yellow. Nose: balanced, complex, expressive, dried flowers, mineral. Palate: full, flavourful, fine bitter notes, good acidity.

JULIO VÁZQUEZ QUINTELA

San Fiz do Varón s/n
32515 San Fiz do Varón (O Carballiño) (Ourense)
☎: +34 645 308 214
www.pazolodeiro.com
bodegaspazolodeiro@hotmail.com

Pazo Lodeiro 2013 B
treixadura, godello, torrontés, loureiro
87
Colour: bright straw. Nose: tropical fruit, floral, wild herbs. Palate: fresh, fruity, easy to drink.

Señorío do Barón 2013 B
treixadura, godello, torrontés, loureiro
87
Colour: bright straw. Nose: fresh fruit, medium intensity, floral, citrus fruit. Palate: correct, easy to drink, good finish.

LA MALETA HAND MADE FINE WINES

Julio Prieto Nespereira, 21
32005 Ourense (Ourense)
☎: +34 988 614 234
lamaletawines.com
hola@lamaletawines.com

Desde la Ladera 2013 B
treixadura, albariño, godello

87

Colour: bright straw. Nose: fresh, fresh fruit, white flowers. Palate: flavourful, fruity, good acidity.

LUIS A. RODRÍGUEZ VÁZQUEZ

Laxa, 7
32417 Arnoia (Ourense)
☎: +34 988 492 977
Fax: +34 988 492 977

A Teixar 2011 B
treixadura, albariño, godello

91

Colour: bright yellow. Nose: powerfull, ripe fruit, sweet spices, creamy oak, fragrant herbs. Palate: rich, flavourful, fresh, good acidity.

A Torna dos Pasas 2011 T
brancellao, caiño, ferrol

88

Colour: cherry, garnet rim. Nose: ripe fruit, wild herbs, earthy notes, spicy, creamy oak. Palate: balanced, flavourful, long, balsamic.

Viña de Martín "Os Pasás" 2012 B
treixadura, albariño, lado, torrontés

90

Colour: bright straw. Nose: wild herbs, ripe fruit, mineral, spicy. Palate: powerful, flavourful, complex.

Viña de Martín Escolma 2009 BFB
treixadura, albariño, lado, torrontés

92

Colour: bright yellow. Nose: powerfull, ripe fruit, sweet spices, fragrant herbs. Palate: rich, smoky aftertaste, flavourful, good acidity.

Viña de Martín Escolma 2009 T
brancellao, caiño, ferrol

88

Colour: light cherry. Nose: grassy, spicy. Palate: fruity, easy to drink, correct.

PAZO CASANOVA

Camiño Souto do Río, 1 Santa Cruz de Arrabaldo
32990 (Ourense)
☎: +34 607 576 923
Fax: +34 988 384 196
www.pazocasanova.com
casanova@pazocasanova.com

Casanova 2013 B
treixadura, godello, albariño, loureiro

89

Colour: bright straw. Nose: medium intensity, citrus fruit, fresh fruit, mineral. Palate: balanced, good acidity, fine bitter notes.

PAZO DE VIEITE

Ctra. Ribadavia – Carballiño, km.6 - Vieite
32419 Leiro (Ourense)
☎: +34 988 488 229
Fax: +34 988 488 229
www.pazodevieite.es
info@pazodevieite.es

Viña Farnadas 2013 B
treixadura, godello, albariño

86

Colour: yellow, greenish rim. Nose: floral, tropical fruit, balanced. Palate: easy to drink, good finish.

PAZO LALON

Pazo Lalón s/n Barro de Gomariz
32427 Leiro (Ourense)
☎: +34 653 131 487
www.eduardobravo.es
eduardogonzalezbravo@gmail.com

Eduardo Bravo 2013 B

88

Colour: bright straw. Nose: fresh fruit, white flowers, dried herbs. Palate: flavourful, fruity, good acidity, fine bitter notes.

PAZO TIZÓN

Rua do Bon Casares, 20
32514 Boboras (Orense)
☎: +34 902 120 915
Fax: +34 916 913 553
www.pazotizon.com
admon@pazotizon.com

Extramundi 2013 B
albariño, treixadura

89

Colour: yellow, greenish rim. Nose: balanced, ripe fruit, faded flowers. Palate: rich, balanced, fine bitter notes.

Pazo Tizon 2012 T
tempranillo, garnacha

87

Colour: dark-red cherry, garnet rim. Nose: sweet spices, cocoa bean, ripe fruit, scrubland. Palate: fruity, flavourful, round tannins.

PAZOS DE ALBOR
Coedo s/n
32454 (Ourense)
☎: +34 626 903 725
monica.albor@hotmail.com

Pazos de Albor 2013 T
mencía

88

Colour: bright cherry. Nose: sweet spices, red berry notes, balsamic herbs. Palate: flavourful, fruity, toasty, round tannins.

Pazos de Albor Treixadura 2013 B
treixadura

88

Colour: yellow, greenish rim. Nose: balanced, citrus fruit, medium intensity. Palate: correct, fine bitter notes.

Pazos de Albor Treixadura Godello Loureira 2013 B
treixadura, godello, loureiro

90

Colour: bright straw, greenish rim. Nose: fresh fruit, citrus fruit, floral, balanced. Palate: fruity, flavourful, good acidity, good finish.

SANCLODIO
Cubilledo-Gomariz
32420 Leiro (Ourense)
☎: +34 686 961 681
www.vinosanclodio.com
sanclodiovino@gmail.com

Sanclodio 2012 B
treixadura, godello, loureiro, torrontés

91

Colour: bright straw. Nose: white flowers, fragrant herbs, fruit expression, mineral. Palate: fresh, fruity, flavourful, balanced, elegant.

TERRA DO CASTELO
Ctra. Ribadavia - Carballiño, Km. 4
32431 Beade (Ourense)
☎: +34 988 471 522
Fax: +34 988 471 502
www.terradocastelo.com
adegas@terradocastelo.com

Terra do Castelo "Sensación" 2013 B
treixadura, torrontés, godello, palomino

89

Colour: bright straw. Nose: white flowers, fragrant herbs, fruit expression. Palate: fresh, fruity, flavourful, balanced.

Terra do Castelo Godello 2013 B
100% godello

87

Colour: bright straw. Nose: white flowers, fragrant herbs, expressive. Palate: fresh, fruity, flavourful, balanced, easy to drink.

Terra do Castelo Treixadura 2013 B
100% treixadura

87

Colour: bright straw. Nose: white flowers, fragrant herbs, fruit expression. Palate: fresh, fruity, flavourful, balanced.

VAL DE SOUTO
Souto, 34
32430 Castrelo de Miño (Ourense)
☎: +34 637 379 563
www.valdesouto.com
info@valdesouto.com

Val de Souto 2013 B
treixadura, godello, loureiro

89

Colour: bright straw. Nose: fresh, fresh fruit, expressive, citrus fruit. Palate: flavourful, fruity, good acidity, balanced.

Val de Souto 2013 T
mencía, brancellao, caíño

86

Colour: light cherry, purple rim. Nose: scrubland, red berry notes, medium intensity. Palate: light-bodied, correct.

Val de Souto Orixes 2013 B
treixadura, godello, loureiro

86

Colour: bright straw. Nose: white flowers, fruit expression, dried herbs, mineral. Palate: fresh, fruity, flavourful, balanced.

VALDEPUGA S.L.
Ctra. Ourense a Cortegada, km 14
32940 Puga Toén (Ourense)
☎: +34 619 018 833
Fax: +34 988 235 817
www.valdepuga.com
valdepuga@grupopuga.com

Terraboa 2012 B
treixadura, godello, loureiro, albariño

84

Valdepuga 2013 B
treixadura, godello, loureiro, albariño

87

Colour: bright straw. Nose: fresh, fresh fruit, white flowers. Palate: fruity, good acidity, balanced.

VIÑA COSTEIRA
Valdepereira, s/n
32415 Ribadavia (Ourense)
☎: +34 988 477 210
Fax: +34 988 470 330
www.vinoribeiro.com
info@pazoribeiro.com

Alén da Istoria 2012 T
caiño, sousón, ferrón, brancellao
84

Colección 68 Costeira Treixadura 2013 B
treixadura, albariño, godello
90
Colour: bright straw. Nose: fresh, fresh fruit, expressive. Palate: flavourful, fruity, balanced, fine bitter notes.

Pazo 2013 B
palomino, torrontés
85

Viña Costeira 2013 B
treixadura, torrontés, albariño, godello
88
Colour: bright straw. Nose: fresh fruit, white flowers, balanced. Palate: correct, good acidity, fine bitter notes, easy to drink.

VIÑA DA CAL
Lg. Astariz, km. 17
32430 Castrelo de Miño (Ourense)
☎: +34 986 226 010
susana@alter-vino.es

Alter 2013 B
treixadura, godello
90
Colour: bright straw. Nose: fresh, fresh fruit, white flowers, expressive. Palate: flavourful, fruity, good acidity, balanced.

Alter 2013 T
brancellao, sousón
87
Colour: cherry, garnet rim. Nose: ripe fruit, wild herbs, earthy notes, spicy. Palate: balanced, flavourful, long, balsamic.

VIÑA MEIN S.L.

Mein, s/n
32420 Leiro (Ourense)
☎: +34 617 326 248
Fax: +34 915 761 019
www.vinamein.com
info.bodega@vinamein.com

Viña Mein 2012 BFB

treixadura, godello, loureiro, albariño

91

Colour: bright straw. Nose: balanced, sweet spices, faded flowers, ripe fruit. Palate: rich, flavourful, long.

Viña Mein 2013 B

91

Colour: bright straw. Nose: white flowers, fragrant herbs, fruit expression. Palate: fresh, fruity, flavourful, balanced, elegant.

VIÑEDOS DO GABIAN

Coto de Gandara, 22
Abelendas das Penas
32433 Carballeda de Avia (Ourense)
☎: +34 636 157 785
pepequecuty@hotmail.com

Gabián 2012 BFB

100% treixadura

91

Colour: bright yellow. Nose: powerfull, ripe fruit, sweet spices, fragrant herbs. Palate: rich, smoky aftertaste, flavourful, fresh, good acidity.

Xanledo 2012 T

caiño, brancellao

91

Colour: light cherry, garnet rim. Nose: expressive, wild herbs, red berry notes, elegant. Palate: balanced, fine tannins, balsamic.

DO. RIBERA DEL DUERO

CONSEJO REGULADOR
Hospital, 6
09300 Roa (Burgos)
☎:+34 947 541 221 - Fax: +34 947 541 116
@: info@riberadelduero.es
www.riberadelduero.es

LOCATION:

Between the provinces of Burgos, Valladolid, Segovia and Soria. This region comprises 19 municipal districts in the east of Valladolid, 5 in the north west of Segovia, 59 in the south of Burgos (most of the vineyards are concentrated in this province with 10,000 Ha) and 6 in the west of Soria.en la parte occidental de Soria.

GRAPE VARIETIES:

White: Albillo.
Red: Tinta del País (Tempranillo – majority with 81% of all vineyards), Garnacha Tinta, Cabernet Sauvignon, Malbec and Merlot.

FIGURES:

Vineyard surface: 21,731 – Wine-Growers: 8,413 – Wineries: 271 – 2013 Harvest rating: Good – Production 13: 59,511,955 litres – Market percentages: 75% domestic - 25% export.

SOIL:

In general, the soils are loose, not very fertile and with a rather high limestone content. Most of the sediment is composed of layers of sandy limestone or clay. The vineyards are located on the interfluvial hills and in the valleys at an altitude of between 700 and 850 m.

CLIMATE:

Continental in nature, with slight Atlantic influences. The winters are rather cold and the summers hot, although mention must be made of the significant difference in day-night temperatures contributing to the slow ripening of the grapes, enabling excellent acidity indexes to be achieved. The greatest risk factor in the region is the spring frosts, which are on many occasions responsible for sharp drops in production. The average annual rainfall is between 450 mm and 500 mm.

VINTAGE RATING

PEÑÍNGUIDE

2009	2010	2011	2012	2013
VERY GOOD	EXCELLENT	VERY GOOD	VERY GOOD	GOOD

3 ASES

Camino de Pesquera, s/n
47360 Quintanilla de Arriba (Valladolid)
☎: +34 983 036 214
www.3asesvino.com
info@3asesvino.com

3 Ases 2011 TC
tempranillo
88
Colour: very deep cherry. Nose: ripe fruit, spicy, creamy oak, toasty, characterful. Palate: powerful, flavourful, toasty, round tannins.

3 Ases 2012 T Roble
tempranillo
85

AALTO BODEGAS Y VIÑEDOS

Paraje Vallejo de Carril, s/n
47360 Quintanilla de Arriba (Valladolid)
☎: +34 620 351 182
Fax: +34 983 036 949
www.aalto.es
aalto@aalto.es

Aalto 2011 T
100% tempranillo
93
Colour: cherry, garnet rim. Nose: red berry notes, ripe fruit, fragrant herbs, sweet spices, creamy oak, mineral. Palate: powerful, flavourful, spicy, concentrated.

Aalto PS 2011 T
100% tempranillo
95
Colour: cherry, garnet rim. Nose: ripe fruit, balsamic herbs, spicy, dry stone, expressive. Palate: balanced, concentrated, flavourful, spicy, long, elegant.

ABADÍA DE ACÓN

Ctra. Hontangas, Km. 0,400
9400 Castrillo de la Vega (Burgos)
☎: +34 947 509 292
Fax: +34 947 508 586
www.abadiadeacon.com
info@abadiadeacon.com

Acón 2007 TR
88
Colour: very deep cherry. Nose: powerfull, fruit preserve, dark chocolate, creamy oak. Palate: good structure, powerful.

Acón 2009 TC
100% tempranillo
91
Colour: very deep cherry. Nose: ripe fruit, spicy, creamy oak, toasty, characterful. Palate: powerful, flavourful, toasty, round tannins.

Acón 2012 T Roble
100% tempranillo
88
Colour: bright cherry. Nose: ripe fruit, sweet spices, creamy oak, expressive. Palate: flavourful, fruity, toasty, round tannins.

Acón 2013 T
100% tempranillo
84

ALEJANDRO FERNÁNDEZ TINTO PESQUERA

Real, 2
47315 Pesquera de Duero (Valladolid)
☎: +34 983 870 037
Fax: +34 983 870 088
www.grupopesquera.com
pesquera@pesqueraafernandez.com

Tinto Pesquera 2011 TC
89
Colour: cherry, garnet rim. Nose: ripe fruit, spicy, creamy oak, toasty. Palate: powerful, flavourful, toasty, lacks balance.

ALIZÁN BODEGAS Y VIÑEDOS

Camino de Pesquera, s/n
47360 Quintanilla de Arriba (Valladolid)
☎: +34 983 306 021
Fax: +34 983 305 948
www.alizan.net
bodegasalizan@alizan.net

Auzau 2009 TC
tempranillo
88
Colour: bright cherry. Nose: ripe fruit, sweet spices, creamy oak, toasty. Palate: fruity, flavourful, toasty, balsamic.

ALTOS DE ONTAÑÓN

Ctra. Roa s/n
09315 Fuentecén (Burgos)
☎: +34 947 532 797
www.ontanon.es
ontanon@ontanon.es

Teón del Condado 2010 TC
tinta del país
89
Colour: bright cherry. Nose: ripe fruit, spicy, creamy oak, dried herbs. Palate: powerful, flavourful, toasty, round tannins.

Teón del Condado 2011 T Roble
tinta del país
90
Colour: bright cherry. Nose: ripe fruit, sweet spices, creamy oak, expressive. Palate: flavourful, fruity, toasty, round tannins.

ALTOS DEL ENEBRO

Regino Sainz de la Maza 13º C
05004 (Burgos)
☎: +34 619 409 097
www.altosdelenebro.es
comercial@altosdelenebro.es

Altos del Enebro 2011 T
100% tinto fino

93

Colour: cherry, garnet rim. Nose: fruit preserve, fruit liqueur notes, spicy. Palate: flavourful, pruney, balsamic.

Tomás González 2011 T
100% tinto fino

91

Colour: cherry, garnet rim. Nose: ripe fruit, spicy, creamy oak, toasty, complex. Palate: powerful, flavourful, toasty, round tannins.

ALTOS DEL TERRAL

Barrionuevo, 11
09400 Aranda de Duero (Burgos)
☎: +34 616 953 451
www.altosdelterral.com
bodega@altosdelterral.com

Altos del Terral 2010 TC
tempranillo

93

Colour: deep cherry, garnet rim. Nose: balanced, complex, wild herbs. Palate: balanced, good structure, flavourful.

Altos del Terral T1 2009 T
tempranillo

91

Colour: cherry, garnet rim. Nose: red berry notes, ripe fruit, spicy, creamy oak, toasty, complex, earthy notes. Palate: powerful, flavourful, toasty, round tannins.

Cuvée Julia Altos del Terral 2010 T
tempranillo

93

Colour: very deep cherry, garnet rim. Nose: expressive, balanced, complex, sweet spices, mineral. Palate: balanced, good acidity, round tannins.

ASTRALES

Ctra. Olmedillo, Km. 7
09313 Anguix (Burgos)
☎: +34 947 554 222
www.astrales.es
administracion@astrales.es

Astrales 2011 T
tempranillo

92

Colour: cherry, garnet rim. Nose: ripe fruit, spicy, creamy oak, toasty, complex, earthy notes. Palate: powerful, flavourful, toasty, harsh oak tannins.

ATALAYAS DE GOLBÁN

Ctra. a Morcuera, s/n
42345 Atauta (Soria)
☎: +34 975 351 349
isanz@avanteselecta.com

Torre de Golban 2009 TR
100% tempranillo

91

Colour: cherry, garnet rim. Nose: ripe fruit, spicy, creamy oak, toasty, complex. Palate: powerful, flavourful, toasty, round tannins.

Torre de Golban 2011 TC
100% tinto fino

90

Colour: cherry, garnet rim. Nose: spicy, toasty, overripe fruit, mineral. Palate: powerful, flavourful, toasty, round tannins.

Viridiana 2013 T
100% tinto fino

90

Colour: bright cherry. Nose: ripe fruit, sweet spices, creamy oak, expressive. Palate: flavourful, fruity, toasty, round tannins.

AVELINO VEGAS-BODEGAS FUENTESPINA

Grupo Calvo Sotelo, 8
40460 Santiuste (Segovia)
☎: +34 921 596 002
Fax: +34 921 596 035
www.avelinovegas.com
ana@avelinovegas.com

Corona de Castilla Prestigio 2011 TC
tempranillo

91

Colour: very deep cherry. Nose: ripe fruit, spicy, creamy oak, toasty, complex. Palate: powerful, flavourful, toasty, round tannins.

F de Fuentespina 2009 TR
tempranillo

90

Colour: cherry, garnet rim. Nose: ripe fruit, spicy, creamy oak, toasty, complex. Palate: powerful, flavourful, toasty, round tannins.

Fuentespina 2011 TC
100% tempranillo

88

Colour: cherry, garnet rim. Nose: powerfull, ripe fruit, toasty. Palate: flavourful, good structure, toasty, round tannins.

Fuentespina 2013 T Roble
tempranillo

87

Colour: bright cherry. Nose: ripe fruit, creamy oak. Palate: flavourful, fruity, toasty, round tannins.

Fuentespina Granate 2013 T
tempranillo

87

Colour: bright cherry. Nose: ripe fruit, sweet spices, creamy oak. Palate: flavourful, fruity, toasty, round tannins.

Fuentespina Selección 2011 T
tempranillo

92

Colour: very deep cherry, garnet rim. Nose: complex, balanced, expressive, creamy oak. Palate: balanced, long, round tannins.

AXIAL
Pla-za Calle Castillo de Capua, 10 Nave 7
50197 (Zaragoza)
☎: +34 976 780 136
Fax: +34 976 303 035
www.axialvinos.com
info@axialvinos.com

Zumaya 2011 TC
100% tempranillo

90

Colour: cherry, garnet rim. Nose: ripe fruit, spicy, creamy oak, toasty, complex. Palate: powerful, flavourful, toasty, round tannins.

Zumaya Tempranillo 2013 T
100% tempranillo

86

Colour: cherry, purple rim. Nose: medium intensity, red berry notes, balanced. Palate: correct, good finish, easy to drink.

BELLORI VINOS
Cobalto, 67 Bajo
47012 (Valladolid)
☎: +34 983 314 522
Fax: +34 983 314 522
www.bellorivinos.com
administracion@bellorivinos.com

Bellori 2013 T
tinto fino

89

Colour: very deep cherry, purple rim. Nose: red berry notes, balanced, expressive, sweet spices. Palate: fruity, fruity aftertestaste.

BODEGA CONVENTO SAN FRANCISCO
Calvario, 22
47300 Peñafiel (Valladolid)
☎: +34 983 878 052
Fax: +34 983 873 052
www.bodegaconvento.com
bodega@bodegaconvento.com

Convento San Francisco 2010 T
100% tinta del país

90

Colour: deep cherry, garnet rim. Nose: toasty, smoky, ripe fruit, balsamic herbs. Palate: flavourful, spicy, ripe fruit, round tannins.

BODEGA COOP. SANTA ANA
Ctra. Aranda - Salas, km. 18,5
09410 Peñaranda de Duero (Burgos)
☎: +34 947 552 011
Fax: +34 947 552 011
www.bodegasantaana.es
bodega@bodegasantaana.es

Castillo de Peñaranda 2011 TC
tempranillo

88

Colour: bright cherry. Nose: ripe fruit, sweet spices, creamy oak. Palate: fruity, flavourful, toasty.

Castillo de Peñaranda 2013 T Roble
tempranillo

86

Colour: bright cherry, purple rim. Nose: ripe fruit, sweet spices, creamy oak, balsamic herbs. Palate: flavourful, fruity, toasty.

Cruz Sagra 2012 T
tempranillo

89

Colour: cherry, garnet rim. Nose: ripe fruit, wild herbs, spicy, creamy oak. Palate: balanced, flavourful, long, balsamic.

BODEGA COOPERATIVA VIRGEN DE LA ASUNCIÓN
Las Afueras, s/n
09311 La Horra (Burgos)
☎: +34 947 542 057
Fax: +34 947 542 057
www.virgendelaasuncion.com
info@virgendelaasuncion.com

Viña Valera 2011 TC
100% tempranillo

88

Colour: cherry, garnet rim. Nose: ripe fruit, spicy, creamy oak, toasty, complex. Palate: powerful, flavourful, toasty, round tannins.

Viña Valera 2013 T Joven
100% tempranillo

87

Colour: very deep cherry, garnet rim. Nose: overripe fruit, warm, dried herbs. Palate: flavourful, ripe fruit, long.

Viña Valera 6 meses Barrica 2012 T Roble
100% tempranillo

86

Colour: bright cherry. Nose: ripe fruit, sweet spices, toasty. Palate: flavourful, fruity, toasty, round tannins.

Viña Valera Reserva 2008 TR
100% tempranillo

88

Colour: very deep cherry, garnet rim. Nose: powerfull, ripe fruit, roasted coffee, dark chocolate. Palate: powerful, toasty, roasted-coffee aftertaste.

Viña Valera Selección 2011 T
100% tempranillo

89

Colour: very deep cherry, garnet rim. Nose: powerfull, ripe fruit, roasted coffee. Palate: powerful, toasty, roasted-coffee aftertaste.

Viña Valera Viñas Viejas 2009 T
100% tempranillo

88

Colour: cherry, garnet rim. Nose: ripe fruit, spicy, toasty. Palate: powerful, flavourful, toasty, round tannins.

Zarzuela 2013 T
100% tempranillo

87

Colour: cherry, purple rim. Nose: red berry notes, ripe fruit, wild herbs. Palate: flavourful, powerful, fruity.

Zarzuela Crianza 2011 TC

88

Colour: cherry, garnet rim. Nose: ripe fruit, spicy, creamy oak, toasty, complex. Palate: powerful, flavourful, toasty, balanced.

Zarzuela Reserva 2008 TR
100% tempranillo

89

Colour: cherry, garnet rim. Nose: red berry notes, ripe fruit, spicy, creamy oak, toasty, earthy notes. Palate: powerful, flavourful, toasty, round tannins.

Zarzuela Selección 2011 T Roble
100% tempranillo

89

Colour: cherry, garnet rim. Nose: ripe fruit, spicy, creamy oak, toasty, complex. Palate: powerful, flavourful, toasty, round tannins.

Zarzuela Tinto 2012 T Roble
100% tempranillo

85

Zarzuela Viñas Viejas 2010 T
100% tempranillo

90

Colour: cherry, garnet rim. Nose: red berry notes, ripe fruit, spicy, creamy oak, toasty, complex, earthy notes. Palate: powerful, flavourful, toasty.

BODEGA CRAYON

Plaza de la Hispanidad 1, 5ºD
09400 Aranda de Duero (Burgos)
☎: +34 661 325 455
info@bodegacrayon.es

Talaia Crayon 2010 T
tempranillo

89

Colour: bright cherry. Nose: ripe fruit, sweet spices, creamy oak, medium intensity. Palate: fruity, flavourful, toasty, balanced.

Talaia Crayon 2012 T
tempranillo

88

Colour: cherry, garnet rim. Nose: ripe fruit, spicy, creamy oak, toasty, complex. Palate: powerful, flavourful, toasty.

BODEGA DE BLAS SERRANO

Ctra. Santa Cruz, s/n
09471 Fuentelcésped (Burgos)
☎: +34 669 313 108
www.bodegasdeblasserrano.com
dbs@bodegasdeblasserrano.com

De Blas Serrano Bodegas 2009 T
tinta del país

90

Colour: very deep cherry, garnet rim. Nose: closed, smoky, ripe fruit, spicy. Palate: good structure, toasty, round tannins.

Mathis 2009 T
tinta del país

92

Colour: very deep cherry, garnet rim. Nose: toasty, closed, ripe fruit, smoky, characterful. Palate: full, good structure, long.

Phylos 2010 T
tinta del país

92

Colour: deep cherry, garnet rim. Nose: expressive, complex, ripe fruit, cocoa bean. Palate: full, spicy, long, round tannins.

BODEGA DÍAZ BAYO

Camino de los Anarinos, s/n
09471 Fuentelcésped (Burgos)
☎: +34 947 561 020
Fax: +34 947 561 204
www.bodegadiazbayo.com
info@bodegadiazbayo.com

FDB 2006 T Barrica
tempranillo

91

Colour: cherry, garnet rim. Nose: balanced, complex, ripe fruit, spicy, wild herbs. Palate: good structure, flavourful, round tannins.

Magunus Maximus 2010 T
tempranillo

88

Colour: cherry, garnet rim. Nose: ripe fruit, spicy, creamy oak, toasty, fine reductive notes. Palate: powerful, flavourful, toasty.

Majuelo de la Hombría 2008 T

92 ❦

Colour: cherry, garnet rim. Nose: balanced, complex, ripe fruit, spicy, mineral. Palate: good structure, flavourful, round tannins.

Nuestro 12 meses 2012 T Barrica
tempranillo

87 ❦

Colour: cherry, garnet rim. Nose: fruit preserve, fruit liqueur notes, spicy. Palate: flavourful, pruney, balsamic.

Nuestro 20 meses 2007 T Barrica
tempranillo

92 ❦

Colour: dark-red cherry. Nose: ripe fruit, spicy, creamy oak, complex, dried herbs. Palate: powerful, flavourful, toasty, round tannins.

Nuestro Crianza 2009 TC
tempranillo

91

Colour: cherry, garnet rim. Nose: ripe fruit, wild herbs, earthy notes, spicy, creamy oak. Palate: flavourful, long, balsamic, balanced.

BODEGA EMINA

Ctra. San Bernardo, s/n
47359 Valbuena de Duero (Valladolid)
☎: +34 983 683 315
Fax: +34 902 430 189
www.emina.es
emina@emina.es

Emina 2011 TC
100% tempranillo

87

Colour: dark-red cherry, garnet rim. Nose: powerfull, ripe fruit, cocoa bean, toasty. Palate: good structure, round tannins, powerful.

Emina Atio 2010 T
100% tempranillo

90

Colour: deep cherry, garnet rim. Nose: medium intensity, expressive, spicy, smoky, cocoa bean. Palate: balanced, round tannins.

Emina Pasión 2013 T Roble
100% tempranillo

85

Emina Prestigio 2010 TR
100% tempranillo

90

Colour: cherry, garnet rim. Nose: spicy, fine reductive notes, aged wood nuances, toasty. Palate: spicy, long, toasty, balanced.

Valdelosfrailes 2013 T Roble
100% tempranillo

86

Colour: bright cherry. Nose: ripe fruit, sweet spices. Palate: flavourful, fruity, toasty, round tannins.

BODEGA HNOS. PÁRAMO ARROYO

Ctra. de Roa Pedrosa
09314 Pedrosa de Duero (Burgos)
☎: +34 947 530 041
www.paramoarroyo.com
bodega@paramoarroyo.com

Eremus 2010 TC
100% tempranillo

89 ❦

Colour: cherry, garnet rim. Nose: ripe fruit, wild herbs, earthy notes, spicy, creamy oak. Palate: balanced, flavourful, long, balsamic.

Eremus 2012 T
100% tempranillo

84 ❦

BODEGA MATARROMERA
Ctra. Renedo-Pesquera, Km. 30
47359 Valbuena de Duero (Valladolid)
☎: +34 983 107 100
Fax: +34 902 430 189
www.grupomatarromera.com
matarromera@matarromera.es

Matarromera 2005 TGR
tempranillo
93
Colour: cherry, garnet rim. Nose: balanced, complex, ripe fruit, spicy. Palate: good structure, flavourful, round tannins.

Matarromera 2010 TR
100% tempranillo
90
Colour: cherry, garnet rim. Nose: ripe fruit, spicy, creamy oak, toasty, complex. Palate: powerful, flavourful, toasty, long.

Matarromera 2011 TC
100% tempranillo
88
Colour: cherry, garnet rim. Nose: powerfull, fruit preserve, sweet spices, creamy oak. Palate: flavourful, round tannins.

Matarromera Edición Limitada 25 Aniversario 2010 T
100% tempranillo
93
Colour: black cherry, garnet rim. Nose: medium intensity, elegant, balanced, ripe fruit, cocoa bean. Palate: full, good structure, complex.

Matarromera Prestigio 2010 TGR
100% tempranillo
92
Colour: cherry, garnet rim. Nose: red berry notes, ripe fruit, spicy, creamy oak, toasty, complex, earthy notes. Palate: powerful, flavourful, toasty, round tannins.

Melior 2013 T Roble
100% tempranillo
84

BODEGA NEXUS
Ctra. Pesquera de Duero a Renedo, s/n
47315 Pesquera de Duero (Valladolid)
☎: +34 983 360 284
Fax: +34 983 345 546
www.bodegasnexus.com
comercial@bodegasnexus.com

Nexus + 2009 T
100% tempranillo
91
Colour: cherry, garnet rim. Nose: spicy, ripe fruit, dried herbs. Palate: complex, good structure, round tannins.

Nexus 2008 TC
100% tempranillo
93
Colour: cherry, garnet rim. Nose: ripe fruit, spicy, creamy oak, toasty, dark chocolate, earthy notes. Palate: powerful, flavourful, toasty, round tannins.

Nexus One 2012 T
100% tempranillo
90
Colour: bright cherry, purple rim. Nose: ripe fruit, sweet spices, creamy oak, expressive. Palate: flavourful, fruity, toasty, round tannins.

Tierras Guindas 2012 T
100% tempranillo
87
Colour: cherry, garnet rim. Nose: spicy, fine reductive notes, wet leather, aged wood nuances, toasty. Palate: spicy, long, toasty.

BODEGA PAGO DE CIRSUS
Ctra. de Ablitas a Ribafora, Km. 5
31523 Ablitas (Navarra)
☎: +34 948 386 427
Fax: +34 948 386 420
www.pagodecirsus.com
laura.dominguez@pagodecirsus.com

Senda de los Olivos Edición Especial 2006 T
tinto fino
89
Colour: pale ruby, brick rim edge. Nose: elegant, spicy, fine reductive notes, wet leather, aged wood nuances, fruit liqueur notes. Palate: spicy, fine tannins, elegant, long.

Senda de los Olivos Vendimia Seleccionada 2011 T
tinto fino
90
Colour: cherry, garnet rim. Nose: ripe fruit, spicy, creamy oak, toasty, complex. Palate: powerful, flavourful, toasty, round tannins.

BODEGA RENACIMIENTO
Santa María, 36
47359 Olivares de Duero (Valladolid)
☎: +34 983 683 315
Fax: +34 902 430 189
www.bodegarento.es
emina@emina.es

Rento 2006 T
100% tempranillo
90
Colour: cherry, garnet rim. Nose: red berry notes, ripe fruit, spicy, creamy oak, toasty, complex, earthy notes. Palate: powerful, flavourful, toasty, round tannins.

BODEGA S. ARROYO

Avda. del Cid, 99
09441 Sotillo de la Ribera (Burgos)
☎: +34 947 532 444
Fax: +34 947 532 444
www.tintoarroyo.com
info@tintoarroyo.com

Tinto Arroyo 2007 TGR
100% tempranillo

89

Colour: pale ruby, brick rim edge. Nose: elegant, spicy, fine reductive notes, wet leather, aged wood nuances, fruit liqueur notes. Palate: spicy, elegant, long.

Tinto Arroyo 2009 TR
100% tempranillo

90

Colour: cherry, garnet rim. Nose: red berry notes, ripe fruit, spicy, creamy oak, toasty, complex, earthy notes. Palate: powerful, flavourful, toasty, round tannins.

Tinto Arroyo 2011 TC
100% tempranillo

89

Colour: cherry, garnet rim. Nose: ripe fruit, spicy, creamy oak, toasty, complex. Palate: powerful, flavourful, toasty, harsh oak tannins.

Tinto Arroyo 2012 T Roble
100% tempranillo

88

Colour: bright cherry. Nose: ripe fruit, sweet spices, creamy oak. Palate: flavourful, fruity, toasty, round tannins.

Tinto Arroyo 2013 T
100% tempranillo

88

Colour: cherry, purple rim. Nose: expressive, fresh fruit, red berry notes, floral. Palate: flavourful, fruity, good acidity, round tannins.

Tinto Arroyo Vendimia Seleccionada 2011 T
100% tempranillo

93

Colour: cherry, garnet rim. Nose: ripe fruit, wild herbs, spicy, balsamic herbs, mineral. Palate: powerful, flavourful, spicy.

Viñarroyo 2013 RD
100% tempranillo

86

Colour: rose, bright. Nose: powerfull, ripe fruit, red berry notes, floral, expressive. Palate: fruity, fresh, easy to drink.

BODEGA SAN MAMÉS, S. COOP.

Ctra. Valladolid, s/n
09315 Fuentecén (Burgos)
☎: +34 947 532 693
Fax: +34 947 532 653
www.bodegasanmames.com
info@bodegasanmames.com

Doble R (5 meses) 2012 T
100% tempranillo

87

Colour: cherry, garnet rim. Nose: ripe fruit, wild herbs, spicy, creamy oak. Palate: balanced, flavourful, long, balsamic.

Doble R 2010 T Roble
100% tempranillo

91

Colour: cherry, garnet rim. Nose: ripe fruit, spicy, creamy oak, toasty, complex, earthy notes. Palate: powerful, flavourful, toasty, round tannins, balanced.

Doble R 2011 TC
100% tempranillo

89

Colour: bright cherry. Nose: ripe fruit, sweet spices, creamy oak, medium intensity. Palate: fruity, flavourful, toasty.

Doble R 2012 T
100% tempranillo

87

Colour: cherry, garnet rim. Nose: dried herbs, ripe fruit, medium intensity. Palate: fruity, easy to drink, flavourful.

Doble R 2013 RD
100% tempranillo

85

BODEGA SAN ROQUE DE LA ENCINA, SDAD. COOP.

San Roque, 73
09391 Castrillo de la Vega (Burgos)
☎: +34 947 536 001
Fax: +34 947 536 183
www.bodegasanroquedelaencina.com
info@bodegasanroquedelaencina.com

Cerro Piñel 2011 TC
100% tempranillo

88

Colour: cherry, garnet rim. Nose: ripe fruit, spicy, warm. Palate: powerful, flavourful, toasty, round tannins.

Cerro Piñel 2012 T
100% tempranillo

86

Colour: cherry, purple rim. Nose: cocoa bean, sweet spices, ripe fruit. Palate: flavourful, toasty.

Monte del Conde 2011 TC
100% tempranillo

88

Colour: cherry, garnet rim. Nose: spicy, creamy oak, toasty, warm. Palate: powerful, flavourful, toasty, round tannins.

Monte del Conde 2013 T
100% tempranillo

86

Colour: deep cherry, purple rim. Nose: ripe fruit, red berry notes, balanced. Palate: correct, fruity, good finish.

Monte Pinadillo 2011 TC
100% tempranillo

89

Colour: bright cherry. Nose: ripe fruit, sweet spices, creamy oak. Palate: fruity, flavourful, toasty.

Monte Pinadillo 2012 T Roble
100% tempranillo

87

Colour: very deep cherry, garnet rim. Nose: toasty, spicy, ripe fruit. Palate: powerful, round tannins, balanced.

Monte Pinadillo 2013 RD
100% tempranillo

86

Colour: light cherry. Nose: powerfull, ripe fruit, red berry notes, floral. Palate: powerful, fruity, fresh.

Monte Pinadillo 2013 T
100% tempranillo

85

BODEGA SEVERINO SANZ
Del Rio, s/n
40542 Montejo De La Vega
De La Serrezuela (Segovia)
☎: +34 944 659 659
Fax: +34 944 531 442
www.bodegaseverinosanz.es
erika@picmatic.es

Alma de Severino 2013 RD
tempranillo

87

Colour: rose, purple rim. Nose: powerfull, ripe fruit, red berry notes, floral. Palate: powerful, fruity, fresh.

Herencia de Llanomingomez 2010 T
tempranillo

91

Colour: black cherry, garnet rim. Nose: expressive, balanced, complex, spicy, aromatic coffee. Palate: good structure, full.

Muron 2011 T
tempranillo

88

Colour: cherry, garnet rim. Nose: ripe fruit, spicy, toasty, smoky. Palate: powerful, flavourful, toasty, round tannins.

Muron 2012 T Roble
tempranillo

91

Colour: bright cherry. Nose: ripe fruit, sweet spices, creamy oak. Palate: flavourful, fruity, toasty, round tannins.

Muron Edición Limitada 2011 T
tempranillo

90

Colour: cherry, garnet rim. Nose: ripe fruit, wild herbs, earthy notes, spicy, creamy oak. Palate: balanced, flavourful, long, balsamic.

Pico del Llano 2013 T
tempranillo

86

Colour: very deep cherry, purple rim. Nose: powerfull, ripe fruit. Palate: fruity, flavourful, round tannins, good acidity.

BODEGA TINTO CARME
Real de Abajo, 4
47359 Valbuena de Duero (Valladolid)
☎: +34 646 242 262
Fax: +34 983 683 014
www.tintocarme.es
info@tintocarme.es

Carme 2012 T
tempranillo

85

BODEGA TOMÁS POSTIGO
Estación, 12
47300 Peñafiel (Valladolid)
☎: +34 983 873 019
Fax: +34 983 880 258
www.tomaspostigo.es
administracion@tomaspostigo.es

Tomás Postigo 2011 TC
tinto fino, cabernet sauvignon, merlot

93

Colour: cherry, garnet rim. Nose: spicy, creamy oak, toasty, complex, ripe fruit. Palate: powerful, flavourful, toasty, round tannins.

BODEGA VIÑA BUENA
Avda. Portugal, 15
09400 Aranda de Duero (Burgos)
☎: +34 947 546 414
Fax: +34 947 506 694
www.vinabuena.com
vinabuena@vinabuena.com

Fuero Real 2011 TC
100% tempranillo

86

Colour: cherry, garnet rim. Nose: ripe fruit, spicy, creamy oak, balsamic herbs. Palate: powerful, flavourful, toasty.

Fuero Real 2013 T
100% tempranillo
85

BODEGA VIÑA VILANO S. COOP.
Ctra. de Anguix, 10
09314 Pedrosa de Duero (Burgos)
☎: +34 947 530 029
Fax: +34 947 530 037
www.vinavilano.com
info@vinavilano.com

Viña Vilano 2010 TR
100% tempranillo
88
Colour: very deep cherry, garnet rim. Nose: powerfull, ripe fruit, roasted coffee, dark chocolate. Palate: powerful, toasty, roasted-coffee aftertaste.

Viña Vilano 2011 TC
100% tempranillo
91
Colour: cherry, garnet rim. Nose: ripe fruit, spicy, creamy oak, toasty, complex. Palate: powerful, flavourful, toasty, round tannins, balanced, elegant.

Viña Vilano 2013 RD
100% tempranillo
86
Colour: rose. Nose: powerfull, ripe fruit, red berry notes, floral, expressive. Palate: powerful, fruity, fresh.

Viña Vilano 2013 T
100% tempranillo
90
Colour: cherry, purple rim. Nose: red berry notes, expressive, balanced, violets. Palate: balanced, good acidity, flavourful, long.

Viña Vilano 2013 T Roble
100% tempranillo
87
Colour: very deep cherry, garnet rim. Nose: powerfull, roasted coffee, dark chocolate. Palate: powerful, toasty, roasted-coffee aftertaste.

BODEGAS ABADÍA LA ARROYADA
La Tejera, s/n
09442 Terradillos de Esgueva (Burgos)
☎: +34 947 545 309
www.abadialaarroyada.es
bodegas@abadialaarroyada.es

Abadía la Arroyada 2009 TC
100% tempranillo
90
Colour: cherry, garnet rim. Nose: ripe fruit, spicy, creamy oak, toasty. Palate: powerful, flavourful, toasty, round tannins.

Abadía la Arroyada 2011 T Roble
100% tempranillo
88
Colour: cherry, garnet rim. Nose: ripe fruit, spicy, creamy oak, toasty. Palate: powerful, flavourful, toasty.

Abadía la Arroyada 2012 T
100% tempranillo
89
Colour: very deep cherry, garnet rim. Nose: dried herbs, red berry notes, ripe fruit, balanced. Palate: flavourful, ripe fruit, long.

BODEGAS ANTÍDOTO
Elias Alvarez nº31, 1ºB
42330 San Esteban de Gormaz (Soria)
☎: +34 676 536 390
www.bodegasantidoto.com
bebervino@hotmail.com

Antídoto 2012 T
tinto fino
89
Colour: cherry, garnet rim. Nose: ripe fruit, wild herbs, earthy notes, spicy, creamy oak. Palate: balanced, flavourful, long, balsamic.

La Hormiga de Antídoto 2012 T
tinto fino
93
Colour: cherry, garnet rim. Nose: ripe fruit, spicy, creamy oak, toasty, complex, dark chocolate, earthy notes. Palate: powerful, flavourful, toasty, round tannins.

Le Rosé de Antídoto 2013 RD
tinto fino, albillo, garnacha
91
Colour: onion pink. Nose: elegant, candied fruit, dried flowers, fragrant herbs, red berry notes. Palate: light-bodied, flavourful, good acidity, long, spicy.

BODEGAS ARROCAL
Eras de Santa María, s/n
09443 Gumiel de Mercado (Burgos)
☎: +34 947 561 290
Fax: +34 947 561 290
www.arrocal.com
arrocal@arrocal.com

Arrocal 2013 T Barrica
100% tempranillo
88
Colour: cherry, garnet rim. Nose: ripe fruit, spicy, creamy oak, toasty. Palate: powerful, flavourful, toasty, balanced.

Arrocal Angel 2010 T
100% tempranillo
93
Colour: cherry, garnet rim. Nose: red berry notes, ripe fruit, spicy, creamy oak, toasty, complex, earthy notes. Palate: powerful, flavourful, toasty, round tannins, balanced.

Arrocal Máximo 2006 T
100% tempranillo

90

Colour: deep cherry, orangey edge. Nose: ripe fruit, spicy, creamy oak, fine reductive notes. Palate: flavourful, spicy, long, balsamic.

Arrocal Passión 2011 T
100% tempranillo

91

Colour: cherry, garnet rim. Nose: ripe fruit, spicy, creamy oak, toasty, complex. Palate: powerful, flavourful, toasty.

Arrocal Selección 2011 T
100% tempranillo

90

Colour: cherry, garnet rim. Nose: ripe fruit, spicy, creamy oak, toasty, complex, dark chocolate, earthy notes. Palate: powerful, flavourful, toasty, balanced.

Rosa de Arrocal 2013 RD

86

Colour: light cherry, bright. Nose: floral, fragrant herbs, balanced. Palate: fruity, easy to drink, correct.

BODEGAS ARZUAGA NAVARRO
Ctra. N-122, km. 325
47350 Quintanilla de Onésimo
(Valladolid)
☎: +34 983 681 146
Fax: +34 983 681 147
www.arzuaganavarro.com
bodeg@arzuaganavarro.com

Amaya Arzuaga Colección Autor 2010 T
94

Colour: cherry, garnet rim. Nose: ripe fruit, spicy, creamy oak, toasty, complex, dark chocolate, mineral. Palate: powerful, flavourful, toasty, round tannins.

AMAYA ARZUAGA
COLECCIÓN 2010

Arzuaga 2012 TC
88

Colour: very deep cherry, garnet rim. Nose: powerfull, ripe fruit, roasted coffee, tar. Palate: powerful, toasty, roasted-coffee aftertaste.

Arzuaga 2010 TR
92

Colour: deep cherry, garnet rim. Nose: red berry notes, fruit expression, sweet spices. Palate: flavourful, good acidity, fresh, fruity, round tannins.

Arzuaga Ecológico 2011 TC
100% tempranillo

90

Colour: very deep cherry, garnet rim. Nose: powerfull, ripe fruit, roasted coffee. Palate: powerful, toasty, roasted-coffee aftertaste.

Arzuaga Reserva Especial 2010 TR
93
Colour: very deep cherry. Nose: ripe fruit, spicy, creamy oak, toasty, characterful. Palate: powerful, flavourful, toasty, round tannins.

Gran Arzuaga 2010 T
93
Colour: cherry, garnet rim. Nose: ripe fruit, spicy, creamy oak, toasty, complex. Palate: powerful, flavourful, toasty, round tannins.

Rosae Arzuaga 2013 RD
100% tempranillo
90
Colour: coppery red. Nose: elegant, candied fruit, dried flowers, fragrant herbs, sweet spices, creamy oak. Palate: light-bodied, flavourful, good acidity, spicy.

Viñedos y Bodegas La Planta 2013 T Roble
100% tempranillo
88
Colour: very deep cherry, garnet rim. Nose: ripe fruit, roasted coffee, dark chocolate. Palate: powerful, toasty, roasted-coffee aftertaste.

BODEGAS ASENJO & MANSO
Ctra. Palencia, km. 58,200
09311 La Horra (Burgos)
☎: +34 669 568 663
Fax: +34 947 505 269
www.asenjo-manso.com
info@asenjo-manso.com

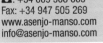

A&M Autor 2009 T
100% tempranillo
90
Colour: very deep cherry. Nose: ripe fruit, spicy, creamy oak, toasty, characterful. Palate: powerful, flavourful, toasty, balanced.

Ceres 2010 TC
100% tempranillo
88
Colour: cherry, garnet rim. Nose: ripe fruit, spicy, creamy oak, toasty, complex. Palate: powerful, flavourful, toasty.

Silvanus 2009 TC
100% tempranillo
89
Colour: bright cherry. Nose: ripe fruit, sweet spices, creamy oak, medium intensity. Palate: fruity, flavourful, toasty.

Silvanus Edición Limitada 2009 T
100% tempranillo
90
Colour: cherry, garnet rim. Nose: ripe fruit, spicy, creamy oak, toasty, complex. Palate: powerful, flavourful, toasty, round tannins.

BODEGAS BADEN NUMEN
Carreterilla, s/n
47359 San Bernardo (Valladolid)
☎: +34 615 995 552
Fax: +34 983 683 041
www.badennumen.es
bodega@badennumen.es

Baden Numen "B" 2012 T
100% tinto fino
91
Colour: cherry, purple rim. Nose: red berry notes, raspberry, fruit expression, fragrant herbs. Palate: flavourful, light-bodied, good acidity, fresh, fruity.

Baden Numen "N" 2011 TC
100% tinto fino
90
Colour: cherry, garnet rim. Nose: red berry notes, ripe fruit, spicy, creamy oak, toasty, earthy notes. Palate: powerful, flavourful, toasty, round tannins.

Baden Numen Oro "AU" 2010 T
100% tinto fino
93
Colour: cherry, garnet rim. Nose: ripe fruit, spicy, creamy oak, toasty, complex, dark chocolate, earthy notes. Palate: powerful, flavourful, toasty, round tannins, elegant.

BODEGAS BALBÁS

La Majada, s/n
09311 La Horra (Burgos)
☎: +34 947 542 111
Fax: +34 947 542 112
www.balbas.es
bodegas@balbas.es

Alitus 2005 TR
91
Colour: cherry, garnet rim. Nose: wild herbs, earthy notes, spicy, creamy oak, ripe fruit, red berry notes. Palate: balanced, flavourful, long, balsamic.

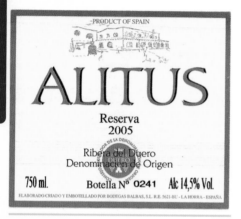

Ardal 2009 TR
90
Colour: cherry, garnet rim. Nose: ripe fruit, spicy, toasty, smoky, dried herbs. Palate: powerful, flavourful, toasty, round tannins.

Ardal 2011 TC
86
Colour: cherry, garnet rim. Nose: ripe fruit, spicy, toasty. Palate: powerful, flavourful, toasty, round tannins.

Balbás 2011 TC
90
Colour: cherry, garnet rim. Nose: ripe fruit, spicy, creamy oak, toasty, complex. Palate: powerful, flavourful, toasty, round tannins.

Ritus 2010 T
92
Colour: cherry, garnet rim. Nose: ripe fruit, wild herbs, earthy notes, spicy, creamy oak. Palate: balanced, flavourful, long, balsamic.

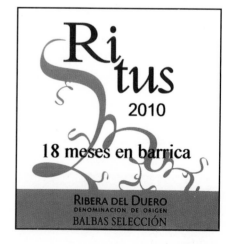

BODEGAS BOHÓRQUEZ

Ctra. Peñafiel, s/n
47315 Pesquera de Duero (Valladolid)
☎: +34 915 643 751
Fax: +34 915 618 602
www.bodegasbohorquez.com
info@bodegasbohorquez.com

Cardela 2010 TC

88

Colour: cherry, garnet rim. Nose: ripe fruit, balsamic herbs, sweet spices, creamy oak. Palate: powerful, flavourful, spicy, toasty.

BODEGAS BRIEGO

Ctra. Cuellar, s/n
47311 Fompedraza (Valladolid)
☎: +34 983 892 156
Fax: +34 983 892 156
www.bodegasbriego.com
info@bodegasbriego.com

Ankal 2011 TC
100% tempranillo

90

Colour: cherry, garnet rim. Nose: red berry notes, ripe fruit, spicy, creamy oak, toasty, complex, elegant. Palate: powerful, flavourful, toasty, round tannins.

Ankal 2012 T Roble
100% tempranillo

89

Colour: bright cherry. Nose: sweet spices, creamy oak, red berry notes. Palate: flavourful, fruity, toasty, round tannins.

Ankal Edición Limitada 2009 TR
100% tempranillo

89

Colour: cherry, garnet rim. Nose: ripe fruit, wild herbs, earthy notes, spicy, creamy oak. Palate: balanced, flavourful, long, balsamic.

Briego Adalid 2009 TR
100% tempranillo

88

Colour: deep cherry, garnet rim. Nose: ripe fruit, dried herbs, smoky. Palate: flavourful, round tannins.

Briego Tiempo 2011 TC
100% tempranillo

90

Colour: cherry, garnet rim. Nose: ripe fruit, wild herbs, earthy notes, spicy, creamy oak. Palate: balanced, flavourful, long, balsamic.

Briego Vendimia Seleccionada 2012 T Roble
100% tempranillo

90

Colour: bright cherry. Nose: sweet spices, creamy oak, overripe fruit. Palate: flavourful, fruity, toasty.

Supernova 2011 TC
100% tempranillo

88

Colour: cherry, garnet rim. Nose: ripe fruit, spicy, toasty, scrubland. Palate: powerful, flavourful, toasty, round tannins.

Supernova Edición Limitada 2009 T
100% tempranillo

90

Colour: black cherry. Nose: ripe fruit, spicy, creamy oak, toasty, complex. Palate: flavourful, toasty, round tannins, easy to drink.

Supernova Roble 2012 T Roble
100% tempranillo

92

Colour: cherry, garnet rim. Nose: ripe fruit, spicy, creamy oak, toasty, complex, dark chocolate, earthy notes. Palate: powerful, flavourful, toasty, round tannins.

BODEGAS BRIONES ABAD

Isabel la Católica, 42
09300 Roa (Burgos)
☎: +34 947 540 613
Fax: +34 947 540 613
www.cantamuda.com
brionesabad@cantamuda.com

Canta Muda 2012 T Roble
100% tempranillo

89

Colour: cherry, garnet rim. Nose: ripe fruit, spicy, creamy oak, toasty, dark chocolate, mineral. Palate: powerful, flavourful, toasty, round tannins.

Canta Muda Finca la Cebolla 2011 T
100% tempranillo

88

Colour: cherry, garnet rim. Nose: spicy, creamy oak, balsamic herbs, dry stone, fruit preserve. Palate: flavourful, spicy, round, elegant.

Canta Muda Parcela 64 2011 T
100% tempranillo

91

Colour: cherry, garnet rim. Nose: ripe fruit, spicy, creamy oak, toasty, mineral, expressive. Palate: powerful, flavourful, toasty, round tannins, balanced.

BODEGAS BRIONES BANIANDRÉS

Camino Valdeguzmán, s/n
09314 Quintanamanvirgo (Burgos)
☎: +34 947 561 385
Fax: +34 947 561 386
www.apricus.es
bodegas@apricus.es

Apricus 2009 TC
100% tempranillo

88

Colour: pale ruby, brick rim edge. Nose: spicy, fine reductive notes, wet leather, aged wood nuances, fruit liqueur notes. Palate: spicy, fine tannins.

Apricus 2012 T Barrica
100% tempranillo

89

Colour: bright cherry. Nose: ripe fruit, sweet spices, creamy oak, expressive. Palate: flavourful, fruity, toasty, round tannins.

Apricus 2012 T Joven
100% tempranillo

90

Colour: cherry, garnet rim. Nose: ripe fruit, balanced, sweet spices. Palate: good structure, fruity, flavourful, round tannins.

BODEGAS CANTAMORA

Travesía de las Eras no2
47315 Pesquera de Duero (Valladolid)
☎: +34 983 870 059
www.bodegascantamora.com
bodegas@bodegascantamora.com

Acebeño 2013 T

87

Colour: bright cherry. Nose: ripe fruit, sweet spices, creamy oak, expressive. Palate: flavourful, fruity, toasty, balsamic.

Tinto Moreño 2010 TC

86

Colour: bright cherry. Nose: ripe fruit, sweet spices, roasted coffee. Palate: flavourful, fruity, toasty, round tannins.

Tinto Moreño Cepas Viejas 2009 TC
100% tempranillo

88

Colour: bright cherry, garnet rim. Nose: expressive, red berry notes, ripe fruit, creamy oak. Palate: good structure, spicy, long.

BODEGAS CEPA 21

Ctra. N-122, Km. 297
47018 Castrillo de Duero (Valladolid)
☎: +34 983 484 083
Fax: +34 983 480 017
www.cepa21.com
bodega@cepa21.com

Cepa 21 2010 T
100% tinto fino

91

Colour: cherry, garnet rim. Nose: red berry notes, ripe fruit, spicy, creamy oak, toasty, complex, earthy notes. Palate: powerful, flavourful, toasty.

Hito 2013 T
100% tinto fino

88

Colour: very deep cherry. Nose: ripe fruit, sweet spices, cocoa bean. Palate: flavourful, fruity, toasty, round tannins.

Malabrigo 2010 T
100% tinto fino

92

Colour: cherry, garnet rim. Nose: ripe fruit, wild herbs, earthy notes, spicy, creamy oak. Palate: balanced, flavourful, long, balsamic.

BODEGAS CRUZ DE ALBA

Síndico, 4 y 5
47350 Quintanilla de Onésimo
(Valladolid)
☎: +34 941 310 295
Fax: +34 941 310 832
www.cruzdealba.es
info@cruzdealba.es

Cruz de Alba 2012 TC
100% tempranillo

88

Colour: very deep cherry, garnet rim. Nose: powerfull, ripe fruit, roasted coffee, dark chocolate. Palate: powerful, toasty, roasted-coffee aftertaste.

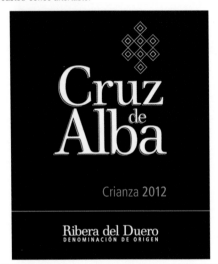

Lucero de Alba 2013 T Roble
100% tempranillo

88

Colour: bright cherry. Nose: ripe fruit, sweet spices, creamy oak. Palate: flavourful, fruity, toasty, round tannins.

BODEGAS CUEVAS JIMÉNEZ - FERRATUS

Ctra. Madrid-Irún, A-I km. 165
09370 Gumiel de Izán (Burgos)
☎: +34 947 679 999
Fax: +34 947 613 873
www.ferratus.es
bodega@ferratus.es

Ferratus 2008 T
100% tempranillo

93

Colour: cherry, garnet rim. Nose: ripe fruit, spicy, creamy oak, toasty, complex, earthy notes. Palate: powerful, flavourful, toasty, round tannins.

Ferratus A0 2013 T Roble
100% tempranillo

90

Colour: cherry, purple rim. Nose: powerfull, red berry notes, ripe fruit, floral, expressive. Palate: powerful, fresh, fruity, unctuous.

Ferratus Sensaciones 2008 T
100% tempranillo

94

Colour: cherry, garnet rim. Nose: red berry notes, ripe fruit, spicy, creamy oak, toasty, complex, fine reductive notes. Palate: powerful, flavourful, toasty, round tannins.

Ferratus Sensaciones Décimo 2003 T
tempranillo

96

Colour: cherry, garnet rim. Nose: ripe fruit, wild herbs, earthy notes, spicy, creamy oak. Palate: balanced, flavourful, long, balsamic, elegant.

BODEGAS DE LOS RÍOS PRIETO

Ctra. Pesquera - Renedo, KM. 1
47315 Pesquera de Duero (Valladolid)
☎: +34 983 880 383
Fax: +34 983 878 032
www.bodegasdelosriosprieto.com
info@bodegasdelosriosprieto.com

Lara Prios Maximus Vino de Autor 2009 T
tempranillo

90

Colour: bright cherry. Nose: ripe fruit, sweet spices, creamy oak, medium intensity. Palate: fruity, flavourful, toasty.

Prios Maximus 2009 TR
tempranillo

86

Colour: cherry, garnet rim. Nose: waxy notes, tobacco, ripe fruit, spicy, aged wood nuances. Palate: fine bitter notes, flavourful, fine tannins.

Prios Maximus 2012 TC
tempranillo

87

Colour: bright cherry. Nose: ripe fruit, sweet spices, creamy oak, balsamic herbs. Palate: fruity, flavourful, toasty, roasted-coffee aftertaste.

Prios Maximus 2013 T Roble
tempranillo

87

Colour: bright cherry. Nose: ripe fruit, sweet spices, creamy oak. Palate: flavourful, fruity, toasty, round tannins.

BODEGAS DEL CAMPO
Camino Fuentenavares, s/n
09370 Quintana del Pidío (Burgos)
☎: +34 947 561 034
Fax: +34 947 561 038
www.pagosdequintana.com
bodegas@pagosdequintana.com

Pagos de Quintana 2010 TC
100% tinto fino
89
Colour: cherry, garnet rim. Nose: ripe fruit, spicy, creamy oak, toasty. Palate: powerful, flavourful, toasty.

Pagos de Quintana Roble 2012 T Roble
100% tinto fino
87
Colour: bright cherry. Nose: ripe fruit, sweet spices, creamy oak. Palate: flavourful, fruity, toasty.

Pagos de Quintana Vendimia Seleccionada 2009 T
100% tinto fino
91
Colour: cherry, garnet rim. Nose: red berry notes, ripe fruit, spicy, creamy oak, toasty, complex, earthy notes. Palate: powerful, flavourful, toasty, round tannins.

BODEGAS DÍEZ LLORENTE
Ctra. Circunvalación, s/n
09300 Roa (Burgos)
☎: +34 615 293 031
Fax: +34 947 540 341
www.diezllorente.com
bodegas@diezllorente.com

Díez Llorente 2009 TR
tempranillo
88
Colour: cherry, garnet rim. Nose: ripe fruit, wild herbs, earthy notes, spicy, creamy oak. Palate: balanced, flavourful, long, balsamic.

Díez Llorente 2011 TC
tempranillo
86
Colour: bright cherry, garnet rim. Nose: ripe fruit, sweet spices, creamy oak. Palate: flavourful, fruity, toasty.

Díez Llorente 2012 T Roble
tempranillo
86
Colour: bright cherry. Nose: ripe fruit, sweet spices, creamy oak. Palate: flavourful, fruity, toasty, round tannins.

Gran Salinero 2009 TR
100% tempranillo
87
Colour: very deep cherry. Nose: powerfull, fruit preserve, spicy, tobacco. Palate: flavourful, ripe fruit, round tannins.

Gran Salinero 2011 TC
100% tempranillo
88
Colour: cherry, garnet rim. Nose: ripe fruit, spicy, creamy oak, toasty. Palate: powerful, flavourful, toasty, round tannins.

Gran Salinero Selección 2012 T Roble
100% tempranillo
89
Colour: bright cherry. Nose: ripe fruit, sweet spices, creamy oak, expressive. Palate: flavourful, fruity, toasty, round tannins.

Señorío de Brenda 2011 TC
tempranillo
87
Nose: ripe fruit, spicy, creamy oak, toasty, wild herbs. Palate: powerful, flavourful, toasty, round tannins.

Señorío de Brenda 2012 T Roble
tempranillo
87
Colour: very deep cherry, garnet rim. Nose: overripe fruit, warm, dried herbs. Palate: flavourful, ripe fruit, long.

Señorío de Brenda 2013 T
tempranillo
86
Colour: cherry, purple rim. Nose: expressive, fresh fruit, red berry notes, floral. Palate: flavourful, fruity, good acidity.

BODEGAS DOMINIO DE CAIR
Ctra. Aranda a la Aguilera. km. 9
09370 La Aguilera (Burgos)
☎: +34 947 545 276
Fax: +34 947 545 383
www.dominiodecair.com
bodegas@dominiodecair.com

Cair 2010 TC
100% tempranillo
93
Colour: cherry, garnet rim. Nose: red berry notes, ripe fruit, dry stone, spicy, creamy oak, balsamic herbs. Palate: elegant, round, powerful, flavourful, spicy, long.

Cair Cuvée 2011 T
90
Colour: cherry, garnet rim. Nose: ripe fruit, spicy, creamy oak, toasty, complex. Palate: powerful, flavourful, toasty, round tannins.

Tierras de Cair 2009 TR
100% tempranillo
92
Colour: very deep cherry. Nose: ripe fruit, spicy, creamy oak, toasty, characterful. Palate: powerful, flavourful, toasty, round tannins.

BODEGAS DURÓN
Ctra. Roa - La Horra, km. 3,800
09300 Roa (Burgos)
☎: +34 902 227 700
Fax: +34 902 227 701
www.solardesamaniego.com
bodega@cofradiasamaniego.com

Durón 2009 TR
87
Colour: ruby red. Nose: spicy, fine reductive notes, wet leather, aged wood nuances, toasty. Palate: spicy, long, toasty.

Durón 2011 TC
100% tinta del país
88
Colour: bright cherry. Nose: ripe fruit, sweet spices, creamy oak, medium intensity. Palate: fruity, flavourful, toasty.

BODEGAS EL INICIO
San Vicente, 22
47300 Peñafiel (Valladolid)
☎: +34 947 515 884
Fax: +34 947 515 886
www.bodegaselinicio.com
rbi@redbottleint.com

Admiración Selección Especial 2009 T
100% tempranillo
90
Colour: cherry, garnet rim. Nose: ripe fruit, wild herbs, spicy, creamy oak. Palate: balanced, flavourful, long, balsamic.

Rivendel 2011 TC
100% tempranillo
88
Colour: very deep cherry, garnet rim. Nose: powerfull, ripe fruit, roasted coffee, dark chocolate. Palate: powerful, toasty, roasted-coffee aftertaste.

Rivendel 2012 T Roble
100% tempranillo
88
Colour: bright cherry. Nose: sweet spices, creamy oak, medium intensity. Palate: fruity, flavourful, toasty.

BODEGAS EMILIO MORO
Ctra. Peñafiel - Valoria, s/n
47015 Pesquera de Duero (Valladolid)
☎: +34 983 878 400
Fax: +34 983 870 195
www.emiliomoro.com
bodega@emiliomoro.com

Emilio Moro 2011 T
100% tinto fino
90
Colour: cherry, garnet rim. Nose: ripe fruit, spicy, creamy oak, toasty, mineral. Palate: powerful, flavourful, toasty, round tannins.

Finca Resalso 2013 T
100% tinto fino
91
Colour: bright cherry. Nose: ripe fruit, sweet spices, creamy oak, expressive. Palate: flavourful, fruity, toasty, round tannins.

Malleolus 2010 T
100% tinto fino
93
Colour: cherry, garnet rim. Nose: ripe fruit, spicy, creamy oak, toasty, complex, dry stone. Palate: powerful, flavourful, toasty, round tannins, balanced.

Malleolus de SanchoMartín 2009 T
100% tinto fino
94
Colour: cherry, garnet rim. Nose: ripe fruit, spicy, creamy oak, toasty, complex, dark chocolate, earthy notes. Palate: powerful, flavourful, toasty, round tannins.

Malleolus de Valderramiro 2009 T
100% tinto fino
92
Colour: very deep cherry, garnet rim. Nose: powerfull, ripe fruit, roasted coffee, dark chocolate. Palate: powerful, toasty, roasted-coffee aftertaste.

BODEGAS EPIFANIO RIVERA
Onésimo Redondo, 1
47315 Pesquera de Duero (Valladolid)
☎: +34 983 870 109
Fax: +34 983 870 109
www.epifaniorivera.com
info@epifaniorivera.com

Erial 2011 T
100% tinto fino
90
Colour: bright cherry. Nose: ripe fruit, sweet spices, creamy oak. Palate: fruity, flavourful, toasty.

Erial TF 2011 T
100% tinto fino

91

Colour: very deep cherry, garnet rim. Nose: spicy, elegant, ripe fruit, mineral. Palate: good structure, full, round tannins.

BODEGAS FÉLIX CALLEJO
Avda. del Cid, km. 16
09441 Sotillo de la Ribera (Burgos)
☎: +34 947 532 312
Fax: +34 947 532 304
www.bodegasfelixcallejo.com
callejo@bodegasfelixcallejo.com

Callejo 2011 TC
100% tempranillo

88

Colour: bright cherry. Nose: sweet spices, creamy oak, expressive. Palate: flavourful, fruity, toasty, round tannins.

Félix Callejo Autor 2011 T
100% tempranillo

93

Colour: cherry, garnet rim. Nose: red berry notes, ripe fruit, balsamic herbs, spicy, creamy oak, balanced. Palate: flavourful, spicy, long, elegant.

Flores de Callejo 2012 T
100% tempranillo

88

Colour: bright cherry. Nose: ripe fruit, sweet spices, creamy oak. Palate: flavourful, fruity, toasty, round tannins.

Majuelos de Callejo 2011 T
100% tempranillo

92

Colour: cherry, garnet rim. Nose: ripe fruit, spicy, creamy oak, toasty, complex. Palate: powerful, flavourful, toasty, round tannins.

Viña Pilar 2013 RD
100% tempranillo

87

Colour: light cherry, bright. Nose: fresh fruit, fragrant herbs, floral. Palate: fruity, long, fine bitter notes.

BODEGAS FUENTENARRO
Ctra. Burgos, s/n Cruce
09311 La Horra (Burgos)
☎: +34 947 542 092
Fax: +34 947 542 083
www.fuentenarro.com
bodegas@fuentenarro.com

Viña Fuentenarro 2005 TGR
tempranillo

87

Colour: ruby red, orangey edge. Nose: spicy, fine reductive notes, wet leather, aged wood nuances, toasty. Palate: spicy, long, toasty.

Viña Fuentenarro 2009 TR
tempranillo

91

Colour: very deep cherry, garnet rim. Nose: powerfull, ripe fruit, roasted coffee, dark chocolate. Palate: powerful, toasty, roasted-coffee aftertaste.

Viña Fuentenarro 2010 TC
tempranillo

91

Colour: cherry, garnet rim. Nose: ripe fruit, wild herbs, earthy notes, spicy, creamy oak. Palate: balanced, flavourful, long, balsamic.

Viña Fuentenarro Cuatro Meses Barrica 2012 T Barrica
tempranillo

89

Colour: bright cherry. Nose: sweet spices, creamy oak, medium intensity. Palate: fruity, flavourful, toasty.

Viña Fuentenarro Vendimia Seleccionada 2010 T
tempranillo

90

Colour: cherry, garnet rim. Nose: ripe fruit, spicy. Palate: flavourful, toasty, round tannins, fruity, good finish.

BODEGAS GARCÍA DE ARANDA

Ctra. de Soria, s/n
09400 Aranda de Duero (Burgos)
☎: +34 947 501 817
Fax: +34 947 506 355
www.bodegasgarcia.com
bodega@bodegasgarcia.com

Edades de Baldíos 2012 T Roble
tempranillo

87

Colour: very deep cherry, garnet rim. Nose: powerfull, ripe fruit, roasted coffee. Palate: powerful, toasty, roasted-coffee aftertaste.

PG Pedro García 2010 TC
tempranillo

91

Colour: cherry, garnet rim. Nose: ripe fruit, spicy, creamy oak, toasty, complex. Palate: powerful, flavourful, toasty, round tannins.

Señorío de los Baldíos 2008 TR
tempranillo

88

Colour: cherry, garnet rim. Nose: ripe fruit, spicy, creamy oak, toasty, complex. Palate: powerful, flavurful, toasty.

Señorío de los Baldíos 2011 TC
tempranillo

88

Colour: cherry, garnet rim. Nose: ripe fruit, spicy, creamy oak, toasty. Palate: powerful, flavourful, toasty, round tannins.

Señorío de los Baldíos 2012 T Roble
tempranillo

84

Señorío de los Baldíos 2013 T
tempranillo

85

Señorío de los Baldíos Don Anastasio 2013 RD
tempranillo

86

Colour: rose, purple rim. Nose: powerfull, ripe fruit, red berry notes. Palate: powerful, fruity, fresh.

BODEGAS GRUPO YLLERA

Autovía A-6, Km. 173,5
47490 Rueda (Valladolid)
☎: +34 983 868 097
Fax: +34 983 868 177
www.grupoyllera.com
grupoyllera@grupoyllera.com

Boada Pepe Yllera 2012 T Roble
100% tempranillo

87

Colour: bright cherry. Nose: ripe fruit, sweet spices, creamy oak. Palate: flavoured, fruity, toasty.

Bracamonte 2009 TC
100% tempranillo

91

Colour: cherry, garnet rim. Nose: red berry notes, ripe fruit, spicy, creamy oak, toasty, complex, earthy notes. Palate: powerful, flavourful, toasty, round tannins.

Bracamonte 2009 TR
100% tempranillo

90

Colour: very deep cherry. Nose: ripe fruit, spicy, creamy oak, toasty, fine reductive notes. Palate: powerful, flavourful, toasty, round tannins.

Bracamonte 2012 T Roble
100% tempranillo

88

Colour: very deep cherry, garnet rim. Nose: powerfull, ripe fruit, spicy, creamy oak. Palate: powerful, toasty, correct.

Viña del Val 2013 T
100% tempranillo

89

Colour: cherry, purple rim. Nose: expressive, fresh fruit, red berry notes, floral. Palate: flavourful, fruity, good acidity.

BODEGAS HACIENDA MONASTERIO
Ctra. Pesquera - Valbuena, km. 36
47315 Pesquera de Duero (Valladolid)
☎: +34 983 484 002
Fax: +34 983 484 079
www.haciendamonasterio.com
bmonasterio@haciendamonasterio.com

Hacienda Monasterio 2009 TR
93

Colour: very deep cherry. Nose: ripe fruit, spicy, creamy oak, toasty, characterful. Palate: powerful, flavourful, toasty, round tannins.

Hacienda Monasterio 2011 T
92

Colour: very deep cherry. Nose: ripe fruit, spicy, creamy oak, toasty, characterful. Palate: powerful, flavourful, toasty, round tannins.

Hacienda Monasterio Reserva Especial 2009 TR
94

Colour: very deep cherry. Nose: balanced, complex, ripe fruit, spicy. Palate: good structure, full, good acidity, round tannins.

BODEGAS HERMANOS PÉREZ PASCUAS
Ctra. Roa, s/n
09314 Pedrosa de Duero (Burgos)
☎: +34 947 530 044
Fax: +34 947 530 002
www.perezpascuas.com
vinapedrosa@perezpascuas.com

Cepa Gavilán 2012 T
100% tinta del país

90

Colour: deep cherry, garnet rim. Nose: red berry notes, ripe fruit, spicy, creamy oak, mineral. Palate: powerful, concentrated, flavourful, balsamic.

Pérez Pascuas Gran Selección 2009 TGR
100% tinta del país

93

Colour: ruby red, garnet rim. Nose: spicy, creamy oak, ripe fruit, balsamic herbs, expressive. Palate: balanced, flavourful, spicy, mineral, long, round tannins.

Viña Pedrosa 2009 TGR
92

Colour: deep cherry, garnet rim. Nose: ripe fruit, balsamic herbs, spicy, creamy oak, fine reductive notes. Palate: balanced, flavourful, spicy, long, fine tannins.

Viña Pedrosa 2011 TR
90% tinta del país, cabernet sauvignon

93

Colour: cherry, garnet rim. Nose: red berry notes, ripe fruit, spicy, creamy oak, dry stone, complex. Palate: powerful, flavourful, toasty, round tannins, balanced, long.

Viña Pedrosa 2012 TC
100% tinta del país

91

Colour: cherry, garnet rim. Nose: ripe fruit, wild herbs, spicy, creamy oak, mineral. Palate: balanced, flavourful, long, toasty.

Viña Pedrosa La Navilla 2011 T
100% tinta del país

94

Colour: cherry, garnet rim. Nose: balsamic herbs, red berry notes, ripe fruit, creamy oak, balanced, mineral. Palate: elegant, concentrated, flavourful, spicy, long.

BODEGAS HERMANOS SASTRE

San Pedro, s/n
09311 La Horra (Burgos)
☎: +34 947 542 108
Fax: +34 947 542 108
www.vinasastre.com
sastre@vinasastre.com

Regina Vides 2011 T
tinta del país

96

Colour: cherry, garnet rim. Nose: ripe fruit, spicy, creamy oak, toasty, complex, dark chocolate, dry stone. Palate: powerful, flavourful, toasty, round tannins, good structure, complex.

Viña Sastre 2011 TC
tinta del país

93

Colour: cherry, garnet rim. Nose: complex, red berry notes, ripe fruit, wild herbs, sweet spices, creamy oak. Palate: powerful, flavourful, round, spicy, balanced.

Viña Sastre 2012 T Roble
tinta del país

91

Colour: bright cherry. Nose: ripe fruit, sweet spices, creamy oak, varietal. Palate: flavourful, fruity, toasty, round tannins.

Viña Sastre Pago de Santa Cruz 2011 T
tinta del país

95

Colour: cherry, garnet rim. Nose: spicy, mineral, red berry notes, ripe fruit, creamy oak, expressive. Palate: powerful, flavourful, spicy, long, balanced, elegant.

Viña Sastre Pesus 2011 T

97

Colour: cherry, garnet rim. Nose: red berry notes, fruit preserve, wild herbs, spicy, creamy oak, expressive. Palate: powerful, flavourful, concentrated, complex, spicy, long, balanced, elegant.

BODEGAS IMPERIALES

Ctra. Madrid - Irun, Km. 171
09370 Gumiel de Izán (Burgos)
☎: +34 947 544 070
Fax: +34 947 525 759
www.bodegasimperiales.com
adminis@bodegasimperiales.com

Abadía de San Quirce 2005 TR
100% tempranillo

90

Colour: ruby red. Nose: spicy, fine reductive notes, wet leather, aged wood nuances, toasty. Palate: spicy, long, toasty.

Abadía de San Quirce 2011 TC
100% tempranillo

93

Colour: cherry, garnet rim. Nose: ripe fruit, spicy, creamy oak, toasty, complex. Palate: powerful, flavourful, toasty, round tannins.

Abadía de San Quirce 2013 T Roble
100% tempranillo

90

Colour: bright cherry. Nose: ripe fruit, sweet spices, creamy oak, expressive. Palate: flavourful, fruity, toasty, round tannins.

Abadía de San Quirce Finca Helena Autor 2008 T
100% tempranillo

91

Colour: very deep cherry. Nose: ripe fruit, spicy, creamy oak, toasty, characterful. Palate: powerful, flavourful, toasty, round tannins.

BODEGAS ISMAEL ARROYO - VALSOTILLO

Los Lagares, 71
09441 Sotillo de la Ribera (Burgos)
☎: +34 947 532 309
Fax: +34 947 532 487
www.valsotillo.com
bodega@valsotillo.com

Mesoneros de Castilla 2011 T Roble
100% tinta del país
87
Colour: cherry, garnet rim. Nose: spicy, toasty, overripe fruit. Palate: powerful, flavourful, toasty, round tannins.

Mesoneros de Castilla 2013 T
100% tinta del país
88
Colour: cherry, purple rim. Nose: expressive, fresh fruit, red berry notes. Palate: flavourful, fruity, good acidity, round tannins.

ValSotillo 2004 TGR
100% tinta del país
92
Colour: very deep cherry. Nose: fruit liqueur notes, old leather, waxy notes, spicy. Palate: fine bitter notes, good acidity, elegant.

ValSotillo 2009 TR
100% tinta del país
90
Colour: cherry, garnet rim. Nose: ripe fruit, spicy, creamy oak, toasty, complex. Palate: powerful, flavourful, toasty, round tannins.

ValSotillo 2011 TC
tinta del país
93
Colour: cherry, garnet rim. Nose: ripe fruit, spicy, creamy oak, toasty, complex, dark chocolate, earthy notes. Palate: powerful, flavourful, toasty, round tannins.

ValSotillo VS 2004 TR
100% tinta del país
93
Colour: deep cherry, orangey edge. Nose: waxy notes, tobacco, ripe fruit, spicy, aged wood nuances. Palate: fine bitter notes, elegant, flavourful, fine tannins.

BODEGAS LA CEPA ALTA

Ctra. de Quintanilla, 28
47359 Olivares de Duero (Valladolid)
☎: +34 983 681 010
Fax: +34 983 681 010
www.lacepaalta.com
laveguilla@gmail.com

Cepa Alta 2009 TC
tempranillo
88
Colour: cherry, garnet rim. Nose: fruit preserve, fruit liqueur notes, spicy. Palate: flavourful, pruney, balsamic.

Cepa Alta 2012 T Roble
tempranillo
85

Laveguilla 2010 TC
tempranillo
92
Colour: cherry, garnet rim. Nose: ripe fruit, spicy, creamy oak, toasty, complex. Palate: powerful, flavourful, toasty, round tannins.

Laveguilla Expresión Tempranillo 2012 T
tempranillo
90
Colour: cherry, garnet rim. Nose: ripe fruit, spicy, creamy oak, toasty. Palate: powerful, flavourful, toasty, round tannins.

BODEGAS LA HORRA

Camino de Anguix, s/n
09311 La Horra (Burgos)
☎: +34 947 613 963
Fax: +34 947 613 963
www.bodegaslahorra.es
rodarioja@roda.es

Corimbo 2011 T
100% tinta del país

91

Colour: bright cherry. Nose: sweet spices, creamy oak, fruit expression. Palate: flavourful, fruity, toasty, round tannins.

Corimbo I 2010 T
100% tinta del país

94

Colour: cherry, garnet rim. Nose: ripe fruit, spicy, creamy oak, complex. Palate: powerful, flavourful, toasty, round tannins, good structure, full.

PRODUCT OF SPAIN   ESTATE BOTTLED

CORIMBO I

EMBOTELLADO EN LA PROPIEDAD

75 cl. e

R.E. 8457-BU

BODEGAS LA HORRA, S.L.
LA HORRA - BURGOS - ESPAÑA

RIBERA DEL DUERO
DENOMINACIÓN DE ORIGEN

ALC.14,5%VOL

BODEGAS LIBA Y DELEITE

Ctra. San Román de
Hornija, P:Km. 1,200
49801 Morales de Toro (Zamora)
☎: +34 615 101 249
www.acontia.es
acontia@acontia.es

Acontia 12 2010 TC
100% tempranillo

90

Colour: cherry, garnet rim. Nose: overripe fruit, dried fruit, sweet spices, toasty. Palate: ripe fruit, warm, powerful.

Acontia 6 2012 T
100% tempranillo

89

Colour: bright cherry. Nose: ripe fruit, sweet spices, creamy oak, expressive. Palate: flavourful, fruity, toasty, round tannins.

BODEGAS LÓPEZ CRISTÓBAL

Barrio Estación, s/n
09300 Roa de Duero (Burgos)
☎: +34 947 561 139
Fax: +34 947 540 606
www.lopezcristobal.com
info@lopezcristobal.com

Bagús 2011 T
100% tempranillo

92

Colour: cherry, garnet rim. Nose: ripe fruit, wild herbs, earthy notes, spicy, creamy oak. Palate: balanced, flavourful, long, balsamic, elegant.

López Cristobal 2010 TR
100% tinta del país

93

Colour: very deep cherry. Nose: ripe fruit, spicy, creamy oak, toasty, balsamic herbs, balanced, expressive. Palate: powerful, flavourful, toasty, round tannins.

López Cristobal 2011 TC

91

Colour: cherry, garnet rim. Nose: ripe fruit, spicy, creamy oak, toasty. Palate: powerful, flavourful, toasty, round tannins.

López Cristobal 2013 T Roble

92

Colour: cherry, garnet rim. Nose: ripe fruit, spicy, creamy oak, toasty, complex. Palate: powerful, flavourful, toasty, round tannins.

BODEGAS MONTEABELLÓN

Calvario, s/n
09318 Nava de Roa (Burgos)
☎: +34 947 550 000
Fax: +34 947 550 219
www.monteabellon.com
info@monteabellon.com

Monteabellón 14 meses en barrica 2011 T
100% tempranillo

89

Colour: cherry, garnet rim. Nose: ripe fruit, wild herbs, earthy notes, spicy, creamy oak. Palate: balanced, flavourful, long, balsamic.

Monteabellón 24 meses en barrica 2008 T
100% tempranillo

92

Colour: pale ruby, brick rim edge. Nose: spicy, fine reductive notes, wet leather, aged wood nuances, fruit liqueur notes. Palate: spicy, fine tannins.

Monteabellón 5 meses en barrica 2013 T
100% tempranillo
86
Colour: bright cherry. Nose: sweet spices, creamy oak, expressive, red berry notes. Palate: flavourful, fruity, toasty.

Monteabellón Finca La Blanquera 2009 T
100% tempranillo
92
Colour: deep cherry. Nose: ripe fruit, spicy, creamy oak, toasty, dried herbs. Palate: powerful, flavourful, toasty, round tannins.

BODEGAS MUNTRA
Ctra. de Castillejo, s/n
09471 Santa Cruz de la Salceda (Burgos)
☎: +34 947 107 630
www.bodegasmuntra.es
info@muntra.es

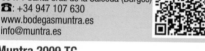

Muntra 2009 TC
100% tempranillo
88
Colour: cherry, garnet rim. Nose: red berry notes, ripe fruit, spicy, creamy oak, toasty. Palate: powerful, flavourful, toasty.

Muntra 2012 T
100% tempranillo
84

Muntra 2012 T Roble
100% tempranillo
86
Colour: bright cherry. Nose: ripe fruit, sweet spices, creamy oak. Palate: flavourful, fruity, toasty.

Muntraçç 2009 TR
100% tempranillo
89
Colour: cherry, garnet rim. Nose: balanced, complex, ripe fruit, spicy, creamy oak. Palate: good structure, flavourful, round tannins.

BODEGAS MUÑOZ Y MAZÓN
Avda. Valle Esgueva, 12
09310 Villatuelda (Burgos)
☎: +34 941 454 050
Fax: +34 941 454 529
www.bodegasriojanas.com
bodega@bodegasriojanas.com

Azuel 2011 TC
100% tempranillo
88
Colour: cherry, garnet rim. Nose: ripe fruit, spicy, creamy oak, toasty, complex. Palate: powerful, flavourful, toasty, round tannins.

Azuel Cosecha 2013 T
100% tempranillo
84

Azuel Roble 2012 T
100% tempranillo
86
Colour: bright cherry. Nose: ripe fruit, sweet spices, creamy oak, medium intensity. Palate: fruity, flavourful, toasty.

BODEGAS ORDÓÑEZ
Bartolomé Esteban Murillo, 11
29700 Vélez- Málaga (Málaga)
☎: +34 952 504 706
Fax: +34 951 284 796
www.grupojorgeordonez.com
info@jorgeordonez.es

Avante 2011 T
100% tinto fino
93
Colour: cherry, garnet rim. Nose: ripe fruit, spicy, creamy oak, toasty, complex. Palate: powerful, flavourful, toasty, round tannins, balanced.

Tineta 2012 T
100% tinto fino
89
Colour: bright cherry. Nose: ripe fruit, sweet spices, creamy oak, expressive, mineral. Palate: flavourful, fruity, toasty.

BODEGAS PAGOS DE MOGAR
Ctra. Pesquera, km. 0,2
47359 Valbuena de Duero (Valladolid)
☎: +34 983 683 011
www.bodegaspagosdemogar.com
comercial@bodegaspagosdemogar.com

Mogar 2012 T Roble
100% tinta del país
87
Colour: cherry, garnet rim. Nose: ripe fruit, spicy, creamy oak, toasty, complex. Palate: powerful, flavourful, toasty.

Mogar Vendimia Seleccionada 2010 TC

100% tinta del país

91

Colour: bright cherry, garnet rim. Nose: ripe fruit, spicy, creamy oak, complex. Palate: powerful, flavourful, round tannins, long.

BODEGAS PASCUAL

Ctra. de Aranda, Km. 5
09471 Fuentelcesped (Burgos)
☎: +34 947 557 351
Fax: +34 947 557 312
www.bodegaspascual.com
export@bodegaspascual.com

Buró de Peñalosa 2008 TR

100% tempranillo

88

Colour: very deep cherry. Nose: ripe fruit, spicy, creamy oak, toasty. Palate: powerful, flavourful, toasty, round tannins.

Buró de Peñalosa 2010 TC

100% tempranillo

89

Colour: very deep cherry. Nose: ripe fruit, creamy oak, smoky. Palate: powerful, flavourful, toasty, round tannins.

Heredad de Peñalosa 2013 RD

100% tempranillo

86

Colour: rose. Nose: balanced, red berry notes, rose petals. Palate: flavourful, powerful, correct, long.

Heredad de Peñalosa 2013 T Roble

100% tempranillo

89

Colour: cherry, purple rim. Nose: red berry notes, raspberry, floral, expressive, creamy oak. Palate: fresh, fruity, flavourful, easy to drink.

BODEGAS PEÑAFIEL

Ctra. N-122, Km. 311
47300 Peñafiel (Valladolid)
☎: +34 983 881 622
Fax: +34 983 881 944
www.bodegaspenafiel.com
bodegaspenafiel@bodegaspenafiel.com

Miros 2012 T Roble

85

Miros de Ribera 2008 TR

100% tempranillo

90

Colour: cherry, garnet rim. Nose: ripe fruit, spicy, creamy oak, toasty, fine reductive notes. Palate: powerful, flavourful, toasty, round tannins, balanced.

Miros de Ribera 2009 TC

88

Colour: ruby red, orangey edge. Nose: spicy, fine reductive notes, wet leather, aged wood nuances, toasty, slightly evolved. Palate: spicy, long, toasty.

BODEGAS PEÑALBA HERRAIZ

Sol de las Moreras, 3 2º
09400 Aranda de Duero (Burgos)
☎: +34 947 508 249
Fax: +34 947 508 249
oficina@carravid.com

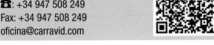

Aptus 2012 T Roble

100% tempranillo

85

Carravid 2011 T

90

Colour: cherry, garnet rim. Nose: ripe fruit, spicy, creamy oak, toasty. Palate: powerful, flavourful, toasty, round tannins.

BODEGAS PINGÓN

Ctra. N-122, Km. 311
47300 Peñafiel (Valladolid)
☎: +34 983 880 623
Fax: +34 983 880 623
www.bodegaspingon.com
carramimbre@bodegaspingon.com

Carramimbre 2010 TC

90

Colour: cherry, garnet rim. Nose: ripe fruit, spicy, toasty, wild herbs. Palate: powerful, flavourful, toasty, round tannins.

CARRAMIMBRE

CRIANZA

RIBERA DEL DUERO
DENOMINACIÓN DE ORIGEN

COSECHADO Y EMBOTELLADO POR
BODEGAS PINGÓN S.A · PEÑAFIEL
(VALLADOLID) · ESPAÑA · R.E.8040-VA

13% vol. 75 cl.

Altamimbre 2011 T
100% tempranillo

89

Colour: cherry, garnet rim. Nose: balanced, complex, ripe fruit, spicy, wild herbs, fine reductive notes. Palate: good structure, flavourful, round tannins.

Carramimbre 2010 TR

92

Colour: cherry, garnet rim. Nose: ripe fruit, wild herbs, earthy notes, spicy, creamy oak. Palate: balanced, flavourful, long, balsamic.

Torrepingón 2010 TC

90

Colour: bright cherry. Nose: ripe fruit, sweet spices, creamy oak, elegant. Palate: fruity, flavourful, toasty, round.

Torrepingón 2010 TR

91

Colour: cherry, garnet rim. Nose: red berry notes, ripe fruit, spicy, creamy oak, earthy notes. Palate: powerful, flavourful, toasty, balanced.

Torrepingón 4 meses 2013 T

88

Colour: bright cherry. Nose: sweet spices, creamy oak, red berry notes, ripe fruit. Palate: flavourful, fruity, toasty.

Torrepingón Selección 2011 T
tempranillo, cabernet sauvignon

92

Colour: cherry, garnet rim. Nose: ripe fruit, spicy, creamy oak, toasty, complex. Palate: powerful, flavourful, toasty.

BODEGAS PORTIA
Antigua Ctra. N-I, km. 170
09370 Gumiel de Izán (Burgos)
☎: +34 947 102 700
Fax: +34 947 107 004
www.bodegasportia.com
info@bodegasportia.com

Ebeia de Portia 2013 T Roble
tempranillo

88

Colour: bright cherry. Nose: ripe fruit, sweet spices, creamy oak, expressive. Palate: flavourful, fruity, toasty, round tannins.

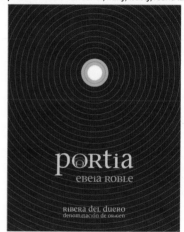

Portia 2011 TC
tempranillo

88

Colour: cherry, garnet rim. Nose: ripe fruit, spicy, toasty, complex, old leather. Palate: powerful, flavourful, toasty, round tannins.

Portia Prima 2011 T
tempranillo

90

Colour: cherry, garnet rim. Nose: ripe fruit, spicy, creamy oak, toasty. Palate: powerful, flavourful, toasty.

Portia Prima 2012 T
tempranillo

87

Colour: cherry, garnet rim. Nose: spicy, toasty, overripe fruit. Palate: powerful, flavourful, toasty, round tannins.

Triennia 2011 T
tempranillo

89

Colour: cherry, garnet rim. Nose: waxy notes, tobacco, ripe fruit, spicy, aged wood nuances. Palate: fine bitter notes, elegant, flavourful.

BODEGAS PRADO DE OLMEDO
Paraje El Salegar, s/n
09370 Quintana del Pidío (Burgos)
☎: +34 947 546 960
Fax: +34 947 546 960
www.pradodeolmedo.com
pradodeolmedo@pradodeolmedo.com

Monasterio de San Miguel 2010 TR
100% tempranillo

90

Colour: cherry, garnet rim. Nose: ripe fruit, spicy, creamy oak, toasty, complex. Palate: powerful, flavourful, toasty, round tannins.

Monasterio de San Miguel 2011 T
100% tempranillo

93

Colour: cherry, garnet rim. Nose: ripe fruit, wild herbs, earthy notes, spicy, creamy oak. Palate: flavourful, long, balsamic, balanced.

Monasterio de San Miguel Selección 2009 T
100% tempranillo

91

Colour: cherry, garnet rim. Nose: red berry notes, ripe fruit, spicy, creamy oak, toasty, complex, earthy notes. Palate: powerful, flavourful, toasty, round tannins.

BODEGAS RAIZ Y PÁRAMO DE GUZMÁN

Ctra. Circunvalación R-30, s/n
09300 Roa (Burgos)
☎: +34 947 541 191
Fax: +34 947 541 192
www.paramodeguzman.es
raizdeguzman@raizdeguzman.es

Raíz de Guzmán 2009 TR
tempranillo

91

Colour: very deep cherry, garnet rim. Nose: powerfull, ripe fruit, dark chocolate. Palate: powerful, toasty, roasted-coffee aftertaste.

Raíz de Guzmán 2011 TC
100% tempranillo

91

Colour: cherry, garnet rim. Nose: ripe fruit, fragrant herbs, spicy, powerfull, creamy oak. Palate: balanced, spicy, correct.

Raíz de Guzmán 2012 T Roble

89

Colour: bright cherry. Nose: ripe fruit, sweet spices, creamy oak. Palate: flavourful, fruity, toasty, round tannins.

Raíz de Guzmán 2013 RD
tempranillo

90

Colour: rose, purple rim. Nose: powerfull, ripe fruit, red berry notes, floral. Palate: powerful, fruity, fresh.

Raiz Profunda 2010 T
tempranillo

94

Colour: cherry, garnet rim. Nose: spicy, creamy oak, toasty, complex, dark chocolate, earthy notes, fruit expression. Palate: powerful, flavourful, toasty, round tannins.

Raiz Roble 2012 T

88

Colour: bright cherry. Nose: ripe fruit, sweet spices, creamy oak, expressive. Palate: flavourful, fruity, toasty, round tannins.

BODEGAS REQUIEM S.L.

Harineras, Nave 5
47300 Peñafiel (Valladolid)
☎: +34 629 060 309
Fax: +34 983 374 746
www.requiem.es

Requiem 2011 TC
100% tempranillo

88

Colour: deep cherry, purple rim. Nose: sweet spices, ripe fruit, cocoa bean. Palate: good structure, round tannins, powerful.

BODEGAS RESALTE DE PEÑAFIEL

Ctra. N-122, Km. 312
47300 Peñafiel (Valladolid)
☎: +34 983 878 160
Fax: +34 983 880 601
www.resalte.com
info@resalte.com

Gran Resalte 2009 T
100% tempranillo

90

Colour: cherry, garnet rim. Nose: ripe fruit, spicy, complex. Palate: powerful, flavourful, toasty, round tannins.

Lecco 2011 TC
100% tempranillo

89

Colour: bright cherry. Nose: ripe fruit, sweet spices, creamy oak. Palate: flavourful, fruity, toasty, round tannins.

Lecco Roble 2013 T
100% tempranillo

88

Colour: bright cherry. Nose: ripe fruit, sweet spices, creamy oak. Palate: flavourful, fruity, toasty.

Peña Roble 2011 TC
100% tempranillo

87

Colour: cherry, garnet rim. Nose: ripe fruit, spicy, creamy oak, toasty, complex. Palate: powerful, flavourful, toasty, round tannins.

Peña Roble 2013 T
100% tempranillo

85

Resalte 2009 TR
100% tempranillo

90

Colour: cherry, garnet rim. Nose: ripe fruit, spicy, creamy oak, toasty, complex, balsamic herbs. Palate: powerful, flavourful, toasty, round tannins, correct.

Resalte 2010 TC
100% tempranillo

90

Colour: very deep cherry. Nose: medium intensity, closed, ripe fruit. Palate: good structure, flavourful, spicy, round tannins.

Resalte Vendimia Seleccionada 2012 T
100% tempranillo

91

Colour: bright cherry. Nose: ripe fruit, sweet spices, creamy oak, expressive. Palate: flavourful, fruity, toasty, round tannins.

BODEGAS REYES

Ctra. Valladolid - Soria, Km. 54
47300 Peñafiel (Valladolid)
☎: +34 983 873 015
Fax: +34 983 873 017
www.bodegasreyes.com
info@teofiloreyes.com

Tamiz 2012 T Roble
tempranillo

88

Colour: bright cherry. Nose: creamy oak, ripe fruit. Palate: flavourful, toasty, spicy, harsh oak tannins.

Teófilo Reyes 2010 TC
tempranillo

91

Colour: cherry, garnet rim. Nose: ripe fruit, spicy, creamy oak, toasty, scrubland. Palate: powerful, flavourful, toasty, round tannins.

BODEGAS RODERO

Ctra. Boada, s/n
09314 Pedrosa de Duero (Burgos)
☎: +34 947 530 046
Fax: +34 947 530 097
www.bodegasrodero.com
rodero@bodegasrodero.com

Carmelo Rodero 2010 TR

92

Colour: very deep cherry, garnet rim. Nose: sweet spices, creamy oak, toasty, dried herbs. Palate: good structure, flavourful, good acidity.

Carmelo Rodero 2011 TC

91

Colour: deep cherry, garnet rim. Nose: closed, spicy, dried herbs, ripe fruit. Palate: flavourful, good structure, round tannins.

Carmelo Rodero 2011 TR

92

Colour: cherry, garnet rim. Nose: red berry notes, ripe fruit, spicy, creamy oak, toasty, complex, earthy notes. Palate: powerful, flavourful, toasty, round tannins.

Carmelo Rodero 2013 T
100% tempranillo

88

Colour: cherry, purple rim. Nose: red berry notes, floral. Palate: flavourful, fruity, good acidity, round tannins.

Carmelo Rodero 9 meses 2013 T
100% tempranillo

88

Colour: bright cherry. Nose: ripe fruit, sweet spices, creamy oak. Palate: flavourful, fruity, toasty, round tannins.

Carmelo Rodero TSM 2011 T

93

Colour: cherry, garnet rim. Nose: red berry notes, ripe fruit, spicy, creamy oak, toasty, complex, earthy notes. Palate: powerful, flavourful, toasty, round tannins.

Pago de Valtarreña 2011 T
100% tempranillo

93

Colour: very deep cherry. Nose: ripe fruit, spicy, creamy oak, toasty, characterful. Palate: powerful, flavourful, toasty, round tannins.

BODEGAS SANTA EULALIA

Malpica, s/n
09311 La Horra (Burgos)
☎: +34 983 586 868
Fax: +34 947 580 180
www.bodegasfrutosvillar.com
bodegasfrutosvillar@bodegasfrutosvillar.com

Conde de Siruela 2009 TR
100% tinta del país

88

Colour: cherry, garnet rim. Nose: spicy, toasty, overripe fruit, mineral. Palate: powerful, flavourful, toasty, round tannins.

Conde de Siruela 2010 TC
100% tinta del país

90

Colour: cherry, garnet rim. Nose: red berry notes, ripe fruit, spicy, creamy oak, toasty, complex, earthy notes. Palate: powerful, flavourful, toasty.

Conde de Siruela 2012 T Roble
100% tinta del país

86

Colour: very deep cherry, garnet rim. Nose: powerfull, ripe fruit, roasted coffee. Palate: powerful, toasty, roasted-coffee aftertaste.

Conde de Siruela 2013 T
100% tinta del país

87

Colour: cherry, purple rim. Nose: expressive, fresh fruit, red berry notes. Palate: flavourful, fruity, good acidity, round tannins.

La Horra 2013 T
100% tinta del país

87

Colour: very deep cherry, garnet rim. Nose: overripe fruit, warm, dried herbs. Palate: flavourful, ripe fruit, long.

Riberal 2009 TC
100% tinta del país

90

Colour: cherry, garnet rim. Nose: red berry notes, ripe fruit, spicy, violets. Palate: flavourful, toasty, round tannins.

Vicenta Mater 2010 T
100% tempranillo
88
Colour: cherry, garnet rim. Nose: ripe fruit, spicy, creamy oak, sweet spices. Palate: powerful, flavourful, toasty.

BODEGAS SEÑORÍO DE NAVA
Ctra Valladolid a Soria, 62
47500 Nava de Roa (Burgos)
☎: +34 947 550 003
Fax: +34 947 550 003
www.senoriodenava.es
snava@senoriodenava.es

Señorío de Nava 2009 TR
100% tempranillo
89
Colour: cherry, garnet rim. Nose: spicy, fine reductive notes, wet leather, aged wood nuances, toasty. Palate: spicy, long, toasty, balanced.

Señorío de Nava 2011 TC
100% tempranillo
88
Colour: dark-red cherry, garnet rim. Nose: ripe fruit, powerfull, spicy. Palate: flavourful, correct, balanced, spicy.

Señorío de Nava 2012 T Roble
86
Colour: very deep cherry, garnet rim. Nose: powerfull, ripe fruit, roasted coffee. Palate: powerful, toasty, roasted-coffee aftertaste.

Señorío de Nava 2013 RD
100% tempranillo
88
Colour: rose, purple rim. Nose: powerfull, ripe fruit, red berry notes. Palate: powerful, fruity, fresh.

Señorío de Nava 2013 T
100% tempranillo
86
Colour: cherry, garnet rim. Nose: medium intensity, ripe fruit, red berry notes. Palate: flavourful, good acidity.

Señorío de Nava Finca San Cobate 2005 TR
100% tempranillo
91
Colour: bright cherry. Nose: ripe fruit, creamy oak, medium intensity, dried herbs, spicy. Palate: fruity, flavourful, toasty.

SN Pink 2013 RD
100% tempranillo
87
Colour: raspberry rose. Nose: elegant, candied fruit, dried flowers, fragrant herbs, red berry notes. Palate: light-bodied, flavourful, good acidity, spicy.

Vega Cubillas 2011 TC
100% tempranillo
85

Vega Cubillas 2012 T Roble
100% tempranillo
86
Colour: bright cherry. Nose: ripe fruit, sweet spices, creamy oak, expressive. Palate: flavourful, fruity, toasty, round tannins.

Vega Cubillas 2013 T
100% tempranillo
85

BODEGAS SERVILIO - ARRANZ
Onésimo Redondo, 39
47315 Pesquera de Duero (Valladolid)
☎: +34 983 870 062
Fax: +34 983 870 062
www.bodegaservilio.com
bodega@bodegaservilio.com

Diego Rivera 2009 TC
100% tempranillo
88
Colour: cherry, garnet rim. Nose: fruit preserve, fruit liqueur notes, spicy. Palate: flavourful, pruney, balsamic.

Diego Rivera 2011 T Roble
100% tempranillo
85

Diego Rivera Vendimia Seleccionada 2007 TC
100% tempranillo
88
Colour: pale ruby, brick rim edge. Nose: spicy, fine reductive notes, aged wood nuances, toasty, ripe fruit. Palate: spicy, long, toasty.

Servilio 2009 TC
100% tempranillo
84

Servilio 2011 T Roble
100% tempranillo
84

Servilio Vendimia Seleccionada 2007 T
100% tempranillo
87
Colour: dark-red cherry, orangey edge. Nose: fruit preserve, candied fruit, cocoa bean. Palate: flavourful, round tannins.

BODEGAS TAMARAL

Crta. N-122 Valladolid-Soria, Km.310,6
47320 Peñafiel (Valladolid)
☎: +34 983 878 017
Fax: +34 983 878 089
www.tamaral.com
info@tamaral.com

Tamaral 2009 TR
tempranillo

93

Colour: cherry, garnet rim. Nose: ripe fruit, spicy, creamy oak, toasty, complex, earthy notes. Palate: powerful, flavourful, toasty, round tannins.

Tamaral 2011 TC
100% tempranillo

92

Colour: cherry, garnet rim. Nose: ripe fruit, wild herbs, earthy notes, spicy, creamy oak. Palate: balanced, flavourful, long, balsamic.

Tamaral 2013 RD
100% tempranillo

87

Colour: light cherry. Nose: powerfull, ripe fruit, red berry notes, floral, expressive. Palate: powerful, fruity, fresh.

Tamaral 2013 T Roble
100% tempranillo

87

Colour: bright cherry. Nose: ripe fruit, sweet spices, creamy oak, medium intensity. Palate: fruity, flavourful, toasty.

Tamaral Finca la Mira 2009 T
100% tempranillo

91

Colour: cherry, garnet rim. Nose: red berry notes, ripe fruit, wild herbs, spicy. Palate: powerful, flavourful, spicy, long, balanced.

BODEGAS TARSUS

Ctra. de Roa - Anguix, Km. 3
09312 Anguix (Burgos)
☎: +34 947 554 218
Fax: +34 947 541 804
www.bodegastarsus.com
tarsus@pernod-ricard.com

Quinta de Tarsus 2010 TC
tinta del país

91

Colour: very deep cherry, garnet rim. Nose: spicy, ripe fruit, balanced. Palate: fruity, flavourful, round tannins.

Tarsus 2009 TR
tinta del país, cabernet sauvignon

90

Colour: deep cherry. Nose: ripe fruit, wild herbs, spicy, creamy oak. Palate: balanced, flavourful, long, balsamic.

Tarsus 2012 T Roble
tinta del país

89

Colour: bright cherry. Nose: ripe fruit, sweet spices, creamy oak, expressive. Palate: flavourful, fruity, toasty, harsh oak tannins.

BODEGAS TIONIO

Carretera de Valoria, Km 7
47315 Pesquera de Duero (Valladolid)
☎: +34 983 870 185
www.tionio.es
bodega@tionio.es

Austum 2013 T
100% tinto fino

88 ♣

Colour: cherry, purple rim. Nose: expressive, fresh fruit, red berry notes. Palate: flavourful, good acidity, round tannins.

Tionio 2010 TR
tinto fino

91

Colour: deep cherry. Nose: characterful, ripe fruit, mineral, dark chocolate, new oak, toasty. Palate: ripe fruit, spicy, round tannins.

Tionio 2011 TC
100% tinto fino

93

Colour: cherry, garnet rim. Nose: ripe fruit, spicy, creamy oak, toasty, complex, mineral, varietal. Palate: powerful, flavourful, toasty, round tannins.

BODEGAS TORREDEROS
Ctra. Valladolid, Km. 289,300
09318 Fuentelisendo (Burgos)
☎: +34 947 532 627
Fax: +34 947 532 731
www.torrederos.com
administracion@torrederos.com

Torrederos 2009 TR
100% tempranillo

90

Colour: very deep cherry. Nose: ripe fruit, spicy, creamy oak, toasty, characterful. Palate: powerful, flavourful, toasty, round tannins.

Torrederos 2011 TC
100% tempranillo

89

Colour: very deep cherry, garnet rim. Nose: closed, medium intensity, ripe fruit, spicy. Palate: flavourful, good structure, round tannins.

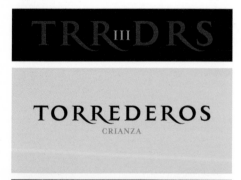

Torrederos 2012 T Roble
100% tempranillo

88

Colour: dark-red cherry, garnet rim. Nose: ripe fruit, sweet spices, expressive. Palate: flavourful, fruity, toasty, round tannins.

Torrederos 2013 RD
100% tempranillo

85

Torrederos Selección 2009 T
100% tempranillo

91

Colour: cherry, garnet rim. Nose: ripe fruit, spicy, creamy oak, toasty, complex, fine reductive notes. Palate: powerful, flavourful, toasty, round tannins.

BODEGAS TORREMORÓN
Ctra. Boada, s/n
09314 Quintanamanvirgo (Burgos)
☎: +34 947 554 075
Fax: +34 947 554 036
www.torremoron.es
torremoron@wanadoo.es

Senderillo 2011 TC
100% tempranillo

89

Colour: cherry, garnet rim. Nose: ripe fruit, spicy, creamy oak, toasty, complex. Palate: powerful, flavourful, toasty, round tannins.

Senderillo 2013 T
100% tempranillo

86

Colour: cherry, purple rim. Nose: powerfull, red berry notes, ripe fruit, floral, expressive. Palate: powerful, fresh, fruity, unctuous.

Torremorón 2010 TC
100% tempranillo

90

Colour: black cherry. Nose: ripe fruit, spicy, creamy oak, toasty. Palate: powerful, flavourful, round tannins, smoky aftertaste.

Torremorón Tempranillo 2013 T
100% tempranillo

84

BODEGAS TRUS

Ctra. Pesquera - Encinas, Km. 3
47316 Piñel de Abajo (Valladolid)
☎: +34 983 872 033
Fax: +34 983 872 041
www.bodegastrus.com
trus@bodegastrus.com

Tramuz 2013 T
tempranillo
90
Colour: bright cherry. Nose: sweet spices, creamy oak, red berry notes. Palate: flavourful, fruity, toasty, round tannins.

Trus 2006 TR
tempranillo
92
Colour: very deep cherry. Nose: ripe fruit, spicy, creamy oak, toasty, characterful. Palate: powerful, flavourful, toasty, round tannins.

Trus 2012 TC
tempranillo
93
Colour: very deep cherry. Nose: toasty, dark chocolate, ripe fruit, lactic notes. Palate: powerful, ripe fruit, long.

Trus 2013 T Roble
tempranillo
90
Colour: deep cherry. Nose: toasty, dark chocolate, red berry notes, ripe fruit. Palate: powerful, toasty, good acidity, balanced.

Trus 6 2010 T
tinto fino
94
Colour: very deep cherry. Nose: powerfull, characterful, mineral, toasty, sweet spices. Palate: powerful, good structure, concentrated, slightly dry, soft tannins.

BODEGAS VALDAYA

Ctra. de Burgos, s/n
09441 Sotillo de la Ribera (Burgos)
☎: +34 947 532 450
www.valdaya.com
info@valdaya.com

Valdaya 2013 T
tempranillo
84

Valdaya 2013 T Roble
tempranillo
86
Colour: cherry, purple rim. Nose: ripe fruit, wild herbs, spicy, creamy oak. Palate: balanced, flavourful, long, balsamic.

BODEGAS VALDEMAR

Camino Viejo de Logroño, 24
01320 Oyón (Álava)
☎: +34 945 622 188
Fax: +34 945 622 111
www.valdemar.es
info@valdemar.es

Fincas de Valdemacuco 2012 T Roble
90
Colour: cherry, garnet rim. Nose: ripe fruit, spicy, creamy oak, toasty. Palate: powerful, flavourful, toasty, round tannins.

Fincas Valdemar 2011 TC
100% tempranillo
90
Colour: cherry, garnet rim. Nose: red berry notes, ripe fruit, spicy, creamy oak. Palate: powerful, flavourful, toasty, round tannins.

BODEGAS VALDUBÓN

Antigua Ctra. N-I, Km. 151
09460 Milagros (Burgos)
☎: +34 947 546 251
Fax: +34 947 546 250
www.valdubon.es
valdubon@valdubon.es

Honoris de Valdubón 2009 T
90
Colour: very deep cherry. Nose: spicy, creamy oak, ripe fruit, fruit preserve. Palate: powerful, flavourful, toasty, round tannins.

Valdubón 2008 TR
tempranillo
88
Colour: ruby red. Nose: spicy, fine reductive notes, wet leather, aged wood nuances, toasty. Palate: spicy, long, toasty.

Valdubón 2011 TC
tempranillo
90
Colour: cherry, garnet rim. Nose: ripe fruit, spicy, creamy oak, toasty, complex. Palate: powerful, flavourful, toasty, round tannins.

Valdubón Diez s/c T
tempranillo
90
Colour: cherry, garnet rim. Nose: red berry notes, ripe fruit, spicy, creamy oak, toasty, complex, earthy notes. Palate: powerful, flavourful, toasty, round tannins.

BODEGAS VALLE DE MONZÓN

Paraje El Salegar, s/n
09370 Quintana del Pidío (Burgos)
☎: +34 947 545 694
Fax: +34 947 545 694
www.vallemonzon.com
bodega@vallemonzon.com

Hoyo de la Vega 2009 TR
tinta del país

89

Colour: cherry, garnet rim. Nose: red berry notes, ripe fruit, spicy, creamy oak, toasty, earthy notes, aged wood nuances. Palate: powerful, flavourful, toasty.

Hoyo de la Vega 2010 TC
tinta del país

88

Colour: cherry, garnet rim. Nose: ripe fruit, spicy, creamy oak, toasty. Palate: powerful, flavourful, toasty.

Hoyo de la Vega 2013 RD
albillo, tinta del país

88

Colour: rose, purple rim. Nose: powerfull, ripe fruit, red berry notes, floral, expressive. Palate: powerful, fruity, fresh.

Hoyo de la Vega 2013 T Roble
tinta del país

86

Colour: bright cherry. Nose: ripe fruit, sweet spices, creamy oak. Palate: flavourful, fruity, toasty.

BODEGAS VALPARAISO

Paraje los Llanillos, s/n
09370 Quintana del Pidío (Burgos)
☎: +34 947 545 286
Fax: +34 947 545 163
www.bodegasvalparaiso.com
info@bodegasvalparaiso.com

Finca El Encinal 2011 TC
100% tempranillo

89

Colour: bright cherry. Nose: sweet spices, creamy oak, ripe fruit. Palate: flavourful, toasty, spicy.

Finca El Encinal 2012 T Roble
100% tempranillo

83

Valparaíso 2011 TC
100% tempranillo

88

Colour: bright cherry. Nose: ripe fruit, sweet spices, medium intensity. Palate: fruity, flavourful, toasty.

Valparaíso 2012 T Roble
100% tempranillo

87

Colour: cherry, garnet rim. Nose: ripe fruit, spicy, creamy oak, toasty, complex. Palate: powerful, flavourful, toasty, round tannins.

BODEGAS VALPINCIA

Ctra. de Melida, 3,5
47300 Peñafiel (Valladolid)
☎: +34 983 878 007
Fax: +34 983 880 620
www.bodegasvalpincia.com
penafiel@bodegasvalpincia.com

Pagos de Valcerracín 2012 T Roble
tempranillo

85

Pagos de Valcerracín 2013 T
tempranillo

86

Colour: cherry, purple rim. Nose: red berry notes, floral. Palate: flavourful, fruity, good acidity, round tannins.

Pagos de Valcerracín Vendimia Seleccionada 2011 TC
tempranillo

89

Colour: cherry, garnet rim. Nose: ripe fruit, spicy, creamy oak, toasty, complex. Palate: powerful, flavourful, toasty, round tannins.

Valpincia 2008 TR
tempranillo

86

Colour: very deep cherry. Nose: ripe fruit, spicy, creamy oak, toasty. Palate: powerful, flavourful, toasty, round tannins.

Valpincia 2011 TC
tempranillo

87

Colour: cherry, garnet rim. Nose: ripe fruit, spicy, creamy oak, toasty, complex. Palate: powerful, flavourful, toasty.

Valpincia 2012 T Roble
tempranillo

87

Colour: cherry, purple rim. Nose: red berry notes, ripe fruit, spicy. Palate: flavourful, fruity, good acidity, round tannins.

Valpincia 2013 T
tempranillo

83

BODEGAS VEGA SICILIA

Ctra. N-122, Km. 323
47359 Valbuena de Duero (Valladolid)
☎: +34 983 680 147
Fax: +34 983 680 263
www.vega-sicilia.com
vegasicilia@vega-sicilia.com

Valbuena 5º 2010 T
98

Colour: cherry, garnet rim. Nose: spicy, toasty, complex, dark chocolate, earthy notes, fruit expression, cocoa bean. Palate: powerful, flavourful, toasty, soft tannins.

Vega Sicilia Reserva Especial 94/96/00 T
97

Colour: cherry, garnet rim. Nose: balanced, complex, ripe fruit, spicy, wet leather, fine reductive notes, cigar. Palate: good structure, flavourful, round tannins.

Vega Sicilia Único 2007 T
94

Colour: bright cherry. Nose: ripe fruit, sweet spices, creamy oak, medium intensity, balsamic herbs, scrubland. Palate: flavourful, toasty, light-bodied, spicy.

BODEGAS VEGARANDA

Avda. Arangón, s/n
09400 Aranda de Duero (Burgos)
☎: +34 626 996 974
www.bodegasvegaranda.com
comercial@bodegasvegaranda.com

Vegaranda 2008 TR
tempranillo
89

Colour: pale ruby, brick rim edge. Nose: spicy, fine reductive notes, wet leather, aged wood nuances, fruit liqueur notes. Palate: spicy, fine tannins, elegant, long.

Vegaranda 2011 TC
tempranillo
84

Vegaranda 2012 T Roble
tempranillo
84

Vegaranda 2013 RD
tempranillo
84

Vegaranda 2013 T
tempranillo
85

BODEGAS VICENTE GANDÍA

Ctra. Cheste a Godelleta, s/n
46370 Chiva (Valencia)
☎: +34 962 524 242
Fax: +34 962 524 243
www.vicentegandia.es
info@vicentegandia.com

Dolmo Tempranillo 2013 TC
100% tempranillo
86

Colour: very deep cherry, garnet rim. Nose: powerfull, ripe fruit, roasted coffee, aromatic coffee. Palate: powerful, toasty, roasted-coffee aftertaste.

BODEGAS VITULIA

Sendín, 49
09400 Aranda de Duero (Burgos)
☎: +34 947 515 051
Fax: +34 947 515 051
www.bodegasvitulia.com
vitulia@bodegasvitulia.com

Hacienda Vitulia Vendimia Seleccionadas 2009 T
92

Colour: cherry, garnet rim. Nose: red berry notes, ripe fruit, spicy, creamy oak, toasty, complex, earthy notes. Palate: powerful, flavourful, toasty, round tannins.

Vitulia 2011 TC
tinto fino
92

Colour: cherry, garnet rim. Nose: ripe fruit, spicy, creamy oak, toasty, complex. Palate: powerful, flavourful, toasty, round tannins.

Vitulia 2012 T Barrica
tinto fino
88 🌷

Colour: bright cherry. Nose: ripe fruit, sweet spices, creamy oak, medium intensity. Palate: fruity, flavourful, toasty.

BODEGAS VIYUELA

Ctra. de Quintanamanvirgo, s/n
09314 Boada de Roa (Burgos)
☎: +34 947 530 072
Fax: +34 947 530 075
www.bodegasviyuela.com
viyuela@bodegasviyuela.com

Viyuela 2011 TC
100% tempranillo
88

Colour: cherry, garnet rim. Nose: ripe fruit, spicy, creamy oak, toasty, complex. Palate: powerful, flavourful, toasty, round tannins.

Viyuela 2013 T Fermentado en Barrica
100% tempranillo

87

Colour: very deep cherry, garnet rim. Nose: overripe fruit, warm, dried herbs, dark chocolate. Palate: flavourful, ripe fruit, long.

BODEGAS VIZCARRA
Finca Chirri, s/n
09317 Mambrilla de Castrejón (Burgos)
☎: +34 947 540 340
Fax: +34 947 540 340
www.vizcarra.es
bodegas@vizcarra.es

Celia Vizcarra 2011 T
94

Colour: cherry, garnet rim. Nose: balanced, complex, ripe fruit, spicy, balsamic herbs. Palate: good structure, flavourful, round tannins, elegant.

Inés Vizcarra 2011 T
93

Colour: cherry, garnet rim. Nose: ripe fruit, wild herbs, mineral, roasted coffee. Palate: balanced, long, balsamic.

Vizcarra 15 meses 2012 T
100% tinto fino

91

Colour: cherry, garnet rim. Nose: ripe fruit, spicy, creamy oak, toasty, complex, earthy notes. Palate: powerful, flavourful, toasty, round tannins, fruity aftestaste.

Vizcarra Senda del Oro 2013 T
100% tinto fino

89

Colour: cherry, purple rim. Nose: expressive, fresh fruit, red berry notes, floral. Palate: flavourful, fruity, good acidity, round tannins.

Vizcarra Torralvo 2011 T
100% tinto fino

93

Colour: cherry, garnet rim. Nose: spicy, creamy oak, mineral, red berry notes, ripe fruit, complex. Palate: powerful, flavourful, toasty, round tannins, balanced.

FINCAS EN MAMBRILLA
DE CASTREJÓN
·BURGOS·

Torralvo

VIZCARRA
TORRALVO

RIBERA DEL DUERO
DENOMINACIÓN
DE ORIGEN

BODEGAS Y VIÑEDOS ACEÑA
Pol. Ind. Las Carretas, calle C, 1
42330 San Esteban de Gormaz (Soria)
☎: +34 667 784 220
www.terraesteban.com
bodega@terraesteban.com

Terraesteban 2011 TC
100% tempranillo

88

Colour: cherry, garnet rim. Nose: ripe fruit, spicy, creamy oak, toasty, complex. Palate: powerful, flavourful, toasty, round tannins.

Terraesteban Author 2011 T Barrica
100% tempranillo

88

Colour: bright cherry. Nose: ripe fruit, sweet spices, creamy oak, medium intensity. Palate: fruity, flavourful, toasty.

BODEGAS Y VIÑEDOS ALIÓN
Ctra. N-122, Km. 312,4 Padilla de Duero
47300 Peñafiel (Valladolid)
☎: +34 983 881 236
Fax: +34 983 881 246
www.bodegasalion.com
alion@bodegasalion.com

Alión 2011 T
100% tinto fino

95

Colour: very deep cherry. Nose: ripe fruit, spicy, creamy oak, toasty, characterful. Palate: powerful, flavourful, toasty, round tannins.

BODEGAS Y VIÑEDOS GALLEGO ZAPATERO
Segunda Travesía de la Olma, 4
09313 Anguix (Burgos)
☎: +34 648 180 777
www.bodegasgallegozapatero.com
info@bodegasgallegozapatero.com

Yotuel 2012 T Roble
100% tinta del país

87

Colour: bright cherry. Nose: ripe fruit, sweet spices, creamy oak. Palate: flavourful, fruity, toasty, harsh oak tannins.

Yotuel Finca La Nava 2011 T
100% tinta del país

91

Colour: cherry, garnet rim. Nose: ripe fruit, spicy, creamy oak, toasty, complex. Palate: powerful, flavourful, toasty, round tannins.

Yotuel Selección 2011 T
100% tinta del país

89

Colour: cherry, garnet rim. Nose: red berry notes, ripe fruit, spicy, creamy oak, toasty, complex, earthy notes. Palate: powerful, flavourful, toasty.

BODEGAS Y VIÑEDOS JUAN MANUEL BURGOS

Aranda, 39
09471 Fuentelcesped (Burgos)
☎: +34 635 525 272
Fax: +34 947 557 443
www.byvjuanmanuelburgos.com
juanmanuelburgos@byvjuanmanuelburgos.com

Avan 2011 TC
tempranillo

87

Colour: cherry, garnet rim. Nose: spicy, creamy oak, toasty, fruit preserve. Palate: powerful, flavourful, toasty.

Avan Cepas Centenarias 2011 TR
tempranillo

94

Colour: cherry, garnet rim. Nose: ripe fruit, spicy, creamy oak, toasty, complex, dark chocolate, earthy notes. Palate: powerful, flavourful, toasty, round tannins.

Avan Concentración 2011 T Barrica
tempranillo

91

Colour: cherry, garnet rim. Nose: spicy, toasty, overripe fruit, mineral. Palate: powerful, flavourful, toasty, round tannins.

Avan Nacimiento 2011 T
tempranillo

91

Colour: bright cherry. Nose: sweet spices, creamy oak, ripe fruit. Palate: flavourful, fruity, toasty, round tannins.

Avan Terruño de Valdehernando 2011 T
tempranillo

92

Colour: very deep cherry, garnet rim. Nose: powerfull, ripe fruit, roasted coffee, dark chocolate. Palate: powerful, toasty, roasted-coffee aftertaste.

Avan Viñedo del Torrubio 2011 T
tempranillo

91

Colour: cherry, garnet rim. Nose: fruit preserve, fruit liqueur notes, spicy. Palate: flavourful, pruney, balsamic.

BODEGAS Y VIÑEDOS LLEIROSO

Ctra. Monasterio, s/n
47359 Valbuena del Duero (Valladolid)
☎: +34 983 683 300
www.bodegaslleiroso.com
bodega@bodegaslleiroso.com

Lleiroso 2009 T
tempranillo

88

Colour: cherry, garnet rim. Nose: balanced, ripe fruit, smoky, toasty. Palate: flavourful, round tannins.

Lleiroso 2009 TC
tempranillo

90

Colour: very deep cherry. Nose: ripe fruit, spicy, creamy oak, toasty, characterful. Palate: powerful, flavourful, toasty, round tannins.

Lvzmillar 2009 TC
tempranillo

90

Colour: cherry, garnet rim. Nose: fruit preserve, fruit liqueur notes, spicy. Palate: flavourful, pruney, balsamic.

Lvzmillar 2013 T
tempranillo

86

Colour: very deep cherry, purple rim. Nose: red berry notes, toasty, powerfull. Palate: correct, good finish, ripe fruit.

BODEGAS Y VIÑEDOS MARTÍN BERDUGO

Ctra. de la Colonia, s/n
09400 Aranda de Duero (Burgos)
☎: +34 947 506 331
Fax: +34 947 506 602
www.martinberdugo.com
bodega@martinberdugo.com

Martín Berdugo 2009 TR
tempranillo
90
Colour: cherry, garnet rim. Nose: red berry notes, ripe fruit, spicy, creamy oak, toasty. Palate: powerful, flavourful, toasty, round tannins.

Martín Berdugo 2010 TC
tempranillo
90
Colour: cherry, garnet rim. Nose: red berry notes, ripe fruit, spicy, creamy oak, toasty, complex. Palate: powerful, flavourful, toasty, harsh oak tannins.

Martín Berdugo 2012 T Barrica
tempranillo
88
Colour: bright cherry. Nose: sweet spices, creamy oak, medium intensity. Palate: fruity, flavourful, toasty.

Martín Berdugo 2013 RD
tempranillo
86
Colour: light cherry. Nose: red berry notes, candied fruit, fragrant herbs. Palate: fresh, fruity, flavourful.

Martín Berdugo 2013 T
tempranillo
88
Colour: cherry, purple rim. Nose: expressive, fresh fruit, red berry notes, floral. Palate: flavourful, fruity, good acidity, round tannins.

MB Martín Berdugo 2008 T
tempranillo
90
Colour: cherry, garnet rim. Nose: red berry notes, ripe fruit, spicy, creamy oak, toasty, complex, earthy notes. Palate: powerful, flavourful, toasty, round tannins.

BODEGAS Y VIÑEDOS MONTECASTRO

Ctra. VA-130, s/n
47318 Castrillo de Duero (Valladolid)
☎: +34 983 484 013
Fax: +34 983 443 939
www.bodegasmontecastro.com
info@bodegasmontecastro.es

Alconte 2010 TC
tempranillo
89
Colour: cherry, garnet rim. Nose: red berry notes, ripe fruit, spicy, complex. Palate: powerful, flavourful, toasty, round tannins.

Montecastro La Roca 2010 T
tempranillo, cabernet sauvignon, garnacha
90
Colour: cherry, garnet rim. Nose: red berry notes, ripe fruit, spicy, creamy oak, toasty, complex, earthy notes. Palate: powerful, flavourful, toasty, round tannins.

Montecastro y Llanahermosa 2009 T
tempranillo, merlot, cabernet sauvignon, garnacha
90
Colour: very deep cherry. Nose: ripe fruit, spicy, creamy oak, toasty, characterful, balsamic herbs. Palate: powerful, flavourful, toasty, round tannins.

BODEGAS Y VIÑEDOS NEO

Ctra. N-122, Km. 274,5
09391 Castrillo de la Vega (Burgos)
☎: +34 947 514 393
Fax: +34 947 515 445
www.bodegasneo.com
ivan@bodegasconde.com

Disco 2013 T
100% tempranillo
88
Colour: bright cherry. Nose: ripe fruit, sweet spices, creamy oak, expressive. Palate: flavourful, fruity, toasty, round tannins.

El Arte de Vivir 2013 T
tempranillo
88
Colour: very deep cherry, garnet rim. Nose: overripe fruit, warm, dried herbs. Palate: flavourful, ripe fruit, long

Neo 2011 T
tempranillo
91
Colour: very deep cherry. Nose: ripe fruit, spicy, creamy oak, toasty, complex. Palate: powerful, flavourful, toasty, round tannins.

Neo Punta Esencia 2011 T
100% tempranillo
93
Colour: bright cherry, garnet rim. Nose: complex, powerfull, spicy, creamy oak. Palate: powerful, balanced, long, round tannins, full.

Sentido 2012 T
100% tempranillo
89
Colour: dark-red cherry, garnet rim. Nose: cocoa bean, creamy oak, toasty, ripe fruit. Palate: powerful, good structure, round tannins.

BODEGAS Y VIÑEDOS ORTEGA FOURNIER
Finca El Pinar, s/n
09316 Berlangas de Roa (Burgos)
☎: +34 947 533 006
Fax: +34 947 533 010
www.ofournier.com
ofournier-ribera@ofournier.com

Alfa Spiga 2007 T
100% tinta del país
92
Colour: cherry, garnet rim. Nose: ripe fruit, wild herbs, earthy notes, spicy, creamy oak. Palate: balanced, flavourful, long, balsamic.

O. Fournier 2007 T
100% tinta del país
92
Colour: very deep cherry. Nose: ripe fruit, spicy, creamy oak, toasty, characterful. Palate: powerful, flavourful, toasty, round tannins.

Spiga 2008 T
100% tinta del país
91
Colour: very deep cherry. Nose: ripe fruit, spicy, creamy oak, toasty, characterful. Palate: powerful, flavourful, toasty, round tannins.

Urban Ribera 2011 T Roble
tinta del país
87
Colour: cherry, garnet rim. Nose: ripe fruit, wild herbs, earthy notes, spicy, creamy oak. Palate: balanced, flavourful, long, balsamic.

BODEGAS Y VIÑEDOS QUMRÁN
Pago de las Bodegas, s/n
47314 Padilla de Duero (Valladolid)
☎: +34 983 882 103
Fax: +34 983 881 514
www.bodegasqumran.es
info@bodegasqumran.es

Proventus 2009 TC
tempranillo
90
Colour: cherry, garnet rim. Nose: ripe fruit, spicy, creamy oak, toasty. Palate: powerful, flavourful, toasty, round tannins.

Proventus 2009 TR
100% tempranillo
92
Colour: bright cherry. Nose: ripe fruit, spicy, creamy oak, toasty, complex. Palate: powerful, flavourful, round tannins, long.

BODEGAS Y VIÑEDOS RAUDA
Ctra. de Pedrosa, s/n
09300 Roa de Duero (Burgos)
☎: +34 947 540 224
Fax: +34 947 541 811
www.vinosderauda.com
informacion@vinosderauda.com

Tinto Roa 2008 TR
100% tinta del país
88
Colour: pale ruby, brick rim edge. Nose: spicy, fine reductive notes, wet leather, aged wood nuances, fruit liqueur notes. Palate: spicy, fine tannins.

Tinto Roa 2010 TC
100% tinta del país

90

Colour: dark-red cherry, garnet rim. Nose: ripe fruit, dark chocolate, spicy. Palate: good structure, long, round tannins.

Tinto Roa 2013 T
100% tinta del país

86

Colour: deep cherry, purple rim. Nose: medium intensity, red berry notes, dried herbs. Palate: correct, good acidity.

BODEGAS Y VIÑEDOS ROBEAL
Ctra. Anguix, s/n
09300 Roa (Burgos)
☎: +34 947 484 706
Fax: +34 947 482 817
www.bodegasrobeal.com
info@bodegasrobeal.com

Buen Miñón 2013 T
tempranillo

87

Colour: cherry, purple rim. Nose: red berry notes, floral. Palate: flavourful, fruity, good acidity, round tannins.

La Capilla 2009 TR
tempranillo

90

Colour: bright cherry. Nose: ripe fruit, sweet spices, creamy oak, medium intensity. Palate: fruity, flavourful, toasty.

La Capilla 2011 TC
tempranillo

87

Colour: cherry, garnet rim. Nose: ripe fruit, spicy, creamy oak, toasty. Palate: powerful, flavourful, toasty, round tannins.

La Capilla Vendimia Seleccionada 2011 T
tempranillo

92

Colour: very deep cherry, garnet rim. Nose: powerfull, ripe fruit, roasted coffee, dark chocolate. Palate: powerful, toasty, roasted-coffee aftertaste.

Valnogal 16 meses 2010 T Barrica
tempranillo

90

Colour: cherry, garnet rim. Nose: ripe fruit, wild herbs, earthy notes, spicy, creamy oak. Palate: balanced, flavourful, long, balsamic.

Valnogal 6 meses 2012 T Roble
tempranillo

88

Colour: cherry, garnet rim. Nose: ripe fruit, spicy, creamy oak, toasty, complex. Palate: powerful, flavourful, toasty, round tannins.

BODEGAS Y VIÑEDOS TÁBULA
Ctra. de Valbuena, km. 2
47359 Olivares de Duero (Valladolid)
☎: +34 608 219 019
Fax: +34 983 107 300
www.bodegastabula.es
armando@bodegastabula.es

Clave de Tábula 2011 T
100% tempranillo

94

Colour: cherry, garnet rim. Nose: ripe fruit, spicy, creamy oak, toasty, complex, dark chocolate, earthy notes. Palate: powerful, flavourful, toasty, round tannins.

Damana 2011 TC
100% tempranillo

90

Colour: very deep cherry, garnet rim. Nose: overripe fruit, warm, dried herbs, dark chocolate. Palate: flavourful, ripe fruit, long.

Damana 5 2012 T
100% tempranillo

88

Colour: bright cherry. Nose: ripe fruit, sweet spices, creamy oak. Palate: flavourful, fruity, toasty.

Gran Tábula 2011 T
100% tempranillo

93

Colour: very deep cherry. Nose: ripe fruit, spicy, creamy oak, toasty, characterful. Palate: powerful, flavourful, toasty, round tannins.

Tábula 2011 T
100% tempranillo

92

Colour: cherry, garnet rim. Nose: red berry notes, ripe fruit, spicy, creamy oak, toasty. Palate: balanced, round, spicy, long.

BODEGAS Y VIÑEDOS VALDERIZ
Ctra. Pedrosa, km 1
09300 Roa (Burgos)
☎: +34 947 540 460
Fax: +34 947 541 032
www.valderiz.com
bodega@valderiz.com

Valdehermoso 2012 TC
100% tinta del país

91

Colour: bright cherry. Nose: ripe fruit, sweet spices, creamy oak, balanced. Palate: fruity, flavourful, toasty, long.

Valdehermoso 2013 T
100% tinta del país

87

Colour: cherry, purple rim. Nose: red berry notes, medium intensity. Palate: easy to drink, good finish, fruity.

Valdehermoso 2013 T Roble
100% tinta del país

89

Colour: deep cherry, purple rim. Nose: balanced, red berry notes, sweet spices. Palate: ripe fruit, round tannins.

Valderiz 2010 T
100% tinta del país

91

Colour: cherry, garnet rim. Nose: ripe fruit, spicy, creamy oak, toasty, complex, earthy notes. Palate: powerful, flavourful, toasty, round tannins.

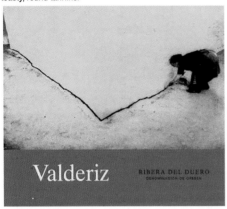

Valderiz Juegalobos 2011 T
100% tinta del país

93

Colour: very deep cherry. Nose: complex, balanced, expressive, ripe fruit, creamy oak, sweet spices. Palate: good structure, round tannins, long.

Valderiz Tomás Esteban 2006 T

94

Colour: dark-red cherry, garnet rim. Nose: elegant, spicy, waxy notes, expressive, ripe fruit. Palate: balanced, long, full, flavourful, complex, varietal.

BODEGAS Y VIÑEDOS VALDUERO
Ctra. de Aranda, s/n
09443 Burgos (Burgos)
☎: +34 947 545 459
Fax: +34 947 545 609
www.bodegasvalduero.com
valduerocom@bodegasvalduero.com

Valduero 2010 TC
100% tempranillo

92

Colour: bright cherry. Nose: ripe fruit, sweet spices, creamy oak, balsamic herbs. Palate: fruity, flavourful, toasty.

BODEGAS Y VIÑEDOS VEGA DE YUSO
Basilón, 9
47350 Quintanilla de Onésimo (Valladolid)
☎: +34 983 680 054
Fax: +34 983 680 294
www.vegadeyuso.com
bodega@vegadeyuso.com

Pozo de Nieve 2012 T Barrica
100% tempranillo

87

Colour: very deep cherry, garnet rim. Nose: balanced, ripe fruit, cocoa bean, sweet spices. Palate: fruity, round tannins.

Tres Matas 2010 TR
100% tempranillo

89

Colour: cherry, garnet rim. Nose: spicy, toasty, overripe fruit, mineral. Palate: powerful, flavourful, toasty, round tannins.

Tres Matas 2011 TC
100% tempranillo

91

Colour: very deep cherry, garnet rim. Nose: powerfull, ripe fruit, toasty. Palate: full, flavourful, round tannins, long.

Tres Matas Vendimia Seleccionada 2009 T
100% tempranillo

91

Colour: cherry, garnet rim. Nose: ripe fruit, spicy, creamy oak, toasty, complex. Palate: powerful, flavourful, toasty, round tannins.

Vegantigua 10 meses 2012 T Barrica
100% tempranillo

87

Colour: cherry, garnet rim. Nose: ripe fruit, spicy, creamy oak, toasty. Palate: powerful, flavourful, toasty.

BODEGAS Y VIÑEDOS VIÑA MAYOR
Ctra. Valladolid - Soria, Km. 325,6
47350 Quintanilla de Onésimo (Valladolid)
☎: +34 983 680 461
Fax: +34 983 027 217
www.vina-mayor.com
rrpp@vina-mayor.com

Dehesas del Rey 2010 TC
tinto fino

89

Colour: cherry, garnet rim. Nose: ripe fruit, spicy, creamy oak, toasty. Palate: powerful, flavourful, toasty, spicy.

Dehesas del Rey 2012 T Joven
tinto fino

87

Colour: cherry, purple rim. Nose: expressive, fresh fruit, red berry notes, floral. Palate: flavourful, fruity, good acidity, easy to drink.

Dehesas del Rey 2013 T

84

Secreto Vendimia Seleccionada 2011 T Roble

92

Colour: cherry, garnet rim. Nose: ripe fruit, spicy, creamy oak, toasty, complex, expressive. Palate: powerful, flavourful, toasty, round tannins.

Viña Mayor 2007 TGR
100% tinta del país

88

Colour: very deep cherry. Nose: ripe fruit, spicy, toasty, characterful. Palate: powerful, flavourful, toasty, round tannins.

Viña Mayor 2010 TR
tinta del país

93

Colour: very deep cherry. Nose: ripe fruit, spicy, creamy oak, complex. Palate: round tannins, balanced.

Viña Mayor 2011 TC
100% tinta del país

89

Colour: dark-red cherry, garnet rim. Nose: ripe fruit, wild herbs, earthy notes, spicy, creamy oak. Palate: balanced, flavourful, long, balsamic.

Viña Mayor 2013 T Roble
100% tinta del país

89

Colour: bright cherry. Nose: ripe fruit, sweet spices, expressive, scrubland. Palate: flavourful, fruity, toasty, round tannins.

Viña Mayor Finca Secreto 2009 TR
100% tinta del país

91

Colour: cherry, garnet rim. Nose: ripe fruit, spicy, creamy oak, toasty. Palate: powerful, flavourful, toasty, round tannins.

BODEGAS ZIFAR
Afueras de D. Juan Manuel, 9-11
47300 Peñafiel (Valladolid)
☎: +34 983 873 147
Fax: +34 983 880 287
www.zifar.com
bodegaszifar@zifar.com

Zifar Selección 2009 T
tempranillo

91

Colour: very deep cherry. Nose: spicy, fine reductive notes, aged wood nuances, toasty, ripe fruit. Palate: spicy, long, toasty.

BODEGUEROS QUINTA ESENCIA
Eras, 37
47520 Castronuño (Valladolid)
☎: +34 605 887 100
Fax: +34 983 866 391
www.bodeguerosquintaesencia.com
ferrin@bodeguerosquintaesencia.com

Al-Nabiz 2012 T
tempranillo

88

Colour: bright cherry. Nose: ripe fruit, sweet spices, creamy oak. Palate: flavourful, fruity, toasty, round tannins.

BOSQUE DE MATASNOS
Sendin, s/n Parc. 5
09400 Aranda de Duero (Burgos)
☎: +34 915 630 590
Fax: +34 915 630 704
www.bosquedematasnos.es
jaimep@bosquedematasnos.es

Bosque de Matasnos 2011 T

94

Colour: cherry, garnet rim. Nose: ripe fruit, spicy, creamy oak, toasty, dark chocolate, earthy notes. Palate: powerful, flavourful, toasty, harsh oak tannins.

Bosque de Matasnos Edición Limitada 2010 T

95

Colour: cherry, garnet rim. Nose: ripe fruit, spicy, toasty, complex, dark chocolate, earthy notes, roasted coffee. Palate: powerful, flavourful, toasty, round tannins.

CAMPOS GÓTICOS

Parcela 622
09313 Anguix (Burgos)
☎: +34 979 165 121
www.camposgoticos.es
clientedirecto@camposgoticos.es

7 Lunas Vendimia Seleccionada 2005 TC
100% tempranillo

91

Colour: dark-red cherry, garnet rim. Nose: balanced, ripe fruit, spicy, balsamic herbs, waxy notes. Palate: flavourful, long, round tannins.

7 Lunas Viñedos de la Joya 2004 T
100% tempranillo

91

Colour: pale ruby, brick rim edge. Nose: balanced, complex, ripe fruit, spicy. Palate: good structure, flavourful, round tannins.

Campos Góticos 2004 TR
100% tempranillo

90

Colour: pale ruby, brick rim edge. Nose: red berry notes, ripe fruit, spicy, creamy oak, toasty, complex, earthy notes. Palate: powerful, flavourful, toasty, round tannins.

Campos Góticos 2005 TC
100% tempranillo

90

Colour: ruby red. Nose: spicy, fine reductive notes, wet leather, aged wood nuances, toasty. Palate: spicy, long, toasty.

Campos Góticos 2009 TC
100% tempranillo

88

Colour: dark-red cherry, garnet rim. Nose: balanced, spicy, toasty. Palate: balanced, correct, round tannins.

Campos Góticos 2010 T Roble
100% tempranillo

89

Colour: bright cherry. Nose: ripe fruit, sweet spices, creamy oak, medium intensity. Palate: fruity, flavourful, toasty.

CARRASVILLA

Ctra. Pesquera VA-101, P.K. 3,700
47300 Peñafiel (Valladolid)
☎: +34 983 218 925
Fax: +34 983 218 926
www.carrasvilla.es
comercial@carrasvilla.es

Terralux 2011 T
100% tempranillo

89

Colour: cherry, garnet rim. Nose: ripe fruit, spicy, toasty. Palate: powerful, flavourful, toasty, round tannins.

CEPAS DE CASTILLA S.L.U.

Ctra. Aranda - Salas, km. 14
09490 San Juan del Monte (Burgos)
☎: +34 947 552 233
Fax: +34 947 552 233
castillalta@gmail.com

Castillalta 2007 TR
100% tempranillo

83

Castillalta 2010 TC
100% tempranillo

88

Colour: bright cherry. Nose: ripe fruit, sweet spices, creamy oak, medium intensity. Palate: fruity, flavourful, toasty.

Castillalta 2013 T
100% tempranillo

85

Enrique I 2010 TC
tinta del país

83

Enrique I 2013 T Joven

86

Colour: cherry, purple rim. Nose: fresh fruit, red berry notes, floral, wild herbs. Palate: flavourful, fruity, good acidity.

CILLAR DE SILOS

Paraje El Soto, s/n
09370 Quintana del Pidio (Burgos)
☎: +34 947 545 126
Fax: +34 947 545 605
www.cillardesilos.es
bodega@cillardesilos.es

Cillar de Silos 2010 TC
100% tempranillo

92

Colour: cherry, garnet rim. Nose: ripe fruit, spicy, creamy oak, toasty, complex, mineral. Palate: powerful, flavourful, toasty, spicy.

Cillar de Silos 2011 TC
100% tempranillo

92

Colour: cherry, garnet rim. Nose: red berry notes, ripe fruit, spicy, toasty, earthy notes, balsamic herbs. Palate: powerful, flavourful, toasty, round tannins, balanced.

El Quintanal 2013 T
100% tempranillo

88

Colour: cherry, purple rim. Nose: red berry notes, raspberry, fruit expression, fragrant herbs, violets. Palate: flavourful, light-bodied, good acidity, fresh, fruity.

Joven de Silos 2013 T
100% tempranillo
88
Colour: cherry, purple rim. Nose: fresh fruit, red berry notes, floral. Palate: flavourful, fruity, good acidity, round tannins.

La Viña de Amalio 2010 T
100% tempranillo
93
Colour: cherry, garnet rim. Nose: red berry notes, ripe fruit, spicy, creamy oak, toasty, complex, earthy notes. Palate: powerful, flavourful, toasty, round tannins, balanced.

Rosado de Silos 2013 RD
100% tempranillo
87
Colour: rose, purple rim. Nose: wild herbs, red berry notes, floral, expressive. Palate: flavourful, fruity, balsamic.

Torresilo 2010 TR
100% tempranillo
93
Colour: cherry, garnet rim. Nose: red berry notes, ripe fruit, spicy, creamy oak, toasty, complex, mineral. Palate: powerful, flavourful, toasty, round tannins, round.

CINEMA WINES
Felipe Gómez, 1
47140 Laguna de Duero (Valladolid)
☎: +34 983 544 696
Fax: +34 983 545 539
www.cinemawines.es
info@cinemawines.es

Cinema 2011 TC
100% tempranillo
88
Colour: very deep cherry, garnet rim. Nose: powerfull, ripe fruit, roasted coffee, dark chocolate. Palate: powerful, toasty, roasted-coffee aftertaste.

Cinema 2012 T Barrica
100% tempranillo
86
Colour: bright cherry. Nose: ripe fruit, sweet spices, creamy oak. Palate: flavourful, toasty, round tannins.

COMENGE BODEGAS Y VIÑEDOS
Camino del Castillo, s/n
47316 Curiel de Duero (Valladolid)
☎: +34 983 880 363
Fax: +34 983 880 717
www.comenge.com
admin@comenge.com

Biberius 2012 T
tempranillo
88
Colour: very deep cherry, garnet rim. Nose: ripe fruit, balanced, sweet spices. Palate: flavourful, good structure, long.

Biberius 2013 T
tempranillo
87
Colour: cherry, purple rim. Nose: red berry notes, floral, wild herbs, spicy. Palate: powerful, flavourful, fruity.

Comenge 2009 T
tempranillo
92
Colour: cherry, garnet rim. Nose: scrubland, ripe fruit, spicy. Palate: good structure, flavourful, round tannins.

Comenge 2010 T
tempranillo
90
Colour: cherry, garnet rim. Nose: ripe fruit, spicy, creamy oak, toasty, complex, fine reductive notes. Palate: powerful, flavourful, toasty, round tannins.

Don Miguel Comenge 2010 T
95
Colour: cherry, garnet rim. Nose: ripe fruit, spicy, creamy oak, toasty, complex, dark chocolate. Palate: powerful, flavourful, toasty, round tannins.

COMPAÑÍA DE VINOS TELMO RODRÍGUEZ
El Monte
01308 Lanciego (Álava)
☎: +34 945 628 315
Fax: +34 945 628 314
www.telmorodriguez.com
contact@telmorodriguez.com

M2 de Matallana 2010 T
tinto fino
92
Colour: bright cherry. Nose: ripe fruit, sweet spices, creamy oak. Palate: flavourful, fruity, toasty, round tannins.

Matallana 2010 T
tinto fino
95
Colour: cherry, garnet rim. Nose: spicy, creamy oak, toasty, complex, dark chocolate, earthy notes. Palate: powerful, flavourful, toasty, round tannins.

CONVENTO DE LAS CLARAS S.L.
Plaza de los Comuneros, 1
47300 Peñafiel (Valladolid)
☎: +34 983 878 168
www.bodegasconventodelasclaras.com
info@bodegasconventodelasclaras.com

Convento Las Claras 2012 T
100% tinto fino
92
Colour: bright cherry. Nose: ripe fruit, sweet spices, creamy oak, expressive. Palate: flavourful, fruity, toasty, round tannins.

Heritage Convento de las Claras 2011 T
100% tinto fino

91

Colour: cherry, garnet rim. Nose: ripe fruit, spicy, creamy oak, toasty, complex, earthy notes. Palate: powerful, flavourful, toasty, round tannins, balanced.

Las Tinajas 2013 RD
100% tinto fino

86

Colour: light cherry. Nose: powerfull, ripe fruit, red berry notes, floral. Palate: powerful, fruity, fresh, easy to drink.

CONVENTO DE OREJA

Avda. Palencia, 1
47010 (Valladolid)
☎: +34 685 990 596
www.conventooreja.net
convento@conventooreja.es

Convento Oreja 2009 TC
100% tinta del país

89

Colour: cherry, garnet rim. Nose: ripe fruit, spicy, creamy oak. Palate: powerful, flavourful, toasty, round tannins.

Convento Oreja 2010 TC
100% tinta del país

89

Colour: cherry, garnet rim. Nose: ripe fruit, spicy, creamy oak, toasty, complex. Palate: powerful, flavourful, toasty.

Convento Oreja 2012 T Roble
100% tinta del país

87

Colour: cherry, garnet rim. Nose: spicy, toasty, overripe fruit, mineral. Palate: powerful, flavourful, toasty, round tannins.

Convento Oreja Memoria 2009 TR
100% tinta del país

91

Colour: cherry, garnet rim. Nose: ripe fruit, spicy, creamy oak, toasty, complex, dark chocolate, earthy notes. Palate: powerful, flavourful, toasty, round tannins.

CORDIS TERRA HISPANIA

Gamonal, 16 2ºC
28031 Madrid (Madrid)
☎: +34 911 610 024
Fax: +34 913 316 047
www.cordisterra.com
info@cordisterra.com

Cuatro Runas 2013 T Roble
tempranillo

86

Colour: bright cherry, garnet rim. Nose: ripe fruit, sweet spices, creamy oak, balsamic herbs. Palate: flavourful, fruity, toasty.

CUESTAROA

Camino de Valdeoliva, 9 Pol. Ind. Norte "El Raso"
28750 San Agustín de Guadalix (Madrid)
☎: +34 918 258 100
www.cuestaroa.es
cuestaroa@cuestaroa.es

Cuesta Roa 2012 T Roble
tinto fino

88

Colour: cherry, garnet rim. Nose: ripe fruit, spicy, creamy oak, toasty. Palate: powerful, flavourful, toasty, harsh oak tannins.

DEHESA DE LOS CANÓNIGOS

Ctra. Renedo - Pesquera, Km. 39
47315 Pesquera de Duero (Valladolid)
☎: +34 983 484 001
Fax: +34 983 484 040
www.bodegadehesadeloscanonigos.com
bodega@dehesacanonigos.com

Dehesa de los Canónigos 2011 T

89

Colour: bright cherry. Nose: sweet spices, creamy oak, medium intensity, earthy notes. Palate: fruity, flavourful, toasty.

Solideo Magnum 2008 TR
87
Colour: cherry, garnet rim. Nose: ripe fruit, spicy, creamy oak, toasty, warm. Palate: powerful, flavourful, toasty, slightly dry, soft tannins.

DEHESA VALDELAGUNA
Ctra. VA-101 a Valoria, Km. 16
47315 Pesquera de Duero (Valladolid)
☎: +34 921 142 325
www.montelaguna.es
montelaguna63@gmail.es

Montelaguna 2010 TC
tempranillo
91
Colour: cherry, garnet rim. Nose: ripe fruit, spicy, creamy oak, toasty, complex. Palate: powerful, flavourful, toasty, round tannins, balanced.

Montelaguna 6 meses 2012 T
tempranillo
89
Colour: deep cherry. Nose: powerfull, characterful, red berry notes, ripe fruit, toasty. Palate: powerful, ripe fruit.

Montelaguna Selección 2010 T
tempranillo
92
Colour: cherry, garnet rim. Nose: ripe fruit, spicy, creamy oak, toasty, complex. Palate: powerful, flavourful, toasty, round tannins.

Ra 09 2009 T
tempranillo
90
Colour: cherry, garnet rim. Nose: roasted coffee, cocoa bean, ripe fruit, dry nuts. Palate: spicy, ripe fruit, fine bitter notes, toasty.

Ra Vendimia Seleccionada 2009 T
92
Colour: cherry, garnet rim. Nose: spicy, toasty, overripe fruit, mineral. Palate: powerful, flavourful, toasty, round tannins.

DOMINIO BASCONCILLOS
Polígono 19 parcela 245
09370 Gumiel de Izán (Burgos)
☎: +34 947 561 022
www.dominiobasconcillos.com
info@dominiobasconcillos.com

Dominio Basconcillos 12 meses 2009 TC
92 ♣
Colour: cherry, garnet rim. Nose: ripe fruit, sweet spices, creamy oak, expressive, elegant. Palate: flavourful, fruity, toasty, round tannins.

Dominio Basconcillos 12 meses 2011 T
100% tinto fino
92 ♣
Colour: bright cherry. Nose: ripe fruit, sweet spices, creamy oak, expressive, lactic notes. Palate: flavourful, fruity, toasty, round tannins.

Dominio Basconcillos Ecológico 6 meses 2012 T
100% tinto fino
89 ♣
Colour: bright cherry. Nose: ripe fruit, sweet spices, creamy oak, medium intensity, toasty. Palate: fruity, flavourful, toasty.

Viña Magna 2009 TR
92
Colour: cherry, garnet rim. Nose: red berry notes, ripe fruit, spicy, creamy oak, complex, earthy notes, cocoa bean. Palate: powerful, flavourful, toasty, round tannins.

Viña Magna 2011 TC
91
Colour: bright cherry, garnet rim. Nose: ripe fruit, sweet spices, creamy oak, balsamic herbs. Palate: fruity, flavourful, toasty, balanced, elegant.

DOMINIO DE ATAUTA

Ctra. a Morcuera, s/n
42345 Atauta (Soria)
☎: +34 975 351 349
www.dominiodeatauta.com
info@dominiodeatauta.com

Dominio de Atauta 2010 T
100% tempranillo
95
Colour: cherry, garnet rim. Nose: ripe fruit, spicy, creamy oak, toasty, complex, dark chocolate, earthy notes. Palate: powerful, flavourful, toasty.

DOMINIO DE ATAUTA

RIBERA DEL DUERO
DENOMINACIÓN DE ORIGEN

Dominio de Atauta 2011 T
100% tempranillo
94
Colour: cherry, garnet rim. Nose: ripe fruit, spicy, creamy oak, toasty, complex, dark chocolate, earthy notes. Palate: powerful, flavourful, toasty, round tannins.

Dominio de Atauta La Mala 2011 TC
tempranillo
96
Colour: cherry, garnet rim. Nose: ripe fruit, spicy, creamy oak, toasty, complex, dark chocolate. Palate: powerful, flavourful, toasty, round tannins.

Dominio de Atauta Llanos del Almendro 2011 T
tempranillo
96
Colour: cherry, garnet rim. Nose: spicy, creamy oak, toasty, complex, dark chocolate, earthy notes, mineral, fragrant herbs. Palate: powerful, flavourful, toasty, round tannins.

Dominio de Atauta Valdegatiles 2011 T
tempranillo
96
Colour: cherry, garnet rim. Nose: spicy, creamy oak, toasty, complex, dark chocolate, earthy notes. Palate: powerful, flavourful, toasty, round tannins.

Parada de Atauta 2011 T
100% tempranillo
94
Colour: bright cherry. Nose: ripe fruit, sweet spices, creamy oak, expressive, mineral, scrubland. Palate: flavourful, fruity, toasty, round tannins.

DOMINIO DE ES

Avenida Manuel de Falla, nº 37 2ºE
26007 Logroño (La Rioja)
☎: +34 676 536 390
bebervino@hotmail.com

Dominio de Es La Diva 2012 T
tinto fino, albillo
95 🌷
Colour: cherry, garnet rim. Nose: ripe fruit, wild herbs, earthy notes, spicy, creamy oak, mineral. Palate: balanced, flavourful, long, balsamic, elegant.

Dominio de Es Viñas Viejas de Soria 2012 T
tinto fino
94 🌷
Colour: cherry, garnet rim. Nose: spicy, creamy oak, toasty, complex, dark chocolate, earthy notes, fruit preserve. Palate: powerful, flavourful, toasty, round tannins.

DOMINIO DE PINGUS S.L.

Hospital, s/n - Apdo. 93, Peñafiel
47350 Quintanilla de Onésimo
(Valladolid)
☎: +34 983 680 189
www.dominiopingus.com
info@pingus.es

Flor de Pingus 2012 T
94
Colour: cherry, garnet rim. Nose: ripe fruit, spicy, creamy oak, toasty, complex, expressive. Palate: powerful, flavourful, toasty, round tannins, balanced.

Pingus 2012 T
98
Colour: cherry, garnet rim. Nose: ripe fruit, wild herbs, spicy, creamy oak, mineral. Palate: flavourful, long, balsamic, balanced, elegant.

PSI 2012 T
95
Colour: cherry, garnet rim. Nose: red berry notes, ripe fruit, spicy, creamy oak, toasty, complex, earthy notes. Palate: powerful, flavourful, toasty, round tannins.

DOMINIO DEL ÁGUILA

Los Lagares, 42
09370 La Aguilera (Burgos)
☎: +34 638 899 236
info@dominiodelaguila.com

Dominio del Aguila 2010 TR
tempranillo

96

Colour: cherry, garnet rim. Nose: ripe fruit, fruit expression, spicy, toasty. Palate: flavourful, powerful, good acidity, fine bitter notes, round tannins.

Pícaro del Aguila 2012 Clarete
tempranillo, blanca del páis

90

Colour: onion pink. Nose: elegant, candied fruit, dried flowers, fragrant herbs. Palate: light-bodied, flavourful, good acidity, long, spicy.

Pícaro del Aguila 2012 T
tempranillo

93

Colour: cherry, garnet rim. Nose: wild herbs, earthy notes, spicy, creamy oak, scrubland, fragrant herbs. Palate: balanced, flavourful, long, balsamic.

DOMINIO ROMANO

Lagares, s/n
47319 Rábano (Valladolid)
☎: +34 983 871 661
Fax: +34 938 901 143
www.dominioromano.es
dominioromano@dominioromano.es

Camino Romano 2012 T
tinto fino

88

Colour: cherry, garnet rim. Nose: spicy, toasty, overripe fruit, mineral. Palate: powerful, flavourful, toasty, round tannins.

Dominio Romano 2012 T
tinto fino

90

Colour: very deep cherry, garnet rim. Nose: powerfull, ripe fruit, roasted coffee, dark chocolate. Palate: powerful, toasty, roasted-coffee aftertaste.

ÉBANO VIÑEDOS Y BODEGAS

Ctra. N-122 Km., 299,6
47318 Castrillo de Duero (Valladolid)
☎: +34 983 106 440
Fax: +34 986 609 313
www.ebanovinedosybodegas.com
ebano@valminorebano.com

Ébano 2009 TC
tempranillo

91

Colour: cherry, garnet rim. Nose: ripe fruit, spicy, toasty. Palate: powerful, flavourful, toasty, round tannins.

Ébano 6 2013 T
tempranillo

87

Colour: very deep cherry, garnet rim. Nose: overripe fruit, warm, dried herbs. Palate: flavourful, ripe fruit, long.

EL LAGAR DE ISILLA

Camino Real, 1
09471 La Vid (Burgos)
☎: +34 947 530 434
Fax: +34 947 504 316
www.lagarisilla.es
bodegas@lagarisilla.es

El Lagar de Isilla 2009 TR
100% tempranillo

92

Colour: cherry, garnet rim. Nose: ripe fruit, spicy, creamy oak, cocoa bean. Palate: powerful, flavourful, toasty, round tannins.

El Lagar de Isilla 2010 TC
100% tempranillo

91

Colour: cherry, garnet rim. Nose: ripe fruit, spicy, creamy oak, toasty, complex. Palate: powerful, flavourful, toasty, round tannins.

El Lagar de Isilla 9 meses Gestación 2011 T Roble
100% tempranillo

89

Colour: cherry, garnet rim. Nose: ripe fruit, spicy, creamy oak, toasty. Palate: powerful, flavourful, toasty, round tannins.

El Lagar de Isilla Vendimia Seleccionada 2009 T
100% tempranillo

90

Colour: ruby red. Nose: spicy, fine reductive notes, wet leather, aged wood nuances, toasty. Palate: spicy, long, toasty.

EL MOSAICO DE BACO

Avda Extremadura, 55
09400 Aranda de Duero (Burgos)
☎: +34 947 512 866
Fax: +34 947 512 866
www.elmosaicodebaco.com
info@elmosaicodebaco.com

Mosaico de Baco 2009 TC
tempranillo
88
Colour: cherry, garnet rim. Nose: ripe fruit, spicy, creamy oak, toasty, complex, wild herbs. Palate: powerful, flavourful, toasty.

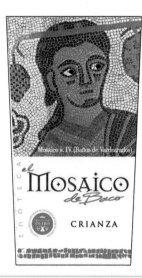

Mosaico de Baco 2012 T Roble
tempranillo
84

Mosaico de Baco 2013 RD
tinto fino, albillo
86
Colour: light cherry. Nose: powerfull, ripe fruit, red berry notes, floral. Palate: powerful, fruity, fresh.

Mosaico de Baco 2013 T
tempranillo
85

Mosaico de Baco Viñas del Monte 2009 T
tinto fino
89
Colour: cherry, garnet rim. Nose: ripe fruit, wild herbs, spicy, creamy oak. Palate: flavourful, long, balsamic.

FINCA TORREMILANOS

Finca Torremilanos
09400 Aranda de Duero (Burgos)
☎: +34 947 512 852
Fax: +34 947 508 044
www.torremilanos.com
reservas@torremilanos.com

Los Cantos de Torremilanos 2012 T
91
Colour: very deep cherry, purple rim. Nose: dry stone, ripe fruit, cocoa bean, creamy oak, expressive. Palate: good structure, full, long, round tannins.

Montecastrillo 2012 T Roble
100% tempranillo
87
Colour: very deep cherry, purple rim. Nose: balanced, expressive, red berry notes, ripe fruit, spicy, toasty. Palate: flavourful, fruity, good finish.

Montecastrillo 2013 RD
tempranillo
86
Colour: light cherry. Nose: red berry notes, floral, expressive, fresh. Palate: fruity, fresh, easy to drink, good finish.

Torre Albéniz 2010 TR
90
Colour: black cherry. Nose: ripe fruit, spicy, toasty, characterful. Palate: powerful, flavourful, toasty, round tannins.

Torremilanos 2010 TR
tempranillo
88
Colour: very deep cherry, garnet rim. Nose: ripe fruit, fruit preserve, sweet spices, cocoa bean. Palate: good structure, full.

Torremilanos 2011 TC
88
Colour: very deep cherry. Nose: ripe fruit, spicy, creamy oak, toasty, complex. Palate: powerful, flavourful, toasty, round tannins.

Torremilanos Colección 2009 TR
tempranillo
92
Colour: black cherry, garnet rim. Nose: expressive, ripe fruit, fruit preserve, new oak, cocoa bean. Palate: good structure, full, round tannins.

FINCA VILLACRECES
Ctra. Soria N-122 Km 322
47350 Quintanilla de Onésimo
(Valladolid)
☎: +34 983 680 437
Fax: +34 983 683 314
www.grupoartevino.com
villacreces@villacreces.com

Finca Villacreces 2011 T
92
Colour: very deep cherry. Nose: ripe fruit, spicy, creamy oak, toasty, characterful, earthy notes. Palate: powerful, flavourful, toasty, round tannins.

Finca Villacreces Nebro 2011 TC
100% tempranillo
96
Colour: cherry, garnet rim. Nose: ripe fruit, spicy, creamy oak, toasty, complex, mineral. Palate: powerful, flavourful, toasty, round tannins.

Pruno 2012 T
91
Colour: deep cherry. Nose: powerfull, characterful, ripe fruit, spicy. Palate: powerful, fine bitter notes, good acidity.

GRANDES BODEGAS
Ctra. de Sotillo de la Ribera, s/n
09311 La Horra (Burgos)
☎: +34 947 542 166
Fax: +34 947 542 165
www.marquesdevelilla.com
bodega@marquesdevelilla.com

Doncel de Mataperras 2009 TR
tinta del país
90
Colour: cherry, garnet rim. Nose: balanced, complex, spicy, fine reductive notes. Palate: good structure, flavourful, round tannins.

Finca La María 2011 T Roble
tinta del país
88
Colour: very deep cherry. Nose: powerfull, fruit preserve, creamy oak. Palate: correct, round tannins, spicy.

Marqués de Velilla 2009 TR
tinta del país
88
Colour: very deep cherry. Nose: ripe fruit, spicy. Palate: flavourful, fruity, round tannins.

Marqués de Velilla 2010 TC
tinta del país
88
Colour: cherry, garnet rim. Nose: ripe fruit, spicy, creamy oak, toasty, complex. Palate: powerful, flavourful, toasty, round tannins.

Marqués de Velilla 2013 T
tinta del país
87
Colour: very deep cherry, purple rim. Nose: ripe fruit, powerfull, wild herbs. Palate: fruity, easy to drink, good finish.

GRUPO VINÍCOLA MARQUÉS DE VARGAS - CONDE SAN CRISTÓBAL
Ctra. Valladolid a Soria, Km. 303
47300 Peñafiel (Valladolid)
☎: +34 983 878 055
Fax: +34 983 878 196
www.marquesdevargas.com
bodega@condesancristobal.com

Conde de San Cristóbal 2011 T
91
Colour: cherry, garnet rim. Nose: ripe fruit, spicy, creamy oak, toasty. Palate: powerful, flavourful, toasty, round tannins.

Conde de San Cristóbal Raíces 2009 TR
90
Colour: cherry, garnet rim. Nose: ripe fruit, spicy, toasty, complex, scrubland. Palate: powerful, flavourful, toasty, round tannins.

HACIENDA URBIÓN
Ctra. Nalda, km. 9
26120 Albelda de Iregua (Rioja)
☎: +34 941 444 233
Fax: +34 941 444 427
www.miguelangelwines.com
info@vinicolareal.com

Vega Vieja 2012 TC
100% tempranillo
85

Vega Vieja 2013 T Roble
100% tempranillo
84

Vega Vieja Cosecha 2013 T
100% tempranillo
83

HACIENDA ZORITA MARQUÉS DE LA CONCORDIA FAMILY OF WINES
Hacienda Abascal, N-122, Km. 321,5
47360 Quintanilla de Onésimo
(Valladolid)
☎: +34 913 878 612
www.the-haciendas.com
abasilio@unitedwineries.com

HZ Abascal Premium 2010 T
100% tempranillo
90
Colour: pale ruby, brick rim edge. Nose: spicy, fine reductive notes, wet leather, aged wood nuances, fruit liqueur notes. Palate: spicy, fine tannins.

HZ Abascal Vineyard 2009 TR
100% tempranillo

89

Colour: cherry, garnet rim. Nose: ripe fruit, spicy, creamy oak, toasty, complex. Palate: powerful, flavourful, toasty, round tannins.

HZ Abascal Vineyard 2011 TC
100% tempranillo

88

Colour: cherry, garnet rim. Nose: ripe fruit, spicy, creamy oak, toasty. Palate: powerful, flavurful, toasty, round tannins.

HAMMEKEN CELLARS
Calle de la Muela, 16
03730 Jávea (Alicante)
☎: +34 965 791 967
Fax: +34 966 461 471
www.hammekencellars.com
cellars@hammekencellars.com

Aventino 200 Barrels 2010 T
100% tempranillo

91

Colour: cherry, garnet rim. Nose: ripe fruit, spicy, creamy oak, toasty, complex. Palate: powerful, flavourful, toasty, round tannins.

Aventino 2006 TR
100% tempranillo

88

Colour: pale ruby, brick rim edge. Nose: ripe fruit, spicy, creamy oak, toasty, complex, fine reductive notes. Palate: powerful, flavourful, toasty, round tannins.

Aventino 2010 TC
100% tempranillo

88

Colour: cherry, garnet rim. Nose: ripe fruit, spicy, creamy oak, toasty, complex. Palate: powerful, flavourful, toasty, round tannins.

Oraculo Collectors Edition 2009 T
100% tempranillo

88

Colour: cherry, garnet rim. Nose: balanced, ripe fruit, spicy. Palate: flavourful, round tannins.

Oraculo Collectors Edition 2010 T
100% tempranillo

90

Colour: cherry, garnet rim. Nose: ripe fruit, wild herbs, earthy notes, spicy, creamy oak. Palate: balanced, flavourful, long, balsamic.

Viña Altamar 2012 T
100% tempranillo

86

Colour: bright cherry. Nose: ripe fruit, sweet spices, expressive. Palate: flavourful, fruity, toasty, round tannins.

HESVERA
Ctra. Peñafiel - Pesquera, Km. 5,5
47315 Pesquera de Duero (Valladolid)
☎: +34 626 060 516
Fax: +34 983 870 201
www.hesvera.es
hesvera@hesvera.es

Hesvera 2010 TC
tempranillo

89

Colour: cherry, garnet rim. Nose: spicy, toasty, overripe fruit. Palate: powerful, flavourful, toasty, round tannins.

Hesvera Cosecha Limitada 2009 T
tempranillo

90

Colour: cherry, garnet rim. Nose: ripe fruit, wild herbs, earthy notes, spicy, creamy oak. Palate: balanced, flavourful, long, balsamic.

Hesvera Seis Meses 2012 T Roble
tempranillo

87

Colour: bright cherry. Nose: ripe fruit, sweet spices, creamy oak, expressive. Palate: flavourful, fruity, toasty, round tannins.

HIJOS DE ANTONIO POLO
La Olma, 5
47300 Peñafiel (Valladolid)
☎: +34 983 873 183
Fax: +34 983 873 783
www.pagopenafiel.com
info@pagopenafiel.com

Pagos de Peñafiel 2009 TC
tempranillo
91
Colour: deep cherry. Nose: ripe fruit, spicy, creamy oak, toasty. Palate: powerful, flavourful, toasty, round tannins.

Pagos de Peñafiel 2009 TR
tempranillo
87
Colour: black cherry. Nose: fruit preserve, creamy oak, sweet spices. Palate: good structure, flavourful, balsamic.

Pagos de Peñafiel 2011 TC
tempranillo
87
Colour: cherry, garnet rim. Nose: toasty, fruit preserve, sweet spices. Palate: slightly acidic, correct, spicy.

Pagos de Peñafiel Vendimia Selección 2009 T Roble
tempranillo
89
Colour: cherry, garnet rim. Nose: ripe fruit, spicy, creamy oak, toasty, complex. Palate: powerful, flavourful, toasty, round tannins.

HORNILLOS BALLESTEROS
Camino Tenerías, 9
09300 Roa de Duero (Burgos)
☎: +34 947 541 071
Fax: +34 947 541 071
hornillosballesteros@telefonica.net

MiBal 2011 TC
tempranillo
89
Colour: bright cherry. Nose: ripe fruit, sweet spices, creamy oak, expressive. Palate: flavourful, fruity, toasty, round tannins.

MiBal 2013 T
tempranillo
85

MiBal Selección 2008 T
tempranillo
88
Colour: cherry, garnet rim. Nose: fruit preserve, fruit liqueur notes, spicy. Palate: flavourful, pruney, balsamic.

Perfil de MiBal 2009 T
tempranillo
91
Colour: cherry, garnet rim. Nose: ripe fruit, wild herbs, earthy notes, spicy, creamy oak. Palate: balanced, flavourful, long, balsamic.

LA MALETA HAND MADE FINE WINES
Julio Prieto Nespereira, 21
32005 Ourense (Ourense)
☎: +34 988 614 234
lamaletawines.com
hola@lamaletawines.com

Finca La Viajera 2010 TC
100% tempranillo
90
Colour: cherry, garnet rim. Nose: red berry notes, ripe fruit, spicy, creamy oak, toasty, complex. Palate: powerful, flavourful, toasty, concentrated.

Finca La Viajera 2013 T
100% tempranillo
89
Colour: cherry, purple rim. Nose: expressive, fresh fruit, red berry notes, floral, spicy. Palate: flavourful, fruity, good acidity, round tannins, concentrated.

Finca La Viajera Vendimia Seleccionada 2010 T
100% tempranillo
92
Colour: cherry, garnet rim. Nose: ripe fruit, spicy, creamy oak, toasty, balsamic herbs, dry stone. Palate: powerful, flavourful, toasty, balanced.

LAN
Paraje del Buicio, s/n
26360 Fuenmayor (La Rioja)
☎: +34 941 450 950
Fax: +34 941 450 567
www.bodegaslan.com
info@bodegaslan.com

Marqués de Burgos 2010 TC
100% tempranillo
87
Colour: bright cherry. Nose: ripe fruit, sweet spices, creamy oak, medium intensity. Palate: fruity, flavourful, toasty.

Marqués de Burgos 2011 T Roble
100% tempranillo
86
Colour: cherry, garnet rim. Nose: red berry notes, ripe fruit, balsamic herbs, spicy, creamy oak. Palate: powerful, flavourful, spicy, balanced.

LEGARIS

Ctra. Peñafiel - Encinas de Esgueva, km. 4,3
47316 Curiel de Duero (Valladolid)
☎: +34 983 878 088
Fax: +34 983 881 034
www.grupocodorniu.com
info@legaris.com

Legaris 2010 TC
100% tinto fino
88
Colour: cherry, garnet rim. Nose: spicy, toasty, overripe fruit. Palate: powerful, flavourful, toasty, round tannins.

Legaris 2010 TR
100% tinto fino
92
Colour: very deep cherry, garnet rim. Nose: complex, expressive, balanced, spicy. Palate: good structure, full, round tannins.

Legaris 2013 T Roble
100% tinto fino
88
Colour: bright cherry. Nose: ripe fruit, sweet spices, creamy oak, expressive. Palate: flavourful, fruity, toasty, round tannins.

Legaris Selección Especial 2009 T
100% tinto fino
90
Colour: cherry, garnet rim. Nose: ripe fruit, spicy, creamy oak, warm. Palate: balanced, flavourful, long, balsamic.

LOESS

El Monte, 7
47195 Arroyo de la Encomienda (Valladolid)
☎: +34 983 664 898
Fax: +34 983 406 579
www.loess.es
loess@loess.es

Loess 2011 T
tinta del país
90
Colour: cherry, garnet rim. Nose: ripe fruit, wild herbs, earthy notes, spicy, creamy oak. Palate: balanced, flavourful, long, balsamic.

MARÍA ASCENSIÓN REPISO BOCOS

Ctra. de Valbuena, 34
47315 Pesquera de Duero (Valladolid)
☎: +34 983 870 178
www.veronicasalgado.es
info@veronicasalgado.es

Verónica Salgado 2011 T Roble
100% tinto fino
88
Colour: bright cherry. Nose: ripe fruit, sweet spices, creamy oak. Palate: flavourful, fruity, toasty, round tannins.

Verónica Salgado Capricho 2010 T
100% tinto fino
93
Colour: cherry, garnet rim. Nose: red berry notes, raspberry, violet drops, balsamic herbs, wild herbs, spicy. Palate: flavourful, fresh, spicy, balsamic, long.

MARQUÉS DE REVILLA

Paraje Tiemblos, Pol 509- Parcela 5146
9441 Sotillo de la Ribera (Burgos)
☎: +34 913 739 689
www.marquesderevilla.com
guiomaro@marquesderevilla.com

Marqués de Revilla 2007 TR
87
Colour: cherry, garnet rim. Nose: ripe fruit, wild herbs, spicy, creamy oak, wet leather, tobacco. Palate: balanced, flavourful, balsamic.

Marqués de Revilla 2009 TC
84

Marqués de Revilla 2011 T Roble
tempranillo, merlot
86
Colour: bright cherry. Nose: ripe fruit, sweet spices, creamy oak, medium intensity. Palate: flavourful, fruity, toasty.

MARQUÉS DE TOMARES

Ctra. de Cenicero, s/n
26360 Fuenmayor (La Rioja)
☎: +34 676 433 820
Fax: +34 941 450 297
www.marquesdetomares.com
info@marquesdetomares.com

TM Ribera Selección de la Familia 2011 TC
90
Colour: cherry, garnet rim. Nose: red berry notes, ripe fruit, spicy, creamy oak, toasty, complex, earthy notes, dry stone. Palate: powerful, flavourful, toasty, round tannins.

MATER VITIS

Calle Doctor Santaolalla, 21 bajo izq
03005 Alicante (Alicante)
☎: +34 965 637 811
www.matervitis.com

Mater Vitis TC
85

Mater Vitis TR
87
Colour: very deep cherry. Nose: ripe fruit, spicy, creamy oak, toasty, characterful. Palate: powerful, flavourful, toasty, round tannins.

Mater Vitis 2012 T Roble
83

Mater Vitis 2013 T
84

MN VINOS

09314 Pedrosa de Duero (Burgos)
☎: +34 947 530 180
www.mnvinos.com
mnvinos@mnvinos.com

MN Vinos 2012 T
100% tinto fino
90
Colour: cherry, garnet rim. Nose: ripe fruit, spicy, creamy oak, toasty, complex, earthy notes. Palate: powerful, flavourful, toasty, round tannins.

MONTEBACO

Finca Montealto
47359 Valbuena de Duero (Valladolid)
☎: +34 983 485 128
www.bodegasmontebaco.com
montebaco@bodegasmontebaco.com

Montebaco 2012 TC
tempranillo
90
Colour: cherry, garnet rim. Nose: ripe fruit, spicy, creamy oak, complex. Palate: powerful, flavourful, toasty, round tannins.

Montebaco Vendimia Seleccionada 2010 T
tempranillo
90
Colour: cherry, garnet rim. Nose: balanced, complex, ripe fruit, spicy. Palate: good structure, flavourful, round tannins.

Semele 2012 TC
91
Colour: bright cherry. Nose: sweet spices, expressive, fruit expression. Palate: flavourful, fruity, toasty, round tannins.

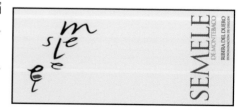

MONTEVANNOS

Paraje Tiemblos, Pol 509 - Parcela 5146
09441 Sotillo de la Ribera (Burgos)
☎: +34 947 534 277
Fax: +34 947 534 016
www.montevannos.es
bodega@montevannos.es

Montevannos 2008 TR
tempranillo, merlot
87
Colour: cherry, garnet rim. Nose: spicy, toasty, overripe fruit, mineral. Palate: powerful, flavourful, toasty, round tannins.

Montevannos 2009 TC
tempranillo, merlot
84

Montevannos 2011 T Roble
tempranillo, merlot
87
Colour: bright cherry. Nose: sweet spices, creamy oak, medium intensity. Palate: fruity, flavourful, toasty.

Montevannos 2013 T
85

Opimius 2007 TR
tempranillo
90
Colour: deep cherry. Nose: balanced, complex, ripe fruit, spicy. Palate: good structure, flavourful, round tannins.

OLID INTERNACIONAL

Juan García Hortelano, 21 7ºC
47014 Valladolid (Valladolid)
☎: +34 983 132 690
www.olidinternacional.com
olid@olidinternacional.com

983 2009 TC
tempranillo
90
Colour: very deep cherry. Nose: ripe fruit, spicy, creamy oak, toasty, characterful. Palate: powerful, flavourful, toasty, round tannins.

983 2012 T Roble
100% tempranillo
90
Colour: cherry, purple rim. Nose: ripe fruit, spicy, creamy oak, toasty, complex, mineral. Palate: powerful, flavourful, toasty.

OSBORNE RIBERA DEL DUERO

Crta. Fuenmayor - Navarrete, km. 2
26360 Fuenmayor (La Rioja)
☎: +34 925 860 990
Fax: +34 925 860 905
www.osborne.es
carolina.cerrato@osborne.es

Señorío del Cid 2012 T Roble
100% tinta del país
87
Colour: very deep cherry, garnet rim. Nose: powerfull, ripe fruit, toasty, balsamic herbs. Palate: powerful, toasty, roasted-coffee aftertaste.

PAGO DE CARRAOVEJAS

Camino de Carraovejas, s/n
47300 Peñafiel (Valladolid)
☎: +34 983 878 020
Fax: +34 983 878 022
www.pagodecarraovejas.com
administracion@pagodecarraovejas.com

Pago de Carraovejas 2011 TR
94
Colour: cherry, garnet rim. Nose: red berry notes, ripe fruit, spicy, creamy oak, toasty, complex, earthy notes. Palate: powerful, flavourful, toasty, round tannins.

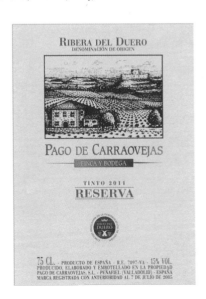

Pago de Carraovejas 2012 TC

93

Colour: cherry, garnet rim. Nose: ripe fruit, spicy, creamy oak, toasty, complex. Palate: powerful, flavourful, toasty, round tannins.

Pago de Carraovejas El Anejón de la Cuesta de las Liebres 2010 T

96

Colour: very deep cherry, garnet rim. Nose: balanced, expressive, fruit expression, spicy, balsamic herbs. Palate: full, flavourful, long, balanced, complex.

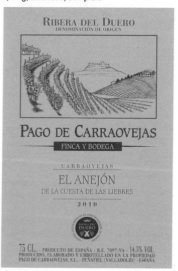

PAGO DE LOS CAPELLANES

Camino de la Ampudia, s/n
09314 Pedrosa de Duero (Burgos)
☎: +34 947 530 068
Fax: +34 947 530 111
www.pagodeloscapellanes.com
bodega@pagodeloscapellanes.com

Pago de los Capellanes 2011 TC
100% tempranillo

92

Colour: cherry, garnet rim. Nose: ripe fruit, spicy, creamy oak, toasty, complex, earthy notes. Palate: powerful, flavourful, toasty, round tannins.

Pago de los Capellanes 2011 TR
100% tempranillo

91

Colour: very deep cherry. Nose: ripe fruit, spicy, creamy oak, toasty, characterful. Palate: powerful, flavourful, toasty, round tannins.

Pago de los Capellanes 2013 T Roble
100% tempranillo

90

Colour: bright cherry. Nose: ripe fruit, sweet spices, creamy oak. Palate: flavourful, fruity, toasty, round tannins.

Pago de los Capellanes Parcela El Nogal 2010 T
100% tempranillo

94

Colour: cherry, garnet rim. Nose: ripe fruit, wild herbs, earthy notes, spicy, creamy oak. Palate: flavourful, long, balsamic.

Pago de los Capellanes Parcela El Picón 2010 T
100% tempranillo

94

Colour: cherry, garnet rim. Nose: spicy, creamy oak, toasty, complex, dark chocolate, earthy notes, fruit expression. Palate: powerful, flavourful, toasty, round tannins.

PAGOS DE MATANEGRA

Ctra. Santa María, 27
09311 Olmedillo de Roa (Burgos)
☎: +34 947 551 310
Fax: +34 947 551 309
www.pagosdematanegra.es
info@pagosdematanegra.es

Matanegra 2012 TC
tempranillo

88

Colour: cherry, garnet rim. Nose: ripe fruit, spicy, toasty, complex. Palate: powerful, flavourful, toasty, round tannins.

Matanegra Media Crianza 2010 T
100% tempranillo

88

Colour: very deep cherry, garnet rim. Nose: powerfull, ripe fruit, roasted coffee, dark chocolate. Palate: powerful, toasty, roasted-coffee aftertaste.

Matanegra Vendimia Seleccionada 2010 T
100% tempranillo

90

Colour: cherry, garnet rim. Nose: ripe fruit, spicy, creamy oak, toasty. Palate: powerful, flavourful, toasty, round tannins.

PAGOS DEL REY
Ctra. Palencia-Aranda, Km. 53
09311 Olmedillo de Roa (Burgos)
☎: +34 947 551 111
Fax: +34 947 551 311
www.pagosdelrey.com
pdr@pagosdelrey.com

Altos de Tamarón 2013 T Roble
tempranillo

86

Colour: bright cherry. Nose: ripe fruit, sweet spices, creamy oak. Palate: flavourful, fruity, toasty, easy to drink, roasted-coffee aftertaste.

Altos de Tamarón 2010 TR
tempranillo

88

Colour: cherry, garnet rim. Nose: balanced, ripe fruit, sweet spices, toasty. Palate: good structure, flavourful, round tannins, toasty.

Altos de Tamarón 2011 TC
tempranillo

87

Colour: cherry, garnet rim. Nose: ripe fruit, sweet spices, creamy oak. Palate: flavourful, fruity, toasty, roasted-coffee aftertaste.

Altos de Tamarón 2013 T
100% tempranillo

87

Colour: cherry, purple rim. Nose: red berry notes, raspberry, floral, expressive. Palate: fresh, fruity, flavourful, easy to drink.

Condado de Oriza 2010 TR
tempranillo

90

Colour: cherry, garnet rim. Nose: red berry notes, ripe fruit, spicy, creamy oak, toasty. Palate: powerful, flavourful, toasty, round tannins.

Condado de Oriza 2011 TC
tempranillo

89

Colour: bright cherry. Nose: ripe fruit, sweet spices, creamy oak. Palate: fruity, flavourful, toasty.

Condado de Oriza 2013 T
tempranillo

87

Colour: cherry, purple rim. Nose: red berry notes, raspberry, wild herbs, floral. Palate: powerful, flavourful, balanced.

Condado de Oriza 2013 T Roble
tempranillo

88

Colour: bright cherry. Nose: ripe fruit, sweet spices, creamy oak, medium intensity. Palate: fruity, flavourful, toasty.

Condado de Oriza 409 2010 T
tempranillo

91

Colour: cherry, garnet rim. Nose: ripe fruit, spicy, creamy oak, toasty, complex, dark chocolate, mineral. Palate: powerful, flavourful, toasty, round tannins.

Moralinos 2013 T

88

Colour: cherry, purple rim. Nose: fresh fruit, red berry notes, floral. Palate: flavourful, fruity, good acidity, round tannins.

PEPE LÓPEZ VINOS Y VIÑEDOS
Avda. Soria, 53 - Bajos Buzón 136
47300 Peñafiel (Valladolid)
☎: +34 983 106 207
Fax: +34 916 048 322
www.arrotos.es
info@arrotos.es

Arrotos 2012 TC
85

Arrotos 2013 T Roble
86
Colour: very deep cherry, garnet rim. Nose: powerfull, ripe fruit, roasted coffee, dark chocolate. Palate: powerful, toasty, roasted-coffee aftertaste.

PICO CUADRO
Del Río, 22
47350 Quintanilla de Onésimo
(Valladolid)
☎: +34 620 547 057
www.picocuadro.com
castrillo@picocuadro.com

Pico Cuadro 2011 T
tinto fino
89
Colour: very deep cherry. Nose: fruit liqueur notes, dark chocolate, aromatic coffee. Palate: ripe fruit, pruney.

Pico Cuadro Original 2010 T
tinto fino
93
Colour: cherry, garnet rim. Nose: ripe fruit, spicy, creamy oak, toasty, complex. Palate: powerful, flavourful, toasty, round tannins.

Pico Cuadro Vendimia Seleccionada 2010 T
tinto fino
91
Colour: cherry, garnet rim. Nose: balanced, complex, ripe fruit, spicy. Palate: good structure, flavourful.

Pico Cuadro Wild 2009 T
tinto fino
91
Colour: cherry, garnet rim. Nose: red berry notes, ripe fruit, spicy, creamy oak, toasty, complex, earthy notes. Palate: powerful, flavourful, toasty, round tannins.

PINNA FIDELIS
Camino Llanillos, s/n
47300 Peñafiel (Valladolid)
☎: +34 983 878 034
Fax: +34 983 878 035
www.pinnafidelis.com
clientes@pinnafidelis.com

Pinna Fidelis 2010 TC
tinta del país
88
Colour: bright cherry. Nose: ripe fruit, sweet spices, creamy oak, expressive. Palate: flavourful, fruity, toasty, round tannins.

Pinna Fidelis 2011 TC
tinta del país
88
Colour: cherry, garnet rim. Nose: ripe fruit, spicy, creamy oak, toasty, complex. Palate: powerful, flavourful, toasty, round tannins.

Pinna Fidelis 2004 TGR
tinta del país
88
Colour: deep cherry, orangey edge. Nose: waxy notes, tobacco, ripe fruit, spicy, aged wood nuances. Palate: fine bitter notes, elegant, flavourful, fine tannins.

Pinna Fidelis 2006 TR
tinta del país
89
Colour: cherry, garnet rim. Nose: ripe fruit, spicy, creamy oak, toasty, complex. Palate: powerful, flavourful, toasty, round tannins.

Pinna Fidelis 2013 T Roble
tinta del país
86
Colour: bright cherry. Nose: ripe fruit, sweet spices. Palate: flavourful, fruity, toasty, round tannins.

Pinna Fidelis Roble Español 2007 T
tinta del país
88
Colour: cherry, garnet rim. Nose: ripe fruit, spicy, toasty, dried herbs. Palate: powerful, flavourful, toasty, round tannins.

Pinna Fidelis Vendimia Seleccionada 2009 T
tinta del país
91
Colour: cherry, garnet rim. Nose: red berry notes, ripe fruit, spicy, creamy oak, toasty, complex, earthy notes. Palate: powerful, flavourful, toasty.

PROTOS BODEGAS RIBERA DUERO DE PEÑAFIEL

Bodegas Protos, 24-28
47300 Peñafiel (Valladolid)
☎: +34 983 878 011
Fax: +34 983 878 012
www.bodegasprotos.com
bodega@bodegasprotos.com

Protos 2010 TR
100% tinto fino

93

Colour: very deep cherry, garnet rim. Nose: ripe fruit, roasted coffee, dark chocolate. Palate: powerful, toasty, roasted-coffee aftertaste, round tannins.

Protos 2011 TC
100% tinto fino

93

Colour: cherry, garnet rim. Nose: ripe fruit, spicy, creamy oak, toasty. Palate: powerful, flavourful, toasty, round tannins.

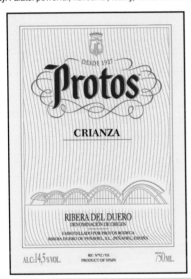

Protos 2009 TGR
100% tinto fino

92

Colour: cherry, garnet rim. Nose: balanced, complex, ripe fruit, spicy, expressive. Palate: good structure, flavourful, round tannins.

Protos 2012 T Roble
100% tinto fino

91

Colour: cherry, garnet rim. Nose: ripe fruit, spicy, creamy oak, toasty, complex, earthy notes. Palate: powerful, flavourful, toasty.

Protos Selección Finca el Grajo Viejo 2011 T
100% tinto fino

94

Colour: cherry, garnet rim. Nose: spicy, creamy oak, toasty, complex, dark chocolate, earthy notes, fruit expression. Palate: powerful, flavourful, toasty, round tannins.

REAL SITIO DE VENTOSILLA

Ctra. CL-619 (Magaz - Aranda) Km. 66,1
09443 Gumiel del Mercado (Burgos)
☎: +34 947 546 900
Fax: +34 947 546 999
www.pradorey.com
bodega@pradorey.com

Adaro de PradoRey 2010 T
100% tempranillo

94

Colour: cherry, garnet rim. Nose: ripe fruit, spicy, creamy oak, toasty, complex, dark chocolate, earthy notes. Palate: powerful, flavourful, toasty, round tannins.

Adaro de PradoRey 2011 TC
100% tempranillo

93

Colour: bright cherry. Nose: ripe fruit, sweet spices, creamy oak. Palate: fruity, flavourful, toasty, balanced, elegant.

Chozo Viejo 2010 TC
tempranillo

89

Colour: cherry, garnet rim. Nose: spicy, toasty, overripe fruit, mineral. Palate: powerful, flavourful, toasty, round tannins.

Chozo Viejo 2013 T Roble
87
Colour: bright cherry. Nose: sweet spices, creamy oak, ripe fruit. Palate: flavourful, fruity, toasty, round tannins.

Lía de PradoRey 2013 RD
100% tempranillo
88
Colour: raspberry rose, bright. Nose: fresh, red berry notes, fresh fruit, medium intensity. Palate: fresh, good acidity, good finish.

PradoRey 2004 TGR
91
Colour: cherry, garnet rim. Nose: ripe fruit, wild herbs, earthy notes, spicy. Palate: balanced, flavourful, long, balsamic.

PradoRey 2013 RD
88
Colour: rose, purple rim. Nose: powerfull, ripe fruit, red berry notes, floral, cocoa bean. Palate: powerful, fruity, fresh, flavourful.

PradoRey 2013 T Roble
88
Colour: deep cherry, purple rim. Nose: ripe fruit, sweet spices, expressive. Palate: flavourful, fruity, toasty, round tannins.

PradoRey Élite 2010 T
100% tempranillo
93
Colour: cherry, garnet rim. Nose: red berry notes, ripe fruit, spicy, creamy oak, complex. Palate: powerful, flavourful, toasty, round tannins.

PradoRey Élite 2011 T
100% tempranillo
94
Colour: cherry, garnet rim. Nose: ripe fruit, spicy, creamy oak, complex, earthy notes, balanced. Palate: powerful, flavourful, toasty, round tannins.

PradoRey Finca La Mina 2009 TR
92
Colour: bright cherry. Nose: ripe fruit, spicy, creamy oak, toasty, complex. Palate: powerful, flavourful, toasty, round tannins.

PradoRey Finca Valdelayegua 2011 TC
91
Colour: cherry, garnet rim. Nose: ripe fruit, spicy, creamy oak, toasty, complex, mineral. Palate: powerful, flavourful, toasty, round tannins, balanced.

RODRÍGUEZ SANZO
Manuel Azaña, 9
47014 (Valladolid)
☎: +34 983 150 150
Fax: +34 983 150 151
www.rodriguezsanzo.com
comunicacion@valsanzo.com

Vall Sanzo 2011 TC
100% tempranillo
90
Colour: bright cherry, garnet rim. Nose: ripe fruit, sweet spices, creamy oak, balanced. Palate: fruity, flavourful, toasty, correct.

ROMATE

Lealas, 26
11404 Jerez de la Frontera (Cádiz)
☎: +34 956 182 212
Fax: +34 956 185 276
www.romate.com
comercial@romate.com

Momo 2010 T
90
Colour: very deep cherry. Nose: powerfull, balsamic herbs, balanced, ripe fruit. Palate: balanced, round tannins, fruity.

RUDELES - TIERRAS EL GUIJARRAL

Trasterrera, 10
42345 Peñalba de San Esteban (Soria)
☎: +34 618 644 633
Fax: +34 975 350 582
www.rudeles.com
info@rudeles.com

Rudeles "23" 2013 T
90
Colour: cherry, purple rim. Nose: powerfull, red berry notes, ripe fruit, floral, expressive. Palate: powerful, fresh, fruity, unctuous.

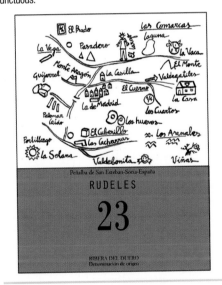

Rudeles Cerro El Cuberillo 2009 T
100% tempranillo
93
Colour: cherry, garnet rim. Nose: red berry notes, ripe fruit, balsamic herbs, mineral, spicy, creamy oak. Palate: balanced, flavourful, spicy, balsamic, long.

Rudeles Finca La Nación 2008 T
89
Colour: bright cherry. Nose: ripe fruit, sweet spices, creamy oak, spicy. Palate: fruity, flavourful, toasty, balanced.

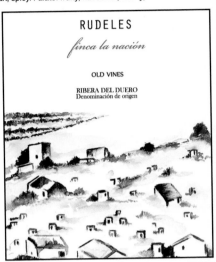

Rudeles Finca La Nación 2011 T
90
Colour: cherry, garnet rim. Nose: red berry notes, ripe fruit, spicy, creamy oak, toasty, earthy notes. Palate: powerful, flavourful, toasty.

Rudeles Selección 2007 T
90
Colour: cherry, garnet rim. Nose: ripe fruit, wild herbs, spicy, creamy oak, fine reductive notes, mineral. Palate: balanced, flavourful, long, balsamic.

SELECCIÓN CÉSAR MUÑOZ

Acera de Recoletos
47004 Valladolid (Valladolid)
☎: +34 666 548 751
www.cesarmunoz.es
info@cesarmunoz.es

Magallanes 2011 TC
tempranillo
89
Colour: bright cherry. Nose: sweet spices, creamy oak, medium intensity, ripe fruit, fruit preserve. Palate: fruity, flavourful, toasty.

SELECCIÓN TORRES

Del Rosario, 56
47311 Fompedraza (Valladolid)
☎: +34 938 177 400
Fax: +34 938 177 444
www.torres.es
mailadmin@torres.es

Celeste 2010 TC
tinto fino
90
Colour: cherry, garnet rim. Nose: ripe fruit, spicy, creamy oak, toasty, complex. Palate: powerful, flavourful, toasty, round tannins.

Celeste 2012 T Roble
tinto fino
87
Colour: bright cherry. Nose: ripe fruit, sweet spices, creamy oak, medium intensity. Palate: fruity, flavourful, toasty.

SEÑORIO DE BOCOS

Camino La Canaleja, s/n
47317 Bocos de Duero (Valladolid)
☎: +34 983 880 988
Fax: +34 983 880 988
www.senoriodebocos.com
bodegas@senoriodebocos.com

Autor de Bocos 2011 T
tempranillo
91
Colour: cherry, garnet rim. Nose: ripe fruit, wild herbs, earthy notes, spicy, creamy oak. Palate: balanced, flavourful, long, balsamic.

Señorio de Bocos 2010 TC
tempranillo
89
Colour: bright cherry. Nose: ripe fruit, sweet spices, creamy oak, expressive. Palate: flavourful, fruity, toasty, round tannins.

Señorio de Bocos 2012 T Roble
tempranillo
86
Colour: deep cherry, purple rim. Nose: red berry notes, ripe fruit, sweet spices. Palate: fruity, easy to drink.

SOLTERRA

Ctra. de Pedrosa, km. 1,5
09300 Roa (Burgos)
☎: +34 915 196 651
Fax: +34 914 135 907
www.cvsolterra.com
m.antonia@cvsolterra.com

Alto de los Zorros 10 meses 2012 T
100% tinto fino
87
Colour: cherry, garnet rim. Nose: red berry notes, ripe fruit, balsamic herbs, toasty, creamy oak. Palate: powerful, flavourful, spicy, toasty.

Alto de los Zorros 2009 TC
100% tinto fino
88
Colour: bright cherry, garnet rim. Nose: ripe fruit, sweet spices, creamy oak, cocoa bean. Palate: flavourful, fruity, toasty, correct.

Alto de los Zorros Autor 2010 TR
100% tinto fino
90
Colour: cherry, garnet rim. Nose: ripe fruit, spicy, creamy oak, toasty, complex. Palate: powerful, flavourful, toasty, balanced.

TERROIR 34

Square Dessy, 18 - 1330 RIX
01330 RIX Bruxelles (Bélgica)
☎: +34 606 941 434
www.terroir34.com
info@terroir34.com

Terroir 34 "Dreams from Limestone" 2012 T
100% tinto fino
88 🥄
Colour: bright cherry, purple rim. Nose: balanced, medium intensity, red berry notes, ripe fruit, sweet spices. Palate: fruity, good finish.

THE GRAND WINES

Ramón y Cajal 7, 1ºA
01007 Vitoria (Alava)
☎: +34 945 158 282
Fax: +34 945 158 283
www.thegrandwines.com
araex@araex.com

Rolland Galarreta 2010 T
91
Colour: bright cherry, garnet rim. Nose: ripe fruit, sweet spices, creamy oak, balsamic herbs, mineral. Palate: fruity, flavourful, toasty, balanced.

TORRES DE ANGUIX

Camino La Tejera, s/n
09313 Anguix (Burgos)
☎: +34 947 554 008
Fax: +34 947 554 129
www.torresdeanguix.com
enologia@torresdeanguix.com

A D'Anguix 2005 T
tinta del país

93

Colour: cherry, garnet rim. Nose: ripe fruit, wild herbs, earthy notes, spicy, creamy oak. Palate: balanced, long, balsamic, elegant.

D'Anguix 2009 T
tinta del país

90

Colour: cherry, garnet rim. Nose: ripe fruit, wild herbs, earthy notes, spicy, creamy oak. Palate: balanced, flavourful, long, balsamic.

R D'Anguix 2013 RD
tinta del país

87

Colour: light cherry, bright. Nose: medium intensity, red berry notes, fresh fruit. Palate: fruity, balanced, good acidity.

T D'Anguix 2004 TGR
tinta del país

89

Colour: pale ruby, brick rim edge. Nose: elegant, spicy, fine reductive notes, wet leather, aged wood nuances, fruit liqueur notes. Palate: spicy, fine tannins, elegant, long.

T D'Anguix 2006 TR
tinta del país

89

Colour: pale ruby, brick rim edge. Nose: balanced, complex, ripe fruit, spicy. Palate: good structure, flavourful, round tannins.

T D'Anguix 2012 T Roble
tinta del país

86

Colour: cherry, garnet rim. Nose: ripe fruit, spicy, creamy oak, toasty. Palate: powerful, flavourful, toasty.

TUDANCA

Isilla, 13
09400 Aranda de Duero (Burgos)
☎: +34 947 506 011
Fax: +34 947 506 012
www.vinostudanca.es
info@vinostudanca.es

Tudanca Vendimia Seleccionada 2009 T
100% tempranillo

89

Colour: cherry, garnet rim. Nose: ripe fruit, fruit preserve, balsamic herbs, spicy, creamy oak. Palate: powerful, flavourful, spicy, long.

UNESDI DISTRIBUCIONES

Aurora, 11
11500 El Puerto de Santa María (Cádiz)
☎: +34 956 541 329
www.unesdi.com
info@unesdi.com

Mataveras 2011 T

89

Colour: bright cherry. Nose: ripe fruit, sweet spices, creamy oak. Palate: flavourful, fruity, toasty, round tannins.

UVAS FELICES

Agullers, 7
08003 Barcelona (Barcelona)
☎: +34 902 327 777
www.vilaviniteca.es

Venta Las Vacas 2012 T

92

Colour: bright cherry. Nose: ripe fruit, sweet spices, creamy oak, expressive. Palate: flavourful, fruity, toasty, round tannins.

VALDEMONJAS VIÑEDOS Y VINOS

Antonio Machado, 14 1ºD
47008 Valladolid (Valladolid)
☎: +34 983 248 294
www.valdemonjas.es
alejandro.moyano@valdemonjas.es

El Primer Beso 2012 T
tempranillo

87

Colour: cherry, garnet rim. Nose: red berry notes, ripe fruit, wild herbs. Palate: powerful, flavourful, good structure.

Entre Palabras 2011 T
tempranillo

89

Colour: bright cherry. Nose: sweet spices, creamy oak, medium intensity, fruit expression. Palate: fruity, flavourful, toasty.

Los Tres Dones 2011 T
tempranillo
91
Colour: cherry, garnet rim. Nose: red berry notes, ripe fruit, spicy, creamy oak, toasty, complex, earthy notes. Palate: powerful, flavourful, toasty, round tannins.

VALLEBUENO
Ctra. Valbuena, 20
47315 Pesquera de Duero (Valladolid)
☎: +34 983 868 116
Fax: +34 983 868 432
www.vallebueno.com
info@taninia.com

Vallebueno 2009 TC
tinta del país
88
Colour: cherry, garnet rim. Nose: spicy, creamy oak, toasty, ripe fruit, fine reductive notes. Palate: powerful, flavourful, toasty.

Vallebueno 2011 T Roble
tinta del país
88
Colour: cherry, garnet rim. Nose: ripe fruit, balsamic herbs, spicy, creamy oak. Palate: powerful, flavourful, concentrated, toasty.

VALTRAVIESO
Finca La Revilla, s/n
47316 Piñel de Arriba (Valladolid)
☎: +34 983 484 030
www.valtravieso.com
valtravieso@valtravieso.com

Valtravieso 2010 TR
89
Colour: cherry, garnet rim. Nose: ripe fruit, spicy, creamy oak, toasty. Palate: powerful, flavourful, toasty.

Valtravieso 2011 TC
90
Colour: cherry, garnet rim. Nose: ripe fruit, spicy, creamy oak, toasty, complex, earthy notes. Palate: powerful, flavourful, toasty, round tannins.

Valtravieso 2012 T Roble
89
Colour: bright cherry. Nose: ripe fruit, sweet spices, creamy oak, expressive. Palate: flavourful, fruity, toasty, round tannins.

Valtravieso VT Tinta Fina 2010 T
100% tinto fino
89
Colour: cherry, garnet rim. Nose: fruit preserve, fruit liqueur notes, spicy. Palate: flavourful, pruney, balsamic.

Valtravieso VT Vendimia Seleccionada 2010 T
90
Colour: cherry, garnet rim. Nose: spicy, fine reductive notes, wet leather, aged wood nuances, toasty, wild herbs. Palate: spicy, long, toasty, balsamic.

VEGA CLARA
Ctra. N-122, Km 328
47350 Quintanilla De Onesimo (Valladolid)
☎: +34 677 570 779
Fax: +34 983 361 005
www.vegaclara.com
vegaclara@vegaclara.com

10 Almendros 2012 T
tempranillo, otras
87
Colour: dark-red cherry. Nose: ripe fruit, spicy, toasty, dried herbs. Palate: powerful, flavourful, toasty, round tannins.

Mario VC 2011 T
tempranillo, cabernet sauvignon
91
Colour: cherry, garnet rim. Nose: ripe fruit, spicy, creamy oak, toasty. Palate: powerful, flavourful, toasty, round tannins.

VEGA REAL
Ctra. N-122, Km. 298,6
47318 Castrillo de Duero (Valladolid)
☎: +34 983 881 580
Fax: +34 983 873 188
www.vegareal.com
visitas@vegareal.net

Vega Real 2009 TC
tempranillo
87
Colour: very deep cherry. Nose: ripe fruit, spicy, creamy oak, toasty, complex. Palate: powerful, flavourful, toasty, round tannins.

Vega Real 2013 T Roble
tempranillo
84

VINO CAMINO SORIA

C. Bahía de Cádiz
28042 Madrid (Madrid)
☎: +34 616 942 873
www.vinocaminosoria.com
joseluis@vinocaminosoria.com

Camino Soria 2011 TC
tempranillo
87
Colour: black cherry, garnet rim. Nose: closed, toasty, sweet spices, ripe fruit. Palate: good structure, flavourful.

VINOS HERCAL

Santo Domingo, 2
09300 Roa (Burgos)
☎: +34 947 541 281
www.somanilla.es
ventas@somanilla.es

Bocca 2012 T Roble
tempranillo
90
Colour: bright cherry. Nose: ripe fruit, sweet spices, creamy oak, expressive. Palate: flavourful, fruity, toasty, round tannins.

Somanilla 2009 TC
tinto fino
92
Colour: cherry, garnet rim. Nose: ripe fruit, earthy notes, spicy, creamy oak. Palate: balanced, flavourful, long, full.

VINOS JOC - JORDI OLIVER CONTI

Mas Marti
17467 Sant Mori (Girona)
☎: +34 607 222 002
www.vinojoc.com
info@vinojoc.com

JOC Tinto Fino 2011 T
tinto fino
88
Colour: dark-red cherry. Nose: ripe fruit, fruit preserve, powerfull, sweet spices. Palate: flavourful, sweet tannins, balsamic.

VINOS SANTOS ARRANZ

Ctra. de Valbuena, s/n
47315 Pesquera de Duero (Valladolid)
☎: +34 983 870 008
Fax: +34 983 870 008
www.lagrima-negra.com
lagrimanegra82@hotmail.com

Lágrima Negra 2011 TC
84

Lágrima Negra 2012 T Roble
87
Colour: deep cherry, garnet rim. Nose: medium intensity, balsamic herbs, ripe fruit, spicy. Palate: fruity, good acidity, balanced.

VINOS TERRIBLES

Avda. Menendez Pelayo 13 B
28009 (Madrid)
☎: +34 914 092 131
www.latintoreriavinoteca.com
esther@vinosterribles.com

Terrible 2013 T Barrica
100% tempranillo
87
Colour: cherry, purple rim. Nose: balanced, expressive, red berry notes, dried herbs, sweet spices. Palate: powerful, toasty, slightly dry, soft tannins.

VIÑA ARNAIZ

Ctra. N-122, km. 281
09463 Haza (Burgos)
☎: +34 947 536 227
Fax: +34 947 536 216
www.garciacarrion.es
atcliente@jgc.es

Castillo de Aza 2008 TR
tinta del país
88
Colour: ruby red. Nose: spicy, fine reductive notes, aged wood nuances, toasty. Palate: spicy, long, toasty.

Castillo de Aza 2012 T Roble
87
Colour: very deep cherry, garnet rim. Nose: powerfull, ripe fruit, roasted coffee, dark chocolate. Palate: powerful, toasty, roasted-coffee aftertaste.

Castillo de Aza 2013 T Joven
tinta del país
87
Colour: cherry, purple rim. Nose: powerfull, red berry notes, ripe fruit, floral, balsamic herbs. Palate: powerful, fresh, fruity.

Mayor de Castilla 2006 TGR
100% tempranillo
89
Colour: pale ruby, brick rim edge. Nose: balanced, complex, ripe fruit, spicy. Palate: good structure, flavourful, round tannins.

Mayor de Castilla 2008 TR
100% tempranillo
87
Colour: bright cherry. Nose: sweet spices, creamy oak, medium intensity. Palate: fruity, flavourful, toasty.

Pata Negra 2008 TR
tinta del país

86

Colour: deep cherry, orangey edge. Nose: fruit preserve, scrubland, spicy, toasty. Palate: powerful, flavourful, roasted-coffee aftertaste.

Pata Negra 2009 T
100% tempranillo

87

Colour: cherry, garnet rim. Nose: balanced, complex, ripe fruit, spicy. Palate: good structure, flavourful, round tannins.

Pata Negra 2011 TC
100% tempranillo

88

Colour: cherry, garnet rim. Nose: ripe fruit, spicy, creamy oak, toasty. Palate: powerful, flavourful, toasty.

Pata Negra 2012 T Roble
100% tempranillo

88

Colour: bright cherry, garnet rim. Nose: ripe fruit, sweet spices, creamy oak. Palate: flavourful, fruity, toasty.

Viña Arnáiz 2010 TC

88

Colour: cherry, garnet rim. Nose: ripe fruit, spicy, creamy oak, toasty, complex. Palate: powerful, flavourful, toasty, round tannins.

Viña Arnáiz 2010 TR

89

Colour: cherry, garnet rim. Nose: ripe fruit, spicy, creamy oak, toasty, complex. Palate: powerful, flavourful, toasty, long.

Viña Arnáiz 2011 TC
100% tempranillo

89

Colour: cherry, garnet rim. Nose: ripe fruit, spicy, creamy oak, complex. Palate: powerful, flavourful, toasty, round tannins.

Viña Arnáiz 2012 T Roble

86

Colour: cherry, garnet rim. Nose: ripe fruit, sweet spices, creamy oak, spicy. Palate: flavourful, fruity, spicy, easy to drink.

VIÑA MAMBRILLA
Ctra. Pedrosa s/n
09317 Mambrilla de Castrejón (Burgos)
☎: +34 947 540 234
Fax: +34 947 540 234
www.mambrilla.com
bodega@mambrilla.com

Alidis 2013 T
100% tempranillo

87

Colour: deep cherry, purple rim. Nose: ripe fruit, balanced. Palate: fruity aftestaste, balsamic.

Alidis 6 meses Barrica 2012 T
100% tempranillo

86

Colour: very deep cherry, garnet rim. Nose: powerfull, ripe fruit, roasted coffee, dark chocolate. Palate: powerful, toasty, roasted-coffee aftertaste.

Alidis Crianza 2011 TC
100% tempranillo

86

Colour: ruby red. Nose: spicy, fine reductive notes, wet leather, aged wood nuances, toasty. Palate: spicy, long, toasty.

Alidis Expresión 2010 T
100% tempranillo

91

Colour: cherry, garnet rim. Nose: ripe fruit, spicy, creamy oak, toasty, complex, balsamic herbs. Palate: powerful, flavourful, toasty.

Alidis Reserva 2010 TR
100% tempranillo

90

Colour: very deep cherry. Nose: ripe fruit, spicy, creamy oak, toasty, characterful. Palate: powerful, flavourful, toasty.

Alidis VS 2010 T
100% tempranillo

89

Colour: cherry, garnet rim. Nose: ripe fruit, wild herbs, spicy, warm. Palate: balanced, flavourful, long.

VIÑA SOLORCA

Ctra. Circunvalación, s/n
09300 Roa (Burgos)
☎: +34 947 541 823
Fax: +34 947 540 035
www.bodegassolorca.com
info@bodegassolorca.com

Barón del Valle 2008 TGR

91

Colour: very deep cherry, garnet rim. Nose: expressive, balanced, cocoa bean, ripe fruit. Palate: good structure, full, round tannins, spicy.

Barón del Valle 2009 TR

89

Colour: very deep cherry, garnet rim. Nose: sweet spices, creamy oak, ripe fruit. Palate: full, flavourful, balanced, spicy.

Barón del Valle 2010 TC

tempranillo

88

Colour: dark-red cherry, garnet rim. Nose: powerfull, toasty, ripe fruit. Palate: concentrated, flavourful, round tannins.

Barón del Valle 2012 T Roble

86

Colour: cherry, garnet rim. Nose: red berry notes, ripe fruit, sweet spices. Palate: correct, flavourful.

VIÑA VALDEMAZÓN

Pza. Sur, 3
47359 Olivares de Duero (Valladolid)
☎: +34 983 680 220
www.valdemazon.com
valdemazon@hotmail.com

Viña Valdemazón Vendimia Seleccionada 2011 T

tempranillo

88

Colour: bright cherry, garnet rim. Nose: ripe fruit, sweet spices, creamy oak, expressive. Palate: fruity, flavourful, toasty, balanced.

VIÑEDOS ALONSO DEL YERRO

Finca Santa Marta - Ctra. Roa-Anguix, Km. 1,8
09300 Roa (Burgos)
☎: +34 913 160 121
Fax: +34 913 160 121
www.alonsodelyerro.es
mariadelyerro@vay.es

"María" Alonso del Yerro 2010 T

tempranillo

93

Colour: cherry, garnet rim. Nose: ripe fruit, wild herbs, earthy notes, spicy, creamy oak. Palate: flavourful, long, balsamic.

Alonso del Yerro 2011 T

100% tempranillo

93

Colour: cherry, garnet rim. Nose: spicy, toasty, overripe fruit, mineral, dark chocolate. Palate: powerful, flavourful, toasty, round tannins.

VIÑEDOS DEL SOTO

Camino Real, 28
09441 Sotillo de la Ribera (Burgos)
☎: +34 947 532 503
Fax: +34 947 532 503
www.vinedosdelsoto.es
info@vinedosdelsoto.es

Aclareo 2012 T

100% tempranillo

85

Horta 2010 TC

100% tempranillo

90

Colour: cherry, garnet rim. Nose: ripe fruit, spicy, creamy oak, toasty, complex. Palate: powerful, flavourful, toasty, round tannins.

Porta Caeli Vino de Autor 2009 T

100% tempranillo

91

Colour: very deep cherry. Nose: ripe fruit, spicy, creamy oak, toasty, characterful. Palate: powerful, flavourful, toasty, round tannins.

VIÑEDOS SINGULARES

Cuzco, 26 - 28, Nave 8
08030 (Barcelona)
☎: +34 934 807 041
Fax: +34 934 807 076
www.vinedossingulares.com
info@vinedossingulares.com

Entrelobos 2012 T

tinto fino

88

Colour: cherry, garnet rim. Nose: ripe fruit, spicy, creamy oak, toasty. Palate: powerful, flavourful, toasty.

VIÑEDOS Y BODEGAS ÁSTER

Finca El Caño Ctra. Aranda-Palencia, Km. 54,9
09313 Anguix (Burgos)
☎: +34 947 522 700
Fax: +34 947 522 701
www.riojalta.com
aster@riojalta.com

Áster 2009 TC
tinta del país
90
Colour: pale ruby, brick rim edge. Nose: spicy, fine reductive notes, wet leather, aged wood nuances, fruit liqueur notes. Palate: spicy, fine tannins.

Áster Finca el Otero 2010 T
tinta del país
93
Colour: cherry, garnet rim. Nose: ripe fruit, spicy, creamy oak, toasty. Palate: powerful, flavourful, toasty.

VIÑEDOS Y BODEGAS GARCÍA FIGUERO

Ctra. La Horra - Roa, Km. 2,2
09311 La Horra (Burgos)
☎: +34 947 542 127
Fax: +34 947 542 033
www.tintofiguero.com
bodega@tintofiguero.com

Figuero Noble 2010 T
100% tempranillo
91
Colour: black cherry. Nose: complex, expressive, balanced, spicy. Palate: fruity, spicy, round tannins.

Figuero Tinus 2011 T
100% tempranillo
93
Colour: cherry, garnet rim. Nose: spicy, toasty, overripe fruit, mineral, dark chocolate. Palate: powerful, flavourful, toasty, round tannins.

Tinto Figuero 12 Meses Barrica 2011 TC
100% tempranillo
90
Colour: cherry, garnet rim. Nose: red berry notes, ripe fruit, spicy, creamy oak, toasty, complex, earthy notes. Palate: powerful, flavourful, toasty.

Tinto Figuero Viñas Viejas 2009 T
100% tempranillo
92
Colour: cherry, garnet rim. Nose: ripe fruit, wild herbs, earthy notes, spicy, creamy oak. Palate: balanced, flavourful, long, balsamic.

VIÑEDOS Y BODEGAS GORMAZ

Ctra. de Soria, s/n
42330 San Esteban de Gormaz (Soria)
☎: +34 975 350 404
Fax: +34 975 351 513
www.hispanobodegas.com
carlos.garcia@hispanobodegas.com

12 Linajes 2009 TR
tempranillo

93

Colour: bright cherry. Nose: ripe fruit, sweet spices, creamy oak, expressive. Palate: flavourful, fruity, toasty.

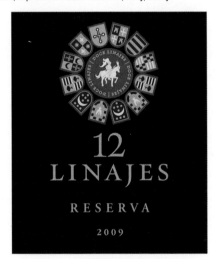

12 Linajes 2011 TC
tempranillo

90

Colour: deep cherry. Nose: ripe fruit, sweet spices, cocoa bean, dried herbs. Palate: fruity, flavourful, round tannins.

12 Linajes 2012 T Roble
tempranillo

87

Colour: bright cherry. Nose: ripe fruit, expressive, balsamic herbs, spicy. Palate: flavourful, fruity, toasty, round tannins

Anier Vendimia Seleccionada 2012 T
100% tempranillo

94

Colour: cherry, garnet rim. Nose: ripe fruit, spicy, creamy oak, complex, dried herbs. Palate: powerful, flavourful, toasty, round tannins.

Catania 2011 TC
tempranillo

91

Colour: cherry, garnet rim. Nose: ripe fruit, spicy, creamy oak, toasty, complex, dry stone. Palate: powerful, flavourful, toasty, balanced, elegant.

Catania 2013 T
tempranillo

87

Colour: cherry, garnet rim. Nose: ripe fruit, scrubland, macerated fruit. Palate: fruity, balanced.

Viña Gormaz 2011 TC
tempranillo

91

Colour: cherry, garnet rim. Nose: ripe fruit, spicy, creamy oak, toasty, complex. Palate: powerful, flavourful, toasty, round tannins, elegant.

WINNER WINES
Avda. del Mediterráneo, 38
28007 Madrid (Madrid)
☎: +34 915 019 042
Fax: +34 915 017 794
www.entornoalvino.com
info@entornoalvino.com

Ibernoble 2008 TR
87

Colour: cherry, garnet rim. Nose: tobacco, spicy, dried herbs, toasty. Palate: correct, fruity.

Ibernoble 2011 T Roble
100% tempranillo

86

Colour: bright cherry. Nose: ripe fruit, sweet spices, creamy oak. Palate: flavourful, toasty, round tannins.

Ibernoble 2011 TC
86

Colour: very deep cherry. Nose: toasty, fruit preserve, powerfull. Palate: correct, round tannins.

Ibernoble 2012 T Roble
85

Viña Gormaz 2013 T
tempranillo

88

Colour: cherry, purple rim. Nose: expressive, fresh fruit, red berry notes, floral. Palate: flavourful, fruity, good acidity.

VIÑEDOS Y BODEGAS RIBÓN
Basilón, 15
47350 Quintanilla de Onésimo
(Valladolid)
☎: +34 983 680 015
Fax: +34 983 680 015
www.bodegasribon.com
info@bodegasribon.com

Tinto Ribón 2011 TC
100% tempranillo

90

Colour: cherry, garnet rim. Nose: ripe fruit, spicy, toasty. Palate: powerful, flavourful, toasty, round tannins, full.

Tinto Ribón 2012 T Roble
100% tempranillo

90

Colour: cherry, purple rim. Nose: expressive, fresh fruit, red berry notes, floral. Palate: flavourful, fruity, good acidity, round tannins.

DO. RIBERA DEL GUADIANA

CONSEJO REGULADOR

Ctra. Sevilla-Gijón, km. 114. Apdo. 299
06200 Almendralejo (Badajoz)
☎:+34 924 671 302
Fax: +34 924 664 703
@: info@riberadelguadiana.eu
www.riberadelguadiana.eu

LOCATION:

Covering the 6 wine-growing regions of Extremadura, with a total surface of more than 87,000 Ha as described below.

SUB-REGIONS AND CLIMATE:

Cañamero. To the south east of the province of Cáceres, in the heart of the Sierra de Guadalupe. It comprises the municipal districts of Alia, Berzocana, Cañamero, Guadalupe and Valdecaballeros. The vineyards are located on the mountainside, at altitudes of between 600 m to 800 m. The terrain is rugged and the soil is slaty and loose. The climate is mild without great temperature contrasts, and the average annual rainfall is 750 mm to 800 mm. The main grape variety is the white Alarije. **Montánchez.** Comprising 27 municipal districts. It is characterised by its complex terrain, with numerous hills and small valleys. The vineyards are located on brown acidic soil. The climate is Continental in nature and the average annual rainfall is between 500 mm and 600 mm. The white grape variety Borba occupies two thirds of the vineyards in the region. **Ribera Alta.** This covers the Vegas del Guadiana and the plains of La Serena and Campo de Castuera and comprises 38 municipal districts. The soil is very sandy. The most common varieties are Alarije, Borba (white), Tempranillo and Garnacha (red). **Ribera Baja.** Comprising 11 municipal districts. The vineyards are located on clayey-limy soil. The climate is Continental, with a moderate Atlantic influence and slight contrasts in temperature. The most common varieties are: Cayetana Blanca and Pardina among the whites, and Tempranillo among the reds. **Matanegra.** Rather similar to Tierra de Barros, but with a milder climate. It comprises 8 municipal districts, and the most common grape varieties are Beba, Montua (whites), Tempranillo, Garnacha and Cabernet Sauvignon (reds). **Tierra de Barros.** Situated in the centre of the province of Badajoz and the largest (4475 Ha and 37 municipal districts). It has flat plains with fertile soils which are rich in nutrients and have great water retention capacity (Rainfall is low: 350 mm to 450 mm per year). The most common varieties are the white Cayetana Blanca and Pardina, and the red Tempranillo, Garnacha and Cabernet Sauvignon.

GRAPE VARIETIES:

WHITE: Alarije, Borba, Cayetana Blanca, Pardina, Macabeo, Chardonnay, Chelva or Montua, Malvar, Parellada, Pedro Ximénez, Verdejo, Eva, Cigüente, Perruno, Moscatel de Alejandría, Moscatel de Grano Menudo, Sauvignon Blanc and Bobal Blanca.
RED: Garnacha Tinta, Tempranillo, Bobal, Cabernet Sauvignon, Garnacha Tintorera, Graciano, Mazuela, Merlot, Monastrell, Syrah, Pinot Noir and Jaén Tinto.

FIGURES:

Vineyard surface: 34,577 – Wine-Growers: 3,193 – Wineries: 25 – 2013 Harvest rating: - – Production 13: 5,429,700 litres – Market percentages: 76% domestic - 24% export.

VINTAGE RATING   PEÑÍNGUIDE

2009	2010	2011	2012	2013
GOOD	VERY GOOD	GOOD	GOOD	AVERAGE

BODEGA CARABAL

Ctra. Alía - Castilblanco, Km. 10
10137 Alía (Cáceres)
☎: +34 917 346 152
Fax: +34 913 720 440
www.carabal.es
info@carabal.es

Carabal Cávea 2008 T
syrah, tempranillo

92

Colour: cherry, garnet rim. Nose: ripe fruit, mineral, balsamic herbs, spicy, creamy oak, expressive. Palate: powerful, rich, flavourful, spicy, long, balanced, elegant.

Carabal Cávea 2009 TC
syrah, tempranillo, cabernet sauvignon, graciano

91

Colour: cherry, garnet rim. Nose: ripe fruit, spicy, creamy oak, toasty, earthy notes. Palate: powerful, flavourful, toasty, round tannins.

Carabal Gulae 2010 TC

93

Colour: cherry, garnet rim. Nose: ripe fruit, spicy, creamy oak, toasty, complex, wild herbs. Palate: powerful, flavourful, toasty, round tannins, balanced.

Carabal Rasgo 2010 T
tempranillo, syrah

89

Colour: cherry, garnet rim. Nose: ripe fruit, balsamic herbs, sweet spices, creamy oak. Palate: powerful, flavourful, spicy.

BODEGA SAN MARCOS

Ctra. Aceuchal, s/n
06200 Almendralejo (Badajoz)
☎: +34 924 670 410
Fax: +34 924 665 505
www.bodegasanmarcos.com
ventas@bodegasanmarcos.com

Campobarro 2005 TR
100% tempranillo

84

Campobarro 2011 TC
100% tempranillo

86

Colour: bright cherry. Nose: ripe fruit, sweet spices, creamy oak, medium intensity. Palate: fruity, flavourful, toasty.

Campobarro Macabeo 2013 B
100% macabeo

85

Campobarro Pardina 2013 B
100% pardina

85

Campobarro Selección 2009 T

86

Colour: cherry, garnet rim. Nose: ripe fruit, spicy, creamy oak, toasty. Palate: powerful, flavourful, toasty.

Campobarro Tempranillo 2013 T
100% tempranillo

85

Heredad de Barros 2005 TR
100% tempranillo

84

Heredad de Barros 2011 TC
100% tempranillo

84

BODEGA VITICULTORES DE BARROS

Ctra. de Barros, s/n
06200 Almendralejo (Badajoz)
☎: +34 924 664 852
Fax: +34 924 664 852
www.viticultoresdebarros.com
bodegas@viticultoresdebarros.com

Emperador de Barros Cayetana 2012 B
cayetana blanca

85

Emperador de Barros Tempranillo 2012 T
tempranillo

84

Vizana 2010 TC
tempranillo

89

Colour: cherry, garnet rim. Nose: ripe fruit, spicy, creamy oak, toasty, complex, balsamic herbs. Palate: powerful, flavourful, toasty, round tannins.

BODEGAS CASTELAR

Avda. de Extremadura, 1
06228 Hornachos (Badajoz)
☎: +34 924 533 073
Fax: +34 924 533 493
www.bodegascastelar.com
bodega@bodegascastelar.com

Castelar 2008 TR
tempranillo, otras

83

Castelar 2010 TC
tempranillo, otras

83

BODEGAS MARCELINO DÍAZ

Mecánica, s/n
06200 Almendralejo (Badajoz)
☎: +34 924 677 548
Fax: +34 924 660 977
www.madiaz.com
bodega@madiaz.com

Puerta Palma 2012 T
tempranillo, cabernet sauvignon, graciano
84

Puerta Palma 2013 B
pardina
84

BODEGAS MARTÍNEZ PAIVA SAT

Ctra. Gijón - Sevilla N-630, Km. 646
Apdo. Correos 87
06200 Almendralejo (Badajoz)
☎: +34 924 671 130
Fax: +34 924 663 056
www.payva.es
info@payva.es

56 Barricas 2008 TC
tempranillo
86
Colour: cherry, garnet rim. Nose: ripe fruit, spicy, creamy oak, toasty. Palate: powerful, flavourful, toasty, round tannins.

Doña Francisquita 2012 T
tempranillo
84

Payva 2007 TR
88
Colour: pale ruby, brick rim edge. Nose: spicy, fine reductive notes, wet leather, aged wood nuances, fruit liqueur notes. Palate: spicy, fine tannins, elegant, long.

Payva 2010 TC
86
Colour: cherry, garnet rim. Nose: ripe fruit, spicy, creamy oak, toasty, grassy. Palate: powerful, flavourful, toasty.

Payva 2013 T
tempranillo
86
Colour: cherry, purple rim. Nose: expressive, fresh fruit, red berry notes, floral. Palate: flavourful, fruity, good acidity, fine bitter notes.

Payva Cayetana Blanca 2012 B
cayetana blanca
87
Colour: bright yellow. Nose: ripe fruit, dried flowers, wild herbs. Palate: fine bitter notes, powerful, flavourful.

BODEGAS ORAN

Granados, 1
06200 Almendralejo (Badajoz)
☎: +34 662 952 800
www.bodegasoran.es
info@bodegasoran.com

Señorío de Orán 2010 TC
tempranillo
85

Señorío de Orán 2013 B
pardina
83

Señorío de Orán Flor 2012 T Roble
tempranillo
85

Viña Roja Tempranillo 2013 T
tempranillo
84

BODEGAS ROMALE

Pol. Ind. Parc. 6, Manz. D
06200 Almendralejo (Badajoz)
☎: +34 924 665 877
Fax: +34 924 665 877
www.romale.com
romale@romale.com

Privilegio de Romale 2008 TR
tempranillo
87
Colour: ruby red, orangey edge. Nose: ripe fruit, balsamic herbs, spicy, fine reductive notes. Palate: powerful, flavourful, spicy.

Privilegio de Romale 2010 TC
tempranillo
86
Colour: cherry, garnet rim. Nose: ripe fruit, spicy, creamy oak, toasty. Palate: powerful, flavourful, toasty.

Privilegio de Romale 2011 T Roble
tempranillo, merlot, cabernet sauvignon
85

BODEGAS RUIZ TORRES

Ctra. EX 116, km.33,8
10136 Cañamero (Cáceres)
☎: +34 927 369 027
Fax: +34 927 369 383
www.ruiztorres.com
info@ruiztorres.com

Attelea 2009 TC
84

Attelea 2012 T Roble
100% tempranillo
84

BODEGAS SANTA MARTA
Cooperativa, s/n
06150 Santa Marta (Badajoz)
☎: +34 924 690 218
Fax: +34 924 690 083
www.bodegasantamarta.com
salesmanager@bodegasantamarta.com

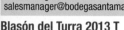

Blasón del Turra 2013 T
tempranillo
85

Blasón del Turra Macabeo 2013 B
macabeo
84

Blasón del Turra Pardina 2013 B
pardina
85

Compass 2012 T Roble
tempranillo
85

Puerta de la Coracha 2012 T
tempranillo
84

Valdeaurum 2011 T
tempranillo
85

BODEGAS TORIBIO
Luis Chamizo, 12 y 21
06310 Puebla de Sancho Pérez (Badajoz)
☎: +34 924 551 449
Fax: +34 924 551 449
www.bodegastoribio.com
info@bodegastoribio.com

Madre del Agua 2010 TC
90
Colour: very deep cherry. Nose: balanced, fruit preserve, spicy, toasty. Palate: balanced, round tannins, long.

Viña Puebla Esenzia 2008 TC
cabernet sauvignon, tempranillo, garnacha
88
Colour: cherry, garnet rim. Nose: spicy, fine reductive notes, wild herbs, toasty. Palate: balanced, good structure, round tannins.

Viña Puebla Macabeo 2012 BFB
macabeo
88
Colour: bright straw. Nose: creamy oak, ripe fruit, fine lees, sweet spices. Palate: powerful, fine bitter notes, toasty, long.

Viña Puebla Selección 2012 T Roble
cabernet sauvignon, tempranillo, garnacha, syrah
88
Colour: deep cherry, purple rim. Nose: powerfull, ripe fruit, fruit preserve, sweet spices, wild herbs. Palate: fruity, flavourful, round tannins.

Viña Puebla Verdejo 2013 B
verdejo
83

COSECHA EXTREMEÑA
Ctra. Villafranca, 23
06360 Fuente del Maestre (Badajoz)
☎: +34 924 530 705
Fax: +34 924 530 705
www.cosechaextremadura.com
admon@cosechaextremadura.com

Señorío de Badajoz 2013 B
macabeo
82

Señorío de Badajoz 2013 T
100% merlot
85

Señorío de Badajoz 2013 T Joven
tempranillo, cabernet sauvignon
84

Señorío de Badajoz Semidulce 2013 B
macabeo
83

LUIS GURPEGUI MUGA
Avda. Celso Muerza, 8
31560 San Adrián (Navarra)
☎: +34 948 670 050
Fax: +34 948 670 259
www.gurpegui.es
bodegas@gurpegui.es

Cinco Viñas 2013 T
tempranillo, garnacha
85

Gurpegui 2013 T
tempranillo, cabernet sauvignon
87
Colour: cherry, purple rim. Nose: powerfull, red berry notes, ripe fruit, floral, expressive. Palate: powerful, fresh, fruity, unctuous.

PAGO LOS BALANCINES

Paraje la Agraria, s/n
06475 Oliva de Mérida (Badajoz)
☎: +34 916 295 841
www.pagolosbalancines.com
info@pagolosbalancines.com

Alunado 2012 BFB
chardonnay

92

Colour: bright straw. Nose: ripe fruit, sweet spices, creamy oak, fragrant herbs. Palate: rich, smoky aftertaste, flavourful, fresh.

Balancines 2012 T Roble
tempranillo, syrah

90

Colour: bright cherry. Nose: ripe fruit, sweet spices, creamy oak, red berry notes. Palate: flavourful, fruity, toasty.

Balancines Blanco Sobre Lías 2013 B
sauvignon blanc, viura

87

Colour: bright yellow. Nose: ripe fruit, candied fruit. Palate: fruity, fine bitter notes, good acidity.

Los Balancines Huno 2011 T
91

Colour: cherry, garnet rim. Nose: ripe fruit, spicy, creamy oak, dark chocolate, earthy notes, balsamic herbs. Palate: powerful, flavourful, toasty, round tannins.

Los Balancines Huno 2012 T
92

Colour: cherry, garnet rim. Nose: ripe fruit, spicy, creamy oak, toasty, earthy notes. Palate: powerful, flavourful, toasty, round tannins.

Los Balancines Matanegra 2012 TC
94

Colour: cherry, garnet rim. Nose: ripe fruit, spicy, creamy oak, toasty, complex, earthy notes. Palate: powerful, flavourful, toasty, round tannins.

Los Balancines Viña de Buenavista 2012 T
tempranillo

94

Colour: bright cherry. Nose: sweet spices, creamy oak, expressive. Palate: flavourful, fruity, toasty, round tannins.

Vaso de Luz 2009 TR
cabernet sauvignon

93

Colour: deep cherry, orangey edge. Nose: spicy, smoky, wet leather, ripe fruit, earthy notes, mineral. Palate: good acidity, fine bitter notes, spicy, ripe fruit.

PALACIO QUEMADO

Ctra. Almendralejo - Alange, km 6,9
06840 Almendralejo (Badajoz)
☎: +34 924 120 082
Fax: +34 924 120 028
www.palacioquemado.com
palacioquemado@alvear.es

"PQ" Primicia 2013 T
100% tempranillo

90

Colour: cherry, garnet rim. Nose: red berry notes, raspberry, fragrant herbs, wild herbs, sweet spices. Palate: fruity, flavourful, balsamic, spicy.

Palacio Quemado 2009 TR
100% tempranillo

86

Colour: bright cherry. Nose: ripe fruit, sweet spices, creamy oak, fine reductive notes, grassy. Palate: fruity, flavourful, toasty.

Palacio Quemado 2011 TC
100% tempranillo

89

Colour: cherry, garnet rim. Nose: ripe fruit, spicy, creamy oak, toasty, complex, dark chocolate, earthy notes. Palate: powerful, flavourful, toasty, round tannins.

Palacio Quemado La Zarcita 2010 T
90

Colour: very deep cherry, garnet rim. Nose: powerfull, red berry notes, raspberry, balsamic herbs, toasty. Palate: powerful, toasty, spicy, long.

Palacio Quemado Los Acilates 2011 T
tempranillo, otras

89

Colour: cherry, garnet rim. Nose: ripe fruit, spicy, creamy oak, toasty, complex, balsamic herbs. Palate: powerful, flavourful, toasty.

PENÍNSULA WINES

Avda. Constitución, 12A
06230 Los Santos de Maimona (Badajoz)
☎: +34 924 572 394
www.doloresmorenas.com
realprovision@hotmail.com

Real Provisión 2009 TC
tempranillo, cabernet sauvignon, syrah

86

Colour: bright cherry. Nose: ripe fruit, sweet spices, creamy oak, medium intensity. Palate: fruity, flavourful, toasty, slightly evolved.

Real Provisión 2012 T
100% tempranillo

84

SOCIEDAD COOPERATIVA SAN ISIDRO DE VILLAFRANCA DE LOS BARROS

Ctra. Fuente del Mestre, 12
06220 Villafranca de los Barros (Badajoz)
☎: +34 924 524 136
Fax: +34 924 524 020
www.cooperativasanisidro.com
info@cooperativasanisidro.com

Valdequemao Macabeo 2013 B
macabeo
84

Valdequemao Macabeo 2013 BFB
macabeo
85

SOCIEDAD COOPERATIVA SANTA MARÍA EGIPCIACA

Ctra. Entrín Bajo, s/n
06196 Corte de Peleas (Badajoz)
☎: +34 924 693 014
Fax: +34 924 693 270
stamegipciaca@terra.es

Conde de la Corte 2012 T
83

Conde de la Corte 2013 B
84

ZALEO-VIÑAOLIVA

Pol. Ind., Las Plcadas II, Parcela 4-17 Aptdo. 149
06200 Almendralejo (Badajoz)
☎: +34 924 677 321
Fax: +34 924 660 989
www.zaleo.es
acoex@bme.es

Zaleo 2013 RD
tempranillo
82

Zaleo Pardina 2013 B
pardina
85

Zaleo Premium 2011 T
tempranillo
87
Colour: cherry, garnet rim. Nose: ripe fruit, spicy, creamy oak, toasty, complex. Palate: powerful, flavourful, toasty, round tannins.

Zaleo Selección 2011 T
tempranillo
86
Colour: bright cherry. Nose: ripe fruit, sweet spices, creamy oak, medium intensity. Palate: fruity, flavourful, toasty.

Zaleo Semidulce 2013 B
pardina
84

Zaleo Tempranillo 2013 T
tempranillo
88
Colour: cherry, purple rim. Nose: expressive, fresh fruit, red berry notes, balsamic herbs. Palate: flavourful, fruity, good acidity.

Zaleo Tempranillo Semidulce 2013 T
tempranillo
83

DO. RIBERA DEL JÚCAR

CONSEJO REGULADOR
Deportes, 4.
16700 Sisante (Cuenca)
☎ :+34 969 387 182 - Fax: +34 969 387 208
@: do@vinosriberadeljucar.com
www.vinosriberadeljucar.com

LOCATION:

The 7 wine producing municipal districts that make up the DO are located on the banks of the Júcar, in the south of the province of Cuenca. They are: Casas de Benítez, Casas de Guijarro, Casas de Haro, Casas de Fernando Alonso, Pozoamargo, Sisante and El Picazo. The region is at an altitude of between 650 and 750 m above sea level.

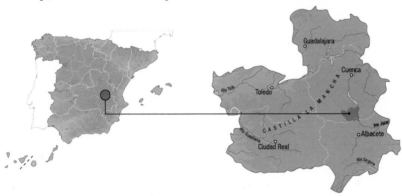

GRAPE VARIETIES:

RED: Cencibel or Tempranillo, Cabernet Sauvignon, Merlot, Syrah, Bobal, Cabernet Franc and Petit Verdot.
WHITE: Moscatel de Grano Menudo and Sauvignon Blanc.

FIGURES:

Vineyard surface: 9,100 – Wine-Growers: 955 – Wineries: 10 – 2013 Harvest rating: Good – Production 13: 623,000 litres – Market percentages: 40% domestic - 60% export.

SOIL:

The most common type of soil consists of pebbles on the surface and a clayey subsoil, which provides good water retention capacity in the deeper levels.

CLIMATE:

Continental in nature, dry, and with very cold winters and very hot summers. The main factor contributing to the quality of the wine is the day-night temperature contrasts during the ripening season of the grapes, which causes the process to be carried out slowly.

VINTAGE RATING · PEÑÍNGUIDE

2009	2010	2011	2012	2013
GOOD	VERY GOOD	VERY GOOD	VERY GOOD	VERY GOOD

PEÑÍNGUIDE to Spanish Wine

BODEGA SAN GINÉS

Virgen del Carmen, 6
16707 Casas de Benítez (Cuenca)
☎: +34 969 382 037
Fax: +34 969 382 998
www.cincoalmudes.es
juancarlos@bodegasangines.es

5 Almudes 2010 TC
tempranillo
84

5 Almudes Tempranillo 2013 T
tempranillo
87
Colour: deep cherry. Nose: ripe fruit, spicy, scrubland. Palate: flavourful, powerful.

Almudes 5 Décadas 2008 TR
tempranillo
85

Las Eras 2010 TC
bobal
90
Colour: cherry, garnet rim. Nose: powerfull, mineral, ripe fruit. Palate: flavourful, spicy, ripe fruit.

BODEGAS Y VIÑEDOS ILLANA

Finca Buenavista, s/n
16708 Pozoamargo (Cuenca)
☎: +34 969 147 039
Fax: +34 969 147 057
www.bodegasillana.com
info@bodegasillana.com

Casa de Illana Alma 2013 B
sauvignon blanc, airén
90
Colour: bright straw. Nose: fresh, fresh fruit, white flowers, expressive. Palate: flavourful, fruity, good acidity, balanced.

Casa de Illana Expression 2013 T
85

Casa de Illana Selección 2009 T
syrah, petit verdot
91
Colour: cherry, garnet rim. Nose: ripe fruit, spicy, creamy oak, toasty, complex, mineral. Palate: powerful, flavourful, toasty, round tannins.

Casa de Illana Tresdecinco 2009 TC
87
Colour: bright cherry. Nose: ripe fruit, sweet spices, creamy oak, medium intensity. Palate: fruity, flavourful, toasty.

Petit Yllana Bobal 2013 T
bobal
88
Colour: cherry, purple rim. Nose: red berry notes, floral, ripe fruit, wild herbs. Palate: flavourful, fruity, good acidity.

Petit Yllana Petit Verdot 2011 T
petit verdot
86
Colour: cherry, garnet rim. Nose: ripe fruit, spicy, creamy oak, toasty. Palate: powerful, flavourful, toasty, round tannins.

ELVIWINES

Finca Clos Mesorah, Ctra. T-300
43775 Falset-Marça (Tarragona)
☎: +34 618 792 963
www.elviwines.com
victor@elviwines.com

Adar de Elviwines 2008 TR
90
Colour: very deep cherry. Nose: ripe fruit, spicy, creamy oak, toasty, characterful, violet drops. Palate: powerful, flavourful, toasty, round tannins.

FINCA LOS MAJANARES

Casillas, 33
16611 Casas de Haro (Cuenca)
☎: +34 625 086 036
Fax: +34 913 658 821
jc@lbbarba.es

Casa La Loma 2013 T
Maceración Carbónica
syrah
88
Colour: cherry, purple rim. Nose: expressive, fresh fruit, red berry notes, floral. Palate: flavourful, fruity, good acidity, round tannins.

NUESTRA SEÑORA DE LA CABEZA S.C.

Tapias, 8
16708 Pozoamargo (Cuenca)
☎: +34 969 387 173
www.casagualda.com
info@casagualda.com

Casa Gualda Sauvignon Blanc 2013 B
sauvignon blanc
86
Colour: bright straw. Nose: fresh, fresh fruit, white flowers. Palate: flavourful, fruity, good acidity, balanced.

Casa Gualda Syrah 2013 T
syrah
85

Casa Gualda Syrah 2013 T
syrah
89
Colour: very deep cherry, garnet rim. Nose: warm, dried herbs, ripe fruit. Palate: flavourful, ripe fruit, long.

Casa Minda 2013 T
tempranillo, bobal, syrah
87
Colour: very deep cherry, garnet rim. Nose: overripe fruit, warm, dried herbs. Palate: flavourful, ripe fruit, long.

Casa Minda Old Roman Way 2011 T
86
Colour: cherry, garnet rim. Nose: powerfull, candied fruit, violet drops. Palate: powerful, fine bitter notes.

TEATINOS
Ctra. Minaya - San Clemente, Km. 10
16610 Casas de Fernando Alonso (Cuenca)
☎: +34 969 383 043
Fax: +34 969 383 153
www.vinoteatino.com
info@vinoteatinos.com

Teatinos B
86
Colour: bright straw. Nose: fresh, fresh fruit, white flowers, expressive. Palate: flavourful, fruity, good acidity, balanced.

Teatinos Bobal RD
bobal
84

Teatinos Dulce Moscatel 2013 Blanco dulce
moscatel
88
Colour: bright straw. Nose: white flowers, ripe fruit, honeyed notes. Palate: fruity, sweetness.

Teatinos Selección 40 Barricas Tempranillo 2008 TR
tempranillo
88
Colour: cherry, garnet rim. Nose: ripe fruit, spicy, creamy oak, toasty, complex, red berry notes. Palate: powerful, flavourful, toasty, round tannins.

Teatinos Signvm 2009 TC
87
Colour: bright cherry. Nose: ripe fruit, sweet spices, creamy oak. Palate: flavourful, fruity, toasty, round tannins.

Teatinos Syrah 2012 T
syrah
87
Colour: very deep cherry, garnet rim. Nose: warm, dried herbs, ripe fruit. Palate: flavourful, ripe fruit, long.

Teatinos Tempranillo 2013 T
tempranillo
89
Colour: cherry, purple rim. Nose: powerfull, red berry notes, ripe fruit, floral, expressive. Palate: powerful, fresh, fruity, unctuous.

DO. Ca. RIOJA

CONSEJO REGULADOR

Estambrera, 52
26006 Logroño (La Rioja)
☎ :+34 941 500 400 - Fax: +34 941 500 672
@: info@riojawine.com
www.riojawine.com

LOCATION:

Occupying the Ebro valley. To the north it borders with the Sierra de Cantabria and to the south with the Sierra de la Demanda, and is made up of different municipal districts of La Rioja, the Basque Country and Navarra. The most western region is Haro and the easternmost, Alfaro, with a distance of 100 km between the two. The region is 40 km wide.es de 40 kilómetros.

SUB-REGIONS:

Rioja Alta. This has Atlantic influences; it is the most extensive with some 20,500 Ha and produces wines well suited for ageing. **Rioja Alavesa.** A mixture of Atlantic and Mediterranean influences, with an area under cultivation of some 11,500 Ha; both young wines and wines suited for ageing are produced. **Rioja Baja.** With approximately 18,000 Ha, the climate is purely Mediterranean; white wines and rosés with a higher alcohol content and extract are produced.

GRAPE VARIETIES:

White: Viura (7,045 Ha), Malvasía, Garnacha Blanca, Chardonnay, Sauvignon Blanc, Verdejo, Maturana Blanca, Tempranillo Blanco and Torrontés.
Red: Tempranillo (majority with 38,476 Ha), Garnacha, Graciano, Mazuelo and Maturana Tinta.

FIGURES:

Vineyard surface: 63,137 – Wine-Growers: 16,706 – Wineries: 799 – 2013 Harvest rating: Good – Production 13: 251,440,000 litres – Market percentages: 63% domestic - 37% export.

SOIL:

Various types: the clayey calcareous soil arranged in terraces and small plots which are located especially in Rioja Alavesa, la Sonsierra and some regions of Rioja Alta; the clayey ferrous soil, scattered throughout the region, with vineyards located on reddish, strong soil with hard, deep rock; and the alluvial soil in the area close to the rivers; these are the most level vineyards with larger plots; here the soil is deeper and has pebbles.

CLIMATE:

Quite variable depending on the different sub-regions. In general, there is a combination of Atlantic and Mediterranean influences, the latter becoming more dominant as the terrain descends from west to east, becoming drier and hotter. The average annual rainfall is slightly over 400 mm.

VINTAGE RATING

PEÑÍNGUIDE

2009	2010	2011	2012	2013
VERY GOOD	EXCELLENT	EXCELLENT	VERY GOOD	GOOD

ALEGRE VALGAÑÓN VIÑAS & VINOS

LR-301, km 4,2
26212 Sajazarra (La Rioja)
☎: +34 609 886 652
oscar@alegrelvalganon.com

Alegre Valgañón 2011 T
88
Colour: bright cherry, garnet rim. Nose: balanced, ripe fruit, cocoa bean. Palate: flavourful, fruity, spicy, round tannins.

La Calleja 2010 T
100% tempranillo
89
Colour: cherry, garnet rim. Nose: ripe fruit, spicy, creamy oak, complex. Palate: flavourful, toasty, round tannins, long.

ALTOS DE RIOJA VITICULTORES Y BODEGUEROS

Ctra. Logroño, s/n
01300 Laguardia (Alava)
☎: +34 945 600 693
Fax: +34 945 600 692
www.altosderioja.com
altosderioja@altosderioja.com

Altos R 2007 TR
100% tempranillo
89
Colour: cherry, garnet rim. Nose: balanced, complex, ripe fruit, spicy, fine reductive notes. Palate: good structure, flavourful, round tannins.

Altos R 2010 TC
100% tempranillo
89
Colour: cherry, garnet rim. Nose: ripe fruit, spicy, creamy oak, toasty, complex. Palate: powerful, flavourful, toasty.

Altos R 2013 B
90
Colour: bright straw. Nose: white flowers, fragrant herbs, fruit expression. Palate: fresh, fruity, flavourful, balanced, elegant.

Altos R Pigeage 2010 T
92
Colour: cherry, garnet rim. Nose: ripe fruit, wild herbs, earthy notes, spicy, creamy oak. Palate: balanced, flavourful, long, balsamic.

Altos R Tempranillo 2011 T
100% tempranillo
89
Colour: cherry, garnet rim. Nose: ripe fruit, spicy, creamy oak, toasty. Palate: powerful, flavourful, toasty, round tannins.

ARBOLEDA MEDITERRÁNEA BODEGAS

Ctra. Samaniego, s/n
01307 Villabuena de Álava (Alava)
☎: +34 902 996 361
www.arboledamediterranean.com
arboleda@arboledamediterranean.com

Amantor 2011 TC
100% tempranillo
88
Colour: cherry, garnet rim. Nose: ripe fruit, wild herbs, spicy, creamy oak. Palate: balanced, flavourful, long.

Amantor Legend 2011 T
90
Colour: cherry, garnet rim. Nose: ripe fruit, spicy, creamy oak, toasty, complex, earthy notes. Palate: powerful, flavourful, toasty, round tannins.

ARBOLEDA MEDITERRÁNEA BODEGAS

Ctra. de Samaniego, 1º Travesía, 5
01307 Villabuena (Álava)

Pérez Basoco "Autor" Vendimia Seleccionada 2011 T
87
Colour: cherry, garnet rim. Nose: ripe fruit, spicy, creamy oak, toasty. Palate: powerful, flavourful, toasty.

Pérez Basoco Blanco Expresión 2013 B
100% viura
85

Pérez Basoco Tinto Expresión 2013 T
86
Colour: cherry, purple rim. Nose: red berry notes, raspberry, floral. Palate: fresh, fruity, flavourful, easy to drink.

ARBOLEDA MEDITERRÁNEA BODEGAS

C. San Ignacio, 26
26313 Uruñuela (La Rioja)

Entregado 2004 TGR
tempranillo, garnacha

88

Colour: deep cherry, orangey edge. Nose: waxy notes, tobacco, ripe fruit, spicy, aged wood nuances. Palate: fine bitter notes, elegant, flavourful, fine tannins.

Entregado 2008 TR
tempranillo, garnacha

86

Colour: light cherry. Nose: spicy, fine reductive notes, wet leather, aged wood nuances. Palate: spicy, long, correct.

Entregado 2011 TC
tempranillo, garnacha

87

Colour: cherry, garnet rim. Nose: ripe fruit, spicy, creamy oak, toasty. Palate: powerful, flavourful, toasty.

Entregado Colección de Autor 2007 T
100% tempranillo

87

Colour: cherry, garnet rim. Nose: ripe fruit, spicy, creamy oak, fine reductive notes. Palate: powerful, flavourful, toasty.

ARIBAU CUVÉE

Doctor Azcarraga, 27-29
26350 Cenicero (La Rioja)
☎: +34 933 134 347
Fax: +34 933 050 112
www.aribaurioja.com
comercial@rotllantorra.com

Aribau Cuvée 2008 TR
87

Colour: cherry, garnet rim. Nose: ripe fruit, spicy, creamy oak, toasty, fine reductive notes. Palate: powerful, flavourful, toasty.

Aribau Cuvée 2009 TC
87

Colour: light cherry, garnet rim. Nose: red berry notes, ripe fruit, wild herbs, sweet spices. Palate: toasty, easy to drink, round tannins.

ARTUKE BODEGAS Y VIÑEDOS

La Serna, 24
01307 Baños de Ebro (Álava)
☎: +34 945 623 323
Fax: +34 945 623 323
www.artuke.com
artuke@artuke.com

Artuke 2013 T Maceración Carbónica
90

Colour: cherry, purple rim. Nose: red berry notes, raspberry, floral, expressive. Palate: fresh, fruity, flavourful, easy to drink, balanced.

Artuke Finca de los Locos 2012 T
94

Colour: cherry, garnet rim. Nose: ripe fruit, wild herbs, earthy notes, spicy, creamy oak. Palate: balanced, flavourful, long, balsamic.

Artuke K4 2012 T
95

Colour: cherry, garnet rim. Nose: spicy, creamy oak, toasty, complex, dark chocolate, earthy notes, fragrant herbs, red berry notes. Palate: powerful, flavourful, toasty, round tannins.

Artuke Vendimia Seleccionada 2013 T
100% tempranillo

86

Colour: bright cherry, purple rim. Nose: toasty, ripe fruit. Palate: flavourful, spirituous, long.

BAIGORRI

Ctra. Vitoria-Logroño, Km. 53
01300 Samaniego (Álava)
☎: +34 945 609 420
www.bodegasbaigorri.com
mail@bodegasbaigorri.com

Baigorri 2012 BFB
89
Colour: bright yellow. Nose: powerfull, sweet spices, creamy oak, fragrant herbs. Palate: rich, smoky aftertaste.

Baigorri 2008 TR
tempranillo
91
Colour: bright cherry. Nose: ripe fruit, sweet spices, creamy oak, expressive. Palate: flavourful, fruity, toasty, round tannins.

Baigorri 2010 TC
tempranillo
91
Colour: cherry, garnet rim. Nose: ripe fruit, spicy, creamy oak, toasty, complex. Palate: flavourful, toasty, round tannins, balanced, complex.

Baigorri 2013 RD
84

Baigorri 2013 T Maceración Carbónica
100% tempranillo
85

Baigorri B70 2009 T
100% tempranillo
93
Colour: bright cherry, garnet rim. Nose: elegant, fresh, red berry notes, spicy. Palate: flavourful, fruity, round tannins.

Baigorri Belus 2009 T
90
Colour: very deep cherry. Nose: balanced, ripe fruit, dried herbs, toasty. Palate: balanced, round tannins.

Baigorri de Garage 2009 T
100% tempranillo
90
Colour: cherry, garnet rim. Nose: spicy, toasty, complex, ripe fruit, fruit preserve. Palate: powerful, flavourful, toasty, round tannins.

Baigorri Garnacha 2010 T
100% garnacha
92
Colour: cherry, garnet rim. Nose: ripe fruit, wild herbs, spicy, creamy oak. Palate: balanced, flavourful, long, balsamic.

BARÓN DE LEY

Ctra. Mendavia - Lodosa, Km. 5,5
31587 Mendavia (Navarra)
☎: +34 948 694 303
Fax: +34 948 694 304
www.barondeley.com
info@barondeley.com

Barón de Ley 2010 TR
90
Colour: ruby red. Nose: balanced, complex, ripe fruit, spicy. Palate: good structure, flavourful, round tannins, balanced, elegant.

Barón de Ley 2013 B
89
Colour: bright straw. Nose: fresh, fresh fruit, white flowers, expressive. Palate: flavourful, fruity, good acidity, fine bitter notes.

Barón de Ley 2013 RD
85

Baron de Ley 3 Viñas 2009 B Reserva
94
Colour: bright golden. Nose: ripe fruit, dry nuts, powerfull, toasty, aged wood nuances. Palate: flavourful, fruity, spicy, toasty, long.

Baron de Ley 7 Viñas 2007 TR
90
Colour: dark-red cherry, garnet rim. Nose: ripe fruit, tobacco, dried herbs. Palate: balanced, round tannins.

Barón de Ley Finca Monasterio 2011 T
91
Colour: cherry, garnet rim. Nose: ripe fruit, spicy, creamy oak, toasty. Palate: powerful, flavourful, toasty, round tannins.

Barón de Ley Rosado de Lágrima 2013 RD
87
Colour: raspberry rose. Nose: elegant, dried flowers, fragrant herbs, red berry notes. Palate: light-bodied, flavourful, good acidity, long.

Barón de Ley Varietales Garnacha 2011 T
100% garnacha
91
Colour: cherry, garnet rim. Nose: earthy notes, spicy, scrubland. Palate: balanced, flavourful, long, balsamic, easy to drink.

Barón de Ley Varietales Graciano 2010 T
100% graciano
90
Colour: cherry, garnet rim. Nose: ripe fruit, wild herbs, earthy notes, spicy, creamy oak. Palate: balanced, flavourful, long, balsamic.

Barón de Ley Varietales Maturana 2011 T
100% maturana
90
Colour: cherry, garnet rim. Nose: ripe fruit, wild herbs, earthy notes, spicy, creamy oak. Palate: balanced, flavourful, long, balsamic.

Barón de Ley Varietales Tempranillo 2010 T
100% tempranillo
92
Colour: cherry, garnet rim. Nose: ripe fruit, spicy, creamy oak, toasty, complex. Palate: powerful, flavourful, toasty, round tannins.

BERARTE VIÑEDOS Y BODEGAS
Mayor, 37
01307 Villabuena De Alava (Alava)
☎: +34 945 609 034
Fax: +34 945 609 034
www.berarte.es
info@berarte.es

Berarte 2009 TR
tempranillo
88
Colour: cherry, garnet rim. Nose: ripe fruit, spicy, creamy oak, toasty, complex. Palate: powerful, flavourful, toasty.

Berarte 2011 TC
tempranillo
86
Colour: bright cherry. Nose: ripe fruit, sweet spices, creamy oak, medium intensity. Palate: fruity, flavourful, toasty.

Berarte 2013 T
tempranillo
84

Berarte Semidulce 2013 B
viura
84

BODEGA ABEL MENDOZA MONGE
Ctra. Peñacerrada, 7
26338 San Vicente de la Sonsierra (La Rioja)
☎: +34 941 308 010
Fax: +34 941 308 010
jarrarte.abelmendoza@gmail.com

Abel Mendoza Graciano Grano a Grano 2011 T
100% graciano
94
Colour: bright cherry. Nose: ripe fruit, sweet spices, expressive, scrubland. Palate: flavourful, fruity, toasty, round tannins, complex.

Abel Mendoza Malvasía 2013 BFB
malvasía
88
Colour: bright yellow. Nose: powerfull, ripe fruit, sweet spices, fragrant herbs. Palate: rich, flavourful, fresh, good acidity.

Abel Mendoza Selección Personal 2011 T
100% tempranillo
93
Colour: cherry, garnet rim. Nose: red berry notes, ripe fruit, spicy, toasty, complex, earthy notes, elegant. Palate: flavourful, toasty, round tannins.

Abel Mendoza Tempranillo Grano a Grano 2011 T
100% tempranillo
94
Colour: cherry, garnet rim. Nose: balanced, elegant, complex, red berry notes, ripe fruit, spicy. Palate: good structure, full, flavourful.

Abel Mendoza Viura 2013 BFB
100% viura
90
Colour: bright yellow. Nose: ripe fruit, sweet spices, creamy oak, fragrant herbs. Palate: rich, smoky aftertaste, flavourful, fresh, good acidity, sweet.

Jarrarte 2009 T
100% tempranillo
89
Colour: cherry, garnet rim. Nose: ripe fruit, balanced, spicy. Palate: good structure, ripe fruit, round tannins.

Jarrarte 2013 T Maceración Carbónica
100% tempranillo

87

Colour: cherry, purple rim. Nose: red berry notes, balanced, expressive. Palate: easy to drink, good finish.

BODEGA CLÁSSICA
Camino del Campo Santo s/n
26338 San Vicente de la Sonsierra
(La Rioja)
☎: +34 941 271 217
Fax: +34 941 272 911
www.bodegaclassica.com
info@bodegaclassica.com

Hacienda López de Haro 2008 TR

89

Colour: cherry, garnet rim. Nose: ripe fruit, spicy, creamy oak, toasty, fine reductive notes. Palate: powerful, flavourful, toasty, round tannins, elegant.

Hacienda López de Haro 2010 TC

88

Colour: cherry, garnet rim. Nose: red berry notes, ripe fruit, spicy, creamy oak, toasty. Palate: powerful, flavourful, toasty, round tannins, balanced.

BODEGA CONTADOR
Ctra. Baños de Ebro, Km. 1
26338 San Vicente de la Sonsierra
(La Rioja)
☎: +34 941 334 228
Fax: +34 941 334 537
www.bodegacontador.com
info@bodegacontador.com

Carmen 2009 TGR
tempranillo, garnacha, graciano, mazuelo

94

Colour: cherry, garnet rim. Nose: ripe fruit, spicy, creamy oak, toasty, complex. Palate: powerful, flavourful, toasty, round tannins.

Contador 2012 T
tempranillo, graciano, mazuelo

99

Colour: cherry, garnet rim. Nose: sweet spices, creamy oak, ripe fruit, toasty, mineral. Palate: powerful, fruity, ripe fruit, fine bitter notes, good acidity.

La Cueva del Contador 2012 T
tempranillo, garnacha

96

Colour: cherry, garnet rim. Nose: spicy, creamy oak, toasty, complex, dark chocolate, red berry notes. Palate: powerful, flavourful, toasty, round tannins.

La Viña de Andrés Romeo 2012 T
100% tempranillo

95

Colour: very deep cherry. Nose: powerfull, dark chocolate, toasty, ripe fruit, fruit expression. Palate: powerful, spicy, ripe fruit, round tannins.

Predicador 2012 B

92

Colour: bright straw. Nose: white flowers, fresh fruit, expressive, fine lees, dried herbs. Palate: flavourful, fruity, good acidity, balanced.

Predicador 2012 T
tempranillo, garnacha

93

Colour: cherry, garnet rim. Nose: ripe fruit, spicy, creamy oak, toasty, complex, red berry notes. Palate: powerful, flavourful, toasty, round tannins.

Predicador 2013 B
garnacha blanca, viura, malvasía

92

Colour: bright straw. Nose: powerfull, sweet spices, creamy oak, fragrant herbs, fruit expression. Palate: rich, flavourful, fresh, good acidity.

Qué Bonito Cacareaba 2013 B
garnacha blanca, viura, malvasía

96

Colour: bright straw. Nose: white flowers, expressive, fine lees, dried herbs, candied fruit, characterful, complex. Palate: flavourful, fruity, good acidity, balanced.

BODEGA IGNACIO PETRALANDA
Avda. La Estación, 44
26360 Fuenmayor (La Rioja)
☎: +34 608 893 732
www.vinoart.es
info@vinoart.es

Nonno 2008 TC
tempranillo, mazuelo

88 ♥

Colour: cherry, garnet rim. Nose: ripe fruit, wild herbs, spicy, creamy oak. Palate: balanced, flavourful, long, balsamic.

BODEGA MUSEO ONTAÑON

Avda. de Aragón, 3
26006 Logroño (La Rioja)
☎: +34 690 858 190
Fax: +34 941 270 482
enoturismo@ontanon.es

Arteso 2008 TC

garnacha, graciano, tempranillo

93

Colour: cherry, garnet rim. Nose: ripe fruit, wild herbs, earthy notes, spicy, creamy oak. Palate: flavourful, long, balsamic, balanced.

Arteso 2010 TC

garnacha, graciano, tempranillo

92

Colour: cherry, garnet rim. Nose: ripe fruit, wild herbs, spicy, creamy oak, expressive. Palate: balanced, flavourful, long, balsamic.

Ontañón 2005 TR

tempranillo, graciano

89

Colour: deep cherry, garnet rim. Nose: waxy notes, old leather, dried herbs. Palate: balanced, ripe fruit, round tannins.

Ontañón 2011 TC

tempranillo, garnacha

89

Colour: bright cherry, purple rim. Nose: balanced, expressive, ripe fruit, spicy, dried herbs. Palate: flavourful, easy to drink.

Vetiver 2012 B

viura

87

Colour: bright straw. Nose: fresh, fresh fruit, white flowers, expressive. Palate: flavourful, fruity, good acidity, balanced.

BODEGA VIÑA EGUILUZ

Camino de San Bartolomé, 10
26339 Abalos (La Rioja)
☎: +34 941 334 064
Fax: +34 941 583 022
www.bodegaseguiluz.es
info@bodegaseguiluz.es

Eguiluz 2006 TR

100% tempranillo

90

Colour: cherry, garnet rim. Nose: spicy, fine reductive notes, aged wood nuances, fruit liqueur notes. Palate: spicy, elegant, long, balanced.

Eguiluz 2010 TC

100% tempranillo

84

Eguiluz 2013 T

100% tempranillo

85

BODEGA Y VIÑEDOS FUENTE VIEJA

Ctra. Calahorra, km 4
26560 Autol (La Rioja)
☎: +34 941 024 484
Fax: +34 941 024 484
www.bodegasfuentevieja.com
info@bodegasfuentevieja.com

Fuente Vieja 2010 TC

88

Colour: cherry, garnet rim. Nose: fruit preserve, fruit liqueur notes, spicy. Palate: flavourful, pruney, balsamic.

Fuente Vieja Garnacha 2012 T

garnacha

88

Colour: cherry, purple rim. Nose: powerfull, red berry notes, ripe fruit, floral, expressive. Palate: powerful, fresh, fruity, unctuous.

Fuente Vieja Graciano 2012 T

graciano

85

Fuente Vieja Tempranillo 2012 T

tempranillo

87

Colour: very deep cherry, garnet rim. Nose: overripe fruit, warm, dried herbs. Palate: flavourful, ripe fruit, long.

Reja de Plata 2011 TC

86

Colour: dark-red cherry, garnet rim. Nose: powerfull, ripe fruit, toasty, spicy, waxy notes. Palate: fruity, balsamic.

BODEGA Y VIÑEDOS SOLABAL

Camino San Bartolomé, 6
26339 Abalos (La Rioja)
☎: +34 941 334 492
Fax: +34 941 308 164
www.solabal.es
solabal@solabal.es

Esculle de Solabal 2010 T

tempranillo

89

Colour: cherry, garnet rim. Nose: ripe fruit, spicy, creamy oak, toasty, complex. Palate: powerful, flavourful, toasty, round tannins, balanced.

Muñarrate de Solabal 2013 B

viura, malvasía

86

Colour: bright straw, greenish rim. Nose: fresh fruit, floral, medium intensity. Palate: correct, sweetness, easy to drink.

Muñarrate de Solabal 2013 RD
85

Muñarrate de Solabal 2013 T
tempranillo
84

Solabal 2008 TR
tempranillo
89
Colour: cherry, garnet rim. Nose: balanced, complex, ripe fruit, spicy. Palate: good structure, flavourful, round tannins, elegant.

Solabal 2011 TC
tempranillo
88
Colour: cherry, garnet rim. Nose: ripe fruit, spicy, creamy oak, toasty. Palate: powerful, flavourful, toasty.

Vala de Solabal 2010 T
tempranillo
92
Colour: cherry, garnet rim. Nose: balanced, complex, ripe fruit, spicy. Palate: good structure, flavourful, round tannins.

BODEGAS 1808
Ctra. El Villar Polígono 7 Biribil, 33
Apdo. 26
01300 Laguardia (Alava)
☎: +34 685 752 384
Fax: +34 945 293 450
www.rioja1808.com
1808@rioja1808.com

1808 Temperamento Natural 2008 TR
tempranillo
90
Colour: cherry, garnet rim. Nose: ripe fruit, spicy, complex. Palate: powerful, flavourful, toasty, round tannins.

1808 Temperamento Natural 2011 TC
tempranillo
88
Colour: bright cherry. Nose: ripe fruit, sweet spices, creamy oak, medium intensity. Palate: fruity, flavourful, toasty.

BODEGAS AGE
Barrio de la Estación, s/n
26360 Fuenmayor (La Rioja)
☎: +34 941 293 500
Fax: +34 941 293 501
www.bodegasage.com
bodegasage@pernod-ricard.com

Siglo 2007 TGR
tempranillo, graciano, mazuelo
88
Colour: dark-red cherry, orangey edge. Nose: balanced, spicy, old leather, varietal, animal reductive notes. Palate: balanced, easy to drink.

Siglo 2009 TR
tempranillo, graciano, mazuelo
87
Colour: dark-red cherry, orangey edge. Nose: ripe fruit, spicy, tobacco. Palate: flavourful, easy to drink, fine tannins.

Siglo Saco 2011 TC
tempranillo, garnacha, mazuelo
87
Colour: cherry, garnet rim. Nose: ripe fruit, spicy, medium intensity. Palate: toasty, round tannins, easy to drink.

BODEGAS ALTOS DEL MARQUÉS
Ctra. Navarrete, 1
26372 Hornos de Moncalvillo (La Rioja)
☎: +34 941 286 728
Fax: +34 941 286 729
www.altosdelmarques.com
info@altosdelmarques.com

Altos del Marqués 2010 TC
100% tempranillo
88
Colour: cherry, garnet rim. Nose: balanced, ripe fruit, spicy. Palate: good structure, flavourful, round tannins.

Altos del Marqués 2012 T
85

BODEGAS ALTÚN

Las Piscinas, 30
01307 Baños de Ebro (Álava)
☎: +34 945 609 317
Fax: +34 945 609 309
www.bodegasaltun.com
altun@bodegasaltun.com

Albiker 2013 T Maceración Carbónica
87
Colour: cherry, purple rim. Nose: fresh fruit, red berry notes, floral, tropical fruit. Palate: flavourful, fruity, good acidity.

Altún 2008 TR
tempranillo
90
Colour: cherry, garnet rim. Nose: red berry notes, ripe fruit, spicy, creamy oak, toasty, complex, earthy notes. Palate: powerful, flavourful, toasty, round tannins, balanced.

Altún 2011 TC
tempranillo
91
Colour: bright cherry. Nose: ripe fruit, sweet spices, creamy oak, expressive, mineral. Palate: flavourful, fruity, toasty, balanced, elegant.

Altún 2012 TC
tempranillo
90
Colour: cherry, garnet rim. Nose: ripe fruit, spicy, creamy oak, toasty, complex, mineral. Palate: powerful, flavourful, toasty, round tannins, balanced.

Ana de Altún 2013 B
86
Colour: bright straw. Nose: fresh, fresh fruit, white flowers, expressive. Palate: flavourful, fruity, good acidity, balanced.

Everest 2011 T
100% tempranillo
93
Colour: cherry, garnet rim. Nose: ripe fruit, spicy, creamy oak, toasty, complex, dark chocolate, earthy notes. Palate: powerful, flavourful, toasty, round tannins, balanced.

Secreto de Altún 2011 T
tempranillo
93
Colour: cherry, garnet rim. Nose: balanced, complex, ripe fruit, spicy, dry stone, balsamic herbs. Palate: good structure, flavourful, round tannins, elegant.

Secreto de Altún 2012 T
tempranillo
92
Colour: bright cherry. Nose: sweet spices, creamy oak, expressive, red berry notes, raspberry. Palate: flavourful, fruity, toasty, balanced.

BODEGAS AMADOR GARCÍA

Avda. Río Ebro, 68 - 70
01307 Baños de Ebro (Álava)
☎: +34 945 290 385
Fax: +34 975 290 373
www.bodegasamadorgarcia.com
pbodegasamadorgarcia@gmail.com

Amador García 2013 BFB
100% viura
88
Colour: bright straw. Nose: white flowers, fragrant herbs, fruit expression. Palate: fresh, fruity, flavourful, balanced, elegant.

Amador García Vendimia Seleccionada 2011 TC
86
Colour: cherry, garnet rim. Nose: fruit preserve, fruit liqueur notes, spicy. Palate: flavourful, pruney, balsamic.

Peñagudo 2011 TC
86
Colour: cherry, garnet rim. Nose: fruit preserve, fruit liqueur notes, spicy. Palate: flavourful, pruney, balsamic.

Peñagudo 2013 B
100% viura
82

Peñagudo 2013 T
85

BODEGAS AMAREN

Ctra. Baños de Ebro, s/n
01307 Villabuena (Álava)
☎: +34 945 175 240
Fax: +34 945 174 566
bodegas@bodegasamaren.com

Amaren 2011 BFB
92
Colour: bright yellow. Nose: powerfull, ripe fruit, sweet spices, creamy oak, fragrant herbs. Palate: rich, smoky aftertaste, flavourful, fresh, good acidity.

Amaren Graciano 2009 T
100% graciano
93
Colour: very deep cherry, garnet rim. Nose: powerfull, ripe fruit, dark chocolate. Palate: powerful, toasty, roasted-coffee aftertaste.

Amaren Tempranillo 2006 TR
100% tempranillo
92
Colour: very deep cherry. Nose: ripe fruit, spicy, creamy oak, toasty, characterful. Palate: powerful, flavourful, toasty, round tannins.

Ángeles de Amaren 2008 T
93
Colour: very deep cherry. Nose: ripe fruit, spicy, creamy oak, toasty, characterful. Palate: powerful, flavourful, toasty, round tannins.

BODEGAS AMÉZOLA DE LA MORA S.A.

Paraje Viña Vieja, s/n
26359 Torremontalbo (La Rioja)
☎: +34 941 454 532
Fax: +34 941 454 537
www.bodegasamezola.es
info@bodegasamezola.es

Iñigo Amézola 2010 BFB
100% viura
90
Colour: bright yellow. Nose: powerfull, ripe fruit, sweet spices, creamy oak, fragrant herbs. Palate: rich, smoky aftertaste, flavourful, fresh, good acidity.

Iñigo Amézola 2010 T Fermentado en Barrica
100% tempranillo
89
Colour: cherry, garnet rim. Nose: ripe fruit, wild herbs, creamy oak. Palate: flavourful, long, balsamic.

Señorío Amézola 2007 TR
87
Colour: ruby red. Nose: spicy, fine reductive notes, wet leather, aged wood nuances, fruit liqueur notes. Palate: spicy, fine tannins.

Solar Amézola 2004 TGR
87
Colour: pale ruby, brick rim edge. Nose: fine reductive notes, wet leather, aged wood nuances, fruit liqueur notes. Palate: spicy, fine tannins, long.

Viña Amézola 2010 TC
88
Colour: cherry, garnet rim. Nose: ripe fruit, spicy, creamy oak, toasty, fine reductive notes. Palate: powerful, flavourful, toasty.

BODEGAS ANTONIO ALCARAZ

Ctra. Vitoria-Logroño, Km. 57
01300 Laguardia (Álava)
☎: +34 658 959 745
Fax: +34 965 888 359
www.antonio-alcaraz.es
rioja@antonio-alcaraz.es

Altea de Antonio Alcaraz 2011 TC
100% tempranillo
88
Colour: bright cherry. Nose: ripe fruit, sweet spices, creamy oak, medium intensity. Palate: fruity, flavourful, toasty.

Antonio Alcaraz 2010 TR
89
Colour: cherry, garnet rim. Nose: ripe fruit, spicy, creamy oak, toasty. Palate: powerful, flavourful, spicy, toasty.

Antonio Alcaraz 2011 TC

88

Colour: deep cherry. Nose: ripe fruit, spicy, toasty. Palate: powerful, flavourful, toasty, round tannins.

Gloria Antonio Alcaraz 2010 TC
100% tempranillo

90

Colour: deep cherry, garnet rim. Nose: elegant, balanced, fragrant herbs, spicy. Palate: easy to drink, correct, ripe fruit.

Les Fonts D'Algar 2011 TC

89

Colour: cherry, garnet rim. Nose: ripe fruit, spicy, creamy oak, toasty, complex. Palate: powerful, flavourful, toasty, round tannins.

Les Fonts D'Algar Selección 2010 T

90

Colour: bright cherry, garnet rim. Nose: balanced, ripe fruit, sweet spices. Palate: long, flavourful, elegant, spicy.

Men to Men 2010 T

90

Colour: cherry, garnet rim. Nose: ripe fruit, spicy, creamy oak, toasty, complex, earthy notes. Palate: powerful, flavourful, toasty, round tannins.

BODEGAS ARTE MENTOR
Camino de Baños de Ebro, 21
01307 Villabuena de Alava (Álava)
☎: +34 902 996 361
www.bodegasmentor.es
info@bodegasmentor.com

Mentor 2010 TC
100% tempranillo

90

Colour: cherry, garnet rim. Nose: red berry notes, ripe fruit, spicy, creamy oak, toasty, earthy notes. Palate: powerful, flavourful, toasty, round tannins.

BODEGAS BAGORDI
Ctra. de Estella, Km. 32
31261 Andosilla (Navarra)
☎: +34 948 674 860
Fax: +34 948 674 238
www.bagordi.com
info@bagordi.com

Bagordi 2008 TR

88

Colour: cherry, garnet rim. Nose: ripe fruit, spicy, creamy oak, fine reductive notes. Palate: powerful, flavourful, toasty.

Bagordi Graciano 2010 TC
100% graciano

86

Colour: cherry, garnet rim. Nose: ripe fruit, spicy, creamy oak, toasty. Palate: powerful, flavourful, toasty.

Usoa de Bagordi 2013 B

85

Colour: cherry, garnet rim. Nose: ripe fruit, wild herbs, spicy, creamy oak. Palate: flavourful, long, balsamic.

Usoa de Bagordi 2013 T

83

Usoa de Bagordi 2010 TC

87

Colour: cherry, garnet rim. Nose: ripe fruit, wild herbs, spicy, creamy oak. Palate: flavourful, long, balsamic.

Usoa de Bagordi 2012 BFB

84

BODEGAS BASAGOITI
Torrent, 38
08391 Tiana (Barcelona)
☎: +34 933 950 811
Fax: +34 933 955 500
www.basagoiti.es
info@parxet.es

Basagoiti 2011 TC
tempranillo, garnacha

89

Colour: cherry, garnet rim. Nose: fruit preserve, fruit liqueur notes, spicy. Palate: flavourful, pruney, balsamic.

Fuera del Rebaño 2012 T
tempranillo

90

Colour: bright cherry. Nose: ripe fruit, sweet spices, creamy oak, medium intensity. Palate: fruity, flavourful, toasty.

Nabari 2013 T
tempranillo, garnacha

84

BODEGAS BENJAMÍN DE ROTHSCHILD & VEGA SICILIA S.A.

Ctra. Logroño - Vitoria, km. 61
01309 Leza (Alava)
☎: +34 983 680 147
Fax: +34 983 680 263
www.vegasicilia.com
vegasicilia@vega-sicilia.com

Macán 2011 T
100% tempranillo
94
Colour: cherry, garnet rim. Nose: ripe fruit, spicy, creamy oak, toasty, complex, dark chocolate, earthy notes. Palate: powerful, flavourful, toasty, round tannins.

Macán Clásico 2011 T
100% tempranillo
93
Colour: cherry, garnet rim. Nose: fruit preserve, fruit liqueur notes, spicy, creamy oak. Palate: flavourful, pruney, balsamic.

BODEGAS BERBERANA

Ctra. El Ciego s/n
26350 Cenicero (La Rioja)
☎: +34 913 878 612
www.berberana.com
abasilio@unitedwineries.com

Berberana Viña Alarde 2008 TR
86
Colour: pale ruby, brick rim edge. Nose: spicy, fine reductive notes, wet leather, aged wood nuances. Palate: spicy, fine tannins, long.

BODEGAS BERCEO

Cuevas, 32-36
26200 Haro (La Rioja)
☎: +34 941 310 744
Fax: +34 948 670 259
www.gurpegui.es
bodegas@gurpegui.es

Berceo "Nueva Generación" 2012 T
tempranillo, garnacha, graciano
90
Colour: dark-red cherry, garnet rim. Nose: toasty, sweet spices, ripe fruit. Palate: balanced, ripe fruit, long.

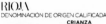

Berceo Selección 2012 T
tempranillo, mazuelo, graciano
90
Colour: deep cherry, garnet rim. Nose: powerfull, creamy oak, toasty, ripe fruit. Palate: correct, fruity aftestaste, long.

Gonzalo de Berceo 2006 TGR
tempranillo, graciano, mazuelo

89

Colour: cherry, garnet rim. Nose: balanced, complex, ripe fruit, spicy. Palate: good structure, flavourful, round tannins.

Gonzalo de Berceo 2009 TR
tempranillo, graciano, mazuelo, garnacha

89

Colour: cherry, garnet rim. Nose: balsamic herbs, fresh, ripe fruit, spicy. Palate: balanced, balsamic, round tannins.

Los Dominios de Berceo "Reserva 36" S/C TR
tempranillo

91

Colour: cherry, garnet rim. Nose: ripe fruit, spicy, creamy oak, toasty, complex, tobacco. Palate: powerful, flavourful, toasty, round tannins.

Los Dominios de Berceo 2013 T
tempranillo

89

Colour: cherry, purple rim. Nose: expressive, red berry notes, floral. Palate: flavourful, fruity, good acidity, round tannins, balanced.

Viña Berceo 2012 TC
tempranillo, garnacha, graciano

89

Colour: dark-red cherry. Nose: ripe fruit, spicy, toasty. Palate: powerful, flavourful, toasty, round tannins.

BODEGAS BERONIA
Ctra. Ollauri - Nájera, Km. 1,8
26220 Ollauri (La Rioja)
☎: +34 941 338 000
Fax: +34 941 338 266
www.beronia.es
beronia@beronia.es

Beronia 2007 TGR
tempranillo, graciano, mazuelo

90

Colour: pale ruby, brick rim edge. Nose: elegant, spicy, fine reductive notes, wet leather, fruit liqueur notes. Palate: spicy, fine tannins, elegant, long.

Beronia 2010 TR
tempranillo, graciano, mazuelo

89

Colour: ruby red. Nose: balanced, complex, ripe fruit, spicy, creamy oak. Palate: good structure, flavourful, round tannins, balanced.

Beronia 2011 TC
tempranillo, garnacha, mazuelo

88

Colour: cherry, garnet rim. Nose: ripe fruit, spicy, creamy oak, toasty. Palate: powerful, flavourful, toasty.

Beronia Graciano 2011 T
graciano

89

Colour: cherry, garnet rim. Nose: ripe fruit, wild herbs, earthy notes, spicy, creamy oak. Palate: balanced, flavourful, long, balsamic.

Beronia Mazuelo 2010 TR
mazuelo

89

Colour: cherry, garnet rim. Nose: expressive, old leather, spicy, scrubland. Palate: correct, fine bitter notes, round tannins.

Beronia Selección 198 Barricas 2008 TR
tempranillo, mazuelo, graciano
91
Colour: cherry, garnet rim. Nose: ripe fruit, spicy, creamy oak, toasty, complex. Palate: powerful, flavourful, toasty, round tannins.

Beronia Tempranillo Elaboración Especial 2012 T
tempranillo
90
Colour: very deep cherry, garnet rim. Nose: powerfull, ripe fruit, roasted coffee, dark chocolate. Palate: powerful, toasty, flavourful, balanced.

Beronia Viñas Viejas 2011 T
tempranillo
89
Colour: cherry, garnet rim. Nose: ripe fruit, spicy, creamy oak, toasty, complex. Palate: powerful, flavourful, toasty, balanced.

III a.C., Beronia 2011 T
tempranillo, graciano, mazuelo
92
Colour: cherry, garnet rim. Nose: ripe fruit, spicy, creamy oak, toasty, complex, dark chocolate, earthy notes. Palate: powerful, flavourful, toasty, round tannins.

BODEGAS BILBAÍNAS
Estación, 3
26200 Haro (La Rioja)
☎: +34 941 310 147
www.bodegasbilbainas.com
info@bodegasbilbainas.com

Bodegas Bilbainas Garnacha 2010 T
100% garnacha
92
Colour: cherry, garnet rim. Nose: ripe fruit, wild herbs, earthy notes, spicy, creamy oak. Palate: balanced, flavourful, long, balsamic.

Bodegas Bilbainas Graciano 2007 T
100% graciano
91
Colour: cherry, garnet rim. Nose: wild herbs, earthy notes, spicy, varietal. Palate: balanced, flavourful, long, balsamic.

La Vicalanda 2008 TGR
100% tempranillo
94
Colour: deep cherry, orangey edge. Nose: waxy notes, tobacco, ripe fruit, spicy, aged wood nuances. Palate: fine bitter notes, elegant, flavourful, fine tannins.

La Vicalanda 2009 TR
100% tempranillo
91
Colour: cherry, garnet rim. Nose: ripe fruit, spicy, creamy oak, toasty. Palate: powerful, flavourful, toasty, round tannins.

Viña Pomal "Alto de la Caseta" 2008 T
100% tempranillo
91
Colour: very deep cherry. Nose: ripe fruit, spicy, creamy oak, toasty, characterful. Palate: powerful, flavourful, toasty, round tannins.

Viña Pomal 2009 TR
100% tempranillo
90
Colour: cherry, garnet rim. Nose: ripe fruit, spicy, creamy oak, toasty, complex. Palate: powerful, flavourful, toasty, round tannins.

Viña Pomal 2012 B
88
Colour: bright yellow. Nose: powerfull, ripe fruit, sweet spices, creamy oak, fragrant herbs. Palate: rich, smoky aftertaste, flavourful, fresh, good acidity.

BODEGAS CAMPILLO
Ctra. de Logroño, s/n
01300 Laguardia (Álava)
☎: +34 945 600 826
Fax: +34 945 600 837
www.bodegascampillo.es
info@bodegascampillo.es

Campillo 2004 TGR
tempranillo, graciano
92
Colour: pale ruby, brick rim edge. Nose: elegant, spicy, fine reductive notes, wet leather, aged wood nuances, fruit liqueur notes. Palate: spicy, fine tannins, elegant, long, balanced.

DO Ca. RIOJA / D.O.P

Campillo 2010 TC
100% tempranillo

90

Colour: cherry, garnet rim. Nose: ripe fruit, spicy, creamy oak, toasty, complex. Palate: powerful, flavourful, toasty, round tannins, balanced.

Campillo 2013 BFB
viura, malvasía, chardonnay

90

Colour: bright straw. Nose: ripe fruit, dried herbs, spicy, creamy oak, expressive. Palate: rich, flavourful, long, balsamic.

Campillo 2013 RD
100% tempranillo

84

Campillo Finca Cuesta Clara 2008 TR
tempranillo peludo

94

Colour: cherry, garnet rim. Nose: ripe fruit, spicy, creamy oak, toasty, complex. Palate: powerful, flavourful, toasty, round tannins, balanced, elegant.

Campillo Reserva Especial 2008 TR
tempranillo, graciano, cabernet sauvignon

90

Colour: cherry, garnet rim. Nose: complex, ripe fruit, spicy. Palate: good structure, flavourful, round tannins, elegant.

Campillo Reserva Selecta 2007 TR
100% tempranillo

92

Colour: deep cherry. Nose: ripe fruit, spicy, creamy oak, toasty, complex, earthy notes. Palate: powerful, flavourful, toasty, round tannins, elegant.

El Niño de Campillo 2012 T
100% tempranillo

90

Colour: cherry, purple rim. Nose: floral, red berry notes, raspberry, fragrant herbs, spicy. Palate: fresh, fruity, flavourful, easy to drink.

BODEGAS CAMPO VIEJO
Camino de la Puebla, 50
26006 Logroño (La Rioja)
☎: +34 941 279 900
www.campoviejo.com
campoviejo@pernod-ricard.com

Alcorta 2009 TR
tempranillo

90

Colour: cherry, garnet rim. Nose: ripe fruit, spicy, creamy oak, toasty, complex, dark chocolate, earthy notes. Palate: powerful, flavourful, toasty, round tannins.

Alcorta 2011 TC
tempranillo

89

Colour: cherry, garnet rim. Nose: red berry notes, ripe fruit, spicy, creamy oak, toasty, earthy notes. Palate: powerful, flavourful, toasty, round tannins.

Azpilicueta 2009 TR
tempranillo, graciano, mazuelo

91

Colour: very deep cherry. Nose: ripe fruit, spicy, creamy oak, toasty, characterful. Palate: powerful, flavourful, toasty, round tannins.

Azpilicueta 2011 TC
tempranillo, graciano, mazuelo

91

Colour: cherry, garnet rim. Nose: ripe fruit, spicy, creamy oak, toasty, complex, red berry notes. Palate: powerful, flavourful, toasty, round tannins.

Azpilicueta 2013 B
viura

90

Colour: bright straw. Nose: fresh, fresh fruit, white flowers, expressive. Palate: flavourful, fruity, good acidity, balanced, long.

Azpilicueta 2013 RD
tempranillo, viura

90

Colour: onion pink. Nose: elegant, candied fruit, dried flowers, fragrant herbs, red berry notes. Palate: light-bodied, flavourful, good acidity, long, spicy, balanced.

Campo Viejo 2008 TGR
tempranillo, graciano, mazuelo

88

Colour: pale ruby, brick rim edge. Nose: spicy, fine reductive notes, aged wood nuances, fruit liqueur notes. Palate: spicy, fine tannins.

Campo Viejo 2011 TC
tempranillo, garnacha, mazuelo

87

Colour: bright cherry. Nose: ripe fruit, sweet spices, creamy oak, medium intensity. Palate: fruity, flavourful, toasty.

Campo Viejo 2012 T
tempranillo, garnacha

87 🌱

Colour: dark-red cherry, garnet rim. Nose: ripe fruit, scrubland, medium intensity. Palate: correct, easy to drink, good finish.

Campo Viejo 2009 TR
tempranillo, graciano, mazuelo

88

Colour: cherry, garnet rim. Nose: ripe fruit, spicy, creamy oak, toasty, complex. Palate: powerful, flavourful, toasty, round tannins.

Dominio Campo Viejo 2011 T
tempranillo, graciano, mazuelo

92

Colour: very deep cherry. Nose: ripe fruit, spicy, creamy oak, toasty, charcterful. Palate: powerful, flavourful, toasty, round tannins.

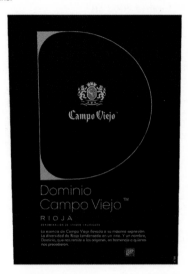

Félix Azpilicueta Colección Privada 2009 T
tempranillo, graciano, mazuelo

92

Colour: dark-red cherry. Nose: ripe fruit, toasty, complex, cocoa bean. Palate: flavourful, long, balanced, round tannins.

Félix Azpilicueta Colección Privada 2013 BFB
viura

89

Colour: bright yellow. Nose: creamy oak, faded flowers, toasty. Palate: rich, spicy, long.

BODEGAS CASA PRIMICIA
Camino de la Hoya, 1
1300 Laguardia (Álava)
☎: +34 945 600 296
Fax: +34 945 621 252
www.bodegasprimicia.com
info@bodegascasaprimicia.com

Casa Primicia Garnacha 2010 TC
100% garnacha

86

Colour: deep cherry, garnet rim. Nose: grassy, wild herbs, spicy. Palate: correct, fruity, good acidity.

Casa Primicia Tempranillo 2010 T
100% tempranillo

87

Colour: cherry, garnet rim. Nose: ripe fruit, spicy, creamy oak, toasty. Palate: toasty, round tannins, ripe fruit.

Julián Madrid 2008 TR

88

Colour: very deep cherry, garnet rim. Nose: powerfull, ripe fruit, cocoa bean. Palate: balanced, round tannins, spicy.

BODEGAS CASTILLO DE MENDOZA, S.L.
Paraje San Juan, s/n
26338 San Vicente de la Sonsierra
(La Rioja)
☎: +34 941 334 496
Fax: +34 941 334 566
www.castillodemendoza.com
comercial@castillodemendoza.com

Castillo de Mendoza 2006 TR
tempranillo

89

Colour: ruby red. Nose: ripe fruit, spicy, creamy oak, wet leather, tobacco. Palate: powerful, flavourful, spicy.

Evento Castillo de Mendoza 2004 T
tempranillo

92

Colour: pale ruby, brick rim edge. Nose: elegant, spicy, fine reductive notes, wet leather, aged wood nuances, fruit liqueur notes. Palate: spicy, fine tannins, elegant, long.

Momilde 2010 TC
tempranillo

89

Colour: cherry, garnet rim. Nose: ripe fruit, spicy, creamy oak, aromatic coffee. Palate: balanced, flavourful, long, toasty.

Noralba Agricultura Ecológica 2011 TC
tempranillo, graciano

90 ♣

Colour: cherry, garnet rim. Nose: ripe fruit, spicy, creamy oak, toasty, complex. Palate: powerful, flavourful, toasty, round tannins.

Vitarán 2011 TC
tempranillo

87

Colour: cherry, garnet rim. Nose: ripe fruit, balsamic herbs, creamy oak, medium intensity. Palate: flavourful, ripe fruit, toasty.

BODEGAS CASTILLO DE SAJAZARRA
Del Río, s/n
26212 Sajazarra (La Rioja)
☎: +34 941 320 066
Fax: +34 941 320 251
www.castillodesajazarra.com
bodega@castillodesajazarra.com

Castillo de Sajazarra 2008 TR

89

Colour: cherry, garnet rim. Nose: ripe fruit, spicy, creamy oak, toasty, complex. Palate: powerful, flavourful, toasty, round tannins.

Digma 2006 TR
100% tempranillo

93

Colour: pale ruby, brick rim edge. Nose: ripe fruit, fragrant herbs, mineral, sweet spices, balanced, elegant. Palate: flavourful, rich, spicy, long, balsamic, elegant.

Digma Graciano 2009 TR
90
Colour: cherry, garnet rim. Nose: ripe fruit, wild herbs, earthy notes, spicy, creamy oak. Palate: balanced, flavourful, long, balsamic.

Digma Tempranillo 2009 TR
100% tempranillo
93
Colour: cherry, garnet rim. Nose: powerfull, red berry notes, ripe fruit, spicy, wild herbs, mineral. Palate: balanced, round, flavourful, spicy, long.

Solar de Líbano 2008 TR
89
Colour: light cherry. Nose: ripe fruit, spicy, creamy oak, toasty, fine reductive notes. Palate: powerful, flavourful, toasty, round tannins, balanced.

Solar de Líbano 2011 TC
88
Colour: bright cherry. Nose: ripe fruit, sweet spices, creamy oak, mineral, medium intensity. Palate: fruity, flavourful, toasty.

Solar de Líbano Vendimia Seleccionada 2010 TC
90
Colour: cherry, garnet rim. Nose: ripe fruit, wild herbs, spicy, creamy oak, mineral. Palate: balanced, flavourful, long, balsamic.

BODEGAS CERROLAZA
Ctra. Navarrete, 1
26372 Hornos de Moncalvillo (La Rioja)
☎: +34 941 286 728
Fax: +34 941 286 729
www.altosdelmarques.com
info@altosdelmarques.com

Aticus 2006 TR
100% tempranillo
86
Colour: pale ruby, brick rim edge. Nose: elegant, spicy, fine reductive notes, wet leather, aged wood nuances, fruit liqueur notes. Palate: spicy, fine tannins, long.

Aticus 2010 TC
100% tempranillo
86
Colour: cherry, garnet rim. Nose: ripe fruit, spicy, creamy oak, toasty, fine reductive notes. Palate: powerful, flavourful, toasty, spicy.

BODEGAS CORRAL
Ctra. de Logroño, Km. 10
26370 Navarrete (La Rioja)
☎: +34 941 440 193
Fax: +34 941 440 195
www.donjacobo.es
info@donjacobo.es

Altos de Corral Single Estate 2004 TR
100% tempranillo
90
Colour: pale ruby, brick rim edge. Nose: ripe fruit, balsamic herbs, spicy, creamy oak. Palate: powerful, flavourful, spicy, long, balanced.

Don Jacobo 1998 TGR
90
Colour: pale ruby, brick rim edge. Nose: elegant, spicy, fine reductive notes, wet leather, aged wood nuances, fruit liqueur notes. Palate: spicy, fine tannins, elegant, long.

Don Jacobo 2005 TR
87
Colour: cherry, garnet rim. Nose: spicy, old leather, ripe fruit. Palate: spicy.

Don Jacobo 2009 TC
87
Colour: cherry, garnet rim. Nose: medium intensity, ripe fruit. Palate: correct, good finish.

Don Jacobo 2013 B
100% viura
84

Don Jacobo 2013 RD
84

BODEGAS COVILA
Camino del Soto, 26
01306 La Puebla de Labarca (Álava)
☎: +34 945 627 232
Fax: +34 945 627 295
www.covila.es
comercial@covila.es

Covila 2009 TR
100% tempranillo
88
Colour: deep cherry. Nose: ripe fruit, wild herbs, spicy, creamy oak. Palate: balanced, flavourful, long, balsamic.

Covila 2011 TC
100% tempranillo
87
Colour: cherry, garnet rim. Nose: ripe fruit, spicy, creamy oak. Palate: powerful, flavourful, toasty.

Pagos de Labarca AEX 2010 T
100% tempranillo
90
Colour: cherry, garnet rim. Nose: red berry notes, ripe fruit, spicy, creamy oak, toasty, complex, earthy notes. Palate: powerful, flavourful, toasty, round tannins.

BODEGAS DAVID MORENO
Ctra. de Villar de Torre, s/n
26310 Badarán (La Rioja)
☎: +34 941 367 338
Fax: +34 941 418 685
www.davidmoreno.es
davidmoreno@davidmoreno.es

David Moreno 2007 TGR
91
Colour: cherry, garnet rim. Nose: balanced, complex, ripe fruit, spicy, balsamic herbs. Palate: good structure, flavourful, round tannins, full, good acidity.

David Moreno 2008 TR
88
Colour: dark-red cherry, garnet rim. Nose: old leather, balsamic herbs, ripe fruit, cocoa bean. Palate: balanced, flavourful.

David Moreno 2011 TC
89
Colour: dark-red cherry, garnet rim. Nose: medium intensity, ripe fruit, dried herbs. Palate: correct, round tannins, fruity aftestaste.

David Moreno 2013 B
100% viura
83

David Moreno 2013 RD
85

David Moreno 2013 T
86
Colour: cherry, purple rim. Nose: medium intensity, red berry notes, balanced. Palate: balsamic, correct.

Dmoreno Selección de la Familia 2010 TC
89
Colour: cherry, garnet rim. Nose: ripe fruit, fruit preserve, toasty. Palate: fruity, round tannins, good finish.

BODEGAS DE CRIANZA MARQUÉS DE GRIÑÓN
Ctra. de El Ciego, s/n
26350 Cenicero (La Rioja)
☎: +34 913 878 612
abasilio@unitedwineries.com

Marqués de Griñón Alea 2010 TC
100% tempranillo
88
Colour: cherry, garnet rim. Nose: ripe fruit, spicy, creamy oak, toasty, balsamic herbs. Palate: powerful, flavourful, toasty, round tannins.

BODEGAS DE FAMILIA BURGO VIEJO

Concordia, 8
26540 Alfaro (La Rioja)
☎: +34 941 183 405
Fax: +34 941 181 603
www.burgoviejo.com
bodegas@burgoviejo.com

Burgo Viejo 2009 TR
84

Burgo Viejo 2011 TC
85

Burgo Viejo 2013 T
83

Licenciado 2009 TR
100% tempranillo
88
Colour: cherry, garnet rim. Nose: red berry notes, ripe fruit, spicy, creamy oak, toasty, fine reductive notes. Palate: powerful, flavourful, toasty, round tannins, balanced.

Palacio de Invierno 2009 TR
100% tempranillo
86
Colour: cherry, garnet rim. Nose: balanced, ripe fruit, spicy, fine reductive notes. Palate: good structure, flavourful, round tannins.

Palacio de Invierno 2011 TC
100% tempranillo
87
Colour: cherry, garnet rim. Nose: ripe fruit, balsamic herbs, sweet spices, creamy oak. Palate: flavourful, spicy, good finish.

Palacio de Invierno 2013 T
100% tempranillo
85

BODEGAS DE LOS HEREDEROS DEL MARQUÉS DE RISCAL

Torrea, 1
03140 Elciego (Álava)
☎: +34 945 606 000
Fax: +34 945 606 023
www.marquesderiscal.com
marquesderiscal@marquesderiscal.com

Arienzo 2010 TC
90
Colour: cherry, garnet rim. Nose: ripe fruit, spicy, creamy oak, scrubland. Palate: balanced, flavourful, long, balsamic.

Barón de Chirel 2010 TR
94
Colour: very deep cherry, garnet rim. Nose: complex, wild herbs, ripe fruit, expressive. Palate: good structure, full, round tannins, long.

Finca Torrea 2010 T
93
Colour: cherry, garnet rim. Nose: ripe fruit, spicy, creamy oak. Palate: flavourful, toasty, round tannins, long, complex.

Marqués de Riscal 2005 TGR
93
Colour: dark-red cherry, garnet rim. Nose: balanced, expressive, ripe fruit, tobacco. Palate: balanced, ripe fruit, long.

Marqués de Riscal 150 Aniversario 2004 TGR
93
Colour: dark-red cherry, orangey edge. Nose: spicy, fine reductive notes, aged wood nuances, toasty. Palate: spicy, long, toasty, fine tannins.

Marqués de Riscal 2010 TR
92
Colour: very deep cherry, garnet rim. Nose: cocoa bean, creamy oak, ripe fruit, scrubland. Palate: good structure, full.

BODEGAS DE SANTIAGO

Avda. del Ebro, 50
01307 Baños de Ebro (Álava)
☎: +34 945 609 201
Fax: +34 945 609 201
www.bodegasdesantiago.es
info@bodegasdesantiago.es

Lagar de Santiago 2011 TC
tempranillo
92
Colour: very deep cherry, garnet rim. Nose: sweet spices, ripe fruit, balanced, spicy. Palate: flavourful, correct.

Lagar de Santiago 2013 B
verdejo, viura

86

Colour: bright straw. Nose: fresh, fresh fruit, white flowers. Palate: flavourful, fruity, good acidity, balanced.

Lagar de Santiago 2013 T
Maceración Carbónica
tempranillo, viura

84

BODEGAS DEL MEDIEVO
Circunvalación San Roque, s/n
26559 Aldeanueva de Ebro (La Rioja)
☎: +34 941 144 138
Fax: +34 941 144 204
www.bodegasdelmedievo.com
info@bodegasdelmedievo.com

Cofrade 2013 T
tempranillo

85

Medievo 2008 TGR
tempranillo, garnacha, mazuelo, graciano

86

Colour: dark-red cherry, orangey edge. Nose: old leather, tobacco. Palate: spicy, correct, reductive nuances.

Medievo 2009 TR
tempranillo, garnacha, mazuelo, graciano

88

Colour: cherry, garnet rim. Nose: ripe fruit, spicy, creamy oak, toasty, complex, earthy notes. Palate: powerful, flavourful, toasty, round tannins.

Medievo 2011 TC
tempranillo, garnacha, mazuelo, graciano

87

Colour: dark-red cherry. Nose: ripe fruit, spicy, toasty, balsamic herbs. Palate: flavourful, toasty, round tannins.

Medievo 2013 BFB
tempranillo blanco

85

Tuercebotas 2012 TC
graciano

89

Colour: cherry, garnet rim. Nose: ripe fruit, wild herbs, spicy, creamy oak, grassy, varietal. Palate: balanced, flavourful, long, balsamic.

Tuercebotas 2013 B
tempranillo blanco

89

Colour: bright straw. Nose: balanced, ripe fruit, tropical fruit, faded flowers. Palate: flavourful, fine bitter notes, long.

BODEGAS DOMECO DE JARAUTA
Camino Sendero Royal, 5
26559 Aldeanueva de Ebro (La Rioja)
☎: +34 941 163 078
Fax: +34 941 163 078
www.bodegasdomecodejarauta.com
info@bodegasdomecodejarauta.com

Viña Marro 2008 TR

87

Colour: cherry, garnet rim. Nose: fruit preserve, fruit liqueur notes, spicy, wild herbs. Palate: flavourful, pruney, balsamic.

Viña Marro 2011 TC
100% tempranillo

90

Colour: cherry, garnet rim. Nose: ripe fruit, spicy, creamy oak, toasty, complex. Palate: powerful, flavourful, toasty, round tannins.

Viña Marro 2013 T
100% tempranillo

84

Viña Marro Ecológico 2011 T
100% tempranillo

88

Colour: bright cherry. Nose: ripe fruit, sweet spices, creamy oak, wild herbs. Palate: fruity, flavourful, toasty.

Viña Marro Vendimia Seleccionada 2012 T
100% tempranillo

89

Colour: bright cherry. Nose: sweet spices, creamy oak, red berry notes, violet drops. Palate: flavourful, fruity, toasty.

BODEGAS DUNVIRO
Ctra. Logroño, Km. 362
26500 Calahorra (La Rioja)
☎: +34 941 130 626
Fax: +34 941 130 626
www.bodegasdunviro.com
info@bodegasdunviro.com

Dunviro 2007 TR

88

Colour: cherry, garnet rim. Nose: ripe fruit, wild herbs, earthy notes, spicy, creamy oak. Palate: balanced, flavourful, long, balsamic.

Dunviro 2011 BFB
viura

88

Colour: bright yellow. Nose: powerfull, ripe fruit, sweet spices, creamy oak, fragrant herbs. Palate: rich, smoky aftertaste, flavourful, fresh, good acidity.

Dunviro 2011 TC
tempranillo, graciano, mazuelo

86

Colour: cherry, garnet rim. Nose: ripe fruit, spicy, creamy oak, toasty. Palate: flavourful, toasty, round tannins.

Dunviro Garnacha 2013 RD
garnacha

86

Colour: light cherry, bright. Nose: fresh fruit, floral, medium intensity. Palate: fresh, easy to drink, correct.

Dunviro Tempranillo 2013 T
tempranillo

83

Dunviro Vendimia Seleccionada Tempranillo 2013 T
tempranillo

86

Colour: cherry, purple rim. Nose: expressive, fresh fruit, red berry notes, floral. Palate: flavourful, fruity, good acidity.

Dunviro Viñas Viejas 2011 TC

87

Colour: dark-red cherry, garnet rim. Nose: balanced, spicy, dried herbs. Palate: fruity, good finish, correct.

Dunviro Viura 2013 B
viura

85

BODEGAS ESCUDERO

Ctra. de Arnedo, s/n
26587 Grávalos (La Rioja)
☎: +34 941 398 008
Fax: +34 941 398 070
www.familiaescudero.com
info@familiaescudero.com

Becquer 2013 BFB

89

Colour: yellow, greenish rim. Nose: ripe fruit, dried flowers, sweet spices. Palate: flavourful, long, balanced, fine bitter notes.

Solar de Becquer 2011 TC

86

Colour: dark-red cherry, garnet rim. Nose: spicy, ripe fruit. Palate: balanced, easy to drink, good finish, toasty.

Solar de Becquer 2013 T

87

Colour: bright cherry, purple rim. Nose: red berry notes, balsamic herbs, medium intensity. Palate: easy to drink, fruity.

Vinsacro Dioro 2010 T
100% vidau

88

Colour: cherry, garnet rim. Nose: ripe fruit, spicy, creamy oak, toasty, complex. Palate: powerful, flavourful, toasty, round tannins.

BODEGAS ESTRAUNZA

Avda. La Poveda, 25
01306 Lapuebla de Labarca (Álava)
☎: +34 944 215 936
Fax: +34 944 219 941
www.bodegasestraunza.com
info@bodegasestraunza.com

Blas de Lezo 2011 TC
tempranillo

86

Colour: bright cherry. Nose: ripe fruit, sweet spices, creamy oak, expressive. Palate: flavourful, fruity, toasty.

Blas de Lezo 2013 T
tempranillo

84

Solar de Estraunza 2005 TGR
tempranillo

88

Colour: pale ruby, brick rim edge. Nose: spicy, fine reductive notes, wet leather, aged wood nuances, fruit liqueur notes. Palate: spicy, fine tannins, long, balanced.

Solar de Estraunza 2007 TR
tempranillo

87

Colour: pale ruby, brick rim edge. Nose: spicy, fine reductive notes, wet leather, aged wood nuances, fruit liqueur notes. Palate: spicy, fine tannins, correct.

Solar de Estraunza 2011 TC
tempranillo

87

Colour: bright cherry. Nose: sweet spices, creamy oak, medium intensity, fruit preserve. Palate: fruity, flavourful, toasty, long, sweet tannins.

Solar de Estraunza 2013 B
viura

84

Solar de Estraunza 2013 RD

86

Colour: onion pink. Nose: elegant, candied fruit, fragrant herbs, medium intensity. Palate: light-bodied, flavourful, good acidity, long, spicy.

Solar de Estraunza 2013 T
tempranillo

84

Solar de Estraunza Selección 2005 T
tempranillo

89

Colour: deep cherry, orangey edge. Nose: waxy notes, tobacco, ripe fruit, spicy, aged wood nuances. Palate: fine bitter notes, flavourful, fine tannins.

Solar de Muskiz 2013 T
tempranillo

83

BODEGAS EXOPTO
Ctra. de Elvillar, 26
01300 Laguardia (Álava)
☎: +34 650 213 993
Fax: +34 941 502 342
www.exopto.net
info@exopto.net

Bozeto de Exopto 2012 T
87

Colour: bright cherry. Nose: ripe fruit, sweet spices, creamy oak, earthy notes. Palate: flavourful, fruity, toasty.

Exopto 2011 T
92

Colour: cherry, garnet rim. Nose: ripe fruit, wild herbs, earthy notes, spicy, creamy oak. Palate: balanced, flavourful, long, balsamic.

Horizonte de Exopto 2012 B
84

Horizonte de Exopto 2012 T
90

Colour: bright cherry. Nose: ripe fruit, sweet spices, creamy oak, expressive. Palate: flavourful, fruity, toasty.

BODEGAS FAUSTINO
Ctra. de Logroño, s/n
01320 Oyón (Álava)
☎: +34 945 622 500
Fax: +34 945 622 106
www.bodegasfaustino.com
info@bodegasfaustino.es

Faustino 2011 TC
100% tempranillo

85

Faustino De Autor Edición Especial 2004 T
100% tempranillo

90

Colour: pale ruby, brick rim edge. Nose: elegant, spicy, fine reductive notes, wet leather, aged wood nuances, fruit liqueur notes. Palate: spicy, fine tannins, elegant, long.

Faustino de Autor Reserva Especial 2006 TR
tempranillo, graciano

87

Colour: very deep cherry. Nose: ripe fruit, spicy, creamy oak, toasty, cigar, wet leather. Palate: powerful, flavourful, toasty, round tannins

Faustino I 2001 TGR
tempranillo, graciano, mazuelo

92

Colour: deep cherry, orangey edge. Nose: waxy notes, tobacco, ripe fruit, spicy, aged wood nuances. Palate: fine bitter notes, elegant, flavourful, fine tannins.

Faustino I 75 Aniversario 2005 TGR
tempranillo, graciano

92

Colour: cherry, garnet rim. Nose: ripe fruit, spicy, creamy oak, toasty, complex, fine reductive notes. Palate: powerful, flavourful, toasty, round tannins.

Faustino V 2009 TR
tempranillo, mazuelo

86

Colour: cherry, garnet rim. Nose: ripe fruit, spicy, creamy oak, toasty, old leather, tobacco. Palate: powerful, flavourful, toasty.

Faustino V 2013 B
viura, chardonnay

86

Colour: bright straw. Nose: fresh, fresh fruit, white flowers. Palate: flavourful, fruity, good acidity, balanced.

Faustino V 2013 RD
100% tempranillo

88

Colour: raspberry rose. Nose: powerfull, ripe fruit, red berry notes, floral, expressive. Palate: powerful, fruity, fresh.

BODEGAS FEDERICO PATERNINA MARQUES DE LA CONCORDIA FAMILY OF WINES
Crta. El ciego s/n.
26350 Cenicero (La Rioja)
☎: +34 913 878 612
www.paternina.com
abasilio@unitedwineries.com

Banda Azul 2010 TC
84

Lacort 2010 TC
88

Colour: bright cherry. Nose: ripe fruit, spicy, toasty. Palate: flavourful, toasty, round tannins, fruity.

Paternina Banda Roja 2008 TR
87

Colour: cherry, garnet rim. Nose: ripe fruit, spicy, creamy oak, toasty, balsamic herbs, fine reductive notes. Palate: powerful, flavourful, toasty.

BODEGAS FINS DE SIGLO

Camino Arenzana de Arriba, 16
26311 Arenzana de Abajo (La Rioja)
☎: +34 941 410 042
Fax: +34 941 410 043
www.bodegasfindesiglo.com
perelada@castilloperelada.com

XIII Lunas 2011 T
87
Colour: bright cherry. Nose: ripe fruit, sweet spices, dried herbs. Palate: fruity, toasty, round tannins, easy to drink.

BODEGAS FOS

Término de Vialba, s/n
01340 Elciego (Álava)
☎: +34 945 606 681
Fax: +34 945 606 608
www.bodegasfos.com
fos@bodegasfos.com

Fos 2008 TR
90
Colour: cherry, garnet rim. Nose: ripe fruit, spicy, creamy oak, toasty, complex. Palate: flavourful, toasty, round tannins.

Fos 2010 TC
90
Colour: cherry, garnet rim. Nose: ripe fruit, spicy, creamy oak, toasty, complex. Palate: powerful, flavourful, toasty, round tannins.

Fos 2013 B
100% viura
90
Colour: bright straw. Nose: white flowers, fresh fruit, expressive, fine lees, dried herbs. Palate: flavourful, fruity, good acidity, balanced.

Fos 2013 T Maceración Carbónica
100% tempranillo
87
Colour: cherry, purple rim. Nose: red berry notes, fruit expression, fragrant herbs. Palate: flavourful, light-bodied, good acidity, fresh, fruity.

Fos Baranda 2011 T
100% tempranillo
93
Colour: deep cherry, garnet rim. Nose: complex, ripe fruit, cocoa bean. Palate: balanced, long, good structure, flavourful.

BODEGAS FRANCO ESPAÑOLAS

Cabo Noval, 2
26009 Logroño (La Rioja)
☎: +34 941 251 300
Fax: +34 941 262 948
www.francoespanolas.com
info@francoespanolas.com

Baron D'Anglade 2009 TR
92
Colour: cherry, garnet rim. Nose: ripe fruit, wild herbs, earthy notes, spicy, creamy oak. Palate: balanced, flavourful, long, balsamic.

RB 2011 TC
100% tempranillo
87
Colour: bright cherry. Nose: ripe fruit, sweet spices, smoky. Palate: fruity, toasty, easy to drink, balanced.

Rioja Bordón 2006 TGR
89
Colour: deep cherry, orangey edge. Nose: waxy notes, tobacco, ripe fruit, spicy, aged wood nuances. Palate: fine bitter notes, elegant, flavourful, fine tannins.

Rioja Bordón 2008 TR
88
Colour: dark-red cherry, orangey edge. Nose: spicy, fine reductive notes, wet leather, aged wood nuances, fruit liqueur notes. Palate: spicy, fine tannins.

Rioja Bordón 2011 TC
86
Colour: dark-red cherry. Nose: ripe fruit, spicy, aged wood nuances, old leather. Palate: correct, fine bitter notes, good finish.

BODEGAS FUIDIO

San Bartolome, 32
01322 Yécora (Álava)
☎: +34 945 601 883
bodegas@fuidio.com

Fuidio 2012 T
tempranillo
86
Colour: cherry, garnet rim. Nose: medium intensity, dried herbs. Palate: correct, round tannins.

Fuidio 2013 B
viura
79

Fuidio Iraley 2011 T
tempranillo
84

BODEGAS GARCÍA DE OLANO

Ctra. Vitoria, s/n
01309 Paganos - La Guardia (Álava)
☎: +34 945 621 146
Fax: +34 945 621 146
www.bodegasgarciadeolano.com
garciadeolano@telefonica.net

3 de Olano 2010 T
100% tempranillo

90

Colour: deep cherry, garnet rim. Nose: ripe fruit, powerfull, sweet spices. Palate: good structure, long, good acidity.

3 de Olano Selección 2010 T
100% tempranillo

93

Colour: bright cherry, garnet rim. Nose: ripe fruit, spicy, creamy oak, toasty, complex. Palate: powerful, flavourful, toasty, round tannins.

Heredad García de Olano 2011 TC
100% tempranillo

89

Colour: cherry, garnet rim. Nose: ripe fruit, spicy, creamy oak, toasty, complex. Palate: powerful, flavourful, toasty, round tannins.

Heredad García de Olano 2013 B
100% viura

84

Heredad García de Olano 2013 T
100% tempranillo

84

Mauleón 2006 TR
100% tempranillo

88

Colour: deep cherry, garnet rim. Nose: powerfull, characterful, balsamic herbs. Palate: good structure, round tannins, fruity aftestaste.

Olanum Vendimia Seleccionada 2009 T Barrica
100% tempranillo

87

Colour: cherry, garnet rim. Nose: red berry notes, fruit liqueur notes, wild herbs, creamy oak. Palate: powerful, flavourful, spicy.

BODEGAS GÓMEZ CRUZADO

Avda. Vizcaya, 6 (Barrio de la Estación)
26200 Haro (La Rioja)
☎: +34 941 312 502
www.gomezcruzado.com
bodega@gomezcruzado.com

Gómez Cruzado 2009 TR

89

Colour: cherry, garnet rim. Nose: balanced, complex, ripe fruit, spicy, fine reductive notes, cigar. Palate: good structure, flavourful.

Gómez Cruzado 2011 TC

90

Colour: bright cherry. Nose: ripe fruit, sweet spices, creamy oak, expressive. Palate: flavourful, fruity, toasty, round tannins.

Gómez Cruzado Cerro Las Cuevas 2012 T
tempranillo

91

Colour: cherry, garnet rim. Nose: ripe fruit, spicy, creamy oak, toasty, complex, dark chocolate, earthy notes. Palate: powerful, flavourful, toasty, round tannins.

Gómez Cruzado Vendimia Seleccionada 2013 T

85

Honorable Gómez Cruzado 2011 T
tempranillo

92

Colour: cherry, garnet rim. Nose: balanced, complex, ripe fruit, spicy, balsamic herbs, mineral. Palate: good structure, flavourful, balanced.

Pancrudo de Gómez Cruzado 2012 T
100% garnacha

90

Colour: cherry, garnet rim. Nose: ripe fruit, spicy, creamy oak, toasty, complex. Palate: powerful, flavourful, toasty, round tannins.

BODEGAS GRAN FEUDO

Ribera, 34
31592 Cintruénigo (Navarra)
☎: +34 948 811 000
Fax: +34 948 811 407
www.granfeudo.com
info@granfeudo.com

Gran Feudo Rioja 2013 T
tempranillo

85

BODEGAS GRUPO YLLERA

Autovía A-6, Km. 173,5
47490 Rueda (Valladolid)
☎: +34 983 868 097
Fax: +34 983 868 177
www.grupoyllera.com
grupoyllera@grupoyllera.com

Coelus 2009 TR
100% tempranillo
86
Colour: ruby red. Nose: ripe fruit, spicy, toasty, fine reductive notes. Palate: powerful, flavourful, classic aged character.

Coelus 2010 TC
100% tempranillo
87
Colour: cherry, garnet rim. Nose: ripe fruit, spicy, creamy oak, toasty. Palate: powerful, flavourful, toasty.

Coelus Joven 2013 T
100% tempranillo
85

BODEGAS HERMANOS PASCUAL MIGUEL

Mayor, 43
01307 Baños de Ebro (Álava)
☎: +34 607 530 227
https://www.facebook.com/BodegasHnosPM
bodegashpm@terra.com

Amicis 2011 T
100% tempranillo
88
Colour: cherry, garnet rim. Nose: ripe fruit, spicy, creamy oak, toasty, complex, cocoa bean. Palate: powerful, flavourful, toasty, round tannins.

HPM 2010 TC
100% tempranillo
85

HPM 2013 T Maceración Carbónica
85

BODEGAS HERMANOS PECIÑA

Ctra. de Vitoria, Km. 47
26338 San Vicente de la Sonsierra
(La Rioja)
☎: +34 941 334 366
Fax: +34 941 334 180
www.bodegashermanospecina.com
info@bodegashermanospecina.com

Chobeo de Peciña 2007 T
100% tempranillo
90
Colour: pale ruby, brick rim edge. Nose: ripe fruit, balsamic herbs, spicy, creamy oak, mineral, fine reductive notes. Palate: powerful, flavourful, spicy, long.

Chobeo de Peciña 2011 BFB
100% viura
83

Gran Chobeo de Peciña 2008 T
100% tempranillo
91
Colour: cherry, garnet rim. Nose: ripe fruit, spicy, creamy oak, toasty. Palate: powerful, flavourful, toasty, round tannins, balanced, elegant.

Señorío de P. Peciña 2003 TGR
87
Colour: pale ruby, brick rim edge. Nose: spicy, fine reductive notes, wet leather, aged wood nuances, fruit liqueur notes. Palate: spicy, fine tannins, aged character.

Señorío de P. Peciña 2007 TR
88
Colour: pale ruby, brick rim edge. Nose: elegant, spicy, fine reductive notes, wet leather, aged wood nuances, fruit liqueur notes. Palate: spicy, fine tannins, elegant, long.

Señorío de P. Peciña 2010 TC
87
Colour: cherry, garnet rim. Nose: red berry notes, ripe fruit, spicy, creamy oak, aged wood nuances. Palate: powerful, flavourful, toasty.

Señorío de P. Peciña 2013 B
100% viura
85

Señorío de P. Peciña Vendimia Seleccionada 2006 TR
89
Colour: deep cherry, orangey edge. Nose: waxy notes, tobacco, ripe fruit, spicy, aged wood nuances. Palate: fine bitter notes, elegant, flavourful, fine tannins.

BODEGAS HOROLA

Plaza Mayor, 5
26320 Baños del Río Tobia (La Rioja)
☎: +34 670 616 840
www.bodegashorola.com
contacto@bodegashorola.com

Horola Garnacha 2012 T
garnacha
89
Colour: bright cherry. Nose: sweet spices, creamy oak, fruit preserve, ripe fruit. Palate: fruity, flavourful, toasty, balanced.

Horola Tempranillo 2012 T
tempranillo
87
Colour: light cherry. Nose: ripe fruit, wild herbs, spicy, creamy oak. Palate: powerful, flavourful, spicy.

Horola Tempranillo 2012 T
Fermentado en Barrica
tempranillo
86
Colour: cherry, garnet rim. Nose: ripe fruit, spicy, creamy oak, toasty. Palate: powerful, flavourful, toasty.

BODEGAS IZADI

Herrería Travesía II, 5
01307 Villabuena de Álava (Álava)
☎: +34 945 609 086
Fax: +34 945 609 261
www.izadi.com
izadi@izadi.com

Izadi 2011 TC
100% tempranillo
90
Colour: very deep cherry, garnet rim. Nose: powerfull, ripe fruit, cocoa bean. Palate: powerful, toasty, ripe fruit, good acidity.

Izadi 2013 BFB
91
Colour: bright straw. Nose: white flowers, fragrant herbs, fruit expression, balsamic herbs, spicy. Palate: fresh, fruity, flavourful, balanced.

Izadi El Regalo 2009 TR
91
Colour: very deep cherry. Nose: toasty, spicy, dark chocolate, wet leather. Palate: spicy, ripe fruit, good finish.

Izadi Expresión 2011 T
100% tempranillo
90
Colour: very deep cherry. Nose: toasty, dark chocolate, ripe fruit. Palate: powerful, concentrated, fine bitter notes, good acidity.

Izadi Larrosa 2013 RD
100% garnacha
89
Colour: salmon. Nose: elegant, candied fruit, dried flowers, fragrant herbs, red berry notes. Palate: light-bodied, flavourful, good acidity, long, spicy.

Izadi Selección 2011 T
93
Colour: cherry, garnet rim. Nose: ripe fruit, spicy, creamy oak, toasty, complex. Palate: powerful, flavourful, toasty, round tannins.

BODEGAS JAVIER
SAN PEDRO ORTEGA

Camino de la hoya nº5
01300 Laguardia (Alava)
☎: +34 639 075 341
administracion@bodegasjaviersanpedro.com

Anahi 2013 B
malvasía, sauvignon blanc, tempranillo blanco
87
Colour: bright yellow. Nose: ripe fruit, citrus fruit, honeyed notes. Palate: sweet, good acidity.

Cueva de Lobos 2011 TC
87
Colour: very deep cherry. Nose: powerfull, ripe fruit, spicy, toasty. Palate: fine bitter notes, good acidity, balanced.

Cueva de Lobos 2013 T
Maceración Carbónica
tempranillo
88
Colour: cherry, purple rim. Nose: red berry notes, violet drops, medium intensity. Palate: flavourful, good acidity, spicy.

La Taconera 2012 T
100% tempranillo
92
Colour: cherry, garnet rim. Nose: spicy, toasty, overripe fruit, mineral, expressive. Palate: powerful, flavourful, toasty, powerful tannins.

Viuda Negra 2011 TC
100% tempranillo
90
Colour: cherry, garnet rim. Nose: ripe fruit, spicy, creamy oak, toasty, complex. Palate: powerful, flavourful, toasty, round tannins.

Viuda Negra 2013 B
tempranillo blanco
94
Colour: bright straw. Nose: ripe fruit, spicy, white flowers, mineral. Palate: flavourful, fruity, fresh, good acidity, round.

Viuda Negra Vendimia Tardía 2013 B

90

Colour: bright yellow. Nose: powerfull, floral, honeyed notes, candied fruit, grapey. Palate: flavourful, sweet, fruity, good acidity, long.

BODEGAS LA CATEDRAL

Avda. de Mendavia, 30
26009 Logroño (La Rioja)
☎: +34 941 235 299
Fax: +34 941 253 703

Rivallana 2009 TR

89

Colour: bright cherry. Nose: ripe fruit, sweet spices, creamy oak, expressive. Palate: flavourful, fruity, toasty, round tannins, balanced.

Rivallana 2012 TC

87

Colour: dark-red cherry. Nose: ripe fruit, toasty, sweet spices. Palate: powerful, flavourful, toasty, round tannins.

Rivallana Segundo Año 2012 T

87

Colour: cherry, garnet rim. Nose: red berry notes, ripe fruit, wild herbs, spicy. Palate: powerful, flavourful, spicy, long.

BODEGAS LA EMPERATRIZ

Ctra. Santo Domingo - Haro, km. 31,500
26241 Baños de Rioja (La Rioja)
☎: +34 941 300 105
Fax: +34 941 300 231
www.bodegaslaemperatriz.com
correo@bodegaslaemperatriz.com

Finca La Emperatriz 2011 TC

92

Colour: bright cherry. Nose: ripe fruit, sweet spices, creamy oak, fruit expression. Palate: flavourful, fruity, toasty, round tannins.

Finca La Emperatriz Garnacha Cepas Viejas 2012 T

100% garnacha

93

Colour: light cherry, garnet rim. Nose: fruit expression, ripe fruit, expressive, creamy oak. Palate: complex, full, round tannins.

Finca La Emperatriz Parcela nº 1 2011 T

100% tempranillo

96

Colour: cherry, garnet rim. Nose: ripe fruit, spicy, creamy oak, toasty, complex, cocoa bean, varietal. Palate: powerful, flavourful, toasty, round tannins.

Finca La Emperatriz Terruño 2010 T

100% tempranillo

95

Colour: cherry, garnet rim. Nose: red berry notes, ripe fruit, spicy, creamy oak, toasty, complex, earthy notes. Palate: powerful, flavourful, toasty, round tannins.

Finca La Emperatriz Viura 2013 B

100% viura

90

Colour: bright straw. Nose: white flowers, fragrant herbs, fruit expression, expressive. Palate: fresh, fruity, flavourful, balanced, elegant.

Finca La Emperatriz 2008 TR

91

Colour: cherry, garnet rim. Nose: ripe fruit, spicy, creamy oak, toasty, complex. Palate: powerful, flavourful, toasty, round tannins.

Finca La Emperatriz Viura
Cepas Viejas 2012 B
100% viura

92
Colour: yellow, greenish rim. Nose: ripe fruit, sweet spices, fragrant herbs. Palate: rich, smoky aftertaste, flavourful.

BODEGAS LACUS
Cervantes, 18
26559 Aldeanueva de Ebro (La Rioja)
☎: +34 649 331 799
Fax: +34 941 144 128
www.bodegaslacus.com
inedito@bodegaslacus.com

Inédito 2012 BFB
garnacha blanca

87
Colour: bright yellow. Nose: powerfull, ripe fruit, sweet spices, creamy oak, fragrant herbs. Palate: rich, smoky aftertaste, flavourful, fresh, good acidity.

Inédito H12 2009 T
86
Colour: cherry, garnet rim. Nose: spicy, toasty, overripe fruit, mineral. Palate: powerful, flavourful, toasty, round tannins.

Inédito S 2011 T
87
Colour: ruby red. Nose: overripe fruit, wild herbs, creamy oak, toasty. Palate: powerful, flavourful, spicy, long.

BODEGAS LAGAR DE ZABALA
Pza. Mayor, 2
26338 San Vicente de la Sonsierra
(La Rioja)
☎: +34 941 334 435
Fax: +34 941 334 435
www.bodegaslagardezabala.com
bodegaslagardezabala@hotmail.com

Lagar de Zabala 2006 TR
100% tempranillo

87
Colour: deep cherry, garnet rim. Nose: closed, ripe fruit, aged wood nuances, medium intensity. Palate: good structure, correct.

Lagar de Zabala 2010 TC
100% tempranillo

80

Lagar de Zabala 2013 B
100% viura

83

Lagar de Zabala 2013 T
84

BODEGAS LAGUNILLA MARQUÉS DE LA CONCORDIA FAMILY OF WINES
Ctra. de Elciego, s/n
26350 Cenicero (La Rioja)
☎: +34 913 878 612
www.unitedwineries.com
abasilio@unitedwineries.com

Lagunilla 2007 TGR
87
Colour: pale ruby, brick rim edge. Nose: elegant, spicy, fine reductive notes, wet leather, aged wood nuances, fruit liqueur notes. Palate: spicy, fine tannins, elegant, long.

Lagunilla 2008 TR
88
Colour: ruby red. Nose: elegant, spicy, fine reductive notes, wet leather, aged wood nuances, fruit liqueur notes. Palate: spicy, fine tannins, long.

Lagunilla 2010 TC
86
Colour: cherry, garnet rim. Nose: ripe fruit, spicy, creamy oak, toasty, complex. Palate: powerful, flavourful, toasty, round tannins.

Lagunilla Optimus 2010 T
tempranillo, syrah, merlot, cabernet sauvignon

90
Colour: very deep cherry. Nose: ripe fruit, spicy, creamy oak, toasty, characterful. Palate: powerful, flavourful, toasty, round tannins.

Lagunilla The Family Collection 2008 TR
88
Colour: cherry, garnet rim. Nose: ripe fruit, spicy, creamy oak, toasty, complex. Palate: powerful, flavourful, toasty, round tannins.

Lagunilla The Family Collection 2010 TC
87
Colour: bright cherry. Nose: ripe fruit, sweet spices, creamy oak, medium intensity. Palate: fruity, flavourful, toasty.

BODEGAS LANDALUCE
Ctra. Los Molinos, s/n
01300 Laguardia (Álava)
☎: +34 944 953 622
www.bodegaslandaluce.es
asier@bodegaslandaluce.es

Capricho de Landaluce 2008 T
100% tempranillo

91
Colour: ruby red. Nose: balanced, complex, ripe fruit, spicy, creamy oak. Palate: good structure, flavourful, round tannins, elegant.

Elle de Landaluce 2010 TC
89
Colour: cherry, garnet rim. Nose: ripe fruit, spicy, creamy oak, toasty, powerfull. Palate: flavourful, toasty, spicy, long.

Elle de Landaluce 2013 B
86
Colour: bright straw. Nose: floral, dried herbs, ripe fruit, medium intensity. Palate: powerful, flavourful, fruity.

Fincas de Landaluce 2009 TR
100% tempranillo
90
Colour: cherry, garnet rim. Nose: ripe fruit, spicy, creamy oak, toasty, complex, fine reductive notes. Palate: powerful, flavourful, toasty, round tannins, balanced.

Fincas de Landaluce 2011 TC
100% tempranillo
89
Colour: bright cherry. Nose: ripe fruit, sweet spices, creamy oak, expressive. Palate: flavourful, fruity, toasty.

Landaluce 2013 T Maceración Carbónica
88
Colour: cherry, purple rim. Nose: red berry notes, raspberry, floral, expressive. Palate: fresh, fruity, flavourful, easy to drink.

BODEGAS LAR DE PAULA
Coscojal, s/n
01309 Elvillar (Álava)
☎: +34 945 604 068
Fax: +34 945 604 105
www.lardepaula.com
info@lardepaula.com

Lar de Paula 2009 TR
100% tempranillo
90
Colour: ruby red. Nose: ripe fruit, wild herbs, balsamic herbs, spicy, creamy oak, fine reductive notes. Palate: powerful, flavourful, balanced.

Lar de Paula Cepas Viejas 2010 T
100% tempranillo
89
Colour: cherry, garnet rim. Nose: ripe fruit, wild herbs, earthy notes, spicy, creamy oak. Palate: balanced, flavourful, long, balsamic.

Lar de Paula Merus 2010 TC
100% tempranillo
88
Colour: cherry, garnet rim. Nose: ripe fruit, spicy, creamy oak, toasty, complex, fine reductive notes. Palate: powerful, flavourful, toasty, round tannins.

Lar de Paula Merus 2012 BFB
viura, malvasía
84

Merus.4 2010 T

100% tempranillo

89

Colour: cherry, garnet rim. Nose: ripe fruit, spicy, creamy oak, toasty, fine reductive notes. Palate: powerful, flavourful, toasty, spicy.

BODEGAS LARRAZ

Paraje Ribarrey. Pol. 12- Parcela 50
26350 Cenicero (La Rioja)
☎: +34 639 728 581
www.bodegaslarraz.com
info@bodegaslarraz.com

Caudum Bodegas Larraz 2008 T

tempranillo

92

Colour: very deep cherry, garnet rim. Nose: dark chocolate, balanced, dried herbs. Palate: good structure, spicy, ripe fruit.

Caudum Bodegas Larraz 2010 T

tempranillo

86

Colour: very deep cherry. Nose: fruit preserve, overripe fruit, sweet spices. Palate: spicy, round tannins.

Caudum Bodegas Larraz Selección Especial 2009 T

tempranillo

89

Colour: cherry, garnet rim. Nose: ripe fruit, spicy, creamy oak, smoky. Palate: powerful, flavourful, toasty, round tannins.

BODEGAS LAS CEPAS

Ctra Najera-Cenicero s/n
26007 Uruñuela (La Rioja)
☎: +34 615 996 878
Fax: +34 941 121 667
www.lascepasriojawine.com
export@lascepasriojawine.com

Cinco Denarios 2012 T

89

Colour: bright cherry, garnet rim. Nose: balanced, scrubland, spicy. Palate: powerful, flavourful, balsamic.

Costalarbol 2012 B

86

Colour: bright straw. Nose: white flowers, fragrant herbs, fruit expression. Palate: fresh, fruity, flavourful, elegant.

Costalarbol 2012 T

87

Colour: bright cherry, garnet rim. Nose: dried herbs, toasty, ripe fruit. Palate: spicy, correct, long.

Costalarbol Graciano 2012 T

100% graciano

90

Colour: bright cherry, purple rim. Nose: balanced, red berry notes, ripe fruit, balsamic herbs. Palate: fruity, good acidity, round tannins.

Cuesta Las Piedras 2012 T

89

Colour: cherry, garnet rim. Nose: ripe fruit, wild herbs, earthy notes, spicy, creamy oak. Palate: balanced, flavourful, long, balsamic.

Dominio de Laertes 2010 TC

90

Colour: bright cherry. Nose: ripe fruit, sweet spices, creamy oak. Palate: flavourful, fruity, toasty, round tannins.

Dominio de Laertes 2012 T

89

Colour: cherry, garnet rim. Nose: red berry notes, ripe fruit, spicy, creamy oak, toasty, complex, earthy notes. Palate: powerful, flavourful, toasty, round tannins.

Legado Decand 2012 T

90

Colour: cherry, garnet rim. Nose: red berry notes, ripe fruit, spicy, creamy oak, toasty, complex, earthy notes, dried herbs. Palate: powerful, flavourful, toasty, round tannins.

BODEGAS LAUNA

Ctra. Vitoria-Logroño, Km. 57
01300 Laguardia (Alava)
☎: +34 946 824 108
Fax: +34 956 824 108
www.bodegaslauna.com
info@bodegaslauna.com

Ikunus 2011 T

100% tempranillo

90

Colour: cherry, garnet rim. Nose: balanced, complex, ripe fruit, spicy. Palate: good structure, flavourful, round tannins.

Launa 2011 TC

89

Colour: bright cherry. Nose: ripe fruit, sweet spices, creamy oak, expressive. Palate: fruity, flavourful, toasty, balanced.

Launa Selección Familiar 2010 TR

91

Colour: bright cherry. Nose: ripe fruit, sweet spices, creamy oak, expressive. Palate: flavourful, fruity, toasty, round tannins, balsamic, balanced.

Launa Selección Familiar 2011 TC
100% tempranillo

90

Colour: cherry, garnet rim. Nose: ripe fruit, wild herbs, earthy notes, spicy, creamy oak. Palate: balanced, flavourful, long, balsamic.

Teo's 2010 T
100% tempranillo

92

Colour: cherry, garnet rim. Nose: ripe fruit, spicy, creamy oak, toasty, complex, balsamic herbs. Palate: powerful, flavourful, toasty, round tannins, elegant.

Teo's 2011 T
100% tempranillo

90

Colour: cherry, garnet rim. Nose: ripe fruit, spicy, creamy oak, toasty, complex, dark chocolate, earthy notes. Palate: powerful, flavourful, toasty, balanced.

BODEGAS LEZA GARCÍA
San Ignacio, 26
26313 Uruñuela (La Rioja)
☎: +34 941 371 142
Fax: +34 941 371 035
www.bodegasleza.com
bodegasleza@bodegasleza.com

Leza García 2008 TR

87

Colour: dark-red cherry. Nose: old leather, ripe fruit, toasty, dark chocolate. Palate: flavourful, round tannins, spicy.

Leza García Tinto Familia 2010 T
100% tempranillo

88

Colour: deep cherry, garnet rim. Nose: balanced, dried herbs, spicy. Palate: ripe fruit, good finish, round tannins.

LG de Leza García 2011 T
100% tempranillo

89

Colour: bright cherry. Nose: ripe fruit, sweet spices, creamy oak, balsamic herbs. Palate: flavourful, fruity, toasty.

Nube de Leza García 2013 RD
100% garnacha

84

Nube de Leza García Semidulce 2013 RD
100% garnacha

85

Valdepalacios 2011 TC

88

Colour: cherry, garnet rim. Nose: ripe fruit, spicy, creamy oak, toasty, complex. Palate: powerful, flavourful, toasty.

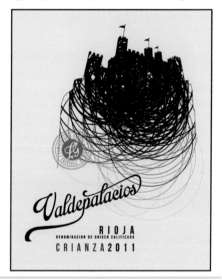

Valdepalacios 2013 B
100% viura

84

Valdepalacios 2013 RD

87

Colour: rose, purple rim. Nose: powerfull, ripe fruit, red berry notes, floral, expressive. Palate: powerful, fruity, fresh.

Valdepalacios Vendimia Seleccionada 2012 T

86

Colour: cherry, garnet rim. Nose: ripe fruit, spicy, creamy oak, toasty. Palate: powerful, flavourful, toasty.

BODEGAS LOLI CASADO

Avda. La Poveda, 46
01306 Lapuebla de Labarca (Álava)
☎: +34 945 607 096
Fax: +34 945 607 412
www.bodegaslolicasado.com
loli@bodegaslolicasado.com

Jaun de Alzate 2009 TR
90
Colour: cherry, garnet rim. Nose: ripe fruit, spicy, creamy oak, toasty, wild herbs. Palate: powerful, flavourful, toasty.

Jaun de Alzate 2010 TC
88
Colour: cherry, garnet rim. Nose: ripe fruit, spicy, creamy oak, toasty. Palate: powerful, flavourful, toasty.

Juan de Alzate Vendimia Seleccionada 2012 T
86
Colour: cherry, garnet rim. Nose: ripe fruit, wild herbs, earthy notes, spicy. Palate: balanced, flavourful, long, balsamic.

Polus 2009 TR
100% tempranillo
89
Colour: pale ruby, brick rim edge. Nose: balanced, complex, ripe fruit, spicy, earthy notes. Palate: good structure, flavourful, round tannins.

Polus 2010 TC
100% tempranillo
87
Colour: cherry, garnet rim. Nose: ripe fruit, spicy, creamy oak, toasty, complex. Palate: powerful, flavourful, toasty.

Polus Tempranillo 2012 T
100% tempranillo
86
Colour: bright cherry. Nose: ripe fruit, sweet spices, creamy oak, fine reductive notes. Palate: flavourful, fruity, toasty.

Polus Viura 2013 B
100% viura
84

BODEGAS LUIS ALEGRE

Ctra. Navaridas, s/n
01300 Laguardia (Álava)
☎: +34 945 600 089
Fax: +34 945 600 729
www.luisalegre.com
luisalegre@bodegasluisalegre.com

Finca la Reñana 2012 BFB
91
Colour: bright yellow. Nose: powerfull, ripe fruit, sweet spices, creamy oak, fragrant herbs. Palate: rich, smoky aftertaste, flavourful, fresh, good acidity.

Gran Vino Pontac 2010 T
92
Colour: black cherry. Nose: complex, spicy, ripe fruit, creamy oak, cocoa bean. Palate: good structure, flavourful, round tannins.

Gran Vino Pontac de Portiles 2011 T
93
Colour: deep cherry, garnet rim. Nose: expressive, complex, spicy, ripe fruit, dried herbs. Palate: good structure, full, spicy.

Koden de Luis Alegre 2012 T
100% tempranillo
90
Colour: very deep cherry. Nose: powerfull, fruit preserve, sweet spices. Palate: balanced, round tannins, ripe fruit.

Luis Alegre Parcela Nº 5 La Minoría 2009 TR
100% tempranillo
91
Colour: cherry, garnet rim. Nose: varietal, spicy, creamy oak, cocoa bean. Palate: good structure, smoky aftertaste, easy to drink.

Luis Alegre Selección Especial 2010 TR
90
Colour: cherry, garnet rim. Nose: ripe fruit, spicy, creamy oak, toasty, complex. Palate: powerful, flavourful, toasty, round tannins.

Viticultura de Precisión 2011 TC
88
Colour: deep cherry, garnet rim. Nose: balanced, creamy oak, sweet spices. Palate: correct, round tannins.

BODEGAS LUIS CAÑAS

Ctra. Samaniego, 10
01307 Villabuena (Álava)
☎: +34 945 623 373
Fax: +34 945 609 289
www.luiscanas.com
bodegas@luiscanas.com

Luis Cañas 2007 TGR
93
Colour: pale ruby, brick rim edge. Nose: spicy, fine reductive notes, wet leather, aged wood nuances, fruit liqueur notes. Palate: spicy, fine tannins.

Luis Cañas 2009 TR
tempranillo, graciano
92
Colour: very deep cherry. Nose: ripe fruit, spicy, creamy oak, toasty. Palate: powerful, flavourful, toasty, round tannins.

Luis Cañas 2011 TC
91
Colour: cherry, garnet rim. Nose: ripe fruit, spicy, creamy oak, toasty, complex. Palate: powerful, flavourful, toasty, round tannins.

Luis Cañas 2013 BFB
91
Colour: bright yellow. Nose: powerfull, ripe fruit, sweet spices, creamy oak, fragrant herbs. Palate: rich, smoky aftertaste, flavourful, fresh, good acidity.

Luis Cañas Hiru 3 Racimos 2007 T
93
Colour: cherry, garnet rim. Nose: ripe fruit, spicy, creamy oak, toasty, complex, dark chocolate, earthy notes. Palate: powerful, flavourful, toasty, round tannins.

Luis Cañas Selección de Familia 2008 TR
94
Colour: cherry, garnet rim. Nose: ripe fruit, spicy, creamy oak, toasty, complex. Palate: powerful, flavourful, toasty, round tannins.

BODEGAS MARQUÉS DE CÁCERES

Ctra. Logroño, s/n
26350 Cenicero (La Rioja)
☎: +34 941 454 000
Fax: +34 941 454 400
www.marquesdecaceres.com

Gaudium Gran Vino 2009 TR
95
Colour: cherry, garnet rim. Nose: ripe fruit, spicy, creamy oak, toasty, complex, dark chocolate, earthy notes. Palate: powerful, flavourful, toasty, round tannins.

Marqués de Cáceres 2005 TGR
92
Colour: deep cherry, orangey edge. Nose: waxy notes, tobacco, ripe fruit, spicy, aged wood nuances. Palate: fine bitter notes, elegant, flavourful, fine tannins.

Marqués de Cáceres 2009 TR
90
Colour: very deep cherry. Nose: ripe fruit, spicy, creamy oak, toasty, characterful. Palate: powerful, flavourful, toasty, round tannins.

Marqués de Cáceres 2010 TC
90
Colour: dark-red cherry, garnet rim. Nose: balanced, ripe fruit, scrubland. Palate: good acidity, spicy, long, easy to drink.

Marqués de Cáceres 2011 TC
88
Colour: cherry, garnet rim. Nose: ripe fruit, spicy, toasty, closed. Palate: powerful, flavourful, round tannins.

Marqués de Cáceres 2013 B
100% viura
87
Colour: bright straw. Nose: fresh, fresh fruit, white flowers, expressive. Palate: flavourful, fruity, good acidity.

Marqués de Cáceres 2013 RD
100% tempranillo
86
Colour: light cherry, bright. Nose: powerfull, ripe fruit, red berry notes, floral. Palate: fruity, fresh, flavourful.

Marqués de Cáceres Antea 2013 BFB
viura, malvasía
88
Colour: bright yellow. Nose: powerfull, ripe fruit, sweet spices, fragrant herbs. Palate: rich, flavourful, fresh, good acidity.

Marqués de Cáceres Ecológico Bio 2013 T
tempranillo, graciano

89 🌱

Colour: light cherry, purple rim. Nose: expressive, fresh fruit, red berry notes, floral. Palate: fruity, good acidity, fruity aftestaste.

Marqués de Cáceres Excellens Cuvee Especial 2011 TC
100% tempranillo

91

Colour: cherry, garnet rim. Nose: ripe fruit, spicy, creamy oak, toasty, complex. Palate: powerful, flavourful, toasty, round tannins.

Marqués de Cáceres Excellens Rose 2013 RD

88

Colour: raspberry rose. Nose: elegant, dried flowers, fragrant herbs, red berry notes. Palate: flavourful, good acidity, long, fine bitter notes.

MC Marqués de Cáceres 2011 T
100% tempranillo

93

Colour: cherry, garnet rim. Nose: ripe fruit, spicy, creamy oak, toasty, complex. Palate: powerful, flavourful, toasty, round tannins.

MC Marqués de Cáceres Cepas Antiguas 2012 T
tempranillo

91

Colour: cherry, garnet rim. Nose: ripe fruit, spicy, creamy oak, toasty, complex, red berry notes. Palate: powerful, flavourful, toasty, round tannins.

Satinela Semi-dulce 2013 B
viura, malvasía

86

Colour: bright straw. Nose: white flowers, fragrant herbs, fruit expression. Palate: fresh, fruity, flavourful, balanced.

BODEGAS MARQUÉS DE TERÁN
Ctra. de Nájera, Km. 1
26220 Ollauri (La Rioja)
☎: +34 941 338 373
Fax: +34 941 338 374
www.marquesdeteran.com
info@marquesdeteran.com

Marqués de Terán 2008 TR

88

Colour: cherry, garnet rim. Nose: fruit preserve, fruit liqueur notes, spicy, wet leather. Palate: flavourful, pruney, balsamic.

Marqués de Terán 2009 TC

88

Colour: cherry, garnet rim. Nose: spicy, creamy oak, toasty, complex, fruit liqueur notes. Palate: powerful, flavourful, toasty, round tannins.

Marqués de Terán Edición Limitada 2007 TR

92

Colour: cherry, garnet rim. Nose: spicy, toasty, overripe fruit, mineral, tobacco, wet leather. Palate: powerful, flavourful, toasty, round tannins.

Marqués de Terán Selección Especial 2011 T

93

Colour: cherry, garnet rim. Nose: ripe fruit, spicy, creamy oak, toasty, complex, dark chocolate, earthy notes. Palate: powerful, flavourful, toasty, round tannins.

Ollamendi 2008 T

88

Colour: ruby red. Nose: spicy, fine reductive notes, wet leather, aged wood nuances, toasty. Palate: spicy, long, toasty.

Versum 2010 T

91

Colour: very deep cherry. Nose: ripe fruit, spicy, characterful, roasted coffee. Palate: powerful, flavourful, toasty, round tannins.

BODEGAS MARTÍNEZ ALESANCO

José García, 20
26310 Badarán (La Rioja)
☎: +34 941 367 075
Fax: +34 941 367 075
www.bodegasmartinezalesanco.com
info@bodegasmartinezalesanco.com

Martínez Alesanco 2005 TGR
88
Colour: pale ruby, brick rim edge. Nose: spicy, fine reductive notes, aged wood nuances, fruit liqueur notes. Palate: spicy, fine tannins, long.

Martínez Alesanco 2009 TR
91
Colour: cherry, garnet rim. Nose: red berry notes, ripe fruit, spicy, creamy oak, toasty. Palate: powerful, flavourful, toasty, round tannins, balanced.

Martínez Alesanco 2011 TC
87
Colour: bright cherry. Nose: ripe fruit, sweet spices, creamy oak, medium intensity. Palate: fruity, flavourful, toasty.

Martínez Alesanco 2013 BFB
84

Martínez Alesanco 2013 RD Fermentado en Barrica
100% garnacha
85

Martínez Alesanco 2013 T
79

Martínez Alesanco Selección 2010 TR
90
Colour: cherry, garnet rim. Nose: red berry notes, ripe fruit, spicy, creamy oak, toasty, complex. Palate: powerful, flavourful, toasty, balanced.

Nada que Ver 2010 TC
maturana
92
Colour: cherry, garnet rim. Nose: ripe fruit, wild herbs, earthy notes, spicy, creamy oak. Palate: balanced, flavourful, long, balsamic.

BODEGAS MARTÍNEZ CORTA

Ctra. Cenicero, s/n
20313 Uruñuela (La Rioja)
☎: +34 670 937 522
www.bodegasmartinezcorta.com
administracion@bodegasmartinezcorta.com

Martínez Corta 2011 TC
tempranillo
86
Colour: very deep cherry. Nose: sweet spices, ripe fruit. Palate: correct, spicy, round tannins.

Martínez Corta Cepas Antiguas 2013 T
tempranillo, garnacha
83

Martínez Corta Cepas Antiguas Selección Privada 2012 T
tempranillo
88
Colour: cherry, garnet rim. Nose: cocoa bean, creamy oak, ripe fruit. Palate: flavourful, toasty, round tannins.

Martínez Corta Selección Especial 2009 T
tempranillo
88
Colour: cherry, garnet rim. Nose: ripe fruit, spicy, creamy oak, toasty, complex. Palate: powerful, flavourful, toasty, round tannins.

Soros 2010 T
tempranillo
87
Colour: cherry, garnet rim. Nose: spicy, creamy oak, toasty, fruit preserve. Palate: powerful, flavourful, toasty, round tannins.

Soros 2011 TC
tempranillo
89
Colour: cherry, garnet rim. Nose: red berry notes, ripe fruit, spicy, creamy oak, toasty, complex, earthy notes. Palate: powerful, flavourful, toasty, round tannins.

Tentación Garnacha 2011 T
100% garnacha
87
Colour: cherry, garnet rim. Nose: ripe fruit, wild herbs, earthy notes, spicy, creamy oak. Palate: balanced, flavourful, long, balsamic.

Tentación Tempranillo 2012 T
tempranillo
86
Colour: bright cherry. Nose: ripe fruit, sweet spices, creamy oak. Palate: flavourful, fruity, toasty, round tannins.

BODEGAS MARTÍNEZ PALACIOS

Real, 22
26220 Ollauri (Rioja)
☎: +34 941 338 023
Fax: +34 941 338 023
www.bodegasmartinezpalacios.com
bodega@bodegasmartinezpalacios.com

Martínez Palacios 2006 TR
89
Colour: pale ruby, brick rim edge. Nose: elegant, spicy, fine reductive notes, wet leather, aged wood nuances, fruit liqueur notes. Palate: spicy, fine tannins, elegant, long.

Martínez Palacios 2009 TC
100% tempranillo
89
Colour: cherry, garnet rim. Nose: ripe fruit, spicy, creamy oak, toasty, complex. Palate: powerful, flavourful, toasty, round tannins.

Martínez Palacios 2013 T
100% tempranillo
84

Martínez Palacios Pago Candela 2008 T
91
Colour: cherry, garnet rim. Nose: balanced, complex, ripe fruit, spicy. Palate: good structure, flavourful, round tannins.

BODEGAS MEDRANO IRAZU S.L.

San Pedro, 14
01309 Elvillar (Álava)
☎: +34 945 604 066
Fax: +34 945 604 126
www.bodegasmedranoirazu.com
fernando@bodegasmedranoirazu.com

Luis Medrano Graciano 2010 T
100% graciano
93
Colour: black cherry, garnet rim. Nose: ripe fruit, wild herbs, earthy notes, spicy, creamy oak. Palate: balanced, flavourful, long, balsamic.

Luis Medrano Tempranillo 2011 TC
100% tempranillo
92
Colour: deep cherry, garnet rim. Nose: spicy, ripe fruit, dry stone, elegant. Palate: good structure, balanced, round tannins, long.

Mas de Medrano Single Vineyard 2011 T
100% tempranillo
90
Colour: cherry, garnet rim. Nose: ripe fruit, spicy, toasty, complex, fine reductive notes. Palate: flavourful, toasty, round tannins.

Medrano Irazu 2008 TR
100% tempranillo
88
Colour: ruby red. Nose: spicy, fine reductive notes, wet leather, aged wood nuances, toasty. Palate: spicy, long, toasty.

Medrano Irazu 2011 TC
100% tempranillo
88
Colour: very deep cherry, garnet rim. Nose: ripe fruit, spicy, varietal, balanced. Palate: fruity, correct, balanced.

Medrano Irazu Reserva de Familia 2007 TR
100% tempranillo
91
Colour: cherry, garnet rim. Nose: ripe fruit, spicy, creamy oak, toasty, complex. Palate: powerful, flavourful, toasty, round tannins.

BODEGAS MITARTE

Avda. La Rioja, 5
01330 Labastida (Álava)
☎: +34 607 343 289
www.mitarte.com
bodegas@mitarte.com

Mitarte 2009 TR
tempranillo
90
Colour: cherry, garnet rim. Nose: ripe fruit, spicy, creamy oak, toasty, balsamic herbs. Palate: powerful, flavourful, toasty, round tannins.

Mitarte 2011 TC
tempranillo
87
Colour: bright cherry, garnet rim. Nose: balanced, ripe fruit, spicy, toasty, fruit preserve. Palate: ripe fruit, round tannins.

Mitarte 2013 BFB
viura
84

Mitarte 2013 RD
84

Mitarte 2013 T
tempranillo
82

Mitarte 2013 T Maceración Carbónica
tempranillo, garnacha, viura
85

Mitarte Vendimia Seleccionada 2011 TC
tempranillo
88
Colour: bright cherry, garnet rim. Nose: ripe fruit, spicy, creamy oak, toasty, complex. Palate: flavourful, toasty, round tannins.

Mitarte Viura 2013 B
100% viura

86

Colour: straw, pale. Nose: medium intensity, fresh fruit, faded flowers, dried flowers. Palate: correct, fine bitter notes.

BODEGAS MONTEABELLÓN
Calvario, s/n
09318 Nava de Roa (Burgos)
☎: +34 947 550 000
Fax: +34 947 550 219
www.monteabellon.com
info@monteabellon.com

Finca Athus 2011 TC
87

Colour: bright cherry. Nose: sweet spices, creamy oak, fruit preserve. Palate: flavourful, toasty, round tannins.

FINCA
ATHUS
RIOJA
Denominación de Origen Calificada
CRIANZA

BODEGAS MONTEALTO
Las Piscinas, s/n
01307 Baños del Ebro (Alava)
☎: +34 918 427 013
www.meddissl.com
contacta@meddissl.com

Robatie 2005 TR
100% tempranillo

87

Colour: very deep cherry. Nose: ripe fruit, spicy, creamy oak, toasty, characterful. Palate: powerful, flavourful, toasty, round tannins.

Robatie 2010 TC
100% tempranillo

89

Colour: bright cherry. Nose: ripe fruit, sweet spices, creamy oak. Palate: flavourful, fruity, toasty.

Robatie 2013 T
88

Colour: cherry, purple rim. Nose: red berry notes, raspberry, floral, expressive. Palate: fresh, fruity, flavourful, easy to drink.

Robatie Vendimia Seleccionada 2007 T
100% tempranillo

90

Colour: cherry, garnet rim. Nose: balanced, complex, ripe fruit, spicy, fine reductive notes. Palate: good structure, flavourful, round tannins.

BODEGAS MONTECILLO
Ctra. Navarrete-Fuenmayor, Km. 2
26360 Fuenmayor (La Rioja)
☎: +34 952 869 000
www.osborne.es
carolina.cerrato@osborne.es

Cumbre Montecillo 2006 T
92

Colour: pale ruby, brick rim edge. Nose: ripe fruit, wild herbs, spicy, creamy oak. Palate: flavourful, spicy, long, balsamic, balanced, elegant.

Montecillo 2007 TR
100% tempranillo

89

Colour: pale ruby, brick rim edge. Nose: elegant, spicy, fine reductive notes, aged wood nuances, wild herbs. Palate: spicy, balsamic, toasty.

Montecillo 2008 TR
100% tempranillo

87

Colour: pale ruby, brick rim edge. Nose: spicy, fine reductive notes, wet leather, aged wood nuances, ripe fruit. Palate: spicy, long, balsamic.

Montecillo 2010 TC
100% tempranillo

86

Colour: light cherry. Nose: ripe fruit, aged wood nuances, fine reductive notes, spicy. Palate: flavourful, spicy, easy to drink.

Viña Cumbrero 2008 TR
100% tempranillo

88

Colour: pale ruby, brick rim edge. Nose: spicy, fine reductive notes, wet leather, aged wood nuances, fruit liqueur notes. Palate: spicy, fine tannins, correct, easy to drink.

Viña Cumbrero 2013 T
100% tempranillo

84

Viña Monty 2008 TR
89

Colour: ruby red. Nose: powerfull, ripe fruit, roasted coffee, creamy oak. Palate: powerful, toasty, flavourful, spicy.

Viña Monty 2010 TC
100% tempranillo
88
Colour: cherry, garnet rim. Nose: ripe fruit, spicy, creamy oak. Palate: powerful, flavourful, toasty.

BODEGAS MORAZA
Ctra. Peñacerrada, s/n
26338 San Vicente de la Sonsierra
(La Rioja)
☎: +34 941 334 473
Fax: +34 941 334 473
www.bodegasmoraza.com
info@bodegasmoraza.com

Alesago 2011 T
100% tempranillo
89
Colour: cherry, garnet rim. Nose: red berry notes, raspberry, floral. Palate: fresh, fruity, flavourful, easy to drink.

Moraza 2011 TC
100% tempranillo
86
Colour: cherry, garnet rim. Nose: ripe fruit, spicy, creamy oak, toasty. Palate: powerful, flavourful, toasty.

Moraza 2013 B
100% viura
84

Moraza 2013 T
100% tempranillo
83 ♥

Moraza Vendimia Seleccionada 2013 T Barrica
100% tempranillo
84

BODEGAS MUGA
Barrio de la Estación, s/n
26200 Haro (La Rioja)
☎: +34 941 311 825
www.bodegasmuga.com
marketing@bodegasmuga.com

Aro 2010 T
95
Colour: very deep cherry, garnet rim. Nose: complex, expressive, cocoa bean, balsamic herbs, ripe fruit, aromatic coffee. Palate: full, round tannins, mineral

Muga 2010 TC
91
Colour: cherry, garnet rim. Nose: ripe fruit, spicy, complex, tobacco, waxy notes. Palate: powerful, flavourful, toasty, round tannins.

Muga 2013 BFB
90
Colour: bright straw. Nose: fresh fruit, tropical fruit, white flowers, elegant. Palate: flavourful, fruity, balanced, long, full.

Muga 2013 RD
88
Colour: raspberry rose. Nose: fresh, medium intensity, floral, citrus fruit. Palate: balanced, fine bitter notes, fruity, fresh.

Muga Selección Especial 2010 TR
92
Colour: ruby red. Nose: ripe fruit, wild herbs, earthy notes, spicy, creamy oak. Palate: balanced, flavourful, long, balsamic, elegant.

Prado Enea 2006 TGR
93
Colour: deep cherry, orangey edge. Nose: spicy, fine reductive notes, wet leather, toasty, cocoa bean, dried herbs. Palate: spicy, long, toasty.

Torre Muga 2010 T
94
Colour: bright cherry. Nose: ripe fruit, spicy, toasty, complex, elegant. Palate: flavourful, toasty, round tannins, spicy, elegant.

BODEGAS NAVAJAS
Camino Balgarauz, 2
26370 Navarrete (La Rioja)
☎: +34 941 440 140
Fax: +34 941 440 657
www.bodegasnavajas.com
info@bodegasnavajas.com

Navajas 2009 TR
88
Colour: dark-red cherry, garnet rim. Nose: cocoa bean, sweet spices, creamy oak, ripe fruit. Palate: flavourful, round tannins.

Navajas 2011 BC
100% viura
88
Colour: bright yellow. Nose: powerfull, ripe fruit, sweet spices, creamy oak, fragrant herbs. Palate: rich, smoky aftertaste, flavourful, fresh, good acidity.

Navajas Graciano 2010 TC
100% graciano
88
Colour: very deep cherry. Nose: smoky, toasty, dried herbs. Palate: fruity, spicy, correct, round tannins.

BODEGAS NAVA-RIOJA S.A.T.
Ctra. Eje del Ebro, s/n
31261 Andosilla (Navarra)
☎: +34 948 690 454
Fax: +34 948 674 491
www.bodegasnavarioja.com
info@bodegasnavarioja.com

Otis Tarda 2011 TC
tempranillo
88
Colour: cherry, garnet rim. Nose: ripe fruit, spicy, creamy oak, toasty, balsamic herbs. Palate: powerful, flavourful, toasty.

Otis Tarda 2013 B
tempranillo blanco
86
Colour: yellow. Nose: ripe fruit, faded flowers. Palate: flavourful, fruity, good acidity, balanced.

Otis Tarda 2013 T
tempranillo
85

BODEGAS NIVARIUS
Ctra. de Nalda a Viguera, 46
26190 Nalda (La Rioja)
☎: +34 941 444 418
www.nivarius.com
contacto@nivarius.com

Nivarius 2013 B
tempranillo blanco, viura
92
Colour: bright straw. Nose: white flowers, fresh fruit, expressive, fragrant herbs. Palate: flavourful, fruity, good acidity, balanced, elegant.

Nivei 2013 B
tempranillo blanco, viura, otras
90
Colour: bright straw. Nose: floral, ripe fruit. Palate: fruity, good acidity.

BODEGAS OBALO

Ctra. 232 A, Km. 26
26339 Abalos (Rioja)
☎: +34 941 744 056
www.bodegaobalo.com
info@bodegasobalo.com

La Tarara 2011 T
100% tempranillo

90

Colour: cherry, garnet rim. Nose: ripe fruit, spicy. Palate: powerful, flavourful, toasty, round tannins, fruity.

Obalo 2009 TR
100% tempranillo

93

Colour: deep cherry, garnet rim. Nose: powerfull, varietal, expressive, toasty. Palate: correct, spicy, flavourful, round tannins.

Obalo 2011 TC
100% tempranillo

93

Colour: bright cherry, garnet rim. Nose: balanced, elegant, cocoa bean, ripe fruit. Palate: good structure, complex, flavourful.

Crianza 2011

obalo

Rioja
Denominación de Origen Calificada

Obalo 2013 T
100% tempranillo

89

Colour: very deep cherry, garnet rim. Nose: powerfull, ripe fruit, roasted coffee, dark chocolate. Palate: powerful, toasty, roasted-coffee aftertaste.

Pinturas 2011 TC
tempranillo

86

Colour: deep cherry, garnet rim. Nose: powerfull, fruit preserve, sweet spices. Palate: correct, powerful.

BODEGAS OLARRA

Avda. de Mendavia, 30
26009 Logroño (La Rioja)
☎: +34 941 235 299
Fax: +34 941 253 703
www.bodegasolarra.es
bodegasolarra@bodegasolarra.es

Añares 2009 TR

88

Colour: cherry, garnet rim. Nose: ripe fruit, spicy, creamy oak, toasty, complex. Palate: powerful, flavourful, toasty, round tannins.

Añares 2012 TC

87

Colour: bright cherry. Nose: ripe fruit, wild herbs, earthy notes, spicy, creamy oak. Palate: balanced, flavourful, long, balsamic.

Cerro Añón 2009 TR

92

Colour: cherry, garnet rim. Nose: ripe fruit, spicy, creamy oak, toasty, complex. Palate: powerful, flavourful, toasty, round tannins, balanced, elegant.

Cerro Añón 2012 TC

90

Colour: cherry, garnet rim. Nose: ripe fruit, spicy, creamy oak, toasty, complex. Palate: powerful, flavourful, toasty.

Otoñal 2009 TR

88

Colour: cherry, garnet rim. Nose: ripe fruit, spicy, creamy oak, toasty, complex, fine reductive notes. Palate: powerful, flavourful, toasty, round tannins, correct.

Otoñal 2012 TC

87

Colour: cherry, garnet rim. Nose: red berry notes, ripe fruit, wild herbs, spicy. Palate: correct, flavourful, spicy, balsamic.

Otoñal 2013 T
100% tempranillo

84

Summa 2009 TR

92

Colour: cherry, garnet rim. Nose: balanced, complex, ripe fruit, spicy. Palate: good structure, flavourful, round tannins, round, unctuous, balanced.

BODEGAS OLARTIA

Pza. Asunción, 8
26003 Rodezno (La Rioja)
☎: +34 941 338 296
Fax: +34 941 338 360
www.bodegasolartia.com
contacto@bodegasolartia.com

Señorío de Olartia 2004 TGR
tempranillo
90
Colour: ruby red. Nose: spicy, fine reductive notes, aged wood nuances, toasty, ripe fruit. Palate: spicy, long, toasty, balsamic, fine tannins.

Señorío de Olartia 2007 TR
tempranillo
86
Colour: deep cherry, garnet rim. Nose: spicy, ripe fruit, toasty, old leather. Palate: flavourful, fine bitter notes.

BODEGAS ONDALÁN

Ctra. de Logroño, 22
01320 Oyón - Oion (Álava)
☎: +34 945 622 537
Fax: +34 945 622 538
www.ondalan.es
ondalan@ondalan.es

100 Abades Graciano Selección 2011 T
100% graciano
89
Colour: cherry, garnet rim. Nose: ripe fruit, wild herbs, earthy notes, spicy. Palate: balanced, flavourful, long, balsamic.

Ondalán 2009 TR
88
Colour: cherry, garnet rim. Nose: ripe fruit, spicy, creamy oak, toasty, complex. Palate: powerful, flavourful, toasty, round tannins.

Ondalán 2011 TC
85

Ondalán 2013 B
100% viura
85

Ondalán 2013 T
84

Ondalán Tempranillo Selección 2011 T
100% tempranillo
89
Colour: bright cherry. Nose: ripe fruit, sweet spices, creamy oak, expressive. Palate: flavourful, fruity, toasty, round tannins.

BODEGAS ONDARRE

Ctra. de Aras, s/n
31230 Viana (Navarra)
☎: +34 948 645 300
Fax: +34 948 646 002
www.bodegasondarre.es
bodegasondarre@bodegasondarre.es

Mayor de Ondarre 2009 TR
90
Colour: cherry, garnet rim. Nose: ripe fruit, wild herbs, earthy notes, spicy, creamy oak. Palate: balanced, flavourful, long, balsamic, elegant.

Señorío de Ondarre 2009 TR
90
Colour: cherry, garnet rim. Nose: balanced, complex, ripe fruit, spicy. Palate: good structure, flavourful, round tannins, balanced.

BODEGAS ORBEN

Ctra. Laguardia, Km. 60
01300 Laguardia (Álava)
☎: +34 945 609 086
Fax: +34 945 609 261
www.grupoartevino.com
izadi@izadi.com

Malpuesto 2012 T
100% tempranillo
94
Colour: black cherry. Nose: toasty, dark chocolate, ripe fruit, sweet spices. Palate: concentrated, powerful, toasty, mineral.

Orben 2011 T
100% tempranillo
93
Colour: cherry, garnet rim. Nose: spicy, creamy oak, toasty, earthy notes. Palate: powerful, flavourful, toasty, round tannins.

BODEGAS ORTUBIA

Camino de Uriso, s/n
26292 Villalba de Rioja (La Rioja)
☎: +34 941 310 842
Fax: +34 941 310 842
www.bodegasortubia.com
ortubia@bodegasortubia.com

1958 de Ortubia 2009 TR
100% tempranillo
90
Colour: bright cherry. Nose: ripe fruit, sweet spices, creamy oak, expressive. Palate: flavourful, fruity, toasty, round tannins.

Ortubia 2007 TR
100% tempranillo
87
Colour: dark-red cherry, garnet rim. Nose: tobacco, spicy. Palate: fruity, easy to drink, spicy, round tannins.

Ortubia 2013 B
100% viura

85

BODEGAS OSTATU
Ctra. Vitoria, 1
01307 Samaniego (Álava)
☎: +34 945 609 133
Fax: +34 945 623 338
www.ostatu.com
info@ostatu.com

Gloria de Ostatu 2007 T
100% tempranillo

93
Colour: very deep cherry. Nose: ripe fruit, spicy, creamy oak, toasty, characterful. Palate: powerful, flavourful, toasty, round tannins.

Laderas Ostatu 2009 T
tempranillo, viura

88
Colour: deep cherry. Nose: spicy, ripe fruit, wet leather. Palate: spicy, ripe fruit.

Lore de Ostatu 2011 B
viura, malvasía

92
Colour: bright yellow. Nose: powerfull, ripe fruit, sweet spices, creamy oak, fragrant herbs. Palate: rich, smoky aftertaste, flavourful, fresh, good acidity.

Ostatu 2008 TR
tempranillo

90
Colour: very deep cherry. Nose: ripe fruit, spicy, creamy oak, toasty, characterful. Palate: powerful, flavourful, toasty, round tannins.

Ostatu 2011 TC
tempranillo, graciano, mazuelo, garnacha

92
Colour: very deep cherry. Nose: ripe fruit, spicy, creamy oak, toasty, characterful. Palate: powerful, flavourful, toasty, round tannins.

Ostatu 2013 B
viura, malvasía

89
Colour: bright straw. Nose: fresh, fresh fruit, white flowers, expressive. Palate: flavourful, fruity, good acidity, balanced.

Ostatu 2013 T
tempranillo, graciano, mazuelo, viura

89
Colour: light cherry. Nose: medium intensity, red berry notes, rose petals. Palate: balanced, fruity, long.

Ostatu Rosé 2013 RD
tempranillo, garnacha, viura

88
Colour: raspberry rose. Nose: dried flowers, fragrant herbs, red berry notes, medium intensity. Palate: flavourful, good acidity, long, fruity aftestaste.

Selección Ostatu 2010 T
tempranillo, graciano

93
Colour: cherry, garnet rim. Nose: ripe fruit, spicy, creamy oak, toasty, complex. Palate: powerful, flavourful, toasty, round tannins.

BODEGAS PACO GARCÍA
Crta. de Ventas Blancas s/n
26143 Murillo de Rio Leza (La Rioja)
☎: +34 941 432 372
Fax: +34 941 432 156
www.bodegaspacogarcia.com
info@bodegaspacogarcia.com

Beautiful Things de Paco García 2010 T

91
Colour: cherry, garnet rim. Nose: ripe fruit, wild herbs, earthy notes, spicy, creamy oak. Palate: balanced, flavourful, long, balsamic.

Paco García 2011 TC
89
Colour: bright cherry. Nose: ripe fruit, sweet spices, toasty. Palate: flavourful, fruity, toasty, round tannins.

Paco García Seis 2013 T
100% tempranillo
88
Colour: bright cherry, garnet rim. Nose: sweet spices, creamy oak, red berry notes, ripe fruit, dried fruit. Palate: flavourful, fruity, toasty.

BODEGAS PALACIO
San Lázaro, 1
1300 Laguardia (Álava)
☎: +34 945 600 057
Fax: +34 945 600 297
www.bodegaspalacio.es
rrpp@bodegaspalacio.es

Bodegas Palacio Especial 2008 TR
91
Colour: cherry, garnet rim. Nose: ripe fruit, spicy, creamy oak, toasty, complex, dark chocolate, earthy notes. Palate: powerful, flavourful, toasty, round tannins.

Cosme Palacio 2011 TC
100% tempranillo
91
Colour: bright cherry. Nose: ripe fruit, spicy, creamy oak, toasty, complex, scrubland. Palate: powerful, flavourful, toasty, round tannins.

Cosme Palacio 1894 2011 B
91
Colour: bright straw. Nose: dried herbs, faded flowers, mineral. Palate: ripe fruit, spicy, long.

Cosme Palacio 2010 TR
100% tempranillo
90
Colour: cherry, garnet rim. Nose: ripe fruit, fruit expression, balanced. Palate: good structure, flavourful, full, toasty.

Cosme Palacio 2012 B
100% viura
88
Colour: bright golden. Nose: candied fruit, citrus fruit, honeyed notes. Palate: fine bitter notes, sweetness.

Cosme Palacio 2012 B Barrica
100% viura
86
Colour: yellow, pale. Nose: ripe fruit, balanced. Palate: rich, ripe fruit, fine bitter notes.

Glorioso 2006 TGR
100% tempranillo
90
Colour: dark-red cherry, orangey edge. Nose: medium intensity, spicy, ripe fruit. Palate: flavourful, fine tannins, good acidity.

Glorioso 2009 TR
100% tempranillo
91
Colour: cherry, garnet rim. Nose: ripe fruit, spicy, creamy oak, toasty, complex. Palate: powerful, flavourful, toasty, round tannins.

Glorioso 2011 TC
100% tempranillo
89
Colour: deep cherry, garnet rim. Nose: ripe fruit, fruit preserve, toasty. Palate: flavourful, correct, round tannins.

Milflores 2013 T
100% tempranillo
87
Colour: light cherry. Nose: expressive, fresh fruit, red berry notes, floral. Palate: flavourful, fruity, good acidity.

BODEGAS PALACIOS REMONDO

Avda. Zaragoza, 8
26540 Alfaro (La Rioja)
☎: +34 941 180 207
Fax: +34 941 181 628
info@palaciosremondo.com

La Montesa 2011 TC
91
Colour: cherry, garnet rim. Nose: wild herbs, earthy notes, spicy, creamy oak. Palate: balanced, flavourful, long, balsamic.

La Montesa 2012 TC
92
Colour: cherry, garnet rim. Nose: spicy, creamy oak, toasty, red berry notes, fragrant herbs. Palate: powerful, flavourful, toasty, round tannins.

La Vendimia 2013 T
88
Colour: bright cherry, garnet rim. Nose: red berry notes, ripe fruit, fresh. Palate: correct, easy to drink, fruity aftestaste.

Plácet Valtomelloso 2011 B
100% viura
93
Colour: bright straw. Nose: powerfull, ripe fruit, sweet spices, creamy oak, fragrant herbs. Palate: rich, smoky aftertaste, flavourful, fresh, good acidity, long.

Propiedad 2010 T
100% garnacha
92
Colour: bright cherry. Nose: ripe fruit, sweet spices, creamy oak, scrubland, balsamic herbs. Palate: flavourful, fruity, toasty, round tannins.

Propiedad 2011 T
100% garnacha
94
Colour: cherry, garnet rim. Nose: wild herbs, earthy notes, spicy, creamy oak, red berry notes. Palate: balanced, flavourful, long, balsamic.

BODEGAS PATROCINIO

Ctra. Cenicero, s/n
26313 Uruñuela (La Rioja)
☎: +34 941 371 319
Fax: +34 941 371 435
www.bodegaspatrocinio.com
info@bodegaspatrocinio.com

Lágrimas de María 2009 TR
100% tempranillo
88
Colour: pale ruby, brick rim edge. Nose: ripe fruit, spicy, creamy oak, toasty. Palate: powerful, flavourful, toasty, round tannins.

Lágrimas de María 2011 TC
100% tempranillo
89
Colour: cherry, garnet rim. Nose: ripe fruit, spicy, creamy oak, toasty, aged wood nuances. Palate: powerful, flavourful, toasty.

Lágrimas de María 2013 RD
100% tempranillo
84

Lágrimas de María 2013 T
100% tempranillo
83

Lágrimas de María Madurado 2012 TC
100% tempranillo
86
Colour: bright cherry. Nose: ripe fruit, sweet spices, creamy oak. Palate: flavourful, fruity, toasty.

Lágrimas de María Viura 2013 B
100% viura
85

Sancho Garcés 2009 TR
100% tempranillo
89
Colour: ruby red. Nose: ripe fruit, fruit liqueur notes, spicy, creamy oak, fine reductive notes. Palate: powerful, spicy, long, balanced.

Sancho Garcés 2011 TC
100% tempranillo
87
Colour: bright cherry. Nose: ripe fruit, sweet spices, creamy oak, medium intensity. Palate: fruity, flavourful, toasty.

Sancho Garcés 2013 T
100% tempranillo
85

Señorío de Uñuela 2009 TR
100% tempranillo
88
Colour: cherry, garnet rim. Nose: ripe fruit, spicy, creamy oak, toasty, complex. Palate: powerful, flavourful, toasty, round tannins.

Señorío de Uñuela 2011 TC
100% tempranillo
89
Colour: cherry, garnet rim. Nose: ripe fruit, spicy, creamy oak, toasty, complex. Palate: powerful, flavourful, toasty.

Señorío de Uñuela 2013 RD
100% tempranillo
85

Señorío de Uñuela Tempranillo 2013 T
100% tempranillo
84

Señorío de Uñuela Viura 2013 B
100% viura
88
Colour: bright straw. Nose: fresh, white flowers, medium intensity. Palate: flavourful, fruity, good acidity, balanced, long.

Zinio 2013 B
100% viura
87
Colour: bright straw. Nose: white flowers, fragrant herbs, fruit expression, citrus fruit. Palate: fresh, fruity, flavourful, elegant.

Zinio 2013 RD
100% tempranillo
85

Zinio Garnacha 2012 T
100% garnacha
87
Colour: cherry, garnet rim. Nose: ripe fruit, spicy, creamy oak, toasty, wild herbs. Palate: powerful, flavourful, toasty.

Zinio Tempranillo Garnacha Orgánico 2009 T
88 🌱
Colour: cherry, garnet rim. Nose: balanced, complex, ripe fruit, spicy, fine reductive notes. Palate: good structure, flavourful, spicy.

Zinio Tempranillo Graciano 2011 T
88
Colour: cherry, garnet rim. Nose: ripe fruit, spicy, creamy oak. Palate: balanced, flavourful, long, balsamic.

Zinio Vendimia Seleccionada 2006 TR
100% tempranillo
88
Colour: pale ruby, brick rim edge. Nose: balanced, complex, ripe fruit, spicy, balsamic herbs. Palate: good structure, flavourful, round tannins.

Zinio Vendimia Seleccionada 2011 TC
100% tempranillo
90
Colour: cherry, garnet rim. Nose: red berry notes, ripe fruit, spicy, creamy oak, toasty. Palate: powerful, flavourful, toasty, round tannins.

BODEGAS PERICA
Avda. de la Rioja, 59
26340 San Asensio (La Rioja)
☎: +34 941 457 152
Fax: +34 941 457 240
www.bodegasperica.com
info@bodegasperica.com

6 Cepas 6 2012 T
100% tempranillo
89
Colour: bright cherry. Nose: ripe fruit, sweet spices, creamy oak, expressive. Palate: flavourful, fruity, toasty, round tannins.

6 Cepas 6 2013 B
87
Colour: bright yellow. Nose: ripe fruit, sweet spices, fragrant herbs. Palate: rich, smoky aftertaste, good acidity.

6 Cepas 6 2013 RD
87
Colour: rose, purple rim. Nose: powerfull, ripe fruit, red berry notes, spicy. Palate: powerful, fruity, fresh.

Mi Villa 2013 T
83

Olagosa 2007 TR
88
Colour: deep cherry. Nose: ripe fruit, spicy, creamy oak, toasty, characterful. Palate: powerful, flavourful, toasty, round tannins.

Olagosa 2011 TC
88
Colour: cherry, garnet rim. Nose: ripe fruit, spicy, creamy oak, toasty, complex. Palate: powerful, flavourful, toasty.

Olagosa 2013 B
88
Colour: bright straw. Nose: white flowers, spicy, balanced. Palate: fruity, spicy, good acidity, fine bitter notes.

Perica Oro 2008 TR

92

Colour: cherry, garnet rim. Nose: ripe fruit, wild herbs, earthy notes, spicy, creamy oak. Palate: balanced, flavourful, long, balsamic.

BODEGAS PUELLES

Camino de los Molinos, s/n
26339 Ábalos (La Rioja)
☎: +34 941 334 415
Fax: +34 941 334 132
www.bodegaspuelles.com
informacion@bodegaspuelles.com

Molino de Puelles Ecológico 2009 T

tempranillo

86

Colour: cherry, garnet rim. Nose: ripe fruit, wild herbs, spicy, creamy oak. Palate: flavourful, long, balsamic.

Puelles 2004 TGR

tempranillo

89

Colour: pale ruby, brick rim edge. Nose: elegant, spicy, fine reductive notes, wet leather, aged wood nuances, fruit liqueur notes. Palate: spicy, fine tannins, elegant, long.

Puelles 2007 TR

tempranillo

86

Colour: ruby red. Nose: ripe fruit, wild herbs, spicy, creamy oak, fine reductive notes. Palate: fine bitter notes, powerful, flavourful.

Puelles 2011 TC

tempranillo

88

Colour: cherry, garnet rim. Nose: ripe fruit, spicy, creamy oak, toasty, complex. Palate: powerful, flavourful, toasty, round tannins.

Puelles 2012 T

tempranillo

84

Puelles 2013 B

viura

86

Colour: bright straw. Nose: fresh, fresh fruit, white flowers, expressive. Palate: flavourful, fruity, good acidity, balanced.

BODEGAS RAMÍREZ DE LA PISCINA

Ctra. Vitoria-Logroño, s/n
26338 San Vicente de la Sonsierra
(La Rioja)
☎: +34 941 334 505
Fax: +34 941 334 506
www.ramirezdelapiscina.es
info@ramirezdelapiscina.com

Ramírez de la Piscina 2005 TGR

100% tempranillo

87

Colour: dark-red cherry. Nose: spicy, fine reductive notes, wet leather, toasty. Palate: spicy, long, toasty.

Ramírez de la Piscina 2007 TR

100% tempranillo

86

Colour: ruby red. Nose: ripe fruit, wild herbs, fine reductive notes, spicy, smoky. Palate: powerful, flavourful, spirituous.

Ramírez de la Piscina 2008 TR

100% tempranillo

88

Colour: cherry, garnet rim. Nose: ripe fruit, wild herbs, spicy, creamy oak. Palate: balanced, flavourful, long, balsamic.

Ramírez de la Piscina 2011 TC

100% tempranillo

87

Colour: deep cherry. Nose: ripe fruit, spicy, creamy oak, toasty. Palate: flavourful, toasty, round tannins.

Ramírez de la Piscina 2013 B

100% viura

84

Ramírez de la Piscina 2013 T

100% tempranillo

86

Colour: cherry, purple rim. Nose: expressive, fresh fruit, red berry notes, floral. Palate: good acidity, light-bodied, good finish.

Ramírez de la Piscina Selección 2009 TR

100% tempranillo

89

Colour: cherry, garnet rim. Nose: ripe fruit, spicy, creamy oak, toasty, complex, balsamic herbs. Palate: powerful, flavourful, toasty.

Ramírez de la Piscina Selección 2010 TC
100% tempranillo

89

Colour: cherry, garnet rim. Nose: red berry notes, ripe fruit, spicy, creamy oak, toasty, complex, earthy notes. Palate: flavourful, round tannins.

BODEGAS RAMÓN BILBAO
Avda. Santo Domingo, 34
26200 Haro (La Rioja)
☎: +34 941 310 295
Fax: +34 941 310 832
www.bodegasramonbilbao.es
info@bodegasramonbilbao.es

Mirto de Ramón Bilbao 2010 T
100% tempranillo

93

Colour: cherry, garnet rim. Nose: ripe fruit, spicy, creamy oak, complex, earthy notes, roasted coffee. Palate: powerful, flavourful, toasty, round tannins.

Ramón Bilbao 2006 TGR

91

Colour: cherry, garnet rim. Nose: red berry notes, ripe fruit, spicy, creamy oak, complex, earthy notes. Palate: powerful, flavourful, round tannins.

Ramón Bilbao 2010 TR

92

Colour: bright cherry. Nose: ripe fruit, sweet spices, medium intensity. Palate: fruity, flavourful, toasty, easy to drink, good acidity, elegant.

Ramón Bilbao 2012 TC
100% tempranillo

88

Colour: deep cherry, garnet rim. Nose: ripe fruit, cocoa bean, sweet spices. Palate: correct, round tannins, toasty.

to Spanish Wine

Ramón Bilbao Edición Limitada 2012 T
100% tempranillo

89

Colour: very deep cherry, garnet rim. Nose: sweet spices, creamy oak, ripe fruit. Palate: correct, fruity, round tannins.

Ramón Bilbao Rosé 2013 RD
100% garnacha

88

Colour: raspberry rose. Nose: medium intensity, white flowers, expressive, fragrant herbs. Palate: fresh, easy to drink, good acidity.

Ramón Bilbao Viñedos de Altura 2012 TC
90

Colour: deep cherry, purple rim. Nose: ripe fruit, spicy, wild herbs. Palate: flavourful, correct, spicy.

BODEGAS REMÍREZ DE GANUZA

Constitución, 1
01307 Samaniego (Álava)
☎: +34 945 609 022
Fax: +34 945 623 335
www.remirezdeganuza.com
cristina@remirezdeganuza.com

Erre Punto 2012 BFB

89

Colour: bright straw. Nose: ripe fruit, balsamic herbs, roasted coffee. Palate: powerful, flavourful, spicy, long, toasty.

Fincas de Ganuza 2007 TR

93

Colour: deep cherry, garnet rim. Nose: elegant, fine reductive notes, ripe fruit, wild herbs. Palate: spicy, good acidity, fine bitter notes.

Remírez de Ganuza 2007 TR

94

Colour: cherry, garnet rim. Nose: complex, balanced, expressive, cocoa bean, ripe fruit, spicy. Palate: balanced, elegant, long, round tannins.

BODEGAS RIOJANAS

Estación, 1 - 21
26350 Cenicero (La Rioja)
☎: +34 941 454 050
Fax: +34 941 454 529
www.bodegasriojanas.com
bodega@bodegasriojanas.com

Canchales 2013 T
100% tempranillo

84

Gran Albina 2008 TR

90

Colour: pale ruby, brick rim edge. Nose: spicy, fine reductive notes, wet leather, aged wood nuances, fruit liqueur notes. Palate: spicy, fine tannins, balanced, elegant.

Gran Albina Vendimia 2009 T
tempranillo, mazuelo, graciano

90

Colour: cherry, garnet rim. Nose: fruit preserve, ripe fruit, spicy, creamy oak. Palate: powerful, flavourful, spicy, long, toasty.

Monte Real 2006 TGR
100% tempranillo

89

Colour: pale ruby, brick rim edge. Nose: spicy, fine reductive notes, wet leather, aged wood nuances, fruit liqueur notes, balanced. Palate: spicy, long, round tannins, correct.

Monte Real 2008 TR
100% tempranillo

88

Colour: bright cherry. Nose: ripe fruit, sweet spices, creamy oak, fine reductive notes. Palate: fruity, flavourful, toasty, balanced.

Monte Real 2011 TC
100% tempranillo

87

Colour: ruby red, garnet rim. Nose: spicy, fine reductive notes, wet leather, aged wood nuances, toasty, balsamic herbs. Palate: spicy, long, toasty, correct.

Monte Real Reserva de Familia 2008 TR
100% tempranillo

89

Colour: cherry, garnet rim. Nose: ripe fruit, spicy, toasty, old leather, tobacco, aged wood nuances. Palate: powerful, flavourful, toasty, round tannins.

Puerta Vieja 2009 TR

88

Colour: cherry, garnet rim. Nose: ripe fruit, spicy, creamy oak, toasty, complex. Palate: powerful, flavourful, toasty, round tannins, balanced.

Puerta Vieja 2011 TC

88

Colour: cherry, garnet rim. Nose: ripe fruit, spicy, creamy oak, toasty. Palate: powerful, flavourful, toasty, balanced.

Puerta Vieja 2013 B
100% viura

85

Puerta Vieja Selección 2011 TC
100% tempranillo

89

Colour: cherry, garnet rim. Nose: ripe fruit, wild herbs, spicy, creamy oak, mineral. Palate: balanced, flavourful, long, balsamic, toasty.

Viña Albina 2013 BFB

87

Colour: bright yellow. Nose: powerfull, ripe fruit, sweet spices, creamy oak. Palate: rich, smoky aftertaste, flavourful, fresh, good acidity.

Viña Albina 2006 TGR

90

Colour: pale ruby, brick rim edge. Nose: elegant, spicy, fine reductive notes, wet leather, aged wood nuances, ripe fruit. Palate: spicy, fine tannins, elegant, long.

Viña Albina 2008 TR

88

Colour: pale ruby, brick rim edge. Nose: ripe fruit, aged wood nuances, spicy, balsamic herbs. Palate: powerful, flavourful, good structure, spicy.

Viña Albina Selección 2008 TR

89

Colour: cherry, garnet rim. Nose: ripe fruit, spicy, creamy oak, toasty. Palate: powerful, flavourful, toasty, round tannins, balanced.

Viña Albina Semidulce 2001 B Reserva

91

Colour: bright golden. Nose: ripe fruit, dry nuts, powerfull, toasty, aged wood nuances. Palate: flavourful, fruity, spicy, toasty, long.

Viña Albina Semidulce 2013 B

85

BODEGAS RIOLANC
Curillos, 36
01308 Lanciego (Álava)
☎: +34 605 954 399
www.riolanc.com
riolanc@riolanc.com

Riolanc Vendimia Seleccionada 2013 T

86

Colour: cherry, purple rim. Nose: fresh fruit, red berry notes, floral. Palate: flavourful, fruity, good acidity, round tannins.

BODEGAS RODA
Avda. de Vizcaya, 5 Bº de la Estación
26200 Haro (La Rioja)
☎: +34 941 303 001
Fax: +34 941 312 703
www.roda.es
rodarioja@roda.es

Cirsion 2010 T
100% tempranillo

96

Colour: cherry, garnet rim. Nose: ripe fruit, spicy, creamy oak, toasty, dark chocolate, mineral. Palate: powerful, flavourful, toasty, round tannins.

Roda 2008 TR

93

Colour: very deep cherry. Nose: ripe fruit, spicy, creamy oak, toasty, characterful. Palate: powerful, flavourful, toasty, round tannins.

Roda 2009 TR

92

Colour: cherry, garnet rim. Nose: ripe fruit, spicy, creamy oak, toasty, complex. Palate: powerful, flavourful, toasty, round tannins.

Roda I 2007 TR
100% tempranillo
94
Colour: bright cherry. Nose: ripe fruit, sweet spices, creamy oak, characterful. Palate: fruity, flavourful, toasty.

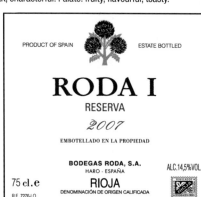

Roda I 2008 T
100% tempranillo
94
Colour: cherry, garnet rim. Nose: ripe fruit, spicy, creamy oak, toasty, complex, dark chocolate, earthy notes. Palate: powerful, flavourful, toasty, round tannins.

Sela 2011 T
90
Colour: bright cherry. Nose: ripe fruit, sweet spices, creamy oak. Palate: flavourful, fruity, toasty, round tannins.

BODEGAS SEÑORÍA DE YERGA
Barrio Bodegas, s/n
26142 Villamediana (La Rioja)
☎: +34 941 435 003
info@senoriodeyerga.com

Castillo de Yerga 2009 TC
87
Colour: ruby red. Nose: powerfull, ripe fruit, roasted coffee, dark chocolate. Palate: powerful, toasty, roasted-coffee aftertaste.

Castillo Yerga 2007 TR
86
Colour: pale ruby, brick rim edge. Nose: spicy, fine reductive notes, wet leather, aged wood nuances, fruit liqueur notes. Palate: spicy, fine tannins, correct.

Señorío de Yerga 2005 TGR
89
Colour: pale ruby, brick rim edge. Nose: spicy, fine reductive notes, wet leather, aged wood nuances, fruit liqueur notes. Palate: spicy, fine tannins, elegant, long.

BODEGAS SIDERALES
Senda del Soto, 10
01306 Lapuebla de Labarca (Alava)
☎: +34 945 627 363
Fax: +34 945 607 257
www.siderales.com
bodega@siderales.com

Sideral 2007 T
100% tempranillo
91
Colour: ruby red. Nose: red berry notes, ripe fruit, spicy, creamy oak, toasty, complex, earthy notes. Palate: powerful, flavourful, toasty, round tannins.

Sideral Edición Limitada 2010 T
100% tempranillo
89
Colour: cherry, garnet rim. Nose: ripe fruit, spicy, creamy oak, toasty. Palate: powerful, flavourful, toasty.

Sideral I 2008 T
100% tempranillo
90
Colour: ruby red. Nose: balanced, complex, ripe fruit, spicy, fine reductive notes. Palate: good structure, flavourful, round tannins, balanced.

BODEGAS SOLAR DE SAMANIEGO
Ctra. De Elciego s/n
01300 Laguardia (Álava)
☎: +34 902 227 700
Fax: +34 902 227 701
www.solardesamaniego.com
bodega@cofradiasamaniego.com

Solar de Samaniego 2007 TGR
87
Colour: dark-red cherry, orangey edge. Nose: waxy notes, balanced, ripe fruit, spicy, old leather. Palate: fruity, fine bitter notes.

Solar de Samaniego 2010 TR
86
Colour: deep cherry, garnet rim. Nose: tobacco, spicy, ripe fruit, dried herbs. Palate: correct, good finish.

Solar de Samaniego 2011 TC
100% tempranillo
87
Colour: bright cherry. Nose: ripe fruit, sweet spices, creamy oak, medium intensity, wild herbs. Palate: fruity, flavourful, toasty.

Valcavada 2008 TR

92

Colour: cherry, garnet rim. Nose: red berry notes, ripe fruit, spicy, creamy oak, toasty, complex, fine reductive notes. Palate: powerful, flavourful, toasty, round tannins.

BODEGAS SOLAR VIEJO

Camino de la Hoya, s/n
01300 Laguardia (Álava)
☎: +34 945 600 113
Fax: +34 945 600 600
www.solarviejo.com
solarviejo@solarviejo.com

Orube 2010 T
tempranillo

91

Colour: bright cherry, garnet rim. Nose: ripe fruit, sweet spices, creamy oak, expressive. Palate: flavourful, fruity, toasty, round tannins.

Solar Viejo 2008 TR
tempranillo, graciano

88

Colour: cherry, garnet rim. Nose: ripe fruit, creamy oak, toasty, dried herbs. Palate: powerful, flavourful, toasty, round tannins.

Solar Viejo 2011 TC
tempranillo

86

Colour: cherry, garnet rim. Nose: ripe fruit, spicy, toasty, medium intensity. Palate: round tannins, easy to drink, correct.

BODEGAS SONSIERRA, S. COOP.

El Remedio, s/n
26338 San Vicente de la Sonsierra
(La Rioja)
☎: +34 941 334 031
Fax: +34 941 334 245
www.sonsierra.com
administracion@sonsierra.com

Pagos de la Sonsierra 2009 TR
tempranillo

90

Colour: pale ruby, brick rim edge. Nose: ripe fruit, wild herbs, spicy, creamy oak. Palate: powerful, flavourful, spicy, long.

Perfume de Sonsierra David Delfín 2010 T
tempranillo

91

Colour: cherry, garnet rim. Nose: ripe fruit, spicy, creamy oak, toasty. Palate: powerful, flavourful, toasty.

Sonsierra 2008 TGR
tempranillo

90

Colour: cherry, garnet rim. Nose: ripe fruit, spicy, creamy oak, toasty, complex, balsamic herbs. Palate: powerful, flavourful, toasty, round tannins, balanced.

Sonsierra 2010 TR
tempranillo

90

Colour: cherry, garnet rim. Nose: balanced, complex, ripe fruit, spicy. Palate: good structure, flavourful, round tannins.

Sonsierra 2011 TC
tempranillo

88

Colour: cherry, garnet rim. Nose: ripe fruit, spicy, creamy oak, toasty, complex. Palate: powerful, flavourful, toasty.

Sonsierra 2013 B
viura

86

Colour: bright straw. Nose: white flowers, fragrant herbs, fruit expression. Palate: fresh, fruity, flavourful, balanced, elegant.

Sonsierra 2013 BFB
viura

88

Colour: bright straw. Nose: white flowers, fresh fruit, expressive, fine lees, dried herbs, toasty. Palate: flavourful, fruity, good acidity, balanced.

Sonsierra 2013 RD
tempranillo

86

Colour: rose, purple rim. Nose: powerfull, ripe fruit, red berry notes, floral, expressive. Palate: powerful, fruity, fresh.

Sonsierra Tempranillo 2013 T
tempranillo

86

Colour: cherry, purple rim. Nose: red berry notes, overripe fruit. Palate: flavourful, fruity, good acidity, round tannins.

Sonsierra Vendimia Seleccionada 2010 TC
tempranillo

89

Colour: cherry, garnet rim. Nose: ripe fruit, wild herbs, earthy notes, spicy, creamy oak. Palate: balanced, flavourful, long, balsamic.

BODEGAS TARÓN

Ctra. de Miranda, s/n
26211 Tirgo (La Rioja)
☎: +34 941 301 650
Fax: +34 941 301 817
www.bodegastaron.com
info@bodegastaron.com

Tarón 2006 TR

89

Colour: cherry, garnet rim. Nose: red berry notes, ripe fruit, spicy, creamy oak, toasty, complex, earthy notes. Palate: powerful, flavourful, toasty, round tannins, balanced.

Tarón 2010 TC
89
Colour: bright cherry. Nose: ripe fruit, sweet spices, creamy oak, expressive. Palate: flavourful, fruity, toasty, round tannins.

Tarón 2013 B
100% viura
87
Colour: bright straw. Nose: white flowers, fragrant herbs, tropical fruit. Palate: fresh, fruity, flavourful, balanced.

Tarón 2013 RD
88
Colour: coppery red, bright. Nose: elegant, dried flowers, fragrant herbs. Palate: light-bodied, flavourful, good acidity, long, spicy.

Tarón 4MB 2011 T
100% tempranillo
91
Colour: cherry, garnet rim. Nose: spicy, creamy oak, toasty, complex, red berry notes, ripe fruit. Palate: powerful, flavourful, toasty.

Tarón Cepas Centenarias 2011 TR
100% tempranillo
93
Colour: cherry, garnet rim. Nose: balanced, complex, ripe fruit, spicy, mineral. Palate: good structure, flavourful, round tannins, balanced.

Tarón Tempranillo 2013 T
100% tempranillo
84

BODEGAS TERMINUS
Camino de Baños, 23
01307 Villabuena de Alava (Álava)
☎: +34 626 636 997
correo@bodegasterminus.com

4D 2013 BFB
100% viura
90
Colour: bright straw. Nose: sweet spices, creamy oak, fragrant herbs, fresh fruit. Palate: rich, flavourful, fresh, good acidity, fine bitter notes.

4D 2013 T Fermentado en Barrica
tempranillo
87
Colour: cherry, garnet rim. Nose: ripe fruit, spicy, creamy oak, toasty. Palate: powerful, flavourful, toasty, round tannins.

BODEGAS TOBÍA
Paraje Senda Rutia, s/n
26214 Cuzcurrita de Río Tirón (La Rioja)
☎: +34 941 301 789
Fax: +34 941 328 045
www.bodegastobia.com
tobia@bodegastobia.com

Daimon 2012 T
88
Colour: cherry, garnet rim. Nose: ripe fruit, wild herbs, earthy notes, spicy, creamy oak. Palate: balanced, flavourful, long, balsamic.

Tobía Selección 2010 TC
91
Colour: cherry, garnet rim. Nose: ripe fruit, wild herbs, earthy notes, spicy, creamy oak. Palate: balanced, flavourful, long, balsamic.

Viña Tobía 2013 RD
garnacha
89
Colour: brilliant rose. Nose: powerfull, ripe fruit, red berry notes, floral, expressive. Palate: powerful, fruity, fresh.

Viña Tobía 2013 B
88
Colour: bright straw. Nose: white flowers, fragrant herbs, fruit expression. Palate: fresh, fruity, flavourful, balanced, elegant.

Viña Tobía 2013 T
tempranillo
85

BODEGAS TORREMACIEL

Ctra. de Autol - Calahorra, km. 6,5
26500 Calahorra (La Rioja)
☎: +34 941 163 021
Fax: +34 941 163 493
www.torremaciel.com
info@torremaciel.com

Marqués de Carabás 2008 TC
tempranillo, graciano

85

Marqués de Carabás 2013 T
tempranillo, graciano

83

Torremaciel 2008 TR
tempranillo, graciano, mazuelo

87

Colour: deep cherry, garnet rim. Nose: old leather, ripe fruit, spicy, dried herbs. Palate: correct, spicy.

Torremaciel 2009 TC
tempranillo, graciano, mazuelo

86

Colour: cherry, garnet rim. Nose: ripe fruit, spicy, creamy oak, toasty, complex. Palate: powerful, flavourful, toasty, round tannins.

Torremaciel 2013 B
viura, malvasía

79

BODEGAS VALDELACIERVA

Ctra. Burgos, Km. 13
26370 Navarrete (La Rioja)
☎: +34 941 440 620
Fax: +34 941 440 787
www.hispanobodegas.com
carlos.garcia@hispanobodegas.com

Alfar 2009 TR
tempranillo

92

Colour: cherry, garnet rim. Nose: balanced, complex, ripe fruit, spicy, fine reductive notes. Palate: good structure, flavourful, round tannins.

Alfar Vendimia Seleccionada 2012 T
tempranillo

91

Colour: deep cherry, garnet rim. Nose: balanced, cocoa bean, violet drops. Palate: flavourful, fruity, balanced.

Valdelacierva 2011 TC
tempranillo

90

Colour: cherry, garnet rim. Nose: ripe fruit, spicy, creamy oak, toasty, complex. Palate: powerful, flavourful, toasty, round tannins.

BODEGAS VALDELANA

Puente Barricuelo, 67
01340 Elciego (Álava)
☎: +34 945 606 055
Fax: +34 945 606 587
www.bodegasvaldelana.com
ana@bodegasvaldelana.com

Agnus de Valdelana de Autor 2011 TC
89
Colour: very deep cherry, garnet rim. Nose: powerfull, ripe fruit, roasted coffee, dark chocolate. Palate: powerful, toasty, roasted-coffee aftertaste.

Agnus de Valdelana de Autor 2012 T
90
Colour: cherry, garnet rim. Nose: ripe fruit, spicy, creamy oak, toasty, complex. Palate: powerful, flavourful, toasty, round tannins.

Avior 2013 T
87
Colour: cherry, purple rim. Nose: red berry notes, raspberry, fragrant herbs. Palate: flavourful, good acidity, fruity.

Duquesa de la Victoria 2009 TR
87
Colour: cherry, garnet rim. Nose: ripe fruit, spicy, creamy oak, toasty, complex. Palate: powerful, flavourful, toasty, round tannins.

Duquesa de la Victoria 2011 TC
91
Colour: cherry, garnet rim. Nose: ripe fruit, spicy, creamy oak, toasty, complex, red berry notes. Palate: powerful, flavourful, toasty, round tannins.

Duquesa de la Victoria 2013 T
86
Colour: cherry, purple rim. Nose: medium intensity, red berry notes, scrubland. Palate: balanced, flavourful, long.

Forlán 2009 TR
90
Colour: deep cherry, garnet rim. Nose: powerfull, ripe fruit, cocoa bean, creamy oak. Palate: full, spicy, balanced.

Forlán 2011 TC
89
Colour: black cherry. Nose: ripe fruit, spicy, creamy oak, toasty, dried herbs. Palate: powerful, flavourful, toasty, round tannins.

Ladrón de Guevara 2009 TR
89
Colour: cherry, garnet rim. Nose: red berry notes, ripe fruit, spicy, creamy oak, toasty, earthy notes. Palate: powerful, flavourful, toasty, round tannins.

Ladrón de Guevara 2011 TC
90
Colour: cherry, garnet rim. Nose: ripe fruit, spicy, creamy oak, toasty, complex. Palate: powerful, flavourful, toasty, round tannins.

Ladrón de Guevara 2013 B
100% viura
85

Ladrón de Guevara 2013 T
87
Colour: cherry, purple rim. Nose: fresh fruit, red berry notes, floral. Palate: flavourful, fruity, good acidity, round tannins.

Ladrón de Guevara de Autor 2011 TC
90
Colour: cherry, garnet rim. Nose: ripe fruit, spicy, creamy oak, toasty, complex. Palate: powerful, flavourful, toasty, round tannins.

Ladrón de Guevara de Autor 2012 T
tempranillo, graciano
91
Colour: cherry, garnet rim. Nose: ripe fruit, spicy, creamy oak, toasty, complex. Palate: powerful, flavourful, toasty, round tannins.

Valdelana 2009 TR
90
Colour: very deep cherry. Nose: ripe fruit, spicy, creamy oak, toasty, characterful. Palate: powerful, flavourful, toasty, round tannins.

Valdelana 2011 TC
91
Colour: bright cherry. Nose: ripe fruit, sweet spices, creamy oak, expressive. Palate: flavourful, fruity, toasty, round tannins.

Valdelana 2013 B
100% malvasía
84

Valdelana 2013 T

87

Colour: cherry, purple rim. Nose: violets, fruit expression, balanced. Palate: easy to drink, good finish, correct.

BODEGAS VALDEMAR

Camino Viejo de Logroño, 24
01320 Oyón (Álava)
☎: +34 945 622 188
Fax: +34 945 622 111
www.valdemar.es
info@valdemar.es

Conde de Valdemar 2006 TGR

88

Colour: cherry, garnet rim. Nose: fruit preserve, fruit liqueur notes, spicy. Palate: flavourful, pruney, balsamic.

Conde de Valdemar 2008 TR

89

Colour: very deep cherry. Nose: ripe fruit, spicy, creamy oak, toasty, characterful. Palate: powerful, flavourful, toasty, round tannins.

Conde de Valdemar 2010 TC

88

Colour: cherry, garnet rim. Nose: ripe fruit, spicy, creamy oak, toasty, complex. Palate: powerful, flavourful, toasty, round tannins.

Conde de Valdemar 2013 RD

84

Conde de Valdemar Finca Alto Cantabria 2013 BFB
100% viura

88

Colour: bright yellow. Nose: ripe fruit, sweet spices, fragrant herbs. Palate: smoky aftertaste, fresh, good acidity.

Conde de Valdemar Selección Especial Tempranillo 2013 T
100% tempranillo

85

Conde de Valdemar Viura 2013 B

85

Inspiración de Valdemar Las Canteras 2010 T

90

Colour: cherry, garnet rim. Nose: ripe fruit, spicy, creamy oak, toasty, complex, mineral. Palate: powerful, flavourful, toasty.

Inspiración Valdemar Edición Limitada 2008 T

90

Colour: pale ruby, brick rim edge. Nose: elegant, spicy, fine reductive notes, wet leather, aged wood nuances, fruit liqueur notes. Palate: spicy, fine tannins, elegant, long.

Inspiración Valdemar Graciano 2005 T
100% graciano

91

Colour: very deep cherry. Nose: ripe fruit, spicy, creamy oak, toasty, characterful. Palate: powerful, flavourful, toasty, round tannins.

Inspiración Valdemar Maturana 2008 T
100% maturana

90

Colour: ruby red. Nose: ripe fruit, spicy, creamy oak, toasty, wild herbs. Palate: powerful, flavourful, toasty.

Inspiración Valdemar Selección 2011 T

87

Colour: cherry, garnet rim. Nose: ripe fruit, spicy, creamy oak, toasty, complex. Palate: powerful, flavourful, toasty, round tannins.

Inspiración Valdemar Tempranillo Blanco 2013 BFB
100% tempranillo blanco

87

Colour: bright yellow. Nose: powerfull, ripe fruit, sweet spices, creamy oak, fragrant herbs. Palate: rich, smoky aftertaste, flavourful, fresh, good acidity.

Valdemar 2013 RD

86

Colour: coppery red. Nose: elegant, candied fruit, dried flowers, fragrant herbs. Palate: light-bodied, good acidity, long, spicy.

BODEGAS VALLEMAYOR

Ctra. Logroño-Vitoria, 38
26360 Fuenmayor (La Rioja)
☎: +34 941 450 142
Fax: +34 941 450 376
www.vallemayor.com
vallemayor@fer.es

Colección Valle Mayor Viña Cerradilla 2010 TC

88

Colour: cherry, garnet rim. Nose: ripe fruit, spicy, creamy oak, toasty, complex. Palate: powerful, flavourful, toasty, round tannins.

Colección Valle Mayor Viña Encineda 2011 T
100% tempranillo

88

Colour: dark-red cherry, garnet rim. Nose: ripe fruit, spicy, dried herbs, balanced. Palate: balanced, ripe fruit, spicy.

Colección Valle Mayor Viña Encineda 2012 T
100% tempranillo

87

Colour: dark-red cherry, garnet rim. Nose: medium intensity, closed, ripe fruit, cocoa bean. Palate: flavourful, round tannins, balanced.

Vallemayor 2005 TGR

89

Colour: light cherry, orangey edge. Nose: spicy, fine reductive notes, wet leather, aged wood nuances, toasty. Palate: spicy, long, toasty.

Vallemayor 2007 TR

88

Colour: cherry, garnet rim. Nose: ripe fruit, spicy, toasty, aged wood nuances, fine reductive notes. Palate: powerful, flavourful, toasty, round tannins.

Vallemayor 2011 TC

86

Colour: cherry, garnet rim. Nose: spicy, tobacco, waxy notes, ripe fruit. Palate: correct, good finish.

Vallemayor 2012 BFB

86

Colour: bright yellow. Nose: powerfull, ripe fruit, sweet spices, creamy oak, fragrant herbs. Palate: rich, smoky aftertaste, flavourful, fresh, good acidity.

Vallemayor 2013 B
100% viura

84

Vallemayor 2013 RD

84

Vallemayor 2013 T
100% tempranillo

82

BODEGAS VALLOBERA S.L.

Camino de la Hoya, s/n
01300 Laguardia (Álava)
☎: +34 945 621 204
Fax: +34 945 600 040
www.vallobera.com
exportacion@vallobera.com

Caudalia 2013 BFB
tempranillo blanco

88

Nose: powerfull, ripe fruit, sweet spices, fragrant herbs. Palate: rich, smoky aftertaste, flavourful, fresh, good acidity.

Finca Vallobera 2011 T
tempranillo

89

Colour: cherry, garnet rim. Nose: red berry notes, ripe fruit, spicy, creamy oak, toasty, complex. Palate: powerful, flavourful, toasty, round tannins.

Pago Malarina 2012 T
tempranillo

87

Colour: cherry, purple rim. Nose: expressive, floral, ripe fruit, fruit expression. Palate: flavourful, fruity, good acidity, round tannins.

Terran 2009 T
tempranillo

91

Colour: cherry, garnet rim. Nose: ripe fruit, spicy, creamy oak, toasty, complex, earthy notes. Palate: powerful, flavourful, toasty, round tannins.

Vallobera 2009 TR
100% tempranillo

89

Colour: cherry, garnet rim. Nose: ripe fruit, spicy, creamy oak, toasty, complex, earthy notes. Palate: powerful, flavourful, toasty, round tannins.

Vallobera 2011 TC

89

Colour: deep cherry, purple rim. Nose: powerfull, balanced, ripe fruit, spicy. Palate: good structure, correct, round tannins.

Vallobera 2013 B
viura, sauvignon blanc

87

Colour: bright straw. Nose: fresh, fresh fruit, white flowers, expressive. Palate: flavourful, fruity, good acidity, balanced.

BODEGAS VICENTE GANDÍA
Ctra. Cheste a Godelleta, s/n
46370 Chiva (Valencia)
☎: +34 962 524 242
Fax: +34 962 524 243
www.vicentegandia.es
info@vicentegandia.com

Altos de Raiza Tempranillo 2012 T
100% tempranillo

84

Raiza Tempranillo 2007 TGR
100% tempranillo

87

Colour: ruby red. Nose: spicy, fine reductive notes, wet leather, aged wood nuances, fruit liqueur notes. Palate: spicy, balsamic, flavourful.

Raiza Tempranillo 2009 TR
100% tempranillo

88

Colour: cherry, garnet rim. Nose: ripe fruit, spicy, creamy oak, toasty, fine reductive notes. Palate: powerful, flavourful, toasty.

Raiza Tempranillo 2010 TC
100% tempranillo

85

BODEGAS VINÍCOLA REAL
Ctra. Nalda, km. 9
26120 Albelda de Iregua (La Rioja)
☎: +34 941 444 233
Fax: +34 941 444 427
www.vinicolareal.com
info@vinicolareal.com

200 Monges Selección Especial 2007 B Reserva

94

Colour: bright straw. Nose: dried herbs, faded flowers, powerfull, sweet spices, creamy oak, saline. Palate: ripe fruit, balanced.

Cueva del Monge 2012 BFB

92

Colour: bright yellow. Nose: powerfull, ripe fruit, sweet spices, creamy oak, fragrant herbs. Palate: rich, smoky aftertaste, flavourful, fresh, good acidity.

Viña Los Valles 50 & 50 2011 TC

90 🌿

Colour: cherry, garnet rim. Nose: ripe fruit, spicy, creamy oak, toasty. Palate: powerful, flavourful, toasty, round tannins, balanced.

Viña Los Valles 70 & 30 2011 TC

87 🌷

Colour: bright cherry. Nose: ripe fruit, sweet spices, creamy oak, balsamic herbs. Palate: fruity, flavourful, toasty.

Viña Los Valles 80 & 20 2011 TC

89 🌿

Colour: cherry, garnet rim. Nose: ripe fruit, spicy, creamy oak, toasty. Palate: powerful, flavourful, toasty, round tannins.

Viña Los Valles Tempranillo 2013 T
100% tempranillo

86

Colour: cherry, purple rim. Nose: fresh fruit, red berry notes, balsamic herbs. Palate: flavourful, fruity, good acidity.

BODEGAS VIÑA BERNEDA
Ctra. Somalo, 59
26313 Uruñuela (La Rioja)
☎: +34 941 371 304
Fax: +34 941 371 304
www.vinaberneda.com
berneda@vinaberneda.com

Berneda Vendimia Seleccionada 2009 TC
100% tempranillo

87

Nose: fine reductive notes, wet leather, ripe fruit. Palate: spicy, long, toasty, good finish, ripe fruit.

Viña Berneda 2010 TC
100% tempranillo
87
Colour: cherry, garnet rim. Nose: medium intensity, spicy, ripe fruit. Palate: easy to drink, correct, good acidity.

Viña Berneda 2013 T Maceración Carbónica
100% tempranillo
84

BODEGAS VIVANCO
Ctra. Nacional 232, s/n
26330 Briones (La Rioja)
☎: +34 941 322 323
www.dinastiavivanco.com
info@vivancoculturadevino.es

Colección Vivanco 4 Varietales 2010 T
91
Colour: bright cherry, garnet rim. Nose: balanced, expressive, ripe fruit, spicy, balsamic herbs. Palate: good structure, long, round.

Colección Vivanco 4 Varietales 2012 T
89
Colour: bright cherry. Nose: ripe fruit, spicy, balsamic herbs. Palate: flavourful, fruity, toasty, round tannins.

Colección Vivanco 4 Varietales Dulce de Invierno 2011 T
94
Colour: cherry, garnet rim. Nose: fruit preserve, ripe fruit, spicy, toasty, aged wood nuances. Palate: powerful, flavourful, sweetness, elegant.

Colección Vivanco Parcelas de Garnacha 2011 T
garnacha
91
Colour: bright cherry, garnet rim. Nose: balanced, ripe fruit, fruit preserve, balsamic herbs, spicy. Palate: balanced, fruity, balsamic.

Colección Vivanco Parcelas de Graciano 2009 T
graciano
91
Colour: black cherry, purple rim. Nose: ripe fruit, scrubland. Palate: correct, round tannins, long, spicy.

Colección Vivanco Parcelas de Maturana 2011 T
maturana
93
Colour: black cherry, garnet rim. Nose: complex, spicy, dried herbs, expressive. Palate: toasty, smoky aftertaste, ripe fruit, long.

Colección Vivanco Parcelas de Mazuelo 2011 T
mazuelo
88
Colour: deep cherry, garnet rim. Nose: spicy, toasty, balanced, dry stone, balsamic herbs, tobacco. Palate: flavourful, fruity, spicy.

Vivanco 2008 TR
89
Colour: dark-red cherry, garnet rim. Nose: toasty, ripe fruit, balanced. Palate: good structure, easy to drink, long, round tannins.

Vivanco 2010 TC
tempranillo
90
Colour: cherry, garnet rim. Nose: ripe fruit, spicy, toasty, complex, balsamic herbs. Palate: flavourful, round tannins, easy to drink.

Vivanco Tempranillo Garnacha 2013 RD
89
Colour: raspberry rose. Nose: red berry notes, candied fruit, raspberry, floral, fragrant herbs. Palate: fresh, fruity, good acidity, balanced.

Vivanco Viura Malvasía Tempranillo Blanco 2013 B
87
Colour: bright straw. Nose: citrus fruit, fresh, wild herbs, floral. Palate: fresh, good finish, fine bitter notes.

BODEGAS Y VIÑAS DEL CONDE
Calle Bodegas, 18
01306 LaPuebla de Labarca (Álava)
☎: +34 673 736 155
www.casadomorales.es
condedealtava@gmail.com

Conde de Altava 2009 TR
100% tempranillo
87
Colour: dark-red cherry, garnet rim. Nose: ripe fruit, fruit preserve, toasty. Palate: flavourful, spicy, correct.

Conde de Altava 2010 TC
100% tempranillo

89

Colour: cherry, garnet rim. Nose: ripe fruit, spicy, creamy oak, toasty, complex, dry stone. Palate: powerful, flavourful, toasty, round tannins.

Conde de Altava 2013 T
100% tempranillo

87

Colour: cherry, purple rim. Nose: fresh fruit, red berry notes, floral. Palate: flavourful, fruity, good acidity, round tannins.

BODEGAS Y VIÑAS SENDA GALIANA

Barrio Bodegas, s/n
26142 Villamediana (La Rioja)
☎: +34 941 435 375
Fax: +34 941 436 072
info@sendagaliana.com

Senda Galiana 2005 TGR
89

Colour: pale ruby, brick rim edge. Nose: elegant, spicy, fine reductive notes, wet leather, aged wood nuances, fruit liqueur notes. Palate: spicy, fine tannins, elegant, long.

Senda Galiana 2007 TR
85

Senda Galiana 2009 TC
84

BODEGAS Y VIÑEDOS ARTADI

Ctra. de Logroño, s/n
01300 Laguardia (Álava)
☎: +34 945 600 119
Fax: +34 945 600 850
www.artadi.com
info@artadi.com

Artadi El Carretil 2012 T
100% tempranillo

98

Colour: cherry, garnet rim. Nose: toasty, complex, dark chocolate, earthy notes, aromatic coffee, fruit expression, red berry notes. Palate: powerful, flavourful, toasty, round tannins.

Artadi La Poza de Ballesteros 2012 T
100% tempranillo

96

Colour: cherry, garnet rim. Nose: spicy, creamy oak, toasty, complex, dark chocolate, candied fruit. Palate: powerful, flavourful, toasty, round tannins.

Artadi Pagos Viejos 2012 T
100% tempranillo

95

Colour: cherry, garnet rim. Nose: ripe fruit, fruit expression, red berry notes, sweet spices, toasty. Palate: powerful, good structure, ripe fruit, long.

Artadi Valdeginés 2012 T
100% tempranillo

97

Colour: very deep cherry. Nose: ripe fruit, spicy, creamy oak, toasty, characterful, balsamic herbs, scrubland. Palate: powerful, flavourful, toasty, round tannins.

Artadi Viña El Pisón 2012 T
100% tempranillo

97

Colour: cherry, garnet rim. Nose: dark chocolate, aromatic coffee, earthy notes, ripe fruit, fruit expression. Palate: flavourful, soft tannins, long.

Artadi Viñas de Gain 2012 T
tempranillo

94

Colour: cherry, garnet rim. Nose: ripe fruit, spicy, creamy oak, toasty, complex. Palate: powerful, flavourful, toasty, round tannins.

BODEGAS Y VIÑEDOS CASADO MORALES, S.L.

Avda. La Póveda 12-14
01306 Lapuebla de Labarca (Alava)
☎: +34 945 607 017
Fax: +34 945 063 173
www.casadomorales.es
info@casadomorales.es

Casado Morales 2006 TGR
89
Colour: cherry, garnet rim. Nose: balanced, complex, ripe fruit, spicy. Palate: good structure, flavourful, round tannins.

Casado Morales 2010 TC
90
Colour: cherry, garnet rim. Nose: ripe fruit, spicy, creamy oak, toasty. Palate: flavourful, toasty, round tannins.

Casado Morales Graciano 2009 T
100% graciano
88
Colour: cherry, garnet rim. Nose: ripe fruit, wild herbs, spicy, creamy oak. Palate: balanced, flavourful, long, balsamic.

Casado Morales Selección Privada 2009 TR
93
Colour: cherry, garnet rim. Nose: ripe fruit, spicy, toasty, complex, earthy notes, elegant. Palate: flavourful, toasty, round tannins.

Nobleza Dimidium 2011 T
100% tempranillo
88
Colour: cherry, garnet rim. Nose: ripe fruit, spicy, creamy oak, toasty. Palate: powerful, flavourful, toasty.

BODEGAS Y VIÑEDOS ILURCE

Ctra. Alfaro - Grávalos (LR-289), km. 23
26540 Alfaro (La Rioja)
☎: +34 941 180 829
Fax: +34 941 183 897
www.ilurce.com
info@ilurce.com

Ilurce 2005 TC
86
Colour: dark-red cherry, orangey edge. Nose: spicy, wet leather, aged wood nuances, toasty. Palate: spicy, long, toasty.

Ilurce 2012 T
100% tempranillo
87
Colour: cherry, garnet rim. Nose: ripe fruit, spicy. Palate: powerful, flavourful, toasty, round tannins, balsamic.

Ilurce 2013 RD
garnacha
90
Colour: rose, purple rim. Nose: powerfull, ripe fruit, red berry notes, floral, expressive. Palate: powerful, fruity, fresh.

Ilurce Graciano 2006 TC
100% graciano
86
Colour: cherry, garnet rim. Nose: wild herbs, dried herbs, spicy. Palate: correct, spicy.

Ilurce Vendimia Seleccionada 2001 TR
87
Colour: dark-red cherry, brick rim edge. Nose: expressive, animal reductive notes, smoky, toasty. Palate: long, good acidity, fine tannins.

Ilurce Vendimia Seleccionada 2005 TC
87
Colour: ruby red. Nose: spicy, fine reductive notes, aged wood nuances, toasty, old leather. Palate: spicy, long, toasty, balsamic.

BODEGAS Y VIÑEDOS LABASTIDA - SOLAGÜEN

Avda. Diputación, 22
01330 Labastida (Álava)
☎: +34 945 331 161
Fax: +34 945 331 118
www.bodegaslabastida.com
info@bodegaslabastida.com

GR II29 2008 TR
87
Colour: cherry, garnet rim. Nose: ripe fruit, spicy, creamy oak, toasty, complex, dried herbs. Palate: powerful, flavourful, toasty, round tannins.

Solagüen 2009 TR
100% tempranillo
89
Colour: deep cherry. Nose: expressive, toasty, ripe fruit. Palate: fruity, flavourful, fruity aftestaste, round tannins.

Solagüen 2011 TC
100% tempranillo
88
Colour: cherry, garnet rim. Nose: ripe fruit, toasty, complex, sweet spices. Palate: flavourful, toasty, round tannins, easy to drink.

Solagüen Cepas Viejas 2013 T
100% garnacha
88
Colour: cherry, purple rim. Nose: expressive, fresh fruit, red berry notes, floral. Palate: flavourful, fruity, good acidity, round tannins.

BODEGAS Y VIÑEDOS MARQUÉS DE CARRIÓN

Ctra. Logroño, s/n
01330 Labastida (Álava)
☎: +34 945 331 643
Fax: +34 945 331 694
www.garciacarrion.es
eromero@jgc.es

Antaño 2010 TR
tempranillo, graciano, mazuelo, garnacha
84

Antaño 2011 TC
tempranillo, graciano, mazuelo, garnacha
82

Antaño 2012 T
tempranillo, garnacha, mazuelo
84

Antaño 2013 B
viura
85

Antaño 2013 RD
tempranillo
84

Antaño Graciano 2010 T
graciano
87
Colour: cherry, garnet rim. Nose: ripe fruit, wild herbs, spicy, creamy oak. Palate: balanced, flavourful, long, balsamic.

Antaño Gran Selección 2011 T
tempranillo
83

Marqués de Carrión 2009 TR
tempranillo, graciano, mazuelo
84

Marqués de Carrión 2010 TC
tempranillo, graciano, mazuelo
84

Pata Negra 2009 TR
tempranillo, graciano, mazuelo
85

Pata Negra 2010 TC
tempranillo, graciano, mazuelo
82

Pata Negra Gran Selección 2011 T
tempranillo
85

Señorio de Garoa 2011 TC
85

BODEGAS Y VIÑEDOS PUENTE DEL EA

Camino Aguachal, s/n
26212 Sajazarra (La Rioja)
☎: +34 941 320 405
Fax: +34 941 320 406
www.puentedelea.com
puentedelea@gmail.com

Eridano 2011 TC
100% tempranillo
87
Colour: cherry, garnet rim. Nose: spicy, varietal, ripe fruit. Palate: good structure, round tannins.

Eridano Edición Especial 2009 TR
88
Colour: cherry, garnet rim. Nose: red berry notes, ripe fruit, spicy, creamy oak, toasty, complex, earthy notes. Palate: powerful, flavourful, toasty, round tannins.

Eridano Vendimia Seleccionada 2012 T
85

Puente del Ea 2012 BFB
100% viura
88
Colour: bright yellow. Nose: powerfull, ripe fruit, sweet spices, creamy oak, fragrant herbs. Palate: rich, flavourful, fresh, good acidity.

Puente del Ea 2013 RD
garnacha, tempranillo
85

Puente del Ea Autor 2010 T
100% tempranillo
88
Colour: bright cherry, garnet rim. Nose: closed, spicy, toasty. Palate: good structure, flavourful, round tannins.

Puente del Ea Garnacha 2010 T
100% garnacha
89
Colour: cherry, garnet rim. Nose: ripe fruit, wild herbs, earthy notes, spicy, creamy oak. Palate: balanced, flavourful, long, balsamic.

Puente del Ea Graciano 2010 T
100% graciano
91
Colour: bright cherry, garnet rim. Nose: powerfull, expressive, ripe fruit, scrubland. Palate: flavourful, fruity, long.

Puente del Ea Tempranillo 2011 T Barrica
100% tempranillo

87

Colour: very deep cherry. Nose: balanced, spicy, varietal, ripe fruit. Palate: ripe fruit, round tannins.

BODEGAS Y VIÑEDOS PUJANZA

Ctra. del Villar, s/n
01300 Laguardia (Álava)
☎: +34 945 600 548
Fax: +34 945 600 522
www.bodegaspujanza.com
info@bodegaspujanza.com

Pujanza Finca Valdepoleo 2011 T
100% tempranillo

94

Colour: cherry, garnet rim. Nose: ripe fruit, fruit expression, sweet spices, creamy oak, toasty. Palate: flavourful.

Pujanza Hado 2012 T
100% tempranillo

92

Colour: cherry, garnet rim. Nose: ripe fruit, spicy, creamy oak, dark chocolate, earthy notes, characterful. Palate: flavourful, toasty, round tannins.

Pujanza Norte 2011 T
tempranillo

95

Colour: very deep cherry, garnet rim. Nose: powerfull, ripe fruit, roasted coffee, dark chocolate, earthy notes. Palate: powerful, toasty, roasted-coffee aftertaste.

BODEGAS Y VIÑEDOS VARAL

San Vicenta, 40
01307 Baños de Ebro (Álava)
☎: +34 945 623 321
Fax: +34 945 623 321
www.bodegasvaral.com
bodegasvaral@bodegasvaral.com

Blanco de Varal 2013 B
100% viura

85

Crianza de Varal 2010 T
100% tempranillo

90

Colour: cherry, garnet rim. Nose: ripe fruit, spicy, creamy oak, toasty, complex. Palate: powerful, flavourful, toasty, round tannins.

Ecos de Varal 2013 T

87 🌷

Colour: cherry, purple rim. Nose: fresh fruit, red berry notes, violets. Palate: fruity, good acidity, round tannins.

Esencias de Varal 2010 T
100% tempranillo

91

Colour: cherry, garnet rim. Nose: red berry notes, ripe fruit, spicy, creamy oak, toasty, complex, earthy notes. Palate: powerful, flavourful, toasty, round tannins.

Joven de Varal 2013 T

87

Colour: cherry, purple rim. Nose: fresh fruit, red berry notes, floral. Palate: flavourful, fruity, good acidity, round tannins.

Varal Vendimia Seleccionada 2009 T
100% tempranillo

89

Colour: dark-red cherry. Nose: ripe fruit, overripe fruit, sweet spices. Palate: flavourful, round tannins, balanced.

BODEGAS Y VIÑEDOS ZUAZO GASTÓN

Las Norias, 2
01320 Oyón (Álava)
☎: +34 945 601 526
Fax: +34 945 622 917
www.zuazogaston.com
zuazogaston@zuazogaston.com

Finca Costanillas 2012 T

88

Colour: bright cherry. Nose: ripe fruit, sweet spices, creamy oak, expressive. Palate: flavourful, fruity, toasty.

Zuazo Gastón 2008 TR

89

Colour: cherry, garnet rim. Nose: complex, ripe fruit, spicy, fine reductive notes. Palate: good structure, flavourful, round tannins.

Zuazo Gastón 2013 B
viura

84

Zuazo Gastón 2011 TC
tempranillo

89

Colour: cherry, garnet rim. Nose: ripe fruit, spicy, creamy oak, toasty. Palate: powerful, flavourful, toasty.

BODEGAS YSIOS

Camino de la Hoya, s/n
01300 Laguardia (Álava)
☎: +34 945 600 640
Fax: +34 945 600 520
www.ysios.com
ysios@pernod-ricard.com

Ysios Edición Limitada 2009 TR
tempranillo
94
Colour: dark-red cherry, garnet rim. Nose: expressive, elegant, cocoa bean, spicy, mineral. Palate: flavourful, round tannins, long.

BODEGAS ZUGOBER

Tejerías, 13-15
01306 Lapuebla de Labarca (Álava)
☎: +34 945 627 228
Fax: +34 945 627 281
www.belezos.com
contacto@belezos.com

Belezos 2001 TGR
89
Colour: pale ruby, brick rim edge. Nose: elegant, spicy, fine reductive notes, wet leather, aged wood nuances, fruit liqueur notes. Palate: spicy, fine tannins, elegant, long.

Belezos 2008 TR
tempranillo
88
Colour: cherry, garnet rim. Nose: ripe fruit, spicy, creamy oak, toasty. Palate: powerful, flavourful, toasty.

Belezos 2010 TC
88
Colour: bright cherry. Nose: ripe fruit, sweet spices, creamy oak, wild herbs. Palate: fruity, flavourful, toasty, correct.

Belezos 2012 BFB
viura
90
Colour: bright yellow. Nose: powerfull, ripe fruit, sweet spices, creamy oak, fragrant herbs. Palate: rich, smoky aftertaste, flavourful, fresh, good acidity.

Belezos Ecológico 2011 T
tempranillo
88 🌱
Colour: cherry, garnet rim. Nose: ripe fruit, fruit preserve, balsamic herbs, spicy, creamy oak, dark chocolate. Palate: powerful, flavourful, correct.

Belezos Vendimia Seleccionada 2010 T
92
Colour: cherry, garnet rim. Nose: ripe fruit, spicy, creamy oak, toasty, complex, dark chocolate, earthy notes. Palate: powerful, flavourful, toasty, round tannins.

Cuna de Maras B
90
Colour: golden. Nose: powerfull, floral, honeyed notes, candied fruit, fragrant herbs. Palate: flavourful, sweet, fresh, fruity, good acidity, long.

Cuna de Maras Malvasia 2013 BFB
83

Raices de Cuna de Maras 2010 T
88
Colour: cherry, garnet rim. Nose: fruit preserve, fruit liqueur notes, spicy. Palate: flavourful, pruney.

Valle de Cuna de Maras 2011 T
92
Colour: cherry, garnet rim. Nose: ripe fruit, spicy, creamy oak, toasty, complex, dark chocolate, earthy notes. Palate: powerful, flavourful, toasty, round tannins.

BOHEDAL

Crta Pancorbo. Camino
de Los Lirios s/n
26214 Cuzcurrita de Río Tirón (La Rioja)
☎: +34 941 328 064
www.banosbezares.com
info@bohedal.com

Bohedal 2013 B
100% viura
88
Colour: bright straw. Nose: fresh, fresh fruit, white flowers, expressive. Palate: flavourful, fruity, good acidity, balanced.

Bohedal 2013 T Joven
100% tempranillo
84

Gran Bohedal 2009 TR
100% tempranillo
87
Colour: cherry, garnet rim. Nose: medium intensity, ripe fruit, spicy. Palate: correct, good acidity, good finish.

Gran Bohedal 2010 TC
100% tempranillo
88
Colour: cherry, garnet rim. Nose: ripe fruit, spicy, creamy oak, complex. Palate: flavourful, toasty, round tannins.

Gran Bohedal 2013 BFB
100% viura
87
Colour: bright yellow. Nose: powerfull, ripe fruit, sweet spices, creamy oak, fragrant herbs. Palate: rich, flavourful, fresh, good acidity.

Hebabe Graciano 2010 T
100% graciano
87
Colour: cherry, garnet rim. Nose: ripe fruit, grassy, herbaceous. Palate: balsamic, fine bitter notes, correct.

Hebabe II 2010 T
100% tempranillo
91
Colour: dark-red cherry. Nose: varietal, balanced, ripe fruit, sweet spices, cocoa bean. Palate: balanced, long, round tannins.

CARLOS SAN PEDRO PÉREZ DE VIÑASPRE
Páganos, 44- Bajo
01300 Laguardia (Álava)
☎: +34 945 600 146
Fax: +34 945 600 146
www.bodegascarlossampedro.com
info@bodegascarlossampedro.com

Carlos San Pedro Colección Familiar 2006 T
tempranillo
91
Colour: cherry, garnet rim. Nose: ripe fruit, spicy, creamy oak, toasty, balsamic herbs, fine reductive notes. Palate: powerful, flavourful, toasty, round tannins.

Viñasperi 2010 TC
tempranillo
86
Colour: bright cherry. Nose: ripe fruit, sweet spices, creamy oak, medium intensity. Palate: fruity, flavourful, toasty.

Viñasperi Corazón 2010 T
tempranillo
85

CARLOS SERRES
Avda. Santo Domingo, 40
26200 Haro (La Rioja)
☎: +34 941 310 279
Fax: +34 941 310 418
www.carlosserres.com
info@carlosserres.com

Carlos Serres 2005 TGR
88
Colour: ruby red. Nose: balanced, complex, ripe fruit, spicy, toasty, fine reductive notes. Palate: good structure, flavourful, round tannins.

Carlos Serres 2007 TR
89
Colour: dark-red cherry, orangey edge. Nose: spicy, aged wood nuances, old leather. Palate: flavourful, ripe fruit, fine tannins.

Carlos Serres 2010 TC
88
Colour: cherry, garnet rim. Nose: medium intensity, grassy, wild herbs, red berry notes. Palate: fruity, easy to drink.

Onomástica 2007 TR
92
Colour: cherry, garnet rim. Nose: complex, ripe fruit, spicy, balanced. Palate: good structure, flavourful, round tannins, elegant.

Onomástica 2009 B Reserva
viura
89
Colour: bright golden. Nose: sweet spices, roasted almonds, creamy oak, dry nuts. Palate: full, rich, toasty, smoky aftertaste.

Serres Tempranillo 2013 T
tempranillo
85

Serres Tempranillo Garnacha 2013 RD
84

Serres Viura 2013 B
viura
84

CASTILLO CLAVIJO
Ctra. de Clavijo, s/n
26141 Alberite (La Rioja)
☎: +34 941 436 702
Fax: +34 941 436 430
www.criadoresderioja.com
info@castilloclavijo.com

Castillo Clavijo 2007 TGR
84

Castillo Clavijo 2008 TR
88
Colour: cherry, garnet rim. Nose: balanced, complex, ripe fruit, spicy, fine reductive notes. Palate: good structure, flavourful, round tannins.

Castillo Clavijo 2010 TC
87
Colour: bright cherry. Nose: ripe fruit, sweet spices, creamy oak, medium intensity. Palate: fruity, flavourful, toasty.

Castillo Clavijo 2012 BFB
100% viura
86
Colour: bright straw. Nose: ripe fruit, sweet spices, dried flowers. Palate: smoky aftertaste, good acidity.

CASTILLO DE CUZCURRITA
San Sebastián, 1
26214 Cuzcurrita del Río Tirón
(La Rioja)
☎: +34 941 328 022
Fax: +34 941 301 620
www.castillodecuzcurrita.com
info@castillodecuzcurrita.com

Señorío de Cuzcurrita 2008 T
100% tempranillo
90
Colour: very deep cherry, garnet rim. Nose: powerfull, ripe fruit, roasted coffee, dark chocolate. Palate: powerful, toasty, roasted-coffee aftertaste.

COMPAÑÍA DE VINOS TELMO RODRÍGUEZ
El Monte
01308 Lanciego (Álava)
☎: +34 945 628 315
Fax: +34 945 628 314
www.telmorodriguez.com
contact@telmorodriguez.com

Altos de Lanzaga 2010 T
tempranillo, graciano, garnacha
96 ♥
Colour: cherry, garnet rim. Nose: ripe fruit, spicy, creamy oak, toasty, complex, dark chocolate, earthy notes, mineral. Palate: powerful, flavourful, toasty, round tannins.

Lanzaga 2010 T
tempranillo, graciano, garnacha
92
Colour: cherry, garnet rim. Nose: scrubland, ripe fruit, toasty, spicy. Palate: flavourful, good acidity, fine tannins.

Las Beatas 2011 T
96 ♥
Colour: bright cherry. Nose: red berry notes, violet drops, mineral, spicy. Palate: spicy, ripe fruit, balsamic, good acidity.

LZ 2013 T
tempranillo, graciano, garnacha
93
Colour: cherry, purple rim. Nose: expressive, fresh fruit, red berry notes, floral. Palate: flavourful, fruity, good acidity, round tannins.

CORDIS TERRA HISPANIA

Gamonal, 16 2°C
28031 Madrid (Madrid)
☎: +34 911 610 024
Fax: +34 913 316 047
www.cordisterra.com
info@cordisterra.com

Vega Valbosque 2011 T
87
Colour: bright cherry. Nose: ripe fruit, sweet spices, creamy oak, medium intensity. Palate: fruity, flavourful, toasty, correct.

CREACIONES EXEO

Costanilla del Hospital s/n
01330 Labastida (Álava)
☎: +34 945 331 230
Fax: +34 945 331 257
www.bodegasexeo.com
export@bodegasexeo.com

Cifras 2011 B
91
Colour: bright straw. Nose: ripe fruit, floral, fragrant herbs, spicy, expressive. Palate: balanced, rich, fruity, flavourful, long.

Cifras 2011 T
garnacha
92
Colour: bright cherry. Nose: ripe fruit, spicy, scrubland. Palate: balanced, flavourful, long, balsamic.

Letras 2011 T
tempranillo
92
Colour: cherry, garnet rim. Nose: ripe fruit, spicy, creamy oak, toasty, complex, earthy notes. Palate: powerful, flavourful, toasty, round tannins.

Letras Minúsculas 2011 T
91
Colour: deep cherry, garnet rim. Nose: ripe fruit, cocoa bean, sweet spices, balsamic herbs. Palate: fruity, good structure, spicy.

CVNE

Barrio de la Estación, s/n
26200 Haro (La Rioja)
☎: +34 941 304 800
Fax: +34 941 304 815
www.cvne.com
marketing@cvne.com

Corona Semidulce 2013 B
90
Colour: bright yellow. Nose: fruit liqueur notes, faded flowers, dried herbs, honeyed notes, citrus fruit. Palate: powerful, flavourful, spicy, sweet.

Cune 2008 TGR
90
Colour: very deep cherry. Nose: ripe fruit, spicy, creamy oak, toasty, characterful. Palate: powerful, flavourful, toasty, round tannins.

Cune 2010 TR
90
Colour: very deep cherry. Nose: ripe fruit, spicy, creamy oak, toasty, characterful. Palate: powerful, flavourful, toasty, round tannins.

Cune 2012 TC
90
Colour: bright cherry. Nose: ripe fruit, sweet spices, creamy oak, expressive. Palate: flavourful, fruity, toasty, round tannins.

Cune 2013 RD
100% tempranillo
85

Cune Semidulce 2013 B
84

Cune White 2013 B
100% viura
90
Colour: bright straw. Nose: fresh, fresh fruit, white flowers, expressive. Palate: flavourful, fruity, good acidity, balanced.

Imperial 2008 TGR
93
Colour: cherry, garnet rim. Nose: balanced, complex, ripe fruit, spicy. Palate: good structure, flavourful, round tannins.

Imperial 2009 TGR
91
Colour: cherry, garnet rim. Nose: ripe fruit, spicy, creamy oak, toasty, dark chocolate. Palate: powerful, flavourful, toasty, round tannins.

Imperial 2009 TR
92
Colour: very deep cherry, garnet rim. Nose: powerfull, ripe fruit, roasted coffee, dark chocolate. Palate: powerful, toasty, roasted-coffee aftertaste.

Monopole 2013 B
100% viura
87
Colour: bright straw. Nose: medium intensity, fresh fruit, white flowers. Palate: fresh, fine bitter notes, good acidity.

DIEZ-CABALLERO
Barrihuelo, 73
01340 Elciego (Álava)
☎: +34 944 630 938
www.diez-caballero.es
diez-caballero@diez-caballero.es

Díez-Caballero 2012 TC
tempranillo
89
Colour: bright cherry. Nose: ripe fruit, sweet spices, creamy oak, expressive. Palate: flavourful, fruity, toasty, correct.

Díez-Caballero 2009 TR
tempranillo
88
Colour: deep cherry. Nose: balanced, complex, ripe fruit, spicy, wild herbs. Palate: good structure, flavourful, round tannins.

Díez-Caballero Vendimia Seleccionada 2010 TR
tempranillo
88
Colour: cherry, garnet rim. Nose: ripe fruit, spicy, creamy oak, toasty, complex, dark chocolate. Palate: powerful, flavourful, toasty, round tannins.

Victoria Díez-Caballero 2010 T
tempranillo
89
Colour: cherry, garnet rim. Nose: balanced, complex, ripe fruit, spicy, balsamic herbs. Palate: good structure, flavourful, round tannins.

DIOSARES S.L.
Ctra. de Navaridas, s/n
01300 Laguardia (Alava)
☎: +34 945 600 678
Fax: +34 945 600 522
www.bodegasdiosares.com
info@bodegasdiosares.com

Dios Ares 2011 TC
100% tempranillo
92
Colour: cherry, garnet rim. Nose: ripe fruit, spicy, creamy oak, toasty, complex, earthy notes. Palate: powerful, flavourful, toasty, round tannins.

DOMINIO DE BERZAL
Término Río Salado, s/n
01307 Baños de Ebro (Álava)
☎: +34 945 623 368
Fax: +34 945 609 090
www.dominioberzal.com
info@dominioberzal.com

Dominio de Berzal 2011 TC
89
Colour: cherry, garnet rim. Nose: ripe fruit, spicy, creamy oak, toasty, complex. Palate: powerful, flavourful, toasty, round tannins.

Dominio de Berzal 2013 B
86
Colour: yellow, pale. Nose: medium intensity, dried herbs. Palate: flavourful, fruity, balanced, fine bitter notes.

Dominio de Berzal 2013 T
Maceración Carbónica
87
Colour: cherry, purple rim. Nose: expressive, fresh fruit, red berry notes, floral. Palate: flavourful, fruity, good acidity, round tannins.

Dominio de Berzal 7 Varietales 2011 T
maturana, graciano, garnacha, merlot
88
Colour: very deep cherry. Nose: ripe fruit, spicy, creamy oak, toasty, characterful. Palate: powerful, flavourful, toasty, round tannins.

Dominio de Berzal Selección
Privada 2011 T
tempranillo
90
Colour: cherry, garnet rim. Nose: ripe fruit, spicy, creamy oak, toasty, complex. Palate: powerful, flavourful, toasty, round tannins.

EGUREN UGARTE
Ctra. A-124, Km. 61
01309 Laguardia (Álava)
☎: +34 945 282 844
Fax: +34 945 271 319
www.egurenugarte.com
info@egurenugarte.com

Anastasio 2007 T
100% tempranillo
88
Colour: cherry, garnet rim. Nose: overripe fruit, dried fruit, sweet spices, toasty. Palate: ripe fruit, warm, powerful.

Cedula Real 2006 TGR
90
Colour: pale ruby, brick rim edge. Nose: spicy, fine reductive notes, wet leather, aged wood nuances, fruit liqueur notes. Palate: spicy, fine tannins.

Cincuenta Ugarte 2010 T
100% tempranillo
87
Colour: cherry, garnet rim. Nose: spicy, toasty, overripe fruit, mineral. Palate: powerful, flavourful, toasty, round tannins.

Martín Cendoya 2009 TR
89
Colour: bright cherry. Nose: ripe fruit, sweet spices, creamy oak, medium intensity. Palate: fruity, flavourful, toasty.

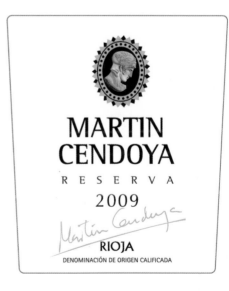

Martín Cendoya Malvasía 2013 B
100% malvasía

86

Colour: bright straw. Nose: white flowers, fragrant herbs, medium intensity, spicy. Palate: fresh, fruity, balanced.

Ugarte 2009 TR

87

Colour: very deep cherry. Nose: ripe fruit, spicy, toasty, characterful. Palate: powerful, flavourful, toasty, round tannins.

Ugarte 2011 TC

87

Colour: cherry, garnet rim. Nose: spicy, creamy oak, toasty. Palate: powerful, flavourful, toasty, round tannins.

Ugarte Cosecha 2011 T

88

Colour: bright cherry. Nose: ripe fruit, sweet spices, creamy oak, expressive. Palate: flavourful, fruity, toasty, round tannins.

Ugarte Tempranillo 2013 T
100% tempranillo

86

Colour: cherry, purple rim. Nose: red berry notes, floral. Palate: flavourful, fruity, good acidity, round tannins.

Ugarte Viura 2013 B
100% viura

85

EL CONJURO DEL CIEGO
Barrihuelo, 77
01340 Elciego (Alava)
☎: +34 945 264 866
Fax: +34 945 264 866
www.elconjurodelciego.com
lur@elconjurodelciego.com

Lur Tempranillo 2009 T
tempranillo

90

Colour: cherry, garnet rim. Nose: ripe fruit, spicy, creamy oak, toasty, complex. Palate: powerful, flavourful, toasty, round tannins.

EL COTO DE RIOJA
Camino Viejo de Logroño, 26
01320 Oyón (Álava)
☎: +34 945 622 216
Fax: +34 945 622 315
www.elcoto.com
cotorioja@elcoto.com

Coto de Imaz 2005 T

88

Colour: dark-red cherry, garnet rim. Nose: closed, spicy, waxy notes. Palate: correct, balanced, spicy, round tannins.

Coto de Imaz 2008 TGR
100% tempranillo

90

Colour: cherry, garnet rim. Nose: balanced, complex, ripe fruit, spicy. Palate: good structure, flavourful, round tannins.

Coto de Imaz 2010 TR
100% tempranillo

89

Colour: cherry, garnet rim. Nose: ripe fruit, spicy, creamy oak, toasty. Palate: toasty, easy to drink.

Coto Mayor 2011 TC
100% tempranillo

90

Colour: very deep cherry. Nose: medium intensity, ripe fruit, dried herbs, spicy. Palate: long, balanced, round tannins.

Coto Real 2011 T
tempranillo, mazuelo, garnacha

90

Colour: very deep cherry. Nose: balanced, dried herbs. Palate: good structure, spicy, long.

El Coto 2011 TC
100% tempranillo

88

Colour: dark-red cherry. Nose: ripe fruit, spicy, creamy oak, toasty. Palate: flavourful, toasty, round tannins, easy to drink.

El Coto 2013 B
100% viura

86

Colour: bright straw. Nose: ripe fruit, floral, dried herbs, medium intensity. Palate: easy to drink, fresh, fruity.

El Coto 2013 RD
100% tempranillo

87

Colour: onion pink. Nose: elegant, candied fruit, dried flowers, fragrant herbs. Palate: light-bodied, flavourful, good acidity, long, spicy.

ELVIWINES
Finca Clos Mesorah, Ctra. T-300
43775 Falset-Marça (Tarragona)
☎: +34 618 792 963
www.elviwines.com
victor@elviwines.com

Herenza 2009 TR
100% tempranillo

91

Colour: light cherry. Nose: red berry notes, ripe fruit, spicy, creamy oak, toasty, complex, earthy notes. Palate: powerful, flavourful, toasty, round tannins, balanced.

EMW GRANDES VINOS DE ESPAÑA
Sánchez Picazo, 53
30332 Balsapintada (Fuente Alamo)
(Murcia)
☎: +34 968 151 520
Fax: +34 968 151 539
www.emw.es
info@emw.es

The Invisible Man 2011 TC

89

Colour: cherry, garnet rim. Nose: ripe fruit, spicy, creamy oak, roasted coffee. Palate: powerful, flavourful, toasty.

FINCA ALLENDE
Pza. Ibarra, 1
26330 Briones (La Rioja)
☎: +34 941 322 301
Fax: +34 941 322 302
www.finca-allende.com
info@finca-allende.com

Allende 2010 T
100% tempranillo

93

Colour: cherry, garnet rim. Nose: spicy, creamy oak, toasty, complex, fruit expression, earthy notes. Palate: powerful, flavourful, toasty, round tannins.

Allende 2011 B

93

Colour: bright yellow. Nose: powerfull, ripe fruit, sweet spices, creamy oak, fragrant herbs. Palate: rich, smoky aftertaste, flavourful, fresh, good acidity.

Allende Dulce 2011 B
100% viura

96

Colour: golden. Nose: powerfull, floral, honeyed notes, candied fruit, fragrant herbs. Palate: flavourful, sweet, fresh, fruity, good acidity, long.

Avrvs 2010 T

97

Colour: cherry, garnet rim. Nose: dark chocolate, ripe fruit, creamy oak, toasty. Palate: powerful, spicy, ripe fruit, fine bitter notes, good acidity, soft tannins.

Calvario 2010 T

95

Colour: cherry, garnet rim. Nose: spicy, toasty, mineral, ripe fruit, overripe fruit. Palate: powerful, flavourful, toasty, round tannins.

Mártires 2012 B
100% viura

96

Colour: bright straw. Nose: white flowers, fresh fruit, expressive, fine lees, dried herbs. Palate: flavourful, fruity, good acidity, balanced.

Mártires 2013 B
100% viura

97

Colour: bright straw. Nose: white flowers, fine lees, dried herbs, ripe fruit, candied fruit, citrus fruit. Palate: flavourful, fruity, good acidity.

FINCA DE LA RICA
Las Cocinillas, s/n
01330 Labastida (Rioja)
☎: +34 628 833 065
www.fincadelarica.com
info@fincadelarica.com

El Buscador de Finca de la Rica 2011 TC
tempranillo, garnacha

88

Colour: dark-red cherry, garnet rim. Nose: spicy, dried herbs, ripe fruit. Palate: fruity, correct, round tannins, fine bitter notes.

El Buscador de Finca de la Rica 2012 TC
tempranillo, garnacha

89

Colour: cherry, garnet rim. Nose: ripe fruit, spicy, creamy oak, toasty, complex. Palate: powerful, flavourful, toasty, round tannins.

El Guía de Finca de la Rica 2012 T
tempranillo, viura

88

Colour: very deep cherry, garnet rim. Nose: ripe fruit, toasty. Palate: flavourful, ripe fruit, long, fruity aftestaste.

El Nómada 2010 T
tempranillo, graciano

92

Colour: deep cherry, garnet rim. Nose: balanced, powerfull, ripe fruit, spicy. Palate: balanced, long, round tannins.

El Nómada 2011 T
tempranillo, graciano

91

Colour: black cherry, garnet rim. Nose: closed, medium intensity, cocoa bean. Palate: complex, full, flavourful, round tannins, powerful.

FINCA DE LOS ARANDINOS
Ctra. LP 137, km. 4,6
26375 Entrena (La Rioja)
☎: +34 941 446 065
Fax: +34 941 446 423
www.fincadelosarandinos.com
bodega@fincadelosarandinos.com

Finca de los Arandinos 2012 TC

88

Colour: dark-red cherry, garnet rim. Nose: fruit preserve, warm, powerfull. Palate: ripe fruit, long, balsamic, round tannins.

Malacapa 2013 T

85

Viero sobre lías 2013 BFB
100% viura

91

Colour: bright yellow. Nose: fragrant herbs, spicy, citrus fruit. Palate: balanced, easy to drink, fine bitter notes.

FINCA EGOMEI

Ctra. Corella, s/n
26540 Alfaro (La Rioja)
☎: +34 948 780 006
Fax: +34 948 780 515
www.bodegasab.com
info@egomei.es

Carpess 2010 T
tempranillo
92
Colour: dark-red cherry, garnet rim. Nose: powerfull, fruit preserve, creamy oak, sweet spices, mineral. Palate: good structure, full, round tannins, long.

Egomei 2010 T
tempranillo, graciano
91
Colour: deep cherry. Nose: ripe fruit, spicy, creamy oak, toasty, complex. Palate: powerful, flavourful, toasty, round tannins.

Egomei Alma 2009 T
tempranillo, graciano
93
Colour: very deep cherry, garnet rim. Nose: powerfull, ripe fruit, creamy oak, spicy, cocoa bean. Palate: powerful, toasty, round tannins, balsamic.

FINCA NUEVA

Las Eras, 16
26330 Briones (La Rioja)
☎: +34 941 322 301
Fax: +34 941 322 302
www.fincanueva.com
info@fincanueva.com

Finca Nueva 2008 TR
100% tempranillo
92
Colour: ruby red, garnet rim. Nose: ripe fruit, spicy, creamy oak, toasty, complex, fine reductive notes. Palate: powerful, flavourful, toasty, round tannins.

Finca Nueva 2010 TC
100% tempranillo
90
Colour: cherry, garnet rim. Nose: ripe fruit, spicy, creamy oak, toasty, complex. Palate: powerful, flavourful, toasty, round tannins.

Finca Nueva 2013 B
100% viura
89
Colour: bright straw. Nose: ripe fruit, citrus fruit, sweet spices. Palate: easy to drink, ripe fruit.

Finca Nueva 2013 RD
89
Colour: coppery red. Nose: elegant, candied fruit, dried flowers, red berry notes. Palate: light-bodied, flavourful, good acidity, long, spicy.

Finca Nueva Tempranillo 2013 T
100% tempranillo
88
Colour: cherry, purple rim. Nose: red berry notes, floral, balsamic herbs. Palate: flavourful, fruity, good acidity, round tannins.

Finca Nueva Viura 2013 BFB
100% viura
89
Colour: bright straw. Nose: fresh, fresh fruit, white flowers. Palate: flavourful, fruity, good acidity, balanced.

FINCA VALPIEDRA

Término El Montecillo, s/n
26360 Fuenmayor (La Rioja)
☎: +34 941 450 876
Fax: +34 941 450 875
www.familiamartinezbujanda.com
info@bujanda.com

Cantos de Valpiedra 2011 T
100% tempranillo
90
Colour: cherry, garnet rim. Nose: ripe fruit, spicy, creamy oak, toasty. Palate: powerful, flavourful, toasty, round tannins.

Finca Valpiedra 2008 TR
93
Colour: cherry, garnet rim. Nose: ripe fruit, spicy, creamy oak, toasty, complex, dark chocolate, earthy notes. Palate: powerful, flavourful, toasty, round tannins.

GÓMEZ DE SEGURA

Barrio El Campillar
01300 Laguardia (Álava)
☎: +34 945 600 227
Fax: +34 945 600 227
www.gomezdesegura.com
bodegas@gomezdesegura.com

Finca Ratón 2009 T
tempranillo
87
Colour: dark-red cherry, garnet rim. Nose: medium intensity, ripe fruit, varietal, spicy, scrubland. Palate: correct, spicy.

Gómez de Segura 2008 TR
tempranillo
88
Colour: cherry, garnet rim. Nose: varietal, ripe fruit, dried herbs. Palate: spicy, correct, balanced.

Gómez de Segura 2011 TC
tempranillo
88
Colour: dark-red cherry. Nose: ripe fruit, spicy, creamy oak, toasty, complex. Palate: powerful, flavourful, toasty, round tannins.

Gómez de Segura 2013 RD
tempranillo
84

Gómez de Segura 2013 B
83

Gómez de Segura 2013 T Maceración Carbónica
tempranillo
84

Gómez de Segura Vendimia Seleccionada 2011 T
tempranillo
89
Colour: cherry, garnet rim. Nose: ripe fruit, wild herbs, earthy notes, spicy, creamy oak. Palate: balanced, flavourful, long, balsamic.

GONZÁLEZ PURAS
Los Carros, 34
26340 San Asensio (La Rioja)
☎: +34 687 936 272
www.bodegasgonzalezpuras.com
info@bodegasgonzalezpuras.com

González Puras 2010 TC
100% tempranillo
87
Colour: cherry, garnet rim. Nose: ripe fruit, spicy, creamy oak, toasty, complex. Palate: flavourful, toasty, round tannins, easy to drink.

González Puras 2013 B
100% viura
85

González Puras 2013 RD
85

GONZÁLEZ TESO
El Olmo, 34-36
01330 Labastida (Álava)
☎: +34 656 745 954
Fax: +34 945 331 321
www.gonzalezteso.com
info@gontes.com

Gontés 2010 TC
89
Colour: cherry, garnet rim. Nose: medium intensity, ripe fruit, wild herbs. Palate: correct, fruity, easy to drink.

Gontés 2013 T
83

Gontés Expresión 2007 T
100% tempranillo
90
Colour: cherry, garnet rim. Nose: balanced, expressive, varietal, spicy, tobacco. Palate: balanced, ripe fruit, round tannins, reductive nuances.

Gontés Media Crianza 2012 T
100% tempranillo
87
Colour: dark-red cherry, garnet rim. Nose: dry stone, powerfull, ripe fruit, wild herbs. Palate: spicy, correct, round tannins.

Olmo 34 2009 T
88
Colour: dark-red cherry. Nose: powerfull, ripe fruit, fruit preserve, sweet spices. Palate: balanced, round tannins.

GRUPO VINÍCOLA MARQUÉS DE VARGAS
Ctra. Zaragoza, Km. 6
26006 Logroño (La Rioja)
☎: +34 941 261 401
Fax: +34 941 238 696
www.marquesdevargas.com
bodega@marquesdevargas.com

Marqués de Vargas 2008 TR
90
Colour: cherry, garnet rim. Nose: spicy, old leather, dried herbs. Palate: flavourful, easy to drink, spicy.

Marqués de Vargas Hacienda Pradolagar 2005 TR
93
Colour: dark-red cherry, orangey edge. Nose: fine reductive notes, fruit liqueur notes, complex, spicy. Palate: full, good acidity, round tannins, classic aged character.

Marqués de Vargas Reserva Privada 2007 TR
92
Colour: ruby red. Nose: spicy, fine reductive notes, aged wood nuances, toasty. Palate: spicy, long, toasty, flavourful, round tannins, balsamic.

HACIENDA GRIMÓN

Gallera, 6
26131 Ventas Blancas (La Rioja)
☎: +34 941 482 184
Fax: +34 941 482 184
www.haciendagrimon.com
info@haciendagrimon.com

Finca La Oración 2011 T
100% tempranillo
91
Colour: cherry, garnet rim. Nose: ripe fruit, spicy, creamy oak, toasty, complex, earthy notes. Palate: powerful, flavourful, toasty, round tannins, balsamic, balanced.

Hacienda Grimón 2011 TC
90
Colour: cherry, garnet rim. Nose: ripe fruit, spicy, creamy oak, toasty, complex, wild herbs. Palate: powerful, flavourful, toasty, balanced.

HACIENDA URBIÓN

Ctra. Nalda, km. 9
26120 Albelda de Iregua (Rioja)
☎: +34 941 444 233
Fax: +34 941 444 427
www.miguelangelwines.com
info@vinicolareal.com

Palacio de Alcántara 2011 TC
100% tempranillo
87
Colour: very deep cherry. Nose: ripe fruit, spicy, toasty. Palate: powerful, flavourful, toasty, round tannins.

Palacio de Alcántara 2013 T
100% tempranillo
82

Palacio de Alcántara PA 20 2013 T
100% tempranillo
86
Colour: very deep cherry. Nose: medium intensity, candied fruit, fragrant herbs. Palate: fine bitter notes, good acidity.

Palacio de Alcántara PA 30 2011 T
100% tempranillo
87
Colour: bright cherry. Nose: ripe fruit, sweet spices, creamy oak. Palate: flavourful, fruity, toasty, round tannins.

Palacio de Alcántara PA 40 2010 T
100% tempranillo
88
Colour: cherry, garnet rim. Nose: ripe fruit, spicy, creamy oak, toasty. Palate: powerful, flavourful, toasty, round tannins.

Urbión Cuvée 2012 T
85

Urbión Vendimia 2010 TC
90
Colour: cherry, garnet rim. Nose: balanced, complex, ripe fruit, spicy, fine reductive notes. Palate: good structure, flavourful, round tannins.

HACIENDA Y VIÑEDO MARQUÉS DEL ATRIO

Ctra. de Logroño NA-134, Km. 86,2
31587 Mendavia (Navarra)
☎: +34 948 379 994
Fax: +34 948 389 049
www.marquesdelatrio.com
info@marquesdelatrio.com

Bardesano 2011 TC
85

Faustino Rivero Ulecia 2009 TR
89
Colour: ruby red. Nose: balanced, complex, ripe fruit, spicy. Palate: good structure, flavourful, round tannins.

Faustino Rivero Ulecia 2011 TC
87
Colour: deep cherry. Nose: ripe fruit, spicy, creamy oak, toasty, complex. Palate: powerful, flavourful, toasty, round tannins.

Marqués del Atrio 2009 TR
87
Colour: bright cherry. Nose: balanced, complex, ripe fruit, spicy. Palate: good structure, flavourful, round tannins.

Marqués del Atrio 2011 TC
88
Colour: cherry, garnet rim. Nose: ripe fruit, spicy, creamy oak, toasty, complex, dark chocolate. Palate: powerful, flavourful, toasty, round tannins.

HERMANOS FRÍAS DEL VAL

Herrerías, 13
01307 Villabuena (Álava)
☎: +34 945 609 172
Fax: +34 945 609 172
www.friasdelval.com
info@friasdelval.com

Don Peduz 2013 T
tempranillo
85

Hermanos Frías del Val 2013 T
tempranillo
85

Hermanos Frías del Val 2009 TR
tempranillo
89
Colour: light cherry. Nose: ripe fruit, spicy, creamy oak, toasty, balsamic herbs. Palate: powerful, flavourful, toasty, round tannins.

Hermanos Frías del Val 2010 TC
tempranillo
88
Colour: bright cherry. Nose: sweet spices, creamy oak, red berry notes, fruit liqueur notes. Palate: flavourful, fruity, toasty, round tannins.

Hermanos Frías del Val 2012 BFB
viura, malvasía
87
Colour: bright yellow. Nose: powerfull, ripe fruit, sweet spices, creamy oak, fragrant herbs. Palate: rich, smoky aftertaste, flavourful, fresh, good acidity.

Hermanos Frías del Val 2013 B
viura, malvasía
86
Colour: bright straw. Nose: fresh, fresh fruit, white flowers, expressive. Palate: flavourful, fruity, good acidity, balanced, easy to drink.

Hermanos Frías del Val Experiencia 2010 T
tempranillo
90
Colour: cherry, garnet rim. Nose: spicy, creamy oak, toasty, complex, dark chocolate, earthy notes, red berry notes, fruit preserve. Palate: powerful, flavourful, toasty, round tannins, elegant.

HNOS. CASTILLO PÉREZ
Camino la Estación, 15
26330 Briones (La Rioja)
☎: +34 667 730 651
www.bodegaszurbal.com
info@bodegaszurbal.com

Zurbal 2009 TR
tempranillo
87
Colour: cherry, garnet rim. Nose: ripe fruit, wild herbs, spicy, creamy oak. Palate: balanced, flavourful, long, balsamic.

Zurbal 2010 T
tempranillo
88
Colour: cherry, garnet rim. Nose: ripe fruit, spicy, creamy oak, toasty. Palate: powerful, flavourful, toasty.

Zurbal 2011 TC
tempranillo
89
Colour: bright cherry. Nose: ripe fruit, sweet spices, creamy oak, medium intensity. Palate: fruity, flavourful, toasty.

Zurbal 2013 B
viura
86
Colour: bright straw. Nose: fresh, fresh fruit, white flowers, citrus fruit. Palate: fruity, good acidity, balanced, correct.

JESÚS FERNANDO GÓMEZ-CRUZADO CÁRCAMO
Polígono Las heras, 9
26330 Briones (La Rioja)
☎: +34 645 309 357
f.gomezcruzado@kzgunea.net

Corral del Sordo 2009 T
91
Colour: cherry, garnet rim. Nose: ripe fruit, spicy, creamy oak, complex. Palate: powerful, flavourful, toasty, round tannins, balsamic.

JOSÉ BASOCO BASOCO
Ctra. de Samaniego, s/n
01307 Villabuena (Álava)
☎: +34 657 794 964
www.fincabarronte.com
info@fincabarronte.com

Betikoa 2013 B Joven
viura
82

Finca Barronte 2011 TC
tempranillo
89
Colour: very deep cherry, purple rim. Nose: powerfull, ripe fruit, dried herbs. Palate: flavourful, balanced.

Finca Barronte Graciano 2011 T
graciano
88
Colour: black cherry. Nose: ripe fruit, dried herbs. Palate: balsamic, correct, ripe fruit, long.

Finca Barronte Tempranillo 2011 T
tempranillo
87
Colour: bright cherry. Nose: ripe fruit, sweet spices, creamy oak. Palate: fruity, toasty, round tannins.

Finca Barronte Vendimia Seleccionada 2013 T
tempranillo
87
Colour: cherry, purple rim. Nose: red berry notes, raspberry, floral, expressive. Palate: fresh, fruity, flavourful, easy to drink.

JUAN CARLOS SANCHA

Cº de Las Barreras, s/n
26320 Baños de Río Tobía (La Rioja)
☎: +34 639 216 011
www.juancarlossancha.com
juancarlossancha@yahoo.es

Ad Libitum Maturana Tinta 2012 T
100% maturana

91

Colour: cherry, garnet rim. Nose: ripe fruit, spicy, creamy oak, toasty, complex, earthy notes. Palate: powerful, flavourful, toasty, round tannins.

Ad Libitum Monastel 2012 T
100% monastel

91

Colour: cherry, garnet rim. Nose: ripe fruit, wild herbs, earthy notes, spicy, creamy oak. Palate: balanced, flavourful, long, balsamic.

Ad Libitum Tempranillo Blanco 2013 B
100% tempranillo blanco

88

Colour: bright straw. Nose: white flowers, fresh fruit, expressive, fine lees, dried herbs. Palate: flavourful, fruity, good acidity, balanced.

Peña El Gato Garnacha de Viñas Viejas 2012 T
100% garnacha

91

Colour: very deep cherry. Nose: ripe fruit, spicy, creamy oak, toasty, characterful. Palate: powerful, flavourful, toasty, round tannins.

LA RIOJA ALTA S.A.

Avda. de Vizcaya, 8
26200 Haro (La Rioja)
☎: +34 941 310 346
Fax: +34 941 312 854
www.riojalta.com
riojalta@riojalta.com

Gran Reserva 904 Rioja Alta 2004 TGR
tempranillo, graciano

95

Colour: pale ruby, brick rim edge. Nose: elegant, spicy, fine reductive notes, wet leather, aged wood nuances, fruit liqueur notes. Palate: spicy, fine tannins, elegant, long.

La Rioja Alta Gran Reserva 890 2001 TGR

94

Colour: pale ruby, brick rim edge. Nose: spicy, fine reductive notes, wet leather, aged wood nuances, fruit liqueur notes, elegant. Palate: spicy, fine tannins, elegant, long.

Viña Alberdi 2007 TC
tempranillo

91

Colour: dark-red cherry, orangey edge. Nose: elegant, spicy, fine reductive notes, aged wood nuances, fruit liqueur notes. Palate: spicy, fine tannins, elegant, long.

Viña Alberdi 2008 TC
tempranillo

92

Colour: cherry, garnet rim. Nose: ripe fruit, spicy, creamy oak, complex. Palate: powerful, flavourful, toasty, round tannins.

Viña Arana 2006 TR
tempranillo, mazuelo

93

Colour: pale ruby, brick rim edge. Nose: spicy, fine reductive notes, wet leather, aged wood nuances, fruit liqueur notes. Palate: spicy, fine tannins.

Viña Ardanza 2005 TR
tempranillo, garnacha

93

Colour: ruby red. Nose: spicy, fine reductive notes, wet leather, aged wood nuances, toasty, ripe fruit. Palate: spicy, long, toasty.

LAN
Paraje del Buicio, s/n
26360 Fuenmayor (La Rioja)
☎: +34 941 450 950
Fax: +34 941 450 567
www.bodegaslan.com
info@bodegaslan.com

Culmen 2010 TR

93

Colour: cherry, garnet rim. Nose: ripe fruit, spicy, creamy oak, toasty, complex, dark chocolate, earthy notes. Palate: powerful, flavourful, toasty, round tannins.

Lan 2007 TGR

90

Colour: cherry, garnet rim. Nose: balanced, complex, ripe fruit, spicy. Palate: good structure, flavourful, round tannins.

Lan 2008 TR

91

Colour: cherry, garnet rim. Nose: ripe fruit, spicy, creamy oak, toasty, complex. Palate: powerful, flavourful, toasty, round tannins.

Lan 2011 TC
tempranillo

88

Colour: bright cherry. Nose: ripe fruit, sweet spices, creamy oak, expressive. Palate: flavourful, fruity, toasty, round tannins.

Lan A Mano 2010 T

93

Colour: very deep cherry, garnet rim. Nose: powerfull, ripe fruit, roasted coffee, dark chocolate. Palate: powerful, toasty, roasted-coffee aftertaste.

Lan D-12 2011 T
100% tempranillo

91

Colour: ruby red. Nose: spicy, fine reductive notes, aged wood nuances, toasty, ripe fruit. Palate: spicy, long, toasty.

Viña Lanciano 2010 TR
90
Colour: bright cherry. Nose: ripe fruit, sweet spices, creamy oak, medium intensity. Palate: fruity, flavourful, toasty.

LONG WINES
Avda. del Puente Cultural, 8 Bloque B Bajo 7
28702 San Sebastián de los Reyes
(Madrid)
☎: +34 916 221 305
Fax: +34 916 220 029
www.longwines.com
adm@longwines.com

Finca Mónica 2011 TC
100% tempranillo
90
Colour: cherry, garnet rim. Nose: creamy oak, ripe fruit, dried herbs, spicy. Palate: fruity, round tannins, balanced.

Finca Mónica Tempranillo 2013 T
100% tempranillo
84

LUBERRI MONJE AMESTOY
Camino de Rehoyos, s/n
01340 Elciego (Álava)
☎: +34 945 606 010
Fax: +34 945 606 482
www.luberri.com
luberri@luberri.com

Biga de Luberri 2011 TC
tempranillo
90
Colour: bright cherry. Nose: ripe fruit, sweet spices, creamy oak, expressive. Palate: flavourful, fruity, toasty, round tannins.

Luberri 2013 T Maceración Carbónica
88
Colour: cherry, purple rim. Nose: red berry notes, raspberry, floral, tropical fruit. Palate: fresh, fruity, flavourful, easy to drink, balanced.

Luberri Cepas Viejas 2008 TC
tempranillo
88
Colour: cherry, garnet rim. Nose: ripe fruit, spicy, creamy oak, toasty. Palate: powerful, flavourful, toasty, round tannins.

Monje Amestoy de Luberri 2007 TR
91
Colour: cherry, garnet rim. Nose: ripe fruit, spicy, creamy oak, toasty, complex. Palate: powerful, flavourful, toasty, round tannins.

Seis de Luberri 2011 T
tempranillo
92
Colour: cherry, garnet rim. Nose: ripe fruit, spicy, creamy oak, toasty, complex. Palate: powerful, flavourful, toasty, round tannins.

LUIS GURPEGUI MUGA
Avda. Celso Muerza, 8
31570 San Adrián (Navarra)
☎: +34 948 670 050
Fax: +34 948 670 259
www.gurpegui.es
bodegas@gurpegui.es

Primi 2013 T
tempranillo, graciano, garnacha
81

MARQUÉS DE LA CONCORDIA
Ctra. El Ciego, s/n
26350 Cenicero (La Rioja)
☎: +34 913 878 612
www.the-haciendas.com
abasilio@unitedwineries.com

Hacienda de Susar 2011 T
88
Colour: cherry, garnet rim. Nose: fruit preserve, fruit liqueur notes, spicy. Palate: flavourful, pruney, balsamic.

Marqués de la Concordia 2008 TR
100% tempranillo
88
Colour: cherry, garnet rim. Nose: ripe fruit, spicy, creamy oak, toasty, complex. Palate: powerful, flavourful, toasty, round tannins.

Marqués de la Concordia 2010 TC
100% tempranillo
89
Colour: cherry, garnet rim. Nose: ripe fruit, wild herbs, spicy, creamy oak. Palate: balanced, flavourful, long.

MARQUÉS DE MURRIETA
Finca Ygay- Ctra. Logroño-Zaragoza, km. 5
26006 Logroño (La Rioja)
☎: +34 941 271 370
Fax: +34 941 251 606
www.marquesdemurrieta.com
rrpp@marquesdemurrieta.com

Capellania 2009 B
100% viura
93
Colour: bright straw. Nose: fresh fruit, expressive, fine lees, dried herbs, dried flowers. Palate: flavourful, fruity, good acidity, balanced.

Castillo Ygay 2005 TGR
95
Colour: cherry, garnet rim. Nose: balanced, complex, ripe fruit, spicy, mineral. Palate: good structure, flavourful, round tannins.

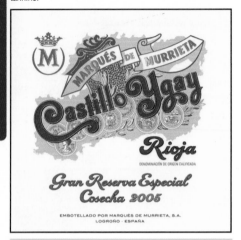

Dalmau 2009 TR
95
Colour: cherry, garnet rim. Nose: ripe fruit, spicy, creamy oak, toasty, complex, dark chocolate, earthy notes. Palate: powerful, flavourful, toasty, round tannins.

Dalmau 2011 TR
96
Colour: cherry, garnet rim. Nose: ripe fruit, spicy, creamy oak, toasty, complex, dark chocolate, earthy notes. Palate: powerful, flavourful, toasty, round tannins.

Marqués de Murrieta 2009 TR
93
Colour: very deep cherry. Nose: ripe fruit, spicy, creamy oak, toasty, characterful. Palate: powerful, flavourful, toasty, round tannins.

MARQUÉS DE REINOSA, S. COOP.
Ctra. Rincón de Soto, s/n
26560 Autol (La Rioja)
☎: +34 941 401 327
Fax: +34 941 390 065
www.marquesdereinosa.com
bodegas@marquesdereinosa.com

Marqués de Reinosa 2009 TR
tempranillo, mazuelo
87
Colour: ruby red. Nose: spicy, fine reductive notes, aged wood nuances, toasty, ripe fruit. Palate: spicy, long, toasty.

Marqués de Reinosa 2011 TC
tempranillo
87
Colour: bright cherry, garnet rim. Nose: scrubland, ripe fruit, spicy. Palate: flavourful, fruity, round tannins.

Marqués de Reinosa 2013 B
viura, verdejo
85

Marqués de Reinosa 2013 RD
garnacha, tempranillo
87
Colour: onion pink. Nose: candied fruit, dried flowers, fragrant herbs. Palate: light-bodied, long, spicy.

MARQUÉS DE TOMARES

Ctra. de Cenicero, s/n
26360 Fuenmayor (La Rioja)
☎: +34 676 433 820
Fax: +34 941 450 297
www.marquesdetomares.com
info@marquesdetomares.com

Convento San Prudencio 2013 T
tempranillo
83

Marqués de Tomares 2001 TGR
89
Colour: dark-red cherry, orangey edge. Nose: old leather, dried herbs, cigar, aged wood nuances. Palate: balanced, spicy, ripe fruit, reductive nuances.

Marqués de Tomares 2009 TR
graciano
89
Colour: very deep cherry. Nose: scrubland, spicy, ripe fruit. Palate: good structure, balanced, round tannins.

Marqués de Tomares Excellence 3F 2013 T
85

Monteleiva 2011 T
100% tempranillo
86
Colour: bright cherry, garnet rim. Nose: medium intensity, ripe fruit, spicy. Palate: fruity, ripe fruit, long.

MARQUÉS DE ULÍA

Paraje del Buicio, s/n
26360 Fuenmayor (La Rioja)
☎: +34 941 450 950
Fax: +34 941 450 567
www.marquesdeulia.com
info@marquesdeulia.com

La Vendimia Marqués de Ulía 2010 TR
89
Colour: bright cherry. Nose: ripe fruit, sweet spices, creamy oak, expressive. Palate: flavourful, fruity, toasty.

Marqués de Ulía 2008 TR
90
Colour: pale ruby, brick rim edge. Nose: ripe fruit, wild herbs, earthy notes, spicy, creamy oak. Palate: balanced, flavourful, long, balsamic.

Marqués de Ulía 2011 TC
tempranillo
90
Colour: cherry, garnet rim. Nose: ripe fruit, spicy, creamy oak, toasty, complex. Palate: powerful, flavourful, toasty, round tannins.

DO Ca. RIOJA / D.O.P

MARQUÉS DE VITORIA
Camino de Santa Lucía, s/n
01320 Oyón (Álava)
☎: +34 945 622 134
Fax: +34 945 601 496
www.marquesdevitoria.com
info@bodegasmarquesdevitoria.es

Ecco de Marqués de Vitoria 2013 T
100% tempranillo
85

Marqués de Vitoria 2005 TGR
100% tempranillo
89
Colour: cherry, garnet rim. Nose: balanced, complex, ripe fruit, spicy, fine reductive notes. Palate: good structure, flavourful, round tannins.

Marqués de Vitoria 2009 TR
100% tempranillo
90
Colour: cherry, garnet rim. Nose: red berry notes, ripe fruit, spicy, creamy oak, toasty, fine reductive notes. Palate: powerful, flavourful, toasty, balanced.

Marqués de Vitoria 2011 TC
100% tempranillo
89
Colour: cherry, garnet rim. Nose: ripe fruit, spicy, toasty. Palate: powerful, flavourful, toasty, round tannins.

Marqués de Vitoria 2013 B
100% viura
85

Marqués de Vitoria 2013 RD
100% tempranillo
87
Colour: light cherry, bright. Nose: balanced, white flowers, fresh fruit, expressive. Palate: correct, good acidity, fine bitter notes, good finish.

MARQUÉS DEL PUERTO
Ctra. de Logroño s/n
26360 Fuenmayor (La Rioja)
☎: +34 941 450 001
Fax: +34 941 450 051
www.bodegamarquesdelpuerto.com
bmp@mbrizard.com

Bentus Vendimia Seleccionada 2005 TR
tempranillo, garnacha, mazuelo, graciano

87

Colour: pale ruby, brick rim edge. Nose: spicy, fine reductive notes, wet leather, aged wood nuances, fruit liqueur notes. Palate: spicy, fine tannins, elegant, long.

Marqués del Puerto 2004 TGR
tempranillo, mazuelo, graciano

86

Colour: pale ruby, brick rim edge. Nose: spicy, fine reductive notes, wet leather, aged wood nuances, fruit liqueur notes. Palate: spicy, elegant, long.

Marqués del Puerto 2006 TR
tempranillo, mazuelo

86

Colour: pale ruby, brick rim edge. Nose: spicy, fine reductive notes, aged wood nuances, wild herbs, fruit liqueur notes. Palate: spicy, long, balsamic.

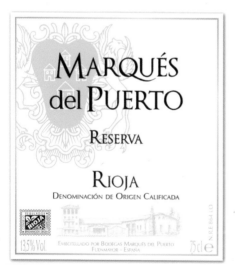

Marqués del Puerto 2010 TC
tempranillo, mazuelo

88

Colour: cherry, garnet rim. Nose: ripe fruit, spicy, creamy oak, toasty, fine reductive notes. Palate: powerful, flavourful, toasty.

Marqués del Puerto 2013 B
100% viura

83

Marqués del Puerto 2013 RD
tempranillo, garnacha

86

Colour: rose, bright. Nose: red berry notes, ripe fruit, rose petals. Palate: flavourful, powerful, ripe fruit.

Román Paladino 2001 TGR
tempranillo, mazuelo, graciano

88

Colour: pale ruby, brick rim edge. Nose: old leather, cigar, waxy notes, spicy, creamy oak, balsamic herbs. Palate: flavourful, elegant, spicy, balanced.

MARTÍNEZ LACUESTA
Paraje de Ubieta, s/n
26200 Haro (La Rioja)
☎: +34 941 310 050
Fax: +34 941 303 748
www.martinezlacuesta.com
bodega@martinezlacuesta.com

Cynthia 2012 T
garnacha

89

Colour: cherry, garnet rim. Nose: ripe fruit, wild herbs, earthy notes, spicy, creamy oak. Palate: balanced, flavourful, long, balsamic.

Martínez Lacuesta 2006 TGR
tempranillo, graciano, mazuelo

88

Colour: pale ruby, brick rim edge. Nose: elegant, spicy, fine reductive notes, wet leather, aged wood nuances, fruit liqueur notes. Palate: spicy, fine tannins, elegant, long.

Martínez Lacuesta 2011 TC
tempranillo, graciano, mazuelo

87

Colour: bright cherry. Nose: ripe fruit, sweet spices, creamy oak, balsamic herbs. Palate: flavourful, fruity, toasty, round tannins.

MATER VITIS
Calle Doctor Santaolalla, 21 bajo izq
03005 Alicante (Alicante)
☎: +34 965 637 811
www.matervitis.com

Palabra de Vino 2009 TR

86

Colour: cherry, garnet rim. Nose: ripe fruit, spicy, powerfull. Palate: powerful, flavourful, toasty, round tannins.

Palabra de Vino 2011 TC

85

Palabra de Vino 2012 T
84

MIGUEL ÁNGEL MURO
Avda. Diputación, 4
01306 Lapuebla de Labarca (Álava)
☎: +34 945 607 081
www.bodegasmuro.com
info@bodegasmuro.es

Amenital 2009 TC
tempranillo, graciano
89
Colour: deep cherry. Nose: ripe fruit, earthy notes, spicy, dried herbs. Palate: balanced, long, balsamic, round tannins.

Miguel Ángel Muro 2013 T
tempranillo, viura
83

Muro 2010 TR
tempranillo, graciano
91
Colour: cherry, garnet rim. Nose: balanced, complex, ripe fruit, spicy. Palate: good structure, flavourful, round tannins.

Muro 2013 B
viura
85

Muro Bujanda 2010 TC
tempranillo
90
Colour: cherry, garnet rim. Nose: ripe fruit, spicy, creamy oak, toasty, complex. Palate: flavourful, toasty, round tannins.

Muro Maturana 2010 T
maturana
90
Colour: cherry, garnet rim. Nose: ripe fruit, wild herbs, spicy, creamy oak. Palate: balanced, flavourful, long, balsamic.

MIGUEL MERINO
Ctra. de Logroño, 16
26330 Briones (La Rioja)
☎: +34 941 322 263
Fax: +34 941 322 294
www.miguelmerino.com
info@miguelmerino.com

Mazuelo de la Quinta Cruz 2011 T
100% mazuelo
88
Colour: deep cherry, garnet rim. Nose: balanced, scrubland, spicy. Palate: fruity, easy to drink.

Miguel Merino 2006 TGR
88
Colour: black cherry, orangey edge. Nose: old leather, animal reductive notes, toasty. Palate: balanced, classic aged character, flavourful.

NUBORI
Avda. del Ebro s/n
26540 Alfaro (La Rioja)
☎: +34 941 183 502
Fax: +34 941 183 157
www.bodegasnubori.com
nubori@nubori.es

Campo Burgo 2008 TR
tempranillo
86
Colour: cherry, garnet rim. Nose: old leather, waxy notes, medium intensity, spicy, aged wood nuances. Palate: correct, round tannins.

Campo Burgo 2009 TC
tempranillo
84

Campo Burgo 2012 T
tempranillo
83

Campo Burgo 2013 RD
garnacha
83

Nubori 2008 TR
tempranillo
84

Nubori 2009 TC
tempranillo
85

Nubori 2013 RD
garnacha
84

Nubori Cuvée Especial 2007 TR
tempranillo
88
Colour: ruby red, orangey edge. Nose: fruit liqueur notes, spicy, creamy oak, balsamic herbs. Palate: spicy, ripe fruit, reductive nuances.

Nubori Vendimia Seleccionada 2006 TR
tempranillo
90
Colour: pale ruby, brick rim edge. Nose: elegant, spicy, fine reductive notes, wet leather, aged wood nuances. Palate: spicy, fine tannins, elegant, long.

OLIVIER RIVIÈRE VINOS
Breton de los Herreros, 14 Entreplanta
26001 Logroño (La Rioja)
☎: +34 690 733 541
www.olivier-riviere.com
olivier@olivier-riviere.com

Ganko 2012 T
94
Colour: cherry, garnet rim. Nose: wild herbs, earthy notes, spicy, ripe fruit, fruit liqueur notes. Palate: flavourful, long, balsamic, balanced, elegant.

Jequitibá 2013 B
viura, garnacha blanca, malvasía
91
Colour: bright straw, greenish rim. Nose: complex, white flowers, citrus fruit, expressive. Palate: balanced, fine bitter notes, long.

Rayos Uva 2013 T
tempranillo, garnacha, graciano
89
Colour: bright cherry. Nose: ripe fruit, sweet spices, creamy oak, expressive. Palate: flavourful, fruity, toasty, round tannins.

PAGO DE LARREA

Ctra. de Cenicero, Km. 0,2
01340 Elciego (Álava)
☎: +34 945 606 063
Fax: +34 945 606 697
www.pagodelarrea.com
bodega@pagodelarrea.com

8 de Caecus 2010 T
100% tempranillo
87
Colour: cherry, garnet rim. Nose: ripe fruit, wild herbs, spicy, creamy oak. Palate: balanced, flavourful, long, balsamic.

Caecus 2009 TR
100% tempranillo
88
Colour: cherry, garnet rim. Nose: balanced, complex, ripe fruit, spicy. Palate: good structure, flavourful, round tannins.

Caecus 2011 TC
100% tempranillo
87
Colour: cherry, garnet rim. Nose: medium intensity, dried herbs, ripe fruit. Palate: fruity, easy to drink.

Caecus 2013 T
86
Colour: cherry, purple rim. Nose: ripe fruit, floral. Palate: powerful, fresh, fruity, unctuous.

Caecus Verderón 2013 BFB
84

PAGOS DEL CAMINO

01300 Laguardia (Alava)
☎: +34 941 444 233
Fax: +34 941 444 427
www.pagosdelcamino.com
info@vinicolareal.com

Dominio de Conte 2010 TR
93
Colour: cherry, garnet rim. Nose: ripe fruit, spicy, creamy oak, toasty, complex. Palate: powerful, flavourful, toasty, slightly dry, soft tannins.

Loriñón 2011 TC
89
Colour: cherry, garnet rim. Nose: overripe fruit, dried fruit, sweet spices, toasty. Palate: ripe fruit, warm, powerful.

PAGOS DEL REY S.L.

Ctra. N-232, PK 422,7
26360 Fuenmayor (La Rioja)
☎: +34 941 450 818
Fax: +34 941 450 818
www.felixsolisavantis.com
jfernandez@pagosdelrey.com

Arnegui 2009 TR
tempranillo
88
Colour: deep cherry. Nose: ripe fruit, spicy, balsamic herbs, creamy oak. Palate: powerful, flavourful, spicy, long.

Arnegui 2011 TC
tempranillo
87
Colour: cherry, garnet rim. Nose: ripe fruit, spicy, creamy oak, toasty. Palate: powerful, flavourful, toasty.

Arnegui 2013 B
viura
85

Arnegui 2013 RD
garnacha
86
Colour: rose, bright. Nose: fresh fruit, rose petals, wild herbs. Palate: fresh, easy to drink, balanced.

Arnegui 2013 T
tempranillo
85

Castillo de Albai 2009 TR
tempranillo
87
Colour: bright cherry. Nose: balanced, complex, ripe fruit, spicy. Palate: good structure, flavourful, round tannins.

Castillo de Albai 2011 TC
tempranillo
85

Castillo de Albai 2013 B
viura
86
Colour: bright straw. Nose: fresh fruit, medium intensity, dried herbs, faded flowers. Palate: fruity, good acidity, fine bitter notes.

Castillo de Albai 2013 RD
100% garnacha
85

Castillo de Albai 2013 T
tempranillo
85

El Círculo 2010 TC
tempranillo
86
Colour: bright cherry. Nose: ripe fruit, wild herbs, spicy, creamy oak. Palate: powerful, flavourful, spicy.

El Círculo 2013 T Joven
tempranillo
83

PAISAJES Y VIÑEDOS
Pza. Ibarra, 1
26330 Briones (La Rioja)
☎: +34 941 322 301
Fax: +34 941 322 302
comunicacio@vilaviniteca.es

Paisajes Cecias 2012 T
90
Colour: cherry, garnet rim. Nose: ripe fruit, spicy, creamy oak, toasty, earthy notes. Palate: powerful, flavourful, toasty.

Paisajes La Pasada 2012 T
93
Colour: cherry, garnet rim. Nose: ripe fruit, wild herbs, earthy notes, spicy, creamy oak. Palate: flavourful, long, balsamic.

Paisajes Valsalado 2012 T
92
Colour: cherry, garnet rim. Nose: fruit preserve, fruit liqueur notes, sweet spices, creamy oak. Palate: flavourful, spicy, long.

PALACIOS VINOTECA
Ctra. de Nalda a Viguera, 46
26190 Nalda (La Rioja)
☎: +34 941 444 418
www.palaciosvinoteca.com
info@palaciosvinoteca.com

Tenue 2013 RD
tempranillo
87
Colour: coppery red. Nose: red berry notes, ripe fruit. Palate: flavourful, fruity, fine bitter notes.

R. LÓPEZ DE HEREDIA VIÑA TONDONIA
Avda. Vizcaya, 3
26200 Haro (La Rioja)
☎: +34 941 310 244
Fax: +34 941 310 788
www.tondonia.com
bodega@lopezdeheredia.com

Viña Tondonia 1999 B Reserva
94
Colour: bright golden. Nose: ripe fruit, dry nuts, powerfull, toasty, aged wood nuances, expressive, elegant. Palate: flavourful, fruity, spicy, toasty, long, balanced.

Viña Tondonia 2002 TR
93
Colour: pale ruby, brick rim edge. Nose: balanced, complex, ripe fruit, spicy, balsamic herbs, fine reductive notes. Palate: good structure, flavourful, round tannins, elegant.

RAMÓN SAENZ BODEGAS Y VIÑEDOS
Mayor, 12
01307 Baños de Ebro (Álava)
☎: +34 945 609 212
bodegasrs@hotmail.com

Cimadago Autor 2012 TC
tempranillo
83

Erramun 2013 RD
tempranillo, viura
85

Erramun 2013 T
tempranillo, viura
79

Mahasti Sonie 2013 B
viura, malvasía
84

REMELLURI
Ctra. Rivas de Tereso, s/n
01330 Labastida (Álava)
☎: +34 945 331 801
Fax: +34 945 331 802
www.remelluri.com
remelluri@remelluri.com

Lindes de Remelluri Labastida 2011 T
92
Colour: cherry, garnet rim. Nose: ripe fruit, wild herbs, spicy, creamy oak, mineral. Palate: balanced, flavourful, long, balsamic.

Lindes de Remelluri San Vicente 2011 T
93
Colour: cherry, garnet rim. Nose: ripe fruit, spicy, creamy oak, toasty, complex. Palate: powerful, flavourful, toasty, round tannins.

Remelluri 2009 TR
94
Colour: cherry, garnet rim. Nose: balanced, complex, ripe fruit, spicy, fine reductive notes. Palate: good structure, flavourful, round tannins, balanced.

Remelluri 2011 B

94

Colour: bright yellow. Nose: ripe fruit, dried flowers, wild herbs, spicy, creamy oak, balanced, expressive. Palate: rich, flavourful, spicy, balsamic, long, elegant.

RESTAURANTE HEVIA

Serrano, 118
28006 Madrid (Madrid)
☎: +34 649 917 608
www.heviamadrid.com
hevia@heviamadrid.com

Hevia 50 2010 TC
tempranillo

88

Colour: cherry, garnet rim. Nose: ripe fruit, wild herbs, spicy, creamy oak. Palate: balanced, flavourful, long, balsamic.

RIOJA VEGA

Ctra. Logroño-Mendavia, Km. 92
31230 Viana (Navarra)
☎: +34 948 646 263
Fax: +34 948 645 612
www.riojavega.com
info@riojavega.com

Rioja Vega 2005 TGR
100% tempranillo

90

Colour: dark-red cherry, garnet rim. Nose: cocoa bean, creamy oak, spicy, ripe fruit. Palate: balanced, ripe fruit, long, round tannins.

Rioja Vega 2009 TR

88

Colour: very deep cherry. Nose: ripe fruit, spicy, creamy oak, toasty, characterful. Palate: powerful, flavourful, toasty, round tannins.

Rioja Vega 2011 TC

88

Colour: very deep cherry. Nose: ripe fruit, spicy, creamy oak, toasty, characterful. Palate: powerful, flavourful, toasty, round tannins.

Rioja Vega 9 Barricas 2011 T
tempranillo, graciano

87

Colour: cherry, garnet rim. Nose: ripe fruit, wild herbs, spicy, creamy oak. Palate: balanced, flavourful, long, balsamic.

Rioja Vega Edición Limitada 2011 TC

91

Colour: cherry, garnet rim. Nose: ripe fruit, spicy, creamy oak, toasty, complex. Palate: powerful, flavourful, toasty, round tannins.

Rioja Vega Tempranillo Blanco 2013 B
tempranillo blanco

92

Colour: bright straw. Nose: ripe fruit, tropical fruit, sweet spices, balsamic herbs, expressive. Palate: powerful, flavourful, fruity, spicy, balanced.

RODRÍGUEZ SANZO

Manuel Azaña, 9
47014 (Valladolid)
☎: +34 983 150 150
Fax: +34 983 150 151
www.rodriguezsanzo.com
comunicacion@valsanzo.com

La Senoba 2010 T

91

Colour: cherry, garnet rim. Nose: ripe fruit, wild herbs, earthy notes, spicy, creamy oak. Palate: flavourful, long, balsamic, elegant, balanced.

Lacrimus 2010 TC

91

Colour: cherry, garnet rim. Nose: spicy, creamy oak, red berry notes, ripe fruit, balanced. Palate: flavourful, long, balsamic, elegant.

Lacrimus 5 2013 T
tempranillo

88

Colour: bright cherry, garnet rim. Nose: ripe fruit, sweet spices, creamy oak. Palate: flavourful, fruity, toasty.

Lacrimus Graciano Rosae 2013 RD
100% graciano

88

Colour: rose, purple rim. Nose: powerfull, ripe fruit, red berry notes, floral, expressive. Palate: powerful, fruity, fresh.

Lacrimus Rex 2012 T
90
Colour: cherry, garnet rim. Nose: ripe fruit, spicy, creamy oak, toasty, complex, mineral. Palate: powerful, flavourful, toasty.

SDAD. COOP. BODEGA SAN MIGUEL
Ctra. de Zaragoza, 7
26513 Ausejo (La Rioja)
☎: +34 941 430 005
Fax: +34 941 430 209
administracion@bodegasanmiguelsc.es

Hebe 2009 TC
100% tempranillo
86
Colour: cherry, garnet rim. Nose: ripe fruit, spicy, creamy oak, toasty, complex, wild herbs. Palate: powerful, flavourful, toasty.

Obrada 2010 TC
88
Colour: bright cherry. Nose: ripe fruit, sweet spices, creamy oak, expressive. Palate: flavourful, fruity, toasty.

Obrada 2013 B
100% viura
85

Obrada 2013 T
100% tempranillo
87
Colour: cherry, purple rim. Nose: expressive, fresh fruit, red berry notes, floral. Palate: flavourful, fruity, good acidity, round tannins.

SEÑORÍO DE ARANA
La Cadena, 20
01330 Labastida (Álava)
☎: +34 944 216 000
Fax: +34 944 121 738
www.senoriodearana.com
info@senoriodearana.com

Sommelier 2007 TR
90
Colour: cherry, garnet rim. Nose: ripe fruit, spicy, creamy oak, toasty, complex, fine reductive notes. Palate: powerful, flavourful, toasty, round tannins.

Sommelier 2011 TC
100% tempranillo
89
Colour: bright cherry. Nose: ripe fruit, sweet spices, creamy oak, expressive. Palate: flavourful, fruity, toasty, round tannins.

Viña del Oja 2004 TR
88
Colour: pale ruby, brick rim edge. Nose: ripe fruit, wild herbs, spicy, creamy oak, fine reductive notes. Palate: flavourful, spicy, balsamic, balanced.

Viña del Oja 2011 TC
86
Colour: cherry, garnet rim. Nose: ripe fruit, spicy, creamy oak, toasty. Palate: powerful, flavourful, toasty.

Viña del Oja 2013 T
84

SEÑORÍO DE SAN VICENTE
Los Remedios, 27
26338 San Vicente de la Sonsierra
(La Rioja)
☎: +34 945 600 590
Fax: +34 945 600 885
www.sierracantabria.com
info@sierracantabria.com

San Vicente 2010 T
tempranillo
96
Colour: very deep cherry. Nose: ripe fruit, spicy, creamy oak, toasty, characterful, fine reductive notes, earthy notes. Palate: powerful, flavourful, toasty, round tannins.

San Vicente 2011 T
tempranillo
95
Colour: cherry, garnet rim. Nose: ripe fruit, spicy, creamy oak, toasty, complex, dark chocolate. Palate: powerful, flavourful, toasty, round tannins.

SEÑORÍO DE SOMALO

Ctra. de Baños, 62
26321 Bobadilla (La Rioja)
☎: +34 941 202 351
Fax: +34 941 202 351
www.bodegasomalo.com
info@bodegasomalo.com

Señorío de Somalo 2001 TGR
90
Colour: pale ruby, brick rim edge. Nose: expressive, fine reductive notes, elegant, fruit liqueur notes. Palate: light-bodied, classic aged character, spicy, round tannins.

Señorío de Somalo 2003 TR
88
Colour: light cherry, brick rim edge. Nose: fine reductive notes, tobacco, fruit liqueur notes. Palate: balanced, easy to drink, fine tannins.

Señorío de Somalo 2011 TC
87
Colour: cherry, garnet rim. Nose: powerfull, ripe fruit, sweet spices. Palate: fruity, easy to drink, good finish.

Señorío de Somalo 2013 B
100% viura
81

Señorío de Somalo 2013 RD
100% garnacha
85

Señorío de Somalo 2013 T
84

Señorío de Somalo Magnum 2001 TGR
91
Colour: pale ruby, brick rim edge. Nose: elegant, spicy, fine reductive notes, aged wood nuances, fruit liqueur notes, smoky. Palate: spicy, fine tannins, elegant, long.

SIERRA CANTABRIA

Amorebieta, 3
26338 San Vicente de la Sonsierra
(La Rioja)
☎: +34 941 334 080
Fax: +34 941 334 371
www.sierracantabria.com
info@sierracantabria.com

Murmurón 2013 T
tempranillo
88
Colour: cherry, purple rim. Nose: fresh fruit, red berry notes, floral. Palate: flavourful, fruity, good acidity.

Sierra Cantabria 2004 TGR
93
Colour: very deep cherry. Nose: ripe fruit, spicy, creamy oak, characterful, aromatic coffee, wet leather. Palate: powerful, flavourful, toasty, round tannins.

Sierra Cantabria 2008 TR
tempranillo
92
Colour: cherry, garnet rim. Nose: ripe fruit, creamy oak, toasty, wet leather. Palate: powerful, flavourful, toasty, round tannins.

Sierra Cantabria 2012 TC
tempranillo
92
Colour: cherry, garnet rim. Nose: ripe fruit, spicy, creamy oak, toasty, complex. Palate: powerful, flavourful, toasty, round tannins.

Sierra Cantabria 2013 RD
89
Colour: brilliant rose. Nose: elegant, candied fruit, dried flowers, fragrant herbs, red berry notes. Palate: light-bodied, flavourful, good acidity, long, spicy.

Sierra Cantabria Garnacha 2011 T
garnacha
93
Colour: cherry, garnet rim. Nose: ripe fruit, wild herbs, earthy notes, spicy, creamy oak. Palate: balanced, flavourful, long, balsamic.

Sierra Cantabria Selección 2012 T
tempranillo
91
Colour: bright cherry. Nose: ripe fruit, sweet spices, creamy oak, expressive. Palate: flavourful, fruity, toasty, round tannins.

SOC. COOP. SAN ESTEBAN P.

Ctra. Agoncillo s/n
26143 Murillo de Río Leza (La Rioja)
☎: +34 941 432 031
Fax: +34 941 432 422
www.bodegassanesteban.com
administracion@bodegassanesteban.com

Tierras de Murillo 2011 TC
100% tempranillo
87
Colour: cherry, garnet rim. Nose: ripe fruit, spicy, toasty, complex. Palate: flavourful, toasty, round tannins, easy to drink.

Tierras de Murillo 2013 RD
100% tempranillo
86
Colour: raspberry rose. Nose: powerfull, ripe fruit, red berry notes, floral, expressive. Palate: powerful, fruity, fresh.

Tierras de Murillo Colección Antique nº 1 2011 T
100% tempranillo

91

Colour: cherry, garnet rim. Nose: ripe fruit, spicy, creamy oak, toasty, complex, dried herbs. Palate: powerful, flavourful, toasty, round tannins.

Tierras de Murillo Tempranillo 2013 T
100% tempranillo

84

Tierras de Murillo Viura 2013 B
100% viura

86

Colour: bright straw. Nose: medium intensity, fresh fruit, floral, citrus fruit. Palate: fresh, easy to drink.

SOLANA DE RAMÍREZ RUIZ
Arana, 24
26339 Abalos (La Rioja)
☎: +34 941 308 049
Fax: +34 941 308 049
www.valsarte.com
consultas@solanaderamirez.com

Solana de Ramírez 2010 TC
87

Colour: bright cherry. Nose: ripe fruit, spicy, creamy oak, toasty. Palate: powerful, flavourful, toasty, round tannins.

Solana de Ramírez 2013 B
85

Solana de Ramírez 2013 RD
85

Solana de Ramírez 2013 T
83

Valsarte 2001 TGR
87

Colour: pale ruby, brick rim edge. Nose: elegant, spicy, wet leather, aged wood nuances, fruit liqueur notes. Palate: spicy, fine tannins, elegant, long.

Valsarte 2008 TR
88

Colour: cherry, garnet rim. Nose: balanced, ripe fruit, sweet spices, creamy oak. Palate: spicy, ripe fruit, round tannins.

Valsarte 2009 TC
100% tempranillo

86

Colour: cherry, garnet rim. Nose: ripe fruit, spicy, creamy oak, toasty, old leather, tobacco. Palate: powerful, flavourful, toasty.

Valsarte Vendimia Seleccionada 2009 T
88

Colour: cherry, garnet rim. Nose: ripe fruit, wild herbs, spicy, creamy oak. Palate: balanced, flavourful, long, balsamic.

SOTO DE TORRES
Camino Los Arenales, s/n
01330 Labastida (Álava)
☎: +34 938 177 400
Fax: +34 938 177 444
www.torres.es
mailadmin@torres.es

Altos Ibéricos 2011 TC
tempranillo

88

Colour: bright cherry. Nose: ripe fruit, sweet spices, creamy oak, medium intensity. Palate: fruity, flavourful, toasty.

SPANISH STORY
Espronceda, 27 1ºD
28003 Madrid (Madrid)
☎: +34 915 356 184
Fax: +34 915 363 796
paul@globalwinefood.com

Spanish Story Garnacha 2012 T
garnacha

86

Colour: cherry, garnet rim. Nose: wild herbs, spicy, ripe fruit. Palate: powerful, full, flavourful.

Spanish Story Tempranillo 2012 T
tempranillo

87

Colour: bright cherry. Nose: ripe fruit, sweet spices, creamy oak. Palate: flavourful, fruity, toasty.

TENTENUBLO WINES
Ctra Vitoria s/n
01300 Laguardia (Alava)
☎: +34 699 236 468
www.tentenublo.com
info@tentenublo.com

Escondite del Ardacho 2012 T
garnacha, tempranillo, alarije

93

Colour: bright cherry. Nose: ripe fruit, sweet spices, creamy oak, expressive, fragrant herbs. Palate: flavourful, fruity, toasty, good acidity, long.

Tentenublo 2011 T
92

Colour: bright cherry. Nose: ripe fruit, sweet spices, creamy oak, spicy. Palate: flavourful, fruity, toasty, round tannins.

Tentenublo 2012 B
100% malvasía
88
Colour: bright straw. Nose: medium intensity, ripe fruit, spicy. Palate: powerful, fine bitter notes, good acidity.

Tentenublo 2012 T
tempranillo, garnacha, viura, alarige
91
Colour: very deep cherry. Nose: ripe fruit, red berry notes, scrubland. Palate: fruity, spicy, ripe fruit, powerful tannins.

THE GRAND WINES
Ramón y Cajal 7, 1ºA
01007 Vitoria (Alava)
☎: +34 945 158 282
Fax: +34 945 158 283
www.thegrandwines.com
araex@araex.com

Rolland Galarreta 2010 T
100% tempranillo
93
Colour: cherry, garnet rim. Nose: red berry notes, ripe fruit, spicy, creamy oak, toasty, complex, mineral. Palate: powerful, flavourful, toasty, round tannins, balanced.

TIERRA DE AGRÍCOLA LA BASTIDA
El Olmo, 16
01330 Labastida (Álava)
☎: +34 945 331 230
Fax: +34 945 331 257
www.tierrayvino.com
info@tierrayvino.com

El Belisario 2010 T
tempranillo
91
Colour: very deep cherry, garnet rim. Nose: powerfull, ripe fruit, roasted coffee. Palate: powerful, toasty, roasted-coffee aftertaste, concentrated.

Fernández Gómez 2013 T
86
Colour: cherry, purple rim. Nose: red berry notes, wild herbs, varietal. Palate: light-bodied, easy to drink.

Tierra 2011 T
tempranillo
89
Colour: cherry, garnet rim. Nose: red berry notes, ripe fruit, spicy, creamy oak, toasty, complex, earthy notes. Palate: flavourful, toasty, round tannins, easy to drink.

Tierra 2013 BFB
87
Colour: bright yellow. Nose: sweet spices, ripe fruit, toasty, creamy oak. Palate: flavourful, fine bitter notes, smoky aftertaste.

Tierra de Fidel 2010 B
viura, malvasía, garnacha, moscatel
90
Colour: bright yellow. Nose: powerfull, characterful, spicy, balanced, ripe fruit. Palate: correct, fine bitter notes, fine bitter notes.

Tierra Fidel 2009 T
89
Colour: very deep cherry, garnet rim. Nose: scrubland, red berry notes, ripe fruit, spicy. Palate: fresh, fruity, good acidity.

TOBELOS BODEGAS Y VIÑEDOS
Ctra. N 124, Km. 45
26290 Briñas (La Rioja)
☎: +34 941 305 630
Fax: +34 941 313 028
www.tobelos.com
tobelos@tobelos.com

Leukade Autor 2011 T
100% tempranillo
87
Colour: very deep cherry. Nose: powerfull, scrubland, dried herbs, spicy. Palate: flavourful, ripe fruit.

Tahón de Tobelos 2010 TR
100% tempranillo
92
Colour: deep cherry. Nose: ripe fruit, spicy, creamy oak, toasty, complex. Palate: flavourful, toasty, round tannins, full.

Tobelos 2013 BFB
89
Colour: bright straw. Nose: white flowers, fresh fruit, expressive, fine lees, dried herbs. Palate: flavourful, fruity, good acidity, balanced.

Tobelos Tempranillo 2010 TC
100% tempranillo
90
Colour: cherry, garnet rim. Nose: red berry notes, ripe fruit, spicy, toasty. Palate: flavourful, toasty, round tannins, fresh.

TORRE DE OÑA
Finca San Martín
01309 Páganos (Álava)
☎: +34 945 621 154
Fax: +34 945 621 171
www.torredeona.com
info@torredeona.com

Finca San Martín 2011 T
tempranillo
89
Colour: ruby red. Nose: spicy, fine reductive notes, wet leather, aged wood nuances, toasty. Palate: spicy, long, toasty.

Torre de Oña 2010 TR
tempranillo, mazuelo

92

Colour: cherry, garnet rim. Nose: ripe fruit, spicy, creamy oak, toasty, complex. Palate: powerful, flavourful, toasty, round tannins.

UVAS FELICES

Agullers, 7
08003 Barcelona (Barcelona)
☎: +34 902 327 777
www.vilaviniteca.es

La Locomotora 2011 TC

88

Colour: cherry, garnet rim. Nose: ripe fruit, spicy, creamy oak, toasty, complex. Palate: powerful, flavourful, toasty, round tannins.

VALENCISO

Ctra. Ollauri-Najera, Km. 0,4
26220 Ollauri (La Rioja)
☎: +34 941 304 724
Fax: +34 941 304 728
www.valenciso.com
valenciso@valenciso.com

Valenciso 2007 TR
100% tempranillo

87

Colour: cherry, garnet rim. Nose: ripe fruit, spicy, creamy oak, toasty. Palate: powerful, flavourful, toasty, round tannins.

VALORIA

Ctra. de Burgos, Km. 5
26006 Logroño (La Rioja)
☎: +34 941 204 059
Fax: +34 941 204 155
www.bvaloria.com
bodega@bvaloria.com

Finca la Pica 1982 T
tempranillo

84

Finca la Pica 2011 TC
tempranillo

85

Viña Valoria 1982 T
tempranillo

90

Colour: light cherry, orangey edge. Nose: waxy notes, tobacco, spicy, aged wood nuances. Palate: fine bitter notes, elegant, fine tannins.

Viña Valoria 2011 TC
tempranillo

86

Colour: dark-red cherry, garnet rim. Nose: toasty, powerfull, ripe fruit. Palate: round tannins, good finish.

VINÍCOLA RIOJANA DE ALCANADRE S.C.

San Isidro, 46
26509 Alcanadre (La Rioja)
☎: +34 941 165 036
Fax: +34 941 165 289
www.riojanadealcanadre.com
vinicola@riojanadealcanadre.com

Aradon 2011 TC
87

Colour: cherry, garnet rim. Nose: red berry notes, ripe fruit, spicy, creamy oak, complex. Palate: powerful, flavourful, toasty, round tannins.

Aradon 2008 TR
86

Colour: ruby red. Nose: ripe fruit, spicy, creamy oak, toasty, characterful, fine reductive notes. Palate: powerful, flavourful, toasty.

Aradon 2013 B
viura
85

Aradon 2013 RD
garnacha
84

Aradon Garnacha Selección 2012 T
garnacha
88

Colour: light cherry. Nose: ripe fruit, wild herbs, spicy, creamy oak. Palate: balanced, flavourful, long, balsamic.

VIÑA BUJANDA

Ctra. Logroño, s/n
01320 Oyón (Alava)
☎: +34 941 450 876
Fax: +34 941 450 875
www.familiamartinezbujanda.com
info@bujanda.com

Viña Bujanda 2007 TGR
100% tempranillo
87

Colour: cherry, garnet rim. Nose: ripe fruit, spicy, toasty, complex. Palate: flavourful, toasty, round tannins, easy to drink.

Viña Bujanda 2009 TR
100% tempranillo
88

Colour: cherry, garnet rim. Nose: balanced, toasty, spicy, varietal. Palate: flavourful, fruity, easy to drink.

Viña Bujanda 2011 TC
100% tempranillo
86

Colour: cherry, garnet rim. Nose: medium intensity, ripe fruit, spicy. Palate: easy to drink, correct.

Viña Bujanda 2013 B
100% viura
85

Viña Bujanda 2013 RD
100% tempranillo
85

Viña Bujanda 2013 T
100% tempranillo
84

VIÑA IJALBA

Ctra. Pamplona, Km. 1
26006 Logroño (La Rioja)
☎: +34 941 261 100
Fax: +34 941 261 128
www.ijalba.com
vinaijalba@ijalba.com

Dionisio Ruiz Ijalba 2012 T
100% maturana
90 🌷

Colour: cherry, garnet rim. Nose: ripe fruit, wild herbs, earthy notes, spicy. Palate: flavourful, long, balsamic, balanced.

Genoli 2013 B
100% viura
87 🌷

Colour: bright straw. Nose: fresh, fresh fruit, white flowers, expressive. Palate: flavourful, fruity, good acidity, balanced.

Ijalba 2009 TR
87 🌷

Colour: ruby red, orangey edge. Nose: spicy, wet leather, aged wood nuances, toasty. Palate: spicy, long, toasty, correct.

Ijalba 2011 TC
86 🌷

Colour: pale ruby, brick rim edge. Nose: fruit preserve, balsamic herbs, premature reduction notes. Palate: powerful, flavourful, spicy.

Ijalba Graciano 2012 TC
100% graciano
88 🌷

Colour: cherry, garnet rim. Nose: fruit preserve, scrubland, balsamic herbs, spicy, creamy oak. Palate: powerful, flavourful, concentrated.

Ijalba Maturana Blanca 2013 B
100% maturana blanca
88 🌷

Colour: bright straw. Nose: fresh, fresh fruit, white flowers, expressive. Palate: flavourful, fruity, good acidity, balanced.

Ijalba Selección Especial 2005 TR

90

Colour: pale ruby, brick rim edge. Nose: ripe fruit, spicy, creamy oak, toasty, complex, dark chocolate, earthy notes, fine reductive notes. Palate: powerful, flavourful, toasty, round tannins.

Livor 2013 T Joven
100% tempranillo

84

Múrice 2011 TC

88

Colour: cherry, garnet rim. Nose: ripe fruit, spicy, creamy oak, toasty, fine reductive notes. Palate: powerful, flavourful, toasty.

Solferino 2012 T

85

VIÑA OLABARRI

Ctra. Haro - Anguciana, s/n
26200 Haro (La Rioja)
☎: +34 941 310 937
Fax: +34 941 311 602
www.bodegasolabarri.com
info@bodegasolabarri.com

Bikandi 2011 TC
100% tempranillo

89

Colour: bright cherry. Nose: ripe fruit, sweet spices, creamy oak, expressive. Palate: flavourful, fruity, toasty, round tannins.

Viña Olabarri 2007 TGR
100% tempranillo

88

Colour: cherry, garnet rim. Nose: ripe fruit, wild herbs, earthy notes, spicy, old leather, tobacco. Palate: balanced, flavourful, long, balsamic.

Viña Olabarri 2009 TR
100% tempranillo

87

Colour: dark-red cherry. Nose: toasty, ripe fruit, balanced. Palate: long, toasty, correct, good acidity, round tannins.

VIÑA REAL

Ctra. Logroño - Laguardia, Km. 4,8
01800 Laguardia (Álava)
☎: +34 945 625 255
Fax: +34 945 625 211
www.cvne.com
marketing@cvne.com

Viña Real 2008 TGR

91

Colour: cherry, garnet rim. Nose: ripe fruit, spicy, creamy oak, toasty, complex. Palate: powerful, flavourful, toasty, round tannins.

Viña Real 2010 TR

93

Colour: cherry, garnet rim. Nose: ripe fruit, spicy, creamy oak, toasty, complex, dark chocolate, earthy notes. Palate: powerful, flavourful, toasty, round tannins.

Viña Real 2012 TC

93

Colour: very deep cherry. Nose: ripe fruit, spicy, creamy oak, toasty, characterful. Palate: powerful, flavourful, toasty, round tannins.

VIÑA SALCEDA

Ctra. Cenicero, Km. 3
01340 Elciego (Álava)
☎: +34 945 606 125
Fax: +34 945 606 069
www.vinasalceda.com
info@vinasalceda.com

Conde de la Salceda 2009 TR
100% tempranillo

91

Colour: cherry, garnet rim. Nose: ripe fruit, wild herbs, earthy notes, spicy, creamy oak. Palate: balanced, flavourful, long, balsamic.

Puente de Salceda 2010 T
100% tempranillo

90

Colour: cherry, garnet rim. Nose: ripe fruit, spicy, creamy oak, toasty, complex. Palate: powerful, flavourful, toasty, balanced.

Viña Salceda 2009 TR

89

Colour: cherry, garnet rim. Nose: balanced, complex, ripe fruit, spicy, balsamic herbs. Palate: good structure, flavourful, round tannins.

Viña Salceda 2011 TC
88
Colour: bright cherry. Nose: ripe fruit, sweet spices, creamy oak. Palate: flavourful, fruity, toasty.

VIÑASPRAL
Camino Del Soto s/n
01309 Elvillar (Álava)
Fax: +34 628 132 151
www.maisulan.com
info@maisulan.com

Maisulan 2009 TC
87
Colour: deep cherry, garnet rim. Nose: fruit preserve, powerfull. Palate: flavourful, spicy, round tannins.

Maisulan 2010 T
87
Colour: cherry, garnet rim. Nose: ripe fruit, spicy, toasty. Palate: toasty, round tannins, easy to drink, fruity.

Maisulan 2012 T
86
Colour: bright cherry, garnet rim. Nose: ripe fruit, sweet spices. Palate: easy to drink, good finish.

Maisulan Los Lagos 2012 T
100% graciano
89
Colour: very deep cherry. Nose: balanced, expressive, scrubland, ripe fruit. Palate: flavourful, slightly tart, round tannins.

Maisulan Sobremoro 2012 T Barrica
100% tempranillo
90
Colour: bright cherry. Nose: ripe fruit, sweet spices, creamy oak, expressive. Palate: flavourful, fruity, toasty, round tannins.

VIÑEDOS DE ALDEANUEVA
Avda. Juan Carlos I, 100
26559 Aldeanueva de Ebro (La Rioja)
☎: +34 941 163 039
Fax: +34 941 163 585
www.aldeanueva.com
va@aldeanueva.com

Azabache 2013 RD
100% garnacha
87
Colour: raspberry rose. Nose: powerfull, ripe fruit, red berry notes, floral, lactic notes. Palate: powerful, fruity, fresh.

Azabache Garnacha 2011 T
100% garnacha
88
Colour: deep cherry, garnet rim. Nose: wild herbs, ripe fruit, spicy, creamy oak. Palate: flavourful, round tannins.

Azabache Tempranillo 2013 T
100% tempranillo
84

Azabache Vendimia Seleccionada 2011 TC
86
Colour: dark-red cherry, garnet rim. Nose: fruit preserve, sweet spices. Palate: flavourful, good structure, easy to drink.

Culto 2010 T
91
Colour: cherry, garnet rim. Nose: creamy oak, toasty, complex, ripe fruit, fruit preserve. Palate: powerful, flavourful, toasty, round tannins.

Fincas de Azabache Garnacha 2011 TC
100% garnacha

88

Colour: cherry, garnet rim. Nose: ripe fruit, spicy, creamy oak, toasty, balsamic herbs. Palate: powerful, flavourful, toasty, balanced.

VIÑEDOS DE ALFARO
Camino de los Agudos s/n
26559 Aldeanueva de Ebro (La Rioja)
☎: +34 941 142 389
Fax: +34 941 142 386
www.vinedosdealfaro.com
info@vinedosdealfaro.com

Conde del Real Agrado 2005 TR
garnacha, tempranillo, mazuelo, graciano

86

Colour: cherry, garnet rim. Nose: ripe fruit, spicy, creamy oak, toasty. Palate: powerful, flavourful, toasty, fine bitter notes.

Conde del Real Agrado 2010 TC
garnacha, tempranillo, mazuelo, graciano

88

Colour: cherry, garnet rim. Nose: ripe fruit, spicy, creamy oak, toasty, wild herbs. Palate: powerful, flavourful, toasty.

Real Agrado 2013 B
viura

85

Real Agrado 2013 RD
garnacha

86

Colour: light cherry, bright. Nose: rose petals, red berry notes, medium intensity. Palate: fresh, fruity, good acidity, easy to drink.

Real Agrado 2013 T
garnacha, tempranillo

87

Colour: cherry, purple rim. Nose: expressive, fresh fruit, red berry notes, floral. Palate: flavourful, fruity, good acidity, round tannins.

Rodiles 2005 T
garnacha, tempranillo, mazuelo, graciano

88

Colour: pale ruby, brick rim edge. Nose: ripe fruit, spicy, creamy oak, toasty, complex, balsamic herbs. Palate: powerful, flavourful, toasty, round tannins.

Rodiles Vendimia Seleccionada 2005 T
graciano

90

Colour: pale ruby, brick rim edge. Nose: spicy, fine reductive notes, wet leather, aged wood nuances, fruit liqueur notes. Palate: spicy, fine tannins, elegant, long, correct.

VIÑEDOS DE PÁGANOS
Ctra. Navaridas, s/n
01309 Páganos (Álava)
☎: +34 945 600 590
Fax: +34 945 600 885
www.sierracantabria.com
info@sierracantabria.com

El Puntido 2006 TGR
tempranillo

93

Colour: cherry, garnet rim. Nose: balanced, complex, ripe fruit, spicy, tobacco, fine reductive notes. Palate: good structure, flavourful, round tannins.

El Puntido 2010 T
tempranillo

95

Colour: bright cherry. Nose: ripe fruit, sweet spices, creamy oak, characterful, balanced. Palate: fruity, flavourful, toasty.

El Puntido 2011 T
tempranillo

95

Colour: very deep cherry. Nose: ripe fruit, spicy, creamy oak, toasty, characterful. Palate: powerful, flavourful, toasty, round tannins.

La Nieta 2011 T
tempranillo

94

Colour: cherry, garnet rim. Nose: spicy, toasty, overripe fruit, mineral. Palate: powerful, flavourful, toasty, round tannins.

La Nieta 2012 T
tempranillo

96

Colour: cherry, garnet rim. Nose: ripe fruit, spicy, creamy oak, toasty, complex, dark chocolate, earthy notes. Palate: powerful, flavourful, toasty, round tannins.

VIÑEDOS DEL CONTINO

Finca San Rafael, s/n
01321 Laserna (Álava)
☎: +34 945 600 201
Fax: +34 945 621 114
www.cvne.com
laserna@contino.com

Contino 2008 TR
92
Colour: very deep cherry. Nose: ripe fruit, spicy, creamy oak, toasty, characterful. Palate: powerful, flavourful, toasty, round tannins.

Contino 2012 B
93
Colour: bright yellow. Nose: citrus fruit, ripe fruit, fragrant herbs, sweet spices, creamy oak. Palate: rich, flavourful, spicy, long, balanced, elegant.

Contino Garnacha 2011 T
100% garnacha
91
Colour: cherry, garnet rim. Nose: ripe fruit, spicy, creamy oak, toasty, complex. Palate: powerful, flavourful, toasty, round tannins.

Contino Graciano 2010 T
100% graciano
92
Colour: cherry, garnet rim. Nose: ripe fruit, wild herbs, earthy notes, spicy, creamy oak. Palate: balanced, flavourful, long, balsamic.

Contino Magnum 2007 TGR
93
Colour: pale ruby, brick rim edge. Nose: spicy, fine reductive notes, wet leather, aged wood nuances, fruit liqueur notes. Palate: spicy, fine tannins.

Contino Viña del Olivo 2010 T
93
Colour: very deep cherry. Nose: ripe fruit, spicy, creamy oak, toasty, characterful. Palate: powerful, flavourful, toasty, round tannins.

VIÑEDOS SIERRA CANTABRIA

Calle Fuente de la Salud s/n
26338 San Vicente de la Sonsierra
(La Rioja)
☎: +34 941 334 080
Fax: +34 941 334 371
www.sierracantabria.com
info@sierracantabria.com

Amancio 2010 T
tempranillo
96
Colour: cherry, garnet rim. Nose: ripe fruit, spicy, creamy oak, toasty, complex, dark chocolate, dry stone, mineral. Palate: powerful, flavourful, toasty, round tannins.

Amancio 2011 T
tempranillo
94
Colour: cherry, garnet rim. Nose: fruit preserve, fruit liqueur notes, spicy, new oak, aged wood nuances. Palate: flavourful, pruney, balsamic.

Finca El Bosque 2011 T
tempranillo
97
Colour: cherry, garnet rim. Nose: spicy, creamy oak, toasty, complex, dark chocolate, fruit expression, mineral. Palate: powerful, flavourful, toasty, round tannins.

Finca El Bosque 2012 T
tempranillo
94
Colour: very deep cherry, garnet rim. Nose: powerfull, ripe fruit, roasted coffee, dark chocolate. Palate: powerful, toasty, roasted-coffee aftertaste.

Sierra Cantabria Colección Privada 2011 T
tempranillo
95
Colour: very deep cherry. Nose: ripe fruit, spicy, creamy oak, toasty, characterful, red berry notes. Palate: powerful, flavourful, toasty, round tannins.

Sierra Cantabria Colección Privada 2012 T
tempranillo
96
Colour: cherry, garnet rim. Nose: ripe fruit, spicy, creamy oak, toasty, complex, dark chocolate, earthy notes. Palate: powerful, flavourful, toasty, round tannins.

Sierra Cantabria Cuvèe Especial 2010 T
tempranillo
94
Colour: bright cherry. Nose: sweet spices, creamy oak, expressive, ripe fruit, red berry notes. Palate: flavourful, fruity, toasty, round tannins.

Sierra Cantabria Organza 2011 B
93
Colour: bright straw. Nose: white flowers, fresh fruit, expressive, fine lees, dried herbs. Palate: flavourful, fruity, good acidity, balanced.

Sierra Cantabria Organza 2012 B
91
Colour: bright yellow. Nose: powerfull, ripe fruit, sweet spices, new oak. Palate: rich, smoky aftertaste, flavourful, fresh, good acidity.

VIÑEDOS SINGULARES
Cuzco, 26 - 28, Nave 8
08030 (Barcelona)
☎: +34 934 807 041
Fax: +34 934 807 076
www.vinedossingulares.com
info@vinedossingulares.com

Jardín Rojo 2012 T
tempranillo
87
Colour: bright cherry. Nose: ripe fruit, sweet spices, balsamic herbs. Palate: flavourful, fruity, toasty, easy to drink.

VIÑEDOS Y BODEGAS DE LA MARQUESA - VALSERRANO
Herrería, 76
01307 Villabuena (Álava)
☎: +34 945 609 085
Fax: +34 945 623 304
www.valserrano.com
info@valserrano.com

Nico by Valserrano 2010 T
91
Colour: bright cherry. Nose: ripe fruit, sweet spices, creamy oak, expressive. Palate: flavourful, fruity, toasty, round tannins.

Valserrano 2008 TGR
89
Colour: dark-red cherry. Nose: balanced, ripe fruit, scrubland, spicy. Palate: balanced, good acidity, round tannins.

Valserrano 2009 TR
90
Colour: dark-red cherry, garnet rim. Nose: balanced, elegant, cocoa bean. Palate: ripe fruit, flavourful, good acidity, spicy.

Valserrano 2011 TC
89
Colour: cherry, garnet rim. Nose: ripe fruit, wild herbs, spicy, creamy oak. Palate: powerful, flavourful, spicy, balanced.

Valserrano 2013 BFB
90
Colour: bright yellow. Nose: powerfull, ripe fruit, sweet spices, fragrant herbs. Palate: rich, flavourful, fresh, good acidity.

Valserrano Finca Monteviejo 2010 T
91
Colour: cherry, garnet rim. Nose: ripe fruit, wild herbs, earthy notes, spicy, creamy oak. Palate: balanced, flavourful, long.

Valserrano Mazuelo 2009 T
100% mazuelo
90
Colour: deep cherry. Nose: ripe fruit, wild herbs, earthy notes, spicy, creamy oak. Palate: balanced, flavourful, long, balsamic.

Valserrano Premium 2008 B Gran Reserva
93
Colour: bright yellow. Nose: powerfull, ripe fruit, sweet spices, creamy oak, fragrant herbs. Palate: rich, smoky aftertaste, flavourful, good acidity.

WINNER WINES

Avda. del Mediterráneo, 38
28007 Madrid (Madrid)
☎: +34 915 019 042
Fax: +34 915 017 794
www.entornoalvino.com
info@entornoalvino.com

Viña Saseta 2004 TGR
100% tempranillo

88

Colour: pale ruby, brick rim edge. Nose: elegant, spicy, fine reductive notes, wet leather, aged wood nuances, fruit liqueur notes. Palate: spicy, fine tannins, long.

Viña Saseta 2007 TR

88

Colour: ruby red. Nose: balanced, complex, ripe fruit, spicy, fine reductive notes. Palate: good structure, flavourful, round tannins.

Viña Saseta 2011 TC

87

Colour: cherry, garnet rim. Nose: ripe fruit, spicy, creamy oak, toasty, complex. Palate: powerful, flavourful, toasty.

Viña Saseta 2013 T
100% tempranillo

84

WOS

Cartago, 2 Escalera derecha 1ºA
28022 (Madrid)
☎: +34 911 263 478
Fax: +34 913 270 601
www.woswinesofspain.com
info@woswinesofspain.com

Sensaciones 2004 TR

89

Colour: pale ruby, brick rim edge. Nose: elegant, spicy, fine reductive notes, wet leather, aged wood nuances, fruit liqueur notes. Palate: spicy, fine tannins, elegant, long.

Sensaciones 2010 TC

86

Colour: cherry, garnet rim. Nose: ripe fruit, spicy, creamy oak, toasty, fine reductive notes. Palate: powerful, flavourful, toasty.

Sensaciones 2011 T
tempranillo

87 ❧

Colour: bright cherry, garnet rim. Nose: balanced, wild herbs, spicy. Palate: fruity, spicy, round tannins, easy to drink.

DO. RUEDA

CONSEJO REGULADOR
Real, 8
47490 Rueda (Valladolid)
☎:+34 983 868 248 - Fax: +34 983 868 135
@: crdo.rueda@dorueda.com
www.dorueda.com

LOCATION:

In the provinces of Valladolid (53 municipal districts), Segovia (17 municipal districts) and Ávila (2 municipal districts). The vineyards are situated on the undulating terrain of a plateau and are conditioned by the influence of the river Duero that runs through the northern part of the region.

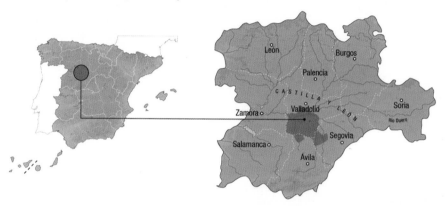

GRAPE VARIETIES:

White: Verdejo (52%), Viura (22%), Sauvignon Blanc (7%) and Palomino Fino (19%).
Red: Tempranillo, Cabernet Sauvignon, Merlot and Garnacha.

FIGURES:

Vineyard surface: 12,942.62 – Wine-Growers: 1,515 – Wineries: 63 – 2013 Harvest rating: Good – Production 13: 70,216,770 litres – Market percentages: 81% domestic - 19% export.

SOIL:

Many pebbles on the surface. The terrain is stony, poor in organic matter, with good aeration and drainage. The texture of the soil is variable although, in general, sandy limestone and limestone predominate.

CLIMATE:

Continental in nature, with cold winters and short hot summers. Rainfall is concentrated in spring and autumn. The average altitude of the region is between 600 m and 700 m, and only in the province of Segovia does it exceed 800 m.

VINTAGE RATING

PEÑÍNGUIDE

2009	2010	2011	2012	2013
VERY GOOD	EXCELLENT	VERY GOOD	VERY GOOD	VERY GOOD

AGRÍCOLA CASTELLANA - BODEGA CUATRO RAYAS

Ctra. Rodilana, s/n
47491 La Seca (Valladolid)
☎: +34 983 816 320
Fax: +34 983 816 562
www.cuatrorayas.org
info@cuatrorayas.org

Azumbre Verdejo Viñedos Centenarios 2013 B

100% verdejo

88

Colour: bright straw. Nose: floral, fragrant herbs, fruit expression, balanced. Palate: easy to drink, flavourful, balsamic, round.

Bitácora Verdejo 2013 B

100% verdejo

85

Cuatro Rayas 2010 BFB

100% verdejo

89

Colour: bright yellow. Nose: citrus fruit, ripe fruit, wild herbs, faded flowers, sweet spices, toasty. Palate: fine bitter notes, unctuous, flavourful.

Cuatro Rayas Ecológico 2013 B

verdejo

88

Colour: bright straw. Nose: powerfull, fresh, fruit expression. Palate: fresh, fruity, flavourful.

Cuatro Rayas Sauvignon 2013 B

100% sauvignon blanc

88

Colour: bright straw. Nose: balanced, fresh fruit, floral, fragrant herbs. Palate: good acidity, correct, fine bitter notes.

Cuatro Rayas Verdejo 2013 B

100% verdejo

88

Colour: bright straw. Nose: fresh, fresh fruit, white flowers. Palate: flavourful, fruity, good acidity.

Cuatro Rayas Viñedos Centenarios 2013 B
100% verdejo

89

Colour: bright straw. Nose: white flowers, fragrant herbs, fruit expression, dry stone. Palate: fresh, fruity, flavourful, elegant.

Dama del Lago 2013 B
verdejo

86

Colour: bright straw. Nose: fresh, fresh fruit, white flowers, fragrant herbs. Palate: flavourful, fruity, easy to drink.

Nave Sur 2013 B
100% verdejo

86

Colour: bright straw. Nose: white flowers, fragrant herbs, fruit expression. Palate: fresh, fruity, flavourful, easy to drink.

Palacio de Vivero 2013 B
100% verdejo

85

Pámpano 2013 B
100% verdejo

85

Vacceos 2010 TC
100% tempranillo

87

Colour: cherry, garnet rim. Nose: smoky, toasty, spicy, ripe fruit. Palate: flavourful, round tannins.

Vacceos 2013 RD
100% tempranillo

86

Colour: coppery red, bright. Nose: medium intensity, fresh, dried flowers, wild herbs. Palate: correct, light-bodied, easy to drink.

Vacceos Tempranillo 2012 T Roble
100% tempranillo

88

Colour: bright cherry. Nose: ripe fruit, sweet spices, creamy oak. Palate: fruity, toasty, round tannins.

Vacceos Verdejo 2013 B
100% verdejo

87

Colour: bright straw. Nose: fresh, fresh fruit, white flowers, expressive. Palate: flavourful, fruity, good acidity, balanced.

Veliterra 2013 B
100% verdejo

84

Visigodo Verdejo 2013 B
100% verdejo

87

Colour: bright straw. Nose: faded flowers, fragrant herbs. Palate: fresh, correct, fine bitter notes, easy to drink.

AGRÍCOLA SANZ
Santísimo Cristo, 107
47490 Rueda (Valladolid)
☎: +34 983 804 132
Fax: +34 983 804 132
www.lacubaderueda.com
info@agricolasanz.com

La Casona de los Condes 2013 B
verdejo

91

Colour: bright straw. Nose: fresh, fresh fruit, white flowers, wild herbs, mineral. Palate: flavourful, fruity, good acidity, balanced.

Viña Sofraga 2013 BR
83

Viña Sofraga 2013 SS
84

ÁLVAREZ Y DÍEZ
Juan Antonio Carmona, 12
47500 Nava del Rey (Valladolid)
☎: +34 983 850 136
Fax: +34 983 850 761
www.alvarezydiez.com
j.benito@alvarezydiez.com

Mantel Blanco 2009 BFB
100% verdejo

91

Colour: bright yellow. Nose: ripe fruit, dry nuts, powerfull, toasty, aged wood nuances. Palate: flavourful, fruity, spicy, toasty, long.

Mantel Blanco Sauvignon Blanc 2013 B
100% sauvignon blanc

87

Colour: bright straw. Nose: white flowers, fresh fruit, expressive, dried herbs. Palate: flavourful, fruity, good acidity.

Mantel Blanco Verdejo 2013 B
100% verdejo

87

Colour: bright straw, greenish rim. Nose: medium intensity, dried herbs, floral. Palate: correct, good finish, easy to drink.

ÁNGEL RODRÍGUEZ VIDAL
Torcido, 1
47491 La Seca (Valladolid)
☎: +34 983 816 302
Fax: +34 983 816 302
martinsancho@martinsancho.com

Martínsancho 2013 B
100% verdejo

90

Colour: bright straw. Nose: fresh fruit, wild herbs, floral, mineral. Palate: flavourful, fruity, good acidity, balanced.

ARBOLEDA MEDITERRÁNEA BODEGAS
Ctra. N-601, km. 151 Pol. Ind. José A. González Caviedes
47410 Olmedo (Valladolid)
☎: +34 902 996 361
www.arboledamediterranean.com
arboleda@arboledamediterranean.com

Enprivado 2013 B
100% verdejo

84

AVELINO VEGAS
Calvo Sotelo, 8
40460 Santiuste (Segovia)
☎: +34 921 596 002
Fax: +34 921 596 035
www.avelinovegas.com
ana@avelinovegas.com

Circe 2013 B
verdejo

88

Colour: bright straw. Nose: fresh, fresh fruit, white flowers. Palate: flavourful, fruity, good acidity, balanced.

Montespina Sauvignon 2013 B Joven
sauvignon blanc

87

Colour: bright straw. Nose: ripe fruit, citrus fruit, wild herbs, floral. Palate: powerful, flavourful, fruity, fine bitter notes.

Montespina Verdejo 2013 B Joven

verdejo

87

Colour: bright straw. Nose: white flowers, fragrant herbs, fruit expression, tropical fruit. Palate: fresh, fruity, flavourful.

AXIAL

Pla-za Calle Castillo de Capua, 10 Nave 7
50197 (Zaragoza)
☎: +34 976 780 136
Fax: +34 976 303 035
www.axialvinos.com
info@axialvinos.com

Esperanza Rueda Verdejo 2013 B

100% verdejo

87

Colour: bright straw, greenish rim. Nose: fresh, fresh fruit, fragrant herbs, citrus fruit. Palate: correct, balanced, easy to drink.

Esperanza Verdejo Viura 2013 B

86

Colour: bright straw. Nose: fresh, fresh fruit, white flowers. Palate: flavourful, fruity, good acidity, easy to drink.

BELLORI VINOS

Cobalto, 67 Bajo
47012 (Valladolid)
☎: +34 983 314 522
Fax: +34 983 314 522
www.bellorivinos.com
administracion@bellorivinos.com

Bellori 2012 BC

100% verdejo

93

Colour: bright yellow. Nose: powerfull, ripe fruit, sweet spices, creamy oak, fragrant herbs. Palate: rich, smoky aftertaste, flavourful, fresh, good acidity.

Bellori 2013 B

100% verdejo

90

Colour: bright straw. Nose: fresh, fresh fruit, white flowers. Palate: flavourful, fruity, good acidity, balanced.

BELONDRADE

Quinta San Diego - Camino del Puerto, s/n
47491 La Seca (Valladolid)
☎: +34 983 481 001
Fax: +34 600 590 024
www.belondrade.com
comunicacion@belondrade.com

Belondrade y Lurton 2012 BFB

verdejo

94

Colour: bright yellow. Nose: powerfull, ripe fruit, sweet spices, creamy oak, fragrant herbs, mineral. Palate: rich, smoky aftertaste, flavourful, fresh, good acidity.

BODEGA 3 PILARES

El Rancho, 3
47491 La Seca (Valladolid)
☎: +34 676 169 122
bodega3pilares@gmail.com

Tres Pilares (3P) 2013 B

100% verdejo

86

Colour: bright straw. Nose: fresh, citrus fruit, fragrant herbs. Palate: fruity, easy to drink, correct.

Valtarre 2013 B

100% verdejo

83

BODEGA ALTAENCINA

Zarcillo, 2
47490 Rueda (Valladolid)
☎: +34 639 780 716
Fax: +34 983 868 905
www.altaencina.com
pablo@altaencina.com

Quivira Verdejo 2013 B

verdejo

86

Colour: bright straw. Nose: fresh, fresh fruit, white flowers. Palate: flavourful, fruity, thin.

BODEGA AYUNTAMIENTO MADRIGAL DE LAS ALTAS TORRES

Plaza Santa María n1
5220 Madrigal de las Altas Torres
(Ávila)
☎: +34 920 320 001
ayuntamientodemadrigal@aytomadrigal.es

Cuna de Ysabel 2013 B

verdejo

87

Colour: bright straw. Nose: fresh, fresh fruit, white flowers, medium intensity, tropical fruit. Palate: flavourful, fruity, good acidity, good finish.

Don Vasco 2013 B
verdejo

86

Colour: bright yellow. Nose: ripe fruit, candied fruit, faded flowers. Palate: flavourful, balsamic, correct.

BODEGA BURDIGALA (F. LURTON & M. ROLLAND)
Camino Magarín, s/n
47529 Villafranca del Duero (Valladolid)
☎: +34 980 082 027
Fax: +34 983 034 040
www.burdigala.es
bodega@burdigala.es

Campo Alegre 2013 B

91

Colour: bright yellow. Nose: floral, wild herbs, balsamic herbs, mineral, spicy. Palate: fresh, fruity, flavourful, balanced, spicy.

BODEGA COOPERATIVA VIRGEN DE LA ASUNCIÓN
Las Afueras, s/n
09311 La Horra (Burgos)
☎: +34 947 542 057
Fax: +34 947 542 057
www.virgendelaasuncion.com
info@virgendelaasuncion.com

Zarzuela Verdejo 2013 B
100% verdejo

86

Colour: bright straw. Nose: fresh, fresh fruit, white flowers. Palate: flavourful, fruity, good acidity, easy to drink.

BODEGA DE ALBERTO
Ctra. de Valdestillas, 2
47321 Serrada (Valladolid)
☎: +34 983 559 107
Fax: +34 983 559 084
www.dealberto.com
info@dealberto.com

De Alberto Verdejo 2013 B
100% verdejo

88

Colour: bright straw. Nose: dried herbs, faded flowers, ripe fruit. Palate: thin, fresh, correct.

Guti Verdejo 2013 B
100% verdejo

86

Colour: bright straw. Nose: fresh, fresh fruit, expressive, wild herbs. Palate: fruity, good acidity, easy to drink.

Monasterio de Palazuelos Sauvignon Blanc 2013 B
100% sauvignon blanc

85

Monasterio de Palazuelos Verdejo 2013 B
100% verdejo

85

BODEGA EL ALBAR LURTON
Camino Magarin, s/n
47529 Villafranca del Duero (Valladolid)
☎: +34 983 034 030
Fax: +34 983 034 040
www.francoislurton.es
bodega@francoislurton.es

Camino del Puerto Verdejo 2013 B
verdejo

85

Hermanos Lurton Cuesta de Oro 2012 BFB

93

Colour: bright yellow. Nose: powerfull, ripe fruit, sweet spices, creamy oak, fragrant herbs. Palate: rich, smoky aftertaste, flavourful, fresh, good acidity, round, elegant

Hermanos Lurton Verdejo 2013 B
verdejo

90

Colour: bright straw. Nose: balanced, fragrant herbs, medium intensity, fresh fruit, dry stone. Palate: easy to drink, good acidity, fine bitter notes.

BODEGA EMINA RUEDA
Ctra. Medina del Campo - Olmedo, Km. 1,5
47400 Medina del Campo (Valladolid)
☎: +34 983 803 346
Fax: +34 902 430 189
www.eminarueda.es
eminarueda@emina.es

Emina Brut Nature ESP
100% verdejo

84

Emina Rosado ESP
100% tempranillo

79

Emina Rueda 2013 B

85

Emina Sauvignon 2013 B
100% sauvignon blanc

86

Colour: bright straw. Nose: white flowers, fragrant herbs, fruit expression. Palate: fresh, fruity, flavourful, fine bitter notes.

Emina Semiseco ESP
100% verdejo

83

Emina Verdejo 2013 B
100% verdejo

87

Colour: bright yellow. Nose: medium intensity, dried flowers, dried herbs. Palate: fruity, fine bitter notes, good acidity.

Melior Verdejo 2013 B
100% verdejo

86

Colour: bright straw. Nose: fruit expression, faded flowers, wild herbs. Palate: fresh, fruity, balsamic.

BODEGA GÓTICA
Ctra. Rueda - La Seca, Km. 1,2
47490 Rueda (Valladolid)
☎: +34 629 458 235
Fax: +34 983 868 387
www.bodegagotica.com
mjhmonsalve@ya.com

Badajo Rueda 2013 B
100% verdejo

85

Camino La Fara Verdejo 2013 B
100% verdejo

84

Monsalve Verdejo 2013 B
100% verdejo

89

Colour: bright straw. Nose: white flowers, fragrant herbs, fruit expression, citrus fruit. Palate: fresh, fruity, flavourful, balanced.

Moyorido 2013 B
100% verdejo

84

Polígono 10 Verdejo 2013 B
100% verdejo

87

Colour: bright yellow. Nose: floral, dried herbs, citrus fruit, fruit expression. Palate: fruity, flavourful, easy to drink.

Trascampanas Sauvignon 2013 B
100% sauvignon blanc

87

Colour: bright straw. Nose: floral, dried herbs, fruit expression. Palate: fresh, fruity, flavourful, thin.

Trascampanas Verdejo 2013 B
100% verdejo

89

Colour: bright yellow. Nose: white flowers, fragrant herbs, fresh fruit, citrus fruit, mineral. Palate: fresh, fruity, flavourful, good finish.

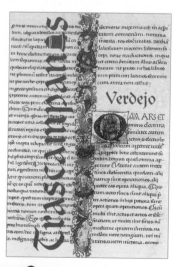

BODEGA HERMANOS DEL VILLAR
Zarcillo, s/n
47490 Rueda (Valladolid)
☎: +34 983 868 904
Fax: +34 983 868 905
www.orodecastilla.com
pablo@orodecastilla.com

Oro de Castilla Sauvignon Blanc 2013 B
sauvignon blanc

86

Colour: bright straw. Nose: fruit expression, wild herbs, floral. Palate: flavourful, fresh, fine bitter notes.

Oro de Castilla Verdejo 2013 B
verdejo

87

Colour: bright straw. Nose: fresh, fresh fruit, white flowers, fragrant herbs. Palate: flavourful, fruity, good acidity.

BODEGA LIBERALIA ENOLÓGICA
Camino del Palo, s/n
49800 Toro (Zamora)
☎: +34 980 692 571
Fax: +34 980 692 571
www.liberalia.es
liberalia@liberalia.es

Enebral 2013 B
100% verdejo

90

Colour: bright straw. Nose: fresh, white flowers, expressive. Palate: flavourful, fruity, good acidity, balanced.

BODEGA MATARROMERA
Ctra. Renedo-Pesquera, Km. 30
47359 Valbuena de Duero (Valladolid)
☎: +34 983 107 100
Fax: +34 902 430 189
www.grupomatarromera.com
matarromera@matarromera.es

Matarromera Verdejo Edición Limitada 25 Aniversario 2012 B
100% verdejo

91

Colour: bright golden. Nose: ripe fruit, sweet spices, creamy oak, balanced, expressive. Palate: fruity, fine bitter notes.

BODEGA REINA DE CASTILLA

Cº de la Moya, s/n Ctra. CL-610 (Entre
La Seca y Serrada)
47491 La Seca (Valladolid)
☎: +34 983 816 667
www.reinadecastilla.es
bodega@reinadecastilla.es

EL Bufón Verdejo 2013 B
100% verdejo

91

Colour: bright straw. Nose: fresh fruit, expressive, fine lees, dried herbs. Palate: flavourful, fruity, good acidity, balanced.

Isabelino 2013 RD
100% tempranillo

86

Colour: light cherry, bright. Nose: red berry notes, floral, medium intensity. Palate: fruity, fresh, easy to drink.

Isabelino Rueda 2013 B

85

Isabelino Verdejo 2013 B
100% verdejo

87

Colour: bright straw. Nose: floral, fresh fruit, dried herbs, medium intensity. Palate: powerful, flavourful, fruity.

Reina de Castilla Sauvignon Blanc 2013 B
100% sauvignon blanc

89

Colour: bright straw. Nose: white flowers, fragrant herbs, fruit expression, expressive. Palate: fresh, fruity, flavourful, balanced, elegant.

Reina de Castilla Verdejo 2013 B
100% verdejo

88

Colour: bright straw. Nose: fragrant herbs, fruit expression, dried flowers, medium intensity. Palate: fresh, fruity, flavourful, balanced.

BODEGA TOMÁS POSTIGO

Estación, 12
47300 Peñafiel (Valladolid)
☎: +34 983 873 019
Fax: +34 983 880 258
www.tomaspostigo.es
administracion@tomaspostigo.es

Tomás Postigo Verdejo 2010 BFB
verdejo

90

Colour: bright yellow. Nose: powerfull, ripe fruit, sweet spices, creamy oak, fragrant herbs. Palate: rich, flavourful, fresh, good acidity.

BODEGA VALDEHERMOSO

Ctra. Nava del Rey - Rueda, km. 12,6
47500 Nava del Rey (Valladolid)
☎: +34 651 993 680
www.valdehermoso.com
valdehermoso@valdehermoso.com

Lagar del Rey Sauvignon Blanc 2013 B
sauvignon blanc

89

Colour: bright yellow. Nose: fresh fruit, wild herbs, fresh. Palate: balanced, flavourful, long, good acidity.

Lagar del Rey Verdejo 100% Lías 2013 B
verdejo

88

Colour: bright straw. Nose: white flowers, fresh fruit, expressive, fine lees, dried herbs. Palate: flavourful, fruity, good acidity, balanced.

Viña Perez Verdejo 2013 B
verdejo

86

Colour: bright straw. Nose: balanced, dried herbs, dried flowers. Palate: correct, easy to drink, light-bodied.

BODEGA VIÑA VILANO S. COOP.

Ctra. de Anguix, 10
09314 Pedrosa de Duero (Burgos)
☎: +34 947 530 029
Fax: +34 947 530 037
www.vinavilano.com
info@vinavilano.com

Viña Vilano Verdejo 2013 B
verdejo

89

Colour: bright straw. Nose: fresh, fresh fruit, white flowers, wild herbs. Palate: flavourful, fruity, balanced.

BODEGAS ABANICO

Pol. Ind Ca l'Avellanet - Susany, 6
08553 Seva (Barcelona)
☎: +34 938 125 676
Fax: +34 938 123 213
www.bodegasabanico.com
info@exportiberia.com

Piedra Blanca 2013 B
100% verdejo

87

Colour: bright straw. Nose: fresh, fresh fruit, white flowers. Palate: good acidity, easy to drink, fine bitter notes.

DO RUEDA / D.O.P

BODEGAS ARROCAL

Eras de Santa María, s/n
09443 Gumiel de Mercado (Burgos)
☎: +34 947 561 290
Fax: +34 947 561 290
www.arrocal.com
arrocal@arrocal.com

Arrocal Verdejo 2013 B
100% verdejo
90
Colour: yellow, greenish rim. Nose: medium intensity, grassy, faded flowers. Palate: correct, fine bitter notes, easy to drink.

BODEGAS AURA

Ctra. Autovía del Noroeste, Km. 175
47490 Rueda (Valladolid)
☎: +34 983 868 286
www.bodegasaura.com
aura@pernod-ricard.com

Aura Verdejo Vendimia Nocturna 2013 B
verdejo
91
Colour: bright straw. Nose: expressive, fresh fruit, balsamic herbs, fragrant herbs, grassy. Palate: flavourful, balsamic, fruity, elegant.

AuraSelección Parcela Avutarda 2013 BFB
100% verdejo
93
Colour: bright yellow. Nose: sweet spices, citrus fruit, balsamic herbs, fruit expression. Palate: rich, flavourful, fresh, good acidity, balanced.

BODEGAS CAÑALVA

Coto, 54
10136 Cañamero (Cáceres)
☎: +34 927 369 405
Fax: +34 927 369 405
www.bodegascanalva.com
info@bodegascanalva.com

Cañalva Verdejo 2013 B
100% verdejo
85

BODEGAS CASTELO DE MEDINA

Ctra. CL-602, Km. 48
47465 Villaverde de Medina (Valladolid)
☎: +34 983 831 932
Fax: +34 983 831 857
www.castelodemedina.com
info@castelodemedina.com

Castelo de la Dehesa 2013 B
87
Colour: bright straw. Nose: fresh, fresh fruit, white flowers, medium intensity. Palate: flavourful, fruity, good acidity, balanced.

Castelo de Medina Sauvignon Blanc 2013 B
100% sauvignon blanc
89
Colour: bright straw. Nose: fresh, fresh fruit, white flowers, expressive. Palate: flavourful, fruity, balanced.

Castelo de Medina Verdejo 2013 B
100% verdejo
89
Colour: bright straw. Nose: floral, wild herbs, fruit expression, expressive. Palate: fresh, fruity, flavourful, balanced.

Castelo de Medina Verdejo Vendimia Seleccionada 2013 B
100% verdejo
90
Colour: bright straw. Nose: white flowers, fragrant herbs, fruit expression. Palate: fresh, fruity, flavourful, fine bitter notes.

Castelo Noble 2012 BFB
90
Colour: bright yellow. Nose: powerfull, ripe fruit, creamy oak, fragrant herbs. Palate: rich, flavourful, fresh, good acidity.

Real Castelo 2013 B
89
Colour: bright straw. Nose: white flowers, fresh fruit, expressive, dried herbs. Palate: flavourful, fruity, good acidity, balanced.

BODEGAS COPABOCA

N-122, Km. 407
47114 Torrecilla de la Abadesa
(Valladolid)
☎: +34 983 486 010
Fax: +34 983 307 729
www.copaboca.com
club@copaboca.com

Copaboca 2013 B
100% verdejo

86

Colour: bright straw. Nose: floral, fruit expression, wild herbs. Palate: fresh, fruity, flavourful, thin, fine bitter notes.

Gorgorito Verdejo 2013 B
100% verdejo

87

Colour: bright straw. Nose: white flowers, fruit expression, dried herbs, mineral. Palate: fresh, fruity, flavourful.

Juan Galindo Lías 2012 B
100% verdejo

90

Colour: bright straw. Nose: white flowers, fresh fruit, expressive, fine lees, dried herbs, spicy. Palate: flavourful, fruity, good acidity, balanced.

BODEGAS DE LOS HEREDEROS DEL MARQUÉS DE RISCAL

Ctra. N-VI, km. 172,600
47490 Rueda (Valladolid)
☎: +34 983 868 029
Fax: +34 983 868 563
www.marquesderiscal.com
comunicacion@marquesderiscal.com

Marqués de Riscal Finca Montico 2013 B
100% verdejo

92

Colour: bright straw. Nose: white flowers, expressive, fine lees, dried herbs, fruit expression. Palate: flavourful, fruity, good acidity, balanced.

Marqués de Riscal Limousin 2012 BFB
100% verdejo

92

Colour: bright straw. Nose: white flowers, fresh fruit, expressive, dried herbs, spicy, creamy oak. Palate: flavourful, fruity, good acidity, balanced.

Marqués de Riscal Limousin 2013 BFB
100% verdejo

91

Colour: bright yellow. Nose: sweet spices, white flowers, balanced. Palate: flavourful, toasty, balanced, good acidity, spicy.

Marqués de Riscal Rueda Verdejo 2013 B
100% verdejo

88

Colour: bright yellow. Nose: citrus fruit, candied fruit, wild herbs. Palate: powerful, flavourful.

Marqués de Riscal Sauvignon 2013 B
100% sauvignon blanc

91

Colour: bright straw. Nose: citrus fruit, floral, dried herbs, powerfull, expressive. Palate: flavourful, balsamic, correct, balanced.

BODEGAS FÉLIX LORENZO CACHAZO

Ctra. Medina del Campo, Km. 9
47220 Pozáldez (Valladolid)
☎: +34 983 822 008
Fax: +34 983 822 008
www.cachazo.com
bodegas@cachazo.com

Carrasviñas Espumoso 2013 BR
100% verdejo

87

Colour: yellow, greenish rim. Nose: faded flowers, fragrant herbs. Palate: correct, easy to drink.

Carrasviñas Verdejo 2013 B
100% verdejo

88

Colour: bright straw. Nose: fresh, fresh fruit, white flowers, expressive. Palate: fruity, good acidity, carbonic notes.

Gran Cardiel Rueda Verdejo 2013 B
100% verdejo

86

Colour: bright straw. Nose: fresh, white flowers, candied fruit. Palate: flavourful, fruity, good acidity, fine bitter notes.

Mania Rueda Verdejo 2013 B
100% verdejo

90

Colour: bright straw. Nose: white flowers, fragrant herbs, fruit expression. Palate: fresh, fruity, flavourful, balanced.

Mania Sauvignon 2013 B
100% sauvignon blanc

87

Colour: bright straw. Nose: medium intensity, wild herbs, citrus fruit. Palate: easy to drink, correct, balanced, fine bitter notes.

BODEGAS FÉLIX SANZ

Santísimo Cristo, 28
47490 Rueda (Valladolid)
☎: +34 983 868 044
Fax: +34 983 868 133
www.bodegasfelixsanz.es
info@bodegasfelixsanz.es

Viña Cimbrón 2012 BFB
100% verdejo

88

Colour: bright yellow. Nose: powerfull, ripe fruit, sweet spices, creamy oak. Palate: rich, smoky aftertaste, fresh.

Viña Cimbrón 2013 RD
tempranillo, garnacha

86

Colour: light cherry, bright. Nose: red berry notes, rose petals, lactic notes. Palate: fruity, easy to drink, good finish.

Viña Cimbrón Sauvignon 2013 B
100% sauvignon blanc

87

Colour: bright straw. Nose: wild herbs, citrus fruit, fresh. Palate: fruity, easy to drink, good finish.

Viña Cimbrón Verdejo 2013 B
100% verdejo

87

Colour: bright straw. Nose: ripe fruit, dried herbs, floral, citrus fruit. Palate: good acidity, correct, fine bitter notes.

Viña Cimbrón Verdejo Selección "80 Aniversario" 2013 B
100% verdejo

90

Colour: bright straw. Nose: ripe fruit, citrus fruit, dried herbs, faded flowers. Palate: powerful, rich, flavourful.

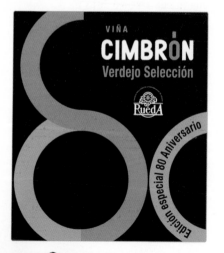

Viña Cimbrón Verdejo Selección 2013 B
100% verdejo

90

Colour: bright straw. Nose: fresh, fresh fruit, white flowers, varietal. Palate: flavourful, fruity, good acidity, balanced.

BODEGAS FRUTOS VILLAR

Ctra. Burgos-Portugal Km. 113,7
47270 Cigales (Valladolid)
☎: +34 983 586 868
Fax: +34 983 580 180
www.bodegasfrutosvillar.com
bodegasfrutosvillar@bodegasfrutosvillar.com

María Molina Rueda 2013 B
verdejo, viura

86

Colour: bright straw. Nose: fresh, fresh fruit, white flowers. Palate: flavourful, fruity, good acidity.

María Molina Verdejo 2013 B
100% verdejo

87

Colour: bright straw. Nose: white flowers, fragrant herbs, fruit expression. Palate: fresh, fruity, flavourful.

Viña Cansina Verdejo 2013 B
100% verdejo

85

Viña Morejona Rueda 2013 B
verdejo, viura

86

Colour: bright straw, greenish rim. Nose: fragrant herbs, varietal, faded flowers. Palate: fruity, correct, good acidity.

Viña Morejona Verdejo 2013 B
100% verdejo

88

Colour: bright straw. Nose: fresh, fresh fruit, white flowers, expressive. Palate: flavourful, fruity, good acidity, balanced.

BODEGAS GARCI GRANDE

Aradillas s/n
57490 Rueda (Valladolid)
☎: +34 983 868 561
Fax: +34 983 868 449
www.hispanobodegas.com
carlos.garcia@hispanobodegas.com

12 Linajes Verdejo 2013 B
verdejo

89

Colour: bright straw. Nose: white flowers, fresh fruit, expressive, dried herbs. Palate: fruity, good acidity, balanced.

Anier Verdejo Vendimia Seleccionada 2013 B
verdejo

92

Colour: bright straw. Nose: fresh, fresh fruit, neat, varietal. Palate: flavourful, fruity, good acidity, balanced.

Señorío de Garci Grande Sauvignon Blanc 2013 B
sauvignon blanc

86

Colour: bright straw. Nose: fresh fruit, floral, wild herbs. Palate: flavourful, fruity, thin.

Señorío de Garci Grande Verdejo 2013 B
verdejo

89

Colour: bright straw. Nose: fresh, white flowers, expressive. Palate: flavourful, fruity, good acidity, balanced.

BODEGAS GARCÍA DE ARANDA
Ctra. de Soria, s/n
09400 Aranda de Duero (Burgos)
☎: +34 947 501 817
Fax: +34 947 506 355
www.bodegasgarcia.com
bodega@bodegasgarcia.com

Oro Blanco Verdejo 2013 B
100% verdejo

86

Colour: bright straw. Nose: fresh fruit, white flowers, wild herbs. Palate: flavourful, fruity, fine bitter notes.

BODEGAS GARCÍAREVALO
Pza. San Juan, 4
47230 Matapozuelos (Valladolid)
☎: +34 983 832 914
Fax: +34 983 832 986
www.garciarevalo.com
garciarevalo@garciarevalo.com

Tres Olmos Lías 2013 B
verdejo

90

Colour: yellow. Nose: white flowers, fresh fruit, expressive, fine lees, dried herbs. Palate: flavourful, fruity, good acidity, balanced.

Tres Olmos Verdejo 2013 B
100% verdejo

88

Colour: bright straw. Nose: white flowers, fresh fruit, expressive, dried herbs. Palate: flavourful, fruity, good acidity, balanced.

BODEGAS GRAN FEUDO
Ribera, 34
31592 Cintruénigo (Navarra)
☎: +34 948 811 000
Fax: +34 948 811 407
www.granfeudo.com
info@granfeudo.com

Gran Feudo Verdejo 2013 B
verdejo

86

Colour: bright straw. Nose: white flowers, fragrant herbs, ripe fruit. Palate: fresh, fruity, flavourful.

BODEGAS GRUPO YLLERA
Autovía A-6, Km. 173,5
47490 Rueda (Valladolid)
☎: +34 983 868 097
Fax: +34 983 868 177
www.grupoyllera.com
grupoyllera@grupoyllera.com

Bracamonte Verdejo 2013 B
100% verdejo

88

Colour: bright straw. Nose: white flowers, fruit expression, wild herbs. Palate: fresh, fruity, flavourful, unctuous.

Bracamonte Verdejo Superior Viñas Viejas 2013 B
100% verdejo

89

Colour: bright straw. Nose: citrus fruit, fruit expression, floral, wild herbs. Palate: fresh, fruity, flavourful, balsamic.

Cantosán BR
100% verdejo
86
Colour: bright straw. Nose: fine lees, floral, fragrant herbs. Palate: powerful, flavourful, good acidity, fine bead.

Cantosán SS
100% verdejo
83

Cantosán BN
100% verdejo
84

Cantosán Reserva Especial ESP
100% verdejo
87
Colour: bright yellow. Nose: medium intensity, fresh fruit, dried herbs, fine lees, floral. Palate: fresh, fruity, flavourful, good acidity, balanced.

Cantosán Verdejo 2013 B
100% verdejo
88
Colour: bright straw. Nose: white flowers, fragrant herbs, fruit expression. Palate: fresh, fruity, flavourful, balanced.

Tierra Buena 2013 B
89
Colour: bright straw. Nose: fresh, fresh fruit, white flowers, balsamic herbs. Palate: flavourful, fruity, good acidity, balanced.

Viña 65 2013 B
88
Colour: bright straw. Nose: fresh, fresh fruit, white flowers. Palate: flavourful, fruity, good acidity.

Viña Garedo 2013 B
88
Colour: bright straw. Nose: dried herbs, floral, fruit expression. Palate: correct, flavourful, thin.

Yllera Rosé 2012 RD
tempranillo, verdejo
84

Yllera Sauvignon Blanc Vendimia Nocturna 2013 B
100% sauvignon blanc
87
Colour: bright straw. Nose: fresh fruit, white flowers, wild herbs. Palate: flavourful, fruity, good acidity.

Yllera Verdejo Vendimia Nocturna 2013 B
100% verdejo
89
Colour: bright straw. Nose: floral, fruit expression, fragrant herbs. Palate: fresh, fruity, easy to drink.

BODEGAS IMPERIALES
Ctra. Madrid - Irun, Km. 171
09370 Gumiel de Izán (Burgos)
☎: +34 947 544 070
Fax: +34 947 525 759
www.bodegasimperiales.com
adminis@bodegasimperiales.com

Abadía de San Quirce Verdejo 2013 B
100% verdejo
88
Colour: bright straw. Nose: white flowers, fragrant herbs, fruit expression. Palate: fresh, fruity, flavurful, balanced, elegant.

BODEGAS JOSÉ PARIENTE

Ctra. de Rueda, km. 2.5
47491 La Seca (Valladolid)
☎: +34 983 816 600
Fax: +34 983 816 620
www.josepariente.com
info@josepariente.com

José Pariente 2012 BFB
100% verdejo

93

Colour: bright yellow. Nose: powerfull, ripe fruit, sweet spices, creamy oak, wild herbs, mineral. Palate: rich, flavourful, fresh, good acidity, roasted-coffee aftertaste.

José Pariente Cuvee Especial 2012 B
100% verdejo

93

Colour: bright yellow. Nose: powerfull, ripe fruit, sweet spices, creamy oak, fragrant herbs. Palate: rich, smoky aftertaste, flavourful, fresh, good acidity.

José Pariente Sauvignon Blanc 2013 B
100% sauvignon blanc

90

Colour: bright straw. Nose: white flowers, fragrant herbs, fruit expression, citrus fruit, mineral. Palate: fresh, fruity, flavourful, balanced, elegant.

José Pariente Verdejo 2013 B
100% verdejo

89

Colour: bright straw. Nose: fresh, fresh fruit, white flowers, expressive, wild herbs. Palate: flavourful, fruity, good acidity, balanced.

BODEGAS MOCEN

Arribas, 7-9
47490 Rueda (Valladolid)
☎: +34 983 868 533
Fax: +34 983 868 514
www.bodegasantano.com
info@bodegasmocen.com

Alta Plata Verdejo 2013 B
verdejo

88

Colour: bright straw. Nose: white flowers, fragrant herbs, fruit expression. Palate: fresh, fruity, flavourful.

Leguillón Verdejo 2013 B
verdejo

89

Colour: bright straw. Nose: fresh, fresh fruit, white flowers, expressive. Palate: flavourful, fruity, good acidity, balanced.

Mocén Sauvignon 2013 B
100% sauvignon blanc

89

Colour: bright straw. Nose: fresh, fresh fruit, expressive, grassy. Palate: flavourful, fruity, good acidity, balanced.

Mocén Verdejo Selección Especial 2013 B
100% verdejo

88

Colour: bright straw. Nose: white flowers, fragrant herbs, fruit expression. Palate: fresh, fruity, flavourful, balanced.

BODEGAS MONTE BLANCO

Ctra. Valladolid, Km. 24,5
47239 Serrada (Valladolid)
☎: +34 941 310 295
Fax: +34 941 310 832
www.bodegas-monteblanco.es
info@bodegas-monteblanco.es

Ramón Bilbao Verdejo 2013 B
100% verdejo

90

Colour: bright straw. Nose: fresh, fresh fruit, white flowers, grassy. Palate: flavourful, fruity, good acidity, balanced.

BODEGAS MONTEABELLÓN

Calvario, s/n
09318 Nava de Roa (Burgos)
☎: +34 947 550 000
Fax: +34 947 550 219
www.monteabellon.com
info@monteabellon.com

Monteabellón Verdejo 2013 B
100% verdejo
88
Colour: bright straw. Nose: white flowers, fragrant herbs, fruit expression. Palate: fresh, fruity, flavourful, thin.

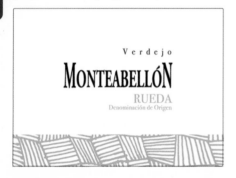

BODEGAS NAIA

Camino San Martín, s/n
47491 La Seca (Valladolid)
☎: +34 628 434 933
www.bodegasnaia.com
info@bodegasnaia.com

Ducado de Altán 2013 B
verdejo, sauvignon blanc
89
Colour: bright straw. Nose: fresh, fresh fruit, white flowers. Palate: flavourful, fruity, good acidity, balanced.

K-Naia 2013 B
verdejo, sauvignon blanc
89
Colour: bright straw. Nose: fresh, fresh fruit, expressive. Palate: flavourful, fruity, good acidity, balanced, fine bitter notes.

Las Brisas 2013 B
verdejo, viura, sauvignon blanc
89
Colour: bright straw, greenish rim. Nose: fragrant herbs, varietal, balanced. Palate: fruity, good acidity, fine bitter notes.

Naia 2013 B
100% verdejo
92
Colour: bright yellow. Nose: faded flowers, fragrant herbs, balanced. Palate: rich, flavourful, full, good acidity.

Naiades 2011 BFB
100% verdejo
96
Colour: bright yellow. Nose: elegant, expressive, sweet spices, dry stone, balanced. Palate: ripe fruit, long, toasty, good acidity, fine bitter notes.

S-Naia 2013 B
100% sauvignon blanc
89
Colour: bright straw. Nose: fresh, fresh fruit, white flowers, expressive. Palate: flavourful, fruity, good acidity, balanced.

BODEGAS NIDIA

Ctra. La Seca 17
47400 Medina del Campo (Valladolid)
☎: +34 983 812 581
danieltorio@laborquo.es

Nidia 2013 B
verdejo
86
Colour: yellow. Nose: faded flowers, fresh fruit. Palate: correct, easy to drink, fine bitter notes, carbonic notes.

BODEGAS NILO

Federico García Lorca, 7
47490 Rueda (Valladolid)
☎: +34 690 068 682
www.bodegasnilo.com
mjose@bodegasnilo.com

Bianca 2013 B
100% verdejo

90

Colour: bright straw. Nose: grassy, medium intensity, fruit expression. Palate: good acidity, balanced, correct.

Bianca Sauvignon Blanc 2013 B
100% sauvignon blanc

89

Colour: bright straw. Nose: fresh, balanced, fragrant herbs, citrus fruit. Palate: correct, fine bitter notes, fresh, good acidity.

BODEGAS ORDÓÑEZ

Bartolomé Esteban Murillo, 11
29700 Vélez- Málaga (Málaga)
☎: +34 952 504 706
Fax: +34 951 284 796
www.grupojorgeordonez.com
info@jorgeordonez.es

Nisia 2013 B
100% verdejo

95

Colour: bright straw. Nose: white flowers, fresh fruit, expressive, fine lees, dried herbs. Palate: flavourful, fruity, good acidity, balanced.

BODEGAS PEÑAFIEL

Ctra. N-122, Km. 311
47300 Peñafiel (Valladolid)
☎: +34 983 881 622
Fax: +34 983 881 944
www.bodegaspenafiel.com
bodegaspenafiel@bodegaspenafiel.com

Alba de Miros 2013 B
100% verdejo

89

Colour: bright straw. Nose: white flowers, fragrant herbs, fruit expression. Palate: fresh, fruity, flavourful, balanced, elegant.

BODEGAS PRADOREY

Ctra. A-VI, Km. 172,5
47490 Rueda (Valladolid)
☎: +34 983 444 048
Fax: +34 983 868 564
www.pradorey.com
bodega@pradorey.com

Chozo Viejo 2013 B
verdejo

88

Colour: bright straw. Nose: fresh, fresh fruit, white flowers, expressive. Palate: flavourful, fruity, good acidity, balanced.

PR 3 Barricas 2009 BFB
100% verdejo

93

Colour: bright golden. Nose: sweet spices, ripe fruit, candied fruit, petrol notes, cocoa bean. Palate: rich, full, complex, long.

Pradorey Sauvignon Blanc 2013 B
100% sauvignon blanc

88

Colour: yellow. Nose: medium intensity, white flowers, citrus fruit. Palate: correct, fine bitter notes, good acidity, good finish.

Pradorey Verdejo 2013 B
100% verdejo

90

Colour: bright straw. Nose: white flowers, fragrant herbs, fruit expression. Palate: fresh, fruity, flavourful.

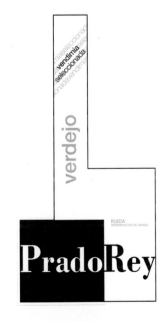

BODEGAS PROTOS S.L.
Ctra. CL 610, Km. 32,5
47491 La Seca (Valladolid)
☎: +34 983 878 011
Fax: +34 983 878 012
www.bodegasprotos.com
bodegasprotos@bodegasprotos.com

Protos Verdejo 2013 B
verdejo
89
Colour: bright straw. Nose: fresh, fresh fruit, white flowers, expressive, grassy. Palate: flavourful, fruity, good acidity, balanced.

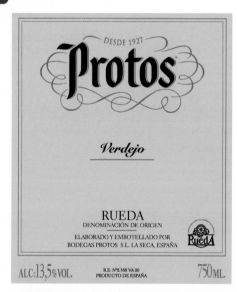

BODEGAS RUEDA PÉREZ
Boyón, 17
47220 Pozáldez (Valladolid)
☎: +34 650 454 657
Fax: +34 983 822 049
www.bodegasruedaperez.es
info@bodegasruedaperez.es

José Galo Verdejo Selección 2013 B
100% verdejo
91
Colour: bright straw. Nose: white flowers, fragrant herbs, fruit expression. Palate: fresh, fruity, flavourful, balanced, elegant.

Viña Burón Verdejo 2013 B
100% verdejo
89
Colour: bright straw. Nose: fresh, fresh fruit, white flowers, wild herbs. Palate: flavourful, fruity, good acidity.

Zapadorado Verdejo 2013 B
100% verdejo
89
Colour: bright straw, greenish rim. Nose: fragrant herbs, fresh fruit. Palate: easy to drink, varietal, fine bitter notes.

BODEGAS SEÑORÍO DE NAVA S.A.
Tejares, 5
47500 Nava del Rey (Valladolid)
☎: +34 987 209 790
Fax: +34 987 209 800
www.senoriodenava.es
snava@senoriodenava.es

Señorío de Nava Rueda 2013 B
verdejo
88
Colour: bright straw. Nose: fresh fruit, white flowers. Palate: flavourful, fruity, good acidity, balanced.

Señorío de Nava Verdejo 100% 2013 B
100% verdejo
87
Colour: bright straw. Nose: fresh, fresh fruit, white flowers, tropical fruit. Palate: flavourful, fruity, good acidity, balanced.

Val de Lamas Verdejo 100% 2013 B
100% verdejo
87
Colour: bright straw. Nose: fresh fruit, citrus fruit, tropical fruit. Palate: fruity, fresh, good acidity.

BODEGAS TAMARAL
Crta. N-122 Valladolid-Soria, Km.310,6
47320 Peñafiel (Valladolid)
☎: +34 983 878 017
Fax: +34 983 878 089
www.tamaral.com
info@tamaral.com

Tamaral Verdejo 2013 B
100% verdejo
87
Colour: bright straw. Nose: fresh, fresh fruit, white flowers. Palate: flavourful, fruity, good acidity.

BODEGAS TEODORO RECIO
Hospital, 6
47491 La Seca (Valladolid)
☎: +34 636 183 494
www.robeser.es
info@robeser.es

Robeser 2013 B
100% verdejo
87
Colour: bright straw. Nose: wild herbs, dried flowers, varietal. Palate: fruity, balanced, correct, fine bitter notes.

BODEGAS TORRES

Miguel Torres i Carbó, 6
08720 Vilafranca del Penedès
(Barcelona)
☎: +34 938 177 400
Fax: +34 938 177 444
www.torres.com
mailadmin@torres.es

Verdeo 2013 B
verdejo
88
Colour: bright straw. Nose: fresh, white flowers. Palate: flavourful, good acidity, balanced.

BODEGAS VAL DE VID

Ctra. Valladolid - Medina, Km. 23,6
47231 Serrada (Valladolid)
☎: +34 983 559 914
Fax: +34 983 559 914
www.valdevid.es
info@valdevid.es

Condesa Eylo 2013 B
100% verdejo
89
Colour: bright straw, greenish rim. Nose: white flowers, fresh, medium intensity. Palate: good acidity, fine bitter notes, balanced.

Eylo Rueda 2013 B
88
Colour: straw, greenish rim. Nose: fragrant herbs, floral, balanced. Palate: flavourful, balanced, fine bitter notes, good acidity.

La Almendrera 2013 B
100% verdejo
89
Colour: bright straw. Nose: fresh, fresh fruit, expressive, varietal. Palate: fruity, good acidity, balanced, balsamic.

Musgo 2013 B
100% verdejo
87
Colour: bright straw, greenish rim. Nose: wild herbs, medium intensity, fresh. Palate: correct, fine bitter notes, easy to drink.

Val de Vid Verdejo 2013 B
100% verdejo
90
Colour: bright straw. Nose: fresh, fresh fruit, white flowers, expressive. Palate: flavourful, fruity, good acidity, balanced.

BODEGAS VALPINCIA

Ctra. de Melida, 3,5
47300 Peñafiel (Valladolid)
☎: +34 983 878 007
Fax: +34 983 880 620
www.bodegasvalpincia.com
penafiel@bodegasvalpincia.com

Valpincia Rueda Verdejo Viura 2013 B
84

Valpincia Verdejo 2013 B
verdejo
86
Colour: bright straw. Nose: fresh, fresh fruit, white flowers. Palate: flavourful, fruity, good acidity, fine bitter notes.

BODEGAS VERACRUZ S.L.

Rodríguez Chico, 4 Bajo 2
47500 Nava del Rey (Valladolid)
☎: +34 983 850 136
Fax: +34 983 850 761
www.bodegasveracruz.com
j.benito@bodegasveracruz.com

Ermita Veracruz 2010 BFB
100% verdejo
88
Colour: bright golden. Nose: ripe fruit, dry nuts, powerfull, toasty, aged wood nuances, roasted coffee. Palate: flavourful, fruity, spicy, toasty, long.

Ermita Veracruz Verdejo 2013 B
100% verdejo
91
Colour: bright straw. Nose: fragrant herbs, fresh fruit, balanced. Palate: fresh, fruity, long, fine bitter notes, good acidity.

Ermita Veracruz Viñas Jóvenes 2013 B
100% verdejo
88
Colour: bright straw. Nose: fresh, fresh fruit, white flowers, dried herbs. Palate: flavourful, fruity, good acidity, balanced.

BODEGAS VERDEAL

Nueva, 8
40200 Cuéllar (Segovia)
☎: +34 921 140 125
Fax: +34 921 142 421
www.bodegasverdeal.com
info@bodegasverdeal.com

Ayre 2013 B
100% verdejo

88

Colour: bright straw. Nose: grassy, fresh fruit, tropical fruit. Palate: easy to drink, good acidity.

Verdeal 2013 B
100% verdejo

92

Colour: bright straw. Nose: fresh, fresh fruit, white flowers, expressive. Palate: flavourful, fruity, good acidity, balanced.

BODEGAS VETUS

Ctra. Toro a Salamanca, Km. 9,5
49800 Toro (Zamora)
☎: +34 945 609 086
Fax: +34 980 056 012
www.bodegasvetus.com
vetus@bodegasvetus.com

Flor de Vetus Verdejo 2013 B
100% verdejo

88

Colour: bright straw. Nose: fresh, white flowers, citrus fruit, tropical fruit. Palate: flavourful, fruity, good acidity, balanced.

BODEGAS VICENTE GANDÍA

Ctra. Cheste a Godelleta, s/n
46370 Chiva (Valencia)
☎: +34 962 524 242
Fax: +34 962 524 243
www.vicentegandia.es
info@vicentegandia.com

Nebla Verdejo 2013 B
100% verdejo

88

Colour: yellow, greenish rim. Nose: medium intensity, varietal. Palate: correct, balanced, good acidity, fine bitter notes.

BODEGAS VIORE

Pol. Ind. Norte – Parcela 5
49800 Toro (Zamora)
☎: +34 941 454 050
Fax: +34 941 454 529
www.bodegasriojanas.com
bodega@bodegasriojanas.com

Expolio 2013 B
verdejo

85

Viore Rueda 2013 B

86

Colour: bright straw. Nose: fresh, fresh fruit, white flowers, expressive. Palate: flavourful, fruity, good acidity, balanced.

Viore Verdejo 2013 B
100% verdejo

89

Colour: bright straw. Nose: white flowers, fragrant herbs, fruit expression, varietal. Palate: fresh, fruity, flavourful, elegant.

BODEGAS VITERRA

Pol. Ind Jerónimo Roure, Parc 45
46520 Puerto de Sagunto (Valencia)
☎: +34 962 691 090
Fax: +34 962 690 963
www.vinamagna.es
direccioncomercial@bodegasviterra.com

Dinastía de Helenio 2013 B
100% verdejo

88

Colour: bright straw. Nose: white flowers, fresh fruit, expressive, fine lees, dried herbs. Palate: flavourful, fruity, good acidity, balanced.

Naxus 2013 B
100% verdejo

87

Colour: bright straw. Nose: white flowers, fragrant herbs, fruit expression, citrus fruit. Palate: fresh, fruity, flavourful.

Optimus 2013 B
100% verdejo

89

Colour: bright straw, greenish rim. Nose: balanced, varietal, fresh fruit. Palate: fruity, flavourful, fine bitter notes, long, easy to drink.

Theseus 2013 B
sauvignon blanc

86

Colour: bright straw. Nose: balsamic herbs, fruit expression, dried flowers, medium intensity. Palate: flavourful, fresh, fruity.

BODEGAS VITULIA

Sendín, 49
9400 Aranda de Duero (Burgos)
☎: +34 947 515 051
Fax: +34 947 515 051
www.bodegasvitulia.com
vitulia@bodegasvitulia.com

Vitulia Verdejo 2013 B
verdejo

85

BODEGAS Y VIÑEDOS ÁNGEL LORENZO CACHAZO

Estación, 53
47220 Pozaldez (Valladolid)
☎: +34 983 822 481
Fax: +34 983 822 012
www.martivilli.com
comercial@martivilli.com

Lorenzo Cachazo 2013 B
86
Colour: bright straw. Nose: fresh fruit, wild herbs, medium intensity. Palate: correct, good acidity, fine bitter notes.

Martivillí Sauvignon Blanc 2013 B
100% sauvignon blanc
86
Colour: bright straw. Nose: fresh fruit, white flowers, dried herbs. Palate: flavourful, fruity, good acidity.

Martivillí Verdejo 2013 B
100% verdejo
87
Colour: bright straw. Nose: fresh, fresh fruit, varietal. Palate: flavourful, fruity, good acidity, balanced.

BODEGAS Y VIÑEDOS MARTÍN BERDUGO

Ctra. de la Colonia, s/n
09400 Aranda de Duero (Burgos)
☎: +34 947 506 331
Fax: +34 947 506 602
www.martinberdugo.com
bodega@martinberdugo.com

Martín Berdugo Verdejo 2013 B
verdejo
86
Colour: bright straw. Nose: fresh, fresh fruit, medium intensity, citrus fruit. Palate: fruity, good acidity, balanced.

BODEGAS Y VIÑEDOS NEO

Ctra. N-122, Km. 274,5
09391 Castrillo de la Vega (Burgos)
☎: +34 947 514 393
Fax: +34 947 515 445
www.bodegasneo.com
ivan@bodegasconde.com

Primer Motivo Verdejo 2013 B
verdejo
88
Colour: bright straw. Nose: fragrant herbs, varietal, fresh fruit, citrus fruit. Palate: good acidity, fine bitter notes, fresh.

BODEGAS Y VIÑEDOS SHAYA

Ctra. Aldeanueva del Codonal s/n
40642 Aldeanueva del Codonal
(Segovia)
☎: +34 968 435 022
Fax: +34 968 716 051
www.orowines.com
info@orowines.com

Arindo 2013 B
100% verdejo
87
Colour: bright straw. Nose: white flowers, ripe fruit. Palate: flavourful, fruity, good acidity, easy to drink, good finish.

Shaya 2013 B
100% verdejo
92
Colour: bright straw. Nose: fresh, fresh fruit, white flowers, expressive. Palate: flavourful, fruity, good acidity, balanced, complex.

Shaya Habis 2011 BFB
100% verdejo
93
Colour: bright straw. Nose: white flowers, fresh fruit, expressive, fine lees, dried herbs. Palate: flavourful, fruity, good acidity, balanced.

BODEGAS Y VIÑEDOS TÁBULA

Ctra. de Valbuena, km. 2
47359 Olivares de Duero (Valladolid)
☎: +34 608 219 019
Fax: +34 983 107 300
www.bodegastabula.es
armando@bodegastabula.es

Damana Verdejo 2013 B
100% verdejo
87
Colour: bright straw. Nose: fresh, citrus fruit, balanced. Palate: easy to drink, fresh, good acidity.

CAMPOS DE SUEÑOS

Avda. Diagonal, 590, 5º 1ª
08021 Barcelona (Barcelona)
☎: +34 660 445 464
www.vinergia.com
vinergia@vinergia.com

Campos de Sueños 2013 B
100% verdejo
89
Colour: bright straw. Nose: fresh, fresh fruit, expressive, grassy. Palate: flavourful, fruity, good acidity, balanced.

COMENGE BODEGAS Y VIÑEDOS

Camino del Castillo, s/n
47316 Curiel de Duero (Valladolid)
☎: +34 983 880 363
Fax: +34 983 880 717
www.comenge.com
admin@comenge.com

Comenge Verdejo 2013 B
verdejo
88
Colour: bright straw. Nose: citrus fruit, balsamic herbs, floral, medium intensity. Palate: fresh, fruity, easy to drink.

COMPAÑÍA DE VINOS TELMO RODRÍGUEZ

El Monte
01308 Lanciego (Álava)
☎: +34 945 628 315
Fax: +34 945 628 314
www.telmorodriguez.com
contact@telmorodriguez.com

Basa 2013 B
verdejo
90
Colour: bright straw. Nose: fresh, white flowers, expressive. Palate: flavourful, fruity, good acidity, balanced.

El Transistor 2012 B
verdejo
94
Colour: bright straw. Nose: ripe fruit, fruit expression, grassy, spicy. Palate: varietal, fruity, fresh, fine bitter notes.

CVNE

Barrio de la Estación, s/n
26200 Haro (La Rioja)
☎: +34 941 304 800
Fax: +34 941 304 815
www.cvne.com
marketing@cvne.com

Monopole S. XXI 2013 B
verdejo
88
Colour: bright straw. Nose: fresh, white flowers, medium intensity, candied fruit. Palate: flavourful, fruity, good acidity, balanced.

DIEZ SIGLOS DE VERDEJO

Ctra. Valladolid Km. 24,5
47231 Serrada (Valladolid)
☎: +34 983 559 910
Fax: +34 983 559 020
www.diezsiglos.es
info@diezsiglos.es

Canto Real 2013 B
100% verdejo
87
Colour: bright straw. Nose: fresh fruit, medium intensity, wild herbs. Palate: correct, easy to drink, good finish.

Diez Siglos 2012 BFB
100% verdejo
89
Colour: bright yellow. Nose: sweet spices, toasty, ripe fruit. Palate: rich, long, spicy, balanced, fine bitter notes.

Diez Siglos 2013 B
100% verijadiego
88
Colour: bright straw. Nose: white flowers, fragrant herbs, fruit expression. Palate: fresh, fruity, flavourful.

Diez Siglos de Verdejo Blush 2013 RD
tempranillo, verdejo
87
Colour: raspberry rose. Nose: medium intensity, balanced, rose petals, fresh fruit. Palate: good acidity.

Nekora 2013 B
100% verdejo
89
Colour: yellow, greenish rim. Nose: fresh, fresh fruit, white flowers, expressive. Palate: flavourful, fruity, good acidity, balanced.

EMILIO GIMENO

Rueda (Valladolid)
☎: +34 686 487 007
emiliogimeno2011@yahoo.es

Emilio Gimeno 2013 B
85

EMW GRANDES VINOS DE ESPAÑA

Sánchez Picazo, 53
30332 Balsapintada (Fuente Alamo)
(Murcia)
☎: +34 968 151 520
Fax: +34 968 151 539
www.emw.es
info@emw.es

El Gordo del Circo 2013 B
100% verdejo
90

Colour: bright straw, greenish rim. Nose: fresh, fresh fruit, white flowers, varietal. Palate: flavourful, fruity, good acidity, balanced.

FINCA CASERÍO DE DUEÑAS

Ctra. Cl. 602, (Medina del Campo - Nava del Rey) km. 50,2
47465 Villaverde de Medina (Valladolid)
☎: +34 915 006 000
Fax: +34 915 006 006
www.caserioduenas.es
rrpp@vina-mayor.es

Viña Mayor Verdejo 2012 BFB
100% verdejo
90

Colour: bright yellow. Nose: powerfull, ripe fruit, sweet spices, creamy oak, fragrant herbs. Palate: rich, smoky aftertaste, flavourful, fresh, good acidity.

Viña Mayor Verdejo 2013 B
100% verdejo
90

Colour: bright straw. Nose: fresh, fresh fruit, white flowers, varietal. Palate: flavourful, fruity, good acidity, balanced.

FINCA MONTEPEDROSO

Término La Morejona, s/n
47490 Rueda (Valladolid)
☎: +34 983 868 977
Fax: +34 983 868 055
www.familiamartinezbujanda.com
acabezas@bujanda.com

Finca Montepedroso Verdejo 2013 B
100% verdejo
90

Colour: bright straw. Nose: white flowers, fresh fruit, expressive, fine lees, dried herbs. Palate: flavourful, fruity, good acidity, balanced.

HAMMEKEN CELLARS

Calle de la Muela, 16
03730 Jávea (Alicante)
☎: +34 965 791 967
Fax: +34 966 461 471
www.hammekencellars.com
cellars@hammekencellars.com

Aventino Verdejo 2013 B
verdejo
85

Viña Altamar Verdejo 2013 B
verdejo
89

Colour: bright straw. Nose: white flowers, fresh fruit, expressive, fine lees, dried herbs. Palate: flavourful, fruity, good acidity, balanced.

HERRERO BODEGA

Camino Real, 55
40447 Nieva (Segovia)
☎: +34 921 124 440
www.herrerobodega.com
info@herrerobodega.com

Atino 2013 B
100% verdejo
86
Colour: bright straw. Nose: fresh, fresh fruit, white flowers. Palate: flavourful, fruity, good acidity, thin.

Erre de Herrero 2013 B
100% verdejo
86
Colour: bright yellow. Nose: white flowers, balanced, varietal, fresh fruit. Palate: correct, good acidity, light-bodied.

Janine Vedel 2013 B
100% sauvignon blanc
87
Colour: bright straw. Nose: white flowers, fruit expression, wild herbs. Palate: fresh, fruity, flavourful, thin.

Robert Vedel Cepas Viejas 2013 B
100% verdejo
88
Colour: bright straw. Nose: white flowers, fragrant herbs, fruit expression. Palate: fresh, fruity, flavourful.

J. GARCÍA CARRIÓN

Jorge Juan, 73
28009 (Madrid)
☎: +34 914 355 556
Fax: +34 915 779 571
www.garciacarrion.com
jbrunet@jgc.es

Castillo de Aza Verdejo 2013 B
verdejo
82

Mayor de Castilla Verdejo 2013 B
verdejo
87
Colour: bright straw. Nose: white flowers, fruit expression, dried herbs. Palate: fresh, fruity, flavourful.

Pata Negra Verdejo 2012 B
87
Colour: bright straw. Nose: fresh, fresh fruit, white flowers. Palate: flavourful, fruity, good acidity.

Pata Negra Verdejo 2013 B
verdejo
84

Solar de la Vega Verdejo 2013 B
verdejo
84

JAVIER SANZ VITICULTOR

San Judas, 2
47491 La Seca (Valladolid)
☎: +34 983 816 669
Fax: +34 983 816 639
www.bodegajaviersanz.com
comunicaciones@bodegajaviersanz.com

Javier Sanz Malcorta Verdejo Singular 2013 B
100% verdejo
90
Colour: bright straw. Nose: white flowers, fragrant herbs, fruit expression, citrus fruit. Palate: fresh, fruity, flavourful, balanced.

Javier Sanz Viticultor Sauvignon 2013 B
sauvignon blanc
88
Colour: bright straw. Nose: fresh, wild herbs, fresh fruit. Palate: flavourful, fruity, fine bitter notes, good acidity.

Javier Sanz Viticultor Verdejo 2013 B
100% verdejo
89
Colour: bright straw. Nose: fresh, fresh fruit, white flowers, expressive. Palate: flavourful, fruity, good acidity, balanced.

JUAN DAVID ALONSO RODRÍGUEZ

Juan de Juni, 4 2ºA
47006 Valladolid (Valladolid)
☎: +34 601 063 001
www.vinedosaequitas.es
vinedosaequitas@gmail.com

Aéquitas 2013 B
verdejo
87
Colour: bright straw. Nose: white flowers, fragrant herbs, fruit expression. Palate: fresh, fruity, flavourful.

LA MALETA HAND MADE FINE WINES

Julio Prieto Nespereira, 21
32005 Ourense (Ourense)
☎: +34 988 614 234
lamaletawines.com
hola@lamaletawines.com

Pizpireta 2013 B
100% verdejo
87
Colour: bright straw. Nose: fresh, fresh fruit, white flowers, wild herbs. Palate: flavourful, fruity, good acidity, balanced.

LA SOTERRAÑA
Ctra. N-601, Km. 151
47410 Olmedo (Valladolid)
☎: +34 983 601 026
Fax: +34 983 601 026
www.bodegaslasoterrana.com
info@bodegaslasoterrana.com

Eresma 2012 B
100% verdejo
89
Colour: bright yellow. Nose: powerfull, sweet spices, creamy oak, fragrant herbs. Palate: rich, smoky aftertaste, flavourful, fresh, good acidity.

Eresma 2013 B
100% verdejo
85

Eresma Sauvignon 2013 B
100% sauvignon blanc
88
Colour: bright yellow. Nose: medium intensity, fresh fruit, citrus fruit. Palate: correct, balanced, fine bitter notes.

Eresma Verdejo 2013 B
100% verdejo
88
Colour: bright straw. Nose: fresh, fresh fruit, white flowers, wild herbs. Palate: flavourful, fruity, good acidity, fine bitter notes.

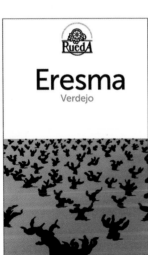

Las Abogadas 2013 B
100% verdejo
87
Colour: bright straw. Nose: fresh, fresh fruit, white flowers, expressive. Palate: flavourful, fruity, good acidity, balanced.

V&R Verdejo 2013 B
100% verdejo
86
Colour: bright straw. Nose: fragrant herbs, white flowers, dried herbs. Palate: flavourful, fresh, easy to drink.

LAN
Paraje del Buicio, s/n
26360 Fuenmayor (La Rioja)
☎: +34 941 450 950
Fax: +34 941 450 567
www.bodegaslan.com
info@bodegaslan.com

Duquesa 2013 B
100% verdejo
87
Colour: bright straw. Nose: fresh, fresh fruit, white flowers. Palate: flavourful, fruity, good acidity.

LLANOS Y AYLLÓN S.L.
Rafael Alberti, 3
47490 Rueda (Valladolid)
☎: +34 627 400 316
www.verdejomaroto.es
ventas@verdejomaroto.es

Maroto Selección Especial 2013 B
87
Colour: straw. Nose: dried flowers, medium intensity, fresh fruit, dry stone. Palate: correct, easy to drink, good acidity.

LOESS
El Monte, 7
47195 Arroyo de la Encomienda (Valladolid)
☎: +34 983 664 898
Fax: +34 983 406 579
www.loess.es
loess@loess.es

Loess 2013 B
verdejo
90
Colour: bright straw. Nose: white flowers, fragrant herbs, fruit expression, expressive. Palate: fresh, fruity, flavourful, balanced, elegant.

Loess Collection 2012 BFB
verdejo
92
Colour: bright yellow. Nose: powerfull, ripe fruit, sweet spices, creamy oak, fragrant herbs. Palate: rich, flavourful, fresh, good acidity.

MARQUÉS DE LA CONCORDIA FAMILY OF WINES*

Avenida Nava del Rey, 8
47490 Rueda (Valladolid)
☎: +34 913 878 612
www.the-haciendas.com
abasilio@unitedwineries.com

Federico Paternina Verdejo 2013 B
100% verdejo
85

Hacienda Zorita Vega de la Reina Verdejo 2013 B
100% verdejo
88
Colour: bright straw. Nose: floral, dried herbs, fruit expression. Palate: balsamic, fruity, flavourful, correct.

MATER VITIS

Calle Doctor Santaolalla, 21 bajo izq
03005 Alicante (Alicante)
☎: +34 965 637 811
www.matervitis.com

Mater Vitis Verdejo 2013 B
verdejo
87
Colour: bright straw. Nose: floral, ripe fruit, fragrant herbs. Palate: flavourful, fruity, good acidity.

MENADE

Ctra. Rueda Nava del Rey, km. 1
47490 Rueda (Valladolid)
☎: +34 983 103 223
Fax: +34 983 816 561
www.menade.es
info@menade.es

Antonio Sanz Sauvignon Blanc 2013 B
100% sauvignon blanc
91
Colour: bright straw. Nose: white flowers, fragrant herbs, fruit expression. Palate: fresh, fruity, flavourful, elegant.

Antonio Sanz Verdejo 2013 B
100% verdejo
90
Colour: bright straw. Nose: fresh, fresh fruit, white flowers, expressive. Palate: flavourful, fruity, good acidity, balanced, elegant.

Menade Sauvignon Blanc 2013 B
100% sauvignon blanc
87
Colour: bright straw. Nose: wild herbs, white flowers, fruit expression, expressive. Palate: flavourful, balsamic, easy to drink.

Menade Verdejo 2013 B
100% verdejo
90
Colour: bright straw. Nose: fresh, fresh fruit, white flowers, expressive. Palate: flavourful, fruity, good acidity, balanced.

V3 2012 BFB
100% verdejo
93
Colour: bright yellow. Nose: ripe fruit, sweet spices, fragrant herbs, expressive. Palate: fruity, flavourful, long, balsamic, balanced, elegant.

MIGUEL ARROYO IZQUIERDO

Calle Real, 34
47419 Puras (Valladolid)
☎: +34 983 626 095
Fax: +34 983 626 095
info@arroyoizquierdo.com

Demimo Sauvignon Blanc 2013 B
sauvignon blanc
86
Colour: bright straw. Nose: medium intensity, wild herbs, balanced. Palate: easy to drink, good finish.

Demimo Verdejo 2013 B
verdejo
87
Colour: bright straw. Nose: medium intensity, ripe fruit, faded flowers. Palate: fruity, correct, good finish.

Miguel Arroyo Izquierdo 2013 B
verdejo
92
Colour: bright yellow. Nose: expressive, fresh fruit, dry stone. Palate: full, flavourful, long, rich, complex, balanced.

MONTEBACO

Finca Montealto
47359 Valbuena de Duero (Valladolid)
☎: +34 983 485 128
www.bodegasmontebaco.com
montebaco@bodegasmontebaco.com

Montebaco Verdejo 2013 B
verdejo
89
Colour: bright straw. Nose: fresh fruit, floral, balanced. Palate: fruity, fine bitter notes, correct, easy to drink.

NUBORI

Avda. del Ebro s/n
26540 Alfaro (La Rioja)
☎: +34 941 183 502
Fax: +34 941 183 157
www.bodegasnubori.com
nubori@nubori.es

Dosmil 2012 B
verdejo
84

NUEVOS VINOS

Alfafara, 12 Entlo.
03803 Alcoy (Alicante)
☎: +34 965 549 172
Fax: +34 965 549 173
www.nuevosvinos.es
josecanto@nuevosvinos.es

Perla Maris Verdejo 2013 B
100% verdejo
88
Colour: bright straw. Nose: ripe fruit, citrus fruit, tropical fruit. Palate: flavourful, fruity, good acidity.

PAGO TRASLAGARES

Autovía Noroeste km 166,4 Apdo. 507
47490 Rueda (Valladolid)
☎: +34 983 667 023
www.traslagares.com
info@traslagares.com

Oro Pálido 2013 B
100% verdejo
82

Traslagares Sauvignon Blanc 2013 B
100% sauvignon blanc
84

Traslagares Verdejo 2013 B
100% verdejo
88
Colour: bright straw. Nose: ripe fruit, floral, wild herbs, expressive. Palate: powerful, flavourful, balanced.

Viña El Torreón Verdejo 2013 B
100% verdejo
81

PAGOS DEL REY S.L

Avda. Morejona, 6
47490 Rueda (Valladolid)
☎: +34 983 868 182
Fax: +34 983 868 182
www.pagosdelrey.com
rueda@pagosdelrey.com

Analivia Rueda 2013 B
verdejo, viura
87
Colour: yellow, greenish rim. Nose: balanced, fresh fruit, fragrant herbs, medium intensity. Palate: fresh, easy to drink.

Analivia Sauvignon Blanc 2013 B
sauvignon blanc
88
Colour: bright straw, greenish rim. Nose: medium intensity, fresh fruit, grassy. Palate: good acidity, fine bitter notes.

Analivia Verdejo 2013 B
verdejo
86
Colour: bright straw. Nose: medium intensity, fragrant herbs, fresh. Palate: easy to drink, good finish.

Blume Rueda 2013 B
verdejo, viura
87
Colour: straw. Nose: fresh, wild herbs, fresh fruit. Palate: easy to drink, good acidity, fine bitter notes, correct.

Blume Sauvignon Blanc 2013 B
sauvignon blanc
88
Colour: bright straw, greenish rim. Nose: fresh fruit, wild herbs, citrus fruit. Palate: flavourful, fresh, balanced, good acidity.

Blume Verdejo 2013 B
verdejo
86
Colour: bright straw. Nose: medium intensity, grassy, fresh. Palate: correct, fine bitter notes.

Moralinos Rueda Verdejo 2013 B
verdejo
87
Colour: bright straw. Nose: white flowers, citrus fruit, balsamic herbs. Palate: flavourful, fruity, easy to drink.

PALACIO DE BORNOS
Ctra. Madrid - Coruña, km. 170,6
47490 Rueda (Valladolid)
☎: +34 983 868 116
Fax: +34 983 868 432
www.palaciodeborno.com
info@taninia.com

Bornos Frizzante Verdejo s/c B
verdejo
86
Colour: bright straw. Nose: white flowers, fresh fruit, jasmine. Palate: fruity, easy to drink, correct, sweetness.

Palacio de Bornos Sauvignon Blanc 2013 B
sauvignon blanc
87
Colour: bright straw. Nose: medium intensity, fresh fruit, dried flowers. Palate: fresh, easy to drink, good finish.

Palacio de Bornos Semidulce 2013 B
sauvignon blanc
85

Palacio de Bornos Verdejo Vendimia Seleccionada 2011 BFB
verdejo
91
Colour: bright yellow. Nose: powerfull, ripe fruit, sweet spices, creamy oak, fragrant herbs. Palate: rich, smoky aftertaste, flavourful, fresh, good acidity.

Palacios de Bornos BN
verdejo
85

Palacios de Bornos BR
verdejo
86
Colour: bright golden. Nose: dry nuts, fragrant herbs, complex, fine lees, sweet spices. Palate: powerful, flavourful, good acidity, fine bead, fine bitter notes.

Palacios de Bornos SS
verdejo
86
Colour: bright straw. Nose: ripe fruit, fine lees, balanced, dried herbs. Palate: good acidity, ripe fruit, long, sweet, flavourful.

Palacios de Bornos La Caprichosa 2012 B
verdejo
91
Colour: bright yellow. Nose: white flowers, fresh fruit, expressive, fine lees, dried herbs. Palate: flavourful, fruity, good acidity, balanced.

Palacios de Bornos Rosado SS
tempranillo
85

Palacios de Bornos Verdejo 2012 BFB
verdejo
89
Colour: bright yellow. Nose: creamy oak, sweet spices, white flowers. Palate: balanced, good acidity, spicy, toasty.

Palacios de Bornos Verdejo 2013 B
verdejo
88
Colour: bright straw. Nose: fresh, fresh fruit, white flowers. Palate: flavourful, fruity, good acidity, balanced, easy to drink.

PALACIO DE VILLACHICA
Ctra. Nacional 122, Km. 433,2
49800 Toro (Zamora)
☎: +34 609 144 711
Fax: +34 983 381 356
www.palaciodevillachica.com
bodegavillachica@yahoo.es

Abside Verdejo 2013 B
100% verdejo
87
Colour: bright straw. Nose: fresh, fresh fruit, white flowers, expressive. Palate: flavourful, fruity, good acidity, balanced.

PALACIOS VINOTECA
Ctra. de Nalda a Viguera, 46
26190 Nalda (La Rioja)
☎: +34 941 444 418
www.palaciosvinoteca.com
info@palaciosvinoteca.com

Trillón 2013 B
verdejo
87
Colour: bright straw. Nose: powerfull, ripe fruit, citrus fruit, tropical fruit. Palate: flavourful, fine bitter notes, good acidity.

PERSEO 7

Montero Calvo, 7
47001 Valladolid (Valladolid)
☎: +34 983 297 830
info@perseo7.com

Perseo 7 2013 B
verdejo
89
Colour: bright straw. Nose: fresh fruit, varietal. Palate: fruity, balanced, good acidity, fine bitter notes.

Perseo 7 Brut ESP
verdejo
84

PREDIO DE VASCARLÓN

Ctra. Rueda, s/n
47491 La Seca (Valladolid)
☎: +34 983 816 325
Fax: +34 983 816 326
www.prediodevascarlon.com
vascarlon@prediodevascarlon.com

Atelier Verdejo 2013 B
verdejo
88
Colour: bright straw. Nose: dried herbs, ripe fruit, floral. Palate: fine bitter notes, powerful, flavourful, long.

Tardevienes 2013 B
verdejo, viura
86
Colour: bright straw. Nose: medium intensity, fragrant herbs, fresh fruit. Palate: correct, easy to drink.

RODRÍGUEZ SANZO

Manuel Azaña, 9
47014 (Valladolid)
☎: +34 983 150 150
Fax: +34 983 150 151
www.rodriguezsanzo.com
comunicacion@valsanzo.com

Dados Verdejo 2012 B
100% verdejo
90
Colour: bright yellow. Nose: powerfull, ripe fruit, sweet spices, creamy oak, balsamic herbs. Palate: rich, flavourful, fresh, good acidity.

Viña Sanzo sobre Lías 2012 B
100% verdejo
92
Colour: bright straw. Nose: white flowers, fresh fruit, expressive, fine lees, dried herbs. Palate: flavourful, fruity, good acidity, balanced.

Viña Sanzo Verdejo Viñas Viejas 2013 B
100% verdejo
88
Colour: bright straw. Nose: fresh, fresh fruit, white flowers. Palate: flavourful, fruity, good acidity, thin.

SOTO Y MANRIQUE V.O.

Arandano, 14
47008 Valladolid (Valladolid)
☎: +34 626 290 408
www.sotoymanriquevo.com
info@sotoymanriquevo.com

Tinita Verdejo 2013 B
verdejo
90
Colour: bright straw. Nose: white flowers, fragrant herbs, fruit expression. Palate: fresh, fruity, flavourful, elegant.

SPANISH STORY

Espronceda, 27 1ºD
28003 Madrid (Madrid)
☎: +34 915 356 184
Fax: +34 915 363 796
paul@globalwinefood.com

Spanish Story Verdejo 2013 B
verdejo
86
Colour: bright straw. Nose: white flowers, fragrant herbs, fruit expression. Palate: fresh, fruity, flavourful.

TERROIR 34

Square Dessy, 18 - 1330 RIX
01330 RIX Bruxelles (Bélgica)
☎: +34 606 941 434
www.terroir34.com
info@terroir34.com

Terroir 34 "Seduction from Cool Stones" 2013 B
100% verdejo

89 🍷

Colour: bright straw. Nose: expressive, fruit expression, white flowers, tropical fruit. Palate: correct, fine bitter notes, good acidity.

THE GRAND WINES

Ramón y Cajal 7, 1ºA
01007 Vitoria (Alava)
☎: +34 945 158 282
Fax: +34 945 158 283
www.thegrandwines.com
araex@araex.com

Rolland Galarreta 2013 B
100% verdejo

91

Colour: bright straw. Nose: fruit expression, floral, wild herbs, spicy. Palate: powerful, flavourful, balsamic, fine bitter notes.

UNESDI DISTRIBUCIONES

Aurora, 11
11500 El Puerto de Santa María (Cádiz)
☎: +34 956 541 329
www.unesdi.com
info@unesdi.com

Palomo Cojo 2013 B
100% verdejo

88

Colour: pale. Nose: fragrant herbs, medium intensity, candied fruit, citrus fruit. Palate: fine bitter notes, correct.

UVAS FELICES

Agullers, 7
08003 Barcelona (Barcelona)
☎: +34 902 327 777
www.vilaviniteca.es

El Perro Verde 2013 B

89

Colour: bright straw. Nose: white flowers, fragrant herbs, fruit expression. Palate: fresh, fruity, flavourful, elegant.

Fenomenal 2013 B

88

Colour: bright straw. Nose: fresh, fresh fruit, white flowers. Palate: flavourful, fruity, good acidity, balanced.

VALDECUEVAS

Ctra. Rueda-Nava del Rey, km 2
47490 Rueda (Valladolid)
☎: +34 983 034 356
Fax: +34 983 034 356
www.valdecuevas.es
bodega@valdecuevas.es

Diwine Verdejo Frizzante 2013 B
verdejo

84

Flor Innata Verdejo 2013 B
100% verdejo

85

Valdecuevas Verdejo 2013 B
100% verdejo

85

VEGA DEL PAS

Ctra. CL-602, Kilómetro 48
47465 Villaverde de Medina (Valladolid)
☎: +34 983 831 884
Fax: +34 983 831 857
www.vegadelpas.com
comunicacion@vegadelpas.com

Vega del Pas Rueda 2013 B

87

Colour: bright straw. Nose: fresh, fresh fruit, white flowers. Palate: flavourful, fruity, good acidity, balanced.

Vega del Pas Rueda Verdejo 2013 B

85

Vega del Pas Sauvignon Blanc 2013 B
100% sauvignon blanc

85

Vega del Pas Verdejo 2013 B
100% verdejo

86

Colour: bright straw. Nose: fresh, fresh fruit, white flowers. Palate: flavourful, fruity, good acidity, thin.

VEGA DEO

Ctra. CL-602, Kilómetro 48
47465 Villaverde de Medina (Valladolid)
☎: +34 983 83 18 84
Fax: +34 983 83 18 57
www.vinosvegadeo.com
comunicacion@vinosvegadeo.com

Vega Deo Rueda 2013 B

86

Colour: bright straw. Nose: fresh fruit, floral, wild herbs. Palate: correct, easy to drink, fine bitter notes.

Vega Deo Rueda Verdejo 2013 B
87
Colour: bright straw. Nose: white flowers, fragrant herbs, fruit expression. Palate: fresh, fruity, flavourful.

Vega Deo Sauvignon Blanc 2013 B
100% sauvignon blanc
87
Colour: bright straw. Nose: fresh, fresh fruit, white flowers, medium intensity. Palate: flavourful, fruity, good acidity, balanced.

Vega Deo Verdejo 2013 B
100% verdejo
85

VICENTE SANZ
Las Flores, 5 Bajo
47240 Valdestillas (Valladolid)
☎: +34 983 551 197
Fax: +34 983 551 197
www.bodegasvicentesanz.com
bodega@bodegasvicentesanz.com

Vicaral Rueda Verdejo 2013 B
100% verdejo
83

VINOS SANZ
Ctra. Madrid - La Coruña, Km. 170,5
47490 Rueda (Valladolid)
☎: +34 983 868 100
Fax: +34 983 868 117
www.vinossanz.com
vinossanz@vinossanz.com

Finca La Colina Sauvignon Blanc 2013 B
100% sauvignon blanc
91
Colour: bright straw. Nose: white flowers, fragrant herbs, fruit expression. Palate: fresh, fruity, flavourful, fine bitter notes. Personality.

Finca La Colina Verdejo Cien x Cien 2013 B
100% verdejo
91
Colour: bright straw. Nose: white flowers, fine lees, dried herbs, mineral, ripe fruit. Palate: flavourful, fruity, good acidity, balanced, round.

Sanz Clásico 2013 B
87
Colour: bright straw. Nose: fresh, wild herbs, dry stone. Palate: correct, good acidity, fine bitter notes.

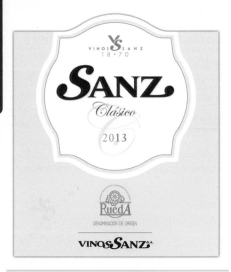

Sanz Sauvignon Blanc 2013 B
100% sauvignon blanc
87
Colour: bright straw. Nose: medium intensity, fresh fruit, fragrant herbs. Palate: fresh, correct, fine bitter notes, light-bodied.

Sanz Verdejo 2013 B
100% verdejo
90
Colour: bright straw. Nose: white flowers, fragrant herbs, fruit expression, mineral. Palate: fresh, fruity, flavourful, balanced, elegant.

VINOS TERRIBLES
Avda. Menendez Pelayo 13 B
28009 (Madrid)
☎: +34 914 092 131
www.latintoreriavinoteca.com
esther@vinosterribles.com

Terrible 2013 B
100% verdejo
88
Colour: bright straw. Nose: fresh, fresh fruit, expressive, citrus fruit. Palate: flavourful, fruity, good acidity, balanced.

VIÑA ARNAIZ
Ctra. N-122, km. 281
09463 Haza (Burgos)
☎: +34 947 536 227
Fax: +34 947 536 216
www.garciacarrion.es
atcliente@jgc.es

Viña Arnaiz 2013 B
sauvignon blanc
84

VIÑEDO VALLELADO SÁNCHEZ
Larga, 33
47238 Alcazarén (Valladolid)
☎: +34 679 797 002
www.verdejocampogrande.com
info@verdejocampogrande.com

Campo Grande 2013 B
verdejo
86
Colour: bright yellow. Nose: ripe fruit, floral, wild herbs. Palate: flavourful, correct, fine bitter notes.

VIÑEDOS DE NIEVA
Camino Real, s/n
40447 Nieva (Segovia)
☎: +34 921 504 628
Fax: +34 921 595 409
www.vinedosdenieva.com
info@vinedosdenieva.com

Blanco Nieva Pie Franco 2010 BFB
100% verdejo
91
Colour: bright golden. Nose: ripe fruit, dry nuts, powerfull, toasty, aged wood nuances. Palate: flavourful, fruity, spicy, toasty, long.

Blanco Nieva Pie Franco 2013 B
100% verdejo
93
Colour: bright straw. Nose: white flowers, fresh fruit, expressive, fine lees, dried herbs. Palate: flavourful, fruity, good acidity, balanced.

Blanco Nieva Sauvignon 2013 B
100% sauvignon blanc
88
Colour: bright straw. Nose: fresh, fresh fruit, white flowers. Palate: flavourful, fruity, good acidity, balanced.

Blanco Nieva Verdejo 2013 B
100% verdejo
91
Colour: bright straw. Nose: fresh, fresh fruit, white flowers, expressive. Palate: flavourful, fruity, good acidity, balanced.

Los Navales Verdejo 2013 B
100% verdejo

88

Colour: bright straw. Nose: fresh, white flowers, tropical fruit. Palate: flavourful, fruity, good acidity, balanced.

VIÑEDOS SINGULARES
Cuzco, 26 - 28, Nave 8
08030 (Barcelona)
☎: +34 934 807 041
Fax: +34 934 807 076
www.vinedossingulares.com
info@vinedossingulares.com

Afortunado 2013 B
verdejo

88

Colour: bright straw. Nose: fresh, fresh fruit, white flowers, expressive. Palate: flavourful, fruity, good acidity, balanced.

DO. SOMONTANO

CONSEJO REGULADOR
Avda. de la Merced, 64
22300 Barbastro (Huesca)
☎ :+34 974 313 031 - Fax: +34 974 315 132
@: erio@dosomontano.com
www.dosomontano.com

LOCATION:
In the province of Huesca, around the town of Barbastro. The region comprises 43 municipal districts, mainly centred round the region of Somontano and the rest of the neighbouring regions of Ribagorza and Monegros.

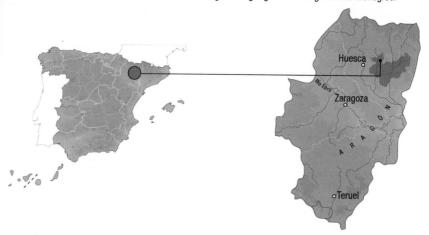

GRAPE VARIETIES:
White: Macabeo, Garnacha Blanca, Alcañón, Chardonnay, Riesling, Sauvignon Blanc and Gewürztraminer.
Red: Tempranillo, Garnacha Tinta, Cabernet Sauvignon, Merlot, Moristel, Parraleta, Pinot Noir and Syrah.

FIGURES:
Vineyard surface: 4,304 – Wine-Growers: 430 – Wineries: 31 – 2013 Harvest rating: Very Good – Production 13: 13,120,700 litres – Market percentages: 68.34% domestic - 31.66% export.

SOIL:
The soil is mainly brownish limestone, not very fertile, with a good level of limestone and good permeability.

CLIMATE:
Characterised by cold winters and hot summers, with sharp contrasts in temperature at the end of spring and autumn. The average annual rainfall is 500 mm, although the rains are scarcer in the south and east

VINTAGE RATING

PEÑINGUIDE

2009	2010	2011	2012	2013
VERY GOOD	VERY GOOD	VERY GOOD	VERY GOOD	VERY GOOD

ALIANZA DE GARAPITEROS

Plaza España, 6 Planta 1ª
50001 (Zaragoza)
☎: +34 976 094 033
Fax: +34 976 094 033
www.alianzadegarapiteros.es
info@alianzadegarapiteros.es

Glárima 2012 T
88
Colour: very deep cherry, garnet rim. Nose: powerfull, ripe fruit, roasted coffee, dark chocolate. Palate: powerful, toasty, roasted-coffee aftertaste.

Glárima 2013 B
91
Colour: bright straw. Nose: fresh, fresh fruit, white flowers, expressive. Palate: flavourful, fruity, good acidity, balanced.

BAL D'ISABENA BODEGAS

Ctra. A-1605, Km. 11,2
22587 Laguarres (Huesca)
☎: +34 605 785 178
Fax: +34 974 310 151
www.baldisabena.com
info@baldisabena.com

Cojón de Gato 2013 B
gewürztraminer, chardonnay
87
Colour: yellow. Nose: fresh, fragrant herbs, citrus fruit, fresh fruit, faded flowers. Palate: fruity, easy to drink, good acidity.

Cojón de Gato 2013 T Roble
merlot, syrah, otras
89
Colour: cherry, purple rim. Nose: red berry notes, fruit preserve, balsamic herbs, spicy, creamy oak. Palate: balanced, good acidity, flavourful, balsamic.

Garnacha de Bal d'Isabena 2013 T
garnacha
88
Colour: bright cherry. Nose: ripe fruit, sweet spices, creamy oak, expressive. Palate: flavourful, fruity, toasty, round tannins.

Ixeia 2013 RD
merlot, garnacha
87
Colour: rose, bright. Nose: medium intensity, red berry notes, balanced. Palate: fruity, flavourful, long.

Ixeia 2013 B
chardonnay
87
Colour: bright yellow. Nose: candied fruit, floral, fragrant herbs. Palate: fresh, fruity, flavourful.

Ixeia 2013 T
cabernet sauvignon, merlot, tempranillo
85

Moristel de Bal d'Isabena 2013 T
moristel
84

Reis d'Isabena 2012 T
merlot, cabernet sauvignon
90
Colour: cherry, garnet rim. Nose: ripe fruit, spicy, creamy oak, toasty, complex, mineral. Palate: powerful, flavourful, toasty, round tannins, balanced.

BATAN DE SALAS DE BEROZ

Pol. Ind. Valle del Cinca, Calle B, 4
22300 Barbastro (Huesca)
☎: +34 974 316 217
Fax: +34 974 310 973
www.deberoz.es
bodega@deberoz.es

Batán de Salas Chardonnay 2013 B
chardonnay
87
Colour: bright straw. Nose: fresh, fresh fruit, white flowers, expressive. Palate: flavourful, fruity, good acidity, balanced.

Batán de Salas Syrah 2013 T
100% syrah
90
Colour: deep cherry, purple rim. Nose: expressive, red berry notes, fresh fruit, spicy. Palate: flavourful, good structure, toasty.

De Beroz Crianza Especial 2008 T
cabernet sauvignon, merlot, syrah
89
Colour: cherry, garnet rim. Nose: ripe fruit, spicy, balsamic herbs, fine reductive notes. Palate: flavourful, spicy, ripe fruit, long.

De Beroz Esencia de Gewürztraminer 2013 B
gewürztraminer
89
Colour: bright straw. Nose: white flowers, fragrant herbs, tropical fruit. Palate: fresh, fruity, flavourful, balanced, elegant.

De Beroz Esencia de Tintos 2013 RD
merlot, syrah
87
Colour: light cherry. Nose: fragrant herbs, candied fruit, red berry notes. Palate: fine bitter notes, ripe fruit.

De Beroz Nuestro Roble 2012 T
tempranillo, merlot

87

Colour: bright cherry. Nose: sweet spices, creamy oak, fruit preserve. Palate: flavourful, fruity, toasty, sweet tannins.

BLECUA
Ctra. de Naval, Km. 3,7
22300 Barbastro (Huesca)
☎: +34 974 302 216
Fax: +34 974 302 098
www.bodegablecua.com
marketing@vinasdelvero.es

Blecua 2004 TR
cabernet sauvignon, merlot, tempranillo, garnacha

95

Colour: ruby red. Nose: ripe fruit, balsamic herbs, mineral, spicy, creamy oak, fine reductive notes, expressive. Palate: fine tannins, flavourful, spicy, long, balanced, elegant.

Blecua 2008 TR
merlot, tempranillo, syrah, cabernet sauvignon

94

Colour: cherry, garnet rim. Nose: ripe fruit, spicy, creamy oak, toasty, complex, dark chocolate, earthy notes. Palate: powerful, flavourful, toasty, round tannins.

BODEGA ALDAHARA
Ctra. Barbastro, 10
22423 Estadilla (Huesca)
☎: +34 620 309 217
www.valdalferche.com
bodega@aldahara.es

Aldahara 2010 TC
cabernet sauvignon, merlot, syrah

83

Aldahara 2013 B
100% chardonnay

84

Aldahara 2013 RD
100% merlot

85

Aldahara 2013 T
tempranillo, merlot, syrah

87

Colour: cherry, purple rim. Nose: fresh fruit, red berry notes, floral. Palate: flavourful, fruity, good acidity.

Aldahara Rasé 2011 T Roble
100% syrah

86

Colour: cherry, garnet rim. Nose: ripe fruit, dried herbs. Palate: spicy, easy to drink, good finish.

Aldahara Rasé 2013 B
100% chardonnay

87

Colour: bright straw. Nose: white flowers, fragrant herbs, tropical fruit. Palate: fresh, fruity, flavourful.

Val d'Alferche Chardonnay 2013 B
100% chardonnay

84

Val d'Alferche Crianza 2010 TC

82

Val d'Alferche Syrah 2011 T
100% syrah

85

BODEGA OTTO BESTUÉ
Ctra. A-138, Km. 0,5
22312 Enate (Huesca)
☎: +34 974 305 157
Fax: +34 974 305 157
www.bodega-ottobestue.com
info@bodega-ottobestue.com

Otto Bestué Cabernet Sauvignon Tempranillo 2013 RD

84

Otto Bestué Chardonnay 2013 B
chardonnay

84

Otto Bestué Finca Rableros 2012 T

88

Colour: cherry, garnet rim. Nose: ripe fruit, wild herbs, spicy, creamy oak. Palate: balanced, flavourful, long, balsamic.

Otto Bestué Finca Santa Sabina 2012 TC
cabernet sauvignon, tempranillo

87

Colour: bright cherry. Nose: ripe fruit, sweet spices, creamy oak, balsamic herbs. Palate: fruity, flavourful, toasty.

BODEGA PIRINEOS
Ctra. Barbastro - Naval, Km. 3,5
22300 Barbastro (Huesca)
☎: +34 974 311 289
Fax: +34 974 306 688
www.bodegapirineos.com
info@bodegapirineos.com

Alquézar de Aguja 2013 RD
tempranillo, cabernet sauvignon

86

Colour: light cherry, bright. Nose: ripe fruit, red berry notes, floral. Palate: powerful, fruity, fresh, correct.

Montesierra 2013 B
macabeo, chardonnay, gewürztraminer
86
Colour: bright straw. Nose: fresh fruit, white flowers, tropical fruit. Palate: flavourful, fruity, good acidity.

Montesierra 2013 RD
tempranillo, cabernet sauvignon, merlot
88
Colour: rose, purple rim. Nose: powerfull, ripe fruit, red berry notes, floral, expressive. Palate: powerful, fruity, fresh, easy to drink.

Pirineos 2013 RD
merlot, cabernet sauvignon
88
Colour: light cherry, bright. Nose: ripe fruit, red berry notes, floral, expressive. Palate: fruity, fresh, balanced.

Pirineos 2013 T
88
Colour: cherry, purple rim. Nose: red berry notes, raspberry, fruit expression, fragrant herbs, sweet spices. Palate: flavourful, light-bodied, good acidity, fresh, fruity.

Pirineos Mesache 2013 B
chardonnay, gewürztraminer, sauvignon blanc
89
Colour: bright straw. Nose: white flowers, fragrant herbs, fruit expression. Palate: fresh, fruity, flavourful, elegant.

Señorío de Lazán 2008 TR
tempranillo, cabernet sauvignon, moristel
89
Colour: cherry, garnet rim. Nose: ripe fruit, spicy, creamy oak, toasty, tobacco, fine reductive notes. Palate: powerful, flavourful, toasty, round tannins.

Señorío de Lazán 2010 TC
tempranillo, cabernet sauvignon, merlot
86
Colour: bright cherry. Nose: ripe fruit, sweet spices, creamy oak, medium intensity. Palate: fruity, flavourful, toasty.

BODEGAS ABINASA
Ctra. N 240, Km. 180
22124 Lascellas (Huesca)
☎: +34 974 319 156
Fax: +34 974 319 156
www.bodegasabinasa.com
info@bodegasabinasa.com

Ana 2010 TC
cabernet sauvignon, merlot
85

Ana 2011 T Roble
merlot, cabernet sauvignon
86
Colour: very deep cherry, garnet rim. Nose: sweet spices, creamy oak, ripe fruit. Palate: flavourful, balsamic.

Ana 2013 RD
merlot
85

Ana Gewürztraminer 2013 B
gewürztraminer
87
Colour: bright straw. Nose: fresh, fresh fruit, white flowers. Palate: flavourful, fruity, good acidity, balanced.

BODEGAS BALLABRIGA
Ctra. de Cregenzán, Km. 3
22300 Barbastro (Huesca)
☎: +34 974 310 216
Fax: +34 974 306 163
www.bodegasballabriga.com
info@bodegasballabriga.com

Auctor Selección Finca Rosellas 2008 T
cabernet sauvignon, merlot, garnacha
88
Colour: pale ruby, brick rim edge. Nose: elegant, spicy, fine reductive notes, wet leather, aged wood nuances, fruit liqueur notes. Palate: spicy, fine tannins, long.

Ballabriga Nunc 2008 TC
merlot, syrah, garnacha, parraleta
92
Colour: cherry, garnet rim. Nose: red berry notes, ripe fruit, spicy, creamy oak, toasty, complex, earthy notes. Palate: powerful, flavourful, toasty, round tannins.

Ballabriga Nunc 2013 B
gewürztraminer, chardonnay, alcañon
86
Colour: bright straw. Nose: medium intensity, fresh fruit, dried flowers. Palate: easy to drink, good finish.

Ballabriga Parraleta 2013 T
100% parraleta
87
Colour: cherry, purple rim. Nose: expressive, fresh fruit, red berry notes, floral, fragrant herbs. Palate: flavourful, fruity, good acidity.

Ballabriga Parraleta Emoción 2008 TC
100% parraleta
91
Colour: cherry, garnet rim. Nose: balanced, complex, ripe fruit, spicy, earthy notes, wild herbs. Palate: good structure, flavourful, round tannins.

Petret 2011 TC
cabernet sauvignon, merlot
89
Colour: bright cherry. Nose: balanced, ripe fruit, wild herbs, spicy. Palate: fruity, good structure, round tannins.

Petret 2013 B
chardonnay, gewürztraminer

85

Petret 2013 RD
cabernet sauvignon, garnacha

89

Colour: light cherry. Nose: elegant, candied fruit, dried flowers, fragrant herbs, red berry notes. Palate: light-bodied, flavourful, good acidity, long.

Señor José 2013 T
100% syrah

88

Colour: cherry, purple rim. Nose: red berry notes, raspberry, floral, expressive. Palate: fresh, fruity, flavourful, easy to drink.

BODEGAS ESTADA
Ctra. A-1232, Km. 6,4
22313 Castillazuelo (Huesca)
☎: +34 628 430 823
www.bodegasestada.com
info@bodegasestada.com

Estada 2012 T Roble
cabernet sauvignon, syrah, tempranillo, garnacha

85

Estada 2020 Vicious 2010 T
cabernet sauvignon, syrah, garnacha, tempranillo

90

Colour: cherry, garnet rim. Nose: ripe fruit, wild herbs, earthy notes, spicy, creamy oak. Palate: balanced, flavourful, long, balsamic.

Estada San Carbás 2013 B
chardonnay

85

Estata 2020 Vicious 2013 BFB
chardonnay

89

Colour: bright yellow. Nose: ripe fruit, sweet spices, creamy oak, fragrant herbs. Palate: rich, smoky aftertaste, flavourful, fresh.

Giménez del Tau 2008 TR
cabernet sauvignon, syrah, tempranillo, garnacha

86

Colour: cherry, garnet rim. Nose: ripe fruit, wild herbs, earthy notes, spicy, creamy oak. Palate: balanced, flavourful, long, balsamic.

Giménez del Tau 2012 T Roble
syrah, tempranillo, cabernet sauvignon, garnacha

86

Colour: bright cherry. Nose: ripe fruit, sweet spices, creamy oak. Palate: flavourful, fruity, toasty.

Giménez del Tau Autor 2007 T
garnacha, tempranillo, cabernet sauvignon

87

Colour: cherry, garnet rim. Nose: ripe fruit, spicy, creamy oak, toasty, fine reductive notes. Palate: powerful, flavourful, toasty.

BODEGAS FÁBREGAS
Cerler, s/n
22300 Barbastro (Huesca)
☎: +34 974 310 498
www.bodegasfabregas.com
info@bodegasfabregas.com

Fábregas Puro Syrah 2008 TC
syrah

85

Mingua 2009 TC
cabernet sauvignon, merlot

86

Colour: cherry, garnet rim. Nose: ripe fruit, spicy, creamy oak, toasty, fine reductive notes. Palate: powerful, flavourful, toasty.

Mingua 2013 B
chardonnay, garnacha blanca

87

Colour: bright straw. Nose: fresh, white flowers. Palate: flavourful, fruity, good acidity, balanced.

Mingua 2013 RD
syrah, garnacha

85

Mingua 2013 T
garnacha, cabernet sauvignon

87

Colour: cherry, purple rim. Nose: expressive, fresh fruit, red berry notes, floral. Palate: flavourful, fruity, good acidity, easy to drink.

Vega Ferrera 2008 TC
cabernet sauvignon, merlot, syrah

84

BODEGAS LASIERRA - BESPEN
Baja, 12
22133 Bespén (Huesca)
☎: +34 652 791 187
Fax: +34 974 260 365
www.bodegaslasierra.es
info@bodegaslasierra.es

Bespén 2010 TC
cabernet sauvignon

86

Colour: dark-red cherry, garnet rim. Nose: ripe fruit, powerfull, dried herbs. Palate: flavourful, correct, balsamic.

Bespén 2013 RD
cabernet sauvignon
85

Bespén 2013 T
tempranillo, merlot
86
Colour: cherry, purple rim. Nose: floral, red berry notes, fruit liqueur notes, sweet spices. Palate: flavourful, fruity, good acidity.

Bespén Chardonnay Macabeo 2013 B
chardonnay, macabeo
86
Colour: bright straw. Nose: white flowers, medium intensity, fresh fruit, balanced. Palate: fruity, fresh, good acidity.

Bespén Vendimia Seleccionada Merlot 2011 T
merlot
86
Colour: cherry, garnet rim. Nose: ripe fruit, spicy, creamy oak, toasty, wild herbs. Palate: powerful, flavourful, toasty.

Bespén Vendimia Seleccionada Syrah 2013 T
syrah
87
Colour: cherry, purple rim. Nose: red berry notes, floral, balanced. Palate: fruity, good acidity, round tannins.

BODEGAS LAUS
Ctra. N-240, km 154,8
22300 Barbastro (Huesca)
☎: +34 974 269 708
Fax: +34 974 269 715
www.bodegaslaus.com
info@bodegaslaus.com

Laus 2009 TC
cabernet sauvignon, merlot
88
Colour: deep cherry, garnet rim. Nose: ripe fruit, wild herbs, spicy. Palate: flavourful, round tannins, balanced.

Laus Flor de Chardonnay 2013 B
chardonnay
91
Colour: yellow, pale. Nose: ripe fruit, white flowers, balanced, elegant. Palate: fruity, rich, full, flavourful.

Laus Flor de Gewürztraminer 2013 B
gewürztraminer
93
Colour: bright straw. Nose: white flowers, fragrant herbs, fruit expression, tropical fruit, expressive, elegant. Palate: balanced, powerful, flavourful, rich, long, elegant.

Laus Flor de Merlot 2013 RD
merlot, cabernet sauvignon
89
Colour: rose, purple rim. Nose: powerfull, ripe fruit, red berry notes, floral, expressive. Palate: powerful, fruity, fresh, balanced.

BODEGAS MELER
Ctra. N-240, km. 154,4 Partida Las Almunietas
22300 (Huesca)
☎: +34 679 954 988
Fax: +34 974 269 907
www.bodegasmeler.com
info@bodegasmeler.com

Meler 95 sobre Aljez Chardonnay 2010 B
chardonnay
90
Colour: bright yellow. Nose: powerfull, ripe fruit, sweet spices, creamy oak, fragrant herbs. Palate: rich, smoky aftertaste, flavourful, fresh, good acidity.

Meler Cabernet 2013 RD
cabernet sauvignon
86
Colour: rose, purple rim. Nose: powerfull, ripe fruit, red berry notes, floral, expressive. Palate: powerful, fruity, fresh.

Meler Chardonnay Edición Limitada 2013 B
chardonnay
88
Colour: bright yellow. Nose: ripe fruit, floral, balanced. Palate: flavourful, fruity, long.

Meler Syrah Edición Limitada 2013 T
syrah
87
Colour: cherry, purple rim. Nose: medium intensity, fresh fruit, red berry notes. Palate: fruity, good acidity, balanced.

Muac de Meler 2011 T
87
Colour: cherry, garnet rim. Nose: ripe fruit, spicy, creamy oak, toasty. Palate: powerful, flavourful, toasty.

BODEGAS MONTE ODINA
Monte Odina, s/n
22415 Ilche (Huesca)
☎: +34 974 343 480
Fax: +34 974 942 750
www.monteodina.com
bodega@monteodina.com

Monte Odina 2009 TR
88
Colour: cherry, garnet rim. Nose: red berry notes, ripe fruit, creamy oak, balsamic herbs, fine reductive notes. Palate: powerful, flavourful, toasty, round tannins.

Monte Odina 2013 RD
cabernet sauvignon, merlot

84

Monte Odina Cabernet Sauvignon 2010 T
100% cabernet sauvignon

88

Colour: cherry, garnet rim. Nose: ripe fruit, wild herbs, earthy notes, spicy, creamy oak. Palate: balanced, flavourful, long, balsamic.

Monte Odina Garnacha Tinta 2013 T
100% garnacha

88

Colour: bright cherry, purple rim. Nose: red berry notes, sweet spices, scrubland, violets. Palate: balanced, fruity aftestaste.

Monte Odina Merlot Cabernet 2013 T

84

Victoria de Monte Odina 2013 B
gewürztraminer

87

Colour: bright straw. Nose: white flowers, fruit expression. Palate: fresh, fruity, flavourful, balanced, elegant.

BODEGAS OBERGO
Ctra. La Puebla, Km. 0,6
22439 Ubiergo (Huesca)
☎: +34 669 357 866
www.obergo.es
bodegasobergo@obergo.es

Obergo "Finca la Mata" 2012 T
merlot, cabernet sauvignon, garnacha

90

Colour: very deep cherry, garnet rim. Nose: complex, powerfull, spicy, ripe fruit, dried herbs. Palate: good structure, long.

Obergo Caramelos 2013 T
garnacha

89

Colour: bright cherry. Nose: ripe fruit, sweet spices, creamy oak, wild herbs, mineral. Palate: flavourful, fruity, toasty.

Obergo Expression 2013 BFB
chardonnay, sauvignon blanc

90

Colour: bright yellow. Nose: powerfull, ripe fruit, sweet spices, creamy oak, fragrant herbs. Palate: rich, smoky aftertaste, flavourful, fresh.

Obergo Merlot 2011 T
merlot

92

Colour: cherry, garnet rim. Nose: ripe fruit, wild herbs, earthy notes, spicy, creamy oak. Palate: balanced, flavourful, long, balsamic.

Obergo Varietales 2011 T
100% cabernet sauvignon

91

Colour: cherry, garnet rim. Nose: ripe fruit, wild herbs, earthy notes, spicy, creamy oak. Palate: balanced, flavourful, long, balsamic.

Obergo Viña Antiqua 2011 T
garnacha

90

Colour: bright cherry. Nose: ripe fruit, wild herbs, earthy notes, spicy, creamy oak. Palate: balanced, flavourful, long, balsamic.

Sueños by Obergo 2013 B
chardonnay

89

Colour: bright straw. Nose: white flowers, fragrant herbs, fruit expression. Palate: fresh, fruity, flavourful, balanced, elegant.

BODEGAS OSCA
La Iglesia, 1
22124 Ponzano (Huesca)
☎: +34 974 319 017
Fax: +34 974 319 175
www.bodegasosca.com
bodega@bodegasosca.com

Mascún Garnacha 2010 T
100% garnacha tintorera

84

Mascún Garnacha 2013 RD
100% garnacha

86

Colour: light cherry. Nose: medium intensity, fresh, wild herbs, dried herbs, fresh fruit. Palate: flavourful, fine bitter notes, good acidity.

Mascún Garnacha Blanca 2013 B
garnacha blanca

85

Mascun Gewurztraminer 2013 B
gewürztraminer

85

Mascún Gran Reserva de la Familia 2006 T
merlot, cabernet sauvignon, syrah, garnacha

88

Colour: ruby red. Nose: elegant, spicy, fine reductive notes, wet leather, aged wood nuances, balsamic herbs. Palate: spicy, fine tannins, elegant, long.

Osca 2010 TC
tempranillo, merlot

87

Colour: bright cherry. Nose: ripe fruit, sweet spices, creamy oak, balsamic herbs. Palate: fruity, flavourful, toasty.

Osca 2013 RD
tempranillo, cabernet sauvignon, moristel
86
Colour: light cherry, bright. Nose: rose petals, red berry notes, medium intensity. Palate: fresh, easy to drink, good finish.

Osca 2013 B
macabeo, garnacha blanca
84

Osca 2013 T
tempranillo, cabernet sauvignon
85

Osca Colección 2009 TR
merlot
87
Colour: cherry, garnet rim. Nose: ripe fruit, spicy, creamy oak, toasty, balsamic herbs. Palate: powerful, flavourful, toasty, round tannins.

Osca Gran Eroles 2008 TR
cabernet sauvignon
87
Colour: bright cherry. Nose: ripe fruit, medium intensity, toasty. Palate: fruity, toasty, good structure, round tannins.

Osca Moristel 2009 TR
moristel
86
Colour: deep cherry. Nose: wild herbs, earthy notes, spicy, creamy oak, ripe fruit. Palate: flavourful, long, balsamic, spicy.

Osca Syrah 2010 TR
syrah
88
Colour: bright cherry. Nose: ripe fruit, sweet spices, creamy oak, medium intensity. Palate: fruity, flavourful, toasty.

BODEGAS RASO HUETE
Joaquín Costa, 23
22423 Estadilla (Huesca)
☎: +34 974 305 357
Fax: +34 974 305 357
www.bodegasrasohuete.com
info@bodegasrasohuete.com

Arnazas 2004 TR
cabernet sauvignon, merlot
82

Arnazas Cabernet-Merlot 2011 TC
cabernet sauvignon, merlot
86
Colour: cherry, garnet rim. Nose: ripe fruit, wild herbs, spicy, creamy oak. Palate: balanced, flavourful, balsamic.

Arnazas Merlot 2007 T Roble
merlot
86
Colour: deep cherry, orangey edge. Nose: wet leather, fruit liqueur notes, dried herbs. Palate: spicy, long, round tannins.

Arnazas Selección 2008 T Roble
syrah, tempranillo, merlot
82

Partida Arnazas 2013 RD
cabernet sauvignon
87
Colour: rose, purple rim. Nose: powerfull, ripe fruit, red berry notes, floral, expressive. Palate: powerful, fruity, fresh.

Partida Arnazas Cabernet-Merlot 2012 T
cabernet sauvignon, merlot
85

BODEGAS SERS
Pza. Mayor, 7
22417 Cofita (Huesca)
☎: +34 652 979 718
www.bodegassers.es
info@bodegassers.es

Sèrs 2007 TGR
cabernet sauvignon, syrah, merlot
93
Colour: cherry, garnet rim. Nose: balanced, complex, ripe fruit, spicy, tobacco, smoky, dried herbs. Palate: good structure, flavourful, round tannins.

Sèrs 2010 TR
cabernet sauvignon, merlot, syrah
90
Colour: cherry, garnet rim. Nose: wild herbs, spicy, creamy oak. Palate: balanced, flavourful, long, ripe fruit.

Sèrs Blanqué 2013 BFB
100% chardonnay
88
Colour: bright straw. Nose: white flowers, fresh fruit, expressive, dried herbs. Palate: flavourful, fruity, good acidity, balanced.

Sèrs Primer 2013 T
100% syrah
87
Colour: cherry, purple rim. Nose: red berry notes, raspberry, fruit liqueur notes, fragrant herbs, spicy. Palate: flavourful, fresh, fruity.

Sèrs Singular 2012 T Barrica
parraleta
90
Colour: cherry, garnet rim. Nose: balanced, spicy, toasty, ripe fruit. Palate: flavourful, ripe fruit, round tannins, long.

Sèrs Temple 2011 TC
cabernet sauvignon, merlot

90

Colour: deep cherry, garnet rim. Nose: medium intensity, spicy, wild herbs, ripe fruit, tobacco. Palate: flavourful, good structure.

BODEGAS SIERRA DE GUARA

Fray Luis Urbano, 27
50002 Lascellas (Zaragoza)
☎: +34 976 461 056
Fax: +34 976 461 558
www.bodegassierradeguara.es
idrias@bodegassierradeguara.es

Idrias Cabernet Sauvignon 2013 T
100% cabernet sauvignon

87

Colour: cherry, garnet rim. Nose: powerfull, scrubland, spicy. Palate: flavourful, long, balsamic.

Idrias Sevil 2008 T

88

Colour: cherry, garnet rim. Nose: ripe fruit, spicy, creamy oak, toasty. Palate: powerful, flavourful, toasty, balanced.

BODEGAS VILLA D'ORTA

Ctra. Alquezar s/n
22313 Huerta de Vero (Huesca)
☎: +34 695 991 967
Fax: +34 974 302 072
www.villadorta.com
villadorta@hotmail.com

Villa D'Orta Bio-lógico 2013 T
cabernet sauvignon, merlot

86

Colour: cherry, garnet rim. Nose: ripe fruit, wild herbs. Palate: balanced, flavourful, long, balsamic.

BODEGAS Y VIÑEDOS OLVENA

Paraje El Ariño, Ctra. N-123 Km. 5
22300 Barbastro (Huesca)
☎: +34 974 308 481
Fax: +34 974 308 482
www.bodegasolvena.com
info@bodegasolvena.com

Olvena 2013 RD
merlot

85

Olvena 2013 T Roble
cabernet sauvignon, tempranillo, merlot

87

Colour: bright cherry. Nose: ripe fruit, sweet spices, creamy oak, expressive. Palate: flavourful, fruity, toasty, balanced.

Olvena Chardonnay 2013 B
chardonnay

89

Colour: bright straw. Nose: fresh, fresh fruit, white flowers, expressive. Palate: flavourful, fruity, good acidity, balanced.

Olvena Chardonnay 2013 BFB
chardonnay

89

Colour: bright yellow. Nose: powerfull, ripe fruit, sweet spices, creamy oak, fragrant herbs. Palate: rich, smoky aftertaste, flavourful, fresh, good acidity.

Olvena Cuatro o Pago de la Libélula 2008 T
tempranillo, merlot, cabernet sauvignon, syrah

89

Colour: cherry, garnet rim. Nose: ripe fruit, wild herbs, earthy notes, spicy, creamy oak. Palate: balanced, flavourful, long, balsamic.

Olvena Gewürztraminer 2013 B
gewürztraminer

84

Olvena Tempranillo 2013 T
tempranillo, merlot

86

Colour: bright cherry, purple rim. Nose: fresh fruit, lactic notes. Palate: easy to drink, good finish, fruity.

CHESA

Autovía A-22, km. 57
22300 Barbastro (Huesca)
☎: +34 649 870 637
Fax: +34 974 313 552
www.bodegaschesa.com
bodegaschesa@hotmail.com

Chesa 2010 TC
merlot, cabernet sauvignon

88

Colour: bright cherry, garnet rim. Nose: powerfull, balsamic herbs, scrubland. Palate: flavourful, balanced, round tannins.

Chesa 2012 T Roble
merlot, cabernet sauvignon

90

Colour: bright cherry, garnet rim. Nose: ripe fruit, sweet spices, violets. Palate: flavourful, fruity, toasty, round tannins, balsamic.

Chesa 2013 RD
cabernet sauvignon

88

Colour: bright cherry. Nose: red berry notes, fresh fruit, balanced, fresh, floral. Palate: good finish, correct, fine bitter notes.

Chesa Gewürztraminer 2013 B
gewürztraminer
85

Chesa Merlot Cabernet 2013 T
merlot, cabernet sauvignon
85

DALCAMP
Pedanía Monte Odina s/n
22415 Monesma de San Juan (Huesca)
☎: +34 973 760 018
Fax: +34 973 760 523
www.castillodemonesma.com
ramondalfo44@gmail.com

Castillo de Monesma 2007 TR
89
Colour: cherry, garnet rim. Nose: ripe fruit, wild herbs, earthy notes, spicy, creamy oak. Palate: balanced, flavourful, long, balsamic.

Castillo de Monesma 2010 TC
cabernet sauvignon
87
Colour: ruby red. Nose: spicy, fine reductive notes, toasty, balsamic herbs. Palate: spicy, long, toasty.

> ## CASTILLO DE MONESMA
> ### CRIANZA
> #### CABERNET SAUVIGNON - MERLOT
> # 2010
> EMBOTELLADO EN LA PROPIEDAD POR DALCAMP S.L.
> 22415 MONESMA DE SAN JUAN - ILCHE - ESPAÑA
> PRODUCT OF SPAIN
> 14%vol   R.E. 40817 - HU   75cl.
> CONTIENE SULFITOS
> ## SOMONTANO
> DENOMINACIÓN DE ORIGEN

Castillo de Monesma 2012 T Roble
83

Castillo de Monesma Gewürztraminer 2013 B
gewürztraminer
86
Colour: bright straw. Nose: white flowers, fragrant herbs, fruit expression. Palate: fresh, fruity, flavourful.

ENATE
Avda. de las Artes, 1
22314 Salas Bajas (Huesca)
☎: +34 974 302 580
Fax: +34 974 300 046
www.enate.es
bodega@enate.es

Enate 2013 RD
cabernet sauvignon
88
Colour: rose, purple rim. Nose: powerfull, ripe fruit, red berry notes, floral, expressive. Palate: powerful, fruity, fresh.

Enate 2006 TR
cabernet sauvignon
93
Colour: deep cherry, garnet rim. Nose: ripe fruit, spicy, creamy oak, toasty, complex, balsamic herbs. Palate: powerful, flavourful, toasty, round tannins.

Enate 2008 TC
tempranillo, cabernet sauvignon
87
Colour: cherry, garnet rim. Nose: ripe fruit, spicy, creamy oak, toasty, wild herbs. Palate: powerful, flavourful, toasty, round tannins.

Enate Cabernet - Cabernet 2010 T
cabernet sauvignon
92
Colour: cherry, garnet rim. Nose: ripe fruit, spicy, creamy oak, toasty, complex, balsamic herbs. Palate: powerful, flavourful, toasty, round tannins, balanced.

ENATE
CABERNET - CABERNET
2010
SOMONTANO
DENOMINACIÓN DE ORIGEN

Enate Cabernet Sauvignon Merlot 2011 T
cabernet sauvignon, merlot

88

Colour: cherry, garnet rim. Nose: ripe fruit, spicy, creamy oak, toasty, scrubland. Palate: powerful, flavourful, toasty, balanced.

Enate Chardonnay 2011 BFB
chardonnay

92

Colour: bright yellow. Nose: powerfull, ripe fruit, sweet spices, creamy oak, fragrant herbs. Palate: rich, smoky aftertaste, flavourful, fresh, good acidity.

ENATE
CHARDONNAY
FERMENTADO EN BARRICA
2011
SOMONTANO
DENOMINACIÓN DE ORIGEN

Enate Chardonnay-234 2013 B
100% chardonnay

90

Colour: yellow. Nose: fresh, fresh fruit, white flowers, expressive. Palate: flavourful, fruity, good acidity, balanced, rich, spicy.

ENATE
CHARDONNAY-234
2013
SOMONTANO
DENOMINACIÓN DE ORIGEN

Enate Gewürztraminer 2013 B
gewürztraminer

91

Colour: bright straw. Nose: fresh fruit, white flowers, varietal. Palate: balanced, easy to drink, fresh, correct, fine bitter notes.

Enate Merlot-Merlot 2010 T
merlot

93

Colour: cherry, garnet rim. Nose: ripe fruit, spicy, creamy oak, toasty, complex, earthy notes, balsamic herbs. Palate: powerful, flavourful, toasty, round tannins.

Enate Reserva Especial 2006 T
cabernet sauvignon, merlot

94

Colour: deep cherry, garnet rim. Nose: scrubland, balanced, spicy. Palate: good structure, balanced, round tannins, long.

Enate Syrah-Shiraz 2010 T
syrah

90

Colour: cherry, garnet rim. Nose: ripe fruit, spicy, creamy oak, complex. Palate: powerful, flavourful, round tannins, fruity aftestaste.

ENATE
SYRAH - SHIRAZ
2010
SOMONTANO
DENOMINACIÓN DE ORIGEN

Enate Tapas 2013 T
tempranillo

86

Colour: cherry, purple rim. Nose: fresh fruit, red berry notes, floral. Palate: fruity, good acidity, easy to drink, good finish.

Enate Uno 2009 T
cabernet sauvignon, syrah, merlot

94

Colour: bright cherry, garnet rim. Nose: expressive, complex, dried herbs, spicy. Palate: full, flavourful, round tannins, spicy.

Enate Uno Chardonnay 2011 B
chardonnay
93
Colour: bright yellow. Nose: powerfull, ripe fruit, sweet spices, creamy oak, fragrant herbs. Palate: rich, smoky aftertaste, flavourful, fresh, good acidity, balanced, elegant.

VIÑAS DEL VERO
Ctra. de Naval, Km. 3,7
22300 Barbastro (Huesca)
☎: +34 974 302 216
Fax: +34 974 302 098
www.vinasdelvero.es
marketing@vinasdelvero.es

Viñas del Vero Cabernet Sauvignon Colección 2011 T
100% cabernet sauvignon
88
Colour: cherry, garnet rim. Nose: ripe fruit, wild herbs, spicy, creamy oak. Palate: flavourful, long, balsamic.

Viñas del Vero Chardonnay Colección 2013 B
100% chardonnay
92
Colour: bright straw. Nose: fresh, fresh fruit, white flowers, fragrant herbs, expressive. Palate: flavourful, fruity, good acidity, balanced, elegant.

Viñas del Vero Clarión 2009 B
93
Colour: bright yellow. Nose: white flowers, expressive, fine lees, mineral. Palate: flavourful, fruity, good acidity, balanced.

Viñas del Vero Clarión Magnum 2008 B
94
Colour: bright yellow. Nose: ripe fruit, spicy, toasty, complex. Palate: rich, full, complex, spicy, fine bitter notes.

Viñas del Vero Gewürztraminer Colección 2013 B
100% gewürztraminer
91
Colour: bright straw. Nose: white flowers, fragrant herbs, fruit expression. Palate: fresh, fruity, flavourful, balanced, elegant.

Viñas del Vero Gran Vos 2008 TR
91
Colour: cherry, garnet rim. Nose: ripe fruit, wild herbs, earthy notes, spicy, creamy oak. Palate: balanced, flavourful, long, balsamic.

Viñas del Vero La Miranda de Secastilla 2012 T
garnacha, syrah, parraleta
89
Colour: cherry, garnet rim. Nose: ripe fruit, spicy, toasty. Palate: powerful, flavourful, toasty, round tannins, fruity.

Viñas del Vero Merlot Colección 2011 T
100% merlot
90
Colour: bright cherry. Nose: ripe fruit, wild herbs, spicy, creamy oak, scrubland. Palate: balanced, flavourful, long, balsamic.

Viñas del Vero Pinot Noir Colección 2013 RD
100% pinot noir
89
Colour: onion pink. Nose: elegant, dried flowers, fragrant herbs, red berry notes. Palate: light-bodied, flavourful, good acidity, long, spicy.

Viñas del Vero Riesling Colección 2013 B
100% riesling
89
Colour: bright straw. Nose: white flowers, expressive, powerfull, citrus fruit. Palate: flavourful, fruity, good acidity, balanced.

Viñas del Vero Secastilla 2011 T
100% garnacha
93
Colour: cherry, garnet rim. Nose: ripe fruit, spicy, creamy oak, toasty, mineral, complex. Palate: powerful, flavourful, toasty, balanced, elegant.

Viñas del Vero Syrah Colección 2011 T
100% syrah
89
Colour: cherry, purple rim. Nose: expressive, red berry notes, floral, spicy. Palate: flavourful, fruity, good acidity, round tannins, easy to drink.

VIÑEDOS DE HOZ
Mayor, 17
22312 Hoz de Barbastro (Huesca)
☎: +34 619 686 765
www.vinosdehoz.com
info@vinosdehoz.com

Hoz 2010 T Roble
cabernet sauvignon, syrah, garnacha
87
Colour: bright cherry. Nose: ripe fruit, sweet spices, creamy oak, balsamic herbs. Palate: flavourful, fruity, toasty.

Hoz 2011 TC
tempranillo, syrah, garnacha
87
Colour: cherry, garnet rim. Nose: ripe fruit, spicy, creamy oak, balsamic herbs. Palate: powerful, flavourful, toasty.

DO. TACORONTE-ACENTEJO

CONSEJO REGULADOR
Ctra. General del Norte, 97
38350 Tacoronte (Santa Cruz de Tenerife)
☎:+34 922 560 107 - Fax: +34 922 561 155
@: consejo@tacovin.com
www.tacovin.com

DO TACORONTE - ACENTEJO / ACENTEJO / D.O.P

LOCATION:
Situated in the north of Tenerife, stretching for 23 km and is composed of 9 municipal districts: Tegueste, Tacoronte, El Sauzal, La Matanza de Acentejo, La Victoria de Acentejo, Santa Úrsula, La Laguna, Santa Cruz de Tenerife and El Rosario.

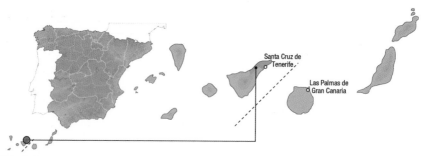

SUB-REGIONS:
Anaga (covering the municipal areas of La Laguna, Santa Cruz de Tenerife and Tegueste) which falls within the limits of the Anaga Rural Park.

GRAPE VARIETIES:
White: Preferred: Güal, Malvasía, Listán Blanco and Marmajuelo.
Authorized: Pedro Ximénez, Moscatel, Verdello, Vijariego, Forastera Blanca, Albillo, Sabro, Bastardo Blanco, Breval, Burra Blanca and Torrontés.
Red: Preferred: Listán Negra and Negramoll.
Authorized: Tintilla, Moscatel Negro, Castellana Negra, Cabernet Sauvignon, Merlot, Pinot Noir, Ruby Cabernet, Syrah, Tempranillo, Bastardo Negro, Listán Prieto, Vijariego Negro and Malvasía Rosada.

FIGURES:
Vineyard surface: 1,120 – Wine-Growers: 1,894 – Wineries: 43 – 2013 Harvest rating: Very Good – Production 13: 1,488,750 litres – Market percentages: 98% domestic - 2% export.

SOIL:
The soil is volcanic, reddish, and is made up of organic matter and trace elements. The vines are cultivated both in the valleys next to the sea and higher up at altitudes of up to 1,000 m.

CLIMATE:
Typically Atlantic, affected by the orientation of the island and the relief which give rise to a great variety of microclimates. The temperatures are in general mild, thanks to the influence of the trade winds, which provide high levels of humidity, around 60%, although the rains are scarce.

VINTAGE RATING

PEÑÍNGUIDE

2009	2010	2011	2012	2013
AVERAGE	GOOD	AVERAGE	VERY GOOD	GOOD

AGRYENCA

Fray Diego, 4
38350 Tacoronte (Tenerife)
☎: +34 922 564 013
Fax: +34 922 564 013
www.agryenca.com
bodega@agryenca.com

Tabaibal 2013 B
listán blanco, gual, verdello
86
Colour: bright yellow. Nose: ripe fruit, sweet spices, violets.
Palate: correct, easy to drink, long, fine bitter notes.

Tabaibal 2013 T
listán negro, negramoll
85

Tabaibal 2013 T Barrica
listán negro, negramoll
86
Colour: bright cherry. Nose: ripe fruit, sweet spices, creamy
oak, expressive, dried herbs. Palate: flavourful, fruity, toasty,
round tannins.

BODEGA DOMÍNGUEZ CUARTA GENERACIÓN

Calvario, 79
38350 Tacoronte
(Santa Cruz de Tenerife)
☎: +34 922 572 435
Fax: +34 922 572 435
www.bodegadominguez.com
info@bodegadominguez.es

Domínguez 2012 T
listán negro, listán blanco, negramoll, tintilla
84

Domínguez Antología 2012 T
negramoll, castellana, baboso negro, verdello
86
Colour: cherry, garnet rim. Nose: ripe fruit, citrus fruit, spicy.
Palate: good structure, balanced, spicy.

Domínguez Blanco de Uva Tinta Semiseco 2012 B
negramoll, malvasía
84

Domínguez con Firma 2010 T
castellana, negramoll
81

Domínguez Malvasía Clásico 2012 B
malvasía, moscatel
87
Colour: bright golden. Nose: fruit preserve, dried fruit, powerfull, pattiserie. Palate: fruity, correct, good finish.

BODEGA EL LOMO

Ctra. El Lomo, 18
38280 Tegueste
(Santa Cruz de Tenerife)
☎: +34 922 545 254
www.bodegaellomo.com
oficina@bodegaellomo.com

El Lomo 2012 T Barrica
listán negro, negramoll, tintilla, castellana
84

El Lomo 2013 B
listán blanco, gual
84

El Lomo 2013 RD
listán negro
82

El Lomo 2013 T Maceración Carbónica
listán negro
86
Colour: cherry, purple rim. Nose: expressive, red berry notes,
balsamic herbs. Palate: flavourful, fruity, good acidity, round
tannins.

El Lomo Afrutado 2013 B
listán blanco, gual
83

El Lomo Baboso 2013 T
baboso negro
85

El Lomo Merlot 2012 T
merlot
86
Colour: cherry, garnet rim. Nose: ripe fruit, wild herbs, earthy
notes, spicy. Palate: balanced, flavourful, long, balsamic.

El Lomo Tempranillo 2012 T
tempranillo
85

BODEGA EL MOCANERO
Ctra. General, 347
38350 Tacoronte
(Santa Cruz de Tenerife)
☎: +34 922 560 762
Fax: +34 922 564 452
www.bodegaelmocanero.com
elmocanero@bodegaelmocanero.com

El Mocanero 2013 T
85

El Mocanero 2013 T Maceración Carbónica
100% listán negro
85

El Mocanero Afrutado 2013 B
100% listán blanco
84

El Mocanero Negramoll 2013 T
100% negramoll
85

BODEGA LA HIJUELA
Cº El Agua s/n Barranco
El Junco, Machado
38290
☎: +34 922 537 284
www.bodegalahijuela.com
bodegalahijuela@hotmail.com

Híboro 2013 T
100% syrah
86
Colour: dark-red cherry, purple rim. Nose: balanced, premature reduction notes, ripe fruit. Palate: good structure, flavourful, balsamic.

BODEGA LA ISLETA
Camino de La Cairosa, 24
38280 Teguste (Santa Cruz de Tenerife)
☎: +34 922 541 805
www.laisleta.es
bodega@laisleta.es

La Isleta 2012 T
listán negro, negramoll
84

La Isleta 2013 B
malvasía, verdello, listán blanco, moscatel
84

La Isleta Baboso Negro 2012 T Barrica
baboso negro
86
Colour: bright cherry. Nose: ripe fruit, sweet spices, creamy oak. Palate: flavourful, fruity, toasty, round tannins.

BODEGAS CRÁTER
San Nicolás, 122
38360 El Sauzal
(Santa Cruz de Tenerife)
☎: +34 922 573 272
www.craterbodegas.com
crater@craterbodegas.com

Cráter 2012 TC
listán negro, negramoll
91
Colour: very deep cherry, garnet rim. Nose: fruit expression, balanced, expressive. Palate: powerful, toasty, smoky aftertaste.

BODEGAS INSULARES TENERIFE
Vereda del Medio, 48
38350 Tacoronte
(Santa Cruz de Tenerife)
☎: +34 922 570 617
Fax: +34 922 570 043
www.bodegasinsularestenerife.es
bitsa@bodegasinsularestenerife.es

Brezal 2013 T
listán negro, negramoll
86
Colour: cherry, purple rim. Nose: fresh fruit, red berry notes, floral, medium intensity. Palate: fruity, good acidity.

Humboldt 1997 Blanco dulce
listán blanco
95
Colour: light mahogany. Nose: sweet spices, cocoa bean, candied fruit, caramel, spicy. Palate: complex, balanced, good acidity, long.

Humboldt Blanco Dulce 2012 B
listán blanco
89
Colour: bright yellow. Nose: floral, honeyed notes. Palate: flavourful, sweet, fresh, fruity, good acidity, balanced, long.

Humboldt Blanco Dulce 2013 B
gual
88
Colour: bright straw. Nose: floral, medium intensity. Palate: flavourful, sweet, fresh, fruity, good acidity, long.

Humboldt Malvasía 2009 B
malvasía
92
Colour: bright golden. Nose: sweet spices, pattiserie, caramel, candied fruit. Palate: full, powerful, complex.

Humboldt Vendimia Tardia 2005 B
listán blanco

92

Colour: old gold. Nose: candied fruit, fruit liqueur notes, honeyed notes, fruit liqueur notes. Palate: unctuous, flavourful, sweet, long.

Humboldt Verdello 2005 Blanco dulce
verdello

94

Colour: old gold. Nose: complex, expressive, pattiserie, cocoa bean, sweet spices. Palate: flavourful, full, concentrated, long.

Viña Norte 2011 TC

86

Colour: very deep cherry, garnet rim. Nose: powerfull, cocoa bean, candied fruit. Palate: correct, spicy.

Viña Norte 2012 T
listán negro, negramoll

87

Colour: cherry, garnet rim. Nose: ripe fruit, wild herbs, spicy. Palate: balanced, flavourful, balsamic, long.

Viña Norte 2012 T Roble
listán negro, negramoll

85

Viña Norte 2013 B
listán blanco

87

Colour: bright straw. Nose: fresh, fresh fruit, white flowers, expressive. Palate: flavourful, fruity, good acidity, balanced.

Viña Norte 2013 T
listán negro, negramoll

86

Colour: cherry, purple rim. Nose: fresh fruit, red berry notes, floral. Palate: flavourful, fruity, good acidity, round tannins.

Viña Norte 2013 T Barrica

87

Colour: cherry, garnet rim. Nose: ripe fruit, wild herbs, earthy notes, spicy, creamy oak. Palate: balanced, flavourful, long, balsamic.

Viña Norte 2013 T Maceración Carbónica
listán negro, negramoll

88

Colour: cherry, purple rim. Nose: red berry notes, raspberry, floral, expressive. Palate: fresh, fruity, flavourful, easy to drink.

Viña Norte Afrutado 2013 T

84

Viña Norte Malvasia Seco 2013 B
malvasía

86

Colour: yellow, greenish rim. Nose: medium intensity, floral, balanced, fresh fruit. Palate: fruity, fine bitter notes, easy to drink.

Viña Norte Negramoll 2013 T
negramoll

86

Colour: very deep cherry. Nose: spicy, toasty, characterful, fruit preserve. Palate: powerful, flavourful, toasty, round tannins.

CÁNDIDO HERNÁNDEZ PÍO

Acentejo, 1
38370 La Matanza
(Santa Cruz de Tenerife)
☎: +34 922 513 288
Fax: +34 922 511 631
www.bodegaschp.es
info@bodegaschp.es

Balcón Canario 2006 TC
listán negro, negramoll, tintilla

84

Balcón Canario 2012 T
listán negro, negramoll, tintilla

83

Balcón Canario 2013 T
listán negro, negramoll, tintilla

86

Colour: cherry, purple rim. Nose: scrubland, spicy. Palate: correct, ripe fruit, round tannins.

Viña Riquelas Afrutado 2013 B
moscatel, verdello, listán blanco

86

Colour: bright straw. Nose: balanced, white flowers, fresh, fresh fruit. Palate: correct, easy to drink, good finish.

Viña Riquelas Blanco Gual 2013 B
gual

88

Colour: bright yellow. Nose: balanced, elegant, expressive, floral, ripe fruit. Palate: rich, flavourful, balanced, long.

Viña Riquelas Negramoll 2012 T
negramoll, listán negro

85

Viña Riquelas Negramoll 2013 T
negramoll, listán negro

85

CARBAJALES
Barranco de San Juan, s/n
38350 Tacoronte
(Santa Cruz de Tenerife)
☎: +34 639 791 608
www.carbajales.es
loscarbajales@gmail.com

Carbajales 2012 T Barrica
85

Carbajales 2013 T Barrica
86
Colour: bright cherry. Nose: ripe fruit, sweet spices, creamy oak, expressive, scrubland. Palate: flavourful, fruity, toasty, round tannins.

FINCA LA HORNACA - HOYA DEL NAVÍO
Camino Hacienda El Pino, 42
38350 Tacoronte
(Santa Cruz de Tenerife)
☎: +34 922 560 676
www.hoyadelnavio.com
info@hoyadelnavio.com

Hoya del Navío 2012 T
87 🍷
Colour: cherry, garnet rim. Nose: ripe fruit, wild herbs, earthy notes, spicy, creamy oak. Palate: balanced, flavourful, long, balsamic.

HACIENDA DE ACENTEJO
Pérez Díaz, 44
38380 La Victoria de Acentejo
(Santa Cruz de Tenerife)
☎: +34 922 581 003
Fax: +34 922 581 831
almac.gutierrez@gmail.com

Hacienda Acentejo 2013 T Barrica
84

Hacienda de Acentejo 2013 T
86
Colour: cherry, purple rim. Nose: medium intensity, fresh, red berry notes. Palate: fruity, balsamic, good finish.

IGNACIO DÍAZ GONZÁLEZ
Capitan Brotons, 1 ATICO
38200 La Laguna
(Santa Cruz de Tenerife)
☎: +34 922 252 610
Fax: +34 922 252 088
arq_idg@hotmail.com

Viña Orlara 2012 B
84

Viña Orlara 2012 T
85

MARBA
Ctra. Portezuelo - Las Toscas (TF-154), 253
38280 Tegueste (Santa Cruz de Tenerife)
☎: +34 639 065 015
Fax: +34 922 638 400
www.bodegasmarba.multiespaciosweb.com
marba@bodegasmarba.es

Marba 2013 B
85

Marba 2013 B Barrica
86
Colour: bright yellow. Nose: sweet spices, creamy oak, ripe fruit, toasty. Palate: rich, smoky aftertaste.

Marba 2013 RD
86
Colour: rose, bright. Nose: expressive, white flowers, violets. Palate: carbonic notes, fruity, good acidity, fine bitter notes.

Marba 2013 T Barrica
86
Colour: cherry, garnet rim. Nose: ripe fruit, wild herbs, earthy notes, spicy, creamy oak. Palate: balanced, flavourful, long, balsamic.

Marba 2013 T Maceración Carbónica
86
Colour: cherry, purple rim. Nose: red berry notes, raspberry, floral, expressive. Palate: fresh, fruity, flavourful, easy to drink.

Marba Afrutado 2013 B
86
Colour: bright straw. Nose: medium intensity, white flowers, balanced, fragrant herbs. Palate: flavourful, easy to drink.

Marba Tradicional 2013 T
84

PRESAS OCAMPO
Los Alamos de San Juan, 5
38350 Tacoronte
(Santa Cruz de Tenerife)
☎: +34 922 571 689
Fax: +34 922 561 700
www.presasocampo.com
enologo@presasocampo.com

Alysius 2012 T Barrica
listán negro, syrah
85

Alysius 2013 T
listán negro, syrah
85

Presas Ocampo 2013 T Maceración Carbónica
listán negro

87

Colour: cherry, purple rim. Nose: medium intensity, dried herbs, ripe fruit. Palate: correct, balanced.

Presas Ocampo Tradicional 2013 T
listán negro, merlot, syrah, tempranillo

86

Colour: cherry, garnet rim. Nose: ripe fruit, wild herbs, earthy notes. Palate: balanced, flavourful, long, balsamic, easy to drink.

VIÑA ESTEVEZ
Pérez Díaz, 80
38380 La Victoria
(Santa Cruz de Tenerife)
☎: +34 608 724 671
elena.vinaestevez@gmail.com

Viña Estévez 2013 T

86

Colour: bright cherry. Nose: ripe fruit, sweet spices, creamy oak. Palate: flavourful, fruity, toasty, round tannins.

DO. TARRAGONA

CONSEJO REGULADOR

Avda. Catalunya, 50
43002 Tarragona
☎:+34 977 217 931 - Fax: +34 977 229 102
@: info@dotarragona.cat
www.dotarragona.cat

LOCATION:

The region is situated in the province of Tarragona. It comprises two different wine-growing regions: El Camp and Ribera d'Ebre, with a total of 72 municipal areas.

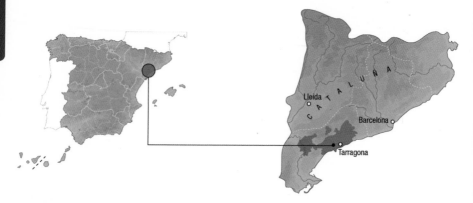

SUB-REGIONS:

El Camp and Ribera d'Ebre (See specific characteristics in previous sections).

GRAPE VARIETIES:

White: Chardonnay, Macabeo, Xarel·lo, Garnacha Blanca, Parellada, Moscatel de Alejandría, Moscatel de Frontignan, Sauvignon Blanc, Malvasía.
Red: Samsó (Cariñena), Garnacha, Ull de Llebre (Tempranillo), Cabernet Sauvignon, Merlot, Monastrell, Pinot Noir, Syrah.

FIGURES:

Vineyard surface: 5,087 – Wine-Growers: 2,100 – Wineries: 34 – 2013 Harvest rating: Very Good – Production 13: 4,000,000 litres – Market percentages: 50% domestic - 50% export.

SOIL:

El Camp is characterized by its calcareous, light terrain, and the Ribera has calcareous terrain and also some alluvial terrain.

CLIMATE:

Mediterranean in the region of El Camp, with an average annual rainfall of 500 mm. The region of the Ribera has a rather harsh climate with cold winters and hot summers; it also has the lowest rainfall in the region (385 mm per year).

VINTAGE RATING

PEÑÍNGUIDE

2009	2010	2011	2012	2013
GOOD	GOOD	VERY GOOD	GOOD	GOOD

ADERNATS

Arrabal de Sant Joan, 7
43887 Nulles (Tarragona)
☎: +34 977 602 622
Fax: +34 977 609 798
www.vinicoladenulles.com
botiga@vinicoladenulles.com

Adernats AdN Macabeo 2013 B
100% macabeo

88

Colour: bright straw. Nose: balanced, fresh fruit, floral. Palate: flavourful, fruity, complex, balanced, good acidity, fine bitter notes.

Adernats Ánima 2012 T
tempranillo, merlot

86

Colour: cherry, garnet rim. Nose: ripe fruit, balsamic herbs, fine reductive notes, spicy, creamy oak. Palate: flavourful, fine bitter notes, balsamic.

Adernats Blanc 2013 B
macabeo, xarel.lo, parellada

85

Adernats Essència 2013 BFB
100% xarel.lo

88

Colour: bright yellow. Nose: powerfull, ripe fruit, sweet spices, creamy oak, fragrant herbs. Palate: rich, flavourful, fresh, good acidity.

Adernats Impuls 2013 T
tempranillo, merlot

83

Adernats Instint 2013 T
tempranillo, merlot

84

Adernats Negre Jove 2013 T
tempranillo, merlot

81

Adernats Rosat 2013 RD
tempranillo, merlot

84

Adernats Seducció 2013 B
macabeo, xarel.lo, chardonnay

88

Colour: bright straw. Nose: white flowers, fragrant herbs, fruit expression. Palate: fresh, fruity, flavourful, balanced.

AGRÍCOLA DE BRAFIM

Major, 50
43812 Brafim (Tarragona)
☎: +34 977 620 061
Fax: +34 977 620 061
www.agricolabrafim.cat
oficina@agricolabrafim.cat

Puig Rodó 2013 RD
ull de llebre

86

Colour: light cherry. Nose: powerfull, ripe fruit, red berry notes, floral, expressive. Palate: powerful, fruity, fresh, flavourful.

Puig Rodó Macabeu 2013 B
macabeo

84

Puig Rodó Negra 2013 T
ull de llebre, merlot

84

Puig Rodó Xarel.lo 2013 B
xarel.lo

85

AGRÍCOLA SANT VICENÇ

Sant Antoni, 29
43748 Ginestar (Ribera d'Ebre)
(Tarragona)
☎: +34 977 409 039
Fax: +34 977 409 006
www.vinsolisuner.com

Suñer 2013 B
macabeo

84

Suñer 2013 RD
merlot

84

Suñer 2013 T
merlot

84

BODEGA COOPERATIVA VILA-RODONA

Ctra. Santes Creus, s/n
43814 Vila-Rodona (Tarragona)
☎: +34 977 638 004
Fax: +34 977 639 075
www.coopvila-rodona.com
copvilar@copvilar.e.telefonica.net

Moscatell Vila-Rodona B
moscatel

86

Colour: bright straw. Nose: powerfull, ripe fruit, faded flowers, honeyed notes. Palate: flavourful, powerful, rich.

Vi Ranci Vila-Rodona MZ
84

Vila-Rodona Mistela Vino de licor
88
Colour: iodine, amber rim. Nose: ripe fruit, balsamic herbs, spicy, creamy oak. Palate: powerful, flavourful, spicy, concentrated, balanced.

CASTELL D'OR
Mare Rafols, 3- 1ºD
08720 Vilafranca del Penedès (Barcelona)
☎: +34 938 905 385
Fax: +34 938 905 455
www.castelldor.com
castelldor@castelldor.com

Flama Roja 2013 B
macabeo, xarel.lo
83

Flama Roja Rosat 2013 RD
tempranillo
84

Flama Roja Vi Negre 2013 T
cabernet sauvignon, merlot
83

CELLER 9+
Cases Noves, 19
43763 La Nou de Gaià (Tarragona)
☎: +34 977 655 940
www.9mes.cat
moisesvirgili@gmail.com

Medol 2013 T
cabernet sauvignon, garnacha, syrah
84

Medol Cartoixa 2013 B
cartoixa
83

Medol Selecció 2012 T
garnacha, cabernet sauvignon
86
Colour: cherry, garnet rim. Nose: ripe fruit, spicy, creamy oak, toasty, balsamic herbs. Palate: powerful, flavourful, toasty.

Serra Alta Cartoixa ESP
cartoixa
88
Colour: bright golden. Nose: fine lees, fragrant herbs, toasty, expressive. Palate: powerful, flavourful, good acidity, fine bead, fine bitter notes.

Serra Alta Cartoixa 2013 B
cartoixa
85 🏆

Serra Alta Tres Caracters 2012 T
garnacha, cabernet sauvignon, merlot
85

CELLER LA BOELLA
Autovía Reus - Tarragona (T-11), km. 12
43110 La Canonja (Tarragona)
☎: +34 977 771 515
www.laboella.com
celler@laboella.com

Mas la Boella Guarda 2010 T
89
Colour: cherry, garnet rim. Nose: ripe fruit, spicy, creamy oak, toasty, complex, balsamic herbs, fine reductive notes. Palate: powerful, flavourful, toasty, balanced.

Mas la Boella Guarda Selecció Magnum 2010 T
100% cabernet sauvignon
90
Colour: cherry, garnet rim. Nose: ripe fruit, wild herbs, earthy notes, spicy, creamy oak. Palate: balanced, flavourful, long, balsamic.

Ullals 2011 T
85

CELLER MAS BELLA
Sant Roc, 8 - Masmolets
43813 Valls (Tarragona)
☎: +34 977 613 092
Fax: +34 977 613 092
www.cellermasbella.com
cellermasbella@gmail.com

Bella Blanc Cartoixa 2013 B
cartoixa
86
Colour: bright yellow. Nose: ripe fruit, sweet spices, creamy oak, fragrant herbs. Palate: rich, smoky aftertaste, flavourful, fresh.

Bella Negre 2010 T
ull de llebre
88
Colour: very deep cherry, garnet rim. Nose: ripe fruit, creamy oak, sweet spices, dried herbs. Palate: good structure, flavourful.

Bella Negre 2011 T
ull de llebre
85

CELLER PEDROLA

Creu, 5
43747 Miravet (Tarragona)
☎: +34 650 093 906
pedrola97@yahoo.es

Camí de Sirga 2012 TC
samsó

85

Camí de Sirga 2013 B
83

Camí de Sirga 2013 T
86

Colour: cherry, garnet rim. Nose: ripe fruit, wild herbs, balsamic herbs. Palate: balanced, flavourful, long, balsamic.

CELLERS UNIÓ

Joan Oliver, 16-24
43206 Reus (Tarragona)
☎: +34 977 330 055
Fax: +34 977 330 070
www.cellersunio.com
info@cellersunio.com

Roureda Blanc de Blancs 2013 B
macabeo, xarel.lo

86

Colour: bright straw. Nose: fresh, fresh fruit, white flowers, expressive. Palate: flavourful, fruity, good acidity, balanced.

Roureda Cabernet Sauvignon 2013 T
cabernet sauvignon

84

Roureda Merlot 2013 RD
merlot

86

Colour: raspberry rose. Nose: red berry notes, fragrant herbs, floral, medium intensity. Palate: fresh, fruity, thin.

DE MULLER

Camí Pedra Estela, 34
43205 Reus (Tarragona)
☎: +34 977 757 473
Fax: +34 977 771 129
www.demuller.es
lab@demuller.es

De Muller Avreo Dulce añejo 1954 OL
garnacha, garnacha blanca

93

Colour: light mahogany. Nose: complex, dry nuts, toasty, acetaldehyde, pungent. Palate: fine solera notes, spicy, long, rich.

De Muller Avreo Seco 1954 Añejo
garnacha, garnacha blanca

92

Colour: light mahogany. Nose: dry nuts, roasted almonds, acetaldehyde, varnish, spicy, aged wood nuances, expressive. Palate: powerful, flavourful, spicy, long.

De Muller Cabernet Sauvignon 2011 TC
cabernet sauvignon

84

De Muller Chardonnay 2013 BFB
chardonnay

89

Colour: bright straw. Nose: white flowers, fresh fruit, expressive, dried herbs, sweet spices. Palate: flavourful, fruity, good acidity, balanced.

De Muller Garnacha Solera 1926 Solera
garnacha

95

Colour: light mahogany. Nose: complex, acetaldehyde, cocoa bean, spicy, varnish, dry nuts. Palate: balanced, long, complex, spicy.

De Muller Merlot 2011 TC
merlot

86

Colour: ruby red. Nose: spicy, fine reductive notes, aged wood nuances, toasty, balsamic herbs. Palate: spicy, long, toasty.

De Muller Moscatel Añejo Vino de licor
moscatel de alejandría

92

Colour: old gold, amber rim. Nose: expressive, smoky, powerfull, candied fruit, rancio notes. Palate: flavourful, balanced, spicy, long.

De Muller Muscat 2013 B
moscatel de alejandría

85

De Muller Rancio Seco Vino de licor
garnacha, mazuelo

91

Colour: light mahogany. Nose: expressive, candied fruit, toasty, rancio notes, varnish, roasted almonds. Palate: flavourful, full, fine bitter notes.

De Muller Syrah 2013 T
syrah

85

Mas de Valls 2012 BN
macabeo, chardonnay, parellada

87

Colour: bright golden. Nose: ripe fruit, balanced, dried herbs. Palate: good acidity, flavourful, ripe fruit, long.

Porpores De Muller 2009 TR
cabernet sauvignon, merlot, tempranillo

88

Colour: cherry, garnet rim. Nose: ripe fruit, wild herbs, earthy notes, spicy, creamy oak. Palate: balanced, flavourful, long, balsamic.

Reina Violant Reserva 2009 BN
chardonnay, pinot noir

89

Colour: bright yellow. Nose: fresh fruit, dried herbs, fine lees, floral, sweet spices, dry nuts. Palate: fresh, fruity, flavourful, good acidity, balanced.

Solimar 2011 TC
merlot, cabernet sauvignon

84

Solimar 2013 B
macabeo, moscatel, sauvignon blanc

87

Colour: bright straw. Nose: white flowers, fragrant herbs, fruit expression. Palate: fresh, fruity, flavourful, balanced.

Solimar 2013 RD
pinot noir, merlot, syrah

84

Trilogía Chardonnay Reserva 2011 BN
chardonnay

88

Colour: bright golden. Nose: fine lees, dry nuts, fragrant herbs, complex, toasty, honeyed notes. Palate: powerful, flavourful, good acidity, fine bitter notes.

Trilogía Muscat Reserva 2012 BR
moscatel de alejandría

88

Colour: bright yellow. Nose: expressive, white flowers, fresh fruit, balanced, powerfull, varietal. Palate: flavourful, fruity, balanced.

Trilogía Pinot Noir Reserva 2010 BN
pinot noir

90

Colour: bright yellow. Nose: ripe fruit, fine lees, balanced, dried herbs. Palate: good acidity, flavourful, ripe fruit, long, elegant.

Vino de Misa Dulce Superior
garnacha blanca, macabeo

91

Colour: old gold. Nose: candied fruit, varnish, sweet spices, cocoa bean. Palate: flavourful, rich, full, long.

HELGA HARBIG CEREZO-BIOPAUMERÀ
Plaça St. Joan, 3
43513 Rasquera (Tarragona)
☎: +34 977 404 711
www.biopaumera.com
biopaumera@biopaumera.com

Adrià de Paumera 2010 T Roble

88 🌸

Colour: dark-red cherry, garnet rim. Nose: wild herbs, balanced, expressive, ripe fruit. Palate: flavourful, balanced, easy to drink, balsamic.

Esther de Paumera 2010 TC

84

MAS DEL BOTÓ
Camí de Porrera a Alforja, s/n
43365 Alforja (Tarragona)
☎: +34 630 982 747
Fax: +34 977 236 396
www.masdelboto.cat
pep@masdelboto.cat

Ganagot 2005 TR

90 🌸

Colour: cherry, garnet rim. Nose: ripe fruit, spicy, creamy oak, complex, earthy notes. Palate: powerful, flavourful, toasty, round tannins.

Ganagot 2006 T

87

Colour: ruby red. Nose: spicy, fine reductive notes, wet leather, aged wood nuances, toasty, scrubland. Palate: spicy, long, toasty.

Ganagot 2007 T

84

Ganagot 2008 T

88

Colour: deep cherry, orangey edge. Nose: balsamic herbs, ripe fruit, spicy, creamy oak. Palate: powerful, flavourful, spicy, balanced.

Mas del Botó 2010 T

87 🌸

Colour: cherry, garnet rim. Nose: ripe fruit, wild herbs, spicy, creamy oak. Palate: flavourful, long, balsamic.

MAS DELS FRARES (FACULTAT D'ENOLOGIA DE TARRAGONA)

Ctra. TV-7211, Km. 7,2
43120 Constantí (Tarragona)
☎: +34 977 520 197
Fax: +34 977 522 156
fincafe@urv.cat

Urv 2011 TC
86
Colour: cherry, garnet rim. Nose: ripe fruit, spicy, creamy oak, toasty, balsamic herbs. Palate: powerful, flavourful, toasty.

Urv Aromatic BR
86
Colour: bright straw. Nose: medium intensity, fresh fruit, dried herbs, fine lees, floral. Palate: fresh, fruity, flavourful, good acidity.

MAS VICENÇ

Mas Vicenç, s/n
43811 Cabra de Camp (Tarragona)
☎: +34 977 630 024
www.masvicens.com
masvicens@masvicens.com

Dent de Lleó 2013 B
chardonnay
85

El Terrat 2013 B
macabeo, moscatel
85

El Vi del Vent Dulce 2013 B
moscatel grano menudo
86
Colour: bright straw. Nose: white flowers, honeyed notes, varietal. Palate: easy to drink, good finish.

Nit de Lluna 2012 TC
ull de llebre, syrah
84

Rombes d'Arlequi 2010 TC
ull de llebre, cabernet sauvignon
88
Colour: cherry, garnet rim. Nose: ripe fruit, spicy, creamy oak, toasty, complex. Palate: powerful, flavourful, toasty, round tannins.

MOLÍ DE RUÉ

Dels Portellets s/n
43792 Vinebre (Tarragona)
☎: +34 977 405 782
Fax: +34 977 405 782
npoquet@moliderue.com

Mims Blanc 2013 B
85

MIMS Rosat 2013 RD
100% syrah
84

Sol i Serena Vino de Licor
100% macabeo
93
Colour: iodine, amber rim. Nose: powerfull, complex, elegant, dry nuts, toasty, dried fruit. Palate: rich, fine bitter notes, long, spicy, balanced, elegant.

SERRA DE LLABERIA

Avda. Vidal i Barraquer, 12, 8º- 4ª
43005 Tarragona (Tarragona)
☎: +34 977 824 122
Fax: +34 977 824 122
www.serradellaberia.com
info@serradellaberia.com

Serra de Llaberia Elisabeth 2005 TR
89
Colour: very deep cherry, garnet rim. Nose: expressive, spicy, scrubland, cocoa bean. Palate: flavourful, good acidity, round tannins.

UNIVERSITAT ROVIRA I VIRGILI

Ctra TV 7211 km 7
43120 Constantí (Tarragona)
☎: +34 977 520 197
Fax: +34 977 522 156
www.urv.cat/vins
fincafe@urv.cat

Universitat Rovira i Virgili 2013 B
86
Colour: bright straw. Nose: fresh, fresh fruit, white flowers, expressive. Palate: fruity, good acidity, balanced.

Universitat Rovira i Virgili 2013 T
85

VINOS PADRÓ

Avda. Catalunya, 64-70
43812 Brafim (Tarragona)
☎: +34 977 620 012
Fax: +34 977 620 486
www.vinspadro.com
info@vinspadro.com

Capitol 2013 B
macabeo, xarel.lo, moscatel
87
Colour: bright straw. Nose: fresh, fresh fruit, white flowers, expressive. Palate: flavourful, fruity, good acidity, balanced.

Ipsis 2011 TC
tempranillo, merlot
88
Colour: cherry, garnet rim. Nose: red berry notes, ripe fruit, spicy, creamy oak, toasty, complex, earthy notes. Palate: powerful, flavourful, toasty, round tannins.

Ipsis Blanc Flor 2013 B
macabeo, xarel.lo, moscatel
85

Ipsis Chardonnay 2013 B
100% chardonnay
87
Colour: bright yellow. Nose: balanced, white flowers, varietal, ripe fruit. Palate: rich, flavourful, long.

Ipsis Muscat 2013 B
84

Ipsis Rosat Llagrima 2013 RD
ull de llebre, merlot
84

Ipsis Tempranillo Merlot 2013 T
ull de llebre, merlot
86
Colour: bright cherry, purple rim. Nose: grassy, fruit expression, balanced. Palate: fruity, flavourful, balanced.

Ipsis Tempranillo Selecció 2011 T
100% tempranillo
88
Colour: cherry, garnet rim. Nose: ripe fruit, spicy, creamy oak, toasty, complex. Palate: powerful, flavourful, toasty, round tannins.

VINYA JANINE

Sant Antoni, 5
43812 Rodonyá (Tarragona)
☎: +34 977 628 305
Fax: +34 977 628 857
www.vinyajanine.com
vjanine@tinet.org

Vinya Janine 2011 T
syrah
84

Vinya Janine 2013 B
xarel.lo, moscatel
86
Colour: bright straw. Nose: floral, dried herbs, balanced. Palate: correct, easy to drink, good finish.

Vinya Janine Merlot 2013 RD
merlot
84

VINYES DEL TERRER

Camí del Terrer, s/n
43480 Vila-Seca (Tarragona)
☎: +34 977 269 229
www.terrer.net
eduard@terrer.net

Blanc del Terrer 2013 B
sauvignon blanc
85

Nus del Terrer 2010 T
93
Colour: cherry, garnet rim. Nose: ripe fruit, wild herbs, earthy notes, spicy, creamy oak, toasty. Palate: balanced, flavourful, long, balsamic.

Nus del Terrer 2011 T
90
Colour: cherry, garnet rim. Nose: ripe fruit, spicy, creamy oak, toasty, scrubland, premature reduction notes. Palate: powerful, flavourful, toasty.

Terrer d'Aubert 2011 T
cabernet sauvignon
89
Colour: black cherry, garnet rim. Nose: ripe fruit, fruit preserve, wild herbs, spicy. Palate: powerful, flavourful, spicy, long.

Terrer d'Aubert 2012 T
cabernet sauvignon
90
Colour: cherry, garnet rim. Nose: red berry notes, ripe fruit, balsamic herbs, mineral. Palate: powerful, flavourful, long, round tannins.

DO. TERRA ALTA
CONSEJO REGULADOR
Ctra. Vilalba, 31
43780 Gandesa (Tarragona)
☎:+34 977 421 278- Fax: +34 977 421 623
@: info@terraaltawine.com
www.doterraalta.com

LOCATION:

In the southeast of Catalonia, in the province of Tarragona. It covers the municipal districts of Arnes, Batea, Bot, Caseres, Corbera d´Ebre, La Fatarella, Gandesa, Horta de Sant Joan, Pinell de Brai, La Pobla de Massaluca, Prat de Comte and Vilalba dels Arcs.

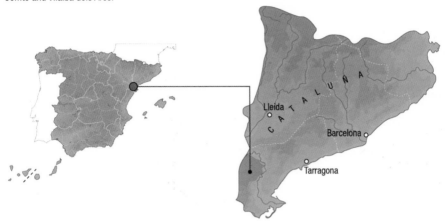

GRAPE VARIETIES:

White: Chardonnay, Garnacha Blanca, Parellada, Macabeo, Moscatel, Sauvignon Blanc, Chenin, Pedro Ximénez. Experimental: Viognier.
Red: Cabernet Sauvigon, Cariñena, Garnacha Tinta, Garnacha Peluda, Syrah, Tempranillo, Merlot, Samsó, Cabernet Franc. Experimental: Petit Verdot, Marselane, Caladoc.

FIGURES:

Vineyard surface: 6,000 – Wine-Growers: 1,300 – Wineries: 49 – 2013 Harvest rating: White: Very Good – Rest: Good – Production 13: 15,027,345 litres – Market percentages: 30% domestic - 70% export.

SOIL:

The vineyards are located on an extensive plateau at an altitude of slightly over 400 m. The soil is calcareous and the texture mainly clayey, poor in organic matter and with many pebbles.

CLIMATE:

Mediterranean, with continental influences. It is characterized by its hot, dry summers and very cold winters, especially in the higher regions in the east. The average annual rainfall is 400 mm. Another vital aspect is the wind: the 'Cierzo' and the 'Garbi' (Ábrego) winds.

VINTAGE RATING

PEÑÍNGUIDE

2009	2010	2011	2012	2013
VERY GOOD	VERY GOOD	GOOD	GOOD	GOOD

7 MAGNIFICS
Miquel Torres i Carbó, 6
08720 Vilafranca del Penedès
(Barcelona)
☎: +34 938 177 400
Fax: +34 938 177 444
www.7magnifics.com
7magnifics@7magnifics.com

Rebels de Batea 2013 B
garnacha blanca
90
Colour: bright straw. Nose: white flowers, citrus fruit, balsamic herbs, expressive. Palate: fresh, fruity, flavourful, balanced.

Rebels de Batea 2013 T
garnacha
89
Colour: cherry, purple rim. Nose: expressive, red berry notes, scrubland. Palate: flavourful, fruity, good acidity, round tannins, easy to drink.

AGRÍCOLA CORBERA D'EBRE
Ponent, 21
43784 Corbera d'Ebre (Tarragona)
☎: +34 977 420 432
Fax: +34 977 420 304
www.agricolacorberadebre.com
coop@corbera.tinet.org

Mirmil-ló Garnacha Blanca 2013 B
garnacha blanca
83

Mirmil-ló Negre 2013 T
garnacha, cariñena, tempranillo, syrah
84

Mirmil-ló Parellada 2013 B
parellada
82

Mirmil-ló Rosat 2013 RD
garnacha
84

Poble Vell Blanco Dulce Natural 2012 B
garnacha blanca
86
Colour: old gold. Nose: fruit liqueur notes, honeyed notes, pattiserie, characterful. Palate: powerful, flavourful, long.

Vall Excels 2011 TC
garnacha, tempranillo
84

AGRÍCOLA SANT JOSEP
Estació, 2
43785 Bot (Tarragona)
☎: +34 977 428 352
Fax: +34 977 428 192
www.santjosepwines.com
info@santjosepwines.com

Brau de Bot 2013 B
84

Brau de Bot 2013 RD
86
Colour: rose, purple rim. Nose: powerfull, ripe fruit, red berry notes, floral, expressive. Palate: powerful, fruity, fresh.

Brau de Bot 2013 T
85

Clot D'Encís 2013 B
garnacha blanca
85

Clot D'Encis 2013 RD
87
Colour: light cherry, bright. Nose: red berry notes, fragrant herbs, balanced. Palate: correct, fine bitter notes, good acidity.

Clot D'Encís 2013 T
84

Clot D'Encis Blanc de Negres 2013 B
100% garnacha
89
Colour: pale. Nose: white flowers, fragrant herbs, fruit expression. Palate: fresh, fruity, flavourful, balanced. Personality.

La Plana d'en Fonoll 2012 T
87
Colour: black cherry, garnet rim. Nose: ripe fruit, spicy, creamy oak, toasty, complex, dried herbs. Palate: toasty, round tannins, balanced.

Llàgrimes de Tardor 2007 TR
86
Colour: cherry, garnet rim. Nose: ripe fruit, spicy, creamy oak, toasty, fine reductive notes. Palate: powerful, flavourful, toasty.

Llàgrimes de Tardor 2009 TC
garnacha, samsó, syrah, cabernet sauvignon
89
Colour: cherry, garnet rim. Nose: ripe fruit, spicy, creamy oak, toasty. Palate: powerful, flavourful, toasty, correct.

Llàgrimes de Tardor 2010 BFB
100% garnacha blanca

91

Colour: bright yellow. Nose: faded flowers, spicy, fragrant herbs, ripe fruit. Palate: fruity, flavourful, rich, toasty.

Llàgrimes de Tardor Mistela Blanca 2012 B
100% garnacha blanca

88

Colour: bright golden. Nose: characterful, fruit liqueur notes, dried fruit, pattiserie, cocoa bean. Palate: flavourful, unctuous.

Llàgrimes de Tardor Mistela Negra 2012 Mistela
100% garnacha

89

Colour: cherry, garnet rim. Nose: ripe fruit, wild herbs, spicy, creamy oak. Palate: balanced, flavourful, long, balsamic, sweet.

ALTAVINS VITICULTORS
Ctra. Vilalba dels Arcs s/n
43786 Batea (Tarragona)
☎: +34 977 430 596
www.altavins.com
altavins@altavins.com

Almodí 2013 T
garnacha

87

Colour: bright cherry. Nose: ripe fruit, sweet spices, creamy oak, balsamic herbs. Palate: flavourful, toasty, round tannins, correct.

Domus Pensi 2008 TC
cabernet sauvignon, garnacha, merlot, syrah

89

Colour: bright cherry. Nose: ripe fruit, sweet spices, creamy oak, expressive. Palate: flavourful, fruity, toasty, round tannins.

Ilercavonia 2013 B
garnacha blanca

88

Colour: bright straw. Nose: fruit expression, tropical fruit, fragrant herbs, floral. Palate: fresh, fruity, flavourful, balanced.

Tempus 2010 TC
garnacha, syrah, cariñena

86

Colour: bright cherry. Nose: ripe fruit, sweet spices, creamy oak, medium intensity, fine reductive notes. Palate: fruity, flavourful, toasty.

BERNAVÍ
Camí de Berrús km.4 –
Finca Mas Vernet
43782 Vilalba dels Arcs (Tarragona)
☎: +34 619 014 194
www.bernavi.com
info@bernavi.com

Bernaví 3D3 2012 T
garnacha, syrah, merlot

85

Bernaví Ca'Vernet 2011 T
cabernet franc, cabernet sauvignon

85

Bernaví Ventuno 2013 RD
garnacha

85

Notte Bianca 2013 B
garnacha blanca, viognier

84

CATERRA
Glorieta, s/n
43783 La Pobla de Massaluca (Tarragona)
☎: +34 608 590 780
Fax: +34 977 439 765
www.caterra.es
catapoma@caterra.es

Font Calenta 2013 B
garnacha blanca, macabeo

84

Font Calenta Negre 2013 T
garnacha, cariñena

82

Hereus Caterra 2013 T
garnacha, cariñena, syrah

83

CELLER BÁRBARA FORÉS
Santa Anna, 29
43780 Gandesa (Tarragona)
☎: +34 620 130 814
Fax: +34 977 421 399
www.cellerbarbarafores.com
info@cellerbarbarafores.com

Bárbara Forés 2013 B
89

Colour: bright yellow. Nose: white flowers, fragrant herbs, fruit expression. Palate: fresh, fruity, flavourful, balanced, elegant.

Bárbara Forés 2013 RD
88
Colour: brilliant rose. Nose: powerfull, ripe fruit, red berry notes, floral, balsamic herbs. Palate: powerful, fruity, fresh, fine bitter notes.

Bárbara Forés Negre 2011 T
89
Colour: cherry, garnet rim. Nose: ripe fruit, wild herbs, earthy notes, spicy, creamy oak. Palate: balanced, flavourful, long, balsamic.

Coma d'En Pou Bàrbara Forés 2011 T
91 🌷
Colour: cherry, garnet rim. Nose: ripe fruit, spicy, creamy oak, toasty, complex, violets, wild herbs. Palate: powerful, flavourful, toasty, round tannins.

El Quintà Bárbara Forés 2012 BFB
garnacha blanca
93 🌷
Colour: bright straw. Nose: powerfull, ripe fruit, sweet spices, creamy oak, fragrant herbs. Palate: rich, smoky aftertaste, flavourful, fresh, good acidity, balanced, elegant.

El Templari Bárbara Forés 2012 T
91 🌷
Colour: light cherry. Nose: wild herbs, earthy notes, spicy, creamy oak, ripe fruit. Palate: balanced, flavourful, long, balsamic, mineral.

Vi Dolç Natural Bárbara Forés 2011 B
garnacha blanca
91 🌷
Colour: golden. Nose: powerfull, floral, honeyed notes, candied fruit, fragrant herbs. Palate: flavourful, sweet, fresh, fruity, good acidity, long.

CELLER BATEA
Moli, 30
43786 Batea (Tarragona)
☎: +34 977 430 056
Fax: +34 977 430 589
www.cellerbatea.com
enolegs@cellerbatea.com

Equinox Batea 2009 B
100% garnacha blanca
90
Colour: old gold, amber rim. Nose: powerfull, characterful, complex, rancio notes, toasty. Palate: full, complex, flavourful, balanced.

L'Aube "Seleccio de Vinyes Velles" 2010 TC
merlot, garnacha, cabernet sauvignon
91
Colour: cherry, garnet rim. Nose: ripe fruit, wild herbs, earthy notes, spicy, creamy oak, fine reductive notes. Palate: flavourful, long, balsamic, balanced, elegant.

Naturalis Mer 2013 B
100% garnacha blanca
90 🌷
Colour: bright straw. Nose: white flowers, fragrant herbs, fruit expression. Palate: fresh, fruity, flavourful, balanced, elegant.

Naturalis Mer 2013 T Roble
garnacha, cabernet sauvignon
90 🌷
Colour: cherry, garnet rim. Nose: ripe fruit, spicy, creamy oak, toasty, mineral, balsamic herbs. Palate: powerful, flavourful, toasty, balanced.

Tipicitat 2010 TC
garnacha, samsó
89
Colour: cherry, garnet rim. Nose: ripe fruit, spicy, creamy oak, toasty, balsamic herbs, fruit preserve. Palate: powerful, flavourful, toasty, round tannins.

Vallmajor 2013 B
100% garnacha blanca
87
Colour: bright straw. Nose: faded flowers, fresh fruit, balanced. Palate: fruity, fresh, easy to drink, flavourful.

Vallmajor Negre 2013 T
86
Colour: dark-red cherry, purple rim. Nose: ripe fruit, powerfull, balanced. Palate: flavourful, fruity, fine bitter notes.

CELLER COMA D'EN BONET
Camí de Les Comes d'En Bonet s/n
43780 Gandesa (Tarragona)
☎: +34 977 232 671
Fax: +34 977 234 665
www.dardell.es
dardell@dardell.es

Dardell 2013 T
garnacha, syrah
83 🌷

Dardell Garnacha Blanca & Viognier 2013 B
garnacha blanca, viognier
85 🌷

ProHom 2012 T
garnacha, syrah, cabernet sauvignon, merlot
85

ProHom 2013 B
garnacha blanca, viognier
87 🌷
Colour: bright straw. Nose: white flowers, fresh fruit, dried herbs. Palate: flavourful, fruity, good acidity, balanced.

CELLER COOPERATIU GANDESA SCCL

Avda. Catalunya, 28
43780 Gandesa (Tarragona)
☎: +34 977 420 017
Fax: +34 977 420 403
www.coopgandesa.com
info@coopgandesa.com

Gandesa Mistela Blanca Vino de licor
garnacha blanca

84

Gandesa Mistela Tinta Mistela
garnacha

87

Colour: ruby red. Nose: dried fruit, fruit liqueur notes, balsamic herbs, spicy, toasty. Palate: sweet, powerful, flavourful, spicy, long.

Gandesola 2012 T
garnacha, tempranillo, cariñena

85

Gandesola 2013 B
garnacha blanca, macabeo, moscatel

85

Somdinou Blanc Jove 2013 B
garnacha blanca, macabeo, moscatel

89

Colour: bright straw. Nose: white flowers, fragrant herbs, fruit expression. Palate: fresh, fruity, flavourful, balanced.

Somdinou Negre Jove 2012 T
garnacha, cariñena, tempranillo

88

Colour: cherry, garnet rim. Nose: dry stone, fragrant herbs, spicy, ripe fruit. Palate: balanced, flavourful, fruity.

Vi de Licor 1919 Rancio
garnacha blanca

90

Colour: light mahogany. Nose: fruit liqueur notes, sweet spices, acetaldehyde, aged wood nuances. Palate: balanced, complex, fine solera notes.

CELLER JORDI MIRÓ

Sant Marc, 96
43784 Corbera d'Ebre (Tarragona)
☎: +34 650 010 639
www.cellerjordimiro.com
jordi@ennak.com

Ennak 2013 T
tempranillo, merlot, syrah, mazuelo

86

Colour: cherry, purple rim. Nose: expressive, red berry notes, floral. Palate: flavourful, fruity, good acidity, round tannins.

Ennak+ 2012 TC
cabernet sauvignon, merlot, tempranillo, mazuelo

88

Colour: cherry, garnet rim. Nose: fruit preserve, fruit liqueur notes, wild herbs, spicy. Palate: flavourful, balsamic, toasty.

Jordi Miró 2013 T Maceración Carbónica
garnacha, syrah

89

Colour: dark-red cherry, purple rim. Nose: red berry notes, ripe fruit, wild herbs, dry stone. Palate: fruity aftestaste, balanced.

Jordi Miró Garnatxa Blanca 2013 B
garnacha blanca

83

CELLER JOSEP VICENS VALLESPÍ

Aragó, 20
43780 Gandesa (Tarragona)
☎: +34 686 135 921
www.vinsjosepvicens.com
celler@vinsjosepvicens.com

Vinyes del Grau 2013 B
garnacha blanca, macabeo

86

Colour: bright straw. Nose: white flowers, fresh fruit, fine lees, dried herbs. Palate: flavourful, fruity, good acidity.

Vinyes del Grau 2013 RD
syrah

86

Colour: light cherry, bright. Nose: powerfull, ripe fruit, red berry notes, floral, expressive. Palate: fruity, fresh, easy to drink.

Vinyes del Grau Gran Coupatge 2013 B
macabeo, viognier

85

Vinyes del Grau Negro 2013 T
garnacha, cariñena

86

Colour: cherry, purple rim. Nose: expressive, fresh fruit, red berry notes, floral, balsamic herbs. Palate: flavourful, fruity, good acidity.

Vinyes del Grau Sauvignon 2013 B
sauvignon blanc

84

Vinyes del Grau Syrah 2009 TC
100% syrah

88

Colour: bright cherry. Nose: ripe fruit, sweet spices, creamy oak, expressive. Palate: flavourful, fruity, toasty, round tannins.

Vinyes del Grau Syrah 2013 T
100% syrah

89

Colour: cherry, purple rim. Nose: powerfull, red berry notes, ripe fruit, violets, floral. Palate: powerful, fresh, fruity, unctuous.

CELLER LA BOLLIDORA
Carrer Tacons, 8
43782 Vilalba dels Arcs (Tarragona)
☎: +34 600 484 900
www.cellerlabollidora.com
info@cellerlabollidora.com

Calitja 2013 B
garnacha blanca, chardonnay

85

Comanda de Vilalba 2011 T
garnacha, merlot, cariñena

84

Naevus 2012 T
garnacha, syrah

85

Plan B 2012 T
garnacha, syrah, cariñena

84

CELLER MARIOL
Rosselló, 442
08025 (Barcelona)
☎: +34 934 367 628
Fax: +34 934 500 281
www.casamariol.com
celler@cellermariol.es

Casa Mariol Cabernet Sauvignon 2010 TC
cabernet sauvignon

85

Casa Mariol Cupatge Dinàmic Chardonnay 2013 B
chardonnay

87

Colour: bright straw. Nose: fresh, fresh fruit, white flowers, dried herbs. Palate: flavourful, fruity, good acidity, balanced.

Casa Mariol Garnatxa Blanca 2013 B

84

Casa Mariol Merlot 2007 TR
merlot

87

Colour: cherry, garnet rim. Nose: scrubland, spicy, toasty. Palate: correct, fruity, flavourful, round tannins, easy to drink.

Casa Mariol Samsó 2010 TC

84

Casa Mariol Syrah 2008 TR
syrah

85

CELLER PIÑOL
Avda. Aragón, 9
43786 Batea (Tarragona)
☎: +34 977 430 505
Fax: +34 977 430 498
www.cellerpinol.com
info@cellerpinol.com

Finca Morenillo 2011 T
100% morenillo

92

Colour: cherry, garnet rim. Nose: ripe fruit, spicy, creamy oak, toasty, complex, earthy notes, balsamic herbs. Palate: powerful, flavourful, toasty, round tannins, elegant.

Josefina Piñol 2012 B
100% garnacha blanca

89

Colour: old gold. Nose: candied fruit, honeyed notes, pattiserie, dried fruit. Palate: unctuous, long, flavourful.

Josefina Piñol Vendimia Tardía 2012 Tinto Dulce
100% garnacha

92

Colour: cherry, garnet rim. Nose: ripe fruit, fruit preserve, balsamic herbs, spicy, toasty. Palate: powerful, flavourful, spicy, long, balanced, elegant, sweet.

L'Avi Arrufí 2009 T

92

Colour: cherry, garnet rim. Nose: ripe fruit, wild herbs, earthy notes, spicy, creamy oak. Palate: flavourful, long, balsamic, balanced, elegant.

L'Avi Arrufí 2012 BFB
100% garnacha blanca

94

Colour: bright straw. Nose: powerfull, ripe fruit, sweet spices, creamy oak, fragrant herbs. Palate: rich, flavourful, fresh, good acidity, toasty, balanced

Mather Teresina Selección de Viñas Viejas 2009 T

93

Colour: cherry, garnet rim. Nose: ripe fruit, spicy, creamy oak, toasty, complex, balsamic herbs. Palate: powerful, flavourful, toasty, round tannins, balanced.

Mather
Teresina
Selecció vinyes velles
D.O.Terra Alta 2009
Celler Piñol

Nuestra Sra. del Portal 2012 T Roble

88

Colour: dark-red cherry, garnet rim. Nose: creamy oak, toasty, cocoa bean. Palate: flavourful, toasty, easy to drink, ripe fruit.

Nuestra Sra. del Portal 2013 B

90

Colour: bright straw. Nose: white flowers, fragrant herbs, citrus fruit, fruit expression, expressive. Palate: fresh, fruity, flavourful, round.

Sa Natura 2011 T

88 🍃

Colour: deep cherry, garnet rim. Nose: spicy, ripe fruit, powerfull, balanced. Palate: flavourful, round tannins.

CELLER TERN, OBRADOR DE VI

Ctra. Vilalba, s/n
43786 Batea (Tarragona)
☎: +34 654 352 964
Fax: +34 977 430 433
www.ternobradordevi.com
ternobradordevi@gmail.com

Tern Arrel de Nou 2012 T

cariñena, garnacha, syrah

86

Colour: cherry, garnet rim. Nose: ripe fruit, creamy oak, roasted coffee. Palate: powerful, flavourful, toasty.

Tern gb Garnatxa Blanca 2013 B

garnacha blanca

89

Colour: bright straw. Nose: fresh, fresh fruit, white flowers, expressive, wild herbs. Palate: flavourful, fruity, good acidity, balanced.

Tern Sirà 2013 T

syrah

86

Colour: cherry, purple rim. Nose: red berry notes, floral, wild herbs. Palate: flavourful, fruity, fine bitter notes.

CELLER XAVIER CLUA

Sant Isidre, 41
43782 Vilalba dels Arcs (Tarragona)
☎: +34 690 641 907
Fax: +34 977 263 067
www.cellerclua.com
rosa@cellerclua.com

Clua Mil.lennium 2009 TC

garnacha, merlot, syrah, cabernet sauvignon

87

Colour: cherry, garnet rim. Nose: ripe fruit, wild herbs, earthy notes, spicy. Palate: balanced, flavourful, long, balsamic.

Il.lusió de Clua 2013 B

100% garnacha blanca

87

Colour: straw. Nose: floral, ripe fruit, balanced. Palate: correct, good acidity, fine bitter notes, easy to drink.

Mas d'en Pol 2010 T Barrica

garnacha, merlot, syrah, cabernet sauvignon

85

Mas d'en Pol 2012 T

83

Mas d'en Pol 2013 B

garnacha blanca, chardonnay, sauvignon blanc

85

CELLERS TARRONÉ

Calvari, 22
43786 Batea (Tarragona)
☎: +34 977 430 109
Fax: +34 977 430 109
www.cellerstarrone.com
info@cellerstarrone.com

Merian 2013 B

100% garnacha blanca

89

Colour: bright straw. Nose: fresh, fresh fruit, white flowers, expressive. Palate: flavourful, fruity, good acidity, balanced.

Merian 2013 T
garnacha, syrah, cabernet sauvignon, merlot
89
Colour: cherry, purple rim. Nose: red berry notes, raspberry, floral, expressive. Palate: fresh, fruity, flavourful, easy to drink.

Merian Dolç Natural 2011 T
garnacha
89
Colour: cherry, garnet rim. Nose: fruit preserve, ripe fruit, spicy, toasty, aged wood nuances. Palate: powerful, flavourful, sweetness, correct.

Torremadrina 2010 TC
garnacha, merlot, syrah, cabernet sauvignon
88
Colour: cherry, garnet rim. Nose: ripe fruit, spicy, creamy oak, toasty, complex. Palate: powerful, flavourful, toasty, round tannins.

Torremadrina Selecció 2005 TR
garnacha, merlot, ull de llebre, cabernet sauvignon
88
Colour: pale ruby, brick rim edge. Nose: spicy, fine reductive notes, wet leather, aged wood nuances, fruit liqueur notes. Palate: spicy, long, toasty, correct.

CELLERS UNIÓ
Joan Oliver, 16-24
43206 Reus (Tarragona)
☎: +34 977 330 055
Fax: +34 977 330 070
www.cellersunio.com
info@cellersunio.com

Clos del Pinell Garnatxa 2011 TC
garnacha
85

Clos del Pinell Garnatxa 2013 RD
garnacha
85

Clos del Pinell Garnatxa 2013 T
garnacha
86
Colour: cherry, purple rim. Nose: red berry notes, fruit expression, fragrant herbs. Palate: flavourful, light-bodied, fresh.

Clos del Pinell Garnatxa Blanca 2013 B
garnacha blanca
84

Gran Copos Garnacha Blanca 2013 B
garnacha blanca
84

Reina Elionor 2010 TR
garnacha, tempranillo, mazuelo
85

COCA I FITÓ
Avda. Onze de Setembre s/n
43736 El Masroig (Tarragona)
☎: +34 619 776 948
Fax: +34 935 457 092
www.cocaifito.com
info@cocaifito.cat

Jaspi Blanc 2013 B
88
Colour: bright straw. Nose: white flowers, fragrant herbs, fruit expression. Palate: fresh, fruity, flavourful.

EDETÀRIA
Finca El Mas - Ctra. Gandesa
a Vilalba del Arcs s/n
43780 Gandesa (Tarragona)
☎: +34 977 421 534
Fax: +34 977 421 534
www.edetaria.com
info@edetaria.com

Edetària 2007 B
garnacha blanca, macabeo
93
Colour: bright golden. Nose: ripe fruit, dry nuts, powerfull, toasty, aged wood nuances. Palate: flavourful, fruity, spicy, toasty, long.

Edetària 2008 B
93
Colour: bright golden. Nose: complex, toasty, cocoa bean, expressive, rancio notes, candied fruit. Palate: rich, spicy, fine bitter notes.

Edetària 2011 B
100% garnacha blanca
95
Colour: bright yellow. Nose: sweet spices, creamy oak, smoky, faded flowers. Palate: ripe fruit, toasty, spicy, rich.

Edetària Dolç 2009 T
90
Colour: cherry, garnet rim. Nose: fruit preserve, ripe fruit, spicy, toasty, aged wood nuances. Palate: powerful, flavourful, sweetness.

Edetària Selecció 2010 T
91
Colour: cherry, garnet rim. Nose: fragrant herbs, ripe fruit, balsamic herbs, spicy, creamy oak. Palate: flavourful, good acidity, round tannins.

Edetària Selecció 2012 B
100% garnacha blanca
91
Colour: bright straw. Nose: white flowers, fresh fruit, dried herbs, sweet spices. Palate: flavourful, fruity, good acidity, balanced.

La Pedrissa de Edetària 2012 T
cariñena
93
Colour: very deep cherry. Nose: ripe fruit, spicy, scrubland, earthy notes. Palate: powerful, good structure, good acidity, fine bitter notes.

Vía Edetana 2011 T
90
Colour: bright cherry. Nose: ripe fruit, sweet spices, creamy oak, balsamic herbs. Palate: flavourful, fruity, toasty, balanced.

Vía Edetana 2012 T
90
Colour: cherry, garnet rim. Nose: ripe fruit, wild herbs, earthy notes, spicy, creamy oak. Palate: balanced, flavourful, long, balsamic.

Vía Edetana 2013 B
91
Colour: straw. Nose: expressive, dry stone, ripe fruit, white flowers. Palate: full, long, spicy, balanced, fine bitter notes.

Vía Edetana Magnum 2012 B Barrica
91
Colour: bright yellow. Nose: dry stone, sweet spices, ripe fruit, balanced. Palate: balanced, long, full.

Vía Terra 2013 B
100% garnacha blanca
89
Colour: bright straw. Nose: fresh fruit, white flowers, balanced. Palate: fruity, flavourful, easy to drink, good acidity, good finish.

Vía Terra 2013 RD
garnacha peluda
86
Colour: rose, purple rim. Nose: powerfull, ripe fruit, red berry notes, floral. Palate: powerful, fruity, fresh, fine bitter notes.

Vía Terra 2013 T
100% garnacha
90
Colour: cherry, purple rim. Nose: expressive, fresh fruit, red berry notes, floral. Palate: flavourful, fruity, good acidity, round tannins.

EL VI A PUNT
Raval del Roser, 3
43886 Vilabella (Tarragona)
☎: +34 625 408 974
www.elviapunt.com
comercial@elviapunt.com

Sine Bag in box (3 litros) 2013 B
100% garnacha blanca
84

ESCOLA AGRÀRIA DE GANDESA
Assis Garrote, s/n
43780 Gandesa (Tarragona)
☎: +34 977 420 164
Fax: +34 977 420 607
www.gencat.cat/agricultura/eca/gandesa
aecagan.daam@gencat.cat

Glau-k 2013 BFB
garnacha blanca
84

L'abella 2013 B
macabeo, moscatel de alejandría
83

L'Elefant 2013 T
ull de llebre, syrah, cabernet sauvignon
83

La Formiga 2013 RD
ull de llebre, syrah, cabernet sauvignon
83

Les Feixes Eixutes 2012 T
garnacha, samsó
86
Colour: deep cherry, garnet rim. Nose: toasty, smoky, ripe fruit. Palate: flavourful, ripe fruit, good finish, spicy.

Murmuri Dulce Natural 2013
garnacha
85

ESTONES
Pl. Sort dels Capellans, Nau Bahaus
43740 Falset (Tarragona)
☎: +34 666 415 735
www.massersal.com
vins@massersal.com

Petites Estones Blanc 2013 B
100% garnacha blanca
87
Colour: bright straw. Nose: fresh, fresh fruit, white flowers, mineral. Palate: flavourful, fruity, good acidity, balanced.

HERÈNCIA ALTÉS

Tarragona, 42
43786 Batea (Tarragona)
☎: +34 977 430 681
www.herenciaaltes.com
nuria@exportiberia.com

Herencia Altés Benufet 2013 B
garnacha blanca

90

Colour: straw. Nose: fresh, white flowers, expressive, dry stone. Palate: flavourful, fruity, good acidity, balanced, long, fine bitter notes.

Herencia Altés Cupatge 2013 T
garnacha, samsó, syrah

85

Herencia Altés Garnatxa Blanca 2013 B
garnacha blanca

89

Colour: bright straw. Nose: fresh, dry stone, balanced, white flowers, dried herbs. Palate: balanced, full, long.

Herencia Altés Garnatxa Negra 2013 T
garnacha

86

Colour: cherry, purple rim. Nose: expressive, fresh fruit, red berry notes, balsamic herbs. Palate: flavourful, fruity, good acidity, fine bitter notes.

Herencia Altés L'Estel 2013 T
garnacha, samsó, syrah

87

Colour: cherry, purple rim. Nose: red berry notes, raspberry, floral, expressive, creamy oak. Palate: fresh, fruity, flavourful, easy to drink, balanced.

Herencia Altés La Serra 2012 T Barrica
garnacha, samsó

91

Colour: bright cherry. Nose: sweet spices, creamy oak, ripe fruit, fruit preserve. Palate: flavourful, fruity, toasty, round tannins.

Herencia Altés Rosat 2013 RD
garnacha

87

Colour: onion pink. Nose: elegant, candied fruit, dried flowers, fragrant herbs, red berry notes. Palate: light-bodied, flavourful, good acidity, long, spicy, fine bitter notes.

I TANT VINS

Passeig del Ferrocarril, 337 Baixos
08860 Castelldefels (Barcelona)
☎: +34 936 628 253
www.aribau.es
albert@aribau.es

I Tant Garnatxa Blanca 2013 B
100% garnacha blanca

89

Colour: bright straw. Nose: fresh, white flowers, grassy. Palate: flavourful, good acidity.

LAFOU CELLER

Plaça Catalunya, 34
43786 Batea (Tarragona)
☎: +34 938 743 511
Fax: +34 938 737 204
www.lafou.net
info@lafou.net

Lafou de Batea 2009 TR

93

Colour: bright cherry. Nose: ripe fruit, sweet spices, creamy oak, medium intensity, scrubland, complex. Palate: fruity, flavourful, toasty, balanced.

Lafou El Sender 2012 TC

91

Colour: cherry, garnet rim. Nose: ripe fruit, spicy, creamy oak, toasty, balsamic herbs, mineral. Palate: powerful, flavourful, toasty, balanced.

Lafou els Amelers 2013 B
100% garnacha blanca

89

Colour: bright straw. Nose: fresh, fresh fruit, white flowers, wild herbs, expressive. Palate: flavourful, fruity, good acidity, balanced.

PAGOS DE HÍBERA - CATEDRAL DEL VI

Pilonet, 8
43594 Pinell de Brai (Tarragona)
☎: +34 977 426 234
Fax: +34 977 426 290
www.catedraldelvi.com
bodega@catedraldelvi.com

Gamberro Garnacha Blanca 2011 B
100% garnacha blanca

90

Colour: bright yellow. Nose: powerfull, ripe fruit, sweet spices, creamy oak, fragrant herbs. Palate: rich, flavourful, fresh, good acidity.

Gamberro Tinto de Guarda 2011 T

89

Colour: cherry, garnet rim. Nose: fruit preserve, fruit liqueur notes, spicy, creamy oak. Palate: pruney, balsamic, powerful, flavourful, toasty.

L'Indià 2012 T
89
Colour: bright cherry. Nose: ripe fruit, sweet spices, creamy oak, mineral, balsamic herbs. Palate: fruity, flavourful, toasty, balanced.

L'Indià 2013 B
100% garnacha blanca
89
Colour: bright straw. Nose: medium intensity, dried flowers, fresh fruit. Palate: fruity, easy to drink, long, balanced, fine bitter notes.

SERRA DE CAVALLS
Bonaire, 1
43594 El Pinell de Brai (Tarragona)
☎: +34 977 426 049
www.serradecavalls.com
sat@serradecavalls.com

Serra de Cavalls 1938 2011 T Fermentado en Barrica
merlot, cabernet sauvignon, syrah
84

Serra de Cavalls 2010 TC
82

Serra de Cavalls 2011 BFB
garnacha blanca
85

Serra de Cavalls 2013 B
garnacha blanca
86
Colour: straw, pale. Nose: faded flowers, medium intensity. Palate: correct, good finish, fine bitter notes.

Serra de Cavalls 2013 T
83

VINS DE MESIES
La Verge, 6
43782 Vilalba dels Arcs (Tarragona)
☎: +34 977 438 196
www.ecovitres.com
info@ecovitres.com

Mesies Garnatxa 2012 T
garnacha
85

Mesies Garnatxa Blanca 2013 B
100% garnacha blanca
82

Mesies Selecció 2009 T
garnacha, samsó, syrah
86 🌷
Colour: black cherry, garnet rim. Nose: complex, balanced, spicy, fine reductive notes, dried herbs. Palate: flavourful, round tannins, lacks balance.

VINS DEL SUD
Raval del Roser, 3
43886 Vilabella (Tarragona)
☎: +34 625 408 974
www.vinsdelsud.com
oriol@vinsdelsud.com

Ciutats 2013 B
83

Ciutats 2013 T
83

VINS DEL TROS
Major, 12
43782 Vilalba dels Arcs (Tarragona)
☎: +34 605 096 447
Fax: +34 977 438 042
www.vinsdeltros.com
info@vinsdeltros.com

Ay de Mí 2012 TC
garnacha, cariñena, syrah
87
Colour: cherry, garnet rim. Nose: fruit preserve, smoky, spicy. Palate: flavourful, fruity, balanced, round tannins.

Cent x Cent 2013 B
garnacha blanca
85

VINS LA BOTERA
Sant Roc, 26
43786 Batea (Tarragona)
☎: +34 977 430 009
Fax: +34 977 430 801
www.labotera.com
labotera@labotera.com

Bruna Dolç 2012 T
garnacha, syrah
91
Colour: cherry, garnet rim. Nose: fruit preserve, ripe fruit, spicy, toasty, aged wood nuances. Palate: powerful, flavourful, sweetness, balanced, elegant.

L'Arnot 2013 T
garnacha, syrah
85

Mudèfer 2011 TC
garnacha, cariñena, syrah, merlot

86

Colour: cherry, garnet rim. Nose: ripe fruit, spicy, creamy oak, roasted coffee. Palate: powerful, flavourful, toasty.

Vila-Closa Chardonnay 2013 BFB
chardonnay

86

Colour: bright yellow. Nose: ripe fruit, dry nuts, toasty, aged wood nuances. Palate: flavourful, fruity, spicy, toasty.

Vila-Closa Garnatxa Blanca 2013 B
100% garnacha blanca

85

Vila-Closa Rubor 2013 RD
garnacha tintorera

87

Colour: rose, purple rim. Nose: powerfull, ripe fruit, red berry notes, floral, rose petals. Palate: powerful, fruity, fresh.

VINYA D'IRTO
Plaça Comerç , 5
43780 Gandesa (Tarragona)
☎: +34 977 421 534
Fax: +34 977 421 534
info@edetaria.com

Vinya d'Irto 2013 B
88

Colour: bright straw. Nose: ripe fruit, fruit expression, floral. Palate: easy to drink, good acidity, fine bitter notes.

Vinya d'Irto 2013 T
88

Colour: cherry, purple rim. Nose: medium intensity, red berry notes, floral. Palate: correct, good acidity, good finish, fruity aftestaste.

DO. TIERRA DE LEÓN

CONSEJO REGULADOR
Alonso Castrillo, 29.
24200 Valencia de Don Juan (León)
☎ :+34 987 751 089 - Fax: +34 987 750 012
@: directortecnico@dotierradeleon.es
www.dotierradeleon.es

LOCATION:

In the southeast of Catalonia, in the province of Tarragona. It covers the municipal districts of Arnes, Batea, Bot, Caseres, Corbera d´Ebre, La Fatarella, Gandesa, Horta de Sant Joan, Pinell de Brai, La Pobla de Massaluca, Prat de Comte and Vilalba dels Arcs.

GRAPE VARIETIES:

White: Chardonnay, Garnacha Blanca, Parellada, Macabeo, Moscatel, Sauvignon Blanc, Chenin, Pedro Ximénez. Experimental: Viognier.
Red: Cabernet Sauvigon, Cariñena, Garnacha Tinta, Garnacha Peluda, Syrah, Tempranillo, Merlot, Samsó, Cabernet Franc. Experimental: Petit Verdot, Marselane, Caladoc.

FIGURES:

Vineyard surface: 1,406 – Wine-Growers: 333 – Wineries: 35 – 2013 Harvest rating: Good – Production 13: 3,084,804 litres – Market percentages: 98% domestic - 2% export.

SOIL:

The vineyards are located on an extensive plateau at an altitude of slightly over 400 m. The soil is calcareous and the texture mainly clayey, poor in organic matter and with many pebbles.

CLIMATE:

Mediterranean, with continental influences. It is characterized by its hot, dry summers and very cold winters, especially in the higher regions in the east. The average annual rainfall is 400 mm. Another vital aspect is the wind: the 'Cierzo' and the 'Garbi' (Ábrego) winds.

VINTAGE RATING · PEÑÍNGUIDE

2009	2010	2011	2012	2013
VERY GOOD	VERY GOOD	GOOD	GOOD	GOOD

BODEGA CIEN CEPAS

Pago de las Bodegas
24225 Corbillo de los Oteros (León)
☎: +34 987 249 071
Fax: +34 987 570 059
cesar@100cepas.es

100 Cepas 2012 T
prieto picudo
88
Colour: cherry, garnet rim. Nose: ripe fruit, spicy, creamy oak, toasty. Palate: powerful, flavourful, toasty, round tannins.

BODEGAS ÁBREGO

Manuel Cadenas, 4
24230 Valdevimbre (León)
☎: +34 987 304 133
bodegasabrego@hotmail.com

Pegalahebra 2012 T
100% prieto picudo
88
Colour: deep cherry, purple rim. Nose: fruit expression, ripe fruit, scrubland. Palate: fruity, easy to drink.

Pegalahebra 2013 RD
100% prieto picudo
84

BODEGAS MARCOS MIÑAMBRES

Camino de Pobladura, s/n
24234 Villamañán (León)
☎: +34 987 767 038
satvined@picos.com

Los Silvares 2009 TR
100% prieto picudo
89
Colour: pale ruby, brick rim edge. Nose: spicy, fine reductive notes, wet leather, aged wood nuances, fruit liqueur notes. Palate: spicy, fine tannins, elegant, long.

BODEGAS MARGÓN

Avda Valencia de Don Juan, s/n
24209 Pajares de los Oteros (León)
☎: +34 987 750 800
Fax: +34 987 750 481
www.bodegasmargon.com
comercial@bodegasmargon.com

Pricum 2013 RD
prieto picudo
89
Colour: light cherry. Nose: elegant, candied fruit, dried flowers, fragrant herbs, red berry notes. Palate: light-bodied, flavourful, good acidity, long, spicy.

Pricum Albarín 2012 B Barrica
albarín
92
Colour: bright yellow. Nose: powerfull, ripe fruit, sweet spices, creamy oak, fragrant herbs. Palate: rich, smoky aftertaste, flavourful, fresh, good acidity, balanced.

Pricum El Voluntario 2010 T
prieto picudo
92
Colour: bright cherry. Nose: ripe fruit, earthy notes, spicy, creamy oak, balsamic herbs. Palate: balanced, flavourful, long, balsamic.

Pricum Paraje del Santo 2010 T
prieto picudo
93
Colour: dark-red cherry, garnet rim. Nose: complex, balsamic herbs, spicy, ripe fruit, varietal. Palate: fruity, balanced, fresh, round tannins.

Pricum Prieto Picudo 2010 T
prieto picudo
91
Colour: deep cherry, garnet rim. Nose: medium intensity, varietal, ripe fruit, scrubland. Palate: good structure, good acidity.

Pricum Primeur 2012 T
prieto picudo
90
Colour: bright cherry. Nose: ripe fruit, sweet spices, creamy oak, expressive, balanced. Palate: flavourful, fruity, toasty, round tannins, balsamic.

Pricum Valdemuz 2010 T
prieto picudo
89
Colour: bright cherry. Nose: ripe fruit, sweet spices, creamy oak, medium intensity. Palate: fruity, flavourful, toasty.

BODEGAS MELWA

Calvo Sotelo 4
24230 Valdevimbre (León)
☎: +34 987 304 149
Fax: +34 987 304 149
melwa45@gmail.com

Valle Gudin 2010 TC
100% prieto picudo
84

Valle Gudin 2013 RD
100% prieto picudo
86
Colour: rose, purple rim. Nose: powerfull, ripe fruit, red berry notes, balsamic herbs. Palate: powerful, fruity, fresh.

BODEGAS VINOS DE LEÓN

La Vega, s/n
24009 León (León)
☎: +34 987 209 712
Fax: +34 987 209 800
www.bodegasvinosdeleon.es
info@bodegasvinosdeleon.es

Don Suero 2009 TR
100% prieto picudo

89

Colour: dark-red cherry, garnet rim. Nose: ripe fruit, sweet spices, creamy oak. Palate: good structure, flavourful, balanced.

Don Suero 2010 TC
100% prieto picudo

86

Colour: cherry, garnet rim. Nose: ripe fruit, spicy, toasty. Palate: flavourful, toasty, round tannins.

Valjunco 2013 B
100% verdejo

83

Valjunco 2013 RD
100% prieto picudo

84

Valjunco 2013 T
prieto picudo

87

Colour: cherry, purple rim. Nose: medium intensity, red berry notes, ripe fruit, balsamic herbs. Palate: fruity, easy to drink, good finish.

BODEGAS VITALIS

Ctra. Villamañan-Astorga, km. 33
24234 Villamañan (León)
☎: +34 987 131 019
www.bodegasvitalis.com
vitalis@bodegasvitalis.com

Vitalis 2009 TC
prieto picudo

87

Colour: cherry, garnet rim. Nose: ripe fruit, spicy, creamy oak, toasty. Palate: powerful, flavourful, toasty, correct.

Vitalis 6 meses 2011 T Roble
prieto picudo

85

Lágrima de Vitalis 2013 B
albarín

88

Colour: straw, greenish rim. Nose: dried flowers, fresh fruit, citrus fruit. Palate: fresh, fruity, good acidity, fine bitter notes.

Lágrima de Vitalis 2013 RD
prieto picudo

85

BODEGAS Y VIÑEDOS CASIS

Las Bodegas, s/n
24325 Gordaliza del Pino (León)
☎: +34 987 699 618
www.bodegascasis.com
anacasis@gmail.com

Casis 2013 T
mencía, prieto picudo

87

Colour: cherry, purple rim. Nose: expressive, fresh fruit, red berry notes, wild herbs. Palate: flavourful, fruity, good acidity.

Casis Prieto Picudo 2011 TC
prieto picudo

87

Colour: bright cherry. Nose: ripe fruit, sweet spices, creamy oak, medium intensity. Palate: fruity, flavourful, toasty.

Casis Prieto Picudo 2013 RD
prieto picudo

85

Casis Verdejo 2013 B
verdejo

80

BODEGAS Y VIÑEDOS LA SILVERA

La Barrera, 7
24209 Pajares de los Oteros (León)
☎: +34 618 174 176
oterobenito@gmail.com

Preto 2013 RD

84

COOPERATIVA DE VALDEVIMBRE

Ctra. de León, s/n
24230 Valdevimbre (León)
☎: +34 987 304 195
Fax: +34 987 304 195
www.vinicoval.com
valdevim@gmail.com

Abadía de Balderedo 2012 T
prieto picudo

85

Abadía de Balderedo 2013 RD
prieto picudo

84

Abadía de Balderedo Verdejo 2013 B
verdejo
85

Señorío de Valdés 2012 T
prieto picudo
83

Señorío de Valdés 2013 RD
prieto picudo
83

GORDONZELLO
Alto de Santa Marina, s/n
24294 Gordoncillo (León)
☎: +34 987 758 030
Fax: +34 987 757 201
www.gordonzello.com
info@gordonzello.com

Gurdos 2013 RD
100% prieto picudo
87
Colour: light cherry, coppery red. Nose: medium intensity, faded flowers. Palate: fruity, flavourful, easy to drink, balanced.

KYra Peregrino 2012 BFB
100% albarín
90
Colour: bright yellow. Nose: powerfull, ripe fruit, sweet spices, creamy oak, fragrant herbs. Palate: rich, smoky aftertaste, flavourful, fresh, good acidity.

Peregrino 2008 TR
100% prieto picudo
89
Colour: ruby red. Nose: ripe fruit, spicy, creamy oak, toasty, fine reductive notes. Palate: powerful, flavourful, toasty, round tannins.

Peregrino 2011 TC
100% prieto picudo
87
Colour: cherry, garnet rim. Nose: ripe fruit, spicy, creamy oak, toasty. Palate: powerful, flavourful, toasty, round tannins.

Peregrino 2013 T
100% prieto picudo
84

Peregrino 14 2011 TC
100% prieto picudo
87
Colour: cherry, garnet rim. Nose: ripe fruit, spicy, toasty. Palate: powerful, flavourful, toasty, round tannins, balsamic.

Peregrino 2012 T Roble
prieto picudo
85

Peregrino 2013 RD
100% prieto picudo
87
Colour: light cherry, bright. Nose: red berry notes, ripe fruit. Palate: flavourful, balanced, easy to drink, fine bitter notes.

Peregrino Albarín 2013 B
100% albarín
87
Colour: bright straw. Nose: medium intensity, varietal, faded flowers, fresh fruit. Palate: correct, good acidity, long.

Peregrino Blanco 2013 B
100% verdejo
85

Peregrino Mil 100 2011 T Barrica
100% prieto picudo
88
Colour: cherry, garnet rim. Nose: ripe fruit, wild herbs, earthy notes, spicy, creamy oak. Palate: balanced, flavourful, long, balsamic.

LEYENDA DEL PÁRAMO
Ctra. de León s/n, Paraje El Cueto
24230 Valdevimbre (León)
☎: +34 987 050 039
Fax: +34 987 050 039
www.leyendadelparamo.com
info@leyendadelparamo.com

El Aprendiz 2013 B
albarín
89
Colour: bright straw. Nose: white flowers, fragrant herbs, fruit expression. Palate: fresh, fruity, flavourful, balanced, elegant.

El Aprendiz 2013 RD
prieto picudo
88
Colour: rose, purple rim. Nose: powerfull, ripe fruit, red berry notes, floral, expressive. Palate: powerful, fruity, fresh, fine bitter notes.

El Aprendiz 2013 T
prieto picudo
87
Colour: bright cherry, purple rim. Nose: fresh, red berry notes, wild herbs. Palate: light-bodied, easy to drink.

El Médico 2011 T Roble
prieto picudo
92
Colour: deep cherry, purple rim. Nose: creamy oak, toasty, ripe fruit, balsamic herbs, varietal. Palate: balanced, spicy, long.

El Músico 2011 T
prieto picudo

93

Colour: cherry, garnet rim. Nose: spicy, creamy oak, toasty, complex, earthy notes, fruit preserve. Palate: powerful, flavourful, toasty.

Flor del Páramo 2013 B
verdejo

87

Colour: bright straw. Nose: fresh fruit, dried herbs, medium intensity. Palate: fruity, easy to drink.

Flor del Páramo 2013 T
prieto picudo

86

Colour: cherry, garnet rim. Nose: ripe fruit, grassy, powerfull. Palate: balsamic, fine bitter notes, slightly green tannins.

Mittel 2013 B
albarín

87

Colour: bright straw. Nose: fresh, fresh fruit, white flowers, expressive. Palate: fruity, good acidity, balanced.

Mittel 2013 RD
prieto picudo

87

Colour: rose, purple rim. Nose: powerfull, ripe fruit, red berry notes, floral, expressive. Palate: powerful, fruity, fresh.

LOS PALOMARES
Los Palomares, 6
24230 Valdevimbre (León)
☎: +34 987 304 218
Fax: +34 987 304 193
www.bodegalospalomares.com
lospalomares@bodegalospalomares.com

3 Palomares 2011 TC
prieto picudo

88

Colour: cherry, garnet rim. Nose: ripe fruit, spicy, creamy oak, toasty, complex, dark chocolate, balsamic herbs. Palate: powerful, flavourful, toasty, round tannins.

3 Palomares 2013 B
verdejo

87

Colour: bright yellow. Nose: fresh, fresh fruit, white flowers, expressive. Palate: flavourful, fruity, good acidity, balanced.

3 Palomares 2013 RD
prieto picudo

85

3 Palomares 2013 T
100% prieto picudo

85

MELGARAJO
Plaza Mayor, 9
47687 Melgar de Abajo (Valladolid)
☎: +34 679 082 971
www.melgarajo.es
melgarajo@melgarajo.es

Melgus 2010 TC
prieto picudo

90

Colour: cherry, garnet rim. Nose: ripe fruit, spicy, creamy oak, toasty, expressive. Palate: powerful, flavourful, toasty, round tannins.

Melgus 2010 TR
prieto picudo

89

Colour: cherry, garnet rim. Nose: balanced, complex, ripe fruit, spicy, balsamic herbs, mineral. Palate: good structure, flavourful, round tannins.

Valdeleña 2013 B
verdejo

84

Valdeleña 2013 RD
prieto picudo

85

SEÑORÍO DE LOS ARCOS
La Iglesia, s/n
24191 Ardoncino (León)
☎: +34 987 226 594
Fax: +34 987 226 594
admin@senoriodelosarcos.es

Vega Carriegos 2010 TC
prieto picudo

89

Colour: cherry, garnet rim. Nose: ripe fruit, spicy, toasty, scrubland. Palate: powerful, flavourful, toasty, round tannins.

Vega Carriegos 2011 T Roble
prieto picudo

87

Colour: dark-red cherry, garnet rim. Nose: ripe fruit, scrubland, spicy. Palate: correct, easy to drink, good finish.

Vega Carriegos 2013 RD
prieto picudo

84

TAMPESTA

La Socollada, s/n
24240 Valdevimbre (León)
☎: +34 666 217 032
Fax: +34 987 351 025
www.tampesta.com
bodegas@tampesta.com

Maneki 2013 B
albarín
89
Colour: bright yellow. Nose: faded flowers, medium intensity, balanced. Palate: flavourful, good acidity, fine bitter notes.

Tampesta 2011 T Roble
prieto picudo
87
Colour: cherry, garnet rim. Nose: scrubland, medium intensity. Palate: fruity, correct, round tannins.

Tampesta 2013 B
albarín
84

Tampesta 2013 RD
prieto picudo
88
Colour: rose, purple rim. Nose: powerfull, ripe fruit, red berry notes, floral, expressive. Palate: powerful, fruity, fresh, fine bitter notes.

Tampesta Finca de los Vientos 2010 T
prieto picudo
88
Colour: cherry, garnet rim. Nose: ripe fruit, spicy, creamy oak, toasty, complex. Palate: powerful, flavourful, toasty.

Tampesta Golán 2010 T
prieto picudo
90
Colour: dark-red cherry, garnet rim. Nose: medium intensity, red berry notes, ripe fruit, spicy. Palate: good structure, flavourful, correct.

Tampesta Imelda 2010 T
prieto picudo
91
Colour: cherry, garnet rim. Nose: ripe fruit, spicy, creamy oak, toasty, complex. Palate: powerful, flavourful, toasty, round tannins.

VINÍCOLA VALMADRIGAL

Constitución, 16
24323 Castrotierra de Valmadrigal
(León)
☎: +34 987 784 249
Fax: +34 987 784 249
bodegavalmadrigal@bodegavalmadrigal.com

Castro Iuvara 2013 B
verdejo
84

Castro Iuvara 2013 B
87
Colour: bright straw. Nose: white flowers, fragrant herbs, fruit expression. Palate: fresh, fruity, flavourful, balanced, elegant.

VIÑEDOS Y BODEGA JULIO CRESPO AGUILOCHE

Ctra. Sahagún-Renedo Km. 6
24326 Joara, Sahagún (León)
☎: +34 987 130 010
Fax: +34 987 130 010
www.bodegasjuliocrespo.com
info@bodegasjuliocrespo.com

Alevosía 2012 T
mencía
84

Premeditación 2011 T
prieto picudo
86
Colour: cherry, garnet rim. Nose: ripe fruit, fruit preserve, woody, balsamic herbs. Palate: powerful, flavourful, spicy, toasty.

VIÑEDOS Y BODEGA PARDEVALLES

Ctra. de León, s/n
24230 Valdevimbre (León)
☎: +34 987 304 222
Fax: +34 987 304 222
www.pardevalles.es
info@pardevalles.es

Pardevalles 2013 RD
prieto picudo
89
Colour: light cherry. Nose: powerfull, ripe fruit, red berry notes, floral, expressive. Palate: powerful, fruity, fresh, fine bitter notes.

Pardevalles Albarín 2013 B
albarín
90
Colour: bright straw. Nose: fresh, fresh fruit, white flowers, citrus fruit, wild herbs. Palate: flavourful, fruity, good acidity, balanced.

Pardevalles Carroleón 2010 T
prieto picudo
92
Colour: cherry, garnet rim. Nose: red berry notes, ripe fruit, spicy, creamy oak, toasty. Palate: powerful, flavourful, toasty, round tannins.

Pardevalles Gamonal 2011 T
prieto picudo
92
Colour: cherry, garnet rim. Nose: ripe fruit, wild herbs, earthy notes, spicy, creamy oak, floral, dry stone. Palate: balanced, flavourful, long, balsamic.

WEINWERK EL LAGARTO
Portugal, 7
49323 Fornillos de Fermoselle (Zamora)
☎: +49 232 459 724
Fax: +49 232 459 721
www.gourmet-lagarto.de
winzer@gourmet-lagarto.de

Luby Godello 2011 B
godello
93
Colour: bright straw. Nose: white flowers, fresh fruit, expressive, fine lees, dried herbs. Palate: flavourful, fruity, good acidity, balanced.

Luby Verdejo Albarín 2012 B
verdejo, albarín
89
Colour: bright straw. Nose: fresh, fresh fruit, white flowers. Palate: flavourful, fruity, good acidity, balanced.

Picú de Weinwerk 2011 T
100% prieto picudo
89
Colour: cherry, garnet rim. Nose: powerfull, ripe fruit, fruit expression, sweet spices, toasty. Palate: flavourful, ripe fruit, mineral, fine tannins.

DO. TIERRA DEL VINO DE ZAMORA

CONSEJO REGULADOR
Plaza Mayor, 1
49708 Villanueva de Campeán (Zamora)
☎:+34 980 560 055 - Fax: +34 980 560 055
@: info@tierradelvino.net
www.tierradelvino.net

LOCATION:

In the southeast part of Zamora, on the Duero river banks. This region comprises 46 municipal districts in the province Zamora and 10 in neighbouring Salamanca. Average altitude is 750 meters.

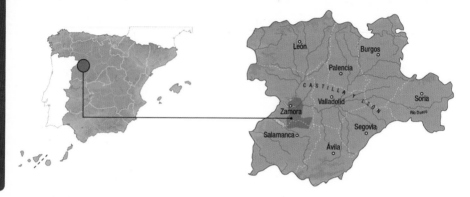

GRAPE VARIETIES:

White: Malvasía, Moscatel de grano menudo and Verdejo (preferential); Albillo, Palomino and Godello (authorized).
Red: Tempranillo (main), Cabernet Sauvignon and Garnacha.

FIGURES:

Vineyard surface: 692 – Wine-Growers: 204 – Wineries: 11 – 2013 Harvest rating: - – Production 13: 530,410 litres – Market percentages: 60% domestic - 40% export.

SOIL:

The character of the territory derives from the river Duero tributaries, so it is predominantly alluvial and clay in the lower strata that might not allow great drainage, though they vary a lot depending on the altitude. There are also some sandy patches on the plain land and stony ones on the hill side.

CLIMATE:

Extreme temperatures as correspond to a dry continental pattern, with very hot summers and cold winters. It does not rain much and average annual rainfall hardly reaches 400 mm.

VINTAGE RATING

PEÑÍNGUIDE

2009	2010	2011	2012	2013
GOOD	N/A	N/A	VERY GOOD	VERY GOOD

ALTER EGO BODEGA DE CRIANZA

Larga, 4
49709 Cabañas de Sayago (Zamora)
☎: +34 670 095 149

Dominio de Sexmil 2008 T
100% tinta del país
91
Colour: cherry, garnet rim. Nose: spicy, toasty, mineral, ripe fruit. Palate: powerful, flavourful, toasty, round tannins.

BODEGA GUILLERMO FREIRE

Cl. Pozo, 33
49150 Moraleja del Vino (Zamora)
☎: +34 655 925 127

Jarreño 2012 T Roble
tempranillo
88
Colour: bright cherry. Nose: ripe fruit, sweet spices, creamy oak, expressive. Palate: flavourful, fruity, toasty, round tannins.

BODEGAS EL SOTO

Ctra. de Circunvalación, s/n
49708 Villanueva de Campeán (Zamora)
☎: +34 980 560 330
Fax: +34 980 560 330
www.bodegaselsoto.com
info@bodegaselsoto.com

Proclama 2013 B
100% malvasía
88
Colour: bright straw. Nose: white flowers, fresh fruit, expressive, fine lees, dried herbs. Palate: flavourful, fruity, good acidity, balanced.

Proclama Selección 2011 T
100% tempranillo
91
Colour: cherry, garnet rim. Nose: spicy, creamy oak, toasty, complex, earthy notes. Palate: powerful, flavourful, toasty, round tannins.

Proclama Tempranillo 2012 T
100% tempranillo
88
Colour: cherry, purple rim. Nose: powerfull, red berry notes, ripe fruit, floral, expressive. Palate: powerful, fresh, fruity, unctuous.

MALANDRÍN

Miguel S. Herrador, 3
47014 (Valladolid)
☎: +34 644 172 122
www.malandrinwines.com
info@malandrinwines.com

Malandrín Tempranillo 2010 T
tempranillo
89
Colour: cherry, garnet rim. Nose: fruit preserve, fruit liqueur notes, spicy. Palate: flavourful, pruney, balsamic.

Malandrín Verdejo 2013 B
verdejo, godello, malvasía
90
Colour: bright straw. Nose: fresh, fresh fruit, white flowers, expressive. Palate: flavourful, fruity, good acidity, balanced.

MICROBODEGA RODRÍGUEZ MORÁN

Del Prado, 14
49719 Villamor de los Escuderos (Zamora)
☎: +34 980 609 047
http://microbodegabio.blogspot.com.es
info@microbodega.es

Alumbro 2013 B
verdejo, godello, albillo
87
Colour: bright straw. Nose: white flowers, expressive, dried herbs. Palate: flavourful, fruity, good acidity, balanced.

Alumbro 2013 T
tempranillo, cabernet sauvignon
88 🌱
Colour: bright cherry. Nose: sweet spices, creamy oak, expressive, red berry notes. Palate: flavourful, fruity, toasty, round tannins.

TESO LA ENCINA BODEGA Y VIÑEDOS

Teso la Encina
49719 Villamor de los Escuderos (Zamora)
☎: +34 639 824 200
www.tesolaencina.es
bodega@tesolaencina.es

Sr. Polo 2013 B
verdejo
89
Colour: bright straw. Nose: fresh, fresh fruit, white flowers. Palate: flavourful, fruity, good acidity, balanced.

VIÑA ESCUDEROS S. COOP.
Ctra. Cubo del Vino, s/n
49719 Villamor de los Escuderos
(Zamora)
☎: +34 980 609 204
Fax: +34 980 609 154
www.vinaescuderos.com
bodega@vinaescuderos.com

Gavión 2012 T Roble
89
Colour: bright cherry. Nose: ripe fruit, sweet spices, creamy oak, expressive. Palate: flavourful, fruity, toasty, round tannins.

Gavión 2007 TR
91
Colour: very deep cherry. Nose: ripe fruit, spicy, creamy oak, toasty, characterful. Palate: powerful, flavourful, toasty, round tannins.

Gavión 2010 TC
88
Colour: bright cherry. Nose: ripe fruit, sweet spices, creamy oak, medium intensity. Palate: fruity, flavourful, toasty.

Gavión 2013 RD
85

Gavión 2013 T
86
Colour: very deep cherry, garnet rim. Nose: warm, dried herbs, ripe fruit. Palate: flavourful, ripe fruit, long.

Gavión Verdejo 2013 B
verdejo
86
Colour: bright straw. Nose: fragrant herbs, fruit expression, expressive. Palate: fresh, fruity, flavourful, balanced, elegant.

VIÑAS DEL CÉNIT
Ctra. de Circunvalación, s/n
49708 Villanueva de Campeán
(Zamora)
☎: +34 980 569 346
www.vinasdelcenit.com
aalberca@avanteselecta.com

Cenit 2010 T
100% tempranillo
95
Colour: cherry, garnet rim. Nose: ripe fruit, spicy, creamy oak, toasty, complex, dark chocolate, earthy notes. Palate: powerful, flavourful, toasty, round tannins.

Via Cenit 2012 T
100% tempranillo
93
Colour: very deep cherry. Nose: ripe fruit, spicy, creamy oak, toasty, characterful. Palate: powerful, flavourful, toasty, round tannins.

DO. TORO

CONSEJO REGULADOR
De la Concepción, 3. Palacio de los Condes de Requena
49800 Toro (Zamora)
☎:+34 980 690 335 - Fax: +34 980 693 201
@: consejo@dotoro.es
www.dotoro.es

LOCATION:

Comprising 12 municipal districts of the province of Zamora (Argujillo, Boveda de Toro, Morales de Toro, El Pego, Peleagonzalo, El Piñero, San Miguel de la Ribera, Sanzoles, Toro, Valdefinjas, Venialbo and Villanueva del Puente) and three in the province of Valladolid (San Román de la Hornija, Villafranca de Duero and the vineyards of Villaester de Arriba and Villaester de Abajo in the municipal district of Pedrosa del Rey), which practically corresponds to the agricultural region of Bajo Duero. The production area is to the south of the course of the Duero, which crosses the region from east to west.

GRAPE VARIETIES:

White: Malvasía and Verdejo.
Red: Tinta de Toro (majority) and Garnacha.

FIGURES:

Vineyard surface: 5,660 – Wine-Growers: 1,250 – Wineries: 57 – 2013 Harvest rating: Very Good– Production 13: 13,000,000 litres – Market percentages: 70% domestic - 30% export.

SOIL:

The geography of the DO is characterised by a gently-undulating terrain. The vineyards are situated at an altitude of 620 m to 750 m and the soil is mainly brownish-grey limestone. However, the stony alluvial soil is better.

CLIMATE:

Extreme continental, with Atlantic influences and quite arid, with an average annual rainfall of between 350 mm and 400 mm. The winters are harsh (which means extremely low temperatures and long periods of frosts) and the summers short, although not excessively hot, with significant contrasts in day-night temperatures.

VINTAGE RATING

PEÑÍNGUIDE

2009	2010	2011	2012	2013
GOOD	VERY GOOD	GOOD	VERY GOOD	VERY GOOD

PEÑÍNGUIDE 25 Years to Spanish Wine

ALVAR DE DIOS HERNANDEZ

Zamora No8
47154 El Pego (Zamora)
☎: +34 629 902 507

eldelarecella@gmail.com

Aciano 2012 T
tinta de Toro

93

Colour: bright cherry. Nose: ripe fruit, sweet spices, creamy oak, medium intensity, complex, expressive. Palate: fruity, flavourful, toasty.

Aciano 2013 T
tinta de Toro

91

Colour: ruby red, purple rim. Nose: red berry notes, fruit liqueur notes, balsamic herbs, wild herbs, spicy. Palate: flavourful, balanced, correct, spicy, balsamic, elegant.

ARXIS

Paseo Zorrilla, 133
47008 Valladolid (Valladolid)
☎: +34 609 662 818
www.multicyclos.com

Arxis 2013 T
100% tinta de Toro

86

Colour: very deep cherry, garnet rim. Nose: warm, dried herbs, ripe fruit. Palate: flavourful, ripe fruit, long.

Arxis Selección 2011 T
100% tinta de Toro

88

Colour: cherry, garnet rim. Nose: ripe fruit, wild herbs, earthy notes, spicy, creamy oak. Palate: balanced, flavourful, long, balsamic.

BODEGA BURDIGALA
(F. LURTON & M. ROLLAND)

Camino Magarín, s/n
47529 Villafranca del Duero (Valladolid)
☎: +34 980 082 027
Fax: +34 983 034 040
www.burdigala.es
bodega@burdigala.es

Campesino 2012 T
tinta de Toro

90

Colour: cherry, garnet rim. Nose: ripe fruit, sweet spices, creamy oak, balanced. Palate: fruity, flavourful, toasty, round.

Campo Alegre 2012 T
tinta de Toro

92

Colour: dark-red cherry. Nose: ripe fruit, spicy, creamy oak, toasty, complex. Palate: powerful, flavourful, toasty, round tannins.

Campo Eliseo 2009 T
tinta de Toro

93

Colour: cherry, garnet rim. Nose: red berry notes, ripe fruit, spicy, creamy oak, toasty, complex, earthy notes. Palate: powerful, flavourful, toasty, round tannins.

BODEGA CAMPIÑA

Ctra. Toro-Veniablo, Km. 6,9
49882 Valdefinjas (Zamora)
☎: +34 980 568 125
Fax: +34 980 059 965
www.bodegacampina.com
info@bodegacampina.com

Campiña 2012 T Roble
100% tinta de Toro

87

Colour: cherry, garnet rim. Nose: ripe fruit, wild herbs, earthy notes, spicy. Palate: balanced, balsamic.

Campiña 2013 T
100% tinta de Toro

85

Campiña Viñas Centenarias 2009 T
100% tinta de Toro

86

Colour: dark-red cherry, garnet rim. Nose: ripe fruit, balanced, spicy. Palate: fruity, spicy, round tannins.

BODEGA CUATRO MIL CEPAS

Rafael Alonso nº 21
49154 El Pego (Zamora)
☎: +34 670 095 149

Cinco de Copas 2012 T Roble
tinta de Toro

87

Colour: bright cherry. Nose: ripe fruit, sweet spices, creamy oak, toasty. Palate: flavourful, fruity, toasty, round tannins.

Díscolo 2010 T
tinta de Toro

88

Colour: cherry, garnet rim. Nose: ripe fruit, spicy, creamy oak, toasty. Palate: powerful, flavourful, toasty, round tannins.

BODEGA CYAN

Ctra. Valdefinjas - Venialbo, Km. 9,2, Finca La Calera
49800 Toro (Zamora)
☎: +34 980 568 029
Fax: +34 980 568 036
www.bodegacyan.es
cyan@matarromera.es

Cyan 2010 TC
100% tinta de Toro

87

Colour: bright cherry. Nose: ripe fruit, sweet spices, medium intensity. Palate: fruity, flavourful, toasty.

Cyan 8 meses 2012 T
100% tinta de Toro

86

Colour: bright cherry. Nose: ripe fruit, sweet spices, creamy oak, fruit preserve. Palate: flavourful, fruity, toasty, round tannins.

Cyan Pago de la Calera 2004 T
100% tinta de Toro

91

Colour: pale ruby, brick rim edge. Nose: elegant, spicy, fine reductive notes, wet leather, aged wood nuances, fruit liqueur notes. Palate: spicy, fine tannins, elegant, long, balanced.

Cyan Prestigio 2006 T
100% tinta de Toro

90

Colour: very deep cherry. Nose: ripe fruit, spicy, toasty, sweet spices. Palate: powerful, flavourful, toasty, round tannins, balanced.

Selección Personal Carlos Moro Cyan 2004 T
100% tinta de Toro

88

Colour: deep cherry. Nose: ripe fruit, spicy, creamy oak, toasty, complex, fine reductive notes. Palate: powerful, flavourful, toasty, round tannins.

BODEGA EL ALBAR LURTON

Camino Magarin, s/n
47529 Villafranca del Duero (Valladolid)
☎: +34 983 034 030
Fax: +34 983 034 040
www.francoislurton.es
bodega@francoislurton.es

Hermanos Lurton 2012 T
tinta de Toro

91

Colour: cherry, garnet rim. Nose: ripe fruit, spicy, creamy oak, toasty, complex. Palate: powerful, flavourful, toasty, balanced.

BODEGA FLORENCIO SALGADO NARROS

Ctra. Toro - Salamanca, Km. 3,20
49800 Toro (Zamora)
☎: +34 649 761 324
bodegasalgadonarros@yahoo.com

Pico Royo 2008 T
tinta de Toro

80

Pico Royo 2013 B
malvasía

85

BODEGA LIBERALIA ENOLÓGICA

Camino del Palo, s/n
49800 Toro (Zamora)
☎: +34 980 692 571
Fax: +34 980 692 571
www.liberalia.es
liberalia@liberalia.es

Liber 2006 TGR
100% tinta de Toro

93

Colour: ruby red. Nose: ripe fruit, complex, balsamic herbs, spicy, creamy oak, balanced.

Liberalia Cabeza de Cuba 2007 TC
tinta de Toro

90

Colour: cherry, garnet rim. Nose: ripe fruit, spicy, creamy oak, dry stone, balsamic herbs. Palate: powerful, flavourful, toasty, balanced.

Liberalia Cero 2013 T
100% tinta de Toro

89

Colour: bright cherry. Nose: ripe fruit, sweet spices, expressive, smoky. Palate: flavourful, fruity, toasty, round tannins.

Liberalia Cinco 2006 TR
100% tinta de Toro

92

Colour: very deep cherry. Nose: powerfull, ripe fruit, fruit liqueur notes, spicy, balsamic herbs, fine reductive notes. Palate: flavourful, concentrated, spicy, long.

Liberalia Cuatro 2009 TC
100% tinta de Toro

89

Colour: cherry, garnet rim. Nose: ripe fruit, spicy, creamy oak, toasty, complex, fine reductive notes. Palate: powerful, flavourful, toasty, balanced.

Liberalia Tres 2013 T Roble
100% tinta de Toro

88

Colour: bright cherry. Nose: ripe fruit, sweet spices, expressive. Palate: flavourful, fruity, round tannins.

BODEGA MARXUACH
Autovía Tordesilla - Zamora, salida 438
Toro (Zamora)
☎: +34 923 541 050
Fax: +34 923 568 425
montelareina@yahoo.es

Marxuach 2008 TC
tinta de Toro

89

Colour: cherry, garnet rim. Nose: ripe fruit, wild herbs, earthy notes, fine reductive notes, mineral. Palate: flavourful, long, balanced, spicy.

BODEGA NUMANTHIA
Real, s/n
49882 Valdefinjas (Zamora)
☎: +34 941 308 065
Fax: +34 945 600 885
www.numanthia.com

Numanthia 2010 T
tinta de Toro

96

Colour: cherry, garnet rim. Nose: ripe fruit, spicy, creamy oak, toasty, complex, dark chocolate, earthy notes. Palate: powerful, flavourful, toasty, round tannins.

Termanthia 2011 T
tinta de Toro

97

Colour: cherry, garnet rim. Nose: aromatic coffee, new oak, scrubland, ripe fruit. Palate: powerful, fine bitter notes, good acidity, fine tannins, spicy.

Termes 2012 T
tinta de Toro

93

Colour: cherry, garnet rim. Nose: ripe fruit, red berry notes, sweet spices. Palate: fruity, good acidity, fine bitter notes.

BODEGA PAGO DE CUBAS
Ctra. Toro Valdefinjas, Km. 6,9
49882 Valdefinjas (Zamora)
☎: +34 980 568 125
Fax: +34 980 059 965
www.bodegapagodecubas.com

Asterisco 2012 TC
100% tinta de Toro

84

Incrédulo 2009 T
100% tinta de Toro

88

Colour: cherry, garnet rim. Nose: ripe fruit, spicy, creamy oak, toasty, complex, tobacco, fine reductive notes. Palate: powerful, flavourful, toasty, round tannins.

Incrédulo 2010 T
100% tinta de Toro

90

Colour: cherry, garnet rim. Nose: ripe fruit, wild herbs, earthy notes, spicy, creamy oak, fine reductive notes. Palate: balanced, flavourful, long, balsamic.

BODEGA VALDIGAL
Capuchinos, 6
49800 Toro (Zamora)
☎: +34 617 356 325
Fax: +34 923 269 209
www.valdigal.com
valdigal@valdigal.com

Valdigal 2011 T
100% tinta de Toro

89

Colour: cherry, garnet rim. Nose: ripe fruit, spicy, creamy oak, toasty. Palate: powerful, flavourful, toasty.

BODEGAS A. VELASCO E HIJOS
Corredera, 23
49800 Toro (Zamora)
☎: +34 980 692 455
www.bodegasvelascoehijos.com
admon@bodegasvelascoehijos.com

Garabitas Premium Vendimia Seleccionada 2009 T
tinta de Toro

88

Colour: very deep cherry, garnet rim. Nose: powerfull, ripe fruit, roasted coffee, dark chocolate. Palate: powerful, toasty, roasted-coffee aftertaste.

Garabitas Selección Viñas Viejas 2011 T
tinta de Toro

86

Colour: dark-red cherry, garnet rim. Nose: toasty, cocoa bean, ripe fruit, tobacco. Palate: correct, balanced, round tannins.

Peña Rejas 2011 TC
tinta de Toro

88

Colour: cherry, garnet rim. Nose: ripe fruit, spicy, creamy oak, toasty, complex. Palate: powerful, flavourful, toasty.

Peña Rejas 2013 T
tinta de Toro

87

Colour: cherry, purple rim. Nose: ripe fruit, wild herbs, expressive. Palate: powerful, flavourful, fruity.

BODEGAS ABANICO
Pol. Ind Ca l'Avellanet - Susany, 6
08553 Seva (Barcelona)
☎: +34 938 125 676
Fax: +34 938 123 213
www.bodegasabanico.com
info@exportiberia.com

Eternum Viti 2011 T
100% tinta de Toro

90

Colour: cherry, garnet rim. Nose: ripe fruit, spicy, creamy oak, toasty, complex. Palate: powerful, flavourful, toasty, round tannins.

Los Colmillos 2011 T
tinta de Toro

91

Colour: cherry, garnet rim. Nose: ripe fruit, spicy, creamy oak, toasty, complex, earthy notes, cocoa bean. Palate: powerful, flavourful, toasty, round tannins.

BODEGAS COVITORO
Ctra. de Tordesillas, 13
49800 Toro (Zamora)
☎: +34 980 690 347
Fax: +34 980 690 143
www.covitoro.com
info@covitoro.com

Arco del Reloj 2009 T
100% tinta de Toro

93

Colour: cherry, garnet rim. Nose: red berry notes, ripe fruit, spicy, creamy oak, toasty, complex, earthy notes. Palate: powerful, flavourful, toasty, round tannins, balanced.

Barón de la Villa 2011 TC
100% tinta de Toro

87

Colour: cherry, garnet rim. Nose: spicy, creamy oak, ripe fruit. Palate: powerful, toasty, round tannins.

Barón de la Villa 2013 T
100% tinta de Toro

86

Colour: cherry, purple rim. Nose: fresh fruit, red berry notes, floral, balsamic herbs. Palate: flavourful, fruity, good acidity.

Cañus Verus Viñas Viejas 2009 T
100% tinta de Toro

89

Colour: cherry, garnet rim. Nose: balanced, complex, ripe fruit, spicy. Palate: good structure, flavourful, round tannins, elegant.

Cermeño 2013 B
malvasía

85

Cermeño 2013 RD
tinta de Toro
87
Colour: rose. Nose: red berry notes, dried flowers, balanced. Palate: fruity, flavourful, good finish, easy to drink.

Cermeño Vendimia Seleccionada 2013 T
100% tinta de Toro
88
Colour: cherry, purple rim. Nose: red berry notes, raspberry, fruit expression. Palate: good acidity, fresh, fruity.

Cien 2013 B
malvasía
86
Colour: bright straw. Nose: fresh, fresh fruit, white flowers. Palate: flavourful, fruity, good acidity, balanced.

Cien 2013 RD
tinta de Toro
85

Cien Roble 2012 T
100% tinta de Toro
84

Gran Cermeño 2010 TC
100% tinta de Toro
89
Colour: cherry, garnet rim. Nose: spicy, ripe fruit. Palate: fruity, good structure, ripe fruit, good finish.

Marqués de la Villa 2010 TC
100% tinta de Toro
88
Colour: cherry, garnet rim. Nose: ripe fruit, spicy, creamy oak, toasty, complex. Palate: powerful, flavourful, toasty.

Marqués de la Villa 2012 T Roble
100% tinta de Toro
86
Colour: cherry, purple rim. Nose: ripe fruit, toasty, spicy. Palate: flavourful, round tannins, spicy.

Marqués de la Villa 2013 B
malvasia
85

Marqués de la Villa 2013 RD
tinta de Toro
87
Colour: rose, purple rim. Nose: powerfull, ripe fruit, red berry notes, floral, expressive. Palate: powerful, fruity, fresh, good finish.

Marqués de la Villa 2013 T
tinta de Toro
85

Vizconde de la Villa 2011 TC
100% tinta de Toro
87
Colour: cherry, garnet rim. Nose: ripe fruit, spicy, creamy oak, toasty. Palate: powerful, flavourful, toasty.

Vizconde de la Villa 2012 T Barrica
tinta de Toro
87
Colour: bright cherry. Nose: ripe fruit, sweet spices, creamy oak, expressive. Palate: flavourful, fruity, toasty, round tannins.

BODEGAS FARIÑA
Camino del Palo, s/n
49800 Toro (Zamora)
☎: +34 980 577 673
Fax: +34 980 577 720
www.bodegasfarina.com
comercial@bodegasfarina.com

Colegiata 2013 RD
100% tinta de Toro
88
Colour: rose, purple rim. Nose: powerfull, ripe fruit, red berry notes, floral. Palate: powerful, fruity, fresh.

Colegiata 2013 T
88
Colour: bright cherry, garnet rim. Nose: ripe fruit, powerfull, wild herbs. Palate: flavourful, toasty, spicy, balsamic.

Gran Colegiata 2008 TR
100% tinta de Toro
90
Colour: deep cherry. Nose: ripe fruit, wild herbs, earthy notes, spicy, creamy oak. Palate: balanced, flavourful, long, balsamic, round tannins.

Gran Colegiata Campus 2008 TC
100% tinta de Toro

93

Colour: very deep cherry. Nose: red berry notes, ripe fruit, spicy, creamy oak, toasty, complex, earthy notes. Palate: powerful, flavourful, toasty, round tannins.

Gran Colegiata Roble Francés 2009 TC
100% tinta de Toro

90

Colour: cherry, garnet rim. Nose: ripe fruit, spicy, creamy oak, toasty, complex. Palate: powerful, flavourful, toasty.

Gran Colegiata Vino de Lágrima 2011 T Roble
100% tinta de Toro

89

Colour: very deep cherry, garnet rim. Nose: powerfull, ripe fruit, roasted coffee, dark chocolate. Palate: powerful, toasty, roasted-coffee aftertaste.

Primero 2013 T Maceración Carbónica

87

Colour: cherry, purple rim. Nose: expressive, fresh fruit, red berry notes, floral, balsamic herbs. Palate: flavourful, fruity, good acidity, easy to drink.

BODEGAS FRANCISCO CASAS
Avda. de Los Comuneros, 67
49810 Morales de Toro (Zamora)
☎: +34 918 110 207
Fax: +34 918 110 798
www.bodegascasas.com
toro@bodegascasas.com

Camparrón 2008 TR
tinta de Toro

90

Colour: cherry, garnet rim. Nose: red berry notes, ripe fruit, toasty, earthy notes, balsamic herbs, sweet spices. Palate: powerful, flavourful, toasty, round tannins, correct.

Camparrón 2011 TC
tinta de Toro

87

Colour: bright cherry. Nose: ripe fruit, sweet spices, creamy oak, medium intensity. Palate: fruity, flavourful, toasty.

Camparrón Albus 2013 B
malvasía

83

Camparrón Novum 2013 T
tinta de Toro

87

Colour: cherry, purple rim. Nose: expressive, fresh fruit, red berry notes, floral. Palate: flavourful, fruity, good acidity, easy to drink.

Camparrón Pinturas de Rubens 2010 T
tinta de Toro

89

Colour: bright cherry. Nose: ripe fruit, sweet spices, medium intensity, violets. Palate: fruity, flavourful, toasty.

Camparrón Seleccion 2013 T
tinta de Toro

87

Colour: cherry, purple rim. Nose: expressive, fresh fruit, red berry notes, floral, wild herbs. Palate: flavourful, fruity, good acidity.

Viña Abba 2009 T
tinta de Toro

86

Colour: cherry, garnet rim. Nose: ripe fruit, spicy, creamy oak, toasty, complex, fine reductive notes. Palate: powerful, flavourful, toasty.

BODEGAS FRONTAURA

Ctra. Pesquera de Duero a Renedo, s/n
47315 Pesquera de Duero (Valladolid)
☎: +34 983 880 488
Fax: +34 983 870 065
www.bodegasfrontaura.com
info@bodegasfrontaura.com

Aponte 2006 T
100% tinta de Toro

93

Colour: ruby red. Nose: red berry notes, ripe fruit, spicy, creamy oak, toasty, complex, earthy notes. Palate: powerful, flavourful, toasty, round tannins, elegant.

Dominio de Valdelacasa 2009 T
100% tinta de Toro

91

Colour: very deep cherry, garnet rim. Nose: powerfull, ripe fruit, roasted coffee, dark chocolate. Palate: powerful, toasty, roasted-coffee aftertaste, balanced.

Frontaura 2006 TC
100% tinta de Toro

90

Colour: deep cherry. Nose: ripe fruit, spicy, creamy oak, toasty, complex. Palate: powerful, flavourful, toasty, round tannins, balanced.

Frontaura 2012 BFB

92

Colour: bright yellow. Nose: sweet spices, creamy oak, fragrant herbs. Palate: rich, smoky aftertaste, flavourful, fresh, good acidity.

Tierras Guindas 2012 T
100% tinta de Toro

87

Colour: deep cherry. Nose: ripe fruit, spicy, creamy oak, toasty. Palate: flavourful, round tannins, easy to drink.

BODEGAS GIL LUNA

Ctra. Toro - Salamanca, Km. 2
49800 Toro (Zamora)
☎: +34 980 698 509
Fax: +34 980 698 294
www.giluna.es
info@giluna.es

Gil Luna 2009 T
100% tinta de Toro

90

Colour: cherry, garnet rim. Nose: red berry notes, ripe fruit, spicy, creamy oak, toasty, complex, earthy notes. Palate: powerful, flavourful, toasty, round tannins.

Tres Lunas 2010 T
100% tinta de Toro

86 🍷

Colour: cherry, garnet rim. Nose: spicy, fine reductive notes, wet leather, aged wood nuances, toasty, fruit preserve. Palate: spicy, long, toasty.

Tres Lunas 2013 T
tinta de Toro

87 🍷

Colour: cherry, purple rim. Nose: ripe fruit, wild herbs, floral, spicy. Palate: powerful, flavourful, long.

Tres Lunas Ecológico 2012 T
100% tinta de Toro

86 🍷

Colour: ruby red. Nose: fine reductive notes, toasty, ripe fruit. Palate: spicy, long, toasty.

Tres Lunas Verdejo 2013 B
100% verdejo

87 🍷

Colour: bright straw. Nose: fresh, fresh fruit, white flowers, expressive. Palate: fruity, good acidity, balanced, easy to drink.

BODEGAS GRUPO YLLERA

Autovía A-6, Km. 173,5
47490 Rueda (Valladolid)
☎: +34 983 868 097
Fax: +34 983 868 177
www.grupoyllera.com
grupoyllera@grupoyllera.com

Garcilaso 2009 TC
100% tempranillo

89

Colour: cherry, garnet rim. Nose: ripe fruit, wild herbs, earthy notes, spicy, creamy oak, fine reductive notes. Palate: flavourful, long, balsamic, spicy.

BODEGAS ITURRIA

Avda. Torrecilla De La Abadesa 2,2E
47100 Tordesillas (Valladolid)
☎: +34 600 523 070
www.bodegas-iturria.com
contact@bodegas-iturria.com

Tinto Iturria 2010 T
tinta de Toro, garnacha

89

Colour: cherry, garnet rim. Nose: balanced, red berry notes, ripe fruit, wild herbs. Palate: ripe fruit, round tannins.

Valdosan 2010 T
tinta de Toro

90

Colour: cherry, garnet rim. Nose: ripe fruit, spicy, creamy oak, toasty, mineral. Palate: powerful, flavourful, toasty, balanced.

BODEGAS LIBA Y DELEITE
Ctra. San Román de Hornija,
P:Km. 1,200
49801 Morales de Toro (Zamora)
☎: +34 615 101 249
www.acontia.es
acontia@acontia.es

Acontia 6 2012 T
tinta de Toro, garnacha
87
Colour: bright cherry. Nose: ripe fruit, sweet spices, medium intensity, balsamic herbs. Palate: fruity, flavourful, toasty.

Acontia Ritual 2010 TC
tinta de Toro, garnacha
87
Colour: cherry, garnet rim. Nose: ripe fruit, spicy, creamy oak, toasty. Palate: powerful, flavourful, toasty.

BODEGAS MATARREDONDA
Ctra. Toro - Valdefinjas, km. 2,5
49800 Toro (Zamora)
☎: +34 980 059 981
Fax: +34 980 059 981
www.vinolibranza.com
libranza@vinolibranza.com

Juan Rojo 2008 T
100% tinta de Toro
89
Colour: cherry, garnet rim. Nose: spicy, creamy oak, toasty, fruit liqueur notes. Palate: powerful, flavourful, toasty.

Libranza 2009 T
100% tinta de Toro
89
Colour: cherry, garnet rim. Nose: red berry notes, ripe fruit, spicy, creamy oak, toasty, complex, earthy notes, fine reductive notes. Palate: powerful, flavourful, toasty.

Libranza 28 2007 T Reserva Especial
100% tinta de Toro
89
Colour: cherry, garnet rim. Nose: spicy, creamy oak, toasty, fruit liqueur notes, earthy notes. Palate: powerful, flavourful, toasty.

Valdefama 2011 T
100% tinta de Toro
86
Colour: cherry, garnet rim. Nose: fruit preserve, fine reductive notes, balsamic herbs, spicy. Palate: powerful, flavourful, spicy.

BODEGAS MONTE LA REINA
Ctra. Toro - Zamora, Km. 436,7
49881 Toro (Zamora)
☎: +34 980 082 011
www.montelareina.es
turismo@montelareina.es

Castillo de Monte la Reina 2009 T Fermentado en Barrica
100% tinta de Toro
88
Colour: cherry, garnet rim. Nose: ripe fruit, spicy, creamy oak, toasty, complex, fine reductive notes. Palate: powerful, flavourful, toasty, round tannins.

Castillo de Monte la Reina 2009 TC
100% tinta de Toro
88
Colour: cherry, garnet rim. Nose: spicy, toasty, overripe fruit, mineral. Palate: powerful, flavourful, toasty, round tannins.

Castillo de Monte la Reina 2012 T Roble
100% tinta de Toro
87
Colour: bright cherry, cherry, garnet rim. Nose: ripe fruit, sweet spices, creamy oak, dried herbs. Palate: flavourful, toasty, round tannins.

Castillo de Monte la Reina Cuvee Privee 2009 T
100% tinta de Toro
91
Colour: cherry, garnet rim. Nose: ripe fruit, spicy, creamy oak, toasty, complex. Palate: powerful, flavourful, toasty, round tannins.

Castillo de Monte la Reina Vendimia Seleccionada 2005 T
tinta de Toro
90
Colour: ruby red. Nose: ripe fruit, wild herbs, spicy, creamy oak, fine reductive notes. Palate: powerful, flavourful, elegant, long.

Castillo de Monte la Reina Verdejo 2013 B
100% verdejo
85

Inaraja 2008 T
100% tinta de Toro
93
Colour: very deep cherry. Nose: ripe fruit, spicy, creamy oak, toasty, complex, mineral. Palate: powerful, flavourful, toasty, round tannins, concentrated.

Tertius 2012 T Roble
85

Tertius 2013 T
tinta de Toro

86

Colour: cherry, purple rim. Nose: red berry notes, floral, ripe fruit. Palate: flavourful, fruity, good acidity, round tannins.

Tertius Verdejo 2013 B
100% verdejo

83

BODEGAS OLIVARA

Eras de Santa Catalina, s/n
49800 Toro (Zamora)
☎: +34 980 693 425
Fax: +34 980 693 409
www.marquesdeolivara.com
marquesdeolivara@marquesdeolivara.com

Olivara 2010 TC
100% tinta de Toro

88

Colour: dark-red cherry. Nose: ripe fruit, spicy, creamy oak, toasty. Palate: powerful, flavourful, toasty, round tannins.

Olivara 2013 T
100% tinta de Toro

85

Olivara Vendimia Seleccionada 2011 T
tinta de Toro

87

Colour: bright cherry. Nose: ripe fruit, spicy, creamy oak. Palate: powerful, flavourful, toasty, round tannins.

BODEGAS ORDÓÑEZ
Bartolomé Esteban Murillo, 11
29700 Vélez- Málaga (Málaga)
☎: +34 952 504 706
Fax: +34 951 284 796
www.grupojorgeordonez.com
info@jorgeordonez.es

Tritón Tinta Toro 2012 T
100% tinta de Toro

89

Colour: cherry, garnet rim. Nose: powerfull, ripe fruit, toasty. Palate: flavourful, fine bitter notes, good acidity.

BODEGAS REJADORADA
Rejadorada, 11
49800 Toro (Zamora)
☎: +34 980 693 089
Fax: +34 980 693 089
www.rejadorada.com
rejadorada@rejadorada.com

Bravo de Rejadorada 2010 T
100% tinta de Toro

93

Colour: cherry, garnet rim. Nose: red berry notes, ripe fruit, spicy, creamy oak, toasty, complex, earthy notes. Palate: powerful, flavourful, toasty, round tannins, long.

Novellum de Rejadorada 2010 TC
100% tinta de Toro

89

Colour: cherry, garnet rim. Nose: ripe fruit, spicy, creamy oak, toasty, complex. Palate: powerful, flavourful, toasty, round tannins.

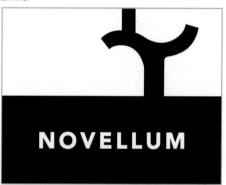

Rejadorada Roble 2012 T Roble
100% tinta de Toro

87

Colour: bright cherry. Nose: ripe fruit, sweet spices, creamy oak, balsamic herbs. Palate: flavourful, fruity, toasty.

Sango de Rejadorada 2009 TR
100% tinta de Toro

92

Colour: cherry, garnet rim. Nose: red berry notes, ripe fruit, spicy, creamy oak, toasty, complex, earthy notes. Palate: powerful, flavourful, toasty, round tannins.

BODEGAS SIETECERROS

Finca Villaester N-122, km. 409
47540 Villaester de Arriba -
Pedrosa del Rey (Valladolid)
☎: +34 983 784 083
Fax: +34 983 784 142
www.bodegasietecerros.com
sietecerros@bodegasietecerros.com

Quebrantarrejas 2013 T
100% tinta de Toro
85

Valdelazarza 2009 TR
100% tinta de Toro
85

Valdelazarza 2010 T Roble
100% tinta de Toro
83

Valdelazarza 2010 TC
100% tinta de Toro
84

BODEGAS SOBREÑO

Ctra. N-122, Km. 423
49800 Toro (Zamora)
☎: +34 980 693 417
Fax: +34 980 693 416
www.sobreno.com
sobreno@sobreno.com

Finca Sobreño 2012 T Roble
100% tinta de Toro
86
Colour: cherry, garnet rim. Nose: ripe fruit, wild herbs, spicy, creamy oak. Palate: long, balsamic.

Finca Sobreño Crianza 2011 TC
tinta de Toro
84

Finca Sobreño Ecológico 2012 T
100% tinta de Toro

84 🏆

Finca Sobreño Ildefonso 2009 T
100% tinta de Toro

90

Colour: cherry, garnet rim. Nose: red berry notes, ripe fruit, spicy, creamy oak, toasty, complex, earthy notes. Palate: powerful, flavourful, toasty, round tannins.

Finca Sobreño Selección Especial 2009 TR
100% tinta de Toro

89

Colour: cherry, garnet rim. Nose: ripe fruit, spicy, creamy oak, toasty, complex. Palate: powerful, flavourful, toasty, round tannins.

BODEGAS TORREDUERO

Pol. Ind. Toro Norte s/n
49800 Toro (Zamora)
☎: +34 941 454 050
Fax: +34 941 454 529
www.bodegasriojanas.com
bodega@bodegasriojanas.com

Marqués de Peñamonte 2008 TR
100% tinta de Toro

88

Colour: bright cherry. Nose: ripe fruit, sweet spices, creamy oak, medium intensity. Palate: fruity, flavourful, toasty.

Marqués de Peñamonte Colección Privada 2011 T
100% tinta de Toro

89

Colour: cherry, garnet rim. Nose: ripe fruit, spicy, creamy oak, toasty, complex, balsamic herbs. Palate: powerful, flavourful, toasty, correct.

Peñamonte 2010 TC
100% tinta de Toro

88

Colour: deep cherry, garnet rim. Nose: ripe fruit, spicy, balanced. Palate: flavourful, correct, round tannins.

Peñamonte 2012 T Barrica
100% tinta de Toro

87

Colour: cherry, garnet rim. Nose: ripe fruit, spicy, creamy oak, toasty, complex, earthy notes. Palate: powerful, flavourful, toasty, correct.

Peñamonte 2013 RD

86

Colour: light cherry. Nose: powerfull, red berry notes, ripe fruit, rose petals. Palate: flavourful, fruity.

Peñamonte 2013 T
tinta de Toro

85

Peñamonte Verdejo 2013 B
100% verdejo

82

BODEGAS VEGA SAUCO

Avda. Comuneros, 108
49810 Morales de Toro (Zamora)
☎: +34 980 698 294
Fax: +34 980 698 294
www.vegasauco.com
info@vegasauco.com

Adoremus 2006 TR
100% tinta de Toro

89

Colour: ruby red. Nose: spicy, fine reductive notes, wet leather, aged wood nuances, fruit liqueur notes, expressive. Palate: spicy, fine tannins, long.

Adoremus 2000 TGR
tinta de Toro

88

Colour: pale ruby, brick rim edge. Nose: elegant, spicy, fine reductive notes, wet leather, aged wood nuances. Palate: spicy, elegant, long, round tannins.

Adoremus 2001 TGR
100% tinta de Toro

87

Colour: deep cherry, orangey edge. Nose: spicy, fine reductive notes, wet leather, aged wood nuances, fruit liqueur notes. Palate: spicy, fine tannins, long.

Adoremus 2009 TR
100% tinta de Toro

90

Colour: cherry, garnet rim. Nose: complex, ripe fruit, spicy. Palate: good structure, flavourful, round tannins.

Vega Saúco El Beybi 2012 T Roble
100% tinta de Toro

86

Colour: cherry, purple rim. Nose: sweet spices, creamy oak, expressive, fruit preserve. Palate: flavourful, fruity, toasty, round tannins.

Vega Saúco El Beybi 2013 T Roble
100% tinta de Toro

87

Colour: bright cherry. Nose: ripe fruit, sweet spices, expressive. Palate: flavourful, fruity, toasty, round tannins.

Vega Saúco Selección 2010 T
88
Colour: cherry, garnet rim. Nose: red berry notes, ripe fruit, spicy, toasty. Palate: powerful, flavourful, toasty, round tannins.

Vega Saúco Selección 2011 T
100% tinta de Toro
86
Colour: deep cherry, garnet rim. Nose: powerfull, fruit preserve, toasty, tobacco. Palate: flavourful, ripe fruit, good finish.

BODEGAS VETUS
Ctra. Toro a Salamanca, Km. 9,5
49800 Toro (Zamora)
☎: +34 945 609 086
Fax: +34 980 056 012
www.bodegasvetus.com
vetus@bodegasvetus.com

Celsus 2012 T
100% tinta de Toro
93
Colour: very deep cherry. Nose: ripe fruit, spicy, creamy oak, toasty, characterful, earthy notes, mineral. Palate: powerful, flavourful, toasty, round tannins.

Flor de Vetus 2012 T
100% tinta de Toro
91
Colour: bright cherry. Nose: ripe fruit, sweet spices, creamy oak, expressive. Palate: flavourful, fruity, toasty, round tannins.

Vetus 2011 T
100% tinta de Toro
92
Colour: cherry, garnet rim. Nose: ripe fruit, spicy, creamy oak, toasty, complex, dark chocolate, earthy notes. Palate: powerful, flavourful, pruney.

BODEGAS Y VIÑEDOS ANZIL
Ctra. Camino El Pego s/n, Ctra. Toro a Villabuena del Puente, km. 9,400
49800 Toro (Zamora)
☎: +34 915 006 000
Fax: +34 915 006 006
www.bodegasanzil.es
rrpp@vina-mayor.es

Finca Anzil Vendimia Seleccionada 2011 T
100% tinta de Toro
91
Colour: cherry, garnet rim. Nose: ripe fruit, spicy, creamy oak, toasty, complex, balsamic herbs, earthy notes. Palate: powerful, flavourful, toasty, round tannins.

Viña Mayor Toro 2012 T
100% tinta de Toro
90
Colour: cherry, garnet rim. Nose: ripe fruit, spicy, balanced, mineral. Palate: powerful, flavourful, round tannins, long.

BODEGAS Y VIÑEDOS MAURODOS
Ctra. N-122, Km. 411 - Villaester
47112 Pedrosa del Rey (Valladolid)
☎: +34 983 784 118
Fax: +34 983 784 018
www.bodegasanroman.com
comunicacion@bodegasmauro.com

Prima 2012 T
90
Colour: bright cherry. Nose: ripe fruit, sweet spices, creamy oak, wild herbs. Palate: flavourful, fruity, toasty, round tannins.

San Román 2011 T
100% tinta de Toro

94

Colour: deep cherry, garnet rim. Nose: ripe fruit, cocoa bean, creamy oak, sweet spices, complex. Palate: balanced, round tannins, spicy, long.

BODEGAS Y VIÑEDOS PINTIA

Ctra. de Morales, s/n
47530 San Román de Hornija
(Valladolid)
☎: +34 983 680 147
Fax: +34 983 680 263
www.bodegaspintia.com
cupos@vega-sicilia.com

Pintia 2011 T
100% tinta de Toro

93

Colour: bright cherry. Nose: sweet spices, creamy oak, expressive, fruit expression. Palate: flavourful, fruity, toasty, round tannins.

BODEGUEROS QUINTA ESENCIA

Eras, 37
47520 Castronuño (Valladolid)
☎: +34 605 887 100
Fax: +34 983 866 391
www.bodeguerosquintaesencia.com
ferrin@bodeguerosquintaesencia.com

Sofros 2012 T
tinta de Toro

89

Colour: cherry, garnet rim. Nose: ripe fruit, spicy, creamy oak, toasty. Palate: powerful, flavourful, toasty, round tannins, roasted-coffee aftertaste.

BOUTIQUE WINES

Jacinto Benavente, 2
47195 Arroyo de la Encomienda
(Valladolid)
☎: +34 639 250 225
Fax: +34 983 211 407
www.contaderowine.com
info@contaderowine.com

Campiña Viñas Centenarias 2009 TC
tinta de Toro

88

Colour: cherry, garnet rim. Nose: balanced, complex, ripe fruit, spicy, fine reductive notes. Palate: good structure, flavourful, round tannins.

Contadero 2013 T
tinta de Toro

86

Colour: very deep cherry, garnet rim. Nose: warm, dried herbs, fruit preserve. Palate: flavourful, ripe fruit, long.

Contadero Viñas Centenarias 2009 T
tinta de Toro

86

Colour: cherry, garnet rim. Nose: ripe fruit, fruit preserve, wild herbs, fine reductive notes. Palate: powerful, flavourful, spicy.

BUIL & GINÉ

Ctra. de Gratallops - Vilella Baixa, Km. 11,5
43737 Gratallops (Tarragona)
☎: +34 977 839 810
Fax: +34 977 839 811
www.builgine.com
info@builgine.com

Buil 2009 TC
tinta de Toro

89

Colour: cherry, garnet rim. Nose: ripe fruit, wild herbs, earthy notes, spicy, creamy oak. Palate: balanced, flavourful, long, balsamic.

CAÑADA DEL PINO

Pol. Ind. 6 - Parcela 83
49810 Morales de Toro (Zamora)
☎: +34 676 701 918
Fax: +34 980 698 318
fincayerro@gmail.com

Finca Yerro 2011 T Roble
tinta de Toro

86

Colour: bright cherry. Nose: ripe fruit, sweet spices, creamy oak, expressive. Palate: flavourful, fruity, toasty.

Piélago 2009 T
tinta de Toro

90

Colour: cherry, garnet rim. Nose: ripe fruit, spicy, toasty, complex, dried herbs. Palate: flavourful, toasty, round tannins.

CARMEN RODRÍGUEZ MÉNDEZ

Ctra. Salamanca, ZA 605, Km. 1,650
49800 Toro (Zamora)
☎: +34 658 788 233
www.carodorum.com
info@carodorum.com

Carodorum 2011 TC
tinta de Toro

90

Colour: cherry, garnet rim. Nose: spicy, creamy oak, toasty, complex, fruit preserve, mineral. Palate: powerful, flavourful, toasty.

Carodorum Selección Especial 2011 TC
tinta de Toro

91

Colour: cherry, garnet rim. Nose: ripe fruit, wild herbs, earthy notes, spicy, creamy oak. Palate: balanced, flavourful, long, balsamic, round.

Carodorum Vendimia Seleccionada 2013 T Roble
tinta de Toro

87

Colour: cherry, purple rim. Nose: ripe fruit, fruit preserve, sweet spices. Palate: good structure, flavourful, round tannins.

COMPAÑÍA DE VINOS TELMO RODRÍGUEZ
El Monte
01308 Lanciego (Álava)
☎: +34 945 628 315
Fax: +34 945 628 314
www.telmorodriguez.com
contact@telmorodriguez.com

Pago La Jara 2010 T
tinta de Toro

94

Colour: cherry, garnet rim. Nose: red berry notes, ripe fruit, spicy, creamy oak, complex, earthy notes. Palate: powerful, flavourful, toasty, round tannins.

CORAL DUERO
Ascensión, s/n
49154 El Pego (Zamora)
☎: +34 980 606 333
Fax: +34 980 606 391
www.rompesedas.com
rompesedas@rompesedas.com

Rompesedas 2007 T
100% tinta de Toro

92

Colour: ruby red. Nose: ripe fruit, wild herbs, earthy notes, spicy, creamy oak, mineral, expressive. Palate: balanced, flavourful, long, balsamic, elegant.

Rompesedas 2012 T Barrica
100% tinta de Toro

89

Colour: bright cherry. Nose: ripe fruit, sweet spices, expressive. Palate: flavourful, fruity, toasty, round tannins.

DIVINA PROPORCIÓN
Camino del Cristo s/n
49800 Toro
☎: +34 980 059 018
www.divinaproporcionbodegas.es
info@divinaproporcionbodegas.es

24 Mozas 2013 T
100% tinta de Toro

89

Colour: cherry, garnet rim. Nose: ripe fruit, spicy, creamy oak, toasty, complex, earthy notes. Palate: powerful, flavourful, toasty, harsh oak tannins.

Abracadabra 2012 T
100% tinta de Toro

90

Colour: deep cherry. Nose: ripe fruit, spicy, creamy oak, toasty, complex. Palate: powerful, flavourful, toasty, round tannins.

Encomienda de la Vega 2011 T
100% tinta de Toro

90

Colour: very deep cherry. Nose: ripe fruit, spicy, toasty. Palate: powerful, flavourful, toasty, round tannins.

Madremia 2012 T
100% tinta de Toro

92

Colour: cherry, garnet rim. Nose: ripe fruit, spicy, creamy oak, toasty, complex, earthy notes. Palate: powerful, flavourful, toasty.

DOMINIO DEL BENDITO
Pza. Santo Domingo, 8
49800 Toro (Zamora)
☎: +34 980 693 306
www.bodegadominiodelbendito.com
info@bodegadominiodelbendito.es

Dominio del Bendito El Primer Paso 2012 T Roble
100% tinta de Toro

90

Colour: bright cherry, garnet rim. Nose: ripe fruit, sweet spices, creamy oak, expressive. Palate: flavourful, fruity, toasty, balanced.

El Titán del Bendito 2011 T
100% tinta de Toro

95 ♥

Colour: cherry, garnet rim. Nose: ripe fruit, spicy, creamy oak, toasty, complex, dark chocolate, earthy notes. Palate: powerful, flavourful, toasty, round tannins, round, balanced, elegant.

ELÍAS MORA

Juan Mora, s/n
47530 San Román de Hornija
(Valladolid)
☎: +34 983 784 029
Fax: +34 983 784 190
www.bodegaseliasmora.com
info@bodegaseliasmora.com

2V Premium 2010 T
tinta de Toro

93

Colour: cherry, garnet rim. Nose: ripe fruit, creamy oak, toasty, complex, earthy notes, expressive. Palate: powerful, flavourful, toasty, round tannins.

Descarte 2012 T
100% tinta de Toro

91

Colour: bright cherry. Nose: ripe fruit, sweet spices, creamy oak, medium intensity. Palate: fruity, flavourful, toasty.

Elías Mora 2009 TR
100% tinta de Toro

92

Colour: cherry, garnet rim. Nose: balanced, complex, ripe fruit, spicy, balsamic herbs. Palate: good structure, flavourful, round tannins, balanced, elegant.

Elías Mora 2011 TC
tinta de Toro

92

Colour: cherry, garnet rim. Nose: ripe fruit, spicy, creamy oak, toasty, complex, balsamic herbs. Palate: powerful, flavourful, toasty, round, elegant.

Gran Elías Mora 2010 TR
100% tinta de Toro

94

Colour: cherry, garnet rim. Nose: ripe fruit, wild herbs, earthy notes, spicy, creamy oak. Palate: flavourful, long, balsamic.

Viñas Elías Mora 2012 T Roble
100% tinta de Toro

90

Colour: cherry, garnet rim. Nose: ripe fruit, spicy, creamy oak, toasty, complex, earthy notes. Palate: powerful, flavourful, toasty, round tannins.

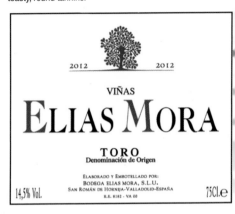

ESTANCIA PIEDRA
Ctra. Toro a Salamanca km. 8
49800 Toro (Zamora)
☎: +34 980 693 900
Fax: +34 980 693 901
www.estanciapiedra.com
piedra@estanciapiedra.com

La Garona 2008 T
tinta de Toro, garnacha
90
Colour: very deep cherry. Nose: ripe fruit, mineral, balsamic herbs, spicy, creamy oak. Palate: powerful, flavourful, balanced, round tannins.

Piedra 2013 RD
tinta de Toro
87
Colour: rose, purple rim. Nose: red berry notes, floral, expressive, fresh, citrus fruit. Palate: powerful, fruity, fresh, easy to drink.

Piedra Platino Selección 2006 TGR
tinta de Toro
91
Colour: cherry, garnet rim. Nose: ripe fruit, spicy, creamy oak, toasty. Palate: powerful, flavourful, toasty, round tannins.

Piedra Roja 2010 TC
tinta de Toro
91
Colour: cherry, garnet rim. Nose: ripe fruit, spicy, creamy oak, toasty, complex. Palate: powerful, flavourful, toasty.

Piedra Viña Azul 2013 T
tinta de Toro
88
Colour: cherry, purple rim. Nose: red berry notes, raspberry, fruit expression. Palate: flavourful, light-bodied, good acidity, fresh, fruity.

FRUTOS VILLAR
Eras de Santa Catalina, s/n
49800 Toro (Zamora)
☎: +34 983 586 868
Fax: +34 983 580 180
www.bodegasfrutosvillar.com
bodegasfrutosvillar@bodegasfrutosvillar.com

Muruve 2010 TC
100% tinta de Toro
88
Colour: cherry, garnet rim. Nose: ripe fruit, spicy, creamy oak, toasty, complex. Palate: powerful, flavourful, toasty.

Muruve 2010 TR
100% tinta de Toro
89
Colour: cherry, garnet rim. Nose: ripe fruit, spicy, creamy oak, toasty, complex. Palate: powerful, flavourful, toasty, round tannins.

Muruve 2013 T
tinta de Toro
86
Colour: cherry, purple rim. Nose: red berry notes, ripe fruit, floral, expressive. Palate: powerful, fresh, fruity.

Muruve Élite 2010 T
100% tinta de Toro
90
Colour: cherry, garnet rim. Nose: ripe fruit, wild herbs, earthy notes, spicy, creamy oak. Palate: balanced, flavourful, long, balsamic.

Puerta de la Majestad 2011 T Roble
100% tinta de Toro
85

HACIENDA TERRA D'URO
Campanas, 4, 1º A
47001 (Valladolid)
☎: +34 983 362 591
Fax: +34 983 357 663
www.terraduro.com
manueldenicolas@gmail.com

Terra D'uro Finca La Rana 2011 T
100% tinta de Toro
89
Colour: cherry, garnet rim. Nose: ripe fruit, wild herbs, earthy notes, spicy, creamy oak. Palate: balanced, flavourful, long, balsamic.

Terra D'uro Selección 2010 T
100% tinta de Toro
91
Colour: cherry, garnet rim. Nose: red berry notes, ripe fruit, balsamic herbs, creamy oak, expressive. Palate: powerful, flavourful, spicy, balanced.

Uro 2010 T
100% tinta de Toro
93
Colour: cherry, garnet rim. Nose: ripe fruit, spicy, creamy oak, toasty, complex, dark chocolate, earthy notes. Palate: powerful, flavourful, toasty, long.

HAMMEKEN CELLARS
Calle de la Muela, 16
03730 Jávea (Alicante)
☎: +34 965 791 967
Fax: +34 966 461 471
www.hammekencellars.com
cellars@hammekencellars.com

Viña Altamar Barrel Select Tempranillo 2010 T
100% tempranillo
89
Colour: bright cherry. Nose: ripe fruit, spicy, creamy oak, toasty, wild herbs. Palate: powerful, flavourful, toasty, round tannins.

Viña Altamar Tempranillo 2013 T
100% tempranillo
87
Colour: cherry, purple rim. Nose: red berry notes, fruit expression, fragrant herbs. Palate: flavourful, good acidity, fresh, fruity.

HEREDAD DE URUEÑA
Ctra. Toro a Medina de Rioseco, km 21,300
47862 Urueña (Valladolid)
☎: +34 915 610 920
Fax: +34 915 634 131
www.heredaduruena.com
direccion@heredaduruena.com

Moises Gran Vino 2009 T
tinta de Toro
92
Colour: cherry, garnet rim. Nose: balanced, complex, ripe fruit, spicy, earthy notes, expressive. Palate: good structure, flavourful, round tannins, elegant.

Toralto 2010 T
tinta de Toro
88
Colour: deep cherry, garnet rim. Nose: toasty, cocoa bean, powerfull. Palate: balanced, good structure, spicy.

LEGADO DE ORNIZ
Real de Pedrosa, 20
47530 San Román de Hornija
(Valladolid)
☎: +34 669 545 976
Fax: +34 983 784 116
www.legadodeorniz.com
info@legadodeorniz.com

Epitafio 2011 T
tinta de Toro
92
Colour: cherry, garnet rim. Nose: red berry notes, ripe fruit, spicy, creamy oak, toasty, complex, earthy notes. Palate: powerful, flavourful, toasty, round tannins.

Triens 2011 T
tinta de Toro
90
Colour: cherry, garnet rim. Nose: ripe fruit, spicy, creamy oak, toasty, complex. Palate: powerful, flavourful, toasty, round tannins.

LONG WINES

Avda. del Puente Cultural, 8 Bloque B Bajo 7
28702 San Sebastián de los Reyes
(Madrid)
☎: +34 916 221 305
Fax: +34 916 220 029
www.longwines.com
adm@longwines.com

El Bos 2012 T
100% tinta de Toro

88

Colour: bright cherry. Nose: ripe fruit, sweet spices, creamy oak, medium intensity. Palate: fruity, flavourful, toasty.

MATSU

Vara del Rey, 5
26003 Logroño (La Rioja)
☎: +34 941 271 217
Fax: +34 941 272 911
www.bodegamatsu.com
comunicacion@vintae.com

Matsu El Pícaro 2013 T
tinta de Toro

88

Colour: cherry, purple rim. Nose: powerfull, red berry notes, ripe fruit, floral, expressive. Palate: powerful, fresh, fruity, unctuous, spicy, long.

Matsu El Recio 2011 T
tinta de Toro

90

Colour: cherry, garnet rim. Nose: ripe fruit, spicy, creamy oak, toasty, complex. Palate: powerful, flavourful, toasty, round tannins.

Matsu El Viejo 2010 T
tinta de Toro

92

Colour: cherry, garnet rim. Nose: balanced, complex, ripe fruit, spicy, creamy oak. Palate: good structure, flavourful, spicy, long.

PAGOS DEL REY

Avda. de los Comuneros, 90
49810 Morales de Toro (Zamora)
☎: +34 980 698 023
www.pagosdelrey.com
nfernandez@felixsolisavantis.com

Bajoz 2011 TC
tinta de Toro

88

Colour: bright cherry. Nose: ripe fruit, sweet spices, creamy oak. Palate: flavourful, fruity, toasty, round tannins.

Bajoz 2013 RD
tinta de Toro

86

Colour: rose, purple rim. Nose: ripe fruit, red berry notes, floral, expressive, fresh. Palate: fruity, fresh, easy to drink, good finish.

Bajoz 2013 T
tinta de Toro

86

Colour: cherry, purple rim. Nose: fresh fruit, wild herbs, balanced. Palate: fruity, easy to drink, good finish.

Bajoz 2013 T Roble
tinta de Toro

87

Colour: very deep cherry, garnet rim. Nose: powerfull, ripe fruit, roasted coffee, dark chocolate. Palate: powerful, toasty, roasted-coffee aftertaste.

Bajoz Malvasía 2013 B
malvasía

85

Finca La Meda 2011 TC
tinta de Toro

90

Colour: bright cherry. Nose: ripe fruit, sweet spices, creamy oak, expressive. Palate: flavourful, fruity, toasty, round tannins.

Finca La Meda 2013 RD
tinta de Toro

85

Finca La Meda 2013 T
tinta de Toro

86

Colour: bright cherry, purple rim. Nose: fresh, medium intensity, red berry notes. Palate: fruity, correct, good acidity.

Finca La Meda 2013 T Roble
tinta de Toro

88

Colour: bright cherry. Nose: ripe fruit, sweet spices, creamy oak, expressive. Palate: flavourful, fruity, toasty.

Finca La Meda Alta Expresión 2011 T
tinta de Toro

91

Colour: bright cherry. Nose: red berry notes, ripe fruit, spicy, creamy oak, toasty, complex. Palate: powerful, flavourful, toasty, round tannins.

Finca La Meda Malvasía 2013 B
malvasía

83

Gran Bajoz 2011 T
tinta de Toro

90

Colour: cherry, garnet rim. Nose: red berry notes, ripe fruit, spicy, creamy oak, toasty, complex, earthy notes. Palate: powerful, flavourful, toasty, round tannins.

Moralinos 2012 T
tinta de Toro

86

Colour: cherry, purple rim. Nose: red berry notes, floral, ripe fruit. Palate: flavourful, fruity, good acidity, round tannins.

PALACIO DE VILLACHICA
Ctra. Nacional 122, Km. 433,2
49800 Toro (Zamora)
☎: +34 609 144 711
Fax: +34 983 381 356
www.palaciodevillachica.com
bodegavillachica@yahoo.es

Palacio de Villachica 2010 TC
100% tinta de Toro

88

Colour: cherry, garnet rim. Nose: ripe fruit, wild herbs, spicy, creamy oak. Palate: balanced, flavourful, long, balsamic.

Palacio de Villachica 2011 T Roble
100% tinta de Toro

85

Palacio de Villachica 2013 T
100% tinta de Toro

85

Palacio de Villachica Selección 2010 T
100% tinta de Toro

89

Colour: cherry, garnet rim. Nose: ripe fruit, spicy, creamy oak, toasty, complex, balsamic herbs, damp earth. Palate: powerful, flavourful, toasty.

QUINOLA SUÁREZ
Paseo de Zorrilla, 11- 4 izq.
47007 Valladolid (Valladolid)
☎: +34 625 227 321
www.quinola.es
garagewine@quinola.es

Quinola Garage Wine 2011 T Roble
100% tinta de Toro

93

Colour: cherry, garnet rim. Nose: ripe fruit, spicy, creamy oak, toasty, complex. Palate: powerful, flavourful, toasty, round tannins.

QUINTA DE LA QUIETUD
Camino de Bardales, s/n
Apdo. Correos 34
49800 Toro (Zamora)
☎: +34 980 568 019
www.quintaquietud.com
info@quintaquietud.com

Corral de Campanas 2012 T
tinta de Toro

90 🌷

Colour: cherry, garnet rim. Nose: ripe fruit, spicy, creamy oak, toasty, complex, earthy notes. Palate: powerful, flavourful, toasty, balanced.

Quinta Quietud 2009 T
tinta de Toro

92 🌷

Colour: ruby red. Nose: fine reductive notes, toasty, old leather. Palate: long, flavourful, spicy, round tannins, complex.

QUINTA
QUIETUD
TORO
Denominación de Origen

RODRÍGUEZ SANZO

Manuel Azaña, 9
47014 (Valladolid)
☎: +34 983 150 150
Fax: +34 983 150 151
www.rodriguezsanzo.com
comunicacion@valsanzo.com

Damalisco 2010 TC
100% tinta de Toro

90

Colour: cherry, garnet rim. Nose: wild herbs, ripe fruit, mineral, spicy, creamy oak. Palate: powerful, flavourful, long, balsamic.

Damalisco 2013 T Roble
100% tempranillo

88

Colour: bright cherry. Nose: ripe fruit, sweet spices, creamy oak. Palate: flavourful, fruity, toasty.

Terras de Javier Rodríguez Toro 2011 T
100% tinta de Toro

93

Colour: cherry, garnet rim. Nose: red berry notes, ripe fruit, spicy, creamy oak, balsamic herbs, mineral. Palate: powerful, flavourful, balanced, spicy.

TESO LA MONJA

Paraje Valdebuey Ctra. ZA-611, Km. 6,3
49882 Valdefinjas (Zamora)
☎: +34 980 568 143
Fax: +34 980 508 144
www.tesolamonja.com
info@sierracantabria.com

Alabaster 2011 T
tinta de Toro

97

Colour: cherry, garnet rim. Nose: spicy, creamy oak, toasty, complex, dark chocolate, fruit expression. Palate: powerful, flavourful, toasty, round tannins.

Alabaster 2012 T
tinta de Toro

95

Colour: cherry, garnet rim. Nose: spicy, toasty, mineral, ripe fruit. Palate: powerful, flavourful, toasty, round tannins.

Almirez 2012 T
tinta de Toro

94

Colour: cherry, garnet rim. Nose: spicy, creamy oak, toasty, complex, red berry notes. Palate: powerful, flavourful, toasty, round tannins.

Romanico 2012 T
tinta de Toro

91

Colour: bright cherry. Nose: ripe fruit, sweet spices, creamy oak, expressive. Palate: flavourful, fruity, toasty, round tannins.

Teso La Monja 2010 T

97

Colour: very deep cherry. Nose: ripe fruit, spicy, creamy oak, toasty, characterful, elegant. Palate: powerful, flavourful, toasty, soft tannins, mineral.

Victorino 2011 T
tinta de Toro

96

Colour: very deep cherry. Nose: ripe fruit, spicy, creamy oak, toasty, characterful. Palate: powerful, flavourful, toasty, round tannins.

Victorino 2012 T
tinta de Toro

98

Colour: cherry, garnet rim. Nose: ripe fruit, spicy, toasty, complex, dark chocolate, earthy notes, new oak. Palate: powerful, flavourful, toasty, round tannins.

TORESANAS

Ctra. Tordesillas, s/n
49800 Toro (Zamora)
☎: +34 983 868 116
Fax: +34 983 868 432
www.toresanas.com
info@taninia.com

Amant 2012 T Roble
tinta de Toro
85

Amant Novillo 2013 T
tinta de Toro
86
Colour: deep cherry, purple rim. Nose: balanced, expressive, balsamic herbs, medium intensity. Palate: fresh, slightly tart, correct.

VALBUSENDA

Ctra. Toro - Peleagonzalo s/n
49800 Toro (Zamora)
☎: +34 980 699 560
Fax: +34 980 699 566
www.bodegasvalbusenda.com
bodega@valbusenda.com

Abios 2013 RD
100% tinta de Toro
84

Abios Tinta de Toro 2013 T
100% tinta de Toro
87
Colour: cherry, purple rim. Nose: powerfull, red berry notes, ripe fruit, floral, expressive. Palate: powerful, fresh, fruity, unctuous.

Valbusenda 2007 TR
100% tinta de Toro
89
Colour: very deep cherry. Nose: ripe fruit, spicy, creamy oak, toasty, balsamic herbs. Palate: powerful, flavourful, toasty, round tannins.

Valbusenda 2009 T Roble
100% tinta de Toro
88
Colour: cherry, garnet rim. Nose: balanced, complex, ripe fruit, spicy, fine reductive notes. Palate: good structure, flavourful, round tannins.

Valbusenda Cepas Viejas 2008 T
100% tinta de Toro
91
Colour: deep cherry. Nose: ripe fruit, spicy, creamy oak, toasty, complex, dry stone. Palate: powerful, flavourful, toasty, round tannins, elegant.

VINOS Y VIÑEDOS DE LA CASA MAGUILA

Ctra. El Piñero s/n Pol. 1 P. 715
49153 Venialbo (Zamora)
☎: +34 980 051 020
Fax: +34 980 081 271
www.casamaguila.com
info@casamaguila.com

Angelitos Negros 2013 T
tinta de Toro
90
Colour: bright cherry. Nose: sweet spices, creamy oak, candied fruit, warm. Palate: flavourful, fruity, toasty, round tannins.

Cachito Mío 2012 T
tinta de Toro
91
Colour: cherry, garnet rim. Nose: ripe fruit, spicy, creamy oak, toasty, complex, balanced. Palate: powerful, flavourful, toasty, round.

Cachito Mío 2013 T
100% tinta de Toro
92
Colour: cherry, garnet rim. Nose: ripe fruit, wild herbs, spicy, creamy oak. Palate: balanced, flavourful, long, balsamic.

VIÑA ZANGARRÓN

San Esteban, s/n
49152 Sanzoles (Zamora)
☎: +34 619 149 062
www.vinovolvoreta.com
info@vinovolvoreta.com

El Vino del Buen Amor 2011 T
100% tinta de Toro

87 ♣

Colour: cherry, garnet rim. Nose: fruit preserve, wild herbs, spicy, creamy oak. Palate: powerful, flavourful, spicy.

El Vino del Buen Amor 2012 T
100% tinta de Toro

88 ♣

Colour: dark-red cherry, purple rim. Nose: powerfull, varietal, creamy oak, toasty. Palate: good structure, varietal, round tannins.

Flores de Cerezo 2013 T
100% tinta de Toro

88 ♣

Colour: cherry, purple rim. Nose: red berry notes, raspberry, floral, expressive. Palate: fresh, fruity, flavourful, easy to drink.

Volvoreta Probus 2011 T Roble
100% tinta de Toro

89 ♣

Colour: bright cherry. Nose: sweet spices, creamy oak, expressive, fruit preserve, balsamic herbs. Palate: flavourful, fruity, toasty.

Volvoreta sin Sulfitos Añadidos 2012 T
100% tinta de Toro

92 ♣

Colour: cherry, garnet rim. Nose: ripe fruit, spicy, mineral, expressive, balsamic herbs. Palate: powerful, flavourful, spicy, long.

VIÑAGUAREÑA

Ctra. Toro a Salamanca, Km. 12,5
49800 Toro (Zamora)
☎: +34 980 568 013
Fax: +34 980 568 134
www.vinotoro.com
info@vinotoro.com

Iduna 2010 BFB
100% verdejo

89

Colour: bright yellow. Nose: powerfull, faded flowers, toasty, sweet spices. Palate: flavourful, fruity, balanced, toasty.

Munia (14 meses en barrica) 2011 T Roble
100% tinta de Toro

89

Colour: cherry, garnet rim. Nose: ripe fruit, spicy, creamy oak, toasty. Palate: powerful, flavourful, toasty, round tannins.

Munia (6 meses en barrica) 2012 T Roble
100% tinta de Toro

87

Colour: bright cherry. Nose: ripe fruit, sweet spices, creamy oak, expressive. Palate: flavourful, fruity, toasty.

Pictor 2010 T Roble
100% tinta de Toro

93

Colour: cherry, garnet rim. Nose: ripe fruit, spicy, creamy oak, toasty, dark chocolate, earthy notes. Palate: powerful, flavourful, toasty, elegant, balanced.

VIÑEDOS ALONSO DEL YERRO

Finca Santa Marta - Ctra. Roa-Anguix, Km. 1,8
09300 Roa (Burgos)
☎: +34 913 160 121
Fax: +34 913 160 121
www.alonsodelyerro.es
mariadelyerro@vay.es

Paydos 2011 T
100% tinta de Toro

92

Colour: cherry, garnet rim. Nose: wild herbs, spicy, creamy oak, ripe fruit, balanced. Palate: powerful, flavourful, complex, spicy, long, balanced.

VIÑEDOS DE VILLAESTER

49800 Toro (Zamora)
☎: +34 948 645 008
Fax: +34 948 645 166
www.familiabelasco.com
info@familiabelasco.com

Taurus 2007 TC
100% tinta de Toro

87

Colour: cherry, garnet rim. Nose: balanced, complex, ripe fruit, spicy. Palate: good structure, flavourful, round tannins.

Taurus 2012 T Roble
100% tinta de Toro

85

Villaester 2004 T
100% tinta de Toro

90

Colour: pale ruby, brick rim edge. Nose: elegant, spicy, fine reductive notes, wet leather, aged wood nuances, fruit liqueur notes. Palate: spicy, fine tannins, elegant, long.

VOCARRAJE

Ctra. San Román, s/n Calle Izq.
49810 Moral de Toro (Zamora)
☎: +34 980 698 172
Fax: +34 980 698 172
www.vocarraje.es
info@vocarraje.es

Abdón Segovia 2011 TC
tinta de Toro
87
Colour: deep cherry, garnet rim. Nose: balanced, spicy, medium intensity, waxy notes. Palate: flavourful, round tannins.

Abdón Segovia 2012 T Roble
tinta de Toro
84

WEINWERK EL LAGARTO

Portugal, 7
49323 Fornillos de Fermoselle (Zamora)
☎: +49 232 459 724
Fax: +49 232 459 721
www.gourmet-lagarto.de
winzer@gourmet-lagarto.de

TeGe Weinwerk 2009 T
91
Colour: cherry, garnet rim. Nose: spicy, toasty, overripe fruit, mineral. Palate: powerful, flavourful, toasty, round tannins.

TeGe Weinwerk 2010 T
tinta de Toro, garnacha
94
Colour: cherry, garnet rim. Nose: ripe fruit, spicy, creamy oak, toasty, complex, earthy notes. Palate: powerful, flavourful, toasty, round tannins.

edición limitada de
Weinwerk

DO. UCLÉS

CONSEJO REGULADOR

Avda. Miguel Cervantes, 93
16400 Tarancón (Cuenca)
☎ :+34 969 135 056 - Fax: +34 969 135 421
@: gerente@vinosdeucles.com
www.vinosdeucles.com

DO UCLÉS / D.O.P

LOCATION:

Midway between Cuenca (to the west) and Toledo (to the northwest), this DO is made up of 25 towns from the first province and three from the second. However, the majority of vineyards are situated in Tarancón and the neighbouring towns of Cuenca, as far as Huete - where La Alcarria starts - the largest stretch of border in the DO.

GRAPE VARIETIES:

Red: Tempranillo, Merlot, Cabernet Sauvignon, Garnacha and Syrah.
White: Verdejo, Moscatel de Grano Menudo, Chardonnay, Sauvignon Blanc and Viura (macabeo).

FIGURES:

Vineyard surface: 1,700 – Wine-Growers: 122 – Wineries: 5 – 2013 Harvest rating: Good – Production 13: 1,650,000 litres – Market percentages: 62% domestic - 38% export.

SOIL:

Despite spreading over two provinces with different soil components, the communal soils are deep and not very productive, of a sandy and consistent texture, becoming more clayey as you move towards the banks of the rivers Riansares and Bendija.

CLIMATE:

The Altamira sierra forms gentle undulations that rise from an average of 600 metres in La Mancha, reaching 1,200 metres. These ups and downs produce variations in the continental climate, which is less extreme, milder and has a Mediterranean touch. As such, rain is scarce, more akin to a semi-dry climate.

VINTAGE RATING   PEÑÍNGUIDE

2009	2010	2011	2012	2013
GOOD	VERY GOOD	VERY GOOD	GOOD	AVERAGE

BODEGA SOLEDAD

Ctra. Tarancón, s/n
16411 Fuente de Pedro Naharro
(Cuenca)
☎: +34 969 125 039
Fax: +34 969 125 907
www.bodegasoledad.com
enologo@bodegasoledad.com

Bisiesto 2012 BFB
chardonnay
87
Colour: bright yellow. Nose: powerfull, ripe fruit, sweet spices, creamy oak, fragrant herbs. Palate: rich, flavourful, fresh, good acidity.

Solmayor 2009 TC
tempranillo
88
Colour: cherry, garnet rim. Nose: ripe fruit, spicy, creamy oak, toasty. Palate: powerful, flavourful, toasty.

Solmayor 2010 T Roble
tempranillo
86
Colour: bright cherry. Nose: ripe fruit, sweet spices. Palate: flavourful, fruity, toasty, round tannins.

Solmayor 2013 T
tempranillo
84

Solmayor Chardonnay 2013 B
chardonnay
85

Solmayor Sauvignon Blanc 2013 B
sauvignon blanc
82

Solmayor Tempranillo 2013 RD
tempranillo
84

BODEGAS FINCA LA ESTACADA

Ctra. N-400, Km. 103
16400 Tarancón (Cuenca)
☎: +34 969 327 099
Fax: +34 969 327 199
www.fincalaestacada.com
enologia@fincalaestacada.com

Finca la Estacada 12 meses barrica 2010 T Barrica
tempranillo
87
Colour: bright cherry. Nose: ripe fruit, sweet spices, creamy oak, medium intensity. Palate: fruity, flavourful, toasty, balsamic.

Finca la Estacada 6 meses barrica 2012 T Roble
tempranillo
88
Colour: bright cherry. Nose: sweet spices, creamy oak, ripe fruit. Palate: flavourful, toasty, spicy.

Finca La Estacada Chardonnay Sauvignon Blanc 2013 B
chardonnay, sauvignon blanc
83

Finca la Estacada Varietales 2009 TC
tempranillo, cabernet sauvignon, syrah, merlot
87
Colour: black cherry. Nose: powerfull, dried herbs, wild herbs, fruit preserve, old leather. Palate: fruity, balsamic, spicy.

La Estacada Syrah Merlot 2012 T Roble
syrah, merlot
90
Colour: deep cherry, garnet rim. Nose: scrubland, ripe fruit, balanced, warm. Palate: balanced, round tannins, balsamic, long.

BODEGAS LA ESTACIÓN S. COOP. DE CLM

Avda Castilla la Mancha, 38
45370 Santa Cruz de la Zarza (Toledo)
☎: +34 925 143 234
Fax: +34 925 125 154
www.bodegaslaestacion.es
enologia@bodegaslaestacion.es

Toc Toc 2012 T
syrah
86
Colour: cherry, garnet rim. Nose: ripe fruit, wild herbs, spicy. Palate: balanced, flavourful, long.

Vicus 12 Meses 2010 TC
tempranillo
85

Vicus 2013 B
macabeo
83

Vicus 2013 T
tempranillo
85

Vicus 6 meses 2012 T
tempranillo
84

BODEGAS VID Y ESPIGA

San Antón, 30
16415 Villamayor de Santiago (Cuenca)
☎: +34 969 139 069
Fax: +34 969 139 069
www.vidyespiga.es
calleja.enologo@gmail.com

Cañada Real 2011 TC
100% tempranillo
85

Cañada Real 2012 T Roble
100% tempranillo
85

Cañada Real 2013 B
sauvignon blanc, verdejo
82

Cañada Real 2013 RD
tempranillo
84

Cañada Real 2013 T
tempranillo
86
Colour: cherry, purple rim. Nose: fresh fruit, red berry notes, floral. Palate: flavourful, fruity, good acidity, round tannins, good finish.

BODEGAS Y VIÑEDOS FONTANA

O'Donnell, 18 1ºG
28009 Madrid (Madrid)
☎: +34 915 783 197
Fax: +34 915 783 072
www.bodegasfontana.com
gemag@bodegasfontana.com

Mesta 2013 B
100% verdejo
86
Colour: bright straw. Nose: fresh, fresh fruit, white flowers, tropical fruit. Palate: flavourful, fruity, good acidity, balanced.

Mesta 2013 RD
100% tempranillo
85

Mesta Tempranillo 2012 T
100% tempranillo
85

Quinta de Quercus 2011 T
100% tempranillo
91
Colour: cherry, garnet rim. Nose: red berry notes, ripe fruit, balsamic herbs, spicy, creamy oak. Palate: powerful, flavourful, balanced, toasty.

DO. UTIEL-REQUENA

CONSEJO REGULADOR

Sevilla, 12. Apdo. 61
46300 Utiel (Valencia)
☎:+34 962 171 062 - Fax: +34 962 172 185
@: info@utielrequena.org
www.utielrequena.org

LOCATION:

In thewest of the province of Valencia. It comprises the municipal districts of Camporrobles, Caudete de las Fuentes, Fuenterrobles, Requena, Siete Aguas, Sinarcas, Utiel, Venta del Moro and Villagordo de Cabriel.

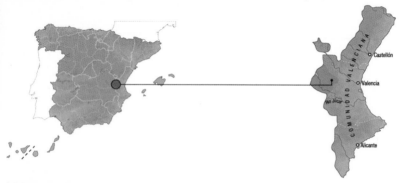

GRAPE VARIETIES:

Red: Bobal, Tempranillo, Garnacha, Cabernet Sauvignon, Merlot, Syrah, Pinot Noir, Garnacha Tintorera, Petit Verdot and Cabernet Franc.
White: Tardana, Macabeo, Merseguera, Chardonnay, Sauvignon Blanc, Parellada,Xarel.lo, Verdejo, Moscatel de Grano Menudo, Viognier and Albariño.

FIGURES:

Vineyard surface: 34,312 – Wine-Growers: 5,604 – Wineries: 95 – 2013 Harvest rating: Very Good – Production 13: 37,718,188 litres – Market percentages: 20% domestic - 80% export.

SOIL:

Mainly brownish-grey, almost red limestone, poor in organic matter andwith good permeability. The horizon of the vineyards are broken by the silhouette of the odd tree planted in the middle of the vineyards,which, bordered bywoods, offer a very attractive landscape.

CLIMATE:

Continental,with Mediterranean influences, coldwinters and slightly milder summers than in other regions of the province. Rainfall is quite scarcewith an annual average of 400 mm.

VINTAGE RATING   PEÑÍNGUIDE

2009	2010	2011	2012	2013
GOOD	VERY GOOD	VERY GOOD	VERY GOOD	GOOD

ARANLEÓN

Ctra. Caudete, 3
46310 Los Marcos (Valencia)
☎: +34 963 631 640
Fax: +34 962 185 150
www.aranleon.com
vinos@aranleon.com

Aranleón Sólo 2011 T
bobal, tempranillo, syrah
90
Colour: cherry, garnet rim. Nose: ripe fruit, spicy, creamy oak, toasty, dark chocolate, earthy notes. Palate: powerful, flavourful, toasty, round tannins.

BODEGA SEBIRAN

Pérez Galdos, 1
46352 Campo Arcis - Requena (Valencia)
☎: +34 962 303 321
Fax: +34 962 301 560
www.sebiran.es
info@sebiran.es

Sebirán "J" 2008 TC
bobal
87
Colour: ruby red. Nose: spicy, fine reductive notes, aged wood nuances, toasty, ripe fruit. Palate: spicy, long, toasty.

Sebirán "T" 2012 T
tempranillo
84

Sebirán "T" 2012 T Fermentado en Barrica
tempranillo
78

Sebirán "T" 2013 B
macabeo
83

Sebirán "T" 2013 RD
bobal
86
Colour: coppery red. Nose: ripe fruit, red berry notes, floral, expressive. Palate: fruity, fresh.

Sebirán "Z" 2008 TC
bobal, tempranillo
88
Colour: cherry, garnet rim. Nose: balanced, ripe fruit, spicy. Palate: good structure, flavourful, round tannins.

BODEGA VERA DE ESTENAS

Junto N-III, km. 266 -
Paraje La Cabeuzela
46300 Utiel (Valencia)
☎: +34 962 171 141
www.veradeestenas.es
estenas@veradeestenas.es

Casa Don Ángel Bobal 2011 T
bobal
93
Colour: cherry, garnet rim. Nose: ripe fruit, spicy, creamy oak, toasty. Palate: powerful, flavourful, toasty, round tannins.

Estenas 2011 TC
bobal, cabernet sauvignon, merlot, tempranillo
88
Colour: cherry, garnet rim. Nose: spicy, wild herbs, overripe fruit. Palate: flavourful, pruney, balsamic.

Estenas 2013 B
macabeo, chardonnay
85

Estenas 2013 T Barrica
bobal, cabernet sauvignon, merlot, tempranillo
87
Colour: deep cherry. Nose: scrubland, red berry notes. Palate: flavourful, ripe fruit.

Estenas Bobal 2013 RD
bobal
85

Martínez Bermell Merlot 2012 T Fermentado en Barrica
merlot
84

Viña Lidón 2013 BFB
chardonnay
88
Colour: bright straw. Nose: white flowers, fresh fruit, expressive, fine lees, dried herbs. Palate: flavourful, fruity, good acidity, balanced.

BODEGA Y VIÑEDOS CARRES

Francho, 1
46352 Casas de Eufema (Valencia)
☎: +34 675 515 729
www.bodegacarres.com
torrescarpio.jl@gmail.com

El Olivastro 2010 T
bobal
88
Colour: cherry, garnet rim. Nose: spicy, toasty, overripe fruit. Palate: powerful, flavourful, toasty, round tannins.

Membrillera 2013 T
bobal

87 🌱

Colour: cherry, purple rim. Nose: powerfull, red berry notes, ripe fruit, floral, expressive. Palate: powerful, fresh, fruity, unctuous.

BODEGAS COVILOR
Antonio Bartual, 21
46313 Cuevas de Utiel (Valencia)
☎: +34 962 182 053
Fax: +34 962 182 055
www.bodegascovilor.com
oficina@bodegascovilor.com

Alto Cuevas 2013 RD
bobal

87

Colour: rose, purple rim. Nose: powerfull, ripe fruit, red berry notes, floral. Palate: powerful, fruity, fresh.

Alto Cuevas Bobal Tempranillo 2011 T
87

Colour: very deep cherry, garnet rim. Nose: powerfull, ripe fruit, roasted coffee, dark chocolate. Palate: powerful, toasty, roasted-coffee aftertaste.

Alto Cuevas Macabeo 2013 B
macabeo

82

Alto Cuevas Tempranillo 2012 T
tempranillo

85

Sucesión Bobal 2011 T
bobal

89

Colour: bright cherry. Nose: ripe fruit, sweet spices, creamy oak, expressive. Palate: flavourful, fruity, toasty, round tannins.

BODEGAS COVIÑAS
Avda. Rafael Duyos, s/n
46340 Requena (Valencia)
☎: +34 962 300 680
Fax: +34 962 302 651
www.covinas.es
covinas@covinas.es

Al Vent Bobal 2012 T
bobal

91

Colour: cherry, garnet rim. Nose: ripe fruit, wild herbs, earthy notes, spicy, creamy oak. Palate: balanced, flavourful, long, balsamic.

Al Vent Bobal 2013 RD
bobal

86

Colour: rose, purple rim. Nose: ripe fruit, red berry notes. Palate: powerful, fruity, fresh.

Al Vent Sauvignon Blanc 2013 B
sauvignon blanc

87

Colour: bright straw. Nose: fresh fruit, white flowers. Palate: flavourful, fruity, good acidity, balanced.

Aula Cabernet Sauvignon 2011 T
cabernet sauvignon

87

Colour: bright cherry. Nose: ripe fruit, sweet spices, creamy oak, medium intensity. Palate: fruity, flavourful, toasty.

Aula Merlot 2011 TC
merlot

89

Colour: cherry, garnet rim. Nose: ripe fruit, wild herbs, earthy notes, spicy, creamy oak. Palate: balanced, flavourful, long, balsamic.

Aula Syrah 2011 TC
syrah

87

Colour: very deep cherry, garnet rim. Nose: powerfull, ripe fruit, roasted coffee, dark chocolate. Palate: powerful, toasty, roasted-coffee aftertaste.

Enterizo 2006 TGR
garnacha

84

Enterizo 2010 TR
garnacha

86

Colour: ruby red. Nose: spicy, fine reductive notes, aged wood nuances, toasty. Palate: spicy, long, toasty.

Viña Enterizo 2010 TC
tempranillo, bobal

86

Colour: cherry, garnet rim. Nose: fruit preserve, fruit liqueur notes, spicy. Palate: flavourful, pruney, balsamic.

Viña Enterizo Bobal 2013 RD
bobal

85

Viña Enterizo Macabeo 2013 B
macabeo

83

Viña Enterizo Tempranillo 2013 T
tempranillo

85

BODEGAS EMILIO CLEMENTE

Camino de San Blas, s/n
46340 Requena (Valencia)
☎: +34 962 323 391
www.eclemente.es
bodega@eclemente.es

Bomelot 2011 T
bobal, merlot

87

Colour: bright cherry. Nose: ripe fruit, sweet spices, creamy oak, expressive. Palate: flavourful, fruity, toasty, round tannins.

BODEGAS HISPANO SUIZAS

Ctra. N-322, Km. 451,7 El Pontón
46357 Requena (Valencia)
☎: +34 661 894 200
www.bodegashispanosuizas.com
info@bodegashispanosuizas.com

Bassus Dulce Bobal-Pinot Noir 2013 RD
pinot noir, bobal

90

Colour: coppery red. Nose: candied fruit, red berry notes, fine lees. Palate: sweetness, fruity, good acidity.

Bassus Pinot Noir 2012 T
pinot noir

91

Colour: cherry, garnet rim. Nose: ripe fruit, spicy, creamy oak, mineral. Palate: powerful, flavourful, toasty, round tannins.

Bassus Premium 2010 T
bobal, petit verdot, cabernet franc, merlot

92

Colour: very deep cherry, garnet rim. Nose: powerfull, ripe fruit, roasted coffee, dark chocolate. Palate: powerful, toasty, roasted-coffee aftertaste.

Bobos Finca Casa la Borracha 2012 T
bobal

93

Colour: cherry, garnet rim. Nose: ripe fruit, spicy, creamy oak, toasty, complex. Palate: powerful, flavourful, toasty, round tannins.

Impromptu 2013 B
sauvignon blanc

92

Colour: bright yellow. Nose: powerfull, ripe fruit, sweet spices, creamy oak. Palate: rich, smoky aftertaste, flavourful, fresh, good acidity.

Quod Superius 2010 T
bobal, cabernet franc, merlot, syrah

93

Colour: cherry, garnet rim. Nose: ripe fruit, spicy, creamy oak, toasty, complex, dark chocolate, earthy notes. Palate: powerful, flavourful, toasty, round tannins.

BODEGAS IRANZO

Ctra. de Madrid, 60
46315 Caudete de las Fuentes (Valencia)
☎: +34 962 319 282
Fax: +34 962 319 282
www.bodegasiranzo.com
comercial@bodegasiranzo.com

Bodegas Iranzo Tempranillo Selección 2012 T
tempranillo

84

Finca Cañada Honda 2011 TC

86 ☙

Colour: bright cherry. Nose: ripe fruit, sweet spices, creamy oak, medium intensity. Palate: fruity, flavourful, toasty.

Finca Cañada Honda 2012 T Barrica

86 ☙

Colour: cherry, garnet rim. Nose: ripe fruit, spicy, creamy oak, toasty, earthy notes. Palate: powerful, flavourful, toasty.

BODEGAS MITOS

Ctra. CV 450, km. 3 El Azagador
46357 Requena (Valencia)
☎: +34 962 300 703
www.bodegasmitos.com
admin@bodegasmitos.com

Mitos 2012 T
cabernet sauvignon, merlot

85

Mitos 2012 T Roble
cabernet sauvignon, merlot, tempranillo

87

Colour: cherry, garnet rim. Nose: ripe fruit, spicy, creamy oak, toasty, complex. Palate: powerful, flavourful, toasty.

Mitos 2012 TC
cabernet sauvignon, tempranillo

83

BODEGAS MURVIEDRO

Ampliación Pol. El Romeral, s/n
46340 Requena (Valencia)
☎: +34 962 329 003
Fax: +34 962 329 002
www.bodegasmurviedro.es
murviedro@murviedro.es

Corolilla 2010 TR
100% bobal

89

Colour: cherry, garnet rim. Nose: red berry notes, ripe fruit, spicy, creamy oak, toasty, complex. Palate: powerful, flavourful, toasty, round tannins.

Corolilla 2011 TC
100% bobal

88
Colour: bright cherry. Nose: ripe fruit, sweet spices, creamy oak, medium intensity. Palate: fruity, flavourful, toasty, balanced.

Cueva de la Culpa 2011 T

93
Colour: cherry, garnet rim. Nose: ripe fruit, spicy, creamy oak, toasty, complex, scrubland. Palate: powerful, flavourful, toasty, round tannins.

DNA Murviedro Classic Bobal 2013 T
100% bobal

85

Murviedro Colección Sauvignon Blanc 2013 B
sauvignon blanc

86
Colour: bright straw, greenish rim. Nose: balanced, ripe fruit, tropical fruit, floral. Palate: correct, fruity, easy to drink, good finish.

Murviedro Colección Tempranillo 2013 T
100% tempranillo

87
Colour: deep cherry. Nose: ripe fruit, red berry notes, spicy. Palate: flavourful, ripe fruit.

Vega Libre 2009 TR

85

BODEGAS PALMERA
Partida Palomera, 345
46300 Utiel (Valencia)
☎: +34 626 706 394
klauslauerbach@hotmail.com

Bobal y Merlot 2012 T
bobal, merlot

84 🍷

Bobal y Tempranillo 2011 T
bobal, tempranillo

87 🍷
Colour: cherry, garnet rim. Nose: ripe fruit, spicy, creamy oak, toasty. Palate: powerful, flavourful, toasty, round tannins.

Capricho 2011 T
cabernet sauvignon, merlot

89 🍷
Colour: cherry, garnet rim. Nose: ripe fruit, spicy, creamy oak, toasty, complex. Palate: powerful, flavourful, toasty, round tannins.

L'Angelet 2011 TC
tempranillo, cabernet sauvignon, merlot

87 🍷
Colour: ruby red. Nose: spicy, fine reductive notes, wet leather, aged wood nuances, toasty, fruit preserve. Palate: spicy, long, toasty.

L'Angelet d'Or 2011 T
bobal, tempranillo, cabernet sauvignon

87 🍷
Colour: very deep cherry, garnet rim. Nose: powerfull, ripe fruit, roasted coffee, dark chocolate. Palate: powerful, toasty, roasted-coffee aftertaste.

Rosado Palmera 2013 RD
bobal

88 🍷
Colour: onion pink. Nose: elegant, candied fruit, dried flowers, fragrant herbs, red berry notes. Palate: light-bodied, flavourful, good acidity, long, spicy.

Viña Cabriel 2011 T
tempranillo, cabernet sauvignon, merlot

84 🍷

BODEGAS PASIEGO
Avda. Virgen de Tejeda, 28
46320 Sinarcas (Valencia)
☎: +34 609 076 575
Fax: +34 962 306 175
www.bodegaspasiego.com
bodega@bodegaspasiego.com

Pasiego Bobal 2010 T

84

Pasiego de Autor 2009 TC
90
Colour: cherry, garnet rim. Nose: ripe fruit, spicy, creamy oak, toasty, dark chocolate. Palate: powerful, flavourful, toasty, round tannins.

Pasiego La Blasca 2008 TC
87
Colour: ruby red. Nose: spicy, fine reductive notes, wet leather, aged wood nuances, toasty. Palate: spicy, long, toasty.

Pasiego La Suertes 2013 B
88
Colour: bright straw. Nose: fresh, fresh fruit, white flowers, expressive. Palate: flavourful, fruity, good acidity, balanced.

BODEGAS SIERRA NORTE
Pol. Ind. El Romeral. Transporte C2
46340 Requena (Valencia)
☎: +34 962 323 099
Fax: +34 962 323 048
www.bodegasierranorte.com
info@bodegasierranorte.com

Cerro Bercial 2008 TR
tempranillo, bobal, cabernet sauvignon
89
Colour: ruby red, brick rim edge. Nose: fruit liqueur notes, earthy notes, spicy, creamy oak, fine reductive notes. Palate: powerful, flavourful, spicy, balsamic, long.

Cerro Bercial 2010 TC
tempranillo, bobal
86
Colour: cherry, garnet rim. Nose: ripe fruit, spicy, creamy oak, toasty. Palate: powerful, flavourful, toasty.

Cerro Bercial 2011 T Barrica
tempranillo, bobal
91
Colour: bright cherry. Nose: ripe fruit, sweet spices, creamy oak, expressive. Palate: flavourful, fruity, toasty, round tannins.

Cerro Bercial 2013 RD
bobal
85

Cerro Bercial Parcela "Ladera los Cantos" 2008 T
bobal, cabernet sauvignon
91
Colour: cherry, garnet rim. Nose: ripe fruit, spicy, creamy oak, toasty, complex, dark chocolate, earthy notes. Palate: powerful, flavourful, toasty, round tannins, balanced.

Cerro Bercial Selección 2012 B
macabeo, sauvignon blanc, chardonnay
89
Colour: bright yellow. Nose: powerfull, ripe fruit, sweet spices, creamy oak, fragrant herbs. Palate: rich, flavourful, fresh, good acidity.

Fuenteseca 2013 B
macabeo, sauvignon blanc
85

Fuenteseca 2013 RD
bobal, cabernet sauvignon
87
Colour: rose, purple rim. Nose: powerfull, ripe fruit, red berry notes, floral. Palate: powerful, fruity, fresh.

Fuenteseca 2013 T
bobal, cabernet sauvignon
86
Colour: cherry, garnet rim. Nose: ripe fruit, fragrant herbs, powerfull. Palate: flavourful, fruity, balanced.

Pasion de Bobal 2012 T Barrica
bobal
90
Colour: bright cherry. Nose: sweet spices, creamy oak, sulphur notes. Palate: flavourful, fruity, toasty, round tannins.

Pasion de Bobal 2013 RD
bobal
88
Colour: coppery red. Nose: elegant, candied fruit, dried flowers, fragrant herbs, red berry notes. Palate: light-bodied, flavourful, good acidity, long, spicy.

Pasion de Moscatel 2013 B
moscatel
84

BODEGAS UTIELANAS
Actor Rambal, 29
46300 Utiel (Valencia)
☎: +34 962 170 801
Fax: +34 962 170 801
www.bodegasutielanas.com
info@bodegasutielanas.com

Vega Infante 2011 TC
85

Vega Infante 2013 B
100% macabeo
85

Vega Infante 2013 RD
100% bobal
87
Colour: rose, purple rim. Nose: powerfull, ripe fruit, red berry notes, floral, expressive. Palate: powerful, fruity, fresh.

Vega Infante 2013 T
100% bobal

82

BODEGAS VICENTE GANDÍA
Ctra. Cheste a Godelleta, s/n
46370 Chiva (Valencia)
☎: +34 962 524 242
Fax: +34 962 524 243
www.vicentegandia.es
info@vicentegandia.com

BO - Bobal Único 2012 T
100% bobal

88

Colour: cherry, garnet rim. Nose: ripe fruit, balsamic herbs, spicy, creamy oak. Palate: powerful, flavourful, long.

Ceremonia 2010 TR

87

Colour: cherry, garnet rim. Nose: ripe fruit, spicy, creamy oak, toasty. Palate: powerful, flavourful, toasty.

Finca del Mar Cabernet Sauvignon 2013 T
100% cabernet sauvignon

82

Finca del Mar Chardonnay 2013 B
100% chardonnay

87

Colour: bright straw. Nose: white flowers, fragrant herbs, citrus fruit, fruit expression. Palate: fresh, fruity, flavourful, balanced.

Finca del Mar Merlot 2012 T
100% merlot

84

Finca del Mar Tempranillo 2012 T
100% tempranillo

85

Generación 1 2010 TR

89

Colour: bright cherry. Nose: ripe fruit, sweet spices, creamy oak. Palate: fruity, flavourful, toasty.

Hoya de Cadenas 2013 B
chardonnay, sauvignon blanc, macabeo

86

Colour: bright straw. Nose: white flowers, fruit expression. Palate: fresh, fruity, flavourful, balanced, elegant.

Hoya de Cadenas 2013 RD
100% bobal

85

Hoya de Cadenas Cabernet Sauvignon 2013 T
100% cabernet sauvignon

85

Hoya de Cadenas Chardonnay 2013 B
chardonnay

86

Colour: bright straw. Nose: fresh, fresh fruit, white flowers. Palate: flavourful, fruity, good acidity, balanced.

Hoya de Cadenas Merlot 2012 T
100% merlot

85

Hoya de Cadenas Reserva Privada 2010 TR

87

Colour: bright cherry. Nose: ripe fruit, sweet spices, creamy oak, medium intensity, fine reductive notes. Palate: fruity, flavourful, toasty.

Hoya de Cadenas Syrah 2012 T
100% syrah

85

Hoya de Cadenas Tempranillo 2010 TR
tempranillo

85

Marqués de Chivé 2010 TR
100% tempranillo

84

Marqués de Chivé 2011 TC
100% tempranillo

84

BODEGAS Y VIÑEDOS DE UTIEL
Finca El Renegado, s/n
46315 Caudete de las Fuentes
(Valencia)
☎: + 34 962 174 029
Fax: +34 962 171 432
www.bodegasdeutiel.com
gestion@bodegasdeutiel.com

Capellana 2013 B
macabeo

84

Capellana 2013 RD
bobal

87

Colour: light cherry. Nose: powerfull, ripe fruit, red berry notes, floral, expressive. Palate: powerful, fruity, fresh.

Capellana 2013 T
tempranillo

83

Capellana Tinto de Autor 2011 TC
cabernet sauvignon, tempranillo

86

Colour: very deep cherry, garnet rim. Nose: powerfull, ripe fruit, roasted coffee, dark chocolate. Palate: powerful, toasty, roasted-coffee aftertaste.

Nodus Bobal 2011 T
bobal

87

Colour: cherry, garnet rim. Nose: ripe fruit, spicy, creamy oak, toasty. Palate: powerful, flavourful, toasty, round tannins, balanced.

Nodus Chardonnay 2012 B
chardonnay

88

Colour: bright golden. Nose: ripe fruit, dry nuts, powerfull, toasty, aged wood nuances. Palate: flavourful, fruity, spicy, toasty, long.

Nodus Merlot Delirium 2010 T
merlot

84

Nodus Tinto de Autor 2010 TC
merlot, syrah, cabernet sauvignon, bobal

88

Colour: very deep cherry, garnet rim. Nose: powerfull, ripe fruit, roasted coffee, dark chocolate. Palate: powerful, toasty, roasted-coffee aftertaste.

CERROGALLINA
Travesía Industria, 5
46352 Campo Arcis (Valencia)
☎: +34 676 897 251
Fax: +34 962 338 135
www.cerrogallina.com
info@cerrogallina.com

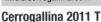

Cerrogallina 2011 T
100% bobal

90

Colour: bright cherry. Nose: ripe fruit, sweet spices, creamy oak, caramel, fruit liqueur notes. Palate: flavourful, fruity, toasty, balanced.

CHOZAS CARRASCAL
Vereda San Antonio POI. Ind. Catastral,
16 Parcelas 136-138
46340 San Antonio de Requena
(Valencia)
☎: +34 963 410 395
Fax: +34 963 168 067
www.chozascarrascal.es
chozas@chozascarrascal.es

Las Dosces 2012 T
90

Colour: cherry, garnet rim. Nose: ripe fruit, wild herbs, spicy, creamy oak. Palate: powerful, flavourful, spicy, ripe fruit.

Las Dosces 2013 B
macabeo, sauvignon blanc

91

Colour: bright straw. Nose: floral, fragrant herbs, fruit expression, spicy. Palate: fresh, flavourful, balsamic.

COMERCIAL GRUPO FREIXENET
Joan Sala, 2
08770 Sant Sadurní D'Anoia
(Barcelona)
☎: +34 938 917 000
Fax: +34 938 183 095
www.freixenet.es
freixenet@freixenet.es

Beso de Rechenna 2010 TC
bobal

89

Colour: cherry, garnet rim. Nose: ripe fruit, spicy, creamy oak, toasty, complex. Palate: powerful, flavourful, toasty, round tannins.

DOMINIO DE LA VEGA
Ctra. Madrid - Valencia, N-III Km. 270,6
46390 Requena (Valencia)
☎: +34 962 320 570
Fax: +34 962 320 330
www.dominiodelavega.com
dv@dominiodelavega.com

Añacal Dominio de la Vega 2013 B
macabeo, sauvignon blanc

81

Añacal Dominio de la Vega 2013 RD
bobal

85

Arte Mayor III 2005/2006/2007 2006/2007/2008 T
bobal

91

Colour: cherry, garnet rim. Nose: ripe fruit, wild herbs, earthy notes, spicy, creamy oak. Palate: balanced, flavourful, long, balsamic.

Dominio de la Vega 2008 TR
bobal, cabernet sauvignon, syrah

87

Colour: very deep cherry. Nose: ripe fruit, spicy, creamy oak, toasty, characterful. Palate: powerful, flavourful, toasty, round tannins.

Dominio de la Vega 2009 TC
bobal, cabernet sauvignon, syrah

87

Colour: bright cherry. Nose: ripe fruit, sweet spices, creamy oak, medium intensity. Palate: fruity, flavourful, toasty.

Dominio de la Vega 2012 T Roble
bobal, syrah, merlot

86

Colour: cherry, garnet rim. Nose: ripe fruit, sweet spices, creamy oak. Palate: flavourful, fruity, toasty.

Dominio de la Vega Bobal 2012 T Roble
bobal

88

Colour: cherry, garnet rim. Nose: fruit preserve, wild herbs, spicy, creamy oak. Palate: powerful, flavourful, spicy.

Dominio de la Vega Dulce 2012 B
sauvignon blanc, chardonnay, macabeo

90

Colour: golden. Nose: powerfull, floral, honeyed notes, candied fruit, fragrant herbs. Palate: flavourful, sweet, fresh, fruity, good acidity, long, balanced.

Dominio de la Vega Sauvignon Blanc 2012 BFB
sauvignon blanc

87

Colour: bright straw. Nose: expressive, fine lees, dried herbs, citrus fruit, ripe fruit, spicy. Palate: flavourful, fruity, good acidity.

FINCA SAN BLAS
Partida de San Blas, s/n
46340 Requena (Valencia)
☎: +34 963 375 617
Fax: +34 963 370 707
www.fincasanblas.com
info@fincasanblas.com

Finca San Blas 2012 B
merseguera, chardonnay

85

Finca San Blas Bobal 2011 T
bobal

87

Colour: cherry, garnet rim. Nose: fruit preserve, fruit liqueur notes, spicy, toasty. Palate: flavourful, pruney, balsamic, concentrated.

HAECKY IMPORT AG FINCA CASA LO ALTO
Ctra. Caudete - Los Isidros
46310 Venta del Moro (Valencia)
☎: +34 962 139 101
www.casa-lo-alto.es
syrah@gawnet.ch

Finca Casa Lo Alto 2010 TR
syrah, garnacha, cabernet sauvignon

87

Colour: bright cherry. Nose: ripe fruit, sweet spices, creamy oak, medium intensity. Palate: flavourful, toasty, powerful.

Finca Casa Lo Alto 2011 TC
tempranillo, garnacha, cabernet sauvignon, syrah

83

Finca Casa Lo Alto 2011 TR
syrah, garnacha, cabernet sauvignon

87

Colour: cherry, garnet rim. Nose: ripe fruit, spicy, creamy oak, toasty, complex. Palate: powerful, flavourful, toasty.

Finca Casa Lo Alto Chardonnay 2012 B
chardonnay

86

Colour: bright yellow. Nose: powerfull, ripe fruit, sweet spices, creamy oak, fragrant herbs. Palate: rich, smoky aftertaste, flavourful, fresh.

LATORRE AGROVINÍCOLA
Ctra. Requena, 2
46310 Venta del Moro (Valencia)
☎: +34 962 185 028
Fax: +34 962 185 422
www.latorreagrovinicola.com
bodega@latorreagrovinicola.com

Duque de Arcas 2011 TC
bobal, tempranillo, cabernet sauvignon

84

Duque de Arcas 2012 TC
tempranillo, cabernet sauvignon

84

Duque de Arcas Bobal 2012 T
bobal

87

Colour: cherry, purple rim. Nose: red berry notes, ripe fruit, balsamic herbs, creamy oak. Palate: flavourful, spicy, long.

Parreño 2013 T
tempranillo, cabernet sauvignon

84

Parreño 2013 B
viura, verdejo

83

Parreño 2013 RD
bobal

83

NOEMIWINES

Rambla, 47
46314 Fuenterrobles (Valencia)
☎: +34 962 183 100
Fax: +34 962 183 100
bodega@noemiwines.com

Exuperio 2013 T
bobal

93

Colour: cherry, garnet rim. Nose: ripe fruit, spicy, toasty, complex, earthy notes. Palate: powerful, flavourful, toasty, round tannins.

PAGO DE THARSYS

Ctra. Nacional III, km. 274
46340 Requena (Valencia)
☎: +34 962 303 354
Fax: +34 962 329 000
www.pagodetharsys.com
pagodetharsys@pagodetharsys.com

Carlota Suria 2007 TR
85

Dominio de Requena 2013 B
100% macabeo
85

Tharsys Único 2008 ESP Reserva
100% bobal
88

Colour: bright golden. Nose: fine lees, dry nuts, fragrant herbs, complex. Palate: powerful, flavourful, good acidity, fine bead, fine bitter notes, balanced.

PRIMUM BOBAL

Constitución, 50 pta. 6
46340 Requena (Valencia)
☎: +34 625 464 377
www.primumbobal.com
vinos@primumbobal.com

Primum Bobal 2012 T
bobal

89

Colour: cherry, purple rim. Nose: powerfull, red berry notes, ripe fruit, floral, sweet spices. Palate: powerful, fresh, fruity, unctuous.

TORRE ORIA

Ctra. Pontón - Utiel, Km. 3
46390 Derramador - Requena
(Valencia)
☎: +34 962 320 289
Fax: +34 962 320 311
www.torreoria.com
marta.fuentes@torreoria.es

Marqués de Requena 2009 TR
86

Colour: ruby red. Nose: spicy, fine reductive notes, wet leather, aged wood nuances, toasty. Palate: spicy, long, toasty.

Marqués de Requena 2010 TC
87

Colour: bright cherry. Nose: ripe fruit, sweet spices, creamy oak, medium intensity. Palate: fruity, flavourful, toasty.

Marqués de Requena 2012 T
88

Colour: cherry, garnet rim. Nose: ripe fruit, spicy, creamy oak, toasty. Palate: powerful, flavourful, toasty.

Marqués de Requena 2013 B
78

VIÑEDOS LA MADROÑERA

Ctra. Nacional 322, km. 430
46354 Los Isidros (Valencia)
☎: +34 963 992 400
Fax: +34 963 992 451
www.constantia.es
bodega@constantia.es

Constantia 2007 TC
cabernet sauvignon, merlot, tempranillo
87

Colour: very deep cherry. Nose: ripe fruit, spicy, creamy oak, toasty. Palate: powerful, flavourful, toasty, round tannins.

Constantia Sine Robore 2011 T
tempranillo, merlot, cabernet sauvignon
88

Colour: cherry, garnet rim. Nose: ripe fruit, spicy, creamy oak, toasty, complex. Palate: powerful, flavourful, toasty, round tannins.

Dulce de Constantia 2011 T
tempranillo, merlot, cabernet sauvignon
88

Colour: cherry, garnet rim. Nose: fruit preserve, wild herbs, faded flowers, sweet spices, toasty. Palate: flavourful, thin, pruney.

Merlot de Constantia 2011 T
merlot
75

VIÑEDOS Y BODEGAS VEGALFARO

Ctra. Pontón - Utiel, Km. 3
46390 Requena (Valencia)
☎: +34 962 320 680
Fax: +34 962 321 126
www.vegalfaro.com
rodolfo@vegalfaro.com

Caprasia Bobal 2012 T
bobal
90
Colour: black cherry, purple rim. Nose: fruit preserve, powerfull, sweet spices, balsamic herbs. Palate: toasty, good structure, full, powerful.

Rebel.lia 2013 B
chardonnay, sauvignon blanc
87
Colour: bright straw. Nose: fresh, fresh fruit, white flowers. Palate: flavourful, fruity, good acidity, balanced.

Rebel.lia 2013 T
garnacha tintorera, bobal, tempranillo
90
Colour: bright cherry. Nose: ripe fruit, sweet spices, creamy oak, expressive. Palate: flavourful, fruity, toasty, round tannins.

Vegalfaro 2011 TC
syrah, merlot, tempranillo
89
Colour: cherry, garnet rim. Nose: ripe fruit, spicy, creamy oak, toasty, complex. Palate: powerful, flavourful, toasty, round tannins.

Vegalfaro Chardonnay 2013 B Roble
chardonnay
87
Colour: bright yellow. Nose: powerfull, ripe fruit, sweet spices, creamy oak. Palate: rich, smoky aftertaste, flavourful, fresh, good acidity.

VITICULTORES SAN JUAN BAUTISTA

Ctra. Cheste - Godelleta, Km. 1
46370 Chiva (Valencia)
☎: +34 962 510 861
www.cherubino.es
cherubino@cherubino.es

Bobal Desanjuan 2011 T
100% bobal
88
Colour: bright cherry, garnet rim. Nose: ripe fruit, sweet spices, creamy oak, expressive. Palate: flavourful, fruity, toasty, round tannins.

Bobal Desanjuan 2013 RD
100% bobal
88
Colour: rose, purple rim. Nose: ripe fruit, red berry notes, floral. Palate: fruity, sweetness, light-bodied.

Clos Desanjuan 2011 T
bobal
89
Colour: bright cherry. Nose: sweet spices, creamy oak, overripe fruit, earthy notes. Palate: fruity, flavourful, toasty.

DO. VALDEORRAS

CONSEJO REGULADOR
Ctra. Nacional 120, km. 463
32340 Vilamartín de Valdeorras (Ourense)
☎ :+34 988 300 295 - Fax: +34 988 300 455
@: consello@dovaldeorras.com
www.dovaldeorras.tv

LOCATION:
The DO Valdeorras is situated in the northeast of the province of Orense. It comprises the municipal areas of Larouco, Petín, O Bolo, A Rua, Vilamartín, O Barco, Rubiá and Carballeda de Valdeorras.

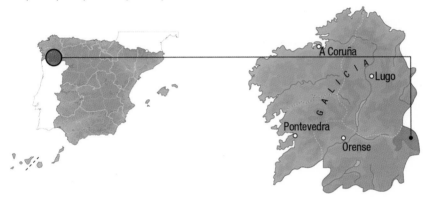

GRAPE VARIETIES:
White: Godello, Dona Blanca, Palomino, Loureira, Treixadura, Dona Branca, Albariño, Torrontes, Lado and Palomino.
Red: Mencía, Merenzao, Grao Negro, Garnacha, Tempranillo (Araúxa), Brancellao, Sousón, Caíño Tinto, Espadeiro, Ferrón, Gran Negro, Garnacha Tintureira and Mouratón.

FIGURES:
Vineyard surface: 1,143 – Wine-Growers: 1,458 – Wineries: 43 – 2013 Harvest rating: - – Production 13: 3,027,124 litres – Market percentages: 90% domestic - 10% export.

SOIL:
Quite varied. There are three types: the first type which is settled on shallow slate with many stones and a medium texture; the second type on deeper granite with a lot of sand and finally the type that lies on sediments and terraces, where there are usually a lot of pebbles.

CLIMATE:
Continental, with Atlantic influences. The average annual temperature is 11°C and the average annual rainfall ranges between 850 mm and 1,000 mm.

VINTAGE RATING   PEÑÍNGUIDE

2009	2010	2011	2012	2013
VERY GOOD	VERY GOOD	EXCELLENT	EXCELLENT	EXCELLENT

ADEGA A COROA

A Coroa, s/n
32350 A Rúa (Ourense)
☎: +34 988 310 648
Fax: +34 988 311 439
www.acoroa.com
acoroa@acoroa.com

A Coroa 2013 B
godello
91
Colour: bright straw. Nose: expressive, citrus fruit, fragrant herbs, faded flowers. Palate: balanced, long, fruity, easy to drink.

ADEGA DA PINGUELA

Camiño do Disco, 18
32350 A Rua de Valdeorras (Ourense)
☎: +34 654 704 753
www.adegadapinguela.com
adega@adegadapinguela.com

Memoria de Ventura Garnacha 2011 T
garnacha tintorera
93
Colour: bright cherry. Nose: ripe fruit, sweet spices, creamy oak, expressive, wild herbs, mineral. Palate: flavourful, fruity, toasty, balsamic.

Memoria de Ventura Godello 2013 B
godello
91
Colour: bright straw. Nose: white flowers, balanced, fruit expression, dry stone, expressive. Palate: flavourful, fruity, full.

Memoria de Ventura Godello Magnum 2013 B
godello
92
Colour: bright straw. Nose: dry stone, white flowers, citrus fruit, fresh fruit. Palate: flavourful, good acidity, fine bitter notes, long.

Memoria de Ventura Mencía 2013 T
mencía
92
Colour: cherry, garnet rim. Nose: red berry notes, wild herbs, dry stone, expressive. Palate: powerful, flavourful, complex, balsamic.

Memoria de Ventura Mencía Magnum 2013 T
mencía
92
Colour: cherry, purple rim. Nose: red berry notes, balsamic herbs, spicy, dry stone, balanced. Palate: powerful, flavourful, concentrated, balsamic.

Vento Godello 2012 B
godello
91
Colour: bright straw. Nose: white flowers, fragrant herbs, fruit expression, mineral. Palate: fresh, fruity, flavourful, balanced, elegant.

Vento Magnum 2012 BFB
godello
93
Colour: bright straw. Nose: ripe fruit, faded flowers, spicy, mineral. Palate: rich, balanced, fine bitter notes.

ADEGA MELILLAS E FILLOS

A Coroa, 22
32350 A Rúa (Ourense)
☎: +34 988 310 510
www.adegamelillas.com
info@adegamelillas.com

Lagar do Cigur 2013 B
godello
89
Colour: bright straw. Nose: fresh, fresh fruit, white flowers, varietal. Palate: flavourful, fruity, good acidity, balanced.

Lagar do Cigur 2011 T Barrica
mencía, tempranillo, merenzao, alicante
88
Colour: cherry, garnet rim. Nose: ripe fruit, spicy, creamy oak, toasty. Palate: powerful, flavourful, toasty.

Lagar do Cigur 2013 T
mencía, tempranillo, alicante
86
Colour: cherry, garnet rim. Nose: earthy notes, spicy, overripe fruit. Palate: flavourful, long, balsamic.

ADEGA O CASAL

Malladín, s/n
32310 Rubiá (Ourense)
☎: +34 689 675 800
www.casalnovo.es
casalnovo@casalnovo.es

Casal Novo Godello 2013 B
godello
91
Colour: bright straw. Nose: white flowers, fresh fruit, expressive, dried herbs. Palate: flavourful, fruity, good acidity, balanced.

Casal Novo Mencía 2013 T
mencía
87
Colour: light cherry, garnet rim. Nose: medium intensity, red berry notes, wild herbs, grassy. Palate: fruity, balanced.

ADEGA O CEPADO

O Patal, 11
32310 Rubia de Valdeorras (Ourense)
☎: +34 686 611 589
www.cepado.com
info@cepado.com

Cepado Godello 2013 B
100% godello
91
Colour: bright straw. Nose: white flowers, fragrant herbs, fruit expression. Palate: fresh, fruity, flavourful, balanced, elegant.

Cepado Mencía 2013 T
100% mencía
88
Colour: deep cherry, purple rim. Nose: powerfull, ripe fruit, fruit preserve, floral. Palate: flavourful, ripe fruit.

ADEGA QUINTA DA PEZA

Ctra. Nacional 120, km.467 Fontei
32350 A Rua de Valdeorras (Ourense)
☎: +34 988 311 537
Fax: +34 981 232 642
www.quintadapeza.es
quintadapeza@gmail.com

Quinta da Peza Godello 2013 B
100% godello
90
Colour: yellow, greenish rim. Nose: fresh, floral, balanced, varietal, citrus fruit, ripe fruit. Palate: flavourful, rich, balanced.

Quinta da Peza Mencía 2013 T
100% mencía
86
Colour: cherry, garnet rim. Nose: red berry notes, ripe fruit, wild herbs. Palate: flavourful, fruity, balsamic, easy to drink.

Quinta da Peza Oro Mencía Barrica 2012 TC
mencía
88
Colour: cherry, garnet rim. Nose: ripe fruit, spicy, creamy oak, toasty, warm. Palate: powerful, flavourful, toasty, round tannins.

ADEGAS RIBOUZO S.A.T.

Valencia do Sil
32349 Vilamartin de Valdeorras (Ourense)
☎: +34 626 323 945
www.adegasribouzo.com
ribouzo@yahoo.es

Marques de Camarasa Mistura T
86
Colour: cherry, garnet rim. Nose: red berry notes, ripe fruit, balsamic herbs, spicy. Palate: powerful, flavourful, concentrated, trated.

Mencía Ribouzo T
mencía
86
Colour: cherry, purple rim. Nose: expressive, fresh fruit, red berry notes, floral. Palate: flavourful, fruity, good acidity.

ALAN DE VAL

San Roque, 36
32350 A Rúa (Ourense)
☎: +34 988 310 431
Fax: +34 988 311 457
www.alandeval.com
alandeval@alandeval.com

A Costiña 2011 T
100% brancellao
91
Colour: cherry, garnet rim. Nose: ripe fruit, violets, scrubland, expressive. Palate: good structure, flavourful, round tannins.

Alan de Val Castes Nobres 2013 T
brancellao
92
Colour: deep cherry, purple rim. Nose: grassy, ripe fruit, expressive. Palate: good structure, balanced, round tannins, balsamic.

Alan de Val Godello 2013 B
100% godello
90
Colour: bright straw. Nose: white flowers, fragrant herbs, fruit expression, balsamic herbs. Palate: fresh, fruity, flavourful, round.

Alan de Val Mencía 2013 T
100% mencía
88
Colour: cherry, purple rim. Nose: wild herbs, fresh fruit, balsamic herbs. Palate: balanced, flavourful, long.

Alan de Val Rosé 2013 RD
brancellao, sausón, caiño
85

Escada Garnacha Tintureira 2012 T
100% garnacha tintorera
89
Colour: very deep cherry, garnet rim. Nose: powerfull, ripe fruit, balanced, balsamic herbs. Palate: flavourful, good structure, long.

Escada Lembranzas 2012 T
100% garnacha tintorera
90
Colour: black cherry, purple rim. Nose: scrubland, ripe fruit, warm, spicy. Palate: flavourful, balanced, powerful, balsamic.

Pedrazais Godello sobre Lías 2013 B
100% godello

93

Colour: bright straw. Nose: white flowers, fragrant herbs, fruit expression, dry stone, earthy notes. Palate: fresh, fruity, flavourful, balanced, elegant.

Pedrazais Mencía 2012 T Barrica
mencía

91

Colour: cherry, garnet rim. Nose: ripe fruit, spicy, creamy oak, complex, earthy notes, balsamic herbs. Palate: powerful, flavourful, toasty.

AVELINA S.A.T.
San Lorenzo, 6
32316 Corgomo, Vilamartin
de Valdeorras (Ourense)
☎: + 34 687 819 099
adega@adegaavelina.com

Casal de Furcos Rocio Godello 2013 B
100% godello

87

Colour: bright straw. Nose: white flowers, fragrant herbs, fruit expression. Palate: fresh, fruity, flavourful, balanced.

Casal de Furcos Rocio Mencía 2013 T
100% mencía

84

BODEGA COOP. VIRGEN DE LAS VIÑAS S.C.G
Campo Grande, 97
32350 A Rua de Valdeorras (Ourense)
☎: +34 988 310 607
Fax: +34 988 312 016
www.cooperativarua.com
market@cooperativarua.com

Amavia 2011 B
godello

90

Colour: bright yellow. Nose: floral, fragrant herbs, citrus fruit, fruit expression, mineral. Palate: rich, fruity, good structure, flavourful, balanced.

Pingadelo 2013 B
100% godello

88

Colour: bright straw. Nose: white flowers, fresh fruit, expressive, fine lees, dried herbs. Palate: flavourful, fruity, good acidity, balanced.

Pingadelo 2013 T
100% mencía

91

Colour: cherry, purple rim. Nose: red berry notes, fruit liqueur notes, balsamic herbs, mineral. Palate: flavourful, fruity, balanced.

BODEGA COOPERATIVA JESÚS NAZARENO
Florencio Delgado Gurriarán, 62
32300 O Barco de Valdeorras (Ourense)
☎: +34 988 320 262
Fax: +34 988 320 242
coopbarco@infonegocio.com

Valdouro 2012 T Barrica

86

Colour: bright cherry. Nose: ripe fruit, sweet spices, creamy oak, toasty. Palate: flavourful, toasty, round tannins.

Villa Abad 2013 T

87

Colour: cherry, purple rim. Nose: ripe fruit, violets, balanced. Palate: flavourful, fruity, good acidity.

Viña Abad Godello 2013 B
godello

89

Colour: bright straw. Nose: fresh, fresh fruit, white flowers, expressive. Palate: flavourful, fruity, good acidity, balanced.

BODEGA ROANDI
O Lagar s/n
32336 Éntoma – O Barco (Ourense)
Fax: +34 988 335 198
www.bodegaroandi.com
info@bodegaroandi.com

Alento Sobre lías 2012 B
godello

88

Colour: bright straw. Nose: white flowers, fine lees, dried herbs, toasty. Palate: flavourful, fruity, good acidity.

Bancales Moral Barrica 2011 T
mencía, sousón, brancellao

89

Colour: cherry, garnet rim. Nose: ripe fruit, spicy, creamy oak, toasty, complex. Palate: powerful, flavourful, toasty, round tannins.

Brinde 2012 ESP
godello

87

Colour: bright straw. Nose: fresh fruit, dried herbs, floral. Palate: fresh, fruity, flavourful, good acidity.

Domus de Roandi 2011 TC
sousón, mencía

89

Colour: cherry, garnet rim. Nose: ripe fruit, spicy, creamy oak, toasty, complex, balsamic herbs. Palate: powerful, flavourful, toasty, round tannins, balanced.

Dona Delfina 2013 B
godello

88

Colour: bright straw. Nose: white flowers, fragrant herbs, fruit expression. Palate: fresh, fruity, flavourful, balanced, elegant.

Flavia 2013 T
mencía, tempranillo, garnacha

89

Colour: cherry, garnet rim. Nose: fruit liqueur notes, red berry notes, wild herbs, dry stone. Palate: fruity, flavourful, balsamic.

BODEGA SANTA MARTA
Ctra. San Vicente s/n
32348 Córgomo-Vilamartin
de Valdeorras (Ourense)
☎: +34 988 324 559
Fax: +34 988 324 559
www.vinaredo.com
gerencia@vinaredo.com

Viñaredo Garnacha Centenaria 2010 T
garnacha tintorera

89

Colour: cherry, garnet rim. Nose: red berry notes, ripe fruit, spicy, creamy oak, toasty, complex, earthy notes, scrubland. Palate: flavourful, toasty, round tannins.

Viñaredo Godello 2013 B
godello

90

Colour: bright straw. Nose: fresh, fresh fruit, white flowers, expressive. Palate: flavourful, fruity, good acidity, balanced.

Viñaredo Mencía 2011 T Barrica
mencía

86

Colour: black cherry, garnet rim. Nose: fruit preserve, spicy, old leather, tobacco. Palate: flavourful, fruity, spicy.

Viñaredo Mencía 2013 T

87

Colour: dark-red cherry, purple rim. Nose: balanced, red berry notes, ripe fruit, scrubland. Palate: balanced, round tannins.

Viñaredo Sousón 2010 T Barrica
sousón

90

Colour: cherry, garnet rim. Nose: ripe fruit, wild herbs, earthy notes, spicy, creamy oak. Palate: balanced, flavourful, long, balsamic.

Viñaredo Tostado 2011 B
100% godello

95

Colour: old gold. Nose: expressive, candied fruit, honeyed notes, varnish, toasty, characterful, complex. Palate: flavourful, full, long.

BODEGAS AVANCIA
Parque Empresarial a Raña, 7
32300 O Barco de Valdeorras (Ourense)
☎: +34 952 504 706
Fax: +34 951 284 796
www.grupojorgeordonez.com
avancia@jorgeordonez.es

Avancia Cuvee de O 2013 B
100% godello

91

Colour: bright straw. Nose: fresh, fresh fruit, white flowers, expressive. Palate: flavourful, fruity, good acidity, balanced.

Avancia Cuvée Mosteiro 2013 T
100% mencía

94

Colour: cherry, garnet rim. Nose: ripe fruit, wild herbs, earthy notes, spicy, creamy oak. Palate: balanced, flavourful, long, balsamic.

Avancia Godello 2013 B
100% godello

94

Colour: bright straw. Nose: white flowers, fresh fruit, expressive, fine lees, dried herbs. Palate: flavourful, fruity, good acidity, balanced.

BODEGAS CARBALLAL
Ctra. de Carballal, km 2,2
32356 Petín de Valdeorras (Ourense)
☎: +34 988 311 281
Fax: +34 988 311 281
bodegascarballal@hotmail.com

Erebo Godello 2013 B
godello

92

Colour: bright straw. Nose: fresh, fresh fruit, white flowers, expressive. Palate: flavourful, fruity, good acidity, balanced.

Erebo Mencía 2013 T
mencía

87

Colour: bright cherry. Nose: ripe fruit, sweet spices, creamy oak, expressive. Palate: flavourful, fruity, round tannins.

BODEGAS D'BERNA

Córgomo
32340 Villamartín de Valdeorras
(Ourense)
☎: +34 988 324 557
Fax: +34 988 324 557
www.bodegasdberna.com
info@bodegasdberna.com

D'Berna Godello 2013 B
100% godello
90
Colour: bright straw. Nose: fresh, fresh fruit, white flowers, expressive, fragrant herbs. Palate: flavourful, fruity, good acidity, balanced.

D'Berna Godello sobre Lías 2011 B
100% godello
90
Colour: bright straw. Nose: white flowers, fresh fruit, expressive, fine lees, dried herbs. Palate: flavourful, fruity, good acidity, balanced.

D'Berna Mencía 2013 T
mencía
88
Colour: dark-red cherry, garnet rim. Nose: ripe fruit, grassy, balanced. Palate: fruity, flavourful, balsamic.

D'Berna Mencía Barrica 2011 T
100% mencía
89
Colour: bright cherry. Nose: ripe fruit, sweet spices, creamy oak, medium intensity. Palate: fruity, flavourful, toasty, balsamic.

BODEGAS GODEVAL

Avda. de Galicia, 20
32300 El Barco de Valdeorras (Ourense)
☎: +34 988 108 282
Fax: +34 988 325 309
www.godeval.com
godeval@godeval.com

Godeval 2013 B
100% godello
91
Colour: bright straw. Nose: white flowers, fresh fruit, expressive, fine lees, dried herbs. Palate: flavourful, fruity, good acidity, balanced.

Godeval Cepas Vellas 2013 B
100% godello
93
Colour: bright straw. Nose: complex, fragrant herbs, white flowers, fresh fruit, varietal, tropical fruit, dry stone. Palate: balanced, fine bitter notes.

BODEGAS SAMPAYOLO

Ctra. de Barxela, s/n
32358 Petín de Valdeorras (Ourense)
☎: +34 679 157 977
www.sampayolo.com
info@sampayolo.com

Garnacha Vella da Chaira do Ramiriño 2011 T
100% garnacha
87
Colour: cherry, garnet rim. Nose: fruit preserve, fruit liqueur notes, spicy. Palate: flavourful, pruney, balsamic.

Sampayolo Godello 2012 B Barrica
100% godello
88
Colour: bright straw. Nose: fragrant herbs, floral, sweet spices. Palate: powerful, flavourful, spicy.

Sampayolo Godello sobre Lías 2013 B
100% godello
90
Colour: bright straw. Nose: white flowers, fresh fruit, expressive, fine lees, dried herbs. Palate: flavourful, fruity, good acidity, balanced.

Sampayolo Lagar de Brimeda 2011 T Barrica
100% mencía
85

Sampayolo Mencía 2013 T
100% mencía
87
Colour: bright cherry. Nose: ripe fruit, sweet spices, creamy oak, expressive. Palate: flavourful, fruity, toasty, round tannins.

CAMPOS DA NÉBOA

Avda. Diagonal, 590, 5º 1ª
08021 Barcelona (Barcelona)
☎: +34 660 445 464
www.vinergia.com
vinergia@vinergia.com

Campos da Néboa Godello 2013 B
100% godello
88
Colour: bright yellow. Nose: white flowers, fragrant herbs, citrus fruit. Palate: fresh, fruity, flavourful, balanced, elegant.

COMPAÑÍA DE VINOS TELMO RODRÍGUEZ

El Monte
01308 Lanciego (Álava)
☎: +34 945 628 315
Fax: +34 945 628 314
www.telmorodriguez.com
contact@telmorodriguez.com

As Caborcas 2011 T
mencía, otras
94
Colour: dark-red cherry, garnet rim. Nose: scrubland, grassy, spicy, complex, smoky. Palate: balanced, fruity, flavourful, easy to drink.

Branco de Santa Cruz 2011 B
godello, otras
95
Colour: bright straw. Nose: white flowers, fresh fruit, expressive, fine lees, dried herbs. Palate: flavourful, fruity, good acidity, balanced.

Gaba do Xil Godello 2013 B
godello
92
Colour: bright straw. Nose: expressive, varietal, grassy. Palate: flavourful, fruity, fresh, fine bitter notes.

ELADIO SANTALLA

Conde Fenosa, 36 Bajo
32300 Barco de Valdeorras (Ourense)
☎: +34 616 169 240
www.bodegaseladiosantalla.com
eladio@bodegaseladiosantalla.com

Hacienda Ucediños 2011 T Barrica
mencía
86
Colour: ruby red. Nose: fruit preserve, balsamic herbs, spicy, creamy oak. Palate: powerful, flavourful, spicy.

Hacienda Ucediños 2012 T
mencía
88
Colour: cherry, garnet rim. Nose: wild herbs, ripe fruit, fruit liqueur notes, spicy. Palate: powerful, flavourful, concentrated, balsamic.

Hacienda Ucediños 2013 B
godello
90
Colour: bright straw. Nose: white flowers, fragrant herbs, fresh fruit, candied fruit. Palate: fresh, fruity, flavourful.

FORNOS GRS C.B.

Av. Barreais, 24
32350 A Rua (Ourense)
☎: +34 629 683 353
Fax: +34 981 151 968
vinafornos@hotmail.com

Viña de Fornos 2013 B
godello
89
Colour: bright straw. Nose: fresh, balanced, varietal, floral. Palate: fruity, balanced, good acidity, good finish.

Viña de Fornos 2013 T
mencía, tempranillo, sousón
89
Colour: cherry, purple rim. Nose: expressive, red berry notes, ripe fruit. Palate: flavourful, fruity, good acidity, round tannins, balsamic.

FRANCK MASSARD

Rambla Arnau de Vilanova, 6
08800 Vilanova i La Geltrú (Barcelona)
☎: +34 938 956 541
Fax: +34 938 956 541
www.epicure-wines.com
info@epicure-wines.com

Audacia 2011 B
godello
92
Colour: bright yellow. Nose: expressive, balanced, wild herbs, ripe fruit, mineral. Palate: rich, full, flavourful.

Audacia 2012 B
godello
90
Colour: bright straw. Nose: white flowers, expressive, fine lees, dried herbs, mineral. Palate: flavourful, fruity, good acidity, balanced.

JOAQUÍN REBOLLEDO

San Roque, 11
32350 A Rúa (Ourense)
☎: +34 988 372 307
Fax: +34 988 371 427
www.joaquinrebolledo.com
info@joaquinrebolledo.com

Joaquín Rebolledo 2012 T Barrica
mencía, tempranillo, sousón, otras
92
Colour: cherry, garnet rim. Nose: ripe fruit, spicy, creamy oak, toasty, complex, earthy notes. Palate: powerful, flavourful, toasty.

Joaquín Rebolledo Godello 2013 B
godello
91
Colour: bright straw. Nose: white flowers, varietal, balanced, fresh, dry stone. Palate: rich, flavourful, long.

Joaquín Rebolledo Mencía 2013 T
mencía
90
Colour: cherry, purple rim. Nose: powerfull, red berry notes, ripe fruit, floral, expressive. Palate: powerful, fresh, fruity, unctuous.

LA MALETA HAND MADE FINE WINES
Julio Prieto Nespereira, 21
32005 Ourense (Ourense)
☎: +34 988 614 234
lamaletawines.com
hola@lamaletawines.com

El Precipicio Godello 2012 B
100% godello
91
Colour: straw, greenish rim. Nose: ripe fruit, wild herbs, varietal, mineral. Palate: spicy, ripe fruit, long.

LA TAPADA
Finca A Tapada
32310 Rubiá de Valdeorras (Ourense)
☎: +34 988 324 197
Fax: +34 988 324 197
bodega.atapada@gmail.com

Guitián Godello 2011 BFB
100% godello
92
Colour: bright yellow. Nose: powerfull, ripe fruit, sweet spices, fragrant herbs, faded flowers. Palate: rich, flavourful, fresh, good acidity.

Guitián Godello 2013 B
100% godello
91
Colour: bright straw. Nose: fruit expression, fragrant herbs, floral, mineral, expressive. Palate: flavourful, fruity, balanced.

Guitián Godello sobre lías 2012 B
100% godello
92
Colour: bright straw. Nose: white flowers, fresh fruit, expressive, fine lees, dried herbs. Palate: flavourful, fruity, good acidity, balanced.

Guitián Godello Vendimia Tardía 2011 B
100% godello
94
Colour: bright golden. Nose: powerfull, honeyed notes, candied fruit, fragrant herbs, citrus fruit, balsamic herbs. Palate: flavourful, sweet, fresh, fruity, good acidity, long. Personality.

MANUEL CORZO RODRÍGUEZ
Chandoiro, s/n
32372 O Bolo (Ourense)
☎: +34 629 893 649
manuelcorzorodriguez@hotmail.com

Viña Corzo Godello 2013 B
godello
90
Colour: bright yellow. Nose: powerfull, ripe fruit, sweet spices, creamy oak, fragrant herbs. Palate: rich, flavourful, fresh, good acidity.

Viña Corzo Mencía 2013 T
mencía
85

RAFAEL PALACIOS
Avda. de Somoza, 22
32350 A Rúa de Valdeorras (Ourense)
☎: +34 988 310 162
Fax: +34 988 310 643
www.rafaelpalacios.com
bodega@rafaelpalacios.com

As Sortes 2012 B
100% godello
96
Colour: bright yellow. Nose: powerfull, ripe fruit, sweet spices, creamy oak, fragrant herbs. Palate: rich, smoky aftertaste, flavourful, fresh, good acidity, balanced.

Louro Godello 2012 B
91
Colour: bright yellow. Nose: toasty, creamy oak, faded flowers, ripe fruit. Palate: rich, good structure, flavourful.

VALDESIL
Ctra. a San Vicente OU 807, km. 3
32348 Vilamartín de Valdeorras (Ourense)
☎: +34 988 337 900
Fax: +34 988 337 901
www.valdesil.com
valdesil@valdesil.com

Montenovo Godello 2013 B
100% godello
92
Colour: bright straw. Nose: fresh, fresh fruit, white flowers, expressive, wild herbs. Palate: flavourful, fruity, good acidity, balanced.

Pezas da Portela 2011 BFB
100% godello
93
Colour: yellow. Nose: elegant, complex, mineral, expressive. Palate: fresh, fruity, good acidity, long, fine bitter notes, good structure.

Valderroa Carballo 2011 T
100% mencía

93

Colour: bright cherry. Nose: ripe fruit, sweet spices, creamy oak, fragrant herbs, dry stone, expressive. Palate: fruity, flavourful, toasty, balanced, elegant.

Valdesil Godello sobre Lías 2007 B
100% godello

95

Colour: bright yellow. Nose: powerfull, ripe fruit, sweet spices, creamy oak, fragrant herbs, dry stone. Palate: rich, flavourful, fresh, good acidity, unctuous, round, elegant.

Valdesil Godello sobre Lías 2008 B
100% godello

92

Colour: bright yellow. Nose: smoky, toasty, spicy. Palate: flavourful, good structure, long, ripe fruit.

Valdesil Godello sobre Lías 2012 B
100% godello

92

Colour: bright straw. Nose: white flowers, fresh fruit, fine lees, dried herbs, dry stone. Palate: flavourful, fruity, good acidity, balanced, elegant.

Valdesil Parcela O Chao 2011 B
100% godello

94

Colour: bright straw. Nose: fragrant herbs, fruit expression, dry stone, mineral, floral. Palate: fresh, fruity, flavourful, balanced, elegant. Personality.

VIÑA SOMOZA
Pombar, s/n
32350 A Rúa (Ourense)
☎: +34 988 311 412
Fax: +34 988 310 918
www.vinosomoza.com
bodega@vinosomoza.com

Neno Viña Somoza Godello Sobre Lias 2013 B
godello

90

Colour: bright straw. Nose: fresh, white flowers, ripe fruit. Palate: flavourful, fruity, good acidity, balanced.

Viña Somoza Godello Selección 2012 B Roble
godello

90

Colour: bright straw. Nose: ripe fruit, sweet spices, creamy oak, fragrant herbs. Palate: rich, flavourful, fresh, good acidity.

VIÑOS DE ENCOSTAS
Florentino López Cuevillas Nº6, 1ºC
32500 O Carballiño (Ourense)
☎: +34 988 101 733
Fax: +34 988 101 733
www.xlsebio.es
miguel@losvinosdemiguel.com

Máis Alá 2012 B
godello

90

Colour: straw, greenish rim. Nose: fresh fruit, citrus fruit, white flowers. Palate: fresh, good acidity, fine bitter notes, balanced, varietal.

VIRXE DE GALIR
Las Escuelas, s/n Estoma
32336 O Barco de Valdeorras (Ourense)
☎: +34 988 335 600
Fax: +34 988 335 592
www.pagosdegalir.es
bodega@pagosdegalir.com

Pagos del Galir Godello 2013 B
100% godello

91

Colour: bright straw. Nose: white flowers, fragrant herbs, fruit expression, mineral. Palate: fresh, fruity, flavourful.

Pagos del Galir Mencía 2012 T Roble
100% mencía

88

Colour: cherry, garnet rim. Nose: ripe fruit, wild herbs, earthy notes, spicy. Palate: balanced, flavourful, long, balsamic.

Pagos del Galir Selección Rosa Rivero 2010 TC
100% mencía

90

Colour: cherry, garnet rim. Nose: ripe fruit, spicy, toasty, complex, scrubland. Palate: powerful, flavourful, toasty, round tannins.

Vía Nova Godello 2013 B
100% godello

88

Colour: bright straw. Nose: medium intensity, fresh fruit, floral, balanced. Palate: balanced, flavourful, fruity.

Vía Nova Mencía 2013 T
100% mencía

89

Colour: dark-red cherry, purple rim. Nose: balanced, varietal, scrubland. Palate: flavourful, fruity, fruity aftestaste.

DO. VALDEPEÑAS

CONSEJO REGULADOR
Constitución, 23
13300 Valdepeñas (Ciudad Real)
☎:+34 926 322 788 - Fax: +34 926 321 054
@: consejo@dovaldepenas.es
www.dovaldepenas.es

LOCATION:

On the southern border of the southern plateau, in the province of Ciudad Real. It comprises the municipal districts of Alcubillas, Moral de Calatrava, San Carlos del Valle, Santa Cruz de Mudela, Torrenueva and Valdepeñas and part of Alhambra, Granátula de Calatrava, Montiel and Torre de Juan Abad.

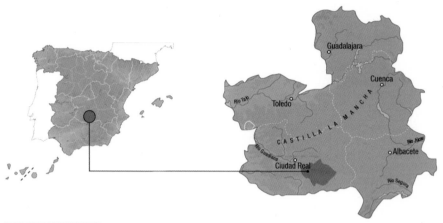

GRAPE VARIETIES:

White: Airén, Macabeo, Chardonnay, Sauvignon Blanc, Moscatel de Grano Menudo and Verdejo.
Red: Cencibel (Tempranillo), Garnacha, Cabernet Sauvignon, Merlot, Syrah and Petit Verdot.

FIGURES:

Vineyard surface: 21,865 – Wine-Growers: 2,691 – Wineries: 26 – 2013 Harvest rating: Good – Production 13: 58,563,992 litres – Market percentages: 59% domestic - 41% export.

SOIL:

Mainly brownish-red and brownish-grey limestone soil with a high lime content and quite poor in organic matter.

CLIMATE:

Continental in nature, with cold winters, very hot summers and little rainfall, which is usually around 250 and 400 mm per year.

VINTAGE RATING   PEÑÍNGUIDE

2009	2010	2011	2012	2013
GOOD	GOOD	GOOD	GOOD	GOOD

BODEGAS FERNANDO CASTRO

Paseo Castelar, 70
13730 Santa Cruz de Mudela
(Ciudad Real)
☎: +34 926 342 168
Fax: +34 926 349 029
www.bodegasfernandocastro.com
fernando@bodegasfernandocastro.com

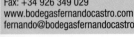

Raíces 2009 TC
100% tempranillo
84

Valdemonte 2013 T
100% tempranillo
75

Venta Real 2005 TGR
100% tempranillo
81

BODEGAS MARÍN PERONA

Castellanos, 99
13300 Valdepeñas (Ciudad Real)
☎: +34 926 313 192
Fax: +34 926 313 347
www.tejeruelas.com
bodega@tejeruela.com

Calar Viejo 2010 TC
tempranillo
82

Marín Perona 2006 TGR
tempranillo
84

Marín Perona 2007 TR
tempranillo
84

Tejeruelas de Viña Aldante 2013 B
airén
82

Tejeruelas de Viña Aldante 2013 T
tempranillo
80

Viña Aldante 2010 TC
86
Colour: bright cherry. Nose: ripe fruit, sweet spices, creamy oak, medium intensity. Palate: fruity, flavourful, toasty, easy to drink.

BODEGAS MEGÍA E HIJOS -CORCOVO

Magdalena, 33
13300 Valdepeñas (Ciudad Real)
☎: +34 926 347 828
Fax: +34 926 347 829
www.corcovo.com
jamegia@corcovo.com

Corcovo 2007 TR
100% tempranillo
88
Colour: bright cherry. Nose: ripe fruit, sweet spices, creamy oak, expressive. Palate: fruity, flavourful, toasty, balanced.

Corcovo 2010 TC
100% tempranillo
90
Colour: cherry, garnet rim. Nose: ripe fruit, spicy, creamy oak, toasty, complex, balanced. Palate: powerful, flavourful, toasty, round tannins.

Corcovo 2013 RD
100% tempranillo
89
Colour: rose, purple rim. Nose: ripe fruit, red berry notes, floral, lactic notes, fragrant herbs. Palate: powerful, fruity, fresh.

Corcovo Airen 2013 B
100% airén
88
Colour: bright straw. Nose: fresh, fresh fruit, white flowers, expressive. Palate: flavourful, fruity, good acidity, balanced.

Corcovo Syrah 2013 T
100% syrah
89
Colour: cherry, purple rim. Nose: powerfull, red berry notes, ripe fruit, floral, expressive. Palate: powerful, fresh, fruity, unctuous, balsamic.

Corcovo Syrah 24 Barricas 2012 T Roble
100% syrah
89
Colour: bright cherry. Nose: ripe fruit, sweet spices, creamy oak, expressive. Palate: flavourful, fruity, toasty, round tannins.

Corcovo Tempranillo 2012 T Roble
100% tempranillo
86
Colour: cherry, garnet rim. Nose: red berry notes, ripe fruit, wild herbs, spicy, creamy oak. Palate: powerful, flavourful, balanced.

Corcovo Verdejo 2013 B
100% verdejo
87
Colour: bright straw. Nose: fragrant herbs, tropical fruit, fresh fruit. Palate: correct, fresh, fruity, flavourful.

Corcovo Verdejo 24 Barricas 2012 B Roble
100% verdejo

89

Colour: bright yellow. Nose: powerfull, ripe fruit, sweet spices, creamy oak, fragrant herbs. Palate: rich, smoky aftertaste, flavourful, fresh, good acidity, balanced.

BODEGAS MIGUEL CALATAYUD

Postas, 20
13300 Valdepeñas (Ciudad Real)
☎: +34 926 348 070
Fax: +34 926 322 150
www.vegaval.com
vegaval@vegaval.com

Vegaval Plata 2008 TGR
tempranillo

85

Vegaval Plata 2009 TR
tempranillo

85

Vegaval Plata 2010 TC
tempranillo

85

Vegaval Plata Tempranillo 2012 T
tempranillo

83

Vegaval Plata Verdejo 2013 B
verdejo

87

Colour: bright straw. Nose: fresh, fresh fruit, white flowers, balanced. Palate: flavourful, fruity, good acidity, elegant.

BODEGAS MUREDA

Ctra. N-IV, Km. 184,1
13300 Valdepeñas (Ciudad Real)
☎: +34 926 318 058
Fax: +34 926 318 058
www.mureda.es
bmoreno@mureda.es

Mureda Cuvée Brut 2008 ESP
airén, macabeo, sauvignon blanc

84

Mureda Cuvée Brut Nature BN
chardonnay, viura

86

Colour: bright straw. Nose: ripe fruit, fine lees, balanced, dried herbs. Palate: good acidity, flavourful, ripe fruit, long.

Mureda Gran Cuvée Brut Nature 2009 ESP Reserva
airén, macabeo, chardonnay

87

Colour: bright yellow. Nose: ripe fruit, fragrant herbs, sweet spices, dry nuts, balanced. Palate: powerful, flavourful, fine bead, good acidity.

BODEGAS NAVARRO LÓPEZ

Autovía Madrid - Cádiz, Km. 193
13300 Valdepeñas (Ciudad Real)
☎: +34 902 193 431
Fax: +34 902 193 432
www.bodegasnavarrolopez.com
laboratorio2@navarrolopez.com

Don Aurelio 2008 TGR
100% tempranillo

84

Don Aurelio 2009 TR
100% tempranillo

85

Don Aurelio 2011 TC
100% tempranillo

86

Colour: cherry, garnet rim. Nose: ripe fruit, spicy, creamy oak, toasty. Palate: powerful, flavourful, toasty.

Don Aurelio 2012 T Barrica
100% tempranillo

85

Don Aurelio 2013 RD
100% tempranillo

87

Colour: raspberry rose. Nose: elegant, candied fruit, dried flowers, fragrant herbs, red berry notes. Palate: light-bodied, flavourful, good acidity, long, spicy.

Don Aurelio Garnacha 2013 T
100% garnacha

88

Colour: cherry, purple rim. Nose: ripe fruit, wild herbs, balsamic herbs. Palate: powerful, fruity, balsamic.

Don Aurelio Tempranillo Selección 2013 T
100% tempranillo

86

Colour: cherry, purple rim. Nose: red berry notes, ripe fruit, floral. Palate: powerful, fresh, fruity.

Don Aurelio Verdejo 2013 B
100% verdejo

84

BODEGAS REAL
Paseo de la Castellana, 144 1º
28046 Madrid (Madrid)
☎: +34 914 577 588
Fax: +34 914 577 210
www.bodegas-real.com
comunicacion@bodegas-real.com

Palacio de Ibor 2007 TR
83

FÉLIX SOLÍS
Autovía del Sur, Km. 199
13300 Valdepeñas (Ciudad Real)
☎: +34 926 322 400
www.felixsolisavantis.com
nfernandez@felixsolisavantis.com

Ayrum 2008 TGR
tempranillo

89

Colour: bright cherry. Nose: ripe fruit, sweet spices, creamy oak, balanced. Palate: fruity, flavourful, toasty, correct.

Ayrum 2010 TR
tempranillo

89

Colour: cherry, garnet rim. Nose: ripe fruit, spicy, creamy oak, toasty, complex. Palate: powerful, flavourful, toasty, round tannins.

Ayrum 2011 TC
tempranillo

87

Colour: bright cherry. Nose: ripe fruit, sweet spices, creamy oak, medium intensity. Palate: fruity, flavourful, toasty.

Ayrum 2013 RD
tempranillo

88

Colour: rose, purple rim. Nose: powerfull, ripe fruit, red berry notes, floral, expressive. Palate: powerful, fruity, fresh.

Ayrum Tempranillo 2013 T
tempranillo

88

Colour: cherry, purple rim. Nose: fresh fruit, red berry notes, floral, balsamic herbs. Palate: flavourful, fruity, good acidity, round tannins.

Ayrum Verdejo 2013 B
verdejo

87

Colour: bright straw. Nose: fresh, fresh fruit, white flowers, expressive. Palate: flavourful, fruity, good acidity, balanced.

Moralinos 2007 TGR

88

Colour: pale ruby, brick rim edge. Nose: elegant, spicy, fine reductive notes, wet leather, aged wood nuances, fruit liqueur notes. Palate: spicy, fine tannins, elegant, long.

Viña Albali 2009 TGR
tempranillo

87

Colour: cherry, garnet rim. Nose: ripe fruit, spicy, creamy oak, toasty, complex. Palate: powerful, flavourful, toasty, round tannins.

Viña Albali 2010 TR
tempranillo

87

Colour: bright cherry. Nose: ripe fruit, sweet spices, creamy oak, medium intensity. Palate: fruity, flavourful, toasty.

Viña Albali 2011 TC
tempranillo

84

Viña Albali 2013 RD
tempranillo

85

Viña Albali Gran Reserva de la Familia 2006 TGR

89

Colour: pale ruby, brick rim edge. Nose: elegant, spicy, fine reductive notes, wet leather, aged wood nuances, ripe fruit. Palate: spicy, fine tannins, elegant, long.

Viña Albali Selección Privada 2009 TGR
tempranillo

88

Colour: pale ruby, brick rim edge. Nose: elegant, spicy, fine reductive notes, wet leather, aged wood nuances, fruit liqueur notes, ripe fruit. Palate: spicy, fine tannins, elegant, long.

Viña Albali Tempranillo 2013 T
tempranillo

85

Viña Albali Verdejo 2013 B
verdejo

86

Colour: bright straw. Nose: fresh, fresh fruit, white flowers, expressive. Palate: flavourful, fruity, good acidity, balanced.

GRUPO DE BODEGAS VINARTIS
A-4, Km. 200,5
13300 Valdepeñas (Ciudad Real)
☎: +34 926 320 300
Fax: +34 926 348 483
www.grupobodegasvinartis.com
ricardo.donado@jgc.es

Pata Negra 2005 TGR
tempranillo

85

Pata Negra 2006 TGR
tempranillo

86

Colour: cherry, garnet rim. Nose: ripe fruit, creamy oak, toasty, complex, roasted coffee, aromatic coffee. Palate: powerful, flavourful, toasty, round tannins.

Pata Negra 2007 TR
tempranillo

84

Pata Negra 2008 TC
tempranillo

83

Pata Negra 2009 TR
tempranillo, mazuelo, graciano, garnacha

84

Pata Negra 2012 T
cabernet sauvignon, tempranillo

82

Pata Negra 2012 T Roble
tempranillo

81

VICENTE NAVARRO Y HERMANOS
Real, 80
13300 Valdepeñas (Ciudad Real)
☎: +34 926 323 354
Fax: +34 926 320 464
bodegasnavarro@hotmail.com

Racimo de Oro 2006 TGR
100% tempranillo

84

Racimo de Oro 2010 T
tempranillo

88

Colour: cherry, garnet rim. Nose: ripe fruit, spicy, creamy oak, toasty. Palate: powerful, flavourful, toasty.

Racimo de Oro 2013 B
100% verdejo

84

DO. VALENCIA
CONSEJO REGULADOR
Quart, 22
46001 Valencia
☎:+34 963 910 096 - Fax: +34 963 910 029
@: info@vinovalencia.org
www.vinovalencia.org

LOCATION:

In the province of Valencia. It comprises 66 municipal districts in 4 different sub-regions: Alto Turia, Moscatel de Valencia, Valentino and Clariano.

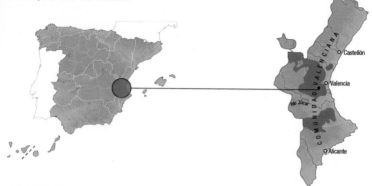

SUB-REGIONS:

There are four in total: **Alto Turia,** the highest sub-region (700 to 800 m above sea level) comprising 6 municipal districts; **Valentino** (23 municipal districts), in the centre of the province; the altitude varies between 250 m and 650 m; **Moscatel de Valencia** (9 municipal districts), also in the central region where the historical wine from the region is produced; and **Clariano** (33 municipal districts), to the south, at an altitude of between 400 m and 650 m.

GRAPE VARIETIES:

White: Macabeo, Malvasía, Merseguera, Moscatel de Alejandría, Moscatel de Grano Menudo, Pedro Ximénez, Plantafina, Plantanova, Tortosí, Verdil, Chardonnay, Semillon Blanc, Sauvignon Blanc, Verdejo, Riesling, Viognier and Gewüztraminer.
Red: Garnacha, Monastrell, Tempranillo, Tintorera, Forcallat Tinta, Bobal, Cabernet Cauvignon, Merlot, Pinot Noir, Syrah, Graciano, Malbec, Mandó, Marselan, Mencía, Merlot, Mazuelo and Petit Verdot.

FIGURES:

Vineyard surface: 13,000 – Wine-Growers: 10,700 – Wineries: 93 – 2013 Harvest rating: Good – Production 13: 84,109,488 litres – Market percentages: 24% domestic - 76% export.

SOIL:

Mostly brownish-grey with limestone content; there are no drainage problems.

CLIMATE:

Mediterranean, marked by strong storms and downpours in summer and autumn. The average annual temperature is 15°C and the average annual rainfall is 500 mm.

VINTAGE RATING

PEÑÍNGUIDE

2009	2010	2011	2012	2013
VERY GOOD	EXCELLENT	EXCELLENT	VERY GOOD	GOOD

ARANLEÓN

Ctra. Caudete, 3
46310 Los Marcos (Valencia)
☎: +34 963 631 640
Fax: +34 962 185 150
www.aranleon.com
vinos@aranleon.com

Aranleón Sólo 2013 B
chardonnay, sauvignon blanc, macabeo

86 🌷

Colour: bright straw. Nose: fresh, fresh fruit, white flowers, expressive. Palate: flavourful, fruity, good acidity, balanced.

Aranleón Sólo 2013 RD
tempranillo

86 🌷

Colour: rose, purple rim. Nose: powerfull, ripe fruit, red berry notes, floral, balsamic herbs. Palate: powerful, fruity, fresh, fine bitter notes.

Blés 2012 T Roble
tempranillo, bobal

86 🌷

Colour: bright cherry. Nose: ripe fruit, sweet spices, creamy oak. Palate: flavourful, fruity, toasty.

Blés Crianza de Aranleón 2011 TC
tempranillo, monastrell, cabernet sauvignon

90 🌷

Colour: cherry, garnet rim. Nose: ripe fruit, spicy, creamy oak, toasty, complex, balsamic herbs. Palate: powerful, flavourful, toasty, round tannins, balanced.

Blés Reserva de Aranleón 2010 TR
monastrell, tempranillo, cabernet sauvignon

89 🌷

Colour: cherry, garnet rim. Nose: red berry notes, ripe fruit, balsamic herbs, spicy, creamy oak, balanced. Palate: powerful, flavourful, complex, spicy, long.

El Árbol de Aranleón 2010 TR
cabernet franc, tempranillo, monastrell, syrah

91 🌷

Colour: cherry, garnet rim. Nose: ripe fruit, fruit liqueur notes, wild herbs, sweet spices, creamy oak. Palate: powerful, flavourful, spicy, long, balanced.

BODEGA EL ANGOSTO

Finca Santa Rosa, Ctra. Fontanars CV-660, km. 23,5
46870 Ontinyent (Valencia)
☎: +34 962 380 648
Fax: +34 962 911 349
www.bodegaelangosto.com
info@bodegaelangosto.com

Almendros 2012 T
marselan, garnacha tintorera, syrah

92

Colour: very deep cherry. Nose: expressive, characterful, warm, candied fruit, creamy oak. Palate: ripe fruit, flavourful, powerful.

Almendros 2013 B
verdejo, sauvignon blanc

92

Colour: bright straw. Nose: white flowers, fresh fruit, expressive, fine lees, dried herbs, creamy oak. Palate: flavourful, fruity, good acidity.

© Paula Sanz Caballero

ANGOSTO | ALMENDROS

Angosto Blanco 2013 B
verdejo, moscatel, sauvignon blanc, chardonnay

91

Colour: bright straw. Nose: white flowers, fresh fruit, expressive, fine lees, dried herbs. Palate: flavourful, fruity, good acidity, balanced.

Angosto Tinto 2012 TC
cabernet franc, syrah, garnacha tintorera

91

Colour: cherry, garnet rim. Nose: ripe fruit, spicy, creamy oak, toasty, complex, dark chocolate, earthy notes. Palate: powerful, flavourful, toasty, balsamic, elegant.

La Tribu 2013 T
monastrell, syrah, garnacha tintorera

89

Colour: bright cherry. Nose: ripe fruit, sweet spices, creamy oak. Palate: flavourful, fruity, toasty, round tannins.

BODEGA EL VILLAR
Avda. del Agricultor, 1
46170 Villar de Arzobispo (Valencia)
☎: +34 962 720 050
Fax: +34 961 646 060
www.elvillar.com
exportacion@elvillar.com

Laderas 2013 B
merseguera, macabeo

83

Laderas Tempranillo 2013 T
tempranillo

83

Laderas Tempranillo Bobal 2013 RD
tempranillo, bobal

85

Tapias 2007 TC
merlot

82

Viña Villar 2008 TC
tempranillo, merlot

86

Colour: cherry, garnet rim. Nose: ripe fruit, spicy, creamy oak, toasty. Palate: powerful, flavourful, toasty.

BODEGA J. BELDA
Avda. Conde Salvatierra, 54
46635 Fontanars dels Alforins (Valencia)
☎: +34 962 222 278
Fax: +34 962 222 245
www.danielbelda.com
info@danielbelda.com

Ca'Belda 2007 T Barrica
monastrell, garnacha tintorera

88

Colour: ruby red. Nose: spicy, fine reductive notes, wet leather, aged wood nuances, toasty. Palate: spicy, long, toasty.

Daniel Belda MC Tempranillo 2013 T
tempranillo

87

Colour: cherry, purple rim. Nose: fresh fruit, red berry notes, floral. Palate: flavourful, fruity, good acidity, round tannins.

Daniel Belda MC Tintorera 2013 T
garnacha tintorera

84

Daniel Belda Verdil 2013 B
verdil

88

Colour: bright straw. Nose: fresh, fresh fruit, white flowers, fruit expression. Palate: flavourful, fruity, good acidity.

Heretat de Belda 2009 T
pinot noir, garnacha tintorera

88

Colour: very deep cherry, garnet rim. Nose: powerfull, ripe fruit, roasted coffee, dark chocolate. Palate: powerful, toasty, roasted-coffee aftertaste.

Migjorn 2007 T
cabernet sauvignon, merlot, garnacha tintorera

84

BODEGAS 40 GRADOS NORTE
Camí Estació de Dalt s/n
46630 La Font de la Figuera (Valencia)
☎: +34 615 167 040
Fax: +34 960 963 724
www.40gradosnorte.com
40gradosnorte@40gradosnorte.com

Cota 830 2009 T
bobal, cabernet sauvignon, tempranillo

86

Colour: ruby red. Nose: spicy, fine reductive notes, wet leather, aged wood nuances, toasty. Palate: spicy, long, toasty, correct.

Mar de So 2010 T
syrah, monastrell, bobal, tempranillo

85

Mar de So Chardonnay 2013 B
chardonnay

84

So de Bobal 2013 T
bobal

84

So de Syrah 2013 T Joven
syrah

84

BODEGAS ARRAEZ

Arcediano Ros, 35
46630 La Font de la Figuera (Valencia)
☎: +34 962 290 031
www.bodegasarraez.com
info@bodegasarraez.com

A2 Verdil 2013 B
verdil
87
Colour: bright straw. Nose: white flowers, fragrant herbs, fruit expression. Palate: fresh, fruity, flavourful, fine bitter notes.

Calabuig 2013 B
macabeo, merseguera
87
Colour: bright straw. Nose: fresh, fresh fruit, white flowers. Palate: flavourful, fruity, good acidity, balanced.

Calabuig 2013 T
tempranillo, monastrell
86
Colour: light cherry, purple rim. Nose: red berry notes, ripe fruit, wild herbs. Palate: fresh, fruity, easy to drink.

Casas de Herencia 2012 T Roble
tempranillo, monastrell
80

Casas de Herencia 2013 B
merseguera, malvasía
82

Eduardo Bermejo 2012 T
tempranillo
85

Eduardo Bermejo 2013 B
87
Colour: bright straw. Nose: fresh, fresh fruit, white flowers, balanced. Palate: flavourful, fruity, good acidity, balanced.

Lagares 2012 TC
cabernet sauvignon
90
Colour: bright cherry. Nose: ripe fruit, sweet spices, creamy oak, expressive. Palate: flavourful, fruity, toasty, round tannins.

Mala Vida 2012 T Roble
tempranillo, monastrell, syrah, cabernet sauvignon
88
Colour: deep cherry. Nose: warm, candied fruit, fruit expression. Palate: flavourful, spicy.

BODEGAS BATALLER

Camí Real, 94-96
46841 Castelló de Rugat (Valencia)
☎: +34 962 813 017
Fax: +34 962 813 017
vinosbenicadell@telepolis.com

Benicadell Tempranillo 2013 T
tempranillo
82

D'Alba Varietal Moscatel 2013 B
moscatel
85

BODEGAS ENGUERA

Ctra. CV - 590, Km. 51,5
46810 Enguera (Valencia)
☎: +34 963 412 450
Fax: +34 962 224 831
www.bodegasenguera.com
oficina@bodegasenguera.com

Blanc d'Enguera 2013 B
verdil, chardonnay, viognier, sauvignon blanc
88
Colour: bright golden. Nose: white flowers, powerfull, ripe fruit, citrus fruit. Palate: flavourful, fruity.

Megala 2011 T
monastrell, syrah, marselan
91
Colour: cherry, garnet rim. Nose: ripe fruit, spicy, creamy oak, toasty, dark chocolate, earthy notes. Palate: powerful, flavourful, toasty, round tannins.

Verdil de Gel 2013 B
verdil
90
Colour: golden. Nose: powerfull, floral, honeyed notes, candied fruit, fragrant herbs. Palate: flavourful, sweet, fresh, fruity, good acidity, long.

BODEGAS LOS PINOS

Casa Los Pinos, s/n
46635 Fontanars dels Alforins
(Valencia)
☎: +34 600 584 397
www.bodegaslospinos.com
bodegaslospinos@bodegaslospinos.com

Brote Blanco de Dominio Los Pinos 2013 BFB
verdil, viognier
85

Brote Tinto de Dominio Los Pinos 2011 TC
monastrell, garnacha, merlot
90
Colour: bright cherry. Nose: ripe fruit, sweet spices, creamy oak, medium intensity. Palate: fruity, flavourful, toasty.

Ca'ls Pins 2013 T Barrica
monastrell, cabernet sauvignon, merlot

87

Colour: bright cherry. Nose: ripe fruit, sweet spices, creamy oak. Palate: flavourful, fruity, toasty.

Dx de Dominio Los Pinos 2012 TC
monastrell, cabernet sauvignon

87

Colour: cherry, garnet rim. Nose: ripe fruit, spicy, creamy oak, toasty, complex. Palate: powerful, flavourful, toasty.

Los Pinos 0 % 2013 T
garnacha, monastrell, syrah

87

Colour: very deep cherry, garnet rim. Nose: overripe fruit, warm, dried herbs. Palate: flavourful, ripe fruit, long.

Los Pinos 1909 2011 TC
monastrell, merlot, cabernet sauvignon

88

Colour: cherry, garnet rim. Nose: fruit preserve, fruit liqueur notes, spicy. Palate: flavourful, pruney, balsamic.

Los Pinos 2012 T Barrica
cabernet sauvignon, syrah, tempranillo

87

Colour: bright cherry. Nose: ripe fruit, sweet spices, creamy oak, expressive, balsamic herbs. Palate: flavourful, fruity, toasty.

Los Pinos Salvat 2013 RD
monastrell, garnacha

87

Colour: rose. Nose: powerfull, ripe fruit, red berry notes, floral, expressive. Palate: powerful, fruity, fresh.

Los Pinos Salvat 2013 T
monastrell, cabernet sauvignon

85

BODEGAS MITOS
Ctra. CV 450, km. 3 El Azagador
46357 Requena (Valencia)
☎: +34 962 300 703
www.bodegasmitos.com
admin@bodegasmitos.com

Mitos 2012 B
macabeo, moscatel

85

Mitos 2013 T
cabernet sauvignon, tempranillo, syrah

85

Mitos 2013 T Roble
cabernet sauvignon, merlot, garnacha

87

Colour: bright cherry. Nose: ripe fruit, sweet spices, creamy oak, expressive. Palate: flavourful, fruity, toasty, round tannins.

BODEGAS MURVIEDRO
Ampliación Pol. El Romeral, s/n
46340 Requena (Valencia)
☎: +34 962 329 003
Fax: +34 962 329 002
www.bodegasmurviedro.es
murviedro@murviedro.es

DNA de Murviedro Classic Tempranillo 2013 T
tempranillo

88

Colour: cherry, garnet rim. Nose: ripe fruit, wild herbs, medium intensity. Palate: powerful, flavourful, balsamic.

DNA de Murviedro Fashion Alba 2013 B
sauvignon blanc, moscatel

89

Colour: bright straw. Nose: white flowers, fragrant herbs, fruit expression. Palate: fresh, fruity, flavourful, fine bitter notes.

DNA de Murviedro Fashion Alma Mística 2013 B
moscatel

85

DNA de Muviedro Classic Viura 2013 B
viura

82

DNA de Muviedro Fashion Rosa Blush 2013 RD
tempranillo, bobal, viura, cabernet sauvignon

87

Colour: light cherry, bright. Nose: rose petals, red berry notes, balanced. Palate: correct, good acidity, fruity, easy to drink.

Estrella de Murviedro Frizzante B
moscatel

84

Estrella de Murviedro Frizzante Rosé 2013 RD
moscatel, tempranillo, bobal

84

Murviedro Colección 2010 TR
monastrell, tempranillo, cabernet sauvignon

89

Colour: cherry, garnet rim. Nose: ripe fruit, spicy, toasty, complex, wild herbs. Palate: powerful, flavourful, toasty, round tannins.

Murviedro Colección 2011 TC
tempranillo

88

Colour: cherry, garnet rim. Nose: ripe fruit, spicy, creamy oak. Palate: balanced, flavourful, long, balsamic.

Murviedro Colección Petit Verdot 2013 T
petit verdot

91

Colour: bright cherry, purple rim. Nose: fragrant herbs, red berry notes, expressive. Palate: balanced, long, spicy.

Murviedro Expresión "Solidarity Cuvée" 2011 TC
monastrell, garnacha

90

Colour: cherry, garnet rim. Nose: ripe fruit, spicy, creamy oak, toasty. Palate: powerful, flavourful, toasty, round tannins.

BODEGAS POLO MONLEÓN
Ctra. Valencia - Ademuz, Km. 86
46178 Titaguas (Valencia)
☎: +34 961 634 148
www.hoyadelcastillo.com
info@hoyadelcastillo.com

Hoya del Castillo 2013 B
88

Colour: bright straw. Nose: fresh, fresh fruit, white flowers. Palate: flavourful, fruity, good acidity, balanced.

BODEGAS SIERRA NORTE
Pol. Ind. El Romeral. Transporte C2
46340 Requena (Valencia)
☎: +34 962 323 099
Fax: +34 962 323 048
www.bodegasierranorte.com
info@bodegasierranorte.com

Mariluna 2012 T
tempranillo, bobal, monastrell

89

Colour: bright cherry. Nose: ripe fruit, sweet spices, creamy oak, expressive. Palate: flavourful, fruity, toasty, round tannins.

Mariluna 2013 B
macabeo, chardonnay, sauvignon blanc

87

Colour: bright straw. Nose: white flowers, fragrant herbs, fruit expression. Palate: fresh, fruity, flavourful, balanced, elegant.

BODEGAS TORREVELLISCA
Ctra. L'Ombria, Km. 1
46635 Fontanars dels Alforins
(Valencia)
☎: +34 962 222 261
Fax: +34 962 222 257
www.bodegas-torrevellisca.es
info@bodegas-torrevellisca.es

Argentum de Zagromonte 2010 TC
tempranillo, cabernet sauvignon

87

Colour: cherry, garnet rim. Nose: spicy, toasty, overripe fruit, warm. Palate: powerful, flavourful, toasty, round tannins.

Aurum de Zagromonte 2010 TC
merlot, cabernet sauvignon

87

Colour: deep cherry, orangey edge. Nose: spicy, fine reductive notes, wet leather, aged wood nuances, fruit liqueur notes. Palate: spicy, fine tannins, long.

Brundisium de Zagromonte 2008 TR
tempranillo, cabernet sauvignon, cabernet franc

86

Colour: very deep cherry, garnet rim. Nose: powerfull, roasted coffee, fruit liqueur notes. Palate: powerful, toasty, roasted-coffee aftertaste.

Embrujo 2013 B
verdejo

80

Embrujo Negro 2013 T
merlot, cabernet sauvignon, tempranillo

83

Palacio de Torrevellisca 2013 T
tempranillo, syrah

79

BODEGAS UTIELANAS
Actor Rambal, 29
46300 Utiel (Valencia)
☎: +34 962 170 801
Fax: +34 962 170 801
www.bodegasutielanas.com
info@bodegasutielanas.com

Sueños del Mediterráneo 2013 B
100% macabeo

88

Colour: bright straw. Nose: fresh, fresh fruit, white flowers, expressive. Palate: flavourful, fruity, good acidity, balanced.

Sueños del Mediterráneo 2013 RD
100% bobal

86

Colour: róse, purple rim. Nose: powerfull, ripe fruit, red berry notes, floral, expressive. Palate: powerful, fruity, fresh.

Sueños del Mediterráneo 2013 T
100% bobal

87

Colour: cherry, purple rim. Nose: powerfull, red berry notes, ripe fruit, floral. Palate: powerful, fresh, fruity, unctuous.

BODEGAS VICENTE GANDÍA
Ctra. Cheste a Godelleta, s/n
46370 Chiva (Valencia)
☎: +34 962 524 242
Fax: +34 962 524 243
www.vicentegandia.es
info@vicentegandia.com

Castillo de Liria 2010 TC
tempranillo, syrah

82

Castillo de Liria 2010 TR
100% tempranillo

83

Castillo de Liria 2012 T

83

Castillo de Liria 2013 B

82

Castillo de Liria 2013 RD
100% bobal

85

Castillo de Liria Moscatel 2013 B
moscatel de alejandría

86

Colour: yellow. Nose: white flowers, expressive, powerfull. Palate: fruity, easy to drink, correct, sweetness.

Castillo de Liria Semi Dulce 2013 B

82

El Miracle 120 2011 T

86

Colour: cherry, garnet rim. Nose: ripe fruit, spicy, creamy oak, wild herbs. Palate: powerful, flavourful, toasty.

El Miracle 120 2013 B

85

El Miracle by Mariscal 2011 T
100% garnacha tintorera

90

Colour: cherry, garnet rim. Nose: ripe fruit, spicy, creamy oak, toasty, complex, dark chocolate. Palate: powerful, flavourful, toasty, round tannins.

El Miracle Tapas 2012 T
100% tempranillo

85

Fusta Nova Moscatel B
100% moscatel de alejandría

86

Colour: bright yellow. Nose: honeyed notes, ripe fruit, balsamic herbs, powerfull. Palate: balanced, flavourful, unctuous.

Fusta Nova Verdejo 2012 B
100% verdejo

84

BODEGAS Y DESTILERÍAS VIDAL
Valencia, 16
12550 Almazora (Castellón)
☎: +34 964 503 300
Fax: +34 964 560 604
www.bodegasvidal.com
info@bodegasvidal.com

Uva D'Or Moscatel B
moscatel

91

Colour: golden. Nose: powerfull, floral, honeyed notes, candied fruit, fragrant herbs. Palate: flavourful, sweet, fresh, fruity, good acidity, long.

BODEGAS Y VIÑEDOS DE UTIEL
Finca El Renegado, s/n
46315 Caudete de las Fuentes (Valencia)
☎: +34 962 174 029
Fax: +34 962 171 432
www.bodegasdeutiel.com
gestion@bodegasdeutiel.com

Actum Colección Macabeo Chardonnay 2013 B
macabeo, chardonnay

86 🌷

Colour: bright straw. Nose: fresh, fresh fruit, white flowers, citrus fruit. Palate: flavourful, fruity, good acidity, balanced.

Actum Colección Syrah Tempranillo 2013 T
syrah, tempranillo

87 🌷

Colour: very deep cherry. Nose: fruit preserve, candied fruit, roasted coffee. Palate: fine bitter notes, powerful, toasty.

Actum Finca El Renegado 2010 T
bobal

87

Colour: cherry, garnet rim. Nose: ripe fruit, spicy, creamy oak, aged wood nuances. Palate: powerful, flavourful, toasty, harsh oak tannins.

Actum Finca El Renegado 2013 B
macabeo

87

Colour: bright straw. Nose: white flowers, fragrant herbs, fruit expression. Palate: fresh, fruity, flavourful.

BODEGUES I VINYES LA CASA DE LAS VIDES

Corral el Galtero, s/n
46890 Agullent (Valencia)
☎: +34 962 135 003
Fax: +34 962 135 494
www.lacasadelasvides.com
bodega@lacasadelasvides.com

Abc 2013 T
85

Acvlivs 2010 T
monastrell, tempranillo, syrah
89
Colour: cherry, garnet rim. Nose: ripe fruit, spicy, creamy oak, toasty, wild herbs. Palate: powerful, flavourful, toasty, round tannins, balanced.

Cup de Cup 2011 T
84

Rosa Rosae 2013 RD
garnacha, cabernet sauvignon
84

Vallblanca 2013 B
verdil, gewürztraminer
86
Colour: bright yellow. Nose: dried flowers, dried herbs, ripe fruit. Palate: fresh, fruity, easy to drink.

BRUNO MURCIANO & DAVID SAMPEDRO GIL

8 Avenida Banda De Musica El Angel
46315 Caudete de las Fuentes
(Valencia)
☎: +34 962 319 096
bru.murciano@yahoo.es

El Novio Perfecto 2013 B
moscatel, viura
87
Colour: bright straw. Nose: fresh, fresh fruit, white flowers, expressive. Palate: flavourful, fruity, sweetness.

CARMELITANO BODEGAS Y DESTILERÍA

Bodolz, 12
12560 Benicasim (Castellón)
☎: +34 964 300 849
Fax: +34 964 304 449
www.carmelitano.com
carmelitano@carmelitano.com

Carmelitano Moscatel 2013 Vino de licor
moscatel de alejandría
88
Colour: bright straw. Nose: candied fruit, citrus fruit, honeyed notes. Palate: flavourful, powerful, sweetness.

CASA LOS FRAILES

Casa Los Frailes, s/n
46635 Fontanares dels Alforins
(Valencia)
☎: +34 962 222 220
Fax: +34 963 363 153
www.bodegaslosfrailes.com
info@bodegaslosfrailes.com

Bilogía 2011 T
monastrell, syrah
86 🍷
Colour: bright cherry. Nose: sweet spices, creamy oak, overripe fruit, wet leather. Palate: flavourful, fruity, toasty, round tannins.

Blanc de Trilogía 2013 B
sauvignon blanc, moscatel, verdil
90 🍷
Colour: bright straw. Nose: white flowers, fragrant herbs, fruit expression, expressive. Palate: fresh, fruity, flavourful, balanced, elegant.

Casa Los Frailes 1771 2012 T
monastrell
88 🍷
Colour: light cherry. Nose: ripe fruit, wild herbs, spicy, dry stone. Palate: balsamic, fruity, spicy.

La Danza de la Moma 2010 T Barrica
monastrell, marselan
90 🍷
Colour: cherry, garnet rim. Nose: ripe fruit, spicy, creamy oak, toasty, premature reduction notes. Palate: powerful, flavourful, toasty, round tannins.

Los Frailes Monastrell 2013 RD
monastrell
84

Los Frailes Monastrell 2013 T
monastrell
84 🍷

Los Frailes Monastrell Garnacha 2012 T Barrica
monastrell, garnacha
84 🍷

Trilogía 2010 T
monastrell, cabernet sauvignon, tempranillo
89
Colour: cherry, garnet rim. Nose: ripe fruit, spicy, creamy oak, toasty, complex. Palate: powerful, flavourful, toasty, round tannins.

CELLER DEL ROURE

Ctra. de Les Alcusses, Km. 11,1
46640 Moixent (Valencia)
☎: +34 962 295 020
javier@cellerdelroure.es

Cullerot 2012 B
89
Colour: yellow. Nose: ripe fruit, floral, dried herbs, citrus fruit. Palate: long, powerful, correct, rich, balanced.

Les Alcusses 2010 T
90
Colour: cherry, garnet rim. Nose: spicy, creamy oak, toasty. Palate: powerful, flavourful, toasty, round tannins.

Maduresa 2009 T
92
Colour: very deep cherry. Nose: ripe fruit, spicy, creamy oak, toasty, characterful. Palate: powerful, flavourful, toasty, round tannins.

Parotet 2011 T
89
Colour: bright cherry. Nose: ripe fruit, sweet spices, creamy oak, balsamic herbs. Palate: flavourful, fruity, toasty, round tannins.

Parotet Vermell 2012 T
92
Colour: cherry, garnet rim. Nose: ripe fruit, spicy, creamy oak, toasty, complex. Palate: powerful, flavourful, toasty, round tannins.

Setze Gallets 2012 T
88
Colour: cherry, garnet rim. Nose: red berry notes, ripe fruit, wild herbs, spicy, toasty. Palate: flavourful, balanced, spicy, long.

CHESTE AGRARIA COOP. V.

La Estación, 5
46380 Cheste (Valencia)
☎: +34 962 511 671
Fax: +34 962 511 732
bodega@chesteagraria.com

Reymos 1918 ESP
84

Reymos Selección ESP
moscatel
84

Sol de Reymos Mistela
moscatel
87
Colour: bright straw. Nose: candied fruit, fruit preserve, citrus fruit. Palate: flavourful, powerful, sweet.

Velada 2013 B
84

Viña Tendida Moscato B
moscatel, garnacha
86
Colour: bright straw. Nose: ripe fruit, citrus fruit, tropical fruit. Palate: flavourful, sweetness, carbonic notes.

Viña Tendida Moscato 2013 RD
moscatel de alejandría, garnacha
85

CLOS COR VÍ

Camino del Cementerio s/n
46640 Moixent (Valencia)
☎: +34 963 746 273
Fax: +34 963 746 842
www.closcorvi.com
lcorbi@ono.com

Clos Cor Ví Riesling + Viognier 2013 B
riesling, viognier
88
Colour: bright straw. Nose: fresh, fresh fruit, white flowers, expressive. Palate: flavourful, fruity, good acidity, balanced.

Clos Cor Ví Riesling 2013 B
riesling
89
Colour: bright straw. Nose: white flowers, fresh fruit, expressive, dried herbs. Palate: flavourful, fruity, good acidity, balanced.

Clos Cor Ví Viognier 2013 B
viognier
85

COOP. SAN PEDRO DE MOIXENT CLOS DE LA VALL

Pza. de la Hispanidad, 4
46640 Moixent (Valencia)
☎: +34 962 260 266
www.closdelavall.com
info@closdelavall.com

Clos de la Vall Autor 2008 T
88
Colour: cherry, garnet rim. Nose: fruit preserve, fruit liqueur notes, spicy, fine reductive notes. Palate: flavourful, pruney, balsamic.

Clos de la Vall Blanc 2013 B
macabeo, moscatel
84

Clos de la Vall Negre 2012 T
tempranillo, monastrell, cabernet sauvignon
84

Clos de la Vall Premium 2008 T
tempranillo, monastrell, cabernet sauvignon
87
Colour: cherry, garnet rim. Nose: balanced, complex, ripe fruit, spicy, aged wood nuances, fine reductive notes. Palate: good structure, flavourful, round tannins.

Clos de la Vall PX 2012 BFB
pedro ximénez
88
Colour: bright yellow. Nose: powerfull, ripe fruit, sweet spices, creamy oak. Palate: rich, smoky aftertaste, flavourful, fresh, good acidity.

Clos de la Vall Único 2011 TC
tempranillo, monastrell, cabernet sauvignon
87
Colour: cherry, garnet rim. Nose: ripe fruit, wild herbs, spicy, aged wood nuances. Palate: flavourful, balsamic, toasty.

Moixaranga 2013 B
macabeo, merseguera
84

Moixaranga 2013 T
tempranillo, monastrell
85

COOPERATIVA LA VIÑA (VINOS DE LA VIÑA)
Portal de Valencia, 52
46630 La Font de la Figuera (Valencia)
☎: +34 962 290 078
Fax: +34 962 232 039
www.ventadelpuerto.com
info@vinosdelavina.com

Casa L'Angel Cepas Viejas 2011 T
89 🌭
Colour: cherry, garnet rim. Nose: red berry notes, ripe fruit, sweet spices, creamy oak. Palate: balanced, flavourful, spicy, balsamic.

Casa L'Angel Cepas Viejas 2012 T
syrah, tempranillo, monastrell
84 🌭

Icono Cabernet Sauvignon 2013 T
cabernet sauvignon
84

Icono Chardonnay 2013 B
chardonnay
89
Colour: bright straw. Nose: fresh, fresh fruit, white flowers, expressive. Palate: flavourful, fruity, good acidity, balanced.

Icono Merlot 2013 T
merlot
85

Icono Syrah 2013 T
syrah
88
Colour: deep cherry. Nose: herbaceous, fresh fruit. Palate: flavourful, fine bitter notes, good acidity.

Juan de Juanes Vendimia Bronce 2013 B
macabeo, chardonnay
84

Juan de Juanes Vendimia Bronce 2013 T
garnacha, tempranillo, syrah
86
Colour: very deep cherry, garnet rim. Nose: overripe fruit, warm, dried herbs. Palate: flavourful, ripe fruit.

Juan de Juanes Vendimia Oro 2011 T
45% syrah, merlot, 12,5% cabernet sauvignon, 12,5% cabernet franc
87
Colour: cherry, garnet rim. Nose: ripe fruit, spicy, creamy oak, toasty. Palate: flavourful, toasty, balsamic.

Juan de Juanes Vendimia Oro 2013 BFB
chardonnay
86
Colour: bright yellow. Nose: powerfull, ripe fruit, sweet spices, creamy oak, fragrant herbs. Palate: rich, smoky aftertaste, flavourful, fresh, good acidity.

Juan de Juanes Vendimia Plata Cabernet Franc 2012 T
cabernet franc
86
Colour: very deep cherry, garnet rim. Nose: powerfull, ripe fruit, roasted coffee, dark chocolate. Palate: powerful, toasty, roasted-coffee aftertaste.

Juan de Juanes Vendimia Plata Petit Verdot 2012 T
petit verdot
83

Venta del Puerto Nº 12 2011 T
90
Colour: cherry, garnet rim. Nose: spicy, creamy oak, toasty. Palate: powerful, flavourful, toasty, round tannins.

Venta del Puerto Nº 18 2010 T Barrica

89

Colour: cherry, garnet rim. Nose: ripe fruit, aged wood nuances, spicy, creamy oak, balsamic herbs. Palate: powerful, flavourful, spicy, long.

HAMMEKEN CELLARS

Calle de la Muela, 16
3730 Jávea (Alicante)
☎: +34 965 791 967
Fax: +34 966 461 471
www.hammekencellars.com
cellars@hammekencellars.com

Besitos Moscato 2013 B
100% moscatel

85

Besitos Moscato 2013 RD

86

Colour: rose. Nose: ripe fruit, red berry notes, honeyed notes. Palate: flavourful, sweetness.

Radio Boca Tempranillo 2013 T
100% tempranillo

90

Colour: bright cherry. Nose: ripe fruit, sweet spices, creamy oak, expressive. Palate: flavourful, fruity, toasty, round tannins.

HERETAT DE TAVERNERS

Ctra. Fontanars - Moixent, Km. 1,8
46635 Fontanares (Valencia)
☎: +34 962 132 437
Fax: +34 961 140 181
www.heretatdetaverners.com
info@heretatdetaverners.com

Heretat de Taverners El Vern 2012 TC
monastrell, tempranillo, cabernet sauvignon, merlot

87

Colour: cherry, garnet rim. Nose: ripe fruit, spicy, creamy oak. Palate: powerful, flavourful, toasty.

Heretat de Taverners Graciano 2010 TC
100% graciano

90

Colour: cherry, garnet rim. Nose: ripe fruit, spicy, creamy oak, toasty. Palate: powerful, flavourful, toasty, round tannins.

Heretat de Taverners Mallaura 2011 TC
tempranillo, cabernet sauvignon, garnacha tintorera, monastrell

88

Colour: bright cherry. Nose: ripe fruit, sweet spices, creamy oak. Palate: fruity, flavourful, toasty.

Punt Dolç T
monastrell, garnacha tintorera

91

Colour: cherry, garnet rim. Nose: fruit preserve, fruit liqueur notes, spicy. Palate: flavourful, pruney, balsamic.

LA BARONÍA DE TURIS COOP. V.

Godelleta, 22
46359 Turis (Valencia)
☎: +34 962 526 011
Fax: +34 962 527 282
www.baroniadeturis.es
baronia@baroniadeturis.es

Luna de Mar 2011 T
merlot, syrah

85

Mistela Moscatel Turís 2013 Vino de Licor
moscatel

87

Colour: bright straw. Nose: citrus fruit, fruit liqueur notes, wild herbs, floral, sweet spices. Palate: powerful, spirituous, flavourful.

PAGO CASA GRAN

Ctra. Moixent - Fontanar, km. 9,5
46640 Mogente (Valencia)
☎: +34 962 261 004
Fax: +34 962 261 004
www.pagocasagran.com
comercial@pagocasagran.com

Casa Benasal 2012 T
garnacha tintorera, syrah, monastrell, otras

89

Colour: cherry, garnet rim. Nose: ripe fruit, sweet spices, creamy oak. Palate: flavourful, fruity, toasty.

Casa Benasal 2013 B
gewürztraminer, moscatel

89

Colour: bright straw. Nose: white flowers, fragrant herbs, fruit expression. Palate: fresh, fruity, flavourful, balanced, elegant.

Casa Benasal 2013 RD
monastrell, syrah

88

Colour: onion pink. Nose: elegant, candied fruit, dried flowers, fragrant herbs, red berry notes. Palate: light-bodied, flavourful, good acidity, long, spicy.

Casa Benasal Crux 2010 T
garnacha tintorera, syrah, monastrell

91

Colour: cherry, garnet rim. Nose: ripe fruit, wild herbs, spicy, creamy oak, balanced. Palate: long, balsamic, powerful, flavourful, spicy.

Casa Benasal Elegant 2010 T
garnacha tintorera, syrah, monastrell

90

Colour: cherry, garnet rim. Nose: ripe fruit, spicy, creamy oak, toasty, complex. Palate: powerful, flavourful, toasty, round tannins.

Falcata 2012 T
garnacha tintorera, syrah, monastrell, otras

89

Colour: cherry, garnet rim. Nose: ripe fruit, spicy, creamy oak, toasty, complex. Palate: powerful, flavourful, toasty, round tannins.

Falcata 2013 B
gewürztraminer, moscatel

89

Colour: bright straw. Nose: white flowers, fresh fruit, fine lees, dried herbs. Palate: flavourful, fruity, good acidity, balanced.

Falcata 2013 RD
monastrell, syrah

88

Colour: rose. Nose: elegant, candied fruit, dried flowers, fragrant herbs. Palate: light-bodied, flavourful, good acidity, long, spicy.

Falcata Arenal 2009 T
garnacha tintorera, monastrell

90

Colour: bright cherry. Nose: ripe fruit, sweet spices, creamy oak, balsamic herbs. Palate: fruity, flavourful, toasty, long, balanced.

Falcata Casa Gran 2011 T
garnacha tintorera, syrah, monastrell

88

Colour: bright cherry. Nose: ripe fruit, sweet spices, creamy oak. Palate: flavourful, fruity, toasty, round tannins.

RAFAEL CAMBRA

Naus Artesanals, 14
46635 Fontanars dels Alforoins
(Valencia)
☎: +34 626 309 327
www.rafaelcambra.es
rafael@rafaelcambra.es

El Bon Homme 2013 T
monastrell, cabernet sauvignon

88

Colour: cherry, garnet rim. Nose: candied fruit, warm. Palate: spicy, ripe fruit.

Rafael Cambra Dos 2012 T
cabernet sauvignon, cabernet franc, monastrell

90

Colour: cherry, garnet rim. Nose: ripe fruit, spicy, creamy oak, toasty. Palate: powerful, flavourful, toasty.

Rafael Cambra Uno 2012 T
monastrell

91

Colour: very deep cherry, garnet rim. Nose: red berry notes, fragrant herbs, floral, sweet spices, mineral. Palate: powerful, flavourful, spicy, balsamic.

Soplo 2011 T
garnacha

89

Colour: cherry, garnet rim. Nose: ripe fruit, spicy, creamy oak, toasty. Palate: powerful, flavourful, toasty, round tannins.

VALSAN 1831

Ctra. Cheste - Godelleta, Km. 1
46370 Chiva (Valencia)
☎: +34 962 510 861
www.cherubino.es
cherubino@cherubino.es

Cuva Vella 1980 Moscatel
moscatel

93

Colour: light mahogany. Nose: pattiserie, sweet spices, cocoa bean, fruit liqueur notes, slightly evolved. Palate: powerful, concentrated, sweetness.

Drassanes 2011 T
bobal, tempranillo, syrah

88

Colour: bright cherry, garnet rim. Nose: ripe fruit, sweet spices, creamy oak, medium intensity. Palate: fruity, flavourful, toasty.

Drassanes 2012 B
chardonnay, semillon, merseguera, moscatel

89

Colour: bright straw. Nose: white flowers, fresh fruit, expressive, fine lees, dried herbs. Palate: flavourful, fruity, good acidity, balanced.

El Novio Perfecto 2013 B
airén, moscatel

87

Colour: bright straw. Nose: fresh, fresh fruit, white flowers, expressive. Palate: flavourful, fruity, sweetness.

Vittore Moscatel 2012 B
moscatel

88

Colour: bright straw. Nose: powerfull, floral, honeyed notes, candied fruit, wild herbs. Palate: flavourful, sweet, fresh, fruity, good acidity, long.

VINÍCOLA ONTENIENSE COOP. V.
Avda. Almansa, 17
46870 Ontinyent (Valencia)
☎: +34 962 380 849
Fax: +34 962 384 419
www.coopontinyent.com
info@coopontinyent.com

Codolla 2013 B
macabeo, merseguera, verdil

79

Ontinium 2012 T Barrica
100% tempranillo

84

Ontinium 2013 B
chardonnay, macabeo, merseguera

84

Ontinium Syrah 2013 T
100% syrah

86

Colour: cherry, purple rim. Nose: red berry notes, ripe fruit, wild herbs, floral. Palate: powerful, flavourful.

Ontinium Tempranillo 2013 T
100% tempranillo

86

Colour: cherry, purple rim. Nose: powerfull, red berry notes, ripe fruit, floral. Palate: powerful, fresh, fruity, unctuous.

Viña Umbria 2013 T
100% monastrell

85

VIÑAS DEL PORTILLO S.L.
P.I. El Llano F2 P4 Apdo. 130
46360 Buñol (Valencia)
☎: +34 962 504 827
Fax: +34 962 500 937
www.vinasdelportillo.es
vinasdelportillo@vinasdelportillo.es

Albufera 2011 T
tempranillo, monastrell

86

Colour: very deep cherry. Nose: overripe fruit, fruit preserve. Palate: sweetness, fine bitter notes.

Alturia 2013 B
malvasía, moscatel, merseguera

87

Colour: bright straw. Nose: citrus fruit, candied fruit, fragrant herbs, white flowers. Palate: fresh, fruity, easy to drink.

VIÑEDOS Y BODEGAS VEGALFARO
Ctra. Pontón - Utiel, Km. 3
46390 Requena (Valencia)
☎: +34 962 320 680
Fax: +34 962 321 126
www.vegalfaro.com
rodolfo@vegalfaro.com

Pasamonte 2013 B
sauvignon blanc

89

Colour: bright straw. Nose: white flowers, fragrant herbs, fruit expression. Palate: fresh, fruity, flavourful, balanced, elegant.

Pasamonte Tintorera 2011 T
garnacha tintorera

91

Colour: cherry, garnet rim. Nose: ripe fruit, wild herbs, spicy, creamy oak. Palate: powerful, flavourful, balsamic, spicy, balanced.

VITICULTORES LO NECESARIO
Calle Fútbol 13
46310 Casas del Rey (Venta del Moro) (Valencia)
☎: +34 636 172 417
www.lonecesario.es
diego@lonecesario.es

Lonecesario 2012 T

89

Colour: very deep cherry, garnet rim. Nose: powerfull, ripe fruit, creamy oak. Palate: powerful, toasty, roasted-coffee aftertaste, balanced.

DO. VALLE DE GÜÍMAR

CONSEJO REGULADOR

Tafetana, 14
38500 Güímar (Santa Cruz de Tenerife)
☎:+34 922 514 709 - Fax: +34 922 514 485
@: consejo@vinosvalleguimar.com
www.vinosvalleguimar.com

LOCATION:

On the island of Tenerife. It practically constitutes a prolongation of the Valle de la Orotava region to the southeast, forming a valley open to the sea, with the Las Dehesas region situated in the mountains and surrounded by pine forests where the vines grow in an almost Alpine environment. It covers the municipal districts of Arafo, Candelaria and Güímar.

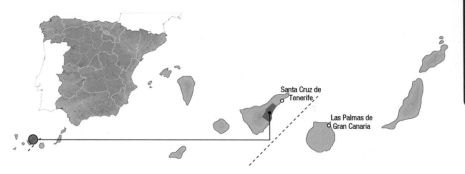

GRAPE VARIETIES:

White: Gual, Listán Blanco, Malvasía, Moscatel, Verdello and Vijariego.
Red: Bastardo Negro, Listán Negro (15% of total), Malvasía Tinta, Moscatel Negro, Negramoll, Vijariego Negro, Cabernet Sauvignon, Merlot, Pinot Noir, Ruby Cabernet, Syrah and Tempranillo.

FIGURES:

Vineyard surface: 270.18 – Wine-Growers: 553 – Wineries: 24 – 2013 Harvest rating: N/A – Production 13: 240,000 litres – Market percentages: 100% domestic.

SOIL:

Volcanic at high altitudes, there is a black tongue of lava crossing the area where the vines are cultivated on a hostile terrain with wooden frames to raise the long vine shoots.

CLIMATE:

Although the influence of the trade winds is more marked than in Abona, the significant difference in altitude in a much reduced space must be pointed out, which gives rise to different microclimates, and pronounced contrasts in day-night temperatures, which delays the harvest until 1st November.

VINTAGE RATING   PEÑÍNGUIDE

2009	2010	2011	2012	2013
AVERAGE	VERY GOOD	GOOD	VERY GOOD	AVERAGE

AGUSTÍN PÉREZ GARCÍA

Urb. Las Cruces, 28
38500 Güímar (Santa Cruz de Tenerife)
☎: +34 922 524 114

Los Cuatro Reales 2013 B
77

Los Cuatro Reales 2013 T
83

ARCA DE VITIS

Chinguaro, 26
38500 Güímar (Santa Cruz de Tenerife)
☎: +34 922 512 552
www.vinocontiempo.com
bodega@vinocontiempo.com

Contiempo Edición Especial 2012 B
malvasía
87
Colour: bright yellow. Nose: balanced, fragrant herbs, faded flowers. Palate: fruity, rich, long, fine bitter notes.

Contiempo Malvasía Dulce 2012 Blanco Dulce
malvasía
86
Colour: bright golden. Nose: candied fruit, faded flowers. Palate: balanced, fruity, rich.

Contiempo Moscatel Afrutado 2013 B
moscatel de alejandría
87
Colour: bright straw. Nose: fresh, fresh fruit, jasmine, varietal. Palate: flavourful, fruity, good acidity, balanced.

Contiempo Tinto de Postre 2012 T
baboso negro, syrah
87
Colour: very deep cherry, garnet rim. Nose: powerfull, fruit liqueur notes, fruit preserve, dried herbs. Palate: full, sweet, flavourful.

Contiempo Vendimia Seleccionada 2012 T
syrah
87
Colour: bright cherry. Nose: ripe fruit, sweet spices, creamy oak, expressive. Palate: flavourful, fruity, toasty, round tannins.

Contiempo Vidueños Seco 2012 B
marmajuelo, malvasía, moscatel
88
Colour: bright yellow. Nose: powerfull, ripe fruit, sweet spices, cocoa bean, faded flowers. Palate: fruity, spicy, long, rich.

BODEGA COMARCAL VALLE DE GÜIMAR

Subida a Los Loros, Km. 4,5
38550 Arafo (Santa Cruz de Tenerife)
☎: +34 922 513 055
Fax: +34 922 510 437
www.bodegavalledeguimar.com
info@bodegacomarcalguimar.com

Brumas de Ayosa 2013 RD
86
Colour: rose, purple rim. Nose: powerfull, ripe fruit, red berry notes, floral, expressive. Palate: powerful, fruity, fresh.

Brumas de Ayosa 2007 BN Reserva
100% listán blanco
84

Brumas de Ayosa 2008 BFB
listán blanco
84

Brumas de Ayosa 2012 BN
listán blanco
86
Colour: bright yellow. Nose: balanced, dried flowers, faded flowers, fresh. Palate: good acidity, balanced, correct.

Brumas de Ayosa 2012 T
listán negro, merlot
85

Brumas de Ayosa 2013 B
listán blanco
85

Brumas de Ayosa Afrutado 2012 SS
100% listán blanco
82

Brumas de Ayosa Afrutado 2013 Semidulce
85

Brumas de Ayosa Malvasía 2013 Blanco dulce
100% malvasía
85

Pico Cho Marcial 2008 B
100% listán blanco
85

Pico Cho Marcial 2013 B
83

Pico Cho Marcial 2013 T
83

Pico Cho Marcial Afrutado 2013 B
84

CÁNDIDO HERNÁNDEZ PÍO

Acentejo, 1
38370 La Matanza
(Santa Cruz de Tenerife)
☎: +34 922 513 288
Fax: +34 922 511 631
www.bodegaschp.es
info@bodegaschp.es

Calius 2008 TR
vijariego negro, castellana, tempranillo, merlot
88
Colour: cherry, garnet rim. Nose: ripe fruit, spicy, creamy oak, toasty, complex. Palate: powerful, flavourful, toasty, round tannins.

Calius 2012 T
vijariego negro, castellana, tempranillo, merlot
85

Calius 2013 T
vijariego negro, castellana, tempranillo, merlot
86
Colour: cherry, purple rim. Nose: fragrant herbs, sweet spices, ripe fruit. Palate: fruity, balanced.

EL BORUJO

Subida Los Loros, km. 4,2
38550 Arafo (Santa Cruz de Tenerife)
☎: +34 636 824 919
www.elborujo.es
jfcofarina@movistar.es

El Borujo 2013 B
88
Colour: bright yellow. Nose: white flowers, fruit expression, balanced. Palate: fruity, flavourful, long, fine bitter notes, balanced.

El Borujo Afrutado 2013 B
50% listán blanco, moscatel de alejandría
86
Colour: bright straw. Nose: fresh, fresh fruit, white flowers. Palate: flavourful, fruity, good acidity, balanced.

El Borujo Afrutado 2013 RD
listán negro
85

Los Loros 2012 BFB
91
Colour: bright yellow. Nose: ripe fruit, sweet spices, balanced, jasmine. Palate: fruity, rich, toasty.

Los Loros 2013 BFB
90
Colour: bright yellow. Nose: spicy, dried flowers, ripe fruit, balanced. Palate: fruity, flavourful, spicy, long.

EL REBUSCO BODEGAS

La Punta, 75 Araya
38530 Candelaria
(Santa Cruz de Tenerife)
☎: +34 608 014 944
www.elrebuscobodegas.es
elrebusco@gmail.com

Dis-Tinto 2013 T
85

La Tentación 2013 B
85

La Tentación Afrutado 2013 B
84

FERRERA

Calvo Sotelo, 44
38550 Arafo (Santa Cruz de Tenerife)
☎: +34 649 487 835
Fax: +34 922 237 359
www.bodegasferrera.com
carmengloria@bodegasferrera.com

Ferrera Afrutado 2013 B
85

SAT VIÑA LAS CAÑAS

Barranco Badajoz
38500 Güimar (Santa Cruz de Tenerife)
☎: +34 922 512 716
vegalascanas@hotmail.com

Amor Alma & Origen 2013 B
83

Amor Alma & Origen 2013 RD
83

Gran Virtud Listán Blanco 2013 B
88
Colour: bright straw. Nose: fresh, fresh fruit, white flowers. Palate: flavourful, fruity, good acidity, fine bitter notes, long.

VIÑA HERZAS

38004 Santa Cruz de Tenerife (Tenerife)
☎: +34 922 511 405
Fax: +34 922 290 064
morraherzas@yahoo.es

Viñas Herzas 2013 B
84

Viñas Herzas 2013 T
82

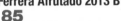

DO. VALLE DE LA OROTAVA

CONSEJO REGULADOR

Parque Recreativo El Bosquito, nº1. Urb. La Marzagana II - La Perdona
38315 La Orotava (Santa Cruz de Tenerife)
☎ :+34 922 309 923 - Fax: +34 922 309 924
@: info@dovalleorotava.com
www.dovalleorotava.com

LOCATION:

In the north of the island of Tenerife. It borders to the west with the DO Ycoden-Daute-Isora and to the east with the DO Tacoronte-Acentejo. It extends from the sea to the foot of the Teide, and comprises the municipal districts of La Orotava, Los Realejos and El Puerto de la Cruz.

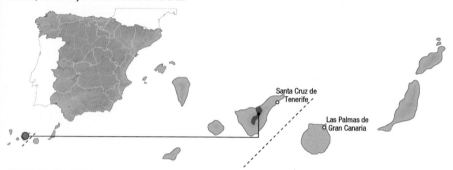

GRAPE VARIETIES:

White: Main: Güal, Malvasía, Verdello, Vijariego, Albillo, Forastera Blanca o Doradilla, Sabro, Breval and Burrablanca. Authorized: Bastardo Blanco, Forastera Blanca (Gomera), Listán Blanco, Marmajuelo, Moscatel, Pedro Ximénez and Torrontés.

Red: Main: Listán Negro, Malvasía Rosada, Negramoll, Castellana Negra, Mulata, Tintilla, Cabernet Sauvignon, Listán Prieto, Merlot, Pinot Noir, Ruby Cabernet, Syrah and Tempranillo.

Authorized: Bastardo Negro, Moscatel Negra, Tintilla and Vijariego Negra.

FIGURES:

Vineyard surface: 365.5 – Wine-Growers: 635 – Wineries: 12 – 2013 Harvest rating: - – Production 13: 531,918 litres – Market percentages: 63% domestic - 37% export.

SOIL:

Light, permeable, rich in mineral nutrients and with a slightly acidic pH due to the volcanic nature of the island. The vineyards are at an altitude of between 250 mm and 700 m.

CLIMATE:

As with the other regions on the islands, the weather is conditioned by the trade winds, which in this region result in wines with a moderate alcohol content and a truly Atlantic character. The influence of the Atlantic is also very important, in that it moderates the temperature of the costal areas and provides a lot of humidity. Lastly, the rainfall is rather low, but is generally more abundant on the north face and at higher altitudes.

VINTAGE RATING

PEÑÍNGUIDE

2009	2010	2011	2012	2013
AVERAGE	GOOD	VERY GOOD	VERY GOOD	VERY GOOD

PEÑÍNGUIDE 25 Years to Spanish Wine

BODEGA TAFURIASTE

Las Candias Altas, 11
38312 La Orotava
(Santa Cruz de Tenerife)
☎: +34 922 336 027
Fax: +34 922 336 027
www.bodegatafuriaste.com
vinos@bodegatafuriaste.com

Tafuriaste Afrutado Semidulce 2013 B
84

Tafuriaste Afrutado Semidulce 2013 RD
100% listán negro
84

BODEGA TAJINASTE

El Ratiño 5, La Perdoma
38315 La Orotava
(Santa Cruz de Tenerife)
☎: +34 922 308 720
Fax: +34 922 105 080
www.tajinaste.net
bodega@tajinaste.net

Can 2012 T
listán negro, vijariego negro
92
Colour: black cherry, purple rim. Nose: ripe fruit, cocoa bean, creamy oak, powerfull, dried herbs. Palate: balanced, round tannins, spicy.

Tajinaste 2013 RD
100% listán negro
84

Tajinaste Tradicional 2012 T
100% listán negro
86
Colour: cherry, garnet rim. Nose: old leather, spicy, ripe fruit. Palate: fruity, spicy, correct.

Tajinaste Vendimia Seleccionada 2012 T
100% listán negro
87
Colour: bright cherry. Nose: sweet spices, creamy oak, cocoa bean. Palate: flavourful, fruity, toasty, round tannins.

BODEGA VALLEORO

Ctra. General La Oratova - Los Realejos, Km. 4,5
38315 La Orotava
(Santa Cruz de Tenerife)
☎: +34 922 308 031
Fax: +34 922 308 233
www.bodegavalleoro.com
info@bodegavalleoro.com

Gran Tehyda 2013 RD
listán negro
86
Colour: rose, bright. Nose: powerfull, red berry notes, rose petals. Palate: balanced, fruity, easy to drink.

Gran Tehyda 2013 T
listán negro
84

Gran Tehyda Vendimia Seleccionada 2012 T Roble
listán negro, merlot, ruby cabernet
86
Colour: bright cherry. Nose: ripe fruit, sweet spices, dried herbs. Palate: flavourful, fruity, toasty, slightly dry, soft tannins.

BODEGAS EL PENITENTE

Camino La Habanera, 288
38300 La Orotava
(Santa Cruz de Tenerife)
☎: +34 922 309 024
Fax: +34 922 321 264
www.bodegaselpenitentesl.es
bodegas@elpenitentesl.es

Arautava 2012 T Fermentado en Barrica
listán negro
87
Colour: bright cherry. Nose: ripe fruit, sweet spices, creamy oak, expressive. Palate: flavourful, fruity, toasty, round tannins.

Arautava 2013 B
listán blanco
89
Colour: bright straw. Nose: expressive, balanced, fresh fruit, elegant. Palate: good acidity, balanced, fine bitter notes, long.

Arautava 2013 T
listán negro
88
Colour: bright cherry. Nose: sweet spices, creamy oak, expressive, fruit expression. Palate: flavourful, fruity, toasty, round tannins.

Arautava Albillo Dulce 2009 B
albillo
93
Colour: bright golden. Nose: expressive, candied fruit, balsamic herbs, spicy, toasty. Palate: balanced, fine bitter notes, long.

Arautava Dulce 2002 B Gran Reserva
listán blanco
94
Colour: old gold, amber rim. Nose: sweet spices, pattiserie, caramel, varnish, candied fruit. Palate: spicy, full, balanced.

Arautava Finca la Habanera 2013 B
albillo
88
Colour: bright yellow. Nose: powerfull, ripe fruit, sweet spices, fragrant herbs. Palate: rich, smoky aftertaste, flavourful, fresh, good acidity.

Bodegas de Miranda 2013 RD
listán negro
84

LA SUERTITA
Real de la Cruz Santa, 35-A
38413 Los Realejos
(Santa Cruz de Tenerife)
☎: +34 669 408 761
bodegalasuertita@yahoo.es

La Suertita 2013 B Barrica
89
Colour: bright yellow. Nose: powerfull, sweet spices, creamy oak, ripe fruit. Palate: rich, spicy, toasty, flavourful.

La Suertita Afrutado 2013 B
85

La Suertita Albillo 2012 B
86
Colour: bright straw. Nose: fresh fruit, balanced, medium intensity. Palate: fruity, easy to drink, good acidity, fine bitter notes.

LOS GÜINES
Pista Los Guines, s/n - El Horno
38410 Los Realejos
(Santa Cruz de Tenerife)
☎: +34 922 343 320
Fax: +34 922 353 855
www.bodegalosguines.com

Los Güines s/c B
83

Los Güines s/c T
80

SECADERO
San Benito
38410 Los Realejos
(Santa Cruz de Tenerife)
☎: +34 665 807 966
www.bodega-secadero.com
pab_estevez@hotmail.com

Cuprum 2012 T Barrica
85

Cuprum Castellana 2013 T
100% castellana
86
Colour: deep cherry, purple rim. Nose: sweet spices, creamy oak. Palate: good structure, ripe fruit, toasty, flavourful.

Cuprum Semiseco 2013 B
84

SOAGRANORTE
Tomas Zerolo, 15
38300 La Orotava
(Santa Cruz de Tenerife)
☎: +34 922 501 300
Fax: +34 922 503 462
www.suertesdelmarques.com
ventas@suertesdelmarques.com

7 Fuentes 2013 T
listán negro, tintilla, vijariego negro
90
Colour: deep cherry, purple rim. Nose: balanced, ripe fruit, balsamic herbs. Palate: fruity, good acidity, fruity aftestaste.

7 Fuentes El Lance 2012 TC
listán negro
91
Colour: cherry, garnet rim. Nose: ripe fruit, wild herbs, earthy notes, spicy. Palate: balanced, flavourful, long, balsamic.

Suertes del Marqués B
88
Colour: bright golden. Nose: toasty, aged wood nuances, wild herbs, candied fruit. Palate: fruity, easy to drink. Personality.

Suertes del Marqués Candio 2011 T
listán negro
91
Colour: cherry, garnet rim. Nose: ripe fruit, spicy, creamy oak, toasty, complex, dried herbs. Palate: powerful, flavourful, toasty, round tannins.

Suertes del Marqués El Ciruelo 2012 T
92
Colour: bright cherry, garnet rim. Nose: wild herbs, elegant, complex, spicy, varietal. Palate: good structure, full, long.

Suertes del Marqués El Esquilón 2012 T
listán negro, tintilla

91

Colour: cherry, garnet rim. Nose: ripe fruit, spicy, complex, scrubland. Palate: flavourful, round tannins, easy to drink.

Suertes del Marqués La Solana 2012 T
100% listán negro

94

Colour: bright cherry, purple rim. Nose: complex, scrubland, balanced, expressive, spicy. Palate: fruity, flavourful, balanced, good acidity.

Suertes del Marqués Los Pasitos 2012 T
baboso negro

92

Colour: bright cherry, garnet rim. Nose: balanced, expressive, wild herbs, ripe fruit. Palate: balanced, round tannins, spicy, long. Personality.

Suertes del Marqués Trenzado 2013 FI
listán blanco, pedro ximénez, baboso blanco, gual

90

Colour: bright straw. Nose: balanced, faded flowers, dried herbs, spicy. Palate: flavourful, long, balanced, good acidity.

Suertes del Marqués Vidonia 2012 B
listán blanco

92

Colour: bright yellow. Nose: complex, spicy, ripe fruit, dry nuts, dried herbs. Palate: flavourful, good structure, full, fine bitter notes.

DO. VINOS DE MADRID

CONSEJO REGULADOR

Ronda de Atocha, 7
28012 Madrid
☎ : +34 915 348 511 / Fax: +34 915 538 574
@ : prensa@vinosdemadrid.es
www.vinosdemadrid.es

LOCATION:

In the south of the province of Madrid, it covers three distinct sub-regions: Arganda, Navalcarnero and San Martín de Valdeiglesias.

SUB-REGIONS:

San Martín. It comprises 9 municipal districts and has more than 3,821 Ha of vineyards, with mainly the Garnacha (red) and Albillo (white) varieties.

Navalcarnero. It comprises 19 municipal districts with a total of about 2,107 Ha. The most typical wines are reds and rosés based on the Garnacha variety.

Arganda. With 5,830 Ha and 26 municipal districts, it is the largest sub-region of the DO. The main varieties are the white Malvar and the red Tempranillo or Tinto Fino.

GRAPE VARIETIES:

White: Malvar, Airén, Albillo, Parellada, Macabeo, Torrontés and Moscatel de Grano Menudo.
Red: Tinto Fino (Tempranillo), Garnacha, Merlot, Cabernet Sauvignon and Syrah.

FIGURES:

Vineyard surface: 8,391 – Wine-Growers: 2,890 – Wineries: 44 – 2013 Harvest rating: Good – Production 13: 5,068,220 litres – Market percentages: 67% domestic - 33% export.

SOIL:

Rather unfertile soil and granite subsoil in the sub-region of San Martín de Valdeiglesias; in Navalcarnero the soil is brownish-grey, poor, with a subsoil of coarse sand and clay; in the sub-region of Arganda the soil is brownish-grey, with an acidic pH and granite subsoil.

CLIMATE:

Extreme continental, with cold winters and hot summers. The average annual rainfall ranges from 461 mm in Arganda to 658 mm in San Martín.

VINTAGE RATING

PEÑÍNGUIDE

2009	2010	2011	2012	2013
GOOD	VERY GOOD	VERY GOOD	GOOD	VERY GOOD

BERNABELEVA

Ctra. Avila Toledo (N-403), Km. 81,600
28680 San Martín de Valdeiglesias
(Madrid)
☎: +34 915 091 909
Fax: +34 917 058 229
www.bernabeleva.com
bodega@bernabeleva.com

Bernabeleva "Arroyo de Tórtolas" 2012 T

garnacha

93 🌷

Colour: light cherry. Nose: ripe fruit, fruit liqueur notes, dry stone, spicy, balanced. Palate: elegant, spicy, mineral, long.

Bernabeleva "Carril del Rey" 2012 T

garnacha

96 🌷

Colour: light cherry. Nose: balanced, red berry notes, ripe fruit, balsamic herbs, mineral. Palate: elegant, good structure, flavourful, full.

Bernabeleva Viña Bonita 2012 T

garnacha

92 🌷

Colour: light cherry, garnet rim. Nose: balanced, fruit preserve, fruit liqueur notes, wild herbs, mineral, spicy. Palate: powerful, flavourful, balsamic.

Cantocuerdas Albillo 2012 B

albillo

93 🌷

Colour: bright yellow. Nose: expressive, balanced, faded flowers, fragrant herbs, dry stone. Palate: balanced, fine bitter notes, good acidity, complex.

Cantocuerdas Moscatel de Grano Menudo 2012 B

moscatel grano menudo

95 🌷

Colour: golden. Nose: powerfully, floral, honeyed notes, candied fruit, fragrant herbs, expressive. Palate: flavourful, sweet, fresh, fruity, good acidity, long, balanced, elegant.

Navaherreros Blanco de Bernabeleva 2012 B

albillo, macabeo

91 🌷

Colour: bright yellow. Nose: smoky, toasty, dry nuts, dried herbs. Palate: flavourful, ripe fruit, balanced, fine bitter notes.

Navaherreros Garnacha de Bernabeleva 2012 T

garnacha

93 🌷

Colour: cherry, purple rim. Nose: elegant, red berry notes, scrubland, dry stone, expressive. Palate: fruity, long, mineral, full, good acidity.

BODEGA ECOLÓGICA LUIS SAAVEDRA

Ctra. de Escalona, 5
28650 Cenicientos (Madrid)
☎: +34 916 893 400
Fax: +34 914 606 053
www.bodegasaavedra.com
info@bodegasaavedra.com

Corucho 2010 TC

90 🌷

Colour: cherry, garnet rim. Nose: ripe fruit, fruit liqueur notes, spicy, mineral. Palate: powerful, flavourful, spicy, long, balanced.

Corucho 2011 T

100% garnacha

87 🌷

Colour: cherry, garnet rim. Nose: ripe fruit, spicy, creamy oak, toasty, earthy notes. Palate: powerful, flavourful, toasty.

Corucho 2012 T Roble

86 🌷

Colour: cherry, purple rim. Nose: red berry notes, wild herbs. Palate: flavourful, fruity, good acidity, round tannins.

Corucho Albillo Moscatel 2013 B

88 🌷

Colour: bright straw. Nose: fresh, fresh fruit, white flowers, fragrant herbs, mineral. Palate: flavourful, fruity, good acidity, balanced.

Corucho Kosher 2010 T

100% garnacha

89 🌷

Colour: light cherry. Nose: red berry notes, fruit liqueur notes, wild herbs, earthy notes. Palate: powerful, flavourful, spicy, elegant.

Luis Saavedra 2009 TC

90

Colour: cherry, garnet rim. Nose: red berry notes, ripe fruit, spicy, creamy oak, toasty, complex, earthy notes. Palate: powerful, flavourful, toasty, round tannins.

BODEGA MARAÑONES

Hilero, 7 - Nave 9
28696 Pelayos de la Presa (Madrid)
☎: +34 918 647 702
www.bodegamaranones.com
bodega@bodegamaranones.com

Labros 2012 T

garnacha

92

Colour: light cherry, garnet rim. Nose: elegant, red berry notes, scrubland, spicy, expressive. Palate: balanced, complex, long, mineral.

DO VINOS DE MADRID / D.O.P

PEÑÍNGUIDE to Spanish Wine

Marañones 2012 T
100% garnacha
94
Colour: light cherry. Nose: ripe fruit, fruit liqueur notes, floral, spicy, wild herbs, mineral. Palate: complex, fine tannins, long, balsamic, balanced.

Peña Caballera 2012 T
100% garnacha
94
Colour: light cherry. Nose: fruit liqueur notes, red berry notes, balsamic herbs, mineral, balanced, elegant. Palate: round, complex, long, elegant, fruity, flavourful.

Picarana 2013 B
albillo
93
Colour: bright yellow. Nose: white flowers, fresh fruit, expressive, floral. Palate: flavourful, fruity, good acidity, balanced.

Piesdescalzos 2012 B
100% albillo
95
Colour: bright yellow. Nose: citrus fruit, fruit expression, fragrant herbs, dry stone, spicy, elegant. Palate: flavourful, complex, balanced, long, spicy, elegant.

Treinta Mil Maravedíes T
garnacha, morenillo
90
Colour: dark-red cherry, garnet rim. Nose: balanced, ripe fruit, balsamic herbs, warm, spicy. Palate: powerful, flavourful, ripe fruit, round tannins.

BODEGA Y VIÑEDOS GOSÁLBEZ ORTI
Real, 14
28813 Pozuelo del Rey (Madrid)
☎: +34 607 625 806
Fax: +34 918 725 399
www.qubel.com
bodega@qubel.com

Mayrit 2012 T Barrica
89
Colour: bright cherry. Nose: sweet spices, creamy oak, red berry notes, balsamic herbs, mineral. Palate: flavourful, fruity, toasty.

Mayrit 2013 B
100% sauvignon blanc
81
Colour: cherry, purple rim. Nose: red berry notes, ripe fruit, balsamic herbs, spicy. Palate: powerful, flavourful, spicy, long.

Qubél 2013 T
89
Colour: cherry, purple rim. Nose: red berry notes, ripe fruit, balsamic herbs, spicy. Palate: powerful, flavourful, spicy, long.

Qubél Nature 2005 T
89
Colour: pale ruby, brick rim edge. Nose: fruit liqueur notes, balsamic herbs, mineral, spicy. Palate: flavourful, round, unctuous, balanced.

BODEGAS ANDRÉS DÍAZ
Palencia, 32-34
28600 Navalcarnero (Madrid)
☎: +34 918 111 391
www.bodegasennavalcarnero.es
info@bodegasennavalcarnero.es

dÓrio Cabernet Sauvignon 2012 T
100% cabernet sauvignon
86
Colour: deep cherry, garnet rim. Nose: scrubland, ripe fruit, spicy. Palate: fruity, flavourful, round tannins.

dÓrio Colección Privada 2011 TC
88
Colour: cherry, garnet rim. Nose: ripe fruit, spicy, creamy oak, toasty, complex. Palate: powerful, flavourful, toasty, round tannins.

dÓrio Garnacha Cepas Viejas 2012 T
100% garnacha
85

dÓrio Tempranillo 2012 T
100% tempranillo
86
Colour: cherry, garnet rim. Nose: ripe fruit, balsamic herbs, creamy oak, roasted coffee. Palate: powerful, flavourful, toasty.

BODEGAS CASTEJÓN
Real, 118
28500 Arganda del Rey (Madrid)
☎: +34 918 710 264
Fax: +34 918 713 343
www.bodegascastejon.com
castejon@bodegascastejon.com

Viña Rey "70 Barricas" 2012 T
100% tempranillo
83

Viña Rey 2013 B
malvar, viura
85

Viña Rey Tempranillo 2013 T
100% tempranillo
83

Viñardul 2007 TR
100% tempranillo
87
Colour: cherry, garnet rim. Nose: ripe fruit, spicy, creamy oak, toasty, complex, earthy notes. Palate: powerful, flavourful, toasty, round tannins.

Viñardul 2011 TC
100% tempranillo
86
Colour: deep cherry, purple rim. Nose: ripe fruit, sweet spices, powerfull. Palate: spicy, ripe fruit, correct.

BODEGAS FELTRER-CAMPOS
C/ Iglesia, 20
28640 Cadalso de los Vidrios (Madrid)
☎: +34 699 124 752
www.bodegasfeltrercampos.com
info@bodegafeltrercampos.com

Feltrer Campos V.2 Selección Varietales 2010 T
cabernet sauvignon, tempranillo, merlot, garnacha
88
Colour: cherry, garnet rim. Nose: red berry notes, ripe fruit, sweet spices, balsamic herbs. Palate: flavourful, spicy, long.

Feltrer Campos V.4 2009 T
tempranillo
85

BODEGAS NUEVA VALVERDE
Domingo de Silos, 6 - bajo
28036 (Madrid)
☎: +34 915 649 495
www.bodegasnuevavalverde.com
info@bodegasnuevavalverde.com

750 2006 TR
merlot, cabernet sauvignon, syrah, garnacha
89
Colour: cherry, garnet rim. Nose: balanced, complex, ripe fruit, spicy, fine reductive notes. Palate: good structure, flavourful, round tannins.

Tejoneras Alta Selección 2009 TC
syrah, cabernet sauvignon, merlot, garnacha
88
Colour: bright cherry. Nose: ripe fruit, sweet spices, creamy oak, medium intensity. Palate: fruity, flavourful, toasty, balanced, concentrated.

BODEGAS ORUSCO
Alcalá, 48
28511 Valdilecha (Madrid)
☎: +34 918 738 006
Fax: +34 918 738 336
www.bodegasorusco.com
esther@bodegasorusco.com

Armonium 2010 T
tempranillo, cabernet sauvignon
89
Colour: cherry, garnet rim. Nose: ripe fruit, wild herbs, earthy notes, spicy, creamy oak. Palate: balanced, flavourful, long, balsamic.

Maín 2011 TC
tempranillo, cabernet sauvignon
86
Colour: dark-red cherry, garnet rim. Nose: toasty, ripe fruit, dark chocolate. Palate: flavourful, fruity, round tannins.

BODEGAS PABLO MORATE - MUSEO DEL VINO
Avda. Generalísimo, 34
28391 Valdelaguna (Madrid)
☎: +34 689 460 060
Fax: +34 918 937 172
www.bodegasmorate.com
bodegasmorate@bodegasmorate.com

Arate Premium Selección 2013 B
malvar, viura
79

Señorío de Morate Gran Selección 2006 TR
tempranillo
85

Señorío de Morate Selección 2008 TC
tempranillo, syrah
83

Señorío de Morate Selección 2012 T Roble
tempranillo, syrah
83

Viña Chozo 2012 B
malvar, macabeo
82

BODEGAS TAGONIUS

Ctra. de Tielmes a Carabaña Km 4,4
28550 Tielmes (Madrid)
☎: +34 918 737 505
Fax: +34 918 746 161
www.tagonius.com
exportacion@tagonius.com

Tagonius 2004 TR
cabernet sauvignon, merlot, syrah, tempranillo
92
Colour: cherry, garnet rim. Nose: red berry notes, ripe fruit, spicy, creamy oak, toasty, complex, earthy notes, fine reductive notes. Palate: powerful, flavourful, toasty, round tannins, elegant.

Tagonius 2005 TR
cabernet sauvignon, merlot, syrah, tempranillo
90
Colour: pale ruby, brick rim edge. Nose: ripe fruit, wild herbs, earthy notes, spicy, creamy oak, waxy notes, tobacco, fine reductive notes. Palate: balanced, flavourful, long, balsamic.

Tagonius 2010 TC
tempranillo, syrah, merlot, cabernet sauvignon
87
Colour: cherry, garnet rim. Nose: ripe fruit, spicy, creamy oak, toasty, complex. Palate: powerful, flavourful, toasty, round tannins.

Tagonius 2011 T Roble
tempranillo, syrah, merlot, cabernet sauvignon
88
Colour: dark-red cherry, garnet rim. Nose: ripe fruit, sweet spices, toasty. Palate: flavourful, correct, easy to drink, round tannins.

Tagonius Blanc 2012 B
malvar
86
Colour: bright straw. Nose: ripe fruit, dry nuts, powerfull, toasty, aged wood nuances, roasted coffee. Palate: flavourful, fruity, spicy, toasty, long.

Tagonius Cosecha 2011 T
tempranillo, cabernet sauvignon, merlot, syrah
84

Tagonius Gran Vino 2004 TR
cabernet sauvignon, syrah, merlot
91
Colour: deep cherry, orangey edge. Nose: elegant, spicy, wet leather, cocoa bean, creamy oak. Palate: spicy, fine tannins, elegant, long, balanced.

Tagonius Merlot 2010 T
merlot
90
Colour: deep cherry, garnet rim. Nose: medium intensity, scrubland, ripe fruit, cocoa bean. Palate: round tannins, flavourful.

Tagonius Syrah 2008 T
syrah
89
Colour: cherry, garnet rim. Nose: ripe fruit, spicy, dried herbs. Palate: powerful, flavourful, toasty, round tannins.

BODEGAS Y VIÑEDOS PEDRO GARCÍA

Soledad, 10
28380 Colmenar de Oreja (Madrid)
☎: +34 918 943 278
byv_pedrogarcia@telefonica.net

Femme Semidulce 2013 B
malvar blanco
83

Isla de San Pedro Barrica Selección 2011 T
merlot, tempranillo
89
Colour: cherry, garnet rim. Nose: ripe fruit, spicy, creamy oak, toasty, dark chocolate. Palate: powerful, flavourful, toasty, round tannins.

La Romera 2012 T Roble
merlot, tempranillo, syrah
87
Colour: bright cherry. Nose: ripe fruit, sweet spices, smoky. Palate: flavourful, fruity, toasty, round tannins.

La Romera 2013 T Joven
merlot, tempranillo, syrah
84

La Romera Esencias 2012 T
cabernet sauvignon, tempranillo
89
Colour: cherry, garnet rim. Nose: ripe fruit, spicy, creamy oak, toasty, complex. Palate: powerful, flavourful, toasty, round tannins.

Pedro García Malvar 2013 B
malvar blanco
85

COMANDO G VITICULTORES

Avda. Constitución, 23
28640 Cadalso de los Vidrios (Madrid)
☎: +34 918 640 602
www.comandog.es
info@comandog.es

La Bruja Avería 2013 T
garnacha

93

Colour: cherry, garnet rim. Nose: ripe fruit, wild herbs, earthy notes, spicy, creamy oak. Palate: balanced, flavourful, long, balsamic.

Las Umbrías 2012 T
garnacha

92

Colour: bright cherry. Nose: balsamic herbs, scrubland, fruit liqueur notes, red berry notes. Palate: easy to drink, slightly dry, soft tannins.

COMERCIAL GRUPO FREIXENET

Joan Sala, 2
8770 Sant Sadurní D'Anoia (Barcelona)
☎: +34 938 917 000
Fax: +34 938 183 095
www.freixenet.es
freixenet@freixenet.es

Heredad Torresano 2010 TC
tinto fino

86

Colour: cherry, garnet rim. Nose: creamy oak, toasty, ripe fruit, fruit preserve. Palate: powerful, flavourful, toasty, round tannins.

Heredad Torresano 2012 T Roble
tinto fino

85

FIGUEROA

Convento, 19
28380 Colmenar de Oreja (Madrid)
☎: +34 918 944 859
Fax: +34 918 944 859
bodegasjesusfigueroa@hotmail.com

Figueroa RD
tempranillo

84

Figueroa 2011 TC

87

Colour: cherry, garnet rim. Nose: ripe fruit, spicy, toasty, complex, scrubland. Palate: powerful, flavourful, toasty, round tannins.

Figueroa 2012 T Roble

87

Colour: cherry, garnet rim. Nose: ripe fruit, wild herbs, spicy, creamy oak. Palate: balanced, flavourful, long, balsamic.

Figueroa 2013 B
airén, macabeo

87

Colour: bright straw. Nose: white flowers, fragrant herbs, fruit expression. Palate: fresh, fruity, flavourful.

Figueroa 2013 T

85

Figueroa Semidulce 2013 B
macabeo

85

IN THE MOOD FOR WINE

Calle Altamirano 12, 6º izq.
28008 Madrid (Madrid)
☎: +34 696 877 811
www.inthemoodforwine.com
contact@inthemoodforwine.com

Chulapa 2010 TC
tempranillo

90

Colour: cherry, garnet rim. Nose: ripe fruit, spicy, toasty, complex, earthy notes, dried herbs. Palate: powerful, flavourful, toasty, round tannins.

LA CASA DE MONROY

José Moya, 12
45940 Valmojado (Toledo)
☎: +34 699 124 752
www.bodegasmonroy.es
info@bodegasmonroy.es

La Casa de Monroy "El Repiso" 2011 TC

89

Colour: cherry, garnet rim. Nose: red berry notes, fruit preserve, balsamic herbs, sweet spices, creamy oak. Palate: powerful, flavourful, ripe fruit.

La Casa de Monroy Garnacha Syrah 2012 T
garnacha, syrah

87

Colour: cherry, garnet rim. Nose: ripe fruit, fruit liqueur notes, wild herbs. Palate: powerful, flavourful, spicy.

La Casa de Monroy Selección Viñas Viejas Garnacha 2011 T
garnacha

91

Colour: light cherry, garnet rim. Nose: fruit liqueur notes, balsamic herbs, dry stone, spicy, creamy oak. Palate: flavourful, balanced, long, spicy.

M de Monroy 2011 T
86
Colour: cherry, garnet rim. Nose: ripe fruit, fruit preserve, scrubland. Palate: powerful, warm, correct.

LAS MORADAS DE SAN MARTÍN
Pago de Los Castillejos Ctra. M-541, Km. 4,7
28680 San Martín de Valdeiglesias
(Madrid)
☎: +34 691 676 570
Fax: +34 974 300 046
www.lasmoradasdesanmartin.es
bodega@lasmoradasdesanmartin.es

Las Moradas de San Martín Initio 2008 T
garnacha
89
Colour: ruby red, orangey edge. Nose: spicy, fine reductive notes, wet leather, toasty, ripe fruit. Palate: spicy, long, toasty, balanced.

Las Moradas de San Martín Senda 2009 T
garnacha
91
Colour: cherry, garnet rim. Nose: ripe fruit, spicy, toasty, dried herbs. Palate: powerful, flavourful, toasty, round tannins.

Las Moradas de San Martín, Libro Siete Las Luces 2008 T
garnacha
90
Colour: cherry, garnet rim. Nose: ripe fruit, spicy, creamy oak, complex, dried herbs. Palate: powerful, flavourful, toasty, round tannins.

PAGOS DE FAMILIA MARQUÉS DE GRIÑÓN
Finca Casa de Vacas CM-4015, Km. 23
45692 Malpica de Tajo (Toledo)
☎: +34 925 597 222
Fax: +34 925 789 416
www.pagosdefamilia.com
service@pagosdefamilia.com

El Rincón 2010 T
91
Colour: cherry, garnet rim. Nose: ripe fruit, spicy, creamy oak, toasty, complex. Palate: powerful, flavourful, toasty.

El Rincón 2008 T
90
Colour: very deep cherry, garnet rim. Nose: toasty, spicy, ripe fruit. Palate: good structure, flavourful, round tannins.

SEÑORÍO DE VAL AZUL
Urb. Valgrande, 37
28370 Chinchón (Madrid)
☎: +34 616 005 565
www.senoriodevalazul.es
evaayuso@arrakis.es

Fabio 2008 T
87
Colour: cherry, garnet rim. Nose: balanced, complex, ripe fruit, spicy, fine reductive notes. Palate: good structure, flavourful, round tannins.

Val Azul 2008 T
cabernet sauvignon, syrah, merlot
87
Colour: dark-red cherry, garnet rim. Nose: balanced, old leather, tobacco, spicy. Palate: correct, spicy.

Val Azul 2010 T
84

UVAS FELICES
Agullers, 7
08003 Barcelona (Barcelona)
☎: +34 902 327 777
www.vilaviniteca.es

El Hombre Bala 2012 T
94
Colour: bright cherry. Nose: red berry notes, fresh fruit, balsamic herbs. Palate: flavourful, fine bitter notes, good acidity.

La Mujer Cañón 2012 T
93
Colour: light cherry. Nose: fruit liqueur notes, dry stone, wild herbs, spicy, expressive. Palate: good acidity, fresh, fruity, flavourful, balanced.

Reina de los deseos 2012 T
94
Colour: light cherry. Nose: ripe fruit, fruit liqueur notes, balsamic herbs, spicy. Palate: powerful, flavourful, spicy, elegant.

VALLEYGLESIAS
Camino Fuente de los Huertos s/n
28680 San Martín de Valdeiglesias
(Madrid)
☎: +34 606 842 636
www.valleyglesias.com
bodega@valleyglesias.com

Minoss 2011 T
87
Colour: bright cherry. Nose: ripe fruit, sweet spices, creamy oak, expressive. Palate: flavourful, fruity, toasty, round tannins.

Valleyglesias Albillo Real 2013 B
88
Colour: bright straw. Nose: fresh, fresh fruit, white flowers, expressive. Palate: flavourful, fruity, good acidity, balanced.

Valleyglesias Garnacha 2012 T
92
Colour: light cherry, garnet rim. Nose: balanced, expressive, balsamic herbs, ripe fruit. Palate: good structure, flavourful, long, spicy.

VINÍCOLA DE ARGANDA SOCIEDAD COOPERATIVA MADRILEÑA
Camino de San Martín de la Vega, 16
28500 Arganda del Rey (Madrid)
☎: +34 918 710 201
Fax: +34 918 710 201
www.vinicoladearganda.com
vinicola@cvarganda.e.telefonica.net

Baladí 2013 BFB
malvar
86
Colour: bright yellow. Nose: powerfull, ripe fruit, sweet spices, creamy oak. Palate: rich, smoky aftertaste, flavourful, fresh.

Pago Vilches 2013 B
malvar
84

Pago Vilches 2013 RD
tempranillo
82

Pago Vilches 2013 T
tempranillo
84

Peruco 2010 TR
tempranillo
86
Colour: cherry, garnet rim. Nose: red berry notes, ripe fruit, spicy, creamy oak, toasty. Palate: powerful, flavourful, toasty.

Viña Rendero T Roble
tempranillo
82

Viña Rendero 2011 TC
tempranillo
83

Viña Rendero Selección Especial 2013 T Roble
tempranillo
85

VINOS JEROMÍN
San José, 8
28590 Villarejo de Salvanés (Madrid)
☎: +34 918 742 030
Fax: +34 918 744 139
www.vinosjeromin.com
comercial@vinosjeromin.com

Dos de Mayo Edición Limitada 2009 TC
100% tempranillo
88
Colour: bright cherry. Nose: ripe fruit, sweet spices, medium intensity, dried herbs, waxy notes. Palate: fruity, flavourful, toasty.

Félix Martínez Cepas Viejas 2010 TR
92
Colour: cherry, garnet rim. Nose: ripe fruit, spicy, creamy oak, toasty, complex, earthy notes. Palate: powerful, flavourful, toasty, round tannins.

Grego 2010 TC
89
Colour: bright cherry. Nose: ripe fruit, sweet spices, creamy oak, medium intensity. Palate: fruity, flavourful, toasty.

Grego 2011 T Roble
87
Colour: bright cherry, garnet rim. Nose: ripe fruit, sweet spices, creamy oak, expressive. Palate: flavourful, fruity, toasty.

Grego Garnacha Centenarias 2011 T Roble
100% garnacha
85

Grego Moscatel Seco 2010 B
100% moscatel grano menudo
87
Colour: bright golden. Nose: ripe fruit, honeyed notes, fruit liqueur notes, sweet spices. Palate: fresh, fruity, easy to drink.

Manu Vino de Autor 2009 TC
90
Colour: cherry, garnet rim. Nose: ripe fruit, spicy, creamy oak, toasty, complex, balsamic herbs, mineral. Palate: powerful, flavourful, toasty, round tannins, elegant.

Puerta Cerrada 2013 B
85

Puerta Cerrada 2013 RD
tempranillo, garnacha, malvar
85

Puerta Cerrada 2013 T
82

Puerta de Alcalá 2010 TC
100% tempranillo
88
Colour: bright cherry. Nose: ripe fruit, sweet spices, creamy oak, expressive. Palate: fruity, flavourful, toasty, balanced.

Puerta de Alcalá 2010 TR
100% tempranillo
89
Colour: cherry, garnet rim. Nose: balanced, ripe fruit, spicy, fine reductive notes. Palate: good structure, flavourful, round tannins.

Puerta de Alcalá 2013 B
100% malvar
85

Puerta de Alcalá 2013 RD
85

Puerta de Alcalá 2013 T
84

Puerta del Sol Malvar Nº1 2013 B
100% malvar
86
Colour: bright yellow. Nose: floral, candied fruit, balsamic herbs. Palate: fresh, fruity, flavourful, balanced.

Puerta del Sol Nº 4 Varietales 2010 TC
86
Colour: cherry, garnet rim. Nose: ripe fruit, scrubland, herbaceous, spicy. Palate: powerful, flavourful, balsamic.

Puerta del Sol Nº2 2013 T Joven
85

Puerta del Sol Nº3 2012 BFB
100% malvar
87
Colour: bright yellow. Nose: powerfull, ripe fruit, sweet spices, creamy oak, fragrant herbs. Palate: rich, flavourful, fresh, roasted-coffee aftertaste.

Puerta del Sol Nº5 Tempranillo 2010 TC
100% tempranillo
86
Colour: dark-red cherry, garnet rim. Nose: ripe fruit, powerfull, warm, spicy, toasty. Palate: correct, easy to drink.

Vega Madroño 2013 B
84

Vega Madroño 2013 RD
tempranillo, garnacha, syrah, merlot
85

VINOS Y ACEITES LAGUNA
Illescas, 5
28360 Villaconejos (Madrid)
☎: +34 918 938 196
Fax: +34 918 938 344
www.lagunamadrid.com
vyalaguna@gmail.com

Alma de Valdeguerra 2013 B
malvar blanco
85

Alma de Valdeguerra 2013 T
tempranillo
86
Colour: cherry, purple rim. Nose: expressive, fresh fruit, red berry notes, floral. Palate: flavourful, fruity, good acidity, easy to drink.

Alma de Valdeguerra Semidulce 2013 B
malvar blanco
84

Alma de Valdeguerra Semidulce 2013 RD
tempranillo
87
Colour: rose, purple rim. Nose: powerfull, ripe fruit, red berry notes, floral. Palate: powerful, fruity, fresh, easy to drink.

Valdeguerra Lacuna 2011 TC
tempranillo
86
Colour: cherry, garnet rim. Nose: ripe fruit, spicy, creamy oak, toasty. Palate: powerful, flavourful, toasty.

VIÑA BAYONA S.A.T.

28359 Titulcia (Madrid)
☎: +34 918 010 445
www.bodegavinabayona.com
vinabayona@bodegavinabayona.com

Viña Bayona 2010 TC
tempranillo, merlot, cabernet sauvignon
84

Viña Bayona 2012 T
tempranillo, merlot
80

VIÑAS EL REGAJAL

Antigua Ctra. Andalucía, Km. 50,5
28300 Aranjuez (Madrid)
☎: +34 913 078 903
Fax: +34 913 576 312
www.elregajal.es
isabel@elregajal.es

El Regajal Selección Especial 2012 T
tempranillo, syrah, cabernet sauvignon, merlot
91
Colour: deep cherry, purple rim. Nose: complex, ripe fruit, dried herbs, sweet spices. Palate: balanced, good structure, flavourful, round tannins.

Las Retamas del Regajal 2012 T
tempranillo, syrah, cabernet sauvignon, merlot
89
Colour: bright cherry. Nose: ripe fruit, sweet spices, creamy oak, wild herbs. Palate: flavourful, fruity, toasty.

DO. YCODEN-DAUTE-ISORA

CONSEJO REGULADOR

La Palmita, 10
38440 La Guancha (Sta. Cruz de Tenerife)
☎ :+34 922 130 246 - Fax: +34 922 828 159
@: ycoden@ycoden.com / promocion@ycoden.com
www.ycoden.com

LOCATION:

Occupying the northeast of the island of Tenerife and comprising the municipal districts of San Juan de La Rambla, La Guancha, Icod de los Vinos, Los Silos, El Tanque, Garachico, Buenavista del Norte, Santiago del Teide and Guía de Isora.

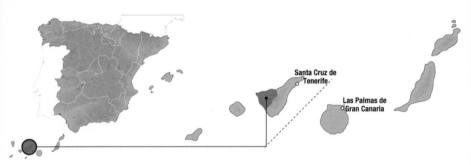

GRAPE VARIETIES:

White: Bermejuela (or Marmajuelo), Güal, Malvasía, Moscatel, Pedro Ximénez, Verdello, Vijariego, Albillo, Bastardo Blanco, Forastera Blanca, Listán Blanco (majority), Sabro and Torrontés.
Red: Tintilla, Listán Negro (majority), Malvasía Rosada, Negramoll Castellana, Bastardo Negra, Moscatel Negra and Vijariego Negra.

FIGURES:

Vineyard surface: 200 – Wine-Growers: 500 – Wineries: 16 – 2013 Harvest rating: - – Production 13: 650,000 litres – Market percentages: 98% domestic - 2% export.

SOIL:

Volcanic ash and rock on the higher grounds, and clayey lower down. The vines are cultivated at very different heights, ranging from 50 to 1,400 m.

CLIMATE:

Mediterranean, characterised by the multitude of microclimates depending on the altitude and other geographical conditions. The trade winds provide the humidity necessary for the development of the vines. The average annual temperature is 19°C and the average annual rainfall is around 540 mm.

VINTAGE RATING

PEÑÍNGUIDE

2009	2010	2011	2012	2013
AVERAGE	VERY GOOD	VERY GOOD	VERY GOOD	GOOD

BODEGA VIÑA ENGRACIA

38430 Icod de los Vinos
(Santa Cruz de Tenerife)
☎: +34 922 810 857
Fax: +34 922 860 895
www.vinosengracia.com
vinosengracia@hotmail.com

Viña Engracia 2013 B
85

Viña Engracia 2013 T
82

BODEGAS ACEVIÑO

La Patita, 63
38430 Icod de los Vinos (Santa Cruz de
Tenerife)
☎: +34 922 810 237
Fax: +34 922 810 237
bodegasacevino@yahoo.es

Aceviño 2013 B
85

Aceviño 2013 B Barrica
84

Aceviño 2013 RD
85

Aceviño 2013 T
84

Aceviño Afrutado 2013 B
85

Aceviño Semiseco 2013 B
85

BODEGAS INSULARES TENERIFE S.A.

Camino Cuevas del Rey, 1
38430 Icod de los Vinos
(Santa Cruz de Tenerife)
☎: +34 922 122 395
Fax: +34 922 814 688
www.bodegasinsularestenerife.es
icod@bodegasinsularestenerife.es

El Ancón 2013 T
listán negro
89
Colour: cherry, purple rim. Nose: expressive, fresh fruit, red berry notes, floral. Palate: flavourful, fruity, good acidity, round tannins.

El Ancón 2013 T Barrica
listán negro, tintilla
89
Colour: bright cherry. Nose: ripe fruit, sweet spices, creamy oak, expressive. Palate: flavourful, fruity, toasty, round tannins.

El Ancón Malvasía Dulce 2009 B
malvasía
93
Colour: bright golden. Nose: candied fruit, faded flowers, varnish, cocoa bean. Palate: full, complex, long, balanced, toasty.

El Ancón Tintilla 2012 T
86
Colour: very deep cherry. Nose: ripe fruit, fruit preserve, sweet spices, cocoa bean. Palate: powerful, fine bitter notes, correct.

Tágara 2013 B
listán blanco
87
Colour: bright straw. Nose: fresh, fresh fruit, expressive, fragrant herbs. Palate: flavourful, fruity, good acidity, balanced.

Tágara Afrutado 2013 B
listán blanco
85

Tágara Malvasía Marmajuelo 2013 B
malvasía, marmajuelo
86
Colour: bright yellow. Nose: white flowers, medium intensity, fresh fruit. Palate: fruity, easy to drink, correct, fine bitter notes.

BODEGAS VIÑAMONTE - IGNIOS ORIGENES

Avda. Villanueva, 34
38440 La Guancha
(Santa Cruz de Tenerife)
☎: +34 630 575 464
www.igniosorigen.com
info@bodegasvinamonte.com

Ignios Origenes Baboso Negro 2012 T
100% baboso negro
89
Colour: light cherry. Nose: grassy, wild herbs, ripe fruit, floral, expressive, saline. Palate: flavourful, fine tannins.

Ignios Origenes Dulce 2011 B
86
Colour: bright yellow, greenish rim. Nose: balanced, medium intensity, white flowers, faded flowers. Palate: rich, good finish.

Ignios Origenes Listán Negro Vendimia Seleccionada 2012 T
100% listán negro
92
Colour: light cherry. Nose: balanced, expressive, sweet spices, ripe fruit, balsamic herbs. Palate: fruity, spicy, easy to drink, good acidity.

Ignios Origenes Marmajuelo 2012 B
100% marmajuelo
89
Colour: bright yellow. Nose: powerfull, ripe fruit, sweet spices, creamy oak, fragrant herbs. Palate: rich, smoky aftertaste, flavourful, fresh, good acidity.

Viñamonte Dulce 2010 T
79

BODEGAS VIÑÁTIGO

Cabo Verde, s/n
38440 La Guancha
(Santa Cruz de Tenerife)
☎: +34 922 828 768
Fax: +34 922 829 936
www.vinatigo.com
vinatigo@vinatigo.com

Viñátigo 2013 SS
86
Colour: bright straw. Nose: fresh, fresh fruit, white flowers, expressive. Palate: flavourful, fruity, good acidity, balanced.

Viñátigo Gual 2012 B
100% gual
88
Colour: bright yellow. Nose: dried herbs, dried flowers, balanced, ripe fruit. Palate: full, fine bitter notes, good acidity.

Viñátigo Listán Blanco 2013 B
100% listán blanco
85

Viñátigo Listán Negro 2013 RD
100% listán negro
84

Viñátigo Listán Negro 2013 T
100% listán negro
86
Colour: cherry, purple rim. Nose: sweet spices, ripe fruit, balanced. Palate: fruity, easy to drink, good finish.

Viñátigo Malvasía Afrutado 2013 B
malvasía
85

Viñátigo Malvasía Clásico Dulce 2008 B
malvasía
88
Colour: golden. Nose: candied fruit, floral, fragrant herbs, toasty. Palate: flavourful, sweet, fresh, fruity, good acidity, long.

Viñátigo Marmajuelo 2013 B
100% marmajuelo
89
Colour: bright yellow. Nose: white flowers, jasmine. Palate: complex, full, long, good acidity, balanced, fine bitter notes.

Viñátigo Negramoll 2012 T
100% negramoll
87
Colour: light cherry. Nose: spicy, toasty, ripe fruit. Palate: fruity, good acidity, balanced.

Viñátigo Tintilla 2012 T Roble
100% tintilla
86
Colour: bright cherry. Nose: ripe fruit, sweet spices. Palate: flavourful, fruity, toasty, round tannins.

Viñátigo Vijariego 2012 BFB
100% vijariego blanco
85

VIÑA LA GUANCHA

El Sol, 3
38440 La Guancha
(Santa Cruz de Tenerife)
☎: +34 922 828 166
Fax: +34 922 828 166
www.zanata.net
zanata@zanata.net

Tara Tintilla 2010 T
tintilla
85

Viña Zanata 2013 RD
listán negro
85

Viña Zanata 2013 T Barrica
listán negro, tintilla, negramoll
85

Viña Zanata Afrutado 2013 B
listán blanco, moscatel, vijariego blanco
84

Viña Zanata Malvasía Seco 2013 B
malvasía
85

Viña Zanata Marmajuelo 2013 B
marmajuelo
84

Viña Zanata Tradicional 2013 B
listán blanco
85

Viña Zanata Tradicional 2013 T
listán negro, tintilla, negramoll
84

DO YECLA

CONSEJO REGULADOR

Poeta Francisco A. Jiménez, s/n - P.I. Urbayecla II
30510 Yecla (Murcia)
☎:+34 968 792 352 - Fax: +34 968 792 352
@: info@yeclavino.com
www.yeclavino.com

LOCATION:

In the northeast of the province of Murcia, within the plateau region, and comprising a single municipal district, Yecla.

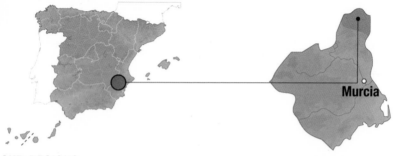

Murcia

SUB-REGIONS:

Yecla Campo Arriba, with Monastrell as the most common variety and alcohol contents of up to 14°, and Yecla Campo Abajo, whose grapes produce a lower alcohol content (around 12° for reds and 11.5° for whites).

GRAPE VARIETIES:

White: Merseguera, Airén, Macabeo, Malvasía, Chardonnay.
Red: Monastrell (majority 85% of total), Garnacha Tinta, Cabernet Sauvignon, Cencibel (Tempranillo), Merlot, Tintorera, Syrah.

FIGURES:

Vineyard surface: 5,824 – Wine-Growers: 493 – Wineries: 8 – 2013 Harvest rating: Very Good – Production 13: 7,179,060 litres – Market percentages: 6.53% domestic - 93.46% export.

SOIL:

Fundamentally deep limestone, with good permeability. The vineyards are on undulating terrain at a height of between 400 m and 800 m above sea level.

CLIMATE:

Continental, with a slight Mediterranean influence, with hot summers and cold winters, and little rainfall, which is usually around 300 mm per annum.

VINTAGE RATING

PEÑÍNGUIDE

2009	2010	2011	2012	2013
GOOD	VERY GOOD	VERY GOOD	VERY GOOD	VERY GOOD

BODEGA TRENZA

Avda. Matías Saenz Tejada, s/n.
Edif. Fuengirola Center - Local 1
29640 Fuengirola (Málaga)
☎: +34 615 343 320
Fax: +34 952 588 467
www.trenzawines.com
info@bodegatrenza.com

La Nymphina 2012 T
100% monastrell
89
Colour: cherry, garnet rim. Nose: ripe fruit, spicy, creamy oak, toasty, complex. Palate: powerful, flavourful, toasty, round tannins.

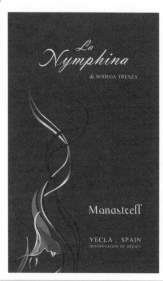

Trenza Family Collection 2008 T
93
Colour: cherry, garnet rim. Nose: ripe fruit, spicy, creamy oak, toasty, complex, dark chocolate, earthy notes. Palate: powerful, flavourful, toasty, round tannins, good acidity, long.

Trenza Family Collection 2010 T
92
Colour: very deep cherry, garnet rim. Nose: cocoa bean, sweet spices, ripe fruit, powerfull. Palate: good structure, flavourful, full.

Trenza Z-Strand 2008 T
88
Colour: deep cherry, garnet rim. Nose: powerfull, warm, ripe fruit, dried herbs. Palate: fruity, round tannins.

Trenza Z-Strand 2009 T
92
Colour: cherry, garnet rim. Nose: ripe fruit, spicy, creamy oak, complex, earthy notes. Palate: powerful, flavourful, round tannins, balanced.

Trenza Z-Strand 2011 T
90
Colour: very deep cherry, garnet rim. Nose: ripe fruit, closed, spicy, complex. Palate: balanced, long, ripe fruit.

BODEGAS BARAHONDA

Ctra. de Pinoso, km. 3
30510 Yecla (Murcia)
☎: +34 968 718 696
Fax: +34 968 790 928
www.barahonda.com
info@barahonda.com

Barahonda 2011 TC
monastrell, syrah, petit verdot
87
Colour: cherry, garnet rim. Nose: ripe fruit, spicy, creamy oak, toasty, complex, warm. Palate: powerful, flavourful, toasty, round tannins.

Barahonda 2013 B
macabeo, verdejo
84

Barahonda 2013 RD
monastrell
86
Colour: rose, purple rim. Nose: powerfull, ripe fruit, red berry notes, floral, expressive. Palate: powerful, fruity, fresh.

Barahonda Barrica 2012 T Barrica
monastrell, syrah
89
Colour: bright cherry. Nose: ripe fruit, sweet spices, expressive, red berry notes. Palate: flavourful, fruity, round tannins.

Barahonda Monastrell 2013 T
monastrell
88
Colour: cherry, purple rim. Nose: powerfull, red berry notes, ripe fruit, floral, expressive. Palate: powerful, fresh, fruity, unctuous.

Campo Arriba 2012 T
monastrell, syrah, garnacha tintorera
88
Colour: bright cherry. Nose: ripe fruit, sweet spices, medium intensity. Palate: fruity, flavourful, toasty.

Carro 2013 T
monastrell, merlot, syrah, tempranillo
87
Colour: cherry, purple rim. Nose: red berry notes, ripe fruit, floral, expressive. Palate: powerful, fresh, fruity.

HC Monastrell 2012 T
monastrell
89
Colour: bright cherry. Nose: ripe fruit, sweet spices, creamy oak, expressive, powerfull. Palate: flavourful, fruity, toasty, round tannins, concentrated.

Tranco 2011 T
monastrell, cabernet sauvignon
86
Colour: bright cherry. Nose: ripe fruit, sweet spices, expressive, scrubland. Palate: flavourful, fruity, toasty, round tannins.

BODEGAS CASTAÑO
Ctra. Fuenteálamo, 3
30510 Yecla (Murcia)
☎: +34 968 791 115
Fax: +34 968 791 900
www.bodegascastano.com
info@bodegascastano.com

Casa Cisca 2012 T
100% monastrell
94
Colour: cherry, garnet rim. Nose: ripe fruit, spicy, creamy oak, toasty, complex, dark chocolate, earthy notes. Palate: powerful, flavourful, toasty, round tannins.

Casa de la Cera 2011 T
93
Colour: very deep cherry. Nose: expressive, balanced, complex, ripe fruit, cocoa bean. Palate: full, ripe fruit, long.

Castaño Colección 2011 T
92
Colour: cherry, garnet rim. Nose: ripe fruit, spicy, complex, earthy notes, balsamic herbs. Palate: powerful, flavourful, toasty, round tannins.

Castaño GSM 2013 T
88
Colour: bright cherry, purple rim. Nose: balanced, medium intensity, balsamic herbs, red berry notes, ripe fruit. Palate: fruity, easy to drink.

Castaño Macabeo Chardonnay 2013 B
88
Colour: bright straw. Nose: fresh, fresh fruit, white flowers, expressive. Palate: flavourful, fruity, good acidity, balanced.

Castaño Monastrell 2013 RD
87
Colour: onion pink. Nose: elegant, fragrant herbs, red berry notes, ripe fruit, floral. Palate: light-bodied, flavourful, good acidity, long, spicy.

Castaño Monastrell 2013 T
100% monastrell
89
Colour: cherry, purple rim. Nose: medium intensity, fresh, red berry notes, floral. Palate: fruity, flavourful, good acidity, easy to drink.

Hécula 2012 T
100% monastrell
88
Colour: bright cherry. Nose: ripe fruit, sweet spices, creamy oak. Palate: flavourful, fruity, toasty, round tannins.

Viña al lado de la Casa 2010 T
89
Colour: bright cherry. Nose: ripe fruit, creamy oak. Palate: fruity, flavourful, toasty.

Viña Detrás de la Casa Syrah 2011 T
syrah
93
Colour: cherry, garnet rim. Nose: ripe fruit, spicy, creamy oak, toasty, complex, earthy notes. Palate: powerful, flavourful, toasty, round tannins.

BODEGAS LA PURÍSIMA
Ctra. de Pinoso, 3 Apdo. 27
30510 Yecla (Murcia)
☎: +34 968 751 257
Fax: +34 968 795 116
www.bodegaslapurisima.com
info@bodegaslapurisima.com

La Purísima 2013 B
sauvignon blanc, macabeo
85

La Purísima 2013 RD
monastrell, syrah
86
Colour: light cherry. Nose: ripe fruit, wild herbs, dried flowers, warm. Palate: powerful, flavourful, fine bitter notes.

La Purísima Monastrell 2013 T
monastrell
88
Colour: bright cherry. Nose: ripe fruit, medium intensity, wild herbs, varietal. Palate: fruity, flavourful, toasty.

La Purísima Old Vines Expressión 2010 T
monastrell, syrah, garnacha
92
Colour: cherry, garnet rim. Nose: scrubland, earthy notes, ripe fruit, spicy. Palate: flavourful, good structure, balanced, round tannins.

La Purísima Syrah 2013 T
syrah

87

Colour: cherry, purple rim. Nose: red berry notes, ripe fruit, floral, wild herbs. Palate: correct, ripe fruit, easy to drink.

Trapío 2010 T
100% monastrell

89

Colour: cherry, garnet rim. Nose: red berry notes, ripe fruit, spicy, creamy oak, toasty, complex, earthy notes. Palate: powerful, flavourful, toasty, round tannins.

DANIEL ALBA BODEGAS

Avda. Córdoba, 25
30510 Yecla (Murcia)
☎: +34 628 687 673
www.danielalbabodegas.com
info@danielalbabodegas.com

La Máquina del Tiempo 2011 T
monastrell, syrah

84

La Máquina Monastrell 2011 T
monastrell, syrah, garnacha tintorera

90

Colour: bright cherry. Nose: ripe fruit, sweet spices, creamy oak, medium intensity, wild herbs. Palate: fruity, flavourful, toasty.

EVINE

Camino Sax, km. 7
30510 Yecla (Murcia)
☎: +34 639 209 553
www.bodegasevine.com
info@bodegasevine.com

Evine 2012 T
85

Kyathos 2008 T
monastrell

90

Colour: bright cherry. Nose: ripe fruit, sweet spices, creamy oak, expressive, balsamic herbs. Palate: flavourful, fruity, round tannins.

Llano Quintanilla 2010 TC
monastrell

86

Colour: cherry, garnet rim. Nose: creamy oak, toasty, complex, fruit preserve. Palate: powerful, flavourful, toasty.

HAMMEKEN CELLARS

Calle de la Muela, 16
3730 Jávea (Alicante)
☎: +34 965 791 967
Fax: +34 966 461 471
www.hammekencellars.com
cellars@hammekencellars.com

Almez Organic Monastrell Shiraz 2013 T
88

Colour: cherry, purple rim. Nose: expressive, red berry notes, floral, balsamic herbs. Palate: flavourful, fruity, good acidity, round tannins.

Finca Rosal November Harvest Monastell 2011 T
monastrell

87

Colour: dark-red cherry, garnet rim. Nose: balsamic herbs, ripe fruit, varietal, spicy. Palate: balanced, flavourful, fruity, long.

Flor del Montgó Organic Monastrell 2013 T
monastrell

89

Colour: cherry, purple rim. Nose: red berry notes, ripe fruit, scrubland, expressive, balanced. Palate: powerful, fresh, fruity, unctuous.

Montgó 2012 T
87

Colour: very deep cherry, garnet rim. Nose: powerfull, fruit preserve, dark chocolate. Palate: full, flavourful, good structure.

LONG WINES

Avda. del Puente Cultural, 8 Bloque B Bajo 7
28702 San Sebastián de los Reyes (Madrid)
☎: +34 916 221 305
Fax: +34 916 220 029
www.longwines.com
adm@longwines.com

Casa del Canto 2009 TR
90

Colour: cherry, garnet rim. Nose: balanced, ripe fruit, toasty, powerfull. Palate: good structure, flavourful, balsamic.

Casa del Canto 2011 T Roble
89

Colour: bright cherry. Nose: ripe fruit, sweet spices, balanced, dried herbs. Palate: flavourful, fruity, toasty, round tannins.

VINOS DE PAGO

The "Vinos de Pago" are linked to a single winery, and it is a status given to that winery on the grounds of unique micro-climatic features and proven evidence of consistent high quality over the years, with the goal to produce wines of sheer singularity. So far, only 16 "Vinos de Pago" labels have been granted for different autonomous regions (Aragón, La Mancha, Comunidad Valenciana and Navarra). The "Vinos de Pago" category has the same status as a DO. This "pago" should not be confused with the other "pago" term used in the wine realm, which refers to a plot, a smaller vineyard within a bigger property. The "Pagos de España" association was formed in 2000 when a group of small producers of single estate wines got together to defend the singularity of their wines. In 2003, the association became Grandes Pagos de España, responding to the request of many colleagues in other parts of the country who wished to make the single-growth concept better known, and to seek excellence through the direct relationship between wines and their places of origin.

PAGO DE AYLES

Situated in the municipality of Mezalocha (Zaragoza), within the limits of the Cariñena appellation. The production area is located within the Ebro basin, principally around the depression produced by the River Huerva. The soils consist of limestone, marl and composites. The climate is temperate continental with low average annual rainfall figures of 350 to 550mm. The varieties authorized for the production of red and rosé wines are: garnacha, merlot, tempranillo and cabernet sauvignon.

PAGO CALZADILLA

Located in the Mayor river valley, in the part of the Alcarria region that belongs to the province of Cuenca, it enjoys altitude levels ranging between 845 and 1005 meters. The vines are mostly planted on limestone soils with pronounced slopes (with up to a 40% incline), so terraces and slant plots have become the most common feature, following the altitude gradients. The grape varieties planted are tempranillo, cabernet-sauvignon, garnacha and syrah.

PAGO CAMPO DE LA GUARDIA

The vineyards are in the town of La Guardia, to the northeast of the province of Toledo, on a high plateau known as Mesa de Ocaña. Soils are deep and with varying degrees of loam, clay and sand. The climate follows a continental pattern, with hot and dry summers and particularly dry and cold winters. The presence of the Tajo River to the north and the Montes de Toledo to the south promote lower rainfall levels than in neighbouring areas, and thus more concentration of aromas and phenolic compounds.

PAGO CASA DEL BLANCO

Its vineyards are located at an altitude of 617 metres in Campo de Calatrava, in the town of Manzanares, right in the centre of the province of Ciudad Real, and therefore with a mediterranean/continental climate. Soils have varying degrees of loam and sand, and are abundant in lithium, surely due to the ancient volcanic character of the region.

PAGO CHOZAS CARRASCAL

In San Antonio de Requena. This is the third Estate of the Community of Valencia, with just 31 hectares. Located at 720 metres above sea level. It has a continental climatology with Mediterranean influence. Low rainfall (and average of 350-400 litres annually), its soils are loam texture tending to clay and sandy. The varieties uses are: bobal, tempranillo, garnacha, cabernet sauvignon, merlot, syrah, cabernet franc and monastrell for red wines and chardonnay, sauvignon blanc and macabeo for white wines.

PAGO DEHESA DEL CARRIZAL

Dehesa del Carrizal was started in 1987 with 8 hectares of vineyard with cabernet sauvignon in Retuerca de Bullaque, to the north of Ciudad Real. Currently the vineyard has 26 hectares, located at 900 metres under the influence of a dry continental climate. The varieties grown are cabernet sauvignon, syrah, merlot and tempranillo for red wines and chardonnay for white wines. These are placed in clay soil formed by pebbles.

PAGO DOMINIO DE VALPEDUSA

Located in the town of Malpica de Tajo (Toledo), its owner, Carlos Falcó (Marqués de Griñón) pioneered the introduction in Spain of foreign grape varieties such as cabernet sauvignon.

PAGO EL TERRERAZO

El Terrerazo, property of Bodegas Mustiguilo, is the first "Vinos de Pago" label granted within the autonomous region of Valencia. It comprises 62 hectares at an altitude of 800 meters between Utiel and Sinarcas where an excellent clone of bobal –that yields small and loose berries– is grown. It enjoys a mediterranean-continental climate and the vineyard gets the influence of humid winds blowing from the sea, which is just 80 kilometres away from the property. Soils are characterized limestone and clay in nature, with abundant sand and stones.

PAGO FINCA ÉLEZ

It became the first of all Vino de Pago designations of origin. Its owner is Manuel Manzaneque, and it is located at an altitude of 1000 metres in El Bonillo, in the province of Albacete. The winery became renown by its splendid chardonnay, but today also make a single-varietal syrah and some other red renderings.

PAGO FLORENTINO

Located in the municipality of Malagón (Ciudad Real), between natural lagoons to the south and the Sierra de Malagón to the north, at an altitude of some 630-670 metres. Soils are mainly siliceous with limestone and stones on the surface and a subsoil of slate and limestone. The climate is milder and dryer than that of neighbouring towns.

PAGO GUIJOSO

Finca El Guijoso is property of Bodegas Sánchez Muliterno, located in El Bonillo, between the provinces of Albacete and Ciudad Real. Surrounded by bitch and juniper woods, the vines are planted on stone (guijo in Spanish, from which it takes its name) soils at an altitude of 1000 metres. Wines are all made from French varieties, and have a clear French lean also in terms of style.

PAGO LOS BALAGUESES

The "Pago de los Balagueses" is located to the south west of the Utiel-Requena wine region, just 20 kilometres away from Requena. At approximately 700 metres over the sea level, it enjoys a continental type of climate with mediterranean influence and an average annual rainfall of around 450 mm. The vines are planted on low hills –a feature that favours water drainage– surrounded by pines, almond and olive trees, thus giving shape to a unique landscape.

PAGO PRADO DE IRACHE

Its vineyard is located in the municipality of Ayegui (Navarra) at an altitude of 450 metres. Climate is continental with strong Atlantic influence and soils are mainly of a loamy nature.

PAGO DE OTAZU

Its vineyards are located in Navarra, between two mountain ranges (Sierra del Perdón and Sierra de Echauri), and is probably the most northerly of all Spanish wine regions. It is a cool area with Atlantic climate and a high day-night temperature contrast. Soils in that part of the country, near the city of Pamplona, are limestone-based with abundant clay and stones, therefore with good drainage that allows vines to sink their roots deeper into the soil.

PAGO SEÑORIO DE ARINZANO

Sie befindet sich im Nordwesten Spaniens, genauer in Estella, Navarra. Ihr Weinstock wächst in einem Tal, das von den letzten Gebirgsausläufern der Pyrenäen gebildet wird, und das vom Fluss Ega, der die Rolle des Moderators der Temperaturen übernimmt, geteilt wird. Ihr Klima besitzt einen atlantischen Einfluss mit einem hohen thermischen Unterschied. Die Weinstöcke dieser Weinbergslagen befinden sich in einer komplexen geologischen Gegend mit unterschiedlichen Anteilen von Schlamm, Mergel, Ton und Degradierung von kalkigem Gestein.

PAGO VERA DE ESTENAS

This is located in the area of Utiel-Requena, in the province of Valencia. It has a Mediterranean climate with a continental influence. Its soils are a dark chalky with a sandy clay loam texture. The average rainfall is 420 millimetres and the varieties planted are bobal, tempranillo, cabernet sauvignon and merlot for red wines and chardonnay for white wines.

PAGO AYLÉS

BODEGA PAGO AYLÉS

Finca Aylés. Ctra. A-1101, Km. 24
50152 Mezalocha (Zaragoza)
☎: +34 976 140 473
Fax: +34 976 140 268
www.pagoayles.com
pagoayles@pagoayles.com

"A" de Aylés 2012 T
merlot, garnacha, tempranillo, cabernet sauvignon

89

Colour: cherry, garnet rim. Nose: fragrant herbs, ripe fruit, dark chocolate, aromatic coffee. Palate: powerful, fine bitter notes, ripe fruit.

"é" de Aylés 2012 TC
tempranillo

88

Colour: very deep cherry. Nose: powerfull, overripe fruit, warm, toasty, spicy. Palate: powerful, ripe fruit, toasty.

"L" de Aylés 2013 RD
garnacha, cabernet sauvignon

87

Colour: light cherry. Nose: red berry notes, ripe fruit. Palate: powerful, good acidity, fine bitter notes.

"Y" de Aylés 2012 T
merlot, garnacha, tempranillo, cabernet sauvignon

92

Colour: deep cherry. Nose: powerfull, characterful, ripe fruit, toasty, spicy. Palate: flavourful, ripe fruit, long, mineral.

Aylés "Tres de 3000" 2011 T
garnacha, cabernet sauvignon, merlot

92

Colour: black cherry. Nose: powerfull, warm, fruit liqueur notes, roasted coffee. Palate: powerful, fine bitter notes, concentrated, sweetness.

PAGO CALZADILLA

PAGO CALZADILLA

Ctra. Huete a Cuenca, Km. 3
16500 Huete (Cuenca)
☎: +34 969 143 020
Fax: +34 969 147 047
www.pagodecalzadilla.com
info@pagodecalzadilla.com

Calzadilla Allegro 2008 T
100% syrah

91

Colour: cherry, garnet rim. Nose: spicy, creamy oak, toasty, dark chocolate, fruit preserve. Palate: powerful, flavourful, toasty, round tannins.

Opta Calzadilla 2009 T

90

Colour: bright cherry. Nose: ripe fruit, sweet spices, creamy oak, mineral. Palate: fruity, flavourful, toasty.

PAGO CAMPO DE LA GUARDIA

BODEGAS MARTÚE

Campo de la Guardia, s/n
45760 La Guardia (Toledo)
☎: +34 925 123 333
Fax: +34 925 123 332
www.martue.com
bodegasenlaguardia@martue.com

Martúe 2010 TC

84

Martúe Chardonnay 2012 B
100% chardonnay

88

Colour: bright yellow. Nose: powerfull, ripe fruit, sweet spices, creamy oak, fragrant herbs. Palate: rich, smoky aftertaste, flavourful, fresh, good acidity.

Martúe Especial 2010 TR

87

Colour: bright cherry. Nose: ripe fruit, sweet spices, creamy oak, grassy, herbaceous. Palate: flavourful, fruity, toasty.

Martúe Syrah 2009 T
100% syrah

88

Colour: bright cherry. Nose: ripe fruit, sweet spices, creamy oak, medium intensity. Palate: fruity, flavourful, toasty.

PAGO CASA DEL BLANCO

PAGO CASA DEL BLANCO

Ctra. Manzanares a Moral de Calatrava , Km. 23,2
13200 Manzanares (Ciudad Real)
☎: +34 917 480 606
Fax: +34 913 290 266
www.pagocasadelblanco.com
quixote@pagocasadelblanco.com

Quixote Cabernet Sauvignon Syrah 2009 T
cabernet sauvignon, syrah

87

Colour: dark-red cherry, garnet rim. Nose: ripe fruit, fruit preserve, dark chocolate, sweet spices. Palate: correct, spicy, balsamic.

Quixote Malbec Cabernet Franc 2009 T
malbec, cabernet franc

89

Colour: cherry, garnet rim. Nose: ripe fruit, wild herbs, earthy notes, spicy, creamy oak, fine reductive notes. Palate: balanced, flavourful, long, balsamic.

Quixote Merlot Tempranillo Petit Verdot 2009 T
merlot, tempranillo, petit verdot

88

Colour: deep cherry, garnet rim. Nose: scrubland, spicy, ripe fruit. Palate: flavourful, balanced.

Quixote Petit Verdot 2009 T
petit verdot

88

Colour: very deep cherry. Nose: ripe fruit, wild herbs, earthy notes, creamy oak. Palate: balanced, flavourful, long, balsamic.

PAGO CHOZAS CARRASCAL

CHOZAS CARRASCAL
Vereda San Antonio POl. Ind. Catastral, 16 Parcelas 136-138
46340 San Antonio de Requena (Valencia)
☎: +34 963 410 395
Fax: +34 963 168 067
www.chozascarrascal.es
chozas@chozascarrascal.es

El Cf de Chozas Carrascal 2012 T
cabernet franc

94 ♣

Colour: cherry, garnet rim. Nose: red berry notes, ripe fruit, balsamic herbs, spicy, mineral. Palate: flavourful, balanced, unctuous, round, spicy, long, elegant.

Las Ocho 2010 T
bobal, monastrell, garnacha, tempranillo

94 ♣

Colour: bright cherry. Nose: ripe fruit, sweet spices, creamy oak, mineral. Palate: fruity, flavourful, toasty, balanced, elegant.

Las Ocho 2012 T

94

Colour: cherry, garnet rim. Nose: spicy, creamy oak, toasty, complex, dark chocolate, earthy notes, red berry notes. Palate: powerful, flavourful, toasty, round tannins.

Las Tres 2013 B
chardonnay, sauvignon blanc, macabeo

93 ♣

Colour: bright yellow. Nose: sweet spices, ripe fruit, balsamic herbs, dried herbs, floral, mineral, creamy oak. Palate: rich, flavourful, spicy, balanced.

PAGO DEHESA DEL CARRIZAL

DEHESA DEL CARRIZAL
Carretera Retuerta a Navas de Estena, Km 5
13194 Retuerta del Bullaque (Ciudad Real)
☎: +34 925 421 773
Fax: +34 925 421 761
www.dehesadelcarrizal.com
bodega@dehesadelcarrizal.com

Dehesa del Carrizal Cabernet Sauvignon 2011 T
100% cabernet sauvignon

90

Colour: deep cherry, garnet rim. Nose: ripe fruit, wild herbs, earthy notes, spicy, creamy oak. Palate: balanced, flavourful, long, balsamic.

Dehesa del Carrizal Chardonnay 2012 B
100% chardonnay

92

Colour: bright golden. Nose: ripe fruit, dry nuts, powerfull, toasty, sweet spices. Palate: flavourful, fruity, spicy, toasty, long, roasted-coffee aftertaste, balanced.

Dehesa del Carrizal Colección Privada 2011 T
syrah, cabernet sauvignon, merlot

92

Colour: very deep cherry, garnet rim. Nose: elegant, balanced, ripe fruit, balsamic herbs. Palate: good structure, round tannins.

Dehesa del Carrizal MV 2011 T
cabernet sauvignon, syrah, merlot, tempranillo

90

Colour: bright cherry. Nose: ripe fruit, sweet spices, creamy oak, medium intensity. Palate: fruity, flavourful, toasty.

Dehesa del Carrizal Syrah 2011 T
100% syrah

91

Colour: bright cherry. Nose: ripe fruit, sweet spices, creamy oak, expressive, warm. Palate: flavourful, fruity, toasty, round tannins.

DO VINOS DE PAGO / D.O.P

PAGO DOMINIO DE VALDEPUSA

PAGOS DE FAMILIA MARQUÉS DE GRIÑÓN

Finca Casa de Vacas CM-4015, Km. 23
45692 Malpica de Tajo (Toledo)
☎: +34 925 597 222
Fax: +34 925 789 416
www.pagosdefamilia.com
service@pagosdefamilia.com

Caliza 2010 T
90
Colour: cherry, garnet rim. Nose: powerfull, ripe fruit, wild herbs, mineral, spicy, creamy oak. Palate: flavourful, balsamic, toasty.

Marqués de Griñón Cabernet Sauvignon 2010 T
100% cabernet sauvignon
93
Colour: deep cherry, garnet rim. Nose: ripe fruit, fruit liqueur notes, balsamic herbs, spicy, creamy oak, expressive. Palate: powerful, flavourful, long, spicy.

Marqués de Griñón Emeritvs 2010 TR
cabernet sauvignon, syrah, petit verdot
94
Colour: cherry, garnet rim. Nose: complex, balanced, ripe fruit, balsamic herbs, mineral, spicy, creamy oak. Palate: elegant, flavourful, spicy, long, round.

Marqués de Griñón Petit Verdot 2010 T
100% petit verdot
92
Colour: bright cherry, garnet rim. Nose: ripe fruit, wild herbs, spicy, creamy oak, powerfull. Palate: fruity, flavourful, toasty, balanced.

Marqués de Griñón Syrah 2007 T
100% syrah
91
Colour: cherry, garnet rim. Nose: balanced, complex, ripe fruit, spicy, fragrant herbs, fine reductive notes. Palate: good structure, flavourful, round tannins.

Svmma Varietalis 2010 T
91
Colour: cherry, garnet rim. Nose: ripe fruit, wild herbs, earthy notes, spicy, creamy oak. Palate: balanced, flavourful, long, balsamic.

PAGO FINCA EL TERRERAZO

MUSTIGUILLO VIÑEDOS Y BODEGA
Ctra. N-340 km. 196
46300 Utiel (Valencia)
☎: +34 962 168 260
Fax: +34 962 168 259
www.bodegamustiguillo.com
info@bodegamustiguillo.com

Finca Terrerazo 2011 T
100% bobal
94
Colour: cherry, garnet rim. Nose: ripe fruit, spicy, creamy oak, toasty, complex, dark chocolate, earthy notes. Palate: powerful, flavourful, toasty, round tannins.

Mestizaje 2013 T
92
Colour: cherry, garnet rim. Nose: ripe fruit, wild herbs, earthy notes, creamy oak. Palate: balanced, flavourful, long, balsamic.

Quincha Corral 2012 T
100% bobal
96
Colour: black cherry. Nose: characterful, red berry notes, dark chocolate, cocoa bean, powerfull, complex. Palate: powerful, concentrated, good acidity, round tannins.

PAGO FINCA ELÉZ

VIÑEDOS Y BODEGA MANUEL MANZANEQUE
Ctra. Ossa de Montiel a El Bonillo, Km. 11,500
2610 El Bonillo (Albacete)
☎: +34 917 153 844
Fax: +34 917 155 564
www.manuelmanzaneque.com
info@manuelmanzaneque.com

Manuel Manzaneque 2013 T
tempranillo, cabernet sauvignon
86
Colour: cherry, garnet rim. Nose: balsamic herbs, red berry notes, ripe fruit. Palate: powerful, flavourful, spicy.

Manuel Manzaneque Chardonnay 2012 B
chardonnay
91
Colour: bright golden. Nose: powerfull, ripe fruit, sweet spices, creamy oak, fragrant herbs, expressive. Palate: rich, flavourful, fresh, fine bitter notes, spicy.

Manuel Manzaneque Chardonnay 2013 B
chardonnay
87
Colour: bright yellow. Nose: ripe fruit, citrus fruit, balsamic herbs, dried flowers. Palate: powerful, rich, flavourful.

Manuel Manzaneque Finca Élez 2007 TC
cabernet sauvignon, merlot, tempranillo
88
Colour: dark-red cherry, garnet rim. Nose: powerfull, expressive, scrubland, ripe fruit. Palate: balanced, spicy, ripe fruit.

Manuel Manzaneque Nuestra Selección 2006 T
cabernet sauvignon, merlot, tempranillo
92
Colour: deep cherry, orangey edge. Nose: tobacco, balsamic herbs, expressive, ripe fruit. Palate: good structure, full, fruity, good acidity.

UN VINO DE
MANUEL MANZANEQUE
Nuestra Selección 2006

DENOMINACIÓN DE ORIGEN
FINCA ELEZ

Manuel Manzaneque Syrah 2007 T
syrah
91
Colour: pale ruby, brick rim edge. Nose: ripe fruit, spicy, creamy oak, toasty, complex, earthy notes, fine reductive notes. Palate: powerful, flavourful, toasty, round tannins.

PAGO FLORENTINO

PAGO FLORENTINO
Ctra. Porzuna - Camino Cristo del Humilladero, km. 3
13420 Malagón (Ciudad Real)
☎: +34 983 681 146
Fax: +34 983 681 147
www.pagoflorentino.com
bodeg@arzuaganavarro.com

Pago Florentino 2010 T
100% cencibel
90
Colour: very deep cherry, garnet rim. Nose: powerfull, ripe fruit, roasted coffee, dark chocolate. Palate: powerful, toasty, roasted-coffee aftertaste.

PAGO
FLORENTINO
DENOMINACION DE ORIGEN PROTEGIDA
VINO DE PAGO
2 0 1 0

PAGO GUIJOSO

BODEGA Y VIÑEDOS FAMILIA CONESA
Ctra. Pozo Aledo, km. 4 Nº 1
30739 Torre Pacheco (Murcia)
☎: +34 967 370 750
Fax: +34 967 370 751
bodega@familiaconesa.com

Flor de Divinus Chardonnay 2012 B
chardonnay
88
Colour: bright yellow. Nose: powerfull, ripe fruit, sweet spices, fragrant herbs. Palate: rich, flavourful, fresh, good acidity.

PAGO LOS BALAGUESES

VIÑEDOS Y BODEGAS VEGALFARO
Ctra. Pontón - Utiel, Km. 3
46390 Requena (Valencia)
☎: +34 962 320 680
Fax: +34 962 321 126
www.vegalfaro.com
rodolfo@vegalfaro.com

Pago de los Balagueses Chardonnay 2012 B
chardonnay
88
Colour: bright yellow. Nose: powerfull, ripe fruit, sweet spices, creamy oak, fragrant herbs. Palate: rich, smoky aftertaste, flavourful, fresh, good acidity.

Pago de los Balagueses Merlot 2012 T
merlot
92
Colour: cherry, garnet rim. Nose: ripe fruit, spicy, creamy oak, toasty, mineral. Palate: powerful, flavourful, toasty, round tannins.

Pago de los Balagueses Syrah 2012 TC
syrah
94
Colour: cherry, garnet rim. Nose: ripe fruit, spicy, creamy oak, toasty, complex, dark chocolate, earthy notes, fruit expression. Palate: powerful, flavourful, toasty, round tannins.

PAGO SEÑORIO DE ARINZANO

PROPIEDAD DE ARÍNZANO
Crta. NA-132, km. 3
31292 Arinzano (Navarra)
☎: +34 948 555 285
Fax: +34 948 555 415
www.arinzano.es
info@arinzano.com

Arínzano Gran Vino 2008 T
tempranillo
95
Colour: bright cherry. Nose: ripe fruit, wild herbs, tobacco, elegant, expressive, complex. Palate: fruity, flavourful, toasty.

Arínzano La Casona 2010 T
tempranillo
94
Colour: cherry, garnet rim. Nose: ripe fruit, spicy, creamy oak, toasty. Palate: powerful, flavourful, toasty, grainy tannins.

PAGO VERA DE ESTENAS

BODEGA VERA DE ESTENAS
Junto N-III, km. 266 - Paraje La Cabeuzela
46300 Utiel (Valencia)
☎: +34 962 171 141
www.veradeestenas.es
estenas@veradeestenas.es

Martínez Bermell Merlot 2013 T
merlot
89
Colour: bright cherry, garnet rim. Nose: balanced, ripe fruit, balsamic herbs, spicy. Palate: balanced, spicy, ripe fruit, long.

VINOS DE CALIDAD

So far, there are only seven wine regions that have achieved the status "Vino de Calidad" ("Quality Wine Produced in Specified Regions"): Cangas, Lebrija, Valtiendas, Granada, Sierra de Salamanca, Valles de Benavente and Islas Canarias, regions that are allowed to label their wines with the VCPRD seal. This quality seal works as a sort of "training" session for the DO category, although it is still quite unknown for the average consumer.

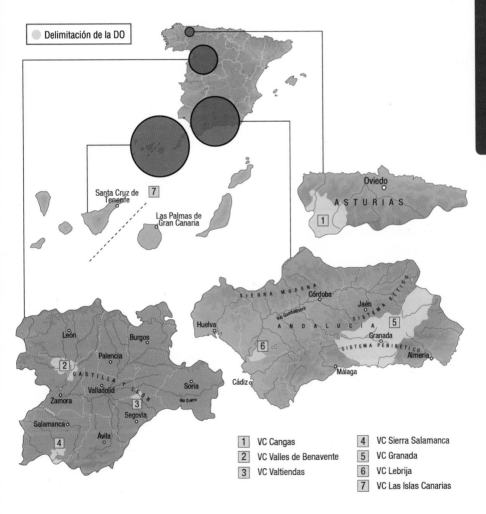

Delimitación de la DO

Santa Cruz de Tenerife 7

Las Palmas de Gran Canaria

Oviedo

ASTURIAS

1

SIERRA MORENA

Córdoba

Jaén

SISTEMA BÉTICO

Río Guadalquivir

Huelva

ANDALUCIA

5

Granada

6

SISTEMA PENIBÉTICO

Almería

León

Burgos

Palencia

2

CASTILLA Y LEÓN

Valladolid

Soria

Zamora

Río Duero

3

Segovia

Málaga

Cádiz

Salamanca

Ávila

4

1	VC Cangas	4	VC Sierra Salamanca
2	VC Valles de Benavente	5	VC Granada
3	VC Valtiendas	6	VC Lebrija
		7	VC Las Islas Canarias

VINO DE CALIDAD / D.O.P. CANGAS

Located to the south-eastern part of the province of Asturias, bordering with León, Cangas del Narcea has unique climatic conditions, completely different to the rest of the municipalities of Asturias; therefore, its wines have sheer singularity. With lower rainfall levels and more sunshine hours than the rest the province, vines are planted on slate, siliceous and sandy soils. The main varieties are albarín blanco and albillo (white), along with garnacha tintorera, mencía and verdejo negro (red).

VINO DE CALIDAD / D.O.P. GRANADA

Wines that come from anywhere within the provincial limits of Granada, it includes nearly 20 wineries and a hundred growers. It enjoys a mediterranean climate with Atlantic influence. Characterized by a rugged topography, the vineyards occupy mostly the highest areas, with an average altitude of around 1200 meters, a feature that provides this territory with an ample day-night temperature differential. The region is promoting white grape varieties such as vijiriega, moscatel and pedro ximénez, as well as red (tempranillo, garnacha, monastrell) and even some French ones, widely planted in the province. Soil structure, although diverse, is based mainly on clay and slate.

VINO DE CALIDAD / D.O.P. LEBRIJA

Recognized by the Junta de Andalucía on March the 11th 2009. The production area includes the towns of Lebrija and El Cuervo, in the province of Sevilla.

The wines ascribed to the "Vino de Calidad de Lebrija" designation of quality will be made solely from the following grape varieties:

– White varieties: moscatel de Alejandría, palomino, palomino fino, sauvignon blanc and that traditionally known as vidueño (montúo de pilas, mollar cano, moscatel morisco, perruno).

– Red varieties: cabernet sauvignon, syrah, tempranillo, merlot and tintilla de Rota.

Types of wines: white, red, generosos (fortified) and generosos de licor, naturally sweet and mistelas.

VINO DE CALIDAD / D.O.P. SIERRA DE SALAMANCA

The "Vino de Calidad" status was ratified to Sierra de Salamanca by the Junta de Castilla y León (Castilla y León autonomous government) in June 2010, becoming the third one to be granted within the region. Sierra de Salamanca lies in the south of the province of Salamanca, and includes 26 towns, all within the same province. Vines are planted mostly on terraces at the top of the hills and on clay soils based on limestone. Authorized varieties are viura, moscatel de grano menudo and palomino (white), as well as rufete, garnacha and tempranillo (red).

VINO DE CALIDAD / D.O.P. VALLES DE BENAVENTE

Recognized by the Junta de Castilla y León in September 2000, the VCPRD comprises nowadays more than 50 municipalities and three wineries in Benavente, Santibáñez de Vidriales and San Pedro de Ceque. The production areas within the region are five (Valle Vidriales, Valle del Tera, Valle Valverde, La Vega and Tierra de Campos) around the city of Benavente, the core of the region. Four rivers (Tera, Esla, Órbigo and Valderadey, all of them tributary to the Duero river) give the region its natural borders.

VINO DE CALIDAD / D.O.P. VALTIENDAS

An area to the north of the province of Segovia relatively known thanks to the brand name Duratón, also the name of the river that crosses a region that has mainly tempranillo planted, a grape variety known there also as tinta del país. The wines are fruitier and more acidic than those from Ribera del Duero, thanks to an altitude of some 900 metres and clay soils with plenty of stones.

VINO DE CALIDAD / D.O.P. ISLAS CANARIAS

Approved in May 2011, the date of publication in the Boletín Oficial de Canarias (BOC), the constitution of its management board took place on 27 December, 2012. The production area covers the entire territory of the Canary Islands, allowing free movement of grapes in the Canary Islands. Its regulations cover broad grape varieties from the Canary Islands, as well as international ones.

VINOS DE CALIDAD CANGAS

CHACÓN BUELTA S.L.

Ctra. General, s/n
33812 Cerredo (Asturias)
☎: +34 985 818 498
chaconbuelta@gmail.com

Nibias Nº 4 2013 B
albarín

91

Colour: bright straw. Nose: balsamic herbs, fresh fruit, floral, fragrant herbs, mineral. Palate: fresh, fruity, flavourful, balanced.

Nibias Nº 5 2012 B
albarín

92

Colour: bright straw. Nose: white flowers, fresh fruit, expressive, fine lees, dried herbs. Palate: flavourful, fruity, good acidity, balanced, fine bitter notes.

VINOS DE CALIDAD DE GRANADA

BODEGA LOS BARRANCOS

Ctra. Cádiar - Albuñol, km. 9,4
18449 Lobras (Granada)
☎: +34 958 343 218
Fax: +34 958 343 412
www.losbarrancos.es
info@losbarrancos.com

Corral de Castro 2012 T
tempranillo, cabernet sauvignon, merlot

85 🌿

BODEGA LOS MARTOS

Alfonso XII, 18
4700 El Ejido (Almería)
☎: +34 630 936 160
Fax: +34 950 482 852
fran.manzano@hotmail.com

Los Martos 2009 TC
tempranillo, syrah

87

Colour: cherry, garnet rim. Nose: overripe fruit, dried fruit, sweet spices, toasty. Palate: ripe fruit, warm, powerful.

Los Martos 2010 TR
tempranillo

86

Colour: cherry, garnet rim. Nose: overripe fruit, dried fruit, sweet spices, toasty. Palate: ripe fruit, warm, powerful.

Los Martos 2012 T
tempranillo, syrah

88

Colour: cherry, garnet rim. Nose: spicy, toasty, overripe fruit, mineral. Palate: powerful, flavourful, toasty, round tannins.

BODEGA VERTIJANA

Paseo de Sierra Nevada, 18
18516 Policar (Granada)
☎: +34 605 074 459
vertijana@vertijana.com

Vertijana 3 2010 TC
tempranillo, cabernet sauvignon, merlot, syrah

90

Colour: dark-red cherry, garnet rim. Nose: balanced, ripe fruit, sweet spices, creamy oak, scrubland. Palate: good structure, ripe fruit, round tannins.

Vertijana 3 2011 TC
tempranillo, cabernet sauvignon, merlot, syrah

89

Colour: bright cherry. Nose: ripe fruit, sweet spices, creamy oak, medium intensity. Palate: fruity, flavourful, toasty.

Vertijana Cabernet Sauvignon 2009 TC
cabernet sauvignon

89

Colour: cherry, garnet rim. Nose: ripe fruit, wild herbs, earthy notes, spicy, creamy oak. Palate: balanced, flavourful, long, balsamic.

Vertijana Syrah 2010 T
syrah

87

Colour: cherry, garnet rim. Nose: spicy, creamy oak, toasty, fruit preserve. Palate: powerful, flavourful, toasty, round tannins.

Vertijana Syrah 2011 T
syrah

86

Colour: cherry, garnet rim. Nose: overripe fruit, dried fruit, sweet spices, toasty. Palate: ripe fruit, warm, powerful.

BODEGAS AL ZAGAL

Paraje Las Cañaillas, s/n
18518 Cogollos de Guadix (Granada)
☎: +34 958 105 605
www.bodegasalzagal.es
info@bodegasalzagal.es

Rey Zagal 2010 TR
88

Colour: cherry, garnet rim. Nose: ripe fruit, spicy, creamy oak, toasty, complex. Palate: powerful, flavourful, toasty, round tannins.

Rey Zagal 2011 T Roble
tempranillo, syrah, cabernet sauvignon, merlot

88

Colour: cherry, garnet rim. Nose: fruit preserve, fruit liqueur notes, spicy. Palate: flavourful, pruney, balsamic.

Rey Zagal 2013 T

87

Colour: very deep cherry, garnet rim. Nose: overripe fruit, warm, dried herbs. Palate: flavourful, ripe fruit, long.

Rey Zagal Sauvignon Blanc 2013 B
sauvignon blanc

83

BODEGAS FONTEDEI
Doctor Horcajadas, 10
18570 Deifontes (Granada)
☎: +34 958 407 957
www.bodegasfontedei.es
info@bodegasfontedei.es

Fontedei Lindaraja 2013 T

90

Colour: bright cherry. Nose: sweet spices, creamy oak, expressive, ripe fruit, red berry notes. Palate: flavourful, fruity, toasty, round tannins.

BODEGAS SEÑORÍO DE NEVADA
Ctra. de Cónchar, s/n
18659 Villamena (Granada)
☎: +34 958 777 092
Fax: +34 958 107 367
www.senoriodenevada.es
info@senoriodenevada.es

Señorío de Nevada 2013 RD
garnacha, tempranillo, cabernet sauvignon

90

Colour: coppery red. Nose: elegant, candied fruit, dried flowers, fragrant herbs, red berry notes. Palate: light-bodied, flavourful, good acidity, long, spicy.

Señorío de Nevada Bronce 2010 T
merlot, cabernet sauvignon

88

Colour: bright cherry. Nose: ripe fruit, sweet spices, creamy oak, expressive. Palate: flavourful, fruity, toasty, round tannins.

Señorío de Nevada Club
de la barrica 2010 T
100% syrah

88

Colour: cherry, garnet rim. Nose: fruit preserve, fruit liqueur notes, spicy. Palate: flavourful, pruney.

Señorío de Nevada Oro Selección 2010 T
cabernet sauvignon, petit verdot

90

Colour: cherry, garnet rim. Nose: spicy, toasty, overripe fruit, mineral. Palate: powerful, flavourful, toasty, round tannins.

Señorío de Nevada Plata 2010 T
syrah, tempranillo, merlot

86

Colour: cherry, garnet rim. Nose: fruit preserve, spicy, toasty, aged wood nuances, overripe fruit. Palate: powerful, flavourful, sweetness.

CUATRO VIENTOS
Finca Cuatro Vientos
Ctra. de Murtas, PK-4
18490 Murtas (Granada)
☎: +34 958 343 325
www.bodegacuatrovientos.es
bodegacuatrovientos@gmail.com

Malafollá 2011 T
100% tempranillo

86

Colour: cherry, garnet rim. Nose: fruit preserve, fruit liqueur notes, spicy. Palate: flavourful, pruney.

Malafollá 2013 B
chardonnay, vijariego blanco

87

Colour: bright straw. Nose: citrus fruit, fresh fruit. Palate: fruity, light-bodied.

Malafollá 2013 RD
tempranillo

83

Marqués de la Contraviesa 2009 TC
tempranillo

86

Colour: cherry, garnet rim. Nose: overripe fruit, dried fruit, sweet spices, toasty. Palate: ripe fruit, warm, powerful.

Marqués de la Contraviesa Syrah 2010 T
syrah

88

Colour: cherry, garnet rim. Nose: ripe fruit, wild herbs, earthy notes, spicy, creamy oak. Palate: balanced, flavourful, long, balsamic.

DOMINGO Y QUILES

Calvo Sotelo, 3
18840 Galera (Granada)
☎: +34 958 739 227
www.bodegasdq.es
domingoyquiles@hotmail.es

Viña Galira 2009 TR
87
Colour: cherry, garnet rim. Nose: fruit preserve, fruit liqueur notes, spicy. Palate: flavourful, pruney, balsamic.

Viña Galira 2010 TC
87
Colour: cherry, garnet rim. Nose: spicy, toasty, overripe fruit, mineral. Palate: powerful, flavourful, toasty, round tannins.

Viña Galira 2013 B
87
Colour: bright straw. Nose: fresh, white flowers, ripe fruit. Palate: flavourful, fruity, good acidity, balanced.

DOMINIO BUENAVISTA

Ctra. de Almería, s/n
18480 Ugíjar (Granada)
☎: +34 958 767 254
Fax: +34 958 990 226
www.dominiobuenavista.com
info@dominiobuenavista.com

Veleta Cabernet Sauvignon 2009 T
cabernet sauvignon
87
Colour: cherry, garnet rim. Nose: spicy, toasty, overripe fruit, mineral. Palate: powerful, flavourful, toasty, round tannins.

Veleta Chardonnay 2013 B
chardonnay
84

Veleta Tempranillo 2009 T
tempranillo
88
Colour: cherry, garnet rim. Nose: fruit preserve, fruit liqueur notes, spicy. Palate: flavourful, pruney, balsamic.

Veleta Tempranillo Privilegio 2009 T
tempranillo
90
Colour: cherry, garnet rim. Nose: ripe fruit, spicy, creamy oak, toasty, complex. Palate: powerful, flavourful, toasty, round tannins.

Veleta Tempranillo Rosé 2013 RD
tempranillo
84

Veleta Vijiriega 2013 B
88
Colour: bright straw. Nose: fresh, fresh fruit, white flowers, expressive. Palate: flavourful, fruity, good acidity, balanced.

HORACIO CALVENTE ALMENDROS

Viñilla, 6
18699 Jete (Granada)
☎: +34 958 644 179
Fax: +34 958 644 179
www.bodegashcalvente.com
info@bodegashcalvente.com

Calvente Finca de Castillejos 2010 T
90
Colour: cherry, garnet rim. Nose: ripe fruit, spicy, creamy oak, toasty, complex, earthy notes. Palate: powerful, flavourful, toasty, round tannins.

Calvente Finca de la Guindalera 2010 TC
89
Colour: cherry, garnet rim. Nose: ripe fruit, spicy, creamy oak, toasty, characterful. Palate: powerful, flavourful, toasty, round tannins.

IRVING

Finca el Duque Ctra. de Huéscar
a Santiago de la Espada. km 13,500
18830 Huéscar (Granada)
☎: +34 653 527 560
Fax: +34 917 150 632
www.irving.es
pedidos@irving.es

Irving 2013 T
86
Colour: very deep cherry, garnet rim. Nose: overripe fruit, warm, dried herbs. Palate: flavourful, ripe fruit, long.

Irving Colección Familiar 2010 T
89
Colour: cherry, garnet rim. Nose: ripe fruit, wild herbs, earthy notes, spicy, creamy oak. Palate: balanced, flavourful, long, balsamic.

Irving Shiraz 2010 T
syrah
91
Colour: deep cherry, garnet rim. Nose: red berry notes, ripe fruit, wild herbs, spicy, balanced, earthy notes. Palate: long, balsamic, powerful, flavourful.

MA AMPARO GARCÍA HINOJOSA

Isaac Albéniz 10 - 2º B
18181 Granada (Granada)
☎: +34 958 277 764
Fax: +34 958 277 764
www.anchuron.es
info@anchuron.es

Anchurón 2009 TR
88
Colour: cherry, garnet rim. Nose: spicy, toasty, overripe fruit.
Palate: powerful, flavourful, toasty, round tannins.

Anchurón 2010 TC
88
Colour: cherry, garnet rim. Nose: spicy, toasty, overripe fruit,
mineral. Palate: powerful, flavourful, toasty, round tannins.

Anchurón 2012 RD
83

Anchurón 2013 B
89
Colour: bright straw. Nose: fresh, fresh fruit, white flowers,
expressive. Palate: flavourful, fruity, good acidity, balanced.

Anchurón Merlot Dulce 2011 T
100% merlot
87
Colour: cherry, garnet rim. Nose: fruit preserve, spicy, toasty,
dried fruit. Palate: powerful, flavourful, sweetness.

MARQUÉS DE CASA PARDIÑAS C.B.

Finca San Torcuato
18540 Huélago (Granada)
☎: +34 630 901 094
Fax: +34 958 252 297
www.marquesdecasapardiñas.com
info@spiracp.es

Marques de Casa Pardiñas 2013 T
92
Colour: cherry, garnet rim. Nose: ripe fruit, wild herbs, earthy
notes, spicy, creamy oak. Palate: balanced, flavourful, long,
balsamic.

NESTARES RINCÓN WINES & FOODS

Finca Juan de Reyes, S/N. Ctra. Haza
del Lino a Cádiar, km.4 (GR-5204)
18430 Torvizcón (Granada)
☎: +34 655 959 500
Fax: +34 958 272 125
www.alpujarride.com
info@alpujarride.com

Nestares Rincón 1.0 2012 T
tempranillo, merlot, syrah
91
Colour: bright cherry. Nose: ripe fruit, sweet spices, creamy
oak, expressive. Palate: flavourful, fruity, toasty, round tannins.

VINOS DE CALIDAD
DE LAS ISLAS CANARIAS

BODEGA TAJINASTE

El Ratiño 5, La Perdoma
38315 La Orotava
(Santa Cruz de Tenerife)
☎: +34 922 308 720
Fax: +34 922 105 080
www.tajinaste.net
bodega@tajinaste.net

Tajinaste 2012 T Roble
100% listán negro
86
Colour: bright cherry. Nose: ripe fruit, sweet spices, creamy
oak, expressive. Palate: flavourful, fruity, toasty, round tannins.

Tajinaste 2013 B
85

Tajinaste Afrutado 2013 B
85

BODEGAS VIÑÁTIGO

Cabo Verde, s/n
38440 La Guancha
(Santa Cruz de Tenerife)
☎: +34 922 828 768
Fax: +34 922 829 936
www.vinatigo.com
vinatigo@vinatigo.com

Viñátigo Baboso 2012 T
100% baboso negro
87
Colour: cherry, garnet rim. Nose: red berry notes, violets, faded flowers. Palate: correct, good acidity, ripe fruit, good finish.

Viñátigo Ensamblaje 2012 T
baboso negro, tintilla, vijariego negro
88
Colour: cherry, garnet rim. Nose: ripe fruit, wild herbs, earthy
notes, spicy, creamy oak. Palate: balanced, flavourful, long,
balsamic.

Viñátigo Ensamblaje 2013 B
marmajuelo, gual, malvasía, vijariego blanco
87
Colour: bright yellow. Nose: dried flowers, medium intensity.
Palate: fruity, balanced, fine bitter notes, good finish.

Viñátigo Vijariego Negro 2012 T
100% vijariego negro
86
Colour: dark-red cherry, orangey edge. Nose: spicy, toasty,
ripe fruit. Palate: fruity, flavourful, easy to drink, good finish.

FERRERA

Calvo Sotelo, 44
38550 Arafo (Santa Cruz de Tenerife)
☎: +34 649 487 835
Fax: +34 922 237 359
www.bodegasferrera.com
carmengloria@bodegasferrera.com

Ferrera 2013 B
85

Ferrera Legendario 2013 T
87
Colour: deep cherry, purple rim. Nose: balanced, red berry notes, ripe fruit, floral, violets. Palate: correct, balanced, long.

MONJE

Camino Cruz de Leandro, 36
38359 El Sauzal
(Santa Cruz de Tenerife)
☎: +34 922 585 027
Fax: +34 922 585 027
www.bodegasmonje.com
monje@bodegasmonje.com

Hollera Monje 2013 T Maceración Carbónica
listán negro
86
Colour: cherry, purple rim. Nose: expressive, fresh fruit, red berry notes, floral. Palate: flavourful, fruity, good acidity, round tannins.

VIÑAS Y VINOS HOYOS DE BANDAMA

Camino a la Caldera, 36 Monte Lentiscal
35300 Santa Brígida (Gran Canaria)
☎: +34 630 472 753
Fax: +34 928 353 893
www.bodegahoyosdebandama.com
maria@bodegahoyosdebandama.com

Caldera 2012 T
86
Colour: cherry, garnet rim. Nose: ripe fruit, wild herbs, spicy. Palate: balanced, flavourful, long, balsamic.

Caldera 2012 T Barrica
cabernet sauvignon, merlot, listán negro, castellana
87
Colour: bright cherry. Nose: ripe fruit, sweet spices, creamy oak, expressive. Palate: flavourful, fruity, toasty, round tannins.

Caldera 2013 B
verdejo, forastera, albillo
86
Colour: bright straw. Nose: fresh, fresh fruit, white flowers. Palate: flavourful, fruity, good acidity, balanced.

Caldera Baboso Negro 2012 T
100% baboso negro
86
Colour: cherry, garnet rim. Nose: saline, wild herbs, ripe fruit. Palate: flavourful, sweet tannins, balanced.

Caldera Semi 2013 B
malvasía, moscatel
85

VINOS DE CALIDAD DE LEBRIJA

BODEGAS GONZÁLEZ PALACIOS

Avda. Jose María Tomassetti, 43
41740 Lebrija (Sevilla)
☎: +34 955 974 084
www.gonzalezpalacios.com
bodegas@gonzalezpalacios.com

Castillo de González Palacios 2013 B
83

Frasquito Flor de Lebrija Reserva s/c
100% palomino
90
Colour: old gold. Nose: ripe fruit, dry nuts, acetaldehyde, pungent, dried herbs, faded flowers. Palate: balanced, powerful, flavourful, spicy, long.

González Palacios Lebrija Old Dulce Vino Generoso
palomino, moscatel
89
Colour: light mahogany. Nose: powerfull, dry nuts, toasty, dark chocolate. Palate: rich, long, fine solera notes, spicy, spirituous.

González Palacios Lebrija Old Vino Generoso s/c
100% palomino
92
Colour: light mahogany. Nose: aged wood nuances, acetaldehyde, pungent, spicy, creamy oak, dry nuts. Palate: flavourful, fine bitter notes, spicy, long, elegant, balanced.

González Palacios M. Fina Vino de licor
100% palomino
91
Colour: bright straw. Nose: ripe fruit, aged wood nuances, spicy, acetaldehyde, dry nuts. Palate: balanced, fine bitter notes, flavourful, good structure.

González Palacios Moscatel s/c B
100% moscatel
89
Colour: golden. Nose: powerfull, floral, honeyed notes, candied fruit, fragrant herbs. Palate: flavourful, sweet, fresh, fruity, good acidity, long.

M. Fina El Poeta Flor de Lebrija
100% palomino
90
Colour: bright yellow. Nose: complex, expressive, pungent, saline, dried flowers. Palate: rich, powerful, fresh, fine bitter notes.

Overo 2011 TC
85

Vino de Pasas El Poeta s/c Vino de licor
100% moscatel
90
Colour: dark mahogany. Nose: spicy, dry nuts, aged wood nuances, sweet spices, dark chocolate, aromatic coffee. Palate: powerful, flavourful, spicy, long.

Valleoscuro 2013 B
verdejo
86
Colour: bright straw. Nose: ripe fruit, citrus fruit. Palate: flavourful, balanced.

Valleoscuro Prieto Picudo 2013 RD
prieto picudo
84

Valleoscuro Prieto Picudo Tempranillo 2013 RD
prieto picudo, tempranillo
87
Colour: rose, purple rim. Nose: powerfull, ripe fruit, red berry notes, floral. Palate: powerful, fruity, fine bitter notes.

VINO DE CALIDAD DE LOS VALLES DE BENAVENTE V.C.P.R.D.

BODEGA EL TESORO
Camino Viñas, s/n
49622 Brime de Urz (Zamora)
☎: +34 636 982 233
bodegaeltesoro@gmail.com

Petavonium 2010 TC
prieto picudo
86
Colour: bright cherry. Nose: ripe fruit, sweet spices, creamy oak, expressive. Palate: flavourful, fruity, toasty, round tannins.

BODEGAS OTERO
Avda. El Ferial, 22
49600 Benavente (Zamora)
☎: +34 980 631 600
Fax: +34 980 631 722
www.bodegasotero.es
info@bodegasotero.es

Otero 2008 TR
prieto picudo
89
Colour: ruby red. Nose: spicy, fine reductive notes, wet leather, aged wood nuances, toasty, ripe fruit. Palate: spicy, long, toasty.

Otero 2009 TC
prieto picudo
87
Colour: very deep cherry. Nose: ripe fruit, spicy, creamy oak, toasty. Palate: powerful, flavourful, toasty, round tannins.

Finca
VALLEOSCURO
✷
*Prieto Picudo
Tempranillo*

Valleoscuro Prieto Picudo Tempranillo 2013 T
prieto picudo, tempranillo
88
Colour: very deep cherry, garnet rim. Nose: overripe fruit, warm, dried herbs. Palate: flavourful, ripe fruit, long.

BODEGAS VERDES
Ctra. Benavente, s/n
49610 Santibáñez de Vidriales (Zamora)
☎: +34 980 648 308
Fax: +34 980 648 308
www.bodegasverdes.galeon.com
bodegasverdes@hispavista.com

Señorío de Vidriales 2012 T
tempranillo, prieto picudo, garnacha
85

Señorío de Vidriales 2013 RD
tempranillo, prieto picudo, malvasía

87

Colour: rose, purple rim. Nose: powerfull, ripe fruit, red berry notes, floral, expressive. Palate: powerful, fruity, fresh.

CASTILLO DE VIDRIALES
Benavente, 37
49622 Quiruelas de Vidriales (Zamora)
☎: +34 628 317 119
www.castillodevidriales.com
castillodevidriales@gmail.com

Valdelacuba 2013 B
verdejo

85

Valdelacuba 2013 RD
prieto picudo

84

VINOS DE CALIDAD DE SIERRA DE SALAMANCA

CÁMBRICO
Paraje El Guijarral s/n
37658 Villanueva del Conde
(Salamanca)
☎: +34 923 281 006
Fax: +34 923 213 605
www.cambrico.com
alberto@cambrico.com

575 Uvas de Cámbrico 2009 TR
90

Colour: cherry, garnet rim. Nose: fruit liqueur notes, wild herbs, sweet spices, creamy oak, dry stone. Palate: powerful, flavourful, balsamic, long.

Viñas del Cámbrico 2012 T
90

Colour: cherry, garnet rim. Nose: ripe fruit, spicy, creamy oak, toasty, complex, mineral. Palate: powerful, flavourful, toasty, spicy, fruity aftestaste.

Viñas del Cámbrico 2013 T
91

Colour: bright cherry. Nose: ripe fruit, creamy oak, expressive. Palate: fruity, toasty, round tannins, balsamic, easy to drink.

COMPAÑÍA DE VINOS LA ZORRA
San Pedro, s/n
37610 Mogarraz (Salamanca)
☎: +34 609 392 591
Fax: +34 923 418 018
www.vinoslazorra.es
estanverdes@vinoslazorra.es

8 Virgenes Serranas 2013 B
rufete blanco, palomino, moscatel grano menudo

91

Colour: bright straw. Nose: faded flowers, dry nuts, balanced. Palate: correct, balsamic, easy to drink, good finish, spicy.

La Vieja Zorra 2012 T Roble
92

Colour: deep cherry, purple rim. Nose: complex, ripe fruit, creamy oak. Palate: flavourful, balsamic, toasty.

La Zorra 2013 T
90

Colour: bright cherry, purple rim. Nose: fruit expression, violets, scrubland, mineral. Palate: balanced, easy to drink, good finish.

La Zorra Raro 2013 T
100% rufete

91

Colour: cherry, purple rim. Nose: red berry notes, raspberry, fruit expression, sweet spices. Palate: flavourful, light-bodied, good acidity, fresh, fruity.

ROCHAL
Salas Pombo, 17
37670 Santibáñez de la Sierra
(Salamanca)
☎: +34 923 435 260
Fax: +34 923 435 260
www.bodegasrochal.com
info@bodegasrochal.com

Zamayón 2013 T
85

Zamayón Calixto Nieto 2010 T
rufete, tempranillo

90

Colour: dark-red cherry, garnet rim. Nose: ripe fruit, sweet spices, creamy oak. Palate: good structure, spicy, long, round tannins.

Zamayón Osiris 2011 T
87

Colour: cherry, garnet rim. Nose: ripe fruit, spicy, creamy oak, toasty, fine reductive notes. Palate: powerful, flavourful, toasty.

VINOS DE CALIDAD VALTIENDAS V.C.P.R.D.

BODEGA PAGO EL ALMENDRO

Camino de la iglesia s/n
40237 Sacramenia (Segovia)
☎: +34 645 962 008
oscar@restaurantemaracaibo.com

Evolet 2012 T
tempranillo
89 🏆

Colour: cherry, garnet rim. Nose: ripe fruit, spicy, creamy oak, toasty, complex, mineral. Palate: powerful, flavourful, toasty, round tannins, balsamic.

Sin Vivir 2011 T
100% tempranillo
90 🏆

Colour: cherry, garnet rim. Nose: ripe fruit, spicy, creamy oak, toasty, complex, fragrant herbs. Palate: powerful, flavourful, toasty, round tannins, balanced.

Vivencias 2011 T
tempranillo
89 🏆

Colour: cherry, garnet rim. Nose: ripe fruit, spicy, creamy oak, toasty, complex. Palate: powerful, flavourful, toasty, round tannins, concentrated.

BODEGAS VAGAL

La Fuente, 19
40314 Valtiendas (Segovia)
☎: +34 921 527 331
www.vagal.es
jose.vagal@gmail.com

Vagal Pago Ardalejos 2011 T
tinta del país
90

Colour: deep cherry, garnet rim. Nose: powerfull, balanced, ripe fruit, sweet spices. Palate: flavourful, long, round tannins.

BODEGAS Y VIÑEDOS ANDREA GUTIÉRREZ FERRERAS

Ctra. La Bañesa, s/n
49618 Fuente Encalada (Zamora)
☎: +34 636 156 320

Valzuquino 2009 TC
tempranillo
86

Colour: very deep cherry, garnet rim. Nose: warm, dried herbs, ripe fruit. Palate: flavourful, ripe fruit, long.

Valzuquino 2012 T
tempranillo
88

Colour: very deep cherry, garnet rim. Nose: warm, dried herbs, ripe fruit, earthy notes. Palate: flavourful, ripe fruit, long.

NAVALTALLAR

Calvario, s/n
40331 Navalilla (Segovia)
☎: +34 638 050 061
www.navaltallar.com
alejandro_costa@navaltallar.com

Navaltallar 2013 T
tempranillo
87

Colour: cherry, purple rim. Nose: powerfull, red berry notes, ripe fruit, floral, balsamic herbs. Palate: powerful, fresh, fruity, unctuous.

Navaltallar Roble 16 2010 TC
tempranillo
87

Colour: cherry, garnet rim. Nose: ripe fruit, spicy, creamy oak, toasty, aged wood nuances. Palate: powerful, flavourful, toasty, round tannins.

Navaltallar Roble 8 2011 T Roble
tempranillo
83

SANZ Y NÚÑEZ S.L.

Ctra. de Valladolid - Soria, 40 H
47300 Peñafiel (Valladolid)
☎: +34 629 563 189
dominiodeperoleja@hotmail.es

Dominio de Peroleja 2011 T Roble
tinto fino
88

Colour: very deep cherry, garnet rim. Nose: powerfull, roasted coffee, dark chocolate, overripe fruit. Palate: powerful, toasty, roasted-coffee aftertaste.

VINOS DE LA TIERRA

The number of "Vino de la Tierra" categories granted so far, 45, means the status is growing in importance, given that growers are only required to specify geographical origin, grape variety and alcohol content. For some, it means an easy way forward for their more experimental projects, difficult to be contemplated by the stern regulations of the designations of origin, as it is the case of vast autonomous regions such as La Mancha, Castilla y León or Extremadura. For the great majority, it is a category able to fostering vineyards with high quality potential, a broader varietal catalogue and therefore the opportunity to come up with truly singular wines, a sort of sideway entrance to the DO status.

The different "Vino de la Tierra" designations have been listed in alphabetical order.

In theory, the "Vino de la Tierra" status is one step below that of the DO, and it is the Spanish equivalent to the French "Vins de Pays", which pioneered worldwide this sort of category. In Spain, however, it has some unique characteristics. For example, the fact that the designation "Vino de la Tierra" is not always the ultimate goal, but it is rather used as a springboard to achieve the highly desired DO category. In addition, as it has happened in other countries, many producers have opted for this type of association with less stringent regulations that allow them greater freedom to produce wine. Therefore, in this section there is a bit of everything: from great wines to more simple and ordinary examples, a broad catalogue that works as a sort of testing (and tasting!) field for singularity as well as for new flavours and styles derived from the use of local, autochthonous varieties.

The new Spanish Ley del Vino (Wine Law) maintains the former status of "Vino de la Tierra", but establishes an intermediate step between this and the DO one. They are the so-called 'Vinos de Calidad con Indicación Geográfica' (Quality Wines with Geographical Indication), under which the region in question must remain for a minimum of five years.

In the light of the tasting carried out for this section, there is a steady improvement in the quality of these wines, as well as fewer misgivings on the part of the wineries about the idea of joining these associations.

VT / I.G.P. 3 RIBERAS

Granted by the administration at the end of 2008 for the wines produced and within the "3 Riberas" geographical indication. The different typologies are: rosé, white, red and noble wines.

VT / I.G.P. ABANILLA

This small wine region comprises the municipalities of Abanilla and Fortuna –in the eastern part of the province of Murcia– and some 1500 hectares, although most of its production is sold to the neighbouring DO Alicante. The region enjoys a hot, dry climate, limestone soils and low rainfall, features all that account for good quality prospects, although there are some differences to be found between the northern and the southern areas within it, given the different altitudes. The grape varieties allowed in the region for red winemaking are: bonicaire, cabernet sauvignon, forcallat tinta, garnacha tintorera, merlot, petit verdot, crujidera and syrah. For white wines, we find chardonnay, malvasía, moravia dulce, moscatel de grano menudo and sauvignon blanc.

VT / I.G.P. ALTIPLANO DE SIERRA NEVADA

With the goal to free Granada's geographical indication exclusively for the "Vino de Calidad" category, in 2009 the VT I.G.P.Norte de Granada changed its name to VT I.G.P.Altiplano de Sierra Nevada. The new geographical indication comprises 43 municipalities in the north of the province of Granada. The authorized grape varieties for white wine production in the region are chardonnay, baladí verdejo, airen, torrontés, palomino, pedro ximénez, macabeo and sauvignon blanc; also tempranillo, monastrell, garnacha tinta, cabernet franc, cabernet sauvignon, pinot noir, merlot, and syrah for red wines.

VT / I.G.P. BAILÉN

Bailén wine region comprises 350 hectares in some municipal districts within the province of Jaén but fairly close to La Mancha. Wines are made mainly from the grape variety known as "molinera de Bailén", that cannot be found anywhere else in the world, but also from other red grape varieties such as garnacha tinta, tempranillo and cabernet sauvignon, as well as the white pedro ximénez.

VT / I.G.P. BAJO ARAGÓN

The most "mediterranean" region within Aragón autonomous community, it borders three different provinces (Tarragona, Castellón and Teruel) and is divided in four areas: Campo de Belchite, Bajo Martín, Bajo Aragón and Matarraña. Soils are mainly clay and limestone in nature, very rich in minerals with high potash content. The climate is suitable for the right maturation of the grapes, with the added cooling effect of the 'Cierzo' (northerly wind), together with the day-night temperature contrast, just the perfect combination for the vines. The main varieties are garnacha (both red and white), although foreign grapes like syrah, cabernet sauvignon, merlot and chardonnay are also present, as well as tempranillo and cariñena.

VT / I.G.P. BARBANZA E IRIA

The last geographical indication to be granted to the autonomous region of Galicia back in 2007, Barbanza e Iria is located within the Ribera de la Ría de Arosa wine region, in the north of the province of Pontevedra. They make both red an white wines from with varieties such as albariño, caíño blanco, godello, loureiro blanco (also known as marqués), treixadura and torrontés (white); and brancellao, caíño tinto, espadeiro, loureiro tinto, mencía and susón (red).

VT / I.G.P. BETANZOS

Betanzos, in the province of La Coruña, became the second VT I.G.P.designation to be granted in Galicia. The vineyards is planted with local white varieties like blanco legítimo, Agudelo (godello) and jerez, as well as red grapes like garnacha, mencía and tempranillo.

VT / I.G.P. CÁDIZ

Located in the south of the province of Cádiz, a vast region with a long history of wine production, the "Vinos de la Tierra de Cádiz" comprises 15 municipalities still under the regulations of the DO regarding grape production, but not winemaking. The authorised white varieties are: garrido, palomino, chardonnay, moscatel, mantúa, perruno, macabeo, sauvignon blanc y pedro ximénez; as well as the red tempranillo, syrah, cabernet sauvignon, garnacha tinta, monastrel, merlot, tintilla de rota, petit verdot and cabernet franc.

VT / I.G.P. CAMPO DE CARTAGENA

Campo de Cartagena is a flatland region close to the Mediterranean Sea and surrounded by mountains of a moderate height. The vineyard surface ascribed to the VT I.G.P.is just 8 hectares. The climate is mediterranean bordering on an arid, desert type, with very hot summers, mild temperatures for the rest of the year, and low and occasional rainfall. The main varieties in the region are bonicaire, forcallat tinta, petit verdot, tempranillo, garnacha tintorera, crujidera, merlot, syrah and cabernet sauvignon (red); and chardonnay, malvasía, moravia dulce, moscatel de grano menudo and sauvignon blanc (white).

VT / I.G.P. CASTELLÓ

Located in the eastern part of Spain, on the Mediterranean coast, the geographical indication Vinos de la Tierra de Castelló is divided in two different areas: Alto Palancia –Alto Mijares, Sant Mateu and Les Useres–, and Vilafamés. The climatic conditions in this wine region are good to grow varieties such as tempranillo, monastrell, garnacha, garnacha tintorera, cabernet sauvignon, merlot and syrah (red), along with macabeo and merseguera (white).

VT / I.G.P. CASTILLA Y LEÓN

Another one of the regional 'macro-designations' for the wines produced in up to 317 municipalities within the autonomous region of Castilla y León. A continental climate with little rainfall, together with diverse soil patterns, are the most distinctive features of a region that can be divided into the Duero basin (part of the Spanish central high plateau) and the mountainous perimeter that surrounds it.

VT / I.G.P. CASTILLA

Castilla-La Mancha, a region that has the largest vineyard surface in the planet (600.000 hectares, equivalent to 6% of the world's total vineyard surface, and to half of Spain's) has been using this Vino de la Tierra label since 1999 (the year the status was granted) for wines produced outside its designations of origin. The main grape varieties are airén, albillo, chardonnay, macabeo (viura), malvar, sauvignon blanc, merseguera, moscatel de grano menudo, pardillo (marisancho), Pedro Ximénez and torrontés (white);and bobal, cabernet sauvignon, garnacha tinta, merlot, monastrell, petit verdot, syrah, tempranillo, cencibel (jacivera), coloraíllo, frasco, garnacha tintorera, moravia agria, moravia dulce (crujidera), negral (tinto basto) and tinto velasco (red).

VT / I.G.P. CÓRDOBA

It includes the wines produced in the province of Córdoba, with the exception of those bottled within the DO Montil-la-Moriles label. All in all, we are talking of some 300 hectares and red and rosé wines made from cabernet sauvignon, merlot, syrah, tempranillo, pinot noir and tintilla de Rota grape varieties.

VT / I.G.P. COSTA DE CANTABRIA

Wines produced in the Costa de Cantabria wine region as well as some inland valleys up to an altitude of 600 meters. The grape varieties used for white winemaking are godello, albillo, chardonnay, malvasía, ondarribi zuri, picapoll blanco and verdejo blanco; and just two for red wines: ondarribi beltza and verdejo negro. The region comprises some 8 hectares of vineyards.

VT / I.G.P. CUMBRES DE GUADALFEO

Formerly known as "Vino de la Tierra de Contraviesa-Alpujarra", this geographical indication is used for wines made in the wine region located in the western part of the Alpujarras, in a border territory between two provinces (Granada and Almería), two rivers (Guadalfeo and Andarax), and very close to the Mediterranean Sea. The grape varieties used for white wine production are montúa, chardonnay, sauvignon blanc, moscatel, jaén blanca, Pedro Ximénez, vijirego y perruno; for red wines, they have garnacha tinta, tempranillo, cabernet sauvignon, cabernet franc, merlot, pinot noir and syrah.

VT / I.G.P. DESIERTO DE ALMERÍA

Granted in the summer of 2003, the wine region comprises a diverse territory in the north of the province of Almería that includes the Tabernas Dessert as well as parts of the Sierra de Alhamilla, Sierra de Cabrera and the Cabo de Gata Natural Park. Harsh, climatic desert conditions follow a regular pattern of hot days and cooler nights that influence heavily the character of the resulting wines. The vineyard's average altitude is 525 meters. The varieties planted are chardonnay, moscatel, macabeo and sauvignon blanc (white); as well as tempranillo, cabernet sauvignon, monastrell, merlot, syrah and garnacha tinta (red).www.vinosdealmeria.es/zonas-viticolas/desierto-de-almeria

VT / I.G.P. EIVISSA

The production area includes the entire island of Ibiza (Eivissa), with the vineyards located in small valleys amongst the mountains –which are never higher than 500 meters– on clay-reddish soil covered by a thin limestone crust. Low rainfall levels and hot, humid summers are the most interesting climatic features. The authorized red varieties are monastrell, tempranillo, cabernet sauvignon, merlot and syrah; macabeo, parellada, malvasía, chardonnay and moscatel make up the white-grape catalogue.

VT / I.G.P. EXTREMADURA

It comprises all the municipalities within the provinces of Cáceres and Badajoz, made up of six different wine regions. In December 1990, the regional government approved the regulations submitted by the Comisión Interprofesional de Vinos de la Tierra de Extremadura, and approved its creation. The varieties used for the production of white wines are alarije, borba, cayetana blanca, chardonnay, chelva, malvar, viura, parellada, Pedro Ximénez and verdejo; for red wines, they have bobal, mazuela, monastrell, tempranillo, garnacha, graciano, merlot, syrah and cabernet sauvignon.

VT / I.G.P. FORMENTERA

This geographical indication comprises the wines produced in the island of Formentera. The dry, subtropical mediterranean climate, characterised by abundant sunshine hours and summers with high temperatures and humidity levels but little rainfall, evidently requires grape varieties well adapted to this type of weather. Red varieties are monastrell, fogoneu, tempranillo, cabernet sauvignon and merlot; malvasía, premsal blanco, chardonnay and viognier make up its white-grape catalogue.

VT / I.G.P. GÁLVEZ

Gálvez wine region, located in the province of Toledo, comprises nine municipalities: Cuerva, Gálvez, Guadamur, Menasalvas, Mazambraz, Polán, Pulgar, San Martín de Montalbán and Totanes. The authorized grape varieties are tempranillo and garnacha tinta.

VT / I.G.P. ILLA DE MENORCA

The island of Menorca, a Biosphere Reserve, has a singular topography of gentle slopes; marl soils with a complex substratum of limestone, sandstone and slate, a mediterranean climate and northerly winter winds are the most significant features from a viticultural point of view. The wines produces in the island should be made exclusively from white grape varieties like chardonnay, macabeo, malvasía, moscatel, parellada or moll; as for the red renderings, cabernet sauvignon, merlot, monastrell, tempranillo and syrah get clearly the upper hand.

VT / I.G.P. LADERAS DE GENIL

Formerly known (up to 2009) as VT I.G.P.Granada Suroeste, the label includes some 53 municipalities in the province of Granada. The region enjoys a unique microclimate very suitable for grape growing, given its low rainfall and the softening effect of the Mediterranean Sea. The white grape varieties used for wine production are vijiriego, macabeo, Pedro Ximénez, palomino, moscatel de Alejandría, chardonnay and sauvignon blanc; as well as the red garnacha tinta, perruna, tempranillo, cabernet sauvignon, merlot, syrah and pinot noir, predominantly.

VT / I.G.P. LAUJAR-ALPUJARRA

This wine region is located at an altitude of 800 to 1500 meters between the Sierra de Gádor and the Sierra Nevada Natural Park. It has some 800 hectares of vines grown on terraces. Soils are chalk soils poor in organic matter, rocky and with little depth. The climate is moderately continental, given the sea influence and its high night-day temperature differential. The predominant grape varieties are jaén blanco, macabeo, vijiriego, Pedro Ximénez, chardonay and moscatel de grano menudo (white); and cabernet sauvignon, merlot, monastrell, tempranillo, garnachas tinta and syrah (red). www.vinosdealmeria.es/bodegas/vino-de-la-tierra-laujar-alpujarra

VT / I.G.P. LIÉBANA

VT I.G.P.Liébana includes the municipalities of Potes, Pesagüero, Cabezón de Liébana, Camaleño, Castro Cillorigo y Vega de Liébana, all of them within the area of Liébana, located in the southwest of the Cantabria bordering with Asturias, León and Palencia. The authorized varieties are mencía, tempranillo, garnacha, garciano, merlot, syrah, pinot noir, albarín negro and cabernet sauvignon (red); and palomino, godello, verdejo, albillo, chardonnay and albarín blanco (white).

VT / I.G.P. LOS PALACIOS

Los Palacios is located in the south-western part of the province of Sevilla, by the lower area of the Guadalquivir river valley. The wines included in this VT I.G.P.are white wines made from airén, chardonnay, colombard and sauvignon blanc.

VT / I.G.P. MALLORCA

The production area of VT I.G.P.Mallorca includes all the municipalities within the island, which has predominantly limestone soils with abundant clay and sandstone, and a mediterranean climate with mild temperatures all-year-round. Red varieties present in the island are callet, manto negro, cabernet sauvignon, fogoneu, merlot, monastrell, syrah, tempranillo and pinot noir; along with the white prensal (moll), chardonnay, macabeo, malvasía, moscatel de Alejandría, moscatel de grano menudo, parellada, riesling and sauvignon blanc.

VT / I.G.P. NORTE DE ALMERÍA

The Vinos de la Tierra Norte de Almería label comprises four municipalities in the Norte de Almería area, right in the north of the province. They produce white, red and rosé wines from grape varieties such as airén, chardonnay, macabeo and sauvignon blanc (white); as well as cabernet sauvignon, merlot, monastrell, tempranillo and syrah for red winemaking and tempranillo and monastrell for rosé.

VT / I.G.P. POZOHONDO

The regulations for VT I.G.P.Pozoblanco were approved by the autonomous government of Castilla-La Mancha in the year 2000. It comprises the municipalities of Alcadozo, Peñas de San Pedro and Pozohondo, all of them in the province of Albacete.

VT / I.G.P. RIBERA DEL ANDARAX

The Ribera del Andarax wine region is located in the middle area of the Andarax river valley at an altitude of 700 to 900 meters. Soils are varied in structure, with abundant slate, clay and sand. It enjoys an extreme mediterranean climate, with low occasional rainfall and high average temperatures. The grape varieties present in the region are predominantly macabeo, chardonnay and sauvignon blanc (white); and cabernet sauvignon, merlot, syrah, garnacha, tempranillo, monastrell and pinot noir (red). www.vinosdealmeria.es/zonas-viticolas/ribera-de-andarax

VT / I.G.P. RIBERA DEL GÁLLEGO-CINCO VILLAS

Ribera del Gállego-Cinco Villas wine region is located in the territory along the Gállego river valley until it almost reaches the city of Zaragoza. Although small, its vineyards are shared between the provinces of Huesca and Zaragoza. Soils are mostly gravel in structure, which affords good drainage. The grape varieties used for wine production are garnacha, tempranillo, carbernet sauvignon and merlot (red), and mostly macabeo for white wines. www.vinosdelatierradearagon.es

VT / I.G.P. RIBERA DEL JILOCA

Ribera del Jiloca, located in the south-eastern part of Aragón along the Jiloca river valley, is a wine region with a great winemaking potential, given its geo-climatic conditions. Vines are mostly planted on slate terraces perched on the slopes of the Sistema Ibérico mountain range, at high altitude, something that affords wines of great quality and singularity. Vines are planted mostly on alluvial limestone terraces of ancient river beds. Garnacha is the predominant grape, followed by macabeo. A dry climate, abundant sunlight hours and cold winters are the features that account for the excellent quality of the local grapes.www.vinosdelatierradearagon.es/empresas/ribera_del_jiloca.php

VT / I.G.P. RIBERA DEL QUEILES

Up to sixteen municipalities from two different provinces (seven from Navarra and nine from Zaragoza) are part of the VT I.G.P.Ribera del Queiles. Wines are exclusively red, made from cabernet sauvignon, graciano, garnacha tinta, merlot, tempranillo and syrah. It has a regulating and controlling body (Comité Regulador de Control y Certificación) and so far just one winery. www.vinosdelatierradearagon.es

VT / I.G.P. SERRA DE TRAMUNTANA-COSTA NORD

Currently, this VT I.G.P.comprises 41,14 hectares an up to eighteen municipal districts in the island of Mallorca, between the cape of Formentor and the southwest coast of Andratx, with mainly brownish-grey and limestone soils. Single-variety wines from malvasía, moscatel, moll, parellada, macabeo, chardonnay and sauvignon blanc (white), as well as cabernet sauvignon, merlot, syrah, monastrell, tempranillo, callet and manto negro (red) stand out.

VT / I.G.P. SIERRA DE ALCARAZ

The Sierra del Alcaraz wine region comprises the municipal districts of Alcaraz, El Ballestero, El Bonillo, Povedilla, Robledo, and Viveros, located in the western part of the province of Albacete, bordering with Ciudad Real. The VT I.G.P. status was granted by the autonomous government of Castilla-La Mancha in the year 2000. The red varieties planted in the region are cabernet sauvignon, merlot, bobal, monastrell, garnacha tinta and garnacha tintorera; along with white moravia dulce, chardonnay, chelva, eva, alarije, malvar, borba, parellada, cayetana blanca and Pedro Ximénez.

VT / I.G.P. SIERRA DE LAS ESTANCIAS Y LOS FILABRES

Located in the namesake mountain region in the province of Almería, this VT I.G.P.was approved along with its regulations in 2008. The grape varieties planted in the region are airén, chardonnay, macabeo, sauvignon blanc and moscatel de grano menudo —also known as morisco–, all of them white; and red cabernet sauvignon, merlot, monastrell, tempranillo, syrah, garnacha tinta, pinot noir and petit verdot.

VT / I.G.P. SIERRA DEL NORTE DE SEVILLA

lThis region, located in the north of the province of Sevilla at the foothills of Sierra Morena, has a landscape of gentle hills and altitudes that range from 250 to almost 1000 metres. The climate in the region is mediterranean, with hot, dry summers, mild winters and a fairly high average rainfall. Since 1998, grape varieties such as tempranillo, garnacha tinta, cabernet sauvignon, cabernet franc, merlot, pinot noir, petit verdot and syrah (red); and chardonnay, Pedro Ximénez, colombard, sauvignon blanc, palomino and moscatel de Alejandría (white) have been planted in the region.

VT / I.G.P. SIERRA SUR DE JAÉN

In this VT I.G.P.there are some 400 hectares planted with vines, although a minor percentage are table grapes. The label includes wines made in the Sierra Sur de Jaén wine region. White wines are made from jaén blanca and chardonnay, and red from garnacha tinta, tempranillo, cabernet sauvignon, merlot, syrah and pinot noir.

VT / I.G.P. TORREPEROGIL

This geographical indication in the province of Jaén, whose regulations were approved in 2006, comprises 300 hectares in the area of La Loma, right in the centre of the province. The climate is mediterranean with continental influence, with cold winters and dry and hot summers. The wines are made mainly from garnacha tinta, syrah, cabernet sauvignon and tempranillo (red); and jaén blanco and Pedro Ximénez (white).

VT / I.G.P. VALDEJALÓN

Established in 1998, it comprises 36 municipal districts in the mid- and lower-Jalón river valley. The vines are planted on alluvial, brownish-grey limestone soils, with low annual average rainfall of some 350 mm. They grape varieties planted are white (macabeo, garnacha blanca, moscatel and airén) and red (garnacha, tempranillo, cabernet sauvignon, syrah, monastrell and merlot). www.vinodelatierravaldejalon.com

VT / I.G.P. VALLE DEL CINCA

Located in the southeast of the province of Huesca, almost bordering with Catalunya, Valle del Cinca is a traditional wine region that enjoys favourable climatic and soil conditions for vine growing: soils are mainly limestone and clay, and the average annual rainfall barely reaches 300 mm (irrigation is usually required). Grape varieties predominantly planted in the region are macabeo and chardonnay (white), along with garnacha tinta, tempranillo, cabernet sauvignon and merlot (red). www.vinosdelatierradearagon.es

VT / I.G.P. VALLE DEL MIÑO-OURENSE

This wine region is located in the north of the province of Ourense, along the Miño river valley. The authorized grape varieties are treixadura, torrontés, godello, albariño, loureira and palomino –also known as xerez– for white wines, and mencía, brancellao, mouratón, sousón, caíño and garnacha for reds.

VT / I.G.P. VALLES DE SADACIA

A designation created to include the wines made from the grape variety known as moscatel riojana, which was practically lost with the phylloxera bug and has been recuperated to produce both "vino de licor" and normal white moscatel. Depending on winemaking, the latter may either be dry, semi-dry or sweet. The vineyards that belong to this VT I.G.P.are mainly located in the south-western part of the region, in the Sadacia and Cidacos river valleys, overall a very suitable territory for vine growing purposes.

VT / I.G.P. VILLAVICIOSA DE CÓRDOBA

One of the most recent geographical indications granted by the autonomous government of Andalucía back in 2008, it includes white and sweet wines made in the Villaviciosa wine region. The authorized varieties are baiadí verdejo, moscatel de Alejandría, palomino fino, palomino, Pedro Ximénez, airén, calagraño Jaén, torrontés and verdejo.

VT 3 RIBERAS

BODEGA ABADÍA DE LA OLIVA

Ctra. Caparroso-Carcastillo, Km. 17,5
31310 Carcastillo (Navarra)
☎: +34 948 725 285
Fax: +34 948 725 285
www.bodegaabadiadelaoliva.com
export@abadiadelaoliva.com

Abadía de la Oliva 2011 T Roble
merlot, cabernet sauvignon, tempranillo
85

Abadía de la Oliva Cosecha Magna 2010 TC
tempranillo, cabernet sauvignon, merlot
88
Colour: bright cherry. Nose: ripe fruit, sweet spices, creamy oak, balsamic herbs. Palate: fruity, flavourful, toasty.

Abadía de la Oliva Garnacha Blanca 2013 B
garnacha blanca
84

Abadía de la Oliva Lacrima Rosa 2013 RD
garnacha
84

Abadía de la Oliva Oak Chardonnay 2012 BC
chardonnay
83

Abadía de la Oliva Tempranillo 2012 T
tempranillo
87
Colour: cherry, garnet rim. Nose: ripe fruit, wild herbs, spicy. Palate: flavourful, ripe fruit, balsamic.

Alma de Abadía de la Oliva Naturalmente Dulce 2012 Moscatel
moscatel grano menudo
88
Colour: bright yellow. Nose: candied fruit, citrus fruit, honeyed notes, sweet spices. Palate: powerful, rich, flavourful, spicy, long, balanced.

Vinum Misae Vino de Licor s/c
garnacha
86
Colour: coppery red. Nose: powerfull, complex, dry nuts, toasty, acetaldehyde. Palate: rich, fine bitter notes, long, spicy.

BODEGA SAN MARTÍN S. COOP.

Ctra. de Sanguesa, s/n
31495 San Martín de Unx (Navarra)
☎: +34 948 738 294
Fax: +34 948 738 297
www.bodegasanmartin.com
enologia@bodegasanmartin.com

Flor de Unx 2013 RD
garnacha
86
Colour: light cherry, bright. Nose: faded flowers, candied fruit. Palate: flavourful, sweetness, easy to drink, ripe fruit.

VT ALTIPLANO DE SIERRA NEVADA

BODEGA VERTIJANA

Paseo de Sierra Nevada, 18
18516 Policar (Granada)
☎: +34 605 074 459
vertijana@vertijana.com

Gentis 2013 T
syrah, garnacha, tempranillo
88
Colour: cherry, purple rim. Nose: red berry notes, raspberry, floral, expressive. Palate: fresh, fruity, flavourful, easy to drink.

BODEGAS MUÑANA

Ctra. Graena a La Peza, Finca Peñas Prietas
18003 Granada (Granada)
☎: +34 958 670 715
Fax: +34 958 670 715
www.bodegasmunana.com
bodegasmunana@gmail.com

Delirio 2013 RD
cabernet sauvignon, tempranillo, syrah
85

Delirio 2013 T
syrah
88
Colour: bright cherry, purple rim. Nose: violets, fruit expression, expressive, varietal. Palate: correct, good acidity, easy to drink.

Muñana 3 Cepas 2010 T
syrah, cabernet sauvignon, merlot, petit verdot
89
Colour: cherry, garnet rim. Nose: ripe fruit, wild herbs, spicy, creamy oak. Palate: balanced, flavourful, long, balsamic.

Muñana Rojo 2010 T
tempranillo, cabernet sauvignon, monastrell

90

Colour: dark-red cherry, garnet rim. Nose: cocoa bean, ripe fruit, fruit preserve, scrubland. Palate: balanced, round tannins.

VT BAJO ARAGÓN

AMPRIUS LAGAR
Los Enebros, 74 – 2ª planta
44002 Teruel (Teruel)
☎: +34 978 623 077
www.ampriuslagar.es
pedrocasas@ampriuslagar.es

Lagar d'Amprius Garnacha 2011 T
100% garnacha

88

Colour: cherry, garnet rim. Nose: fruit preserve, scrubland, sweet spices, mineral. Palate: powerful, flavourful, long.

Lagar d'Amprius Syrah Garnacha 2010 T

86

Colour: cherry, garnet rim. Nose: fruit preserve, spicy, wild herbs. Palate: balsamic, powerful, ripe fruit.

BODEGA COOP. NTRA. SRA. DEL OLIVAR
Avda. José Antonio, 18
50131 Lecera (Zaragoza)
☎: +34 976 835 016
www.bodegacooperativadelecera.es
admin@bodegacooperativadelecera.es

Valssira 2010 T
garnacha

85

Valssira 2011 T
garnacha

86

Colour: dark-red cherry, garnet rim. Nose: powerfull, fruit preserve, cocoa bean, sweet spices. Palate: good structure, long, pruney.

Valssira 2013 T Fermentado en Barrica
garnacha

86

Colour: bright cherry, purple rim. Nose: toasty, red berry notes, ripe fruit, powerfull. Palate: correct, balanced, fruity aftestaste.

BODEGAS BRECA
Ctra. Monasterio de Piedra, s/n
50219 Munébrega (Zaragoza)
☎: +34 976 895 071
Fax: +34 976 895 171
www.grupojorgeordonez.com
breca@jorgeordonez.es

Garnacha de Fuego 2013 T
100% garnacha

88

Colour: cherry, garnet rim. Nose: ripe fruit, wild herbs, earthy notes. Palate: balanced, flavourful, long, balsamic.

BODEGAS CRIAL LLEDÓ
Arrabal de la Fuente, 23
44624 Lledó (Teruel)
☎: +34 978 891 909
Fax: +34 978 891 995
www.crial.es
crial@bodegascrial.com

Crial 2013 B

85

Crial 2013 RD
garnacha

85

Crial 2013 T

84

Crial Lledó 2009 TC

85

BODEGAS SIERRA DE GUARA
Fray Luis Urbano, 27
50002 Lascellas (Zaragoza)
☎: +34 976 461 056
Fax: +34 976 461 558
www.bodegassierradeguara.es
idrias@bodegassierradeguara.es

Evohé Garnacha Blanca 2013 B
100% garnacha blanca

87

Colour: bright straw. Nose: white flowers, fresh fruit, expressive, fine lees, dried herbs. Palate: flavourful, fruity, good acidity, balanced.

Evohé Garnacha Viñas Viejas 2013 T
100% garnacha

89

Colour: cherry, purple rim. Nose: red berry notes, ripe fruit, wild herbs, spicy. Palate: flavourful, fruity, balsamic, correct.

CELLER D'ALGARS

Cooperativa, 9
44622 Arenys De Lledó (Teruel)
☎: +34 699 145 906
Fax: +34 978 853 147
www.enigmma.es
info@cellerdalgars.com

Dogma 2009 T
garnacha, syrah, cabernet sauvignon
85

Musas 2013 B
garnacha blanca, macabeo, chenin blanc
87
Colour: bright golden. Nose: wild herbs, ripe fruit, floral, spicy. Palate: balanced, powerful, flavourful.

Plans d'Algars 2013 BFB
chenin blanc, garnacha blanca, macabeo
88
Colour: bright yellow. Nose: powerfull, ripe fruit, sweet spices, creamy oak, fragrant herbs. Palate: rich, flavourful, fresh, good acidity.

COOPERATIVA DEL CAMPO SAN PEDRO

Avda. Reino de Aragón, 10
44623 Cretas (Teruel)
☎: +34 978 850 309
Fax: +34 978 850 309
www.cooperativasanpedro.es
info@cooperativasanpedro.es

Belví 2011 T
78

Belví 2013 B
100% garnacha blanca
82

Belví 2013 RD
100% garnacha peluda
85

Emperle 2013 B
84

Emperle 2013 T
70

COOPERATIVA SAN LORENZO MAELLA

Avda. de Aragón 110
50710 Maella (Zaragoza)
☎: +34 976 638 004
Fax: +34 976 639 215
www.magalia.org
admon@magalia.org

Magalia 2013 B
84

Magalia 2013 T Roble
100% garnacha
86
Colour: bright cherry. Nose: ripe fruit, sweet spices, creamy oak. Palate: flavourful, fruity, toasty, round tannins, long.

Magalia Selección 2012 T
89
Colour: cherry, garnet rim. Nose: ripe fruit, wild herbs, spicy, creamy oak, mineral. Palate: balanced, flavourful, long, balsamic.

DOMINIO MAESTRAZGO

Royal III, B12
44550 Alcorisa (Teruel)
☎: +34 978 840 642
Fax: +34 978 840 642
www.dominiomaestrazgo.com
bodega@dominiomaestrazgo.com

Dominio Maestrazgo 2011 T Roble
garnacha, tempranillo, syrah
89
Colour: ruby red. Nose: spicy, fine reductive notes, aged wood nuances, toasty, wild herbs. Palate: spicy, long, toasty, correct.

Dominio Maestrazgo Garnacha Blanca 2012 B
garnacha blanca
86
Colour: bright straw. Nose: ripe fruit, balsamic herbs, dried flowers, dried herbs. Palate: powerful, flavourful, long.

Dominio Maestrazgo Syrah 2011 T Barrica
syrah
89
Colour: bright cherry. Nose: sweet spices, creamy oak, ripe fruit, mineral. Palate: flavourful, toasty, spicy, balanced.

Rex Deus 2010 T Roble
garnacha, syrah
92
Colour: cherry, garnet rim. Nose: ripe fruit, spicy, creamy oak, toasty, complex, earthy notes. Palate: powerful, flavourful, toasty, round tannins, balanced, elegant.

Santolea 2012 T
garnacha, tempranillo
86
Colour: cherry, garnet rim. Nose: fruit preserve, fruit liqueur notes, balsamic herbs, dry stone, creamy oak. Palate: powerful, flavourful, correct.

MAS DE TORUBIO

Plaza del Carmen, 4
44623 Cretas (Teruel)
☎: +34 669 214 845
www.masdetorubio.com
masdetorubio@hotmail.com

Xado 2012 T Roble
garnacha, cabernet sauvignon
85

Xado Blanco sobre Lías 2013 B
100% garnacha blanca
86

Colour: bright straw. Nose: white flowers, fruit expression, fragrant herbs, fine lees, citrus fruit. Palate: fresh, balsamic, spicy, easy to drink.

VT CÁDIZ

BODEGAS BARBADILLO

Luis de Eguilaz, 11
11540 Sanlúcar de Barrameda (Cádiz)
☎: +34 956 385 500
Fax: +34 956 385 501
www.barbadillo.com
barbadillo@barbadillo.com

Castillo de San Diego 2013 B
palomino
84

Gibalbín 2011 TC
tempranillo, merlot, petit verdot
87

Colour: cherry, garnet rim. Nose: ripe fruit, wild herbs, spicy, creamy oak. Palate: balanced, flavourful, long, balsamic.

Gibalbín 2013 T
tempranillo, syrah, cabernet sauvignon, tintilla
85

Gibalbín 8 meses 2011 T
merlot, tempranillo, petit verdot
86

Colour: bright cherry. Nose: ripe fruit, sweet spices, creamy oak, wild herbs. Palate: flavourful, fruity, toasty.

Maestrante 2013 B
palomino
83

CORTIJO DE JARA

Medina, 79
11402 Jerez de la Frontera (Cádiz)
☎: +34 679 488 992
Fax: +34 956 338 163
www.cortijodejara.com
puertanueva.sl@cortijodejara.es

Cortijo de Jara 12 meses 2012 T
syrah, merlot, tempranillo
84

Cortijo de Jara 6 meses 2012 T
tempranillo, merlot, syrah
85

FINCA MONCLOA

Manuel María González, 12
11403 Jerez de la Frontera (Cádiz)
☎: +34 956 357 000
Fax: +34 956 357 043
www.gonzalezbyass.com
nacional@gonzalezbyass.com

Finca Moncloa 10 Barricas 2011 T
92

Colour: cherry, garnet rim. Nose: powerfull, ripe fruit, balsamic herbs, spicy. Palate: powerful, flavourful, long.

Finca Moncloa 2011 T
91

Colour: bright cherry. Nose: ripe fruit, sweet spices, creamy oak, medium intensity. Palate: fruity, flavourful, toasty, balanced.

Tintilla de Rota de Finca Moncloa 2011 T
tintilla de rota
92

Colour: cherry, garnet rim. Nose: fruit preserve, ripe fruit, spicy, toasty, aged wood nuances, acetaldehyde, warm. Palate: powerful, flavourful, sweetness.

MIGUEL DOMECQ

Finca Torrecera, Ctra. Jerez - La Ina, Km. 14,5
11595 Torrecera (Cádiz)
☎: +34 856 030 033
Fax: +34 856 030 033
www.migueldomecq.com
comercial@migueldomecq.com

Alhocen Syrah Merlot 2010 TR
syrah, merlot
89

Colour: cherry, garnet rim. Nose: balanced, complex, ripe fruit, spicy, earthy notes. Palate: good structure, flavourful, correct.

Entrechuelos 2012 T Roble
cabernet sauvignon, syrah, merlot, tempranillo
84

Entrechuelos Chardonnay 2013 B
100% chardonnay
87
Colour: straw, greenish rim. Nose: balanced, ripe fruit, dried flowers. Palate: easy to drink, flavourful, fine bitter notes.

Entrechuelos Premium 2010 T
cabernet sauvignon, merlot, syrah, tempranillo
90
Colour: cherry, garnet rim. Nose: ripe fruit, spicy, creamy oak, toasty, complex, earthy notes. Palate: powerful, flavourful, toasty, round tannins.

Entrechuelos Tercer Año 2011 T
cabernet sauvignon, merlot, syrah, tempranillo
86
Colour: bright cherry. Nose: ripe fruit, sweet spices, creamy oak, medium intensity. Palate: fruity, flavourful, toasty.

VT CAMPO DE CARTAGENA

BODEGAS SERRANO
Finca La Cabaña, 30 Pozo Estrecho
30594 Cartagena (Murcia)
☎: +34 659 280 231
Fax: +34 968 556 298
www.bodegasserrano.es
info@bodegasserrano.es

Darimus 2011 T Barrica
cabernet sauvignon
84

Darimus Syrah Dulce 2013 T
syrah
88
Colour: cherry, purple rim. Nose: ripe fruit, dried fruit, wild herbs, floral, sweet spices, toasty. Palate: powerful, flavourful, sweet, fruity, balanced.

Galtea ESP
malvasía, moscatel, chardonnay
83

Viña Galtea Moscatel Semiseco 2013 B
moscatel
86
Colour: bright straw. Nose: white flowers, fragrant herbs, honeyed notes. Palate: fresh, fruity, flavourful, ripe fruit.

VT CASTELLÓN

BODEGA LES USERES
Ctra. Vall d'AlbaLes - Les Useres, Km. 11
12118 Les Useres (Castellón)
☎: +34 964 388 525
Fax: +34 964 388 526
www.bodegalesuseres.com
info@bodegalesuseres.es

33 Route 2012 T
tempranillo, bonicaire
85

33 Route 2013 B
macabeo, chardonnay
83

33 Route 2013 RD
bonicaire, garnacha
84

86 Winegrowers 2009 TR
tempranillo, cabernet sauvignon
84

L'Alcalatén 2012 T
tempranillo
86
Colour: bright cherry. Nose: ripe fruit, sweet spices, creamy oak. Palate: flavourful, fruity, toasty, balanced.

BODEGA MAS DE RANDER
Trinquete, 3 Bajo
12560 Benicassim (Castellón)
☎: +34 964 302 416
www.masderander.com
masderander@masderander.com

Syrah Mas de Rander 2012 T
100% syrah
88
Colour: cherry, garnet rim. Nose: ripe fruit, wild herbs, earthy notes, spicy. Palate: balanced, flavourful, long, balsamic.

Temps Mas de Rander 2010 T
cabernet sauvignon, merlot, syrah
80

BODEGA VICENTE FLORS

Pda. Pou D'en Calvo, s/n
12118 Les Useres (Castellón)
☎: +34 671 618 851
www.bodegaflors.com
bodega@bodegaflors.com

Clotàs Monastrell 2011 T
monastrell
87
Colour: very deep cherry, garnet rim. Nose: powerfull, expressive, ripe fruit, fruit preserve, violet drops, spicy. Palate: good structure, flavourful.

Flor de Clotàs 2011 T
tempranillo
88
Colour: cherry, garnet rim. Nose: ripe fruit, wild herbs, spicy, mineral. Palate: powerful, flavourful, spicy, fine tannins.

Flor de Taronger 2013 RD
80

BODEGAS Y VIÑEDOS BARÓN D'ALBA

Partida Vilar La Call, 10
12118 Les Useres (Castellón)
☎: +34 608 032 884
Fax: +34 964 313 455
www.barondalba.com
barondalba@gmail.com

Clos D' Esgarracordes 2013 RD
merlot, garnacha, monastrell
80

Clos D'Esgarracordes 2011 T Barrica
monastrell, garnacha, tempranillo, cabernet sauvignon
90
Colour: cherry, garnet rim. Nose: ripe fruit, wild herbs, earthy notes, spicy, creamy oak. Palate: balanced, flavourful, long, balsamic.

Clos D'Esgarracordes 2013 B
macabeo, viognier
86
Colour: bright straw. Nose: dried flowers, dried herbs, balanced. Palate: fruity, spicy.

Llevant by Clos D' Esgarracordes 2013 B
macabeo, moscatel, viognier
87
Colour: bright straw. Nose: faded flowers, dried herbs, earthy notes. Palate: flavourful, rich, spicy, long.

DI VINOS & VIÑAS

General Calvo Lucía, 5
12400 Segorbe (Castellón)
☎: +34 629 282 758
www.dibodegas.com
info@dibodegas.com

Diversiones 2009 T
89
Colour: ruby red. Nose: balanced, complex, ripe fruit, spicy, fine reductive notes. Palate: good structure, flavourful, round tannins, balanced.

La Perdición Selección 2011 T
ull de llebre, merlot, bonicaire
88
Colour: cherry, garnet rim. Nose: ripe fruit, spicy, creamy oak, toasty, complex. Palate: powerful, flavourful, toasty, round tannins.

Odisea 2012 T Roble
ull de llebre, bonicaire, merlot, cabernet sauvignon
84

ALENUR

Paseo de la Libertad 6 1º A
02001 Albacete (Albacete)
☎: +34 967 242 982
www.alenur.com
info@alenur.com

Alenur 2012
100% tempranillo
80

Alenur Tempranillo 2011 T
100% tempranillo
84

VT CASTILLA

ALTOLANDÓN

Ctra. N-330, km. 242
16330 Landete (Cuenca)
☎: +34 677 228 974
Fax: +34 962 300 662
www.altolandon.com
altolandon@altolandon.com

L´Ame Malbec 2010 T
100% malbec
89
Colour: very deep cherry, garnet rim. Nose: powerfull, ripe fruit, roasted coffee, dark chocolate. Palate: powerful, toasty, roasted-coffee aftertaste.

BODEGA DEHESA DE LUNA

Ctra. CM-3106, km. 16
2630 La Roda (Albacete)
☎: +34 967 442 434
www.dehesadeluna.com
contacto@dehesadeluna.com

Dehesa de Luna 2012 T
tempranillo, syrah, cabernet sauvignon

89

Colour: cherry, garnet rim. Nose: red berry notes, ripe fruit, scrubland, spicy, creamy oak. Palate: powerful, flavourful, toasty.

Dehesa de Luna Selección Tempranillo 2012 T
tempranillo

90

Colour: cherry, garnet rim. Nose: ripe fruit, wild herbs, spicy, creamy oak. Palate: powerful, flavourful, spicy, long, balsamic.

Luna Lunera Tempranillo 2013 T
tempranillo

86

Colour: cherry, purple rim. Nose: fresh fruit, red berry notes, floral, wild herbs. Palate: flavourful, fruity, good acidity.

BODEGA GARCÍA DE LA ROSA (AGROCONGOSTO S.L.)

Podadores, 12 Pol. La Carbonera,
45350 Noblejas (Toledo)
☎: +34 616 124 947
Fax: +34 925 140 605
www.bodegagarciadelarosa.es
carlosgarciarosa@bodegagarciadelarosa.es

Castillo Palomares 2013 B
airén

75

Nóbriga 2010 T
tempranillo, syrah

87

Colour: cherry, garnet rim. Nose: ripe fruit, spicy, creamy oak, toasty, fine reductive notes. Palate: powerful, flavourful, toasty.

BODEGA HACIENDA LA PRINCESA

Ctra. San Carlos del Valle, km. 8
13300 Valdepeñas (Ciudad Real)
☎: +34 655 665 050
www.haciendalaprincesa.com
haciendalaprincesa@telefonica.net

Hacienda La Princesa Chardonnay 2013 B
100% chardonnay

83 ✿

Hacienda La Princesa Debir Sucunza 2010 TC
tempranillo, merlot

85

Hacienda La Princesa Gala 2010 T
tempranillo

89

Colour: cherry, garnet rim. Nose: ripe fruit, spicy, creamy oak, toasty. Palate: powerful, flavourful, toasty, round tannins.

BODEGA LOS ALJIBES

Finca Los Aljibes
2520 Chinchilla de Montearagón (Albacete)
☎: +34 967 260 015
Fax: +34 967 261 450
www.fincalosaljibes.com
info@fincalosaljibes.com

Aljibes 2010 T
cabernet franc, merlot, cabernet sauvignon

89

Colour: cherry, garnet rim. Nose: ripe fruit, spicy, creamy oak, toasty, complex. Palate: powerful, flavourful, toasty, round tannins.

Aljibes Cabernet Franc 2011 T
cabernet franc
89
Colour: cherry, garnet rim. Nose: red berry notes, ripe fruit, balsamic herbs, dry stone, creamy oak. Palate: spicy, long, balanced, elegant.

Aljibes Petit Verdot 2011 T
petit verdot
89
Colour: cherry, garnet rim. Nose: ripe fruit, dry stone, dark chocolate, cocoa bean, toasty. Palate: powerful, flavourful, balsamic, long, balanced.

Aljibes Syrah 2010 T
syrah
88
Colour: cherry, garnet rim. Nose: ripe fruit, floral, wild herbs, roasted coffee. Palate: powerful, flavourful, roasted-coffee aftertaste.

La Galana Garnacha Tintorera 2012 TC
garnacha tintorera
88
Colour: cherry, garnet rim. Nose: red berry notes, ripe fruit, mineral, fragrant herbs, spicy. Palate: powerful, flavourful, balanced, elegant.

Selectus 2010 T
syrah, cabernet franc, cabernet sauvignon, merlot
90
Colour: cherry, garnet rim. Nose: ripe fruit, spicy, creamy oak, toasty, dark chocolate, earthy notes. Palate: powerful, flavourful, toasty, round tannins, balanced, elegant.

Viña Aljibes 2011 T
cabernet sauvignon, merlot, petit verdot, garnacha tintorera
86
Colour: very deep cherry, garnet rim. Nose: powerfull, ripe fruit, roasted coffee. Palate: powerful, toasty, roasted-coffee aftertaste.

Viña Aljibes 2013 B
sauvignon blanc, chardonnay
88
Colour: bright straw. Nose: complex, citrus fruit, wild herbs, floral, expressive. Palate: fresh, fruity, easy to drink.

Viña Aljibes 2013 RD
syrah
88
Colour: rose, purple rim. Nose: powerfull, ripe fruit, red berry notes, floral, expressive. Palate: powerful, fruity, fresh.

Viña Galana Garnacha Tintorera 2012 T
garnacha tintorera
87
Colour: cherry, garnet rim. Nose: ripe fruit, spicy, creamy oak, toasty. Palate: powerful, flavourful, toasty.

Viña Galana Verdejo 2013 B
verdejo
85

BODEGA TRENZA
Avda. Matías Saenz Tejada, s/n.
Edif. Fuengirola Center - Local 1
29640 Fuengirola (Málaga)
☎: +34 615 343 320
Fax: +34 952 588 467
www.trenzawines.com
info@bodegatrenza.com

Sedosa Tempranillo Syrah 2013 T
tempranillo, syrah
84

Sedosa Verdejo Sauvignon Blanc 2013 B
84

BODEGA Y VIÑEDOS FAMILIA CONESA
Ctra. Pozo Aledo, km. 4 Nº 1
30739 Torre Pacheco (Murcia)
☎: +34 967 370 750
Fax: +34 967 370 751
bodega@familiaconesa.com

Finca La Sabina Tempranillo 2011 T
tempranillo
85

BODEGAS ANHELO
Jabalón, 14
13350 Moral de Calatrava
(Ciudad Real)
☎: +34 626 929 262
www.bodegasanhelo.com
j.sanchez@bodegasanhelo.com

Campo Anhelo Riesling 2013 B
100% riesling
87
Colour: bright straw. Nose: fresh, fresh fruit, white flowers, citrus fruit. Palate: flavourful, fruity, good acidity, balanced.

Campo Anhelo Tempranillo 2012 T Roble
100% tempranillo
85

BODEGAS ARÚSPIDE
Ciriaco Cruz, 2
13300 Valdepeñas (Ciudad Real)
☎: +34 926 347 075
Fax: +34 926 347 875
www.aruspide.com
export@aruspide.com

Ágora 2013 T Maceración Carbónica
100% tempranillo
85

Ágora Ciento 69 2013 RD
malbec
85

Ágora Lágrima 2013 B
airén, verdejo
83

Ágora S/C T Roble
tempranillo
86
Colour: cherry, purple rim. Nose: toasty, sweet spices. Palate: fruity, spicy, correct, easy to drink.

Ágora Viognier 2013 B
100% viognier
85

Ardales 2011 T
tempranillo
86
Colour: cherry, garnet rim. Nose: powerfull, fruit preserve, sweet spices, creamy oak. Palate: correct, round tannins.

Ardales 2013 B
airén
87
Colour: bright straw. Nose: fragrant herbs, fresh, expressive, tropical fruit. Palate: fruity, flavourful, good acidity.

Autor de Arúspide Chardonnay 2012 B
chardonnay
86
Colour: bright yellow. Nose: tropical fruit, floral, expressive. Palate: correct, spicy, ripe fruit.

Autor de Arúspide Tempranillo 2008 T
tempranillo
87
Colour: dark-red cherry, garnet rim. Nose: fruit preserve, cocoa bean, tobacco. Palate: balanced, spicy, toasty, round tannins, balsamic.

El Linze 2010 B
100% viognier
88
Colour: bright straw. Nose: ripe fruit, tropical fruit, balsamic herbs, floral, spicy, fragrant herbs. Palate: fresh, fruity, flavourful, correct.

El Linze 2011 T
87
Colour: dark-red cherry, garnet rim. Nose: powerfull, fruit preserve, wild herbs. Palate: balanced, long, round tannins.

Pura Savia 2012 T
tempranillo
86
Colour: dark-red cherry, garnet rim. Nose: scrubland, ripe fruit, spicy. Palate: flavourful, correct, round tannins.

BODEGAS BALMORAL
Mayor, 32 - 1º
02001 (Albacete)
☎: +34 967 508 382
Fax: +34 967 235 301
www.vinedosbalmoral.com
info@vinedosbalmoral.com

Edoné Cuvée de María 2011 ESP
100% chardonnay
84

Edoné Gran Cuvée 2010 ESP Gran Reserva
85

Edoné Rosé 2010 ESP
85

Maravides 2011 T
tempranillo, syrah, merlot, cabernet sauvignon
90
Colour: cherry, garnet rim. Nose: ripe fruit, spicy, creamy oak, toasty, complex. Palate: powerful, flavourful, toasty, round tannins, balanced, elegant.

Maravides Chardonnay 2012 B
87
Colour: bright straw. Nose: white flowers, fragrant herbs, fruit expression, ripe fruit. Palate: fresh, fruity, flavourful, powerful.

Maravides Mediterraneo 2012 T
89
Colour: very deep cherry, garnet rim. Nose: powerfull, ripe fruit, creamy oak, balsamic herbs. Palate: powerful, toasty.

Maravides Syrah 2012 T
100% syrah
88
Colour: cherry, garnet rim. Nose: ripe fruit, spicy, creamy oak, toasty, complex, dark chocolate, earthy notes. Palate: powerful, flavourful, toasty, round tannins.

BODEGAS BARREDA

Ramalazo, 2
45880 Corral de Almaguer (Toledo)
☎: +34 915 435 387
Fax: +34 915 435 387
www.bodegas-barreda.com
nacional@bodegas-barreda.com

Torre de Barreda Amigos 2010 T
tempranillo, syrah, cabernet sauvignon

89

Colour: cherry, garnet rim. Nose: powerfull, fruit preserve, balsamic herbs, creamy oak, balanced. Palate: powerful, flavourful, spicy.

Torre de Barreda Cabernet Sauvignon 2013 T
cabernet sauvignon

88

Colour: cherry, garnet rim. Nose: ripe fruit, wild herbs, balsamic herbs. Palate: powerful, flavourful, long, spicy.

Torre de Barreda PañoFino 2010 T
tempranillo

91

Colour: cherry, garnet rim. Nose: red berry notes, ripe fruit, spicy, creamy oak, toasty, complex, mineral. Palate: powerful, flavourful, toasty, round tannins, balanced, elegant.

Torre de Barreda Syrah 2012 T
syrah

89

Colour: cherry, garnet rim. Nose: red berry notes, ripe fruit, floral, fragrant herbs. Palate: powerful, flavourful, correct.

Torre de Barreda Tempranillo 2011 T
tempranillo

86

Colour: cherry, garnet rim. Nose: powerfull, ripe fruit, sweet spices. Palate: flavourful, spicy, long.

BODEGAS CORONADO

Ctra. San Isidro, s/n
16620 La Alberca de Záncara (Cuenca)
☎: +34 676 463 483
www.bodegascoronado.com
informacion@bodegascoronado.com

Charcón 2013 T
100% cencibel

82

Charcón Sauvignon Blanc 2013 B
100% sauvignon blanc

85

Viña Charcón 2011 TC
merlot, petit verdot, syrah
85

Viña Charcón Selección 2011 T Roble
86
Colour: bright cherry. Nose: ripe fruit, sweet spices, creamy oak. Palate: flavourful, fruity, toasty.

Viña Charcón Syrah 2013 T Roble
syrah
85

BODEGAS CRIN ROJA
Paraje Mainetes
02651 Fuenteálamo (Albacete)
☎: +34 938 743 511
Fax: +34 938 737 204
www.crinroja.es
info@crinroja.es

Crin Roja Cabernet Sauvignon Syrah 2013 T
85

Crin Roja Macabeo 2013 B
100% macabeo
84

Crin Roja Tempranillo 2013 T
100% tempranillo
84

Las Corazas 2013 RD
84

Las Corazas Macabeo 2013 B
100% macabeo
84

Las Corazas Tempranillo 2013 T Roble
100% tempranillo
85

Montal Macabeo Airen 2013 B
86
Colour: bright straw. Nose: fruit expression, citrus fruit, floral, dried herbs. Palate: fresh, fruity, easy to drink.

Montal Monastrell-Syrah 2010 T
monastrell, syrah
88
Colour: bright cherry, brick rim edge. Nose: ripe fruit, sweet spices, creamy oak, cocoa bean. Palate: fruity, flavourful, toasty, balanced, round tannins.

BODEGAS D4
Camino Matallana, s/n
16211 El Picazo (Cuenca)
☎: +34 639 345 940
www.bodegasd4.com
valsavi@hotmail.es

D4 2012 TC
tempranillo, petit verdot, bobal, cabernet sauvignon
89
Colour: bright cherry, garnet rim. Nose: ripe fruit, sweet spices, creamy oak, balsamic herbs. Palate: fruity, flavourful, toasty.

BODEGAS DEL MUNI
Victor Andrés Belaunde, 2 4ºC
28016 Madrid (Madrid)
☎: +34 925 152 511
Fax: +34 925 152 511
www.bodegasdelmuni.com
info@bodegasdelmuni.com

Corpus del Muni 2012 T Roble
tempranillo, syrah, garnacha, petit verdot
88
Colour: bright cherry. Nose: ripe fruit, sweet spices, creamy oak, expressive. Palate: flavourful, fruity, toasty, round tannins, balanced.

Corpus del Muni Blanca Selección 2013 B
chardonnay, sauvignon blanc, verdejo
86
Colour: bright straw. Nose: fragrant herbs, citrus fruit, candied fruit, floral. Palate: fresh, fruity, flavourful.

Corpus del Muni Lucía Selección 2007 TC
tempranillo
89
Colour: cherry, garnet rim. Nose: balanced, complex, ripe fruit, spicy, toasty. Palate: good structure, flavourful, spicy, long.

Corpus del Muni Selección Especial 2009 T
tempranillo
90
Colour: bright cherry. Nose: ripe fruit, sweet spices, creamy oak, expressive. Palate: flavourful, fruity, round tannins.

Corpus del Muni Vendimia Seleccionada 2013 T Joven
tempranillo
88
Colour: cherry, purple rim. Nose: red berry notes, ripe fruit, balsamic herbs. Palate: powerful, flavourful, easy to drink, balanced.

BODEGAS EGUREN

Avda. del Cantábrico, s/n
1012 Vitoria (Álava)
☎: +34 945 282 844
Fax: +34 945 271 319
www.egurenugarte.com
info@egurenugarte.com

Condado de Eguren Tempranillo 2012 T
100% tempranillo
86
Colour: ruby red. Nose: spicy, fine reductive notes, toasty, balsamic herbs. Palate: spicy, long, toasty.

Kame 2009 T
88
Colour: bright cherry. Nose: ripe fruit, sweet spices, creamy oak, balsamic herbs. Palate: fruity, flavourful, toasty, balanced.

Kame 2013 B
100% verdejo
88
Colour: bright straw. Nose: floral, fragrant herbs, white flowers, expressive. Palate: powerful, flavourful, fruity.

Kame Muscat 2013 B
100% moscatel
85

Mercedes Eguren Cabernet Sauvignon 2012 T
100% cabernet sauvignon
86
Colour: bright cherry. Nose: ripe fruit, sweet spices, creamy oak, balsamic herbs. Palate: flavourful, fruity, toasty.

Mercedes Eguren Cabernet Sauvignon 2013 RD
cabernet sauvignon
84

Mercedes Eguren Sauvignon Blanc 2013 B
sauvignon blanc
87
Colour: bright straw. Nose: fresh, fresh fruit, white flowers, fragrant herbs. Palate: flavourful, fruity, good acidity, easy to drink.

Mercedes Eguren Shiraz Tempranillo 2012 T
87
Colour: very deep cherry, garnet rim. Nose: powerfull, ripe fruit, roasted coffee. Palate: powerful, toasty, flavourful.

Pazos de Eguren Tempranillo 2013 T
100% tempranillo
85

Reinares 2013 B
100% viura
84

Reinares 2013 RD
100% tempranillo
82

Reinares Tempranillo 2013 T
100% tempranillo
82

BODEGAS FINCA LA ESTACADA

Ctra. N-400, Km. 103
16400 Tarancón (Cuenca)
☎: +34 969 327 099
Fax: +34 969 327 199
www.fincalaestacada.com
enologia@fincalaestacada.com

Secua Cabernet-Syrah 2010 T
cabernet sauvignon, syrah
88
Colour: cherry, garnet rim. Nose: ripe fruit, spicy, creamy oak, toasty, balsamic herbs. Palate: powerful, flavourful, toasty, balsamic, spicy, correct.

BODEGAS HERMANOS TORRES DE MADRIGUERAS

Pablo Picasso, 63
2230 Madrigueras (Albacete)
☎: +34 967 484 428
Fax: +34 967 485 416
www.furorwines.com
export@furorwines.com

Furor Tempranillo Syrah 2013 T
tempranillo, syrah
88
Colour: cherry, purple rim. Nose: expressive, fresh fruit, red berry notes, floral. Palate: flavourful, fruity, good acidity.

BODEGAS MAS QUE VINOS

Camino de los Molinos, s/n
45312 Cabañas de Yepes (Toledo)
☎: +34 925 122 281
Fax: +34 925 137 003
www.bodegasercavio.com
masquevinos@fer.es

El Señorito 2010 T
100% tempranillo
92
Colour: cherry, garnet rim. Nose: red berry notes, ripe fruit, expressive, balsamic herbs, creamy oak, balanced. Palate: powerful, flavourful, spicy, long.

Ercavio 2013 B
airén

87

Colour: bright straw. Nose: white flowers, fragrant herbs, fruit expression. Palate: fresh, fruity, flavourful.

Ercavio 2013 RD
tempranillo

89

Colour: onion pink. Nose: elegant, candied fruit, dried flowers, fragrant herbs, red berry notes. Palate: light-bodied, flavourful, good acidity, long, spicy, balanced.

Ercavio 31 Noviembre 2013
T Maceración Carbónica
tempranillo, garnacha

90

Colour: cherry, purple rim. Nose: expressive, fresh fruit, red berry notes, floral. Palate: flavourful, fruity, good acidity, fine bitter notes.

Ercavio Tempranillo 2012 T Roble
tempranillo

88

Colour: bright cherry. Nose: ripe fruit, sweet spices, creamy oak, expressive. Palate: flavourful, fruity, toasty, round tannins, powerful.

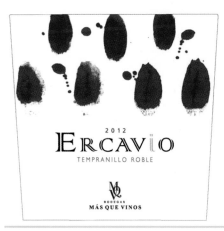

La Malvar de Ercavio 2013 B
malvar blanco

90

Colour: bright straw. Nose: citrus fruit, fruit expression, floral, fragrant herbs, mineral, sweet spices. Palate: spicy, long, balanced, fine bitter notes.

BODEGAS MONTALVO WILMOT
Ctra. Ruidera, km. 10,2 Finca Los Cerrillos
13710 Argamasilla de Alba
(Ciudad Real)
☎: +34 926 699 069
www.montalvowilmot.com
info@montalvowilmot.com

Montalvo Wilmot Cabernet de Familia 2007 T
100% cabernet sauvignon

87

Colour: ruby red. Nose: spicy, fine reductive notes, wet leather, toasty, grassy. Palate: spicy, long, toasty, easy to drink.

Montalvo Wilmot Chardonnay 2011 B
100% chardonnay

82

Montalvo Wilmot Colección Privada 2010 T Roble

87

Colour: bright cherry. Nose: ripe fruit, sweet spices, creamy oak, medium intensity. Palate: fruity, flavourful, toasty.

Montalvo Wilmot Quintos de la Tejera 2013 T
100% tempranillo

86

Colour: cherry, purple rim. Nose: fresh fruit, red berry notes, floral, lactic notes, sweet spices. Palate: flavourful, fruity, good acidity.

Montalvo Wilmot Syrah 2012 T Roble
100% syrah

87

Colour: cherry, garnet rim. Nose: fruit liqueur notes, sweet spices, roasted coffee. Palate: powerful, flavourful, toasty.

Montalvo Wilmot Tempranillo-Cabernet 2012 T Roble

88

Colour: bright cherry. Nose: ripe fruit, sweet spices, creamy oak. Palate: flavourful, fruity, toasty.

Montalvo Wilmot Verdejo Colección 2013 B
100% verdejo

81

BODEGAS MUREDA

Ctra. N-IV, Km. 184,1
13300 Valdepeñas (Ciudad Real)
☎: +34 926 318 058
Fax: +34 926 318 058
www.mureda.es
bmoreno@mureda.es

Mureda 100 2009 T
tempranillo
87
Colour: dark-red cherry, garnet rim. Nose: ripe fruit, fruit preserve, spicy, toasty. Palate: good structure, round tannins, full.

Mureda Merlot 2013 T
merlot
84

Mureda Syrah 2013 T
syrah
88
Colour: cherry, purple rim. Nose: fresh fruit, red berry notes, floral, balsamic herbs. Palate: flavourful, fruity, good acidity.

Mureda Tempranillo 2013 T
tempranillo
89
Colour: cherry, purple rim. Nose: expressive, fresh fruit, red berry notes, floral. Palate: flavourful, fruity, good acidity, round tannins.

BODEGAS NAVARRO LÓPEZ

Autovía Madrid - Cádiz, Km. 193
13300 Valdepeñas (Ciudad Real)
☎: +34 902 193 431
Fax: +34 902 193 432
www.bodegasnavarrolopez.com
laboratorio2@navarrolopez.com

Para Celsus 2013 T
100% tempranillo
85

Premium 1904 2011 T
88
Colour: cherry, garnet rim. Nose: ripe fruit, spicy, creamy oak, toasty. Palate: powerful, flavourful, toasty.

Rojo Garnacha 2013 T
garnacha
87
Colour: light cherry, purple rim. Nose: fruit liqueur notes, wild herbs, balanced. Palate: powerful, flavourful, balsamic.

Rojo Tempranillo 2013 T
100% tempranillo
86
Colour: cherry, purple rim. Nose: powerfull, red berry notes, ripe fruit, floral, balsamic herbs. Palate: powerful, fresh, fruity, unctuous.

Tierra Calar 2013 B
macabeo
83

Tierra Calar 2013 T
100% tempranillo
85

BODEGAS RASGÓN

Autovía Madrid-Cádiz, km. 193
13300 Valdepeñas (Ciudad Real)
☎: +34 926 647 194
Fax: +34 926 647 044
www.rasgon.com
bodegas@rasgon.com

Rasgón 2013 RD
tempranillo
84

Rasgón Barrica 2012 T
85

Rasgón de María 2013 T
syrah
83

Rasgón Macabeo 2013 B
macabeo
83

Rasgón Syrah 2013 T
syrah
85

Rasgón Tempranillo 2013 T
tempranillo
84

BODEGAS REAL

Paseo de la Castellana, 144 1º
28046 Madrid (Madrid)
☎: +34 914 577 588
Fax: +34 914 577 210
www.bodegas-real.com
comunicacion@bodegas-real.com

Finca Marisánchez 2009 T Roble
87
Colour: bright cherry. Nose: ripe fruit, sweet spices. Palate: flavourful, fruity, toasty, round tannins.

Finca Marisánchez Chardonnay 2013 B
100% chardonnay
85

Vega Ibor Tempranillo 2010 TC
100% tempranillo

86

Colour: cherry, purple rim. Nose: fresh fruit, grassy, spicy. Palate: good acidity, correct.

BODEGAS RÍO NEGRO
Ctra. CM 1001, Km. 37,400
19230 Cogolludo (Guadalajara)
☎: +34 913 022 646
Fax: +34 917 660 019
www.fincarionegro.com
info@fincarionegro.es

Finca Río Negro 2011 T
tempranillo, syrah, merlot, cabernet sauvignon

91

Colour: cherry, garnet rim. Nose: ripe fruit, spicy, creamy oak, toasty, complex, earthy notes, cocoa bean. Palate: powerful, flavourful, toasty, round tannins.

BODEGAS ROMERO DE ÁVILA SALCEDO
Avda. Constitución, 4
13240 La Solana (Ciudad Real)
☎: +34 926 631 426
www.bodegasromerodeavila.com
sales@bras1960.com

Bondad 3 meses en Barrica 2011 T
tempranillo, syrah

85

Bondad Syrah Tempranillo 2010 T Roble
tempranillo, syrah

82

Bondad Tempranillo 2011 T
tempranillo

84

Bondad Verdejo 2013 B
verdejo

83

Testigo T
tempranillo, syrah, cabernet sauvignon

85

BODEGAS SAN ISIDRO DE PEDRO MUÑOZ
Ctra. El Toboso, 1
13620 Pedro Muñoz (Ciudad Real)
☎: +34 926 586 057
Fax: +34 926 568 380
www.viacotos.com
mail@viacotos.com

Carril de Cotos 2011 TC
100% tempranillo

85

Carril de Cotos Airén 2013 B
100% airén

83

Carril de Cotos Cabernet Sauvignon 2011 T Barrica
cabernet sauvignon

86

Colour: bright cherry. Nose: ripe fruit, sweet spices, creamy oak, balsamic herbs. Palate: flavourful, fruity, toasty.

Carril de Cotos Semidulce B
100% airén

84

Carril de Cotos Tempranillo 2013 T
100% tempranillo

87

Colour: deep cherry, purple rim. Nose: fruit expression, violets, powerfull. Palate: balanced, ripe fruit, easy to drink.

BODEGAS TERRA VINIS
Españoleto, 20 1ºD
28010 (Madrid)
☎: +34 911 168 338
Fax: +34 911 168 335
www.terraviniswines.com
export@tradeworldcompany.com

Actium Cabernet Sauvignon 2013 T
cabernet sauvignon

83

Actium Syrah 2013 T
syrah

84

Actium Tempranillo 2013 T
tempranillo

85

BODEGAS TIERRAS DE ORGAZ

Orgaz, 12
45460 Manzaneque (Toledo)
☎: +34 666 417 377
www.bodegastierrasdeorgaz.com
jcserrano@bodegastierrasdeorgaz.com

Bucamel 2009 T
tempranillo

89

Colour: bright cherry. Nose: ripe fruit, sweet spices, creamy oak, medium intensity. Palate: fruity, flavourful, toasty.

Mernat 2009 T
merlot, syrah, cabernet sauvignon, tempranillo

90

Colour: cherry, garnet rim. Nose: ripe fruit, wild herbs, earthy notes, spicy, creamy oak. Palate: balanced, flavourful, long, balsamic.

Mernat 2013 B
viognier

91

Colour: bright straw. Nose: white flowers, fresh fruit, expressive, fine lees, dried herbs. Palate: flavourful, fruity, good acidity, balanced.

BODEGAS VENTA MORALES

Paraje Casa Alfaqui, 1
03650 Rodriguillo (Pinoso)
☎: +34 965 978 603
www.bodegasvolver.com
export@bodegasvolver.com

Venta Morales 2013 T
tempranillo

89

Colour: cherry, purple rim. Nose: powerfull, red berry notes, warm. Palate: flavourful, fruity, long.

BODEGAS VILLAVID, D.N.J. S. COOP. DE CLM

Niño Jesús, 25
16280 Villarta (Cuenca)
☎: +34 962 189 006
Fax: +34 962 189 125
www.villavid.com
export@villavid.com

Villavid Bobal 2012 T Roble
100% bobal

86

Colour: very deep cherry, garnet rim. Nose: powerfull, ripe fruit, roasted coffee, dark chocolate. Palate: powerful, toasty, roasted-coffee aftertaste.

Villavid Syrah 2012 T Roble
100% syrah

84

Villavid Tempranillo 2012 T Roble
100% tempranillo

87

Colour: dark-red cherry, purple rim. Nose: ripe fruit, red berry notes, floral, balanced, sweet spices. Palate: balanced, ripe fruit.

BODEGAS VITIVINOS

Camino de Cabezuelas, s/n
2270 Villamalea (Albacete)
☎: +34 967 483 114
Fax: +34 967 483 964
www.vitivinos.com
info@vitivinos.com

Llanos del Marqués Tempranillo 2013 T
tempranillo

82

BODEGAS VOLVER

Ctra de Pinoso a Fortuna s/n
3658 Rodriguillo - Pinoso (Alicante)
☎: +34 966 185 624
Fax: +34 965 075 376
www.bodegasvolver.com
export@bodegasvolver.com

Paso a Paso Tempranillo 2013 T
tempranillo

89 🌱

Colour: cherry, purple rim. Nose: powerfull, balsamic herbs, spicy, creamy oak. Palate: toasty, balanced, concentrated.

Paso a Paso Verdejo 2013 B
verdejo

85

BODEGAS Y VIÑEDOS CASTIBLANQUE

Isaac Peral, 19
13610 Campo de Criptana (Ciudad Real)
☎: +34 926 589 147
Fax: +34 926 589 148
www.bodegascastiblanque.com
info@bodegascastiblanque.com

Baldor Old Vines 2009 T
100% cabernet sauvignon

86

Colour: cherry, garnet rim. Nose: ripe fruit, wild herbs, spicy, creamy oak. Palate: balanced, flavourful, long, balsamic.

Baldor Tradición Chardonnay 2013 B Joven
100% chardonnay

89

Colour: bright straw. Nose: ripe fruit, sweet spices, creamy oak, fragrant herbs. Palate: flavourful, fresh, good acidity.

Baldor Tradición Syrah 2009 T
100% syrah
86
Colour: dark-red cherry, orangey edge. Nose: old leather, ripe fruit, fruit preserve. Palate: correct, balanced.

Ilex 2012 RD
100% syrah
84

Ilex 2012 T
84

Ilex Coupage 2012 T
86
Colour: cherry, purple rim. Nose: medium intensity, red berry notes, ripe fruit, floral, spicy. Palate: ripe fruit, correct, easy to drink.

Ilex Verdejo 2013 B
100% verdejo
82

La Triste Figura 2012 T
84

Sloamente Cabernet Sauvignon 2008 T
100% cabernet sauvignon
86
Colour: deep cherry, purple rim. Nose: fruit expression, balanced, medium intensity, spicy. Palate: correct, ripe fruit, easy to drink.

BODEGAS Y VIÑEDOS CERRO DEL ÁGUILA
Avda. de Toledo, 23
45127 Ventas con Peña Aguilera (Toledo)
☎: +34 625 443 153
bodegascerrodelaguila@gmail.com

Puerto Carbonero 2011 T
garnacha, syrah
90
Colour: cherry, garnet rim. Nose: ripe fruit, spicy, creamy oak, toasty, complex, mineral. Palate: powerful, flavourful, toasty, round tannins, balanced.

Vereda del Lobo 2011 T
syrah
91
Colour: cherry, garnet rim. Nose: ripe fruit, spicy, creamy oak, toasty, complex, earthy notes. Palate: powerful, flavourful, toasty, round tannins, elegant.

BODEGAS Y VIÑEDOS FONTANA
O'Donnell, 18 1ºG
28009 Madrid (Madrid)
☎: +34 915 783 197
Fax: +34 915 783 072
www.bodegasfontana.com
gemag@bodegasfontana.com

Gran Fontal 2011 TR
100% tempranillo
91
Colour: cherry, garnet rim. Nose: red berry notes, ripe fruit, spicy, creamy oak, toasty, violets. Palate: powerful, flavourful, toasty, round tannins, balanced.

BODEGAS Y VIÑEDOS PINUAGA
Ctra. N-301 Km. 95,5
45880 Corral de Almaguer (Toledo)
☎: +34 629 058 900
Fax: +34 914 577 117
www.bodegaspinuaga.com
info@bodegaspinuaga.com

Finca Salazar 2013 B
sauvignon blanc
85

Finca Salazar 2013 T
100% tempranillo
86
Colour: cherry, purple rim. Nose: expressive, fresh fruit, red berry notes, floral. Palate: flavourful, fruity, good acidity, round tannins.

Pinuaga 200 Cepas 2011 T
100% tempranillo
89
Colour: black cherry, garnet rim. Nose: creamy oak, sweet spices, ripe fruit, cocoa bean, aromatic coffee. Palate: spicy, long, round tannins.

Pinuaga Colección 2012 T
100% tempranillo
87
Colour: bright cherry. Nose: ripe fruit, sweet spices, creamy oak, medium intensity. Palate: fruity, flavourful, toasty.

Pinuaga La Senda 2012 T
86
Colour: bright cherry, garnet rim. Nose: balanced, ripe fruit, scrubland. Palate: good structure, round tannins.

Pinuaga Nature 3 Meses barrica 2012 T
100% tempranillo
87
Colour: bright cherry, garnet rim. Nose: red berry notes, balsamic herbs, sweet spices. Palate: correct, good finish, balanced.

BODEGAS Y VIÑEDOS TAVERA S.L.

Ctra. Valmojado - Toledo, Km. 22
45182 Arcicóllar (Toledo)
☎: +34 637 847 777
www.bodegastavera.com
info@bodegatavera.com

Nereo Garnacha 2011 T
100% garnacha
84

Nereo Garnacha 2013 RD
100% garnacha
85

Nereo Syrah Tempranillo 2011 T
83

Nereo Tempranillo Syrah Garnacha 2010 T
87
Colour: cherry, garnet rim. Nose: ripe fruit, spicy, toasty, complex, balsamic herbs. Palate: powerful, flavourful, toasty, round tannins.

Tavera Vendimia Seleccionada 2009 T
tempranillo, syrah, garnacha
87
Colour: dark-red cherry, garnet rim. Nose: ripe fruit, scrubland, warm. Palate: correct, good acidity, balanced, fine tannins.

BODEGAS ZIRIES

Menasalbas, 18
45120 San Pablo de los Montes (Toledo)
☎: +34 679 443 792
www.lobecasope.com
flequi@ziries.es

Melé 2011 T
100% garnacha
89
Colour: light cherry. Nose: balanced, cocoa bean, dried herbs, fruit liqueur notes. Palate: good structure, flavourful, spicy, balsamic.

Navalegua 2013 T Barrica
100% garnacha
87 🌷
Colour: cherry, purple rim. Nose: wild herbs, red berry notes, spicy. Palate: correct, easy to drink, good finish.

Ziries 2012 T
100% garnacha
88 🌷
Colour: deep cherry. Nose: spicy, creamy oak, toasty, ripe fruit, fruit preserve. Palate: powerful, flavourful, toasty, round tannins.

CAMINO ALTO

Polillo, 4
45860 Villacañas (Toledo)
☎: +34 925 200 878
Fax: +34 925 200 849
www.bodegascaminoalto.com
info@bodegascaminoalto.com

Camino Alto 2012 T Roble
100% tempranillo
84 🌷

Camino Alto Petit Verdot 2012 T Roble
100% petit verdot
84 🌷

CAPILLA DEL FRAILE

Finca Capilla del Fraile, s/n
45600 San Bartolomé de las Abiertas (Toledo)
☎: +34 925 599 329
www.capilladelfraile.com
info@capilladelfraile.com

Capilla del Fraile 2008 T
88
Colour: deep cherry. Nose: spicy, violet drops, ripe fruit. Palate: ripe fruit, spicy.

Capilla del Fraile 2009 T
88
Colour: cherry, garnet rim. Nose: spicy, toasty, overripe fruit, mineral. Palate: powerful, flavourful, toasty, round tannins.

CARRASCAS

Ctra. El Bonillo - Ossa de Montiel P.K. 11,4
02610 El Bonillo (Albacete)
☎: +34 967 965 880
Fax: +34 967 965 879
www.carrascas.com
info@carrascas.com

Carrascas 2012 B
sauvignon blanc, chardonnay
90
Colour: bright yellow. Nose: ripe fruit, sweet spices, cocoa bean, toasty. Palate: flavourful, balanced, spicy, long.

Carrascas 2012 T
syrah, tempranillo
89
Colour: bright cherry. Nose: sweet spices, creamy oak. Palate: flavourful, fruity, toasty, round tannins.

Origen de Carrascas 2012 BFB
chardonnay, sauvignon blanc

91

Colour: bright yellow. Nose: ripe fruit, balsamic herbs, spicy, smoky, toasty, elegant. Palate: powerful, flavourful, rich, long, toasty, balanced.

Tiento de Carrascas 2012 T
merlot, cabernet sauvignon

92

Colour: cherry, garnet rim. Nose: ripe fruit, spicy, creamy oak, toasty, complex, dark chocolate, earthy notes. Palate: powerful, flavourful, toasty, round tannins.

CASA CARRIL CRUZADO
Ctra. Iniesta-Villagarcía
del Llano km, 13
16236 Villagarcía del Llano (Cuenca)
☎: +34 967 571 154
www.carrilcruzado.com
bodega@carrilcruzado.com

Carril Cruzado Chardonnay Sauvignon Blanc 2013 B
chardonnay, sauvignon blanc

84

Carril Cruzado Petit Verdot 2013 RD
100% petit verdot

83

Carril Cruzado Syrah 2007 T
100% syrah

78

CASAQUEMADA
Ctra. Ruidera, Km. 5,5
13710 Argamasilla de Alba
(Ciudad Real)
☎: +34 628 621 187
www.casaquemada.es
casaquemada@casaquemada.es

Alba de Casa Quemada 2012 T
syrah

90

Colour: cherry, garnet rim. Nose: ripe fruit, spicy, creamy oak, toasty, complex, mineral, balsamic herbs. Palate: powerful, flavourful, toasty, round tannins, elegant.

Anea de Casaquemada 2007 T
syrah

89

Colour: very deep cherry. Nose: ripe fruit, spicy, creamy oak, toasty, characterful. Palate: powerful, flavourful, toasty, round tannins, balanced.

Brincho 2011 T
tempranillo

89

Colour: deep cherry, garnet rim. Nose: ripe fruit, powerfull, dried herbs. Palate: good structure, round tannins, spicy.

Hacienda Casaquemada 2009 T
tempranillo

90

Colour: cherry, garnet rim. Nose: ripe fruit, spicy, creamy oak, toasty, complex. Palate: powerful, flavourful, toasty, round tannins.

COMERCIAL GRUPO FREIXENET
Joan Sala, 2
08770 Sant Sadurní D'Anoia
(Barcelona)
☎: +34 938 917 000
Fax: +34 938 183 095
www.freixenet.es
freixenet@freixenet.es

Mía 2013 B
macabeo, parellada, moscatel, xarel.lo

84

Mía 2013 T
tempranillo

85

Oroya 2013 B
airén, macabeo, moscatel

85

COOP. AGRARIA SANTA QUITERIA
Baltasar González Sáez, 34
2694 Higueruela (Albacete)
☎: +34 967 287 012
Fax: +34 967 287 031
www.tintoralba.com
direccion@tintoralba.com

Tintoralba Sauvgnon Blanc - Verdejo 2013 B
sauvignon blanc, verdejo

85

CORTIJO TRIFILLAS
Finca Trifillas Ctra. Rincón del Moro, km. 10
2410 Liétor (Albacete)
☎: +34 967 680 009
Fax: +34 967 681 165
www.cortijodetrifillas.com
info@cortijotrifillas.com

CT 2013 B
verdejo, sauvignon blanc

84

CT Cabernet Sauvignon 2011 T
100% cabernet sauvignon
89
Colour: bright cherry. Nose: ripe fruit, sweet spices, creamy oak, medium intensity, wild herbs, lactic notes. Palate: fruity, flavourful, toasty.

CT Garnacha Tintorera 2013 T
garnacha tintorera
84

CT Petit Verdot 2011 T
100% petit verdot
85

CT Rosado 2013 RD
85

CT Tempranillo + Merlot 2013 T
87
Colour: cherry, purple rim. Nose: fresh fruit, red berry notes. Palate: flavourful, fruity, good acidity, round tannins.

CT Tempranillo-Petit Verdot-Cabernet Sauvignon 2011 T
tempranillo, petit verdot, cabernet sauvignon
87
Colour: deep cherry, garnet rim. Nose: spicy, creamy oak, ripe fruit. Palate: balanced, round tannins, fruity.

COSECHEROS Y CRIADORES
Diputación, s/n
01320 Oyón (Álava)
☎: +34 945 601 944
Fax: +34 945 622 488
www.familiamartinezbujanda.com
nacional@cosecherosycriadores.com

Infinitus Cabernet Sauvignon 2013 T
cabernet sauvignon
86
Colour: cherry, purple rim. Nose: red berry notes, ripe fruit, balsamic herbs, herbaceous. Palate: powerful, flavourful.

Infinitus Cabernet Sauvignon Tempranillo 2012 T
cabernet sauvignon, tempranillo
85

Infinitus Gewürztraminer 2013 B
gewürztraminer
87
Colour: bright straw. Nose: white flowers, fragrant herbs, fruit expression, ripe fruit. Palate: fresh, fruity, flavourful, balanced.

Infinitus Malbec 2013 T
malbec
86
Colour: cherry, purple rim. Nose: fruit preserve, balsamic herbs, balanced, fragrant herbs. Palate: flavourful, spicy, balsamic.

Infinitus Merlot 2013 T
merlot
85

Infinitus Moscatel Semidulce 2013 B
moscatel
87
Colour: golden. Nose: powerfull, floral, honeyed notes, candied fruit, fragrant herbs. Palate: flavourful, sweet, fresh, fruity, good acidity.

Infinitus Syrah 2013 T
syrah
87
Colour: cherry, purple rim. Nose: red berry notes, floral, fragrant herbs, expressive. Palate: powerful, flavourful, easy to drink.

Infinitus Tempranillo 2013 T
tempranillo
88
Colour: cherry, purple rim. Nose: expressive, fresh fruit, red berry notes, floral. Palate: flavourful, fruity, good acidity, easy to drink.

Infinitus Tempranillo Cabernet Franc 2013 RD
tempranillo, cabernet franc
86
Colour: rose, purple rim. Nose: powerfull, ripe fruit, red berry notes, floral, expressive. Palate: powerful, fruity, fresh.

Infinitus Viura Chardonnay 2013 B
viura, chardonnay
84

DEHESA DE LOS LLANOS
Ctra. Peñas de San Pedro, Km. 5,5
02006 (Albacete)
☎: +34 967 243 100
Fax: +34 967 243 093
www.dehesadelosllanos.es
info@dehesadelosllanos.es

Mazacruz 2011 T Roble
syrah, tempranillo, merlot
90
Colour: cherry, garnet rim. Nose: balsamic herbs, warm, ripe fruit. Palate: balanced, good acidity, full, long, spicy, round tannins.

Mazacruz 2013 B

verdejo, sauvignon blanc

88

Colour: bright straw. Nose: white flowers, dried herbs, fruit expression, citrus fruit. Palate: flavourful, fruity, good acidity, balanced.

Mazacruz Cima 2009 T

petit verdot, merlot, cabernet sauvignon, graciano

89

Colour: deep cherry, garnet rim. Nose: ripe fruit, scrubland, spicy, mineral. Palate: good structure, spicy, long.

Mazacruz Cima 2012 B

verdejo, sauvignon blanc

90

Colour: bright yellow. Nose: powerfull, ripe fruit, sweet spices, creamy oak, fragrant herbs. Palate: rich, flavourful, fresh, good acidity.

DEHESA Y VIÑEDOS DE NAVAMARÍN

Ctra. Comarcal 313, Km. 1
02160 Lezuza (Albacete)
☎: +34 967 376 005
Fax: +34 967 376 003
www.aldonzavinos.com
pedrojnavarro@aldonzavinos.com

Aldonza Navamarín 2009 T

88

Colour: cherry, garnet rim. Nose: ripe fruit, spicy, creamy oak, fine reductive notes. Palate: flavourful, long, balsamic, spicy.

Aldonza Pisces 2009 T

86

Colour: cherry, garnet rim. Nose: grassy, balanced, ripe fruit. Palate: correct, easy to drink, good finish.

Aldonza Selección 2009 TR

87

Colour: cherry, garnet rim. Nose: ripe fruit, wild herbs, earthy notes, spicy, creamy oak. Palate: long, balsamic, easy to drink, good finish.

DOMINIO DE EGUREN

Camino de San Pedro, s/n
01309 Páganos (Álava)
☎: +34 945 600 117
Fax: +34 945 600 590
www.eguren.com
info@eguren.com

Códice 2012 T

100% tempranillo

91

Colour: cherry, purple rim. Nose: fresh fruit, red berry notes, floral. Palate: flavourful, fruity, good acidity, round tannins.

DOMINIO DE PUNCTUM ORGANIC & BIODYNAMIC WINES

Finca Fabian, s/n - Aptdo. 71
16660 Las Pedroñeras (Cuenca)
☎: +34 912 959 998
Fax: +34 912 959 997
www.dominiodepunctum.com
export@dominiodepunctum.com

Finca Fabian 2013 RD

100% garnacha

86

Colour: onion pink. Nose: floral, candied fruit, fragrant herbs. Palate: fresh, fruity, balsamic.

Finca Fabian Chardonnay 2013 B

100% chardonnay

87

Colour: bright straw. Nose: fragrant herbs, citrus fruit, ripe fruit, expressive. Palate: fresh, fruity, flavourful, balanced.

Finca Fabian Tempranillo 2013 T

100% tempranillo

87

Colour: cherry, purple rim. Nose: red berry notes, floral, wild herbs, earthy notes. Palate: flavourful, good acidity, balsamic.

Punctum 2013 RD

100% bobal

87

Colour: onion pink. Nose: elegant, candied fruit, dried flowers, fragrant herbs, red berry notes. Palate: light-bodied, flavourful, good acidity, long, spicy, easy to drink.

Punctum Chardonnay Selección 2013 B

88

Colour: bright straw. Nose: fresh, fresh fruit, white flowers, fragrant herbs. Palate: flavourful, fruity, good acidity, balanced.

Punctum Tempranillo Petit Verdot 2012 T Roble

89

Colour: bright cherry. Nose: ripe fruit, sweet spices, creamy oak, fragrant herbs. Palate: flavourful, fruity, toasty, round tannins, balanced.

Punctum Tempranillo Petit Verdot 2013 T

86

Colour: bright cherry, purple rim. Nose: red berry notes, dried herbs, medium intensity. Palate: easy to drink, flavourful, balanced.

ENCOMIENDA DE CERVERA

Arzobispo Cañizares, 1
13270 Almagro (Ciudad Real)
☎: +34 926 102 099
www.encomiendadecervera.com
info@encomiendadecervera.com

1758 Selección Petit Verdot 2012 T
petit verdot

89

Colour: cherry, garnet rim. Nose: ripe fruit, spicy, creamy oak, toasty, balsamic herbs. Palate: powerful, flavourful, toasty.

Maar de Cervera Cencibel 2010 TC
cencibel

88

Colour: dark-red cherry, garnet rim. Nose: balanced, expressive, ripe fruit. Palate: spicy, round tannins, good finish.

Poker de Tempranillos 2010 TC
100% tempranillo

87

Colour: bright cherry. Nose: ripe fruit, sweet spices, creamy oak, medium intensity. Palate: fruity, flavourful, toasty.

Señorío de Almagro 2012 T
tempranillo, syrah, petit verdot, cabernet sauvignon

86

Colour: cherry, garnet rim. Nose: ripe fruit, spicy, creamy oak. Palate: powerful, flavourful, spicy, long.

Vulcanus Cabernet Sauvignon 2011 TC
cabernet sauvignon

86

Colour: dark-red cherry, garnet rim. Nose: wild herbs, ripe fruit, toasty. Palate: correct, easy to drink, round tannins.

FÉLIX SOLÍS

Autovía del Sur, Km. 199
13300 Valdepeñas (Ciudad Real)
☎: +34 926 322 400
www.felixsolisavantis.com
nfernandez@felixsolisavantis.com

Consigna 2013 RD
tempranillo

80

Consigna Cabernet Sauvignon 2013 T
cabernet sauvignon

81

Consigna Chardonnay 2013 B
chardonnay

81

Consigna Merlot 2013 T
100% merlot

84

Consigna Semidulce Airén 2013 B
airén

83

Consigna Shiraz 2013 T
syrah

83

Consigna Tempranillo 2013 T
tempranillo

84

Orquestra 2013 RD
tempranillo

84

Orquestra Cabernet Sauvignon 2013 T
cabernet sauvignon

84

Orquestra Chardonnay 2013 B
chardonnay

85

Orquestra Merlot 2013 T
merlot

85

Orquestra Tempranillo 2013 T
tempranillo

84

FINCA CASA ALARCÓN

Ctra. Montealegre del Castillo, km 4,5
02660 Caudete (Albacete)
☎: +34 965 828 266
Fax: +34 965 229 405
www.casalarcon.com
export@casalarcon.com

Blau 2011 T
monastrell

85

Casa Alarcón 2013 RD
100% syrah

84

Casa Alarcón Sauvignon Blanc 2013 B
100% sauvignon blanc

87

Colour: bright straw, greenish rim. Nose: fresh fruit, balsamic herbs, fresh, balanced. Palate: fruity, balanced, good acidity, fine bitter notes, easy to drink.

Casa Alarcón Viognier 2013 B
100% viognier

86

Colour: bright yellow. Nose: dried herbs, dried flowers, medium intensity. Palate: fruity, flavourful, fine bitter notes.

Don Jaime 2011 T
tempranillo, cabernet sauvignon, petit verdot

86

Colour: dark-red cherry, garnet rim. Nose: premature reduction notes, wild herbs, ripe fruit, fruit preserve. Palate: correct, fruity.

Dua 2012 T
tempranillo, cabernet sauvignon

85

Nea 2010 T
petit verdot

85

Tria 2010 T
syrah

86

Colour: cherry, garnet rim. Nose: medium intensity, red berry notes, ripe fruit. Palate: correct, easy to drink, good finish.

FINCA CONSTANCIA
Camino del Bravo, s/n
45543 Otero (Toledo)
☎: +34 914 903 700
Fax: +34 916 612 124
www.www.fincaconstancia.es
lslara@gonzalezbyass.es

Altos de la Finca 2011 T
petit verdot, syrah

91

Colour: cherry, garnet rim. Nose: ripe fruit, wild herbs, earthy notes, spicy, creamy oak, mineral. Palate: balanced, flavourful, long, balsamic.

Finca Constancia Graciano Parcela 12 2012 T
graciano

89

Colour: deep cherry, garnet rim. Nose: balanced, ripe fruit, scrubland, sweet spices. Palate: good structure, spicy.

Finca Constancia Selección 2012 T
syrah, cabernet sauvignon, petit verdot, tempranillo

90

Colour: cherry, purple rim. Nose: elegant, sweet spices, toasty, balsamic herbs, ripe fruit. Palate: balanced, spicy, good acidity.

Finca Constancia Tempranillo Parcela 23 Dulce 2012 T
tempranillo

87

Colour: black cherry, garnet rim. Nose: fruit preserve, sweet spices, dried herbs. Palate: good structure, flavourful, round tannins.

Finca Constancia Verdejo Parcela 52 2013 B
verdejo

88

Colour: bright golden. Nose: macerated fruit, tropical fruit, spicy, creamy oak, balsamic herbs. Palate: powerful, flavourful, toasty.

FINCA EL REFUGIO
Ctra. CM 3102, km. 14,6
13630 Socuéllamos (Ciudad Real)
☎: +34 913 562 746
www.fincaelrefugio.es
info@fincaelrefugio.es

Legado Finca El Refugio Cabernet Merlot 2011 T Roble

87

Colour: cherry, garnet rim. Nose: ripe fruit, wild herbs, sweet spices, creamy oak. Palate: powerful, flavourful, spicy, balanced.

Legado Finca El Refugio Petit Verdot 2011 T
petit verdot

84

Legado Finca El Refugio Syrah 2011 T
syrah

86

Colour: bright cherry, garnet rim. Nose: sweet spices, creamy oak, expressive, fruit preserve. Palate: flavourful, fruity, toasty.

Legado Finca El Refugio Tempranillo 2011 T Roble
tempranillo

85

Legado Finca El Refugio Verdejo 2012 B
verdejo

85

Quorum de Finca El Refugio Private Collection 2011 T

88

Colour: bright cherry. Nose: ripe fruit, sweet spices, creamy oak, wild herbs. Palate: flavourful, fruity, toasty, round tannins, balanced.

FINCA LA BLANCA
Princesa, 84
45840 Puebla de Almoradiel (Toledo)
☎: +34 669 995 315
Fax: +34 968 897 675
www.fincalablanca.es
export@fincalablanca.es

Marinada 2013 B
airén, moscatel

82

FINCA LA LAGUNILLA

Avda. Reyes Católicos 31 5ºA
03003 Alicante (Albacete)
☎: +34 965 928 857
www.fincalalagunilla.com
info@fincalalagunilla.com

Casa Corredor Cabernet Sauvignon 2010 T
cabernet sauvignon
86
Colour: cherry, garnet rim. Nose: ripe fruit, spicy, wild herbs. Palate: flavourful, balsamic, long.

Casa Corredor Syrah 2010 T
syrah
85

Casa Corredor Tempranillo 2011 T
tempranillo
87
Colour: cherry, garnet rim. Nose: ripe fruit, spicy, creamy oak, toasty. Palate: powerful, flavourful, toasty.

FINCA LORANQUE

Finca Loranque
45593 Bargas (Toledo)
☎: +34 669 476 849
www.fincaloranque.com
fincaloranque@fincaloranque.com

Finca Loranque Tempranillo Syrah 2008 T
tempranillo, syrah
86
Colour: dark-red cherry, garnet rim. Nose: powerfull, toasty, spicy, waxy notes. Palate: balanced, round tannins, ripe fruit.

Lacruz de Finca Loranque Cabernet Sauvignon 2008 T
100% cabernet sauvignon
88
Colour: cherry, garnet rim. Nose: ripe fruit, spicy, creamy oak, toasty, complex. Palate: powerful, flavourful, toasty, round tannins.

Lacruz de Finca Loranque Syrah 2008 T
100% syrah
86
Colour: cherry, garnet rim. Nose: ripe fruit, creamy oak, earthy notes, slightly evolved. Palate: powerful, flavourful, toasty, round tannins.

Lacruz de Finca Loranque Tempranillo 2012 T
100% tempranillo
84

Loranque El Grande 2007 T
100% syrah
88
Colour: cherry, garnet rim. Nose: fruit preserve, fruit liqueur notes, floral, balsamic herbs, sweet spices. Palate: powerful, flavourful, balanced, toasty.

FINCA LOS ALIJARES

Avda. de la Paz, 5
45180 Camarena (Toledo)
☎: +34 918 174 364
Fax: +34 918 174 364
www.fincalosalijares.com
gerencia@fincalosalijares.com

Finca Los Alijares Garnacha 2013 T
100% garnacha
86
Colour: cherry, purple rim. Nose: expressive, fresh fruit, red berry notes. Palate: flavourful, fruity, good acidity.

Finca Los Alijares Graciano 2011 TC
100% graciano
89 🌱
Colour: cherry, garnet rim. Nose: ripe fruit, wild herbs, earthy notes, spicy, creamy oak, dark chocolate. Palate: balanced, flavourful, long, balsamic.

Finca Los Alijares Moscatel 2013 B
moscatel grano menudo
85 🌱

Finca Los Alijares Moscatel Semidulce 2013 B
moscatel grano menudo
86 🌱
Colour: yellow. Nose: white flowers, characterful, fresh, varietal. Palate: fruity, easy to drink, correct, sweetness.

Finca Los Alijares Viognier 2013 B
100% viognier
84 🌱

HAMMEKEN CELLARS

Calle de la Muela, 16
03730 Jávea (Alicante)
☎: +34 965 791 967
Fax: +34 966 461 471
www.hammekencellars.com
cellars@hammekencellars.com

Apanillo Semi 2013 T
100% tempranillo
85

Capa Tempranillo 2013 T
84

Capa Verdejo 2013 B
100% verdejo
85

Castillo del Rocío Old Vines Tempranillo 2013 T
100% tempranillo
88
Colour: deep cherry, purple rim. Nose: expressive, fresh fruit, red berry notes, spicy. Palate: fruity, easy to drink, balanced, good acidity.

Cepunto Oro 2012 T
100% tempranillo
86
Colour: cherry, purple rim. Nose: medium intensity, scrubland, red berry notes, ripe fruit. Palate: fruity, varietal.

Conde Pinel Oak Aged 2013 T Barrica
89
Colour: dark-red cherry, garnet rim. Nose: balanced, sweet spices, wild herbs. Palate: balanced, good acidity, round tannins.

Conde Pinel Tempranillo 2013 RD
tempranillo, syrah
83

Conde Pinel Tempranillo 2013 T
87
Colour: dark-red cherry, garnet rim. Nose: red berry notes, medium intensity, balanced, spicy. Palate: fruity, flavourful.

Condes Patricia Tempranillo 2013 T
84

Dos Puntos 2013 B
85

Dos Puntos Tempranillo 2013 T
88
Colour: bright cherry, purple rim. Nose: balanced, fruit expression, red berry notes, violets. Palate: fruity, flavourful.

El Paso del Lazo 2013 RD
100% tempranillo
83

El Paso del Lazo Tempranillo 2013 T
88
Colour: cherry, purple rim. Nose: expressive, fresh fruit, red berry notes, floral, spicy. Palate: flavourful, fruity, good acidity, round tannins.

El Paso del Lazo Viura Verdejo 2013 B
84

El Tocador Tempranillo 2013 T
85

El Tocador Verdejo 2013 B
100% verdejo
84

Flor del Montgó Tempranillo 2013 T
100% tempranillo
87
Colour: dark-red cherry, purple rim. Nose: fruit preserve, ripe fruit. Palate: fruity, flavourful, balsamic, round tannins.

La Niña de Columbus Shiraz 2013 T
100% syrah
85

Lumos Tempranillo 2013 T
100% tempranillo
88
Colour: dark-red cherry, purple rim. Nose: red berry notes, varietal, earthy notes, dried herbs. Palate: fruity, good structure, long, good acidity.

Montgo Tempranillo 2012 T
100% tempranillo
88
Colour: cherry, garnet rim. Nose: ripe fruit, spicy, creamy oak, toasty. Palate: powerful, flavourful, toasty.

Picos del Montgó 2013 T
88
Colour: bright cherry, purple rim. Nose: medium intensity, red berry notes, floral, balanced. Palate: fruity, good acidity, spicy.

JESÚS DEL PERDÓN - BODEGAS YUNTERO

Pol. Ind., Ctra. Alcázar de San Juan s/n
13200 Manzanares (Ciudad Real)
☎: +34 926 610 309
Fax: +34 926 610 516
www.yuntero.com
yuntero@yuntero.com

Lazarillo 2013 B
verdejo
84

Lazarillo 2013 T Joven
tempranillo
84

JESÚS Mª RECUERO MARTÍNEZ BODEGAS RECUERO

La Puebla, 14
45810 Villanueva de Alcardete (Toledo)
☎: +34 608 285 321
Fax: +34 925 167 278
www.bodegasrecuero.com
info@bodegasrecuero.com

Recuero 2011 T
tempranillo
88
Colour: bright cherry. Nose: sweet spices, creamy oak, fruit preserve. Palate: flavourful, fruity, toasty, round tannins.

Recuero Guarda Familiar 2009 T
tempranillo
89
Colour: very deep cherry, garnet rim. Nose: cocoa bean, varnish, sweet spices, ripe fruit, powerfull. Palate: balsamic, full, flavourful, round tannins.

Red Vintage Antier 2011 T
rufete, piñuelo, otras
81

Sigilo Moravia 2011 T
moravia
89
Colour: cherry, purple rim. Nose: expressive, ripe fruit, spicy, balanced. Palate: good structure, round tannins.

Terra Sigillata 2007 T
syrah, tempranillo, pinot noir
84

White Vintage Antier 2012 B
verdejo, otras
88
Colour: bright yellow. Nose: dried flowers, faded flowers, ripe fruit, balanced. Palate: balanced, ripe fruit, long.

LAZO BODEGAS Y VIÑEDOS

Finca La Zorrera, s/n
02436 Férez (Albacete)
☎: +34 622 766 900
www.lazotur.com
info@lazotur.com

Cabeza del Hierro 2011 T
monastrell, otras
87
Colour: cherry, garnet rim. Nose: fruit preserve, waxy notes, fine reductive notes, spicy, aged wood nuances. Palate: powerful, flavourful, long, toasty.

Fianza Selección Syrah 2011 T
syrah
88
Colour: cherry, garnet rim. Nose: ripe fruit, spicy, creamy oak, toasty, wild herbs. Palate: powerful, flavourful, toasty.

Fianza Syrah 2011 T
syrah
87
Colour: cherry, garnet rim. Nose: ripe fruit, spicy, creamy oak, mineral. Palate: powerful, flavourful, toasty, harsh oak tannins.

Lacerta 2012 T
monastrell, bobal
88
Colour: cherry, garnet rim. Nose: ripe fruit, spicy, creamy oak, toasty, earthy notes, balsamic herbs. Palate: powerful, flavourful, toasty.

MANO A MANO

Ctra. CM-412, Km. 100
13248 Alhambra (Ciudad Real)
☎: +34 926 694 317
www.manoamano.com
info@bodegamanoamano.com

Mano a Mano 2012 T
100% tempranillo
90
Colour: bright cherry. Nose: ripe fruit, sweet spices, creamy oak. Palate: flavourful, fruity, toasty, round tannins.

Manon 2012 T
100% tempranillo
87
Colour: very deep cherry. Nose: overripe fruit, sweet spices, toasty. Palate: powerful, sweetness.

Venta la Ossa Syrah 2011 T
100% syrah
93
Colour: very deep cherry. Nose: sweet spices, red berry notes. Palate: powerful, concentrated, spicy, fine bitter notes.

Venta la Ossa Tempranillo 2011 TC
100% tempranillo
93
Colour: very deep cherry. Nose: ripe fruit, spicy, creamy oak, toasty, characterful. Palate: powerful, flavourful, toasty, round tannins.

Venta la Ossa TNT 2012 T
94
Colour: cherry, garnet rim. Nose: ripe fruit, spicy, creamy oak, toasty, complex, dark chocolate, earthy notes. Palate: powerful, flavourful, toasty, round tannins.

MIGUEL ANGEL AGUADO ZAZO
Eras, 5
45165 San Martín de Montalbán (Toledo)
☎: +34 653 821 659
Fax: +34 925 417 206
www.bodegasmiguelaguado.com
info@bodegasmiguelaguado.com

Pasión de Castillo de Montalban 2012 ESP
macabeo
83

San Martineño 2008 TR
cabernet sauvignon, garnacha
84

San Martineño 2013 B
macabeo
83

San Martineño 2013 RD
garnacha
85

San Martineño Garnacha 2013 T
garnacha
84

San Martineño Garnacha Dulce 2013 RD
garnacha
83

MONT REAGA
Ctra. N-420, Km. 333,200
16649 Monreal del Llano (Cuenca)
☎: +34 645 769 801
Fax: +34 967 182 518
www.mont-reaga.com
mont-reaga@mont-reaga.com

Blanco de Montreaga 2010 B
100% sauvignon blanc
88
Colour: bright golden. Nose: ripe fruit, dry nuts, powerfull, toasty, aged wood nuances. Palate: flavourful, fruity, spicy, toasty, long.

Fata Morgana Tinto dulce
100% merlot
90
Colour: very deep cherry. Nose: dried fruit, fruit preserve, acetaldehyde, aged wood nuances, creamy oak. Palate: powerful, flavourful, sweet, toasty, unctuous.

Isola de MontReaga 2013 B
82

Isola de MontReaga 2013 T
84

Las Liras 2005 TGR
100% cabernet sauvignon
89
Colour: pale ruby, brick rim edge. Nose: spicy, fine reductive notes, wet leather, aged wood nuances, fruit liqueur notes, powerfull. Palate: spicy, long, correct.

Montreaga Clásico 2005 T
100% syrah
88
Colour: cherry, garnet rim. Nose: ripe fruit, spicy, creamy oak, toasty, fine reductive notes. Palate: powerful, flavourful, toasty, round tannins.

MontReaga El Secreto 2004 T
90
Colour: dark-red cherry, orangey edge. Nose: ripe fruit, spicy, creamy oak, toasty, complex, earthy notes. Palate: powerful, flavourful, toasty, round tannins, balanced.

MontReaga La Esencia 2006 T
100% syrah
90
Colour: cherry, garnet rim. Nose: balanced, complex, ripe fruit, spicy, creamy oak, balsamic herbs. Palate: good structure, flavourful, round tannins.

MontReaga Tempo 2009 T
85

Tempo La Espera 2005 T
87
Colour: deep cherry, orangey edge. Nose: balanced, complex, ripe fruit, spicy, creamy oak. Palate: good structure, flavourful, round tannins.

OSBORNE MALPICA DE TAJO

Ctra. Malpica - Pueblanueva, km. 6
45692 Malpica del Tajo (Toledo)
☎: +34 925 860 990
Fax: +34 925 860 905
www.osborne.es
carolina.cerrato@osborne.es

Solaz 2013 RD
syrah, mencía
84

Solaz 2013 B
verdejo, viura
83

Solaz Coupage 2012 T
syrah, tempranillo
85

Solaz Tempranillo Cabernet Sauvignon 2012 T
tempranillo, cabernet sauvignon
83

PAGO DE VALLEGARCÍA

Finca Vallegarcía, s/n
13194 Retuerta del Bullaque
(Ciudad Real)
☎: +34 925 421 407
Fax: +34 925 421 822
www.vallegarcia.com
comercial@vallegarcia.com

Hipperia 2010 T
91
Colour: cherry, garnet rim. Nose: ripe fruit, scrubland, spicy, creamy oak, mineral. Palate: flavourful, powerful, balsamic, toasty, long.

Petit Hipperia 2011 T
89
Colour: cherry, garnet rim. Nose: ripe fruit, balsamic herbs, mineral, spicy, creamy oak. Palate: powerful, flavourful, spicy.

Vallegarcía Syrah 2010 T
100% syrah
92
Colour: very deep cherry. Nose: warm, sweet spices, earthy notes, mineral. Palate: powerful, ripe fruit, fine bitter notes.

Vallegarcía Viognier 2012 BFB
100% viognier
93
Colour: bright yellow. Nose: citrus fruit, ripe fruit, fragrant herbs, white flowers, spicy, creamy oak. Palate: rich, flavourful, balanced, elegant. Personality.

PAGO DEL VICARIO

Ctra. Ciudad Real - Porzuna, (CM-412) Km. 16
13196 Ciudad Real (Ciudad Real)
☎: +34 926 666 027
Fax: +34 926 666 029
www.pagodelvicario.com
info@pagodelvicario.com

Pago del Vicario 50-50 2009 T
tempranillo, cabernet sauvignon
88
Colour: cherry, garnet rim. Nose: ripe fruit, wild herbs, earthy notes, spicy, creamy oak. Palate: balanced, flavourful, long, balsamic.

Pago del Vicario Agios 2007 T
tempranillo, garnacha
86
Colour: black cherry, orangey edge. Nose: wet leather, animal reductive notes, spicy, dark chocolate. Palate: good structure, round tannins.

Pago del Vicario Blanco de Tempranillo 2013 B
tempranillo
86
Colour: straw, pale. Nose: dry nuts, faded flowers, wild herbs. Palate: fine bitter notes, correct.

Pago del Vicario Corte Dulce 2007 B
chardonnay, sauvignon blanc
81

Pago del Vicario Merlot Dulce 2010 T
merlot
84

Pago del Vicario Monagós 2007 T
syrah, graciano
87
Colour: cherry, garnet rim. Nose: ripe fruit, spicy, toasty, smoky, tobacco. Palate: powerful, flavourful, toasty, round tannins.

Pago del Vicario Penta 2011 T
tempranillo, merlot, syrah, cabernet sauvignon
86
Colour: cherry, garnet rim. Nose: ripe fruit, wild herbs, earthy notes, spicy. Palate: flavourful, long, balsamic.

Pago del Vicario Petit Verdot 2013 RD
petit verdot
86
Colour: rose. Nose: powerfull, ripe fruit, red berry notes, floral. Palate: powerful, concentrated, balsamic.

Pago del Vicario Talva 2007 BFB
chardonnay, sauvignon blanc
83

QUINTA DE AVES

Ctra. CR-P-5222, Km. 11,200
13350 Moral de Calatrava
(Ciudad Real)
☎: +34 915 716 514
Fax: +34 915 711 151
www.quintadeaves.es
info@quintadeaves.es

Quinta de Aves Alauda Chardonnay 2012 B
100% chardonnay

86

Colour: bright yellow. Nose: ripe fruit, candied fruit, lees reduction notes. Palate: fruity, good acidity, fine bitter notes.

Quinta de Aves Alauda Moscatel Sauvignon 2012 B

84

Quinta de Aves Noctua Ensamblaje 2011 T

87

Colour: bright cherry. Nose: sweet spices, creamy oak, fruit preserve, balsamic herbs. Palate: flavourful, fruity, toasty.

Quinta de Aves Noctua Syrah 2012 T
100% syrah

86

Colour: cherry, garnet rim. Nose: fruit preserve, scrubland, floral, spicy. Palate: powerful, flavourful, ripe fruit.

RODRÍGUEZ DE VERA

Ctra. de Pétrola, km. 3, A
02695 Chinchilla de Montearagón
(Albacete)
☎: +34 696 168 873
www.rodriguezdevera.com
info@rodriguezdevera.com

Jumenta 2012 T Roble
100% cabernet sauvignon

83

Rodríguez de Vera 2010 T
100% merlot

82

Rodríguez de Vera 2012 BFB
100% chardonnay

84

Sorrasca 2010 T

85

THE GRAND WINES

Ramón y Cajal 7, 1ºA
01007 Vitoria (Alava)
☎: +34 945 158 282
Fax: +34 945 158 283
www.thegrandwines.com
araex@araex.com

Gran Sello 2013 T

86

Colour: cherry, garnet rim. Nose: red berry notes, ripe fruit, balsamic herbs, medium intensity. Palate: powerful, flavourful, easy to drink.

Gran Sello Colección Privada Tempranillo Syrah Garnacha 2012 T

89

Colour: very deep cherry. Nose: balanced, expressive, balsamic herbs, spicy. Palate: good structure, elegant, balanced, round tannins.

TINEDO

Ctra. CM 3102, Km. 30
13630 Socuéllamos (Ciudad Real)
☎: +34 646 433 414
www.tinedo.com
pvelasco@tinedo.com

Cala N 1 2011 T
tempranillo, syrah, cabernet sauvignon, graciano

88 🌺

Colour: cherry, garnet rim. Nose: red berry notes, ripe fruit, wild herbs, dry stone. Palate: powerful, flavourful, balanced.

Cala N 2 2010 T
tempranillo, graciano, roussanne

89 🌺

Colour: cherry, garnet rim. Nose: ripe fruit, spicy, creamy oak, toasty, complex, mineral. Palate: powerful, flavourful, toasty, round tannins.

UNION CAMPESINA INIESTENSE

San Idefonso, 1
16235 Iniesta (Cuenca)
☎: +34 967 490 120
Fax: +34 967 490 777
www.cooperativauci.com
aurora@cooperativauci.com

Señorío de Iniesta 2012 T Roble
tempranillo, syrah

85

Señorío de Iniesta 2013 B
sauvignon blanc

82

Señorío de Iniesta 2013 RD
bobal

85 🌺

Señorío de Iniesta 2013 T
tempranillo, syrah, petit verdot

83 🏵

Señorío de Iniesta Tempranillo 2013 T
tempranillo

84

UVAS FELICES
Agullers, 7
08003 Barcelona (Barcelona)
☎: +34 902 327 777
www.vilaviniteca.es

Sospechoso 2011 T
89

Colour: bright cherry. Nose: ripe fruit, sweet spices, creamy oak. Palate: flavourful, fruity, toasty, round tannins.

Sospechoso 2013 RD
84

VINÍCOLA DE CASTILLA
Pol. Ind. Calle I, s/n
13200 Manzanares (Ciudad Real)
☎: +34 926 647 800
Fax: +34 926 610 466
www.vinicoladecastilla.com
nacional@vinicoladecastilla.com

Olimpo 2010 T Barrica
tempranillo, syrah, petit verdot

84

Olimpo Privilegio 2011 BFB
moscatel, chardonnay, sauvignon blanc

85

Pago Peñuelas 2010 T
tempranillo

85

Pago Peñuelas 2013 B
verdejo

85

VINOS COLOMAN S.A.T.
Goya, 17
13620 Pedro Muñoz (Ciudad Real)
☎: +34 926 586 410
Fax: +34 926 586 656
www.satcoloman.com
coloman@satcoloman.com

Pedroteño 2013 T
tempranillo

84

Pedroteño Airén 2013 B
airén

80

VINOS Y BODEGAS
Ctra. de las Mesas, Km. 1
13630 Socuéllanos (Ciudad Real)
☎: +34 926 531 067
Fax: +34 926 532 249
www.vinosybodegas.com
export@vinosybodegas.com

Amelasio Cabernet 2012 T
100% cabernet sauvignon

85

Amelasio Merlot 2012 T
100% merlot

86

Colour: cherry, garnet rim. Nose: ripe fruit, wild herbs, spicy. Palate: balanced, flavourful, long, balsamic.

Amelasio Sauvignon Blanc 2013 B
sauvignon blanc

84

Amelasio Syrah 2012 T
100% syrah

87

Colour: bright cherry. Nose: red berry notes, ripe fruit, balanced, floral, sweet spices. Palate: fruity, easy to drink, good finish.

Amelasio Tempranillo 2012 T
100% tempranillo

86

Colour: cherry, garnet rim. Nose: sweet spices, ripe fruit, varietal. Palate: correct, ripe fruit, easy to drink.

Mirador de Castilla 12 meses 2008 T
cabernet sauvignon, tempranillo, merlot, syrah

85

Mirador de Castilla 6 meses 2009 T
cabernet sauvignon, merlot, tempranillo, syrah

85

Ro Reserva de oro 2007 T
cabernet sauvignon, tempranillo

88

Colour: cherry, garnet rim. Nose: ripe fruit, spicy, creamy oak, toasty, complex. Palate: powerful, flavourful, toasty, round tannins.

Templum Cabernet Sauvignon 2012 T
100% cabernet sauvignon

84

Templum Merlot 2012 T
100% merlot

87

Colour: dark-red cherry, garnet rim. Nose: powerfull, ripe fruit, wild herbs, dried herbs. Palate: good structure, round tannins.

Templum Sauvignon blanc 2013 B
sauvignon blanc

86

Colour: bright straw. Nose: white flowers, fragrant herbs, fruit expression. Palate: fresh, fruity, flavourful.

Templum Syrah 2012 T
syrah

87

Colour: cherry, garnet rim. Nose: ripe fruit, fragrant herbs, spicy. Palate: powerful, flavourful, balanced.

Templum Tempranillo 2012 T
100% tempranillo

85

Villa Cachita 2008 T
cabernet sauvignon, tempranillo

85

VIÑA RUDA
Ctra CM-400 Km 0,5
13700 Tomelloso (Ciudad Real)
☎: +34 926 038 585
Fax: +34 926 038 540
www.vinaruda.com
comercial@vinaruda.com

Ruda Airen 2012 BFB
airén

85

Ruda Airen 2013 B
airén

84

Ruda Ensamblaje 2012 T

85

Ruda Tempranillo 2012 T
tempranillo

84

VIÑEDOS MEJORANTES S.L.
Ctra. de Villafranca, km. 2
45860 Villacañas (Toledo)
☎: +34 925 200 023
Fax: +34 925 200 023
www.portillejo.es
portillejo@portillejo.com

Monte Gudello 2012 T
tempranillo, cabernet sauvignon

83

Monte Gudello 2013 B
airén

82

VIÑEDOS Y BODEGAS MUÑOZ
Ctra. Villarrubia, 11
45350 Noblejas (Toledo)
☎: +34 925 140 070
Fax: +34 925 141 334
www.bodegasmunoz.com
c.calidad@bodegasmunoz.com

Finca Muñoz Barrel Aged 2010 T Roble
tempranillo

88

Colour: pale ruby, brick rim edge. Nose: ripe fruit, spicy, creamy oak, toasty. Palate: powerful, flavourful, toasty.

Finca Muñoz Cepas Viejas 2010 T
100% tempranillo

91

Colour: cherry, garnet rim. Nose: ripe fruit, spicy, creamy oak, toasty, complex, earthy notes. Palate: powerful, flavourful, toasty, round tannins.

Legado Muñoz Chardonnay 2013 B
chardonnay

87

Colour: bright golden. Nose: dried herbs, dried flowers, ripe fruit, sweet spices. Palate: flavourful, fruity, good acidity.

Legado Muñoz Garnacha 2012 T
garnacha

86

Colour: bright cherry. Nose: ripe fruit, sweet spices, creamy oak, medium intensity. Palate: flavourful, fruity, toasty.

Legado Muñoz Merlot 2011 T
merlot

85

Legado Muñoz Tempranillo 2013 T
tempranillo

83

VT CASTILLA/ CAMPO DE CALATRAVA

AMANCIO MENCHERO MÁRQUEZ
Legión, 27
13260 Bolaños de Calatrava
(Ciudad Real)
☎: +34 926 870 076
www.vinos-menchero.com
amanciomenchero@hotmail.com

Cuba 38 2013 T
tempranillo, cabernet sauvignon

83

Quarta Cabal 2013 B
airén

82

BODEGAS NARANJO

Felipe II, 5
13150 Carrión de Calatrava
(Ciudad Real)
☎: +34 926 814 155
Fax: +34 926 815 335
www.bodegasnaranjo.com
info@bodegasnaranjo.com

Lahar de Calatrava 2012 B
tempranillo

85

VT CASTYLE

ABADÍA RETUERTA

Ctra. N-122 Soria, km. 332,5
47340 Sardón de Duero (Valladolid)
☎: +34 983 680 314
Fax: +34 983 680 286
www.abadia-retuerta.com
info@abadia-retuerta.es

Abadía Retuerta Le Domaine 2013 B

91

Colour: yellow, greenish rim. Nose: sweet spices, creamy oak, ripe fruit, floral. Palate: balanced, good structure, good acidity, fine bitter notes.

Abadía Retuerta Pago Garduña Syrah 2011 T
100% syrah

95

Colour: cherry, purple rim. Nose: red berry notes, violets, mineral, cocoa bean, spicy, creamy oak, expressive. Palate: powerful, flavourful, spicy, long, balanced, elegant.

Abadía Retuerta Pago Negralada 2011 T
100% tempranillo

95

Colour: black cherry, garnet rim. Nose: balsamic herbs, creamy oak, toasty, spicy, ripe fruit, mineral. Palate: powerful, flavourful, spicy, long.

Abadía Retuerta Pago Valdebellón 2011 T
100% cabernet sauvignon

94

Colour: black cherry, purple rim. Nose: red berry notes, ripe fruit, wild herbs, dry stone, spicy, toasty. Palate: powerful, flavourful, balsamic, spicy, elegant.

Abadía Retuerta Petit Verdot PV 2011 T
100% petit verdot

92

Colour: black cherry, garnet rim. Nose: red berry notes, ripe fruit, wild herbs, spicy, creamy oak. Palate: flavourful, balsamic, fruity aftestaste, balanced.

Abadía Retuerta Selección Especial 2010 T

91

Colour: cherry, garnet rim. Nose: balsamic herbs, ripe fruit, spicy, creamy oak, earthy notes. Palate: powerful, flavourful, spicy, long.

AGRÍCOLA CASTELLANA - BODEGA CUATRO RAYAS

Ctra. Rodilana, s/n
47491 La Seca (Valladolid)
☎: +34 983 816 320
Fax: +34 983 816 562
www.cuatrorayas.org
info@cuatrorayas.org

Caballero de Castilla 2013 RD
100% tempranillo

83

Caballero de Castilla Tempranillo 2012 T Roble
100% tempranillo

86

Colour: bright cherry. Nose: ripe fruit, sweet spices, creamy oak. Palate: flavourful, fruity, toasty, round tannins.

Caballero de Castilla Verdejo 2013 B
100% verdejo

83

Dolce Bianco Verdejo 2013 Semidulce
100% verdejo

85

Pecatis Tuis Verdejo 2013 B
100% verdejo

85

ALFREDO MAESTRO TEJERO

Avda. Escalona, 42
47300 Peñafiel (Valladolid)
☎: +34 687 786 742
www.alfredomaestro.com
alfredo@alfredomaestro.com

46 Cepas 2012 T
100% merlot

90

Colour: bright cherry. Nose: sweet spices, macerated fruit, expressive. Palate: flavourful, fruity, spicy, round tannins.

Amanda Rosado de Lágrima 2012 RD
100% garnacha tintorera

86

Colour: rose, purple rim. Nose: powerfull, floral, candied fruit, red berry notes, slightly evolved. Palate: powerful, fruity, fresh, good acidity.

Castrillo de Duero 2012 T
100% tempranillo

87

Colour: bright cherry. Nose: ripe fruit, sweet spices, creamy oak. Palate: flavourful, fruity, toasty.

El Marciano 2012 T
garnacha

93

Colour: bright cherry. Nose: ripe fruit, sweet spices, creamy oak, damp earth, mineral, toasty. Palate: flavourful, fruity, toasty, round tannins, balanced.

Gran Fausto 2009 T
100% tempranillo

92

Colour: pale ruby, brick rim edge. Nose: elegant, spicy, fine reductive notes, wet leather, aged wood nuances, fruit liqueur notes. Palate: spicy, fine tannins, elegant, long.

Lovamor 2012 B
100% albillo

90

Colour: old gold. Nose: ripe fruit, dried herbs, faded flowers, mineral. Palate: powerful, flavourful, spicy, rich, sweetness.

Valle del Botijas 2011 T

89

Colour: cherry, garnet rim. Nose: ripe fruit, spicy, creamy oak, toasty. Palate: powerful, flavourful, toasty.

Viña Almate 2012 T
100% tempranillo

93

Colour: cherry, garnet rim. Nose: ripe fruit, spicy, creamy oak, toasty, mineral, balsamic herbs, balanced. Palate: powerful, flavourful, toasty, elegant.

Viña Almate Finca La Guindalera 2011 T
100% tempranillo

92

Colour: cherry, garnet rim. Nose: ripe fruit, spicy, toasty, earthy notes, complex, expressive. Palate: powerful, flavourful, toasty, round tannins, good structure.

Viña Almate Finca La Olmera 2011 T
100% tempranillo

92

Colour: bright cherry. Nose: ripe fruit, sweet spices, creamy oak, balsamic herbs, dry stone, mineral. Palate: fruity, flavourful, toasty, elegant.

Viña Almate Garnacha 2011 T
100% garnacha

94

Colour: cherry, garnet rim. Nose: fruit liqueur notes, red berry notes, wild herbs, balsamic herbs, mineral, balanced, expressive. Palate: flavourful, balsamic, spicy, round. Personality.

ALVAR DE DIOS HERNANDEZ

Zamora No8
47154 El Pego (Zamora)
☎: +34 629 902 507
eldelarecella@gmail.com

Vagüera 2012 B
albillo real, albillo común, albillo rojo, moscatel
92
Colour: bright yellow. Nose: fresh fruit, expressive, fine lees, dried herbs, faded flowers. Palate: flavourful, fruity, good acidity, balanced.

Vagüera 2013 B
albillo real, albillo común, albillo rojo, moscatel
89
Colour: bright straw. Nose: faded flowers, medium intensity, wild herbs. Palate: correct, fine bitter notes.

AVELINO VEGAS

Calvo Sotelo, 8
40460 Santiuste (Segovia)
☎: +34 921 596 002
Fax: +34 921 596 035
www.avelinovegas.com
ana@avelinovegas.com

Nicte 2013 RD
100% prieto picudo
88
Colour: rose, purple rim. Nose: powerfull, ripe fruit, red berry notes, floral, expressive. Palate: powerful, fruity, fresh.

AXIAL

Plaza Calle Castillo de Capua, 10 Nave 7
50197 (Zaragoza)
☎: +34 976 780 136
Fax: +34 976 303 035
www.axialvinos.com
info@axialvinos.com

La Granja 360 Verdejo Viura 2013 B
84

BEATRIZ HERRANZ

Cuesta de las Descargas, 11 bis
28005 Madrid (Madrid)
☎: +34 655 890 949
www.barcodelcorneta.com
info@barcodelcorneta.com

Barco del Corneta 2012 B
100% verdejo
91
Colour: bright straw. Nose: fruit expression, balsamic herbs, wild herbs, varietal, creamy oak. Palate: flavourful, fresh, fruity, spicy, balanced, elegant.

BELONDRADE

Quinta San Diego - Camino del Puerto, s/n
47491 La Seca (Valladolid)
☎: +34 983 481 001
Fax: +34 600 590 024
www.belondrade.com
comunicacion@belondrade.com

Quinta Apolonia Belondrade 2013 B
verdejo
90
Colour: bright straw. Nose: fresh, fresh fruit, white flowers. Palate: flavourful, fruity, good acidity, balanced.

Quinta Clarisa Belondrade 2013 RD
tempranillo
88
Colour: rose, purple rim. Nose: powerfull, ripe fruit, red berry notes, floral, expressive. Palate: powerful, fruity, fresh.

BITEL S.L.

Ctra Villabañez, 5
47130 Tudela de Duero (Valladolid)
☎: +34 983 403 907
www.paguscopa.com
paguscopa@paguscopa.com

Pagus Copa 2010 T
garnacha
86
Colour: cherry, garnet rim. Nose: ripe fruit, spicy, creamy oak, toasty. Palate: powerful, flavourful, toasty.

BODEGA ALISTE

Pza. de España, 4
49520 Figueruela de Abajo (Zamora)
☎: +34 676 986 570
www.vinosdealiste.com
javier@hacedordevino.com

Estrela 2011 T
89
Colour: cherry, garnet rim. Nose: spicy, creamy oak, complex, fruit preserve, cocoa bean, roasted coffee. Palate: powerful, flavourful, toasty, round tannins.

Marina de Aliste 2012 T
90
Colour: deep cherry, garnet rim. Nose: powerfull, characterful, ripe fruit, spicy. Palate: good structure, spicy, ripe fruit, long.

BODEGA DE ALBERTO

Ctra. de Valdestillas, 2
47321 Serrada (Valladolid)
☎: +34 983 559 107
Fax: +34 983 559 084
www.dealberto.com
info@dealberto.com

CCCL 2009 T
88
Colour: cherry, garnet rim. Nose: ripe fruit, sweet spices, creamy oak. Palate: powerful, flavourful, spicy, long.

Finca Valdemoya 2013 RD
tempranillo
87
Colour: rose, purple rim. Nose: powerfull, ripe fruit, red berry notes, floral, expressive. Palate: powerful, fruity, fresh, balanced.

Finca Valdemoya Tempranillo 2011 T
87
Colour: cherry, garnet rim. Nose: ripe fruit, spicy, creamy oak, toasty. Palate: powerful, flavourful, toasty.

BODEGA DON JUAN DEL AGUILA

Real de Abajo, 100
05110 El Barraco (Ávila)
☎: +34 920 281 032
www.donjuandelaguila.es
bodegadonjuandelaguila@gmail.com

Gaznata 2012 T
garnacha
86
Colour: cherry, garnet rim. Nose: ripe fruit, fruit liqueur notes, fragrant herbs, dry stone. Palate: powerful, flavourful, balanced.

Gaznata 2013 RD
garnacha
83

Gaznata Concrete 2011 T
garnacha
85

Gaznata Finca Cipri 2012 T
91
Colour: pale ruby, brick rim edge. Nose: fruit liqueur notes, ripe fruit, balsamic herbs, spicy, balanced. Palate: powerful, flavourful, spicy, balsamic, elegant.

Gaznata Finca Mariano 2012 T
garnacha
90
Colour: light cherry. Nose: fruit liqueur notes, wild herbs, dry stone, spicy. Palate: powerful, flavourful, spicy, mineral.

BODEGA EMINA RUEDA

Ctra. Medina del Campo - Olmedo, Km. 1,5
47400 Medina del Campo (Valladolid)
☎: +34 983 803 346
Fax: +34 902 430 189
www.eminarueda.es
eminarueda@emina.es

Emina Chardonnay 2013 B
100% chardonnay
87
Colour: bright straw. Nose: citrus fruit, tropical fruit, white flowers, wild herbs. Palate: fresh, fruity, good acidity, balanced.

Emina Gewürztraminer 2013 B
100% gewürztraminer
88
Colour: bright straw. Nose: citrus fruit, fruit expression, floral, fragrant herbs, varietal. Palate: fresh, fruity, flavourful, good acidity, balanced.

Emina Moscatel 2013 B
100% moscatel
84

BODEGA FINCA CÁRDABA

Coto de Cárdaba, s/n
40314 Valtiendas (Segovia)
☎: +34 921 527 470
Fax: +34 921 527 470
www.fincacardaba.com
info@fincacardaba.com

Finca Cárdaba 2009 TC
tinta del país
90
Colour: cherry, garnet rim. Nose: ripe fruit, spicy, creamy oak, toasty, complex, expressive. Palate: powerful, flavourful, toasty, round tannins, elegant.

Finca Cárdaba 6 meses 2011 T Roble
tinta del país
88
Colour: bright cherry. Nose: ripe fruit, sweet spices, creamy oak, balsamic herbs. Palate: flavourful, fruity, toasty.

Finca Cárdaba Selección 2006 T
tinta del país

91

Colour: deep cherry, orangey edge. Nose: ripe fruit, wild herbs, spicy, creamy oak. Palate: flavourful, long, balsamic, balanced.

Viña Sancha 2013 RD
tinta del país

87

Colour: rose, purple rim. Nose: powerfull, ripe fruit, red berry notes, floral, expressive. Palate: powerful, fruity, fresh.

BODEGA FINCA FUENTEGALANA
Ctra. M-501, Alcorcón -
Plasencia, km. 65
05429 Navahondilla (Ávila)
☎: +34 646 843 231
www.fuentegalana.com
info@fuentegalana.com

Toros de Guisando 2012 T

87

Colour: bright cherry. Nose: sweet spices, creamy oak, ripe fruit, fruit preserve. Palate: flavourful, fruity, toasty.

Toros de Guisando Coupage 2009 T

86

Colour: cherry, garnet rim. Nose: ripe fruit, wild herbs, spicy, creamy oak. Palate: balanced, flavourful, long, balsamic.

Toros de Guisando Merlot 2010 TC
merlot

89

Colour: cherry, garnet rim. Nose: ripe fruit, wild herbs, earthy notes, spicy, creamy oak. Palate: balanced, flavourful, long, balsamic.

Toros de Guisando Syrah 2009 T
syrah

85

BODEGA LIBERALIA ENOLÓGICA
Camino del Palo, s/n
49800 Toro (Zamora)
☎: +34 980 692 571
Fax: +34 980 692 571
www.liberalia.es
liberalia@liberalia.es

Liberalia Uno 2013 Blanco dulce
moscatel grano menudo, albillo

88

Colour: bright straw. Nose: honeyed notes, grapey, fragrant herbs, white flowers. Palate: powerful, flavourful, fruity, long, sweet.

BODEGA PAGO DE CALLEJO
Avda. del Cid, km. 16
09441 Sotillo de la Ribera (Burgos)
☎: +34 947 532 312
Fax: +34 947 532 304
www.noecallejo.blogspot.com
callejo@bodegasfelixcallejo.com

El Lebrero 2012 B
albillo

90

Colour: bright golden. Nose: citrus fruit, ripe fruit, dried herbs, floral, spicy, creamy oak. Palate: flavourful, spicy, powerful.

Finca Valdelroble 2011 T Barrica
tempranillo, merlot, syrah

91 ♣

Colour: cherry, garnet rim. Nose: ripe fruit, spicy, creamy oak, toasty, complex, earthy notes. Palate: powerful, flavourful, toasty, balanced.

BODEGA Y VIÑEDOS FERNÁNDEZ RIVERA
Real, 2
47315 Pesquera de Duero (Valladolid)
☎: +34 983 870 037
Fax: +34 983 870 088
www.dehesalagranja.com
lagranja@dehesalagranja.com

Dehesa La Granja 2007 T
100% tempranillo

88

Colour: pale ruby, brick rim edge. Nose: spicy, wet leather, aged wood nuances, fruit liqueur notes, wild herbs. Palate: spicy, balsamic, long, toasty.

BODEGAS ABABOL

Tomás Bayón, 56
47491 La Seca (Valladolid)
☎: +34 635 504 720
Fax: +34 983 034 995
www.bodegasababol.com
labodega@bodegasababol.com

Ababol 2012 T
tempranillo
83

Ababol Verdejo sobre Lías 2012 B
100% verdejo
88
Colour: bright yellow. Nose: expressive, white flowers, ripe fruit, balanced. Palate: rich, flavourful, fruity, long.

Gran Ababol 2010 BFB
verdejo
86
Colour: bright golden. Nose: ripe fruit, dry nuts, powerfull, toasty, aged wood nuances. Palate: flavourful, fruity, spicy, toasty, long.

BODEGAS ALDEASOÑA

Ctra. Peñafiel - San Idelfonso, s/n
40235 Aldeasoña (Segovia)
☎: +34 983 878 052
Fax: +34 983 873 052
bodega@bodegaconvento.com

El Lagar de Aldeasoña 2008 T
aragonés
90
Colour: cherry, garnet rim. Nose: ripe fruit, spicy, creamy oak, toasty, complex, dark chocolate, earthy notes. Palate: powerful, flavourful, toasty, round tannins, balanced.

BODEGAS ALTA PAVINA

Camino de Santibáñez, s/n
47328 La Parrilla (Valladolid)
☎: +34 983 681 521
www.altapavina.com
info@greatwinesfromspain.net

Alta Pavina Pago La Pavina 2011 T
88
Colour: cherry, garnet rim. Nose: red berry notes, ripe fruit, wild herbs, dry stone, spicy, creamy oak. Palate: powerful, flavourful, balsamic, spicy.

Alta Pavina Pinot Noir Citius 2009 TC
100% pinot noir
86
Colour: pale ruby, brick rim edge. Nose: fruit liqueur notes, citrus fruit, scrubland, spicy, creamy oak. Palate: powerful, flavourful, long.

BODEGAS ARRAYÁN

Finca La Verdosa, s/n
45513 Santa Cruz del Retamar (Toledo)
☎: +34 916 633 131
Fax: +34 916 632 796
www.arrayan.es
comercial@arrayan.es

Garnacha de Arrayán 2012 T
garnacha
95
Colour: deep cherry. Nose: red berry notes, scrubland, balsamic herbs, sweet spices. Palate: flavourful, fruity, fresh, fine bitter notes, fine tannins.

BODEGAS CANOPY

Ctra. Toledo-Valmojado, km. 23
45180 Camarena (Toledo)
☎: +34 619 244 878
Fax: +34 925 283 680
achacon@bodegascanopy.com

KAOS 2009 T
garnacha
91
Colour: cherry, garnet rim. Nose: fruit liqueur notes, candied fruit, sweet spices. Palate: spicy, ripe fruit, pruney.

BODEGAS CASTELO DE MEDINA

Ctra. CL-602, Km. 48
47465 Villaverde de Medina (Valladolid)
☎: +34 983 831 932
Fax: +34 983 831 857
www.castelodemedina.com
info@castelodemedina.com

Castelo Rosé Garnacha 2013 RD
garnacha
88
Colour: onion pink. Nose: elegant, candied fruit, dried flowers, fragrant herbs. Palate: light-bodied, flavourful, good acidity, long, spicy.

Syté 2008 T
90
Colour: cherry, garnet rim. Nose: ripe fruit, spicy, creamy oak, toasty, complex. Palate: powerful, flavourful, toasty, round tannins.

Vega Busiel 2010 T
86
Colour: cherry, garnet rim. Nose: ripe fruit, spicy, creamy oak, toasty. Palate: powerful, flavourful, toasty, round tannins.

Viña Castelo 2013 RD
garnacha
86
Colour: rose, purple rim. Nose: red berry notes, floral, wild herbs. Palate: powerful, fruity, fresh, correct.

BODEGAS DE LOS HEREDEROS DEL MARQUÉS DE RISCAL

Ctra. N-VI, km. 172,600
47490 Rueda (Valladolid)
☎: +34 983 868 029
Fax: +34 983 868 563
www.marquesderiscal.com
comunicacion@marquesderiscal.com

Riscal 1860 2012 T Roble
88
Colour: cherry, garnet rim. Nose: ripe fruit, spicy, creamy oak, toasty. Palate: powerful, flavourful, toasty, easy to drink.

BODEGAS FRUTOS VILLAR

Ctra. Burgos-Portugal Km. 113,7
47270 Cigales (Valladolid)
☎: +34 983 586 868
Fax: +34 983 580 180
www.bodegasfrutosvillar.com
bodegasfrutosvillar@bodegasfrutosvillar.com

Don Frutos Verdejo 2013 B
100% verdejo
85

BODEGAS GARCÍA NIÑO

Avda. Julio, s/n
09410 Arandilla (Burgos)
☎: +34 636 970 508
Fax: +34 916 126 072
www.bodegasgarcianino.es
fernando@bodegasgarcianino.es

Altorredondo 2011 T
100% tempranillo
88
Colour: cherry, garnet rim. Nose: ripe fruit, spicy, creamy oak, toasty, balsamic herbs. Palate: powerful, flavourful, toasty.

Pago de Costalao 24 meses 2009 TR
100% tempranillo
89
Colour: cherry, garnet rim. Nose: fruit preserve, balsamic herbs, damp earth, spicy. Palate: powerful, flavourful, rich, spicy, long.

BODEGAS GODELIA

Antigua Ctra. N-VI, NVI, Km. 403,5
24547 Pieros-Cacabelos (León)
☎: +34 987 546 279
Fax: +34 987 548 026
www.godelia.es
info@godelia.es

Libamus 2011 T
mencía
88
Colour: black cherry, purple rim. Nose: fruit preserve, wild herbs, sweet spices, dark chocolate, creamy oak. Palate: sweet, rich, powerful, flavourful, toasty.

BODEGAS GRUPO YLLERA

Autovía A-6, Km. 173,5
47490 Rueda (Valladolid)
☎: +34 983 868 097
Fax: +34 983 868 177
www.grupoyllera.com
grupoyllera@grupoyllera.com

Cuvi 2012 T Roble
100% tempranillo
87
Colour: bright cherry. Nose: ripe fruit, sweet spices, creamy oak. Palate: flavourful, fruity, toasty, roasted-coffee aftertaste.

Yllera 30 Aniversario 2011 TC
100% tempranillo
90
Colour: cherry, garnet rim. Nose: ripe fruit, wild herbs, spicy, creamy oak. Palate: balanced, flavourful, long, balsamic.

Yllera Dominus Gran Selección Viñedos Viejos 2005 T
100% tempranillo

91

Colour: pale ruby, brick rim edge. Nose: elegant, spicy, fine reductive notes, wet leather, aged wood nuances, fruit liqueur notes. Palate: spicy, fine tannins, elegant, long.

Yllera Privée BR
82

Yllera Vendimia Seleccionada 2009 TR
100% tempranillo

91

Colour: cherry, garnet rim. Nose: balanced, complex, ripe fruit, spicy, fine reductive notes. Palate: good structure, flavourful, round tannins, balanced.

BODEGAS LEDA
Mayor, 48
47320 Tudela de Duero (Valladolid)
☎: +34 983 520 682
www.bodegasleda.com
info@bodegasleda.com

Más de Leda 2011 T
100% tempranillo

89

Colour: cherry, garnet rim. Nose: ripe fruit, fruit preserve, wild herbs, mineral, spicy, creamy oak. Palate: powerful, rich, spicy, long.

BODEGAS MAURO
Ctra. Villabañez, km. 1
47320 Tudela de Duero (Valladolid)
☎: +34 983 521 972
Fax: +34 983 521 973
www.bodegasmauro.com
comunicacion@bodegasmauro.com

Mauro Vendimia Seleccionada 2009 T
100% tempranillo

93

Colour: cherry, garnet rim. Nose: ripe fruit, spicy, creamy oak, toasty, complex, mineral. Palate: powerful, flavourful, toasty, round tannins, balanced, elegant.

Terreus 2011 T
100% tempranillo

95

Colour: black cherry, purple rim. Nose: red berry notes, ripe fruit, balsamic herbs, mineral, spicy, creamy oak, toasty. Palate: powerful, flavourful, fruity, spicy, long, balanced, elegant, round.

BODEGAS MENTO
Calvario, 13
47320 Tudela de Duero (Valladolid)
☎: +34 983 521 233
www.bodegasmento.com
info@bodegasmento.com

Luisita 2014 RD
tempranillo

88

Colour: light cherry. Nose: lactic notes, raspberry, red berry notes, fragrant herbs, floral. Palate: fresh, fruity, easy to drink.

Mento 2007 T Roble
tempranillo

86

Colour: pale ruby, brick rim edge. Nose: ripe fruit, balsamic herbs, spicy, creamy oak, fine reductive notes. Palate: powerful, flavourful, spicy.

Mento 2009 T Roble
tempranillo

88

Colour: cherry, garnet rim. Nose: ripe fruit, wild herbs, spicy, creamy oak. Palate: flavourful, spicy, long.

Mento 2010 T Roble
tempranillo

87

Colour: bright cherry. Nose: ripe fruit, sweet spices, creamy oak, medium intensity. Palate: fruity, flavourful, toasty.

BODEGAS PEÑASCAL

Ctra. Valladolid a Segovia (N-601)
km. 7,3 Pol. 2 Parcela 273
47140 Laguna de Duero (Valladolid)
☎: +34 983 546 080
www.penascal.es
rrpp@vina-mayor.com

Cuesta del Aire Sauvignon Blanc Verdejo 2013 B
83

Cuesta del Aire Tempranillo Shiraz 2013 RD
86
Colour: raspberry rose. Nose: red berry notes, candied fruit, balsamic herbs, floral. Palate: fresh, fruity, easy to drink.

Cuesta del Aire Tempranillo Shiraz 2013 T
85

Peñascal RD
83

Peñascal frizzante 5.5 B
verdejo
86
Colour: pale. Nose: white flowers, fresh fruit, citrus fruit. Palate: sweet, flavourful.

Ponte Vecchio Moscato RD
85

Tríptico 2009 T
87
Colour: bright cherry. Nose: sweet spices, creamy oak, ripe fruit. Palate: flavourful, toasty, spicy, harsh oak tannins.

BODEGAS SANTA RUFINA

Pago Fuente La Teja. Pol. Ind. 3 - Parcela 102
47290 Cubillas de Santa Marta
(Valladolid)
☎: +34 983 585 202
Fax: +34 983 585 202
www.bodegassantarufina.com
info@bodegassantarufina.com

Bosque Real Cabernet 2012 T
100% cabernet sauvignon
80

Bosque Real Merlot 2012 T
100% merlot
84

Bosque Real Verdejo 2013 B
100% verdejo
85

BODEGAS TRITÓN

Pol.1 Parc. 146/148 Paraje Cantagrillos
49708 Villanueva de Campeán
(Zamora)
☎: +34 968 435 022
Fax: +34 968 716 051
www.orowines.com
info@orowines.com

Entresuelos 2011 T
100% tempranillo
90
Colour: very deep cherry, garnet rim. Nose: powerfull, ripe fruit, roasted coffee, dark chocolate. Palate: powerful, toasty, roasted-coffee aftertaste.

Entresuelos 2012 T
100% tempranillo
90
Colour: deep cherry, garnet rim. Nose: smoky, toasty, ripe fruit. Palate: balanced, easy to drink, fruity.

Rejón 2011 T
100% tempranillo
94
Colour: cherry, garnet rim. Nose: spicy, creamy oak, toasty, complex, dark chocolate, earthy notes, warm, overripe fruit. Palate: powerful, flavourful, toasty, round tannins.

Rejón 2012 T
100% tempranillo
95
Colour: cherry, garnet rim. Nose: ripe fruit, spicy, creamy oak, toasty, complex. Palate: powerful, flavourful, toasty, round tannins.

Tridente Mencía 2011 T
100% mencía
93
Colour: cherry, garnet rim. Nose: wild herbs, earthy notes, spicy, red berry notes, ripe fruit. Palate: balanced, flavourful, long, balsamic.

Tridente Prieto Picudo 2012 T
100% prieto picudo
92
Colour: cherry, garnet rim. Nose: ripe fruit, spicy, creamy oak, toasty, complex, scrubland. Palate: powerful, flavourful, toasty, round tannins.

Tridente Tempranillo 2011 T
100% tempranillo
94
Colour: cherry, garnet rim. Nose: spicy, creamy oak, toasty, complex, dark chocolate, earthy notes, overripe fruit. Palate: powerful, flavourful, toasty, round tannins.

Tridente Tempranillo 2012 T
100% tempranillo

92

Colour: bright cherry. Nose: sweet spices, creamy oak, ripe fruit, fruit preserve. Palate: flavourful, fruity, toasty, round tannins.

BODEGAS VEGA DE TERA
Bajura de los Carreteros, s/n
49627 Sitrama de Tera (Zamora)
☎: +34 606 411 428
www.bodegasvegadetera.com
miguel.regil@bodegasvegadetera.com

Vega de Tera 12 meses 2012 T
tempranillo

86

Colour: cherry, garnet rim. Nose: fruit preserve, balsamic herbs, damp earth, creamy oak. Palate: powerful, flavourful, spicy, long.

Vega de Tera 2012 T Roble
tempranillo

87

Colour: very deep cherry, garnet rim. Nose: powerfull, ripe fruit, roasted coffee, dark chocolate. Palate: powerful, toasty, roasted-coffee aftertaste.

Vega de Tera 2013 B
verdejo

86

Colour: bright yellow. Nose: citrus fruit, ripe fruit, floral, fragrant herbs. Palate: powerful, flavourful, correct.

Vega de Tera 2013 RD
prieto picudo

85

Vega de Tera 2013 T
tempranillo, prieto picudo

86

Colour: cherry, garnet rim. Nose: ripe fruit, red berry notes, balsamic herbs, expressive. Palate: powerful, flavourful, balanced.

Vega de Tera 24 meses 2011 T
tempranillo

88

Colour: cherry, garnet rim. Nose: ripe fruit, spicy, creamy oak, toasty, balsamic herbs. Palate: powerful, flavourful, toasty.

BODEGAS VINOS DE LEÓN
La Vega, s/n
24009 León (León)
☎: +34 987 209 712
Fax: +34 987 209 800
www.bodegasvinosdeleon.es
info@bodegasvinosdeleon.es

Palacio de León Cuvée 2011 T
100% tempranillo

87

Colour: bright cherry. Nose: ripe fruit, sweet spices, creamy oak, medium intensity. Palate: fruity, flavourful, toasty, balanced.

Palacio de León Tempranillo 2012 T
100% tempranillo

83

BODEGAS VITERRA
Pol. Ind Jerónimo Roure, Parc 45
46520 Puerto de Sagunto (Valencia)
☎: +34 962 691 090
Fax: +34 962 690 963
www.vinamagna.es
direccioncomercial@bodegasviterra.com

Ennius 2013 B
100% verdejo

81

Ennius 2013 T
100% tempranillo

82

Ennius Rosado Frizzante 2013 RD
100% tempranillo

84

BODEGAS VIZAR
Avda. Ramón Pradera, 14
47009 Valladolid (Valladolid)
☎: +34 983 682 690
Fax: +34 983 682 125
www.bodegasvizar.es
info@bodegasvizar.es

Vizar Selección Especial 2010 T

94

Colour: cherry, garnet rim. Nose: ripe fruit, spicy, creamy oak, toasty, complex, earthy notes. Palate: powerful, flavourful, toasty, round tannins.

Vizar Syrah 2010 T
100% syrah

89

Colour: bright cherry. Nose: ripe fruit, sweet spices, creamy oak, expressive. Palate: flavourful, fruity, toasty, round tannins.

VIZAR

AÑADA: *2010*
PARCELA: *El Redondal*
UVA: *100% Syrah*
CRIANZA: *14 meses Roble Francés*
ALCOHOL.: *13,5 %*
PRODUCCIÓN: *3.000 botellas*

BODEGAS Y VIÑEDOS EL CODONAL

Pza. de la Constitución, 3
40462 Aldeanueva del Codonal
(Segovia)
☎: +34 921 582 063
www.bodegaselcodonal.com
pedro.gomez@bodegaselcodonal.com

Codonal Vinum Nobile 2012 B
100% verdejo

87

Colour: bright yellow. Nose: powerfull, sweet spices, creamy oak. Palate: rich, smoky aftertaste, flavourful.

BODEGAS Y VIÑEDOS LA MEJORADA

Monasterio de La Mejorada
47410 Olmedo (Valladolid)
☎: +34 606 707 041
www.lamejorada.es
contacto@lamejorada.es

La Mejorada Las Cercas 2010 T

95

Colour: cherry, garnet rim. Nose: ripe fruit, cocoa bean, spicy, creamy oak, toasty, mineral, expressive. Palate: powerful, flavourful, balanced, balsamic, elegant.

La Mejorada Las Cercas 2011 T Roble

94

Colour: cherry, garnet rim. Nose: red berry notes, ripe fruit, fragrant herbs, spicy, toasty, creamy oak, mineral. Palate: powerful, flavourful, balsamic, balanced.

La Mejorada Las Norias 2010 T Roble
tempranillo

92

Colour: cherry, garnet rim. Nose: ripe fruit, wild herbs, earthy notes, spicy, creamy oak. Palate: balanced, flavourful, long, balsamic.

La Mejorada Tiento 2009 T

91

Colour: deep cherry, garnet rim. Nose: ripe fruit, dark chocolate, sweet spices, toasty, creamy oak. Palate: powerful, flavourful, balsamic, toasty, balanced.

La Mejorada Tiento 2011 T

92

Colour: cherry, garnet rim. Nose: ripe fruit, spicy, creamy oak, toasty, complex, dark chocolate, earthy notes. Palate: powerful, flavourful, toasty, round tannins.

Villalar Oro 2010 T Roble
tempranillo

90

Colour: bright cherry. Nose: ripe fruit, sweet spices, creamy oak, expressive. Palate: flavourful, fruity, toasty.

BODEGAS Y VIÑEDOS RODRIGO MÉNDEZ S.L.

Pza. de Compostola, 22
36201 Vigo (Pontevedra)
☎: +34 699 446 113
goliardovino@gmail.com

El Barredo 2011 T
pinot noir, mencía

90

Colour: black cherry, garnet rim. Nose: scrubland, ripe fruit, old leather. Palate: flavourful, correct, balsamic.

CLUNIA

Camino Torre, 1
09410 Coruña del Conde (Burgos)
☎: +34 607 185 951
Fax: +34 948 818 574
ppavez@principedeviana.com

Clunia Syrah 2011 T
100% syrah

92

Colour: cherry, purple rim. Nose: red berry notes, ripe fruit, violets, expressive, spicy. Palate: flavourful, long, fruity aftestaste, full.

Clunia Syrah 2012 T
100% syrah

93

Colour: cherry, garnet rim. Nose: red berry notes, ripe fruit, balsamic herbs, spicy, creamy oak. Palate: balanced, fruity, spicy, correct.

Clunia Tempranillo 2011 T
100% tempranillo

93

Colour: cherry, purple rim. Nose: red berry notes, elegant, mineral, balsamic herbs, creamy oak. Palate: flavourful, good structure, long, balanced.

Finca El Rincón de Clunia 2010 T
100% tempranillo

95

Colour: deep cherry, purple rim. Nose: ripe fruit, cocoa bean, creamy oak, expressive, elegant. Palate: rich, good structure, long, balsamic, good acidity, balanced.

Finca El Rincón de Clunia 2011 T
100% tempranillo

94

Colour: cherry, purple rim. Nose: red berry notes, violet drops, balsamic herbs, mineral, powerfull. Palate: flavourful, rich, spicy, balanced.

COMANDO G VITICULTORES

Avda. Constitución, 23
28640 Cadalso de los Vidrios (Madrid)
☎: +34 918 640 602
www.comandog.es
info@comandog.es

El Tamboril 2012 B
garnacha blanca, garnacha gris

93

Colour: bright yellow. Nose: white flowers, fine lees, dried herbs, candied fruit. Palate: flavourful, fruity, balanced.

Rumbo al Norte 2012 T
garnacha

96

Colour: bright cherry. Nose: fresh, red berry notes, earthy notes, balsamic herbs. Palate: flavourful, light-bodied, spicy, slightly dry, soft tannins.

Tumba del Rey Moro 2012 T
garnacha

94

Colour: cherry, garnet rim. Nose: ripe fruit, wild herbs, earthy notes, spicy, creamy oak. Palate: balanced, flavourful, long, balsamic.

COMPAÑÍA DE VINOS TELMO RODRÍGUEZ

El Monte
01308 Lanciego (Álava)
☎: +34 945 628 315
Fax: +34 945 628 314
www.telmorodriguez.com
contact@telmorodriguez.com

Pegaso "Barrancos de Pizarra" 2011 T
garnacha

93

Colour: cherry, garnet rim. Nose: spicy, creamy oak, toasty, dark chocolate, earthy notes. Palate: powerful, flavourful, toasty, round tannins.

Pegaso "Granito" 2011 T
garnacha

94

Colour: light cherry. Nose: elegant, balanced, spicy, ripe fruit, cocoa bean. Palate: balanced, long, balsamic, round.

DANI LANDI

Constitución, 23
28640 Cadalso de los Vidrios (Madrid)
☎: +34 696 366 555
www.danilandi.com
daniel@danilandi.com

El Reventón 2012 T
garnacha

95

Colour: bright cherry. Nose: expressive, elegant, red berry notes, scrubland, fragrant herbs. Palate: good acidity, spicy, grainy tannins.

Las Uvas de la Ira 2012 B
albillo

92

Colour: bright golden. Nose: ripe fruit, citrus fruit, sweet spices. Palate: ripe fruit, round.

DEHESA DE CADOZOS

José Bardasano Baos, 9 4º
28016 Madrid (Madrid)
☎: +34 915 280 134
Fax: +34 915 280 238
www.cadozos.com
nmaranon@cadozos.com

Cadozos 2007 T

88

Colour: cherry, garnet rim. Nose: complex, ripe fruit, spicy, wild herbs, damp earth. Palate: good structure, flavourful, spirituous.

Sayago 830 2011 TC

91

Colour: cherry, garnet rim. Nose: ripe fruit, spicy, creamy oak, toasty, scrubland. Palate: powerful, flavourful, toasty.

DOMINIO DOSTARES

P.I. Bierzo Alto, Los Barredos, 4
24318 San Román de Bembibre (León)
☎: +34 987 514 550
Fax: +34 987 514 570
www.dominiodostares.com
info@dominiodetares.com

Cumal 2010 T
100% prieto picudo

93

Colour: dark-red cherry, garnet rim. Nose: ripe fruit, fruit liqueur notes, fragrant herbs, dry stone, spicy, creamy oak. Palate: balanced, spicy, balsamic, long, fruity aftestaste.

LLanos de Cumal 2011 T
prieto picudo
89
Colour: bright cherry. Nose: ripe fruit, sweet spices, creamy oak, wild herbs. Palate: fruity, flavourful, toasty.

Tombú 2013 RD
100% prieto picudo
87
Colour: rose, purple rim. Nose: powerfull, ripe fruit, dried herbs. Palate: powerful, fruity, fresh, correct.

ERMITA DEL CONDE
Camino de la Torre, 1
09410 Coruña del Conde (Burgos)
☎: +34 916 441 583
Fax: +34 914 860 598
www.ermitadelconde.com
info@ermitadelconde.com

Ermita del Conde 2011 T
tempranillo
92
Colour: black cherry, garnet rim. Nose: ripe fruit, sweet spices, creamy oak, toasty. Palate: fruity, flavourful, long.

Ermita del Conde Albillo Centenario 2011 B
albillo
94
Colour: bright yellow. Nose: elegant, dry stone, fragrant herbs, floral, spicy, creamy oak. Palate: balanced, flavourful, spicy, long. Personality.

Pago del Conde 2010 T
tempranillo
94
Colour: black cherry, garnet rim. Nose: mineral, red berry notes, balsamic herbs, spicy, creamy oak, balanced. Palate: powerful, flavourful, long, spicy, elegant.

Pago del Conde 2011 T
tempranillo
92
Colour: cherry, garnet rim. Nose: ripe fruit, spicy, creamy oak, toasty, complex. Palate: powerful, flavourful, toasty, round tannins.

FINCA LA RINCONADA
Avda. Fuencarral, 98
28108 Alcobendas (Madrid)
☎: +34 914 901 871
Fax: +34 916 620 430
www.barcolobo.com
info@barcolobo.com

Barcolobo 12 meses Barrica 2011 T
tempranillo, cabernet sauvignon, syrah
93
Colour: cherry, garnet rim. Nose: ripe fruit, spicy, creamy oak, toasty, complex, mineral. Palate: powerful, flavourful, toasty, round tannins, long.

Barcolobo Lacrimae Rerum 2013 RD
tempranillo
90
Colour: rose, purple rim. Nose: powerfull, ripe fruit, red berry notes, floral, expressive. Palate: powerful, fruity, fresh.

Barcolobo Verdejo 2012 B
verdejo
89
Colour: bright golden. Nose: ripe fruit, powerfull, aged wood nuances, roasted coffee. Palate: flavourful, fruity, spicy, toasty, long.

FINCA LAS CARABALLAS
Camino Velascálvaro, s/n
47400 Medina del Campo (Valladolid)
☎: +34 650 986 185
www.lascaraballas.com
esmeralda@lascaraballas.com

Finca Las Caraballas 2013 B
89
Colour: bright yellow, greenish rim. Nose: floral, ripe fruit, balanced, expressive. Palate: rich, flavourful, balanced, fine bitter notes.

FINCA TORREMILANOS
Finca Torremilanos
09400 Aranda de Duero (Burgos)
☎: +34 947 512 852
Fax: +34 947 508 044
www.torremilanos.com
reservas@torremilanos.com

Peñalba-López 2012 B
89 ⚘
Colour: bright yellow. Nose: faded flowers, ripe fruit. Palate: flavourful, rich, spicy, long.

FORTUNA WINES
Sanjurjo Badia, 22 - 3B
36207 Vigo (Pontevedra)
☎: +34 691 561 471
www.fortunawines.es
info@fortunawines.es

Alaia (4 Ever Alaia) 2011 T Roble
prieto picudo, tempranillo, merlot
87
Colour: bright cherry. Nose: ripe fruit, sweet spices, creamy oak, expressive. Palate: flavourful, fruity, toasty.

Olaia 2013 B
verdejo
85

 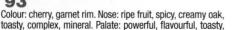

GARNACHA ALTO ALBERCHE

Camino del Pimpollar, s/n
05100 Navaluenga (Ávila)
☎: +34 616 416 542
Fax: +34 920 286 522
www.bodegagarnachaaltoalberche.com
sietenavas@live.com

7 Navas 2011 T Roble
100% garnacha
90
Colour: cherry, garnet rim. Nose: ripe fruit, wild herbs, earthy notes, spicy, creamy oak. Palate: balanced, flavourful, long, balsamic.

7 Navas 2013 T
100% garnacha
90
Colour: cherry, purple rim. Nose: red berry notes, ripe fruit, dry stone, wild herbs. Palate: fresh, fruity, flavourful, balsamic.

7 Navas Finca Catalino 2010 T
100% garnacha
93
Colour: cherry, garnet rim. Nose: ripe fruit, spicy, creamy oak, toasty, complex, balsamic herbs. Palate: powerful, flavourful, toasty, round tannins.

7 Navas Finca Faustina 2009 T
100% garnacha
93
Colour: ruby red. Nose: fruit liqueur notes, spicy, creamy oak, fine reductive notes, expressive. Palate: powerful, flavourful, spicy, long.

7 Navas Selección 2010 T
100% garnacha
93
Colour: cherry, garnet rim. Nose: ripe fruit, fruit liqueur notes, scrubland, dry stone, spicy, balanced. Palate: flavourful, fruity, complex, good acidity, correct.

GOYO GARCÍA VIADERO

Urb. Valdelvira
09140 Quintanaortuño (Burgos)
☎: +34 619 268 242
goyoviadero@gmail.com

Goyo García "Finca el Peruco" 2011 T
tempranillo, albillo
90
Colour: cherry, garnet rim. Nose: ripe fruit, wild herbs, earthy notes, spicy, creamy oak. Palate: balanced, flavourful, long, balsamic.

HACIENDA ZORITA MARQUÉS DE LA CONCORDIA FAMILY OF WINES

Ctra. Zamora - fermoselle, km. 58
49220 Fermoselle (Zamora)
☎: +34 980 613 163
Fax: +34 980 613 163
www.the-haciendas.com
agarcia@the-haciendas.com

Hacienda Zorita Magister 2011 T
91
Colour: cherry, garnet rim. Nose: ripe fruit, spicy, creamy oak, toasty, balsamic herbs, complex. Palate: powerful, flavourful, toasty.

Hacienda Zorita Natural Reserve 2011 T
syrah
90
Colour: cherry, garnet rim. Nose: ripe fruit, spicy, creamy oak, toasty, complex, dark chocolate, earthy notes. Palate: powerful, flavourful, toasty, round tannins.

HEREDAD DE URUEÑA

Ctra. Toro a Medina de Rioseco, km 21,300
47862 Urueña (Valladolid)
☎: +34 915 610 920
Fax: +34 915 634 131
www.heredaduruena.com
direccion@heredaduruena.com

Forum 2012 RD
tinta de Toro, tempranillo
82

Forum Etiqueta Negra 2011 T
tinta de Toro, tempranillo
92
Colour: cherry, garnet rim. Nose: red berry notes, ripe fruit, balsamic herbs, spicy, creamy oak, characterful. Palate: powerful, flavourful, balanced, round tannins.

Santo Merlot 2011 T
merlot
89
Colour: cherry, garnet rim. Nose: ripe fruit, wild herbs, earthy notes, spicy, creamy oak. Palate: balanced, flavourful, long, balsamic.

Santo Syrah 2011 T
syrah
88
Colour: cherry, garnet rim. Nose: ripe fruit, fruit preserve, wild herbs, sweet spices. Palate: powerful, flavourful, spicy, long.

Santo Tempranillo 2011 T
tempranillo
90
Colour: bright cherry. Nose: ripe fruit, sweet spices, creamy oak, mineral. Palate: fruity, flavourful, toasty, balanced.

LEYENDA DEL PÁRAMO

Ctra. de León s/n, Paraje El Cueto
24230 Valdevimbre (León)
☎: +34 987 050 039
Fax: +34 987 050 039
www.leyendadelparamo.com
info@leyendadelparamo.com

Flor del Páramo 2013 RD
prieto picudo
87
Colour: rose. Nose: red berry notes, raspberry, balsamic herbs, expressive. Palate: fine bitter notes, fresh, fruity, flavourful.

LONG WINES

Avda. del Puente Cultural, 8 Bloque B Bajo 7
28702 San Sebastián de los Reyes (Madrid)
☎: +34 916 221 305
Fax: +34 916 220 029
www.longwines.com
adm@longwines.com

Afán 2013 B
85

Afán 2013 RD
tempranillo, syrah
85

Afán 2013 T
84

LOS PALOMARES

Los Palomares, 6
24230 Valdevimbre (León)
☎: +34 987 304 218
Fax: +34 987 304 193
www.bodegalospalomares.com
lospalomares@bodegalospalomares.com

Impresiones 2013 B
100% verdejo
84

Impresiones 2013 RD
prieto picudo
85

MALDIVINAS

Los Pinillas, 1
28032 (Madrid)
☎: +34 913 710 587
www.maldivinas.es
carlos@maldivinas.es

Combate 2013 B
albillo
92
Colour: bright straw. Nose: fresh, fresh fruit, white flowers, balsamic herbs, expressive, mineral. Palate: flavourful, fruity, good acidity, balanced, elegant.

Doble Punta 2012 T
garnacha
90
Colour: ruby red. Nose: ripe fruit, spicy, creamy oak, toasty, fragrant herbs, mineral. Palate: powerful, flavourful, toasty, round tannins.

La Movida 2012 T
garnacha
94
Colour: ruby red. Nose: fruit liqueur notes, wild herbs, spicy, creamy oak, floral, dry stone. Palate: fresh, fruity, flavourful, spicy, balsamic, balanced.

La Movida Granito 2012 T
garnacha
93
Colour: light cherry. Nose: fruit liqueur notes, fruit preserve, wild herbs, dry stone, earthy notes, spicy. Palate: powerful, flavourful, balanced.

La Movida Laderas 2012 T
garnacha
91
Colour: light cherry. Nose: fruit liqueur notes, balsamic herbs, mineral, sweet spices. Palate: flavourful, spicy, balsamic, elegant.

MELGARAJO

Plaza Mayor, 9
47687 Melgar de Abajo (Valladolid)
☎: +34 679 082 971
www.melgarajo.es
melgarajo@melgarajo.es

Valdeleña 2011 T Roble
prieto picudo
86
Colour: bright cherry. Nose: ripe fruit, sweet spices, creamy oak. Palate: flavourful, fruity, toasty.

Valdeleña 2012 T
prieto picudo
83

Valdeleña 2012 T Roble
prieto picudo

84

Valdeleña Tinto de Autor 2011 T
prieto picudo

89

Colour: cherry, garnet rim. Nose: ripe fruit, spicy, creamy oak, toasty, complex. Palate: powerful, flavourful, toasty, round tannins.

OSSIAN VIDES Y VINOS
Cordel de las Merinas s/n
40447 Nieva (Segovia)
☎: +34 983 878 020
www.ossian.es
ossian@ossian.es

Capitel 2012 BFB
100% verdejo

91

Colour: bright yellow. Nose: floral, citrus fruit, ripe fruit, sweet spices, roasted coffee, mineral, balsamic herbs. Palate: powerful, flavourful, long, toasty.

Ossian 2012 BFB
100% verdejo

93

Colour: bright yellow. Nose: citrus fruit, ripe fruit, wild herbs, spicy, creamy oak, balanced. Palate: rich, powerful, flavourful, spicy, long, elegant.

OSSIAN

AGRICULTURA ECOLÓGICA

2012

VIÑAS VIEJAS VERDEJO 100% FERMENTADO Y CRIADO EN BARRICAS FRANCESAS EN EL ANTIGUO MONASTERIO DEL PARRAL 40447-SEGOVIA-ESPAÑA

Quintaluna 2013 B
verdejo

90

Colour: straw, greenish rim. Nose: elegant, expressive, floral, ripe fruit, dried herbs. Palate: flavourful, balanced, fine bitter notes, long.

Verdling 2011 B
verdejo

89

Colour: bright straw. Nose: white flowers, tropical fruit, citrus fruit, fragrant herbs. Palate: fresh, fruity, easy to drink.

QUINTA SARDONIA
Casa, s/n - Granja Sardón
47340 Sardón de Duero (Valladolid)
☎: +34 986 621 001
Fax: +34 986 621 084
www.terrasgauda.com

Quinta Sardonia QS 2009 T
tinto fino, cabernet sauvignon, syrah, malbec

89 🍷

Colour: cherry, garnet rim. Nose: ripe fruit, fruit preserve, balsamic herbs, powerfull, spicy, creamy oak. Palate: rich, powerful, flavourful, warm.

Quinta Sardonia QS 2010 T
tinto fino, cabernet sauvignon, syrah, malbec

93 🍷

Colour: deep cherry, garnet rim. Nose: complex, elegant, ripe fruit, spicy, balsamic herbs, expressive. Palate: full, complex, balanced.

Quinta Sardonia QS2 2011 T
tinto fino, cabernet sauvignon, merlot, syrah

91

Colour: very deep cherry, garnet rim. Nose: ripe fruit, sweet spices, scrubland, balanced. Palate: good structure, flavourful, varietal, long.

RAMIRO WINE CELLAR
Camino Viejo de Simancas, km. 3,5
47008 Valladolid (Valladolid)
☎: +34 639 306 279
www.ramirowinecellar.com
bodegasramiros@hotmail.com

Ramiro's 2009 T
tempranillo

93

Colour: cherry, garnet rim. Nose: balanced, ripe fruit, spicy, creamy oak, toasty, balsamic herbs, mineral. Palate: flavourful, good structure, spicy, long, elegant.

RODRÍGUEZ SANZO
Manuel Azaña, 9
47014 (Valladolid)
☎: +34 983 150 150
Fax: +34 983 150 151
www.rodriguezsanzo.com
comunicacion@valsanzo.com

Parajes Verdejo Viognier 2011 B

91

Colour: bright golden. Nose: ripe fruit, dry nuts, powerfull, toasty, aged wood nuances. Palate: flavourful, fruity, spicy, toasty, long.

Sanzo Verdejo Frizzante 2013 B
100% verdejo

86

Colour: bright straw. Nose: citrus fruit, dried flowers, wild herbs. Palate: fresh, fruity, easy to drink.

T * Sanzo 3 Tempranillos 2012 T

89

Colour: cherry, garnet rim. Nose: ripe fruit, spicy, creamy oak. Palate: powerful, flavourful, toasty, balanced.

RUDELES - TIERRAS EL GUIJARRAL
Trasterrera, 10
42345 Peñalba de San Esteban (Soria)
☎: +34 618 644 633
Fax: +34 975 350 582
www.rudeles.com
info@rudeles.com

Valdebonita Albillo 2013 B
100% albillo

88

Colour: bright straw. Nose: white flowers, fragrant herbs, fruit expression. Palate: fresh, fruity, flavourful, elegant.

Valdebonita Garnacha 2012 T
100% garnacha

89

Colour: ruby red, garnet rim. Nose: red berry notes, fruit liqueur notes, balsamic herbs, spicy. Palate: powerful, flavourful, fruity, correct.

SOTO Y MANRIQUE V.O.
Arandano, 14
47008 Valladolid (Valladolid)
☎: +34 626 290 408
www.sotoymanriquevo.com
info@sotoymanriquevo.com

Naranjas Azules Garnacha 2013 RD
garnacha

89

Colour: raspberry rose. Nose: balanced, expressive, fresh fruit, floral, dried herbs. Palate: fruity, flavourful, balanced, elegant.

VINOS DE ARGANZA
Río Ancares
24560 Toral de los Vados (León)
☎: +34 987 544 831
Fax: +34 987 563 532
www.vinosdearganza.com
admon@vinosdearganza.com

Lagar de Robla 2012 T Roble
100% mencía

89

Colour: very deep cherry, garnet rim. Nose: medium intensity, varietal, wild herbs, ripe fruit. Palate: flavourful, balanced.

Lagar de Robla Premium 2012 T
100% mencía

90

Colour: bright cherry. Nose: ripe fruit, sweet spices, creamy oak, balsamic herbs, varietal. Palate: flavourful, fruity, toasty.

Palacio de Arganza 2007 T
mencía, cabernet sauvignon, tempranillo

87

Colour: very deep cherry, garnet rim. Nose: dried herbs, fine reductive notes, ripe fruit, fruit liqueur notes, spicy. Palate: fruity, round tannins, good finish.

Palacio de Arganza 2011 T
mencía, cabernet sauvignon, tempranillo

85

VINOS MALAPARTE

Avda. Camilo José Cela, 2
40200 Cuéllar (Segovia)
☎: +34 921 105 204
www.vinosmalaparte.es
info@vinosmalaparte.es

Malaparte Espantalobos 2011 T
tempranillo
90
Colour: cherry, garnet rim. Nose: red berry notes, ripe fruit, fragrant herbs, sweet spices, creamy oak, mineral, expressive. Palate: powerful, flavourful, toasty, long.

Malaparte Montón de Piñas 2010 T
tempranillo
93
Colour: cherry, garnet rim. Nose: ripe fruit, spicy, creamy oak, toasty, complex, earthy notes, balsamic herbs. Palate: powerful, flavourful, toasty, round tannins, balanced.

VIÑA ALBARES

Camino Real, s/n
24310 Albares de la Ribera (León)
☎: +34 987 519 147
www.vinaalbareswine.com
info@vinaalbareswine.com

Quinta del Obispo 2013 RD
mencía, tempranillo, syrah, merlot
87
Colour: light cherry, bright. Nose: powerfull, ripe fruit, red berry notes, floral, expressive, dried herbs. Palate: powerful, fruity, fresh.

Quinta del Obispo Chardonnay - Gewürztraminer 2013 B
chardonnay, gewürztraminer
89
Colour: bright straw. Nose: white flowers, fragrant herbs, fruit expression. Palate: fresh, fruity, flavourful, balanced, elegant.

Quinta del Obispo Gewürztraminer 2013 B
gewürztraminer
87
Colour: bright straw. Nose: white flowers, fragrant herbs, tropical fruit. Palate: fresh, fruity, flavourful.

Quinta del Obispo Mencía 2013 T
mencía
87
Colour: bright cherry, garnet rim. Nose: powerfull, wild herbs, spicy. Palate: varietal, fruity, flavourful.

VIÑA DEL SOPIÉ

La Seca
47491 La Seca (Valladolid)
☎: +34 948 645 008
Fax: +34 948 645 166
www.destileriaslanavarra.com
info@familiabelasco.com

Viña del Sopié Verdejo 100% 2013 B
100% verdejo
87
Colour: bright straw. Nose: fresh, fresh fruit, white flowers. Palate: flavourful, fruity, good acidity.

Viña del Sopié Verdejo 2013 B
verdejo, viura
84

VIÑAS DEL CÉNIT

Ctra. de Circunvalación, s/n
49708 Villanueva de Campeán (Zamora)
☎: +34 980 569 346
www.vinasdelcenit.com
aalberca@avanteselecta.com

Venta Mazarrón 2012 T
100% tempranillo
93
Colour: very deep cherry, garnet rim. Nose: powerfull, ripe fruit, roasted coffee, dark chocolate. Palate: powerful, toasty, roasted-coffee aftertaste.

Villano 2012 T
tempranillo
88
Colour: cherry, purple rim. Nose: red berry notes, ripe fruit, aromatic coffee, dark chocolate, creamy oak. Palate: powerful, flavourful, roasted-coffee aftertaste.

VIÑEDOS DE VILLAESTER

49800 Toro (Zamora)
☎: +34 948 645 008
Fax: +34 948 645 166
www.familiabelasco.com
info@familiabelasco.com

Avutarda 2012 T
tempranillo, cabernet sauvignon
88
Colour: deep cherry, garnet rim. Nose: ripe fruit, wild herbs, spicy, creamy oak. Palate: powerful, flavourful, spicy, long.

WEINWERK EL LAGARTO

Portugal, 7
49323 Fornillos de Fermoselle (Zamora)
☎: +49 232 459 724
Fax: +49 232 459 721
www.gourmet-lagarto.de
winzer@gourmet-lagarto.de

Ruby Luby de Weinwerk 2012 T
88
Colour: bright cherry. Nose: ripe fruit, sweet spices, creamy oak, expressive. Palate: flavourful, fruity, toasty, round tannins.

VT CORDOBA

BODEGAS JESÚS NAZARENO

Avda. Cañete de las Torres, 33
14850 Baena (Córdoba)
☎: +34 957 670 225
Fax: +34 957 690 873
www.bjn1963.com
bjn@bjn1963.com

Castillo de Baena 2008 T Roble
80

NAVISA INDUSTRIAL VINÍCOLA ESPAÑOLA

Avda. José Padillo, s/n
14550 Montilla (Córdoba)
☎: +34 957 650 554
Fax: +34 957 651 747
www.navisa.es
navisa@navisa.es

Valpina 2011 TC
tempranillo, syrah, cabernet sauvignon
85

VT COSTA DE CANTABRIA

BODEGA NATES

Bº Llamosa, s/n
39761 Nates (Cantabria)
☎: +34 616 111 907
www.bodegasnates.net
comercial@bodegasnates.es

Nates 2013 B
88
Colour: bright straw. Nose: white flowers, fragrant herbs, fruit expression. Palate: fresh, fruity, flavourful, balanced, elegant

SEÑORÍO DEL PAS

Bº San Martín, 19-A
39638 San Martín de Villafufre (Cantabria)
☎: +34 630 543 351
www.senoriodelpas.es
info@senoriodelpas.es

Señorío del Pas 2012 B
84

VT CUMBRES DE GUADALFEO

BODEGA GARCÍA DE VERDEVIQUE

Cortijo Los García de Verdevique s/n
18439 Castaras (Granada)
☎: +34 958 957 925
www.bodegasgarciadeverdevique.com
info@bodegasgarciadeverdevique.com

García de Verdevique 2010 ESP
vijiriego
75

Los García de Verdevique 2008 T
tempranillo, cabernet sauvignon, syrah
90
Colour: cherry, garnet rim. Nose: balanced, complex, ripe fruit, spicy, fragrant herbs, earthy notes. Palate: good structure, flavourful, round tannins.

Los García de Verdevique 2013 B Barrica
vijiriego
78

DOMINIO BUENAVISTA

Ctra. de Almería, s/n
18480 Ugíjar (Granada)
☎: +34 958 767 254
Fax: +34 958 990 226
www.dominiobuenavista.com
info@dominiobuenavista.com

Don Miguel Dulce 2010 T
87
Colour: cherry, garnet rim. Nose: fruit preserve, dried fruit, smoky, aromatic coffee, toasty. Palate: powerful, flavourful, toasty, long.

Nolados 2009 T
90
Colour: cherry, garnet rim. Nose: ripe fruit, spicy, creamy oak, toasty, complex, earthy notes, characterful. Palate: powerful, flavourful, toasty, round tannins.

Sweet Melodies Dulce Natural 2013 B
100% viognier
85

VT EIVISSA

CAN RICH
Camí de Sa Vorera, s/n
07820 Sant Antoni (Illes Balears)
☎: +34 971 803 377
Fax: +34 971 803 377
www.bodegascanrich.com
info@bodegascanrich.com

BES Can Rich 2013 RD
monastrell
79

Can Rich 2013 B
chardonnay, malvasía
87
Colour: bright straw. Nose: fresh, fresh fruit, white flowers. Palate: flavourful, fruity, good acidity, balanced.

Can Rich 2013 RD
tempranillo, merlot
82

Can Rich Dulce Vino de licor
malvasía
85

Can Rich Ereso 2012 BFB
chardonnay
85

Can Rich Negre 2010 T
tempranillo, merlot
87
Colour: cherry, garnet rim. Nose: ripe fruit, wild herbs, earthy notes, spicy. Palate: balanced, flavourful.

Can Rich Selección 2008 T
cabernet sauvignon, merlot, tempranillo
87
Colour: cherry, garnet rim. Nose: spicy, tobacco, ripe fruit. Palate: balanced, round tannins, balsamic.

Lausos Cabernet Sauvignon 2007 T
cabernet sauvignon
90
Colour: cherry, garnet rim. Nose: ripe fruit, wild herbs, earthy notes, spicy, creamy oak. Palate: balanced, flavourful, long, balsamic.

Yviça 2013 T
monastrell, merlot, tempranillo
86
Colour: cherry, purple rim. Nose: fresh fruit, red berry notes, balsamic herbs. Palate: flavourful, fruity, easy to drink.

SA COVA
Bodega Sa Cova s/n
07816 Sant Mateu D'Albarca
(Illes Balears)
☎: +34 971 187 046
Fax: +34 971 312 250
www.sacovaibiza.com
sacova@sacovaibiza.com

Clot d'Albarca 2009 TR
syrah, merlot
90
Colour: cherry, garnet rim. Nose: ripe fruit, spicy, creamy oak, toasty, complex, earthy notes. Palate: powerful, flavourful, toasty, round tannins.

Sa Cova 2013 RD
monastrell
86
Colour: coppery red, bright. Nose: faded flowers, fragrant herbs. Palate: correct, fine bitter notes, fruity.

Sa Cova 9 2010 T
monastrell, syrah, merlot
88
Colour: bright cherry. Nose: ripe fruit, sweet spices, creamy oak, medium intensity. Palate: fruity, flavourful, toasty.

Sa Cova Blanc de Blanc 2013 B
malvasía, macabeo
84

Sa Cova Privat 2009 T
syrah, monastrell
89
Colour: cherry, garnet rim. Nose: ripe fruit, spicy, creamy oak. Palate: powerful, flavourful, toasty, round tannins.

TOTEM WINES
Camino Viejo de San Mateu, s/n
07814 Santa Gertrudis (Illes Balears)
☎: +34 685 838 875
Fax: +34 971 198 344
www.totemwines.com
patrice@totemwines.com

Ibizkus 2012 T
monastrell
88
Colour: cherry, garnet rim. Nose: medium intensity, spicy, wild herbs. Palate: fruity, good structure, round tannins.

Ibizkus 2013 RD
monstruosa, syrah, tempranillo
88
Colour: raspberry rose. Nose: elegant, dried flowers, fragrant herbs, red berry notes. Palate: flavourful, good acidity, long, spicy.

Tótem 2011 T
monastrell

91

Colour: cherry, garnet rim. Nose: ripe fruit, spicy, creamy oak, toasty, complex, earthy notes. Palate: powerful, flavourful, toasty, round tannins.

VINOS CAN MAYMÓ

Casa Can Maymó
07816 Sant Mateu d'Albarca (Ibiza)
☎: +34 971 805 100
Fax: +34 971 805 100
www.bodegascanmaymo.com
info@bodegascanmaymo.com

Can Maymó Merlot 2010 T
merlot

86

Colour: cherry, garnet rim. Nose: medium intensity, wild herbs. Palate: correct, good finish.

Can Maymó 2011 T Barrica
tempranillo, merlot

87

Colour: bright cherry. Nose: ripe fruit, sweet spices, creamy oak. Palate: flavourful, fruity, toasty, round tannins.

Can Maymó 2013 B

87

Colour: bright straw. Nose: fresh, fresh fruit, expressive, jasmine. Palate: fruity, good acidity, balanced, easy to drink.

Can Maymó 2013 RD
syrah

89

Colour: onion pink. Nose: elegant, dried flowers, fragrant herbs, red berry notes. Palate: light-bodied, flavourful, good acidity, long, spicy.

Can Maymó Tradición 2011 T
monastrell, tempranillo, merlot, syrah

85

VT EXTREMADURA

BODEGA DE MIRABEL

Buenavista, 31
10220 Pago de San Clemente (Cáceres)
☎: +34 927 323 254
bodegademirabel@hotmail.com

Mirabel 2010 T

92

Colour: cherry, garnet rim. Nose: ripe fruit, wild herbs, earthy notes, spicy, creamy oak. Palate: balanced, flavourful, long, balsamic.

Pago de Mirabel 2013 T
100% garnacha

95

Colour: cherry, garnet rim. Nose: ripe fruit, spicy, creamy oak, toasty, complex, earthy notes. Palate: powerful, flavourful, toasty, round tannins.

Tribel de Mirabel 2013 T

88

Colour: cherry, purple rim. Nose: balanced, medium intensity. Palate: flavourful, fruity, good structure.

BODEGA MARQUÉS DE VALDUEZA

Fortuny, 19 1° Dcha
28010 (Madrid)
☎: +34 913 191 508
Fax: +34 913 084 034
www.marquesdevaldueza.com
contact@marquesdevaldueza.com

Marqués de Valdueza Etiqueta Roja 2010 T
cabernet sauvignon, syrah

84

Marqués de Valdueza Gran Vino de Guarda 2007 T
cabernet sauvignon, syrah, merlot

92

Colour: cherry, garnet rim, orangey edge. Nose: balanced, complex, ripe fruit, spicy, balsamic herbs, fine reductive notes. Palate: good structure, flavourful, round tannins.

Marqués de Valdueza Gran Vino de Guarda 2008 T
cabernet sauvignon, syrah

93

Colour: ruby red, orangey edge. Nose: spicy, toasty, scrubland, ripe fruit, mineral. Palate: spicy, long, toasty, balanced, round tannins.

BODEGA SAN MARCOS

Ctra. Aceuchal, s/n
06200 Almendralejo (Badajoz)
☎: +34 924 670 410
Fax: +34 924 665 505
www.bodegasanmarcos.com
ventas@bodegasanmarcos.com

Campobravo 2013 RD
100% syrah

86

Colour: rose, purple rim. Nose: powerfull, ripe fruit, red berry notes, floral, expressive. Palate: powerful, fruity, fresh, easy to drink.

BODEGAS CAÑALVA

Coto, 54
10136 Cañamero (Cáceres)
☎: +34 927 369 405
Fax: +34 927 369 405
www.bodegascanalva.com
info@bodegascanalva.com

Cañalva Coupage Especial 2010 TC
89

Colour: cherry, garnet rim. Nose: ripe fruit, wild herbs, earthy notes, spicy, creamy oak. Palate: balanced, flavourful, long, balsamic, round tannins.

Cañalva Macabeo 2013 B
100% macabeo
83

Cañalva Selección 2009 T
88

Colour: cherry, garnet rim. Nose: fruit preserve, fruit liqueur notes, spicy, wild herbs, fine reductive notes. Palate: flavourful, pruney, balsamic.

Esencia de Luz 2013 B
100% moscatel de alejandría
80

Fuente Cortijo 2010 TC
100% tempranillo
87

Colour: ruby red. Nose: spicy, toasty, ripe fruit, balsamic herbs. Palate: spicy, long, toasty.

Luz 2013 RD
100% garnacha
84

Luz 2013 Semidulce
84

BODEGAS CARLOS PLAZA

Sol s/n
06196 Cortegana (Badajoz)
☎: +34 924 687 932
Fax: +34 924 667 569
www.bodegascarlosplaza.com
export@bodegascarlosplaza.com

Carlos Plaza 2013 B
100% pardina
88

Colour: bright straw. Nose: white flowers, fragrant herbs, fruit expression. Palate: fresh, fruity, flavourful, elegant

.

Carlos Plaza 2013 T
90

Colour: very deep cherry, garnet rim. Nose: warm, dried herbs, ripe fruit. Palate: flavourful, ripe fruit, long.

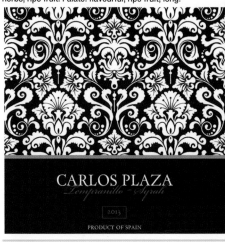

CARLOS PLAZA
Tempranillo - Syrah
2013
PRODUCT OF SPAIN

Carlos Plaza Selección 2011 T
88

Colour: bright cherry. Nose: ripe fruit, sweet spices, creamy oak, expressive. Palate: flavourful, fruity, toasty, round tannins.

La Llave Roja 2011 T
87

Colour: very deep cherry, garnet rim. Nose: powerfull, ripe fruit, sweet spices. Palate: powerful, toasty, roasted-coffee aftertaste.

La Llave Roja 2013 T
90

Colour: deep cherry. Nose: ripe fruit, red berry notes. Palate: flavourful, ripe fruit.

BODEGAS CASTELAR

Avda. de Extremadura, 1
6228 Hornachos (Badajoz)
☎: +34 924 533 073
Fax: +34 924 533 493
www.bodegascastelar.com
bodega@bodegascastelar.com

Castelar Blanco V 2013 B
verdejo
82

BODEGAS DE OCCIDENTE

Granados, 1 Bajo
06200 Almendralejo (Badajoz)
☎: +34 662 952 801
www.bodegasdeoccidente.com
info@bodegasdeoccidente.es

Buche 2012 T
tempranillo
87
Colour: bright cherry. Nose: ripe fruit, sweet spices, creamy oak. Palate: flavourful, fruity, toasty, round tannins.

BODEGAS HABLA

Ctra. A-V, km. 259
10200 Trujillo (Cáceres)
☎: +34 927 659 180
Fax: +34 927 659 180
www.bodegashabla.com
habla@bodegashabla.com

Habla de la Tierra 2011 T
tempranillo, cabernet sauvignon
84

Habla nº 12 2011 T
syrah
91
Colour: cherry, garnet rim. Nose: ripe fruit, wild herbs, spicy. Palate: powerful, flavourful, correct, round.

BODEGAS ORAN

Granados, 1
06200 Almendralejo (Badajoz)
☎: +34 662 952 800
www.bodegasoran.es
info@bodegasoran.com

Entremares 2013 B
pardina, cayetana blanca, eva, montua
84

BODEGAS SANTA MARTA

Cooperativa, s/n
06150 Santa Marta (Badajoz)
☎: +34 924 690 218
Fax: +34 924 690 083
www.bodegasantamarta.com
salesmanager@bodegasantamarta.com

Calamón Semidulce 2013 B
pardina
85

Calamón Semidulce 2013 RD
tempranillo
84

BODEGAS TORIBIO

Luis Chamizo, 12 y 21
06310 Puebla de Sancho Pérez (Badajoz)
☎: +34 924 551 449
Fax: +34 924 551 449
www.bodegastoribio.com
info@bodegastoribio.com

Golosina Eva Semidulce 2013 B
eva beba
85

Golosina Garnacha Semidulce 2013 RD
garnacha
85

Mú + Madera 2013 T Roble
tempranillo, cabernet sauvignon
86
Colour: cherry, purple rim. Nose: medium intensity, red berry notes, balanced. Palate: fruity, easy to drink, balsamic, correct.

Mú 2013 B
eva, macabeo, verdejo
83

Mú 2013 T
tempranillo, macabeo
86
Colour: cherry, purple rim. Nose: expressive, fresh fruit, red berry notes, floral, wild herbs. Palate: flavourful, fruity, good acidity, round tannins.

Tori-Bio 2012 T
tempranillo
87
Colour: very deep cherry, garnet rim. Nose: warm, dried herbs, ripe fruit. Palate: flavourful, ripe fruit, long.

Torivín 2013 T
tempranillo, cabernet sauvignon, garnacha, syrah
85

Torivín 4x4 2012 T Roble
cabernet sauvignon, tempranillo, garnacha, syrah
87
Colour: dark-red cherry, garnet rim. Nose: toasty, spicy, smoky, dried herbs. Palate: spicy, balsamic, ripe fruit.

Torivín ADN 2010 T Roble
tempranillo, syrah, cabernet sauvignon
86
Colour: cherry, garnet rim. Nose: wild herbs, ripe fruit, spicy. Palate: balanced, flavourful, round tannins.

Torivín Natura 2012 T
tempranillo

87

Colour: dark-red cherry, purple rim. Nose: ripe fruit, balanced. Palate: flavourful, round tannins, ripe fruit.

Torivín Pi 2012 TC
cabernet sauvignon, tempranillo, garnacha, syrah

88

Colour: cherry, garnet rim. Nose: ripe fruit, spicy, complex. Palate: powerful, flavourful, toasty, round tannins.

Viña Puebla 12 meses Barrica 2010 TC
tempranillo, syrah, cabernet sauvignon

87

Colour: bright cherry. Nose: ripe fruit, sweet spices, wild herbs. Palate: flavourful, fruity, toasty, round tannins.

Viña Puebla Macabeo 2013 B
macabeo

84

Viña Puebla Tempranillo 2013 T
tempranillo

87

Colour: cherry, purple rim. Nose: expressive, fresh fruit, red berry notes, floral. Palate: flavourful, fruity, good acidity, round tannins.

BODEGAS VIÑA EXTREMEÑA

Lago de Alange, s/n
06200 Almendralejo (Badajoz)
☎: +34 924 670 158
Fax: +34 924 670 159
www.vinexsa.com
info@vinexsa.com

Monasterio de Tentudia 2008 TR
100% tempranillo

86

Colour: very deep cherry. Nose: ripe fruit, spicy, creamy oak, toasty, fine reductive notes. Palate: powerful, flavourful, toasty.

Monasterio de Tentudia Premium 2010 T
84

Terra Magna 2006 TR
86

Colour: cherry, garnet rim. Nose: ripe fruit, spicy, creamy oak, toasty, fine reductive notes. Palate: powerful, flavourful, toasty.

COLOMA VIÑEDOS Y BODEGAS

Ctra. EX-363, km. 5,6
06170 Alvarado (Badajoz)
☎: +34 924 440 028
Fax: +34 924 440 409
www.bodegascoloma.com
coloma@bodegascoloma.com

Coloma Castillo "Torre Bermeja" Graciano 2011 TC
100% graciano

88

Colour: cherry, garnet rim. Nose: ripe fruit, wild herbs, spicy, creamy oak. Palate: balanced, flavourful, long, balsamic.

Coloma Garnacha Roja 2012 T
100% garnacha roja

87

Colour: very deep cherry, garnet rim. Nose: red berry notes, fruit liqueur notes, balsamic herbs. Palate: flavourful, ripe fruit, long.

Coloma Garnacha Selección 2012 T
100% garnacha

86

Colour: bright cherry. Nose: ripe fruit, sweet spices, creamy oak. Palate: flavourful, fruity, toasty.

Coloma Merlot Selección 2011 T Barrica
100% merlot

85

Coloma Muscat 2013 B
100% moscatel grano menudo

84

Evandria Pinot Noir 2012 RD
100% pinot noir

84

LUIS GURPEGUI MUGA

Avda. Celso Muerza, 8
31560 San Adrián (Navarra)
☎: +34 948 670 050
Fax: +34 948 670 259
www.gurpegui.es
bodegas@gurpegui.es

Pintoresco 2013 T
tempranillo

87

Colour: cherry, purple rim. Nose: expressive, fresh fruit, red berry notes, floral. Palate: flavourful, fruity, good acidity, fine bitter notes.

MCR, S.L.
Ctra. Badajoz, 75
06200 Almendralejo (Badajoz)
☎: +34 924 677 337
www.bodegasmcr.com

Inés del Alma Mía 2013 B
100% chardonnay

88

Colour: bright straw. Nose: white flowers, fine lees, dried herbs, ripe fruit. Palate: flavourful, fruity, good acidity.

VIÑA PLACENTINA
Avda. Martín Palomino, 49
10600 Plasencia (Cáceres)
☎: +34 927 116 250
Fax: +34 927 418 102
www.vinaplacentina.com
info@vinaplacentina.com

Viña Placentina Etiqueta Negra 2007 TR
100% cabernet sauvignon

85

Viña Placentina Etiqueta Roja 2010 TC

82 🌣

Viña Placentina Pago de los Ángeles 2005 TGR
100% cabernet sauvignon

86 🌣

Colour: pale ruby, brick rim edge. Nose: spicy, fine reductive notes, wet leather, aged wood nuances, fruit liqueur notes. Palate: spicy, fine tannins, long.

VIÑEDOS Y BODEGAS FUENTES
Ctra. Alange, Km. 17,700
06200 Almendralejo (Badajoz)
☎: +34 635 654 871
bodegasfuentes@gmail.com

Leneus Vino Ecológico 2013 T Roble
100% tempranillo

83 🌣

Vino Ecológico Cayetana 2013 B
100% cayetana blanca

85

VT FORMENTERA

CAP DE BARBARIA
Ctra. d'Es Cap, km. 5,8
07860 Formentera (Baleares)
☎: +34 647 707 572
www.capdebarbaria.com
info@capdebarbaria.com

Cap de Barbaria 2009 T
cabernet sauvignon, merlot, monastrell, fogoneu

92

Colour: cherry, garnet rim. Nose: powerfull, toasty, creamy oak, scrubland, ripe fruit. Palate: full, round tannins.

Cap de Barbaria 2010 TR
cabernet sauvignon, merlot, monastrell, fogoneu

94

Colour: dark-red cherry. Nose: expressive, balanced, balsamic herbs, ripe fruit. Palate: full, round tannins, spicy, long, balsamic.

Ophiusa 2011 T
cabernet sauvignon, merlot, monastrell, fogoneu

90

Colour: bright cherry. Nose: ripe fruit, sweet spices, creamy oak, expressive, scrubland. Palate: flavourful, fruity, toasty, round tannins.

TERRAMOLL
Ctra. de La Mola, Km. 15,5
07872 Formentera (Illes Balears)
☎: +34 971 327 293
Fax: +34 971 327 293
www.terramoll.es
jabalde@terramoll.es

Es Monestir 2010 TC
monastrell

91

Colour: cherry, garnet rim. Nose: ripe fruit, spicy, creamy oak, complex, earthy notes. Palate: powerful, flavourful, toasty, round tannins.

Rosa de Mar 2013 RD
cabernet sauvignon, merlot, monastrell

87

Colour: coppery red, bright. Nose: fragrant herbs, white flowers, fresh fruit. Palate: fresh, fruity, fine bitter notes.

Savina 2012 B
garnacha, viognier, moscatel grano menudo, moll

88

Colour: bright yellow. Nose: powerfull, white flowers, wild herbs, ripe fruit. Palate: balanced, fine bitter notes, long.

Terramoll Primus 2007 TC
merlot, cabernet sauvignon

88

Colour: cherry, garnet rim. Nose: smoky, toasty, sweet spices, wild herbs. Palate: powerful, ripe fruit, balsamic.

Terramoll Primus 2013 BFB
viognier

88

Colour: bright straw. Nose: ripe fruit, sweet spices, creamy oak, fragrant herbs. Palate: rich, flavourful, fresh, good acidity.

VT ILLA DE MENORCA

BINITORD
Santa Catarina, 1
07760 Ciutadella de Menorca
(Illes Balears)
☎: +34 654 909 714
www.binitord.com
info@binitord.com

Binitord Blanc 2013 B
chardonnay, merlot, syrah, macabeo

88

Colour: straw. Nose: balanced, fresh, white flowers, dried herbs. Palate: fresh, easy to drink, fine bitter notes.

Binitord Negre 2011 T
cabernet sauvignon, syrah, merlot

86

Colour: cherry, garnet rim. Nose: ripe fruit, wild herbs, spicy. Palate: balanced, flavourful, balsamic.

Binitord Rosat 2013 RD
tempranillo

84

Binitord Roure 2010 T
cabernet sauvignon, tempranillo, syrah

87

Colour: bright cherry, garnet rim. Nose: spicy, ripe fruit, scrubland. Palate: fruity, balsamic.

Ciutat de Parella 2010 T
cabernet sauvignon, tempranillo, syrah

86

Colour: bright cherry. Nose: ripe fruit, sweet spices. Palate: flavourful, fruity, toasty, round tannins.

BODEGAS MENORQUINAS
Camí de Tramuntana, Km. 1
07740 Es Mercadal (Illes Balears)
☎: +34 618 253 253
www.bodegasmenorquinas.com
bodegasmenorquinas@msn.com

Fusió Blanc 2013 B
macabeo, parellada, moscatel

87

Colour: bright yellow. Nose: fresh fruit, wild herbs. Palate: flavourful, fine bitter notes, easy to drink, good acidity.

Fusió Negre 2013 T
merlot, cabernet sauvignon

86

Colour: light cherry. Nose: medium intensity, red berry notes, dried herbs. Palate: light-bodied, easy to drink.

Fusió Rosat 2013 RD
macabeo, merlot

86

Colour: coppery red, bright. Nose: medium intensity, fresh fruit, dried herbs. Palate: fresh, easy to drink, good finish.

CRISPÍN MARIANO VADELL
(Menorca)
☎: +34 971 375 391
Fax: +34 971 375 467
bodegasmenorquinas@mns.net

Ferrer de Munt Palau 2005 T

86

Colour: deep cherry, orangey edge. Nose: sweet spices, toasty, ripe fruit. Palate: fruity, flavourful, round tannins.

Ferrer de Munt Palau 2009 T

84

Ferrer de Munt Palau VI VERMELL 2003 T

84

FINCA SA MARJALETA
Calle Alfons V nº 10
07760 Ciutadella de Menorca
(Illes Balears)
☎: +34 971 385 737
Fax: +34 971 385 737
www.marjaleta.com
marjaleta@telefonica.net

Lamontanum 2011 T
100% syrah

92

Colour: cherry, garnet rim. Nose: ripe fruit, wild herbs, earthy notes, spicy, creamy oak. Palate: balanced, flavourful, long, balsamic.

Lamontanum 2012 T
91
Colour: deep cherry, purple rim. Nose: cocoa bean, sweet spices, ripe fruit, creamy oak. Palate: balanced, good structure, flavourful.

Lamontanum 2013 B
100% viognier
90
Colour: bright yellow. Nose: medium intensity, white flowers, dried flowers. Palate: fruity, ripe fruit, balanced, long, spicy.

SA FORANA
Cugullonet Nou
07712 Sant Climent - Mahón
(Illes Balears)
☎: +34 607 242 510
www.saforana.com
saforana@saforana.com

600 Metros Sa Forana 2013 T
ull de llebre, cabernet sauvignon, syrah
90
Colour: cherry, purple rim. Nose: expressive, red berry notes, faded flowers, wild herbs. Palate: fruity, flavourful, fruity aftestaste.

Sa Forana 2012 T
cabernet sauvignon, merlot, syrah
87
Colour: deep cherry. Nose: medium intensity, old leather, ripe fruit, balsamic herbs. Palate: flavourful, round tannins.

VINYA SA CUDIA
Cos de Gracia, 7
07702 Mahón (Illes Balears)
☎: +34 686 361 445
Fax: +34 971 353 607
www.vinyasacudia.com
fincasacudia@gmail.com

Favaritx Blanc 2013 B
100% malvasía
86 🌺
Colour: straw. Nose: faded flowers, citrus fruit, fresh fruit. Palate: flavourful, fine bitter notes, easy to drink.

Favaritx Negre 2013 T
100% cabernet sauvignon
82 🌺

VT LADERAS DEL GENIL

BODEGAS FONTEDEI
Doctor Horcajadas, 10
18570 Deifontes (Granada)
☎: +34 958 407 957
www.bodegasfontedei.es
info@bodegasfontedei.es

Abadía 2013 B
sauvignon blanc, chardonnay
89
Colour: bright yellow. Nose: expressive, balanced, floral, spicy. Palate: balanced, fine bitter notes, rich.

BODEGAS SEÑORÍO DE NEVADA
Ctra. de Cónchar, s/n
18659 Villamena (Granada)
☎: +34 958 777 092
Fax: +34 958 107 367
www.senoriodenevada.es
info@senoriodenevada.es

Viña Dauro 2013 B
viognier
89
Colour: bright yellow. Nose: fresh, fresh fruit, white flowers, fragrant herbs. Palate: flavourful, fruity, good acidity, balanced.

VT LAUJAR/ALPUJARRA

VALLE DE LAUJAR
Ctra. de Laujar a Berja, Km. 2,2
04470 Laujar de Andarax (Almería)
☎: +34 950 514 200
Fax: +34 950 608 001

Finca Matagallo 2011 T
83

Viña Laujar 2013 B
100% Jaen blanca
84

Viña Laujar Cota 950 2011 B
82

Viña Laujar Macabeo 2013 B
100% macabeo
84

Viña Laujar Syrah 2010 T
100% syrah
84

VT LIÉBANA

BODEGA PICOS DE CABARIEZO

Barrio Cabariezo, s/n
39571 Cabezón de Liébana (Cantabria)
☎: +34 942 735 177
Fax: +34 942 735 176
www.vinosylicorespicos.com
info@vinosylicorespicos.es

Picos de Cabariezo 2012 T Roble
88
Colour: cherry, garnet rim. Nose: ripe fruit, spicy, mineral, scrubland. Palate: balanced, flavourful, long, balsamic.

Picos de Cabariezo 2013 T

85

BODEGA RÍO SANTO

Cillorigo de Liébana
39584 Esanos (Santander)
☎: +34 636 987 865
Fax: +34 942 732 188
www.riosanto.es
info@riosanto.es

Lusia 100% Mencía 2013 T
100% mencía
89
Colour: very deep cherry, purple rim. Nose: fruit expression, balanced, floral. Palate: fruity, easy to drink, balsamic.

Lusia 2012 T Roble
92
Colour: very deep cherry. Nose: spicy, ripe fruit, dried herbs. Palate: balanced, round tannins, balsamic.

VT MALLORCA

4 KILOS VINÍCOLA

1ª Volta, 168 Puigverd
07200 Felanitx (Illes Balears)
☎: +34 971 580 523
Fax: +34 971 580 523
www.4kilos.com
fgrimalt@4kilos.com

12 volts 2012 T
callet, merlot, cabernet sauvignon, syrah
92
Colour: bright cherry. Nose: sweet spices, ripe fruit, wild herbs, creamy oak. Palate: good structure, flavourful, round tannins.

4 Kilos 2012 T
callet, merlot, fogoneu
93
Colour: cherry, garnet rim. Nose: expressive, ripe fruit, spicy. Palate: good structure, full, balanced, round tannins, ripe fruit.

ÁN NEGRA VITICULTORS S.L.

3ª Volta, 18 - Apdo. 130
07200 Faianitx (Illes Balears)
☎: +34 971 584 481
Fax: +34 971 584 482
www.animanegra.com
info@annegra.com

Quíbia 2013 B
89
Colour: bright straw. Nose: candied fruit, citrus fruit, faded flowers. Palate: flavourful, good acidity.

ANTONIO NADAL BODEGAS Y VIÑEDOS

Cami de Son Roig, s/n
07350 Binissalem (Illes Balears)
☎: +34 630 914 511
Fax: +34 971 515 060
www.bodegasantonionadal.es
info@bodegasantonionadal.es

Fresc 2013 B
macabeo
82

Primerenc 2012 T
manto negro, callet, monastrell, tempranillo
88
Colour: cherry, garnet rim. Nose: ripe fruit, scrubland, spicy. Palate: balanced, round tannins, ripe fruit.

Tres Uvas 2012 T
manto negro, callet, monastrell, tempranillo
89
Colour: bright cherry. Nose: ripe fruit, sweet spices, expressive. Palate: flavourful, fruity, round tannins.

ARMERO I ADROVER

Camada Real s/n
07200 Mallorca (Illes Balears)
☎: +34 971 827 103
Fax: +34 971 580 305
www.armeroiadrover.com
luisarmero@armeroiadrover.com

Armero Adrover Chardonnay Prensal 2013 B
chardonnay
87
Colour: bright straw. Nose: fresh, fresh fruit, white flowers. Palate: flavourful, fruity, good acidity, balanced.

BINIGRAU

Fiol, 33
07143 Biniali (Illes Balears)
☎: +34 971 512 023
Fax: +34 971 886 495
www.binigrau.es
info@binigrau.es

B - Binigrau 2010 T
80% manto negro, callet, 20% merlot

93

Colour: bright cherry, garnet rim. Nose: spicy, scrubland, ripe fruit, complex. Palate: ripe fruit, long, balsamic, round tannins.

Binigrau Chardonnay 2012 BFB
100% chardonnay

92

Colour: bright yellow. Nose: powerfull, ripe fruit, sweet spices, creamy oak, fragrant herbs. Palate: rich, smoky aftertaste, flavourful, fresh, good acidity.

Binigrau Dolç 2010 T
manto negro, merlot

88

Colour: bright cherry, garnet rim. Nose: balanced, expressive, sweet spices, ripe fruit, candied fruit. Palate: flavourful, long, spicy.

E - Binigrau 2013 RD

88

Colour: light cherry, bright. Nose: expressive, balanced, fresh, red berry notes, white flowers. Palate: good acidity, fine bitter notes, long.

E - Binigrau 2013 T

89

Colour: light cherry, garnet rim. Nose: medium intensity, dried herbs, ripe fruit, expressive. Palate: fruity, good acidity.

Nou Nat 2013 B

91

Colour: bright straw. Nose: white flowers, fragrant herbs, fruit expression, elegant. Palate: fresh, fruity, flavourful, balanced, elegant.

Obac' 11 2011 TC
manto negro, callet, merlot, syrah

90

Colour: cherry, garnet rim. Nose: ripe fruit, wild herbs, earthy notes, spicy, creamy oak. Palate: balanced, flavourful, long, balsamic.

Obac' 12 2012 T
manto negro, callet, syrah, cabernet sauvignon

91

Colour: cherry, garnet rim. Nose: spicy, toasty, overripe fruit, mineral, dried herbs. Palate: powerful, flavourful, toasty, round tannins.

VI DE LA TERRA MALLORCA

obac'12

Binigrau

ELABORAT PER BINIGRAU VINS I VINYES

BODEGA CASTELL MIQUEL

Ctra. Alaró-Lloseta, Km. 8,7 Apart. Correos 11
07340 Alaró (Baleares)
☎: +34 971 510 698
Fax: +34 971 510 669
www.castellmiquel.com
info@castellmiquel.com

Castel Miquel Shiraz Stairway to Heaven 2010 TR

syrah

87

Colour: cherry, garnet rim. Nose: medium intensity, ripe fruit, closed. Palate: balanced, good acidity, fruity.

Castell Miquel Cabernet Sauvignon Stairway to Heaven 2010 TR

100% cabernet sauvignon

89

Colour: light cherry, orangey edge. Nose: balanced, expressive, ripe fruit, spicy, scrubland. Palate: flavourful, good structure.

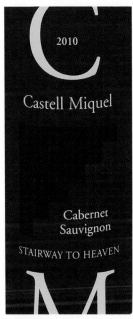

Castell Miquel Monte Sion 2010 T

88

Colour: bright cherry, garnet rim. Nose: balanced, medium intensity, ripe fruit, dried herbs. Palate: flavourful, long, balsamic.

BODEGA MARUCCIA

Camino Son Mendivil Buzon 30
07620 Llucmajor (Baleares)
☎: +34 971 660 134
www.maruccia.com
info@maruccia.com

Amada Tessa 2011 T

merlot, syrah

90

Colour: cherry, garnet rim. Nose: ripe fruit, spicy, creamy oak, toasty, complex. Palate: powerful, flavourful, toasty, round tannins.

Berilo de Callet 2011 T

callet, cabernet sauvignon

88

Colour: cherry, garnet rim. Nose: balanced, dried herbs, ripe fruit. Palate: rich, round tannins, correct, balsamic.

Oro del Huevo 2012 B

chardonnay, prensal

88

Colour: bright yellow. Nose: balanced, ripe fruit, faded flowers, sweet spices. Palate: rich, fruity.

Zafiro de Galdent 2011 T

cabernet sauvignon

88

Colour: bright cherry, garnet rim. Nose: balanced, dried herbs, scrubland, ripe fruit, spicy. Palate: fruity, flavourful.

BODEGA MESQUIDA MORA

Camí Pas des Frare,s/n (antigua carretera Porreres Sant Joan)
07260 Porreres (Illes Balears)
☎: +34 687 971 457
www.mesquidamora.com
info@mesquidamora.com

Acrollam Blanc 2013 B

prensal, chardonnay

85

Acrollam Rosat 2013 RD

merlot, cabernet sauvignon

85

Sincronía 2013 B

prensal, parellada, chardonnay

90

Colour: bright yellow. Nose: ripe fruit, faded flowers, dried herbs, petrol notes. Palate: powerful, flavourful, long, spicy.

Sincronía 2013 RD

cabernet sauvignon, callet, manto negro

83

Sincronía 2013 T
callet, manto negro, cabernet sauvignon, merlot

89

Colour: cherry, purple rim. Nose: red berry notes, ripe fruit, balsamic herbs, balanced. Palate: fresh, fruity, balsamic, balanced.

Sòtil 2012 T
callet, manto negro, cabernet sauvignon

90

Colour: cherry, garnet rim. Nose: red berry notes, ripe fruit, spicy, creamy oak, toasty, complex, earthy notes. Palate: powerful, flavourful, toasty, round tannins.

BODEGAS ÁNGEL
Ctra. Sta María - Sencelles, km. 4,8
07320 Santa María del Camí
(Illes Balears)
☎: +34 971 621 638
Fax: +34 971 621 638
www.bodegasangel.com
info@bodegasangel.com

Ángel Blanc de Blanca 2013 B
88

Colour: bright straw. Nose: dried herbs, faded flowers, fresh. Palate: fruity, fine bitter notes, good acidity.

Ángel Cabernet Sauvignon 2010 T
cabernet sauvignon

89

Colour: cherry, garnet rim. Nose: ripe fruit, wild herbs, earthy notes, spicy, creamy oak. Palate: balanced, flavourful, long, balsamic.

Ángel Gran Selecció 2010 T Roble
cabernet sauvignon, merlot, manto negro

91

Colour: bright cherry. Nose: ripe fruit, sweet spices, creamy oak, expressive. Palate: flavourful, fruity, toasty, round tannins.

Ángel Lau Rosa 2013 RD
86

Colour: light cherry, bright. Nose: medium intensity, fresh fruit, wild herbs. Palate: flavourful, fruity, long, fine bitter notes.

Ángel Syrah 2010 T
syrah

89

Colour: bright cherry, garnet rim. Nose: fruit expression, sweet spices, creamy oak. Palate: flavourful, ripe fruit, long.

Ángel Viognier 2012 BFB
100% viognier

89

Colour: bright yellow. Nose: ripe fruit, sweet spices, faded flowers. Palate: flavourful, fruity, long.

BODEGAS CA'N VIDALET
Ctra. Alcudia - Pollença Ma 2201, Km. 4,85
07460 Pollença (Illes Balears)
☎: +34 971 531 719
Fax: +34 971 535 395
www.canvidalet.com
info@canvidalet.com

Ca'n Vidalet Blanc de Blancs 2013 B
87

Colour: bright straw. Nose: fresh, fresh fruit, white flowers, expressive. Palate: flavourful, fruity, good acidity, balanced.

Ca'n Vidalet Blanc de Negres 2013 RD
87

Colour: onion pink. Nose: elegant, dried flowers, fragrant herbs, red berry notes. Palate: flavourful, good acidity, long, fine bitter notes.

Ca'n Vidalet So del Xiprer 2010 T
merlot, cabernet sauvignon, syrah

89

Colour: cherry, garnet rim. Nose: ripe fruit, wild herbs, earthy notes, spicy, creamy oak. Palate: balanced, flavourful, long, balsamic.

Ca'n Vidalet So del Xiprer-Gran Selección 2008 T
92

Colour: cherry, garnet rim. Nose: ripe fruit, spicy, creamy oak, toasty, complex, earthy notes, varietal. Palate: powerful, flavourful, toasty, round tannins.

Ca'n Vidalet Terra Fusca 2010 T
100% syrah

91

Colour: cherry, garnet rim. Nose: balanced, complex, ripe fruit, dried herbs. Palate: flavourful, fruity, long.

BODEGAS JOSÉ LUIS FERRER
Conquistador, 103
07350 Binissalem (Illes Balears)
☎: +34 971 511 050
Fax: +34 971 870 084
www.vinosferrer.com
secretaria@vinosferrer.com

José L. Ferrer DUES Mantonegro Cabernet 2012 T
manto negro, cabernet sauvignon

84

José L. Ferrer DUES Moll Chardonnay 2013 B
moll, chardonnay

86

Colour: bright yellow. Nose: medium intensity, faded flowers. Palate: fruity, correct, fine bitter notes.

José L. Ferrer DUES Syrah Callet 2011 T
syrah, callet

89

Colour: cherry, garnet rim. Nose: sweet spices, ripe fruit, balanced. Palate: fruity, balsamic, spicy.

BODEGAS SON PUIG S.L.
Finca Son Puig, s/n
07194 Puigpunyent (Illes Balears)
☎: +34 971 614 184
Fax: +34 971 614 184
www.sonpuig.com
info@sonpuig.com

Gran Sonpuig 2010 T
merlot, cabernet sauvignon, tempranillo, callet

88

Colour: cherry, garnet rim. Nose: dried herbs, old leather, spicy. Palate: fruity, flavourful, round tannins.

Sonpuig 2012 BFB
chardonnay, prensal, sauvignon blanc

89

Colour: bright yellow. Nose: ripe fruit, sweet spices, dried flowers. Palate: rich, flavourful, fresh, good acidity, long.

Sonpuig 2010 T
merlot, cabernet sauvignon, tempranillo, callet

86

Colour: cherry, garnet rim. Nose: old leather, ripe fruit, spicy. Palate: fruity, correct.

Sonpuig Blanc D'Estiu 2012 B
prensal, chardonnay, sauvignon blanc

88

Colour: bright yellow. Nose: expressive, balanced, ripe fruit, faded flowers. Palate: flavourful, balanced, fine bitter notes.

Sonpuig Estiu 2012 T
merlot, cabernet sauvignon, tempranillo

86

Colour: cherry, garnet rim. Nose: ripe fruit, wild herbs, spicy. Palate: balanced, flavourful, long, balsamic.

CA'N VERDURA VITICULTORS
S'Era, 6
07350 Binissalem (Balears)
☎: +34 695 817 038
tomeuverdura@gmail.com

L'Origen 2011 T
manto negro

91

Colour: light cherry. Nose: ripe fruit, balanced, expressive, wild herbs, fruit preserve. Palate: flavourful, fruity, round tannins.

CELLER TIANNA NEGRE
Camí des Mitjans
07340 Binissalem (Illes Balears)
☎: +34 971 886 826
www.tiannanegre.com
info@tiannanegre.com

Tianna Bocchoris Blanc 2013 B
prensal, sauvignon blanc, giró

91

Colour: yellow. Nose: fresh, fresh fruit, white flowers, expressive, sweet spices. Palate: flavourful, fruity, good acidity, balanced, rich.

CELLERS UNIÓ
Joan Oliver, 16-24
43206 Reus (Tarragona)
☎: +34 977 330 055
Fax: +34 977 330 070
www.cellersunio.com
info@cellersunio.com

Roua Mediterranea Blanc de Blancs 2013 B
prensal, macabeo, chardonnay

90

Colour: bright straw. Nose: fresh fruit, white flowers, citrus fruit, wild herbs. Palate: balanced, fine bitter notes, good acidity.

Roua Mediterranea Collita Seleccionada 2011 T
merlot, syrah, cabernet sauvignon, callet

87

Colour: dark-red cherry, orangey edge. Nose: ripe fruit, fruit liqueur notes, sweet spices, dark chocolate. Palate: flavourful, balsamic.

COMERCIAL GRUPO FREIXENET

Joan Sala, 2
08770 Sant Sadurní D'Anoia (Barcelona)
☎: +34 938 917 000
Fax: +34 938 183 095
www.freixenet.es
freixenet@freixenet.es

Susana Sempre 2012 T Roble
manto negro, cabernet sauvignon, syrah, merlot

86

Colour: cherry, garnet rim. Nose: ripe fruit, fruit preserve, sweet spices. Palate: fruity, round tannins.

Susana Sempre 2013 B

86

Colour: bright yellow. Nose: medium intensity, white flowers, fresh fruit. Palate: fruity, easy to drink, light-bodied.

Susana Sempre Maior Negre 2010 T

90

Colour: bright cherry, garnet rim. Nose: medium intensity, balanced, ripe fruit, balsamic herbs. Palate: fruity, flavourful, spicy.

Susana Sempre Manto Negro 2012 T

87

Colour: bright cherry, garnet rim. Nose: scrubland, faded flowers, ripe fruit. Palate: flavourful, easy to drink, good finish.

ES VERGER

S'Hort des Verger s/n
07190 Esporles (Illes Balears)
☎: +34 971 619 220
Fax: +34 971 715 732
esvergerolivi@yahoo.es

Els Rojals 2009 TC
87 🌷

Colour: bright cherry, garnet rim. Nose: scrubland, toasty, spicy. Palate: flavourful, round tannins, easy to drink.

Ses Marjades 2009 T
90 🌷

Colour: cherry, garnet rim. Nose: expressive, red berry notes, ripe fruit, violets. Palate: good structure, spicy, fruity aftestaste.

FINCA SON BORDILS

Ctra. Inca - Sineu, Km. 4,1
07300 Inca (Illes Balears)
☎: +34 971 182 200
Fax: +34 971 182 202
www.sonbordils.es
info@sonbordils.es

Bisbals de Son Borrdils 2007 T
87

Colour: bright cherry, orangey edge. Nose: ripe fruit, fruit liqueur notes, spicy, tobacco, scrubland. Palate: flavourful, spicy, long.

Finca Son Bordils Blanc de raïm Blanc 2013 B
90

Colour: bright straw. Nose: fresh, fresh fruit, white flowers, expressive. Palate: flavourful, fruity, good acidity, balanced.

Finca Son Bordils Cabernet Sauvignon 2007 T
100% cabernet sauvignon

88

Colour: dark-red cherry, orangey edge. Nose: varietal, ripe fruit, scrubland, cocoa bean. Palate: good structure, balsamic, long.

Finca Son Bordils Chardonnay 2013 B
88

Colour: bright yellow. Nose: medium intensity, floral, fresh fruit, varietal. Palate: fruity, fine bitter notes, balanced.

Finca Son Bordils Muscat 2013 B
100% moscatel grano menudo

90

Colour: bright yellow. Nose: fresh, varietal, white flowers, expressive. Palate: fruity, flavourful, good acidity, balanced, fine bitter notes.

Finca Son Bordils Negre 2009 T
89
Colour: dark-red cherry. Nose: ripe fruit, wild herbs, earthy notes, spicy, creamy oak. Palate: balanced, flavourful, long, balsamic.

Finca Son Bordils Rosat de Monastrell 2013 RD
88
Colour: light cherry, bright. Nose: medium intensity, dried herbs, red berry notes, fresh. Palate: full, fruity, good acidity, fine bitter notes.

Finca Son Bordils Syrah 2007 T
100% syrah
88
Colour: bright cherry, garnet rim. Nose: medium intensity, red berry notes, ripe fruit, faded flowers, sweet spices. Palate: fruity, flavourful.

Myotragus 2010 T
syrah, cabernet sauvignon, manto negro, callet
88
Colour: dark-red cherry, garnet rim. Nose: powerfull, ripe fruit, dried herbs. Palate: good structure, flavourful, round tannins.

Son Bordils Merlot 2007 T
100% merlot
90
Colour: dark-red cherry. Nose: ripe fruit, wild herbs, earthy notes, spicy, creamy oak. Palate: balanced, flavourful, long, balsamic.

SON CAMPANER
Pou Bauza 19B
07350 Binissalem (Mallorca)
☎: +34 971 870 004
www.soncampaner.es
info@soncampaner.es

Son Campaner Athos 2011 T
syrah, cabernet sauvignon
91
Colour: cherry, garnet rim. Nose: ripe fruit, spicy, creamy oak, scrubland. Palate: powerful, flavourful, toasty, round tannins.

Son Campaner Blanc de Blancs 2013 B
macabeo, chardonnay
88
Colour: bright straw. Nose: fresh, fresh fruit, white flowers, expressive. Palate: flavourful, fruity, good acidity, balanced.

Son Campaner Blanc de Negres 2013 RD
87
Colour: raspberry rose. Nose: dried herbs, fragrant herbs, faded flowers. Palate: fresh, correct, balanced, fine bitter notes.

Son Campaner Chardonnay Selecció 2013 B
chardonnay
87
Colour: bright yellow. Nose: powerfull, ripe fruit, sweet spices, creamy oak, fragrant herbs. Palate: rich, smoky aftertaste, flavourful, fresh, good acidity.

Son Campaner Merlot 2011 T
merlot
90
Colour: cherry, garnet rim. Nose: ripe fruit, wild herbs, earthy notes, spicy, creamy oak. Palate: balanced, flavourful, long, balsamic.

Son Campaner Terra Rossa 2011 T
callet, merlot, cabernet sauvignon, syrah
91
Colour: light cherry, garnet rim. Nose: expressive, medium intensity, red berry notes, ripe fruit. Palate: fruity, round tannins, easy to drink.

DO VINOS DE LA TIERRA / I.G.P.

SON PRIM PETIT

Ctra. Inca - Sencelles, Km. 4,9
07140 Sencelles (Balears)
☎: +34 971 872 758
www.sonprim.com
ventas@sonprim.com

Cup Son Prim 2011 T Barrica
91
Colour: bright cherry, garnet rim. Nose: ripe fruit, medium intensity, dried herbs, sweet spices. Palate: flavourful, full, good structure.

Son Prim Cabernet Sauvignon 2011 T
cabernet sauvignon
92
Colour: bright cherry, garnet rim. Nose: powerfull, varietal, scrubland, ripe fruit. Palate: flavourful, good structure, round tannins.

Son Prim Merlot 2011 T
merlot
90
Colour: cherry, garnet rim. Nose: ripe fruit, spicy, toasty, complex, balsamic herbs. Palate: powerful, flavourful, toasty, round tannins.

Son Prim Syrah 2011 T
syrah
89
Colour: bright cherry. Nose: ripe fruit, sweet spices, medium intensity. Palate: flavourful, fruity, toasty, round tannins.

TERRA DE FALANIS

2o Volta, 157. Apartado de Correos 28
07200 Felanitx (Illes Balears)
☎: +34 971 584 481
Fax: +34 971 584 482
www.terradefalanis.com
info@terradefalanis.com

Bla Bla Bla 2012 B
100% prensal
85

Muac 2011 T
86
Colour: cherry, garnet rim. Nose: medium intensity, fruit liqueur notes, earthy notes, scrubland. Palate: light-bodied, spicy, fine bitter notes.

VINOS Y VIÑEDOS TRAMUNTANA

Jesús, 13 Baja
07003 Palma de Mallor (Baleares)

Ca'N Xanet 2011 T
91
Colour: cherry, garnet rim. Nose: ripe fruit, fruit preserve, toasty, spicy. Palate: balanced, long, round tannins.

Cadmo 2011 T
92
Colour: dark-red cherry, garnet rim. Nose: smoky, toasty, ripe fruit. Palate: flavourful, good structure, fruity, balsamic.

Cumas 2011 T
94
Colour: light cherry, garnet rim. Nose: balanced, elegant, expressive, ripe fruit, scrubland. Palate: full, flavourful, long.

Sibila 2011 T
GORGOLLOSA
93
Colour: light cherry. Nose: elegant, ripe fruit, spicy. Palate: complex, long, spicy, good acidity, fine bitter notes.

VINS NADAL

Ramón Llull, 2
07350 Binissalem (Illes Balears)
☎: +34 971 511 058
Fax: +34 971 870 150
www.vinsnadal.com
albaflor@vinsnadal.com

Coupage 110 Vins Nadal 2010 T Barrica
manto negro, merlot, cabernet sauvignon
90
Colour: cherry, garnet rim. Nose: ripe fruit, spicy, creamy oak, toasty, complex. Palate: powerful, flavourful, toasty, round tannins.

Merlot 110 Vins Nadal 2009 T Barrica
merlot
89
Colour: cherry, garnet rim. Nose: spicy, creamy oak, scrubland. Palate: flavourful, good structure, round tannins.

Rosat 110 Vins Nadal 2013 RD
manto negro
87
Colour: light cherry. Nose: fruit expression, white flowers, fresh. Palate: fruity, easy to drink, good finish.

VINYES MORTITX

Ctra. Pollença Lluc, Km. 10,9
07315 Escorca (Illes Balears)
☎: +34 971 182 339
Fax: +34 871 100 053
www.vinyesmortitx.com
info@vinyesmortitx.com

Flaires de Mortitx 2013 RD
monastrell, merlot, cabernet sauvignon
85

L'Ergull de Mortitx 2012 BFB
malvasía, chardonnay, moscatel
88
Colour: yellow. Nose: ripe fruit, sweet spices, creamy oak, faded flowers. Palate: rich, flavourful, fresh, good acidity.

L'U Blanc 2012 B
malvasía, chardonnay
90
Colour: bright yellow. Nose: powerfull, ripe fruit, sweet spices, creamy oak. Palate: rich, smoky aftertaste, flavourful, fresh, good acidity.

L'U Negre 2009 T
syrah, cabernet sauvignon, tempranillo
87
Colour: cherry, garnet rim. Nose: ripe fruit, spicy, toasty. Palate: powerful, flavourful, toasty, round tannins.

Mortitx Blanc 2013 B
malvasía, moscatel, chardonnay, riesling
86
Colour: bright straw. Nose: fresh, fresh fruit, white flowers, medium intensity. Palate: good acidity, good finish, correct.

Mortitx Negre 2011 T
syrah, merlot, cabernet sauvignon, monastrell
86
Colour: cherry, garnet rim. Nose: ripe fruit, wild herbs, spicy. Palate: easy to drink, correct, fine bitter notes.

Mortitx Rosat 2013 RD
syrah, merlot, monastrell, cabernet sauvignon
85

Mortitx Syrah 2010 T
syrah
88
Colour: bright cherry. Nose: ripe fruit, sweet spices, creamy oak, expressive. Palate: flavourful, fruity, round tannins, good finish.

Rodal Pla de Mortitx 2010 T
syrah, cabernet sauvignon, merlot
90
Colour: cherry, garnet rim. Nose: ripe fruit, wild herbs, earthy notes, spicy, creamy oak. Palate: balanced, flavourful, long.

VT MURCIA

BODEGA VIÑA ELENA S.L.

Estrecho Marín, s/n
30520 Jumilla (Murcia)
☎: +34 968 781 340
www.vinaelena.com
info@vinaelena.com

Estancia del Silencio 2012 T
monastrell
87
Colour: bright cherry. Nose: ripe fruit, expressive, dried herbs. Palate: flavourful, fruity, toasty, round tannins.

VT RIBERA DEL ANDARAX

PAGOS DE INDALIA

Paseo de los Baños, 2
04458 Padules (Almería)
☎: +34 950 510 728
www.pagosdeindalia.com
juanma@pagosdeindalia.com

Flor de Indalia 2013 B
vermentino, macabeo
88
Colour: bright straw. Nose: white flowers, dried herbs, ripe fruit, spicy. Palate: powerful, rich, flavourful, balsamic.

Indalia Pinot Noir 2012 T
pinot noir
90
Colour: light cherry, garnet rim. Nose: medium intensity, ripe fruit, fruit preserve. Palate: correct, spicy, long.

Indalia Syrah 2012 T
100% syrah
88
Colour: cherry, garnet rim. Nose: fruit preserve, fruit liqueur notes, spicy, damp earth, scrubland. Palate: flavourful, pruney, balsamic.

Indalia Vendimia Seleccionada 2011 T
tempranillo, cabernet sauvignon, cabernet franc
89
Colour: deep cherry, garnet rim. Nose: ripe fruit, fruit preserve, dried herbs, warm. Palate: flavourful, round tannins.

Lacabra & Labota 2011 T Roble
tempranillo, cabernet sauvignon, syrah
87
Colour: bright cherry. Nose: ripe fruit, sweet spices, creamy oak, earthy notes, balsamic herbs. Palate: flavourful, fruity, toasty.

VT RIBERA DEL GÁLLEGO/ CINCO VILLAS

BODEGA PEGALAZ

Ctra. A-1202, Km. 7
22806 Santa Eulalia de Gállego
(Zaragoza)
☎: +34 625 643 440
www.pegalaz.com
bodegaspegalaz@gmail.com

Firé 2008 T
cabernet sauvignon, merlot, tempranillo
89
Colour: pale ruby, brick rim edge. Nose: balanced, complex, ripe fruit, spicy, fine reductive notes. Palate: good structure, flavourful, round tannins, balanced.

BODEGAS EJEANAS

Avda. Cosculluela, 23
50600 Ejea de los Caballeros
(Zaragoza)
☎: +34 976 663 770
Fax: +34 976 663 770
www.bodegasejeanas.com
pilar@bodegasejeanas.com

Uva Nocturna Garnacha Plus 2007 T
100% garnacha
87
Colour: cherry, garnet rim. Nose: balanced, complex, ripe fruit, spicy, wild herbs, fine reductive notes. Palate: good structure, flavourful, round tannins.

Uva Nocturna Merlot 2012 T
100% merlot
88
Colour: cherry, garnet rim. Nose: wild herbs, balsamic herbs, fruit preserve, sweet spices. Palate: flavourful, balsamic, spicy.

Uva Nocturna Syrah 2012 T
100% syrah
86
Colour: cherry, garnet rim. Nose: powerfull, red berry notes, ripe fruit, balsamic herbs. Palate: flavourful, long, balanced.

Vega de Luchán 2009 T Barrica
86
Colour: cherry, garnet rim. Nose: ripe fruit, spicy, creamy oak, toasty. Palate: powerful, flavourful, toasty.

Vega de Luchán 2013 RD
merlot, cabernet sauvignon
86
Colour: rose. Nose: ripe fruit, fragrant herbs, floral. Palate: powerful, flavourful, balsamic, long.

Vega de Luchán Dulce 2009 B
moscatel, verdejo
89
Colour: golden. Nose: powerfull, floral, honeyed notes, candied fruit, fragrant herbs, balsamic herbs. Palate: flavourful, sweet, fresh, fruity, good acidity, long.

EDRA BODEGA Y VIÑEDOS

Ctra A - 132, km 26
22800 Ayerbe (Huesca)
☎: +34 679 420 455
www.bodega-edra.com
edra@bodega-edra.com

Edra Xtra Syrah 2010 T
syrah
88
Colour: cherry, garnet rim. Nose: ripe fruit, spicy, creamy oak, toasty, complex. Palate: powerful, flavourful, toasty, round tannins.

VT RIBERA DEL QUEILES

BODEGA DEL JARDÍN

San Juan, 14
31520 Cascante (Navarra)
☎: +34 948 850 055
Fax: +34 948 850 097
www.bodegadeljardin.es
info@bodegadeljardin.es

1 Pulso 2010 T
tempranillo, garnacha
87
Colour: cherry, garnet rim. Nose: ripe fruit, wild herbs, spicy, creamy oak. Palate: balanced, flavourful, long, balsamic.

2 Pulso 2010 T
tempranillo, cabernet sauvignon, merlot
88
Colour: deep cherry, garnet rim. Nose: balanced, ripe fruit, wild herbs, spicy. Palate: balanced, round tannins.

3 Pulso 2010 T
tempranillo, garnacha
87
Colour: very deep cherry, garnet rim. Nose: fruit preserve, roasted coffee, spicy. Palate: good structure, flavourful, round tannins.

EDRA BODEGA Y VIÑEDOS

Ctra A - 132, km 26
22800 Ayerbe (Huesca)
☎: +34 679 420 455
www.bodega-edra.com
edra@bodega-edra.com

Edra Grullas de Paso 2011 T
merlot, cabernet sauvignon, tempranillo

86

Colour: light cherry, orangey edge. Nose: ripe fruit, scrubland, damp undergrowth, creamy oak. Palate: green, spicy, flavourful.

GUELBENZU

Paraje La Lombana s/n
50513 Vierlas (Zaragoza)
☎: +34 948 202 200
Fax: +34 948 202 202
www.guelbenzu.com
info@taninia.com

Guelbenzu Azul 2011 T
tempranillo, cabernet sauvignon, merlot

89

Colour: cherry, garnet rim. Nose: ripe fruit, spicy, creamy oak, toasty, balsamic herbs. Palate: powerful, flavourful, toasty.

Guelbenzu Evo 2010 TR
cabernet sauvignon, merlot, tempranillo

88

Colour: very deep cherry, garnet rim. Nose: powerfull, old leather, wild herbs. Palate: good structure, flavourful.

Guelbenzu Vierlas 2012 T
syrah

88

Colour: cherry, garnet rim. Nose: ripe fruit, spicy, creamy oak. Palate: powerful, flavourful, toasty, round tannins.

VT SIERRA NORTE DE SEVILLA

COLONIAS DE GALEÓN

Plazuela, 39
41370 Cazalla de la Sierra (Sevilla)
☎: +34 955 710 092
Fax: +34 955 710 093
www.coloniasdegaleon.com
info@coloniasdegaleon.com

Colonias de Galeón 2012 T Roble

85

Colonias de Galeón 2013 T Maceración Carbónica

86 ♥

Colour: cherry, purple rim. Nose: red berry notes, fruit liqueur notes, fragrant herbs, expressive. Palate: fresh, fruity, flavourful.

Ocnos 2012 BFB

85 ♥

Petit Ocnos sobre Lías 2012 B
100% chardonnay

84 ♥

Silente Selección 2008 T Roble

89 ♥

Colour: bright cherry. Nose: ripe fruit, sweet spices, creamy oak, scrubland, fine reductive notes. Palate: fruity, flavourful, toasty, round.

VT VALDEJALÓN

EPILENSE DE VINOS Y VIÑEDOS, THE GARAGE WINE

San Agustín, 7
50019 Epila (Zaragoza)
☎: +34 669 148 771
www.thegaragewine.com
info@thegaragewine.com

Frontonio 2010 T
garnacha

89

Colour: cherry, garnet rim. Nose: ripe fruit, wild herbs, earthy notes, spicy, creamy oak. Palate: balanced, flavourful, long, balsamic.

Latidos de Vino I Love 2013 T
garnacha

88

Colour: cherry, purple rim. Nose: expressive, fresh fruit, red berry notes, floral. Palate: flavourful, fruity, good acidity.

Latidos I Love Moscatel 2013 B
moscatel

88

Colour: golden. Nose: powerfull, floral, honeyed notes, candied fruit, fragrant herbs. Palate: flavourful, sweet, fresh, fruity, good acidity, long.

Supersónico Natural Red Wine 2013 T
garnacha

88

Colour: dark-red cherry, garnet rim. Nose: powerfull, ripe fruit, spicy, dried herbs. Palate: fruity, powerful, round tannins.

Telescópico Blanco Cósmico 2013 B
viognier, garnacha blanca, macabeo

90

Colour: bright yellow, greenish rim. Nose: white flowers, sweet spices, ripe fruit. Palate: correct, fine bitter notes, good finish, flavourful.

VIÑEDOS DE MANCUSO
Mayor, 10
01300 Laguardia (Álava)
☎: +34 651 845 176
Fax: +34 976 620 539
www.mancuso.es
info@navascuesenologia.es

Mancuso 2006 T
garnacha

93

Colour: cherry, garnet rim. Nose: fruit liqueur notes, aromatic coffee, characterful, complex. Palate: ripe fruit, long, fine tannins.

Moncaíno de Mancuso 2008 T
garnacha

88

Colour: cherry, garnet rim. Nose: ripe fruit, wet leather, toasty, spicy. Palate: sweetness, spirituous, spicy.

VT VALLE DEL CINCA

FINCA VALONGA
Monte Valonga, s/n
22533 Belver de Cinca (Huesca)
☎: +34 974 435 127
Fax: +34 974 339 101
www.valonga.com
bodegas@valonga.com

Busardo Selección 2010 T Roble
garnacha, tempranillo, syrah

86

Colour: cherry, garnet rim. Nose: spicy, creamy oak, toasty, fruit preserve. Palate: powerful, flavourful, toasty.

Monte Valonga Merlot 2011 T
merlot

82

Valonga Saso Alto 2010 T
garnacha

87

Colour: deep cherry, orangey edge. Nose: ripe fruit, grassy, spicy, fine reductive notes. Palate: powerful, flavourful, spicy, long.

TABLE WINES / WINES

Just outside the "Vino de Calidad" status, we find the "Vino de Mesa" ("Table Wine") category, which are those not included in any of the other categories (not even in the "Vino de la Tierra" one, regarded as "Vino de Mesa" by the Ley del Vino ("Wine Law"). The present editions of our Guide has up to 41 table wines rated as excellent, something which is quite telling, and force us to a change of mind in regard to the popular prejudice against this category, traditionally related –almost exclusively– to bulk, cheap wines.

In this section we include wines made in geographical areas that do not belong to any designation of origin (DO as such) or association of Vino de la Tierra, although most of them come indeed from wines regions with some vine growing and winemaking tradition.

We do not pretend to come up with a comprehensive account of the usually overlooked vinos de mesa (table wines), but to enumerate here some Spanish wines that were bottled with no geographic label whatsoever.

The wineries are listed alphabetically within their Autonomous regions. The reader will discover some singular wines of –in some cases– excellent quality that could be of interest to those on the look out for novelties or alternative products to bring onto their tables.

ALEMANY I CORRIO

Melió, 78
08720 Vilafranca del Penedès
(Barcelona)
☎: +34 938 180 949
sotlefriec@sotlefriec.com

Núvols 2013 B
93
Colour: bright yellow. Nose: powerfull, ripe fruit, sweet spices, creamy oak, fragrant herbs. Palate: rich, smoky aftertaste, flavourful, fresh, good acidity.

ALFREDO MAESTRO TEJERO

Avda. Escalona, 42
47300 Peñafiel (Valladolid)
☎: +34 687 786 742
www.alfredomaestro.com
alfredo@alfredomaestro.com

A dos Tiempos 2012 T
92
Colour: cherry, garnet rim. Nose: spicy, creamy oak, toasty, complex, balsamic herbs, fruit liqueur notes. Palate: powerful, flavourful, toasty, good acidity. Personality.

La Viñuela 2011 T
91
Colour: cherry, garnet rim. Nose: spicy, creamy oak, toasty, earthy notes, fruit liqueur notes. Palate: powerful, flavourful, toasty, round tannins.

ARTIGA FUSTEL

Progres, 21 Bajos
08720 Vilafranca del Penedès
(Barcelona)
☎: +34 938 182 317
Fax: +34 938 924 499
www.artiga-fustel.com
info@artiga-fustel.com

Monasterio de Santa Cruz 2013 T
86
Colour: cherry, purple rim. Nose: powerfull, red berry notes, ripe fruit, floral, expressive. Palate: fresh, fruity, easy to drink.

BODEGA BALCONA

Ctra. Bullas-Avilés, Km. 8
30180 Bullas (Murcia)
☎: +34 968 652 891
www.partal-vinos.com
info@partal-vinos.com

Casa de la Cruz 2005 T
80

BODEGA CASTELL MIQUEL

Ctra. Alaró-Lloseta, Km. 8,7 Apart. Correos 11
07340 Alaró (Baleares)
☎: +34 971 510 698
Fax: +34 971 510 669
www.castellmiquel.com
info@castellmiquel.com

Castel Miquel Sauvignon Blanc Stairway to Heaven 2013 B
100% sauvignon blanc
86
Colour: bright straw. Nose: fresh, fresh fruit, fragrant herbs. Palate: fruity, good acidity, balanced, good finish.

Castell Miquel Stairway to Heaven 2013 RD
87
Colour: rose, bright. Nose: red berry notes, balanced, medium intensity. Palate: fresh, good acidity, easy to drink.

BODEGA DE BLAS SERRANO

Ctra. Santa Cruz, s/n
09471 Fuentelcésped (Burgos)
☎: +34 669 313 108
www.bodegasdeblasserrano.com
dbs@bodegasdeblasserrano.com

DBS Albillo Mayor 2010 B
albillo mayor
92
Colour: bright straw. Nose: spicy, wild herbs, expressive, complex. Palate: long, full, good acidity, fine bitter notes.

BODEGA F. SCHATZ

Finca Sanguijuela, s/n
29400 Ronda (Málaga)
☎: +34 952 871 313
Fax: +34 952 871 313
www.f-schatz.com
bodega@f-schatz.com

Acinipo 2005 TC
100% lemberger
90
Colour: ruby red. Nose: ripe fruit, wild herbs, earthy notes, spicy, creamy oak, fine reductive notes. Palate: balanced, flavourful, long, balsamic.

Acinipo 2006 T
100% lemberger
87
Colour: cherry, garnet rim. Nose: fruit liqueur notes, cocoa bean, balanced. Palate: ripe fruit, long, balsamic.

Acinipo 2007 T
100% lemberger
84

Acinipo 2008 T
100% lemberger

91

Colour: dark-red cherry, garnet rim. Nose: balanced, expressive, cocoa bean, ripe fruit, smoky. Palate: elegant, round tannins, spicy.

Acinipo 2009 T
100% lemberger

89

Colour: deep cherry, garnet rim. Nose: balanced, scrubland, ripe fruit, wild herbs, tobacco. Palate: fruity, balsamic, long.

Acinipo 2010 T
100% lemberger

88

Colour: deep cherry, garnet rim. Nose: fine reductive notes, dried herbs, ripe fruit. Palate: spicy, round tannins, good acidity.

Acinipo 2011 T
100% lemberger

89

Colour: light cherry, garnet rim. Nose: ripe fruit, spicy, tobacco. Palate: flavourful, ripe fruit, long, good structure.

Schatz Rosado 2013 RD
100% muskattrolinger

86

Colour: rose. Nose: ripe fruit, fruit preserve, wild herbs, floral. Palate: powerful, flavourful, balsamic.

BODEGA FINCA FUENTEGALANA
Ctra. M-501, Alcorcón - Plasencia, km. 65
05429 Navahondilla (Ávila)
☎: +34 646 843 231
www.fuentegalana.com
info@fuentegalana.com

Toros de Guisando 2013 RD
syrah

85

BODEGA KIENINGER
Los Frontones, 67 (Apdo. Correos 215)
29400 Ronda (Málaga)
☎: +34 952 879 554
www.bodegakieninger.com
martin@bodegakieninger.com

7 Vin Blaufraenkisch 2012 T
100% blaufraenkisch

93

Colour: cherry, garnet rim. Nose: expressive, ripe fruit, earthy notes, balsamic herbs. Palate: fruity, long, good acidity, balanced. Personality.

7 Vin Zweigelt 2012 TC
100% zweigelt

91

Colour: bright cherry. Nose: ripe fruit, sweet spices, creamy oak, expressive, floral. Palate: flavourful, fruity, round tannins, easy to drink.

BODEGA LA ENCINA
Pedro Más, 23
03408 La Encina (Alicante)
☎: +34 610 410 945
Fax: +34 962 387 808
www.bodegalaencina.com
bodegalaencina@ono.com

Albalat 2012 T
monastrell, garnacha

84

Cero 2011 T
garnacha

85

Cero 2013 T
garnacha, merlot, monastrell

83

BODEGA LIBERALIA ENOLÓGICA
Camino del Palo, s/n
49800 Toro (Zamora)
☎: +34 980 692 571
Fax: +34 980 692 571
www.liberalia.es
liberalia@liberalia.es

Ariane 2012 ESP
verdejo, moscatel

85

BODEGA MAS L'ALTET
Mas L'Altet Partida de la Creu, s/n
03838 Alfafara (Alicante)
☎: +34 609 759 708
www.bodegamaslaltet.com
nina@bodegamaslaltet.com

Avi de Mas L'Altet 2010 T
89

Colour: cherry, garnet rim. Nose: overripe fruit, dried fruit, sweet spices, toasty. Palate: ripe fruit, warm, powerful.

Nineta de Mas L'Altet 2011 T
90

Colour: cherry, garnet rim. Nose: spicy, toasty, overripe fruit, mineral. Palate: powerful, flavourful, toasty, round tannins.

BODEGA PARDO TOLOSA

Villatoya, 26
02215 Alborea (Albacete)
☎: +34 963 517 067
Fax: +34 963 517 091
www.bodegapardotolosa.com
export@bodegapardotolosa.com

Mizaran Macabeo 2013 B
100% macabeo
85

Sensibel 2013 T
78

BODEGA ROANDI

O Lagar s/n
32336 Éntoma – O Barco (Ourense)
Fax: +34 988 335 198
www.bodegaroandi.com
info@bodegaroandi.com

Brinde de Rosas Rosado 2012 ESP
mencía, sousón, brancellao
85

Dona Delfina 2013 RD
mencía, sousón, brancellao
86
Colour: rose, purple rim. Nose: powerfull, ripe fruit, red berry notes, floral. Palate: powerful, fruity, fresh.

BODEGA VERA DE ESTENAS

Junto N-III, km. 266 - Paraje La Cabeuzela
46300 Utiel (Valencia)
☎: +34 962 171 141
www.veradeestenas.es
estenas@veradeestenas.es

Casa Don Ángel Malbec 1-2 T
91
Colour: cherry, garnet rim. Nose: ripe fruit, wild herbs, earthy notes, spicy, creamy oak. Palate: balanced, flavourful, long, balsamic.

BODEGA VICENTE FLORS

Pda. Pou D'en Calvo, s/n
12118 Les Useres (Castellón)
☎: +34 671 618 851
www.bodegaflors.com
bodega@bodegaflors.com

Clotàs 2010 T
89
Colour: very deep cherry, garnet rim. Nose: old leather, spicy, ripe fruit. Palate: good structure, spicy, long.

Clotàs Monastrell 2010 T
monastrell
88
Colour: dark-red cherry. Nose: fine reductive notes, wet leather, toasty, ripe fruit, dried herbs. Palate: spicy, long, toasty.

Flor de Taronger 2012 T
tempranillo, monastrell, garnacha, cabernet sauvignon
86
Colour: cherry, garnet rim. Nose: ripe fruit, wild herbs, powerfull. Palate: spicy, balsamic, flavourful.

BODEGAS ARZUAGA NAVARRO

Ctra. N-122, km. 325
47350 Quintanilla de Onésimo (Valladolid)
☎: +34 983 681 146
Fax: +34 983 681 147
www.arzuaganavarro.com
bodeg@arzuaganavarro.com

Fan D.Oro 2013 BFB
chardonnay
88
Colour: bright yellow. Nose: powerfull, sweet spices, creamy oak, fragrant herbs. Palate: rich, smoky aftertaste, flavourful, fresh, good acidity.

BODEGAS AUSÍN

Cuesta de Santa María s/n
05460 Gavilanes (Avila)
☎: +34 692 621 708
www.bodegasausin.com
info@bodegasausin.com

Julia 2013 RD
88
Colour: bright cherry. Nose: red berry notes, ripe fruit, rose petals, faded flowers. Palate: rich, powerful, balanced.

Mmadre 2011 T
90
Colour: cherry, garnet rim. Nose: ripe fruit, spicy, creamy oak, toasty, mineral. Palate: powerful, flavourful, toasty, round tannins, balanced.

BODEGAS AVANCIA

Parque Empresarial a Raña, 7
32300 O Barco de Valdeorras (Ourense)
☎: +34 952 504 706
Fax: +34 951 284 796
www.grupojorgeordonez.com
avancia@jorgeordonez.es

Avancia Rosé 2013 RD
100% mencía
86
Colour: light cherry. Nose: red berry notes, characterful. Palate: flavourful, sweetness.

BODEGAS BENTOMIZ

Finca Almendro - Pago Cuesta Robano
29752 Sayalonga (Málaga)
☎: +34 658 845 285
www.bodegasbentomiz.com
info@bodegasbentomiz.com

Ariyanas David Dulce 2012 T
merlot
89
Colour: cherry, garnet rim. Nose: fruit preserve, ripe fruit, spicy, toasty, aged wood nuances. Palate: powerful, flavourful, sweetness, balanced.

BODEGAS DELEA A MARCA

Finca La Herreria
21590 Villablanca (Huelva)
☎: +34 683 121 635
www.deleaamarca.com
info@deleaamarca.com

Delea a Marca 2011 T
cabernet sauvignon, petit verdot
84

Delea a Marca 2011 T
syrah
83

Delea a Marca 2011 T
merlot
82

Delea a Marca 2013 B
vermentino
87
Colour: bright straw. Nose: fresh, fresh fruit, white flowers, expressive. Palate: flavourful, fruity, good acidity, balanced.

Delea a Marca 2013 RD
merlot, syrah, petit verdot
84

Delea a Marca Chardonnay Barrique 2012 B
chardonnay
88
Colour: bright yellow. Nose: powerfull, ripe fruit, sweet spices, creamy oak, fragrant herbs. Palate: rich, smoky aftertaste, flavourful, fresh.

BODEGAS FONTEDEI

Doctor Horcajadas, 10
18570 Deifontes (Granada)
☎: +34 958 407 957
www.bodegasfontedei.es
info@bodegasfontedei.es

Prado Negro 2010 T
tempranillo, garnacha, cabernet sauvignon
86
Colour: very deep cherry. Nose: balsamic herbs, ripe fruit, warm, spicy. Palate: powerful, ripe fruit, long.

Prado Negro 2011 T
tempranillo, merlot, garnacha, cabernet sauvignon
86
Colour: cherry, garnet rim. Nose: fruit preserve, fruit liqueur notes, spicy. Palate: flavourful, pruney.

BODEGAS MARCOS MIÑAMBRES

Camino de Pobladura, s/n
24234 Villamañán (León)
☎: +34 987 767 038
satvined@picos.com

M. Miñambres 2010 T
prieto picudo, cencibel
87
Colour: black cherry. Nose: ripe fruit, wild herbs, earthy notes, spicy. Palate: balanced, flavourful, long, balsamic.

M. Miñambres Albarín 2013 B
100% albarín
88
Colour: yellow, pale. Nose: dried flowers, fragrant herbs, medium intensity, varietal. Palate: flavourful, fruity, correct, fine bitter notes.

BODEGAS MARQUÉS DE VIZHOJA

Finca La Moreira s/n
36438 Arbo (Pontevedra)
☎: +34 986 665 825
Fax: +34 986 665 960
www.marquesdevizhoja.com
informacion@marquesdevizhoja.com

Marqués de Vizhoja 2013 B
84

BODEGAS MONTALVO WILMOT

Ctra. Ruidera, km. 10,2 Finca Los Cerrillos
13710 Argamasilla de Alba
(Ciudad Real)
☎: +34 926 699 069
www.montalvowilmot.com
info@montalvowilmot.com

Montalvo Rosado 2013 RD
84

BODEGAS SIERRA DE GUARA

Fray Luis Urbano, 27
50002 Lascellas (Zaragoza)
☎: +34 976 461 056
Fax: +34 976 461 558
www.bodegassierradeguara.es
idrias@bodegassierradeguara.es

Idrias 2013 RD
100% tempranillo
86
Colour: light cherry. Nose: powerfull, ripe fruit, red berry notes, floral. Palate: powerful, fruity, fresh.

Idrias Abiego 2012 T
90
Colour: cherry, garnet rim. Nose: ripe fruit, spicy, creamy oak, toasty, complex, dark chocolate, earthy notes. Palate: powerful, flavourful, toasty, round tannins, balanced.

Idrias Chardonnay 2013 B
100% chardonnay
88
Colour: bright straw. Nose: white flowers, fresh fruit, expressive, fine lees, dried herbs. Palate: flavourful, fruity, good acidity, balanced.

BODEGAS VICENTE GANDÍA

Ctra. Cheste a Godelleta, s/n
46370 Chiva (Valencia)
☎: +34 962 524 242
Fax: +34 962 524 243
www.vicentegandia.es
info@vicentegandia.com

Hoya de Cadenas Tempranillo 2013 T
100% tempranillo
85

Hoya de Cadenas Verdejo 2013
100% verdejo
85

Sandara Blanco 2013 ESP
verdejo, sauvignon blanc, viura
83

Sandara Rosado 2013 ESP
100% bobal
84

Whatever it Takes by David Bowie 2012 T
100% syrah
86
Colour: cherry, purple rim. Nose: red berry notes, ripe fruit, wild herbs, spicy. Palate: powerful, flavourful, concentrated.

Whatever it Takes by George Clooney 2012 T
100% cabernet sauvignon
85

Whatever it Takes by Penelope Cruz 2012 B
86
Colour: bright yellow. Nose: ripe fruit, balsamic herbs, floral, medium intensity. Palate: powerful, rich, flavourful, easy to drink.

Whatever it Takes by Pierce Brosnan 2012 T
100% tempranillo
86
Colour: cherry, garnet rim. Nose: medium intensity, ripe fruit, balanced. Palate: correct, easy to drink, good finish.

BODEGAS Y VIÑEDOS CASIS

Las Bodegas, s/n
24325 Gordaliza del Pino (León)
☎: +34 987 699 618
www.bodegascasis.com
anacasis@gmail.com

Condelize Pedro Casis 2013 B
chardonnay
80

Condelize Pedro Casis 2013 RD
mencía, prieto picudo, syrah
83

BODEGAS Y VIÑEDOS CASTIBLANQUE

Isaac Peral, 19
13610 Campo de Criptana
(Ciudad Real)
☎: +34 926 589 147
Fax: +34 926 589 148
www.bodegascastiblanque.com
info@bodegascastiblanque.com

Lagar de Ensancha s/c T
82

Solamente s/c B
83

Solamente s/c RD
100% syrah
75

Solamente Tempranillo s/c T
100% tempranillo
83

Zumo de Amor s/c T
84

BODEGAS Y VIÑEDOS CERRO DEL ÁGUILA
Avda. de Toledo, 23
45127 Ventas con Peña Aguilera
(Toledo)
☎: +34 625 443 153
bodegascerrodelaguila@gmail.com

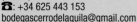

Malabra 2012 T
garnacha, syrah, cencibel
89
Colour: cherry, garnet rim. Nose: scrubland, damp earth, spicy, fruit liqueur notes. Palate: powerful, warm, flavourful.

Vereda del Lobo 2012 T
garnacha, syrah, cencibel
90
Colour: cherry, garnet rim. Nose: wild herbs, earthy notes, creamy oak, red berry notes, ripe fruit, sweet spices. Palate: balanced, flavourful, long, balsamic.

BODEGAS Y VIÑEDOS MENGOBA
Avda. del Parque, 7
24544 San Juan de Carracedo (León)
☎: +34 649 940 800
www.mengoba.com
gregory@mengoba.com

Estaladiña 2012 T
merenzao
90
Colour: cherry, garnet rim. Nose: spicy, toasty, fruit preserve. Palate: powerful, flavourful, toasty, round tannins.

BRUNO MURCIANO & DAVID SAMPEDRO GIL
8 Avenida Banda De Musica El Angel
46315 Caudete de las Fuentes
(Valencia)
☎: +34 962 319 096
bru.murciano@yahoo.es

El Sueño de Bruno 2012 T
bobal
88
Colour: bright cherry. Nose: ripe fruit, sweet spices, creamy oak, earthy notes. Palate: flavourful, round tannins, fine bitter notes.

La Malkerida 100% Bobal 2013 T
bobal
88
Colour: very deep cherry. Nose: overripe fruit, spicy, grassy. Palate: powerful, sweetness, spicy.

CAN RICH
Camí de Sa Vorera, s/n
07820 Sant Antoni (Illes Balears)
☎: +34 971 803 377
Fax: +34 971 803 377
www.bodegascanrich.com
info@bodegascanrich.com

Can Rich Blanco 2010 BN
malvasía
86 🌷
Colour: bright yellow. Nose: candied fruit, faded flowers, honeyed notes, toasty. Palate: flavourful, good acidity, fine bitter notes.

Can Rich Rosado 2011 BN
syrah
83 🌷

CARRIEL DELS VILARS
Mas Can Carriel
17753 Els Vilars (Girona)
☎: +34 972 563 335
www.carrieldelsvilars.com
carrieldelsvilars@hotmail.com

Blanc Petillant Carriel dels Vilars 2012 B
macabeo, xarel.lo, parellada, garnacha blanca
86 🌷
Colour: bright golden. Nose: ripe fruit, balanced, spicy, varnish, wild herbs. Palate: fruity, sweetness, correct.

Carriel dels Vilars 2011 BN
macabeo, xarel.lo, parellada, garnacha blanca
88
Colour: bright golden. Nose: dark chocolate, spicy, fine lees, powerfull, expressive. Palate: flavourful, toasty, long, fine bead, fine bitter notes.

Carriel dels Vilars 2012 T
garnacha, syrah, cabernet sauvignon, samsó
70

Mistela de Chardonnay PX Roble
chardonnay
90
Colour: mahogany. Nose: complex, fruit liqueur notes, dried fruit, pattiserie, toasty, elegant. Palate: sweet, rich, unctuous, powerful.

Rosat Escumòs Carriel dels Vilars 2008 ESP
macabeo, xarel.lo, garnacha, garnacha blanca
84

CAVAS DEL AMPURDÁN

Pza. del Carme, 1
17491 Perelada (Girona)
☎: +34 932 233 022
Fax: +34 932 231 370
www.blancpescador.com
perelada@castilloperelada.com

Blanc Pescador Premium Blanco de aguja
84

Blanc Pescador Vino de aguja B
82

Cresta Azul de Aguja B
84

Cresta Rosa Premium Rosado de aguja
85

Cresta Rosa Vino de Aguja RD
84

Pescador Rosé Rosado de aguja
84

CELLER COOPERATIU D'ESPOLLA

Ctra. Roses, s/n
17773 Espolla (Gerona)
☎: +34 972 563 178
www.celleespolla.com
info@celleespolla.com

Babalà Vi Blanc Simpàtic 2013 B
cariñena blanca, moscatel de alejandría
85

CELLER L'ARC

San Roc, 5
46844 Beniatjar (Valencia)
☎: +34 699 148 159
www.cellerlarc.com
detallsrg@gmail.com

Archvs 2012 T
merlot
86
Colour: cherry, garnet rim. Nose: spicy, toasty, overripe fruit. Palate: powerful, round tannins.

Oppinum 2012 T
syrah
84

Sarment 2013 T
merlot
75

CELLER LA MUNTANYA

Rotonda Quatrecamins,
Cami L'Alquerieta, Nave B
03830 Muro de Alcoy (Alicante)
☎: +34 965 531 248
www.cellerlamuntanya.com
info@cellerlamuntanya.com

Albir 2011 B
malvasía, merseguera, verdil
90
Colour: bright straw, greenish rim. Nose: white flowers, fresh fruit, wild herbs, fine lees. Palate: fruity, long, balanced, good acidity.

Almoroig 2008 T
monastrell, garnacha tintorera, garnacha
88
Colour: dark-red cherry, orangey edge. Nose: spicy, fine reductive notes, aged wood nuances, fruit preserve. Palate: spicy, fine tannins, balsamic.

Celler La Muntanya 2010 TC
monastrell, garnacha, garnacha tintorera, bonicaire
91
Colour: dark-red cherry, garnet rim. Nose: balanced, scrubland, spicy, ripe fruit, warm. Palate: full, flavourful, round tannins.

Celler La Muntanya Dolç Natural 2011 B
malvasía
94
Colour: old gold. Nose: ripe fruit, balsamic herbs, spicy, pattiserie, toasty. Palate: spirituous, fine bitter notes, powerful, flavourful, long, toasty, balanced.

Lliure Albir 2011 B
garnacha blanca, verdil, malvasía
91
Colour: bright yellow. Nose: ripe fruit, sweet spices, dried flowers. Palate: ripe fruit, spicy, balanced.

Minifundi 2010 T
monastrell, garnacha, garnacha tintorera, bonicaire
90
Colour: cherry, garnet rim. Nose: ripe fruit, spicy, creamy oak, toasty, complex, wild herbs. Palate: powerful, flavourful, toasty, round tannins.

Paquito El Chocolatero 2010 T
monastrell, garnacha tintorera, garnacha
88
Colour: bright cherry. Nose: ripe fruit, sweet spices, creamy oak, cocoa bean. Palate: flavourful, fruity, toasty, round tannins, balsamic, fine bitter notes.

CELLER MARIOL

Rosselló, 442
08025 (Barcelona)
☎: +34 934 367 628
Fax: +34 934 500 281
www.casamariol.com
celler@cellermariol.es

Jo! Verdejo 2013 B

verdejo

87

Colour: yellow, greenish rim. Nose: ripe fruit, tropical fruit, floral. Palate: flavourful, ripe fruit, fine bitter notes, balanced.

CLAVERÍA BARRABÉS VITICULTORES

Mayor, 1
22420 Almunia de San Juan (Huesca)
☎: +34 686 178 400
www.dominiodelfanfarrioso.com
dominiodelfanfarrioso@gmail.com

Dominio del Fanfarrioso Macabeo 2012 B

macabeo

86

Colour: bright straw. Nose: wild herbs, fresh, dry nuts. Palate: correct, fine bitter notes, fruity.

Dominio del Fanfarrioso Tempranillo 2011 T Barrica

tempranillo

88

Colour: cherry, garnet rim. Nose: ripe fruit, wild herbs, earthy notes, spicy, creamy oak. Palate: balanced, flavourful, long, balsamic.

CLOS DELS CIMS

08474 Gualba (Barcelona)
☎: +34 678 889 808
romerolluis@hotmail.com

Clos dels Cims 2013 T

syrah

86 🌑

Colour: cherry, garnet rim. Nose: fruit liqueur notes, scrubland, spicy. Palate: powerful, flavourful, balsamic.

CORTIJO DE JARA

Medina, 79
11402 Jerez de la Frontera (Cádiz)
☎: +34 679 488 992
Fax: +34 956 338 163
www.cortijodejara.com
puertanueva.sl@cortijodejara.es

Cortijo de Jara 2013 B

83

COSMIC

Plaça M. Teresa Palleja, 3
17707 Agullana (Girona)
☎: +34 639 338 176
www.cosmic.cat
info@cosmic.cat

Cosmic Cabernet Franc 2013 T

cabernet franc

88 🌷

Colour: bright cherry, purple rim. Nose: balanced, mineral, ripe fruit, expressive. Palate: flavourful, good structure, fruity aftestaste, spicy.

Cosmic Passiò 2013 T

marcelan

88 🌑

Colour: very deep cherry, purple rim. Nose: complex, powerfull, ripe fruit. Palate: flavourful, full, long, round tannins.

Cosmic Sauvignon Blanc 2012 B

sauvignon blanc

87 🌑

Colour: bright yellow. Nose: balanced, wild herbs, ripe fruit. Palate: flavourful, ripe fruit, fine bitter notes.

DANIEL RAMOS

San Pedro de Alcántara, 1
5170 El Tiemblo (Ávila)
☎: +34 687 410 952
www.danielramos.wine
dvrcru@gmail.com

Zerberos A + P 2011 T Roble

garnacha

91

Colour: cherry, garnet rim. Nose: ripe fruit, spicy, creamy oak, toasty, complex, earthy notes. Palate: powerful, flavourful, toasty, mineral.

Zerberos Arena 2011 T Roble

garnacha

92

Colour: cherry, garnet rim. Nose: fruit liqueur notes, scrubland, spicy, creamy oak, mineral. Palate: powerful, flavourful, spicy.

Zerberos Sauvignon 2012 B

90

Colour: bright golden. Nose: faded flowers, spicy, pattiserie, fine lees, complex, citrus fruit. Palate: rich, flavourful, fine bitter notes.

Zerberos Pizarra 2011 T Roble

garnacha

93

Colour: cherry, garnet rim. Nose: ripe fruit, fruit liqueur notes, balsamic herbs, spicy, creamy oak, balanced, expressive, dry stone. Palate: powerful, flavourful, spicy, elegant.

Kπ Amphorae 100% 2013 T
garnacha
88
Colour: cherry, garnet rim. Nose: ripe fruit, wild herbs, earthy notes, spicy, mineral. Palate: balanced, flavourful, long, balsamic, fine bitter notes.

Kπ White 2013 B
sauvignon blanc
85

DOMINIO DEL BENDITO
Pza. Santo Domingo, 8
49800 Toro (Zamora)
☎: +34 980 693 306
www.bodegadominiodelbendito.com
info@bodegadominiodelbendito.es

La Chispa Negra 2008 T
92
Colour: cherry, garnet rim. Nose: fruit preserve, ripe fruit, spicy, toasty, aged wood nuances, acetaldehyde. Palate: powerful, flavourful, sweetness.

Perlarena 2013 RD
87
Colour: raspberry rose. Nose: dried flowers, fragrant herbs, red berry notes. Palate: light-bodied, flavourful, good acidity, long, spicy.

DOMINIO DEL UROGALLO
Las Barzaniellas s/n, Limés
33817 Cangas de Narcea (Asturias)
☎: +34 626 568 238
www.dominiodelurogallo.com
info@dominiodelurogallo.com

Dominio del Urogallo Cadario 2012 T
91
Colour: cherry, garnet rim. Nose: ripe fruit, wild herbs, earthy notes, spicy, creamy oak. Palate: balanced, flavourful, long, balsamic.

Dominio del Urogallo La Zorrina 2012 T
carrasquín, otras
88
Colour: cherry, garnet rim. Nose: ripe fruit, spicy, creamy oak, toasty, earthy notes, fine reductive notes. Palate: powerful, flavourful, toasty, balsamic.

Dominio del Urogallo Retoitoiro 2012 T
verdejo negro, otras
92
Colour: cherry, garnet rim. Nose: fruit liqueur notes, spicy, creamy oak, fragrant herbs, mineral. Palate: powerful, flavourful, toasty, round tannins.

Flor del Narcea Naturalmente Dulce 2011 B
albillo, verdin, petit manseng
93
Colour: bright golden. Nose: ripe fruit, dry nuts, balsamic herbs, honeyed notes. Palate: rich, powerful, flavourful, balanced, fine bitter notes, elegant.

Pésico 2012 B
100% blanco verdin
92
Colour: bright straw, greenish rim. Nose: dry nuts, dried flowers, balanced. Palate: balanced, rich, long, full.

Pésico 2012 T
albarín tinto, carrasquín, verdejo negro, mencía
90
Colour: cherry, garnet rim. Nose: ripe fruit, fruit preserve, wild herbs, spicy. Palate: powerful, flavourful, spicy, long.

EDRA BODEGA Y VIÑEDOS
Ctra A - 132, km 26
22800 Ayerbe (Huesca)
☎: +34 679 420 455
www.bodega-edra.com
edra@bodega-edra.com

Edra Blancoluz 2013 B
viognier
88
Colour: bright yellow. Nose: powerfull, ripe fruit, sweet spices, fragrant herbs. Palate: rich, smoky aftertaste, flavourful, fresh, good acidity.

ENVINATE
Gran Vía, 2 1ºC
27600 Sarría (Lugo)
☎: +34 682 207 160
asesoria@envinate.es

Albahra 2013 T
garnacha tintorera
93
Colour: cherry, garnet rim. Nose: red berry notes, ripe fruit, balsamic herbs, wild herbs, spicy. Palate: fruity, flavourful, spicy, balsamic, correct.

Puzzle 2012 T
garnacha, touriga nacional, monastrell
91
Colour: cherry, purple rim. Nose: red berry notes, fruit preserve, wild herbs, spicy. Palate: flavourful, fruity, spicy.

T. Amarela 2013 T
trincadeira preta
93
Colour: cherry, purple rim. Nose: red berry notes, ripe fruit, floral, balsamic herbs, spicy, expressive. Palate: flavourful, spicy, balsamic, long, balanced.

Táganan 2013 B
malvasía, marmajuelo, albillo, vijariego blanco

92

Colour: bright golden. Nose: ripe fruit, petrol notes, dried flowers, wild herbs, spicy, smoky. Palate: powerful, flavourful, spicy, long.

Táganan 2013 T
negramoll, listán negro, baboso negro, vijiriego

93

Colour: cherry, garnet rim. Nose: ripe fruit, spicy, toasty, complex, mineral. Palate: powerful, flavourful, balsamic, toasty, balanced.

Táganan Parcela Amogoje 2013 B
malvasía, marmajuelo, albillo, vijariego blanco

93

Colour: bright straw. Nose: fine lees, dried herbs, wild herbs, spicy, pungent. Palate: flavourful, fruity, good acidity, balanced.

Táganan Parcela Margaelagua 2013 T
negramoll, listán negro, baboso negro, vijiriego

94

Colour: cherry, garnet rim. Nose: wild herbs, red berry notes, ripe fruit, spicy, expressive, dry stone. Palate: powerful, flavourful, spicy, balsamic.

EQUIPO NAVAZOS
11403 Jerez de la Frontera (Cádiz)
www.equiponavazos.com
equipo@navazos.com

La Bota de Florpower "Mas allá" 2010 B
palomino

95

Colour: bright yellow. Nose: petrol notes, lees reduction notes, fragrant herbs. Palate: flavourful, long, spicy, good acidity.

ESPERANZA MOLINERO
Encinas de Esgueva (Valladolid)
☎: +34 665 112 051
juandelafuentesutil@hotmail.com

La Viña de Valfrío 2013 RD
tempranillo

87

Colour: deep cherry. Nose: powerfull, ripe fruit, red berry notes, floral, balsamic herbs. Palate: powerful, ripe fruit, long, unctuous.

HERETAT ANTIGUA, CASA SICILIA 1707
Paraje Alcaydias, 4
03660 Novelda (Alicante)
☎: +34 965 605 385
Fax: +34 965 604 763
www.casasicilia1707.es
administracion@casasicilia1707.es

Ad Gaude 2007 T

87

Colour: cherry, garnet rim. Nose: wild herbs, dried herbs, ripe fruit, fruit preserve. Palate: correct, balanced.

Ad Gaude Heretat 2008 T

87

Colour: bright cherry. Nose: ripe fruit, sweet spices, expressive, wild herbs. Palate: flavourful, fruity, toasty, round tannins.

JORGE ORDÓÑEZ & CO
Bartolome Esteban Murillo, 11
29700 Velez-Málaga (Málaga)
☎: +34 952 504 706
Fax: +34 951 284 796
www.jorgeordonez.es
info@jorgeordonez.es

Botani 2013 ESP
100% moscatel de alejandría

88

Colour: bright straw. Nose: white flowers, ripe fruit. Palate: good acidity, balanced.

Ordóñez & Co. Nº4 Esencia B

93

Colour: bright golden. Nose: varietal, candied fruit, citrus fruit. Palate: sweet, powerful, long.

KAIROS
Dels Nostris, 26-A
08185 Lliçà de Vall (Barcelona)
☎: +34 938 437 036
Fax: +34 938 439 671
www.kairosvino.com
kairos@vinodegaraje.com

Kairos 2013 B

83

LAGAR DE BESADA
Pazo, 11
36968 Xil-Meaño (Pontevedra)
☎: +34 986 747 473
Fax: +34 986 747 826
www.lagardebesada.com
info@lagardebesada.com

Henoba Vino de Autor 2009 T
100% tempranillo

87

Colour: very deep cherry. Nose: ripe fruit, sweet spices, creamy oak, medium intensity. Palate: fruity, flavourful, toasty.

TABLE WINE / WINES

MAS COMTAL

Mas Comtal, 1
08793 Avinyonet del Penedès
(Barcelona)
☎: +34 938 970 052
Fax: +34 938 970 591
www.mascomtal.com
mascomtal@mascomtal.com

Antistiana Incrocio Manzoni 2012 B
100% Incroccio manzoni

90

Colour: bright straw. Nose: fresh, fresh fruit, white flowers, expressive. Palate: flavourful, fruity, good acidity, balanced.

Gran Angular Cabernet Franc 2011 TC
100% cabernet franc

91

Colour: cherry, garnet rim. Nose: spicy, creamy oak, complex, dark chocolate, earthy notes, red berry notes, ripe fruit. Palate: powerful, flavourful, toasty, round tannins, elegant.

Lyric Vino de Licor AM
100% merlot

94

Colour: iodine, amber rim. Nose: powerfull, complex, elegant, dry nuts, toasty, acetaldehyde. Palate: rich, fine bitter notes, fine solera notes, long, spicy, balanced.

Mas Comtal Pizzicato Frizzante 2013 RD
muscato de Hamburgo

86

Colour: light cherry, bright. Nose: white flowers, expressive. Palate: fresh, fruity, easy to drink, correct.

MAS DE LA REAL DE SELLA

Calle Sella, 44
03570 Villajoyosa (Alicante)
☎: +34 699 308 250
Fax: +34 965 890 819
www.masdelarealdesella.es
info@masdelarealdesella.es

Mas de Sella Carreró 2010 TR
cabernet franc, garnacha tintorera, marselan, syrah

93

Colour: cherry, garnet rim. Nose: ripe fruit, wild herbs, earthy notes, spicy, creamy oak, expressive. Palate: balanced, flavourful, long, balsamic.

Mas de Sella Selección 2012 T
garnacha tintorera, syrah, marselan, cabernet franc

91

Colour: bright cherry. Nose: ripe fruit, sweet spices, creamy oak, medium intensity, scrubland. Palate: fruity, flavourful, toasty.

MAS DE TORUBIO

Plaza del Carmen, 4
44623 Cretas (Teruel)
☎: +34 669 214 845
www.masdetorubio.com
masdetorubio@hotmail.com

Cloteta Garnacha Indígena 2013 T
100% garnacha peluda

90

Colour: cherry, garnet rim. Nose: red berry notes, wild herbs, dry stone, floral, creamy oak. Palate: fresh, fruity, spicy, balsamic.

MN VINOS

9314 Pedrosa de Duero (Burgos)
☎: +34 947 530 180
www.mnvinos.com
mnvinos@mnvinos.com

Rita Hetvin Vino de Licor 2011 T
100% tinto fino

92

Colour: cherry, garnet rim. Nose: fruit preserve, ripe fruit, spicy, toasty, aged wood nuances. Palate: powerful, flavourful, sweetness.

MUSTIGUILLO VIÑEDOS Y BODEGA

Ctra. N-340 km. 196
46300 Utiel (Valencia)
☎: +34 962 168 260
Fax: +34 962 168 259
www.bodegamustiguillo.com
info@bodegamustiguillo.com

Finca Calvestra 2013 B
100% merseguera

93

Colour: bright straw. Nose: fresh, fresh fruit, white flowers, expressive, mineral. Palate: flavourful, fruity, good acidity, balanced.

Mestizaje 2013 B
merseguera, viognier, malvasía

93

Colour: bright straw. Nose: fresh, fresh fruit, white flowers. Palate: flavourful, fruity, good acidity, balanced.

PAGO DE LA ROGATIVA

Paraje de La Rogativa. Finca " Casas de Alfaro" Polígono 30 Parcela 9
30440 Moratalla (Murcia)
☎: +34 615 689 083
www.pagodelarogativa.es
info@pagodelarogativa.es

Viñedo de la Rogativa 2012 T
tempranillo, cabernet sauvignon

90

Colour: cherry, garnet rim. Nose: ripe fruit, balsamic herbs, spicy, creamy oak. Palate: powerful, flavourful, spicy, long.

PAGO DE THARSYS

Ctra. Nacional III, km. 274
46340 Requena (Valencia)
☎: +34 962 303 354
Fax: +34 962 329 000
www.pagodetharsys.com
pagodetharsys@pagodetharsys.com

Pago de Tharsys Merlot 2008 T
100% merlot

88

Colour: ruby red. Nose: spicy, fine reductive notes, wet leather, aged wood nuances, toasty. Palate: spicy, long, toasty, good finish.

Pago de Tharsys Nuestro Bobal 2010 T

88

Colour: cherry, garnet rim. Nose: ripe fruit, wild herbs, earthy notes, spicy, creamy oak. Palate: balanced, flavourful, long, balsamic.

Pago de Tharsys Vendimia Nocturna 2013 B
albariño

86

Colour: bright straw. Nose: white flowers, fragrant herbs, fruit expression. Palate: fresh, fruity, flavourful.

PAGO DEL MARE NOSTRUM

Ctra. A-348, Km. 85-86
04460 Fondón (Almería)
☎: +34 926 666 027
Fax: +34 926 666 029
www.pagodelvicario.com
info@pagodelvicario.com

1500 H Coupage 2007 T
pinot noir, tempranillo, merlot, cabernet sauvignon

88

Colour: black cherry, orangey edge. Nose: tobacco, balsamic herbs, dried herbs, spicy. Palate: fruity, balanced, fine tannins.

1500 H Pinot Noir 2007 T
pinot noir

88

Colour: dark-red cherry, orangey edge. Nose: medium intensity, ripe fruit, fruit liqueur notes, toasty, spicy, old leather. Palate: spicy, fine tannins.

PALACIO DE CANEDO

La Iglesia, s/n
24546 Canedo (León)
☎: +34 987 563 366
Fax: +34 987 567 000
www.pradaatope.es
info@pradaatope.es

Pardoxin Dulce Natural 2011 B
godello

91

Colour: yellow. Nose: honeyed notes, candied fruit, fragrant herbs. Palate: flavourful, sweet, fresh, fruity, good acidity, long.

PÉREZ CARAMÉS

Peña Picón, s/n
24500 Villafranca del Bierzo (León)
☎: +34 987 540 197
Fax: +34 987 540 314
www.perezcarames.com
info@perezcarames.com

Casar de Santa Inés 1998 T

87 ♣

Colour: pale ruby, brick rim edge. Nose: spicy, fine reductive notes, wet leather, aged wood nuances, fruit liqueur notes. Palate: spicy, fine tannins, elegant, long.

Casar de Santa Inés 2012 T

81 ♣

SEÑORÍO DE VALDESNEROS

Avda. La Paz, 4
34230 Torquemada (Palencia)
☎: +34 979 800 545
www.bodegasvaldesneros.com
sv@bodegasvaldesneros.com

Amantia 2012 T
tempranillo

88

Colour: coppery red. Nose: ripe fruit, red berry notes, balsamic herbs, dried flowers. Palate: fresh, fruity, flavourful, sweet.

SEXTO ELEMENTO

C/Caliches, 13
46310 Venta del Moro (Valencia)
☎: +34 637 414 137
www.vinosextoelemento.com
bodega@@vinosextoelemento.com

6º Elemento 2006 T
100% bobal

88

Colour: cherry, garnet rim. Nose: ripe fruit, earthy notes, spicy, creamy oak, scrubland, fine reductive notes. Palate: balanced, flavourful, long, balsamic.

6º Elemento 2011 T
100% bobal

89

Colour: cherry, garnet rim. Nose: ripe fruit, spicy, creamy oak, toasty. Palate: powerful, flavourful, toasty, roasted-coffee aftertaste.

TRESGE WINERY
Ctra. Picaña, 18, 10
46200 Paiporta (Valencia)
☎: +34 676 599 583
www.gratiaswines.com
gratias@gratiaswines.com

Gratias Máximas 2012 T
100% bobal

88

Colour: cherry, garnet rim. Nose: ripe fruit, spicy, creamy oak, toasty. Palate: powerful, flavourful, toasty.

Gratias Rosé 2013 RD
100% bobal

87

Colour: light cherry. Nose: candied fruit, dried flowers, fragrant herbs, red berry notes. Palate: light-bodied, flavourful, good acidity, long, balsamic.

VALQUEJIGOSO
Ctra, Villamanta - Méntrida, s/n
28610 Villamanta (Madrid)
☎: +34 912 163 917
Fax: +34 918 136 842
www.valquejigoso.com
aureliogarcia@valquejigoso.com

Valquejigoso V2 2007 T
94 🏵

Colour: cherry, garnet rim. Nose: ripe fruit, spicy, creamy oak, toasty, complex, dark chocolate, earthy notes. Palate: powerful, flavourful, toasty, round tannins.

Valquejigoso V2 2009 T
94 🏵

Colour: very deep cherry. Nose: ripe fruit, spicy, creamy oak, toasty, characterful. Palate: powerful, flavourful, toasty, round tannins.

VINS DE TALLER
Nou, 5
17469 Siurana d'Empordà (Girona)
☎: +34 972 525 578
Fax: +34 972 525 578
www.vinsdetaller.com
info@vinsdetaller.com

Vins de Taller Baseia 2013 B
90

Colour: bright straw. Nose: white flowers, fine lees, dried herbs. Palate: flavourful, fruity, good acidity, balanced, spicy, rich.

Vins de Taller Geum 2013 T
merlot

91

Colour: light cherry. Nose: ripe fruit, wild herbs, earthy notes, spicy, creamy oak. Palate: balanced, flavourful, long, balsamic.

Vins de Taller LEA Dulce Natural 2012 BFB
cortese

91

Colour: bright golden. Nose: honeyed notes, candied fruit, dried herbs, floral, expressive. Palate: powerful, flavourful, rich, unctuous, spicy.

Vins de Taller Phlox 2013 B
88

Colour: bright yellow. Nose: faded flowers, balanced, dried herbs. Palate: fruity, flavourful, long, fine bitter notes.

Vins de Taller Siurà 2010 T
87

Colour: cherry, garnet rim. Nose: ripe fruit, wild herbs, earthy notes, spicy, creamy oak. Palate: balanced, flavourful, long, balsamic.

VINS DEL COMTAT
Turballos, 11
03820 Cocentaina (Alicante)
☎: +34 667 669 287
Fax: +34 965 593 194
www.vinsdelcomtat.com
vinsdelcomtat@gmail.com

Viognier de Vins del Comtat 2013 B
viognier

88

Colour: bright straw. Nose: fresh, fresh fruit, white flowers, expressive. Palate: flavourful, fruity, good acidity, balanced.

VINYA NATURA
Herrero, 32- 5º 12
12005 Castellón (Castellón)
☎: +34 670 056 497
www.vinyanatura.com
info@vinyanatura.com

Barranc de l'Infern 2010 T
100% merlot

86

Colour: dark-red cherry, garnet rim. Nose: powerfull, green pepper, wild herbs, ripe fruit. Palate: good structure, flavourful.

Barranc de l'Infern 2013 B
macabeo, chardonnay

89

Colour: bright straw. Nose: fresh, fresh fruit, expressive, fragrant herbs, citrus fruit. Palate: flavourful, fruity, good acidity, balanced.

L'Equip 2013 T
tempranillo, cabernet sauvignon
84

VINYES DEL TIET PERE
Raval del Roser, 3
43886 Vilabella (Tarragona)
☎: +34 625 408 974
www.camidelafont.com
oriol@camidelafont.com

Cami de la Font "Vinyes del tiet Pere" 2013 B
100% macabeo
81

VINYES MORTITX
Ctra. Pollença Lluc, Km. 10,9
07315 Escorca (Illes Balears)
☎: +34 971 182 339
Fax: +34 871 100 053
www.vinyesmortitx.com
info@vinyesmortitx.com

Dolç de Gel Mortitx 2011 B
moscatel, riesling
88
Colour: bright yellow. Nose: white flowers, candied fruit. Palate: flavourful, full, sweet, rich, long.

VIÑAS EL REGAJAL
Antigua Ctra. Andalucía, Km. 50,5
28300 Aranjuez (Madrid)
☎: +34 913 078 903
Fax: +34 913 576 312
www.elregajal.es
isabel@elregajal.es

Galia 2011 T
tempranillo, garnacha
93
Colour: cherry, purple rim. Nose: red berry notes, ripe fruit, wild herbs, sweet spices, creamy oak, toasty, dry stone. Palate: powerful, flavourful, spicy, long, balanced.

VIÑEDOS Y BODEGAS MAYO GARCÍA
La Font 116
12192 Vilafamés (Castellón)
☎: +34 964 329 312
www.mayocasanova.com
mail@mayogarcia.com

Magnanimvs Platino Vino de Autor 2011 T
cabernet sauvignon, merlot, syrah
87
Colour: cherry, garnet rim. Nose: wild herbs, earthy notes, spicy, creamy oak. Palate: flavourful, toasty, easy to drink.

Magnanimvs Rubí 2010 TC
cabernet sauvignon, merlot, syrah
89
Colour: very deep cherry, garnet rim. Nose: powerfull, ripe fruit, roasted coffee, sweet spices. Palate: powerful, toasty, roasted-coffee aftertaste.

VIÑOS DE ENCOSTAS
Florentino López Cuevillas Nº6, 1ºC
32500 O Carballiño (Ourense)
☎: +34 988 101 733
Fax: +34 988 101 733
www.xlsebio.es
miguel@losvinosdemiguel.com

Wish 2011 T
caiño, ferrol, sousón, bastardo negro
93
Colour: cherry, garnet rim. Nose: ripe fruit, spicy, creamy oak, toasty, complex, earthy notes, scrubland. Palate: powerful, flavourful, toasty, round tannins.

SPARKLING WINES

SPARKLING WINES-TRADITIONAL METHOD

All the wines included in this section are made by the so-called traditional method of a second fermentation in the bottle, the same one used in Cava –and Champagne– production, but in areas outside those ascribed to Cava or any other Spanish DO. They represent a tiny part of all the sparkling wines made in Spain and their figures and quality are understandably far away from those of Cava.

AGROALIMENTARIA VIRGEN DEL ROCÍO

Avda. de Cabezudos, 1
21730 Almonte (Huelva)
☎: +34 959 406 146
www.raigal.es
administracion@raigal.com

Raigal BN
zalema
84

BODEGAS BARBADILLO

Luis de Eguilaz, 11
11540 Sanlúcar de Barrameda (Cádiz)
☎: +34 956 385 500
Fax: +34 956 385 501
www.barbadillo.com
barbadillo@barbadillo.com

Barbadillo Beta BR
palomino, chardonnay
86
Colour: bright yellow. Nose: fragrant herbs, floral, medium intensity, fresh. Palate: correct, fine bitter notes, easy to drink, good acidity.

BODEGAS GRUPO YLLERA

Autovía A-6, Km. 173,5
47490 Rueda (Valladolid)
☎: +34 983 868 097
Fax: +34 983 868 177
www.grupoyllera.com
grupoyllera@grupoyllera.com

Yllera 5.5 Rosé Frizzante ESP
tempranillo, verdejo
86
Colour: raspberry rose. Nose: candied fruit, jasmine, dried herbs. Palate: fresh, fruity, easy to drink.

Yllera 5.5 Verdejo Frizzante ESP
100% verdejo
87
Colour: bright straw. Nose: white flowers, candied fruit, balsamic herbs, medium intensity. Palate: fresh, fruity, easy to drink.

FINCA LA BLANCA

Princesa, 84
45840 Puebla de Almoradiel (Toledo)
☎: +34 669 995 315
Fax: +34 968 897 675
www.fincalablanca.es
export@fincalablanca.es

D'Lucio Blanco 2013 ESP
airén, macabeo
82

D'Lucio Rosado 2013 ESP
tempranillo, garnacha
83

LOBBAN WINES

Creueta, 24
08784 St. Jaume Sesoliveres (Barcelona)
☎: +34 667 551 695
www.lapamelita.com
info@lapamelita.com

La Pamelita 2006 Tinto Espumoso
80

La Rosita 2009 ESP
84

PALACIO DE CANEDO

La Iglesia, s/n
24546 Canedo (León)
☎: +34 987 563 366
Fax: +34 987 567 000
www.pradaatope.es
info@pradaatope.es

Xamprada 2009 ESP Reserva
godello, chardonnay
83 ☘

Xamprada Extra Brut 2011 ESP
godello, chardonnay
84 ☘

Xamprada Extra Brut Rosado 2012 ESP
mencía, godello
81 ☘

Xamprada Rosado Semiseco 2012 ESP
mencía, godello
80 ☘

Xamprada Semiseco 2011 ESP
godello, chardonnay
82 ☘

RAVENTÓS I BLANC

Plaça del Roure, s/n
08770 Sant Sadurní D'Anoia (Barcelona)
☎: +34 938 183 262
Fax: +34 938 912 500
www.raventos.com
raventos@raventos.com

Enoteca Personal Manuel Raventos 1998 BN
96
Colour: bright golden. Nose: dry nuts, fragrant herbs, complex, fine lees, macerated fruit, sweet spices, expressive. Palate: powerful, flavourful, good acidity, fine bead, fine bitter notes, elegant.

Enoteca Personal Manuel Raventos 1999 BN

95

Colour: bright golden. Nose: fine lees, dry nuts, fragrant herbs, complex, candied fruit. Palate: powerful, flavourful, good acidity, fine bead, fine bitter notes.

Enoteca Personal Manuel Raventos 2000 BN

94

Colour: bright golden. Nose: fine lees, dry nuts, fragrant herbs, complex, toasty. Palate: powerful, flavourful, good acidity, fine bead, fine bitter notes, elegant.

Enoteca Personal Manuel Raventos 2001 BN

macabeo, xarel.lo, parellada, chardonnay

93

Colour: bright golden. Nose: dry nuts, complex, sweet spices, pattiserie, expressive. Palate: powerful, flavourful, good acidity, fine bead, elegant, roasted-coffee aftertaste.

L'Hereu 2012 ESP Reserva

macabeo, xarel.lo, parellada

90

Colour: bright yellow. Nose: fine lees, dry nuts, fragrant herbs, complex, toasty, citrus fruit. Palate: powerful, flavourful, good acidity, fine bead, fine bitter notes.

Raventós i Blanc De La Finca 2011 BN Gran Reserva

parellada, xarel.lo, macabeo

91

Colour: bright golden. Nose: dry nuts, fragrant herbs, complex, fine lees, sweet spices, expressive. Palate: powerful, flavourful, good acidity, fine bead, fine bitter notes, elegant.

Raventós i Blanc De La Finca Magnum 2011 ESP

parellada, macabeo, xarel.lo

92

Colour: bright yellow. Nose: fine lees, dry nuts, fragrant herbs, complex. Palate: powerful, flavourful, good acidity, fine bead, fine bitter notes, elegant.

Raventós i Blanc De Nit 2012 BN Reserva

macabeo, xarel.lo, parellada, monastrell

91

Colour: coppery red. Nose: floral, jasmine, candied fruit, wild herbs, spicy. Palate: fresh, fruity, flavourful, correct, balanced.

GLOSARY & INDEXES

TERMINOLOGY RELATED TO COLOUR

AMBER. The first step in the oxidative ageing of sherry generoso wines, brandies, whiskies and rum, somewhere between yellow and coppery red.

BEADS. The slow rising string of bubbles in a sparkling wine.

BRICK RED. An orangey hue, similar to that of a brick, used to describe reds aged in bottle for more than 10 years or in barrel for longer than six.

BRILLIANT. Related to a young and neat wine.

CANDY CHERRY. This is used to define a colour lighter than a red but darker than a rosé.

CLEAN. Utterly clean, immaculate.

CLOUDY. Lacking clarity.

COPPERY. A reddish nuance that can be appreciated in whites aged in wood for a long period, generally amontillados and some palo cortados.

CHERRY. Commonly used to express red colour. It can take all sort of degrees from 'light' all the way to 'very dark' or almost 'black cherry'.

DARK. This often refers to a tone slightly lighter than 'deep' and synonymous to "medium-intensity".

DEEP. A red with a very dark colour, which hardly lets us see the bottom of the glass.

DULL. A wine lacking in liveliness, usually with an ochre hue.

GARNET RED. A common nuance in medium to light reds. If the wine is an intense cherry red it could have a garnet rim only if it comes from cooler regions; if it is more luminous and open than the violet rim of a dark wine, it generally would be a young wine.

GOLDEN. Gold in colour with yellow –predominantly– to reddish tones.

GLIMMER. A vague brilliance.

IODINE. A tone similar to iodine tincture stains (old gold and brownish) displayed by rancio and generoso wines have after their long oxidative ageing.

LIVELY. A reflection of the youth of a wine through bright, brilliant colours.

MAHOGANY. Describes the second stage of ageing in brandies, rum and generoso sherry (fortified) wines. A hue between brown and yellow displayed by wines when long aged.

OCHRE. Yellow-orangey hue, the last colour phase of a table wine, generally found in wines with a long oxidative ageing; it is a sign of their decline.

OILY. A wine that appears dense to the eye, usually sweet and with high alcohol content.

OLD GOLD. Gold colour with the brownish tones found in amontillados and a bit lighter than the mahogany nuance predominant in oloroso sherry.

ONION SKIN. A touch lighter than salmon colour.

OPAQUE. A wine with such depth of colour we cannot see the bottom of the glass. Generally found in very old pedro ximénez and therefore akin to caramelised notes.

OPEN. Very pale, not at all intense.

ORANGEY EDGE. Intermediate phase between a deep red and brick red found towards the rim in red wines of a medium age. It generally appears sooner in wines with higher alcohol content and it is also typical of wines made from pinot noir.

RASPBERRY. Sort of pinkish colour with a bluish rim, it is the optimal colour for rosé wines since it denotes freshness, youth and a good acidity.

RIM. Also known as 'edge', it refers to the lighter colour the wine displays at the edge of the oval when we hold the glass at 45°, as opposed to the 'core' or main body of colour right in the centre. If it is a young red, it will show normally violet or raspberry nuances; when slightly older, it will be a deeper red or garnet, and if has been in the bottle for more than five years it might be anything from ruby to tawny through brick red and orangey.

RUBY. Slightly orangey hue with a yellow nuance found in old wines that have lost part of their original cherry colour.

SALMON. A tone slightly redder than pink found in rosé wines with less acidity and more alcohol.

STEELY. Pale colour with metallic reflections (reminiscent of those from steel) found in some whites.

STRAW-COLOURED. This term should be understood as straw yellow, the colour found in the majority of young white wines, halfway between yellow and green. It can also be described as "lemony".

TERMINOLOGY RELATED TO AROMA

ACETONE. Very close notes to those of nail varnish, typical of very old eau de vie.

ALCOHOL. It is not a pejorative term for an excess of alcohol –in which case we would refer to it as burning–, but just a predominant, non-aggressive note.

ALDEHYDE. A sensory note of oxidized, slightly rancid alcohol, typical of old wines with high alcohol content that have undergone oxidative ageing.

ANIMAL. Not a positive note, generally the result of long storage in bottle, also referred to as 'wet dog' or 'wet hide' and normally associated with a lack of hygiene. If it is found in younger vintages, then it could be a symptom of "brett" (see brett).

ATTIC. An aroma associated with that of old dry wood and dust typical of attics, mainly found in fortified wines aged in wood and in very old wines aged for a long period in old barrels which happen to have also been bottled for more than ten years.

BALSAMIC. A trait usually associated to wood-aged wines in hot regions, where high temperatures accelerate their evolution. It also refers to the aroma of dry herbs such as eucalyptus and bay leaf, as well as incense and tar.

BLACK FRUIT. It refers to the sort of toasted aromas of very ripe grapes, those almost 'burnt skin' notes found in reds that have undergone a long vatting period in contact with the skins.

"BRETT". This is the abbreviation for a new term (brettanomyces) to describe an old problem: the aroma of stables, henhouse, and wet new leather generally found along with reductive off-odours in wines that have been in the bottle for more than ten years. These aromas were considered part of the sensory complexity of old wines and therefore tolerated. Nowadays, due to better olfactory research and more hygienic working conditions in the wineries, they are easily detected and considered more a defect. In addition, today brett is often found in younger wines as this particular bacteria or yeast usually develops better in wines with higher ph levels. The increase in the ph of wines is quite common these days due to global warming, riper grapes and the use of fertilizers over the past thirty-five years.

BROOM. An aroma reminiscent

of Mediterranean shrubs, only a bit dryer.

CANDIED FRUIT. This is a sweet nuance, somewhere between toasted and jammy, which is found in whites with a long oxidative ageing and in some sweet white wines.

CAROB. Anybody who has chewed or smelt one of those beans cannot would easily recall its typical blend of sweetness and toasted notes, as well as the slightly rustic nuance. It is usually found in old brandy aged in soleras of pedro ximénez and in deep, concentrated wines made from very ripe grapes.

CEDAR. The somewhat perfumed aroma of cedar, a soft wood commonly found in Morocco.

CHARACTERFUL. Used to express the singularity of a wine above the rest. It may refer to winemaking, terroir or the peculiarities of its ageing.

CITRUS. An aroma reminiscent of lemon, orange and grapefruit.

CLASSIC RIOJA. A note named after the more traditional and popular style of Rioja, with predominantly woody notes (normally from very old wood) along with a typical character of

sweet spices and occasionally candle wax nuances instead of fruit, given the oxidative character provided by long ageing periods.

CLEAR. A wine with no defects, neither in the nose nor in the palate.

CLOSED. A term to describe a faint or not properly developed nose. Almost always found in concentrated wines from a good vintage, which evolve very slowly in the bottle, but it can also be found in wines recently bottled.

COCOA. Delicate, slightly toasted aroma found in wines aged in wood for a moderately long time that have evolved very well in the bottle.

COMPLEX. A wine abundant in aromas and flavours related either to grape variety, soil or ageing, although none of those features is particularly prominent.

CREAMY. Aroma of finely toasted oak (usually French) with notes of caramelised vanilla.

DATES. A sweet aroma with hints of dates and a raisiny nuance.

EARTHY. An aroma somewhere between clay and dust typical of red wines ma-

de from ripe grapes and with high alcohol content. It can also refer in some wines to a mineral nuance.

ELEGANT. A harmonious combination of fine, somewhat restrained aromatic notes related to perfumed wood, and a light, pleasantly balanced richness or complexity (see complex).

ETHEREAL. This is used to describe spirits, fortified wines and wines with a certain intensity of alcohol in their oxidative evolution; the strength of the alcohol reveals the rancid-type aromas. It has a lot to do with age.

EVOLUTION NOTES. Generally used to describe wines aged prematurely by either oxygen or heat, e.g., a wine that has been left in a glass for several hours.

FINE. A synonym for elegant.

FINE LEES. This is an aroma between herbaceous and slightly toasty that is produced by the contact of the wine with the lees (dead yeasts cells) after the fermentation has taken place, a process called autolysis that helps to make the wine more complex and to give it a richer aroma.

FLOR. This is a pungent, saline aroma typically found in sherry wines, particularly fino, manzanilla and, to a lesser degree, amontillado. It is caused by a film-forming yeast known as 'flor' in Spanish (literally flower), which transfers to the wine its singular smell and flavour.

FLORAL. Reminiscent of the petals of certain flowers –such as roses and jasmine–noticeable in certain northern withes or in quality reds after a bottle-ageing spell that also delivers some spicy notes.

FRAGRANT HERBS. An aroma similar to soaps and perfumes made from lavender, rosemary, lemon, orange blossom or jasmine. It is found in white wines that undergo pre-fermentative cold skin maceration.

FRESH. A wine with lively aroma and hardly any alcohol expression.

FRESH FRUIT. These are fruity notes produced by a slow grape-ripening cycle typical of mild climates.

FRUIT EXPRESSION. Related to different flavours and aromas reminiscent of various fruits and fine herbs.

FRUITY. Fruit notes with a fine herbal character and even hints of green grass.

HERBACEOUS. A vague note of vine shoots, scrub and geranium

leaf caused by an incomplete maturation of the grape skin.

INTENSE. A powerful aroma that can be immediately referred to as such when first nosing the wine.

IODINE. This refers to iodine tincture, a combination of the sweetish smell of alcohol, toasted notes, liniment and varnish or lacquer.

JAM. Typical notes of very ripe black fruit slightly caramelised by a slow oxidative ageing in oak barrels. Very similar to forest fruit jam (prunes, blackberries, blueberries, redcurrants, cherries…). Found in red wines –generally from southern regions– with a high concentration of fruit notes giving that they are made resorting to long vatting periods, which provide longer contact with the skins.

MACERATION. These are aromas similar to those produced during fermentation and that –logically– found in young wines.

MEDITERRANEAN. An aroma where various prominent notes (sweetness, alcohol, burning and raisiny notes, caramel…) produced by grapes grown in hot regions blend in to characterize the wines.

MINERAL NOTES. Used to des-

cribe wines that have a subtle nose with plenty of notes reminiscent of flint, slate, hot stones or dry sand.

MUSK. A term to describe the sweet and grapey notes typical of highly aromatic varieties such as moscatel, riesling and gewürztraminer.

ROASTED COFFEE. (See terms of taste).

SUBDUED FRUIT. It generally refers to aromas produced by a fast ripening of the grapes typical of warm climates.

NUTS. Notes generally found in white wines with oxidative ageing; the oxygen in the air gives rise to aromas and flavours reminiscent of nuts (bitter almond, hazelnut, walnut…). When ageing spells are longer and –most importantly– take place in older casks, there will appear notes that are closer to fruits like figs, dates and raisins.

ORANGE PEEL. Typical fruity aroma found in certain white wines with, above all, a vibrant spicy character.

ORGANIC NOTES. A way to define the fermentative aromas – essentially related to yeast– and typical of young white wines and also fortified generoso wines from the sherry region.

OVERRIPE FRUIT. An aroma typical of young wines that are already slightly oxidized and reminiscent of grape bunches with some signs of rot –noble or not–, or simply bruised or recently pressed grapes.

OXIDATIVE EVOLUTION. Notes related to the tendency of a wine to age by the action of oxygen that passes through the pores of the cask or barrel (micro-oxidation), or during racking.

PATISSERIE. An aroma between sweet and toasted with hints of caramelised sugar and vanilla typical of freshly baked cakes. It is found in wines –generally sweet– that have been aged in oak for a long time and it is caused by both oxidative evolution and the aromatic elements (mainly vanillin) found in oak.

PEAT. A slightly burnt aroma that occurs when the notes of ripe grapes blend in with the toasted aromas of new oak in wines with a high alcohol content.

PHENOLIC. A short and derivative way to describe polyphenols (a combination of the tannins and anthocyanins, vegetal elements of the grape), it describes aromas of grape skins macerated for a long time that yield notes somewhere between ink and a pressed bunch of grapes.

PORT. This is the sweet aroma of wine made from somewhat raisiny or overripe grapes and reminiscent of the vintage Ports made with a short oxidative ageing.

PUNGENT. A prominent aromatic note produced by the combination of alcohol, wood and flor notes and typical of –particularly– fino sherry wines.

RANCIO. This is not a defect but a note better known as "sherryfied" and brought about by oxidative ageing.

RED FRUIT. An aromatic note that refers to forest red fruits (blackberries, redcurrants, mulberries) as well as slightly unripe cherries and plums.

REDUCTION. A wine aroma caused by the lack of oxygen during long bottle ageing, which gives rise to notes like tobacco, old leather, vanilla, cinnamon, cocoa, attic, dust, etc.

REDUCTION OFF-ODOURS. This is a negative set of aromas, halfway between boiled cabbage and boiled eggs, produced by the lees in wines that have not been properly aerated or racked.

REDUCTIVE TANK OFF-ODOURS. A smell between metal and boiled fruit typical of wines stored in large vats at high temperatures. The sulphur added – probably in excess– combines with the wine and reduces its freshness and the expression of fruit notes. This phenomenon is largely found in the production of bulk wines.

RIPE GRAPE SKIN. The aroma that a very ripe grape gives off when squeezed, similar to that of ink or of ripe grape bunches just pressed.

SALINE. This is the note acquired by a fino that has aged in soleras under flor yeast.

SEASONED WOOD. It refers to notes that may appear in wines aged in barrel for a long period –more than four or five years– which have lost the fine toasted aromas and flavours of new oak.

SHRUB. An aroma typically herbal found in Mediterranean regions, a mixture of rosemary, thyme and other typically semi-arid herbs. It refers to the dry, herbaceous note found generally in white and red wines from warmer regions.

SOLERA. An aroma close to the damp, seasoned, aged aroma of an old bodega for oloroso wines.

SPICY. It refers to the most common household spices

(pepper, cloves, cinnamon) that appear in wines that undergo long and slow oxidative ageing in oak casks or barrels.

SPIRITUOUS. Both a flavour and an olfactory feature related to high alcohol content but without burning sensations. It is an almost 'intellectual' term to define alcohol, since that product is nothing else but the "spirit of wine".

STEWED FRUIT. Notes of stewed or 'cooked' fruit appear in wines made from well-ripened –not overripe– grapes and are similar to those of jam.

TAR. The pitchy, petrolly aromas of very toasted wood, associated with concentrated red wines with lots of colour, structure and alcohol.

TERROIR. An aromatic note determined by the soil and climate and therefore with various nuances: mountain herbs, minerals, stones, etc.

TOASTED SUGAR. Sweet caramelised aromas.

TOFFEE. A note typical of the milk coffee creams (lactic and toasted nuances mixed together) and present in some crianza red wines.

TROPICAL NOTES. The sweet white fruit aromas present in white wines made from grapes that have ripened very quickly and lack acidity.

TRUFFLE. Similar note to that of a mixture of damp earth and mushrooms.

UNDERGROWTH. This is the aromatic nuance between damp earth, grass and fallen leaves found in well-assembled, wood-aged reds that have a certain fruity expression and good phenolic concentration.

VANILLA. A typical trait of wines –also fortified– aged in oak, thanks to the vanillin, an element contained in that type of wood.

VARIETAL EXPRESSION. This is the taste and aroma of the variety or varieties used to make the wine.

VARNISH. A typical smell found in very old or fortified wines due to the oxidation of the alcohol after a long wood-ageing period. The varnished-wood note is similar to the aroma of eau de vie or spirits aged in wood.

VARNISHED WOOD. A sharp note typical of wines aged in wood for a long period, during which the alcohol oxidises and gives off an aroma of acetone, wood or nail varnish.

VISCOUS. The sweet taste and aromatic expression of wines with high alcohol content.

VOLATILE. A note characteristic of wines with high volatile acidity, i.e., just the first sign of them turning into vinegar. It is typical of poorly stabilized young wines or aged wines either with a high alcohol content or that have taken on this note during the slow oxidative wood-ageing phase, although we should remember it is a positive trait in the case of generoso wines.

WINE PRESS. The aroma of the vegetal parts of the grape after fermentation, vaguely reminiscent of pomace brandy, grapeskins and ink.

WITHERED FLOWERS. This is a sort of 'toasty' nuance typical of good champagnes made with a high percentage of pinot noir and some cavas which have aged perfectly in the bottle and on their lees for a long time.

WOODY. It describes an excess of notes of wood in a wine. The reason could be either a too long ageing period or the wine's lack of structure.

YEASTY. The dry aroma of bread yeast that can be perceived in young cavas or champagnes, or wines that have just been bottled.

TERMINOLOGY RELATED TO THE PALATE

ALCOHOL. A gentle, even sweet note of fine spirits; it is not a defect.

ALCOHOLIC EDGES. A slight excess of alcohol perceived on the tongue, but which does not affect the overall appreciation of the wine.

AMPLE. A term used to describe richness. It is a sensation generally experienced on the attack.

BITTER. A slight, non-aggressive note of bitterness, often found in some sherry wines (finos, amontillados) and the white wines from Rueda; it should not be regarded as a negative feature, quite on the contrary, it helps to counterbalance soft or slightly sweet notes.

CARAMELISED. A very sweet and toasted note typical of some unctuous wines aged in oloroso or pedro ximénez casks.

DENSE. This is related to the body of the wine, a thick sensation on the palate.

FATNESS. "Gordo" (fat) is the adjective used in Jerez to describe a wine with good body; it is the antonym of "fino" (light).

FLABBY. Used to describe a wine low in acidity that lacks freshness.

FLAVOURFUL. A pronounced and pleasant sensation on the palate produced by the combination of various sweet nuances.

FULL. A term used to describe volume, richness, some sweetness and round tannins; that is, a wine with a fleshy character and an almost fat palate.

LIGHT. The opposite of meaty, dense or concentrated; i.e., a wine with little body.

LONG. This refers to the persistence of the flavour after the wine has been swallowed.

MEATY. A wine that has body, structure and which can almost literally be "chewed".

NOTES OF WOOD. Well-defined notes somewhere between woody and resin generally found in wines matured in younger casks.

OILY. This is the supple, pleasantly fat sensation produced by glycerine. It is more prominent in older wines –thanks to the decrease in acidity– or in certain varieties such as riesling, gewürztraminer, chardonnay, albariño and godello.

OXIDATIVE AGEING. It refers to the influence of the air in the evolution of wine. Depending on the level of oxygen in the air, oxidation will take place in wine to a greater or lesser extent. Oxidative ageing happens when the air comes in contact with the wine either during racking –which ages the wine faster– or through the pores of the wood.

PASTY. This is not a pejorative term, simply a very sweet and dense taste.

ROASTED COFFEE. The sweet and toasted note of caramelised sugar typically found in wines aged in oak barrels –generally burnt inside–, or else the taste of very ripe (sometimes even overripe) grapes.

ROUGH TANNINS. Just unripe tannins either from the wood or the grape skins.

ROUND. This is an expression commonly used to describe a wine without edges, supple, with volume and body.

SWEETENED. Related to sweetness, only with an artificial nuance.

SWEETNESS. A slightly sweet note that stands out in a wine with an overall dry or tannic character.

SOFT TANNINS. Both alcohol and adequately ripened grapes help to balance out the natural bitter character of the tannins. They are also referred to as fat or oily tannins.

TANNIC. This is term derived from tannin, a substance generally found in the skin of the grape and in the wood that yields a somewhat harsh, vegetal note. In wines, it displays a slightly harsh, sometimes even grainy texture.

UNCTUOUS. This refers to the fat, pleasant note found in sweet wines along with their somewhat sticky sweetness.

VELVETY. A smooth, pleasant note on the palate typical of great wines where the tannins and the alcohol have softened down during ageing.

VIGOROUS. A wine with high alcohol content.

WARM. The term speaks of alcohol in a more positive way.

WELL-BALANCED. A term that helps to define a good wine: none of the elements that are part of it (alcohol, acidity, dry extract, oak) is more prominent than the other, just pure balance.

PEÑÍNGUIDE **to Spanish Wine**

PEÑÍNGUIDE 25 Years **to Spanish Wine**

PEÑÍNGUIDE 25 years to Spanish Wine

PEÑÍNGUIDE **to Spanish Wine**

PEÑÍNGUIDE 25 to Spanish Wine

PEÑÍNGUIDE to Spanish Wine

PEÑÍNGUIDE to Spanish Wine

PEÑÍNGUIDE **to Spanish Wine**

WINE	PAGE

PEÑÍNGUIDE 25 years to Spanish Wine

WINES

PEÑÍNGUIDE to Spanish Wine

WINES

PEÑÍNGUIDE to Spanish Wine

 PENÍNGUIDE **to Spanish Wine**

PEÑÍNGUIDE to Spanish Wine

WINES

PEÑÍNGUIDE 25 Years to Spanish Wine

WINES

PEÑÍNGUIDE 25 Years to Spanish Wine

PEÑÍNGUIDE 25 Years to Spanish Wine

WINES

U

WINES

WINES

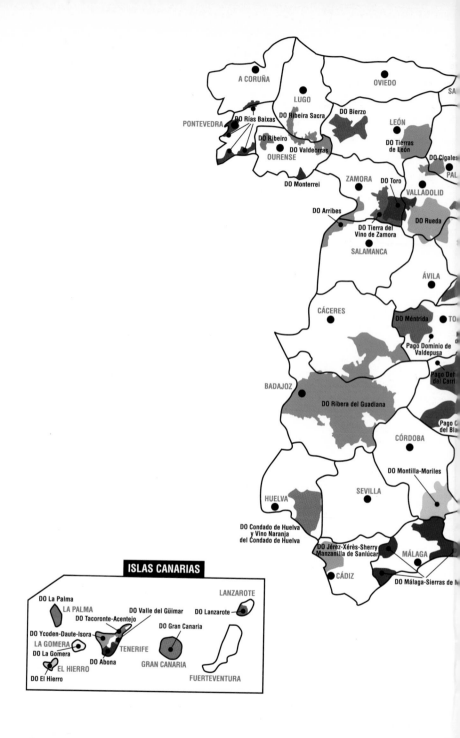

A CORUÑA

OVIEDO

SA

LUGO

DO Bierzo

DO Ribeira Sacra

LEÓN

PONTEVEDRA

DO Rías Baixas

DO Tierras
de León

DO Ribeiro

DO Valdeorras

OURENSE

DO Cigales

PAL

DO Monterrei

ZAMORA

DO Toro

VALLADOLID

DO Arribes

DO Tierra del
Vino de Zamora

DO Rueda

SALAMANCA

ÁVILA

CÁCERES

DO Méntrida

TO

Pago Dominio de
Valdepusa

Pago Deh
del Carri

BADAJOZ

DO Ribera del Guadiana

Pago C
del Bla

CÓRDOBA

DO Montilla-Moriles

HUELVA

SEVILLA

DO Condado de Huelva
y Vino Naranja
del Condado de Huelva

DO Jérez-Xérès-Sherry
Manzanilla de Sanlúcar

MÁLAGA

CÁDIZ

DO Málaga-Sierras de N

ISLAS CANARIAS

LANZAROTE

DO La Palma

LA PALMA

DO Valle del Güimar

DO Lanzarote

DO Tacoronte-Acentejo

DO Ycoden-Daute-Isora

DO Gran Canaria

LA GOMERA

DO La Gomera

TENERIFE

EL HIERRO

DO Abona

GRAN CANARIA

DO El Hierro

FUERTEVENTURA

...colina

Bizkaiko Txacolina

...ILBAO DO Getariako Txakolina

SAN SEBASTIÁN

VITORIA

Pago Señorío de Arínzano   DO Navarra

PAMPLONA

...S

Pago de Otazu

Pago Prado de Iráche

DOCa Rioja

HUESCA

DO Empordá

LLEIDA   GIRONA

DO Somontano   DO Pla de Bages   DO Catalunya

SORIA

DO Campo de Borja   ZARAGOZA

DO Costers del Segre   DO Alella

DO Ceriñena   BARCELONA

DO Calatayud   Pago de Aylés   DO Penedés

DO Conca de Barbera

DO Tarragona

DO Ca. Priorat

DO Montsant

TARRAGONA

GUADALAJARA

DO Terra Alta

Pago Calzadilla

TERUEL   CASTELLÓN

Pago Chozas Carrascal

CUENCA   Pago Los Balagueses   Pago El Terrerazo

DO Uclés

DO Manchuela   VALENCIA

DO Ribera del Júcar

DO Binissalem Mallorca   DO Pla y Llevant

ALBACETE   DO Utiel Requena   PALMA DE MALLORCA

Pago Guijoso   DO Valencia

DO Almansa

Pago Finca Élez   DO Yecla   DO Alicante

DO Jumilla   ALICANTE

DO Bullas

MURCIA

...DA

ALMERÍA

DO CAVA

GIRONA

LLEIDA

ZARAGOZA   BARCELONA

VITORIA-GASTEIZ   TARRAGONA

PAMPLONA

LOGROÑO

BADAJOZ   VALENCIA

ANDALUCÍA
1 - Norte de Almería
2 - Sierra de las Estancias y los Filabres
3 - Desierto de Almería
4 - Ribera del Andarax
5 - Laujar-Alpujarra
6 - Contraviesa-Alpujarra/Cumbres de Guadalfeo
7 - Granada Suroeste/Laderas de Genil
8 - Norte de Granada/Altiplano de Sierra Nevada
9 - Sierra Sur de Jaén
10 - Bailén
11 - Torreperogil
12 - Córdoba
13 - Villaviciosa de Córdoba
14 - Sierra Norte de Sevilla
15 - Los Palacios
16 - Cádiz

ARAGÓN
17 - Ribera del Gállego-Cinco Villas
18 - Ribera del Jiloca
19 - Valdejalón
20 - Bajo Aragón
21 - Valle del Cinca

CANTABRIA
22 - Liébana
23 - Costa de Cantabria

CASTILLA-LA MANCHA
24 - Castilla
25 - Pozohondo
26 - Sierra de Alcaraz
27 - Gálvez

CASTILLA Y LEÓN
28 - Castilla y León

EXTREMADURA
29 - Extremadura

GALICIA
30 - Betanzos
31 - Barbanza e Iria
32 - Val Do Miño-Ourense

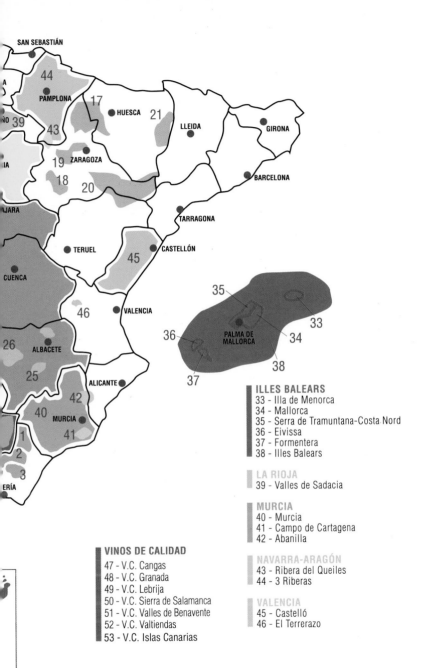

ILLES BALEARS
33 - Illa de Menorca
34 - Mallorca
35 - Serra de Tramuntana-Costa Nord
36 - Eivissa
37 - Formentera
38 - Illes Balears

LA RIOJA
39 - Valles de Sadacia

MURCIA
40 - Murcia
41 - Campo de Cartagena
42 - Abanilla

NAVARRA-ARAGÓN
43 - Ribera del Queiles
44 - 3 Riberas

VALENCIA
45 - Castelló
46 - El Terrerazo

VINOS DE CALIDAD
47 - V.C. Cangas
48 - V.C. Granada
49 - V.C. Lebrija
50 - V.C. Sierra de Salamanca
51 - V.C. Valles de Benavente
52 - V.C. Valtiendas
53 - V.C. Islas Canarias